West's Paralegal Today

The Legal Team at Work

Comprehensive Edition

West's Paralegal Today

THE LEGAL Team AT WORK

COMPREHENSIVE EDITION

Roger LeRoy Miller
School of Law
University of Miami

Mary S. Urisko
Madonna University, Michigan
Assistant Professor, Paralegal Program

West Publishing Company
St. Paul/Minneapolis • New York • Los Angeles • San Francisco

Copy Editor Beverly Peavler

Composition Parkwood Composition Service

Index Bob Marsh

Cover Photographs *Top left:* © Ed Malitsky, Liaison International. *Top right:* © PBJ Pictures, Liaison International. *Lower left:* © Larry Williams, Masterfile. *Lower right:* © J.A. Kraulis, Masterfile.

Credits and Acknowledgments Photo credits and acknowledgments appear following the index

West's Commitment to the Environment

In 1906, West Publishing Company began recycling materials left over from the production of books. This began a tradition of efficient and responsible use of resources. Today, up to 95 percent of our legal books and 70 percent of our college and school texts are printed on recycled, acid-free stock. West also recycles nearly 22 million pounds of scrap paper annually—the equivalent of 181,717 trees. Since the 1960s, West has devised ways to capture and recycle waste inks, solvents, oils, and vapors created in the printing process. We also recycle plastics of all kinds, wood, glass, corrugated cardboard, and batteries, and have eliminated the use of Styrofoam book packaging. We at West are proud of the longevity and the scope of our commitment to the environment.

Production, Prepress, Printing and Binding by West Publishing Company.

British Library Cataloguing-in-Publication Data. A catalogue record for this book is available from the British Library.

Printed in the United States of America

03 02 01 00 99 98 97 96 8 7 6 5 4 3 2 1 0

Library of Congress Cataloging-in-Publication Data

Miller, Roger LeRoy.
West's paralegal today: the legal team at work : the comprehensive edition / Roger LeRoy Miller, Mary S. Urisko.
p. cm.
Includes index.
ISBN 0–314–06588–1 (hardcover : alk. paper)
1. Legal assistants—United States. 2. Legal assistants—United States—Handbooks, manuals, etc.. I. Urisko, Mary S. II. Title.
KF320.L4M556 1996
340′ .023′73—dc20 95–23789
CIP

Dedication

To the other Roger,
for all of your support and help
over these many years. Thanks.
RLM

To my grandmother, Dorothy Gidner Mesick,
and her sister, Marjora Gidner Garrity,
for their knowledge and inspiration.
MSU

Contents in Brief

Contents

Part One
The Paralegal Profession 1

Chapter 1
Today's Professional Paralegal 3

CHAPTER 3 The Regulation of Legal Professionals 79

CHAPTER 4
Ethics and Professional Responsibility 123

CHAPTER 5
Working in a Law Office 153

PART TWO INTRODUCTION TO LAW 193

CHAPTER 6 Sources of American Law 195

CHAPTER 7

The Court System and Alternative Dispute Resolution 229

CHAPTER 9
Corporate Law and Government Regulation 316

CHAPTER 11
Trial Procedures 423

CHAPTER 12
Criminal Law and Procedures 457

CHAPTER 13
Administrative Law and Procedures 497

CHAPTER 16
Computers and the Legal Profession 603

CHAPTER 18
Legal Analysis and Writing 701

PART FOUR
SUBSTANTIVE LAW: EXTENDED COVERAGE 757

CHAPTER 19
Special Forms of Business Organization 758

CHAPTER 23
Wills, Trusts, and Estates 868

PREFACE

One of the fastest-growing occupations in America today is that of the paralegal, or legal assistant. It seems fitting, then, that you and your students should have a new textbook that reflects the excitement surrounding paralegal studies today. *West's Paralegal Today: Comprehensive Edition*, we believe, imparts this excitement to your students. They will find paralegal studies accessible and interesting. This book is modern, colorful, and visually attractive, which encourages learning. We are certain that you and your students will find this text extremely effective.

West's Paralegal Today makes the paralegal field come alive for the student. We use real-world examples, present numerous boxed-in features, and support the text with the most extensive supplements package ever offered for an introductory paralegal textbook. We have even developed a special series of teaching videos that show paralegals dealing with on-the-job situations.

West Publishing Company has been providing authoritative materials to the entire legal field for over 120 years. *West's Paralegal Today* draws on the expertise of a company that has had a long history of encouraging excellence in legal education.

All of the basic areas of paralegal studies are covered in *West's Paralegal Today*, including careers, ethics, regulation, pretrial preparation, trial procedures, criminal law, administrative law, legal interviewing, legal investigation, the use of computers in legal work, and legal research and writing. In addition, there are a number of chapters on substantive law.

THE MOST MODERN AND UP-TO-DATE TEXT AVAILABLE

We have attempted to make sure that *West's Paralegal Today* is the most modern and up-to-date text available in today's marketplace. Specifically, your students will find the latest information, forms, documents, charts, and diagrams relating to currently required legal procedures.

For example, in the chapters on litigation procedures, your students will read about the new requirements concerning service of process and discovery in federal court cases under the 1993 revision of the Federal Rules of Civil Procedure. We include illustrations of the new federal forms for waiver of service and discovery planning as well. Additionally, all information with respect to ethics and regulation reflects the most current laws, ethical guidelines, ethical opinions, and court rulings concerning this important aspect of paralegal practice.

A PRACTICAL, REALISTIC APPROACH

There sometimes exists an enormous gulf between classroom learning and on-the-job realities. We have tried to bridge this gulf in *West's Paralegal Today* by offering a text that is full of practical advice and "hands-on" activities. Exercises at the end of each chapter provide opportunities for your students to apply the concepts and skills discussed in the chapter. Many of the book's other key features, which you will read about below, were designed specifically to give your students a glimpse of the types of situations and demands that they may encounter on the job as professional paralegals. A special appendix at the end of the text (Appendix A) contains practical advice and tips for how to learn legal concepts and procedures, advice and tips that your students can also apply later, on the job.

West's Paralegal Today also realistically portrays paralegal working environments and on-the-job challenges. Ethical dimensions of the practice of law frame paralegals' work experiences to a significant extent. Because of this, we have made a special effort to show how seemingly abstract ethical rules affect the day-to-day tasks performed by attorneys and paralegals in the legal workplace.

KEY FEATURES

West's Paralegal Today offers the following special features, which are set apart and used both to instruct and to pique the interest of your paralegal students.

Developing Paralegal Skills

Each chapter in this text includes two or three of these boxed-in features. These special features present hypothetical examples of paralegals at work to help your students develop crucial paralegal skills. Some examples are the following:

- Erecting an Ethical Wall (Chapter 4).
- Federal Court Rules—Creating a Complaint Checklist (Chapter 10).
- The Prosecutor's Office—Warrant Division (Chapter 12).
- Conducting an Intake Interview (Chapter 14).
- Creative Investigating (Chapter 15).

Ethical Concerns

Every chapter presents, in the page margins, three or more *Ethical Concerns*. These features typically take a student into a hypothetical situation that clearly presents an ethical problem. When possible, students are told what they should and should not do in particular situations being discussed. Some examples are the following:

- Saying "If I were you . . . " and the UPL (Chapter 3).
- Deadlines and the Duty of Competence (Chapter 10).
- Telephone Calls and Confidentiality (Chapter 15).
- Avoiding Plagiarism (Chapter 17).

The Legal Team at Work

These features stress the growing importance of the team approach to legal representation today. They illustrate how attorneys, paralegals, and other staff members work as a team to serve most effectively the needs of clients. Some examples are the following:

- Communication and Teamwork (Chapter 5).
- Holding the Client's Many Hands (Chapter 10).
- In the Courtroom (Chapter 11).
- Humanizing Legal Practice (Chapter 14).

Featured-guest Articles

In most chapters, we have included a contributed article written by an educator or an expert in the field. These articles offer your students practical tips for some aspect of paralegal work relating to the topic covered in the chapter. Some examples are the following:

- "Paralegal Career Planning and Development," by Denise Templeton, president and chief executive officer of Templeton & Associates, a legal-support services firm, and one of the founders of the Minnesota Association of Legal Assistants, the American Association for Paralegal Education, and the National Federation of Paralegal Associations (Chapter 2).
- "Ten Tips on Ethics and the Paralegal," by Michael A. Pener, instructor at Johnson County Community College, Overland Park, Kansas (Chapter 4).
- "Ten Tips for Drafting Interrogatories," by James W. H. McCord, director of paralegal programs at Eastern Kentucky University, Richmond, Kentucky (Chapter 10).
- "Keeping Current on Computer Technology," by Jan Richmond, instructor at St. Louis Community College, St. Louis, Missouri (Chapter 16).

Paralegal Profiles

Another key feature of *West's Paralegal Today* is the inclusion of profiles of paralegals who are currently working in specific areas of law. These profiles open with a short biography of the paralegal and then present the paralegal's own answers to questions asked by the interviewer. The paralegal tells of his or her greatest challenges on the job, gives suggestions on what he or she thinks students should concentrate on when studying to become a paralegal, and offers tips for being a successful paralegal in his or her line of work. This feature gives your students insights into various legal specialties and the diversity of paralegal working environments.

Today's Professional Paralegal

Near the end of every chapter we have included a feature entitled *Today's Professional Paralegal*. This important feature exposes your students to situations that they are likely to encounter on the job and offers guidance on how certain types of problems can be resolved. Some examples are the following:

- Managing Conflict (Chapter 5).
- Arbitrating Commercial Contracts (Chapter 7).

- Drafting *Voir Dire* Questions Like a Pro (Chapter 10).
- Locating a Witness (Chapter 15).

Other Special Pedagogical Features

We have included in *West's Paralegal Today* a number of additional pedagogical features, including those discussed below.

Chapter Objectives

Every chapter opens with five or six chapter objectives. Your students will know immediately what is expected of them as they read each chapter.

Chapter Outlines

In every chapter, just following the *Chapter Objectives*, a *Chapter Outline* lists both the first-level and second-level headings within the chapter. These outlines allow you and your students to tell at a glance what topics are covered in the chapters.

Vocabulary and Margin Definitions

Legal terminology is often a major challenge to beginning paralegal students. We have used an important pedagogical device—margin definitions—to help your students understand legal terms. Whenever an important term is introduced, it is done so in boldface type and defined. In addition, the term is listed and defined in the margin of the page, alongside the paragraph in which the boldfaced term appears.

At the end of each chapter, all terms that have been boldfaced within the chapter are listed in alphabetical order in a section called *Key Terms and Concepts*. The page on which the term is defined is given after each term. Your students can briefly examine this list to make sure that they understand all of the important terms introduced in the chapter. If they do not understand a term completely, they can immediately refer to the page number given and review the term.

All boldfaced terms are again listed and defined in the *Glossary* at the end of the text. Spanish equivalents to many important legal terms in English are given in a separate glossary.

Concept Summaries

We have added special summaries of legal concepts in those chapters that focus on substantive law (Chapters 6, 8, 9, and 19–24), as well as in the chapter covering the court system (Chapter 7). These summaries allow the student to review essential legal concepts in various areas of the law. For example, Chapter 8 introduces the student to contract law, sales law, torts, property law, and intellectual property. To help the student review and retain the legal concepts and principles involved in each of these areas of law, we present a concept summary for each area.

Exhibits and Forms

When appropriate, we present exhibits illustrating important forms or concepts relating to paralegal work. Many exhibits are filled in with hypothetical data. In all, there are over 170 exhibits and forms in *West's Paralegal Today*, including those listed below:

- A Sample Retainer Agreement (Chapter 5).
- A Sample Complaint (Chapter 10).
- Major Procedural Steps in a Criminal Case (Chapter 12).
- An Investigation Plan (Chapter 15).

In Chapter 18, we present a *special fold-out exhibit* (Exhibit 18-1), which shows the major components of a court case, including excerpts from the court's opinion. Important sections, terms, and phrases in the sample case are defined or discussed in margin annotations.

CHAPTER-ENDING MATERIALS FOR REVIEW AND STUDY

Every chapter contains numerous chapter-ending pedagogical materials. These materials are designed to provide a wide variety of assignments for your students. The chapter-ending pedagogy begins with the *Key Terms and Concepts,* which we have already mentioned. Next are the materials described below.

Chapter Summary

Every chapter ends with a series of numbered paragraphs that summarize the major points made in the chapter. These summaries can be used by students to review and test their knowledge of the topics covered in the chapter.

Questions for Review

In every chapter, following the *Chapter Summary*, are ten relatively straightforward questions for review. These questions are designed to test the student's knowledge of the basic concepts discussed in the chapter.

Ethical Questions

Because of the importance of ethical issues in paralegal training, we have also included at the end of each chapter two to four ethical questions. Each question presents a hypothetical situation, which is followed by one or two questions about what the paralegal should do to solve the dilemma.

Practice Questions and Assignments

The "hands-on" approach to learning paralegal skills is emphasized in the practice questions and assignments. There are two to four of these questions and assignments at the end of each chapter. A particular situation is presented, and the student is asked to actually carry out an assignment.

Questions for Critical Analysis

Every chapter has from two to four questions for critical analysis. These questions are designed to elicit critical analysis and discussion of issues relating to the topic covered in the chapter.

Role-playing Exercises

Every chapter has two or three role-playing exercises in which your students are asked to work together to act out the roles of particular paralegals or others (such as attorneys or clients) in specific, well-defined situations.

Projects

There are two to four projects at the end of every chapter. These are specific work tasks that your students can carry out. Often, these projects involve obtaining information from sources that paralegals may deal with on the job, such as a library, a court, a prosecutor's office, or a police department.

Annotated Selected Readings

From five to ten selected readings, fully annotated, are also included in the end-of-chapter materials. These readings give your student a wide range of additional materials from which to draw information about topics that are discussed in the chapter.

APPENDICES

To make this text a reference source for your students, we have included the appendices listed below:

A Mastering *West's Paralegal Today:* How to Study Legal Concepts and Procedures
B Electronic Legal Research Using the Internet
C The NALA Code of Ethics and Professional Responsibility
D The NALA Model Standards and Guidelines for the Utilization of Legal Assistants
E The NFPA Model Code of Ethics and Professional Responsibility
F The ABA Model Standards and Guidelines for the Utilization of Legal Assistants
G Paralegal Ethics and Regulation: How to Find State-specific Information
H Paralegal Associations
I State and Major Local Bar Associations
J Information on the NALA's Certified Legal Assistant (CLA) and Certified Legal Assistant Specialist (CLAS) Examinations
K Specialty Certification Standards for Legal Assistants in Texas
L The Constitution of the United States
M Spanish Equivalents for Important Legal Terms in English

SUPPLEMENTAL TEACHING/LEARNING MATERIALS

West's Paralegal Today is accompanied by what is arguably the largest number of teaching and learning supplements available for any text of its kind. We understand that instructors face a difficult task in finding the time necessary to teach the materials that they wish to cover during each term. In conjunction with a number of our colleagues, we have developed supplementary teaching materials that we believe are the best available today. Each component of the supplements package is described below.

Instructor's Manual

Written by text co-author Mary Urisko, the *Instructor's Manual* includes the following:

- Sample course syllabi.
- Chapter/lecture outlines.
- Teaching suggestions.
- Lists of supplemental materials.
- Answers to text exercises and questions.
- Suggested teaching uses for videos.
- Transparency masters.
- Handouts.

Computerized Instructor's Manual

For those instructors who wish to modify the *Instructor's Manual* by adding their own notes or who wish to print out some of the class-enrichment materials, we provide a fully computerized version of the *Instructor's Manual*. You may order the manual in any popular format.

Study Guide

Prepared by Kathleen Reed and Bradene Moore of the University of Toledo, the *Study Guide* provides the following:

- Chapter objectives are presented in a checklist form so that students can review systematically the areas they have learned and determine which areas need more study.
- Chapter outlines provide succinct, easy-to-read summaries of the chapters and help students review the material. Study suggestions are included within the outlines, including tips on how to remember key information.
- Review questions in true-false, fill-in-the-blank, and multiple-choice formats provide students with an extensive review of the terminology and concepts presented in each chapter of the text. There are between thirty and fifty review questions for each chapter.
- Additional practice questions, questions for critical analysis, and ethical questions reinforce the concepts and procedures presented in the chapters.

Three-ring Binder

This binder holds all of the printed supplements that accompany the text.

Test Bank

Text co-author Mary Urisko has developed an extensive test bank that contains approximately fifty questions per chapter in multiple-choice and essay formats.

Computerized Test Bank

The test bank is available on the latest version of WESTEST, a highly acclaimed computerized testing system. WESTEST is offered for IBM PCs and compatible microcomputers or the Macintosh family of microcomputers. WESTEST allows instructors to do the following:

- Add or edit questions, instructions, and answers.
- Select questions by previewing the question on the screen.
- Let the system select questions randomly.
- Select questions by question number.
- View summaries of the test or test-bank chapters.
- Set up the page layout for exams.
- Print exams in a variety of formats.

Transparency Acetates

More than three dozen transparency acetates covering many important exhibits are available free to adopters.

State-specific Supplements

State-specific supplements are available for California, Florida, New York, and Texas. These supplements are keyed to each chapter in the text and point out state-specific information when it differs from the text's discussion. For example, Chapter 7 of the supplement provides a detailed description of the state court system.

West's Law Finder

West's Law Finder is a brief (seventy-seven page) pamphlet that describes various legal-research sources and how they can be used. Classroom quantities are available.

Sample Pages, Third Edition

This 225-page, soft-cover pamphlet introduces all of West's legal-research materials. The accompanying *Instructor's Manual* gives ideas for effectively using the material in the classroom. Classroom quantities are available.

Citation-At-A-Glance

This handy reference card provides a quick, portable reference to the basic rules of citation for the most commonly cited legal sources, including judicial opinions, statutes, and secondary sources, such as legal encyclopedias and legal periodicals. *Citation-At-A-Glance* uses the rules set forth in *A Uniform System of Citation,* Fifteenth Edition (1991). A free copy of this valuable supplement is included with every student text.

Guide to *Shepard's Citations*

How to Shepardize: Your Guide to Complete Legal Research through Shepard's Citations—1993 WESTLAW Edition is a sixty-four-page pamphlet that helps students understand the research technique of Shepardizing case citations. The pamphlet is available in classroom quantities (one copy for each student who purchases a new text).

Strategies for Paralegal Educators

Strategies and Tips for Paralegal Educators, a pamphlet by Anita Tebbe of Johnson County Community College, provides teaching strategies specifically designed for paralegal educators. It concentrates on how to teach and is organized in three parts: the WHO of paralegal education—students and teachers; the WHAT of paralegal education—goals and objectives; and the HOW of paralegal education—methods of instruction, methods of evaluation, and other aspects of teaching. A copy of this pamphlet is available to each adopter. Quantities for distribution to their adjunct instructors are available for purchase at a minimal price. A coupon in the pamphlet provides ordering information.

Handbook of Cases

A booklet entitled *Handbook of Selected Court Cases Relating to Paralegal Issues* presents excerpts from twenty court opinions relating to paralegal issues, such as the unauthorized practice of law, paralegal compensation, and conflict of interest. The cases have been pulled from court decisions reported by West Publishing Company's WESTLAW Division. Each case excerpt is preceded by a full citation to the case and an introduction, in our own words, to the paralegal issue being addressed by the court and the court's decision on the issue. The ninety-six-page booklet is available for students on the instructor's request.

Videotape of Selected Role-playing Exercises

This videotape shows individuals acting out selected end-of-chapter role-playing exercises from *West's Paralegal Today.* Students can view this tape, in or out of the classroom, to get ideas on how to perform role-playing exercises generally or to evaluate how effectively others have acted out a particular role-playing exercise. A separate pamphlet containing teaching suggestions is available.

Data Disk

Forms needed to complete selected end-of-chapter practice questions and projects are provided on a data disk. Exercises that can be completed using the data disk are marked in the text with the following logo:

WESTLAW

West's on-line computerized legal-research system offers students "hands-on" experience with a system commonly used in law offices. Qualified adopters can receive ten free hours of WESTLAW. WESTLAW can be accessed with Macintosh and IBM PCs and compatibles. A modem is required.

WESTMATE Tutorial

This interactive tutorial guides students through the process of accessing legal resources on WESTLAW by using WESTMATE, the special software that West has created for that purpose. There are two versions of the tutorial, one for DOS and one for Windows.

Video Library

West is proud to present an extensive video library for use in the classroom. This library includes the following videotapes:

- **The Making of a Case**. This videotape, which is narrated by Richard Dysart, star of *L.A. Law,* introduces the student to the meaning and importance of case law. It explains how cases are published and, in the process, provides an introduction to significant aspects of our legal system.
- **West's Legal Research Videos**. These videos teach the basis and rationale for legal research. The videos cover the three types of legal research tools—Primary Tools, Secondary Tools, and Finding Tools—as well as law reporters, digests, computer assistance, statutes, special searches, and CD-ROM libraries.
- **I Never Said I Was a Lawyer**. This videotape, which was produced by the Colorado Bar Association Committee on Legal Assistants, uses a variety of scenarios to inspire discussion and give students experience dealing with ethical dilemmas.
- **Drama of the Law II: Paralegal Issues**. This video series of five separate dramatizations is intended to stimulate classroom discussion about various issues and problems faced by paralegals on the job today. An *Instructor's Manual* is available.
- **Arguments to the United State Supreme Court**. In this video, accomplished lawyers, professors, and judges play various roles as the case *Federal Trade Commission v. The American United Tobacco Company* is argued before a mock United States Supreme Court. The arguments center on the fol-

lowing question: Should commercial speech be protected as free speech? One of the mock United States Supreme Court justices is Stephen G. Breyer, who has since been appointed to the Supreme Court.

- **Business Litigation**. This videotape, which was produced by the American Bar Association, is designed to show the various parts of a trial. Various segments have been taken from a mock trial to illustrate the actions that take place during a trial. The case involves a lost shipment of computer parts. The parties in this case are business firms. The plaintiff, BMI, is suing the defendant, Minicom, for breach of contract.
- **Trial Techniques: A Products Liability Case**. This video, which was produced by the American Bar Association, is designed to show the types of arguments used by plaintiffs and defendants in product-liability lawsuits. Various segments have been taken from a mock trial to illustrate these arguments. The specific case involves Mr. Lockette (the plaintiff), who is suing the World-Wide Motorcycle Company (the defendant) for injuries he sustained in a motorcycle accident. The plaintiff claims that the defendant defectively manufactured the motorcycle by failing to install a crash bar on the motorcycle as part of its standard equipment.

ACKNOWLEDGMENTS

Numerous careful and conscientious individuals have helped us in this undertaking. We particularly wish to thank the paralegal educators listed below. In their reviews of the manuscript for *West's Paralegal Today*, these professionals offered us penetrating criticisms, comments, and suggestions for improving the text. While we haven't been able to follow each request, each of the reviewers will see that many of his or her suggestions have been taken to heart.

Laura Barnard
Lakeland Community College, Ohio

Jeptha Clemens
Northwest Mississippi Community College

Donna Hamblin Donathan
Marshall University Community College, Ohio

Vera Peaslee Haus
McIntosh College, New Hampshire

Susan Howery
Yavapai College, Arizona

Wendy Edson
Hilbert College, New York

Pamela Faller
College of the Sequoias, California

Gary Glascom
Cedar Crest College, Pennsylvania

Dolores Grissom
Samford University, Alabama

Jean A. Hellman
Loyola University, Chicago

Marlene L. Hoover
El Camino College, California

Jane Kaplan
New York City Technical College, New York

Jennifer Allen Labosky
Davidson County Community College, North Carolina

Dora J. Lew
California State University, Hayward

Mary Hatfield Lowe
Westark Community College, Arkansas

Gerald A. Loy
Broome Community College, New York

Linda Mort
Kellogg Community College, Michigan

H. Margaret Nickerson
William Woods College, Missouri

Martha Nielsen
University of California, San Diego

Elizabeth L. Nobis
Lansing Community College, Michigan

Joy D. O'Donnell
Pima Community College, Arizona

Vera Peaslee
McIntosh College, New Hampshire

Francis D. Polk
Ocean County College, New Jersey

Ruth-Ellen Post
Rivier College, New Hampshire

Elizabeth Raulerson
Indian River Community College, Florida

Kathleen Mercer Reed
University of Toledo, Ohio

Lynn Retzak
Lakeshore Technical Institute, Wisconsin

Evelyn L. Riyhani
University of California, Irvine

Melanie A. P. Rowand
California State University, Hayward

Vitonio F. San Juan
University of La Verne, California

Susan F. Schulz
Southern Career Institute, Florida

A special thanks is due to the following paralegal educators, our featured guests in *West's Paralegal Today,* for enhancing the quality of our book with their tips and illuminating insights into paralegal practice:

Anna Durham Boling
Athens Area Technical Institute, Georgia

Andrea Nager Chasen
Private Law Practice

John DeLeo
Central Pennsylvania Business School, Pennsylvania

Wendy B. Edson
Hilbert College, New York

Daniel F. Hinkel
National Center for Paralegal Training, Georgia

Deborah A. Howard
University of Evansville, Indiana

Susan D. Kligerman
Philadelphia Institute and Fairleigh Dickinson University

Judy A. Long
Rio Hondo College, California

James W. H. McCord
Eastern Kentucky University, Kentucky

Michael A. Pener
Johnson County Community College, Kansas

Kathleen Mercer Reed
University of Toledo's Community and Technical College, Ohio

Jan Richmond
St. Louis Community College, Missouri

Melanie A. P. Rowand
California State University, Hayward

Vitonio F. San Juan
University of La Verne, California

Denise Templeton
President and chief executive officer of Templeton & Associates

Richard M. Terry
Baltimore City Community College, Maryland

Pamela Poole Weber
Seminole Community College, Florida

E. J. Yera
Holmes Regional Medical Center, Florida

Additionally, we would like to extend our gratitude to those on-the-job paralegals who agreed to appear in the *Paralegal Profiles* of *West's Paralegal Today.*

We are also indebted to the following individuals, whose efforts contributed significantly to the quality of *West's Paralegal Today:* Roger Meiners, Jefferson Weaver, Darin Zenov, and Laura Valade, for their research assistance; Jennifer Sparks, for her many helpful comments and criticisms; and Elizabeth Cameron, for her numerous insights into the daily workings of the law office and the paralegal's role in legal work, as well as samples of forms used in the litigation and settlement processes. We also wish to thank Lavina Leed Miller and Barbara Curtiss for their editorial assistance, and Marie-Christine Louiseau and Elliot Simon for their proofreading assistance. We are also grateful to Suzanne Jasin for her valuable contributions to this project, as well as to Beverly Peavler, whose expert copy-editing skills will not go unnoticed. Additionally, we extend our thanks to Richard F. X. Urisko for his guidance in regard to federal court litigation and the 1993 amendments to the Federal Rules of Civil Procedure, Jennifer Wanty Coté for her endless knowledge of the paralegal field and paralegal ethics, and Barbara Habermas for her editorial assistance.

In preparing *West's Paralegal Today,* we were the beneficiaries of the expertise brought to the project by an incredibly skilled and dedicated editorial, production, and printing and manufacturing team at West Publishing Company. Our editor, Elizabeth Hannan, successfully guided the project through each phase and put together a supplements package that is without parallel in the teaching and learning of paralegal skills. Patty Bryant, the developmental editor, was also incredibly helpful in putting together the *West's Paralegal Today* teaching/learning package. Additionally, we sincerely appreciate the efforts of our project editor, Bill Stryker, who designed what we feel is the most visually attractive paralegal text on the market, and Beth Kennedy, the production supervisor on the project. Finally, we particularly wish to thank our editor in chief, Clyde Perlee, Jr., whose expert supervision and guidance during each stage of the project kept us all on track.

We know that we are not perfect. If you or your students have suggestions on how we can improve this book, write to us. That way, we can make *West's Paralegal Today* an even better book in the future. We promise to answer every single letter that we receive.

Roger LeRoy Miller
Mary S. Urisko

PART ONE

THE PARALEGAL PROFESSION

1

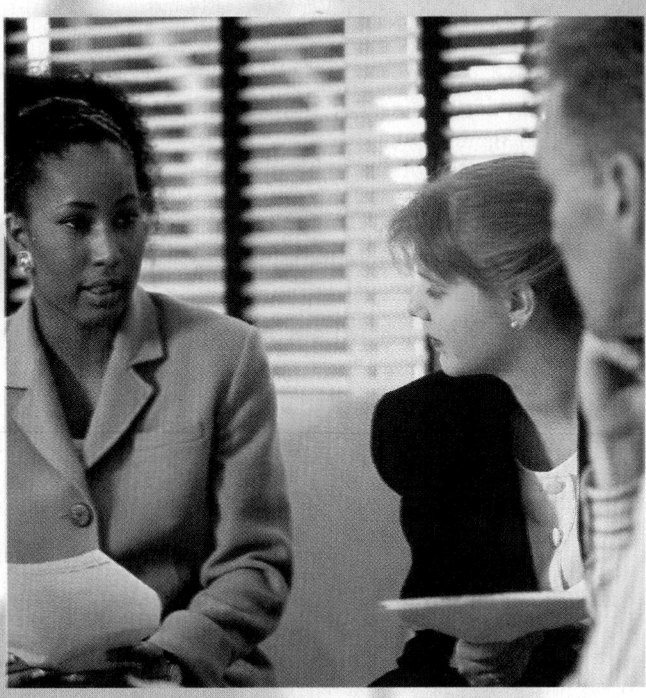

Today's Professional Paralegal

CHAPTER OBJECTIVES

After completing this chapter, you will know:

- **What a paralegal is and does.**
- **How and why the paralegal profession developed.**
- **The professional organizations that exist for paralegals and the benefits of membership in them.**
- **The education and training available to paralegals.**
- **The skills that are useful for a paralegal to have.**
- **Some important personal attributes of the professional paralegal.**

CHAPTER OUTLINE

INTRODUCTION

AMERICAN BAR ASSOCIATION (ABA)
A voluntary national association of attorneys. The ABA plays an active role in developing educational and ethical standards for attorneys and in pursuing improvements in the administration of justice.

The paralegal profession was first recognized as a profession in 1968 by the **American Bar Association (ABA),** a voluntary national association of attorneys (lawyers). In that year, the ABA formed the Special Committee on Lay Assistants for Lawyers. During the early 1970s, the committee met to study and discuss how lawyers could most effectively use nonlawyers in their practices. The paralegal profession continued to grow throughout the 1970s and 1980s, and it is now one of the fastest-growing occupations in the United States. You will read more about paralegal employment statistics, including paralegal salaries, in Chapter 2.

For the individual who seeks interesting and challenging work, the paralegal profession offers many opportunities. Paralegals deal with real people and real problems. Even when the paralegal is in a library doing legal research, the real world is not too far away. When locating and analyzing court cases, the paralegal will find that each case tells a story of its own, involving specific people and circumstances. Through their legal work, paralegals learn much about human nature, the law, and how the law applies to real-life problems.

Some of the most frequently asked questions concerning the paralegal profession are the following: What is a paralegal? What is the difference between a paralegal and a legal assistant? What do paralegals do? You will learn the answers to these questions in this chapter. You will also read about the evolution of the paralegal profession, paralegal education, and the kinds of skills and personal qualities that will help you become a successful paralegal.

WHAT IS A PARALEGAL?

PARALEGAL (OR LEGAL ASSISTANT)
A person sufficiently trained or experienced in the law and legal procedures to assist, under an attorney's supervision, in the performance of substantive legal work that would otherwise be performed by an attorney. Often referred to as a legal assistant.

Generally, a **paralegal,** or a **legal assistant,** is a person sufficiently trained in law and legal procedures to assist attorneys in the delivery of legal services to the public. More specifically, the ABA's Standing Committee on Ethics and Responsibility defines a *legal assistant* as follows:

> The terms legal assistant and paralegal are used interchangeably, which means persons who, although not members of the legal profession, are qualified through education, training, or work experience, who are employed or retained by a lawyer, law office, governmental agency, or other entity in a capacity or function which involves the performance, under the direction and supervision of an attorney, of specifically delegated substantive legal work, which work, for the most part, requires a sufficient knowledge of legal concepts such that, absent that legal assistant, the attorney would perform the task.[1]

1. The ABA's definition is very similar to the definitions created by two of the largest national paralegal associations, the National Association of Legal Assistants (NALA) and the National Federation of Paralegal Associations (NFPA). These two organizations will be discussed shortly.

Several elements in the ABA's definition merit attention. First, the ABA states that the terms *legal assistant* and *paralegal* are used interchangeably. In this book, we follow this practice and use the terms synonymously.

Second, the ABA's definition states that a legal assistant may be qualified through "education, training, or work experience." The emphasis is on the ability to perform specified tasks, regardless of whether that ability was acquired through education or on-the-job experience. The definition acknowledges the fact that persons can acquire, through on-the-job training and experience, the knowledge and skills necessary to perform paralegal tasks. In fact, the first paralegals—and the founders of many paralegal associations—were highly qualified and skilled legal secretaries.

Third, the phrase "under the direction and supervision of an attorney" is a key element in the definition of a legal assistant. Legal assistants, or paralegals, are not attorneys; they are attorneys' assistants. Although paralegals perform work that traditionally has been performed only by attorneys, they do so under attorneys' supervision—that is, the ultimate responsibility for paralegal work falls on attorneys. Moreover, there are certain types of legal work that paralegals by law may not undertake. For example, a paralegal may not give legal advice, set legal fees, or (with rare exceptions) represent a client in court. (You will read more about what tasks paralegals may and may not perform in Chapter 3.)

Finally, the definition emphasizes that attorneys delegate "substantive legal work" to paralegals, legal work that, "absent the legal assistant," attorneys themselves would handle. This is an important element in the definition of a paralegal because it indicates that although paralegals are not attorneys, they do the kinds of work traditionally undertaken only by attorneys.

WHAT DO PARALEGALS DO?

Throughout this book, you will read about the different ways in which paralegals assist attorneys, and it would be impossible to list them all in this brief space. The following list is thus just a sampling of some of the types of tasks that paralegals typically perform.

- *Draft legal documents*—such as legal correspondence, documents to be filed with the courts, and interoffice memoranda.
- *Calendar and track important deadlines*—such as the dates when certain documents must be filed with the court.
- *Assist attorneys in preparing for trial*—by preparing exhibits, documents, and trial notebooks that the attorney will need to have on hand at trial. Some paralegals also assist attorneys during trials.
- *Interview clients and witnesses*—to gather relevant facts and information about a lawsuit, for example.
- *Conduct legal investigations*—to gather facts about a case by interviewing clients and witnesses and obtaining relevant records (such as medical records or the police report of an accident).
- *Organize and maintain client files*—or (as is often the situation) supervise the organization and maintenance of client files.
- *Conduct legal research*—to find, analyze, and summarize court decisions, statutes, or regulations applicable to a client's case.

The specific kinds of tasks that paralegals perform vary, of course, from office to office. If you work in a one-attorney office, for example, you will probably not have much secretarial or clerical assistance. In other words, your job might overlap to some extent with that of the legal secretary. Your tasks might range from conducting sophisticated legal research and investigations to photocopying documents to answering the telephone while the secretary is out to lunch.

If you work in a larger law firm, you will have more support staff (secretaries, file clerks, and others) to whom you can delegate work. Your work might also be more specialized. Instead of working on a number of cases relating to different areas of the law, you might concentrate solely on certain types of cases. If you work in a law firm's real-estate department, for example, you will deal only with legal matters relating to that area of the law. In the next chapter, you will read about the variety of environments in which paralegals work.

ETHICAL CONCERN

Paralegal Expertise and Legal Advice

Paralegals often become very knowledgeable in a specific area of the law. If you specialize in environmental law, for example, you will become very knowledgeable about environmental claims. In working with a client on a matter involving an environmental agency, you might therefore be tempted to advise the client on which type of action would be most favorable to the client. Never do so. As will be discussed in detail in Chapters 3 and 4, only attorneys may give legal advice, and paralegals who give legal advice risk penalties for the unauthorized practice of law. Whatever legal advice is given to the client must come either directly from the attorney or, if from you, must reflect exactly (or nearly exactly) what the attorney said with no embellishment on your part. After consulting with your supervising attorney, for example, you can say to the client that Mr. X (the attorney) "advises that you do all that you can to settle the claim as soon as possible."

HISTORY OF THE PARALEGAL PROFESSION

The paralegal profession initially developed in response to the need for a legal professional to fill a position somewhere between that of an attorney and that of a legal secretary. To some extent, law clerks fill this need. A **law clerk** is a law student who gains practical experience in the law by working for a law firm. Law clerks are often hired on a temporary basis (for the summer, for example, when they are not attending school, or to assist on a specific project).[2]

LAW CLERK
In the context of law-office work, a law student who works as an apprentice, during the summer or part-time during the school year, with an attorney or law firm to gain practical legal experience.

The problem faced by law firms is that if they need permanent, full-time legal assistance, hiring a law student on a temporary or part-time basis will not fill this need. Another option is, of course, to hire a law-school graduate as an **associate attorney** (a hired attorney who, unlike a partner in a partnership, has no ownership rights in a firm) on a full-time basis, but this might be too great an expense for the firm's budget to bear.

ASSOCIATE ATTORNEY
An attorney who is hired by a law firm as an employee and who has no ownership rights in the firm.

Competent and experienced legal secretaries began to fill the need faced by many law firms to have full-time assistance at a lower cost. The first paralegals were legal secretaries who had become, through on-the-job experience, extremely competent and skilled in legal procedures. They learned how to do legal research and investigation, draft documents to be filed with the court, and perform other tasks that today's paralegals are trained to undertake. Eventually, legal assistants succeeded in defining themselves as a distinct professional group within the field of law. Paralegal professional associations and paralegal education programs further advanced the professional status of paralegals. Today, individuals who want to become legal assistants can enter a paralegal program and receive specialized training.

2. The term *law clerk* is also used to designate an attorney who does legal research and writing for a judge or a justice.

Paralegal Associations and Professional Growth

One feature that distinguishes a profession from other occupations is that the members of a profession form professional associations for the following purposes:

- To establish a forum (place) in which issues relating to their profession can be discussed, experiences can be shared, and communication networks can be established.
- To establish guidelines to regulate their activities, such as ethical codes of conduct.
- To determine the level of skills or educational preparation necessary to the type of work performed by the members of the profession.
- To establish or sponsor educational programs to train potential professional practitioners or provide continuing education for those members who are already practicing their profession.

The evolution of the *paralegal profession* is thus directly related to the formation of paralegal associations. The earliest paralegal associations were formed at the state and local levels. The formation of national paralegal associations in the mid-1970s significantly furthered the professional interests and goals of paralegals.

State and Local Paralegal Associations. By the early 1970s, there were numerous local paralegal associations. If you look at Appendix H at the end of this book, you will see that today every state has a paralegal association, and several states have many regional or local organizations within their borders. Practicing paralegals typically belong to their local (and/or state) paralegal association, as well as one of the national paralegal associations discussed below. Most **state bar associations**—associations of attorneys at the state level—also allow paralegals to become associate members of their organizations.

STATE BAR ASSOCIATION
An association of attorneys within a state. Membership in the state bar association is mandatory in over two-thirds of the states—that is, before an attorney can practice law in a state, he or she must be admitted to that state's bar association.

NATIONAL FEDERATION OF PARALEGAL ASSOCIATIONS (NFPA)
One of the two largest national paralegal associations in the United States; formed in 1974. NFPA is actively involved in paralegal professional developments.

AFFILIATE
An entity that is connected (affiliated) with another entity. State and local branches of national or regional paralegal associations are often referred to as affiliates.

NATIONAL ASSOCIATION OF LEGAL ASSISTANTS (NALA)
One of the two largest national paralegal associations in the United States; formed in 1975. NALA offers a certification program for paralegals and is actively involved in paralegal professional developments.

The National Federation of Paralegal Associations (NFPA). The **National Federation of Paralegal Associations (NFPA),** which was founded in 1974, was created to represent paralegals at U.S. Senate hearings that were considering the question of whether paralegals should be regulated. NFPA represented the few local paralegal organizations that existed in 1974. As of 1994, its membership consisted of fifty-nine paralegal associations from around the country reaching over 17,000 legal assistants. The member associations of NFPA are referred to as affiliated associations, or **affiliates,** of NFPA.

The National Association of Legal Assistants (NALA). The **National Association of Legal Assistants (NALA)** was formed in 1975. Unlike NFPA, NALA has individual members. As of 1994, NALA had 3,751 individual members and 85 affiliated associations, reaching over 15,000 legal assistants nationwide. While both NALA and NFPA encourage the growth of the profession, they differ on the direction that the profession should take, as you will learn in Chapter 3.

> **ETHICAL CONCERN**
>
> **Ethics and the Effective Utilization of Paralegals**
>
> As you will read in Chapter 3, the ethical codes and guidelines regulating attorneys urge attorneys to use paralegals effectively—because the effective use of paralegals in legal representation benefits the public by providing quality legal services at lower cost. Paralegal ethical codes and guidelines also reflect this commitment. As a paralegal, you will share in this ethical responsibility. What can you do to promote the effective use of paralegal services? One thing you can do is to join a paralegal association and work together with other association members toward this goal. Another thing you can do is to encourage your supervising attorney to delegate substantive work to you. For example, you might volunteer to take on certain tasks so that you can display your competence. Some attorneys do not yet realize how many tasks paralegals can competently perform and how beneficial it is for them (freeing up their time for other work and lowering clients' bills) to delegate substantive work to paralegals.

Other National Paralegal Associations. As the profession grew, other national professional organizations were formed. Professional Legal Assistants, Inc. (PLA), was chartered in 1985. Other national paralegal professional associations include the Legal Assistant Management Association, the American Paralegal Association, and the National Association for Independent Paralegals. The names and addresses of these and other paralegal associations, including state associations, are given in Appendix H.

Benefits of Professional Membership. As a paralegal, you will find that membership in a paralegal association presents numerous benefits. Among other things, membership offers the following kinds of opportunities:

- To meet and network with others in your profession.
- To receive professional publications that keep you up to date on the latest issues in the profession.
- To continue your training and education through seminars, workshops, and other programs.
- To participate in meetings to develop policy relating to current issues affecting the paralegal profession.
- To indicate to potential employers that you are active in professional affiliations—a plus for the paralegal job candidate.

Economics and the Paralegal Profession

In the modern competitive environment for legal services, clients shop around for legal services, and the cost of those services is an important factor in determining which lawyer or law firm will be hired. Lawyers can provide lower-cost legal services to their clients when they use paralegals because they can bill their clients at lower rates for paralegal work. As you will read in Chapter 5, in which this topic is explored more fully, the billable rate for a paralegal (the hourly rate charged to clients for work done on their behalf) is substantially less than that for an attorney.

Clients, then, benefit from the use of paralegals because the clients pay less for legal services. Lawyers who delegate substantive legal work to paralegals also benefit from this practice because it frees up their time and allows them to concentrate on the areas of legal work that demand their expertise. They can also take on more clients and thus increase the firm's profits.

PARALEGAL EDUCATION

No law (as yet) requires paralegals to meet specific educational requirements. The paralegal will find, though, that the job market demands a certain amount of education and training. You will have difficulty finding employment as a paralegal without having completed a paralegal training course or without having obtained a degree in the field. Depending on your educational background and experience, you can spend anywhere from several months to several years obtaining a paralegal certificate or a degree.

Educational Options

Educational options for paralegals include certificate programs and degree programs. These programs are available through colleges and universities, community colleges, business schools, and trade schools.

Certificate Programs. Many paralegals choose the certificate program. Depending on the student's educational background, certificate programs can take up to eighteen months to complete. A student who already has a bachelor's degree can attend a program offered through a college or university. Normally, this type of program takes one year to complete. The certificate that is awarded to the student who successfully completes this type of program is referred to as a **postbaccalaureate certificate,** or postgraduate certificate.

Another option is to attend a certificate program offered by a private, for-profit business school, trade school, or college. Typically, this type of program requires a high school diploma for admission. The length of time to complete such a program ranges from three to eighteen months. After the program is completed, the student receives a **paralegal certificate.**

POSTBACCALAUREATE CERTIFICATE
A postgraduate certificate awarded by a college or university to an individual who, having already completed a bachelor's degree program, successfully completes a paralegal program of study.

PARALEGAL CERTIFICATE
A certificate awarded to an individual with a high school diploma or its equivalent who has successfully completed a paralegal program of study at a private, for-profit business school or trade school.

Degree Programs. Degree options include an associate's degree or a bachelor's degree. The **associate's degree** is a two-year degree, which normally is obtained from a two-year community college. The degree requirements are typically split evenly between general education courses (such as English, math, science, history, and social sciences) and law courses. A total of approximately 60 semester hours is required to complete an associate's degree.

A **bachelor's degree** requires the completion of about 120 semester hours. From 50 to 60 of these hours are spent in general education courses similar to those required for the associate's degree. In addition, students take courses in their major area—legal-assistant studies—and often select a minor field. Minors that complement a legal-assistant major include computer-information systems, business administration, communications, and public administration. These minors are helpful because they provide paralegals with useful skills and information relating to computer technology, business firms, and government agencies. Certain minors, particularly minors in environmental studies and computer-information systems, help to boost the legal assistant's marketability in today's job market, which increasingly requires knowledge and skills in these areas. Additionally, paralegals who combine a bachelor's degree in a field such as nursing with a paralegal certificate are highly sought after.

ASSOCIATE'S DEGREE
An academic degree signifying the completion of a two-year course of study, normally at a community college

BACHELOR'S DEGREE
An academic degree signifying the completion of a four-year course of study at a college or university.

Curriculum—A Procedural Focus

A legal assistant's education includes the study of both substantive law and procedural law. **Substantive law** includes all laws that define, describe, regulate, and create legal rights and obligations. For example, a law prohibiting employment discrimination on the basis of age falls into the category of substantive law. **Procedural law** establishes the methods of enforcing the rights established by substantive law. Questions about what documents need to be filed to begin a lawsuit, when the documents should be filed,

SUBSTANTIVE LAW
Law that defines the rights and duties of individuals with respect to each other, as opposed to procedural law, which defines the manner in which these rights and duties may be enforced.

PROCEDURAL LAW
Rules that define the manner in which the rights and duties of individuals may be enforced.

which court will hear the case, which witnesses will be called, and so on are all questions of procedural law. In brief, substantive law defines our legal rights and obligations; procedural law specifies what methods, or procedures, must be employed to enforce those rights and obligations.

Although paralegal students study both substantive law and procedural law, the emphasis is on procedural law. Law students, in contrast, focus mostly on substantive law. A law student might, for example, take a semester-long course in bankruptcy law. During that semester, the law student would study closely the substantive law governing bankruptcy—federal bankruptcy laws and court decisions interpreting those laws. A paralegal student might also take a semester-long course in bankruptcy. The paralegal student would study the general rules relating to bankruptcy, but the emphasis would be on bankruptcy forms and procedures. For example, the paralegal would learn which forms should be used for which types of bankruptcy proceedings, how to draft those forms, when the forms should be submitted to the bankruptcy court, and generally what procedures apply to specific types of bankruptcy actions.

The reason for the difference in the education of attorneys and paralegals has to do with their professional work. Attorneys are taught to analyze and solve legal problems so that they can advise clients on substantive legal matters. Legal assistants, in contrast, are trained in procedures so that they can assist in implementing attorneys' solutions to legal problems.

The ABA's Role in Paralegal Education

The ABA has played an active role in paralegal educational programs since the early 1970s. By 1973, the ABA had drafted and formally adopted a set of educational standards for paralegal training programs. Programs that meet these standards and that are approved by the ABA are usually referred to as **ABA-approved programs.** Today, the ABA approval commission consists of members of the ABA as well as representatives from NALA, NFPA, and the American Association for Paralegal Education, an association formed by paralegal educators and educational institutions. Of the paralegal education programs in existence today (over 650), the ABA has approved about 150. Paralegal schools are not required to be ABA-approved. ABA approval is a voluntary process that gives extra credentials to those schools that successfully apply for it.

ABA-Approved Program
A legal or paralegal educational program that satisfies the standards for paralegal training set forth by the American Bar Association.

Certification

Certification involves recognition by a private professional group or a state agency that an individual has met specified standards of proficiency. Note that certification, as used here, is not the same as receiving a paralegal certificate. A paralegal certificate means that the paralegal has successfully completed a specific course of studies. A *certified paralegal,* in contrast, is one who has demonstrated his or her knowledge and competence in the field by taking and passing an examination administered by a private professional group or a state agency.

Certification
Formal recognition by a private group or a state agency that an individual has satisfied the group's standards of proficiency, knowledge, and competence; ordinarily accomplished through the taking of an examination.

Certified Legal Assistant (CLA)
A legal assistant whose legal competency has been certified by the National Association of Legal Assistants (NALA) following an examination that tests the legal assistant's knowledge and skills.

NALA Certification. A certification program for paralegals offered by NALA is called the **Certified Legal Assistant (CLA)** Certification Program.

THE LEGAL TEAM AT WORK

Paralegal Education and the Concept of Teamwork

Throughout this book, you will encounter such terms and phrases as *teamwork, team effort*, and *team player.* Additionally, in a number of chapters, you will see features, such as this one, that emphasize the teamwork approach to legal representation. Law-office professionals have always worked as a team in the sense that the attorneys and support personnel all worked on behalf of clients. Today's law firms, however, increasingly recognize that effective teamwork means more than simply a joint effort. It also means allocating the workload in such a way that the expertise of the attorney, the paralegal, and others on the team is used *effectively.*

If an attorney delegated only secretarial tasks to his or her paralegal, that paralegal's training and skills would be underutilized. Similarly, if an attorney drafted routine legal documents rather than delegating the work to a paralegal capable of doing that work, the attorney would not be effectively using his or her own time. In the team approach to legal representation, the paralegal assists with the procedural aspects of a case while the attorney concentrates on those tasks that require an extensive knowledge of substantive law (or that can be undertaken legally only by an attorney).

For example, when a client goes to a law firm for advice on whether or how to incorporate a business, the attorney advises the client on the advantages and disadvantages of incorporation in view of the client's particular business situation, lets the client know what the attorney's assistance will cost, and so on. If the client decides to incorporate, the paralegal will assist in drafting the necessary documents, filing the documents with the relevant state office, and carrying out other tasks associated with the incorporation process. The lawyer and the legal assistant thus combine their efforts to function as a legal team.

Paralegals who wish to become certified by NALA may apply to take the CLA exam. The CLA exam provides recognition of the legal assistant's abilities and competence. This voluntary, comprehensive, two-day exam is given three times a year. The exam covers basic areas, such as communication skills (verbal and written), judgment and analytical skills, ethics, and human relations, as well as legal research and legal terminology. It also covers substantive and procedural law. Each person taking the exam must pass a section on the U.S. legal system, as well as four other areas of substantive law. The legal assistant can choose from a list of eight sections: litigation, estate planning and probate, real estate, criminal law, bankruptcy, contracts, business organizations, and administrative law.

In addition to the CLA exam, NALA offers exams for those who wish to become certified by NALA as specialists in certain areas of practice. To become a **Certified Legal Assistant Specialist (CLAS)**, a legal assistant must demonstrate special competence in a particular field. Specialty exams are offered in the following areas: bankruptcy, civil litigation, probate and estate planning, corporate and business law, criminal law and procedure, and real estate. Appendix J offers further information on NALA certification procedures and requirements.

CERTIFIED LEGAL ASSISTANT SPECIALIST (CLAS)
A legal assistant whose competency in a legal specialty has been certified by the National Association of Legal Assistants (NALA) following an examination of the legal assistant's knowledge and skills in the specialty area.

Note that certification as a CLA or a CLAS is not required to work as a paralegal. The CLA and CLAS exams are voluntary exams that give extra credentials to those who take and pass them.

State Certification. Many states are now considering the development of state-administered or statewide voluntary certification programs, and some states are beginning to implement such programs. In 1994, for example, the Texas Bar Association Board of Legal Specialization established a voluntary certification program that permits paralegals in Texas to become certified as specialists in the following three areas: civil-trial law, personal-injury law, and family law. To become certified paralegal specialists in these areas, paralegals must meet minimum standards for certification. These standards and further information on the Texas certification program are included in Appendix K at the end of this book.

In July 1994, the California Alliance of Paralegal Associations (CAPA) and NALA formally agreed to develop and administer a voluntary statewide certification program for paralegals in California. Under the 1995 pilot-tested program, California paralegals may become certified in several specialty areas, including the following: civil litigation, corporate law, real-estate law, probate and estate-planning law, and environmental law. The CAPA will work closely with NALA in implementing the program, and to qualify for the California certification examination, a paralegal must be certified by NALA as a CLA. Other states are also implementing statewide voluntary certification programs. The Louisiana State Paralegal Association, for example, developed a voluntary certification program for paralegals in that state.

PARALEGAL SKILLS

Paralegals need and use a variety of skills on the job. Depending on your personality traits, some skills will be easier than others for you to learn. For example, if you tend to be an organized person, you will have little difficulty in acquiring and applying the organizational skills required of the paralegal. Throughout this book, you will read in detail about the specific skills that you will need in your work as a paralegal. Here, we describe the general types of skills that paralegal work requires.

Organizational Skills

Being a well-organized person is a plus for a legal assistant. Law offices are busy places. There are many phone calls to be answered and returned, witnesses to get to court and on the witness stand on time, documents to be filed, and checklists and procedures to be followed. If you are able to organize files, create procedures and checklists, and keep things running smoothly, you will be doing a great service to the legal team and to clients.

If organization comes naturally to you, you are ahead of the game. If not, now is the time to learn and practice organizational skills. You will find plenty of opportunities to do this as a paralegal student—by organizing your notebooks, devising an efficient tracking system for homework assignments, creating a study or work schedule and following it, and so on. Other suggestions

DEVELOPING PARALEGAL SKILLS

Preparing for the CLA Exam

Rita Barron received her postbaccalaureate paralegal certificate over a year ago. She has been working as a legal assistant since graduation. Rita plans to take the Certified Legal Assistant (CLA) exam in four months and has decided to talk to Jill Sanderson, a CLA who works in the same office as Rita, about the exam. Rita wants to ask Jill if she has any suggestions on how Rita could best prepare for it.

Rita arranges to have lunch with Jill the next day. Rita asks Jill how she prepared for the CLA exam. "Well," says Jill, "I formed a study group with several other paralegals who were preparing for the exam. It was great. We divided up the work among ourselves. We met once a week, and each member of the group shared with the other members his or her assignment for that week. For example, I remember that one week, I had to prepare a thorough outline of all of the procedures involved in a real-estate closing. I made copies of the outline for everyone in the group. Our joint efforts paid off: we all passed the exam with flying colors."

FORMING A STUDY GROUP

Inspired by Jill's study-group approach, Rita contacted several former classmates who were also planning to take the exam. They agreed to form a study group and then devised a plan for dividing among themselves the substantive-law subjects, such as bankruptcy law and real-estate law, that they had to cover. Each member was to prepare an outline on one of the subjects for the others. The group would review and discuss the outlines the following week, when they met. They would also ask each other questions and take some practice tests.

Rita brought copies of her outline of bankruptcy law to the next meeting, passed them out to the other members, and received their outlines in return. She was disappointed to see that two of the group's five members, Leslie and Eric, had not put in much time or effort.

EVALUATING THE STUDY GROUP

On her way home, Rita reevaluates the study group. She knows that she is committed to taking and passing the CLA exam, but she feels that not all of the other members of the study group are as serious about it as she is. She decides to talk to Jill again.

When Rita mentions the problem to Jill, Jill says, "You know, I should have warned you about this kind of problem. A study group can be great, but unless everybody knows exactly what they are supposed to do and puts in the effort, it won't work. You need to make sure that assignments are clear. At the end of each meeting, each person should clearly state, in his or her own words, what exactly that person will work on during the week. If you realize that you've got weak study-group members, drop out of the group. Otherwise, you'll end up teaching them more than they teach you. Unless you have a good study group, you might try another alternative: pay the money and take a professional review course. If you don't want to spend the money on a review course, you could try a self-study course, using your own notes or a CLA review book."

for organizing your time and work, both as a student and as a paralegal on the job, are included in Appendix A at the end of this book.

You will also find in any university or public library an abundance of books that offer guidelines on how to organize efficiently your work, your use of time, and your life generally.

Analytical Skills

Legal assistants also need analytical skills, especially when engaging in tasks relating to trials, legal investigations, legal research and writing, and certain other assignments. Analysis is usually defined as the separation of a whole into its parts. Legal professionals need to be able to take complex theories and fact patterns and break them down into smaller, more easily understandable components. As you will read in Chapters 17 and 18, an important aspect of legal research and writing involves analysis. Analysis is used to decipher the meaning of the law as set forth in the decisions handed down by the courts and in statutes passed by legislatures.

Analysis also involves, to some extent, the ability to synthesize—or put together—facts and legal concepts in such a way that they form a single unit, or "picture." For example, if you are conducting a legal investigation, you will uncover numerous facts and opinions about a certain event, such as an automobile accident. You will learn how the client believed the accident occurred, how any available witnesses described it, and what facts are indicated or implied by medical records or police reports. As a paralegal, you will want to discern how the facts and opinions you have gathered fit together into patterns or sequences. Further, you will want to discern how the facts fit into the legal strategy that your supervising attorney plans to pursue.

Computer Skills

In today's law office, computer skills are essential. At a minimum, you should have experience with word processing—generating and revising documents using a computer. Although computers have reduced the need for excellent typing skills, the ability to type rapidly and accurately is still a plus for the legal assistant. If you work for a small law firm, as many entry-level paralegals do, you will probably not have much secretarial or clerical assistance. Even if you work for a larger firm and have such assistance, you will still draft and revise numerous documents yourself.

Advances in computer technology continue to affect dramatically how business firms, including law firms, conduct their operations. Large law firms today are using sophisticated computer equipment and software to handle tasks ranging from document control to client billing procedures. Although smaller law firms are not always so extensively computerized, increasingly they are also investing in computer systems and legal software to reduce the time costs involved in legal work and to compete with larger firms. In Chapter 16, you will read in greater detail about computers and how they are used in the legal profession. Many experienced paralegals say that if they were paralegal students today, they would devote more time to studying computer technology and learning computer skills.

Interpersonal Skills

The ability to communicate and interact effectively with other people is an important asset for the paralegal. Paralegals work closely with their supervising attorneys, and the ability to cultivate a positive working relationship helps to get the work done more efficiently. Paralegals also work with legal secretaries and other support staff in the law office, with attorneys and paralegals from other firms, with court personnel, and with numerous other people. Paralegals frequently interview clients and witnesses. As you will read in Chapter 14, if you can relate well to the person whom you are interviewing, your chances of obtaining useful information from that person are increased.

There may be times when you will have to deal with clients who are experiencing difficulties in their lives, such as divorce or the death of a loved one. These people will need to be handled with sensitivity, tact, understanding, and courtesy. There will also be times when you will have to deal with people in your office who are under a great deal of stress or who for some other reason are demanding and less than courteous to you. You will need to know how to respond to these people in ways that promote positive working relationships. You will read more about these important "people skills" in Chapter 5 and other chapters in this text.

Communication Skills

Good communication skills are critical when working in the legal area. In fact, it is sometimes said that the legal profession is a "communications profession" because effective legal representation depends to a great extent on how well a legal professional can communicate with clients, witnesses, court judges and juries, opposing attorneys, and others. Poor communication can damage a case, destroy a client relationship, and harm the legal professional's reputation. Good communication, in contrast, wins cases, clients, and sometimes promotions.

Communication skills include reading and analytical skills, speaking skills, listening skills, and writing skills. We look briefly at each of these skills here.

Reading Skills. Reading skills involve more than just being able to decipher the meaning of written letters and words. Reading skills also involve understanding the *meaning* of a sentence, paragraph, section, or page. As a legal professional, you will need to be able to read and understand many different types of written materials, including statutes and court decisions. You will therefore need to become familiar with legal terminology and concepts so that you understand the meaning of these legal writings. You will also need to develop the ability to read documents *carefully* so that you do not miss important distinctions—such as the difference in meaning that can result from the use of "and" instead of "or."

Oral Communication. Paralegals must also be able to speak well. In addition to using good grammar, legal assistants need to be precise and clear in communicating ideas or facts to others. For example, when you discuss facts

DEVELOPING PARALEGAL SKILLS

Working under the Supervision of a Lawyer

Carl Coates works as a legal assistant. Today, his supervising attorney, Geraldine Mallon, has asked him to come into her office to talk about an offer to purchase real estate that she wants him to prepare. The purchase offer is to be prepared for a client named Joseph Morgenstern. Geraldine currently handles all of the legal matters for Morgenstern's business. Now that he is about to purchase his dream home, Morgenstern wants the contract, if accepted, by the seller, to be "water tight."

THE ASSIGNMENT

Carl enters Geraldine's office. She asks him to have a seat at the nearby conference table and hands him a file. It contains some handwritten notes, a copy of a real-estate listing describing the property, and a standard purchase-offer form. They review the details of the offer that Morgenstern wants to make on the house. Carl indicates that although he studied real-estate transactions as part of his paralegal program, he has had no on-the-job experience with them.

Geraldine instructs him carefully in the details of the offer. Morgenstern wants to offer $250,000 for the house. He wants to put down $10,000 as *earnest money* (a deposit toward the purchase price of real estate to indicate that the offer is made seriously). This money will go toward his down payment at the *closing* (the final step in the purchase and sale of real estate). He also wants to specify in his offer that the kitchen appliances, all of the light fixtures, including the dining room chandelier, and all of the window treatments will be included in the sale of the home. The sale would be conditioned on two events: First, the house must pass a building inspection to Morgenstern's satisfaction. Second, Morgenstern must be able to obtain financing from a lending institution for the purchase.

PREPARING THE FIRST DRAFT OF THE PURCHASE OFFER

Geraldine then instructs Carl to use the purchase-offer form that is on one of the diskettes in the diskette "forms file"—model forms that can be loaded

learned in an investigation with your supervising attorney, your oral report must communicate exactly what you found, or it could mislead the attorney. A miscommunication in this context could have serious consequences if it led the attorney to take an action detrimental to the client's interests. Oral communication also has a nonverbal dimension—that is, we communicate our thoughts and feelings through gestures, facial expressions, and other "body language" as well as through words. You will read more about both verbal and nonverbal forms of communication in Chapter 5.

Listening Skills. Good listening skills are extremely important in the context of paralegal work. Paralegals must follow instructions meticulously. To understand the instructions that you receive, you must listen carefully. Asking follow-up questions will help you to clarify anything that you do not understand. Also, repeating the instructions will not only ensure that you

DEVELOPING PARALEGAL SKILLS, Continued

onto the computer and modified as necessary to customize them for a particular client's preferences. Geraldine feels that it will adequately protect Morgenstern's interests. Carl is to prepare the offer by copying the form from the diskette onto his computer's hard drive and then filling in all of the information that they have discussed, as well as the property description and any other information that the form requires. Carl understands the assignment and goes to his office to prepare the offer.

He begins by keying into the computerized form the real-estate listing, which gives a legal description of the property. He inserts the legal description in the appropriate section of the offer. He continues to the next section and inserts the amount being offered, the amount of earnest money to be deposited, and the two conditions. Carl continues to type in information until the purchase offer is completed.

REVIEWING AND REVISING THE PURCHASE OFFER

Carl then takes the offer to Geraldine for her review. She asks him to sit down, and they review the offer together. Carl has prepared it correctly, and Geraldine compliments him on his accurate work. While Carl is in Geraldine's office, Morgenstern calls. He tells Geraldine that he also wants to offer to buy the bar stools in the kitchen, which match the countertop perfectly. He will offer the seller $700 for the bar stools. Carl will now have to revise the offer to reflect this change.

Carl returns to his office to make the changes on the form, which is easy to do on the computer. He simply opens the document and inserts Morgenstern's offer to buy the bar stools in the appropriate place on the form. Carl prints out a copy of the revised offer and gives it to Geraldine for her review. She approves Carl's insertion and asks him to call Morgenstern to let him know that the offer is ready for his signature.

Carl is pleased with his work. He knows that the next time he assists Geraldine in drafting an offer to purchase real estate, he will be more confident in his ability to draft the offer accurately, and Geraldine will have to spend less of her time instructing him in the details.

understand them but also give the attorney a chance to add anything that he or she may have forgotten to tell you initially. Listening skills are particularly important in the interviewing context. In Chapters 14 and 15, you will read in greater detail about different types of listening skills and techniques that will help you conduct effective interviews with clients or witnesses.

Writing Skills. Finally, it is important for paralegals to have excellent writing skills. Legal assistants draft letters, memoranda, and a variety of legal documents. Letters to clients, witnesses, court clerks, and others must be clear and well organized and must follow the rules of grammar and punctuation. Legal documents must also be free of errors. Lawyers are generally scrupulously attentive to detail in their work, and they expect legal assistants to be equally so. Remember, you represent your supervising attorney when you write. You will learn more about writing skills in Chapter 18.

FEATURED GUEST: WENDY B. EDSON

Ten Tips for Effective Communication

Biographical Note

Wendy B. Edson received her master's degree in library science (M.L.S.) from the University of Rhode Island and served as law librarian at the Buffalo, New York, firm of Phillips, Lytle, Hitchcock, Blaine and Huber. In 1978, she joined the legal-assistant faculty at Hilbert College, in Hamburg, New York, and helped to develop an ABA-approved bachelor's program in 1992. She teaches paralegalism and legal ethics, legal research, law and literature, and volunteerism. She also developed and coordinates the internship program. Edson reviews and publishes on the topics of paralegal education, legal research, and community service. She has lectured to legal professionals on legal research, teaching skills, internships, and community service.

Words! They are the building blocks of human communication. How we deliver and receive words can inspire or discourage, fascinate or repel. But how do we become skilled at maneuvering the *two-way* traffic of interpersonal communication? As in driving, we need to follow the "rules of the road." The rules of the road in regard to communication traffic are embodied in the following ten tips.

1 Establish Communication Equality. Communication equality does not require that individuals hold equal status in an office or organization but requires that each party believe in *equal rights* to speak and listen. Observe someone whom you consider to be a good communicator. You will note that he or she demonstrates equality by actively listening and responding appropriately to whoever is speaking. Problems in the employment context often reflect communication ailments rooted in inequality. A firm belief in communication equality, despite job titles, will help to create a cooperative, productive working environment.

2 Plan for Time and Space. Effective communication requires *time.* Imagine your reaction to a request to work overtime if your supervising attorney took thirty seconds to order you to do the work versus taking two minutes to explain the reason for the request and listening to your response. In the first situation, the attorney saved one and a half minutes but scored "zero" in terms of communication skills. In today's rushed world, it is easy to overlook the importance of communication skills in morale building and creating a cooperative, efficient work force.

Effective communicators are aware of how the physical environment in which a conversation takes place can affect the communication process. Communication is always enhanced when the parties have reasonable privacy and are not continually interrupted. Another important factor is physical comfort. Choosing an inappropriate time and place for communication denies the importance of the matters being discussed and may send the wrong messages to both the speaker and the listener.

3 Set the Agenda. Skilled communicators prepare an *agenda*—whether written or mental—of matters to be discussed in order of their priority. Frequently, both parties bring their respective agendas to a discussion, which means that priorities may need to be negotiated. A subordinate who brings up the topic of desired vacation time when the supervisor is preoccupied with a major project clearly demonstrates that his or her priorities are different from those of the supervisor.

Successful communication requires that the parties first negotiate a *common agenda*—that is, determine jointly the agenda for a particular discussion or meeting and what topics should take priority. Then, the topics can be dealt with one by one, in terms of their relative importance, to the satisfaction of both parties. *Agenda awareness* prevents parties from jumping from topic to topic without successfully resolving anything.

4 Fine-tune Your Speaking Skills. Observe an individual whom you consider to be a good speaker, whether before a group of persons or on a one-on-one basis. What skills does that individual demonstrate? Effective speakers work hard to express thoughts clearly; sometimes, they refer to notes or lists to refresh their memories. Skilled speakers also try to

FEATURED GUEST, Continued

communicate accurately and to talk about matters that they know will interest their listeners. They cultivate *communication empathy*—the sincere effort to put themselves in their listener's shoes. As you speak to others, pause occasionally and ask yourself: "Would I enjoy listening to what I am saying and how I am saying it?"

5 Cultivate Listening Skills. Listening is not just refraining from speaking while another person is talking but an *active* process—the other half of the communication partnership. An active listener does not interrupt the speaker. If you sense that the speaker is engaging in a monologue, responsive behavior—including body language, attentiveness, and appropriate remarks—can steer the conversation back to a dialogue without cutting off the speaker.

An active listener realizes that listening is an investment in effective communication. By truly responding to what is being said, rather than regarding listening time as insignificant or time to plan his or her own remarks, the skilled listener establishes a bond of trust with the speaker. Active listeners avoid preconceived ideas about topics being discussed and assume that they do not know all the answers.

6 Watch for Body Language. Body language is nonverbal communication that reflects our emotional state. Physical positions, such as leaning forward or away from the speaker while listening, can reinforce or negate our spoken responses. Body attitudes, whether relaxed (comfortable posture, leaning forward, uncrossed arms and legs, relaxed neck and shoulders) or tense (stiff posture, backing away, crossed arms and legs, stiff neck and shoulders) vividly illustrate our response before we utter a word. Eye contact is one of the most important tools in the body-language toolkit for communication. Interviewers, social workers, and police officers—as well as most other people—commonly interpret steady and responsive eye contact to mean sincerity on the part of the speaker or listener.

7 Put Note Taking in Perspective. Overinvolvement in note taking detracts from the communication process because opportunities to listen actively, speak responsively, and be sensitive to body language are reduced. The speaker may ramble while the listener records the ramblings in extensive notes.

When it is necessary to take notes, it is helpful to establish some rapport with the speaker or listener before launching the note-taking process. Alternatively, follow-up notes can be a workable solution to the problem. The note taker can devote the interview time to communication and, after the interview, record his or her general impressions of the interview and identify specific issues that need to be discussed further.

8 Recognize the Role of Criticism. *Constructive criticism* focuses on specific actions or behaviors rather than personalities. It is objective rather than subjective. Criticism that is stated calmly and objectively ("There are not enough measurements on the Ferris scale drawing") is much more palatable for the person being criticized than is criticism in the form of a personal attack ("You did a terrible job"). By placing emphasis on actions instead of personalities, the parties can more easily work toward a satisfactory solution. If both the critic and the person being criticized can remain calm and can separate actions from personalities, then criticism will usually produce the desired result and *mutual* satisfaction.

"EYE CONTACT IS ONE OF THE MOST IMPORTANT TOOLS IN THE BODY-LANGUAGE TOOLKIT FOR COMMUNICATION."

9 Aim for Satisfactory Closure. Closure means "wrapping up" the communication. Successful communicators know that handling closure properly can leave a participant with a good feeling even if the solution was not exactly what he or she initially desired. Summarizing the discussion and checking for agreement or a need for further discussion will encourage all participants to follow the tenth tip.

10 Commit to Communicate. Excellent speakers and listeners have positive, self-confident attitudes that problems can be solved if the "rules of the road" are followed. Skilled communicators cultivate open minds, self-knowledge, and the ability to tolerate differences and empathize with others. They are committed to exercising their rights and responsibilities as speakers and listeners in the communication process.

PERSONAL ATTRIBUTES OF THE PROFESSIONAL PARALEGAL

There are many different attributes that help paralegals succeed in their careers. The paralegal who is responsible, reliable, committed to hard work, objective, ethical, and generally considerate of others will have an easy time meeting the challenges presented by his or her work. These attributes define an individual's personality and character, and they are also important in paralegal practice.

Responsibility and Reliability

The paralegal must be responsible and reliable. The practice of law involves helping people with their legal problems. A paralegal's mistake, such as missing a deadline for filing a certain document with the court, could cause a client to lose his or her legal rights (and possibly cause a lawsuit to be brought against the attorney).

Attorneys frequently mention how they *rely* on their paralegals to perform certain tasks for them. The responsible paralegal is reliable. He or she completes tasks accurately and on time. Paralegals often mention how important trust is to efficient teamwork in the legal office. Each team member must be able to trust the other members of the legal team to do their share of the work—or the team effort fails.

Commitment

Being committed to your work and the goals of the legal team is important, too. Many tasks can take hours, days, weeks, or even months to perform, and you must be committed to giving your best effort until the job is completed. Commitment to your work involves persistence.

For example, if you are trying to track down heirs to a will and you are having difficulty locating them, you must try everything possible to find them before you give up the search. You will need to review county birth and marriage records to try to locate them through their siblings and spouses. If that does not work, you will need to contact state agencies, such as the motor vehicle department, to try to obtain addresses from their driver's licenses or vehicle-registration records. You might also have to advertise in newspapers. Being diligent in your search means that you keep going until you have exhausted virtually every possible information source.

Objectivity

Another personal attribute of professional behavior is objectivity. To the extent that personal emotions or biases interfere with the goal of serving the client's interest, the paralegal must set these emotions or biases aside. For example, your sympathy for a client's plight should not prevent you from acknowledging factual evidence that is harmful to the client's position.

Lawyers and paralegals sometimes find themselves working on behalf of clients whom, for one reason or another, they dislike or do not respect. You may dislike having to deal with one of your firm's overly aggressive business clients, for example, or with a criminal defendant charged with spousal abuse, which is extremely offensive to you. But these feelings should not affect the quality of the services rendered. The job of the attorney and the paralegal is to see that the client's interests are not harmed by their personal views or assumptions.

The Ability to Keep Confidences

One of the requirements of being a paralegal is the ability to keep client information confidential. The word *requirement* is used here because being able to keep confidences is not just a desirable attribute in a paralegal, but a mandatory one. As you will read in Chapters 3 and 4, attorneys are ethically and legally obligated to keep all information relating to the representation of a client strictly confidential unless the client consents to the disclosure of the information.[3] The attorney may share this information only with people who are also working on behalf of the client and who therefore need to know the information. Paralegals share in this duty imposed on all attorneys. If a paralegal reveals confidential client information to anyone outside the group working on the client's case, the lawyer (and the paralegal) may face legal consequences (including being sued by the client) if the client suffers harm as a result of the paralegal's actions.

Keeping client information confidential means that you, as a paralegal, cannot divulge such information even to your spouse, family members, or closest friends. You should not talk about a client's case in hallways, elevators, or other areas in which others may overhear your conversation. Keeping work-related information confidential is an important part of being a responsible and reliable paralegal.

Other Attributes

Other attributes of the professional paralegal include accuracy, efficiency, attentiveness to detail, discretion, diplomacy, and the ability to work under pressure. Each of these attributes is considered to be appropriate in a law office because it enhances the firm's ability to serve the client's needs most effectively.

When deadlines are nearing and the pace of office work becomes somewhat frantic, it may be difficult to meet the challenge of acting professionally. For example, you may have to complete a brief (a document filed with a court to support an attorney's argument) by noon. It is 11 A.M., and you still have a considerable portion of the brief to complete. When the pressure is on, it is important to remain calm and focus on completing your task quickly and accurately to ensure quality work.

THE FUTURE OF THE PROFESSION

Since its beginnings over twenty-five years ago, the paralegal profession has been in a state of constant change, and by all indications, it will continue to undergo change during the 1990s and beyond. Legal services are costly, and

3. Exceptions to the confidentiality rule are made in certain circumstances, as will be discussed in Chapter 4.

PARALEGAL PROFILE Bankruptcy Specialist

GARY BRYER, a paralegal who specializes in the area of bankruptcy, works for the large Philadelphia law firm of Dechert, Price & Rhoads. Bryer's educational background includes two years of college at the Philadelphia Community College, where he studied journalism. He received his paralegal certificate from the Philadelphia Institute for Paralegal Training in May 1988. Since then, Bryer has been employed by several law firms, working solely in the area of bankruptcy and creditors' rights. Bryer is an active participant in the Philadelphia Association of Paralegals (PAP). In 1992, he was elected to the PAP's board of directors, and he has chaired or co-chaired PAP committees on bankruptcy and banking. He has taught paralegal classes (on a part-time basis) for local paralegal programs. He has also authored a series of articles on consumer bankruptcy and six articles exploring the topic of paralegal job searching.

What do you like best about your work?

"The thing I like best is drafting documents and pleadings. I also enjoy investigative work and training other paralegals. The field of bankruptcy is very fast paced, detailed, and focused on deadlines. Bankruptcy work is team oriented, although each team member enjoys a great deal of autonomy as well. I relish both the pressure and the independence."

What is the greatest challenge that you face in your area of work?

"The most challenging aspect of my job is coordinating a project from start to finish. Coordinating a project includes interacting with in-house services, as well as contracting with outside services. Just filing an ordinary complaint or motion with the court includes coordinating the efforts of numerous individuals—the responsible attorney and other attorneys working on the case, secretaries, document copiers, mail clerks, and delivery or courier services. Each project requires significant oversight. It can be difficult to work for eight to ten attorneys, each of whom has a separate agenda, and still meet deadlines."

What advice do you have for would-be paralegals in your area of work?

"My advice for those paralegals is to have a clear understanding that they support attorneys in the practice of law. They also need to know that paralegal work is important. Paralegals exist because they can provide substantive legal services at a lower cost than attorneys' services. Paralegals need to consciously determine what types of tasks they might enjoy day in and day out. There are many paralegals who don't like the fast-paced and pressured life of a bankruptcy paralegal. Some paralegals prefer transactional work, such as filling in forms or preparing tax returns. The area of law in which you work should reflect your personality and temperament. An entry-level position allows you the time to get to know the everyday basic duties, and later there will be many opportunities to take on further responsibilities. A paralegal can never be too completely prepared for a task. Finally, paralegals must learn to delegate and accept responsibility."

> **"THE AREA OF LAW IN WHICH YOU WORK SHOULD REFLECT YOUR PERSONALITY AND TEMPERAMENT."**

What are some tips for success as a paralegal in your area of work?

"A tip for success as a bankruptcy paralegal would be to learn the rules of the court system with which you work and keep abreast of the law. Another tip for success is to become actively involved in your field. Paralegals who are professionally active and involved eventually move into the better-paying and more responsible positions. Another tip is to complete every task that you work on efficiently and conscientiously—no matter how mundane the task may be. Most importantly, if you are flexible, thorough, and accommodating, you will be a welcome addition to any department or firm."

TODAY'S PROFESSIONAL PARALEGAL

A Winning Combination

Steven Latham is a legal assistant in the law offices of Melinda T. Oakwood. Melinda is a sole practitioner, which means that she owns her practice and practices alone. She shares office space with several other attorneys in an office building, however. Her practice is a general law practice, and she handles a variety of legal matters, including divorces, wills, real-estate matters, and personal-injury lawsuits.

Steven has worked for Melinda for seven years; it was his first job after graduating from a legal-assistant program. He is given a great deal of responsibility because he has shown Melinda that he is responsible and reliable in handling the work that she assigns to him. His work is always turned in on time, and it is always accurate.

LEARNING ON THE JOB

If Steven has questions, he always asks Melinda. When Steven first started working for Melinda, she told him that the only "stupid question" was the one that was not asked. She also told him that he should spend more time on assignments to be sure that they were thoroughly and accurately performed rather than rushing through projects and increasing the risk of inaccuracies. "It does me no good to spend time reviewing work that I have to give back to you to correct. I'd rather have it right the first time," Melinda told him. Steven had a strong sense of commitment, so he always saw a project through, even if it seemed to take forever.

Steven was also very lucky to have a supervising attorney who liked to teach him how to perform new assignments. Melinda had been a teacher for ten years before she went to law school. When Steven had a new type of document to prepare, for example, Melinda would give him a sample of the document and very good instructions. When Steven had to prepare the same document for a different case, Melinda would explain the differences between the first and second assignments and why the differences mattered, from a legal perspective.

IMPROVING PARALEGAL SKILLS

Melinda was also lucky to have Steven as her paralegal. He had many personal attributes that helped him on the job. He learned quickly and performed his work competently and efficiently. He also paid great attention to detail, unlike the paralegal that Melinda had had before Steven, who would send out letters and fail to include the documents that should have accompanied the letters. Melinda could also always count on Steven to keep client information confidential. That was especially important in the small town in which they lived and worked.

Steven already had good computer, organizational, and analytical skills when Melinda hired him. He did need to work at improving his communication skills, however, particularly his listening skills. Over time, he learned to listen carefully to Melinda's instructions and directions and to question her when he was not exactly certain of them.

THE RESULT: A WINNING LEGAL TEAM

Eventually, Melinda and Steven developed a solid working relationship. It took time for Steven to develop some of the skills that he needed, but Melinda was patient and a good teacher. It also took time to develop a trusting relationship in which Melinda could confidently delegate significant assignments to Steven, knowing that he would complete them accurately and on time. Now Steven and Melinda work efficiently and productively together. They like and rely on each other and enjoy their work. Theirs is a winning combination of talents and skills.

the public is demanding access to more affordable legal services. This means that the role of the paralegal in delivering lower-cost legal services will most likely continue to expand. According to the U.S. Department of Labor's Bureau of Labor Statistics, paralegal employment is expected to grow much faster than the average for all occupations through the year 2005.[4]

4. *Occupational Outlook Handbook*, 1994–95 ed. (Washington, D.C.: Government Printing Office, 1994), p. 232.

By the early 1990s, many state bar associations had created special sections for legal assistants. Admission to state bar associations added greater recognition to the contribution made by legal assistants to the legal profession. Paralegal associations, state bar associations, state legislatures, the American Bar Association, and other groups are now debating whether some or all paralegals should be licensed by the state to work as paralegals. You will read more about this pressing issue confronting the paralegal profession in Chapter 3.

In brief, the paralegal profession is a dynamic, changing, and growing field within the legal arena. Although legal assistants initially worked only in the law-firm context, today's job opportunities for paralegals include working for corporations, government agencies, and other organizations—as you will learn in the following chapter. Those who enter the profession today will find not only a variety of career options but also the opportunity to help chart the course that the profession will take in the future.

KEY TERMS AND CONCEPTS

ABA-approved program 10
affiliate 7
American Bar Association (ABA) 4
associate attorney 6
associate's degree 9
bachelor's degree 9
certification 10
Certified Legal Assistant (CLA) 10
Certified Legal Assistant Specialist (CLAS) 11
law clerk 6
legal assistant 4
National Association of Legal Assistants (NALA) 7
National Federation of Paralegal Associations (NFPA) 7
paralegal 4
paralegal certificate 9
postbaccalaureate certificate 9
procedural law 9
state bar association 7
substantive law 9

CHAPTER SUMMARY

1. The professional status of paralegals was first acknowledged by the American Bar Association in 1968. Since then, the paralegal profession has continued to grow, and it is now one of the fastest-growing occupations in the United States.

2. Many legal professionals use the terms *paralegal* and *legal assistant* interchangeably. A paralegal, or a legal assistant, can be defined as a person sufficiently trained in law and legal procedures to assist attorneys in the delivery of legal services to the public. Paralegal expertise may be attained through on-the-job experience or through paralegal training programs. Paralegals are not attorneys but attorneys' assistants. Attorneys supervise paralegal work and assume ultimate responsibility for it. Paralegals perform many of the tasks involved in legal representation that have traditionally been handled by attorneys. Certain tasks, however (such as giving legal advice, setting fees for legal services, and representing clients in court), can only be handled by attorneys.

3. Typical tasks performed by paralegals include drafting legal documents, calendaring and tracking important deadlines, assisting attorneys in trial preparations and at trial, interviewing clients and witnesses, organizing and maintaining client files, conducting legal investigations, and conducting legal research.

4. The first paralegals were legal secretaries who, through on-the-job experience, developed the skills and expertise now taught in paralegal training programs. The paralegal profession evolved rapidly because paralegals filled the growing need for lower-cost, permanent, and competent legal assistance.

5. The formation of paralegal associations was a significant step in the growth of the paralegal profession. By the early 1970s, numerous local paralegal organizations were in existence. By the mid-1970s, the National Federation of Paralegal Associations (NFPA) and the National Association of Legal Assistants (NALA)—the two leading national paralegal associations—had been formed. Paralegal professional associations provide a forum in which professional issues can be discussed, establish guidelines to regulate professional conduct, determine skill levels and educational requirements, and possibly establish or sponsor educational programs. Professional membership provides the following opportunities for paralegals: to meet and network with others in the profession, to receive publications issued by paralegal associations, to engage in continuing legal education, to participate in planning relating to current and future developments in the profession, and to indicate to potential employers an involvement in paralegal professional development.

6. Paralegal educational options include certificate programs and degree programs. A person who has a bachelor's degree can receive a postbaccalaureate certificate by completing a program offered by a college or university, which usually takes one year. Paralegal certificates can be obtained through programs of varying lengths, offered by business schools, trade schools, and other for-profit occupational training centers. Degree options include an associate's degree and a bachelor's degree. The curriculum in paralegal programs emphasizes procedural law, while the curriculum in law schools emphasizes substantive law. The training of paralegals and attorneys thus is complementary, which enhances the effectiveness of attorney-paralegal teamwork in legal representation.

7. The American Bar Association has played an active role in paralegal education programs since the early 1970s. Paralegal programs that meet standards established by the ABA (currently, about one-fourth of all paralegal programs) are called ABA-approved programs.

8. Certification involves recognition by a private professional group or a state agency that a person has met specified standards of proficiency. The National Association of Legal Assistants (NALA) has developed a certification program for paralegals. After meeting specified requirements (including passing an examination), a paralegal can become certified by NALA as a Certified Legal Assistant (CLA) or a Certified Legal Assistant Specialist (CLAS). The possibility of state certification programs is being discussed in most states. By 1994, the state of Texas had adopted a voluntary certification program, and the California Alliance of Paralegal Associations agreed with NALA to develop a voluntary statewide certification program for paralegals in California.

9. Paralegals need to have a variety of skills. It is especially important for paralegals to have good organizational, analytical, computer, interpersonal, and communication skills.

10. Certain personal attributes are also important in paralegal practice. These attributes include responsibility, reliability, commitment to hard work, objectivity, the ability to keep confidences, accuracy, efficiency, attentiveness to detail, discretion, diplomacy, and the ability to work under pressure.

QUESTIONS FOR REVIEW

1. When and by which organization was the paralegal profession first recognized as a profession?

2. What is a paralegal? What are some of the key elements in the ABA's definition of a legal assistant? Is there any difference between a paralegal and a legal assistant?

3. What kinds of tasks do paralegals perform?

4. Why did the paralegal profession evolve? What needs within the legal profession do paralegals meet?

5. Name the two largest national paralegal associations in the United States. When and why were they formed? What are the benefits of belonging to a paralegal association?

6. What type of educational programs and training are available to paralegals? Must a person meet specific educational requirements to work as a paralegal?

7. How does the paralegal's education and training differ from the education and training of an attorney? What is the particular expertise of the paralegal?

8. What does *certification* mean? What is a CLA? What is a CLAS?

9. List and describe the skills that are useful in paralegal practice. Do you have these skills?

10. List and describe some of the personal attributes of a professional paralegal. Do you feel that persons who do not have these attributes can cultivate them? If so, how?

ETHICAL QUESTIONS

1. Carla Seegen is an experienced legal assistant who is also a licensed realtor. She sold real estate for eight years before becoming a paralegal. Carla works in a small law firm and has recently been assigned to work for Mike McAllister, who is a new attorney and the son of one of the firm's founding partners, John McAllister. Mike is asked to handle a real-estate closing for the firm's biggest client. Mike is unfamiliar with the client's business. Furthermore, he studied property law only briefly in law school and has no experience in real-estate transactions. Carla soon learns of Mike's lack of knowledge and experience because he does not ask her to draft the appropriate documents and undertake the kinds of tasks that are necessary for the closing. Whenever she mentions these things to Mike, however, or offers to show him what must be done, Mike becomes annoyed. Carla likes her job and knows that if she continues to annoy Mike, she may be fired. At the same time, she is concerned about the client's welfare and legal protection. Should she talk to one of the partners about the problem? Should she discuss the issue with John McAllister, Mike's father? How would you handle the situation?

2. Paula Abrams works for a law firm in a small, midwestern community. Her husband works as a sales representative for Benedetto Home Stores, a large home-supply store in the community. One day, Sal Benedetto consults with Paula's supervising attorney about the possibility of entering bankruptcy proceedings. Apparently, Benedetto Home Stores is facing a financial crisis, and Sal sees bankruptcy as the only solution. Paula's husband, Joseph, has worked for Benedetto for ten years, earns a good income, and has a good benefits package. Their combined incomes support them, their three children, and Paula's mother. Paula wants to tell Joseph about the apparently impending bankruptcy of Benedetto Home Stores so that he can begin to look for another job as soon as possible. Paula knows that she has an ethical responsibility to keep this client information strictly confidential. Yet she also feels that she has an ethical responsibility to her family. Should Paula tell Joseph? What would you do if you were Paula?

PRACTICE QUESTIONS AND ASSIGNMENTS

1. Which of the following tasks might legal assistants do?

a. Draft legal documents.
b. Try cases in court.
c. Calendar important deadlines.
d. Give legal advice.
f. Set legal fees.
g. Interview clients and witnesses.
h. Perform legal investigations.

2. Refer to Appendix H and Appendix I at the end of this book and find the answers to the following questions:

a. What is the address and telephone number of the state bar association in your state?
b. Is there an affiliate of the National Association of Legal Assistants or the National Federation of Paralegal Associations in your city? Where is the nearest affiliate of either of these organizations located?
c. Are there any regional or local paralegal associations in your area? If so, what are their names, addresses, and phone numbers?

QUESTIONS FOR CRITICAL ANALYSIS

1. Samantha Black is a newly hired paralegal at the law firm of Howe & Howe. She has been asked by one of the partners in the firm to retrieve quickly from WESTLAW (a computerized legal-research service) a case decision handed down yesterday by the United States Supreme Court. Samantha was trained to use LEXIS, another computerized legal-research service, but she does not know how to use WESTLAW. Considering that the firm will be charged for on-line time, what should Samantha do?

2. Bob Remis, a paralegal at the law firm of Robinson & Randolph, has been given assignments by two attorneys. Bob cannot possibly complete both assignments within the alloted time frame. How can Bob best communicate this problem to the attorneys?

ROLE-PLAYING EXERCISES

1. Assume that in the scenario presented in Ethical Question 1, Carla Seegen decides to discuss her problem with Mike McAllister's father. One student should play the role of Carla trying to explain the problem she is having to John McAllister, Mike's father. Remember, she does not want to lose her job, and if she alienates John McAllister, she might do so. The student playing Carla's role will therefore need to be very tactful in her approach. The other student should play the role of John McAllister. He is an outgoing person who likes to control others, including his son, Mike. John McAllister played an aggressive role in Mike's education, urging Mike to continue his law studies even though Mike was not all that interested in a career in law. If time permits, reverse roles.

2. Role-play the interviewer and the job applicant in a situation in which a paralegal is applying for a first job. The student playing the role of the interviewer should ask the applicant the questions listed below. The person playing the role of the applicant should answer the questions as honestly and forthrightly as possible.

a. Why did you decide to become a paralegal?

b. If you had to name one paralegal task that you would enjoy more than any other, what would that task be?

c. What personal attributes or skills do you possess that you think will help you succeed as a paralegal?

d. Other than the training you received in your paralegal studies, do you have other experiences and training that will help you in your work as a paralegal?

PROJECTS

1. Write or call the National Association of Legal Assistants and the National Federation of Paralegal Associations (see Appendix H for the addresses and telephone numbers of these associations). See if they have affiliates in your area. Also, see if there are any state or local paralegal organizations in your area. Contact them for membership information. Do they accept student members?

2. Arrange an interview with an experienced paralegal, such as a graduate of your program or another paralegal that you may know. Ask the paralegal what he or she thinks are the most important skills and characteristics that paralegals should have.

ANNOTED SELECTED READINGS

BERNARDO, BARBARA. *Paralegal: An Insider's Guide to One of the Fastest-Growing Occupations of the 1990s.* 2d ed. Princeton, N.J.: Peterson's Guides, 1993. An outstanding introduction to the paralegal profession and overview of what legal assistants do.

EDWARDS, IVANA. "Insights from Litigation Attorneys." *Legal Assistant Today,* September/October 1993. An article consisting of interviews with attorneys from various parts of the country on the qualities and skills they look for in litigation paralegals.

GREENE, ARTHUR G., ed. *Leveraging with Legal Assistants: How to Maximize Team Performance, Improve Quality, and Boost Your Bottom Line.* Chicago: American Bar Association, Section on Law Practice Management, 1993. An analysis of how attorneys can benefit from the effective utilization of legal assistants. Chapter 2 (entitled "Expanding the Role of the Legal Assistant—Why Do It?") is particularly instructive in regard to the economic benefits, for attorneys and clients alike, of effectively incorporating paralegals in the delivery of legal services.

HAMMACK, DEBRA D. "Utilization: The Legal Assistant's Perspective." *Facts and Findings: The Journal for Legal Assistants,* February 1994. An article that emphasizes how attorney-paralegal teamwork can lead to lower-cost legal services for clients.

MORROW, REBECCA. "Power to the Paralegal." *Legal Assistant Today,* March/April 1994. An overview of why clients are demanding less costly legal services and the consequent expanded demand for paralegal services.

NATIONAL ASSOCIATION OF LEGAL ASSISTANTS, INC. *NALA Manual for Legal Assistants.* 2d ed. St. Paul.: West Publishing Co., 1992. A manual that provides good, detailed background reading on a variety of paralegal skills.

WINSTON, STEPHANIE. *The Organized Executive.* New York: W. W. Norton & Co., 1994. An informative book on how to get organized, including discussions on streamlining your paperwork, evaluating your time, filing, and using your computer to get organized.

2

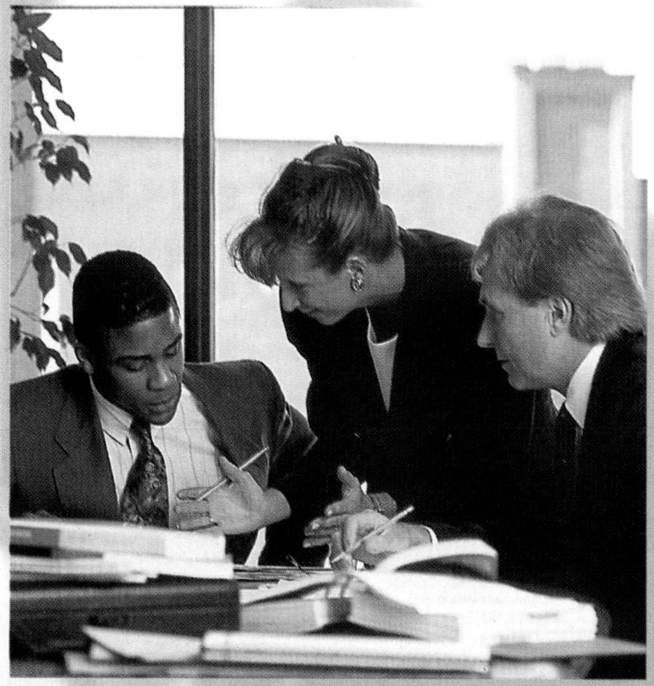

Careers in the Legal Community

Chapter Objectives

After completing this chapter, you will know:

- What types of firms and organizations hire paralegals.
- Some areas of law in which paralegals specialize.
- What paralegals can expect to earn.
- How paralegals are compensated for overtime work.
- How to prepare a career plan and pursue it.
- What is involved in a job search and how to go about it.

Chapter Outline

Introduction

As a paralegal, you will enjoy a broad spectrum of employment opportunities. In the past two decades, attorneys have begun to realize how the use of paralegals in the law office can help them achieve the goal of providing quality legal services at lower cost to clients. Paralegals perform a number of tasks that in the past only attorneys handled. By turning over these tasks to paralegals, whose hourly fees are lower than those of attorneys, law firms can represent more clients, and clients pay less for their services.

The fact that you are entering a growth profession presents further opportunities. As mentioned in Chapter 1, the first paralegals were legal secretaries who had acquired, through experience, the necessary skills and abilities to assist attorneys in substantive legal work within the law-firm environment. As the paralegal profession developed, so did opportunities for paralegals in other employment settings. Corporations began to realize how paralegals could be used effectively in their legal departments. Government agencies created positions for paralegals. Banks, insurance companies, and other types of firms and institutions began to hire paralegals to assist with work that required legal training. Today, most paralegals continue to work for law firms, as will be discussed shortly, but they are increasingly assuming greater responsibilities as attorneys realize the benefits of delegating substantive legal work to paralegals.

This chapter provides a point of departure for your career planning. In the pages that follow, you will read about where paralegals work, some special areas of paralegal practice, and how paralegals are compensated. You will also learn about the essential steps involved in planning for a successful career and how to go about finding a job.

Where Paralegals Work

Paralegal employers fall into three broad categories: law firms, corporations and other business organizations, and government agencies. This section describes the general characteristics of each of these three basic types of working environments.

Law Firms

When paralegals first established themselves within the legal community in the 1960s, they assisted lawyers in a law-firm setting. Today, as indicated in Exhibit 2.1, law firms continue to hire more paralegals than do any other organizations.

Law firms vary in size from the small, one-attorney office to the huge "megafirm" with hundreds of attorneys. As you can see in Exhibit 2.2 on page 34, the majority of paralegals working for law firms are employed by firms

EXHIBIT 2.1
Where Paralegals Work

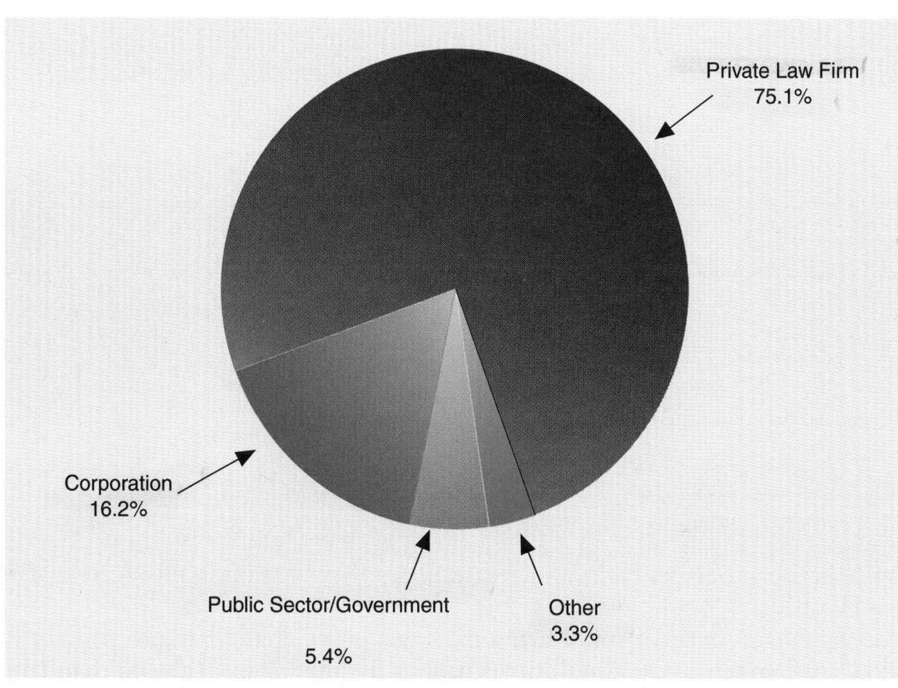

Source: Carol Milano, "Salary Survey Results," *Legal Assistant Today*, May/June 1993, p. 58.

having fewer than twenty attorneys, and 32.7 percent are employed by firms having four or fewer attorneys.[1]

Working for a Small Firm. Many paralegals begin their careers working for small law practices, such as one-attorney firms or firms with just a few attorneys. To some extent, this is because of the greater number of small law firms, relative to large law firms. It may also be due to geographic location. For example, a paralegal who lives in a relatively rural environment, such as a small community, may find that his or her only option is to work for a small legal practice.

Working for a small firm offers many advantages to the beginning paralegal, and you should be aware of them. If the firm is a general law practice, you will have the opportunity to gain experience in many different areas of the law. You will be able to learn whether you enjoy working in one area (such as family law) more than another area (such as personal-injury law) in the event that you later decide to specialize. Some paralegals also prefer the often more personal and less formal environment of the small law office, as

1. One of the difficulties in describing law-firm environments is that the terms *small law firm* and *large law firm* mean different things to different people. In a large metropolitan city, for example, a firm with fifteen attorneys might qualify as a small law firm. In a smaller, more rural community, however, a firm with fifteen attorneys would be considered a very large law firm. In this text, we refer to law firms with fifteen or fewer attorneys as small law firms and firms with over fifteen attorneys as large firms.

EXHIBIT 2.2
Paralegal Employment in Various Sizes of Law Firms

NUMBER OF ATTORNEYS IN FIRM	PERCENTAGE OF ALL LAW FIRM PARALEGALS EMPLOYED BY FIRM
0–4	32.7%
5–9	14.4%
10–19	16.3%
20–29	7.6%
30–75	18.4%
Over 75	10.6%

Source: Carol Milano, "Salary Survey Results," *Legal Assistant Today*, May/June 1993, p. 58.

well as the variety of tasks and greater flexibility that often characterize the small office.

A characteristic of small firms that may prove challenging to you has to do with compensation. Small firms pay, on average, lower salaries than larger firms do. As Exhibit 2.3 indicates, paralegal income is closely related to firm size. Generally, the larger the firm, the higher the paralegal salaries. Small firms also find it hard to afford the employee benefits packages, including insurance and pension plans, that large firms often provide for their employees.

Paralegals who work for small firms may also have less support staff to assist them. This means that if you work in a small law office, your job may involve a substantial amount of secretarial or clerical work.

Working for a Large Firm. In contrast to the (typically) more casual environment of the small law office, larger law firms usually are more formal. If you work for a larger firm, your responsibilities will probably be limited to specific types of tasks and more well defined. For example, you may work for a department that handles (or for an attorney who handles) only certain types of cases, such as real-estate transactions. Office procedures and employment policies will also be more clearly defined and may be set forth in a written employment manual.

The advantages of the large firm include greater opportunities for promotions and career advancement, higher salaries and better benefits packages (typically), more support staff for paralegals, and (often) more sophisticated computer technology and greater access to research resources.

You may view certain characteristics of large law firms as either advantages or disadvantages, depending on your personality and preferences. For example, if you prefer the more specialized work and more formal working environment of the large law firm, then you will view these characteristics as advantages. If you prefer to handle a greater variety of tasks and enjoy the more personal, informal atmosphere of the small law office, then you might view the specialization and formality of the large law firm as disadvantages.

EXHIBIT 2.3
Paralegal Compensation

BY FIRM SIZE

Number of Attorneys in Firm	Average Paralegal Salary
0–4	$28,411
5–9	$30,251
10–19	$32,177
20–29	$33,312
30–75	$33,218
Over 75	$36,809

BY TYPE OF EMPLOYER

Employer	Salary
Private law firm	$30,581
Corporation	$34,915
Public Sector/ Government	$29,241
Other	$27,877

BY YEARS OF EXPERIENCE

Years of Experience	Salary
0–2	$24,549
3–5	$27,644
6–10	$32,983
11–15	$33,989
Over 15	$38,909

BY LOCATION OF FIRM

Location	Salary
Metropolitan	$32,999
Urban	$30,023
Rural	$26,043

BY AREA OF PRACTICE

Area of Practice	Salary	Area of Practice	Salary
Administrative/Legislative	$32,478	Family Law	$26,238
Banking and Finance	$47,767	Intellectual Property	$38,219
Bankruptcy	$30,444	Litigation—Defense	$37,683
Corporate Law	$35,861	Litigation—Plaintiff	$30,112
Criminal Law	$26,871	Personal Injury	$27,873
Employment and Labor	$34,249	Real Estate	$31,815
Environmental	$29,141	Workers' Compensation	$26,195
Estate and Probate	$30,382	Other	$33,516

Source: Authors' estimates based on data reported in Carol Milano, "Salary Survey Results," *Legal Assistant Today,* May/June 1993, p. 48ff., and Bureau of Labor Statistics, *Monthly Labor Review,* various issues.

Corporations and Other Business Organizations

Over the past three decades, as mentioned earlier, paralegals have been given opportunities to work in business environments outside of law firms. Many of these businesses (such as insurance companies and banks) engage in activities that are highly regulated by government. Others (such as title insurance companies and law-book publishers) are in some way related to the practice of law.

An increasing number of paralegals work for corporate legal departments. Most major corporations hire in-house attorneys to handle corporate legal affairs. Some extremely large corporations have hundreds of attorneys on their payrolls. Paralegals who work for corporations ordinarily work under the supervision of in-house attorneys and assist them in such tasks as the following:

- Scheduling corporate meetings (discussed in Chapter 9); drafting meeting notices, agendas, and minutes; and assembling documents necessary for meetings.

DEVELOPING PARALEGAL SKILLS

Contracts Administrator

Martha Parnell, a legal assistant, works as a contracts administrator for the Best Engines Corporation. Martha's job is to take calls from buyers who want to negotiate contracts with Best Engines. The corporation uses preprinted forms containing provisions that Best Engines prefers to have in its contracts, terms that are advantageous to Best Engines. Some customers, however, buy large quantities of engines to use in factories, to pump oil from oil wells, or to pump oil through pipelines. These customers usually want to negotiate contracts that are less favorable to the seller (Best Engines) and that provide the buyer with more rights.

Martha's telephone rings. One of the company's sales representatives is on the line. He has a customer's attorney on hold who wants to negotiate the indemnity provision. The indemnity provision in the preprinted contract form requires the buyer to pay Best Engines for any losses arising under or resulting from the contract.

DEALING WITH A CUSTOMER'S REQUEST

The sales representative wants to know if Martha has time now for a conference call with the customer's attorney. Martha hesitates because she is in the middle of preparing another contract. The sales representative prods her. He tells her that this company is a major oil company that wants to purchase over $15 million worth of engines to use in a pipeline-expansion project. Martha agrees to talk to the attorney now.

The sale representative conferences the oil company's attorney into the call and introduces him to Martha. The oil company's attorney wants the indemnity provision reversed, so that Best Engines would be obligated to reimburse the oil company for any losses. He asks Martha if this could be accomplished. Martha tells him that Best Engines does not usually negotiate the indemnity provision, but because the oil company wants to make a sub-

- Preparing case files, drafting documents, and doing other work related to lawsuits in which the corporation is involved.
- Collecting and interpreting technical information for corporate reports to a regulatory agency (such as the Environmental Protection Agency).
- Drafting documents necessary to register for patent, trademark, or copyright protection for a corporate product.
- Researching laws and regulations that might affect corporate actions or policies.
- Preparing and reviewing corporate contracts.
- Working with outside counsel.

As noted in Exhibit 2.1, 16.2 percent of paralegals are now working in corporate or other business environments. On average, paralegals working for corporations receive higher salaries than those working for law firms, as indicated in Exhibit 2.3. Paralegals who work for corporations normally work more regular hours and experience less stress than paralegals who work for

DEVELOPING PARALEGAL SKILLS, Continued

stantial purchase, she will look into it. She asks him if the oil company would be willing to accept any other variations of the indemnity provision, such as splitting the indemnity or leaving it out entirely, so that state law would govern the issue. The attorney tells Martha that the oil company might agree to either of these possibilities.

CONSULTING WITH THE SUPERVISING ATTORNEY

Martha walks down the hall to her supervising attorney's office. She talks to the attorney, Joyce Ross, about modifying the indemnity provision. Joyce tells Martha that they will have to discuss it with the general counsel (the attorney who heads the corporate legal department) and get back to the customer's attorney later. Joyce picks up the phone and calls the general counsel's office. He is in the office but has just taken another call. His secretary asks Joyce what her call relates to, and Joyce explains the situation. The general counsel's secretary arranges a time for Joyce and Martha to meet with him.

MEETING WITH THE GENERAL COUNSEL

Later that day, Joyce and Martha go to the general counsel's office for the meeting. They sit down in his office, and Joyce explains the situation. The general counsel asks Martha several questions about the oil company's position on the indemnity provision. Would the oil company agree to eliminate the indemnity provision and rely on state law? Would the oil company be willing to split the indemnity? Would the indemnity provision be limited to certain types of losses, or would all losses, including personal injuries, be included?

After Martha answers his questions, the general counsel tells Joyce and Martha that he will have to consult with both the vice president of marketing and the president of Best Engines and that he will call Martha as soon as he can to let her know the corporation's decision.

law firms. For example, unlike in law firms, in the corporate environment paralegals are not required to generate a specific number of "billable hours" per year (hours billed to clients for paralegal services performed—discussed in Chapter 5) because there are no clients to bill—the corporation is the client.

Government Agencies

A small but growing number of paralegals (around 5.4 percent) are employed by the government. Most paralegals who work for the government work for administrative agencies, such as the Environmental Protection Agency and the Social Security Administration. Paralegals who work for government agencies may be engaged in administrative appeals work (see Chapter 13), general or specialized legal research, the examination of documents (such as loan applications), and many other types of tasks. Your best source of information about employment positions in a particular administrative agency is the agency itself. The names, addresses, and phone numbers of selected federal agencies are listed in Exhibit 13.5 in Chapter 13. See also the featured-guest article in Chapter 9 entitled "Paralegal Positions in Government."

Paralegals who work for government agencies normally work regular working hours, tend to work fewer total hours per year (have more vacation time) than paralegals in other environments, and, like paralegals who work for corporations, do not have to worry about billable hours. Additionally, paralegals who work for the government usually enjoy comprehensive employment benefits. Salaries, however, are on average lower than those offered by traditional law firms and other employers in the private sector, as indicated in Exhibit 2.3.

PARALEGAL SPECIALTIES

While many paralegals work for small firms that offer a wide range of legal services, other paralegals have found it useful and satisfying to specialize in one area of law. There are numerous opportunities for the paralegal who wishes to concentrate his or her efforts on a particular area and become a specialist. Here we discuss just a few of these specialty areas.

Litigation Assistance

LITIGATION
The process of working a lawsuit through the court system.

LITIGATION PARALEGALS
Paralegals who specialize in assisting attorneys in the litigation process.

PLAINTIFF
A party who initiates a lawsuit.

DEFENDANT
A party against whom a lawsuit is brought.

Working a lawsuit through the court system is called **litigation.** Paralegals who specialize in assisting attorneys in the litigation process are called **litigation paralegals.** Litigation paralegals work in general law practices, small litigation firms, litigation departments of larger law firms, or corporate legal departments. Litigation paralegals often specialize in a certain type of litigation, such as personal-injury litigation (discussed below) or product-liability cases (which involve injuries caused by defective products). Some litigation paralegals may also work primarily on behalf of **plaintiffs** (those who bring lawsuits) or on behalf of **defendants** (those against whom lawsuits are brought). Lawyers in a personal-injury practice, for example, often represent plaintiffs. Lawyers in a criminal-law practice represent criminal defendants—those accused of crimes.

You will read in detail about litigation procedures and the important role played by paralegals in the ligitation process in Chapters 10 and 11. We indicate below just a sampling of the kinds of work that a paralegal might perform during the litigation process:

- Interview a client to obtain detailed information about a case.
- Locate and interview witnesses.
- Contact relevant medical personnel and institutions, employers, or other sources of factual information relating to a case.
- Prepare documents to initiate (or defend against) a lawsuit and file them with the court, draft interrogatories (written questions to be answered under oath by the opposing party), attend depositions (recorded question-and-answer sessions in which an attorney questions a party or a witness), and summarize deposition transcripts.
- Prepare exhibits for trial, arrange to have all needed equipment and supplies in the courtroom at the time of the trial, create a trial notebook for the attorney to refer to during the trial, and prepare the client and witnesses for trial.

• Assist at trial and in any posttrial procedures, such as those required for appealing the case to a higher court.

Personal-injury Law

Much litigation involves claims brought by persons who have been injured in automobile accidents or other incidents as a result of the negligence of others. *Negligence* is a *tort,* or civil wrong, and someone who has been injured as a result of another's negligence is entitled under tort law to obtain compensation from the wrongdoer. (Tort law, including negligence, is discussed in Chapter 8.)

Paralegals who specialize in the area of personal-injury litigation often work for law firms that concentrate their efforts on personal-injury litigation. Personal-injury paralegals are also hired by insurance companies to investigate claims. Defendants in personal-injury cases are typically insured by automobile or other insurance, and a defendant's insurance company will therefore have an interest in the outcome of the litigation.

A paralegal working on a personal-injury case would typically perform the following types of tasks:

• Interview a client (plaintiff) to obtain details about an accident and the injuries sustained by the client.
• Interview witnesses to the accident to gather as much information about the accident as possible.
• Obtain medical reports from physicians and hospitals describing the plaintiff's injuries.
• Obtain employment data to verify the amount of lost wages that should be claimed as damages—if the client's current or future employment is affected by the injury.
• Obtain a copy of the police report, and, if necessary, consult with police officers and investigators who worked on the case.
• Generally, provide litigation assistance.

Criminal Law

Law is sometimes classified into the two categories of civil law and criminal law. **Civil law** is concerned with the duties that exist between persons or between citizens and their governments, excluding the duty not to commit crimes. Contract law, for example, is part of civil law. The whole body of *tort law,* which has to do with the infringement by one person of the legally recognized rights of another (see Chapter 8), is an area of civil law.

CIVIL LAW
The branch of law dealing with the definition and enforcement of all private or public rights, as opposed to criminal matters.

Criminal law, in contrast, is concerned with wrongs committed against the public as a whole. Criminal acts are prohibited by federal, state, or local statutes. In a criminal case, the government seeks to impose a penalty on a person who has commited a crime. In a civil case, one party tries to make the other party comply with a duty or pay for the damage caused by the failure to so comply.

CRIMINAL LAW
The branch of law that governs and defines those actions that are crimes and that subjects persons convicted of crimes to punishment imposed by the government.

As you will read in Chapter 12, which discusses criminal law and procedures in detail, a person accused of a crime is prosecuted by a *public prosecutor.* Public prosecutors (such as district attorneys) are government officials and are paid by the government. Accused persons may be defended by private attorneys or, if they cannot afford to hire counsel, by *public defenders*—attorneys paid for by the state to ensure that criminal defendants are not deprived of their constitutional right to counsel.

Paralegals who specialize in the area of criminal law may work for public prosecutors, public defenders, or criminal-defense attorneys. Criminal litigation is similar to civil litigation in many respects, and the kinds of work performed by litigation paralegals (described above) also apply in the criminal-law context. In addition to providing general litigation assistance, a paralegal working in the area of criminal law might perform the following tasks:

- As a public prosecutor's legal assistant, draft search warrants, which authorize law-enforcement officers to search a person or place.
- As a public prosecutor's legal assistant, draft arrest warrants, which authorize law-enforcement officers to arrest and take into custody a criminal suspect.
- As a defense attorney's legal assistant, assist a criminal defendant in making arrangements to post bail (so that the defendant can be released from custody until further proceedings are held—see Chapter 12).
- As a public prosecutor's legal assistant, act as a liaison between the police department and the public prosecutor's office.
- Generally, help to make sure that a criminal defendant's constitutional rights are not violated by any action undertaken by police officers or attorneys handling the case.

Corporate Law

CORPORATE LAW
Law that governs the formation, financing, merger and acquisition, and termination of corporations, as well as the rights and duties of those who own and run the corporation.

Corporate law consists of the laws that govern the formation, financing, merger and acquisition, and termination of corporations, as well as the rights and duties of those who own and run the corporation. You will read in detail about the meaning of these terms in Chapter 9.

Paralegals who specialize in corporate law may work for a corporation, in its legal department, or for a law firm that specializes in corporate law. The demand for paralegals who are experienced in the area of corporate law is expanding. If you refer back to Exhibit 2.3 on paralegal compensation, you will see that paralegals specializing in this area also receive, on average, higher salaries or wages than paralegals in most other specialty areas.

Here are just a few of the tasks that a paralegal working in the area of corporate law might be asked to undertake:

- Prepare articles of incorporation and file them with the appropriate state office (usually the secretary of state's office).
- Draft corporate bylaws (rules that govern the internal affairs of the corporation).
- Prepare minutes of corporate meetings and maintain a minutes binder.
- Draft shareholder proposals.
- Review or prepare documents relating to the sale of corporate securities (stocks and bonds); assist a supervising attorney in making sure that federal and state requirements relating to the sale of corporate securities are met.
- Assist with legal work relating to corporate mergers and acquisitions, such as researching a corporation's financial status.
- File papers necessary to terminate a corporation's legal existence.

DEVELOPING PARALEGAL SKILLS

Obtaining a Police Report

Maria Sanchez works as a paralegal in a one-attorney office. The attorney, Bob Billings, has just finished a meeting with a client who was arrested and charged with drunk driving and involuntary manslaughter (see Chapter 12). Bob will be defending the client, Jim Hannon, at the preliminary hearing.

Bob calls Maria into his office. He asks her to go to the police station to pick up a copy of the police report for the accident. He tells her the date of the accident was August 11, 1995, and that it occurred on Square Lake Road in Livingston, Minnesota. She will need to go to the Livingston Police Department. Bob also gives Maria the names of the parties involved in the accident and Hannon's driver's license number. Maria will need all of this information to obtain a copy of the police report. Additionally, Bob gives her a check, drawn on the law firm's account and made payable to the City of Livingston, in the amount of ten dollars to pay for the police report.

Maria drives to the police station. She enters the building and approaches the front desk. "May I help you?" asks the officer sitting at the front desk. "Yes. Where can I obtain a copy of the police report for a car accident?" asks Maria. "Did the accident occur in Livingston, and did the Livingston police respond?" asks the officer. "It happened here, and I believe that the Livingston police were at the scene," answers Maria. "Then fill out this form and I will get the report for you," instructs the officer.

Maria fills out the form and returns it to the officer. The officer keys the information into her computer and then prints out a copy of the police report. The officer hands the copy to Maria and takes her check. Maria thanks the officer and returns to the office.

Bankruptcy Law

Bankruptcy law is a body of law that allows debtors to obtain relief from their debts. Bankruptcy law is federal law, and bankruptcy proceedings take place in federal courts (see the discussion of the federal court system in Chapter 7). The twin goals of bankruptcy law are (1) to protect a debtor by giving him or her a fresh start, free from creditors' claims; and (2) to ensure that creditors who are competing for a debtor's assets are treated fairly. Bankruptcy law provides for several types of relief, and both individuals and business firms may petition for bankruptcy.

BANKRUPTCY LAW
The body of federal law that governs bankrupcy proceedings. The twin goals of bankruptcy law are (1) to protect a debtor by giving him or her a fresh start, free from creditors' claims; and (2) to ensure that creditors who are competing for a debtor's assets are treated fairly.

Both large and small law firms practice bankruptcy law. A corporation undergoing bankruptcy proceedings (often in the form of a "reorganization," as provided for under bankruptcy law) may hire, on a temporary basis, a paralegal experienced in bankruptcy law to assist in the process. If you are working on behalf of a debtor who seeks bankruptcy relief, you might perform the following types of tasks:

- Interview the debtor (which may be an individual or a corporate representative) to obtain information relating to the debtor's income, debts, and assets.
- Review creditors' claims and verify their validity.

- Prepare the necessary documents for submission to the bankruptcy court.
- Attend bankruptcy proceedings.
- Assist in defending the debtor against any legal actions concerning the bankruptcy proceedings.

Employment and Labor Law

As will be discussed in Chapter 9, laws governing employment relationships are referred to collectively as *employment and labor law.* Employment and labor law includes laws governing health and safety in the workplace, labor unions and union-management relations, employment discrimination, wrongful employment termination, pension plans, retirement and disability income (Social Security), employee privacy rights (to a limited extent), the minimum wage that must be paid, and overtime wages.

Paralegals who are experienced in one or more of these areas of employment and labor law may work for law firms, corporations and other business entities, or government agencies. Often, paralegals specialize in just one area of employment law. For example, many paralegals work in the area of workers' compensation. Under state **workers' compensation statutes,** employees who are injured on the job are compensated from state funds (obtained by taxes paid by employers). Paralegals working in this area of employment law assist persons injured on the job in obtaining compensation from the state workers' compensation board. As you will read in Chapter 13, some government agencies, including many state workers' compensation boards, allow paralegals to represent clients before agency hearings, which are conducted by agencies to settle disputes, or in negotations with the agencies.

WORKERS' COMPENSATION STATUTES
State laws establishing an administrative procedure for compensating workers for injuries that arise in the course of their employment.

Numerous other areas of employment and labor law are regulated by administrative agencies, and paralegals working in those areas need to be familiar with the relevant agency's requirements and procedures. Here are just a few agencies that are involved in regulating the workplace and with which employment-law paralegals should be familiar:

- *National Labor Relations Board (NLRB)*—A federal agency that implements federal laws governing union organizational activities, union elections, and labor-management relations generally.
- *Occupational Safety and Health Administration (OSHA)*—A federal agency that implements federal laws governing safety in the workplace. OSHA establishes safety standards that employers must follow. State agencies also establish safety and health standards.
- *Equal Employment Opportunity Commission (EEOC)*—A federal agency that administers and enforces federal laws prohibiting employment discrimination on the basis of race, color, national origin, gender, religion, age, or disability. Before an employee can sue an employer for discrimination in violation of these federal laws, the employee must comply with EEOC procedures for handling such complaints. Only if the EEOC does not satisfactorily settle the claim may the employee file suit.
- *Labor Management Services Administration (LMSA)*—A federal agency that implements the provisions of the federal Employee Retirement Income Security Act (ERISA), which imposes certain requirements on employers in regard to pension funds.

Paralegals working in the area of employment and labor law often have extensive contact with these and other administrative agencies. If you work as a paralegal in the law-firm or corporate environment, you might undertake the following types of tasks, each of which may involve rules and procedures established by government agencies:

- Conduct research on labor law to determine how the law applies to a labor-management contract or dispute.
- Draft a contract setting forth the terms of a labor-management agreement.
- Assist in informal negotiations to settle a dispute between an employee and an employer or between a labor union and a firm's managers.
- Assist in formal dispute-settlement proceedings before one of the above-mentioned government agencies.
- Inform a client of the procedures involved in submitting a claim of employment discrimination to the EEOC and assist the client in preparing the necessary documents.
- Prepare the documents needed to initiate (or defend against) a lawsuit for employment discrimination in violation of federal or state law and generally assist in the litigation process.
- Contact and work with the state workers' compensation board on behalf of a client who is seeking compensation for injuries incurred during the course of employment.
- Draft employment policies to make sure that a business client (or a corporate employer) complies with federal and state laws prohibiting employment discrimination.
- Assist a business client (or a corporate employer) in benefits planning to ensure compliance with the requirements of ERISA and any other laws regulating employee benefits, such as health, life, or disability insurance.

Estate Planning and Probate Administration

Estate planning and probate administration both have to do with the transfer of an owner's property, or *estate,* on the owner's death. Through **estate planning,** the owner decides, *before* death, how his or her property will be transferred to others. The owner may make a **will,** for example, to designate the persons to whom his or her property shall be transferred. The formal requirements for a valid will are set forth in state statutes, and because these requirements may differ from state to state, paralegals working in this area should be familiar with their state's law governing wills. If the property passes by will, depending on the size of the estate and other factors, the genuineness of the will may have to be proved **(probated)** in **probate court** (a county or other court that handles probate procedures). Probate administration thus involves the procedures relating to the transfer of property *after* the owner's death.

The process of probate may take many months and, in some cases, more than a year. The *personal representative* (a person named in the will to handle the affairs of the deceased after his or her death) or an *administrator* (a person appointed by the court if no personal representative is named in the will) satisfies all obligations (pays debts, taxes, etc.) of the deceased. The personal representative or administrator also arranges to have the deceased's

ESTATE PLANNING
Making arrangements, during a person's lifetime, for the transfer of that person's property or obligations to others on the person's death. Estate planning often involves executing a will, establishing a trust fund, or taking out a life-insurance policy to provide for others, such as a spouse or children, on one's death.

WILL
A document directing what is to be done with the maker's property upon his or her death.

PROBATE
The process of "proving" the validity of a will and ensuring that the instructions in a valid will are carried out.

PROBATE COURT
A court that probates wills; usually a county court.

property distributed among the heirs in accordance with the will's provisions. Because the probate process can be time consuming, many people arrange to have at least some of their property transferred in ways other than by will.

One estate-planning possibility involves the establishment of a **trust,** a legal arrangement in which the property owner transfers legal title to his or her property to a *trustee.* The trustee (which may be a relative or trusted friend of the property owner, an attorney, a law firm, or a banking institution) has a duty imposed by law to hold the property for the use or benefit of another (the *beneficiary* of the trust). A trust created during the owner's life is called a living trust. A trust provided for in a will comes into existence on the owner's death. Estate planning often involves life insurance. A person who wants to provide for a spouse and children after his or her death, for example, may obtain a life-insurance policy listing the spouse and children as beneficiaries. On the death of the insured person, the beneficiaries receive the amount specified in the policy.

Paralegals who specialize in the area of estate planning and probate frequently work for law firms, but they may also be employed by other firms or agencies, such as banks, as well as by probate courts. If you work in this area, these are some of the tasks that you might perform:

- Interview clients to obtain information relating to their assets, how and to whom they want to transfer their property on death, and what arrangements they want to have made for the guardianship of minor children.
- Draft wills and other documents required to set up a trust fund.
- Make sure that all procedural requirements are met during the probate process—that the proper documents are submitted to the court in a timely fashion, for example.
- Gather information relating to the debts and assets of the deceased, and assist in settling all financial and other obligations of the deceased.
- Locate heirs, if necessary.
- Explain probate procedures to family members or other heirs of the deceased and keep them informed of the status of the proceedings.

ETHICAL CONCERN

Serving the Interests of Bereaved Clients

One of the hardest events to cope with is the loss of a loved one, yet it is precisely at this time that bereaved persons must also cope with funeral arrangements and legal formalities. These formalities may include checking with an attorney, locating a will if one was made, tending to the decedent's financial affairs, and so on. Undertaking these activities can be costly, and financial needs may cause further stress. These are factors that paralegals should keep in mind when dealing with clients during the probate process. Probate proceedings always take time, but the amount of time may be reduced by the paralegal who files the necessary forms in a timely fashion and follows up on the status of the proceedings to make sure that there are no unnecessary delays. Your kind or sympathetic words may be appreciated by a bereaved client; but you can best serve his or her interests by doing your job efficiently and responsibly and by undertaking any action you can to speed up the probate process.

TRUST
An arrangement in which title to property is held by one person (a trustee) for the benefit of another (a beneficiary).

Intellectual-property Law

Intellectual property consists of the products of individuals' minds—products that result from intellectual, creative processes. Those who create intellectual property acquire certain rights over the use of that property, and these rights are protected by law. Literary and artistic works are protected by *copyright law. Trademark law* protects business firms' distinctive marks or mottos. Inventions are protected by *patent law.*

INTELLECTUAL PROPERTY
Property that consists of the products of individuals' minds—products that result from intellectual, creative processes. Copyrights, patents, and trademarks are examples of intellectual property.

Although it is an abstract term for an abstract concept, intellectual property is nonetheless wholly familiar to virtually everyone. The book you are reading is copyrighted. Undoubtedly, the personal computer you use is trademarked and patented. The software you use on that computer might be copyrighted. The primary benefit of intellectual-property rights to the owner is that he or she controls the commercial use of the property. The owner, for example, may sell the intellectual property rights to another, may collect royalties on the use of the property (such as a popular song) by others, and may prevent all but one publisher from reproducing the property (such as a novel). In Chapter 8, you will read in greater detail about laws governing intellectual property.

Many law firms (or special departments of large law firms) specialize in intellectual-property law, such as patent law, while other firms provide a spectrum of legal services to their clients, of which intellectual-property law is only a part. Corporate legal departments may be responsible for registering copyrights, patents, or trademarks with the federal government.[2] Paralegal specialists in the area of intellectual property frequently undertake the following kinds of work:

- Interview clients who want to register for copyright, trademark, or patent protection of certain intellectual property, such as a new computer program, a product name, or an invention.
- Conduct research to find out whether someone has already applied for patent or trademark protection of an invention or product that the firm's client (or a corporate employer) wants to develop or register.
- Draft the documents that are necessary to apply for patent, trademark, or copyright protection.
- Draft contracts that provide for another's authorized use of a copyrighted, patented, or trademarked product.
- Assist in litigation resulting from the *infringement* (unlawful use of) copyright, trademark, or patent rights.

Environmental Law

Environmental law consists of all laws that have been created to protect the environment. Environmental law involves the regulation of air and water pollution, natural-resource management, endangered-species protection, hazardous-waste disposal and the clean-up of hazardous-waste sites, pesticide control, and nuclear-power regulation.

ENVIRONMENTAL LAW
All state and federal laws or regulations enacted or issued to protect the environment and preserve environmental resources.

Employers of paralegal specialists in environmental law include administrative agencies (such as the federal Environmental Protection Agency, the state's natural-resource department, and the local zoning board), environmental-law departments of large law firms, law firms that specialize in environmental law, and corporations. Corporations with legal departments often employ environmental specialists. For example, a corporation may employ a paralegal as an *environmental coordinator* to assist the corporation in proper compliance with environmental regulations.

Here are some of the types of tasks that paralegal specialists in the area of environmental law frequently perform:

- Coordinate a corporate employer's environmental programs and policies and ensure that the corporation is complying properly with environmental regulations.
- Obtain permits from local, state, or federal environmental agencies to use land in certain ways (such as clearing trees or filling wetlands).

2. Copyrights are registered with the U.S. Copyright Office, Library of Congress, Washington, DC 20559. Patents and trademarks are registered with the Patent and Trademark Office, U.S. Department of Commerce, Washington, DC 20231.

ETHICAL CONCERN

Questions about Child Custody

Divorcing clients frequently ask whether they can take their children out of the state while the mediation or divorce proceedings are under way. For example, suppose that Kerry Lynn, a paralegal, receives a call from a client who wants to know if it would be all right to take her children to her mother's home in another state over the weekend. Kerry tells the client that there is no problem with that. Normally, there would be no problem, but what Kerry doesn't know is that in this case, just two days ago, the court ordered that the children could not leave the state. The client, relying on Kerry's answer, violates the order. Kerry has both given legal advice to a client (which only attorneys may do) and has caused the client to suffer adverse legal consequences as a result of that advice. In your work as a paralegal, you may face similar questions from divorcing parents. You should always let the client know that as a paralegal, you cannot give legal advice, which you would be doing if you answered such questions.

- Prepare forms and documents relating to the disposal of hazardous waste created by a corporate client's (or corporate employer's) manufacturing plants.
- Assist in litigation or other legal actions relating to violations of environmental laws. Paralegals play an important role in coordinating different aspects of the litigation (which may involve multiple violators) and in managing case files, which are often voluminous.
- Attend conferences with administrative-agency personnel or hearings conducted by an agency to assist in the settlement of a dispute.
- As an environmental agency employee, investigate and process claims of violations and assist in settling claims.

Real-estate Law

REAL ESTATE
Land and things permanently attached to the land, such as houses, buildings, and trees and foliage.

Real estate, or *real property,* consists of land and all things permanently attached to the land, such as houses, buildings, and trees and foliage. Because of the value of real estate (for most people, a home is their most expensive purchase), attorneys frequently assist persons or business firms that buy or sell real property to make sure that nothing important is overlooked. Paralegals who specialize in the area of real estate may find employment in a number of environments, including small law firms that specialize in real-estate transactions, real-estate departments in large law firms, corporations or other business firms that frequently buy or sell real property, banking institutions (which finance real-estate purchases), title companies, or real-estate agencies. You will read in greater detail about real-property law in Chapter 8. Here we list just a few of the tasks that paralegals working in this area might perform:

- Interview clients who want to buy or sell real property.
- Draft contracts for the sale of real estate.
- Conduct *title* examinations. (The title to real property represents the right to own and possess the property, and title examinations are conducted to see if there are any defects in the title.)
- Review title abstracts, which summarize the ownership history of real property.
- Draft mortgage agreements.
- Provide information to banking institutions involved in financing clients' real-estate purchases.
- Prepare *deeds* (a deed is a written document that transfers title from one person to another).
- Make sure that property transfers are recorded in the appropriate public office (usually the county register of deeds office).
- Schedule *closings* (the closing is the final step in the purchase of real estate—see Chapter 8).
- Attend closings (when permitted by state law to do so).

Family Law

FAMILY LAW
Law relating to family matters, such as marriage, divorce, child support, and child custody.

Family law, as the term implies, deals with family matters, such as marriage, divorce, alimony, child support, and child custody. Family law is governed primarily by state statutes. If you specialize in this area, you will need to

PARALEGAL PROFILE

Real-estate and Litigation Paralegal

DORA LEW received her bachelor of arts and master of arts degrees in Spanish language and literature from the University of California, Berkeley. After teaching Spanish for three years at that university and then two years at a private high school for girls, Lew became a secretary for a real-estate company, which immediately recognized her talents and gave her more responsibility. The company also put her through a master of business administration (MBA) program in international business at Armstrong University. Lew now works as a real-estate paralegal at the law firm of Landels, Ripley and Diamond.

What do you like best about your work?

"I enjoy the field of real estate because I am able to bring in all of my experience from the past to my current position. While working for Brobeck, Phlager and Harrison, I became the senior paralegal specializing in multimillion-dollar real-estate closings and related tasks. That experience helps me in my present job. I find I am able to utilize my experiences as a teacher, my experience in real estate, business, and the law. I have even used my Spanish in many situations when doing *pro bono* work. I also like the independence I have in my position."

What is the greatest challenge that you face in your area of work?

"I find that the most challenging aspect of my work is satisfying the twin goals of cost-efficiency and the generation of a superior work product. To meet these goals, it is important to "get it right" the first or second time. During the 1980s, clients called the attorneys to explain what they needed done, and then the attorneys would assign the work to paralegals. Now, clients are so cost-conscious that they often call me directly to skip a step. Of course, I run any client requests by the attorney, who may do some of the necessary work."

"BRINGING TO YOUR POSITION ALL EXPERIENCES THAT YOU HAVE HAD WILL ADD TO YOUR VALUE AS A PARALEGAL."

What advice do you have for would-be paralegals in your area of work?

"My advice is to be as detail-oriented as possible and to be the best you can be in all things that you do. Bringing to your position all experiences that you have had will add to your value as a paralegal. I would also advise paralegal students to get work experience. Without work experience, students can't get an idea of office culture and environment, which are important aspects of a job. When you start a job, for example, you're expected to know certain procedures, such as how to request supplies and fill out time sheets. Although you might have read about these procedures, you can only truly learn them through actual work experience."

What are some tips for success as a paralegal in your area of work?

"Anticipation is the biggest tip I can give to a paralegal who hopes to be successful. If you anticipate your supervising attorney's needs, the problems that may arise in a case, and so on, you're always prepared to deal with the case more efficiently and effectively."

become familiar with your state's requirements concerning marriage and divorce procedures, child support, and related issues.

As a family-law specialist, you might work for a small family-law practice, a family-law department in a large law firm, or with a state or local agency, such as a community services agency, that assists persons who need

DEVELOPING PARALEGAL SKILLS

Conducting a Title Examination

Kim Murphy is a paralegal working for the real-estate law firm of Clark & Clark. Today Kim is going to the Winston County Register of Deeds office to examine the title to the Spartan Shopping Center located in Winston County. One of Clark & Clark's clients is negotiating a sale of the shopping center, and Kim's supervising attorney must prepare an "abstract of title," which is a history of who owned the property, when past transfers were made, and other significant events. The abstract will be used to assure the buyer that he or she will receive good, clear, and marketable title to the property.

Kim arrives at the county offices. She takes the elevator to the third floor, where the Register of Deeds office is located. Kim approaches the counter, and a clerk asks her, "What do you need today?" Kim recognizes the clerk, Sam McGrath, who has worked there for as long as Kim has worked for Clark & Clark. He often assists Kim and is very helpful.

"Sam, I need the title records for the Spartan Shopping Center, located at 611 Harris Road, Dunham Township, Winston County," responds Kim. "Okay. I'll be right back with them for you, Kim," says Sam. He goes to a wall full of filing cabinets, opens a drawer, and looks for the title records of the Spartan Shopping Center.

EXAMINING OWNERSHIP RECORDS

Kim looks in a book on the counter, called the *Liber*, in which all of the deeds that are filed with the county are recorded. She locates the Spartan Shopping Center and then takes the *Liber* to a nearby table. She begins to read the ownership history of the property.

Sam brings the file folder containing copies of the deeds to Kim's table. She begins to read through each document. Kim looks at the copies to see if

help with family-related problems. As a paralegal working in the area of family law, you might perform such tasks as the following:

- Interview a divorcing client to obtain information relating to the couple's assets and liabilities.
- Research state laws governing child custody and assist in making child-custody arrangements for a divorcing couple.
- Draft a settlement agreement.
- Prepare the necessary documents to be filed with the court in a divorce suit and assist in the litigation process.
- Prepare a client for divorce proceedings.
- Assist a client—particularly a spouse who has never handled household financial affairs—in financial planning.

PARALEGAL COMPENSATION

What do paralegals earn? This is an important question for anyone contemplating a career as a paralegal. You can get some idea of what paralegals

DEVELOPING PARALEGAL SKILLS, Continued

each one contains the same description of the property—to ensure that the entire parcel of land was conveyed (transferred) with each sale. Kim sees that it was. Kim also checks to make sure that the seller of the Spartan Shopping Center is the owner of the property.

CHECKING FOR LIENS

Next Kim looks for any *liens* (rights of creditors against the property for the payment of debts) that might have been filed against the property. Kim notes the mortgage lien, which is normal and expected. Typically, when the purchase of real property is financed by a mortgage loan, the lending institution places a lien on the property until the buyer has made all payments due under the terms of the loan contract. She also notes that the Internal Revenue Service (IRS) has placed a tax lien on the property. A tax lien means that the current owner is behind in the payment of taxes and that the IRS may *foreclose on* (take temporary ownership of) the shopping center, sell it, and use the proceeds to pay the overdue taxes. Any remaining proceeds will be returned to the shopping center's owner. If someone buys the shopping center and the IRS forecloses on it, the buyer could lose some, and perhaps all, of the money that he or she paid for the property.

THE CONSEQUENCES OF THE TAX LIEN FOR THE CLIENT

Kim realizes that the tax lien will make the property unsellable. Once the abstract is prepared, the buyer's attorney will learn about the lien and warn the buyer not to purchase the property because of the obvious risk. This tax lien must be resolved before Clark & Clark's client can sell the property.

Kim makes a copy of the tax-lien documents and then continues to review the file. When she has finished reviewing it, she returns it to Sam, thanks him for his help, and returns to the office to inform her supervising attorney of the tax lien.

make, on average, from paralegal compensation surveys. Following a discussion of these surveys, we look at some other components of paralegal compensation, including job benefits and how paralegals are compensated for overtime work.

Compensation Surveys

If you refer back to Exhibit 2.3, you can see that paralegal income is affected by a number of factors. We have already mentioned how the average income of paralegals is affected by firm size (smaller or larger) and the type of employer (law firm, corporation, or government). Other income-determining factors include years of experience working as a paralegal, as well as the area of practice. Note that the average salary of a paralegal working in the area of corporate law is $35,861, approximately $9,623 more than that of a paralegal working in the area of family law. Average salaries are also affected by location. The average salary for paralegals who work in metropolitan areas (major cities) is approximately $6,956 more than that of paralegals working in rural areas (small communities).

Exhibit 2.3 indicates *national* averages. To have a clearer picture of what your potential future income will be, you need to look at the average paralegal income in the state where you live or plan to work. As you can see in Exhibit 2.4, paralegals working in Alaska earn, on average, over $23,590 more than paralegals working in Wyoming.

Keep in mind that salary statistics do not tell the whole story. Although paralegals earn more in California than in a midwestern state such as Nebraska (as shown in Exhibit 2.4), the cost of living is higher in California than in Nebraska. This means that your real income—the amount of goods and services that you can purchase with your income—may, in fact, be the same in both states despite the differences in salary. Salary statistics also do not reveal another important component of compensation—job benefits.

Job Benefits

Part of your total compensation package as an employee will consist of various job benefits. These benefits may include paid holidays, sick leave, group insurance coverage (life, disability, medical, dental), pension plans, and possibly others. Benefits packages vary from firm to firm. For example, one employer may pay the entire premium for your life and health insurance, while another employer may require you to contribute part of the cost of the insurance. Usually, the larger the firm, the greater the value of the benefits package.

- **When evaluating any job offer, you need to consider the benefits that you will receive and what these benefits are worth to you.**

You will read more about the importance of job benefits later in this chapter, in the context of evaluating a job offer.

Salaries versus Hourly Wages

Most paralegals (about 85 percent)[3] are salaried employees. In other words, they receive a specified annual salary regardless of the number of hours they actually work. Other paralegals are paid an hourly wage rate for every hour worked. Paralegals are frequently asked to work overtime, and how they are compensated for overtime work usually depends on whether they are salaried employees or are paid hourly wages. Many firms compensate their salaried paralegals for overtime work through year-end **bonuses,** which are special payments made to employees in recognition of their devotion to the firm and the high quality of their work. Some firms allow salaried employees to take compensatory time off work (for example, an hour off work for every hour worked beyond usual working hours). Employees who are paid an hourly wage rate are normally paid overtime wages.

BONUS
An end-of-the-year payment to a salaried employee in appreciation for that employee's overtime work, work quality, diligence, or dedication to the firm.

Federal Law and Overtime Pay

A major issue in the paralegal profession in regard to compensation has to do with overtime pay. Some paralegals who receive year-end bonuses question whether their bonuses sufficiently compensate them for the amount of

3. Carol Milano, "Salary Survey Results," *Legal Assistant Today,* May/June 1993, p. 48; Bureau of Labor Statistics, *Monthly Labor Review;* and authors' estimates.

EXHIBIT 2.4
Paralegal Compensation by State

STATE	AVERAGE SALARY	STATE	AVERAGE SALARY
Alabama	$33,942	Montana	$22,896
Alaska	$41,583	Nebraska	$24,187
Arizona	$40,167	Nevada	$32,911
Arkansas	$36,254	New Hampshire	$30,186
California	$37,001	New Jersey	$28,224
Colorado	$28,156	New Mexico	$27,666
Connecticut	$34,069	New York	$35,714
Delaware	$48,145	North Carolina	$27,265
District of Columbia	$30,471	North Dakota	$25,166
Florida	$29,472	Ohio	$29,119
Georgia	$31,876	Oklahoma	$28,772
Hawaii	$31,890	Oregon	$32,150
Idaho	$22,365	Pennsylvania	$27,137
Illinois	$32,014	Rhode Island	$28,408
Indiana	$25,208	South Carolina	$24,941
Iowa	$26,567	South Dakota	$28,908
Kansas	$32,795	Tennessee	$31,239
Kentucky	$26,451	Texas	$33,181
Louisiana	$28,728	Utah	$25,469
Maine	$35,113	Vermont	$24,752
Maryland	$27,090	Virginia	$28,001
Massachusetts	$24,607	Washington	$31,693
Michigan	$29,305	West Virginia	(not available)
Minnesota	$32,641	Wisconsin	$28,120
Mississippi	$26,407	Wyoming	$17,993
Missouri	$29,996		

Source: Authors' estimates based on data reported in Carol Milano, "Salary Survey Results," *Legal Assistant Today*, May/June 1993, p. 48ff., and Bureau of Labor Statistics, *Monthly Labor Review*, various issues.

overtime they have worked. The debate over overtime pay is complicated by the fact that the Fair Labor Standards Act (Wage-Hour Law) of 1938 requires employers to pay employees **overtime wages**—one and a half times their normal hourly rate for all hours worked beyond forty hours per week. The act exempts certain types of employees from this overtime-pay requirement, however. *Exempt employees* include those who qualify under the terms of the act as holding "administrative," "executive," or "professional" positions.

OVERTIME WAGES
Wages paid to workers who are paid an hourly wage rate to compensate them for overtime work (hours worked beyond forty hours per week). Under federal law, overtime wages are at least one-and-a-half times the regular hourly wage rate.

The issue, then, is whether paralegals are exempt or nonexempt employees under the Fair Labor Standards Act. If they are exempt, they need not be paid an hourly overtime rate. If they are nonexempt, by law they must be paid overtime wages. Many firms argue that their paralegals are professionals and thus exempt from the act. Other firms, fearing possible liability for unfair labor practices, are beginning to pay overtime wages to their paralegals. Paralegals seem to be split fairly evenly on the issue. A poll taken in 1993 by the National Federation of Paralegal Associations indicated that 51 percent of paralegals supported exempt status and 49 percent preferred to be nonexempt employees (and thus receive overtime wages).

In early 1994, a federal court addressed this issue for the first time. The case arose when twenty-three paralegals who worked for Page & Addison, a law firm in Dallas, Texas, sought $40,000 in back wages for overtime hours that they had worked. The Department of Labor, which enforces the Fair Labor Standards Act, had concluded that the paralegals were nonexempt employees and thus subject to the act's overtime provisions. The federal court, however, disagreed, finding that paralegals could be classified as exempt (or professional) employees because they perform important work and exercise discretion and independent judgment.[4] Although the court decision in the *Page & Addison* case is significant, it does not mean that all paralegals will be classified as exempt employees. Very likely, the Labor Department and courts hearing future cases, should cases arise, will evaluate the claims relating to overtime pay on a case-by-case basis and take into consideration the specific types of tasks undertaken by the paralegals involved.

PLANNING YOUR CAREER

Career planning involves essentially three steps. The first step is defining your long-term goals. The second step involves adjusting your long-term goals to meet the realities of the job market. We look at these two steps of career planning in this section. Later in this chapter, we discuss the third step: reevaluating your career after you have had some on-the-job experience as a paralegal.

Defining Your Long-term Goals

From the outset, you will want to define, as clearly as possible, your career goals, and this requires some personal reflection and self-assessment. What are you looking for in a career? Why do you want to become a paralegal? Is income the most important factor? Is job satisfaction (doing the kind of work you like) the most important factor? Is the environment in which you work the most important factor? What profession could best utilize your special talents or skills? Asking yourself these and other broad questions about your personal preferences and values will help you define more clearly your overall professional goals.

Do not be surprised to find that your long-term goals change over time. As you gain more experience as a paralegal and your life circumstances change, you may decide that your former long-term goals are no longer as satisfying. Also, at the outset of your career, you cannot know what opportunities might present themselves in the future. Career planning is an ongoing challenge for paralegals, just as it is for all persons. Throughout your career as a paralegal, you will probably meet other paralegals who have made career changes. Many paralegals, for example, decided to become paralegals after several years of working in another profession, such as nursing, business administration, or accounting. Changes within the profession, your own experiences, and new opportunities constantly affect the career choices before you. The realities you face during your career may play a significant role in modifying your long-term goals.

Short-term Goals and Job Realities

Long-term goals are just that—goals that we hope to achieve over the long run. It may take many years or even a lifetime to attain certain long-term

4. *U.S. Department of Labor v. Page & Addison, P.C.*, U.S. District Court, Dallas, Texas, No. 91-2655, March 15, 1994.

goals that we set for ourselves. Short-term goals are the steps that we take to realize our long-term goals. As an entry-level paralegal, one of your short-term goals is simply to find a job.

Ideally, you will find a job that provides you with a salary commensurate with your training and abilities, a level of responsibility that is comfortable (or challenging) for you, and excellent job benefits. The realities of the job market are not always what we would wish them to be, however. You should be prepared for the possibility that you might not find the "right" employer or the "perfect" job for you when you first start your job search. You may be lucky from the outset, but then again, it may take several attempts before you find the employer and the job that best suits your needs, skills, and talents. Remember, though, that even if you do not find the perfect job at the outset, you can gain valuable skills and experience in *any* job environment—skills and experience that can help you achieve long-term goals in the future.

LOCATING POTENTIAL EMPLOYERS

Looking for a job is time consuming and requires attention to detail, persistence, and creativity. Your paralegal education is preparing you, among other things, to do investigative research. The investigative skills that you will use on the job as a paralegal are the ones that you should apply when looking for a job.

You should begin compiling employer information for your job search while you are still engaged in paralegal studies. Many of the resources you will need are available at the college or university that you attend or through your paralegal program. In a well-organized job search, you will locate and contact those organizations that offer the benefits, the salary, the opportunities for advancement, the work environment, and perhaps the legal specialty of your choice.

Although a **trade journal** (such as your state bar association's newsletter) or a local newspaper may list available jobs, you should also apply to firms and other organizations that have not yet advertised a vacancy. You want your job application to be immediately available to the potential employer when an opening does occur. To accomplish this, you want to have your application on file with the employer before a position opens up. After all, there is little need for a firm to advertise in the "Help Wanted" section of a newspaper or trade magazine when it has a number of qualified candidates already in its personnel file. Most firms, if they are interested in your qualifications, will normally keep your application on file for six months.

TRADE JOURNAL
A newsletter, magazine, or other periodical that provides a certain trade or profession with information (products, trends, or developments) relating to that trade or profession.

Where do you begin your investigation? How do you know which law firms practice the type of law that interests you? Does the law firm of your choice employ paralegals? The following sources for employer information will be helpful in answering all of these questions.

Directories

Numerous directories list potential employers. The *Martindale-Hubbel Law Directory*, which is available at most law libraries, lists the names, addresses, telephone numbers, area of legal practice, and other data for many lawyers and law firms throughout the United States. The directory is an excellent resource for the paralegal interested in employment with a law firm.

FEATURED GUEST: DENISE TEMPLETON

Paralegal Career Planning and Development

Biographical Note

Denise Templeton is the president and chief executive officer of Templeton & Associates, a legal support services firm based in Minneapolis, Minnesota. She has been involved with the paralegal profession since she graduated from the Institute for Paralegal Training in Philadelphia in 1972. Her professional career has included work as a legal assistant in both the public and private sectors, as well as seven years as the director of the legal assistant program at the University of Minnesota. In 1985, she founded the Minnesota Legal Assistant Institute, a private postsecondary certificate program. Templeton is also a founder of the Minnesota Association of Legal Assistants, the American Association for Paralegal Education, and the National Federation of Paralegal Associations (NFPA). She is currently on the NFPA Advisory Council.

In the early 1970s, the paralegal field was just beginning to be officially recognized, and its parameters were undefined. The larger law firms and corporate legal departments were the first to grasp the concept that legal assistants could free busy attorneys by taking over the more routine legal tasks. This enabled law firms to get more work done in the same amount of time and at a constant level of quality. Because paralegals were a less expensive resource than attorneys, clients were able to pay less for legal services without sacrificing quality.

Then, as now, the majority of paralegals were employed in the litigation area [relating to lawsuits]. Over time, more specialty areas have opened up, and today's paralegal can be involved in anything from real estate to environmental law. Many opportunities are available now, and many more will be created in the future. People are entering the paralegal field in greater numbers each year. The successful legal assistant knows the importance of adopting a career-development strategy. My strategy includes six basic components: (1) self-awareness, (2) knowledge of the field, (3) openness to opportunity, (4) professional development, (5) support systems, and (6) periodic review.

SELF-AWARENESS

Self-awareness involves creating a vision. You must envision what you want and expect from a paralegal career based on your knowledge of yourself and what is important to you in your work. As you develop your career path, think about where you want to start and where you want to be in the long run. There are many possibilities in terms of both work environments and types of work. As a beginner, you may seek a large, structured office and a position that is clearly defined. One of the larger law firms or a corporate legal department may provide you with this framework. You may, however, sense that a smaller, less structured environment would be more comfortable for you. Your duties may be more varied. In any event, analyze your previous experience and prioritize your goals. Decide which goal is most important for you.

KNOWLEDGE OF THE FIELD

In tandem with self-assessment, consider the realities of the paralegal field itself. Again, because of the many options available in terms of legal specialties and work environments, the paralegal field can accommodate many types of people.

Some areas of law require more intensity, time, and dedication than others. If you are already juggling the demands of a job and a family,

You may also find the Yellow Pages of your telephone book useful in locating potential employers. Look under "Attorneys" for the names of attorneys and law firms in your area. If you want to work in a special area, such as real estate, you might look under other listings, such as "Title Companies." Many larger libraries have the Yellow Pages for major cities across the country, which allows you to broaden the geographic scope of your search.

FEATURED GUEST, Continued

for example, overtime may be a serious problem. Talk to people working in the area that interests you. Learn about the advantages and disadvantages of working in that area. The more you learn about that area, the more accurate and complete will be your picture of what to expect and how the position fits in with your vision.

OPENNESS TO OPPORTUNITY

By keeping an open mind and being aware of changing interests, you will be able to create new opportunities for yourself and take advantage of opportunities that arise as your career develops. Even if you have already created your vision of the ideal paralegal career path, stay open to possibilities that may present themselves. If you are trained in probate practice (which deals with the transfer of property on a person's death), for example, you may find that real estate is a compatible specialty. By making your interest in real-estate practice known to your supervisor, you demonstrate a willingness to expand your legal knowledge. Ultimately, you may work for a corporation in its real-estate management or development division. The idea of cross-training becomes increasingly more acceptable as firms develop a more flexible work force. When the economy takes a turn for the worse, those who have multiple skills can be reassigned rather than laid off.

PROFESSIONAL DEVELOPMENT

Closely aligned with openness to opportunity is staying aware of developments in your profession. Developing and maintaining professional contacts and reading paralegal publications regularly are great ways to keep up with trends in your field. This knowledge can help you decide when and how to make turns in your career path. Also, the critical skill of networking plays an important role for any professional, including the paralegal. From the beginning, keep a current list of the people you meet and the area in which they work. Become an active member of your local paralegal association. If there is no paralegal association in your community, then start one. Read the periodicals published by national paralegal associations and bar associations, and read materials that will keep you up to date on what is happening locally and nationally with paralegals. Ask paralegals and attorneys what they read, and attend continuing-education seminars to expand your knowledge base.

SUPPORT SYSTEMS

The value of having people give you encouragement and constructive criticism cannot be overstated. When you share ideas and concerns with others involved in your work, you will have a more balanced perspective on your work. Balance is an important ingredient in life.

"TODAY'S PARALEGAL CAN BE INVOLVED IN ANYTHING FROM REAL ESTATE TO ENVIRONMENTAL LAW."

When you are working in an intense, deadline-oriented atmosphere, balance can be painfully elusive. That is why having friends and participating in activities both inside and outside the legal profession is important to your well-being. Promise yourself that you will take regular vacations with family and friends and keep yourself healthy, happy, and productive.

PERIODIC REVIEW

Remember, change is the only constant in life. Many opportunities exist now that were not possible when the paralegal field was new. Many new opportunities will arise in the future. By taking the time periodically to take stock of your own changing needs and desires, as well as the evolution of the field, you can decide which career step to take next and when to take it. For those paralegals who take charge of their own destinies, there are many ways to grow and prosper as legal professionals.

Once you have the telephone number of the firm, you can usually obtain the name of the individual in charge of hiring by calling the organization and speaking with the receptionist. When you send your job application, address it to the individual responsible for screening the legal staff if at all possible. If you cannot find out the name of the individual in charge of hiring, send your letter to the attention of the legal-assistant manager, the personnel director, or one of the attorneys you located in the *Martindale-Hubbel Law Directory.*

There are also numerous guides to employment with the federal government. The reference librarian in your city or university library can direct you to these sources, some of which are listed in the *Annotated Selected Readings* section at the end of Chapter 13.

Computerized Legal Services and the Internet

You might search for an employer using computerized legal services such as those offered through WESTLAW or LEXIS (discussed in Chapter 16), if you have access to these services. Through WESTLAW, for example, you can access *West's Legal Directory,* which contains detailed information on U.S. and Canadian attorneys and law firms, state and federal attorneys and offices, and corporate general counsel.

You can also access *West's Legal Directory* and other valuable sources of information through the Internet. The Internet is an international computerized network that connects over 35,000 educational, corporate, and research computer networks around the world. If you are enrolled in a college or university, it may be connected directly to the Internet. Although the college or university pays thousands of dollars a year for this hookup, access to the Internet is "free" to students and faculty. How to do research using the Internet is discussed in Appendix B at the end of this book.

Job-placement Services

Throughout the job search, make full use of your school's placement service. Many paralegal programs provide job-placement services, and ABA-approved schools are required to provide ongoing placement services for students. Placement offices are staffed with personnel trained to assist you in finding a job, as well as in preparing job-search tools, such as your résumé and a list of potential employers.

Another option is to contact a local paralegal association (or the state bar association's paralegal division, if one exists) to learn the names of any legal-placement services in your area. The names and addresses of paralegal associations and bar associations in each state are listed in Appendix H and Appendix I, respectively, at the end of this book.

Networking

Career opportunities often go unpublished. Many firms post notices within their own organization before publishing in the "Help Wanted" section of a newspaper or a periodical. This opens doors to their own employees before the general public. It also spares employers from having to wade through hundreds of employment applications for a vacant position. If you have connections within an organization, you may be told that a position is opening before other paralegal candidates are aware that an opportunity exists.

Paralegals looking for jobs often learn of available positions through networking. For paralegals, **networking** is the process of making personal connections with other paralegals, paralegal instructors, attorneys, and others who are involved in (or who know someone who is involved in) the paralegal or legal profession. You should begin networking while you are still attending your paralegal program. Cultivate relationships with your instructors. Let them know your career interests, and ask them for their advice. See if

NETWORKING
Making personal connections and cultivating relationships with people in a certain field, profession, or area of interest.

your local paralegal association allows students to be members. If it does, attend meetings and become acquainted with other paralegals, who may know of job opportunities.

Also cultivate connections during your internship as a paralegal. One of the benefits of internships or of working part-time in a law firm while studying to be a paralegal is that it allows you to establish connections that may be useful in your job search, and the firm itself may offer you a full-time job when you graduate. Throughout your career, you will find that networking can provide valuable job leads.

MARKETING YOUR SKILLS

Once you have located potential employers, the next step in your job search is to market your skills and yourself effectively to those employers. Marketing your skills involves three stages: the application process, interviewing for jobs, and following up on job interviews.

You should keep in mind throughout your job search the fact that each personal contact you make, whether it results in employment or not, has potential for your future. A firm may not hire you today, for example, because you lack experience. But it may hire you a year from now if by then you have the experience that it is seeking. Therefore, always keep track of the contacts you make during your search, be patient, and be professional. You may be surprised how many doors will open for you, if not today, then tomorrow.

The Application Process

As a paralegal looking for professional employment, you will need to assemble and present professional application materials. The basic materials you should create are a résumé, a cover letter, a list of professional references, and a portfolio. The following discussion explains each of these documents and gives some practical tips on how to create them.

The Résumé. For almost all job applications, you must submit a personal *résumé,* which summarizes your employment and educational background. Your résumé is an advertisement, and you should invest the time to make that advertisement effective. Because personnel officers in law firms, corporations, and government agencies may receive a hundred or more résumés for each position they advertise, your résumé should create the best possible impression if you want to gain a competitive edge over other job seekers.

Either generate your résumé yourself, using a computer and a laser printer, or have a professional résumé-preparation service do it for you. Format each page so that the reader is able to scan it quickly and catch the highlights. You might vary the type size, but never use a type size or style that is difficult to read.

Your name, address, and telephone number belong at the beginning of your résumé. The résumé should be simple, brief, and clear. As a general rule, it should contain only information that is relevant to the job that you are seeking. A one-page résumé is usually sufficient, unless two pages are required to list relevant educational background and work experience. Exhibit 2.5 on page 58 shows a sample résumé.

> **ETHICAL CONCERN**
>
> **"Gilding the Lily"**
>
> When applying and interviewing for a job, be honest about your skills and job qualifications. Even though you are trying to impress a prospective employer, never succumb to the temptation to "gild the lily" by exaggerating your experience and qualifications. Suppose that you are interviewing for a job and the interviewer asks you about your GPA. Wanting to impress the interviewer, you say that your GPA was 3.8 when in fact it was 3.4. This "little white lie" may cost you the job. Prospective employers usually check your credentials, including your transcripts. Any misrepresentation, no matter how minor it may seem, will create a negative impression. Professional responsibility requires, among other things, that you be honest and pay scrupulous attention to detail—not only on the job but also during the job-application process.

EXHIBIT 2.5
A Sample Résumé

ELENA LOPEZ
1311 North Shore Drive
Nita City, NI 48804
(616) 555-0102

EMPLOYMENT OBJECTIVE
Paralegal in a private law firm that specializes in personal-injury practice.

EDUCATION
1994 Postbaccalaureate Certificate, Midwestern Professional School for Paralegals, Green Bay, WI 54311.

Focus: Litigation Procedures; Legal Investigation, Research, and Writing. GPA 3.8

1993 Bachelor of Arts degree, University of Wisconsin, Madison, WI 53706. Political Science major; GPA 3.5.

PARALEGAL EXPERIENCE
Paralegal with the Caldwell Legal Clinic, 3189 Plainview, Nita City, Nita 48801. June 1994 to the present.

Responsibilities: General legal research and writing, and trial preparation in personal-injury cases.

Paralegal with the Free Legal Aid Society, 122 W. Fourth St., Green Bay, WI 54311. June 1993 through May 1994.

Responsibilities: Part-time assistance to legal-aid attorneys in their representation of indigent clients in matters such as divorce, abuse, child custody, paternity, and landlord/tenant disputes.

Research Assistant with the Political Science Department, University of Wisconsin. January 1990 to May 1993.

Responsibilities: Research on the international implications of an end to the Cold War and the changing face of the former Soviet Union.

AFFILIATIONS
Paralegal Association of Wisconsin
National Association of Legal Assistants

Headings. Divide your résumé into logical sections with headings. Examples of headings are as follows:

- Employment Objective.
- Employment History.

- Legal Work Experience.
- Related Work Experience.
- Professional Affiliations and Membership.
- Selected Accomplishments.

Whenever you list dates, such as educational and employment dates, list them chronologically, in reverse order. In other words, list your most recent educational or work history first. When discussing your education, list the names, cities, and states of the colleges or universities that you have attended and the degrees that you have received. You may want to indicate your major and minor concentrations and those courses that are most related to your professional goal, such as "Major: Paralegal Studies" or "Minor: Political Science."

Scholarships or honors should also be indicated. If you have a high grade point average (GPA), you should include it in your résumé. Under the heading "Selected Accomplishments," you might indicate your ability to speak a foreign language or other special skill, such as computer skills.

When listing your work experience, specify what your responsibilities have been in each position that you have held. Also, include any volunteer work that you have done.

Do Not Include Personal Data. Avoid including personal data (such as age, marital status, number of children, gender, or hobbies) in your résumé. Employers are prohibited by law from discriminating against employees or job candidates on the basis of race, color, sex, national origin, religion, age, or disability. You can help them fulfill this legal obligation by not including in your résumé any information that could serve as a basis for discrimination. For the same reason, you would be wise not to include a photograph of yourself with your résumé. Also, most prospective employers are not interested in information such as personal preferences, pastimes, or hobbies.

Use a Computer, If Possible. If you have access to a computer, create a file for your résumé so that you can easily update it and tailor it to specific job openings. (If you do not have a computer, keep a printout of the résumé for future use or revision.) For instance, you may wish to modify your listing under the "Related Work Experience" heading, depending on whether you are responding to an advertisement for a mortgage processor with a local bank or a paralegal position with a prominent law firm. When making changes on your résumé, be careful not to introduce formatting or other errors.

When you create your own résumé on a computer, use a laser printer and good-quality paper, such as white bond or even parchment paper. You want your résumé to look as professional and aesthetically attractive as possible.

Proofread Your Results. Carefully proofread your résumé. Use the spelling checker and grammar checker on your computer, but do not rely on them totally. Also have a friend or teacher review your résumé for punctuation, syntax, grammar, spelling, and content. If you find an error, you need to fix it, even if it means having new résumés printed. A mistake on your résumé tells the potential employer that you are a careless worker, and this message may ruin your chances of landing a job.

The Cover Letter. To encourage the recruiter to review your résumé, you need to capture his or her attention with a *cover letter* that accompanies the résumé. Because the cover letter often represents your first contact with an employer, it should be written carefully and precisely. It should be brief, perhaps only two or three paragraphs in length. Exhibit 2.6 shows a sample cover letter.

Whenever possible, you should learn the name of the individual in charge of hiring (by phone, if necessary) and direct your letter to that person. If you do not know the name of the individual responsible for reviewing résumés, use a generic title that is neither sexist nor condescending. A female recruiter may be offended if you begin your letter with "Dear Sir" ("Dear Sir or Madam" might be a better choice), and an individual whose title is "Director" may be offended by "Dear Personnel Clerk."

Your cover letter should point out a few things about yourself and your qualifications for the position that might persuade a recruiter to examine your résumé. As a recently graduated paralegal, for example, you might draw attention to your high academic standing at school, your eagerness to specialize in the same area of law as the employer (perhaps listing some courses relating to that specialty), and your willingness to relocate to the employer's city. Your job is to convince the recruiter that you are a close match to the mental picture that he or she has of the perfect candidate for the job. Make sure that the reader knows when and where you can be reached. Often this is best indicated in the closing paragraph of the letter, as shown in Exhibit 2.6.

As with your résumé, you should read through your letter several times and have someone else read it also to make sure that it is free from mistakes and reads easily. You should use the same type of paper for your cover letter as you use for your résumé.

List of Professional References. If a firm is interested in your application, you will probably be asked to provide a list of references—people whom the firm can contact to obtain information about you and your abilities. A paralegal instructor who has worked closely with you on an academic project, an internship supervisor who has first-hand knowledge of your work, or a past employer who has observed your problem-solving ability would all make excellent references. You should have at least three professionally relevant references, but no more than five references are necessary (if an interviewer needs additional references, he or she will ask for them). Never include the names of family members, friends, or others who will be clearly biased in your favor.

For each person included on your list of references, include his or her current institutional affiliation or business firm, address, and telephone number. Also, when creating your list of references, always remember the following rule:

- **Never list a person's name as a reference unless you have first obtained that person's permission to do so.**

After all, it will not help you win the position if one of your references is surprised by the call or is permanently unavailable, such as a paralegal instructor who is out of the country for the year. Such events raise a red flag to the interviewer and indicate that you are not concerned with details.

Obtaining permission from legal professionals to use their names as references also gives you an opportunity to discuss your plans and goals with them, and they may be able to advise you and assist you in your networking.

EXHIBIT 2.6
A Sample Cover Letter

Elena Lopez
1311 North Shore Drive
Nita City, NI 48804
(616) 555-0102

August 22, 1995

Mr. Allen P. Gilmore
Jeffers, Gilmore & Dunn
553 Fifth Avenue, Suite 101
Nita City, NI 48801

Dear Mr. Gilmore:

I am responding to your advertisement in the University of Nita Law Journal for a paralegal to assist you in personal-injury litigation.

My bachelor of arts degree is from the University of Nita. I am a recent graduate of the Midwestern Professional School for Paralegals. My paralegal courses included litigation procedures, legal research, legal investigation, and legal writing. I hope to specialize in the area of personal-injury law.

I would like very much to meet with you or your representative to learn more about the position that you have available. I am enclosing a copy of my résumé and a list of professional references.

If you wish to contact me, I can be reached during the day at (616) 555-6932 and after five o'clock at the number given above.

Sincerely yours,

Elena Lopez

Elena Lopez

Encs.

Additionally, it gives you a chance to discuss with them the kinds of experience and skills that a prospective employer may ask them about.

Your Portfolio. When a potential employer asks you for an interview, have your **portfolio** of selected documents ready to give to the interviewer. The portfolio should contain another copy of your résumé, a list of references, letters of recommendation written by previous employers or instructors, samples of legal documents that you have written, college or university transcripts, and any other relevant professional information, such as proof of

Portfolio
A job applicant's collection of selected personal documents (such as school transcripts, writing samples, and certificates) for presentation to a potential employer.

professional certification or achievement. This collection of documents should be well organized and professionally presented. Depending on the size of your portfolio, a cover sheet, a table of contents, and a commercial binder may be appropriate.

The interviewer may be very interested in your research and writing skills. Therefore, your portfolio should contain several samples of legal writing. If you are looking for your first legal position, go through your paralegal drafting assignments and pull out those that reflect your best work. Then, working with an instructor or other mentor, revise and improve those samples for inclusion in the portfolio. Documents that you have drafted while an intern or when working as a part-time or a full-time paralegal might also be used. These documents make excellent writing samples because they involve real-life circumstances. Be careful in doing this, however, and always remember to do the following:

- **On any sample document, completely blacken out (or "white out") any identifying reference to the client unless you have the client's permission to disclose his or her identity or the information is not confidential.**

Always include a résumé, as well as a list of references, in your portfolio, even though you already sent your résumé to the prospective employer with your cover letter. Interviewers may not have the résumé at hand at the time of the interview, and providing a second copy with your portfolio is a thoughtful effort on your part.

Some interviewers may examine your portfolio carefully. Others may retain it to examine later, after the interview has concluded. Still others may not be interested in it at all. If there is some particular item in your portfolio that you would like the interviewer to see, make sure you point this out before leaving the interview.

The Interview

Interviews with potential employers may be the most challenging (and most stressful) aspect of your search for employment. The interview ordinarily takes place after the employer has reviewed your cover letter and résumé. Often, if the employer is interested in your application, a secretary or a legal assistant will contact you to schedule an interview.

Every interview will be a unique experience. Some interviews will go very well, but you may still be a second choice and lose out to another candidate. Nonetheless, you have made a good contact, and you may be able to use this interviewer as a resource for information about other jobs. Remember what went right about the interview, and try to use that information at the next one. Other interviews may go poorly. There are good lessons to be learned from poor interviews, however.

You will also find that some interviewers are more skilled at interviewing than others. Some have a talent for getting applicants to open up and discuss candidly their work and backgrounds. Others are confrontational and put the already nervous candidate on the defensive. Still others may be unprepared for the interview. They may not have had time to check the job requirements, for example, or when the position is available. Unfortunately, as the person being interviewed, you have no control over who will interview you. The following discussion will help you prepare for a first paralegal job interview and will also serve as a refresher for you when seeking a career change.

Before the Interview. You can do many things prior to the interview to enhance your chances of getting the job. First of all, you should do your "homework." Learn as much about the employer as possible. Check with your instructors or other legal professionals to find out if they are familiar with the firm or the interviewer. When you are called for an interview, learn the full name of the interviewer, so that you will be able to address the interviewer by name during the interview and properly address a follow-up letter. During the interview, use Mr. or Ms. unless directed by the interviewer to be less formal.

Anticipate and review in your mind the possible questions that you might be asked during the interview. Then prepare (and possibly rehearse with a friend) your answers to these questions. For example, if you did not graduate from high school with your class but later fulfilled the requirements to graduate and received a general equivalency diploma (GED), you might well be asked why you dropped out of school. If you have already prepared an answer for this question, it may save you the embarassment of having to decide, on the spot, how to reduce a complicated story to a brief sentence or two.

Timing is an extremely important factor. When preparing for an interview, you should therefore do the following:

- **Arrive for the interview at least ten minutes early and allow plenty of extra time to get there. If the firm is located in an area that is unfamiliar to you, make sure that you know how to get there, how long it will take to get there, and, if you are driving, whether parking space is available nearby.**

Appearance is also important. Wear a relatively conservative suit or dress to the interview, and limit your use of jewelry or other flashy accents. You can find further tips on how to prepare for a job interview by checking your local bookstore or the library for books dealing with careers and job hunting.

At the Interview. During the interview, pay attention and listen closely to the interviewer's questions, observations, and comments. The interviewer asks questions to learn whether the candidate will fit comfortably into the firm, whether the candidate is organized and competent and will satisfactorily perform the job, and whether the candidate is reliable and will apply himself or herself to mastering the tasks presented. Your answers should be directly related to the questions, and you should not stray from the point. If you are unsure of what the interviewer means by a certain question, ask for clarification.

Interviewers use certain question formats to elicit certain types of responses. Four typical formats for questions are closed-ended questions, open-ended questions, pressure questions, and hypothetical questions.

Closed-ended Questions. The **closed-ended question** is phrased in such a way that it calls for a simple "Yes" or "No" answer plus, perhaps, a brief explanation. "What was your GPA?" is a closed-ended question. The

CLOSED-ENDED QUESTION
A question that is phrased in such a way that it elicits a simple "Yes" or "No" answer.

EXHIBIT 2.7
Closed-ended Questions

Q. If you were offered this position, would you be willing to relocate to this city?

A. Yes. I've already subscribed to a local newspaper to learn about housing prices and availability.

Q. Have you ever assisted at a real-estate closing?

A. No, I have not. I did take a course in real-estate law and procedures while in paralegal school, however.

Q. Do you have any medical training?

A. No, although in my previous job I assisted attorneys with personal-injury cases and learned some medical terminology.

Q. Do you plan to go to law school?

A. No.

Q. Do you have any experience in the area of bankruptcy law?

A. No. I've never worked in that area.

interviewer may ask several of these questions in quick succession to see how alert you are and how quickly you respond. Exhibit 2.7 illustrates some other closed-ended questions.

OPEN-ENDED QUESTION
A question that is phrased in such a way that it elicits a relatively detailed discussion of an experience or topic.

Open-ended Questions. An **open-ended question** is one that requires the candidate to discuss, in some detail, a specific topic or experience. "Why did you decide to become a paralegal?" is an example of an open-ended question. See Exhibit 2.8 for other examples.

HYPOTHETICAL QUESTION
A question based on hypothesis, conjecture, or fiction. Interviewers sometimes use hypothetical questions to observe how an interviewee might handle a difficult situation.

Hypothetical Questions. The **hypothetical question** is an effective method of determining how you might handle difficult situations. Often, hypothetical questions are directly related to a situation that realistically could occur during the course of your work as a paralegal. On some occasions, however, the hypothetical question may appear farfetched, such as "If you were stranded on a desert island with only two books, which two would you choose?" Although you may think that such a question is irrelevant, the interviewer may learn a surprising amount of information about your personality and character from your answer. Exhibit 2.9 on page 66 offers a sampling of hypothetical questions.

PRESSURE QUESTION
A question intended to make the interviewee uncomfortable and respond emotionally. Pressure questions are sometimes used by interviewers to observe how the interviewee handles uncomfortable or unpleasant situations.

Pressure Questions. One line of questioning, using **pressure questions,** is intended to see how you deal with uncomfortable situations or unpleasant discussions and to elicit emotional responses. Pressure questions are intended to throw you off balance and to allow the interviewer to observe how you communicate and act under stress. Often, what you say is less important than how you say it. Maintain your poise and answer the question in a way that is comfortable for you. (See Exhibit 2.10 on page 66 for sample pressure questions.)

Q. Why are you interested in working for this firm?

A. Well, actually there are several reasons why I want to work for your organization. First of all, I am interested in civil practice, and in particular, personal-injury law. Second, your law firm has an excellent reputation. Third, I hope to . . .

Q. Why are you changing jobs?

A. As you may have heard, the Caldwell Legal Clinic is closing some of its branch offices, including the office in which I worked. They offered me a job in their New York City office, but I don't want to live in New York. Also, . . .

Q. What was your favorite paralegal subject in school?

A. Well, that's difficult to say. I really enjoyed learning about litigation procedures, but I also enjoyed studying about legal investigation and legal research. Also, the area of . . .

Q. What was your least favorite paralegal subject?

A. I'm not sure how to answer that question. Generally, I liked all of my courses, but if I had to choose . . .

EXHIBIT 2.8
Open-ended Questions

Pressure questions should be distinguished from questions that are illegal. Questions that are at least objectionable and that may be illegal include those directed at your marital status, family, religion, race, color, national origin, age, health or disability, or arrests. You do not have to answer such questions unless you choose to do so. Exhibit 2.11 on page 67 shows some examples of these types of questions.

"Do You Have Any Questions?" As odd as it may seem, one of the most difficult moments is when the interviewer turns the questioning around by asking, "Now then, do you have any questions?" Be prepared for this question. Before the interview, take time to list your concerns. Take the list to the interview with you. Questioning the interviewer gives you an opportunity to learn more about the firm and how it uses paralegal services. Questioning the interviewer also may also give the interviewer an opportunity to see how you might interview a client on behalf of the firm. Exhibit 2.12 on page 67 lists some sample questions that you might ask the interviewer. Note that you should not raise the issue of salary at the first interview unless you are offered the job.

After the Interview. You should not expect to be hired as the result of a single interview, although occasionally this does happen. Often, two and maybe three interviews take place before you are offered a job. After leaving the interview, jot down a few notes to provide a refresher for your memory

EXHIBIT 2.9
Hypothetical Questions

Q. If you were asked at four o'clock on a Wednesday afternoon to continue working until eight o'clock that night to complete a rather lengthy document that had to be filed with the court on Thursday morning, what would be your response?

A. I would certainly stay, as needed. I understand that there are certain tasks that must be completed within a given time frame and that this may entail evening or even weekend work.

Q. Suppose that you are working with another paralegal as part of a team. How would you handle a situation in which your work product was claimed by the other paralegal as his or her own work?

A. Well, that would certainly be an unpleasant situation. I keep very good records of the work I do, how long it takes me to accomplish the task, and the name of the attorney for whom I did the work. I would have to confront . . .

Q. What would you do if a client asked you to keep certain information secret from your supervising attorney?

A. Hmm. That's another difficult situation. First, I would explain to the client that I am obligated to disclose to my supervising attorney any information that is relevant to the legal representation of the client. Then I would encourage the client to never tell me . . . .

should you be called back for a second (or third) interview. You will impress the interviewer if you are able to "pick up where you left off" from a discussion initiated several weeks ago. Also list the names and positions of the people you met during the interview or just before or after it.

The Follow-up Letter

A day or two after the interview, but not longer than a week later, you should send a *follow-up letter* to the interviewer. In this brief letter, you can reiterate your availability and interest in the position, thank the interviewer for his or her time in interviewing you, and perhaps refer to a discussion that took place during the interview.

You may have left the interview with the impression that the meeting

EXHIBIT 2.10
Pressure Questions

Q. You mentioned that you are a member of the Nature Conservancy. I've heard that those people are nothing but a bunch of pompous enviro-morons. Why are you affiliated with them?

A. (Chuckling at the absurdity of the question.) No, I am definitely not a crackpot. I am a concerned citizen, and, as I am sure you are aware, I have the right to choose those organizations that best reflect my interests.

Q. I see. Well I guess you would like to see all of the lumberjacks on the West Coast unemployed and destitute, too?

A. On the contrary, I feel that the lumber industry is at a critical juncture in its development. The lumbering tradition can be preserved with more advanced nursery practices. Both the timber industry and lumbering jobs can be preserved without destroying the limited timber resources that provide critical habitats to endangered species, such as the spotted owl. I know of an interesting article on this very subject written by a local environmental attorney, perhaps you know him. . . .

EXHIBIT 2.11
Objectionable or Illegal Questions

Q. Are you married?

A. Yes, but is my marital state relevant to this job?

Q. Do you have any children yet?

A. No I don't. Do you think this line of questioning is appropriate?

Q. Just one more question. Are you or your husband a member of the Republican party?

A. That's a private matter. Please realize that my family and political life will not interfere with my ability to do excellent work for your firm.

Q. You're quite a bit more mature than other applicants. Will you be thinking of retiring in the next ten years?

A. I may be, but I don't understand how my age relates to my ability to perform this job.

went badly. But the interviewer may have a different sense of what happened at the meeting. Interviewers have different styles, and what you interpreted to be a bad interview may just have been a reflection of that interviewer's particular approach or style. You simply have no way of being certain, so follow through and make yourself available for the job or at least for another meeting. For an example of a follow-up letter, see Exhibit 2.13 on page 68.

Record Keeping

In addition to keeping your portfolio materials up to date, you need to create a filing system to stay abreast of your job-search activities. You should keep copies of your letters and any responses to them in your files. You might also want to keep lists or notes on addresses, telephone numbers, dates of contacts, advantages and disadvantages of employment with the various firms that you have contacted or by which you have been interviewed, topics dis-

EXHIBIT 2.12
Questioning the Interviewer

QUESTIONS THAT YOU MIGHT WANT TO ASK THE INTERVIEWER INCLUDE THE FOLLOWING:

- What is the method by which the firm assigns duties to paralegals?
- How do paralegals function within the organization?
- What clerical support staff is available for paralegals?
- Does the job involve travel? How will travel expenses be covered?
- What computer technology is used by the firm?
- Does the firm support paralegal continuing-education and training programs?
- Will client contact be direct or indirect?
- Does the firm have an in-house library and access to computerized research services that paralegals can use?
- Will the paralegal be assigned work in a given specialty, such as real-estate or family law?
- When does the job begin?
- What method is used to review and evaluate paralegal performance?
- How are paralegals supervised and by whom?

acceptable, then you have no problem. If you think it is too low, then the situation becomes more delicate. If you have no other job offer and really need a job, you may not want to foreclose this job opportunity by saying that the salary is too low. You might instead tell the prospective employer that the job interests you and that you will consider the offer seriously. Also, remember that salary is just one factor in deciding what a job is worth to you. In addition to salary, you need to consider job benefits and other factors, including those listed in Exhibit 2.14 on page 70.

Some prospective employers do not suggest a salary or a salary range but rather ask the job applicant what kind of salary he or she had in mind. You should be prepared for this question and should have done your research on paralegal salaries in the area.

- **Unless you are already familiar with the firm's salary structure, you should research the compensation given to paralegals in similar job situations in your community before you discuss salary with a prospective employer.**

Suppose that you have found in your research that paralegals in the community usually start at $20,000 but that many with your education and training start at $25,000. If you ask for an annual salary of $30,000, then you may be unrealistically expensive—and the job offer may be lost. If you ask for $25,000, then you are still "in the ballpark"—and you may win the job offer.

Negotiating salaries can be difficult. On the one hand, you want to obtain a good salary and do not want to underprice your services. On the other hand, overpricing your services may extinguish an employment opportunity or eliminate the possibility of working for an otherwise suitable employer. Your best option might be to state a salary *range* that is acceptable to you. That way, you are not pinned down to a specific figure. Note, though, that if you indicate an acceptable salary range, you invite an offer of the lowest salary—so the low end of the salary range should be the threshold amount that you will accept.

REEVALUATING YOUR CAREER

Once you have gained experience working as a paralegal, you can undertake the third step in career planning: reevaluation. Assume that you have worked for a long enough period (two to four years, for example) to have acquired experience in certain types of paralegal work. At this point, you should reevaluate your career goals and reassess your abilities based on your accumulated experience.

Career Advancement

Paralegals who want to advance in their careers normally have two options: (1) being promoted or transferring to another department within the firm or (2) moving to another firm—and perhaps another specialty.

Larger firms often provide career paths for their paralegal employees. Moving from the entry-level position of *legal-assistant clerk* to the position of *legal-assistant manager,* for example, may be one career track within a

EXHIBIT 2.14
Salary Negotiations: What Is the Job Worth to You?

BENEFITS
What benefits are included? Will the benefits package include medical insurance? Life insurance? Disability insurance? Dental insurance? What portion, if any, of the insurance premium will be deducted from your wages? Is there an employee pension plan? How many paid vacation days will you have? Will the firm cover your paralegal association fees? Will the firm assist you in tuition and other costs associated with continuing paralegal education? Will the firm assist in day-care arrangements and/or costs? Will you have access to a company automobile? Does the firm help with parking expenses (important in major cities)?

CAREER OPPORTUNITIES
Does the position offer you opportunities for advancement? You may be willing to accept a lower salary now if you know that it will increase as you move up the career ladder.

COMPENSATION
Will you receive an annual salary or be paid by the hour? If you will receive an annual salary, will you receive annual bonuses? How are bonuses determined? Is the salary negotiable? (In some large firms and in government agencies, it may not be.)

COMPETITION
How stiff is the competition for this job? If you really want the job and are competing with numerous other candidates for the position, you might want to accept a lower salary just to land the job.

JOB DESCRIPTION
What are the paralegal's duties within the organization? Do you have sufficient training and experience to handle these duties? Are you underqualified or overqualified for the job? Will your skills as a paralegal be utilized effectively? How hard will you be expected to work? How much overtime work will likely be required? How stressful will the job be?

JOB FLEXIBILITY
How flexible are the working hours? If you work eight hours overtime one week, can you take a (paid) day off the following week? Can you take time off during periods when the workload is less?

LOCATION
Do you want to live in this community? What is the cost of living in this area? Remember, a $40,000 salary in New York City, where housing and taxes are very expensive, may not give you as much *real* income as a $25,000 salary in a smaller, mid-sized community in the Midwest.

PERMANENCE
Is the job a permanent or temporary position? Usually, hourly rates for temporary assistance are higher than for permanent employees.

TRAVEL
Will you be required to travel? If so, how often or extensively? How will travel expenses be handled? Will you pay them up front and then be reimbursed by the employer?

large law firm. A career track with a state government agency might begin at a *legal-technician* level and advance to a *legal-specialist* level.

Creating Opportunities

Smaller firms, in contrast, usually have no predetermined career path or opportunities for promotion and career advancement. If you are the only paralegal in a small law firm, there will be no specified career path within the firm for you to follow. If you find yourself in this situation, you might consider staying with the firm and creating your own position or career ladder. Moving up the ladder is often a matter of bringing in someone new to assist you with your paralegal responsibilities. Are you prevented from taking on more complicated tasks (which you are capable of performing)

TODAY'S PROFESSIONAL PARALEGAL

Witness Coordination

Barbara Lyons works as a paralegal for a busy litigation firm. Today she is assisting with a medical-malpractice trial. Susan Weiss, the attorney for whom Barbara works, has asked Barbara to coordinate Susan's witnesses. It is 8:30 A.M., and Barbara and Susan are waiting in the courtroom for Dr. Max Brennan, the first witness that Susan will call today.

PLANNING A WITNESS'S ARRIVAL TIME

While they are waiting, Susan fills Barbara in on how the trial went yesterday and what she expects to happen today. Susan tells Barbara that she expects Dr. Brennan to be on the stand testifying from 9 A.M. until at least the lunch break. Then she expects that he will be cross-examined for an hour or two after lunch. Susan wants Barbara to have the next witness, Laura Lang, at the courthouse and ready to testify by 11 A.M., though, in the event that Dr. Brennan is excused earlier than expected.

Barbara had previously arranged with the witness to arrive at the courthouse by 11 A.M. but is concerned that Lang will not be on time. Even though Barbara met with Lang two times to review her testimony and prepare her for the trial experience, she was always late. Barbara tells this to Susan. Susan tells Barbara to go out into the hallway at 9 A.M. and call Lang. "Tell her that things are moving along more quickly than planned and to be here at ten o'clock. That should help to make sure that she will be here by eleven."

A WITNESS IS DELAYED

It is 8:35 A.M., and Dr. Brennan has not yet arrived. Susan asks Barbara to go out to the hallway and call him, first in his car and then his office, to find out where he is. Barbara opens her trial notebook to the witness section. Dr. Brennan's page is first because he is the first witness scheduled to appear. She locates the number for his car phone, jots it down on a scrap of paper, and leaves the courtroom. As she starts dialing Dr. Brennan's number, she sees him walk out of the elevator. Barbara puts the phone back and greets Dr. Brennan. "Sorry I'm running late, but I had an emergency this morning and I had to stop by the hospital before I came here," explains Dr. Brennan.

"I'm just glad to see you!" exclaims Barbara. "Let's go into the courtroom. You are the first witness, and Susan wants to see you," instructs Barbara. Barbara and Dr. Brennan enter the courtroom. Susan and Dr. Brennan talk briefly before the judge enters the courtroom. The court is called to order, and the trial resumes. Barbara sits at the counsel table while Susan questions Dr. Brennan on the stand. At 9:00 A.M., Barbara leaves the courtroom and calls Laura Lang.

TAKING PRECAUTIONS—ARRANGING FOR A WITNESS TO ARRIVE EARLY

Lang answers the phone. "Hello Ms. Lang. It's Barbara Lyons from Smith, White & White. Susan Weiss asked me to call you and tell you that the trial is moving faster than we anticipated. Susan would like you to be here at ten o'clock instead of eleven, if that's possible," advises Barbara. "Oh. Well, I suppose I can be there by then," responds Lang. "Do you remember how to get here?" asks Barbara. "Yes, I have the directions," answers Lang. "Good. I'll see you soon then, at ten o'clock," says Barbara. She returns to the courtroom.

At 9:55 A.M., Barbara leaves the courtroom again to wait in the hallway for Laura Lang. By 10:15 A.M., Lang has still not arrived. Barbara opens the courtroom door to listen. The testimony is going faster than Susan had anticipated, and Barbara can tell that Susan will probably be ready to put Lang on the stand in another thirty minutes or so. Barbara closes the courtroom door. She goes to the pay phone and dials Lang's telephone number. There is no answer. I hope that she is on her way, thinks Barbara.

A TIMELY ARRIVAL

Now it is 10:45 A.M., and Lang is still not there. Barbara opens the courtroom door again and can tell that there is only about five minutes left in Dr. Brennan's testimony. She dials Lang's number again. No answer. Barbara continues to wait in the hallway, and a few minutes later, Lang appears. Barbara breathes a sigh of relief. She opens the courtroom door, catches Susan's eye, and nods her head.

because of your heavy workload, much of which could be handled by a paralegal with less experience? Suggest a plan to your employer that shows how you can provide more complex legal services if you delegate many of your existing responsibilities to a new paralegal employee. One of the advantages of working for a small firm is the lack of any set, formal structure for promotions. If the firm is expanding, the paralegal may have significant input into how and to whom responsibilities will be assigned as new personnel are hired.

Other Options

There are many other alternatives. You may apply for a job with another firm that offers you a better position or more advancement opportunities. You may learn a new specialty or return to school for further education. You might volunteer to speak to paralegal classes and seminars and, in so doing, establish new contacts and contribute to paralegal professional development. Researching and writing law-related articles for your paralegal association's newsletter or trade magazine improves your professional stature in the legal community as well. Any of these activities will increase your visibility both inside and outside the firm. In a broad sense, these activities are part of networking. The people you meet when engaging in these activities may offer you employment opportunities that you did not even know existed but that are perfect for you.

KEY TERMS AND CONCEPTS

bankruptcy law 41
bonus 50
civil law 39
closed-ended question 63
corporate law 40
criminal law 39
defendant 37
environmental law 45
estate planning 43
family law 46
hypothetical question 64
intellectual property 44
litigation 37
litigation paralegal 37
networking 56
open-ended question 64
overtime wages 51
plaintiff 37
portfolio 61
pressure question 64
probate 43
probate court 43
real estate 46
trade journal 53
trust 44
will 43
workers' compensation statutes 42

CHAPTER SUMMARY

1. The job opportunities available in today's paralegal employment market are extraordinarily varied. Traditionally, paralegals worked for law firms, and most paralegals continue to work in the law-firm environment. Increasingly, however, paralegals are finding employment in corporate legal departments, as well as other business institutions, such as banks and insurance companies. A small but growing number of paralegals work for government agencies at the federal or state level.

2. Paralegals often specialize in particular areas of law, including the following: litigation assistance, personal-injury law, criminal law, corporate law, bankruptcy law, employment and labor law, estate planning and probate administration, intellectual-property law, environmental law, real-estate law, and family law.

3. Salaries and wage rates for paralegal employees vary substantially. Factors affecting compensation include geographical location, firm size, and type of employer (law firm, corporation, or government agency). Most paralegals are salaried—that is, they are paid a specified amount per year, regardless of the number of hours worked. Overtime work is compensated through year-end bonuses or in some other way, such as equivalent time off work. Some paralegals are paid hourly wages for all hours worked and overtime wages for all hours worked exceeding forty hours per week.

4. Career planning involves three steps: defining your long-term career goals, adjusting your goals to fit job realities (and creating short-term goals), and reevaluating your career and career goals after you have had some on-the-job experience.

5. When looking for employment, you should apply the investigative skills that you learned in your paralegal training. You can locate potential employers by reviewing published and posted information about law firms and other possible employers, including information contained in legal trade journals, newspapers, and directories. Using computerized legal services or the Internet is an efficient means of finding useful information. You should also stay in contact with your school's placement service. Many paralegals learn of jobs through networking with other professionals. You can begin networking while you are still a paralegal student.

6. In marketing your skills as a paralegal, you will need to submit an application to potential employers. The application papers you create should include a résumé, a cover letter, a list of professional references, and a portfolio. The résumé presents a clear and concise summary of your employment and educational history. The cover letter briefly mentions some of your most important qualifications and draws attention to the résumé. The portfolio, which you provide at the job interview, contains an additional copy of the résumé, letters of recommendation, samples of legal writing, transcripts, and other relevant documents.

7. In preparing for a job interview, you should learn as much about the firm as possible. You should also anticipate questions that might be asked and prepare answers in advance. Make sure that you know how to get to the prospective employer's office, and arrive about ten minutes early. During the interview, listen closely to the questions that are asked. Some questions will be closed-ended, requiring a "Yes" or "No" answer. Other questions will be open-ended, calling for a lengthier response. Hypothetical questions and pressure questions are often used to test your communication skills and to see how you react to difficult or stressful situations. Illegal questions need not be answered. After the interview, send a follow-up letter to the interviewer. The letter should thank the interviewer for his or her time and reaffirm your interest in the position.

8. Career goals change over time, as do job opportunities. Advancing in your career may mean educating your employer in your abilities so that you can take on more responsibility, or it may mean looking for a job in a different department of the same firm or with another firm. Active participation in paralegal professional organizations or in paralegal education is a way to achieve higher visibility in the profession and to learn of new professional opportunities.

QUESTIONS FOR REVIEW

1. Name and describe the basic types of organizations that hire paralegals. What percentage of paralegals work for each type of organization?

2. From your perspective, what would be the advantages and disadvantages of working for each of the following organizations?

a. A small law firm.

b. A large law firm.

c. A corporation.

d. A government agency.

3. List and ... cialties dis... area or area...

4. How a... average par... what speci... salaries?

5. What ... What are ... wage? Wh... compensat...

6. How c... Of the met... potential ... would be r...

7. List and define the materials that are needed for the job-application process.

8. What should you do before a job interview? What types of questions may be asked during a job interview? What is the purpose of each type of question? What steps should you take after a job interview?

9. When are salary arrangements discussed during the job-application process? What factors other than salary should you consider when determining what a job is worth?

10. What are some ways in which you can advance in your paralegal career?

ETHICAL QUESTIONS

1. Tom Brown is a legal assistant in a busy litigation firm. As Tom is walking in the door at 8:30 A.M., he passes Mike Walker, his supervising attorney, who is on his way to court to begin a trial. As they pass, Mike says to Tom, "I need a motion and a brief for the *Jones* case. I've left the file on your desk." Mike walks out the door and down the street to court. Can Tom competently prepare the motion and brief? Why or why not? What should Tom do?

2. Laura Bronson has just started her first job with the firm of Thompson & Smith, a general law practice. Laura is asked to prepare articles of incorporation for one of the firm's corporate clients. Laura did not take corporate law while studying to be a paralegal and has never prepared articles of incorporation before. Should Laura accept the assignment? If she does accept it, what obligations does she have?

3. Dennis Walker works at a very busy law firm. On each side of his desk, there are one-foot-high stacks of work, leaving only enough room for a small work space in the center of the desk and a spot for the telephone. His floor is likewise stacked high with legal documents. Dennis constantly misses deadlines and is often in trouble for turning work in late or doing work incorrectly. Dennis has tried to get organized but feels that it is impossible to do so because he has such a heavy workload. What are Dennis's ethical obligations in this situation?

PRACTICE QUESTIONS AND ASSIGNMENTS

1. Which of the following are tasks that might be assigned to a litigation paralegal:

   a. Interviewing a client.
   b. Drafting a will.
   c. Drafting a complaint.
   d. Preparing articles of incorporation.
   e. Collecting technical data to submit to the Environmental Protection Agency.
   f. Attending a deposition.
   g. Preparing a witness for trial.
   h. Reviewing an information checklist for a divorce case.
   i. Assisting at trial.
   j. Preparing a trial notebook.

DATA DISK

2. Using the information in this chapter, prepare a résumé.

3. Using the information in this chapter, prepare a cover letter for an entry-level job with the general practice law firm of Hector & Micks, 220 Washington Blvd., Suite 125, Chicago, IL 12345.

QUESTIONS FOR CRITICAL ANALYSIS

1. Do you think that the way paralegals are paid (by annual salary or hourly wages) affects their attitudes about their work? Would you prefer one of these options over the other? If so, why?

2. What are your long-term goals? Do your short-term goals relate logically to the attainment of your long-term goals?

ROLE-PLAYING EXERCISES

1. Lisa Johns, a twenty-five-year-old graduate (at the top of her class) of the Detroit Institute for Paralegal Studies, is interviewing for her first paralegal job. The partner in the law firm that is interviewing Lisa is Vernon Hambly III. Vernon is a "stuffed-shirt" type with a 1950s mentality. He does not believe that women want to work after they have children. The paralegal to be hired will work for Vernon, and he wants to make sure that whoever he hires will not leave him to have a family. Eyeing Lisa's engagement ring, he asks Lisa if she is married and if she has children or plans to have children—illegal questions. Working in pairs, role-play this scenario. Vernon should ask Lisa the illegal questions, and Lisa must respond to the questions. Lisa should choose a direct, yet tactful, way of responding to the questions.

If time permits, the person playing the role of Vernon should try eliciting indirectly Lisa's views on marriage and children. Vernon might say, for example, that he has had to spend a great deal of time away from his wife and family to develop his successful law practice, and then say something like, "I don't know how you feel about that type of lifestyle, but . . . " Reverse roles if time allows.

DATA DISK

2. Using the facts presented in this chapter's exhibits showing Elena Lopez's résumé and cover letter to attorney Allen Gilmore, and assuming that Gilmore has requested an interview with Lopez, act out their roles during the interview. Gilmore should ask open-ended, closed-ended, hypothetical, and pressure questions, as illustrated in the exhibits within this chapter. Elena should base her answers on the facts given in the answers contained in the exhibits.

PROJECTS

1. Locate a copy of the *Martindale-Hubbel Law Directory* in your school's library or your local law library. Find three law firms in your area that practice areas of law in which you are interested. Write down the names and addresses of the firms. Also try to find the name of the hiring partners or human resources managers whom you could contact about a job in the future. Start your job file today!

2. Find out if your school has a placement office. If so, does it offer professional assistance or workshops in résumé preparation and interviewing? Find out at what point in your education you may use these services. Make a note of this information and keep it in your job file.

3. Contact your local paralegal professional associations. The names of these associations should be available in the state bar association directory found in most law libraries. Find out which organizations will accept student members and what networking opportunities are available.

4. Ask your program director if your school has a legal-assistant student club and how you can get involved in it. Network with other students, and consider how the club may be used to network on a broader scale—that is, to network with graduates, attorneys, and potential employees.

ANNOTATED SELECTED READINGS

BERNARDO, BARBARA. *Paralegal: An Insider's Guide to One of the Fastest-Growing Occupations of the 1990s.* 2d ed. Princeton, N.J.: Peterson's Guides, 1993. An excellent guide to the paralegal profession. A "must read" for anyone interested in the paralegal profession.

DEWITT, A. L. "Writing an Effective Resume." *Legal Assistant Today,* July/August 1994. An article that contains helpful guidelines on how to create a résumé that gets results. The article also provides sample résumés.

ESTRIN, CHERE B. *Paralegal Career Guide.* New York: John Wiley & Sons, 1992. A book that is full of suggestions for paralegals, including tips on how to be successful on the job, deal with challenging on-the-job situations, climb the career ladder, negotiate for deserved raises, and make career changes.

MILANO, CAROL. "Evaluating Your Benefits: 1993 Legal Assistant Today Benefits Survey Results." *Legal Assistant Today,* July/August 1993. An article that indicates what legal assistants can expect in terms of fringe benefits from law firms and corporate legal departments.

PATRICK, DIANE. "To Be or Not to Be (Exempt): A Closer Look at the Paralegal Overtime Issue." *Legal Assistant Today,* September/October 1992. An article that describes the tests used by courts to determine whether an employee is exempt or nonexempt from the provisions of the Fair Labor Standards Act. The article also discusses the issue of how being nonexempt affects a paralegal's status as a professional.

STEINBERG, CAROL. "Balancing Parenthood and a Paralegal Career." *Legal Assistant Today,* July/August 1993. An article that discusses the opportunities for paralegals for part-time work, flexible hours, freelance assignments, and job sharing. It provides tips on how to work out these arrangements with employers and discusses the issues involved in balancing a career and a family.

3

THE REGULATION OF LEGAL PROFESSIONALS

Chapter Objectives

After completing this chapter, you will know:

- **Why and how legal professionals are regulated.**
- **Some important ethical rules governing the conduct of attorneys and how these rules affect paralegal practice.**
- **Some of the consequences of attorney regulation for legal professionals and for the public.**
- **The extent to which the paralegal profession is regulated.**
- **The kinds of activities that paralegals are and are not legally permitted to perform.**
- **Some of the pros and cons of direct regulation in the form of paralegal licensing.**

Chapter Outline

INTRODUCTION

As discussed in the previous chapter, paralegals preparing for a career in today's legal arena have a variety of career options. Regardless of which career path you choose to follow, you should have a firm grasp of your state's ethical rules governing the legal profession. When you work under the supervision of an attorney, as most paralegals do, you and the attorney become team members. You will work together on behalf of clients and share in the ethical and legal responsibilities arising as a result of the attorney-client relationship.

In preparing for a career as a paralegal, you must know what these responsibilities are, why they exist, and how they affect you. The reason why the first part of this chapter is devoted to the regulation of attorneys is because the ethical duties imposed on attorneys by state laws also affect paralegals. If a paralegal violates one of the rules governing attorneys, that violation may result in serious consequences for the client, for the attorney, and for the paralegal.

Although attorneys are subject to direct regulation by the state, paralegals are not. Paralegals are regulated *indirectly*, however, both by attorney ethical codes and by state laws that prohibit nonlawyers from practicing law.[1] As the paralegal profession develops, professional paralegal organizations, the American Bar Association, and state bar associations of attorneys continue to issue guidelines that also serve to regulate paralegals indirectly.

THE IMPLICATIONS OF PROFESSIONAL STATUS

PROFESSION
An occupation requiring knowledge of the arts or sciences and advanced study in a specialized field, such as the law.

A **profession** is usually defined as an occupation or trade that requires a basic knowledge of the arts and sciences as well as advanced study in a specialized field. Historically, professions have been distinguished from other types of occupations by the fact that, in addition to acquiring expert knowledge in their fields of study as demonstrated by the passing of examinations, professionals are subject to standards of expertise and behavior established by their peers—other members of their profession.

SELF-REGULATION
The regulation of the conduct of a professional group by members of the group themselves. Self-regulation usually involves the establishment of ethical or professional standards of behavior with which members of the group must comply.

Professional groups usually engage in a degree of **self-regulation** by establishing ethical or professional codes to regulate their conduct while serving the public. Note that if professionals simply acquired knowledge but never offered their expert advice to the public, there would be no need to regulate professions. The need for regulation arises only when the members of the public (individuals without such specialized knowledge) rely on professionals for expert advice. The fact that individuals rely on (and pay for) professional services imposes a duty on professionals to serve those individuals' best interests.

1. Some legal professionals maintain that statutes that prohibit nonlawyers from practicing law constitute a form of direct regulation, because paralegals who violate such statutes may be directly sanctioned (in the form of criminal penalties) under those laws. In this chapter, we use the term *direct regulation* to mean state regulation of a specified professional group, particularly through state licensing requirements.

At the heart, then, of the concept of a professional is *service to others.* In their professional capacity, lawyers strive to make sure that their clients' interests are protected under the law; physicians seek to heal and comfort patients; accountants work hard to ensure that their clients have the best accounting advice possible; and so on. In regard to the legal profession, an attorney's advice and work product can greatly affect the client's welfare. The quality of an attorney's work can determine, for example, whether a client will be imprisoned, be compensated for pain and suffering, receive a fair share of marital assets and liabilities in a divorce proceeding, or acquire rights to the exclusive proceeds of his or her invention. Because so much is at stake, attorneys are regulated both internally by members of the profession and externally by the state.

The quality of a paralegal's work can also have serious consequences for clients, so paralegals who work for attorneys are also subject to (indirect) regulation by attorney rules of conduct. Whether paralegals should also be regulated directly by state laws—through licensing requirements, for example—is a question that has elicited a great deal of controversy, as you will see later in this chapter.

THE REGULATION OF ATTORNEYS

The term *regulate* derives from the Latin term *regula,* meaning "rule." According to Webster's dictionary, to *regulate* means "to control or direct in agreement with a rule." To a significant extent, attorneys are self-regulated because they themselves establish the majority of the rules governing the profession—rules that are enforced by state authorities.

The rules governing attorneys protect the public interest in two ways. First, by establishing educational and licensing requirements, they ensure that anyone practicing law is competent to do so. Second, by defining specific ethical requirements for attorneys, they protect the public against unethical attorney behavior that may affect clients' welfare. We discuss these requirements and rules below. First, however, you should know how these rules are created and enforced.

Who Are the Regulators?

Key participants in determining what rules should govern attorneys and the practice of law, as well as how these rules should be enforced, are bar associations, state supreme courts, state legislatures, and, in some cases, the United States Supreme Court. Procedures for regulating attorneys vary, of course, from state to state. What follows is a general discussion of who the regulators may be.

Bar Associations. Lawyers themselves determine the requirements for entering the legal profession and the rules of conduct they will follow. Traditionally, lawyers have joined together in professional groups, or bar associations, at the local, state, and national levels to discuss issues affecting the legal profession and to decide on standards of professional conduct.

Although membership in local and national bar associations is always voluntary, membership in the *state* bar association is mandatory in over two-thirds of the states. In these states, before an attorney can practice law, he or she must be admitted to the state's bar association. Approximately half of the lawyers in the United States are members of the American Bar Association (ABA), the voluntary national bar association discussed in Chapter 1. As you will read shortly, the ABA plays a key regulatory role by proposing model (uniform) codes, or rules of conduct, for adoption by the various states.

State Supreme Courts. Each state's highest court, often called the state supreme court, is normally the ultimate regulatory authority in that state. The judges who sit on the bench of the highest state court decide what conditions (such as licensing requirements, discussed below) must be met before an attorney can practice law within the state and under what conditions that privilege will be suspended or revoked. In many states, the state supreme court works closely with the state bar association. The state bar association may recommend rules and requirements to the court. If the court so orders, these rules and requirements become law within the state. Under the authority of the courts, state bar associations often perform routine regulatory functions, including the initiation of disciplinary proceedings against attorneys who fail to comply with professional requirements.

State Legislatures. State legislatures regulate the legal profession by enacting legislation affecting attorneys—statutes prohibiting the unauthorized practice of law, for example. In a few states, the states' highest courts delegate significant regulatory responsibilities to the state legislatures, which may include the power to bring disciplinary proceedings against attorneys.

The United States Supreme Court. On rare occasions, the United States Supreme Court has decided issues relating to attorney conduct. For example, until a few decades ago, state ethical codes, or rules governing attorney conduct, prohibited lawyers from advertising their services to the public. These restrictions on advertising were challenged as an unconstitutional limitation on attorneys' rights to free speech, and ultimately, the United States Supreme Court decided the issue. In a case decided in 1977, *Bates v. State Bar of Arizona*,[2] the Supreme Court ruled that truthful advertising of the availability and price of routine legal services was protected speech under the First Amendment to the U.S. Constitution and that provisions of state ethical codes forbidding such advertising were therefore unconstitutional.

Licensing Requirements

LICENSING
A government's official act of granting permission to an individual, such as an attorney, to do something that would be illegal in the absence of such permission.

The **licensing** of attorneys, which gives them the right to practice law, is accomplished at the state level. Each state has different requirements that individuals must meet before they are allowed by law to practice law and give legal advice. Generally, however, there are three basic requirements:

2. 433 U.S. 350, 97 S.Ct. 2691, 53 L.Ed.2d 810 (1977). (See Chapter 17 for a discussion of how to read case citations.)

1. A prospective attorney must have obtained a bachelor's degree from a university or college and must have graduated from an accredited law school (in many states, the school must be accredited by the ABA), which requires an additional three years of study. There are rare exceptions to this requirement.
2. A prospective attorney must pass a state bar examination—a very rigorous and thorough examination that tests the candidate's knowledge of the law and (in some states) the state's ethical rules governing attorneys. The examination covers both state law (law applicable to the particular state in which the attorney is taking the exam and wishes to practice) and multistate law (law applicable in most states, including federal law).
3. The candidate must pass an extensive personal-background investigation to verify that he or she is a responsible individual and otherwise qualifies to engage in an ethical profession. An illegal act committed by the candidate in the past, for example, might disqualify the individual from being admitted to the profession.

Only when these requirements have been met can an individual be admitted to the state bar and legally practice law within the state.

Licensing requirements for attorneys are the result of a long history of attempts to restrict entry into the legal profession. The earliest of these restrictions date to the colonial era. During the 1700s, local bar associations began to form agreements to restrict entry into their associations to those who fulfilled certain educational and apprenticeship requirements. At the same time, to curb unnecessary litigation and the detrimental effects of incompetent legal practitioners, courts began to require that individuals representing clients in court proceedings had to be licensed by the court to do so.

Beginning in the mid-1850s, restrictions on who could (or could not) practice law were given statewide effect by state statutes prohibiting the **unauthorized practice of law (UPL)**. Court decisions relating to unauthorized legal practice also date to this period. By the 1930s, virtually all states had enacted legislation prohibiting anyone but licensed attorneys from practicing law. As you will see in subsequent sections, many of the regulatory issues facing the legal profession—and particularly paralegals—are directly related to these UPL statutes.

UNAUTHORIZED PRACTICE OF LAW (UPL)
Engaging in actions defined by a legal authority, such as a state legislature, as constituting the "practice of law" without legal authorization to do so.

Ethical Codes and Rules

The legal profession is regulated by the licensing requirements just discussed. Additionally, the profession is regulated through ethical codes and rules adopted by each state—in most states, by order of the state supreme court. These codes of professional conduct—the names of the codes vary from state to state—evolved over a long period of time. As early as 1836, for example, at least one attorney was concerned with the need to establish ethical standards for lawyers. That attorney was David Hoffman, a professor of law at the University of Maryland. He created for his students a publication containing fifty resolutions concerning "professional deportment." Other law professors began to follow suit, and in 1887, the Alabama Bar Association—the first state bar to do so—published a "Code of Ethics." The code consisted of fifty-six rules, which were included under two general duties: the "Duty of Attorneys to Courts and Judicial Officers" and the

"Duty of Attorneys to Each Other, to Clients, and the Public." The introduction to this code is presented in Exhibit 3.1.

A major step toward ethical regulation was taken in 1908, when the ABA approved the Canons of Ethics, which consisted of thirty-two ethical principles based on the Alabama model. In the following decades, various states adopted these canons as law.

Today's state ethical codes are based, for the most part, on two subsequent revisions of the ABA canons: the Model Code of Professional Responsibility (published in 1969) and the Model Rules of Professional Conduct (published in 1983 to replace the Model Code). Although most of the states have now adopted the 1983 revision, the 1969 code is still in effect in some states, so you should be familiar with the basic format and content of both the Model Code and the Model Rules.

The Model Code of Professional Responsibility. The ABA Model Code of Professional Responsibility, often referred to as simply the Model Code, consists of the nine canons listed in Exhibit 3.2. In the Model Code, each canon is followed by sections entitled "Ethical Considerations" (ECs) and "Disciplinary Rules" (DRs). The ethical considerations are "aspirational" in character—that is, they suggest ideal conduct, not behavior that is necessarily required by law. For example, Canon 6 ("A lawyer should represent a client competently") is followed by EC 6–1, which states (in part) that a lawyer "should strive to become and remain proficient in his practice." In

EXHIBIT 3.1
Alabama Code of Ethics of 1899 (Excerpt)

Code of Ethics
Adopted by
ALABAMA STATE BAR ASSOCIATION

* * * *

A comprehensive summary of the duties specifically enjoined by law upon attorneys, which they are sworn " not to violate," is found in section 791 of the Code of Alabama.

These duties are:
"Ist. To support the constitution and laws of this State and the United States.

"2d. To maintain the respect due to courts of justice and judicial officers.
"3d. To employ, for the purpose of maintaining the causes confided to them, such means only as are consistent with truth, and never seek to mislead the judges by any artifice or false statement of the law.
"4th. To maintain inviolate the confidence, and, at every peril to themselves, to preserve the secrets of their clients.
"5th. To abstain from all offensive personalities, and to advance no fact prejudicial to the honor or reputation of a party or a witness, unless required by the justice of the cause with which they are charged.
"6th. To encourage neither the commencement nor continuance of an action or proceeding from any motive of passion or interest.
"7th. Never to reject, for any consideration personal to themselves, the cause of the defenseless and oppressed."

EXHIBIT 3.2
The ABA Model Code of Professional Responsibility (Canons Only)

CANON 1
A lawyer should assist in maintaining the integrity and competence of the legal profession.

CANON 2
A lawyer should assist the legal profession in fulfilling its duty to make legal counsel available.

CANON 3
A lawyer should assist in preventing the unauthorized practice of law.

CANON 4
A lawyer should preserve the confidences and secrets of a client.

CANON 5
A lawyer should exercise independent professional judgment on behalf of a client.

CANON 6
A lawyer should represent a client competently.

CANON 7
A lawyer should represent a client zealously within the bounds of the law.

CANON 8
A lawyer should assist in improving the legal system.

CANON 9
A lawyer should avoid even the appearance of professional impropriety.

contrast, disciplinary rules are mandatory in character—an attorney may be subject to disciplinary action for breaking one of the rules. For example, DR 6–101 (which follows Canon 6) states that a lawyer "shall not . . . [n]eglect a legal matter entrusted to him."

The Model Rules of Professional Conduct. The 1983 revision of the Model Code—referred to as the Model Rules of Professional Conduct or, more simply, as the Model Rules—represented a thorough revamping of the code. The Model Rules replaced the canons, ethical considerations, and disciplinary rules of the Model Code with a set of rules organized under eight general headings, as outlined in Exhibit 3.3 on the next page. Each rule is followed by comments shedding additional light on the rule's application and how it compares with the Model Code's treatment of the same issue.

The Model Rules—A Sampling

The ethical codes of conduct play an essential role in the regulation of legal professionals. To understand how the profession is regulated, you therefore need to have some knowledge of the duties imposed on attorneys (and indirectly, paralegals) by these codes.

The state ethical codes are fairly uniform because they are patterned after either the Model Code or the Model Rules (except in California, whose code follows neither the Model Code nor the Model Rules). Because most state codes are guided by the Model Rules of Professional Conduct, the rules discussed in this and the next chapter are drawn from the Model Rules. Keep in mind, though, that it is the code of conduct *adopted by your state* that is the governing authority on attorney conduct in your state. You will thus want to obtain and keep in your office (or on your desk) a copy of your state's ethical code.

EXHIBIT 3.3
The ABA Model Rules of Professional Conduct (Headings Only)

CLIENT-LAWYER RELATIONSHIP			
1.1	Competence	1.9	Conflict of Interest: Former Client
1.2	Scope of Representation	1.10	Imputed Disqualification: General Rule
1.3	Diligence	1.11	Successive Government and Private Employment
1.4	Communication	1.12	Former Judge or Arbitrator
1.5	Fees	1.13	Organization as Client
1.6	Confidentiality of Information	1.14	Client under a Disability
1.7	Conflict of Interest: General Rule	1.15	Safekeeping Property
1.8	Conflict of Interest: Prohibited Transactions	1.16	Declining or Terminating Representation
COUNSELOR			
2.1	Advisor	2.3	Evaluation for Use by Third Persons
2.2	Intermediary		
ADVOCATE			
3.1	Meritorious Claims and Contentions	3.6	Trial Publicity
3.2	Expediting Litigation	3.7	Lawyer as Witness
3.3	Candor toward the Tribunal	3.8	Special Responsibilities of a Prosecutor
3.4	Fairness to Opposing Party and Counsel	3.9	Advocate in Nonadjudicative Proceedings
3.5	Impartiality and Decorum of the Tribunal		
TRANSACTIONS WITH PERSONS OTHER THAN CLIENTS			
4.1	Truthfulness in Statement to Others	4.3	Dealing with Unrepresented Person
4.2	Communication with Person Represented by Counsel	4.4	Respect for Rights of Third Persons
LAW FIRMS AND ASSOCIATIONS			
5.1	Responsibilities of a Partner or Supervisory Lawyer	5.4	Professional Independence of a Lawyer
5.2	Responsibilities of a Subordinate Lawyer	5.5	Unauthorized Practice of Law
5.3	Responsibilities Regarding Nonlawyer Assistants	5.6	Restrictions on Right to Practice
PUBLIC SERVICE			
6.1	*Pro Bono Publico* Service	6.3	Membership in Legal Services Organization
6.2	Accepting Appointments	6.4	Law Reform Activities Affecting Client Interests
INFORMATION ABOUT LEGAL SERVICES			
7.1	Communications Concerning a Lawyer's Services	7.4	Communication of Fields of Practice
7.2	Advertising	7.5	Firm Names and Letterheads
7.3	Direct Contact with Prospective Clients		
MAINTAINING THE INTEGRITY OF THE PROFESSION			
8.1	Bar Admission and Disciplinary Matters	8.4	Misconduct
8.2	Judicial and Legal Officials	8.5	Jurisdiction
8.3	Reporting Professional Misconduct		

We look here at some of the Model Rules that have significant implications for both attorneys and paralegals. The rules on competence, confidentiality of client information, conflict of interest, and fees (client billing practices) are especially important to paralegals. These rules have thus been singled out for special attention in the following chapter, so we touch upon them only briefly here.

BREACH
To violate a legal duty by an act or a failure to act.

Competence. The first of the Model Rules states one of the most fundamental duties of attorneys—the duty of competence. Rule 1.1 of the Model Rules reads as follows:

> A lawyer shall provide competent representation to a client. Competent representation requires the legal knowledge, skill, thoroughness and preparation reasonably necessary for representation.

Competent legal representation is a basic requirement of the profession, and **breaching** (failing to perform) this duty may subject attorneys to one or more of the sanctions discussed later. As a paralegal, you should realize that when you undertake work on an attorney's behalf, you share in this duty. If your supervising attorney asks you to research a particular legal issue for a client, for example, you must make sure that your research is careful and thorough—because the attorney's reputation (and the client's welfare) may depend on your performance. You should also realize that careless performance of the research, if it results in substantial injury to the client's interests, may subject you personally to liability for negligence (discussed below), not to mention the loss of a job or career opportunities.

The duty of competence, because it is so fundamental and so broadly conceived, overlaps with numerous other duties, including the duty of diligence.

Diligence. Model Rule 1.3 states that "[a] lawyer shall act with reasonable diligence and promptness in representing a client." Comment 2 to this rule is particularly instructive:

> Perhaps no professional shortcoming is more widely resented than procrastination. A client's interests often can be adversely affected by the passage of time or the change of conditions; in extreme instances, as when a lawyer overlooks a statute of limitations, the client's legal position may be destroyed. Even when the client's interests are not affected in substance, however, unreasonable delay can cause a client needless anxiety and undermine confidence in the lawyer's trustworthiness.

The paralegal plays a vital role in making sure that a client's case or legal matter is handled efficiently and in a timely manner. Attorneys and paralegals often work on several cases at the same time, some of which may take years to resolve. A major challenge for paralegals and attorneys is making sure that no unnecessary delays occur.

As indicated in the comment quoted above, a particularly serious problem occurs when an attorney fails to initiate action on behalf of a client within the time period established by a statute of limitations. State **statutes of limitations** establish fixed time limits within which different types of lawsuits must be filed. After the time allowed under a statute of limitations has expired, the client's right to sue is extinguished, and no action can be brought, no matter how strong the case was originally.

ETHICAL CONCERN

Missed Deadlines

As a paralegal, you will find that one of your most useful allies is a calendar. Consistently entering important deadlines on a calendaring system (computerized or otherwise) will help to ensure that you and your supervising attorney do not breach the duty of competence simply because a document was not filed with the court on time. For example, if a *complaint* (the document that initiates a lawsuit, discussed in Chapter 10) is served on one of your firm's clients, you must file with the court the client's *answer* to the complaint within a specified number of days. If you fail to file the answer during that period, the court could enter a judgment in favor of the party bringing the lawsuit. As you might imagine, the consequences of this judgment—called a *default judgment*—can be extremely harmful for the client. As a paralegal, you need to be aware of the seriousness of the consequences of missed deadlines for your clients, especially the consequences of failing to file an answer on time.

STATUTE OF LIMITATIONS
A statute setting the maximum time period within which certain actions can be brought or rights enforced. After the period of time has run, normally no legal action can be brought.

DEVELOPING PARALEGAL SKILLS

Competently Assessing the Statute of Limitations

Mark Crosby, a paralegal, works in a law firm that handles medical-malpractice cases. After a client interview, one of the first things that Mark and the attorney for whom he works, Tim Hannon, do is determine if the statute of limitations has expired in the case. For most medical-malpractice cases in their state, the statute of limitations is two years. The most important task is to determine when the statute begins to run—or, in legal terminology, when the action "accrues." In Tim and Mark's state, the action accrues at the time of the act (or the failure to act) that caused the injury.

FACTUAL BACKGROUND OF THE CLIENT'S CASE

Today, October 3, 1995, Mark and Tim are reviewing a case after a client interview. A fifty-five-year-old woman went to see her physician on September 11, 1993. She had hit her thigh on a couch while moving furniture, and shortly thereafter, her thigh became very painful. Her physician told her that she had bruised her thigh but that otherwise she was fine. The physician did not examine her thigh for a mass, and he did not request that any biopsies or other diagnostic tests be taken. The pain did not subside, and the woman subsequently returned to see her physician on several occasions over the next several weeks—on September 15, on October 8, on October 23, and again on November 5. It was not until the November 5 visit that the doctor became worried about the discoloration. He felt a mass and suspected that it was cancerous. Her physician had biopsies taken and, when they confirmed his belief, referred her to a cancer specialist for further diagnosis and treatment.

DETERMINING WHEN THE STATUTE OF LIMITATIONS EXPIRES

The woman died from cancer in April 1994. Her family is distraught and wants to sue the physician for failing to detect the mass on the woman's September 11, 1993, visit to the physician. Mark and Tim must determine if the two-year statute of limitations has expired. To do this, they must determine the date on which the act or omission that caused the injury occurred—that is, the date on which the physician should reasonably have detected the suspicious mass. That date was not, in all likelihood, September 11 or 15, because the physician could reasonably have assumed that the thigh discoloration and pain were caused by hitting the couch. When she returned on October 8, however, the physician should have suspected that something else was wrong and undertaken further examination and tests. Mark and Tim thus conclude that the date that the statute began to run is most likely October 8, 1993. That means that the two-year statute of limitations will not expire until October 8, 1995. Because today is October 3, 1995, they must act quickly to file the lawsuit before the statute expires.

Communication. Model Rule 1.4 establishes the attorney's duty to keep the client reasonably informed. The rule reads as follows:

> (a) A lawyer shall keep a client reasonably informed about the status of a matter and promptly comply with reasonable requests for information.
> (b) A lawyer shall explain a matter to the extent reasonably necessary to permit the client to make informed decisions regarding the representation.

As a paralegal, you need to be aware that keeping clients reasonably informed about the progress being made on their cases goes beyond courtesy and the cultivation of a client's goodwill—it is a *legal* duty of attorneys. The meaning of "reasonably informed" varies, of course, depending on the client and on the nature of the work being done by the attorney. In some cases, a phone call every week or two will suffice to keep the client informed. In other cases, the attorney may ask the paralegal to draft a letter to a client explaining the status of the client's legal matter. Generally, as a paralegal, you should discuss with your supervising attorney how each client should be kept informed of the status of his or her case.

Some firms institute a regular monthly mailing to update clients on the status of their claims or cases. Copies of all letters to a client should, of course, be placed in the client's file. Additionally, the client's file should contain a written record of each phone call made to or received from a client. That way, there is a "paper trail"—in case it is ever necessary to provide evidence of communication with the client. (Actually, this is a good practice for all phone calls relating to a client's matter.) Monthly bills to clients (see Chapter 5) also are a means of communicating to clients what work has been done on their cases.

Fees. Model Rule 1.5 begins with the statement, "A lawyer's fees shall be reasonable." The rule goes on to indicate what factors should be considered in determining the reasonableness of a fee. The factors include the time and labor required to perform the legal work, the fee customarily charged in the locality for similar legal services, and the experience and ability of the lawyer performing the services. A major ethical concern of the legal profession has to do with the reasonableness of attorneys' fees and the ways in which clients are billed for legal services. We will look at some of the ethical problems relating to fees and client billing procedures in the next chapter.

In regard to fees, paralegals should also become familiar with Rule 5.4 of the Model Rules. That rule states, "A lawyer or law firm shall not share legal fees with a nonlawyer." For this reason, paralegals cannot become partners in a law partnership (because the partners share the firm's income), nor can they have a fee-sharing arrangement with an attorney in any way.

One of the reasons for this rule is that it protects the attorney's independent judgment concerning legal matters. For example, if an attorney became partners with two or three nonattorneys, the nonattorneys would have a significant voice in determining the firm's policies. In this situation, a conflict might arise between a policy of the firm and the attorney's duty to exercise independent professional judgment in regard to a client's case. The rule against fee splitting also protects against the possibility that nonlawyers would, indirectly through attorneys, be able to engage in the practice of law, which no one but an attorney can do.

Confidentiality of Information. Rule 1.6 of the Model Rules concerns attorney-client confidentiality. All information relating to the representation of a client must be kept confidential unless the client consents to disclosure. What this means for paralegals is that they also must assume responsibility for keeping confidential all knowledge relating to clients' cases. This rule, because of its significance for legal practice, will be examined in detail in the following chapter.

DEVELOPING PARALEGAL SKILLS

Prohibition on Fee Splitting

Robert Minson has worked as a paralegal for Peter H. Stonequist III for ten years. Robert has on several occasions referred cases to Peter that have been big winners. Robert has another one of those cases, and he is going into Peter's office to tell him about it.

"Peter, I have another case that you might be interested in handling—do you have a minute?" asks Robert. Peter responds, "Certainly, Robert, please come in. What kind of case is it?" Robert says, "Well, it's a personal-injury case. One of my father's friends was involved in a car accident a few months ago and was badly injured. He wants to sue the person who caused the accident, and I told my father that I'd see if you were interested in taking on the case." Robert and the attorney discuss the case, and Peter agrees with Robert that his father's friend might have a strong case against the driver of the other car.

"You know, Robert, you have referred many cases to me over the years, and I'd like to compensate you in some way for contributing to the firm's business," says Peter. Robert suggests that maybe they can work out a commission arrangement. "That presents a problem, Robert," replies Peter. "Lawyers are not allowed to split fees with nonlawyers, and they aren't allowed to pay referral fees, either. I value the business that you bring in, as well as the quality of your work, but I'm not allowed to give you a commission on your referrals because that would, in effect, be splitting fees with a nonlawyer, which I can't legally do. I've thought about it many times. Believe me, if I could, I'd make you a partner, but again, the ethical rules prohibit lawyers from entering into a partnership with nonlawyers."

"I see," Robert says. Peter, noting Robert's disappointment, then tells Robert that although attorneys cannot legally split fees with nonlawyers, there is no prohibition against increasing paralegals' salaries and bonuses when the firm is profitable. "When it's time for your performance review, your overall contribution to the firm's profitability will be considered," Peter explains to Robert. Robert smiles and replies that he certainly wouldn't object to that!

Conflict of Interest. Attorneys must be fully committed to serving their clients' best interests. If an attorney engages in an activity that adversely affects a client's interests (such as simultaneously representating opposing parties in a legal proceeding), the attorney faces a conflict of interest. Model Rules 1.7, 1.8, 1.9, and 1.10 all pertain to conflict-of-interest situations. These rules and their implications for paralegal practice will also be discussed at length in the next chapter.

Safekeeping of Property. Rule 1.15 imposes strict requirements on attorneys in relation to the safekeeping of property (documents, money, or other items) that they hold in trust for clients. The rule begins as follows:

> A lawyer shall hold property of clients or third persons that is in a lawyer's possession in connection with a representation separate from the lawyer's

> own property. Funds shall be kept in a separate account. . . . Other property shall be identified as such and appropriately safeguarded.

As a paralegal, you may be responsible for safeguarding evidence in the form of documents or other property belonging to the firm's clients or others, such as witnesses. It is extremely important that these documents or other property not be mislaid or lost, or fall into the wrong hands. You may also be involved in handling client funds, particularly if you work for a small law firm. You will read more about how client funds are handled in Chapter 5.

Expediting of Litigation. Rule 3.2 states that "[a] lawyer shall make reasonable efforts to expedite litigation consistent with the interests of the client." As you will learn in Chapters 10 and 11, litigation procedures often involve numerous delays. Typically, the attorneys for both sides file a number of *motions* (requests to the court) to obtain relevant evidence from the other party or from **third parties** (persons not directly involved in the lawsuit)—or for a variety of other reasons. Rule 3.2 prohibits attorneys from using motions and other permitted procedural devices to delay the litigation—to give them more time to conduct their investigations, for example. Many paralegals assist attorneys in work relating to litigation, and you should know that the rule generally requires that any actions causing a delay in litigation proceedings must serve some substantial purpose.

THIRD PARTIES
In the context of legal proceedings, parties who are not directly involved in the proceeding—that is, parties other than the plaintiff and defendant and their attorneys.

Candor toward the Tribunal. Rule 3.3 imposes a duty of candor on attorneys, which means, among other things, that attorneys must not make false statements, offer false evidence, or fail to disclose information that should be disclosed to a *tribunal* (a court or other official hearing body). To ensure that the attorney for whom you work does not violate this duty of candor, you need to take special care when conducting research, preparing exhibits, drafting documents to be submitted in courts, and undertaking similar tasks. Submitting false or inaccurate evidence, for example, could lead to serious consequences, including the court's dismissal of the client's case.

This duty also requires attorneys to disclose to the court any law or court decision "known to the lawyer to be directly adverse to the position of the client and not disclosed by opposing counsel." The underlying rationale for this rule is that an attorney's legal argument before a court is essentially a discussion of how the applicable law relates to the facts of his or her client's case. The attorney is obligated to disclose to the court what the applicable law is, even if it is adverse to his or her client's position.

You should keep Rule 3.3 in mind when you conduct legal research. For example, if you are researching the law on an issue that your supervising attorney is litigating, you should bring to the attorney's attention any statute, regulation, or court decision governing the issue—*even if it supports the opponent's argument*—that surfaces during your research. The attorney can then acknowledge this authority when arguing the client's case in court—and indicate why the authority should not apply in your client's circumstances.

Fairness to Opposing Party and Counsel. Rule 3.4 describes a number of actions that are prohibited as unfair to the opposing party or that party's attorney. The rule begins as follows:

> A lawyer shall not:
> (a) unlawfully obstruct another party's access to evidence or unlawfully alter, destroy or conceal a document or other material having potential evidentiary value [value as evidence]. A lawyer shall not counsel or assist another person to do any such act.
> (b) falsify evidence, counsel or assist a witness to testify falsely, or offer an inducement to a witness that is prohibited by law.

If, as a paralegal, you are ever requested, for whatever reason, to conceal or to falsify evidence or to prevent the opposing party from obtaining evidence in the attorney's possession, do not do so. The rule speaks for itself: any such action is clearly prohibited and could result in serious consequences for both you and your supervising attorney.

Responsibilities Regarding Nonlawyer Assistants. Rule 5.3 of the Model Rules of Professional Conduct defines the responsibilities of attorneys in regard to nonlawyer assistants. This rule states, in part, that "a lawyer having direct supervisory authority over the nonlawyer shall make reasonable efforts to ensure that the person's conduct is compatible with the professional obligations of the lawyer." The comment to this rule reads, in part, as follows:

> A lawyer should give . . . assistants appropriate instruction and supervision concerning the ethical aspects of their employment, particularly regarding the obligation not to disclose information relating to representation of the client, and should be responsible for their work product. The measures employed in supervising nonlawyers should take account of the fact that they do not have legal training and are not subject to professional discipline.

Rule 5.3 further states that "a lawyer shall be responsible for the conduct of [a nonlawyer] that would be a violation of the rules of professional conduct if engaged in by a lawyer." In sum, Rule 5.3 requires that attorneys not only supervise their assistants' work but also bear responsibility for their assistants' actions that violate professional ethical standards.[3]

Sanctions for Violations

REPRIMAND
A disciplinary sanction in which an attorney is rebuked for his or her misbehavior. Although a reprimand is the mildest sanction for attorney misconduct, it is nonetheless a serious one and may significantly damage the attorney's reputation in the legal community.

SUSPENSION
A serious disciplinary sanction in which an attorney who has violated an ethical rule or a law is prohibited from practicing in the state for a specified or an indefinite period of time.

Attorneys who violate the rules governing professional conduct are subject to disciplinary proceedings brought by the state bar association, state supreme court, or state legislature—depending on the state's regulatory scheme. In most states, unethical attorney actions are reported (by clients, legal professionals, or others) to the ethics committee of the state bar association, which is obligated to investigate each complaint thoroughly. For serious violations, the state bar association or the court initiates disciplinary proceedings against the attorney. Sanctions range from a **reprimand** (a formal "scolding" of the attorney—the mildest sanction[4]) to **suspension** (a more serious sanction by

3. Note that attorneys and law firms may also be liable for paralegal *torts* (wrongful acts) under agency law (discussed in Chapter 9).
4. Even this mildest sanction can seriously damage an attorney's reputation within the legal community. In some states, state bar associations publish in their monthly journals the names of violators and details of the violations for all members of the bar to read (see the discussion of attorney disciplinary proceedings in the feature entitled *Today's Professional Paralegal* at the end of this chapter).

DEVELOPING PARALEGAL SKILLS

Inadequate Supervision

Michael Patton is a paralegal in a firm consisting of two attorneys, himself, and two secretaries. The two attorneys have been in practice together since they graduated from law school ten years ago. The firm, a general law practice, is located in a rural community.

Michael has a great deal of experience in divorce law and has just finished drafting a complaint for Muriel Chapman, one of the two attorneys. Later that day, Michael reviews the complaint. He thinks that it is complete, but he has a question about the temporary alimony that the plaintiff is requesting. He walks to Muriel's office and knocks on the door. Muriel, who is on the phone, waves him in. Muriel hangs up the phone and looks up. Michael says, "I have a question about the amount of temporary alimony the plaintiff is requesting in this case. Was it $5,000 per year or was that the total amount?"

Muriel responds, "That is the total amount." "Okay. I'll insert the $5,000 and bring the complaint back for you to review," answers Michael. But Muriel thinks otherwise and says, "Don't bother to bring it back. I know that you know as much about this as I do. Just call her and have her come in to sign it." Michael hesitates and responds, "I'd feel more comfortable if you reviewed it."

"I'll be in court or at depositions or meetings for most of the next couple of days," Muriel replies. "The client wants her divorce filed as soon as possible, so I will have to rely on you," instructs Muriel. Michael, still not comfortable with Muriel's request, says, "Actually, it will take me just a couple of minutes to insert the $5,000 figure. Could you take a moment to review it before you leave?" "Okay," responds Muriel. "You know, Michael, you are rather persistant in making me do 'the right thing.' Bring the complaint back, and I'll review it before I leave."

which the attorney is prohibited from practicing law in the state for a given period of time, such as one month or one year, or for an indefinite period of time) to **disbarment** (revocation of the attorney's license to practice law in the state—the most serious sanction).

In addition to these sanctions, attorneys (and their paralegals) may be subject to civil liability for negligence. As will be discussed in Chapter 8, *negligence* (called **malpractice** when committed by a professional, such as an attorney) is a *tort* (a wrongful act) that is committed when an individual fails to perform a legally recognized duty. Tort law allows one who is injured by another's wrongful or careless act to bring a civil lawsuit against the wrongdoer for compensation (money **damages**). Of course, a client is permitted to bring a lawsuit against an attorney only if the client has suffered harm because of the attorney's failure to perform a legal duty. Attorneys and paralegals are also subject to potential criminal liability under criminal statutes prohibiting fraud, theft, and other crimes.

DISBARMENT
A severe disciplinary sanction in which an attorney's license to practice law in the state is revoked because of unethical or illegal conduct.

MALPRACTICE
Professional misconduct or negligence—the failure to exercise due care—on the part of a professional, such as an attorney or a physician.

DAMAGES
Money sought as a remedy for a civil wrong, such as a breach of contract or a tortious act.

ATTORNEY REGULATION AND THE PRACTICE OF LAW

The corollary to licensing requirements for attorneys is, of course, that only attorneys are legally permitted to practice law. Statutes prohibiting all persons but licensed attorneys from practicing law have always presented problems for those legal practitioners who either could not or did not wish to satisfy state requirements for licensing. In the last few decades, however, these statutes have also presented problems for paralegals. No matter how expert a paralegal may be in terms of legal knowledge and skills, he or she cannot give legal advice to clients or otherwise engage in the unauthorized practice of law (UPL) as defined by state laws.

As mentioned earlier in this chapter, the reason attorneys are regulated by the state is to protect the public from the harms that could result from incompetent legal advice and representation. Licensing requirements for attorneys thus serve the public interest. But they also give lawyers something of a monopoly over the delivery of legal services that, in turn, may have detrimental effects for those who cannot afford to pay attorneys for their services. A knowledge of how legal professionals and the courts have responded to this problem and other consequences of UPL statutes will help you understand some of the key regulatory issues facing paralegals today.

Pro Bono Legal Services

Historically, the legal profession has always justified its restrictions on entry into the profession by citing the ethical goal served by the restrictions—the protection of the public from incompetent counsel. Another goal of the legal profession, however, and one that is clearly expressed in state ethical codes, is to ensure that Americans, particularly the needy, are not deprived of access to legal services. The legal profession has responded to the need to lower the costs of legal services in several ways, including *pro bono* work (defined below) and the increased utilization of paralegals. The question of how legal services can be made available to a wider segment of the American population, however, continues to challenge the legal profession.

The Model Code acknowledged this goal in EC 2–25 (an Ethical Consideration following Canon 2 of the code), which states, in part, that "[e]very lawyer, regardless of professional prominence or professional workload, should find time to participate in serving the disadvantaged." EC 8–3 states that "[t]hose persons unable to pay for legal services should be provided needed services."

The Model Rules place greater emphasis on the responsibility of lawyers to help the disadvantaged. The Preamble to the Model Rules includes the following statement:

> A lawyer should be mindful of deficiencies in the administration of justice and of the fact that the poor, and sometimes persons who are not poor, cannot afford adequate legal assistance, and should therefore devote professional time and civil influence in their behalf. A lawyer should aid the legal profession in pursuing these objectives and should help the bar regulate itself in the public interest.

Model Rule 6.1 follows up on this concern by stating that "[a] lawyer should render public interest legal service" through providing legal services ***pro bono publico*** (for the benefit of the public) "at no fee or a reduced fee to persons of limited means."

PRO BONO PUBLICO
Legal services provided for free or at a reduced fee by an attorney or paralegal to persons of limited financial means in need of legal assistance.

Lawyers and law firms normally take very seriously their ethical obligation to perform *pro bono* work, and in this way, the legal profession has broadened the public's access to legal services. The legal profession has also made legal services more affordable by creating legal clinics and prepaid or group legal services, by reducing restrictions on advertising so that the public could compare legal services and prices, and by increasing the use of paralegal expertise.

As a paralegal, you may be involved in your firm's *pro bono* work. Alternatively, you may volunteer your assistance as a paralegal to attorneys working on behalf of needy clients at no fee or at a reduced fee.

The Increased Use of Paralegals

To an extent, the growth of the paralegal profession coincides with the increasing number and complexity of laws and regulations created during the past few decades. Each new government agency created to protect the public interest—in consumer protection, environmental preservation, or employee health and safety, for example—has generated, in turn, numerous rules and compliance requirements. The result has been more work for lawyers.

For example, suppose that an attorney has a client who is having difficulty obtaining disability benefits from a state or federal agency. To assist that client in obtaining the benefits, the attorney will have to spend hours going through the paperwork involved. The attorney will have to make sure that the correct forms are used and that all procedures are followed exactly. Alternatively, the attorney can delegate these tasks to a paralegal. As mentioned in Chapter 1, the particular expertise of the paralegal is his or her knowledge of legal procedures. Increasingly, attorneys are relying on paralegals to perform services that attorneys no longer have time to handle.

The use of paralegals to do work that was once solely the province of attorneys benefits clients because the hourly rate for paralegals is, of course, substantially lower than that for attorneys. For this reason, bar associations (and courts, when approving fees) encourage attorneys to delegate work to paralegals whenever feasible to lower the costs of legal services for clients—and thus provide greater access to legal services.

The Question of the Independent Paralegal

Another response to the need for more affordable legal services was the rise of the **independent paralegal**, or *legal technician.* A small number of paralegals practice independently—that is, they are not under an attorney's supervision. The independent-paralegal movement began in California over twenty years ago when a group of individuals with various degrees of legal training launched the so-called *Wave Project.*

INDEPENDENT PARALEGAL
A paralegal who offers services directly to the public, normally for a fee, without attorney supervision. Independent paralegals assist consumers by supplying them with forms and procedural knowledge relating to simple or routine legal procedures.

This project involved the establishment of a chain of do-it-yourself divorce centers, in which paralegals, for a fee ranging between \$50 and \$75, supplied members of the public with the necessary forms and procedural knowledge to obtain a divorce without having to use the services of an attorney. Over the following twenty years, Wave divorce centers handled thousands of divorces and saved the public millions of dollars. The repercussions of the Wave Project were felt around the country as paralegals in some other states began to set up businesses (which were usually called typing services, form-preparation services, or something similar) for the purpose of assisting members of the public in relatively simple legal tasks, such as preparing a will or obtaining a simple divorce.

Lawsuits brought by bar associations, clients, or other parties against independent paralegals for the unauthorized practice of law have focused attention on an issue of concern to all paralegals, including those working under attorney supervision: What kinds of tasks or activities can paralegals undertake without violating UPL statutes? We turn now to examination of that question. Later in the chapter, you will read about another question of concern to legal professionals that has come about, in part, as a result of independent paralegal practice: Should paralegals, particularly those who offer services directly to the public, be regulated by the state through licensing requirements?

THE UNAUTHORIZED PRACTICE OF LAW

What kinds of activities constitute the unauthorized practice of law? This is a serious question for practicing paralegals because paralegals judged to have engaged in the unauthorized practice of law are subject to fines and possibly imprisonment. UPL actions are complicated by the fact that state statutes stipulating that only licensed attorneys can engage in the practice of law rarely indicate with any specificity what constitutes the "practice of law."

Definitional Problems: What Is the Practice of Law?

Some state statutes do not define the phrase *practice of law* at all. Other statutes essentially define the practice of law as being "what attorneys do." Still others attempt a definition of the practice of law and then add to that definition a phrase, such as "and any other action connected with law," that essentially nullifies the narrower definition.

The ABA's Model Code and Model Rules are also vague in this respect. For example, the Ethical Consideration (EC) 3–5 to Canon 3 of the Model Code reads as follows:

> It is neither necessary nor desirable to attempt the formulation of a single, specific definition of what constitutes the practice of law. Functionally, the practice of law relates to the rendition of services for others that call for the professional judgment of a lawyer. The essence of the professional judgment of the lawyer is his educated ability to relate the general body and philosophy of law to a specific legal problem of a client; and thus, the public interest will be better served if only lawyers are permitted to act in matters involving professional judgment.

Model Rule 5.5 essentially states that the practice of law varies from state to state, that restricting the practice of law to attorneys benefits the public interest, and that attorneys can delegate functions to paralegals as long as attorneys supervise the work and retain responsibility for it. Both the Model Code and the Model Rules also specifically prohibit lawyers from assisting in the "unauthorized practice of law."

Court Decisions

In the past two decades, the courts have had to address such questions as the following:

- If an independent paralegal advises a customer on what forms are necessary to obtain a simple, uncontested divorce, how those forms should be filed with the court, how the court hearing should be scheduled, and so on, do those activities constitute the practice of law?
- If a paralegal starts his or her own business and works as a freelance paralegal for attorneys, does that constitute the unauthorized practice of law? (**Freelance paralegals** are distinct from independent paralegals because freelancers work for attorneys, and attorneys assume responsibility for the paralegals' work products.)
- If a paralegal working as an employee of a law firm does substantial research on behalf of clients, prepares legal documents for an attorney's signature, or interviews witnesses, do those activities constitute the practice of law?

FREELANCE PARALEGAL
A paralegal who operates his or her own business and provides services to attorneys on a contractual basis. A freelance paralegal works under the supervision of an attorney, who assumes responsibility for the paralegal's work product.

In deciding such questions, courts have used different criteria. In some cases, courts have decided that the practice of law equates to "what attorneys usually do"—or something equally vague. In other cases, the courts have established some general standards, or tests, to use in determining whether a particular action constitutes the unauthorized practice of law. In *The Florida Bar v. Sperry,*[5] a case decided in 1962, the Florida Supreme Court held that giving advice or performing services constituted the practice of law if that advice or those services affected "important rights of a person under the law."[6] Other courts have been guided by whether a legal task requires a lawyer's special training and expert skills. If so, the professional judgment of a lawyer is required and only a lawyer can legally perform such a task. Generally, the determination of what kinds of actions constitute the unauthorized practice of law has been decided by the courts on a case-by-case basis.

We look here at how the courts have addressed the first two questions listed above. The third question—what tasks paralegals working as employees are or are not legally permitted to do—will be examined later in this chapter.

5. 140 So.2d 587 (Fla. 1962).
6. Although the Florida Supreme Court *enjoined* (prohibited) the paralegal from continuing to prepare patent applications for members of the public, the United States Supreme Court *vacated* (nullified) the Florida court's decision in *Sperry v. State of Florida ex rel. The Florida Bar* [373 U.S. 379, 83 S.Ct. 1322, 10 L.Ed.2d 428 (1963)]. The United States Supreme Court held that the Florida court could not enjoin a nonlawyer registered to practice before the U.S. Patent Office from preparing patent applications in Florida. (See Chapter 13 for a discussion of how some administrative agencies, such as the U.S. Patent Office, authorize paralegals to represent clients in actions governed by those agencies.)

THE LEGAL TEAM AT WORK
Teamwork and the Risk of UPL

One of the valuable functions of the paralegal as a member of the legal team is communicating with the the firm's clients. In some areas of legal practice, clients need more than just legal advice. They may need to be encouraged, consoled, and so on. For example, if you become a paralegal in a family-law practice, many of the firm's clients will be undergoing difficult times emotionally. They may also face economic problems. A spouse who has never been involved in the family's finances, for example, may have no idea of the extent of the value of the marital property to be distributed (the value of the home, investments, and other assets). He or she may never have balanced a checkbook before or paid routine bills. As a paralegal, you will have frequent contact with the client, and you will probably have numerous opportunities to communicate with and assist the client in regard to one matter or another.

Your challenge is to know which kinds of statements you may legally make and which kind of statements may subject you to liability for the unauthorized practice of law. Because each client's circumstances are unique, so will be many of the questions you are asked. Unless you are absolutely certain that answering a particular question will not constitute the unauthorized practice of law, discuss the issue with your supervising attorney. Ask the attorney how you should answer the client's questions before giving the client any answer.

Independent Paralegal Practice. In *The Florida Bar v. Brumbaugh,*[7] a case decided in 1978, the Florida Supreme Court was faced with an issue involving the first of the questions mentioned above—whether independent paralegals who prepared forms and lent other assistance to consumers were engaging in the unauthorized practice of law. The case was brought by the Florida Bar Association. The bar association alleged that Ms. Brumbaugh, who prepared legal documents for people who sought a simple, uncontested divorce, was engaging in the practice of law in violation of the state's UPL statute. Brumbaugh prepared all the necessary court documents and told her customers how to file the documents with the court, how to schedule the court hearings, and—in a conference the day before the hearing—what would occur at the hearing.

In its decision, the court held that Brumbaugh could sell legal forms and other printed information regarding divorces and other legal procedures, that she could fill in the forms as long as the customer provided the information in writing, and that she could advertise her services. She could not, however, advise customers of their legal rights; tell them which forms should be used, how they should be filled out, and where to file them; or how to present their cases in court.

A year later, the same court decided *The Florida Bar v. Furman,*[8] which involved a woman who performed legal services very similar to those performed by Brumbaugh. The court held that the woman, Ms. Furman, had

7. 355 So.2d 1186 (Fla. 1978).
8. 376 So.2d 378 (Fla. 1979).

engaged in the unauthorized practice of law by failing to comply with the decision in *Brumbaugh.* The *Furman* case received substantial publicity when Furman disobeyed a later *injunction* (a court order to cease engaging in the prohibited activities) and was sentenced to prison for **contempt of court** (failing to cooperate with a court order).

CONTEMPT OF COURT
The intentional obstruction or frustration of the court's attempt to administer justice. A party to a lawsuit may be held in contempt of court (punishable by a fine or jail sentence) for refusing to comply with a court's order.

Numerous other courts have addressed this issue. Some courts have allowed independent paralegals to assist consumers by providing them with self-help law kits and typing forms but have not allowed paralegals to go a step further by selecting or filling out forms for their customers or in any way advising customers of legal rights. Clearly, the lines drawn are very fine in some instances—such as the line between handing a customer a kit containing forms and selecting forms for the customer. Because the consequences of violating state UPL statutes can be so serious, we cannot emphasize enough the following advice:

- **Any paralegal who contemplates working as an independent paralegal must thoroughly investigate the relevant state laws and court decisions on the unauthorized practice of law before offering any services directly to the public and then rigorously abide by the letter of the law.**

Paralegals Freelancing for Attorneys. In 1992, the New Jersey Supreme Court's Committee on the Unauthorized Practice of Law rendered its opinion (Opinion 24) on the second question raised above—whether paralegals doing freelance work for attorneys are engaging in the unauthorized practice of law. The opinion stated that freelance paralegals lacked adequate attorney supervision and therefore were engaging in the unauthorized practice of law. When a group of freelance paralegals appealed the issue to the New Jersey Supreme Court, however, that court stated that it could find no reason why freelance paralegals could not be just as adequately supervised by the attorneys for whom they worked as those paralegals working in attorneys' offices. The New Jersey Supreme Court's decision regarding Opinion 24 is discussed in greater detail in this chapter's featured-guest article entitled "Opinion 24 of the New Jersey Supreme Court's UPL Committee."

THE INDIRECT REGULATION OF PARALEGALS

Independent paralegal practice and the increased use of paralegals to assist attorneys, whether as freelancers or as employees, have created a pressing need to define with greater precision the paralegal's role and the ethical responsibilities a paralegal has as a legal professional. Paralegal associations, bar associations, courts, and state legislatures are all grappling with these issues and with the general question of how and to what extent the paralegal profession should be regulated.

The ethical codes for attorneys discussed above indirectly regulate the conduct of paralegals also. Paralegal conduct is also regulated indirectly by standards created by paralegal professional groups. In their search for professional status, paralegal associations have formed ethical codes specifically

FEATURED GUEST: SUSAN D. KLIGERMAN

Opinion 24 of the New Jersey Supreme Court's UPL Committee

Biographical Note

Susan D. Kligerman was appointed to the New Jersey Supreme Court Standing Committee on Paralegal Education and Regulation in 1993. She is co-chair of the New Jersey State Bar Association Paralegal Committee and has served on the committee since 1987. She is the national seminar coordinator for the National Federation of Paralegal Associations and board advisor and immediate past president of the South Jersey Paralegal Association. As a paralegal, Kligerman specialized in personal-injury litigation for ten years and is now president of Paralegal Enterprises, Inc., in Mt. Laurel, New Jersey. Paralegal Enterprises provides paralegal consulting services for attorneys. She teaches paralegal ethics and litigation courses at the Philadelphia Institute and at Fairleigh Dickinson University.

Paralegals who do freelance work for attorneys in New Jersey were relieved and encouraged in 1993 when the New Jersey Supreme Court decided that paralegals freelancing[a] for attorneys were not engaging in the unauthorized practice of law (UPL). Since 1989, when the court's Unauthorized Practice of Law Committee (UPL Committee) began investigating freelance paralegal practices in New Jersey, freelancers had awaited the UPL Committee's opinion—and later the New Jersey Supreme Court's decision—on the issue.

a. Although the term *independent paralegal* was used by the UPL Committee and the court to designate paralegals who offer their services to attorneys as freelancers, independent paralegals are more commonly defined as paralegals who deliver services directly to the public—that is, paralegals who do *not* work under the supervision of attorneys. In this article, I have therefore replaced the term *independent paralegal* with *freelance paralegal* to avoid possible confusion.

THE NATURE OF THE ISSUES

New Jersey paralegals first learned that an investigation into the practices of freelance paralegals was being conducted by the UPL Committee in 1989. The committee was concerned about the amount of supervision an attorney could provide if the freelance paralegal was not physically performing the paralegal work at the attorney's office. The investigation focused on several important issues. One issue had to do with whether freelance paralegals were sufficiently qualified to perform legal services for attorneys, given the fact that they did not have to disclose their educational background or demonstrate their proficiency to the extent that employees normally must.

Another issue focused on whether freelance paralegals' communciations with clients could be adequately supervised. Also of concern was whether freelancers were disclosing potential conflicts of interest to the attorneys for whom they worked. Finally, an interesting aspect of the investigation had to do with whether freelance paralegals who had substantial expertise in a specialized legal area could be adequately supervised by an attorney who lacked such expertise.

THE UPL COMMITTEE'S HEARINGS AND OPINION 24

Local, state, and national paralegal and bar associations were notified of the UPL Committee's inquiry, and these associations provided extensive information on paralegals to the UPL Committee. In fact, the committee received so much information about the paralegal profession and freelance paralegals that it decided to conduct public hearings on the issue of whether freelance paralegals were engaging in the unauthorized practice of law.

At hearings held in September 1989, freelance paralegals, traditional paralegals (those working in law firms), and representatives of local and national paralegal associations testified. Most individuals offering testimony stated that freelance paralegals were performing work under the supervision of attorneys,

FEATURED GUEST, Continued

regardless of the fact that they were not physically located in the attorneys' offices. Further, attorneys were responsible for the work of paralegals, and therefore freelance paralegals were not engaged in the unauthorized practice of law. The UPL Committee issued Opinion 24 in November 1990. The committee found that paralegals performing freelance services for attorneys were engaging in the unauthorized practice of law and thus should be prohibited from continuing to offer their services to attorneys.

Subsequently, eleven New Jersey freelance paralegals sought and received a *stay* (suspension) of the opinion and appealed the decision to the New Jersey Supreme Court. The National Federation of Paralegal Associations (NFPA) and the American Association of Paralegal Educators jointly filed an *amicus curiae* brief,[b] as did the National Association of Legal Assistants (NALA).

THE NEW JERSEY SUPREME COURT'S DECISION

Oral arguments were held before the supreme court on February 4, 1992. On May 14, 1992, the court issued its decision, *In re Opinion No. 24 of the Committee on the Unauthorized Practice of Law.*[c] The court did not agree with the UPL Committee's conclusion that freelance paralegals were engaging in the unauthorized practice of law and found no distinction between a freelance paralegal retained by an attorney to perform specified services and a paralegal who is employed by an attorney.

In both situations, paralegals could be adequately supervised by attorneys. The court pointed out the public benefits stemming from paralegal services and the need to encourage the further development of such services. The court stressed, however, that a freelance paralegal has an independent obligation to refrain from illegal conduct and to work under an attorney's supervision.

IMPLICATIONS OF THE DECISION FOR PARALEGALS

The New Jersey Supreme Court's decision had significant implications for paralegals across the nation, particularly those who do freelance work for attorneys. The decision was also significant because in it, the court called for the establishment of a standing committee on paralegal education and regulation—the first of its kind. The purpose of the committee was to establish guidelines encouraging New Jersey attorneys to utilize paralegal services and to create a set of principles that, together with the state's ethical code, would guide paralegals. On March 30, 1993, the New Jersey Supreme Court Standing Committee on Paralegal Education and Regulation was established, and members were appointed.

"[A] FREELANCE PARALEGAL HAS ONE INDEPENDENT OBLIGATION... TO WORK UNDER AN ATTORNEY'S SUPERVISION."

New Jersey Supreme Court Chief Justice Wilentz stated in his letter of appointment that "important in the court's decision to create this standing committee were (a) its conclusion that there is currently in New Jersey a lack of standards for regulating freelance paralegals and (b) the absence of any sort of licensing procedure to regulate paralegals generally."[d] The justice also indicated the court's concern about the lack of educational or ethical standards for paralegals.

The justice charged the committee with recommending appropriate educational, disciplinary, and regulatory standards for paralegals following a study of the issues. The results of the committee's activities pertaining to education and regulation of the paralegal profession may have a significant impact on paralegal practice not only in New Jersey but also in other states that are searching for guidance on these issues.

b. *Amicus curiae* means, literally, "friend of the court." An *amicus curiae* brief is a document filed with the court, on behalf of one of the parties, by a person or organization that is not a party to the lawsuit.

c. 128 N.J 114, 607 A.2d 962 (1992).

d. The regulation of paralegals through licensing procedures is discussed later in this chapter.

for paralegals, as well as guidelines defining what a paralegal is, what paralegal activities are legally permissible, and what paralegal activities constitute the unauthorized practice of law. The American Bar Association and several states have also adopted such guidelines.

These codes and guidelines, as well as formal opinions issued by various state bar associations and committees, regulate the paralegal profession indirectly by providing ethical guidance to paralegals. They also assist attorneys and the courts in defining the role of the legal assistant and in determining what tasks paralegals can and cannot perform, as well as the responsibilities of attorneys in relation to work conducted by their legal assistants.

In this section, you will learn about the ways in which paralegals are regulated indirectly by attorney ethics, paralegal codes and guidelines, and liability under state civil or criminal statutes for malpractice, the unauthorized practice of law, or other wrongful acts. The controversial issue of whether paralegals should be directly regulated by the state—through licensing requirements, for example—will be addressed at the end of the chapter.

Attorney Ethics and Paralegal Practice

The ethical codes governing attorney conduct apply directly only to attorneys, and only attorneys are subject to disciplinary proceedings for violating the ethical duties required by state codes. If a paralegal's action or inaction causes an attorney to breach a professional duty, the paralegal will not be subject to sanctions by the legal profession. Whereas attorneys can be disbarred and lose their licenses, paralegals have no licenses to be revoked.

Nonetheless, the ethical standards of the legal profession *indirectly* regulate paralegal activities because part of a paralegal's job is to ensure that he or she does not violate the professional rules governing attorneys. Furthermore, as mentioned earlier, the fact that attorneys assume legal responsibility not only for their own ethical violations but also for those of their legal assistants indirectly regulates paralegal behavior. An attorney will not want to hire or maintain as an employee a paralegal whose incompetence or unfamiliarity with professional ethics could result in disciplinary sanctions or a lawsuit against the attorney.

The fact that paralegals are subject to tort liability for negligence is a further incentive for paralegals to adhere to the ethical standards regulating attorney conduct. If a paralegal's breach of a professional duty causes a client to suffer substantial harm, the client may sue not only the attorney but also the paralegal. Although many law firms' liability insurance policies cover paralegals as well as attorneys, if this is not the situation and if the paralegal has not secured malpractice insurance independently, just one lawsuit could ruin the paralegal financially—as well as destroy that paralegal's reputation in the legal community.

> **ETHICAL CONCERN**
>
> ### Social Events and Confidentiality
>
> Assume that you are at a party with some other paralegals. You tell a paralegal whom you know quite well of some startling news—that a client of your firm, a prominent city official, is being investigated for drug dealing. Although your friend promises to keep this information strictly confidential and secret, she nonetheless relays it to her husband, who in turns tells his co-worker, who in turn tells his friend, and so on. Within a few days, the news has reached the press, and the resulting media coverage results in irreparable harm to the official's reputation and standing in the community. If it can be proved that the harm is the direct result of your breach of the duty of confidentiality, the official could sue both you and the attorney for whom you work for damages.

Paralegal Ethical Codes

In addition to indirect regulation through attorney ethical codes, paralegals are becoming increasingly self-regulated. Recall from Chapter 1 that the two major national paralegal associations in the United States—the National Federation of Paralegal Associations (NFPA) and the National Association of

Legal Assistants (NALA)—were formed to define and represent paralegal professional interests on a national level. Soon after they were formed, both associations adopted ethical codes defining the ethical responsibilities of legal assistants.

These ethical codes, which are discussed below, establish ethical guidelines for paralegals. Both codes maintain that it is the responsibility of every paralegal to adhere to specified ethical standards. Note that compliance with these codes is not mandatory for paralegals. In other words, if a paralegal does not abide by a paralegal association's code of ethics, the association cannot initiate disciplinary proceedings against the paralegal. The association can, however, expel the paralegal from the association, which may have significant implications for the paralegal's future career opportunities.

The NFPA Code of Ethics. In 1977, NFPA adopted its first code of ethics, called the Affirmation of Responsibility. The Affirmation set forth six ethical standards for paralegals, the sixth of which called for commitment on the part of NFPA members to professional development. The Affirmation of Responsibility was revised in 1981 and again in 1991. In 1993, NFPA replaced the Affirmation with its Model Code of Ethics and Professional Responsibility. The 1993 code reflects the influence of the Model Code of Professional Responsibility discussed earlier in this chapter by presenting ethical precepts as "canons" and by following each canon with a series of "Ethical Considerations" (ECs). NPFA's 1993 code of ethics is presented in its entirety in Exhibit 3.4 on the following two pages.

The NALA Code of Ethics. In 1975, NALA issued its Code of Ethics and Professional Responsibility, which has since undergone two revisions, the latest in 1988.[9] The NALA code is also phrased as a series of canons. Exhibit 3.5 on page 106 presents the code in its entirety.

Guidelines for the Utilization of Paralegals

The growth of the paralegal profession during the 1970s and 1980s raised a number of definitional issues concerning the role and function of paralegals within the legal arena. What are paralegals? What kinds of tasks do they perform? What are their professional responsibilities? How can attorneys best utilize paralegal services? What responsibilities should attorneys assume in respect to their assistants' work? Individual attorneys, state bar associations, and the courts were all struggling with such questions. In response to these concerns, NALA, the ABA, and several states have adopted guidelines for the utilization of legal assistants.

The NALA Model Standards and Guidelines. In 1984, NALA adopted its Model Standards and Guidelines for the Utilization of Legal Assistants. This

9. NALA is currently considering a revision of its Code of Ethics and Professional Responsibility.

EXHIBIT 3.4

The NFPA Model Code of Ethics and Professional Responsibility

PREAMBLE

The National Federation of Paralegal Associations, Inc. ("NFPA") is a professional organization comprised of paralegal associations and individual paralegals throughout the United States. Members of NFPA have varying types of backgrounds, experience, education, and job responsibilities which reflect the diversity of the paralegal profession. NFPA promotes the growth, development and recognition of the paralegal profession as an integral partner in the delivery of legal services.

NFPA recognizes that the creation of guidelines and standards for professional conduct are important for the development and expansion of the paralegal profession. In May 1993, NFPA adopted this Model Code of Ethics and Professional Responsibility ("Model Code") to delineate the principles for ethics and conduct to which every paralegal should aspire. The Model Code expresses NFPA's commitment to increasing the quality and efficiency of legal services and recognizes the profession's responsibilities to the public, the legal community, and colleagues.

Paralegals perform many different functions, and these functions differ greatly among practice areas. In addition, each jurisdiction has its own unique legal authority and practices governing ethical conduct and professional responsibilities.

It is essential that each paralegal strive for personal and professional excellence and encourage the professional development of other paralegals as well as those entering the profession. Participation in professional associations intended to advance the quality and standards of the legal profession is of particular importance. Paralegals should possess integrity, professional skill and dedication to the improvement of the legal system and should strive to expand the paralegal role in the delivery of legal services.

CANON 1.

A PARALEGAL[1] SHALL ACHIEVE AND MAINTAIN A HIGH LEVEL OF COMPETENCE.

EC-1.1 A paralegal shall achieve competency through education, training, and work experience.

EC-1.2 A paralegal shall participate in continuing education to keep informed of current legal, technical and general developments.

EC-1.3 A paralegal shall perform all assignments promptly and efficiently.

CANON 2.

A PARALEGAL SHALL MAINTAIN A HIGH LEVEL OF PERSONAL AND PROFESSIONAL INTEGRITY.

EC-2.1 A paralegal shall not engage in any ex parte[2] communications involving the courts or any other adjudicatory body in an attempt to exert undue influence or to obtain advantage for the benefit of only one party.

CANON 2.

EC-2.2 A paralegal shall not communicate, or cause another to communicate, with a party the paralegal knows to be represented by a lawyer in a pending matter without the prior consent of the lawyer representing such other party.

EC-2.3 A paralegal shall ensure that all timekeeping and billing records prepared by the paralegal are thorough, accurate, and honest.

EC-2.4 A paralegal shall be scrupulous, thorough and honest in the identification and maintenance of all funds, securities, and other assets of a client and shall provide accurate accountings as appropriate.

EC-2.5 A paralegal shall advise the proper authority of any dishonest or fraudulent acts by any person pertaining to the handling of the funds, securities or other assets of a client.

CANON 3.

A PARALEGAL SHALL MAINTAIN A HIGH STANDARD OF PROFESSIONAL CONDUCT.

EC-3.1 A paralegal shall refrain from engaging in any conduct that offends the dignity and decorum of proceedings before a court or other adjudicatory body and shall be respectful of all rules and procedures.

EC-3.2 A paralegal shall advise the proper authority of any action of another legal professional which clearly demonstrates fraud, deceit, dishonesty, or misrepresentation.

EC-3.3 A paralegal shall avoid impropriety and the appearance of impropriety.

CANON 4.

A PARALEGAL SHALL SERVE THE PUBLIC INTEREST BY CONTRIBUTING TO THE DELIVERY OF QUALITY LEGAL SERVICES AND THE IMPROVEMENT OF THE LEGAL SYSTEM.

EC-4.1 A paralegal shall be sensitive to the legal needs of the public and shall promote the development and implementation of programs that address those needs.

EC-4.2 A paralegal shall support bona fide efforts to meet the need for legal services by those unable to pay reasonable or customary fees; for example, participation in pro bono projects and volunteer work.

EC-4.3 A paralegal shall support efforts to improve the legal system and shall assist in making changes.

EXHIBIT 3.4
Continued

CANON 5.

A PARALEGAL SHALL PRESERVE ALL CONFIDENTIAL INFORMATION[3] PROVIDED BY THE CLIENT OR ACQUIRED FROM OTHER SOURCES BEFORE, DURING, AND AFTER THE COURSE OF THE PROFESSIONAL RELATIONSHIP.

EC-5.1 A paralegal shall be aware of and abide by all legal authority governing confidential information.

EC-5.2 A paralegal shall not use confidential information to the disadvantage of the client.

EC-5.3 A paralegal shall not use confidential information to the advantage of the paralegal or of a third person.

EC-5.4 A paralegal may reveal confidential information only after full disclosure and with the client's written consent; or, when required by law or court order; or, when necessary to prevent the client from committing an act which could result in death or serious bodily harm.

EC-5.5 A paralegal shall keep those individuals responsible for the legal representation of a client fully informed of any confidential information the paralegal may have pertaining to that client.

EC-5.6 A paralegal shall not engage in any indiscreet communications concerning clients.

CANON 6.

A PARALEGAL'S TITLE SHALL BE FULLY DISCLOSED.[4]

EC-6.1 A paralegal's title shall clearly indicate the individual's status and shall be disclosed in all business and professional communications to avoid misunderstandings and misconceptions about the paralegal's role and responsibilities.

EC-6.2 A paralegal's title shall be included if the paralegal's name appears on business cards, letterhead, brochures, directories, and advertisements.

CANON 7.

A PARALEGAL SHALL NOT ENGAGE IN THE UNAUTHORIZED PRACTICE OF LAW.

EC-7.1 A paralegal shall comply with the applicable legal authority governing the unauthorized practice of law.

CANON 8.

A PARALEGAL SHALL AVOID CONFLICTS OF INTEREST AND SHALL DISCLOSE ANY POSSIBLE CONFLICT TO THE EMPLOYER OR CLIENT, AS WELL AS TO THE PROSPECTIVE EMPLOYERS OR CLIENTS.

EC-8.1 A paralegal shall act within the bounds of the law, solely for the benefit of the client, and shall be free of compromising influences and loyalties. Neither the paralegal's personal or business interest, nor those of other clients or third persons, should compromise the paralegal's professional judgment and loyalty to the client.

EC-8.2 A paralegal shall avoid conflicts of interest which may arise from previous assignments whether for a present or past employer or client.

EC-8.3 A paralegal shall avoid conflicts of interest which may arise from family relationships and from personal and business interests.

EC-8.4 A paralegal shall create and maintain an effective recordkeeping system that identifies clients, matters, and parties with which the paralegal has worked, to be able to determine whether an actual or potential conflict of interest exists.

EC-8.5 A paralegal shall reveal sufficient nonconfidential information about a client or former client to reasonably ascertain if an actual or potential conflict of interest exists.

EC-8.6 A paralegal shall not participate in or conduct work on any matter where a conflict of interest has been identified.

EC-8.7 In matters where a conflict of interest has been identified and the client consents to continued representation, a paralegal shall comply fully with the implementation and maintenance of an Ethical Wall.[5]

1 "Paralegal" is synonymous with "Legal Assistant" and is defined as a person qualified through education, training, or work experience to perform substantive legal work that requires knowledge of legal concepts and is customarily, but not exclusively performed by a lawyer. This person may be retained or employed by a lawyer, law office, governmental agency or other entity or may be authorized by administrative, statutory or court authority to perform this work.

2 "Ex Parte" denotes actions or communications conducted at the instance and for the benefit of one party only, and without notice to, or contestation by, any person adversely interested.

3 "Confidential Information" denotes information relating to a client, whatever its source, which is not public knowledge nor available to the public. ("Non-Confidential Information" would generally include the name of the client and the identity of the matter for which the paralegal provided services.)

4 "Disclose" denotes communication of information reasonably sufficient to permit identification of the significance of the matter in question.

5 "Ethical Wall" refers to the screening method implemented in order to protect a client from a conflict of interest. An Ethical Wall generally includes, but is not limited to, the following elements: (1) prohibit the paralegal from having any connection with the matter; (2) ban disussions with or the transfer of documents to or from the paralegal; (3) restrict access to files; and (4) educate all members of the firm, corporation or entity as to the separation of the paralegal (both organizationally and physically) from the pending matter. For more information regarding the Ethical Wall, see the NFPA publication entitled "The Ethical Wall–Its Application to Paralegals."

EXHIBIT 3.5
The NALA Code of Ethics and Professional Responsibility

PREAMBLE

It is the responsibility of every legal assistant to adhere strictly to the accepted standards of legal ethics and to live by general principles of proper conduct. The performance of the duties of the legal assistant shall be governed by specific canons as defined herein in order that justice will be served and the goals of the profession attained.

The canons of ethics set forth hereafter are adopted by the National Association of Legal Assistants, Inc. as a general guide, and the enumeration of these rules does not mean there are not others of equal importance although not specifically mentioned.

CANON 1: A legal assistant shall not perform any of the duties that lawyers only may perform nor do things that lawyers themselves may not do.

CANON 2: A legal assistant may perform any task delegated and supervised by a lawyer so long as the lawyer is responsible to the client, maintains a direct relationship with the client, and assumes full professional responsibility for the work product.

CANON 3: A legal assistant shall not engage in the practice of law by accepting cases, setting fees, giving legal advice or appearing in court (unless otherwise authorized by court or agency rules).

CANON 4: A legal assistant shall not act in matters involving professional legal judgment as the services of a lawyer are essential in the public interest whenever the exercise of such judgment is required.

CANON 5: A legal assistant must act prudently in determining the extent to which a client may be assisted without the presence of a lawyer.

CANON 6: A legal assistant shall not engage in the unauthorized practice of law and shall assist in preventing the unauthorized practice of law.

CANON 7: A legal assistant must protect the confidences of a client, and it shall be unethical for a legal assistant to violate any statute now in effect or hereafter to be enacted controlling privileged communications.

CANON 8: It is the obligation of the legal assistant to avoid conduct which would cause the lawyer to be unethical or even appear to be unethical, and loyalty to the employer is incumbent upon the legal assistant.

CANON 9: A legal assistant shall work continually to maintain integrity and a high degree of competency throughout the legal profession.

CANON 10: A legal assistant shall strive for perfection through education in order to better assist the legal profession in fulfilling its duty of making legal services available to clients and the public.

CANON 11: A legal assistant shall do all other things incidental, necessary, or expedient for the attainment of the ethics and responsibilities imposed by statute or rule of court.

CANON 12: A legal assistant is governed by the American Bar Association Model Code of Professional Responsibility and the American Bar Association Model Rules of Professional Conduct.

document addresses and provides guidance on the three issues discussed below, each of which is of paramount importance to paralegals (and other legal professionals) today. (See Appendix D for the complete text of the 1988 revision of the NALA Model Standards and Guidelines.)

Definition of a Legal Assistant. Section II of the document (Section I is the preamble) defines a *legal assistant* as follows:

> Legal assistants* are a distinguishable group of persons who assist attorneys in the delivery of legal services. Through formal education, training, and

> experience, legal assistants have knowledge and expertise regarding the legal system and substantive and procedural law which qualify them to do work of a legal nature under the supervision of an attorney.
>
> *Within this occupational category some individuals are known as paralegals.

NALA clarifies the meaning of its footnote to this definition in a comment to Section II:

> This definition has been used to foster a distinction between a legal assistant as one working under the direct supervision of an attorney and a broader class of paralegals who perform tasks of a similar nature, but not necessarily under the supervision of an attorney. In applying the standards and guidelines, it is important to remember that they in turn were developed to apply to the legal assistant as defined therein.

Generally, NALA's position is that paralegals who assist attorneys fall into one professional category (to which the NALA guidelines apply) and independent paralegals into another. NPFA's definition of a legal assistant, in contrast, makes no such distinction (see footnote 1 in the NPFA Model Code of Ethics and Professional Responsibility in Exhibit 3.4). Like the ABA's definition of a legal assistant (presented in Chapter 1), NPFA's definition treats the terms *legal assistant* and *paralegal* synonymously.

Standards and Qualifications. Section III states that "[a] legal assistant should meet certain minimum qualifications" and sets out six standards that "may be used to determine an individual's qualifications as a legal assistant." The standards range from formal paralegal educational requirements to on-the-job training as a legal assistant.

Guidelines on Paralegal Performance. Section IV, the lengthiest section of the document, indicates the types of tasks that paralegals are and are not legally permitted to perform. The document cites specific provisions of the Model Code and the Model Rules, state codes, and court decisions that shed light on what constitutes the unauthorized practice of law. We will examine these guidelines in more detail shortly.

The ABA Model Guidelines. The ABA adopted its Model Guidelines for the Utilization of Legal Assistant Services in 1991. The ABA Standing Committee on Legal Assistants, which drafted the guidelines, based them on the NALA guidelines, various state codes and guidelines on the use of paralegals, and relevant state court decisions. The document consists of ten guidelines, each of which is followed by a lengthy comment on the derivation, scope, and application of the guideline. The ten guidelines are presented in Exhibit 3.6 on the next page. (For reasons of space, Exhibit 3.6 presents only the guidelines; for the comments, refer to the version of the Model Guidelines in Appendix F of this text.)

State Guidelines. Over one-third of the states have adopted some form of guidelines concerning the use of legal assistants by attorneys, the respective responsibilities of attorneys and legal assistants in performing legal work, the types of tasks paralegals may perform, and other ethically challenging

EXHIBIT 3.6
The ABA Model Guidelines for the Utilization of Legal Assistant Services (Comments Not Included)

Guideline 1: A lawyer is responsible for all of the professional actions of a legal assistant performing legal assistant services at the lawyer's direction and should take reasonable measures to ensure that the legal assistant's conduct is consistent with the lawyer's obligations under the ABA Model Rules of Professional Conduct.

Guideline 2: Provided the lawyer maintains responsibility for the work product, a lawyer may delegate to a legal assistant any task normally performed by the lawyer except those tasks proscribed to one not licensed as a lawyer by statute, court rule, administrative rule or regulation, controlling authority, the ABA Model Rules of Professional Conduct, or these Guidelines.

Guideline 3: A lawyer may not delegate to a legal assistant:

(a) Responsibility for establishing an attorney-client relationship.
(b) Responsibility for establishing the amount of a fee to be charged for a legal service.
(c) Responsibility for a legal opinion rendered to a client.

Guideline 4: It is the lawyer's responsibility to take reasonable measures to ensure that clients, courts, and other lawyers are aware that a legal assistant, whose services are utilized by the lawyer in performing legal services, is not licensed to practice law.

Guideline 5: A lawyer may identify legal assistants by name and title on the lawyer's letterhead and on business cards identifying the lawyer's firm.

Guideline 6: It is the responsibility of a lawyer to take reasonable measures to ensure that all client confidences are preserved by a legal assistant.

Guideline 7: A lawyer should take reasonable measures to prevent conflicts of interest resulting from a legal assistant's other employment or interests insofar as such other employment or interests would present a conflict of interest if it were that of the lawyer.

Guideline 8: A lawyer may include a charge for the work performed by a legal assistant in setting a charge for legal services.

Guideline 9: A lawyer may not split legal fees with a legal assistant nor pay a legal assistant for the referral of legal business. A lawyer may compensate a legal assistant based on the quantity and quality of the legal assistant's work and the value of that work to a law practice, but the legal assistant's compensation may not be contingent, by advance agreement, upon the profitability of the lawyer's practice.

Guideline 10: A lawyer who employs a legal assistant should facilitate the legal assistant's participation in appropriate continuing education and *pro bono publico* activities.

areas of legal practice. Although the guidelines of some states reflect the influence of the NALA standards and guidelines, the state guidelines focus largely on state statutory definitions of the practice of law, state codes of ethics regulating the responsibilities of attorneys, and state court decisions. As a paralegal, you should make sure that you become familiar with your state's guidelines.

What Paralegals Cannot (and Should Not) Do

The NALA Model Standards and Guidelines and the ABA Model Guidelines hold paralegals to the ethical standards governing attorneys—that is, paralegals cannot do what attorneys cannot do. These guidelines also indicate the kinds of activities that *only* attorneys are permitted to do, as determined by court interpretations of UPL statutes. Guideline VI of the NALA Model Standards and Guidelines states, in part, that legal assistants may *not* perform any of the following actions:[10]

- Establish attorney-client relationships.
- Set legal fees.
- Give legal opinions or advice.
- Represent a client before a court (with some exceptions).

These activities, because they lie at the heart of the attorney-client relationship, have traditionally been regarded by the courts as activities that can only be undertaken by an attorney.

The first two prohibitions listed above are relatively straightforward. The second two prohibitions are less so, however, for the reasons discussed below.

Legal Opinions and Advice. In regard to giving legal opinions and advice, Guideline 3 of the ABA Model Guidelines echoes NALA Guideline VI by stating that a lawyer "may not delegate to a legal assistant" the responsibility "for a legal opinion rendered to a client." Clearly, giving legal advice goes to the essence of legal practice. After all, a person would not seek out a legal expert if he or she did not want legal advice on some matter. Although a paralegal may *communicate* an attorney's legal advice to a client, the paralegal may not *give* legal advice.

Although other nonlawyers often give advice affecting others' legal rights or obligations, paralegals may not do so. For example, when an individual receives a speeding ticket, a friend or relative who is a nonlawyer might suggest that the person should argue the case before a judge and explain his or her side of the story. When a paralegal gives such advice, however, he or she may be accused of engaging in the unauthorized practice of law. Legal assistants are prohibited from giving even simple, common-sense advice because of the understandably greater weight given to the advice of someone who has legal training. Although as a legal assistant you may have developed great expertise in a certain area of law, you must refrain from advising clients in respect to their legal obligations or rights.

For example, suppose that you are a bankruptcy specialist and know that a client who wants to petition for bankruptcy has two realistic options to pursue under bankruptcy law. Should you tell the client about these options and their consequences? No, you should not. In effect, advising someone of his or her legal options is very close to advising a person of his or her legal rights and may therefore—in the view of many courts, at least—constitute the practice of law. Also, even though you may qualify what you say by telling the client that he or she needs to check with the attorney, this does not alter the fact that you are giving advice to the client, advice on which the client might rely.

What constitutes the giving of legal advice is not always easy to pin down. As you will read below, paralegals are permitted to advise clients on

10. Although the NFPA Model Code of Ethics and Professional Responsibility does not specify the kinds of tasks that paralegals may not perform, it does state, in Canon 7, that a paralegal "shall not engage in the unauthorized practice of law."

ETHICAL CONCERN

Saying "If I were you. . ." and the UPL

Any time a paralegal says, "If I were you, I would . . . ," the paralegal is, in effect, engaging in the unauthorized practice of law—giving legal advice that could result in a client's decision to take (or not to take) a certain action. For example, suppose that a client calls your law office, and you take the call. The client, Mrs. Rabe, is an older woman who is very upset about the fact that an insurance company has not paid on a $1,000 life insurance policy that she purchased covering the life of her grandson, who has just died. Mrs. Rabe tells you all of the details, and you feel that even though she might win a lawsuit against the insurance company, she would probably spend a lot more than $1,000 in the process. Mrs. Rabe wants to know if your supervising attorney will see her about the case, and when you tell her the attorney is out of town, she presses you for advice. Finally, you say, "Well, if I were you, I'd take the case to small claims court. You would not have to hire an attorney, it would be less costly, and you might recover some of the money." What you do not realize (and thus do not tell Mrs. Rabe) is that if she sues the insurance company, she might win not just the $1,000 payment but also substantial punitive damages for the insurance company's wrongful behavior—and might also benefit by other penalties imposed under the state's insurance statute.

a number of matters, and drawing the line between permissible and impermissible advice may at times be difficult. To be on the safe side (and avoid potential liability for the unauthorized practice of law), a good rule of thumb is the following:

- **Never advise a client or other person on any matter if the advice may alter the legal position or legal rights of the one to whom the advice is given.**

Whenever you are pressured to render legal advice—as you surely will be at one time or another, by your firm's clients or others—simply say that you cannot give legal advice because it is against the law to do so. Paralegals find that this frank and honest statement usually solves the problem.

The Representation of Clients. The rule that only attorneys—with limited exceptions—can represent others in court has a long history. Recall from the discussion of attorney regulation earlier in this chapter that attorney licensing was initially required only for court representation. In the last few decades, the ethical reasoning underlying this rule has been called into question by two developments.

First, in 1975, the United States Supreme Court held that people have a constitutional right to represent themselves in court.[11] Some people have questioned why a person can represent himself or herself in court but cannot hire a person more educated in the law to do so unless that person is a licensed attorney. Second, the fact that paralegals are allowed to represent clients before some federal and state government agencies, such as the federal Social Security Administration and state welfare departments (see Chapter 13), has called into question the ethical underpinnings of this rule. Nonetheless, as a paralegal, you should know that you are not allowed to appear in court on behalf of your supervising attorney—although local courts in some states are carving out exceptions to this rule for *limited* purposes.

What Paralegals Can (and Should) Do

Other than the above-mentioned activities, paralegals can perform virtually any legal task as long as the work is supervised by an attorney. Guideline 2 of the ABA Model Guidelines indicates the breadth of paralegal responsibilities:

> Provided the lawyer maintains responsibility for the work product, a lawyer may delegate to a legal assistant any task normally performed by the lawyer except those tasks proscribed to one not licensed as a lawyer by statute, court rule, administrative rule or regulation, controlling authority, the ABA Model Rules of Professional Conduct, or these Guidelines.

Paralegals working for attorneys may interview clients and witnesses, investigate legal claims, draft legal documents for attorneys' signatures, attend will executions (in some states), appear at real-estate closings (in some states), and undertake numerous other types of legal work, as long as the work is supervised by attorneys. When state or federal law allows them to do so, paralegals can also represent clients before government agencies.

11. *Faretta v. California*, 422 U.S. 806, 95 S.Ct. 2525, 45 L.Ed.2d 562 (1975).

Paralegals are allowed to perform freelance services for attorneys and, depending on state law and the type of service, perform limited independent services for the public.

Legal assistants are also permitted to give information to clients on many types of matters relating to a case or other legal matter. When arranging for client interviews, they let clients know what kind of information is needed and what documents to bring to the office. They inform clients about legal procedures and what the client should expect to experience during the progress of a legal proceeding. For example, in preparing for trial, legal assistants instruct clients on trial procedures, what they should wear to the trial, and so on. Clearly, as a legal assistant, you will be permitted to give clients all kinds of information. Nonetheless, you must make sure that you know where to draw the line between giving permissible types of advice and giving "legal advice"—advice that only attorneys are licensed to give under state laws.

The specific types of tasks that paralegals are legally permitted to undertake are described throughout this book—and it would be impossible to list them all here. Generally, Guideline 2 of the ABA makes it clear that paralegals can engage in a wide spectrum of legal activities:

- **Apart from tasks that only attorneys can legally perform, paralegals may perform almost any type of legal work as long as the attorney authorizes the work and assumes responsibility for the paralegal's work product.**

Ethical Responsibilities of All Legal Assistants. NALA Guideline V summarizes the ethical responsibilities of all legal assistants:

> Legal assistants should:
> 1. Disclose their status as legal assistants at the outset of any professional relationship with a client, other attorneys, a court or administrative agency or personnel thereof, or members of the general public;
> 2. Preserve the confidences and secrets of all clients; and
> 3. Understand the attorney's Code of Professional Responsibility and these guidelines in order to avoid any action which would involve the attorney in a violation of that Code, or give the appearance of professional impropriety.

Because of the close working relationship between an attorney and a paralegal, a client may have difficulty perceiving that the paralegal is not also an attorney. To avoid misleading clients and others, the NALA guidelines strongly emphasize the importance of disclosing to clients and others the fact that a paralegal is not an attorney. When you are first introduced to a client, you should make sure that the client knows that you are not a lawyer. Similarly, in correspondence with clients or others, you should indicate your nonattorney status by typing "Paralegal" or "Legal Assistant" after your name.

The ABA Model Guidelines also emphasize the importance of disclosing the nonattorney status of paralegals. Guideline 4 places this responsibility on attorneys:

> It is the lawyer's responsibility to take reasonable measures to ensure that clients, courts, and other lawyers are aware that a legal assistant, whose services are utilized by the lawyer in performing legal services, is not licensed to practice law.

ETHICAL CONCERN

Disclosure of Paralegal Status

UPL problems often result from telephone conversations between a client or a potential client and a paralegal. For example, a client's call to an attorney may be transferred to the attorney's paralegal if the attorney is not in the office. The paralegal may assume that the client knows that he or she is not an attorney and may speak freely with the client about a legal matter, advising the client that the attorney will be in touch with the client shortly about the matter. The client, however, may assume that the paralegal is an attorney and may make inferences based on the paralegal's comments that result in actions with harmful consequences—in which event, the paralegal might be charged with the unauthorized practice of law. To avoid such problems, you should always make sure that a client or a potential client knows that you are a paralegal and not an attorney.

The NPFA Model Code of Ethics and Professional Responsibility also stresses the importance of disclosing paralegal status (in Canon 6) and of keeping client information confidential (in Canon 5).

THE DIRECT REGULATION OF PARALEGALS

One of the major issues facing legal professionals and other interested groups today is whether paralegals should be subject to direct regulation by the state through licensing requirements. Unlike certification, which was discussed in Chapter 1, *licensing* involves direct and *mandatory* regulation, by the state, of an occupational or professional group. When licensing requirements are established for a professional group, such as for attorneys, a license is required before a member of the group can practice his or her profession.

GENERAL LICENSING
A type of licensing in which all individuals within a specific profession or group (such as paralegals) must meet licensing requirements imposed by the state before they may legally practice their profession.

A few states have considered implementing a **general licensing** program, which would require all paralegals to meet certain educational requirements and other specified criteria before being allowed to practice their profession. The problem with general licensing has been that to license a professional group, the licensing body must first define the group to be licensed. This is difficult to do in respect to paralegals because of the diversity of paralegal tasks and the broad range of services they perform.

LIMITED LICENSING
A type of licensing in which a limited number of individuals within a specific profession or group (such as independent paralegals within the paralegal profession) must meet licensing requirements imposed by the state before those individuals may legally practice their profession.

As an alternative to general licensing, over half the states are considering **limited licensing**, which would limit licensing requirements to those paralegals (independent paralegals, or legal technicians) who wish to provide specified legal services directly to the public. With limited licensing, qualified paralegals would be authorized to handle routine legal services traditionally rendered only by attorneys, such as advising clients on simple divorces, will executions, bankruptcy petitions, incorporation, real-estate transactions, selected tax matters, and other specified services as designated by the state licensing body. Currently, only the state of Washington has adopted a form of limited licensing. That state now permits qualifying paralegals to become licensed in one specialty area—real estate.

Direct Regulation—The Pros and Cons

The two national paralegal organizations, NFPA and NALA, are divided on whether paralegals should be directly regulated by the state. Although there are numerous other participants in the debate—including other paralegal associations, state bar associations, the American Bar Association, the courts, and various interest groups—the arguments for and against regulation set forth by NFPA and NALA indicate the basic contours of the debate.

NPFA's Position. NPFA endorses the implementation of regulation of the paralegal profession on a state-by-state basis insofar as its implementation expands the utilization of paralegals to deliver cost-efficient legal services. If it can be demonstrated that there is a public need for lower-cost legal services, NFPA is in favor of the regulation of paralegals, providing the paralegals meet certain minimum criteria.

NFPA contends that the licensing of paralegals would accomplish several goals. First, attorneys and the public would benefit because only demonstrably qualified paralegals would be licensed to practice as paralegals. Second, attorneys' search costs in finding competent assistance would be reduced. Third, the licensing of paralegals would be a step forward in the development of the paralegal profession. Fourth, licensing would permit paralegals to legally perform specified tasks, and therefore they would not be at risk for the unauthorized practice of law to the extent they are today. And finally, the licensing of paralegals would give consumers greater access to low-cost legal assistance for routine legal matters. NPFA argues that the latter issue (access to legal services) provides a compelling reason to expand the role of paralegals.

NFPA proposes a two-tiered system of licensing: general licensing and specialty licensing. General licensing by a state board or agency would require all paralegals within the state to satisfy stipulated requirements in regard to education, experience, and continuing education; it would also subject practicing paralegals to disciplinary procedures by the licensing body. Specialty licensing would require paralegals who wish to practice in a specialized area to demonstrate, by an examination, their proficiency in that area.

NALA's Position. While NALA supports voluntary certification, it believes that imposing licensing requirements on paralegals would be premature. Currently, paralegals perform a wide range of tasks and work in a variety of settings. In NALA's opinion, to impose mandatory, uniform requirements on a group of professionals whose function is not yet sufficiently defined would limit paralegal opportunities—it would close the door to those paralegals who could not meet the requirements for licensing and might prohibit activities that paralegals are currently authorized to undertake. NALA looks at certification and the development of paralegal education programs as being, at least at this point in time, a reasonable alternative to licensing. Furthermore, NALA emphasizes that most paralegals work under the supervision of attorneys and are thus already subject to regulation via attorney codes.

NALA's objections to specific limited-licensing proposals for independent paralegals (legal technicians) do not reflect opposition to the idea of limited licensing for independent paralegals so much as disagreement with specific aspects of the proposed regulatory schemes.

The Debate Continues

To date, no state has adopted licensing requirements, except for the state of Washington, in which the licensing is limited to real-estate paralegals, as mentioned above. To a great extent, this is because it has been difficult to reach consensus on such issues as who should be regulated, who should do the regulating, what types of services should be regulated, and what proficiency or educational standards should be required.

In 1992, the American Bar Association created the Commission on Nonlawyer Practice to examine the issue of how legal professionals can provide high-quality legal services to all consumers. Since its formation, the commission has been holding hearings around the country on the issue, and based on its findings, it will eventually make recommendations for the

PARALEGAL PROFILE

Freelance Paralegal

PATRICIA HERRING received her associate's degree in liberal arts from Suffolk Community College in New York. She also received a paralegal certificate from Adelphi University, and she is currently pursuing her bachelor's degree through the New York State Regent's Department Empire State Program. After working for law firms for six years and becoming a highly skilled paralegal, Herring turned to freelance work. Herring's professional affiliations have included board memberships in the Long Island Paralegal Association and service as a primary representative in the National Federation of Paralegal Associations. She is currently a member of the New York State Bar Association Paralegal Subcommittee and the Nassau County Bar Association Subcommittee on Paralegals. Herring has been a guest lecturer for local paralegal schools and has taught civil litigation at New York Technical University.

What do you like best about your work?

"The thing I like best about my job as a freelancer is that, to some extent, I can choose the clients and attorneys with whom I wish to work and the type of work I do. I specialize in all aspects of estate administrations and trusts, including some of the tax work, and have four or five main clients. I also do some legal research and litigation-support work. I also feel that freelancing is slightly more lucrative than working as an employee, and I like having access to different firms and seeing how they operate. All and all, there's just a greater diversity of contacts and types of work."

"I...HAVE NOT REGRETTED FOR A MINUTE MY DECISION TO PURSUE THIS PROFESSION."

What is the greatest challenge that you face in your area of work?

"My greatest challenge is keeping current on all the changes in the law. Because I do not work for a law firm, there are many resources that I do not have at my fingertips. I have therefore invested heavily in both legal publications and continuing legal education to maintain my standards as a specialist. In addition, I maintain contacts with my colleagues and have taken steps to form a small networking group of paralegals to further share resources and information."

What advice do you have for would-be paralegals in your area of work?

"I would recommend that anyone interested in a paralegal career be 'people oriented' because most paralegals maintain heavy client contact. It is also helpful to start out as a generalist because it gives you broader exposure to the various areas of law. Once you identify the areas that interest you, you can hopefully begin to specialize and direct your career along those lines."

What are some tips for success as a paralegal in your area of work?

"I recommend that individuals who are contemplating a move into freelance work test the waters by initially providing services on the side while they are still employed and have a dependable income. The entrepreneurial step into freelancing requires strong client contacts and administrative skills. Additionally, a first-time freelancer will be faced with issues relating to retainer agreements, fee structures, and payments. When a freelancer is retained by a law firm or an attorney with whom she has not had any prior experience, it is generally beneficial to form a retainer agreement so that all of the parties are clear regarding the services to be provided and the fees to be charged for those services. I find myself fortunate to be in this field and have not regretted for a minute my decision to pursue this profession."

ABA's consideration. Representatives of both NALA and NPFA are members of this commission.

Because the debate touches on a vital public concern—the need to have access to lower-cost legal services—the implications of paralegal licensing

TODAY'S PROFESSIONAL PARALEGAL

Working for the Attorney Discipline Board

Denise James is a legal assistant who works for the attorney discipline board in her state. She has an interesting job that entails a variety of responsibilities. One of Denise's job responsibilities is to contact attorneys to sit on the attorney discipline board's hearing panel. She goes to the list of attorneys who have volunteered to sit on the panel and calls a number of them to make arrangements for the hearing panels. She sends out background information on, and summaries of, the cases they will be hearing. On the day of the hearing, she meets the attorneys, escorts them to the hearing room, provides them with hearing examiners' robes, and assists them in getting the hearing started.

PREPARING "NOTICES OF DISCIPLINE"

Another of Denise's duties is to prepare the "notices of discipline" that are published every month in the state bar association journal, a monthly publication that is sent to all licensed attorneys in the state. These notices identify which attorneys have been subject to disciplinary actions and for what reasons. To prepare this month's notices, Denise pulls out all of the "final orders of discipline" that were entered this month. She then reads through and summarizes each order.

SUMMARIZING DISCIPLINARY PROCEEDINGS

Denise reads a final order sanctioning an attorney. The attorney, who commingled a client's funds with her own personal funds, was suspended. The funds involved consisted of a check received as a result of the settlement of a personal-injury lawsuit. The attorney deposited the check in her personal checking account and then used the money to pay her monthly bills. She did not issue a check to the client for the money until three months later. The client continually called the attorney's office and demanded the settlement check. The attorney kept stalling and then simply refused to return the client's phone calls.

Denise summarizes the disciplinary proceedings against the attorney as follows: "[Attorney's name], P12345, Binghamton, by Attorney Discipline Board, Binghamton County, Hearing Panel #6, effective June 3, 1995. Respondent commingled client funds by using the client's money, received in a settlement, to pay her personal bills, then paid the client three months later. The hearing panel found respondent's conduct to be in violation of Court Rule 1.15 and the state rules of professional conduct. A suspension was issued, and costs were assessed in the amount of $751.53."

There is never a dull moment working for the attorney discipline board. The unfortunate part is that Denise sees many cases in which clients have lost legal rights because their cases were neglected for a variety of reasons.

reach beyond legal professionals. In a sense, the paralegal profession is facing a question faced by attorneys over a century ago—how to ensure that the public is protected against incompetent legal services without unnecessarily restricting entry into (and thus competition within) the profession delivering those services.

THE CHANGING REGULATORY LANDSCAPE

An interesting aspect of the UPL committee's investigation into New Jersey freelance paralegal practices (discussed in this chapter's featured-guest article) was that prior to undertaking its investigation in 1989, the committee was unaware that paralegal associations even existed. Only when it began to investigate paralegal practices did it learn that paralegal associations existed both in New Jersey and at the national level. It also learned at that time that the New Jersey State Bar Association had a subcommittee on paralegals. This lack of awareness underscores how rapidly the paralegal profession has developed. At times, even the courts have been caught off guard, as was the New Jersey court.

New professional or business practices often outdistance the law, and it takes a while for the law to catch up. For example, the technological developments of the past two decades, particularly the computer revolution, resulted in new business practices, new types of crimes, and other activities that were not covered by existing laws. It has taken the law some time to adapt old laws or establish new ones to govern such situations. Similarly, the development of the paralegal profession has created a need to establish guidelines for a new type of legal professional—one not adequately regulated by existing laws.

When you begin working as a paralegal, you will be a member of a profession that may be entering its most dynamic phase of development. As a paralegal, you will have an opportunity to become personally involved in shaping the future of your profession. You will also need to keep closely attuned to regulatory developments that affect your work, because these developments are occurring so rapidly.

KEY TERMS AND CONCEPTS

breach 87
contempt of court 99
damages 93
disbarment 93
freelance paralegal 97
general licensing 112
independent paralegal 95
licensing 82
limited licensing 112
malpractice 93
pro bono publico 95
profession 80
reprimand 92
self-regulation 80
statute of limitations 88
suspension 92
third parties 91
unauthorized practice of law (UPL) 83

CHAPTER SUMMARY

1. A professional is one who has acquired a basic knowledge of the arts and sciences in addition to specialized knowledge in a particular area. Historically, professional groups have engaged in self-regulation by establishing minimum levels of competency for membership in the profession and ethical or professional codes to regulate the conduct of those belonging to the profession. Because clients seek out and pay lawyers for their legal expertise and because the professional judgment of a lawyer can significantly affect a client's welfare, lawyers are ethically (and legally) obligated to act in the client's best interests.

2. Key participants in the regulation of attorneys are state bar associations, state supreme courts, state legislatures, the United States Supreme Court (very occasionally), and the American Bar Association, which establishes model rules and guidelines relating to attorney conduct to be adopted by the various states. Attorneys are regulated both through licensing requirements and through ethical codes of conduct. To obtain a license to practice law in most states, an attorney must receive a bachelor's degree from a college or university, graduate from an accredited law school, take and pass a state bar examination, and pass an extensive background inspection.

3. All states but California have adopted a version of either the 1969 Model Code of Professional Responsibility or the 1983 revision of the Model

Code, called the Model Rules of Professional Conduct, both of which were published by the American Bar Association. The majority of the states have adopted the Model Rules. The Model Code and Model Rules spell out the ethical and professional duties governing attorneys and the practice of law.

4. Ethical rules governing attorney behavior relate to competence, diligence, communication with clients, fees, confidentiality of client information, conflicts of interest, safekeeping of property, expediting of litigation, and other areas or activities. Attorneys who violate these duties may be subject to sanctions in the form of a reprimand, a suspension, or a disbarment. Additionally, attorneys are subject to potential liability for malpractice or for violation of criminal statutes.

5. In the 1970s and 1980s, the need for low-cost legal services became pressing as more laws were created and laws became more complex. The legal profession responded to this need by emphasizing that all attorneys have an ethical duty to provide legal services *pro bono publico* (for the benefit of the public) at reduced cost or at no cost. The profession also responded by creating legal clinics and prepaid or group services, reducing restrictions on advertising, and delegating more work to paralegals at a lower hourly rate for the client. The rise of the independent paralegal, a paralegal who provides services directly to the public, was another response to the demand for low-cost legal services.

6. The fact that both paralegals working for attorneys and independent paralegals engage in work that traditionally only attorneys have performed raises concerns about the unauthorized practice of law. Lawsuits against independent paralegals, particularly, focused attention on the unauthorized practice of law. Determining what constitutes the unauthorized practice of law is complicated by the fact that state UPL statutes generally offer only vague or very broad definitions of what constitutes the practice of law. Generally, the paralegal must be extremely cautious when contemplating the possibility of working without attorney supervision.

7. Paralegals are regulated indirectly by attorney ethical rules, by ethical codes created by paralegal professional associations, and by guidelines on the utilization of paralegals, which define the status and function of paralegals and the scope of their authorized activities. The American Bar Association and several states have also adopted guidelines on the utilization of paralegals. These codes and guidelines provide paralegals, attorneys, and the courts with guidance on the paralegal's role in the practice of law. Paralegals are also regulated indirectly by their potential liability under civil or criminal statutes.

8. Court decisions, state attorney ethical rules, paralegal ethical codes and guidelines, and the guidelines on the use of legal assistants that have been adopted by the American Bar Association and several states all express a general consensus that paralegals, under attorneys' supervision, may perform virtually any legal task that attorneys can, with four exceptions. A paralegal may not (1) establish an attorney-client relationship, (2) set the fees to be charged for an attorney's services, (3) represent a client in court (with a few exceptions), or (4) give legal advice or opinions.

9. Court decisions in some states have established that independent paralegals, or legal technicians, do not engage in the unauthorized practice of law when they sell do-it-yourself kits to consumers and assist consumers in pursuing their legal rights by typing forms for them—so long as paralegals do not help consumers select forms and do not in any way advise consumers in regard to their legal rights. Again, because the line between authorized and unauthorized practice in respect to this type of work is very blurred, paralegals who want to work as independents should be extremely careful.

10. A major concern today for both legal professionals and the public is whether paralegals should be directly regulated by the state through licensing requirements. General licensing would establish minimum standards that every paralegal would have to meet in order to practice as a paralegal in the state. Limited licensing would require paralegals wishing to offer routine legal services directly to the public in certain areas, such as family law and bankruptcy law, to demonstrate their proficiency in that area. The pros and cons of direct regulation through licensing are being debated vigorously by the leading paralegal associations, state bar associations, state courts, state legislatures, and public-interest groups.

QUESTIONS FOR REVIEW

1. How is the legal profession regulated? Who are the regulators?

2. Why is regulation needed? How is regulation accomplished?

3. What are the two primary sets of ethical rules that guide the legal profession in the United States? What additional sets of rules are there?

4. How has attorney regulation affected the practice of law? What are some of the ways in which attorneys respond to the need for lower-cost legal services?

5. How is the paralegal profession regulated by attorney ethical codes?

6. How is the paralegal profession regulated by paralegal codes of ethics?

7. What types of tasks may legally be performed by paralegals?

8. What types of tasks may normally be performed only by attorneys?

9. Should paralegals be licensed? Why or why not? Should only independent paralegals be licensed? Why or why not?

10. How can paralegals influence the debate over

ETHICAL QUESTIONS

1. Anton Snow, a paralegal, has been asked to research the cases decided by courts in his state to see if he can find a case in which a landlord was held liable for crimes caused by a third party (someone other than the landlord or the tenant) on leased premises. Anton finds a case in which the trial court held that a landlord was liable for harms suffered by a plaintiff when she was mugged and robbed in an apartment complex's parking lot. The trial court stated that landlords have a duty to make sure that common areas (areas used in common by the tenants and their guests, including parking lots) are safe. Anton does not take the time to update the case. He therefore fails to find out that the state court of appeals later reversed the trial court's decision. The court of appeals held that landlords can be held liable for crimes caused by third parties on leased premises only if "prior similar incidents" (similar crimes) had occurred on the premises—so that the landlord had notice of the problem. Thus, the trial court's decision, which Anton gives to his supervising attorney, is no longer "good law." The supervising attorney, relying on Anton's research, advises the client accordingly. Discuss the potential problems that the client, the attorney, and Anton might face as a result of Anton's failure to update the trial court's decision.

2. Norma Sollers works as a paralegal for a small law firm. She is a trusted, experienced employee who has worked for the firm for twelve years. One morning, Linda Lowenstein, one of the attorneys, calls in from her home and asks Norma to sign Linda's name to a document that must be filed with the court that day. Norma has just prepared the final draft of the document and placed it on Linda's desk for her review and signature. Linda explains to Norma that because her child is sick, she does not want to the leave the child to come into the office. Norma knows that she should not sign Linda's name—only the client's attorney can sign the document. She mentions this to Linda, but Linda says, "Don't worry. No one will ever know that you signed it instead of me." How should Norma handle this situation?

3. Matthew Hinson is an independent paralegal. He provides divorce forms and typing and filing services to the public at very low rates. Samantha Eggleston uses his services. She returns with the forms filled out, but she has one question: How much in monthly child-support payments will she be entitled to receive? How may Matthew legally respond to this question?

PRACTICE QUESTIONS AND ASSIGNMENTS

1. Joel Marino has been through a very difficult year financially and had consulted several times with a bankruptcy attorney, Roxanne Baker. At one point, he even asked Baker to prepare the necessary forms to file with the bankruptcy court—then, at the last minute, he decided not to file the papers. Although Baker has sent Marino monthly bills for four months, Marino refuses to pay her. Now Marino calls Baker and asks her if she will help him file for a divorce. Baker says that she will be happy to help him, but first he must pay his outstanding bill. Marino explains that he is having a hard time financially, but Baker insists that unless he pays what he owes her, she will not perform further legal services for him. Marino becomes very upset and says to Baker, "I thought that lawyers had some sort of obligation to help the poor? Why don't I count?" What obligation to represent Marino in these circumstances does Baker have?

2. According to this chapter's text, which of the following tasks may a paralegal legally perform?

a. Draft a complaint at an attorney's request.

b. Interview a witness to a car accident.

c. Represent a client before an administrative agency.

d. Investigate the facts of a car-accident case.

e. Work as a freelance paralegal for attorneys.

f. Work as an independent paralegal providing legal services directly to the public.

3. Review the facts in Ethical Question 3 above. What do the following ethical codes say about the unauthorized practice of law, and how would these statements apply to Hinson's situation?

a. The NFPA Model Code of Ethics and Professional Responsibility (see Exhibit 3.4).

b. The NALA Code of Ethics and Professional Responsibility (see Exhibit 3.5).

Do your answers differ? If so, how?

QUESTIONS FOR CRITICAL ANALYSIS

1. Examine the definition of a legal assistant as stated in the NALA Model Standards and Guidelines for the Utilization of Legal Assistants and quoted in this chapter. Next review the definition of a legal assistant given in footnote 1 of the NFPA's Model Code of Ethics and Professional Responsibility (presented in Exhibit 3.4). How are the definitions similar? How do they differ? What differences in the approach and philosophy of each organization does this usage suggest?

2. What would be the advantages of licensing requirements for paralegals? What would be the disadvantages? Do you agree with NALA that legal assistants are already sufficiently regulated?

ROLE-PLAYING EXERCISES

1. Using the facts from Ethical Question 3 above, role-play the situation in which the client, Samantha Eggleston, asks the independent paralegal, Matthew Hinson, how much child support she will be entitled to receive. The paralegal, Matthew, should answer the client's (Samantha's) questions without engaging in the unauthorized practice of law. Samantha should be persistent in attempting to get Matthew to answer her question. If time permits, reverse roles.

2. Using the facts provided in Ethical Question 2, one person should play the role of Norma Sollers after she is asked to sign the document. The other person should play the role of Linda Lowenstein, the attorney. The person playing Norma should be direct and honest but slightly intimidated about objecting to Linda's request. Norma should politely persuade Linda to review and sign the document herself. The person playing Linda's role should be very assertive and undaunted by Norma's worries. If time permits, reverse the roles.

Projects

1. Find out what the requirements are for becoming licensed to practice law as an attorney in your state. Do they differ from the requirements mentioned in the text? If so, how?

2. Obtain a copy of your state's rules of professional responsibility for attorneys. How do they compare with the ABA Model Rules?

3. Find out how attorneys are disciplined in your state. Learn about the various degrees of discipline that are imposed. If the disciplinary hearings are open to the public, try to attend one. What is your impression?

Annotated Selected Readings

James, Christopher. "Software and Hard Choices: Interactive Legal Software Should Be Considered before Independent Paralegals Are Licensed." *Oregon State Bar Bulletin*, July 1992. A thoughtful article on the use of interactive software to create wills and other documents and on whether the use of such software by independent paralegals and other nonlawyers constitutes the practice of law.

Garwin, Arthur. "(Para) Legal Aid: What Sort of Assignments Can You Delegate to Nonlawyer Assistants?" *American Bar Association Journal*, July 1993. An article describing the tasks that lawyers may delegate to paralegals.

Latorraca, Dominic. "Regulation of Paralegals: An Upcoming Issue." *The Colorado Lawyer*, March 1993. An informative article, the purpose of which is to inform the Colorado Bar of the issues involved with paralegal regulation and the steps being taken in this direction by other states.

Meehan Rudy, Theresa. "Has the Time Arrived for State-by-State Licensing? No: Another Roadblock." *American Bar Association Journal*, December 1992. An article that provides an interesting review of the argument that licensing paralegals will not provide consumers of legal services with what they want—lower costs—but will serve to raise the costs by limiting entry into the profession.

Merle, Isgett L. *Litigation and Administrative Practice Course Handbook Series: The Role of the Legal Assistant: What Constitutes the Unauthorized Practice of Law?* New York: Practising Law Institute, 1991. A good discussion of what actions constitute the unauthorized practice of law and the role of ethics in the legal profession.

Morrison, Andrew S. "Is Divorce Mediation the Practice of Law? A Matter of Perspective." *California Law Review*, May 1987. An interesting article discussing whether or not acting as a divorce mediator constitutes the practice of law.

Resnick, Rosalind. "Legal Techs Face Regulation: Rules Mulled Nationwide." *National Law Journal*, June 22, 1992. An article that discusses the movement to license legal technicians, the pros and cons of such licensing according to others in the legal profession, and possible alternatives for providing low-cost legal services to the public.

Talamanta, Ryan J. "We Can't All Be Lawyers . . . Or Can We? Regulating the Unauthorized Practice of Law in Arizona." *Arizona Law Review*, Winter 1992. An in-depth review of the UPL rules in Arizona, the importance of regulating unlicensed practitioners, enforcement problems, and problems in defining what constitutes the practice of law. The article contains suggestions for reforming Arizona rules and stresses the need to keep "quality high and costs low" and to ensure that the public gets the legal services that many are currently unable to afford.

Withem, Karen. "The Independents Movement." *Legal Assistant Today*, September/October 1993. An informative article that discusses the pros and cons of allowing independent paralegals to provide legal services directly to the public. It also covers issues relating to licensing and the unauthorized practice of law.

4

ETHICS AND PROFESSIONAL RESPONSIBILITY

Chapter Objectives

After completing this chapter, you will know:

- The meaning of ethics and the function of personal and professional ethics in the legal context.
- How the ethical rules governing confidentiality, competence, and conflict of interest affect legal practice and paralegals.
- Which professional rules are most often violated, how violations can occur, and how to avoid them.
- What the "double billing" of clients means and the ethical implications of this practice.

Chapter Outline

INTRODUCTION

In Chapter 3, you read about many of the professional rules that govern the conduct of attorneys and, indirectly, paralegals working under their supervision. You also learned that violations of these rules may expose attorneys (and paralegals) to serious legal consequences. As a paralegal, one of your foremost professional responsibilities is to follow these rules meticulously.

If you are like most paralegals, you will find that following the rules sometimes is easier said than done. For example, what do you do when you perceive that adhering to a professional ethical rule in a given situation would violate your personal ethical standards? What is the "ethical" thing to do in such a situation? The opening section of this chapter addresses just this question and suggests that the answer lies in understanding how ethics—both personal and professional—function in the legal context.

The remainder of this chapter looks at some of the more challenging areas for paralegals in respect to ethics and professional responsibility. These areas relate to confidentiality, competence, conflict of interest, and legal fees (client billing practices).

ETHICS AND PARALEGAL PRACTICE

LEGAL ETHICS
The principles, values, and rules of conduct that govern legal professionals.

PERSONAL ETHICS
The moral principles and values that individuals apply in their daily lives and decision making.

ETHICS
Moral principles and values applied to social behavior.

If you are like most paralegals, you may find that some of the ethical conflicts you face cannot be resolved by the ethical rules of the legal profession, or **legal ethics**. Rather, the solutions will rest on your **personal ethics**—your own personal moral or ethical convictions. Generally, people who have a clear idea of their ethical values and priorities are best able to cope with ethical challenges. As you enter the paralegal profession, it is thus a good idea to examine carefully the meaning of ethics and your own personal ethical standards and priorities.

Ethics can be defined as that branch of philosophy that focuses on morality and the way in which moral principles are applied to daily life. Ethics has to do with fundamental questions such as the following: What is fair? What is just? What is the right thing to do in this situation? Essentially, ethics has to do with any question relating to the fairness, justness, rightness, or wrongness of an action.

Ethics is not an abstract or a static concept. On the contrary, ethics affects and gives meaning to our everyday lives and the decisions we make. We constantly apply our values and moral convictions to our actions and decisions, frequently without even being aware of the fact that we are doing so. The clothes we buy, the music we prefer, the way we treat our friends, the books we choose to read—these and a thousand other everyday activities and decisions, if you analyze them carefully, ultimately relate, at least in part, to ethical values and goals. Your interest in paralegal work may even be rooted in some moral belief or ethical conviction that you hold.

Personal Ethics and Professional Responsibility

As a paralegal, you will be expected to abide by the ethical rules governing the legal profession, which you *must* do. But in a broader sense, ethical behavior means more than merely abiding by a particular profession's rules of conduct. A paralegal could follow each of the rules governing the legal profession meticulously and still act unethically in a broader sense.

For example, suppose that Joan, a paralegal, is looking for a job. Her father knows an attorney who is looking for a paralegal, and Joan interviews for the job. The attorney mistakenly assumes, from comments made to him by Joan's father, that Joan has more experience as a paralegal than she actually has. Joan realizes this but does nothing to correct the mistaken assumption. The employer hires Joan and never learns of Joan's implicit misrepresentation. In fact, Joan does excellent work, and no one suffers any harmful consequences from her deceptive action (or inaction). Joan has not violated any ethical rule governing the legal profession, but has she acted ethically? Many people would conclude that she has not.

Violating a professional ethical rule, such as the duty of competence or the duty of confidentiality, may expose attorneys and paralegals to legal liability. Violating a personal ethical standard usually does not, unless a professional rule is violated at the same time. There is no law, for example, that requires you to "go that extra mile" for your supervising attorney and his or her client, even when it involves working overtime. Nor is there any law that requires you to be kind to a grieving client or sensitive to the views of your co-workers.

Honesty, personal integrity, consideration for others, a commitment to excellence, dedication to hard work—these and other attributes that will be expected of you as a paralegal are not mandated by law but rooted in personal ethical convictions. Generally, paralegals are expected to have made a personal ethical commitment to their profession and to the rules that govern it.

Conflicts between Personal and Legal Ethics

As a paralegal, you may encounter situations in which your personal ethical views conflict with one or more of the ethical rules that govern the legal profession, or legal ethics. Personally, for example, you may believe that there is nothing wrong with discussing confidential information about a client with your spouse—you trust your spouse implicitly and know that the information will go no further. As a legal professional, however, you have a duty to refrain from disclosing confidential information to anyone who is not working on the case, including your spouse, unless the client consents to the disclosure—as will be discussed later in this chapter.

Paralegals sometimes face similar ethical conflicts when asked by friends for legal advice. For example, suppose that a good friend asks you for legal advice concerning an issue about which you are particularly well informed. Your friend is having financial difficulties and asks you for advice on whether she should file for bankruptcy and what the consequences would be if she did. You doubt that she would ever hold you responsible for any unexpected detriment she might suffer if she followed your advice. Given the circumstances, and the fact that you want to help a friend, you feel that the "right" thing to do is answer her questions. But clearly, if you advised your friend on her legal rights, you would be engaging in the unauthorized practice of law, which is prohibited in all states and a crime under many state statutes.

THE LEGAL TEAM AT WORK
Teamwork and Professional Responsibility

Much of the work traditionally done by attorneys—including legal research and investigations, client interviews, the drafting of documents, and other tasks—can be handled by paralegals at a much lower hourly cost to the client. In the interests of lowering the cost of legal services to the public, the American Bar Association and many state bar associations have issued guidelines that encourage attorneys to make effective use of paralegal services.

The efficient delivery of legal services to the public is also a goal of the paralegal profession. This goal is reflected in the ethical codes of both the National Federation of Paralegal Associations (NFPA) and the National Association of Legal Assistants (NALA). For example, Canon 10 of the NALA Code of Ethics and Professional Responsibility reads, "A legal assistant shall strive for perfection through education in order to better assist the legal profession in fulfilling its duty of making legal services available to clients and the public." Canon 4 of the NPFA Model Code of Ethics and Professional Responsibility states, "A paralegal shall serve the public interest by contributing to the delivery of quality legal services and the improvement of the legal system." The NPFA code, in its preamble, states generally that paralegals "should strive to expand the paralegal role in the delivery of legal services."

An increasing number of law firms have adopted a teamwork approach to legal representation. As team members, paralegals participate substantially in the legal work involved in handling clients' cases. Some attorneys, however, are uncertain about the expertise paralegals possess and the many ways in which paralegal services can be used. As a result, those attorneys do not fully utilize paralegals to perform work that paralegals are trained to do. As a paralegal, you may face such a situation. What should you do if this happens? Do you have any ethical obligation to "educate" your supervising attorney in how your services can be effectively utilized in a team approach to legal work? Do the ethical canons quoted in the above paragraph obligate paralegals to take the initiative in such situations? Many paralegals believe that it is their professional responsibility to try to show their employers—by taking on additional projects, for example, or by going that "extra mile" to ensure quality work—how valuable they can be as team members and how the team approach to legal representation can best meet the needs of both attorneys and clients.

Perhaps one of the most serious personal ethical conflicts occurs when you are asked to work on behalf of a client whose actions you cannot condone. For example, what if you are asked to assist an attorney who is defending an alleged cold-blooded killer or drug dealer? You are morally uncomfortable about being a member of a defense team working on behalf of such a client. What is your ethical responsibility in this situation? On the one hand, you have a professional responsibility to assist the attorney in defending the client's rights. On the other hand, you feel that, by assisting in the client's defense, you may be implicitly condoning unethical (and criminal) behavior. When facing these kinds of ethical conflicts, you must place legal ethics in the larger context of the American system of justice and examine how legal ethics function within that context.

Legal Ethics and the Adversarial System of Justice

American and English courts follow the **adversarial system of justice**, in which the parties act as adversaries, or opponents. Parties to a lawsuit come before the court as contestants. In a sense, a courtroom is like a battlefield in which the parties to a lawsuit conduct a "legal battle." One side "wins" and the other "loses."

ADVERSARIAL SYSTEM OF JUSTICE
A legal system in which the parties to a lawsuit are opponents, or adversaries, and present their cases in a light most favorable to themselves. The court arrives at a just solution based on the evidence presented by the parties, or contestants, and determines who wins and who loses.

The parties do not come together in the courtroom with the idea of working out a compromise solution to their problems or of looking at the dispute from each other's point of view (although to avoid the time and expense of a lawsuit or of continuing a lawsuit, parties often do settle for a compromise solution out of court). Nor are they unbiased in their presentation of the facts to the court. Rather, they take sides and present the facts of the case in a light most favorable to their respective positions. The adversarial system of justice is founded on the assumption that the court (the judge—and the jury, if it is a jury trial), based on the evidence presented by the parties, will arrive at a true and just solution to the matter.

The Concept of Advocacy and Legal Ethics. Attorneys are **advocates** for their clients—that is, they present and argue their clients' cases before the courts. Their job is not to judge the rightness or wrongness of their clients' actions but to help their clients obtain a favorable judgment. Although attorneys argue on behalf of their clients, they are also officers of the court. As such, they must act with integrity and comply with ethical rules when presenting a client's case or evidence relating to the case. An attorney who does not fulfill this responsibility may be held in contempt of court.

ADVOCATE
As a verb, to assist, defend, or plead (argue) a cause for another. As a noun, a person (such as an attorney) who assists, defends, or pleads (argues) for another (such as a client) before a court.

Attorneys are essential to the legal process because they know the law. They have the necessary expertise to help a client put forth the best argument possible in support of the client's position. Although parties to a dispute have the right to represent themselves in court (instead of having attorneys represent them),[1] few persons do so—and with good reason: unless they are knowledgeable in the law and know how the law can be used in support of their claims, they will be at a serious disadvantage. As the oft-quoted adage states, "Only a fool has himself or herself for a client."

Many of the ethical rules governing attorneys, who are key participants in the litigation process, are rooted in this adversarial framework. To advocate effectively a client's cause, for example, an attorney must be able to communicate openly with his or her client. The rule of confidentiality facilitates such communication by protecting clients against unauthorized disclosures of confidential information. The rules governing conflicts of interest, which are designed both to protect clients and to ensure fairness in legal representation, also stem from the concept of advocacy. Other rules that you will read about in this text, including the rules governing court procedures and evidence, also relate to the adversarial nature of our justice system.

Professional Responsibility and Adversarial Justice. Now, consider again the situation mentioned above, in which you are asked to assist an attorney

1. See *Faretta v. California,* 422 U.S. 806, 95 S.Ct. 2525, 45 L.Ed.2d 562 (1975). (See Chapter 17 for an explanation of how to read legal citations.)

who is defending someone whose purported behavior you cannot ethically condone. Your professional responsibility is to fulfill your supervising attorney's request. Furthermore, if you look at the question in the larger context, the question takes on a different meaning. Ultimately, the issue is, do you believe that it is right for people to be allowed to have their "day in court" and to have legal advice and guidance in presenting their cases? Do you believe that every person has a right to the "due process of law"?[2] Do you believe that it should be up to the court, and not to the attorneys (or their paralegals), to decide on truth and pronounce judgments?

If you answer "yes" to these questions, then you will probably be able to assist your supervising attorney in good conscience. Your participation on the defense team does not suggest that you condone the wrongdoing allegedly committed by the client but that you believe in the American system of justice. By assisting your supervising attorney in finding evidence and legal theories in support of your client's claim, you are helping the court do its job—that of dispensing justice in a fair and equitable manner.

ETHICAL CHALLENGES IN PARALEGAL PRACTICE

Even if you have memorized every one of the professional rules governing the legal profession, you can still quite easily violate a rule unintentionally, as mentioned earlier. In fact, you should realize that paralegals rarely breach professional duties intentionally. A busy paralegal, for example, can easily overlook a deadline for filing a document with the court and thus breach the duty of competence. If the firm's client suffers significant harm as a result of a breach of the professional duty, it will not matter whether the breach was intentional or unintentional. In either case, the supervising attorney (and the paralegal) may face undesirable consequences, including a lawsuit for negligence.

To minimize the chances that you will unintentionally violate a rule, you need to know not only what the rules are but also how they apply to the day-to-day realities of your job. Consider, for example, a task that paralegals routinely perform: drafting and filing with the court a complaint (the document that initiates a lawsuit, discussed in Chapter 10). Just this one task involves a host of ethical responsibilities, including the following:

- *The duty of confidentiality.* Before the complaint is filed with the court (and becomes a public record), the paralegal must take care to make sure that the document is not seen by an office visitor, another client, or anyone else who is not authorized to know of the complaint or its contents.
- *The duty of competence.* The information in the complaint must be accurate, and the complaint must be filed with the proper court within the proper time period.

2. This right is guaranteed by the Fifth and Fourteenth Amendments to the U.S. Constitution, which provide that no person can be deprived of life, liberty, or property without due process of law. As will be discussed in Chapter 12, *due process of law* means that the government must follow a set of reasonable, fair, and standard procedures in any action against a citizen.

• *The attorney's duty to supervise the paralegal's work.* Before the complaint is filed, the paralegal should make sure that the attorney signs it.
• *An obligation to record accurately time spent and costs incurred on a client's behalf.* The time spent in drafting and filing the complaint, as well as any expenses incurred by the firm in copying or filing the document, must be accurately recorded so that the client can be billed properly.

Professional duties—and the possibility of violating those duties—are involved in virtually every task you will perform as a paralegal. Certain areas, however, deserve special attention here because they present more problems than others. These areas relate to confidentiality, competence, conflict of interest, and client billing practices.

ETHICAL CONCERN

Always Be Prepared

The professionally responsible paralegal will anticipate what will be needed in a given situation and prepare for those needs. How would you feel, for example, if, while attending a trial with your supervising attorney, you realized that you had forgotten to bring with you an important document—the written, sworn statement of a key witness? You interviewed the witness and typed up the statement for the witness to sign, and you are fairly sure that what the witness is now saying on the stand is inconsistent with what she said earlier during your interview. But you cannot prove it because you do not have the witness statement with you. Forgetting to include the statement in the materials you brought to the courtroom was an oversight, but it may be a costly one. As a result of your negligence, your supervising attorney may lose the case, the client may suffer substantial harm and sue the attorney for malpractice (breach of the duty of competence), and you may lose your job!

Confidentiality

The rule of confidentiality is one of the oldest and most important rules of the legal profession, primarily because it would be difficult for a lawyer to represent a client without such a rule. A client must be able to confide in his or her attorney so that the attorney can best represent the client's interest. Because confidentiality is one of the easiest rules to violate, a thorough understanding of the rule is essential.

The Rule. Rule 1.6 of the Model Rules of Professional Conduct,[3] which states the rule governing confidentiality, is presented in Exhibit 4.1. Note that paragraph (a), which states the general rule, does not make any qualifications about *what* kind of information is confidential. It simply states that a lawyer may not reveal "information relating to representation of a client." Does this mean that if a client tells you that he is the president of a local company, you have to keep that information confidential, even when the whole community knows that fact? For example, could you tell your spouse that "Mr. X is the president of XYZ Corporation"? It may seem permissible, because that fact is, after all, public knowledge. But in so doing, you must not indicate, by words or conduct, that Mr. X is a client of your firm. In such a situation, it is hard to know just what assumptions might be made based on what you have said. Consider another example. Suppose that one evening at dinner you told your spouse that you had met Mr. X that day. Your spouse might reasonably assume that your firm was handling some legal matter involving Mr. X. Because it may be difficult to decide what information is or is not confidential, a good rule of thumb is the following:

- **Paralegals should regard all information about a client or a client's case as confidential information.**

Exceptions to the Rule. In Exhibit 4.1 on the following page, you can see that Rule 1.6 provides for four exceptions, each of which we discuss here.

Client Consents to Disclosure. As stated in paragraph (a) of Rule 1.6, an attorney may reveal confidential information *if* the client consents to the

3. See Chapter 3 for a discussion of the origin and significance of these rules.

EXHIBIT 4.1
Rule 1.6 of the Model Rules of Professional Conduct

MODEL RULE 1.6

Rule 1.6 of the Model Rules of Professional Conduct:

(a) A lawyer shall not reveal information relating to representation of a client unless the client consents after consultation, except for disclosures that are impliedly authorized in order to carry out the representation, and except as stated in paragraph (b).
(b) A lawyer may reveal such information to the extent the lawyer reasonably believes necessary:
(1) to prevent the client from committing a criminal act that the lawyer believes is likely to result in imminent death or substantial bodily harm; or
(2) to establish a claim or defense on behalf of the lawyer in a controversy between the lawyer and the client, to establish a defense to a criminal charge or civil claim against the lawyer based upon conduct in which the client was involved, or to respond to the allegations in any proceeding concerning the lawyer's representation of the client.

disclosure. For example, suppose that an attorney is drawing up a will for a client, and the client is making his only son the sole beneficiary under the will and leaving nothing to his daughter. The daughter calls and wants to know how her father's will reads. The attorney cannot divulge this confidential information to the daughter because the client has not consented to such disclosure. Now suppose that the client told the attorney that if his daughter calls the attorney to find out if she inherited anything under the will, the attorney is to "go ahead and tell her that she gets nothing." In this situation, the attorney could disclose the information because the client consented to the disclosure.

Impliedly Authorized Disclosures. Paragraph (a) of Rule 1.6 also states that an attorney may make "disclosures that are impliedly authorized in order to carry out the representation." The latter exception is clearly necessary. Legal representation of clients necessarily involves the attorney's assistants, and they must have access to the confidential information to do their jobs. If a paralegal is working on the client's case, for example, he or she must know what the client told the attorney about the legal matter and must have access to information in the client's file concerning the case.

Client Intends a Harmful Act. Paragraph (b) of Rule 1.6 provides for two other exceptions. The first exception applies when a client reveals that he or she intends to commit a criminal act that may cause bodily harm or death to another. In this situation, the policy underlying the rule of confidentiality (protection of the client's legal rights) is outweighed by the policy of protecting another from imminent bodily harm or death.

The problem with this exception is that it is sometimes difficult to determine whether the client really intends to do what he or she said. Also, it is not always clear whether a client's intended behavior is in fact a criminal act that will result in bodily harm or death to another. If you are ever confronted with a situation in which you suspect that a client is about to harm another, discuss the matter immediately with your supervising attorney—and he or she will decide what should be done.

Defending against a Client's Legal Action. The second exception in paragraph (b) of Rule 1.6 is particularly important for attorneys and paralegals. The classic example of this exception is a client's malpractice suit against an attorney. In this situation, it is essential for the lawyer to reveal confidential information to prove that he or she was not negligent. Note, though, that the attorney is permitted to disclose confidential information only to the extent that it is essential to defend against the lawsuit.

Violations of the Confidentiality Rule. Paralegals, like other professionals, spend a good part of their lives engaged in their work. Naturally, they are tempted to discuss their work at home, with spouses and family members, or with others, such as co-workers and good friends. As a paralegal, perhaps one of the greatest temptations you will face is the desire to discuss a particularly interesting case, or some aspect of a case, with someone you know. You can deal with this temptation in two ways: you can decide, as a matter of policy, never to discuss *anything* concerning your work; or you can limit your discussion to issues and comments that will not reveal the identity of your client. The latter approach is, for many paralegals, a more realistic solution, but it requires great care. Something you say may reveal a client's identity, even though you are not aware of it.

Conversations Overheard by Others. Violations of the confidentiality rule may happen simply by oversight. For example, suppose that you and the legal secretary in your office are both working on the same case and continue, as you walk down the hallway toward the elevator, a conversation about the case that you started in the office. You pause before the elevator, not realizing that your conversation is being overheard by someone around the corner from you. You have no way of knowing the person is there, and you have no way of knowing whether the confidential information that you inadvertently revealed will have any adverse effect on your client's interests. One way to avoid the possibility of unwittingly revealing confidential information to third parties is to follow this rule of thumb:

- **Never discuss confidential information when you are in a common area, such as a hallway, an elevator, or a cafeteria, where a conversation might be overheard.**

Telephone Calls and Confidentiality. Similarly, you need to take preventive measures whenever you talk to or about a client on the telephone by making sure that your conversation will not be overheard by a third party. You may be sitting in your private office, but if your door is open, someone may overhear the conversation. Telephone calls can be particularly problematic if your work area is in or near a reception room. For example, assume that you work for a sole practitioner. Your job combines the functions of receptionist, legal secretary, and paralegal. Your desk is in the reception area of the office, and a client enters the room. While the client is waiting to see

DEVELOPING PARALEGAL SKILLS

Client Intends to Commit a Crime

Samantha Serles, a legal assistant, is meeting with a client whom her firm is defending. The client, Jim Storm, has been accused of murdering his mother-in-law. Samantha, who also has a degree in psychology and who previously worked with prison inmates, is going to the county jail to evaluate his mental state and to consider whether he needs further psychiatric evaluation.

MEETING THE CLIENT

Samantha arrives at the county jail. She goes through the security check and is admitted. The guard escorts her to the room where the inmates are allowed to meet with their lawyers. A few minutes later, the guard brings Jim into the room. He is dressed in a gray uniform. He looks worn out and has dark circles under his bloodshot eyes. Samantha introduces herself to Jim once again. He quietly says hello and stares down at the table. Samantha asks the guard to leave. The guard steps back into the hall and waits outside the windowed room.

THE CLIENT'S CONFESSION AND THREATS AGAINST HIS FORMER WIFE

Samantha begins to talk to Jim. She asks him how things are going and how he feels. He rolls his eyes at her questions and says, "How do you think I feel being locked up in this place?" She decides to try to talk to him about the crime. "Jim," she says, "have you thought any more about how your mother-in-law died and about what happened that night?" "Yeah," he says. "I've thought about it plenty. I killed her, you know. But they aren't going to be able to prove that I did it."

Samantha just listens as he continues: "I hated her. She talked my wife into divorcing me, and then she and my ex-wife turned my kids against me. I'm going to get even with my ex-wife for that, too. I've been talking to some guys in here. They told me how I can have her taken care of while I'm in here. Then I won't have to take the rap for that one either."

THREATS OF HARM AND THE CONFIDENTIALITY RULE

Samantha has seen enough of Jim to know that he needs psychiatric evaluation. She also knows that he might very well be able to hire someone from the inside to kill his ex-wife. She recalls the exception to the confidentiality rule that permits a lawyer to disclose confidential information if it is necessary to prevent death or bodily harm to another. Upon her return to her office, she immediately meets with her supervising attorney. She informs him of Jim's confession and threats against his ex-wife and that she thinks Jim is serious about his threats. The attorney says that he will look into the situation at once.

the attorney, another client calls you on the phone. You cannot even greet the caller by name without revealing confidential information to the client in your office. Similarly, if you are engaged in a phone conversation and someone enters the office, you must immediately be very guarded in what you say while the visitor is present.

Paralegals should take special care when using cellular phones. Cellular phones often are not secure because conversations on such phones can be tapped. As a precaution, you should thus never disclose confidential information when talking on cellular phones.

Other Ways of Violating the Confidentiality Rule. There are hundreds of other ways in which you can reveal confidential information without intending to do so. A file or document sitting on your desk, if observed by a third party, may reveal the identity of a client or enough information to suggest the client's identity. A computer screen, if visible to those passing by your desk, could convey information to someone who is not authorized to know that information. As a paralegal, you will need to be particularly careful to prevent such inadvertent disclosures of confidential information. For example, you should develop a habit of always making sure that your computer screen is blank before you leave your desk. Some law offices are now attaching a special kind of computer screen cover. This device makes it impossible for anyone to view the screen from an angle. Only the person directly facing the computer can see the document on the screen.

Consequences of Violations. To best understand the importance of the confidentiality doctrine, you need to consider what might occur if an attorney or other legal professional divulges confidential client information to third parties. Consider an example. Kara, a paralegal, works for a law firm specializing in probate administration. A client of the firm has died, and the deceased client's three sons (his heirs) have asked the firm to handle the legal procedures necessary to transfer the client's property to the heirs. Kara is working closely with the attorney who is handling the matter.

In the course of her work, Kara learns that the heirs are planning to put the deceased client's home up for sale. Kara reveals this information to some friends of hers who have been looking for some time for just that kind of house. Her friends contact one of the sons, and an aunt—the deceased client's sister—overhears the conversation regarding the sale of the house. One of the other sons has promised the aunt that the house will not be sold, and the aunt becomes furious and writes a new will, excluding the sons as beneficiaries to her substantial fortune.

Although this is an extreme example, the point is that no matter how innocent or well intended an action may be, if it results in a breach of confidentiality, the consequences for your firm's client (and therefore for you and the attorney) may be very serious. In the scenario just described, for example, if the sons report the breach of confidentiality to the state bar association's ethics committee, the attorney could be subject to one of the disciplinary actions discussed in Chapter 3. Because the breach of confidentiality caused the sons to suffer substantial harm, they might also bring a malpractice lawsuit against the attorney and Kara, seeking damages in the amount of the lost fortune. Of course, the moment that Kara breached the confidentiality rule, she also placed her job—and perhaps her professional career—in jeopardy.

ETHICAL CONCERN

Misdialed Fax Numbers and Confidentiality

Sending a fax is a simple operation, but it presents a potential pitfall for the paralegal. What if you accidentally key in a wrong number? If that wrong number happens to be someone else's fax number, confidential information will end up in the hands of a third party. Sometimes, faxes are sent to the wrong person because the client has several fax numbers and the wrong one is selected. For example, you may have more than one fax number for a large corporation. If you inadvertently sent a fax to the corporate president, when you intended to send it to the firm's accountant (who had consulted with your supervising attorney about his employment relationship with the firm), the breach of confidentiality could significantly harm the accountant's interests. One way to guard against misdialing fax numbers is by double-checking the recipient's number registered on the fax machine after you have dialed the number.

Confidentiality and the Attorney-client Privilege

ATTORNEY-CLIENT PRIVILEGE
A rule of evidence requiring that confidential communications between a client and his or her attorney (relating to their professional relationship) be kept confidential, unless the client consents to disclosure.

All information relating to a client's representation is considered confidential information. Some confidential information also qualifies as *privileged* information, or information subject to the **attorney-client privilege**. The attorney-client privilege comes into play during the litigation process. As you will read in Chapter 10, prior to a trial, each attorney is permitted to obtain information relating to the case from the opposing attorney, as well as other persons, such as witnesses. This means that attorneys must exchange a certain amount of information relating to their clients. An attorney need not divulge privileged information, however—unless the client consents to the disclosure or a court orders the disclosure. Similarly, if an attorney is called to the witness stand during a trial, the attorney may not disclose privileged information unless the court orders him or her to do so.

What Kind of Information Is Privileged? State statutes and court cases define what constitutes privileged information. Generally, any communications concerning a client's *legal* rights or problem fall under the attorney-client privilege. For example, suppose that an attorney's client is a criminal defendant. The client tells the attorney that she was actually in the vicinity of the crime site at the time of the crime, but to her knowledge, no one noticed her presence there. This is privileged information that the attorney may only disclose with the client's consent or on a court's order to do so.

Other types of information, although confidential, are not necessarily privileged. For example, information relating to a client's identity is usually not privileged. Nor, as a rule, is information concerning client fees. Furthermore, information concerning the client's personal or business affairs is also not privileged unless it is related to the legal claim. For example, suppose that a client who is bringing a malpractice suit against a physician mentions to the attorney that he is divorcing his wife. Unless the client's divorce is related in some way to the malpractice suit being handled by the attorney, the information about the divorce normally is not considered privileged.

WORK PRODUCT
An attorney's mental impressions, conclusions, and legal theories regarding a case being prepared on behalf of a client. Work product normally is regarded as privileged information.

Certain materials relating to an attorney's preparation of a client's case for trial are protected as privileged information under what is known as the **work product** doctrine. Usually, information concerning an attorney's legal strategy for conducting a case is classified as work product and, as such, may be subject to the attorney-client privilege. Legal strategy includes the legal theories that the attorney plans to use in support of the client's claim, how the attorney interprets the evidence relating to the claim, and so on. Certain evidence gathered by the attorney to support the client's claim, however, such as financial statements relating to the client's business firm, would probably not be classified as work product. Because it is often difficult to tell what types of information (including work product) qualify as privileged, paralegals should consult closely with their supervising attorneys whenever issues arise that may require that such a distinction be made.

When the Attorney-client Privilege Arises. The attorney-client privilege comes into existence the moment a client communicates with an attorney concerning a legal matter. People sometimes mistakenly assume that there is no duty to keep client information confidential unless an attorney agrees to represent a client and the client signs a retainer agreement. This is not so.

- **The privilege—and thus the duty of confidentiality—arises even though the lawyer decides not to represent the client and even when the client is not charged any fee.**

Duration of the Privilege. The client is the holder, or "owner," of the privilege, and only the client can waive (or set aside) the privilege. Unless waived by the client, the privilege lasts indefinitely. In other words, the privilege continues even though an attorney has completed the client's legal matter and is no longer working on the case.

As with all confidential information relating to a client's case, privileged information is subject to the exceptions to the confidentiality rule discussed above. For example, if the attorney learns from a client that the client plans to harm physically another person, this information is not protected by the privilege. If a client challenges the attorney's competence, through a malpractice suit, for example, the privilege may be impliedly waived.

The Duty of Competence

As stated in the previous chapter, attorneys have a duty to represent their clients competently. Most breaches of the duty of competence are inadvertent, like most breaches of the confidentiality rule. Often, breaches of the duty of competence have to do with missed deadlines. Paralegals frequently work on several cases simultaneously, and keeping track of every deadline in every case can be challenging—especially for paralegals who are pressed for time.

Organization is the key to making sure that all deadlines are met. All important dates relating to every case or client should be entered on a calendar. Larger firms typically use computerized calendaring and tickler systems. Smaller firms also normally have calendaring procedures and tickler systems in place. In addition to making sure that all deadlines are entered into the appropriate systems, you may want to have your own personal calendar for tracking the dates relevant to the cases on which you are working—and then make sure that you *consistently* use it. You should develop a habit of checking your calendar every morning when you arrive at work or some other convenient time. Also, you should check frequently with your attorney about deadlines that he or she may not have mentioned to you.

The duty of competence can also be breached in numerous other ways. For example, erroneous information might be included (or crucial information omitted) in a legal document to be filed with the court. If the attorney fails to notice the error before signing the document, and the document is delivered to the court containing the erroneous information, a breach of the duty of competence has occurred. Depending on its legal effect, this breach may expose the attorney and the paralegal to liability for negligence. To prevent these kinds of violations, you need to be especially careful in drafting and proofreading documents.

Generally, if you are ever unsure about what to include in a document, when it must be completed or filed with the court, how extensively you should research a legal issue, or any other aspect of an assignment, you should ask your supervising attorney for special instructions. You should

> **ETHICAL CONCERN**
>
> **Typographical Errors and the Duty of Competence**
>
> Legal documents, because they can seriously affect the legal rights and welfare of clients, must be carefully drafted and proofread. Even a simple typographical error in a legal document can have significant consequences. For example, assume that on October 20, Tom Jansen, an attorney, asks his paralegal, Jim Halloran, to draft a letter to a client informing the client that the statute of limitations governing the type of lawsuit that the client wants to bring will expire on November 12. When drafting the letter, Halloran inadvertently keys in "November 21" instead of "November 12." The client comes to the office on November 18 and asks the attorney to file the lawsuit, but by then it is too late. Three days later, the client files suit—against Tom Jansen. The client, claiming that he might have obtained $150,000 in damages in the lawsuit (which he can no longer bring because of the paralegal's negligence), is now seeking that amount from Jansen. The simple typographical error was very costly indeed!

also make sure that your work is adequately supervised by your attorney, to reduce the chances that the work will contain costly mistakes or errors.

Obtaining Adequate Supervision. Because attorneys are held legally responsible for the work of their assistants, it may seem logical to assume that attorneys will take time to supervise that work carefully. In fact, paralegals may find it difficult to ensure that their work is adequately supervised. For one thing, most paralegals are kept very busy, and making sure that everything they do is properly supervised can be time consuming. Similarly, a busy attorney often does not want to take the time to read through every document drafted by his or her paralegal—particularly if the attorney knows that the paralegal is competent. Nonetheless, as a paralegal, you have a duty to assist your supervising attorney in fulfilling ethical obligations, including the attorney's obligation to supervise your work.

Here are some ideas that may work for you when trying to obtain adequate supervision:

- Keep communication channels open. The more you communicate with your supervising attorney, the more likely it is that the attorney will take a more active role in directing your activities.
- Place reminders on your supervising attorney's calendar requesting feedback on certain projects.
- Place reminders on your personal calendar to discuss particular issues or questions with your supervising attorney.
- When submitting drafts, particularly final drafts, of a legal document to your supervising attorney, attach a note asking him or her to review the document (or its revised sections) carefully before signing it.
- If the attorney has to be out of the office when you need supervision (which is often the case), make sure that you work around the attorney's schedule. Take advantage of opportunities when he or she is available to review your work.

The Problem of "Overload" and Adequate Supervision. Another problem facing paralegals is "overload"—too much work to do and too many projects to handle. Paralegals in this situation find it particularly challenging to ensure that their work is properly supervised. No matter how committed you are to your work and job, there is a limit to how much work you can handle and still make sure that your work is thorough, accurate, and adequately supervised. If you ever feel that your ethical responsibilities as a paralegal—or your supervising attorney's ethical responsibilities to his or her client—are suffering because of a work overload, you should discuss the problem with your supervising attorney.

Conflict of Interest

CONFLICT OF INTEREST
A situation in which two or more duties or interests come into conflict, as when an attorney attempts to represent opposing parties in a legal dispute.

A **conflict of interest** exists whenever a person's duties (or interests) come into conflict. In the legal context, a classic example of a conflict of interest exists when an attorney simultaneously represents two adverse parties in a legal proceeding. Clearly, in such a situation, the attorney's loyalties must be divided. It would be as if a football player agreed to play on both teams during a game—half of the time with one team and half of the time with the other. To ensure that clients' interests are not harmed by an attorney's divided loyalties, professional codes or rules of ethics prohibit lawyers from representing clients when doing so would result in a conflict of interest. Rule 1.7 of the Model Rules of Professional Conduct states the general rule: "A lawyer shall not represent a client if the representation of the client will be directly adverse to another client."

Simultaneous Representation. If an attorney decides that representing two parties in a legal proceeding will not adversely affect either party's interest, then the attorney is permitted to do so—but only if both parties agree. Normally, attorneys avoid this kind of situation because what might start out as a simple, uncontested proceeding may evolve into a legal battle. Divorce proceedings, for example, may begin amicably but end up in heated disputes over child-custody arrangements or property division. The attorney then faces a conflict of interest: assisting one party will necessarily be adverse to the interests of the other. Note that because of the potential for a conflict of interest in divorce proceedings, some courts do not permit attorneys to represent both spouses, even if the spouses consent to such an arrangement.

Similar conflicts arise when the "family attorney" is asked to handle a family matter and the family members eventually disagree on what the outcome of the matter should be. For example, consider a situation in which two adult children request the family lawyer to handle the procedures required to settle their deceased parent's estate. The parent's will favors one of the children, and the other child decides to challenge the will's validity. The attorney cannot represent both sides in this dispute without facing a conflict of interest.

Attorneys representing corporate clients may face conflicts of interest when corporate personnel become divided on an issue. For example, assume that ABC Corporation has retained Carl Finn, an attorney, to represent the corporation. Finn typically deals with the corporation's president, Julie Johnson, when rendering legal assistance and advice. At times, however, Finn deals with other corporate personnel, including Seth Harrison, the corporation's accountant. Harrison and Johnson disagree with each other on several major issues, and eventually Johnson arranges to have Harrison fired. Harrison wants attorney Finn to represent him in a lawsuit against the corporation for wrongful termination of his employment. Finn now faces a conflict of interest.

Former Clients. A conflict of interest may also involve former clients. Model Rule 1.9 states that "[a] lawyer who has formerly represented a client in a matter shall not thereafter represent another person in the same or substantially related matter in which that person's interests are materially adverse to the interests of the former client unless the former client consents after consultation." The rule regarding former clients is closely related to the rule on preserving the confidentiality of a client. The rationale behind the rule is that an attorney, in representing a client, is entrusted with certain information that may be unknown to others, and that information should not be used against the client—even after the represention has ended.

For example, assume that a year ago an attorney defended a company against a lawsuit for employment discrimination brought by one of the company's employees. During the course of the representation, the attorney learned a great deal about the company. Now, someone who was injured while using one of that same company's products consults with the attorney about the possibility of bringing a product liability lawsuit against the company. The attorney normally must refuse to represent this person. Because the attorney has confidential information about the company that could be used to harm the company's interest, a conflict of interest exists.

Job Changes and Former Clients. The rule concerning former clients does not prohibit an individual from working at a firm or agency that may represent interests contrary to those of a former client. If that were the situation, many of those who have worked for very large firms would be unable ever to change jobs. Generally, the rules vary, depending on the specific circumstances. In some situations, when a conflict of interest results from a job change, the new employer can avoid violating the rules governing conflict of interest through the use of screening procedures. The new employer can erect an impenetrable screen, or ethical wall, around the new employee so that the new employee remains in ignorance about the case giving rise to the conflict of interest.

Walling-off Procedures. Law offices usually have special procedures for "walling off" an attorney or other legal professional from a case when a conflict of interest exists. The firm may announce in a written memo to all employees that a certain attorney or paralegal should not have access to certain files, for example, and may set out procedures to be followed to ensure that access to those files is restricted. Computer documents relating to the case may be protected by warning messages or in some other way. Commonly, any hard-copy files relating to the case are flagged with a sticker to indicate that access to the files is restricted. Firms normally take great care to establish such procedures and observe them carefully, because if confidential information is used in a way harmful to a former client, the firm may be sued by the client and have to pay steep damages. In defending against such a suit, the firm will need to demonstrate that it took reasonable precautions to protect that client's interests.

Issue Conflicts. Model Rule 1.7 mentions yet another situation involving a conflict of interest. The rule states that an attorney "shall not represent a client if the representation of that client may be materially limited by the lawyer's responsibilities to another client or to a third person, or by the lawyer's own interests." An exception is made if the client consents to the representation after the attorney discloses the potential conflict of interest.

This rule has been problematic because it is not always clear what kinds of actions might "materially limit" an attorney's representation of a client. To clarify the rule, the American Bar Association (ABA) issued an opinion on the matter.[4] The ABA opinion stated that an attorney cannot represent a client with respect to a substantive legal issue if the client's position is

4. American Bar Association Formal Opinion 93-377, October 16, 1993.

DEVELOPING PARALEGAL SKILLS

Erecting an Ethical Wall

Lana Smith, a paralegal, is meeting with her supervising attorney, Fred Martin, in his office. "I asked you to meet with me because the firm is hiring a new attorney, Sandra Piper," Fred tells Lana. "Sandra is coming from Nunn & Bush. There is a conflict of interest because she represented the plaintiff in *Tymes v. Seski Manufacturing Co.*, and we're representing the defendant in that case. Because of the conflict of interest, we will need to set up some screening procedures to wall Sandra off from this case. Are you familiar with ethical walls?" Lana answers, "Yes, I know about them from my paralegal training program." "Good. Have you ever set one up before?" asks Fred. "No, I haven't," answers Lana. "Then we'll work together on it," replies Fred.

PHYSICAL LOCATION

"The first thing that you need to do is draft a memo to the office manager explaining the existence of the conflict of interest. I want you to suggest that Sandra's office should be located on a different floor from ours, maybe on the twenty-first floor. Be sure to explain the importance of the physical separation from a court's perspective. That is, explain that a court would look for proof that Sandra did not have access to the case files and that we did not have easy access to Sandra because we were physically separated," explains Fred.

COMPUTER PASSWORDS

"Next, I want you to request that the office manager's staff assign a special computer password to all computer files relating to the *Tymes* case and that only our team be given the password. This will restrict access to the documents on the computer and should also satisfy a court that Sandra was not involved in the case," says Fred.

INFORMING THE FIRM'S PERSONNEL

"We also need to prepare a memo to the firm. In the memo, we need to explain the conflict of interest and state the case name and who is involved. The memo must instruct the other members of the firm that they are to maintain a blanket of silence regarding this case whenever they talk to Sandra," instructs Fred.

CONFLICTS STICKERS

"In terms of our procedures, we need to collect all of the files on the case and place conflicts stickers on them. You should be able to find these stickers in the supply room. They are in fluorescent colors and have "ACCESS RESTRICTED" in bold letters on them. You need to place these stickers on all of the files. Then I want you to develop a procedure for keeping track of all the files, so that we do not give any of them to Sandra or anyone who works with her," says Fred. Lana asks Fred some questions and then leaves to begin her assignment.

directly contrary to that of another client being represented by the lawyer—or the lawyer's firm—in a case being brought within the same jurisdiction (the geographic area or subject matter over which a specific court has authority to decide legal disputes).

For example, suppose that Abrams, an attorney, is representing a client, Becker, who is suing a restaurant. Becker, while entering the restaurant, slipped on some ice just outside the door and broke his leg. The question before the court is whether the restaurant had a duty to warn its customers of the icy condition of the sidewalk. Now suppose that Abrams is asked by Gemini Office Supplies, Inc., to defend Gemini in a lawsuit brought by a customer who slipped on a patch of ice just outside the store's entrance. The suit would be brought in the same court as the one hearing the Becker case. The substantive legal issue is the same in both cases—whether a business firm has a duty to warn customers of dangerous (icy) conditions on the sidewalks outside their entrances.

An issue conflict exists because if Abrams succeeds in winning one case, the court's decision could serve as a precedent that the court might have to follow in deciding the other case. (As you will read in Chapter 6, courts are normally obligated to follow *precedents*—previous court decisions on issues similar to those before the court—made within their jurisdiction.) In this situation, if Becker won, Gemini Office Supplies would lose, and vice versa.

Other Conflict-of-interest Situations. There are several other types of situations that may give rise to a conflict of interest. Gifts from clients may create conflicts of interest, because they may tend to bias the judgment of the attorney or paralegal. Some types of gifts are specifically prohibited. Rule 1.8(c) of the Model Rules of Professional Conduct, for example, prohibits an attorney from preparing for a client wills or other documents that give the attorney or a member of the attorney's family a gift—unless the attorney is a relative of the client. Note that the rule does not prohibit an attorney from receiving gifts; rather, it prohibits an attorney from drafting the documents that convey gifts to himself or herself. As a paralegal, you may be offered gifts from appreciative clients at Christmas or other times. Generally, such gifts pose no ethical problems. If a client offers you a gift that has substantial value, however, you should discuss the issue with your supervising attorney.

Occasionally, conflicts of interest may arise when two family members who are both attorneys or paralegals are involved in the representation of adverse parties in a legal proceeding. Model Rule 1.8(i) prohibits an attorney from representing a client if the adverse party to the dispute is being represented by a member of the attorney's family (such as a spouse, parent, child, or brother or sister). If you, as a paralegal, are married to another paralegal or an attorney, you should inform your firm of this fact if you ever suspect that a conflict of interest might result from your spousal relationship.

CONFLICTS CHECK
A procedure for determining whether an agreement to represent a potential client will result in a conflict of interest.

Conflicts Checks. Whenever a potential client consults with an attorney, the attorney will want to make sure that no potential conflict of interest exists before deciding whether to represent the client. This is a standard procedure in the law office and one that is frequently undertaken by paralegals. Before you can run a **conflicts check**, you need to know the name of the prospective client, the other party or parties that may be involved in the client's legal matter, and the legal issue involved. Normally, every law firm has some established procedure for conflicts checks, and in larger firms, there is usually a computerized database containing the names of former clients and the other information you will need in checking for conflicts of interest.

Ethics and Client Billing Practices

The legal profession generally bills clients by the hour. Attorneys (and paralegals) track the time that they spend on each client's case and record that time on time sheets. For some types of work, other types of fee arrangements may be made, but in many firms the major determinant of the firm's income is how many billable hours are generated by the firm's attorneys. (**Billable hours** are the hours or fractions of hours that attorneys and paralegals spend in client-related work that requires legal expertise and that can be billed directly to clients.)

BILLABLE HOURS
The time spent on legal work for a client that requires the legal expertise of an attorney or a paralegal and that is charged directly to the client.

Increasingly, and particularly in offices that have adopted the teamwork approach to legal work, work undertaken by paralegals and others on behalf of a client is also billed to the client at an hourly rate. You will read in greater detail about fee arrangements, how clients are billed, and the distinction between billable and nonbillable hours in Chapter 5. Here, the focus is on some of the ethical implications of billing clients by the hour.

The "Double Billing" of Clients. To understand why hourly billing can present ethical problems, consider the following situation. Suppose that you are asked to travel to another city to interview a witness in a case for Client A. You spend three hours traveling in an airplane, travel time that is necessary in working on behalf of Client A. You spend two hours in the airplane summarizing a document relating to a case for Client B. Who should pay for those two hours, Client A, Client B, or both? In this situation, you could argue—as many attorneys do in similar circumstances—that you generated five billable hours, three on Client A's work and two on Client B's case. This is an example of how **double billing**—billing more than one client for the same time—can occur.

DOUBLE BILLING
Billing more than one client for the same billable time.

As mentioned, a law firm's income is determined to a great extent by how many billable hours are generated by the firm's attorneys and paralegals. Billable hours determine, in part, the amount of profit that will be distributed to the firm's owners. Attorneys who work as employees for the firm realize that part of their value to the firm (and thus promotions and salary increases) will be measured by how many billable hours they generate. Paralegals also face pressure to generate billable hours and are often expected to work a specified number of billable hours per year (see Chapter 5). Clearly, the double billing of clients is one way to meet these pressures. Lawyers, however, as mentioned in the preceding chapter, have a duty to charge their clients "reasonable fees."

Overlapping Research. Double billing also occurs when a firm bills a new client for work that was done for a previous client. For example, suppose that an attorney is working on a case for Client B that is very similar to a

FEATURED GUEST: MICHAEL A. PENER

Ten Tips on Ethics and the Paralegal

Biographical Note

Michael A. Pener developed the paralegal program at Johnson County Community College, in Kansas, in 1977. It was approved by the American Bar Association (ABA) in 1980. He was the program's first director and continued as director until 1987, when be became one of its full-time instructors. Pener is one of the founders of the American Association for Paralegal Education (AAfPE). He served on its initial board of directors and, in 1985 and 1986, as its president. He is a member of the Ethics Advisory Services Committee and Legal Assistant Committee of the Kansas Bar Association (KBA). Since 1992, he has been serving as one of the AAfPE's representatives on the Approval Commission of the ABA Standing Committee on Legal Assistants.

As a legal-assistant educator and practicing attorney, I have developed several ethics-related "truths" for my students that I think are essential for their professional survival as working legal assistants. Each of these truths is important, and the legal assistant must adhere to all of them if he or she wants to avoid, or lessen the impact of, situations involving ethical problems. While I believe the following tips will keep you out of trouble, no list of this type is ever complete without your own input—so use it to develop ethical "rules" appropriate for your work and legal practice area.

1 Obtain Copies of State and Local Ethical Rules. Keep up with current state ethical rules for attorneys and paralegals and continually review their application in cases, disciplinary proceedings, and ethical opinions of local, state, and national lawyer associations. Specifically, there are now many guidelines on major areas of concern to the legal profession, including the use of legal assistants by lawyers, confidentiality, the unauthorized practice of law, conflicts of interest, and legal competence.

2 Attend Continuing Legal Education (CLE) Programs on Legal Ethics. In many states, lawyers are required to have CLE hours on legal ethics. Attending CLE programs not only reminds you of what the rules require but also helps you remain current in ethical developments within the profession.

3 Network with Other Legal Assistants. Network with other legal assistants through local paralegal organizations and education programs and through the National Federation of Paralegal Associations and the National Association of Legal Assistants. Both of the national organizations have professional ethical codes and are involved in court cases affecting paralegals.

4 Make No Assumptions about Others. In an ideal world, all legal professionals would act ethically at all times. In such a world, there would be no need for rules to govern attorney behavior and no need for disciplinary actions. As a paralegal, you may encounter situations in which you suspect unethical behavior on the part of someone with whom you work. Ignoring unethical behavior will not necessarily make it go away. Always keep your professional ethical

case handled by the firm a year ago for Client A. The firm charged Client A $2,000 for the legal services. Because much of the research, writing, and other work done on Client A's case can transfer over to Client B's case, the firm is able to complete the work for Client B in half the time. In this situation, would it be fair to bill Client B $2,000 also? After all, $1,000 of that amount represents hours spent on Client A's case (and for which Client A has already been billed). At the same time, would it be fair to Client A to

FEATURED GUEST, Continued

requirements in mind. At times, this may mean you need to discuss the matter with someone in authority.

5 Double-check Your Work. Expect the unexpected, especially when dealing with unfamiliar matters or with strangers. Don't assume that the documents you produce will be checked for accuracy by others. As a legal assistant, you will need to pay the utmost attention to detail and double-check everything you do to make sure it is accurate. Also, make sure that all written communications are sent to the proper person.

6 Review All Documents That You Receive. When documents are being exchanged in the drafting stage with opposing counsel or during negotiations, always review the documents that you receive in their entirety.

7 Anticipate and Prepare for Ethical Problems. Anticipate and prepare for situations in your work and professional relationships that may give rise to ethical problems. In this chapter, you will encounter a number of "real-life" situations that test your understanding and application of legal ethics. Study them carefully, because they most likely will happen to you. Also, note that clients want to know how their legal matters are progressing but lawyers are sometimes too busy to attend to their clients' needs in this respect. Legal assistants may end up communicating more frequently with the clients than attorneys do. If the lawyer for whom you work puts you in this role, you should feel complimented by the lawyer's confidence in you. Watch out, however, for a client who becomes too dependent on you and your judgment. Very soon, he or she may be asking you for your "legal opinion." If you respond to such a question, you will get into trouble very quickly.

8 Use Caution When Notarizing Documents or Signing Documents as a Witness. If you are a notary public, only notarize documents signed in your presence. As a notary public you have a statutory requirement to perform the duties of your appointed office. Failure to act as required may subject you to personal liability. This means that you must refuse a lawyer's request to notarize a document that was not signed in your presence. Similarly, never sign any document as a witness without first reviewing it to make sure that your signature is properly requested.

9 Maintain a Balance Between Personal and Legal Ethics. Maintain a proper balance between your personal ethics and legal ethics. This may be the most difficult thing for you to do. You may be a party to confidential communications that concern unethical, and even immoral, behavior on the part of clients. Your law firm may have a policy or engage in an activity that is acceptable by legal ethical standards but that you personally consider to be unethical. Professionally, you must accept this. If you personally cannot, then you may have no other choice but to seek employment elsewhere.

10 Rely on Your Common Sense and Intuition. Use your common sense and intuition. Develop a sense of what is right and wrong behavior in any given situation and then seek the answer to any legal ethical problem that you encounter.

"DON'T ASSUME THAT THE DOCUMENTS YOU PRODUCE WILL BE CHECKED FOR ACCURACY BY OTHERS."

bill Client B less for essentially the same services? Would it be fair to the firm if it was not allowed to profit from cost efficiencies generated by overlapping work?

Some firms today are tackling this ethical problem by what is known as "value-added" billing or "value billing"—in effect, splitting the benefits derived from cost efficiencies between the client and the firm. For example, the attorney in the above example might split the savings created by the

DEVELOPING PARALEGAL SKILLS

A Client Complains about a Bill

Joni Winston, a paralegal in a one-attorney law practice, answers the telephone. "Law offices of Mary Perkins," says Joni. "Is Ms. Perkins there?" asks a man's voice on the other end of the line. "No, I'm sorry, she's out of the office now. May I take a message?" asks Joni. "Yes. Please tell her that Jim Hendry called, regarding the bill for my father's estate," says Hendry.

"Mr. Hendry, this is Joni Winston, Ms. Perkins's legal assistant. I worked on your father's estate. Do you remember talking with me?" asks Joni. "Yes, I do," responds Hendry. "Would you like to give me the details about the problem with the bill? I would be happy to talk to Ms. Perkins about it," says Joni.

THE CLIENT'S COMPLAINT: DOUBLE BILLING

"I have received a bill for almost $1,000," Hendry tells Joni. "You tell Ms. Perkins that I think that she double billed on a couple of these items, and if I don't hear from her by 5 P.M. today, I am going to report her to the bar association for double billing." In response, Joni asked, "Mr. Hendry, what specifically do you feel that you were double-billed for?"

"Well," Hendry says, "the first page of the bill has an entry for filing Letters of Authority with the court. The same entry appears at the bottom of the second page. Was this done twice, or am I being billed for the same work twice?"

RESOLVING THE PROBLEM

"Mr. Hendry, I understand why you are upset. I will talk to Ms. Perkins about your concerns and I will call you back by the end of the day," responds Joni.

Joni pulls out Hendry's file and reviews the billing sheets and the bill that was sent to him. When Mary returns, Joni takes the file into Mary's office and discusses the problem with Mary. They notice that indeed Hendry was billed twice for filing the Letters of Authority. Mary says to Joni, "This entry is a mistake. The Letters of Authority were only filed once. The second entry should have indicated that it was for preparing the estate tax returns. The amount charged would be the same."

Mary calls Hendry and explains to him that a mistake was made. She had a temporary secretary working for her and the secretary mislabeled the second entry as "Filing Letters of Authority with the Court" when it should have been "Preparing Estate Tax Return." The amount billed remains the same. Mary assures him that all future bills will be checked carefully before they are sent out.

overlapping research ($1,000) with Client B by billing Client B $1,500 instead of $2,000. Other firms still bill their clients for the time spent on previous work that transfers over to new clients' cases.

The American Bar Association's Response. The American Bar Association addressed this ethical "gray area" in the legal profession—double billing—in

PARALEGAL PROFILE

Litigation Paralegal and Paralegal Cordinator

JILL BURTON has a bachelor of arts degree in paralegal studies from Eastern Kentucky University. In 1980, when Burton received her degree, there were only six students in her class. Since that time, however, the program has expanded significantly. Burton started her career with the law firm of Middleton and Reutlinger, located in Louisville, Kentucky, where she worked in the area of litigation. After three years, Burton took a position with the largest law firm in Kentucky, Brown, Todd, and Heyburn, where she currently works. In 1985, Burton assumed the role of paralegal coordinator for the firm. Her job involves hiring and training paralegals and acting as liaison between the attorneys and the paralegals. In 1993, she became the firm's legal-support manager, which involves administrative work and handling office automation.

What do you like best about your work?

"The thing I enjoy the most is that each new case I work on has a new set of facts and witnesses. I work on complex business litigation, which produces a lot of paper, and I enjoy managing all the documents. I particularly enjoy the challenge of creating and tracking the paper trail as the puzzle pieces fall together. Also, the attorneys for whom I work are super advocates for paralegals. They consistently encourage me to express my views and solicit my ideas, making me feel like an integral part of the team."

What is the greatest challenge that you face in your work?

"Really, the greatest challenge I face is convincing our attorneys to use paralegals effectively. Some of our more senior paralegals tend to become frustrated with the level of assignments they receive. New associates can also present a challenge in that they are not comfortable in relying on a paralegal for assistance. I have tried to overcome this problem by arranging for a lunch meeting with our paralegals and new associates each fall. This gives the paralegals an opportunity to share their educational backgrounds, levels of experience, and areas of expertise with the new associates. Generally, the associates are pleasantly surprised to find out that the firm has on its staff paralegals who are so talented and experienced and who are anxious to help the associates."

"A SUCCESSFUL LITIGATION PARALEGAL . . . HAS A 'CAN-DO' ATTITUDE."

What advice do you have for would-be paralegals in your area of work?

"I recommend that new paralegals take on any tasks that they are assigned, and I would encourage them to avoid telling the attorney that they don't know how to do the task. I feel that new paralegals should always accept assignments and then rely on experienced paralegals, or other resources, to help get the job done. Good writing skills are extremely important, and I would encourage any would-be paralegals to take as many English and writing classes in school as possible."

What are some tips for success as a paralegal in your area of work?

"First, develop a good working relationship with other members of the litigation team. This will go a long way in getting the attorneys to let you take an active role in the litigation. Learn the facts of each case on which you are working so that you are in a position to anticipate what needs to be done without constant supervision and instruction. Be creative and look for areas in which you can apply your analytical skills. Many paralegals make the mistake of working like hourly employees who leave when the clock says it is time to go home. Be prepared to work the hours needed to get the job done even if it means leaving the office at 10 P.M. A successful litigation paralegal is one who is dedicated and resourceful and who has a 'can-do' attitude."

TODAY'S PROFESSIONAL PARALEGAL

What to Do When Your Values Clash with Those of Your Client

Sandy Brownell works as a legal assistant for a sole practitioner of law, Joe Harding. Joe has been asked to defend Dr. Wyeth Ebon, who has gained notoriety in the past few years by assisting terminally ill patients in committing suicide. Aiding a person in committing suicide is illegal under the state's criminal statutes. Dr. Ebon has been charged with the crime of assisting in the suicide of Daniel Currie, who had an advanced case of Alzheimer's disease.

AN ETHICAL DILEMMA

Joe calls Sandy into his office and tells her that he will conduct an initial client interview with Dr. Ebon tomorrow at 9 A.M. Joe wants Sandy to sit in on the interview because if he accepts the case, she will be working closely with him on it. Sandy is uncomfortable with the idea of working with Dr. Ebon, but she realizes that she has no other option. After all, she works for a sole practitioner, and she is the only legal assistant in the office. She tells Joe that she will see him at nine o'clock the next morning.

On returning to her office, Sandy cannot get Dr. Ebon off her mind. She knows that she has to work on the case; Joe expects her to. Yet she does not believe in assisted suicide for anyone, not even for the terminally ill. In her opinion, assisting another in committing suicide is ethically unjustifiable under any circumstances. By helping Joe prepare Dr. Ebon's defense, will she be compromising her own ethical beliefs and standards? As a professional, how should she deal with this situation?

RESOLVING THE DILEMMA

Once Sandy reminds herself of her professional status, the answer becomes clear. It is not up to her to judge Dr. Ebon's actions. Even though she does not agree with Dr. Ebon, she knows that as a criminal defendant, he has a right to counsel, an important constitutional right of all Americans. As a legal professional, she has an obligation to ensure that the constitutional rights of criminal defendants, including the right to counsel, are not violated. Sandy concludes that it is her professional duty to help the attorney prepare to defend Dr. Ebon against the criminal charges.

Having analyzed the situation and decided where her professional duties lay, Sandy arrives at the initial client interview with an open mind, ready to assist Joe.

an ethical opinion issued in 1993. In its first formal opinion on the issue, the ABA stated that attorneys are prohibited from charging more than one client for the same hours of work. Additionally, the ABA rejected the notion that the firm, and not the client, should benefit from cost efficiencies created by the firm's work for previous clients. "The lawyer who has agreed to bill solely on the basis of time spent is obliged to pass the benefit of these economies on to the client."[5] Although ABA opinions do not become legally binding on attorneys until they are adopted by the states as law, they do carry much weight in the legal profession.

A FINAL NOTE

Learning to think and act in a professionally responsible manner takes time and practice. Yet there is little room for learning legal ethics by "trial and

5. American Bar Association Formal Opinion 93–379, December 6, 1993.

error" in the legal workplace. In this chapter, you have read about some of the most common ways in which paralegals can unintentionally violate professional rules. The *Ethical Concerns* throughout this book will offer you further insights into some of the ethical problems that can arise in various areas of paralegal performance. Understanding how violations can occur will help you anticipate and guard against them as you begin your paralegal career. Once on the job, you can continue your preventive tactics by asking questions whenever you are in doubt and by making sure that your work is adequately supervised.

KEY TERMS AND CONCEPTS

CHAPTER SUMMARY

1. Ethics can be defined as the study of morality and how moral principles and convictions apply to various real-world situations. Questions involving the rightness, fairness, or justness of an action are, in essence, ethical questions. Our choices and decisions are ultimately affected, consciously or unconsciously, by our ethical values and goals. Personal ethics are not quite the same as legal ethics—the body of professional rules governing legal professionals. Ethical conduct in the legal arena requires an attorney or a paralegal, at a minimum, to abide by the ethical rules of the profession.

2. When facing ethical conflicts, paralegals may find it helpful to view legal ethics in the larger context of the American system of justice. Many of the ethical rules governing attorneys are rooted in the adversarial justice system and the concept of advocacy.

3. A basic professional responsibility of every paralegal is making sure that professional rules of conduct are not violated. Because most ethical violations occur inadvertently, paralegals must be on guard against accidentally breaching a rule. To avoid ethical violations, paralegals should become thoroughly familiar with the rules governing legal professionals in their states and how those rules apply to their day-to-day tasks in the workplace.

4. One of the most important professional rules of conduct is the confidentiality rule. All information relating to a client's representation must be kept in confidence and not revealed to third parties who are not authorized to know the information. Some client information is so sensitive and confidential that it is regarded as privileged information. An attorney may reveal privileged information only if the client consents, if a court orders the attorney to reveal the information, or in special circumstances, as when revealing the information is necessary to protect another from bodily harm or death.

5. One of the most common ethical pitfalls for paralegals is inadvertently breaching the rule of confidentiality. The rule is breached whenever information concerning a client's case is told to (or overheard by) third parties. Paralegals need to constantly guard against revealing confidential information to third parties when talking to others in person or on the phone; when sending faxes; when using files, documents, or computer screens while visitors are present in the office; and generally at all times both on and off the job.

6. Violation of the duty of competence may lead to a lawsuit against the attorney (and perhaps the paralegal) for negligence. The duty is violated whenever a client suffers harm as a result of the attorney's incompetent action or inaction. The paralegal can protect against inadvertently violating the duty of competence by exercising good organizational skills (making sure all important deadlines are met, for example), checking and double-checking documents to make sure that they are accurate, and making sure that his or her work is adequately supervised by the attorney.

7. Attorneys are prohibited from representing a client if the attorney's representation of that client will adversely affect the interests of another client, including former clients. An attorney may represent both sides in a legal proceeding only if the attorney feels that neither party's rights will be adversely affected and only if both clients are aware of the conflict of interest and consent to the representation. Paralegals also fall under this rule. If a firm is handling a case that one of the firm's attorneys or paralegals cannot work on, owing to a conflict of interest, that attorney or paralegal must be "walled off" from the case—that is, prevented from having any access to files or other information relating to the case. Normally, whenever a prospective client consults with an attorney, a conflicts check is done to ensure that if the attorney or firm accepts the case, no conflict of interest will exist.

8. An important ethical concern in the legal profession today concerns the double billing of clients. Double billing occurs when a law firm bills two or more clients for the same billable time. Double billing includes billing two clients for overlapping work, such as when a firm uses the research or other legal work done on a previous client's case for a present client and bills both clients for the time spent in performing that research or other legal work. In 1993, the American Bar Association, in its first ethical opinion on double billing, stated that it is unethical to ever bill two clients for the same billable hours or legal work. The ABA also stated that any cost efficiencies created by using previous work for a present client should be passed on to the client.

QUESTIONS FOR REVIEW

1. What does the term *ethics* mean? How are ethical values reflected in everyday life?

2. What is the difference between personal ethics and legal ethics?

3. What is meant by the "adversarial system of justice"? How do legal ethics reflect the values underlying the adversarial justice system?

4. What does the rule of confidentiality require? What are the exceptions to the rule?

5. What is the attorney-client privilege? What is its relationship to the rule of confidentiality? What is work product?

6. What are some potential consequences of violating the confidentiality rule?

7. What does the duty of competence involve? How can violations of the duty of competence be avoided?

8. What is a conflict of interest? What kinds of situations can give rise to conflicts of interest?

9. How do law firms "wall off" an attorney or a paralegal when a conflict of interest exists?

10. What is double billing? What is value billing? What are some ethical implications of double billing? How has the American Bar Association addressed this issue?

ETHICAL QUESTIONS

1. Roberta Miller works as a paralegal, secretary, and receptionist for an attorney who is a sole practitioner. She is drafting an opinion letter to a client, Gina Thomas, advising her to file for bankruptcy. The telephone rings, and she turns away from her computer to answer it, leaving the opinion letter on the screen.

As she hangs up the phone, James Archer, another client enters the reception area and asks to see her supervising attorney. She leaves her desk and the computer screen with the letter on it. While she is gone, Archer looks in the direction of the computer, and the letter to Gina Thomas catches his eye. Gina Thomas is a neighbor of his, so he reads the letter. Has an ethical violation occurred? If so, by whom and of what rule? How could the violation have been avoided?

2. Mike Robbins works for Sarah Jones, a sole practitioner. Sarah's first appointment on Monday morning is with Jeffrey Sutherland. When Sutherland leaves the office, Sarah calls Mike in and asks him to draft a complaint to initiate Sutherland's divorce action. She expresses her disbelief over the divorce of two clients whom she has known for so long. Later that week, Sutherland's wife, Melanie, calls to make an appointment with Sarah to discuss the possibility of a divorce. May Sarah represent both Jeffrey and Melanie Sutherland? Why or why not? What ethical rule is involved?

PRACTICE QUESTIONS AND ASSIGNMENTS

1. Kathryn Borstein works for the legal department of a large manufacturing corporation as a legal assistant. In the process of interviewing a middle-management accountant with the company relating to an employment-discrimination lawsuit, Kathryn discovers that a few of the top executives cheat on their income-tax returns by not declaring a portion of their bonuses. Kathryn becomes disenchanted with her job with the corporation for other reasons and finds a new one with a law firm. Her supervising attorney in the law firm is involved in a case against her former employer. The attorney tells Kathryn that the only way to deal with these big corporations is to get whatever dirt you can on them and then threaten to go to the press. He wants to know if she can give him any such information. Can she tell him any of the "dirt" about the executives who cheat on their income taxes? Why or why not? What ethical rules are involved in her decision?

2. A legal assistant in your law firm is working on a research project for a class that she is taking. She spends two hours doing personal research for her project on a computerized legal-research service that charges the firm several dollars per minute of on-line time. The legal assistant bills the two hours to a major client's file, assuming that no one will ever learn what she has done. You happen to be sitting at the terminal next to her, and you notice that she bills the time to one of the firm's clients. What should you do? What would you do if you learned that your supervising attorney had billed personal research time to a client's file?

3. Marc Sims, a paralegal, is instructed by his supervising attorney, Sam Felder, to file a complaint in federal court. Because the federal courthouse is an hour's drive from their office, Sam also tells Marc to take Sam's cellular phone with him and to make a number of follow-up calls relating to other clients' cases while Marc is driving to and from the courthouse. Sam instructs Marc to record the exact amount of time that he spends driving, so that Sam can bill the client for this travel time. Sam also asks Marc to keep track of the time he spends making the telephone calls concerning the other clients' cases, so that Sam can also bill those clients for the time Marc spends making calls on their behalf. Is it ethical of Sam to bill Marc's time in this way? If Marc follows Sam's instructions, will he be acting unethically in any way?

QUESTIONS FOR CRITICAL ANALYSIS

1. As noted in this chapter, in a 1993 ethical opinion, the ABA concluded that the client, and not the law firm, should benefit from any cost efficiencies created by the firm's use of previous research and other work products for a present client. Do you agree with the ABA's conclusion on this issue? How would you argue against the ABA's position? How would you argue in support of it?

2. In your view, are personal ethics and legal ethics totally distinct? How, generally, do (or should) personal and legal ethical standards interrelate?

3. If it were up to you to devise a set of ethical standards for the legal profession, would they be any different from those presented and discussed in this chapter and the preceding chapter? If so, in what ways?

ROLE-PLAYING EXERCISES

1. You work as a paralegal for a sole practitioner. You and the legal secretary both work in a large reception area. A client is waiting in the reception area to see the attorney. Assume that the following events occur:

> The legal secretary brings you a fax of a real-estate contract that she just received from a client, Mrs. Henley. Then she transfers the client to you. Mrs. Henley tells you that your supervising attorney had promised to review the real-estate contract prior to the *closing* (the final step in the sale of real estate) and that the closing will take place at 4 P.M. today. Before becoming a paralegal, you worked as a realtor and are very experienced in real-estate closings. Mrs. Henley knows this and insists that you review and approve the contract if the attorney does not have time to review it.

You should work in pairs. One should assume the role of the paralegal and the other the role of the client. The person playing the part of the paralegal should answer the client's requests without violating any ethical rules governing the practice of law that were discussed in Chapter 3 or in this chapter. If time allows, reverse roles.

2. Using the facts given in Practice Question 1, role-play the conversation in which Kathryn Borstein's new supervising attorney asks her to disclose information about her former employer. Working in pairs, one of you should assume the role of Kathryn and the other the role of the attorney. Kathryn must tell the attorney that she cannot disclose confidential information gained as a result of her previous employment. If time allows, reverse roles.

PROJECTS

1. Find out if your state's ethical rules on attorney-client confidentiality are the same as those presented in the ABA Model Rules. Start by looking in your state's court rules.

2. Compare your state's ethical rules on conflict of interest with the American Bar Association Model Rules on this issue. How are they similar? How are they different? Start by looking in your state's court rules.

3. Go to your school's library or to a local public library. Find materials on the ethical standards of professions other than the legal profession. What ethical concerns do the rules of other professions cover? How are the rules of other professions similar to or different from the legal profession's ethical rules?

4. Review your state's ethical rules on billing practices. Is double billing prohibited? How is value billing treated?

ANNOTATED SELECTED READINGS

ENOCH, CRAIG. "Incivility in the Legal System? Maybe It's the Rules." *SMU Law Review*, January/February 1994.

An interesting discussion of the rules of professional conduct and "hardball" tactics.

HILANDER, SALLY K. "What's Right? Dilemmas Easier with a Solid Core of Values." *Montana Lawyer,* October 1993. An interesting discussion of the six core values—including trustworthiness, respect, and responsibility—by which "lawyers and everyone else can judge their ethical behavior."

KALISH, STEPHEN E. "The Side-Switching Staff Person in a Law Firm: Uncomplimentary Assumptions and an Ethics Curtain." *Hamline Law Review,* Fall 1991. A good article discussing the ethical conflicts of interest created when paralegals or other staff members change jobs and, in effect, "switch sides" in a lawsuit or other legal proceeding.

PERRY, PHILLIP M. "Should You Rat on Your Boss?" *Legal Assistant Today,* March/April 1993. The whistleblower's guide to survival. A good article discussing what to do when your supervising attorney tells you to do something unethical or illegal.

PITULLA, JOANNE. "Truth in Billing." *American Bar Association Journal,* December 1992. An informative discussion concluding that certain billing practices, such as the double billing of clients and the billing of costs as fees, are ethically indefensible.

ROSS, WILLIAM G. "The Ethics of Hourly Billing by Attorneys," *Rutgers Law Review,* Fall 1991. A detailed article discussing the problem of unethical billing and focusing on the specific problem areas, including the billing of paralegals' time.

TOKUITSU, CYNTHIA. "How to Avoid the Top Ten Mistakes Paralegals Make on the Job." *Legal Assistant Today,* November/December 1991. An article that reviews the mistakes that paralegals and lawyers have identified as the top ten. Included among these mistakes is breaching the confidentiality rule. The article discusses how breaches of confidentiality can be avoided.

5

WORKING IN A LAW OFFICE

Chapter Objectives

After completing this chapter, you will know:

- How law firms organize and structure their businesses.
- The various lines of authority and accountability in a typical law partnership.
- How confidentiality considerations frame the law-office experience.
- Some typical employment policies and how paralegals are compensated and evaluated.
- The importance of an efficient filing system in legal practice and some typical filing procedures.
- How clients are billed for legal services.
- The importance of communication skills in the legal profession.

Chapter Outline

INTRODUCTION

The wide variety of law-office environments makes it impossible to describe in any detail how the particular firm with which you find employment will be run. Typically, though, that firm will have specific policies and procedures relating to how many hours per day or per week you will be required to work, how you are to document the time you spend on various projects, how office supplies are maintained, how vacation time accrues, the employee benefits to which you are entitled, and so on. In some firms, particularly large law firms, these policies and procedures may be spelled out in a written document, such as an **employment policy manual**. In smaller firms, policies and procedures are often less formal and may be based largely on habit or tradition. Because most paralegals are employed by private law firms, this chapter focuses on the organization, management, and procedures characteristic of private law firms.

EMPLOYMENT POLICY MANUAL
A firm's handbook or written statement that specifies the policies and procedures that govern the firm's employees and employer-employee relationships.

Part of working in a law office also involves knowing how to communicate and relate well with others. The latter part of this chapter discusses the importance of communication skills in the context of legal work.

THE ORGANIZATIONAL STRUCTURE OF LAW FIRMS

As mentioned in Chapter 2, law firms range in size from the small, one-attorney firm to the huge megafirm that consists of hundreds of attorneys. Regardless of their differences in size, though, in terms of business organization, law firms typically organize their businesses as sole proprietorships, partnerships, or professional corporations. Because the way in which a business is organized affects the law-office environment, we look briefly at each of the three major organizational forms here. You will read in detail about these types of business organizations, and others less widely used, in Chapter 9.

Sole Proprietorships

SOLE PROPRIETORSHIP
The simplest form of business, in which the owner is the business. Anyone who does business without creating a formal business entity has a sole proprietorship.

PERSONAL LIABILITY
An individual's personal responsibility for debts or obligations. The owners of sole proprietorships and partnerships are personally liable for the debts and obligations incurred by their business firms. If their firms go bankrupt or cannot meet debts as they become due, the owners will be personally responsible for paying the debts.

Many law firms, particularly smaller firms, are **sole proprietorships**. Sole proprietorships are the simplest business form and are often used by attorneys when they first set up legal practices. In a sole proprietorship, one individual—the sole proprietor—owns the business. The sole proprietor is entitled to any profits made by the firm but is also personally liable for all of the firm's debts or obligations. **Personal liability** means that the personal assets of the business owner (such as a home, automobile, savings or investment accounts, and other property) may have to be sacrificed to pay business obligations if the business fails.

An attorney who practices law as a sole proprietor is often called a *sole (solo) practitioner.* Although a sole practitioner may at times hire an associate attorney to help with the legal work, the associate will be paid a specific sum for his or her time and will not share in the profits or losses of the firm itself.

Working for a sole practitioner is a good way for a paralegal to learn about law-office procedures because the paralegal will typically perform a wide variety of tasks. Many sole practitioners hire one person to perform the functions of secretary, paralegal, administrator, and manager. Paralegals holding this kind of position would probably handle the following kinds of tasks: receiving and date-stamping the mail, organizing and maintaining the filing system, interviewing clients and witnesses, bookkeeping (receiving payments from clients, preparing and sending bills to clients, and so on), conducting investigations and legal research, drafting legal documents, assisting the attorney in trial preparation and perhaps in the courtroom, and numerous other tasks, including office administration.

As mentioned in Chapter 2, working for a sole practitioner who runs a small general practice is a good way to learn about procedures relating to different areas of legal work. You will have an opportunity to find out which area of law you most enjoy—and you may want to pursue a career as a specialist in that area with another firm. If you work for a sole practitioner who specializes in one area of law, you will have an opportunity to develop expertise in that area of law. In sum, working in a small law firm gives you a broad overview of law-office procedures and legal practice. This knowledge will help you throughout your career.

Partnerships

The majority of law firms are either partnerships or professional corporations. In a **partnership**, two or more individuals undertake to do business jointly as **partners**. A partnership may consist of just a few attorneys or over a hundred attorneys. In a partnership, each partner owns a share of the business and shares jointly in the firm's profits or losses. Like sole proprietors, partners are personally liable for the debts and obligations of the business if the business fails.

In smaller partnerships, the partners may participate equally in managing the partnership. They will likely meet periodically to make decisions relating to clients, policies, procedures, and other matters of importance to the firm. In larger partnerships, managerial decisions are usually made by a committee consisting of some of the partners, one of whom may be designated as the **managing partner**.

The partnership may hire associate attorneys, but, as in a sole proprietorship, the associates will not have ownership rights in the firm. Normally, an associate hopes to become a partner, and if the associate's performance is satisfactory, the partners may invite the associate to become a partner in the firm.

Professional Corporations

A **professional corporation (P.C.)** is owned by **shareholders**, so called because they purchase the corporation's stock, or shares, and thus own a share of the business. The shareholders share in the profits and losses of the firm in proportion to how many shares they own. Their personal liability, unlike that of partners, is limited to the amount of their investment. In other words, they normally are not personally liable for corporate debts and obligations.

PARTNERSHIP
An association of two or more persons to carry on, as co-owners, a business for profit.

PARTNER
A person who has undertaken to operate a business jointly with one or more other persons. Each partner is a co-owner of the business firm.

MANAGING PARTNER
The partner in a law firm who makes decisions relating to the firm's policies and procedures and who generally oversees the business operations of the firm.

PROFESSIONAL CORPORATION (P.C.)
A business form in which shareholders (those who purchase the corporation's stock, or shares) own the firm and share in the profits and losses of the firm in proportion to how many shares they own. Their personal liability, unlike that of partners, is limited to the amount of their investment.

SHAREHOLDER
One who purchases corporate stock, or shares, and who thus becomes an owner of the corporation.

As you will read in Chapter 9, this limited personal liability is one of the key advantages of the corporate form of business.

In many respects, the professional corporation is run like a partnership, and the distinction between these two forms of business organization is often more a legal formality than an operational reality. Because of this, attorneys who organize their business as a professional corporation are nonetheless sometimes referred to as partners. For the sake of simplicity, in this chapter we will refer to anyone who has ownership rights in the firm as a partner.

DEVELOPING PARALEGAL SKILLS

Types of Practice

Jane Upton, a student in a legal-assistant program, is looking for a job for her internship course. She has some questions about some of the job postings, which she is discussing with Lorraine Burwitz, a friend who graduated from the program two years ago. "With which type of firm should I do my internship?" asks Jane. "There are so many different types and sizes of firms to consider. How do I sort it all out?"

Lorraine responds, "You need to think about the different types of practices. First, there are private law firms—you know, sole practitioners, partnerships, and professional corporations. Then there are corporations and government legal departments and offices."

Jane pulls out a job posting for a sole practitioner. It reads: "General law practice seeks legal-assistant student with strong word-processing skills. Areas of law include family law, probate, real estate, some litigation. Must be dependable and willing to take initiative. Contact the law offices of Mary T. Jones, (616) 555-9000." Jane asks Lorraine whether Mary Jones, because she is the only person listed, is a sole practitioner. "Right," responds Lorraine. "If it were a partnership, the name would read something like the name of the firm I work for, which is Culpepper, Hines, Tobin & Thomas." "What about a professional corporation? Would the name be something like Culpepper, Hines, Tobin & Thomas, P.C.?" asks Jane. "It might in some states," answers Lorraine. "In other states, though," Lorraine continues, "the names of professional corporations are followed by other initials, such as P.A., for professional association."

"What about working for these various types of firms? How does that differ?" asks Jane. "Sole practitioners usually want someone who can act as both a paralegal and a secretary and who isn't afraid to ask questions and assume a lot of responsibility. Working for a sole practitioner can be a good way to get a lot of experience," explains Lorraine. "In larger partnerships and P.C.s, paralegals tend to specialize, and you don't get to work in as many different areas. It really depends on what you feel comfortable with, but for my internship, I chose a sole practitioner's office for the varied experience. I didn't know yet which area of law I wanted to work in," says Lorraine. Jane liked that idea and decided to apply to the offices of Mary T. Jones.

LAW-OFFICE PERSONNEL

When you take a job as a legal assistant, one of the first things you will want to learn is the relative status of the office personnel. Particularly, you will want to know who has authority over you and to whom you are accountable. You also want to know who will be accountable to you—whether you have an assistant or a secretary (or share an assistant or a secretary with another paralegal), for example. In a small firm, you will have no problem learning this information. If you work for a larger law firm, however, the lines of authority may be more difficult to perceive. Your supervisor will probably instruct you, either orally or in writing, on the relative status of the firm's personnel. If you are not sure about who has authority over whom and what kinds of tasks are performed by various employees, you should ask your supervisor.

The lines of authority and accountability vary from firm to firm, depending on the firm's size and its organizational and management preferences. A sample organizational chart for a smaller law partnership is shown in Exhibit 5.1. The ultimate decision makers in the hypothetical firm represented by that chart are the partners. Next in authority are the associate attorneys and summer associates (law clerks—see Chapter 1). The paralegals in this firm are supervised by both the attorneys (in regard to legal work) and the office manager (in regard to office procedural and paralegal staffing matters). In

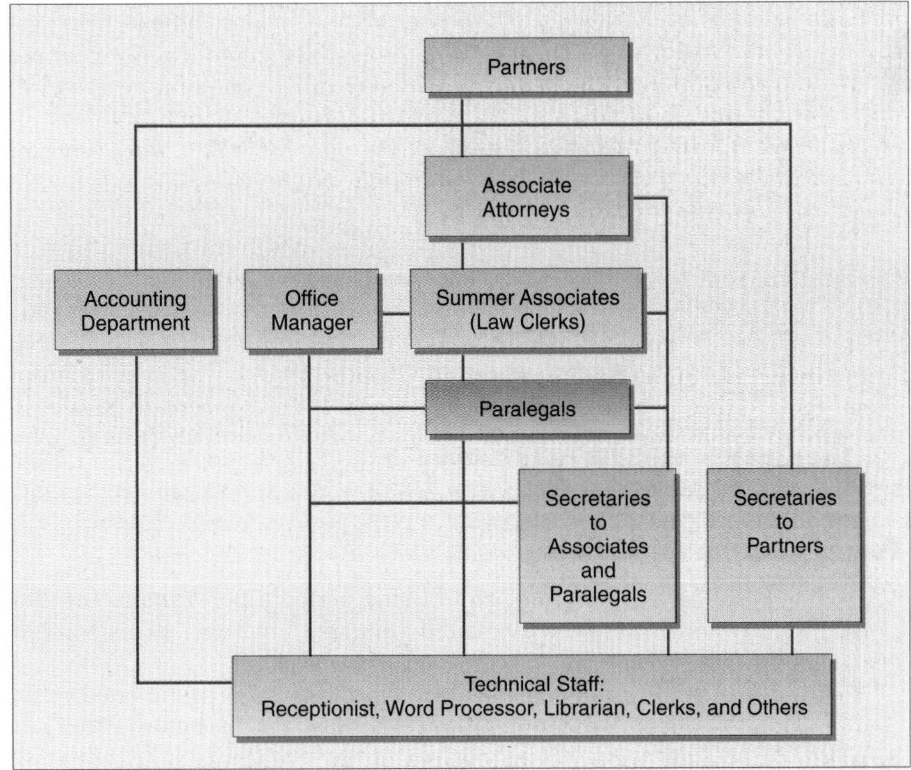

EXHIBIT 5.1
A Sample Organizational Chart for a Law Partnership

LEGAL-ASSISTANT MANAGER
An employee who is responsible for overseeing the paralegal staff and paralegal professional development.

LEGAL ADMINISTRATOR
An administrative employee of a law firm who manages the day-to-day operations of the firm. In smaller law firms, legal administrators are usually called office managers.

OFFICE MANAGER
An administrative employee who manages the day-to-day operations of a business firm. In larger law firms, office managers are usually called legal administrators.

SUPPORT PERSONNEL
Those employees who provide clerical, secretarial, or other support to the legal, paralegal, and administrative staff of a law firm.

larger firms, there may be a **legal-assistant manager**, who coordinates and oversees paralegal staffing and various programs relating to paralegal educational and professional development.

Law-firm personnel include, in addition to attorneys and paralegals, administrative personnel. In larger firms, the partners may hire a **legal administrator** to run the business end of the firm. The legal administrator might delegate some of his or her authority to an **office manager** and other supervisory employees. In smaller firms, such as that represented by the chart in Exhibit 5.1, an office manager handles the administrative aspects of the firm. Generally, the legal administrator or office manager makes sure that the office runs smoothly, that sufficient supplies are on hand, that office procedures are established and followed, and so on. In a small firm, the office manager might also handle client billing procedures. The hypothetical firm represented by the chart in Exhibit 5.1 has an accounting department to perform this function.

The **support personnel** in a large law office may include secretaries, receptionists, bookkeepers, file clerks, messengers, and others. Depending on their functions and specific jobs, support personnel may fall under the supervision of any number of the other personnel in the firm. In a very small firm, just one person—the legal secretary, for example—may perform all of the above-mentioned functions.

EMPLOYMENT POLICIES

Every law firm has basic rules or policies—which may be written or unwritten—that govern the basic conditions of employment and indicate what the firm expects of employees. There will be an established policy, for example, on how much vacation time you are entitled to during the first year, second year, and so on. There will also be a policy governing which holidays are observed by the firm, how much sick leave you can take, when you are expected to arrive at the workplace, and what will serve as grounds for the employer to terminate your employment.

Employment policies and benefits packages vary from firm to firm. A foremost concern of paralegals (and employees generally) is how much they will be paid for their work, how they will be paid (that is, whether they will receive salaries or hourly wages), and what job benefits they will receive. These issues were discussed in detail in Chapter 2, so we will not examine them here. Rather, we look at two other key areas of concern to paralegals in regard to employment policies: performance evaluations and termination procedures.

Performance Evaluations

Many law firms have a policy of conducting periodic performance evaluations. Usually, performance is evaluated annually, but some firms conduct evaluations every six months.

Because paralegal responsibilities vary from firm to firm, no one evaluation checklist applies to every paralegal. Some of the factors that may be considered during a performance evaluation are indicated in Exhibit 5.2.

PARALEGAL PROFILE Paralegal Supervisor

JOEL WIRCHIN received his bachelor of arts degree from the State University of New York at Albany. He then enrolled in the lawyer's assistant program at Adelphi University. He is now working on a master's degree in public administration. Wirchin is currently the director of paralegal services for Sullivan and Cromwell, a law firm specializing in corporate transactions and litigation. Wirchin started at Sullivan and Cromwell as a senior legal assistant and moved into administrative work about four and a half years ago. Prior to working at Sullivan and Cromwell, he worked in the legal department of a pharmaceutical company.

What do you like best about your work?

"I like working in an administrative position, especially because of the variety of duties involved. It is a very people-oriented job, and I consider that to be one of my greatest talents—working with others. I think I'm making a positive difference in the lives of the people whom I manage."

What is the greatest challenge that you face in your area of work?

"The biggest challenge for me is the varied scope of my work. I find it very challenging to manage and deal with such a large staff. The New York office, in which I work, employs about forty-five paralegals. I am in charge of seventy paralegals worldwide, and my duties include hiring, training, evaluating, and budgeting responsibilities, to name just a few. I also travel occasionally, mainly to Sullivan and Cromwell's office in Washington, D.C. One of my greatest challenges is working with lawyers and clients when urgent or particularly demanding circumstances arise. I feel as though I have to create miracle after miracle."

What advice do you have for would-be paralegals in your area of work?

"My advice to paralegals who are interested in administrative work is to pay close attention to the work environment—not just to the lawyers but to the law firm itself. I feel you should keep one eye on the client work and one eye on how decisions are made. This will help the paralegal get a feel for the business transactions and, really, the business of the law firm. If I were a student now, I'd focus on shooting higher and being more selective when planning my career and selecting potential employers."

"I THINK I'M MAKING A POSITIVE DIFFERENCE IN THE LIVES OF THE PEOPLE WHOM I MANAGE."

What are some tips for success as a paralegal in your area of work?

"Paralegals should convey a positive, upbeat attitude. It is, of course, important to be smart, organized, and analytical, but it's also important to inspire confidence in others. Also, a paralegal's attitude comes through in his or her performance evaluation."

Typically, under each factor is a series of options—ranging from "very good" to "unsatisfactory" or something similar—for the supervisor or attorney to check. When you begin work as a paralegal, you should learn at the outset what exactly your duties will be and what performance is expected of you. This way, you will be able to prepare for your first evaluation from the moment you begin working. You will not have to wait six months or a year before you learn that you were supposed to be doing something that you failed to do.

EXHIBIT 5.2
A Sample Evaluation Checklist

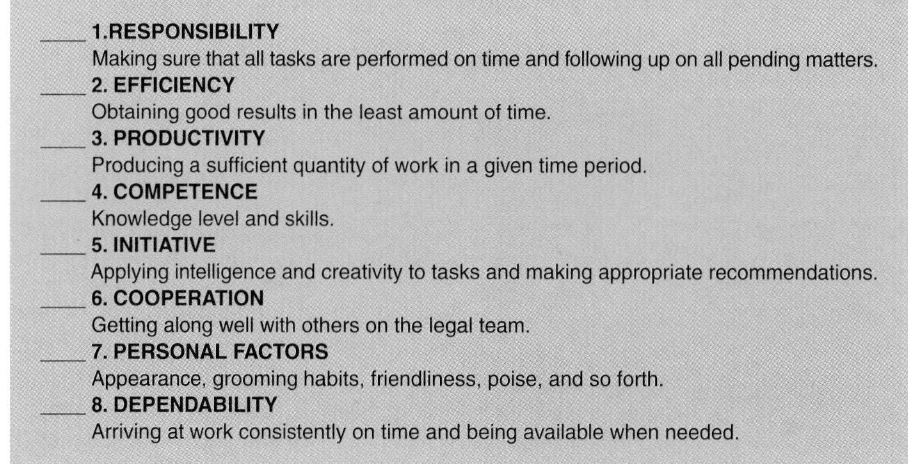
____ 1.RESPONSIBILITY
Making sure that all tasks are performed on time and following up on all pending matters.
____ 2. EFFICIENCY
Obtaining good results in the least amount of time.
____ 3. PRODUCTIVITY
Producing a sufficient quantity of work in a given time period.
____ 4. COMPETENCE
Knowledge level and skills.
____ 5. INITIATIVE
Applying intelligence and creativity to tasks and making appropriate recommendations.
____ 6. COOPERATION
Getting along well with others on the legal team.
____ 7. PERSONAL FACTORS
Appearance, grooming habits, friendliness, poise, and so forth.
____ 8. DEPENDABILITY
Arriving at work consistently on time and being available when needed.

In the busy legal workplace, you will probably not have much time available to discuss issues with your supervisor that do not relate to immediate needs. And even if you do find a moment, you may feel awkward in broaching a discussion about your performance or about problems that you face in the workplace. Performance evaluations are designed specifically to allow both the employer and the employee to exchange their views on such issues.

During performance reviews, you can learn how the firm rates your performance. You can gain valuable feedback from your supervisor, learn more about your strengths and weaknesses, and identify the areas in which you need to improve your skills or work habits. You can also give feedback to your supervisor on how you feel about the workplace. For example, if you think that your expertise is not being fully utilized, this would be a good time to discuss that issue and perhaps suggest some ways in which your knowledge and experience could be put to better use.

Employment Termination

Virtually all policy manuals deal with the subject of employment termination. If you work for a firm that has prepared such a manual for its employees, the manual will likely specify what kind of conduct serves as a basis for firing employees. For example, the manual might specify that if an employee is absent more than twelve days a year for two consecutive years, the employer has grounds to terminate the employment relationship. The manual will also probably describe employment-termination procedures. For example, the firm might require that it be notified one month in advance if an employee decides to leave the firm; if the employee fails to give one month's notice, he or she may forfeit accumulated vacation time or other benefits on termination.

Traditionally, employment relationships have been governed by the common law doctrine of employment at will. Under this doctrine, employers may hire and fire employees "at will"—that is, for any reason or no reason. Today, courts have created several exceptions to this doctrine, and state and federal statutes now regulate numerous aspects of the employment relationship. Under federal law (and many state statutes), employers may not fire employees for discriminatory reasons—because of the employee's age or race, for example. These and other laws regulating employment relationships will be discussed in Chapter 9.

CONFIDENTIALITY AND LAW-OFFICE PROCEDURES

The duty of confidentiality, which was discussed at length in Chapter 4, also deserves special mention in this chapter because of the extent to which it frames law-office work and procedures. Law-firm personnel, from the owner or owners to the supply-room clerk, must keep confidential all information relating to the firm's clients. All information received from or about clients, including client files and documents, is considered confidential.

Note that all business firms require their workers to keep certain information confidential. If you were a payroll clerk for a large corporation, for example, you would be dealing with sensitive information—the amount of money that various corporate employees earn. Very likely, your employer would request that you keep all such information confidential. If you failed to do so, you could lose your job—but your breach of confidentiality would normally not violate any law. A law firm, in contrast, is legally obligated to keep client information confidential.

- **A breach of confidentiality by a paralegal or other employee can cause the firm to incur potentially extensive liability.**

The confidentiality rule lends a unique quality to the law-office environment. Many of the typical law-office procedures that you will read about later in this chapter reflect the need to protect client confidentiality. This is particularly true of filing procedures.

For example, for filing purposes, clients are often identified by alphabetical or numerical combinations, or by computerized bar codes, rather than by recognizable names. Also, files must be located in an office area to which visitors do not have access, and the storage and destruction of old files must be accomplished in such a way as to protect confidentiality. In some circumstances, such as conflict-of-interest situations (discussed in Chapter 4), procedures must be in place to prevent even members of the same firm from accessing certain files. Confidentiality needs also affect telephone and E-mail procedures, fax and mailing procedures, copier use, the disposal of trash, and a number of other routine law-office procedures.

FILING PROCEDURES

The paperwork generated by law offices is enormous. And, for the most part, the paperwork consists of important and confidential documents that must be safeguarded yet be readily retrievable when they are needed. Efficient filing procedures are thus essential. Otherwise, important files and documents may be lost or unavailable when needed. Documents must also be filed in such a way as to protect client confidentiality, as just discussed.

Larger firms normally have specific procedures concerning the creation, maintenance, use, and storage of office files. If you take a job with a large firm, a supervisor will probably spend some time training you in routine office procedures, including filing procedures. The trend today, particularly in larger firms, is toward computerized filing systems. You will read about the application of computer technology to document management and filing later in this text, in Chapter 16. If you work for a small firm, filing procedures may be less formal, and you may even assume the responsibility for organizing and developing an efficient filing system. In either situation, you must take the initiative, if necessary, to learn about existing filing procedures.

Generally, law offices maintain several types of files. Typically, a law firm's filing system will include client files, work-product files and reference materials, forms files, and personnel files.

Client Files

The heart of any legal practice is its filing system. Law firms could not operate without having some kind of system for organizing and maintaining client files. If a document is misfiled or a file is missing, valuable time may have to be spent tracking down the document or file. If a file is lost, the client may suffer irreparable harm. Each law firm, regardless of its size, must take special care in maintaining its case files so that the files are protected, kept confidential, and yet immediately at hand when needed.

To illustrate client filing procedures, we present below the phases in the "life cycle" of a hypothetical client's file. The name of the client is Katherine Baranski, who has just retained one of your firm's attorneys to represent her in a lawsuit that she is bringing against Tony Peretto. Because Baranski is initiating the lawsuit, she is referred to as the plaintiff. Peretto, because he has to defend against Baranski's claims, is the defendant. The name of the case is *Baranski v. Peretto.* Assume that you will be working on the case and that your supervising attorney has just asked you to open a new case file. Assume also that you have already verified, through a "conflicts check" (discussed in Chapter 4), that no conflict of interest exists.

Opening a New Client File. The first step that you (or a secretary, at your request) will take in opening a new file is to assign the case a file number. For reasons of both efficiency and confidentiality, many firms identify their client files by numbers or some kind of numerical and/or alphabetical sequence instead of the clients' names.

The range of possibilities is virtually limitless. One frequently used technique is to identify the file by the date on which it is created. For example, a file opened on January 12, 1996, could be identified as follows: 96-0112. The advantage of identifying files by date is that the age of the file is readily apparent. Additionally, the initials of the **responsible billing partner** (the partner responsible for overseeing the case) might be added to the file number. If attorney Allen Gilmore was the responsible partner for the Baranski case, the

RESPONSIBLE BILLING PARTNER
The partner in a law firm who is responsible for overseeing a particular client's case and the billing of that client.

file label might read 96-0112-AG. To ensure confidentiality, some law firms identify the responsible billing partner by a number instead of the attorney's initials. Assuming that Allen Gilmore's identifying number was six, then the file number for the Baranski file would be 96-0112-06.

Another technique is to combine letters of the names of the plaintiff and defendant in such as way as to obscure their identities. The *Baranski v. Peretto* case file might be identified by the letters BARAPE—the first four letters of the plaintiff's name followed by the first two letters of the defendant's name.

Typically, law firms maintain a master client list on which clients' names are entered alphabetically and cross-referenced to the clients' case numbers. If file numbers consist of numerical sequences, there is also a master list on which the file numbers are listed in numerical order and cross-referenced to the clients' names.

Adding Subfiles. As the work on the Baranski case progresses and more documents are generated or received, the file will expand. To ensure that documents will be easy to locate, you will create subfiles. A special subfile might be created for client documents (such as a contract, will, stock certificate, or photograph) that the firm needs for reference or for evidence at trial. As correspondence relating to the Baranski case is generated, you will probably add a correspondence subfile. You will also want a subfile for your or the attorney's notes on the case, including research results.

As you will read in Chapters 10 and 11, litigation involves several stages. The first stage involves *pleadings.* The pleadings include the plaintiff's *complaint,* a document filed with the court to initiate a lawsuit, and the defendant's *answer,* or response to the complaint. Prior to trial, attorneys for both sides will engage in a process called *discovery*. The purpose of discovery is to gather ("discover") as much evidence as possible—from opposing parties, witnesses, and other sources—to support the claims of the parties.

As the Baranski litigation progresses through the pleadings and discovery stages, subfiles for documents relating to each stage will be added to the Baranski file. By the discovery stage of litigation, for example, the Baranski file might contain the subfiles shown in Exhibit 5.3 on the next page. Numerous other subfiles may be created during the course of the litigation.

Documents are typically filed within each subfile in reverse chronological order, with the most recently dated document on the top. Usually, to safeguard the documents, they are punched at the top with a two-hole puncher so that they can be secured within the file with a clip. Note, though, that original client documents should not be punched or altered in any way. They should always be left loose within the file. For example, if you were holding in the file a property deed belonging to a client, you would not want to alter that document in any way.

Color Coding, Tabs, and Indexes. Many law firms find it useful to color-code subfiles so that they can be readily identified. For example, pink file folders (or pink stickers on the file labels) might be used routinely for pleadings subfiles, orange folders for discovery subfiles, yellow folders for

EXHIBIT 5.3
A Sample Client File

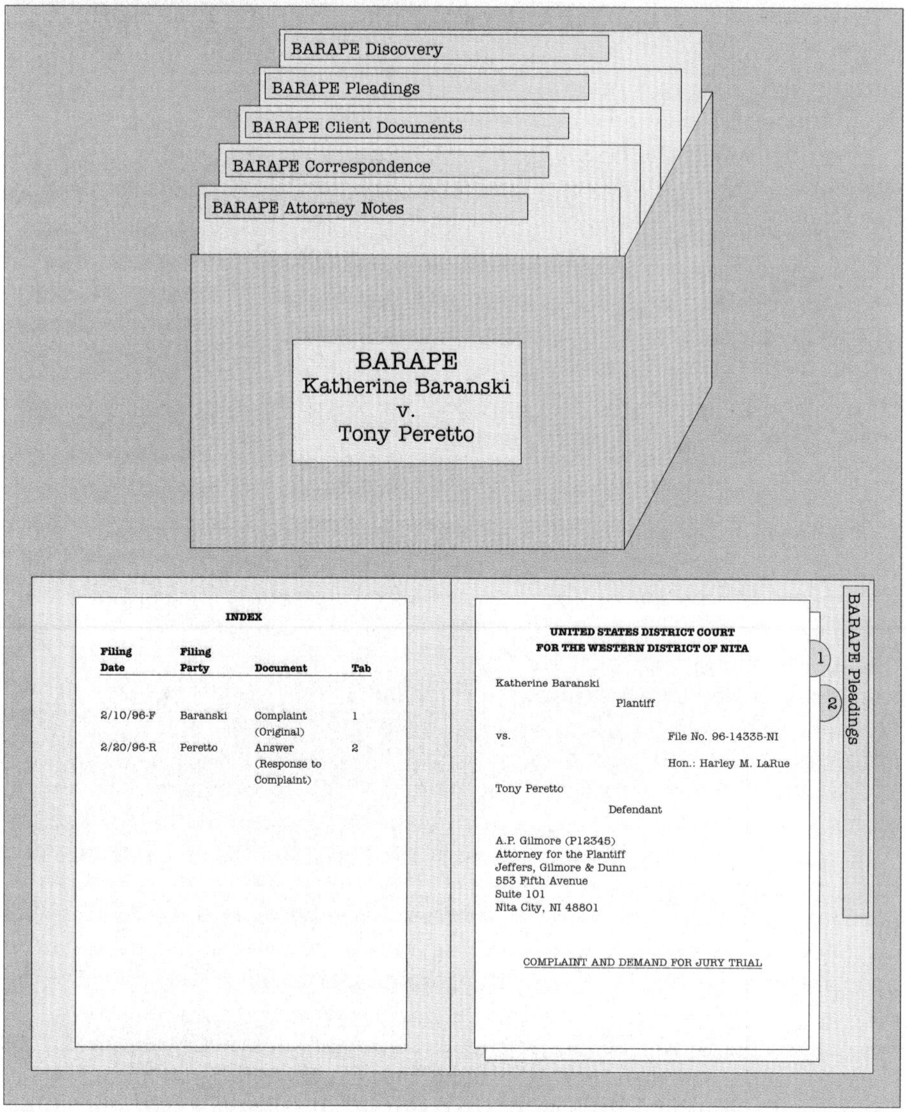

BARAPE Discovery
BARAPE Pleadings
BARAPE Client Documents
BARAPE Correspondence
BARAPE Attorney Notes

BARAPE
Katherine Baranski
v.
Tony Peretto

INDEX

Filing Date	Filing Party	Document	Tab
2/10/96-F	Baranski	Complaint (Original)	1
2/20/96-R	Peretto	Answer (Response to Complaint)	2

UNITED STATES DISTRICT COURT
FOR THE WESTERN DISTRICT OF NITA

Katherine Baranski
Plantiff

vs. File No. 96-14335-NI

Hon.: Harley M. LaRue

Tony Peretto
Defendant

A.P. Gilmore (P12345)
Attorney for the Plantiff
Jeffers, Gilmore & Dunn
553 Fifth Avenue
Suite 101
Nita City, NI 48801

COMPLAINT AND DEMAND FOR JURY TRIAL

1
2
BARAPE Pleadings

correspondence, and so on. Color coding may also be used in other ways—to indicate the responsible attorney for certain files, for example. Some firms use different colors of paper for different documents so that they can be quickly identified. For example, all *copies* of original documents might be made on pink paper.

A subfile is sometimes further subdivided by adding tabs to various documents within the subfile. An index attached to the inside cover of the subfile indicates what documents can be found at what tab number. Exhibit 5.3 also shows a sample index for the pleadings file in the Baranski case. Note that the sample index shown in the exhibit also includes relevant dates, such as when the complaint was filed with the court (indicated by an "F" following the date) and when the answer was received (indicated by an "R" following the date).

File Use and Storage. Typically, files are stored in a central file room or area. Most firms require that office staff use "out cards" when removing files from the storage area. An **out card** is a piece of cardboard, about the size of a manila folder, with lines on it to indicate the date, the name of the file, and the initials of the user. When a file is removed, the card is inserted in the file's place. Even if a file is removed for only a few minutes, an out card should be used. The consistent use of out cards helps to avoid the time cost and frustration involved in trying to locate missing files. An alternative to an out card is an *out folder,* in which documents can be filed temporarily until the file is returned to storage.

OUT CARD
A large card inserted in a filing cabinet in the place of a temporarily removed file. The out card notifies others who may need the file of the name of the person who has the file and the time and date that the file was removed.

The problem with out cards and out folders is that people either do not use them at all or fail to initial them. A perpetual challenge for most law firms is trying to devise a "foolproof" system for quickly locating files that have been removed from the file storage area. Valuable staff time is often spent in tracking down files that are not where they should be. As you will read in Chapter 16, computerized file-management systems can provide firms with a solution to this problem.

Note that documents should never be removed from a client file or subfile. Rather, the entire file or subfile should be removed for use. This ensures that important documents will not be separated from the file and possibly mislaid or lost. Many paralegals and other users make copies of documents in the file for their use. For example, if you are working on the Baranski case and need to review the complaint, which is located in the pleadings file, you might remove the pleadings file temporarily from the storage area (inserting an out card or folder), copy the complaint, and immediately return the file to storage.

Closing a File. Assume that the Baranski case has been settled out of court and that no further legal work on Baranski's behalf needs to be done. For a time, her file will be retained in the inactive files, but when it is fairly certain that no one will need to refer to it very often—if ever—it will be closed. Closed files are often stored in a separate area of the building or even off-site. There are warehouses that specifically cater to attorneys and other professionals who need storage space for confidential files. Such warehouses make sure that the files are secure and protected from dampness or other environmental problems that could damage their contents. Many larger law firms store the content of old files on microfilm.

Specific procedures for closing files vary from firm to firm. Typically, when a case is closed, original documents provided by the client (for example, a deed to property) are returned to the client, and extraneous materials, such as extra copies of documents or cover letters, are destroyed.

Destroying Old Files. Law firms do not have to retain client files forever, and at some point, the Baranski file will be destroyed. Law firms exercise great care when destroying client files because a court or government agency may impose a heavy fine on a law firm that destroys a file that should have been retained for a longer period of time. How long a particular file must be retained depends on many factors, including the nature of the client's legal matters and governing statutes, such as the statute of limitations.

State statutes of limitations for legal-malpractice actions vary from state to state—from six months to ten years after the attorney's last contact with the client. When the statute of limitations in your state expires is thus an important factor in determining how long to retain a client file because an attorney or law firm will need the information contained in the client's file to defend against a malpractice action. If the file has been destroyed, the firm will not be able to produce any documents or other evidence to refute the plaintiff's claim.

Only when the retention time for a client file has expired should the file be destroyed. Old files are normally destroyed by shredding them so that confidentiality is preserved.

Work-product Files and Reference Materials

Many law firms keep copies of research projects, legal memoranda, and pleadings and other case-related materials prepared by the firm's attorneys and paralegals so that these documents can be referred to in future projects. In this way, legal personnel do not have to start all over again when working on a claim similar to one dealt with in the past. These work-product files, or legal information files, are typically filed in the firm's library in alphabetical order by legal topic, with subtopics. For example, the topic of "Automobile Negligence" would include in subfiles copies of complaints, answers, legal research, and other documents relating to cases involving automobile negligence.

When a firm has its own library, someone is normally assigned the job of overseeing the library and making sure that it is kept current. This person probably also maintains a card catalog, creating new cards for new additions to the library and keeping a log of who has which book or other reference materials.

Forms Files

FORMS FILE
A reference file containing copies of the firm's commonly used legal documents and informational forms. The documents in the forms file serve as a model for drafting new documents.

Every law firm keeps on hand various forms that it commonly uses. These forms may be kept in various files or, as is often the case, stored in a **forms file**. A forms file might include retainer-agreement forms, forms used for filing lawsuits in specific courts, bankruptcy forms indicating the type of information that must be obtained from clients petitioning for bankrupcy, forms used in real-estate matters, and numerous others. Often, to save time, copies of pleadings (or other documents) relating to specific types of cases are kept for future reference. Then, when the attorney or paralegal works on a similar case, the pleadings (or other documents) from the previous case can be used as a model, or guide. These forms may be kept either in a forms file or in a work-product file.

As will be discussed in Chapter 16, there is an abundance of legal software that contains forms for use in litigation and other legal specialties. Computerized forms have simplified legal practice by allowing legal personnel to generate customized documents within minutes.

DEVELOPING PARALEGAL SKILLS

Client File Confidentiality

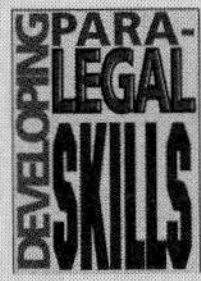

At the law firm of Jenkins & Fitzgerald, P.C., the client files are organized so that there is a separate folder, or subfile, for each of the following: attorney notes (research), client documents, pleadings, and discovery. All of the subfiles are kept in a large, red, accordion-shaped folder, which expands to accommodate a great number of documents. On each subfile, as well as on the large red folder, is written the name of the case, such as *Hanks v. Hardy,* the court's docket (or file) number, the firm's file number, and the client's name.

Robert James, a paralegal with the firm, was assigned a research project on *Sims v. Purdy Contracting, Inc.*, a case involving a personal-injury suit for millions of dollars against the firm's client, Mr. Purdy. Robert took the pleadings and research folders with him to the county bar association's law library to do some research. He set the files down on a table and went to the shelves to find a case reporter. While Robert was looking for the reporter, in an area several aisles away from the table on which he had left the files, Lori Langer walked by and noticed the file. Lori was an attorney and was currently doing work on behalf of Clark Construction Company, a large contractor who was considering giving Mr. Purdy's company a big job. Lori looked at the folders and saw Purdy's name, the docket number, and a law firm's file number.

Curious about the lawsuit, Laurie wrote down the docket number, left the library, and went to the court clerk's office. There she requested a copy of the court's file on the case, which was public information. Laurie read through the complaint. She could see that the plaintiff, Sims, sought a substantial amount in money damages. Laurie decided to call Mr. Clark to see if he was aware of the lawsuit. She knew that he would be hesitant to award a subcontract to Purdy if he knew that Purdy was being sued for so much money. This kind of case could bankrupt Purdy, and he might not be able to finish the job.

Later that week, Robert's supervising attorney, Lane Perkins, called Robert into his office. "It seems that Mr. Purdy lost out on a major contract with Clark Construction Company because Mr. Clark found out about Purdy's lawsuit," said Lane. "Clark told Purdy that Clark's attorney had seen a file with Purdy's name on it at the law library. Purdy is furious over the breach of client confidentiality. I have discussed this matter with my partners, and we do not hold you responsible. But we have learned a lesson: our filing system needs to be modified. We will be changing the system so that the case names and client names no longer appear on the outside of any of the files."

Personnel Files

The firm's personnel files usually contain a complete employment record for each employee of the firm, including the employee's original employment application and résumé, performance reviews, general progress notes, and attendance records. These records are usually kept in a locked file at all times, and old personnel files are rarely stored off-site—because they

FEATURED GUEST: KATHLEEN MERCER REED

Ten Tips for Creating and Maintaining an Efficient File System

Biographical Note

Kathleen Mercer Reed holds a bachelor of science degree in legal administration from the University of Toledo and has a law degree. She currently works as an assistant professor and as the Coordinator of Legal Assistant Technology at the University of Toledo's Community and Technical College, the same program from which she received her associate's degree in 1985. A member of many legal-assistant advisory committees, Reed is a former president of the Toledo Association of Legal Assistants. She is active in national paralegal education issues and a frequent speaker on the paralegal profession.

File maintenance is one of the most important aspects of legal work. Without an organized case file, the attorney is unable to make sure that the case is on track and deadlines are being met. This can mean unhappy clients and a resulting loss of business. Generally, attorneys rely on their paralegals to assume responsibility for the essential task of maintaining (or supervising the maintenance of) the files. Filing systems vary. In some firms, they are highly structured and efficient; in other firms, they may be virtually nonexistent. If you are ever faced with the challenge of setting up (or reorganizing) a file system, here are some tips to consider.

1 Set Aside Time for Planning. The major problem relating to filing systems is the time factor. Law offices are extremely busy places. Time is money in the law firm. Everyone wants to get on with the important job of performing work for the client. But filing systems *must* be planned. You need to recognize this fact and allow time for the planning process.

2 Create a System That Is Simple, Yet Effective. Remember that you and the attorney will not be the only ones working with the file. Secretaries, receptionists, and file clerks may also need to use client files. Don't create a system that generates confusion about where certain documents are to be filed or where they can be found. Try to establish a simple, logical system that can be readily understood by everybody.

3 Make Sure That the Files are Clearly Labeled. Each file should be clearly labeled so that it can be easily located. Files are more easily recognized when the labels are consistently placed on files and consistently typed, printed, or handwritten.

4 Don't Be Afraid to Create as Many Files as You Need. Don't hesitate to create additional files, especially subfiles, if you think that they are necessary. Generally, the more subfiles you create, the better organized your file will be—and the easier it will be to retrieve specific documents.

5 Make Sure That the Filing System Ensures Client Confidentiality. When setting up your file system, make sure that the system protects client confidentiality to the greatest possible extent. Some law firms are eliminating alphabetical systems (files in which the client's name is clearly identified on the file folder) and are using numeric filing sys-

must be close at hand if someone requests a job reference for a previous employee.

FINANCIAL PROCEDURES

Like any other business firm, a law firm needs to at least cover its expenses or it will fail. In the business of law, the product is legal services, which are

FEATURED GUEST, Continued

tems instead. Numerical file systems eliminate the risk of one client seeing another client's name when the file is opened. Remember, a firm can breach a client's right to confidentiality simply by divulging (inadvertently or otherwise) the fact that the client consulted the firm, even as a potential client.

6 Set Up Efficient Case-opening Procedures. A client file should be set up within twenty-four hours of the initial client interview and sent back to the attorney assigned to the file. This means that conflict-of-interest checks and initial file organization must be done quickly. A thorough conflict-of-interest check must be done to prevent the necessity of spending hours on a plaintiff's case only to find out that another attorney in the law firm is representing the defendant in that same case. At the same time, the file must be given to the attorney promptly so that he or she can begin working for the client and avoid missing any deadlines.

7 Establish an Efficient Check-out System. No matter how well organized your file is, you can't work on the file if you can't find it! In a very small law office, this may not be a great concern. But the larger the firm, the more difficult it becomes to locate files—because more people have access to them. A file that you or an attorney needs urgently may be sitting on a partner's desk, but you do not know this. You need to establish and enforce some kind of sign-out system, such as placing "out cards" or "sign-out cards" in the file whenever a file folder is removed.

8 Establish Proper Procedures for Closing and Storing Files. Closed files must be properly stored and maintained for several reasons. First, a client may contact the firm—sometimes months after his or her case has been closed—to obtain documents or information from the client's file. Second, work that you did on past cases can be a great resource when working on current cases, and if old files are easily accessible, you will not have to "reinvent the wheel" whenever you work on a case that is similar to a case already in the firm's files. Third and most important, there are state and national standards governing file retention. Find out how long your law firm is *legally required* to store and maintain closed files. For all of these reasons, closed files must be maintained with as much integrity as active files.

9 Establish Proper Procedures for Destroying Files. Client confidentiality must be maintained even when destroying very old closed files. One lawyer was shocked to find out that the paper from his closed files had been made into

"TRY TO ESTABLISH A SIMPLE, LOGICAL SYSTEM THAT CAN BE READILY UNDERSTOOD BY EVERYBODY."

note pads and donated to a local school! There are a number of companies nationwide that deal exclusively with the destruction of confidential files. Use one of them or encourage your firm to invest in a paper shredder.

10 Keep in Mind the Ultimate Goal of Your Filing System. When setting up and maintaining a filing system, you should always keep in mind your primary goal—to help the firm deliver legal services more efficiently and economically. With an organized case file, the attorney can make sure that the case is on track and that deadlines are being met. Clients are happier, and malpractice actions are avoided. Additionally, by getting involved in file organization, your job as a paralegal is made easier. You not only stay well informed on file contents but also don't have to waste time searching for needed files or documents.

sold to clients for a price. A foremost concern of any law firm is therefore to establish a clear policy on fee arrangements and efficient procedures to ensure that each client is billed appropriately for the time and costs associated with serving that client. Efficient billing procedures require, in turn, that attorneys and paralegals keep accurate records of the time that they spend working on a given client's case or other legal matter.

ETHICAL CONCERN

Handling Clients' Questions about Fees

Suppose that you work as a paralegal for a sole practitioner, Marina Tesner, who is just setting up practice. You know that the attorney is soliciting new clients and that she relies on you, when she is out of the office, to make sure that potential clients are not turned away for any reason. One day, while Tesner is out of town, a man named Henry Roth calls the office. He is purchasing a home and wants to consult with an attorney before signing the final papers four days from now. You explain that Ms. Tesner is out of the office but will return in two days and could see him then. Roth says that he would wait for a couple of days if he knew what Tesner would charge for her services. Should you tell him that Ms. Tesner usually bills clients $125 an hour for her services, which is a low billable rate for your community? No, you should not. As discussed in Chapter 3, professional ethical codes prohibit anyone but an attorney from setting legal fees. If you told Roth what he wanted to know, you may be engaging in the unauthorized practice of law.

Fee Arrangements

Normally, fee arrangements are discussed and agreed on at the outset of any attorney-client relationship. Recall from Chapter 3 that the practice of law is usually defined to include the establishment of legal fees, and thus only attorneys make fee arrangements with clients. Basically, there are three forms of fee arrangements: fixed fees, hourly fees, and contingency fees.

Fixed Fees. The client may agree to pay a **fixed fee** for a specified legal service. Certain procedures, such as incorporation and simple divorce filings, are often handled on a fixed-fee basis because the attorney can estimate fairly closely how much time will be involved in completing the work. For example, an attorney may charge $500 for a simple will or $1,000 for an uncontested divorce involving no children or property.

Hourly Fees. With the exception of litigation work done on a contingency-fee basis (discussed below), most law firms charge clients hourly rates for legal services. Hourly rates vary widely from firm to firm. Some litigation firms, for example, can charge extremely high hourly rates ($500 an hour or more) for their services because of their reputation for obtaining favorable settlements or court judgments for their clients. In contrast, an attorney just starting up a practice as a sole practitioner will have to charge a lower, more competitive rate (which may be as low as $75 per hour) to attract clients.

Today's law firms are increasingly billing clients for hourly rates for paralegal services. Because the hourly rate for paralegals is lower than that for attorneys, clients benefit from attorneys' use of paralegal services. Clients normally appreciate the flexibility of being able to contact paralegals, knowing that they will be charged less than the hourly rate for attorneys. At the initial client interview, the attorney usually explains to the client the kinds of work that will be undertaken by paralegals and the lower rates that will be charged for their services. The estimated 1995 average billable rate for paralegals is $77.[1]

Note that although your services might be billed to the client at a certain rate, say $75, that does not mean that the firm will actually pay you $75 an hour as wages. The billable rate for paralegal services, as for attorney services, has to take into account the firm's expenses for overhead (rent, utilities, employee benefits, supplies, and so on). The estimated 1995 average annual salary for paralegals who work for private law firms is $30,851. If you divide this salary by fifty-two weeks, you will see that paralegals, on average, earn $588.10 per week. If you divide this figure by forty (hours per week), the average hourly wage rate for paralegals is $14.70—substantially lower than the average *billable* hourly rate.

Contingency Fees. A common practice among litigation attorneys, especially those representing plaintiffs in certain types of cases (such as personal-

FIXED FEE
A fee paid to the attorney by his or her client for having rendered a specified legal service, such as the creation of a simple will.

1. Authors' estimate based on the 1993 paralegal compensation survey conducted by *Legal Assistant Today* (see Carol Milano, "Salary Survey Results," *Legal Assistant Today,* May/June 1993, p. 48); the Legal Assistant Management Association's *1994 Compensation Survey;* and Bureau of Labor Statistics, *Monthly Labor Review,* various issues.

injury or negligence cases) is to charge the client on a contingency-fee basis. A **contingency fee** is contingent (dependent) on the outcome of the case. If the plaintiff wins the lawsuit and recovers damages or settles out of court, the attorney will be entitled to a certain percentage of the amount recovered. If the plaintiff loses the lawsuit, the attorney gets nothing—although the client normally will reimburse the attorney for the costs and expenses involved in preparing for trial (costs and expenses are discussed below, in regard to billing procedures).

CONTINGENCY FEE
A legal fee that consists of a specified percentage (such as 30 percent) of the amount the plaintiff recovers in a civil lawsuit. The fee must be paid only if the plaintiff prevails in the lawsuit (recovers damages).

Often, the attorney's contingency fee is one-fourth or one-third of the amount recovered. The agreement may provide for modification of the amount depending on how and when the dispute is settled. For example, an agreement that provides for a contingency fee of 25 percent of the amount recovered for a plaintiff may state that the amount will be reduced to a lower percentage if the case is settled out of court. In this situation, the agreement might provide that if the case is settled before trial, the attorney's fee will be one-tenth of the amount recovered in the settlement.

While some people maintain that the use of contingency fees is ethically questionable (because it may motivate attorneys to resort to aggressive tactics just to win a case), the legal profession deems it ethical because it allows broader access to legal services. Contingency-fee arrangements allow clients who otherwise could not afford legal services to have their claims settled, in or out of court, by competent attorneys.

Note that contingency-fee agreements only apply if an attorney represents the client in a *civil* lawsuit. In a civil case, the plaintiff frequently seeks money damages from the defendant to compensate the plaintiff for harms suffered. If the plaintiff "wins" the case, the attorney's fee will be a percentage of the amount awarded. Criminal cases, in contrast, are brought by the state (through the district attorney, county attorney, or other attorney working for the government)—as you will read in Chapter 12. If the court finds the defendant guilty, the state imposes a penalty (a fine and/or imprisonment) on him or her. If the defendant is deemed innocent in the eyes of the court, no money is awarded to the defendant. In criminal cases, contingency fees are thus not an option.

Retainer Agreements

Whenever a client seeks legal advice from an attorney, fee arrangements are normally discussed at the initial client interview. Most law firms require each client to agree, in a signed writing called a **retainer agreement**, to whatever fee arrangements have been made. (Some states also require, by law, that fee arrangements be stated in writing.) The agreement specifies that the client is *retaining* (hiring) the attorney and/or firm to represent the client in a legal matter and states that the client agrees to the fee arrangements set forth in the agreement. Exhibit 5.4 shows a sample retainer agreement.

RETAINER AGREEMENT
A signed document stating that the attorney or the law firm has been hired by the client to provide certain legal services and that the client agrees to pay for those services in accordance with the terms set forth in the retainer agreement.

Client Trust Accounts

Law firms often require new clients to pay a **retainer**—an initial advance payment to the firm to cover part of the fee and various costs that will be incurred on the client's behalf (such as mileage or other travel expenses,

RETAINER
An advance payment made by a client to a law firm to cover part of the legal fee and/or costs that will need to be incurred on that client's behalf.

phone and fax charges, and so on). Former clients of the firms, if they have paid their bills promptly, may not be required to pay retainer fees.

As mentioned in Chapter 3, every law firm maintains a bank account into which funds advanced to the firm by its clients are deposited. This account is usually referred to as a **trust account** (or *escrow account*).

TRUST ACCOUNT
A bank or escrow account in which one party (the trustee, such as an attorney) holds funds belonging to another person (such as a client); a bank account into which funds advanced to a law firm by a client are deposited.

- **It is extremely important that the funds held in a trust account be used only for expenses relating to the costs of serving that client's needs. Misuse of such accounts constitutes a breach of the firm's duty to its client.**

An attorney's personal use of the funds, for example, can lead to disciplinary action and possible disbarment, as well as criminal penalties. Commingling (mixing together) a client's funds with the firm's funds also constitutes abuse. If you handle a client's trust account, you should be especially careful to document fully your use of the funds to protect yourself and your firm against the serious problems that may arise if there are any discrepancies in the account.

Billing and Timekeeping Procedures

As a general rule, a law firm bills its clients monthly. Each client's bill reflects the amount of time spent on the client's matter by the attorney or other legal personnel. In the context of legal work, client billing serves both a financial function (collecting payment for services rendered) and a communicative function (keeping the client informed of work being done on the client's behalf—which is an ethical obligation of the profession).

Generally, client bills are prepared by a legal secretary or a bookkeeper or, in larger firms, by someone in the accounting department. The bills are based on the fee arrangements and the time slips collected from the firm's attorneys and paralegals. The time slips (discussed below) indicate how many hours are to be charged to each client at what hourly rate.

The *legal fees* billed to clients will be based on the number of billable hours generated for work requiring legal expertise. The *costs* billed to clients will include expenses incurred by the firm (such as court fees, travel expenses, phone and fax charges, express-delivery charges, and copying costs) on the client's behalf. If an attorney is retained on a contingency-fee basis, the client is not billed monthly for legal fees. The client is normally billed monthly for any costs incurred on the client's behalf, however.

Typically, a preliminary draft of the client's bill will be given to the responsible billing partner for that client. The responsible billing partner then reviews and possibly modifies the client's bill. The final draft of the bill is then generated and sent to the client. Exhibit 5.5 illustrates a sample client bill in its final form.

Most law firms today have computerized their billing procedures, using time-and-billing software designed specifically for law-office use. Billing procedures using time-and-billing software will be discussed in detail in Chapter 16, in the context of computer programs used in law offices. Here we look at traditional timekeeping and billing procedures to illustrate the basic principles involved in client billing.

ETHICAL CONCERN
Trust Accounts

Suppose that a legal professional who has access to funds held in trust for clients borrows money from those funds for temporary personal use. Would such borrowing be unethical? Would it be illegal? The answer to both questions is a resounding "Yes!" By law, anyone who takes for personal use any property (including money) that is legally entrusted to his or her care commits a form of theft called embezzlement. It does not matter whether the person who used the funds *intended* to replace them the next day, week, or month. The fact is, a crime has been committed.

EXHIBIT 5.4
A Sample Retainer Agreement

RETAINER AGREEMENT

I, Katherine Baranski, agree to employ Allen P. Gilmore and his law firm, Jeffers, Gilmore & Dunn, as my attorneys to prosecute all claims for damages against Tony Peretto and all other persons or entities that may be liable on account of an automobile accident that caused me to sustain serious injuries. The accident occurred on August 4, 1995, at 7:45 A.M., when Tony Peretto ran a stop sign on Thirty-eighth Street at Mattis Avenue and, as a result, his car collided with mine.

I agree to pay my lawyers a fee that will be one-fourth (25 percent) of any sum recovered in this case, regardless of whether the sum is received through settlement, lawsuit, arbitration, or any other way. The fee will be calculated on the sum recovered, after costs and expenses have been deducted. The fee will be paid when any money is actually received in this case. I agree that Allen P. Gilmore and his law firm have an express attorney's lien on any recovery to ensure that their fee is paid.

I agree to pay all necessary costs and expenses, such as court filing fees, court reporter fees, expert witness fees and expenses, travel expenses, long distance telephone and facsimile costs, and photocopying charges. I understand that these costs and expenses will be billed to me by my attorney on a monthly basis and that I am responsible for paying these costs and expenses, even if no recovery is received.

I agree that this agreement does not cover matters other than those described above. It does not cover an appeal from any judgment entered, any efforts necessary to collect money due because of a judgment entered by a court, or any efforts necessary to obtain other benefits, such as insurance.

I agree to pay a carrying charge amounting to the greater of two dollars ($2.00) or two percent (2%) per month on the average daily balance of bills on my account that are thirty days overdue. If my account is outstanding by more than sixty (60) days, all work by the attorney shall cease until the account is paid in full or a monthly payment plan is agreed on.

This contract is governed by the law of the state of Nita.*

I AGREE TO THE TERMS AND CONDITIONS STATED ABOVE:

Date: 2 / 4 / 96 Katherine Baranski

Katherine Baranski

I agree to represent Katherine Baranski in the matter described above. I will receive no fee unless a recovery is obtained. If a recovery is obtained, I will receive a fee as described above.

I agree to notify Katherine Baranski of all developments in this matter promptly, and I will make no settlement of this matter without her consent.

I AGREE TO THE TERMS AND CONDITIONS STATED ABOVE:

Date: 2 / 4 / 96 Allen P. Gilmore

Allen P. Gilmore
Jeffers, Gilmore & Dunn
553 Fifth Avenue
Suite 101
Nita City, Nita 48801

*A hypothetical state.

DEVELOPING PARALEGAL SKILLS

Creating a Trust Account

Louise Larson is a paralegal who has just begun working for Don Jones. Don is just starting his own law practice as a sole practitioner after many years of working with a medium-sized law firm in which he had nothing to do with the firm's financial management. Don has hired Louise to help him with legal matters, as well as with the practical aspects of running a law office. One of Louise's first assignments is to establish a client trust account.

Don explains that the rules of professional responsibility require that client funds not be commingled with the lawyer's funds. "They must be kept in separate accounts. It's too easy to 'borrow' a client's money when all the money is in the same account."

"What kinds of funds go into the client trust account?" asks Louise. "Attorneys receive money from clients for a variety of reasons," explains Don. "Sometimes, we request an advance from clients to cover costs relating to the client's case. Sometimes we receive checks in settlement of a lawsuit. Generally, any money that we receive from clients in payment for legal services rendered goes into the firm's account. Everything else will go into the client's trust account."

Don instructs Louise to get the necessary forms from the bank to open a client trust account. Louise obtains the forms, and the account is set up. "Now that we have the account, I want you to devise a bookkeeping method for keeping track of the money we receive and the deposits that are made into the client trust account. We also need to keep a record of the payments that are made to the clients," Don says. Louise purchases an appropriate ledger from an office-supply store. The ledger allows her to record each amount received from a client and each payment or disbursement made to a client. Louise also creates a file for the deposit slips, which prove that she deposited the money into the trust account, and a file for the canceled checks, which prove that the client was paid. In addition, she sets up a file for the monthly bank statements on the trust account, which she will have to reconcile monthly. The bookkeeping system appears to have all the features needed to meet the professional requirement that client funds be kept in a separate account to protect Jones from any potential claims that he misused or commingled client funds.

TIME SLIP
A record documenting, for billing purposes, the hours (or fractions of hours) that an attorney or a paralegal worked for each client, the date on which the work was done, and the type of work that was undertaken.

Documenting Time and Expenses. Accurate timekeeping by attorneys and paralegals is crucial because clients cannot be billed for time spent on their behalf unless that time is documented. Attorneys and paralegals normally keep track of the time they spend on each client's work by filling out **time slips**. Each time slip documents in hours and fractions of hours (commonly in tenths or quarters of an hour) the amount of time spent on a particular day on a particular task for a particular client. Exhibit 5.6 on page 176 shows a sample time slip.

When working on a client's matter, an attorney or paralegal usually records on the time slip—in addition to the time spent—his or her initials,

EXHIBIT 5.5
A Sample Client Bill

Jeffers, Gilmore & Dunn
553 Fifth Avenue
Suite 101
Nita City, NI 48801

BILLING DATE: February 28, 1996

Thomas Jones, M.D.
508 Oak Avenue
Nita City, Nita 48802

RE: Medical-Malpractice Action Brought against Dr. Jones, File No. 15789

DATE	SERVICES RENDERED	PROVIDED BY	HOURS SPENT	TOTAL
1/30/96	Initial client consultation	APG (attorney)	1.00	$150.00
1/30/96	Client interview	EML (paralegal)	1.00	74.00
1/30/96	Document preparation	EML (paralegal)	1.00	74.00
2/5/96	Interview: Susanne Mathews (nurse)	EML (paralegal)	1.50	111.00
	TOTAL FOR LEGAL SERVICES			**$409.00**
DATE	EXPENSES			
2/5/96	Hospital charges for a copy of the medical documents			$75.00
	TOTAL FOR EXPENSES			**$75.00**
	TOTAL BILL TO CLIENT			**$484.00**

the date, the client number, and a description of the type of legal services performed. (This description will appear on the client's bill.) Any costs incurred on behalf of clients are entered on **expense slips**. Exhibit 5.7 shows a sample expense slip.

EXPENSE SLIP
A slip of paper on which any expense, or cost, that is incurred on behalf of a client (such as the payment of court fees or long-distance telephone charges) is recorded.

Keep a Personal Time Diary. One of the challenges you will face as a paralegal is keeping track of the number of hours or fractions of hours that you spend on work for various clients. Suppose, for example, that you fill out time slips at the end of each day. You may assume that you will remember accurately how you spent your time. In fact, it is very easy to forget details, such as interruptions due to telephone calls.

EXHIBIT 5.6
A Sample Time Slip

TIME SLIP

Name of timekeeper__________ Client name/number__________
File number__________ Time allocated __________
Hourly rate__________ Billable/nonbillable__________
Date service rendered__________
Brief description of legal service:__________

PERSONAL TIME DIARY
A journal or notebook used by paralegals and attorneys to record and track the hours (or fractions of hours) worked and the tasks completed on behalf of each client.

To ensure that you never have difficulties in accounting accurately for your time, you should keep a **personal time diary**—a journal or notebook in which you note how you spend your time. Have the time diary at hand at all times and make entries in the diary whenever you start and end a particular task for a particular client. You should include in each entry the client's name (or identifying number), a precise description of the task, and the time you spent on the task. If you are interrupted by a phone call, make a note of the minutes you spent on the phone so that those minutes are not charged to the client. Also note in your time diary when you change from one task to another and from one client's work to another client's work.

If you consistently account for your time in a personal time diary, you will find that filling out time slips at the end of the day (or week) presents few problems. Another advantage of keeping a time diary is that if a client ever challenges a bill, you will be able to produce an exact record of the work you performed for the client, when it was performed, and how long it took to complete it.

As an alternative to keeping a time diary, you might keep with you a pad of time slips thorughout the day and record your time as you complete each task. The advantage of having a personal time diary is that you can enter more detail than the time-slip format may allow.

Billable versus Nonbillable Hours. The time recorded on time slips is charged either to a client (billable hours) or to the firm (nonbillable hours). As mentioned in Chapter 4, billable time generally includes the hours or fractions of hours that attorneys and paralegals spend in client-related work that requires legal expertise. For example, the time you spend researching or investigating a client's claim is billable time. So is the time spent in conferences with or about a client, drafting documents on behalf of a client, interviewing clients or witnesses, and traveling (to and from the courthouse to file documents, for example).

Time spent on other tasks, such as administrative work, staff meetings, or performance reviews, is nonbillable time. For example, suppose that you spend thirty minutes photocopying forms for the forms file, time sheets, or a procedures manual for the office. That thirty minutes would not be considered billable time.

EXHIBIT 5.7
A Sample Expense Slip

EXPENSE SLIP

Name____

Client name and file number__________________________

Billable/nonbillable____________

Date of expense________________

Brief description of expense incurred:_________________

____

____

Quantity and rate (if applicable)_____________________

Generally, law firms have a legitimate reason for wanting to maximize their billable hours:

- **The financial well-being of a law firm depends to a great extent on how many billable hours are generated by its employees.**

Nonbillable time ultimately cuts into the firm's profits. Of course, as mentioned earlier, nonbillable time is factored into the hourly rate charged for legal services. But to remain competitive, a law firm cannot charge too high an hourly rate. Therefore, the more billable hours generated by the firm's legal professionals, the more profitable the business will be.

Law firms normally tell their paralegals and associate attorneys how many billable hours they are expected to produce and the consequences of not being able to meet that number. Some firms expect associate attorneys to produce a minimum of 2,200 billable hours per year; other firms require fewer hours or more hours. Depending on the firm, a paralegal may be expected to generate between 1,250 and 2,000 billable hours per year.[2]

Attorneys and paralegals face substantial pressure to produce billable hours for the firm. As a paralegal, you may be subject to this pressure and must learn how to handle it. For example, suppose that your employer expects you to produce 1,800 billable hours per year. Discounting vacation time and holidays (assuming a two-week vacation and ten paid holidays), this equates to 37.5 hours weekly. Assuming that you work forty hours a week, you will have 2.5 hours a week for such nonbillable events as interoffice meetings, performance reviews, coffee breaks, tidying up your desk, reorganizing your work area, or chatting with others in the office. As you can imagine, unless you are willing to work more than eight hours a day, you may have difficulty meeting the billable-hours requirement.

2. According to the 1993 paralegal compensation survey conducted by *Legal Assistant Today,* paralegals were expected to generate, on average, 1,519 billable hours per year. See Carol Milano, "Salary Survey Results," *Legal Assistant Today,* May/June 1993, p. 48. According to the Legal Assistant Management Association's *1994 National Compensation Survey,* the average paralegal's billable hours were approximately 1,500.

HANDLING THE MAIL

As a paralegal, you will probably not be involved in handling incoming and outgoing mail. You should be familiar, though, with how the firm's mail is handled. Many law offices have established specific procedures for handling the mail to reduce the risk of losing or misplacing valuable documents. Typically, the receptionist receives the incoming mail, sorts it, and stamps the first page of each piece of mail with the date the document was received. A policy in many firms is to attach the envelope to the document received. The envelope contains the postmark and thus provides proof, should it be necessary, of the date on which the document was sent.

In addition to mail, law firms receive documents via fax, express-delivery services, and personal couriers. A firm will typically handle these documents in the same manner as incoming mail.

Many firms have a log book in which incoming documents are recorded. The following types of information are usually entered into the log book:

- The date received.
- The attorney or other person to whom the document is addressed.
- The client or legal matter to which the document relates, if any.
- A brief description of the document.

A log book is an invaluable reference, especially if a document is missing and a question arises as to whether it was ever received. After "logging in" incoming documents, the receptionist distributes them, perhaps by placing the documents in separate mailboxes (one for each attorney or employee) near the front desk or perhaps in some other manner. In many law firms, attorneys, paralegals, and others have in-boxes and out-boxes on their desks for incoming and outgoing documents, as well as for interoffice written communications.

If you work for a larger firm, a mail clerk or other person picks up and distributes the outgoing and incoming routinely, perhaps twice a day. Larger firms usually also have "runners" (or "messengers")—clerks or others who deliver documents to or from opposing counsel, courts, or other sources within a specific geographical area. If you work for a small firm, you may do some or all of these tasks.

ETHICAL CONCERN

Billable Hours

Timekeeping requirements present numerous ethical pitfalls for attorneys and paralegals. A problem occurs when you work on behalf of several clients during the same time period. Suppose that you need to go to the county courthouse to file a document for a client's case. While at the courthouse, you have to wait for ten minutes to see the court clerk, so you read through a document for another client. On your way back to the office, you stop by the library to obtain a copy of a case pertaining to yet another client's claim. In all, you have spent two hours, but how do you allocate these 120 minutes accurately to the three clients served? As you can see, part of the ethical problem in regard to billable hours is not intentionally "padding" the client's bill or double billing but devising techniques for allocating time fairly when you work on several cases during the same time period. Whenever you face questions of how to allocate your time, discuss the issue with your office manager or supervising attorney. Law firms often have established policies on how to calculate billable hours, and you need to make sure that you learn about and abide by these policies.

COMMUNICATION SKILLS AND THE LEGAL PROFESSION

The legal profession is essentially a communications profession. Legal representation involves communicating with clients, opposing counsel, third parties (witnesses and others from whom information must be obtained), court personnel, and many others. Legal representation also involves generating, receiving, and safeguarding legal documents relating to clients' cases or legal matters. As a legal professional, you will be directly involved in this communications enterprise. You will frequently be communicating with others in person, on the telephone, or in writing.

Furthermore, each worker in a law firm—whether it be a partner, a legal assistant, or legal secretary—is a member of the legal team whose overall goal is to serve clients' needs efficiently and effectively. Maximum efficiency and effectiveness can only be attained through cooperative work efforts, which in turn depend on the ability of team members to communicate openly and productively with one another.

In the broadest sense, **communication skills** involve all of the skills used in conveying concepts or information to another person. Writing skills are communication skills, as are speaking, reading, and listening skills. This section explains what communication means and how communication skills can be applied to the kinds of situations that you will encounter as a paralegal.

COMMUNICATION SKILLS
All skills that assist in the communication process. Speaking, reading, writing, and listening skills are all communication skills.

The Communication Process

The **communication process** involves the sending and receiving of messages. The term *message* is commonly used to mean a transmission of information only, as in "He left a message for you." As used here, however, the term refers not to the words or other symbols used in communication but rather to the *meaning* of those words and symbols. If the person receiving a message does not understand its meaning, the communication process is incomplete, and no communication has occurred.

COMMUNICATION PROCESS
The process of sending and receiving verbal and nonverbal messages.

Miscommunication and communication failure occur frequently in all walks of life, and the law office is no exception. As a paralegal, you might have difficulty communicating with a certain attorney or other staff member. Your supervising attorney, for example, might not give very clear instructions, and thus you would not be sure what was expected of you. Similarly, you might have difficulty communicating instructions to your secretary or to a co-worker. How can you make sure, in these situations, that communication is actually occurring? One way is to give—or ask for—feedback.

Feedback from the listener (or the person to whom a message is directed) is an essential part of the communication process. Feedback indicates whether a message has been received and understood as intended. When your supervising attorney gives you instructions, for example, you might give feedback in the form of statements summarizing the instructions or questions asking for clarification. You might want to give feedback to the attorney in the form of a memo summarizing the instructions. If you have worked with an attorney for years, you probably face few communication difficulties, and your feedback might consist of merely a nod of the head and an "Okay."

FEEDBACK
A response from the person to whom a message has been sent indicating whether the receiver received and understood the message.

The ultimate feedback to instructions is, of course, the resulting work product. If you are instructed to draft a document containing certain information, the document that you produce will be the final "test" of whether the instructions were communicated effectively.

Effective communication requires skills in both sending messages and receiving messages.

Sending Messages. As a message sender in the communication process, your responsibility is to phrase your intended message in words that will be understood by the listener or reader. For attorneys and paralegals, this often means avoiding the use of legal terminology when communicating with people other than legal professionals.

For example, assume that your supervising attorney asks you to write a rough draft of a letter to a client, which the attorney will then rework and put in final form. The attorney says, "Essentially, explain to the client that his oral contract to buy Green Acres from Jethro Hull is unenforceable under the Statute of Frauds." Unless the client is a lawyer, you would probably avoid the use of the phrase *Statute of Frauds.* Instead, you might say the following: "State law requires contracts for the purchase or sale of land to be in writing. Unfortunately, because your contract with Jethro Hull was made orally, it is not enforceable for this reason." If you do use a legal term or phrase that might not be familiar to the client or other person whom you are addressing, be sure to define the term or phrase.

In the context of legal work, your responsibility as a message sender will also entail accuracy and precision. Many paralegals spend a good part of their time drafting or summarizing legal documents. An inaccurate or ambiguous provision in a legal document could have important legal ramifications. Attorneys are known for their utmost attention to detail when writing legal documents, and they expect their paralegals to exercise the same degree of care. You will read more about the importance of written communications in the legal arena and how to write effectively in Chapter 18.

Receiving Messages. The other half of the communication process—receiving messages—requires good reading and listening skills. When conducting legal research, for example, you will be reading various documents to learn what laws apply to a given client's legal matter. You may need to read the written opinions of judges on previous similar or related issues. Additionally, legal research frequently requires you to decipher the often difficult language of statutes enacted by legislatures or regulations issued by government agencies.

When reading a legal document, you must make sure that you understand their meaning, or the "message" being conveyed by the documents. If you are assigned to do research for a client's case, your supervising attorney may rely on your research results in deciding how to advise the client or in determining what legal strategy to pursue. If you misread or misinterpret the meaning of a particular court case or statute, it could have serious consequences for the client.

As a paralegal, you will also find that good listening skills are essential. You will need to listen carefully to instructions and give appropriate feedback so there is no chance for miscommunication. You may be responsible for interviewing clients and witnesses to obtain information—information that could be crucial to the outcome of a client's case. You will read about specific types of listening and how to listen effectively in Chapter 14, in the context of legal interviewing.

Nonverbal Communication

VERBAL COMMUNICATION
The sending and receiving of messages using spoken or written words.

Sending and receiving messages also may involve a nonverbal dimension. Generally, the use of language to convey messages is referred to as **verbal communication.** Written documents fall into the category of verbal communication; so do the words we say, in person or on the phone, to others. **Nonverbal communication**, in contrast, results from the use of body language (such as gestures), voice tones, and other expressions that do not involve language. Nonverbal messages are often subtle, and sometimes we may even be unaware that we are sending or receiving them. The paralegal who is sensitive to nonverbal as well as verbal messages is in a better position to control the communication process to his or her advantage.

NONVERBAL COMMUNICATION
The sending and receiving of messages without using language. Nonverbal communication includes body language (such as facial gestures) and utterances or sounds that do not consist of words.

Body Language. Using body language to reinforce or complement verbal messages can significantly enhance communication. For example, suppose that you are being introduced to a new legal assistant in the law firm for which you work. You say, "Nice to meet you," and you are genuinely pleased. But your expression is deadpan, you do not offer to shake hands, and you look more or less at the floor as you are saying these words. Now, imagine the same situation, but this time add a smile, a firm handshake, and eye contact to your verbal message. These nonverbal messages reinforce your verbal message and enhance the chances that your verbal communication was interpreted accurately. The meanings commonly attached to some specific gestures and other body movements are summarized in Exhibit 5.8 on the next page.

Tonal Qualities. Tonal qualities can also enhance verbal communication. Voice volume (shouting versus whispering, for example) alters the quality of messages, as do different levels of pitch (highness or lowness of sound). For example, consider how the message conveyed in the following question is changed, depending on which word is stressed:

> "WHY didn't you ask the supervisor?"
> "Why DIDN'T you ask the supervisor?"
> "Why didn't YOU ask the supervisor?"
> "Why didn't you ask the SUPERVISOR?"

Irony and sarcasm are also conveyed by voice tones, usually in conjunction with a smile, sneer, or other facial expression or body movement. For example, assume that an attorney has just given her legal assistant a complex research task. Ten minutes later, the attorney walks by the paralegal's desk and, smiling, asks, "Well, have you finished the research yet?" The paralegal responds, also with a smile, "Oh, sure!" The message in this exchange had little to do with the actual words being spoken.

Personal Appearance. The clothes we wear, the way we wear our hair, and other things relating to personal appearance also send nonverbal messages to others about our personalities and values. Assume, for example, that Jana Johnson, a paralegal, is just starting a new job for a well-known and very respectable law firm. During her interview with the firm, she observed that the attorneys and office staff wore fashionable but conservative clothing, so she does likewise on her first day of work. By dressing "appropriately," she has made a statement: she has indicated her willingness to adapt to the customs and traditions of the firm.

Time. Being late or early to work, to meetings, or to appointments can convey important messages to those concerned. If you consistently arrive at

EXHIBIT 5.8
Nonverbal Cues and Their Effects

Gesture/Action	Message Commonly Attached to Gesture/Action
Maintaining eye contact	Interested, sincere, honest, or (if glaring) hostile and intimidating
Avoiding eye contact, looking away from speaker	Uninterested, suspicious, insincere, dishonest
Leaning away from speaker	Uninterested, showing dislike
Tapping fingers on desk	Uninterested, impatient
Continuing to read or work on task	Uninterested
Sighing, grimacing	Bored, disgusted
Failing to acknowledge greeting or other remark	Inconsiderate, unfriendly
Making agitated hand or arm movements	Worried, distressed
Smiling	Friendly, interested, supportive
Sneering	Sarcastic, disgusted, arrogant
Frowning	Concerned, displeased, concentrating
Raising eyebrows	Surprised, showing disbelief
Shrugging shoulders	Uninterested, uncaring
Glaring	Angry

work fifteen to twenty minutes late, for example, your supervisor may doubt that you are very interested in your job. Your actions indicate a lack of respect for a basic job requirement—punctuality.

Barriers to Communication

Anything that interferes with the communication process can result in miscommunication or communication failure. As a paralegal, you have a vital interest in communicating effectively with others. Becoming aware of the communication barriers discussed below is the first step in overcoming these obstacles to effective communication.

Noise and Distractions. Some listening barriers consist of sound or other activities that are distracting. If you are trying to hear what your supervising attorney is saying while someone nearby noisily opens and closes file drawers, these sounds will distract your attention. Loud radios, ringing phones or faxes, or people walking back and forth in the immediate area may also distract you. Whenever you find that you cannot listen because of these kinds of distractions, find a quiet place to hold your conversation—if you really want to listen effectively. When you interview clients, for example, you

DEVELOPING PARALEGAL SKILLS

Curbing Interruptions

It is 12:30 P.M., and Bob Jacobson, a legal assistant, is sitting in the office with his supervising attorney, Myra Ames. Bob is beginning to read through a new and important statute that has been passed and that will have an impact on a case on which they are working. Just then, the phone rings. It is a client, Mr. Tams, who wants to know when he can pick up the purchase agreement that Myra is preparing for him. She tells him it will be ready by three o'clock that afternoon.

While this conversation is going on, Bob continues in his attempt to read the statute. He tries to concentrate but finds it difficult, and he has to reread the same paragraph over and over. Finally, Myra hangs up the phone. "Sorry for the interruption, Bob," she apologizes. "But I have to take clients' calls. Now, where were we?"

"Look at Section 3," Bob tells her. "I think that is what we were afraid of. Having to comply with those kinds of requirements will be very costly for Mr. Sander's dry-cleaning business." Myra's phone rings again. "Sorry, Bob, I have to get it," says Myra, as she picks up the phone.

"Hello Mr. Sander. Yes, we do have a copy, and Bob and I are looking at it right now. Yes, I saw that provision, and we are concerned, too. We will analyze it for you and send you a letter explaining how it applies to your company. Thank you, too," says Myra, as she hangs up the phone.

The phone interruptions continue until Myra's assistant, Carole, returns from lunch. Myra asks Carole to please hold all calls that aren't urgent until she and Bob have finished their meeting. Finally, Myra and Bob are able to concentrate on reading the statute without interruption. After they've read it, they discuss the impact of the statute on Mr. Sander's dry-cleaning business. Myra asks Bob to draft a letter to Mr. Sander explaining the effect of the statute. "We never could have accomplished this with my phone ringing. It would have taken us all day. Sometimes you have to turn it off!" remarks Myra.

should conduct the interview in a quiet environment, such as a conference room, to prevent interruptions.

Preoccupation. Preoccupation is an obvious barrier to effective listening. If we are preoccupied with other mental tasks, such as planning tomorrow's agenda, it is difficult to devote our full attention to what someone is saying. In the law office, legal professionals are often involved in several tasks at once, and you should not be surprised if, now and then, someone to whom you are talking seems preoccupied. While you cannot control other people's listening behavior, you can control your own. When someone starts talking to you and you realize that you are not listening attentively because you are preoccupied with another matter, take action. Either put the preoccupying matter "on the shelf" for the moment and give the speaker your full attention or let the speaker know that now is not a good time for you to listen.

Selective Listening. Selective listening occurs when the listener hears only what he or she wants to hear. Selective listening often occurs as a result of personal attitudes or biases. For example, in a paternity lawsuit (a lawsuit brought by a mother to establish that the defendant is her child's father and should thus pay child support), a judge who is sympathetic toward the plight of single mothers might unconsciously "screen out" elements of the testimony given on the defendant's behalf.

Expectations. Our expectations can strongly influence the messages we receive from others. For example, assume that a client on whose case you are working calls the firm and asks for your supervising attorney. The attorney is out of the office, so you take the call. The client asks if the pretrial hearing date has been set yet, and you tell him that it has not. The client, frustrated and impatient at the amount of time involved in litigation, says to you, "Well, you tell Mack that I want this matter settled as soon as possible!"

You know that your supervising attorney (Mack) has recommended to the client that it would be to the client's advantage to settle the lawsuit out of court. In view of this context, you assume that the client has just agreed to settle the case. What the client meant to communicate, though, was that he wanted to "get this show on the road." When your supervising attorney returns to the office, you give him the message. He calls the client to discuss the possibility of a settlement. The client is, understandably, baffled. This simple example illustrates how expectations can interfere with the communication process.

Lack of Interest. Inevitably, we are all involved from time to time in conversations that we simply do not find interesting. What do you do when you are totally uninterested in what someone is saying to you? Should you feign interest, just to show respect? The chances are that if you try to seem interested, you will send nonverbal messages (glazed-over eyes, a tapping foot, sighs) that will betray your lack of interest. Assuming that you value your relationship with that person, a better approach would be to pursue one of the following options:

- End the conversation as courteously as possible.
- Steer the conversation to a subject that interests both you and the speaker.
- Make a conscious effort to become actively engaged in the listening process by asking questions that will draw the speaker out and let you get to know him or her better.

Timing and Message Overload. An important factor in the communication process is the timing of the message. Often, a person sending a message has no way of knowing whether the message will be received at a "good" or "bad" time. If you call someone on the phone, for example, the person may have a moment of leisure and may enjoy talking to you at that moment. Alternatively, the person may be in the midst of a personal or a work-related crisis and in no mood to talk.

- **As a courtesy, you should normally ask the person you are calling if this is a good time to speak.**

As a paralegal, you will often receive messages from various sources at times that are inconvenient for you. If you are concentrating on a particular task, your preoccupation with the task will make it difficult to listen attentively to someone at just that moment.

Sometimes, the sheer quantity of messages being received by one person can be overwhelming. Suppose, for example, that you are in the midst of drafting an important document relating to a case that your supervising attorney is handling. Your attorney stops at your desk to give you some instructions relating to another case. At the same time, your phone rings; a witness to an accident wants to know the trial date and wants to know how to prepare for the trial. The fax machine comes to life; the faxed memo contains information that you need to act on within the next few minutes. The office manager signals to you that he is off to lunch. In this and similar situations, the receiver of a message may want to listen attentively but simply cannot, because there are too many messages being received simultaneously.

To overcome communication problems caused by message overload, you should first assess the situation calmly and prioritize the messages. Then take action. Tell the witness to hold the line or that you will call him or her back shortly. Ignore the fax for a moment or two. Give your complete attention to your supervising attorney. If it appears that the attorney's instructions will take more than a minute or so to convey, mention the urgent need to tend to the fax and let him or her help determine what should take priority—the attorney's instructions or the fax memo.

Communication Skills and Conflict Resolution

Conflict is inevitable. We all have our own set of personal needs, goals, and agendas, and it is only natural that at some point, these needs, goals, and agendas will come into conflict with those of others. The law office is not exempt from the human experience, and as you begin your career as a paralegal, you should expect to encounter conflict as a normal element in the legal workplace.

- **One way to reduce or minimize conflict is to focus on issues rather than on personalities. For example, how often do you say "I disagree with you" rather than "I disagree with that idea [opinion, statement, conclusion]"? This may seem like a subtle distinction, but it is a significant one in communication behavior.**

We all have our own opinions. If someone disagrees with our views on an issue, we sometimes take it personally and become defensive of our opinions. Before we know it, an emotional element has entered the picture. Hostile words or attitudes may result, and they can lead to communication failure. Separating issues from personalities helps you to view opinions, including your own, more openly and objectively.

Another way of dealing with conflict is to address the problem openly. Communicating openly with others requires, first of all, the ability to listen effectively so that you can identify others' needs, goals, and perhaps motivations. It also requires the ability to assert your needs and opinions and, at times, your rights as an individual or as a member of the legal team. If you feel uncomfortable with a particular arrangement or sense a conflict between

THE LEGAL TEAM AT WORK
Communication and Teamwork

Increasingly, law firms are recognizing the expertise of paralegals and the value of the teamwork approach to legal representation. Teamwork requires, above all, open communication channels among team members. For example, assume that an attorney, you, and a legal secretary are working as a team on a particular client's case. You will need to communicate clearly, both verbally and in writing, with the attorney about what you have learned concerning the client's case or related developments. You will need to keep informed of the secretary's work relating to the case. As a team player, you will need to rely on the others' judgments and they on yours. If conflicts among you surface, you will need to be able to negotiate your differences for the sake of the client.

Additionally, you will need to communicate effectively with clients. You will have to be able to listen carefully to what a client says, even in casual conversations. Many paralegals have noted that they often learn important facts or information relating to a case during casual phone calls or office chats with clients. Clients frequently need reassurance and support. They also need to be informed about the various steps in a lawsuit or a legal proceeding and be ready for each step. In preparing for a career as a paralegal, you should keep in mind that the more effectively you communicate, the greater your chances for a successful career will be.

your goals and needs and those of others, the wisest course of action may be to assert your concern immediately to prevent the situation from worsening. Suppressing your feelings may result in growing hostility toward those responsible for the arrangement.

ASSERTIVE COMMUNICATION
Stating one's opinions confidently but tactfully and with concern for the thoughts, feelings, and rights of the listener.

Note that being assertive is different from being aggressive. **Assertive communication** occurs when one person takes the initiative and lets others know his or her thoughts and feelings on issues. As a paralegal, you will have to be an assertive communicator. Other members of the legal team will rely on your input, and you will need to be forthcoming with your ideas and conclusions. You cannot play a passive role. At the same time, you do not want to let your communication cross the line between assertiveness and aggressiveness. **Aggressive communication** involves placing your own thoughts and feelings above those of others and being inattentive to others' opinions. Respecting the views of others is essential in any kind of cooperative work arrangement, including working together as a legal team.

AGGRESSIVE COMMUNICATION
Stating one's opinions without concern for the thoughts, feelings, or rights of the listener.

LAW-OFFICE CULTURE AND POLITICS

As a paralegal, you will find that each law firm you work for is unique. Even though two firms may be the same size and have similar organizational structures, they will have different cultures, or "personalities." The culture of a given legal workplace is ultimately determined by the attitudes of the firm's owners (the partners, for example) in regard to the fundamental goals of the firm.

TODAY'S PROFESSIONAL PARALEGAL

Managing Conflict

On Cheryl Hardy's first day at her new job as a legal assistant at Comp-Lease, Inc., a computer leasing corporation, Cheryl is introduced to the department staff by her boss, Dennis Hoyt. Dennis then takes her to meet the legal team. When she meets Jackie, the team secretary, Jackie gives her a frosty "Hello," without a handshake or smile, and then looks down at the desk. Cheryl does not understand why Jackie seems hostile. She has just met Jackie and has not done or said anything to offend her.

After her lunch break, Cheryl is given her first lease package to prepare. The work consists of drafting a lease (rental) agreement and giving it to the secretary to input into the computer and print out the agreement form. Cheryl prepares the draft and gives it to Jackie. Cheryl is very polite and tells Jackie not to rush because the agreement does not have to be sent out for two days. When Cheryl asks Jackie for the lease two days later, it is not done. Jackie tells Cheryl to check with her after lunch to see how it is coming. "Great," thinks Cheryl to herself, as she walks back to her desk. "My first week on the job and I'll be in trouble because of Jackie."

ANALYZING THE PROBLEM

Cheryl knows that she must do something about the situation with Jackie. She decides to talk to a co-worker, Sandy, about the problem. At lunch, Cheryl explains to Sandy that Jackie has resented her from the minute that she walked in the door. "She probably does resent you," agreed Sandy. "You see, Jackie has always wanted to be a paralegal. The company has a policy that you have to have a degree or a certificate, even if you have experience, and so she cannot move into a paralegal position without some education. She has not been able to attend a paralegal training program because of family obligations and the expense involved. I'm sure that she knows that you were a legal secretary and that you worked your way through school. When Dennis told us that he had hired a new paralegal, he made your experience and education quite clear."

"So that is why she reacted the way she did to me," says Cheryl. "Thanks, that clears up the situation a lot." Sandy says, "If you need help in getting your lease out today, just let me know. Our team secretary can probably help out." Cheryl ends up using Sandy's secretary that day and on several other occasions because Jackie always leaves Cheryl's work until last, no matter how early Cheryl gives it to her. "This has got to stop," thinks Cheryl one day. "I wonder how I can win her over."

SOLVING THE PROBLEM

Cheryl has an idea. She invites Jackie to lunch. Jackie talks about her interest in becoming a paralegal, her frustration with the company's policy, and her inability to get a certificate or degree because of her family obligations and the cost of going back to school. Cheryl tells Jackie that she was in a similar situation and that she got a scholarship from her school to pay for most of her education. She tells Jackie that she might be able to get one too. She encourages Jackie by telling her, truthfully, that she is obviously bright enough to be a paralegal. Cheryl gives Jackie the name and phone number of Lois Allison, the director of the program that Cheryl attended. "Why don't you call her and tell her that I referred you? Explain that you are in the same situation that I was in when I started. She can tell you what might be available," suggested Cheryl.

When Cheryl returns to her office from lunch, she calls Lois Allison. She explains Jackie's situation and tells Lois that Jackie might be calling to get information on the program and scholarships. Lois replies that she will be happy to talk to Jackie and to help her if she can.

Later that afternoon, when Cheryl gives Jackie a lease package to prepare, Jackie prepares it right away. She even brings it into Cheryl's office, which she does not have to do. "I just want to thank you for going out of your way for me," says Jackie. "I called Lois Allison, and she wants me to come in and fill out some application forms. She thinks that I might qualify for a scholarship. So I might get to go to school after all."

Cheryl smiles. "I am glad that Lois could help you," she says. She feels happy knowing that she and Jackie are off to a better start in their relationship because she has resolved the conflict between them.

Additionally, you will find that each firm has a political infrastructure that may have little to do with the lines of authority and accountability that are spelled out in the firm's employment manual or other formal policy statement. An up-and-coming younger partner in the firm, for example, may in fact exercise more authority than one of the firm's older partners who is about to retire. There may be rivalry between associate attorneys for promotion to partnership status, and you may be caught in the middle of it. If you are aware (and you may not be) of the rivalry and your position relative to it, you may find yourself tempted to take sides—which could jeopardize your own future with the firm.

Unfortunately, paralegals have little way of knowing about the culture and politics of a given firm until they have worked for the firm a while. Of course, if you know someone who works or has worked for a firm and value that employee's opinion, then you might gain some advance knowledge about the firm's environment from that source. Otherwise, when you start to work for a firm, you will need to learn for yourself about interoffice politics. One way to do this is to listen carefully whenever a co-worker discusses the firm's staff and ask discreet questions to elicit information from co-workers about office politics and unwritten policies. This way, you can both prepare yourself to deal with these issues and protect your own interests. Ultimately, after you've worked for the firm for a time, you will be in a position to judge whether the firm you have chosen is really the "right firm" for you.

KEY TERMS AND CONCEPTS

aggressive communication 186
assertive communication 186
communication process 179
communication skills 179
contingency fee 171
employment policy manual 154
expense slip 175
feedback 179
fixed fee 170
forms file 166
legal administrator 158
legal-assistant manager 158
managing partner 155
nonverbal communication 181
office manager 158
out card 165
partner 155
partnership 154
personal liability 154
personal time diary 176
professional corporation (P.C.) 155
responsible billing partner 162
retainer 171
retainer agreement 171
shareholder 155
sole proprietorship 154
support personnel 158
time slip 174
trust account 172
verbal communication 180

CHAPTER SUMMARY

1. In terms of business organization, a law firm may take the form of a sole proprietorship (in which one individual owns the business), a partnership (in which two or more individuals—called partners—jointly own the business), or a professional corporation (in which two or more individuals—called shareholders—own the business). The sole proprietor is entitled to all the firm's profits, bears the burden of any losses, and is personally liable for the firm's debts or other obligations. Partners share jointly the profits or losses of the firm and are subject to personal liability for all of the firm's debts or other obligations. The owner-shareholders of a professional corporation, like partners, share the firm's profits or losses but, unlike partners, are not liable for the firm's debts or other obligations beyond the amount they invested in the corporation.

2. Law-firm personnel include the owners of the firm (partners, for example); associate attorneys, who are hired as employees and do not have ownership rights in the business; summer associates, or temporary law clerks; paralegals; administrative personnel, who are supervised by the legal administrator or office manager; and support personnel, including receptionists, secretaries, clerks, and others. Paralegals should learn, upon first taking a job in a law firm, the relative status of law-firm personnel. Particularly, they should learn to whom they are accountable and who, in turn, is accountable to them.

3. Confidentiality is a major concern and a fundamental policy of every law firm. A breach of confidentiality by anyone in the law office can subject the firm to extensive legal liability. The requirement of confidentiality lends a unique character to the law-office experience and shapes, to a significant extent, law-office procedures.

4. Other employment policies relate to compensation and employee benefits, performance evaluations, employment termination, and other rules of the workplace, such as office hours. Usually (particularly in larger firms), these policies are spelled out in an employment manual or other writing.

5. Every law firm follows certain procedures in regard to its filing system. In larger firms, these procedures may be written up in a procedural book. In smaller firms, procedures may be more casual and based on habit or tradition. A typical law firm has client files, work-product files and reference materials, forms files, and personnel files. Proper file maintenance is crucial to a smoothly functioning law firm. An efficient filing system helps to ensure that important documents will not be lost or misplaced and will be available when needed. Filing procedures must also maximize client confidentiality and the safekeeping of documents and other evidence.

6. A foremost concern of any law firm is to establish a clear policy on fee arrangements and efficient billing procedures, so that each client is billed appropriately. Types of fee arrangements include fixed fees, hourly fees, and contingency fees. As a rule, clients pay hourly fees and are billed monthly for the time spent by attorneys or other legal personnel on the clients' cases or projects. Clients who are represented on a contingency-fee basis, however, do not pay legal fees until the case or legal matter has been decided or completed. All costs incurred on behalf of clients, including those retained on a contingency-fee basis, normally are billed to the client monthly.

7. Firms require attorneys and paralegals to document how they use their time by filling out and submitting time slips. Because the firm's income depends on the number of billable hours produced by the firm's legal personnel, firms usually require attorneys and paralegals to generate a certain number of billable hours per year. This requirement subjects legal personnel to significant pressure.

8. The legal profession is a communications profession, and good communications skills are essential to legal practice. The communications process involves two events: the sending of a message and the receiving of that message. If a message is couched in language that the receiver cannot understand, the communication process is incomplete, and communication failure results. A knowledge of how to send messages (which requires good writing and speaking skills) is crucial in legal work. Just as important is knowing how to understand messages (which requires good reading and listening skills). Much communication takes place nonverbally, and the paralegal should also be familiar with what messages are conveyed by different types of gestures, expressions, and other actions or utterances.

9. Anything that interferes with the communication process is a barrier to communication. Communication barriers include noises and distractions, preoccupation with other thoughts, selective listening (hearing only those things we want to hear), expectations (hearing what we expect to hear), lack of interest in what the speaker is saying, and message overload (receiving too many messages simultaneously).

10. Communication skills are helpful in managing or reducing conflict. A willingness to focus on issues instead of personalities is one way of reducing or preventing conflict. Open and assertive communication also helps to alleviate conflict.

11. Each law office has its own culture, or personality, which is largely shaped by the attitudes of the firm's owners and the qualities they look for when hiring personnel. Each firm also has a political infrastructure that is not apparent to outsiders. Law-office culture and politics make a great difference in terms of job satisfaction and comfort. Wise paralegals will learn as soon as possible after taking a job, from co-workers or others, about these aspects of the legal workplace.

QUESTIONS FOR REVIEW

1. What are the three basic organizational structures of law firms?

2. What is the difference between an associate and a partner? Who handles the administrative tasks of a law firm? Who supervises the work of paralegals in a law firm?

3. Name some of the topics that might be included in an employment policy manual. How do firms evaluate paralegal performance?

4. Why is maintaining confidentiality so important in law offices? How does the confidentiality requirement affect law-office procedures and practices?

5. What kinds of files do law firms maintain? What procedures are typically followed in regard to client files?

6. How does a law firm arrange its fees with its clients? How do lawyers and legal assistants keep track of their time? What is the difference between billable and nonbillable hours?

7. What procedures are routinely followed for handling the mail?

8. Describe the communication process. What are nonverbal messages, and how do we send them?

9. What are some of the reasons for miscommunication or communication failure?

10. How can communication skills be used to reduce or prevent conflict? What is the difference between assertive and aggressive communication?

ETHICAL QUESTIONS

1. Beth Goldberg, a paralegal with a large litigation firm, is talking to her husband, Steven. Steven has just come home from the high school play with their children. Steven tells her that they sat next to the Bergmans at the play. Mr. Bergman, a local businessperson and a coach for the youth hockey team, had told Steven previously that he wanted to meet Steven's son, Josh, who played on the all-state championship team. When Steven introduced Josh to Mr. Bergman at the play, however, Mr. Bergman was not at all friendly to Josh or, for that matter, to Steven.

Beth responds, "I am not surprised. I am working on a product-liability lawsuit against his company, which appears to have been grossly negligent in the way it designed and manufactured one of the tools it sells. The company will probably have to pay hefty damages to our client, who lost a finger while using the defective tool. I just met with Mr. Bergman yesterday to take care of some pretrial paperwork."

What has Beth done that is ethically improper? What, if anything, can she do to rectify the situation?

2. Sam Martin, an attorney, receives a settlement check for a client's case. It is made out jointly to Sam and his client. Sam signs it and deposits it in his law firm's bank account because he wants to take out his fee before he gives the client his portion of the money. May Sam do this? Why or why not?

3. Tom Baker, a paralegal, has been doing research for a client using WESTLAW (a computerized research service discussed in Chapter 16). Tom's supervising attorney tells him to bill the WESTLAW charges that he just incurred on behalf of one client to another client's account. The client to be billed is a large and prosperous corporation. After he prepares a memo summarizing his WESTLAW research, he is instructed to bill his time in preparing the memo to yet another client number. What should Tom do?

PRACTICE QUESTIONS AND ASSIGNMENTS

1. Obtain a page from the "want ads" in your local newspaper or from another source that advertises for legal professionals. Try to determine from the ads whether the firms advertising openings are organized as sole proprietorships, partnerships, or professional corporations.

2. Identify the type of billing that is being used in each of the following examples:

a. The client is billed $150 per hour for a partner's time, $100 per hour for an associate attorney's time, and $70 per hour for a legal assistant's time.

b. The attorney's fee is one-third of the amount that the attorney recovers for the client, either through a pretrial settlement or through a trial.

c. The client is charged $175 to change the name of the client's business firm.

3. Try an experiment the next time your supervisor or professor gives you an assignment. Try repeating the instructions to the person giving them. See if your interpretation of the instructions matched exactly the intended instructions.

QUESTIONS FOR CRITICAL ANALYSIS

1. Many law firms require their legal assistants to meet a quota of billable hours. Often, legal assistants can only generate the number of billable hours required per week by working more than the number of hours that they are paid to work. This can lead to the temptation to "pad the bill." Can you think of ways to meet the quota without breaching ethical standards?

2. Nonverbal communication can enhance and clarify what is being said verbally. For this reason, face-to-face conversations are normally more effective than other types of communication. In the following situations, should face-to-face communication be preferred to written communication? Why or why not?

a. Interviewing a witness.

b. Notifying a client of a trial date.

c. Solving a problem with a legal secretary.

d. Summarizing research results for an attorney.

ROLE-PLAYING EXERCISES

1. Using the facts from Ethical Question 3 above, role-play the scene between Tom Baker and his supervising attorney, who has just asked him to bill research time on WESTLAW on behalf of one client to another client's account. You should work in pairs. One should assume the role of the legal assistant and the other the role of the attorney. The person playing the part of the attorney should insist that Tom bill the other client's account. The person playing the part of the legal assistant, Tom, should try, tactfully, to refuse. If time allows, reverse roles.

2. Review this chapter's feature entitled *Today's Professional Paralegal.* Role-play the scene when the paralegal (Cheryl) takes the legal secretary (Jackie) to lunch to try to resolve the problem posed by Jackie's resentment of Cheryl. You should work in pairs. One person should assume the role of the paralegal and the other the role of the secretary. The person playing the role of the paralegal should practice using good communication skills to resolve the problem. If time allows, reverse roles.

PROJECTS

1. Locate a copy of the May/June 1993 issue of *Legal Assistant Today.* Read the article entitled "Building a Strong Working Relationship with New Associates" by Cynthia Tokumitsu. Write a one-page review of the article and include your impressions of how you would handle the type of situation described in the article.

2. The next time you encounter a conflict at the office or at home, "listen" carefully for nonverbal cues to determine the real messages being conveyed. Summarize in a brief report the causes of the conflict (both apparent and real), how the conflict was handled, and whether the conflict could have been prevented or alleviated through the effective use of communication skills.

ANNOTATED SELECTED READINGS

BASSETT, JULIE. "Solving the Five Most Common Personnel Problems." *Legal Assistant Today*, July/August 1993. An interesting article that discusses the real-world problems associated with the law office, including burnout, personality conflicts, and the difficulty in balancing deadlines and priorities.

BIKE, REBECCA S. "Strategies for Training Legal Assistants in the Law Firm." *Legal Assistant Today*, January/February 1993. An article that discusses the increased use of in-house training programs for legal assistants and provides tips on how to establish one. According to the article, employers feel that legal assistants who have completed a formal legal-assistant education program are not always fully trained in all of the daily skills needed.

ESTRIN, CHERE B. "Formal Evaluations," in *Paralegal Career Guide.* New York: John Wiley & Sons, 1992. An insightful chapter on how attorneys evaluate paralegals and how paralegals can prepare for performance reviews.

HELOU, PAUL. "The Inside Story: Working with Prominent Attorneys." *Legal Assistant Today*, March/April 1993. An eye-opening article that provides a positive view of working for prominent or famous attorneys. It gives numerous insights into what it is like to work in a law office run by well-known attorneys.

MELLO, JOHN P. "Paralegal Billing Trends." *Legal Assistant Today,* September/October 1993. An article that reviews billing trends for paralegals and indicates that although most law firms set some type of billing goals for paralegals, practices vary widely. The article also explores related issues, including the pressure associated with billable hours, the relationship between billable hours and salary, and padding the bill.

NATIONAL ASSOCIATION OF LEGAL ASSISTANTS, INC., *Manual for Legal Assistants,* 2d ed. St. Paul: West Publishing Co., 1992. A useful work, sometimes referred to as the *NALA Manual.* Chapter 1 discusses communication skills in detail and offers numerous examples and techniques applicable to the law-office environment. Chapter 4 provides helpful, real-world advice on interpersonal relationships in the law office.

PART TWO

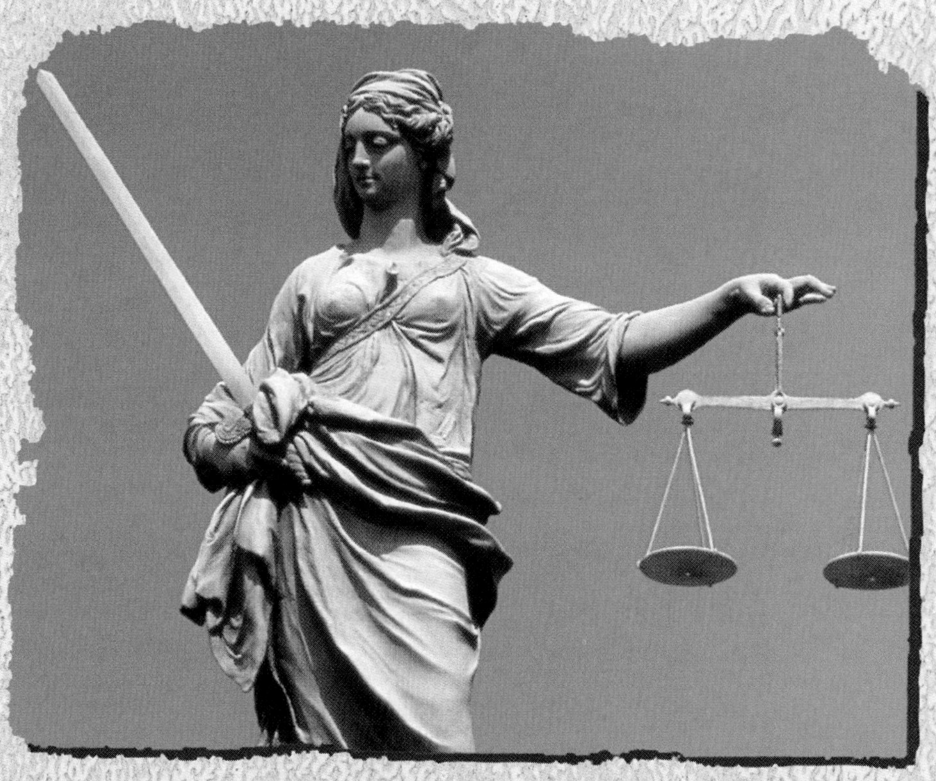

INTRODUCTION TO LAW

6

SOURCES OF AMERICAN LAW

Chapter Objectives

After completing this chapter, you will know:

- How English law influenced the development of the American legal system.
- What the common law tradition is and what types of legal reasoning judges use when deciding court cases.
- The difference between remedies at law and equitable remedies.
- Some of the terms that are commonly found in case law.
- The meaning and relative importance in the American legal system of constitutional law, statutory law, and administrative law.
- How national law and international law differ and why these bodies of law sometimes guide judicial decisions in American courts.

Chapter Outline

What Is Law?

The Common Law Tradition

Early English Courts of Law

The Doctrine of *Stare Decisis*

Stare Decisis and Legal Reasoning

Remedies at Law versus Remedies in Equity

The Common Law Today

The Terminology of Case Law

Common Law and the Paralegal

Constitutional Law

The Federal Constitution

State Constitutions

Constitutional Law and the Paralegal

Statutory Law

Statutory Law and the Common Law

Statutory Law and the Paralegal

Administrative Law

Agency Creation and Function

Administrative Law and the Paralegal

National and International Law

National Law

International Law

International Law and the Paralegal

INTRODUCTION

Like the legal systems of many other countries, the American legal system is based on tradition. For the most part, the colonists who first came to America were governed by English law. As a result, the law of England continued to be the paramount model for American jurists and legislators after the colonists declared their independence from England in 1776. English common law from medieval times onward thus became part of the American legal tradition as well, modified as necessary to suit conditions unique to America.

This chapter opens with a discussion of the nature of law and then examines the common law tradition. The remainder of the chapter focuses on other important sources of American law, including constitutional law, statutory law, and administrative law. You will read how the law of other countries and international law affect judicial decision making in American courts. Another component of the American legal system—the court system—will be examined in Chapter 7.

WHAT IS LAW?

Paralegals spend their entire careers dealing with legal matters. But even the most seasoned paralegal might be hard pressed to give you a useful definition of *law*. What is law? There is no one answer to this question because how law is defined depends on the speaker's personal philosophy about such things as morality, ethics, and truth. As a result, there have been and will continue to be different definitions of *law*. Although the various definitions differ in their particulars, they all are based on the following general observation concerning the nature of **law**:

LAW
A body of rules of conduct with legal force and effect, prescribed by the controlling authority (the government) of a society.

- **Law consists of a body of rules of conduct with legal force and effect, prescribed by the controlling authority (the government) of a society.**

In the United States, these "rules of conduct" are embodied in numerous sources, including the common law, constitutions, statutes, and administrative law.

THE COMMON LAW TRADITION

Because of our colonial heritage, much of American law is based on the English legal system. After the United States declared its independence from England, American jurists continued to be greatly influenced by English law and English legal writers. Indeed, much of American law in such areas as contracts, torts (types of civil wrongs), property law, and criminal law derives in large part from the English legal system.

Early English Courts of Law

In 1066, the Normans conquered England, and William the Conqueror and his successors began the process of unifying the country under their rule.

One of the means they used to this end was the establishment of the king's courts, or *curia regis*. Before the Norman Conquest, disputes had been settled according to the local legal customs and traditions in various regions of the country. The king's courts sought to establish a uniform set of customs for the country as a whole. What evolved in these courts was the beginning of the **common law**—a body of general rules that prescribed social conduct and applied throughout the entire English realm.

COMMON LAW
A body of law developed from custom or judicial decisions in English and U.S. courts and not attributable to a legislature.

Courts developed the common law rules from the principles behind judges' decisions in actual legal controversies. Judges attempted to be consistent. When possible, they based their decisions on the principles suggested by earlier cases. They sought to decide similar cases in a similar way and considered new cases with care because they knew that their decisions would make new law. Each interpretation became part of the law on the subject and served as a legal **precedent**. Later cases that involved similar legal principles or facts could be decided with reference to that precedent. The courts were guided by traditions and legal doctrines that evolved over time.

PRECEDENT
A court decision that furnishes an example or authority for deciding subsequent cases in which identical or similar facts are presented.

In the early years of the common law, there was no single place or publication in which legal opinions could be found. In the late thirteenth and early fourteenth centuries, however, decisions of each year were gathered together and recorded in *Year Books*. These books were informal, containing only notes of cases made by lawyers and law students, and were not organized according to different legal topics. They were not official reports, did not include every case, and sometimes did not include cases until two or three years after the cases had been decided. Nevertheless, the *Year Books* were useful to lawyers and judges. In the sixteenth century, the *Year Books* were discontinued, and other compilations of cases became available.

The Doctrine of *Stare Decisis*

The practice of deciding new cases with reference to former decisions, or precedents, eventually became a cornerstone of the English and American judicial systems. It forms a doctrine called ***stare decisis***[1] ("to stand on decided cases"). Under this doctrine, judges are obligated to follow the precedents established by higher courts within their jurisdictions.

STARE DECISIS
A flexible doctrine of the courts, recognizing the value of following prior decisions (precedents) in cases similar to the one before the court; the courts' practice of being consistent with prior decisions based on similar facts.

The doctrine of *stare decisis* performs many useful functions. It helps the courts to be more efficient because if other courts have carefully reasoned through a similar case, their legal reasoning and opinions can serve as guides. *Stare decisis* also creates consistency. It makes the law more stable and predictable, because if the law on a given subject is well settled, someone bringing a case to court can usually rely on the court to make a decision based on what the law has been.

Departures from Precedent. Sometimes a court will depart from the rule of precedent if it decides that the precedent should no longer be followed. If a court decides that a ruling precedent is simply incorrect or that technological or social changes have rendered the precedent inapplicable, the court

1. Pronounced *ster*-ay dih-*si*-ses.

might rule contrary to the precedent. Cases that overturn precedent often receive a great deal of publicity.

In *Brown v. Board of Education of Topeka*[2] (decided in 1954), for example, the United States Supreme Court expressly overturned precedent when it concluded that separate educational facilities for whites and African Americans, which had been upheld as constitutional in numerous previous cases,[3] were inherently unequal. The Supreme Court's departure from precedent in *Brown* received a tremendous amount of publicity as people began to realize the ramifications of this change in the law. It also spearheaded the civil rights movement, which led to further lawsuits involving claims of racial discrimination.

Cases of First Impression. Sometimes, there is no precedent on which to base a decision. For example, in 1986, a New Jersey court had to decide whether a surrogate-parenting contract should be enforced against the wishes of the surrogate parent (the natural mother).[4] This was the first such case to reach the courts, and there was no precedent in any jurisdiction to which the court could look for guidance. Developments in technology, which often outpace the law, sometimes result in cases for which there is no precedent. For example, suppose that an employer monitors an employees' electronic mail (E-mail), and the employee claims that this is an invasion of privacy. There may be no controlling state or federal law that deals with the employee's complaint.

When deciding cases such as these, called **cases of first impression**, or when there are conflicting precedents, courts may consider a number of factors, including legal principles and policies underlying previous court decisions or existing statutes, fairness, social values and customs, **public policy** (a governmental policy based on widely held societal values), and data and concepts drawn from the social sciences. Which of these sources is chosen or receives the greatest emphasis will depend on the nature of the case being considered and the particular judge hearing the case.

Judges always strive to be free of subjectivity and personal bias in deciding cases. Each judge, however, has his or her own unique personality, set of values or philosophical leanings, and intellectual attributes—all of which necessarily frame the decision-making process.

ETHICAL CONCERN

Legal Research and *Stare Decisis*

One of the challenges faced by legal professionals is keeping up with the ever-changing law. For example, suppose that you are asked to do research on a case involving issues similar to those in a case you researched just three months ago. If you apply your previous research results to the current client's case, you need to verify that your earlier research still applies—that is, that previous case decisions are still "good law." In three months' time, an appeals court might have created a new precedent, and failure to update your research (how to do this is explained in Chapter 17) can lead to serious consequences for the client—and for you and the attorney, if the client decides to sue the attorney for negligence (specifically, for breaching the duty of competence).

CASE OF FIRST IMPRESSION
A case presenting a legal issue that has not yet been addressed by a court in a particular jurisdiction.

PUBLIC POLICY
A governmental policy based on widely held societal values.

LEGAL REASONING
The process of reasoning by which a judge harmonizes his or her decision with previous judicial decisions.

Stare Decisis and Legal Reasoning

The reasoning process by which a judge harmonizes his or her decision with previous judicial decisions is called **legal reasoning**. When applying, overrul-

2. 347 U.S. 483, 74 S.Ct. 686, 98 L.Ed. 873 (1954). (Legal citations are briefly explained later in this chapter and discussed in detail in Chapter 17.)
3. See, for example, *Plessy v. Ferguson,* 163 U.S. 537, 16 S.Ct. 1138, 41 L.Ed. 256 (1896). In *Plessy,* the United States Supreme Court upheld a Louisiana statute providing for separate railway cars for whites and African Americans. The Court held that the statute did not violate the U.S. Constitution, which mandates equal protection under the laws, because the statute provided for equal facilities for African Americans. Lower courts interpreted this decision to apply to other types of facilities as well, and the "separate-but-equal doctrine" prevailed until the *Brown* decision in 1954.
4. *In re Baby M,* 217 N.J.Super. 313, 525 A.2d 1128 (1987).

ing, or creating precedent, judges use many forms of reasoning, including those discussed below.

Deductive Reasoning. Generally, a judge writes an opinion in the form of a **syllogism**—that is, deductive reasoning consisting of a major premise, a minor premise, and a conclusion. For example, a plaintiff (a suing party) comes before the court alleging assault. An **assault** is a wrongful action, or tort, in which one person makes another fearful of immediate physical harm. The plaintiff claims that the defendant (the party who is sued) threatened her while she was sleeping. Although the plaintiff was unaware at the time that she was being threatened, her roommate heard the defendant make the threat and told her about it. The judge might point out that "under the common law, an individual must be *aware* of a threat of danger for the threat to constitute civil assault" (major premise); "the plaintiff in this case was unaware of the threat at the time it occurred" (minor premise); and "therefore, the circumstances do not amount to a civil assault" (conclusion).

SYLLOGISM
A form of deductive reasoning consisting of a major premise, a minor premise, and a conclusion.

ASSAULT
Any word or action intended to make another person fearful of immediate physical harm; a reasonably believable threat.

Linear Reasoning. A second important form of commonly employed legal reasoning is more linear in nature. This kind of reasoning might be thought of as a knotted rope, with each knot tying together separate pieces of rope to form a tight length. As a whole, the rope represents a logical, linear progression of thought connecting various points, and the last knot represents the conclusion.

For example, imagine that a tenant in an apartment building sues the landlord for damages for an injury resulting from an allegedly dimly lit stairway. The landlord, who was on the premises the evening the injury occurred, testifies that none of the other nine tenants who used the stairway that night complained about the lights. The court concludes that the tenant is not entitled to compensation on the basis of the stairway's lighting. The reasoning might progress as follows:

1. The landlord testifies that none of the tenants who used the stairs on the evening in question complained about the lights.
2. The fact that none of the tenants complained is the same as if they had said the lighting was sufficient.
3. That there were no complaints does *not* prove that the lighting was sufficient but supports the conclusion that the landlord had no reason to believe that it was not.
4. The landlord's belief was reasonable, because no one complained.
5. Therefore, the landlord acted reasonably and was not negligent in providing adequate lighting.

Reasoning by Analogy. Another important form of reasoning that judges use in deciding cases is reasoning by analogy. To reason by **analogy** is to compare the facts in the case at hand to the facts in other cases and, to the extent that the *patterns* are similar, apply the same rule to the case at hand. To the extent that the facts are unique, or "distinguishable," different rules may apply.

ANALOGY
In logical reasoning, an assumption that if two things are similar in some respects, they will be similar in other respects also. Often used in legal reasoning to infer the appropriate application of legal principles in a case being decided by referring to previous cases involving different facts but considered to come within the policy underlying the rule.

For example, in a previously decided case, a woman dining at a restaurant choked on a chicken bone and died. Her husband sued the restaurant, claiming that it had a duty to its patrons to ensure that its employees were skilled in the Heimlich maneuver, a medical technique used to assist a person who is choking. The judge in that case held that the restaurant had no such duty to its patrons because to impose such a duty would unduly burden the restaurant owner.

Now assume that a judge is hearing a case in which a patron at a restaurant had a heart attack while dining and died. The patron's wife sued the restaurant, claiming that it had a duty to ensure that its employees were skilled in cardiopulmonary resuscitation (CPR), a medical technique used to assist heart-attack victims. The judge hearing the current case analogizes the facts of the current case to those of the earlier case and concludes that the restaurant had no duty to require that its employees be skilled in CPR.

There Is No One "Right" Answer. Rarely does a case present the situation of a "good" person suing a "bad" person, and rarely is there a single correct answer to a legal question. Good arguments can often be made to support either side of a legal controversy. In most cases, both parties have acted in good faith in some measure or have acted in bad faith to some degree. Also, even though judges must *apply* (not create) the law, legal rules tend to be expressed in general terms. The law is not an exact science, and judges have some flexibility in interpreting and applying the law. Judges can sometimes be very creative in their legal reasoning in the interests of preventing injustice.

Remedies at Law versus Remedies in Equity

In the early English king's courts, the kinds of remedies that the courts could grant were severely restricted. If one person wronged another in some way, the king's court could award as compensation only land, items of value, or money. The courts that awarded these things became known as **courts of law**, and the three remedies awarded by these courts—land, items of value, and money—became known as **remedies at law**.

Even though this system helped to standardize the ways in which disputes were settled, those parties who wanted a remedy other than economic compensation could not be helped. Because the courts of law could not grant noneconomic remedies, many disappointed litigants became very frustrated with the court system. Some of the more persistent parties petitioned the king for relief. Most of these petitions were decided by an adviser to the king, called a **chancellor**. The chancellor, who was also the head of the Church of England, was said to be the "keeper of the king's conscience." When the chancellor thought that the claim was a fair one for which there was no adequate remedy at law, he would fashion new and unique remedies, called **remedies in equity**, to resolve the case. In this way, a new body of rules and remedies came into being and eventually led to the establishment of formal courts of chancery, or **courts of equity**.

Equity is that branch of law, founded on what might be described as notions of justice and fair dealing, that seeks to supply a remedy when there is no adequate remedy available at law. Once the courts of equity were established, plaintiffs could pursue their claims in either courts of law (if they sought money damages) or courts of equity (if they sought equitable remedies). Plaintiffs had to specify whether they were bringing an "action at law"

COURT OF LAW
A court in which the only remedies that could be granted were things of value, such as money damages. In the early English King's Court, courts of law were distinct from courts of equity.

REMEDY AT LAW
A remedy available in a court of law. Money damages are awarded as a remedy at law.

CHANCELLOR
An advisor to the king in medieval England. Individuals petitioned the king for relief when they could not obtain an adequate remedy in a court of law, and these petitions were decided by the chancellor.

REMEDY IN EQUITY
A remedy allowed by courts in situations where remedies at law are not appropriate. Remedies in equity are based on settled rules of fairness, justice, and honesty.

COURT OF EQUITY
A court that decides controversies and administers justice according to the rules, principles, and precedents of equity.

or an "action in equity," and they chose their courts accordingly. Only one remedy could be granted for a particular wrong.

Equitable Principles and Maxims. Courts of equity often supplemented the common law by making decisions based on considerations of justice and fairness. Today, the same court can award both legal and equitable remedies so plaintiffs may request both equitable and legal relief in the same case. Yet judges continue to be guided by so-called **equitable principles and maxims** when deciding whether to grant equitable remedies. Maxims are propositions or general statements of rules of law that courts often use in arriving at a decision. Some of the more influential maxims of equity are listed in Exhibit 6.1.

EQUITABLE PRINCIPLES AND MAXIMS
Propositions or general statements of rules of law that are frequently involved in equity jurisdiction.

The last maxim listed in the exhibit ("Equity aids the vigilant, not those who slumber on their rights") has become known as the equitable doctrine of **laches**. The doctrine of laches encourages people to bring lawsuits while the evidence is still fresh. What constitutes a reasonable time, of course, varies depending on the circumstances of the case. The time period for pursuing a particular claim against another party is now usually fixed by a statute of limitations, as discussed in Chapter 3. After the time allowed under the statute of limitations has expired, further action on that claim is barred.

LACHES
The equitable doctrine that bars a party's right to legal action if the party has neglected for an unreasonable length of time to act upon his or her rights.

For torts, or civil wrongs, the statute of limitations varies from state to state. It may be two years, three years, or even longer for certain types of wrongs. The statute of limitations for contracts involving the sale of goods is normally four years. In regard to criminal actions, the duration of the statute of limitations is often directly related to the seriousness of the offense. The statute of limitations for petty theft (the theft of an item of insignificant value), for example, may be a year while the statute of limitations for armed robbery might be twenty years. (For certain crimes, such as treason and first-degree murder, there is no statute of limitations.)

Equitable Remedies. A number of equitable remedies are available. As mentioned above, equitable remedies are normally granted only if the court concludes that the remedy at law (money damages) is inadequate. Three

EXHIBIT 6.1
Equitable Principles and Maxims

EQUITABLE PRINCIPLES AND MAXIMS:

- Whoever seeks equity must do equity. (Anyone who wishes to be treated fairly must treat others fairly.)
- One who seeks the aid of an equity court must come to the court with clean hands. (The plaintiffs must have acted fairly and honestly.)
- Equity will not suffer a right to exist without a remedy. (Equitable relief will be awarded when there is a right to relief and there is no adequate legal remedy.)
- Equity regards substance rather than form. (Equity is more concerned with fairness and justice than with legal technicalities.)
- Equity aids the vigilant, not those who slumber on their rights. (Individuals who fail to assert their legal rights until after a reasonable period of time has passed will not be helped.)

equitable remedies—specific performance, rescission, and injunction—are briefly discussed here.

SPECIFIC PERFORMANCE
An equitable remedy requiring exactly the performance that was specified in a contract; usually granted only when money damages would be an inadequate remedy and the subject matter of the contract is unique (for example, real property).

Specific Performance. A judge's decree of **specific performance** is an order to perform what was promised. This remedy was, and still is, only available when the dispute before the court involves a contractual transaction involving something unique and money damages are inadequate. Contracts for the sale of goods that are readily available on the market rarely qualify for specific performance. Money damages ordinarily are adequate in such situations because substantially identical goods can be bought or sold in the market.

If the goods are unique, however, a court of equity may decree specific performance. For example, paintings, sculptures, and rare books and coins are so unique that money damages will not enable a buyer to obtain substantially identical substitutes in the market. The same principle applies to contracts relating to sales of land or interests in land, because each parcel of land is unique.

RESCISSION
A remedy whereby a contract is terminated and the parties are returned to the positions they occupied before the contract was made.

Rescission. In certain situations, if the legal remedy of money damages is unavailable or inadequate, the equitable remedy of rescission may be given. **Rescission**[5] is an action to undo a contract—to return the parties to the positions they occupied prior to the contract. If a customer agrees to purchase a vacuum cleaner because the seller misrepresents its quality, for example, the buyer might want merely to rescind, or cancel, the agreement if he or she discovers the fraud before any money changes hands. If the money has already changed hands, rescission would also involve restitution—returning to each party any money or other items of value that had been exchanged by the parties.

INJUNCTION
A court decree ordering a person to do or refrain from doing a certain act or activity.

Injunction. An **injunction** is a court order directing the defendant to do or to refrain from doing a particular act. For example, an injunction may be obtained to stop a neighbor from burning trash in his or her yard or to prevent an estranged husband from coming near his wife. Persons who violate injunctions are typically held in *contempt of court* (discussed in Chapter 3) and punished with a jail sentence or a fine.

The Merging of Law and Equity. During the nineteenth century, most states adopted rules of procedure that combined courts of law and equity—although some states, such as Arkansas, still retain the distinction. Today, a plaintiff, or a petitioner in equity (the person bringing the action), may request both legal and equitable remedies in the same action, and the trial court judge may decide whether to grant either or both forms of relief.

Despite the merging of the courts, remnants of the procedures used when law and equity courts were separate still exist. Courts still distinguish between remedies at law and equitable remedies, and differences in procedure sometimes also depend on whether the civil lawsuit involves an action in equity or an action at law. For example, in actions at law, a party has the

5. Pronounced reh-*sih*-zhen.

DEVELOPING PARALEGAL SKILLS

A Case for Specific Performance

Louise Lassen is a wealthy heiress. She collects art in various forms, such as sculptures, paintings, and photography, because she enjoys art. She displays her collection throughout her home, which has become known as something of a gallery. She is so wealthy that she no longer collects art for investment purposes; she does not need the money.

A CONTRACT IS FORMED

Louise attends an auction at Sotheby's in New York. She purchases a one-of-a-kind painting, for which she pays $1.5 million. The painting is among an art collection currently on a nationwide tour, and one of the conditions of the purchase contract, or agreement, is that the tour must be completed before Louise may take possession of the painting. The tour is expected to be completed in six months.

Louise is thrilled about the purchase, and when she returns home, she contacts her architect and interior decorator. She asks them to come to her home to design a room in which to display the painting. They design a garden room around the theme of the painting, and construction begins.

THE CONTRACT IS BREACHED

Six months pass, and Louise has heard nothing regarding the arrangements for the delivery of the painting. She contacts Sotheby's. Sotheby's gets in touch with the seller. It appears that the seller has decided that he no longer needs to sell the painting because he raised so much money when it was on tour. Sotheby's conveys this information to Louise. Louise contacts the law firm of Murdoch & Larson. One of the attorneys, Jan Murdoch, and her legal assistant, Bob Humboldt, meet with Louise. Louise wants to have the painting that she bought; she wants the contract to be enforced.

AVAILABLE REMEDIES

The attorney explains that Louise could seek an order of specific performance, by which the judge would order the seller to perform what was promised in the contract—delivery of the painting. As an alternative, Louise could ask for compensatory damages to compensate her for the cost of the painting and of designing and building the new room. Louise decides to file suit. After the meeting, the attorney asks Bob to meet with Louise to collect all of the paperwork documenting the purchase of the painting from Sotheby's and the costs of having the garden room constructed.

Bob collects the documents and later sits down at his word processor to prepare a memo to place in the file. Bob concludes that they have a good case for winning an order for specific performance. The painting is unique, so the first requirement for a remedy of specific performance is met. The second requirement, that any remedy at law must be inadequate, is also met because money damages would not compensate Louise for her loss of the painting. Hopefully, the judge will grant an order of specific performance. If not, Louise could seek compensation in money damages for the cost of building her garden room and other costs incurred in the attempt to acquire the painting.

ETHICAL CONCERN

The Statute of Limitations and the Duty of Competence

The duty of competence requires, among other things, that attorneys and paralegals be aware of the statute of limitations governing a client's legal matter. Assume, for example, that a client of your firm, a restaurant owner, wants to sue a restaurant-supply company for breaking a contract for the sale of dishes. If the attorney asks you to look into the matter, the first thing you should check is your state's statute of limitations covering contracts for the sale of goods. If the time period has already expired, then your attorney will need to advise the client accordingly. If the time period is about to expire, then you and your supervising attorney need to act quickly to make sure that the complaint (the document that initiates a lawsuit) is filed before the time period expires.

right to demand a jury trial, but actions in equity are not decided by juries. (A judge may, however, call in a jury to serve in an advisory capacity.) The procedural differences between an action at law and an action in equity are summarized in Exhibit 6.2, which is applicable to most states.

The Common Law Today

The common law developed in England and still used in the United States consists of the rules of law announced in court decisions. These rules of law include interpretations of constitutional provisions, of statutes enacted by legislatures, and of regulations created by administrative agencies, such as the Environmental Protection Agency. Today, this body of law is referred to variously as the common law, judge-made law, or **case law.** The common law governs all areas not covered by *statutory law,* which (as will be discussed shortly) generally consists of those laws enacted by state legislatures and by the federal Congress.

To summarize and clarify common law rules and principles, the American Law Institute (ALI) drafted and published compilations of the common law called Restatements of the Law. The ALI, which was formed in the 1920s, consists of practicing attorneys, legal scholars, and judges. There are Restatements of the Law in several common law areas, including contracts and torts. The Restatements, which generally summarize the common law rules followed by most states, do not in themselves have the force of law but are an important secondary source of legal analysis and opinion on which judges often rely in making their decisions. You will read more about the Restatements of the Law in Chapter 17, in the context of legal research.

The Terminology of Case Law

Throughout the remainder of this text, you will encounter various terms that have traditionally been used to describe parties to lawsuits, case titles, and the types of decisions that judges author. Although details on how to research case law will be given in Chapter 17, it is worthwhile at this point to explain some of the basic terminology of case law.

CASE LAW
Rules of law announced in court decisions.

Case Titles. The title of a case, which is sometimes referred to as the *style* of the case, indicates the names of the parties to the lawsuit. Note that a case

EXHIBIT 6.2
Procedural Differences between an Action at Law and an Action in Equity

PROCEDURE	ACTION AT LAW	ACTION IN EQUITY
Initiation of lawsuit	By filing a petition	By filing a complaint
Decision	By jury or judge	By judge (no jury)
Result	Judgment	Decree
Remedy	Monetary damages	Injunction, decree of specific performance, or rescission

title, such as *Baranski v. Peretto,* includes only the parties' surnames, not their first names. The *v.* in the case title stands for *versus,* which means "against." In the trial court (the court in which the lawsuit was first brought and tried), Baranski was the plaintiff, so Baranski's name appears first in the case title. If the case is appealed to a higher court for review, however, the appeals court sometimes places the name of the party appealing the decision first, so that the case may be called *Peretto v. Baranski.* Because some appeals courts retain the trial court order of names, it is often impossible to distinguish the plaintiff from the defendant in the title of a reported appeals court decision. You must carefully read the facts of the case to identify the parties. Otherwise, the discussion by the appeals court will be difficult to understand.

Usually, whenever attorneys or paralegals refer to a court decision, they give not only the title of the case but also the case citation. The **citation** indicates in which reports or reporters the case can be found (reports and reporters are volumes in which cases are published, or "reported"). For example, a citation to 251 Kan. 728 following a case title would indicate that the case could be found in volume 251 of the Kansas reports at page 728. You will read in further detail about how to read case citations and locate case law in Chapter 17, in the context of legal research.

CITATION
A citation indicates where a particular constitutional provision, statute, reported case, or article may be found.

The Parties. The **parties** to a lawsuit are the plaintiff, who initiates the lawsuit, and the defendant, against whom the lawsuit is brought. Lawsuits frequently involve multiple parties—that is, more than one plaintiff or defendant. For example, a person who is injured by a defective product might sue both the manufacturer of the product as well as the retailer from whom the product was purchased to obtain compensation for injuries caused by the product. In this situation, the manufacturer and the retailer would be *co-defendants.*

PARTY
A plaintiff or defendant in a lawsuit. Some cases involve multiple parties (more than one plaintiff or defendant).

Judges and Justices. The terms *judge* and *justice* are usually synonymous and represent two designations given to judges in various courts. All members of the United States Supreme Court, for example, are referred to as justices. Justice is also the formal title usually given to judges of appeals courts, although this is not always the case. Justice is commonly abbreviated to J., and justices to JJ. A Supreme Court case might refer to Justice Kennedy as Kennedy, J., or to Chief Justice Rehnquist as Rehnquist, C.J.

In a trial court, a case is heard by one judge. In an appeals court, normally a panel of three or more judges (or justices) sits on the bench. Most decisions reached by appeals courts are explained in written court opinions.

Decisions and Opinions. The **opinion** contains the court's reasons for its decision, the rules of law that apply, and the judgment. There are four different types of opinions. When all judges or justices unanimously agree on an opinion, the opinion is written for the entire court and can be deemed a *unanimous opinion.* When there is not a unanimous opinion, a *majority opinion* is written, outlining the views of the majority of the judges or justices deciding the case. The name of the judge or justice immediately preceding the unanimous or majority opinion indicates the author of the opinion—that is, the judge or justice who wrote the opinion on behalf of the others.

OPINION
A statement by the court expressing the reasons for its decision in a case.

Often, a judge or justice who feels strongly about making or emphasizing a point that was not made or emphasized in the unanimous or majority opinion writes a *concurring opinion,* which appears just following the unanimous or majority opinion. In a concurring opinion, the judge or justice agrees (concurs) with the decision given in the majority opinion but for different reasons. In other than unanimous opinions, a *dissenting opinion* is may also be written by a judge or justice who does not agree with the majority. The dissenting opinion, which follows the concurring opinion, if any, is important because it may form the basis of the arguments used years later in overruling the precedential majority opinion. The names of the judges or justices authoring any concurring or dissenting opinions are also indicated at the beginning of those opinions.

ETHICAL CONCERN

What to Do When Someone Asks You about Remedies

Suppose you learn that Lewis, one of your friends, recently broke his hip when he fell off a new ladder while painting his house. He fell because one of the steps wasn't securely attached and came loose as he was climbing the ladder. He had to pay $1,000 of the medical costs out of pocket. Also, his doctor told him that he probably wouldn't be able to work at his construction job for at least two months and maybe longer. Knowing that you are trained in law, Lewis asks you whether he can obtain compensation for the out-of-pocket medical expenses and for the lost wages. Should you advise him that he could sue the ladder's manufacturer and the owner of the hardware store that sold him the ladder for money damages, a remedy at law? No, you should not. Such a statement could subject you to liability for the unauthorized practice of law. The best thing to do in this situation is simply tell Lewis that because you are a paralegal, you cannot give legal advice, but that he should check with an attorney to see what remedies he might pursue to compensate him for his injuries.

Common Law and the Paralegal

As a paralegal, you will find that a basic understanding of the common law tradition will serve you well whenever you need to research and analyze case law. The doctrine of *stare decisis,* the different types of judicial reasoning, and the distinction between legal and equitable remedies—these concepts are all critical when applied to real-life situations faced by clients.

For example, suppose that a client wants to sue another party for breaching a contract to perform computer consulting services. In this situation, the common law of contracts would apply to the case. (As you will read in Chapter 8, contracts for the sale of *goods* are governed by statutory law in virtually all of the states.) If you were asked to research the case, you would search for previous cases dealing with similar issues to see how those cases were decided. You would want to know of any precedents set by a higher court in your jurisdiction—and, of course, by the United States Supreme Court—on that issue. Even in an area governed by statutory law, such as sales contracts, you will want to find out how the courts have interpreted and applied the relevant state statute or statutory provision.

In addition to lawsuits involving contract law, the common law also applies to *tort law* (the law governing civil wrongs, such as negligence or assault and battery, as opposed to criminal wrongs). As a paralegal, you may be working on behalf of clients bringing or defending against the following types of actions, all of which involve tort law:

- *Personal-injury lawsuits*—actions brought by plaintiffs to obtain compensation for injuries allegedly caused by the wrongful acts of others, either intentionally or through negligence.
- *Malpractice lawsuits*—actions brought by plaintiffs against professionals, such as physicians and attorneys, to obtain compensation for injuries allegedly caused by professional negligence (breach of professional duties).
- *Product-liability lawsuits*—actions brought by plaintiffs to obtain compensation for injuries allegedly caused by defective products.

Numerous other areas, such as property law and employment law, are also still governed to some extent by the common law. Depending on the nature of your job as a paralegal, you may be dealing with many cases that are governed by the common law.

SUBSTANTIVE LAW CONCEPT SUMMARY

The Common Law Tradition

The Nature of the Common Law	The common law tradition originated in medieval England with the creation of the king's courts. Portions of the decisions rendered by these courts were collected into volumes and referred to by judges in rendering subsequent decisions. The practice of deciding new cases with reference to former decisions, or precedents, forms the doctrine of *stare decisis,* which is often referred to as the cornerstone of the common law tradition. The doctrine obligates judges to follow precedents established by higher courts within their jurisdictions.
Legal Reasoning	Legal reasoning is the reasoning process by which judges harmonize their decisions with decisions that have been made previously. Types of legal reasoning include the following: **1.** *Deductive reasoning*—A form of reasoning that involves a major premise (a rule of law), a minor premise (a specific action or event), and a conclusion based on the relationship between the major and minor premises (how the law relates to the action or event). **2.** *Linear reasoning*—A logical, linear progression of thought connecting various points that lead to a reasoned conclusion. **3.** *Reasoning by analogy*—A form of reasoning in which the facts in a present case are compared with those in previously decided cases. To the extent the fact patterns of the present case are similar to those in a previously decided case, the rule of the previous cases will be applied to the present case.
Remedies at Law and Remedies in Equity	In medieval England, two types of courts emerged: courts of law and courts of equity. Courts of law granted remedies at law (such as money damages). Courts of equity arose in response to the need for other types of remedies. Remedies in equity, which are normally only available when the remedy at law (money damages) is inadequate, include the following: **1.** *Specific performance*—A court decree ordering a party to perform a contractual promise. Specific performance may be granted when a contract involves something unique, such as a painting or parcel of land. **2.** *Injunction*—A court order directing someone to do or refrain from doing a particular act. **3.** *Rescission*—An action to undo a contract and return the parties to their precontractual positions; all duties under the contract are abolished.
Case Law Terminology	**1.** *Case title and citation*—A case title consists of the surnames of the parties, such as *Baranski v. Peretto.* The "v." stands for versus. The citation indicates the volume and page number of the reporter in which the case can be found. **2.** *Party*—The plaintiff or the defendant. Some cases involve multiple parties—that is, more than one plaintiff or defendant. **3.** *Judge and justice*—These terms are often used synonymously. The term *justice* is traditionally used to designate judges who sit on the bench of federal appellate courts and the United States Supreme Court. Usage of the terms in state courts varies. **4.** *Opinion*—A document containing the court's reasons for its decision, the rules of law that apply, and the judgment. If the opinion is not unanimous, a majority opinion—reflecting the view of the majority of the judges or justices—will be written. There may also be concurring and dissenting opinions.

CONSTITUTIONAL LAW

In addition to the common law, courts have numerous other sources of law to consider when making their decisions, including constitutional law. The federal government and the states have separate constitutions that set forth the general organization, powers, and limits of their respective governments.

The Federal Constitution

The U.S. Constitution, as amended, is the supreme law of the land. A law in violation of the Constitution (including its amendments), no matter what its source, will be declared unconstitutional if it is challenged. For example, if a state legislature enacts a law that conflicts with the federal Constitution, a person or business firm that is subject to that law may challenge its validity in a court action. If the court agrees with the complaining party that the law is unconstitutional, it will declare the law invalid and refuse to enforce it.

The U.S. Constitution sets forth the powers of the three branches of the federal government and the relationship between the three branches. The need for a written declaration of the rights of individuals eventually caused the first Congress of the United States to submit twelve amendments to the Constitution to the states for approval. Ten of these amendments, commonly known as the **Bill of Rights**, were adopted in 1791 and embody a series of protections for the individual—and in some cases, business entities—against various types of interference by the federal government.[6]

BILL OF RIGHTS
The first ten amendments to the Constitution.

Constitutional Rights. Summarized below are the protections guaranteed by the Bill of Rights. The full text of the Constitution, including its amendments, is presented in Appendix L at the end of this book.

1. The First Amendment guarantees the freedoms of religion, speech, and the press and the rights to assemble peaceably and to petition the government.
2. The Second Amendment guarantees the right to keep and bear arms.
3. The Third Amendment prohibits, in peacetime, the lodging of soldiers in any house without the owner's consent.
4. The Fourth Amendment prohibits unreasonable searches and seizures of persons or property.
5. The Fifth Amendment guarantees the rights to indictment by grand jury and to due process of law, and prohibits compulsory self-incrimination and double jeopardy. (These terms and concepts will be defined in Chapter 12, which deals with criminal law and procedure.) The Fifth Amendment also prohibits the taking of private property for public use without just compensation.
6. The Sixth Amendment guarantees the accused in a criminal case the right to a speedy and public trial by an impartial jury and the right to counsel. The accused has the right to cross-examine witnesses against him or her and to solicit testimony from witnesses in his or her favor.

6. One of these proposed amendments was ratified 203 years later (in 1992) and became the Twenty-seventh Amendment to the Constitution. See Appendix L.

7. The Seventh Amendment guarantees the right to a trial by jury in a civil case involving at least twenty dollars.[7]

8. The Eighth Amendment prohibits excessive bail and fines, as well as cruel and unusual punishment.

9. The Ninth Amendment establishes that the people have rights in addition to those specified in the Constitution.

10. The Tenth Amendment establishes that those powers neither delegated to the federal government nor denied to the states are reserved for the states.

The Courts and Constitutional Law. You should realize that the rights secured by the Bill of Rights are not absolute. The broad principles enunciated in the Constitution are given form and substance by the courts. For example, even though the First Amendment guarantees the freedom of speech, we are not, in fact, free to say anything we want. In interpreting the meaning of the First Amendment's guarantee of free speech, the United States Supreme Court has made it clear that certain types of speech will not be protected. For example, speech that harms the good reputation of another is deemed a tort, or civil wrong. If the speaker is sued, he or she may be ordered by a court to pay damages to the harmed person.

Courts often have to balance the rights and freedoms enunciated in the Bill of Rights against the other rights, such as the right to be free from the harmful actions of others. Ultimately, it is the United States Supreme Court, as the final interpreter of the Constitution, that both gives meaning to our constitutional rights and determines their boundaries.

State Constitutions

Each state also has a constitution that sets forth the general organization, powers, and limits of the state government. The Tenth Amendment to the U.S. Constitution, which defines the powers and limitations of the federal government, reserves all powers not granted to the federal government to the states. Unless they conflict with the U.S. Constitution, state constitutions are supreme within the states' respective borders.

Constitutional Law and the Paralegal

Many paralegals assist attorneys in handling cases that involve constitutional provisions or rights. For example, a corporate client might claim that a regulation issued by a state administrative agency, such as the state department of natural resources, is invalid because it conflicts with a federal law or regulation. (Administrative agencies are discussed later in this chapter.) You may be assigned the task of finding out which regulation takes priority. Many cases arise in which the plaintiff claims that his or her First Amendment rights have been violated. Suppose that a plaintiff's religious beliefs forbid working on a certain day of the week. If he or she is required to work on that day, the plaintiff may claim that the employer's requirement violates the First Amendment, which guarantees the free exercise of religion.

7. Twenty dollars was forty days' pay for the average person when the Bill of Rights was written.

SUBSTANTIVE LAW CONCEPT SUMMARY

Constitutional Law

The Nature of Constitutional Law	Constitutional law is all law that is based on the provisions in the U.S. Constitution and the various state constitutions. The U.S. Constitution is the supreme law of the land. State constitutions are supreme within state borders to the extent that they do not conflict with the U.S. Constitution or a federal law.
The Bill of Rights	The Bill of Rights consists of the first ten amendments to the U.S. Constitution. The amendments embody a series of protections for the individual—and in some cases, business entities—against various types of government actions.
The Courts and Constitutional Law	The rights secured by the Constitution are not absolute. Ultimately, the United States Supreme Court interprets and defines the boundaries of rights guaranteed by the Constitution. In doing so, the Court balances constitutional rights against other rights, such as the right to be protected from the harmful acts of others.

No matter what kind of work you do as a paralegal, you will find that a knowledge of constitutional law will be beneficial. This is because the authority and underlying rationale for the substantive and procedural laws governing many areas of law are ultimately based on the Constitution. For example, a knowledge of constitutional law is helpful to paralegals working in the area of criminal law, because criminal procedures are essentially designed to protect the constitutional rights of accused persons—as you will read in Chapter 12.

STATUTORY LAW

STATUTE
A written law enacted by a legislature under its constitutional lawmaking authority.

STATUTORY LAW
Laws enacted by a legislative body.

ORDINANCE
An order, rule, or law enacted by a municipal or county government to govern a local matter unaddressed by state or federal legislation.

Laws passed by the federal Congress and the various state legislatures are called **statutes**. These statutes make up another source of law, which, as mentioned earlier, is generally referred to as **statutory law**. When a legislature passes a statute, that statute is ultimately included in the federal code of laws or the relevant state code of laws. The California Code, for example, contains the statutory law of the state of California.

Statutory law also includes local ordinances. An **ordinance** is a statute (law, rule, or order) passed by a municipal or county government unit to govern matters not covered by federal or state law. Ordinances commonly have to do with city or county land use (zoning ordinances), building and safety codes, and other matters affecting the local unit. Persons who violate ordinances may be fined or jailed, or both. No state statute or local ordinance may violate the U.S. Constitution or the state constitution.

Today, legislative bodies and administrative agencies assume an ever-increasing share of lawmaking. Much of the work of modern courts consists of interpreting what the rulemakers intended to accomplish when a particular law was drafted and enacted and deciding how the law applies to a specific set of facts.

DEVELOPING PARALEGAL SKILLS

State versus Federal Regulation

Stephanie Wilson works as a paralegal in the legal department of National Pipeline, Inc. National Pipeline's business is transporting natural gas to local utility companies, factories, and other sites throughout the United States. Last month, there was an explosion on one of its pipelines. The pipeline ran under a residential street in a suburb of Minneapolis, Minnesota. The explosion occurred in the middle of the night, set several homes on fire, and resulted in one death.

FEDERAL PREEMPTION

In 1968, the federal government passed the Natural Gas Pipeline Safety Act (NGPSA), which regulates the safety and maintenance of pipelines. The federal act has been effective in reducing the number of injuries and deaths associated with pipeline leaks and explosions. The Minnesota legislature decided, however, that it should further regulate the pipeline industry within its state to increase pipeline safety.

The vice presidents of engineering and operations at National Pipeline have always believed that the NGPSA preempted state law. *Preemption* occurs when the federal government indicates its intention to regulate an area of national concern, such as aviation. A state may not pass a law that regulates a field of law that is preempted by federal law. The vice presidents remember that several years ago, in 1979, another state tried to pass a pipeline safety act, which failed because of federal preemption.

The two vice presidents of engineering and operations meet with Stephanie's supervising attorney, Randall Holman, and ask Randall to research the issue to determine if it would be possible to challenge the proposed state legislation on the ground of federal preemption. Randall is very busy with other matters, so he assigns the research task to Stephanie.

FINDING THE FEDERAL STATUTE AND RELEVANT CASE LAW

Stephanie begins her research in the company's law library. She locates the NGPSA in the federal statutory code. The first section of the statute contains definitions of the terms used in the statute. The next section covers federal safety standards. A subsection states the minimum standards required, factors to be considered, state standards, and reporting requirements. As Stephanie reads it, she notices the following clause:

> No state agency may adopt or continue in force any such standards applicable to interstate transmission facilities. . . .

Great, thinks Stephanie. This applies to us because we *transmit* natural gas *interstate,* or among states. Our pipeline crosses the United States. Now I will see if there are any cases in which the courts have interpreted this statute. She finds a case from a federal appeals court in which the court held that the NGPSA preempted New York state requirements regarding a pipeline project.

Stephanie copies the relevant portions of the statute and the case. She takes them back to her office and prepares a memo summarizing the results of her research and discussing National Pipeline's chances of successfully challenging the proposed Minnesota legislation.

Statutory Law and the Common Law

CODIFY
To collect and organize systematically and logically a body of concepts, principles, decisions, or doctrines.

As mentioned earlier, the common law governs all areas not covered by statutory law. In the early years of this nation, the body of statutory law was relatively small compared to the body of common law principles and doctrines. The body of statutory law has expanded greatly since then, however, and continues to grow. To some extent, this expansion has resulted from the enactment of statutes that essentially **codify** (systematize, or arrange in a logical order) common law doctrines. For example, criminal law was at one time governed extensively by common law. Over time, common law doctrines were codified, expanded on, and enacted in statutory form. Today, criminal law is primarily statutory law.

The expansion of statutory law has also resulted from the need to regulate business and other activities for various purposes. For example, many federal and state statutes have been enacted in an attempt to protect consumers, employees, investors, and other groups from business practices that are potentially harmful to the rights or interests of these groups. Numerous statutes and regulations exist to protect the environment, and a whole body of law, antitrust law, is based on statutes passed to protect the public's interest in a freely competitive society. Another reason why the body of statutory law has expanded is to address the need for uniform laws among the states, such as the laws governing commercial transactions.

Even when legislation has been substituted for common law principles, a court's interpretation and application of a statute may become a precedent that lower courts in the jurisdiction must follow. Furthermore, courts often look to the common law when determining how to interpret a statute, on the theory that the people who drafted the statute intended to codify an existing common law rule. In a sense then, common law and statutory law are never totally separate bodies of law, because the courts must interpret and apply statutory law.

Statutory Law and the Paralegal

As a paralegal, you may often be involved in cases that involve violations of statutory law. If you work for a small law firm, you may become familiar with the statutory law governing a wide spectrum of activities. If you specialize in one area, such as bankruptcy law, you will become very familiar with the federal statutory law governing bankruptcy and bankruptcy procedures. Here are just a few examples of the areas in which you might work that are governed extensively by statutory law:

- *Corporate law*—governed by state statutes.
- *Patent, copyright, and trademark law*—governed by federal statutes.
- *Employment law*—governed to an increasing extent by federal statutes concerning discrimination in employment, workplace safety, labor unions, pension plans, Social Security, and other aspects of employment. Each state also has statutes governing certain areas of employment, such as safety standards in the workplace and employment discrimination.
- *Antitrust law*—governed by federal statutes prohibiting specific types of anticompetitive business practices.

SUBSTANTIVE LAW CONCEPT SUMMARY **Statutory Law**	
The Nature of Statutory Law	Statutory law consists of all laws enacted by the federal Congress, a state legislature, a county, a municipality, or some other governing unit. Laws passed by Congress and state legislatures are called *statutes* and are published in federal or state statutory codes. Laws passed by local governing units (counties or cities) are called *ordinances*.
Statutory Law and the Common Law	The common law governs all areas not covered by statutory law. As the body of statutory law grows to meet different needs, the common law governs fewer areas. Even if an area is governed by a statute, the common law plays an important role, however, because statutes are interpreted and applied by the courts, and their decisions may become precedents that must be followed by lower courts within the jurisdiction.

- *Consumer law*—governed by state and federal statutes protecting consumers against deceptive trade practices (such as misleading advertising), unsafe products, and generally any activities that threaten consumer health and welfare.
- *Wills and probate administration* (relating to the transfer of property on the property owner's death)—governed by state statutes.

You will read about some of these areas of law in later chapters. A paralegal working in an area (or on a case) governed by statutory law needs to know how to both locate and interpret the relevant state or federal statutes. You will learn how to find and analyze statutory law in Chapters 17 and 18.

ADMINISTRATIVE LAW

There is virtually no way that the federal Congress or a state legislature can oversee the actual implementation of all the laws that it enacts. To assist them in their governing responsibilities, legislatures at all levels of government often delegate such tasks to **administrative agencies**, particularly when the issues relate to highly technical areas. By creating and delegating some of its authority to an administrative agency, a legislature may indirectly monitor a particular area in which it has passed legislation without becoming bogged down in the details relating to enforcement—details that are best left to specialists.

ADMINISTRATIVE AGENCY
A federal or state government agency established to perform a specific function. Administrative agencies are authorized by legislative acts to make and enforce rules relating to the purpose for which they were established.

Agency Creation and Function

To create an administrative agency at the federal level, Congress passes **enabling legislation**, which specifies the name, purpose, composition, and powers of the agency being created. The Occupational Safety and Health Act of 1970, for example, provided for the creation of the Occupational Safety and Health Administration to administer and implement the provisions of the act, to issue rules as necessary to protect employees from dangerous

ENABLING LEGISLATION
Statutes enacted by Congress that authorize the creation of an administrative agency and specify the name, composition, and powers of the agency being created.

PARALEGAL PROFILE

Legal Assistant in a General Law Practice

KAREN DUNN works as a legal assistant in a small law firm. She has worked for several law firms in the past, all of them small (the largest had thirteen lawyers). Dunn started her career in law as a legal secretary when she was nineteen years old. After working as a legal secretary for eleven years, she was promoted to the position of legal assistant and eventually passed the Certified Legal Assistant exam. Dunn's responsibilities at her current job include handling various documents associated with the litigation process. She performs these tasks with a minimum of supervision and works extensively with clients, particularly in the area of domestic relations. Dunn has been actively involved in the National Association of Legal Assistants (NALA) and served as NALA's president for two terms, the second term ending in July 1994.

What do you like best about your work?

"The thing that I like best about my job is the variety. The law is challenging and always different. I also enjoy the fact that everything done in a law firm is important and affects somebody's life. I find this exciting and challenging. Even a routine task, such as handling a contract for the sale of real estate, can be extremely important for the buyer and seller."

What is the greatest challenge that you face in your area of work?

"One of the challenges of my job is dealing with clients because something is usually wrong; that is the reason that they are in the office. If I am am drawing up a will, I am dealing with people who find it stressful because they are forced to think about the end of their life. I enjoy gaining their confidence and trust and easing their concerns about the legal process. I find that I can often help them and gain their trust through difficult situations. For example, in one situation I dealt with a very difficult divorce client. I found the client challenging but continually tried to make the process easier for that person. Even though I didn't particularly like the person, I enjoyed getting a note from the client after the case was over in which the client thanked me for my assistance.

"I also find that people tend to confide in legal assistants. They tell the legal assistant things that they wouldn't take the time to tell the lawyer. Sometimes these are things that are very important to the client's case. Perhaps this is because with a lawyer, they feel they are being charged high rates per hour, and they are also intimidated by the fact that they are speaking with a lawyer."

"THE LAW IS CHALLENGING AND ALWAYS DIFFERENT."

What advice do you have for would-be paralegals in your area of work?

"My advice is to prepare well and learn as many skills as you can. For example, don't be afraid of keyboards. Also, I strongly recommend that you be willing to learn everything and anything."

What are some tips for success as a paralegal in your area of work?

"My tips for success as a paralegal include the following: pay attention to detail, know what you like to do, and come to grips with the fact that legal assistants don't make the final decisions. Legal assistants are not the stars. If they are comfortable with this, then they will be comfortable and happy in their career choice. Also, don't be afraid to try new things. For example, ask an attorney to give you a shot at doing an answer or a motion. Don't wait for something to be assigned to you. The more you experiment and learn, the more interesting assignments you will get in the future."

conditions in the workplace, and to enforce the act's provisions and the agency's rules.

There are dozens of federal administrative agencies, each of which has been established to perform specific governing tasks. For example, the federal Environmental Protection Agency coordinates and enforces federal environmental laws. The Food and Drug Administration enforces federal laws relating to the safety of foods and drugs. The Federal Trade Commission issues and enforces rules relating to unfair advertising or sales practices. Each state also has a number of administrative agencies, many of which parallel agencies at the federal level. For example, state environmental laws are implemented by state environmental agencies, such as a state's department of natural resources. The rules, orders, and decisions of administrative agencies at all levels of government constitute what is known as **administrative law**.

ADMINISTRATIVE LAW
A body of law created by administrative agencies—such as the Securities and Exchange Commission and the Federal Trade Commission—in the form of rules, regulations, orders, and decisions in order to carry out their duties and responsibilities.

Administrative Law and the Paralegal

Paralegals frequently deal with administrative agencies. If you work for a law firm that has many corporate clients, you may be involved extensively in researching and analyzing agency regulations and their applicability to certain business activities. If you work for a corporate legal department, you will probably assist the attorneys in the department in a vital task—determining which agency regulations apply to the corporation and whether the corporation is complying with those regulations. If you work for an administrative agency, you may be involved in drafting new rules, in analyzing survey results to see if a new rule is necessary, in mediating disputes between a private party and an agency, in investigations to gather facts about agency compliance, and numerous other tasks. In any law practice, you may be asked to assist clients who are involved in disputes with administrative agencies.

Paralegals who do *pro bono* work (work for free or at a reduced charge) or who work for legal aid societies or legal services corporations often become very familiar with administrative process when helping clients obtain needed benefits, such as Social Security benefits, from state or federal administrative agencies. You may work with local agencies in assisting the homeless obtain medical assistance, for example. As you will read in Chapter 13, some administrative agencies, including the Social Security Administration, allow

SUBSTANTIVE LAW CONCEPT SUMMARY

Administrative Law

The Nature of Administrative Law	Administrative law consists of the rules, orders, and decisions of administrative agencies at all levels of government.
Agency Creation and Function	Federal administrative agencies are created by enabling legislation enacted by the U.S. Congress, which specifies the name, composition, and powers of each agency created. State administrative agencies are created by state legislatures. Administrative agencies administer and enforce legislation and issue rules to implement the goals of specific legislation.

paralegals to represent clients at administrative agency hearings and other procedures.

We list below a few federal government agencies and describe how paralegals may be involved with administrative law and procedures relating to those agencies. You will learn in greater detail about the tasks paralegals perform in the area of administrative law in Chapter 13.

- *Equal Employment Opportunity Commission (EEOC).* If a client wants to pursue a claim against his or her employer for employment discrimination, the client must first contact the EEOC. The EEOC will investigate and try to settle the claim, and only if the problem cannot be resolved by the EEOC will the client be entitled to sue the employer directly. You may be involved in contacting the EEOC and assisting the client in complying with procedures required by the EEOC for handling complaints of employment discrimination.
- *Internal Revenue Service (IRS).* If you work for a corporate law department, you might be asked to assist corporate counsel in handling corporate taxes and related IRS requirements. If you work in a law firm, a corporate client may request legal assistance in settling a dispute with the IRS or in complying with tax laws.
- *Securities and Exchange Commission (SEC).* If you work for a corporation that sells shares of stock in its company to the public, you may be asked to assist in drafting the documents necessary to fulfill registration requirements under federal securities law. If you work for a law firm, you may perform similar tasks for corporate clients. You may also assist in the defense of a client who has been charged with "insider trading" in violation of securities law (which prohibits the purchase or sale of securities, for personal gain, based on knowledge available only to corporate officers or employees and not to the general public).
- *Food and Drug Administration (FDA).* Any firm that places foods or drugs on the market must make sure that those products are safe and properly labeled. If you work for a corporation or on behalf of a corporate client that markets food or drug products, you may be involved in procedures required by the FDA for product testing and labeling or for seeking FDA approval to market a firm's product.

NATIONAL AND INTERNATIONAL LAW

Because business and other activities are becoming increasingly global in scope, numerous cases now brought before American courts relate to issues involving foreign parties or governments. The laws of other nations and international doctrines or agreements may affect the outcome of these cases, and thus those laws, doctrines, and agreements are also sources of law that guide judicial decisions in American courts. Many paralegals, particularly those who work for law firms that service clients operating in foreign countries, may need to become familiar with the legal systems of other nations during the course of their careers. For example, if you work in a firm in Texas, New Mexico, Arizona, or California, you may assist in the representation of Mexican clients. In this situation, you will want to have some familiarity with Mexican law and any international agreements that regulate U.S.–Mexican relations, such as the North American Free Trade Agreement.

National Law

The law of a particular nation is referred to as **national law**. The laws of nations differ from country to country because each country's laws reflect that nation's own unique cultural, historical, economic, and political background. Broadly speaking, however, there are two types of legal systems used by the various countries of the globe. We have already discussed one of these systems—the common law system of England and the United States. Generally, those countries that were once colonies of Great Britain retained their English common law heritage after they achieved their independence. Today, common law systems exist in several countries, including Ireland, Canada, Australia, New Zealand, and India.

NATIONAL LAW
Law that pertains to a particular nation (as opposed to international law).

In contrast to Great Britain and the common law countries, most of the other European nations base their legal systems on Roman civil law, or "code law." The term *civil law,* as used here, refers not to civil as opposed to criminal law but to *codified* law—an ordered grouping of legal principles enacted into law by a legislature or governing body. In a **civil law system**, the primary source of law is a statutory code, and case precedents are not judicially binding, as they normally are in a common law system. This is not to say that precedents are unimportant in a civil law system. On the contrary, judges in such systems commonly refer to previous decisions as sources of legal guidance. The difference is that judges in a civil law system are *not bound* by precedent; in other words, the doctrine of *stare decisis* does not apply.

CIVIL LAW SYSTEM
A system of law derived from that of the Roman Empire and based on a code rather than case law; the predominant system of law in the nations of continental Europe and the nations that were once their colonies.

Today, the civil law system is followed in most of the continental European countries, as well as in the Latin American, African, and Asian countries that were once colonies of the continental European nations. Japan and South Africa also have civil law systems. Ingredients of the civil law system are found in the Islamic courts of predominantly Muslim countries. In the United States, the state of Louisiana, because of its historical ties to France, has in part a civil law system. The legal systems of Puerto Rico, Québec, and Scotland are similarly characterized as having elements of the civil law system.

International Law

Relationships between countries are also regulated by international law. **International law** can be defined as a body of written and unwritten laws observed by independent nations and governing the acts of individuals as well as governments. The key difference between national law and international law is the fact that national law can be enforced by government authorities, whereas international law is enforced primarily for reasons of courtesy or expediency. In essence, international law is the result of centuries-old attempts to reconcile the traditional need of each nation to be the final authority over its own affairs with the desire of nations to benefit economically from trade and harmonious relations with one another. Although no independent nation can be compelled to obey a law external to itself, nations

INTERNATIONAL LAW
The law that governs relations among nations. International customs and treaties are generally considered to be two of the most important sources of international law.

FEATURED GUEST: DANIEL F. HINKEL

Pro Bono for Paralegals

Biographical Note

Daniel F. Hinkel is a graduate of the University of Illinois College of Law and is licensed to practice law in Indiana and Georgia. He is a practicing real-estate attorney with a law firm in Atlanta, Georgia, and an instructor of real estate for the National Center for Paralegal Training, also in Atlanta. Hinkel has written numerous articles on real-estate and construction law. He is the author of *Practical Real Estate Law* and *Essentials of Practical Real Estate Law,* both published by West Publishing Company, and *Georgia Construction Mechanics' and Materialmen's Liens,* which is published by the Harrison Company.

My grandfather's creed for living was "Work hard and be generous to people in need." Long before my grandfather, the Romans had a word for it, *pro bono publico*, roughly translated from the Latin to mean "for the public good." Attorneys have always considered it a professional obligation to volunteer legal services for the poor. Most state bar associations have adopted either voluntary or compulsory *pro bono* participation by their memberships. The rules of professional conduct that govern attorneys in most states include a public-service obligation as one of the ethical requirements of being an attorney. *Pro bono* participation, however, should not be limited to attorneys. A paralegal should consider voluntary *pro bono* participation a necessary part of his or her professional life as well.

LEGAL NEEDS OF THE POOR

The criminal legal needs of the poor are generally satisfied by state and federal constitutional requirements which provide that anyone accused of a crime has a right to counsel. Through a public-defender program or court-appointed attorneys, the legal needs of poor persons accused of crimes are generally met.

One of the major problems of the American justice system is the unmet civil legal needs of the poor. The right to legal counsel in civil cases is less well defined; and it is generally provided by a number of quasi-governmental or voluntary associations that usually depend upon full-time paid staff and volunteers to provide the necessary legal services.

It is estimated that a poor household is faced with from one to six legal problems a year and that most of these problems are not solved. Some of the common and serious civil legal problems faced by the poor relate to housing, securing public benefits (such as Social Security), consumer issues (such as consumer fraud and debt-collection problems), health needs, difficulties with utility companies, family disputes, and discrimination. It is within these problem areas that *pro bono* participants are most greatly needed.

PRO BONO OPPORTUNITIES

Voluntary *pro bono* activities are usually performed within the structure of a nonprofit legal-aid or legal-service organization. Most states have legal service organizations, which have offices in various cities within the state to pro-

can and do voluntarily agree to be governed in certain respects by international law for the purpose of facilitating international trade and commerce and civilized discourse.

Traditional sources of international law are the customs that have been historically observed by nations in their dealings with each other. Other sources include treaties and international organizations and conferences.

FEATURED GUEST, **Continued**

vide services to the poor. In addition, city and county governments may establish neighborhood legal-service centers. Private, nonprofit organizations may also provide specialized legal services to certain groups, such as elderly persons, migrant workers, battered women, and abused children. A list of organizations that welcome and encourage *pro bono* participation can generally be obtained from the state bar association.

PRO BONO WORK CAN MAKE A DIFFERENCE

Donating your time to provide legal services to the poor is the right thing to do, and it can make you feel good about yourself and your profession. A paralegal participating in *pro bono* activities makes a difference in his or her clients' lives. For example, assisting an indigent person in obtaining deserved and needed Social Security benefits or protecting a family from an unlawful eviction from their apartment can be a gratifying work experience. In a small way, paralegals who work with the legal needs of the poor help to resolve some of the pressing social issues of our time, and in many instances *pro bono* work may have a far greater real value than compensated work.

Pro bono participation also provides the paralegal with an opportunity to develop and improve skills in specialty areas. The *pro bono* experience may also offer a paralegal an opportunity to work in areas of the law in which he or she would not otherwise have the opportunity to work.

GETTING STARTED

Many private law firms and corporate legal departments have implemented a *pro bono* policy or program. Generally, these *pro bono* policies or programs state the firm's commitment to *pro bono* work and encourage the firm's attorneys and paralegals to participate in *pro bono* activities. A law firm or corporation with a *pro bono* program will probably have a *pro bono* coordinator who is responsible for managing the *pro bono* efforts of the firm and its employees. This coordinator can help the paralegal match his or her talents and interests with the *pro bono* opportunities available within the community. The assignment of a paralegal to a *pro bono* project should be cleared in advance with the coordinator. Most firms with such programs count time spent on authorized *pro bono* matters as part of the total productive hours required of a paralegal for purposes of performance evaluations and compensation.

"A PARALEGAL SHOULD CONSIDER VOLUNTARY *PRO BONO* PARTICIPATION A NECESSARY PART OF HIS OR HER PROFESSIONAL LIFE."

Paralegals employed with firms that do not have *pro bono* programs should investigate and identify *pro bono* opportunities. Once a *pro bono* opportunity has been identified, the paralegal should discuss this opportunity with his or her supervisor and obtain permission to participate. Hopefully, the firm will consider time spent on the *pro bono* matter the same as other firm time spent in determining performance evaluations and compensation.

Treaties. Treaties and international organizations regulate, to an increasing extent, relationships among nations. A **treaty** is an agreement between two or more nations that creates rights and duties binding on the parties to the treaty, just as a private contract creates rights and duties binding on the parties to the contract. To give effect to a treaty, the supreme power of each nation that is a party to the treaty must ratify it. For example, the U.S.

TREATY
An agreement, or compact, formed between two independent nations.

DEVELOPING PARALEGAL SKILLS

Immigration Practice

Maggie Sufuentes is a paralegal with the law firm of Ramirez & Sanchez in Miami, Florida, which specializes in immigration law. Maggie's parents immigrated to the United States from Cuba, and Maggie was born in this country. Her parents spoke Spanish at home, and Maggie is bilingual.

Maggie plays a crucial role in her firm. Although both of the attorneys with whom she works are Hispanic, their families have been in the United States for several generations, so their Spanish is not as good as Maggie's. They also do not understand as well as Maggie does what kinds of problems face those who newly immigrate from other countries to the United States.

Maggie's job is to meet with new clients and find out what legal problems they have and obtain necessary factual background. Then Maggie arranges for an attorney to join her and the client to discuss the client's specific legal questions. The attorney, after briefly reviewing Maggie's intake sheet and checklist, advises the client on his or her legal options.

MEETING WITH A CLIENT

Today, Maggie meets with Bianca Martinez. Maggie only knows the client's name and that she speaks Spanish. Maggie introduces herself to Bianca in Spanish and explains her role as the legal assistant. Their entire conversation takes place in Spanish.

Maggie learns that Bianca is from Cuba and that she has been staying with some relatives in Miami for one year and now wants to remain in the country. On further questioning, Maggie finds out that Bianca flew here from Havana, Cuba, and that she has a one-year visitor's visa. She was able to obtain the visa because her father is a lawyer in Havana, and he has connections. Bianca is now nineteen years old, attended a university in Havana for one year, and has never worked because she has always been in school. She likes children and would be interested in working with children or caring for children as a nanny—if she could get a work permit.

Maggie also asks Bianca why she has come to the office. Bianca tells her that she wants to immigrate to the United States. She tells Maggie how much better the standard of living is in America and how she wants to enjoy the political freedom that citizens have in this country. Maggie talks to Bianca about her own parents and their experiences in Cuba, during and after Fidel Castro's revolution. They discuss the conditions of life in Cuba, and Bianca feels secure knowing that she and Maggie have so much in common.

ATTORNEY CONSULTATION—ADVISING THE CLIENT

Maggie excuses herself from the interview and returns in a few minutes with attorney Sanchez. He reviews Bianca's background information, and they discuss her options. They decide that the best way for her to stay in the United States is to obtain an immigrant visa under the Cuban Adjustment Act of 1980. Once Bianca becomes a permanent resident of the United States, she may attend a college or university.

Maggie arranges an appointment with Bianca for tomorrow. Bianca will return with her visa, and they will begin work on college applications, an immigrant visa application, and other documents.

SUBSTANTIVE LAW CONCEPT SUMMARY

National and International Law

National Law	National law is the law of a particular nation. Each nation's law is different because it has evolved from different customs and traditions. Most countries have adopted one of the following types of legal systems: **1.** *The common law system*—Great Britain and the United States have a common law system. Generally, countries that were once colonies of Great Britain retained their English common law heritage after achieving independence. Under the common law, case precedents are judicially binding. **2.** *The civil law system*—Many of the continental European countries and nations that were formerly their colonies have civil law systems. Based on Roman codified law, civil law (or code law) is an ordered grouping of legal principles enacted into law by a legislature or governing body. The primary source of law is a statutory code. Although important, case precedents are not judicially binding.
International Law	International law is a body of laws that governs relationships among nations. International laws allow nations to enjoy harmonious relations with each other and to benefit economically from international trade. Sources of international law include international customs and traditions developed over time, treaties among nations, and international organizations and conferences.

Constitution requires approval by two-thirds of the Senate before a treaty executed by the president will be binding on the U.S. government. Bilateral agreements, as the term implies, occur when two nations form an agreement that will govern their commercial exchanges or other relations with one another. Multilateral agreements are formed by several nations. The European Union, for example, which regulates commercial activities among its European member nations, is the result of a multilateral trade agreement. Other multilateral agreements have led to the formation of regional trade associations, such as the North American Free Trade Agreement, which was formed by Canada, Mexico, and the United States

International Organizations and Conferences. International organizations and conferences also play an important role in the international legal arena. International organizations and conferences adopt resolutions, declarations, and other types of standards that often require a particular behavior of nations. The General Assembly of the United Nations, for example, has adopted numerous resolutions and declarations that embody principles of international law and has sponsored conferences that have led to the formation of international agreements. The United States is a member of more than one hundred multilateral and bilateral organizations, including at least twenty through the United Nations.

International Law and the Paralegal

Communications technology, improved transportation facilities, and international organizations and treaties—all have helped to form a global environment of business. What this means for attorneys and paralegals is that an

TODAY'S PROFESSIONAL PARALEGAL

Legal and Paralegal Practice in England

Linda Lowden, a legal assistant with the large New York firm of Stone & Stone, has just received an exciting new assignment. She is going to work in the firm's London, England, office for several months to perform "due-diligence" work for a joint venture involving an American client, USA-Tech, Inc., and a British company, BritTech, Inc. Due-diligence work is the background research that is done on a company's financial records to make sure that these records accurately reflect the true financial situation of the company.

PARALEGALS IN ENGLAND

Linda arrives at Heathrow airport and is greeted by RuthAnne Coddens, a legal executive with whom she will be working. In England, legal assistants are called legal executives. On the drive into London, RuthAnne explains that legal executives have been used for many years in England and are very well accepted. They are required to earn a degree and to obtain work experience prior to accepting employment as legal executives. Once they are employed, they assist attorneys by preparing legal documents, interviewing clients, and representing clients in the inferior (lower) courts. Legal executives work for solicitors' firms.

ATTORNEYS IN ENGLAND

"What is a solicitor's firm?" asks Linda. RuthAnne explains that in England, lawyers practice either as solicitors or as barristers. Solicitors advise clients on legal matters and prepare briefs, contracts, wills, and other legal documents for their clients. Barristers, in contrast, only represent clients in court. They are not allowed to form law partnerships, which is why most legal executives work for solicitors' firms. RuthAnne drops Linda off at the apartment where she will be living for the next several months.

LINDA'S WORK BEGINS

On Monday, RuthAnne picks Linda up for work, and they drive to London offices of Stone & Stone. Linda begins her day with a tour of the offices. She meets the people with whom she will be working. She also talks to Stephen Markham, the attorney for BritTech, on the phone and arranges to meet with him at BritTech's offices the next day. Finally, by the end of the day, she settles into her temporary office and begins to organize a plan for tackling the due-diligence work that she has come to London to perform.

She begins her due-diligence research the next day by going to BritTech and talking to Stephen Markham. She requests that she be given access to BritTech's financial records so that she can review them and, if necessary, make copies to be examined by a certified public accountant. She also needs to verify the number of years that BritTech has been in business, which she can tell from its financial data.

TITLE SEARCHES AND INSURANCE POLICIES

As a result of her preliminary review of the financial records, Linda finds that the company owns all of the real estate on which its manufacturing operations are located. The next step is to perform title searches on the property to be certain that there are no liens on (legal claims to) the property. Linda returns to the office to find out how to go about a title search in London. She completes the title searches, finds nothing unusual, and forwards the results to her supervising attorney in New York.

The next step is to go to BritTech and look at the insurance policies for the business. It is important to verify that they exist and to look at the type of coverage they provide. Linda returns once more to the offices of BritTech and spends many days reviewing and copying the company's insurance policies.

LINDA COMPLETES HER TASK

Linda has now been in London for four months. Her research has gone well. She has one more major project. It is to review court dockets for litigation pending against BritTech. For this project, she needs the assistance of RuthAnne, who is familiar with the courts in London. She can tell Linda which courts would be handling cases in which BritTech would be a defendant and in which BritTech could lose large sums of money if the plaintiffs won. Linda and RuthAnne begin their tour of the courts in London. After two weeks, they find one case that may have significant financial consequences for BritTech, should the company lose the case. They get a copy of the documents relating to the case from the file, and Linda sends them to New York for further analysis of the potential liability. She is now ready to return home.

increasing amount of legal work involves an international dimension. As a paralegal, you may be asked to assist your supervising attorney in many tasks that involve an international dimension, including the following:

- Research the law of a foreign country on a particular issue, such as labor law, to determine whether a corporate client (or your corporate employer) with business operations overseas is complying with the laws of the host country.
- Assist a client who has a manufacturing plant overseas in forming employment policies that are consistent with the national law of the host country and (if U.S. employees work at the plant) with U.S. employment laws.
- Determine whether a client's patented product will be protected under the patent laws of a specific foreign country or whether an international treaty provides for such protection.
- Determine what special contractual provisions should be included in a client's contract for the international sale of goods to protect the client's interest.
- Send communications via mail, express delivery services, telephone, or facsimile (fax) machines to the foreign offices of an American firm or a foreign firm with which an American client has business dealings.

KEY TERMS AND CONCEPTS

administrative agency 213
administrative law 215
analogy 199
assault 199
Bill of Rights 208
case law 204
case of first impression 198
chancellor 200
citation 205
civil law system 217
codify 212
common law 197
court of equity 200
court of law 200
enabling legislation 213
equitable principles and maxims 201
injunction 202
international law 217
laches 201
law 196
legal reasoning 198
national law 217
opinion 205
ordinance 210
party 205
precedent 197
public policy 198
remedies at law 200
remedies in equity 200
rescission 202
specific performance 202
***stare decisis* 197**
statute 210
statutory law 210
syllogism 199
treaty 219

CHAPTER SUMMARY

1. Law has been defined variously over the ages, yet all definitions of law rest on the following assumption about the nature of law: law consists of a body of rules of conduct with legal force and effect, prescribed by the controlling authority (the government) of a society.

2. A major source of American law is the common law, which originated in medieval England with the creation of the king's courts. The common law tradition was established in America during the colonial era and was continued in the United States after the Revolutionary War. A cornerstone of the common law tradition is the doctrine of *stare decisis,* which means "to stand on decided cases." Under this doctrine, judges are expected to abide by the law as established by previous court decisions—although occasionally a court will depart from precedent if the precedent is based on a clearly erroneous application of the law or if the political, economic, or cultural environment has changed so significantly that the precedent is no longer relevant.

3. In attempting to make their decisions consistent with previous case law (or with statutory law), judges engage in a process called legal reasoning. Legal reasoning can take several forms, including the following: deductive reasoning (which involves drawing a conclusion based on the relationship between a major premise and a minor premise); linear reasoning (which involves linking a series of events together in a logical progression, as in progressing from one knot to the next on a knotted rope); and reasoning by analogy (which involves applying legal principles applied in a previous case that is similar to a case being decided).

4. Two parallel court systems emerged in medieval England: courts of law and courts of equity. Courts of law granted remedies at law, which consisted primarily of money damages. Courts of equity granted remedies in equity (equitable remedies), which were sought by plaintiffs for whom remedies at law could not provide adequate relief. Remedies in equity include specific performance (an order to perform the specific terms of a contract), rescission (the cancellation of a contract so that the parties are returned to their precontractual status), and injunction (an order to refrain from engaging in certain conduct).

5. Today, the common law governs all areas that are not covered by statutory law. Because the body of statutory law has expanded greatly in the last century, the scope of activities governed by common law has diminished. Nonetheless, many statutes embody common law concepts, and the courts continue to establish precedents when interpreting particular statutes or ordinances.

6. Another important source of American law is constitutional law—the law established by the U.S. Constitution and the constitutions of the various states. The U.S. Constitution, as amended, is the supreme law of the land. A law in violation of the Constitution or one of its amendments, no matter what its source, will be declared unconstitutional and will not be enforced. A state constitution, so long as it does not conflict with the U.S. Constitution, is the supreme law within the state's borders.

7. Statutory law consists of statutes enacted by the U.S. Congress and state legislatures and ordinances passed by local governing bodies. Statutory law takes precedence over the common law.

8. Administrative law consists of the rules and regulations issued and enforced by administrative agencies at both the state and federal levels. Administrative agencies are created by legislatures to administer and enforce legislation and to issue rules to implement the goals of specific legislation. Examples of federal administrative agencies are the Environmental Protection Agency, the Occupational Safety and Health Administration, and the Food and Drug Administration.

9. Because of the international scope of much of today's business and other dealings, the laws of other nations (national law) and the law governing relationships between nations (international law) also affect the outcome of cases brought in American courts. Many nations—generally, the continental European countries and the nations that were once colonies of those European countries—have civil law systems, in which the primary source of law is a statutory code. Many other nations—including England and the United States, as well as other countries that were formerly colonies of England—have common law systems, in which case precedents play a leading role.

QUESTIONS FOR REVIEW

1. What is law? Why are there so many definitions of law?

2. Where, when, and how did the common law tradition begin?

3. What does *stare decisis* mean? Why is it said that the doctrine of *stare decisis* became the cornerstone of English and American law?

4. What is the difference between courts of law and courts of equity? Why did courts of equity evolve?

5. Name and describe three types of legal reasoning used by judges when deciding court cases.

6. What kinds of remedies could be granted by a court of law? Name three remedies that could be granted by a court of equity.

7. What is constitutional law? If a state constitution conflicts with the U.S. Constitution, which constitution takes priority?

8. What is a statute? How is statutory law created? How does the enactment of statutes affect the common law?

9. What is an administrative agency? How are such agencies created?

10. Explain the difference between national law and international law. What are some important sources of international law?

ETHICAL QUESTIONS

1. Lon Thompson is a paralegal who works for a New York law firm. One of the firm's clients wants to open a chain of restaurants (with bars) in Michigan, and Lon has been asked to research the Michigan statutes to find out what the legal drinking age is in that state. Lon looks in the hardbound volume of the Michigan statutes and sees that the legal drinking age is eighteen. Lon forgets to check the "pocket part"—which is inserted into a "pocket" in the inside back cover of the book. The pocket part contains amendments, indicates if a statute has been repealed, and generally updates the law as described in the volume. Because of this oversight, Lon does not learn that the legal drinking age in Michigan was recently raised to twenty-one. He tells his supervising attorney that the legal drinking age in Michigan is eighteen, and the attorney passes that information on to the client. Has Lon violated any ethical rule? If so, which one? What consequences might the attorney face as a result of Lon's oversight? What consequences might Lon face?

2. John Scott, an attorney, has asked his legal assistant, Nanette Lynch, to do some research. Nanette is to research the state statutes to find out how many persons are required to witness a will. Nanette looks up the relevant state statute and finds it difficult to understand because it is so poorly written. After studying the statute for a while, Nanette decides that two witnesses are required and conveys this information to John. Actually, the statute requires that three persons witness a will or it will not be valid. John, relying on Nanette's conclusion, has two persons witness a client's will the next day. Have John and Nanette violated any ethical rules? Explain.

3. Marilyn Clark works as a paralegal in a small general law practice. After work one day, she receives a telephone call from her Aunt May, who is in distress. Her Aunt May and Uncle Bill went to open their summer cottage and found that beavers had made a dam in the lake, which caused severe flooding on their property and in their basement. Uncle Bill is threatening to take his rifle and put an end to the beavers and their mess. Aunt May, an environmentalist, does not want Uncle Bill to shoot the beavers, so she asks Marilyn if it is illegal to shoot beavers. How should Marilyn answer this question?

PRACTICE QUESTIONS AND ASSIGNMENTS

1. Look at the Constitution in Appendix L of this text. Locate the language in the Bill of Rights that gives U.S. citizens the following rights and protections:

a. The right to freely exercise one's religion.
b. Protection against unreasonable searches and seizures.
c. Protection against self-incrimination.
d. The right to counsel in criminal prosecutions.
e. The right to free speech.

2. Identify the type of law (common law, constitutional law, statutory law, or administrative law) that applies in each of the following scenarios:

a. Jean Gorman strongly disagrees with the U.S. government's decision to declare war on a foreign country. She places an antiwar sign in the window of her home. The city passes an ordinance that bans all such signs.
b. An official of the state department of natural resources learns that the Ferris Widget Company has violated the state's Hazardous Waste Management Act. The official issues a complaint against the company for not properly handling and labeling its toxic waste.
c. Mrs. Sams was walking down a busy street when two teenagers on rollerblades crashed into her because they weren't watching where they were going. As a result of the teenagers' conduct, Mrs. Sams broke her hip, and according to her doctor, she will never walk normally again. She sues the teenagers for damages.
d. Joseph Barnes is arrested and charged with the crime of murder.

QUESTIONS FOR CRITICAL ANALYSIS

1. Courts are able to overturn precedents and thus change the common law, but they normally do not have the same authority to overrule statutory law. Do you think that judges should also be able to overrule statutory law? Explain.

2. The rights guaranteed by the U.S. Constitution would be of little significance if they were not enforced by the government. In view of this fact, is a written constitution really necessary? Would the rights and privileges enjoyed by Americans be any different if we did not have a written constitution?

ROLE-PLAYING EXERCISES

1. Role-play the scenario described in Ethical Question 3, in which paralegal Marilyn Clark's Aunt May is pressuring Marilyn for answers. The student who plays the role of Aunt May should be aggressive and try every tactic possible to get an answer from Marilyn. The student who plays the role of Marilyn should be considerate and respectful of Aunt May but at the same time should avoid giving her aunt any legal advice.

2. Assume that Rosa Jennings has worked as a paralegal for many years. One day, while visiting with one of her neighbors, Lori Dolan, Lori asks her some general questions about American law. Lori wants to know, for example, what the Bill of Rights is and what is meant by the common law tradition. Working in pairs, act out the roles of Rosa Jennings and Lori Dolan. The person playing the role of Rosa, the paralegal, should explain to Lori the sources of American law as described in this chapter and make sure that any legal terms are carefully defined so that Lori can understand them. The person playing the role of Lori should be very inquisitive and ask for details.

PROJECTS

1. Read through the sample court case presented as Exhibit 18.1 in Chapter 18. See if you can identify the type of legal reasoning—deductive, linear, or analogical—used by the judge who authored the opinion.

2. Look in the White Pages of your local telephone directory for listings under the name of your state. Write down the names of three administrative agencies listed there and see if you can determine from their names what areas or activities they regulate. Write down your conclusions.

3. Find out if your state's courts use different procedures for cases involving equity matters than they use for cases that do not. Are there any trial courts in your state that cannot grant equitable remedies?

ANNOTATED SELECTED READINGS

GLANVILLE, RANULF DE. *Treatise on the Laws and Customs of the Realm of England*. Trans. from the Latin by G. D. G. Hall. Oxford: Clarendon Publications, 1965. A treatise written by a twelfth-century English jurist on the practice of the royal court during the reign of Henry II. It describes the documents used at that time to initiate a case and the procedures that were followed once a case was underway.

MILLER, ROGER LEROY, AND GAYLORD A. JENTZ, *Business Law Today: The Essentials: Text and Summarized Cases—Legal, Ethical, Regulatory, and International Environment*. 3d ed. St. Paul: West Publishing Co., 1994. A concise and very readable explanation of the law governing contracts, torts, crimes, and numerous other areas. Actual court cases are presented, in summarized form, to illustrate various points of law.

RAACK, DAVID, W. "A History of Injunctions in England before 1700," *Indiana Law Journal*, Fall 1986. A fascinating review of the history of the remedy of injunction, beginning with its forerunners in Roman law and continuing with its use in the early common law courts. Excellent, easy reading.

FILIPPATOS, PARISIS G. "The Doctrine of *Stare Decisis* and the Protection of Civil Rights and Liberties in the Rehnquist Court." *Boston College Third World Law Journal*, Summer 1991. An examination of the Rehnquist Court's conservatism and its reluctance to follow the doctrine of *stare decisis* in two cases decided by the Court in the early 1990s: *Patterson v. MacLean Credit Union* and *Webster v. Reproductive Health Services.*

MARSHALL, LAWRENCE C. "Let Congress Do It: The Case for an Absolute Rule of Statutory *Stare Decisis.*" *Michigan Law Review*, November 1989. A discussion of the use of *stare decisis* by the United States Supreme Court to justify its decisions, with examples from the Warren and Rehnquist Courts.

7

The Court System and Alternative Dispute Resolution

Chapter Objectives

After completing this chapter, you will know:

- The requirements that must be met before a lawsuit can be brought in a particular court by a particular party.
- The difference between jurisdiction and venue.
- The types of courts that make up a typical state court system and the different functions of trial courts and appellate courts.
- The organization of the federal court system and the relationship between state and federal jurisdiction.
- How cases reach the United States Supreme Court.
- The various ways in which disputes can be resolved outside the court system.

Chapter Outline

INTRODUCTION

As explained in Chapter 6, American law is based on numerous elements—the case decisions and legal principles that form the common law, federal and state constitutions, statutes passed by federal and state legislatures, administrative law, and, to an extent, the laws of other nations and international law. But the laws would be meaningless without the courts to interpret and apply them, and for this reason the court system is a vital component of the American legal system.

Paralegals working in all areas of the law, and particularly litigation paralegals, need to have a basic understanding of the different types of courts that make up the American court system. Even though there are fifty-two court systems—one for each of the fifty states, one for the District of Columbia, and a federal system—similarities abound. Keep in mind that the federal courts are not superior to the state courts. They are simply an independent court system, which derives its authority from Article III, Section 2, of the U.S. Constitution.[1]

In the first part of this chapter, we examine the basic structure of the American court system. Because of the costs, both in time and money, and the potential publicity attending court trials, many individuals and firms today are turning to alternative methods of dispute resolution that allow parties to resolve their disputes outside of court. In some cases, parties are required by the courts to try to resolve their disputes by one of these methods before they can take their cases to court. In the latter part of this chapter, we provide an overview of these alternative methods of dispute resolution and the role that attorneys and paralegals play in facilitating out-of-court dispute settlements.

THE AMERICAN SYSTEM OF JUSTICE

Before a lawsuit can be brought before a court, certain requirements must be met. We first examine these important requirements and some of the basic features of the American system of justice. We then look at the state and federal court systems.

Types of Jurisdiction

JURISDICTION
The authority of a court to hear and decide a specific action.

In Latin, *juris* means "law," and *diction* means "to speak." Thus, "the power to speak the law" is the literal meaning of the term **jurisdiction**. Before any court can hear a case, it must have jurisdiction over the person against whom the suit is brought or over the property involved in the suit. The court must also have jurisdiction over the subject matter.

Jurisdiction over Persons. Generally, a court can exercise personal jurisdiction (*in personam* jurisdiction) over residents of a certain geographical

1. See Appendix L for the full text of the U.S. Constitution.

area. A state trial court, for example, normally has jurisdictional authority over residents of a particular area of the state, such as a county or district. A state's highest court (often called the state supreme court)[2] has jurisdictional authority over all residents within the state.

In some cases, under the authority of a long-arm statute, a court can exercise personal jurisdiction over nonresidents as well. A **long-arm statute** is a state law permitting courts to exercise jurisdiction over nonresident defendants. Before a court can exercise jurisdiction over a nonresident under a long-arm statute, though, it must be demonstrated that the nonresident had sufficient contacts (*minimum contacts*) with the state to justify the jurisdiction. For example, if an individual has committed a wrong within the state, such as causing an automobile injury or selling defective goods, a court can usually exercise jurisdiction even if the person causing the harm is located in another state. Similarly, a state may exercise personal jurisdiction over a nonresident defendant who is sued for breaching a contract that was formed within the state.

LONG-ARM STATUTE
A state statute that permits a state to obtain jurisdiction over nonresident individuals and corporations. Individuals or corporations, however, must have certain "minimum contacts" with that state for the statute to apply.

In regard to corporations, the minimum-contacts requirement is usually met if the corporation does business within the state. A Maine corporation that has a branch office or manufacturing plant in Georgia, for example, has sufficient minimum contacts with the state of Georgia to allow a Georgia court to exercise jurisdiction over the Maine corporation. If the Maine corporation advertises and sells its products in Georgia, those activities may also suffice to meet the minimum-contacts requirements.

Jurisdiction over Property. A court can also exercise jurisdiction over property that is located within its boundaries. This kind of jurisdiction is known as *in rem* jurisdiction, or "jurisdiction over the thing." For example, suppose that a a dispute arises over the ownership of a boat in dry dock in Fort Lauderdale, Florida. The boat is owned by an Ohio resident, over whom a Florida court cannot normally exercise personal jurisdiction. The other party to the dispute is a resident of Nebraska. In this situation, a lawsuit concerning the boat could be brought in a Florida state court on the basis of the court's *in rem* jurisdiction.

Jurisdiction over Subject Matter. Jurisdiction over subject matter is a limitation on the types of cases a court can hear. In both the state and federal court systems, there are courts of *general jurisdiction* and courts of *limited jurisdiction*. The basis for the distinction lies in the subject matter of cases heard. For example, **probate courts**—state courts that handle only matters relating to the transfer of a person's assets and obligations on that person's death, including matters relating to the custody and guardianship of children—have limited subject-matter jurisdiction. A common example of a federal court of limited subject-matter jurisdiction is a bankruptcy court. **Bankruptcy courts** handle only bankruptcy proceedings, which are governed by federal bankruptcy law (bankruptcy law allows debtors to obtain

PROBATE COURT
A court having jurisdiction over proceedings concerning the settlement of a person's estate.

BANKRUPTCY COURT
A federal court of limited jurisdiction that hears only bankruptcy proceedings.

2. As will be discussed shortly, a state's highest court is often referred to as the state supreme court, but there are exceptions. For example, in New York, the supreme court is a trial court.

relief from their debts when they cannot make ends meet). In contrast, a court of general jurisdiction can decide virtually any type of case.

The subject-matter jurisdiction of a court is usually defined in the statute or constitution creating the court. In both the state and federal court systems, a court's subject-matter jurisdiction can be limited not only by the subject of the lawsuit, but also by the amount of money in controversy, by whether a case is a felony (a more serious type of crime) or a misdemeanor (a less serious type of crime), or by whether the proceeding is a trial or an appeal.

Original and Appellate Jurisdiction. The distinction between courts of original jurisdiction and courts of appellate jurisdiction normally lies in whether the case is being heard for the first time. Courts having **original jurisdiction** are courts of the first instance, or **trial courts**—that is, courts in which lawsuits begin, trials take place, and evidence is presented. In the federal court system, the *district courts* are trial courts. In the various state court systems, the trial courts are known by different names. The key point here is that normally, any court having original jurisdiction is known as a trial court. Courts having **appellate jurisdiction** act as reviewing courts, or **appellate courts**. In general, cases can be brought before them only on appeal from an order or a judgment of a trial court or other lower court. State and federal trial and appellate courts will be discussed more fully later in this chapter.

ORIGINAL JURISDICTION
The power of a court to take a case, try it, and decide it.

TRIAL COURT
A court in which most cases usually begin and in which questions of fact are examined.

APPELLATE JURISDICTION
The power of a court to hear and decide an appeal; that is, the power and authority of a court to review cases that already have been tried in a lower court and the power to make decisions about them without actually holding a trial. This process is called appellate review.

APPELLATE COURT
A court that reviews decisions made by lower courts, such as trial courts; a court of appeals.

Jurisdiction of the Federal Courts

Because the federal government is a government of limited powers, the jurisdiction of the federal courts is limited. Article III of the U.S. Constitution established the boundaries of federal judicial power. Section 2 of Article III states that "[t]he judicial Power shall extend to all Cases, in Law and Equity, arising under this Constitution, the Laws of the United States, and Treaties made, or which shall be made, under their Authority."

Federal Questions. Whenever a plaintiff's cause of action is based, at least in part, on the U.S. Constitution, a treaty, or a federal law, then a **federal question** arises, and the case comes under the judicial power of federal courts. Any lawsuit involving a federal question can originate in a federal court. People who claim that their constitutional rights have been violated can begin their suits in a federal court.

FEDERAL QUESTION
A question that pertains to the U.S. Constitution, acts of Congress, or treaties. A federal question provides jurisdiction for federal courts. This jurisdiction arises from Article III, Section 2, of the Constitution.

Diversity Jurisdiction. Federal district courts can also exercise original jurisdiction over cases involving **diversity of citizenship**. Such cases may arise between (1) citizens of different states, (2) a foreign country and citizens of a state or of different states, or (3) citizens of a state and citizens or subjects of a foreign country. The amount in controversy must be more than $50,000 before a federal court can take jurisdiction in such cases. For purposes of diversity-of-citizenship jurisdiction, a corporation is a citizen of the state in which it is incorporated and of the state in which its principal place of business is located. A case involving diversity of citizenship can be filed

DIVERSITY OF CITIZENSHIP
Under Article III, Section 2, of the Constitution, a basis for federal court jurisdiction over a lawsuit between citizens of different states.

in the appropriate federal district court, or, if the case starts in a state court, it can sometimes be transferred to a federal court.

As an example of diversity jurisdiction, assume that the following events have taken place. Maria Ramirez, a citizen of Florida, was walking near a busy street in Tallahassee, Florida, one day when a large crate flew off a passing truck and hit and seriously injured her. She incurred numerous medical expenses and could not work for six months. She now wants to sue the trucking firm for $300,000 in damages. The trucking firm's headquarters are in Georgia, although the company does business in Florida.

In this situation, Maria could bring suit in a Florida court because she is a resident of Florida, the trucking firm does business in Florida, and that is where the accident occurred. She could also bring suit in a Georgia court, because a Georgia court could exercise jurisdiction over the trucking firm, which is headquartered in that state. As a third alternative, Maria could bring suit in a federal court because the requirements of diversity jurisdiction have been met—the lawsuit involves parties from different states, Florida and Georgia, and the amount in controversy (the damages Maria is seeking) exceeds $50,000.

Note that in a case based on a federal question, a federal court will apply federal law. In a case based on diversity of citizenship, however, a federal court will normally apply the law of the state in which the court sits.

EXHIBIT 7.1
Exclusive and Concurrent Jurisdiction

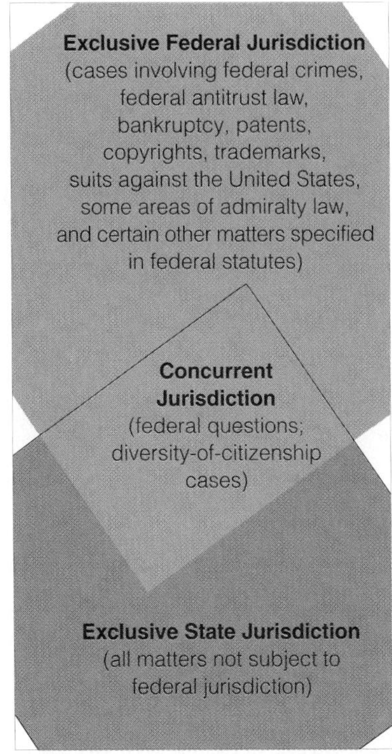

Exclusive versus Concurrent Jurisdiction. When both federal and state courts have the power to hear a case, as is true in suits involving diversity of citizenship (such as Maria's case described above), **concurrent jurisdiction** exists. When cases can be tried only in federal courts or only in state courts, **exclusive jurisdiction** exists. Federal courts have exclusive jurisdiction in cases involving federal crimes, bankruptcy, patents, and copyrights (discussed in Chapter 9); in suits against the United States; and in some areas of admiralty law (law governing transportation on the seas and ocean waters). States also have exclusive jurisdiction in certain subject matters—for example, in divorce and adoptions. The concepts of concurrent and exclusive jurisdiction are illustrated in Exhibit 7.1.

CONCURRENT JURISDICTION
Jurisdiction that exists when two different courts have the power to hear a case. For example, some cases can be heard in either a federal or a state court.

EXCLUSIVE JURISDICTION
Jurisdiction that exists when a case can be heard only in a particular court.

When concurrent jurisdiction exists, a plaintiff bringing a lawsuit has a choice: he or she may bring the case in either a state court or a federal court. Normally, an attorney will look at several factors before advising a client on which court would be most advantageous. These factors include convenience (the physical location of the court), how long it would take in either type of court to get the case to trial (state courts often have heavier caseloads, and thus the wait may be longer), and the temperaments and judicial philosophies of the judges of the courts.

Venue

Jurisdiction has to do with whether a court has authority to hear a case involving specific persons, property, or subject matter. **Venue**[3] is concerned with the most appropriate location for a trial. For example, two state courts may have

VENUE
The geographical district in which an action is tried and from which the jury is selected.

3. Pronounced *ven*-yoo.

DEVELOPING PARALEGAL SKILLS

Choice of Courts: State or Federal?

Joan Dunbar is a legal assistant in a law firm. Her supervisor, Susan Radtke, is a well-known lawyer who specializes in employment law. They are meeting with a new client who wants to sue her former employer for sex discrimination. The client complained to her employer when she was passed over for a promotion, and she was fired as a result of her complaint. The client appears to have a strong case because several of her former co-workers have agreed to testify that they heard the employer say on several occasions that he would never promote a woman to a managerial position in his firm.

Susan explains to the client that both state law and federal law prohibit sex discrimination, and therefore the client's case could be brought in either a state court or a federal court. The client asks Susan about the advantages and disadvantages of each of these options.

THE PROS AND CONS OF FILING THE SUIT IN A STATE COURT

Susan asks Joan to get the newspaper and magazine clippings file on the county court. When Joan returns with it, Susan removes a newspaper article from the file entitled "Plaintiff's County, USA." Their county has earned this reputation nationwide because of the large number of million-dollar and multimillion-dollar jury verdicts that the county court awards to plaintiffs each year. The client asks if this means that she is assured of winning her case if she files in this court. "No," Susan responds. "But it will help. The disadvantage to filing here is that the county's docket is so backlogged that you are looking at three to five years before you go to trial." The client, who is unemployed, explains to Susan that she does not want to wait that long to obtain a decision, and the claimed damages, in her case.

THE PROS AND CONS OF FILING THE SUIT IN A FEDERAL COURT

Susan explains that if the client filed in federal court, the case could go to trial within six months to a year. "The disadvantage here," continues Susan, "is that you might not have a county jury that favors plaintiffs and apparently dislikes defendants, especially corporate ones." The client likes the idea of having her case decided as quickly as possible, but she also wants to win at trial and obtain damages. The client decides to let Susan choose the court. "Just remember that while I want to maximize the amount of damages awarded, it's more important that I receive damages as soon as possible. My unemployment compensation won't last forever."

MAKING THE DECISION

The client leaves, and Susan and Joan discuss the case. They both agree that because the client has a strong case, she could probably win in either court. Because of the client's concern about time, Susan decides to file the case in a federal court, even though the damages awarded might not be as high as they would be in the county court. Susan then discusses with Joan the legal theories that the complaint should contain.

the authority to exercise jurisdiction over a case, but it may be more appropriate or convenient to hear the case in one court than in the other.

Basically, the concept of venue reflects the policy that a court trying a suit should be in the geographic neighborhood (usually the county) in which the incident leading to the lawsuit occurred or in which the parties involved in the lawsuit reside. Pretrial publicity or other factors, though, may require a change of venue to another community, especially in criminal cases in which the defendant's right to a fair and impartial jury has been impaired. For example, in 1992, when four Los Angeles police officers accused of beating Rodney King were brought to trial, the attorneys defending the police officers requested a change of venue from Los Angeles to Simi Valley, California. The attorneys argued that to try the case in a Los Angeles court would prejudice the police officers' right to a fair trial. The court agreed and granted the request.

Standing to Sue

To bring a lawsuit before a court, a party must have **standing to sue**, or a sufficient "stake" in a matter to justify seeking relief through the court system. In other words, a party must have a legally protected and tangible interest at stake in the litigation in order to have standing. The party bringing the lawsuit must have suffered a harm as a result of the action about which he or she complained. For example, assume that a friend of one of your firm's clients was injured in a car accident caused by defective brakes. The client's friend would have standing to sue the automobile manufacturer for damages. The client, however, would not have standing because the client was not injured and therefore has no legally recognizable stake in the controversy.

STANDING TO SUE
The requirement that an individual must have a sufficient stake in a controversy before he or she can bring a lawsuit. The plaintiff must demonstrate that he or she either has been injured or threatened with injury.

Note that in some cases, a person will have standing to sue on behalf of another person. For example, suppose that a child suffered serious injuries as a result of a defectively manufactured toy. Because the child is a minor, a lawsuit could be brought on his or her behalf by another person, such as the child's parent or legal guardian.

Standing to sue also requires that the controversy at issue be justiciable. A **justiciable**[4] **controversy** is one that is real and substantial, as opposed to hypothetical or academic. For example, in the above example, the child's parent could not sue the toy manufacturer merely on the ground that the toy was defective. The issue would become justiciable only if the child had actually been injured due to the defect in the toy as marketed. In other words, the parent normally could not ask the court to determine what damages might be obtained *if* the child had been injured, because this would be merely a hypothetical question.

JUSTICIABLE CONTROVERSY
A controversy that is real and substantial as opposed to hypothetical or academic.

Judicial Procedures

Litigation in court, from the moment a lawsuit is initiated until the final resolution of the case, must follow specifically designated procedural rules. The procedural rules for federal court cases are set forth in the Federal Rules of

4. Pronounced jus-*tish*-a-bul.

Civil Procedure. State rules, which are often similar to the federal rules, vary from state to state—and even from court to court within a given state. Rules of procedure also differ in criminal and civil cases. Paralegals who work for trial lawyers need to be familiar with the procedural rules of the relevant courts. Because judicial procedures will be examined in detail in Chapters 10 through 12, we do not discuss them here.

PROCEDURAL LAW CONCEPT SUMMARY

The American System of Justice

Jurisdiction	**1.** *Jurisdiction over persons, or* in personam *jurisdiction*—The geographic boundaries within which a court has the right and power to decide cases concerning a defendant. State long-arm statutes may allow state courts to exercise jurisdiction over nonresident defendants. **2.** *Jurisdiction over property, or* in rem *jurisdiction*—The geographic boundaries within which a court has the right and power to decide cases concerning a defendant's property. **3.** *Jurisdiction over subject matter*— a. Limited jurisdiction—Exists when a court is limited to a specific subject matter, such as probate or divorce proceedings. b. General jurisdiction—Exists when a court can hear any kind of case. **4.** *Original jurisdiction*—Exists with courts that have the authority to hear a case for the first time (trial courts). **5.** *Appellate jurisdiction*—Exists with courts of appeal and review; generally, appellate courts do not have original jurisdiction. **6.** *Federal jurisdiction*—Arises in the following situations: a. When a federal question is involved (when the plaintiff's cause of action is based at least in part on the U.S. Constitution, a treaty, or a federal law). b. In diversity-of-citizenship cases between (1) citizens of different states, (2) a foreign country and citizens of a state or different states, or (3) citizens of a state and citizens or subjects of a foreign country. The amount in controversy must exceed $50,000. **7.** *Concurrent jurisdiction*—Exists when two different courts have authority to hear the same case. **8.** *Exclusive jurisdiction*—Exists when only state courts or only federal courts have authority to hear a case.
Venue	The most appropriate location for a trial. The concept of venue reflects the policy that a court trying a suit should be in the geographic neighborhood (usually the county) in which the incident leading to the lawsuit occurred or in which the parties involved in the lawsuit reside.
Standing to Sue	A party must have a sufficient "stake" in a controversy (a legally protected and tangible interest in the litigation) to justify seeking relief through the court system.
Judicial Procedures	Rules governing procedures relating to lawsuits and proceedings before the courts. Civil litigation in the federal courts is governed by the Federal Rules of Civil Procedure. Each state has its own procedural rules, and each court within a state has specific court rules that must be followed.

The American System of Justice and the Paralegal

Paralegals should be familiar with the concepts of jurisdiction, venue, and standing to sue because these concepts affect pretrial litigation procedures. For example, a defendant in a lawsuit may claim that the court in which the plaintiff filed the lawsuit cannot exercise jurisdiction over the matter—or over the defendant or the defendant's property. If you are working on behalf of the defendant, you may be asked to draft a motion to dismiss the case on this ground. You may also be asked to draft a legal memorandum in support of the motion, outlining the legal reasons why the court cannot exercise jurisdiction over the case. (Motions to dismiss and supporting documents are discussed in Chapter 10.) Additionally, a party to a lawsuit may request that a case filed in a state court should be "removed" to a federal court (if there is a basis for federal jurisdiction) or vice versa. You may also be asked to draft a document requesting a change of venue (or objecting to an opponent's request for change of venue) or to dismiss the case because the plaintiff lacks standing to sue.

If you work for a plaintiff's attorney, you might be asked to draft a complaint to initiate a lawsuit. Once the attorney reviews the facts with you, he or she may expect you to know whether concurrent jurisdiction exists. If concurrent jurisdiction exists, the attorney may expect you to ask whether the suit should be filed in a state or a federal court. If concurrent jurisdiction does not exist, the attorney may assume that you know in which court the case will be filed and that you know how to prepare the compaint for the appropriate court.

Recall from Chapter 1 that paralegal education and training emphasizes procedural law. A paralegal can be a valuable member of a legal team if he or she has substantial knowledge of the procedural requirements relating to litigation and to different types of legal proceedings. You will read in detail about litigation procedures in Chapters 10 through 12 and administrative procedures in Chapter 13.

> **ETHICAL CONCERN**
>
> **Meeting Procedural Deadlines**
>
> One of the paralegal's most important responsibilities is making sure that court deadlines are met. For example, suppose that your supervising attorney asks you to file with the court a motion to dismiss (a document requesting the court to dismiss a lawsuit for a specific reason). You know that the deadline for filing the motion is three days away. You plan to deliver the motion to the court the next day, so you don't place a reminder note on your calendar. In the meantime, you place the motion in the client's file. The next morning, you arrive at work and immediately are called to help your supervising attorney with last-minute trial preparations on another case. You are busy all afternoon interviewing witnesses in still another case. You have totally forgotten about the motion to dismiss and do not think of it again until a week later—when the deadline for filing the motion has passed. Because you forgot to file the motion, your supervising attorney has breached the duty of competence. How can you make sure that you remember important deadlines? The answer is simple: *always* enter deadlines on the office calendaring system and *always* check your calendar several times a day.

STATE COURT SYSTEMS

Each state has its own system of courts, and no two state systems are the same. As Exhibit 7.2 on the next page indicates, there may be several levels, or tiers, of courts within a state court system: (1) state trial courts of limited jurisdiction, (2) state trial courts of general jurisdiction, (3) appellate courts, and (4) the state's highest court (often called the state supreme court). Judges in the state court system are usually elected by the voters for a specified term.

Generally, any person who is a party to a lawsuit has the opportunity to plead the case before a trial court and then, if he or she loses, before at least one level of appellate court. Finally, if a federal statute or federal constitutional issue is involved in the decision of a state supreme court, that decision may be further appealed to the United States Supreme Court.

Trial Courts

Trial courts are exactly what their name implies—courts in which trials are held and testimony taken. You will read in detail about trial procedures in

EXHIBIT 7.2
State Court Systems

State court systems vary widely from state to state, and it is therefore impossible to show a "typical" state court system. This exhibit is typical of the court systems in several states, however, including Texas, California, Arizona, and Nevada.

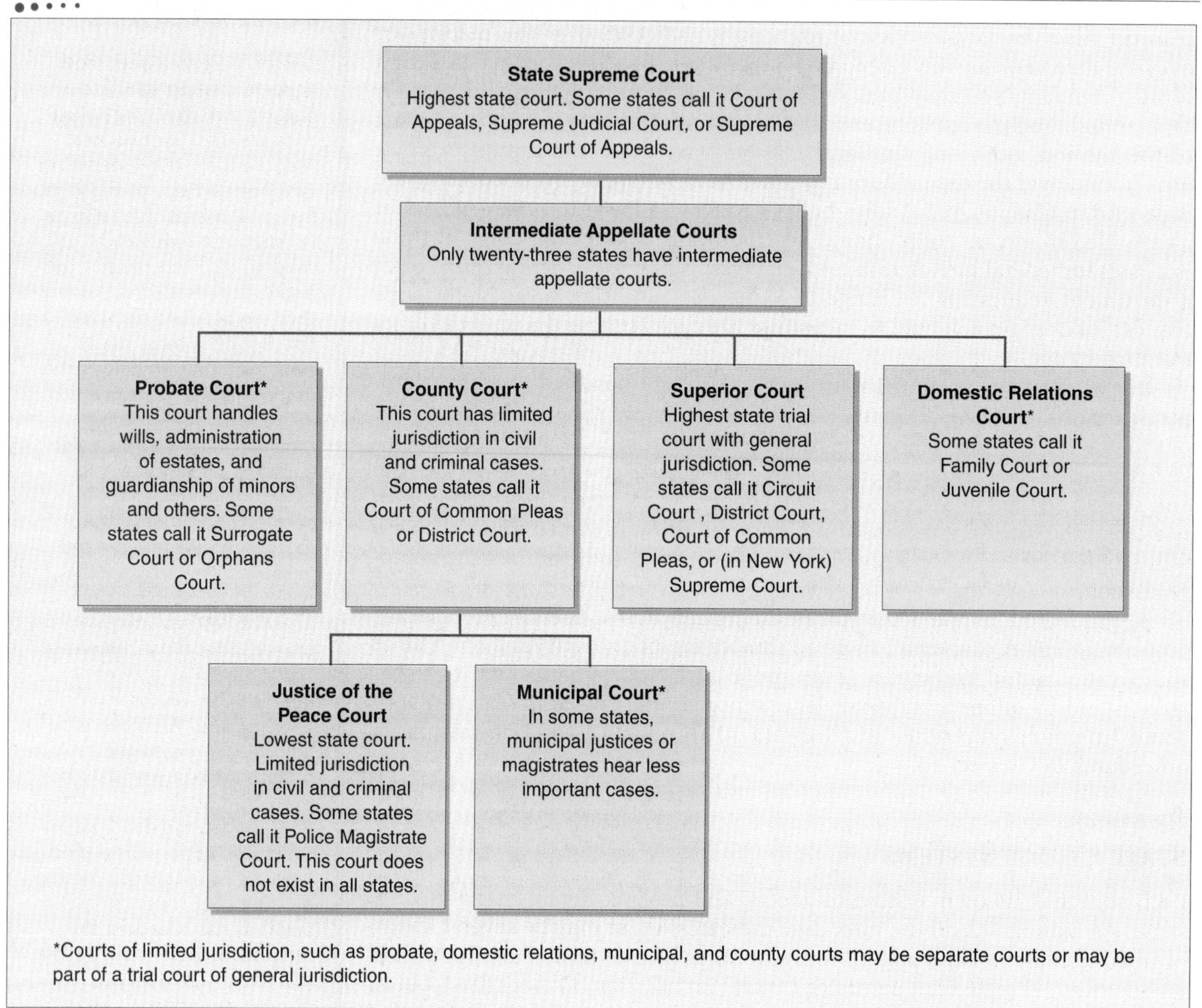
State Supreme Court
Highest state court. Some states call it Court of Appeals, Supreme Judicial Court, or Supreme Court of Appeals.
Intermediate Appellate Courts
Only twenty-three states have intermediate appellate courts.
Probate Court*
This court handles wills, administration of estates, and guardianship of minors and others. Some states call it Surrogate Court or Orphans Court.
County Court*
This court has limited jurisdiction in civil and criminal cases. Some states call it Court of Common Pleas or District Court.
Superior Court
Highest state trial court with general jurisdiction. Some states call it Circuit Court , District Court, Court of Common Pleas, or (in New York) Supreme Court.
Domestic Relations Court*
Some states call it Family Court or Juvenile Court.
Justice of the Peace Court
Lowest state court. Limited jurisdiction in civil and criminal cases. Some states call it Police Magistrate Court. This court does not exist in all states.
Municipal Court*
In some states, municipal justices or magistrates hear less important cases.
*Courts of limited jurisdiction, such as probate, domestic relations, municipal, and county courts may be separate courts or may be part of a trial court of general jurisdiction.

Chapter 11. In that chapter, we follow a hypothetical case through the various stages of a trial. Briefly, a trial court is presided over by a judge, who issues a decision on the matter before the court. If the trial is a jury trial (many trials are held without juries), the jury will decide the outcome of factual disputes, and the judge will issue a judgment based on the jury's conclusion. During the trial, the attorney for each side introduces evidence (such as relevant documents, exhibits, and testimony of witnesses) in support of his or her client's position. Each attorney is given an opportunity to

cross-examine the opposing party and challenge evidence introduced by the opposing party.

State trial courts have either general or limited jurisdiction. Trial courts that have general jurisdiction as to subject matter may be called county, district, superior, or circuit courts.[5] The jurisdiction of these courts is often determined by the size of the county in which the court sits. State trial courts of general jurisdiction have jurisdiction over a wide variety of subjects, including both civil disputes (such as landlord-tenant matters or contract claims) and criminal prosecutions.

Courts with limited jurisdiction as to subject matter are often called special inferior trial courts or minor judiciary courts. Courts of limited jurisdiction include domestic relations courts, which handle only divorce actions and child-custody cases; local municipal courts, which mainly handle traffic cases; and probate courts, which, as previously mentioned, handle the administration of wills, estate-settlement problems, and related matters.

Courts of Appeals

Generally, courts of appeals (appellate courts, or reviewing courts) are not trial courts. In some states, however, trial courts of general jurisdiction may have

5. The name in Ohio is Court of Common Pleas; the name in New York is Supreme Court.

DEVELOPING PARALEGAL SKILLS

State Court Litigation

David Garner is a legal assistant in a busy law firm. David's supervising attorney, Helen Schmidt, has called him into a meeting. She wants him to draft complaints for a couple of new cases. The first case is a medical-malpractice case against an orthopedist whose allegedly careless treatment of the client's knee injury resulted in unnecessary complications and expensive surgery. The client is all right now, but she lost two months of work while she was recovering. She feels that she is entitled to damages to cover her medical expenses and her lost wages. Her total damages are about $7,000.

Because the state has, for the most part, a two-tiered trial court system, David suggests to Helen that they file the case in the local district court, the lowest-level trial court with jurisdiction. These courts have jurisdiction over civil cases in which the amount in controversy (the damages sought by the plaintiff) is under $10,000. Helen agrees that the district court has jurisdiction to hear the case.

The second case is a product-liability case against a local automobile manufacturer. The plaintiffs are the parents of a young man whose death was allegedly caused by a defective steering mechanism in a car produced by the auto manufacturer. The plaintiffs are seeking damages in the millions. Helen tells David to prepare this case to be filed with the county circuit court, because this court has jurisdiction over civil cases that exceed $10,000 in damages.

limited jurisdiction to hear appeals from the minor judiciary—for example, from small claims courts or traffic courts. Every state has at least one court of appeals, which may be an intermediate appellate court or a state supreme court.

Intermediate Appellate Courts. Twenty-three states have intermediate appellate courts. The subject-matter jurisdiction of these courts of appeals is substantially limited to hearing appeals. Appellate courts do not retry cases (conduct new trials, in which evidence is submitted to the court and witnesses are examined). Rather, an appellate court panel of three or more judges reviews the record of the case on appeal, which includes a transcript of the trial proceedings, and determines whether the trial court committed an error. Appellate courts look at questions of law and procedure but usually not at questions of fact.

Normally, an appellate court will defer to a trial court's finding of fact because the trial court judge and jury were in a better position to evaluate testimony; they could directly observe witnesses' gestures, demeanor, and nonverbal behavior generally during the trial. At the appellate level, the judges review the written transcript of the trial, which does not include these nonverbal elements. An appellate court will challenge a trial court's finding of fact only when the finding is clearly erroneous (that is, when it is contrary to the evidence presented at trial) or when there is no evidence to support the finding. For example, if a jury concluded that a manufacturer's product harmed the plaintiff but no evidence was submitted to the court to support that conclusion, the appellate court would hold that the trial court's decision was erroneous. The options exercised by appellate courts will be further discussed in Chapter 11.

State Supreme Courts. The highest appellate court in a state is usually called the supreme court but may be called by some other name. For example, in both New York and Maryland, the highest state court is called the Court of Appeals. The decisions of each state's highest court on all questions of state law are final. Only when issues of federal law are involved can a decision made by a state's highest court be overruled by the United States Supreme Court.

State Court Systems and the Paralegal

Because each state has its own unique system of courts, you will need to become familiar with the court system of your particular state. What is the official name of your state's highest court, or supreme court? How many intermediate state appellate courts are in your state, and to which of these courts should appeals from your local trial court or courts be appealed? What courts in your area have jurisdiction over what kinds of disputes?

In addition to knowing the names of your state's courts and their jurisdictional authority, you will also need to become familiar with the procedural requirements of specific courts. Paralegals frequently assist their attorneys in drafting legal documents to be filed in state courts, and the required procedures for filing these documents may vary from court to court. You will read more about court procedures in Chapters 10 and 11.

As indicated earlier and illustrated in Exhibit 7.1, state courts exercise exclusive jurisdiction over all matters that are not subject to federal jurisdiction. Family law and probate law (discussed in Chapter 2), for example,

PROCEDURAL LAW CONCEPT SUMMARY

State Court Systems

Trial Courts	State trial courts have either general or limited jurisdiction. Those with limited jurisdiction hear cases on a particular subject matter, such as divorce or probate. Those with general jurisdiction can hear any type of case.
Intermediate Appellate Courts	State appellate courts are generally without original jurisdiction. These courts determine whether an error was made by the trial court. Appellate courts ordinarily examine questions of law and procedure, while deferring to the trial court's findings of fact. Only if the appellate court determines that the trial court's finding of fact was clearly erroneous (contrary to the evidence presented at trial) or unsupported by evidence will it challenge the trial court's findings.
Supreme Courts	A state's highest court is its supreme court (although it may have some other title). Decisions of a state's highest court on all questions of state law are final. If a federal question is at issue, however, the case may be appealed to the United States Supreme Court.
State Court Judges and Justices	Judges and justices who sit on the benches of state courts are normally elected by the voters for specified terms.

are two areas in which state courts exercise exclusive jurisdiction. If you work in these or other areas of the law over which state courts exercise jurisdiction, you will need to be familiar with procedural requirements established by state (or local) courts relating to those areas.

THE FEDERAL COURT SYSTEM

The federal court system is basically a three-tiered model consisting of (1) U.S. district courts (trial courts of general jurisdiction) and various courts of limited jurisdiction, (2) U.S. courts of appeals (intermediate courts of appeals), and (3) the United States Supreme Court. Exhibit 7.3 on page 243 shows the organization of the federal court system.

According to the language of Article III of the U.S. Constitution, there is only one national Supreme Court. All other courts in the federal system are considered "inferior." Congress is empowered to create other inferior courts as it deems necessary. The inferior courts that Congress has created include those on the first and second tiers in our model—the district courts and various courts of limited jurisdiction, as well as the U.S. courts of appeals.

Unlike state court judges, who are usually elected, federal court judges are appointed by the president of the United States, subject to the approval of the U.S. Senate. Federal judges receive lifetime appointments (because under Article III they "hold their Offices during good Behavior").

U.S. District Courts

At the federal level, the equivalent of a state trial court of general jurisdiction is the district court. There is at least one federal district court in every

PARALEGAL PROFILE Specialist in Domestic-violence Law

ELIZABETH LAREW has a bachelor of arts degree from Indiana University, with a major in women's studies. She received her paralegal certificate from Sonoma State University in California and currently works at a battered women's shelter at the YWCA of Sonoma County. She works directly with the residents of the center, listens to their problems, and assesses their legal needs. She actively participates in a statewide organization working for new laws that will benefit abused women and their children.

What do you like best about your work?

"The thing I like best about my job is being able to provide options for people, which allows them to make choices for change. Depending on a shelter resident's legal needs, I may refer the resident to an attorney or other service. I frequently help residents prepare to mediate or bring court actions relating to family-law disputes. I lend my support to the women by going to the proceedings with them. I also offer indirect assistance to the residents of the shelter by working on their behalf with the courts, law-enforcement personnel, mediators, social-services representatives, and other groups. I am able to watch battered women, against all odds, break the cycle of violence and begin new lives for themselves and their children."

What is the greatest challenge that you face in your area of work?

"The judicial system. Helping women through the system can be very challenging. In a judicial system that at one time legally sanctioned "wife beating," attempting to attain justice, protection, and respect for battered women is very challenging. Each step along the way is difficult."

What advice do you have for would-be paralegals in your area of work?

"I recommend that persons interested in my area of work get in touch with the local domestic-violence program and read as much as they can about domestic-violence law. There are many complexities within this area of law, and the more information you have, the better. I also recommend that students take internships to expose themselves to this type of work."

"NETWORKING AND A GOOD SUPPORT SYSTEM ARE ESSENTIAL."

What are some tips for success as a paralegal in your area of work?

"Success as a paralegal working in the area of domestic-violence law includes staying in touch with other domestic-violence programs through legislative work, conferences, and meetings. Networking and a good support system are essential. Don't plan on 'saving the world,' because the successes are small in comparison to the enormity of the problem, but even a seemingly small victory can save lives."

state. The number of judicial districts can vary over time, primarily owing to population changes and corresponding caseloads. Currently, there are ninety-six judicial districts.

U.S. district courts have original jurisdiction in federal matters. Federal cases typically originate in district courts. There are other trial courts with original, but special (or limited) jurisdiction, such as the federal bankruptcy courts and others shown in Exhibit 7.3.

EXHIBIT 7.3
The Organization of the Federal Court System

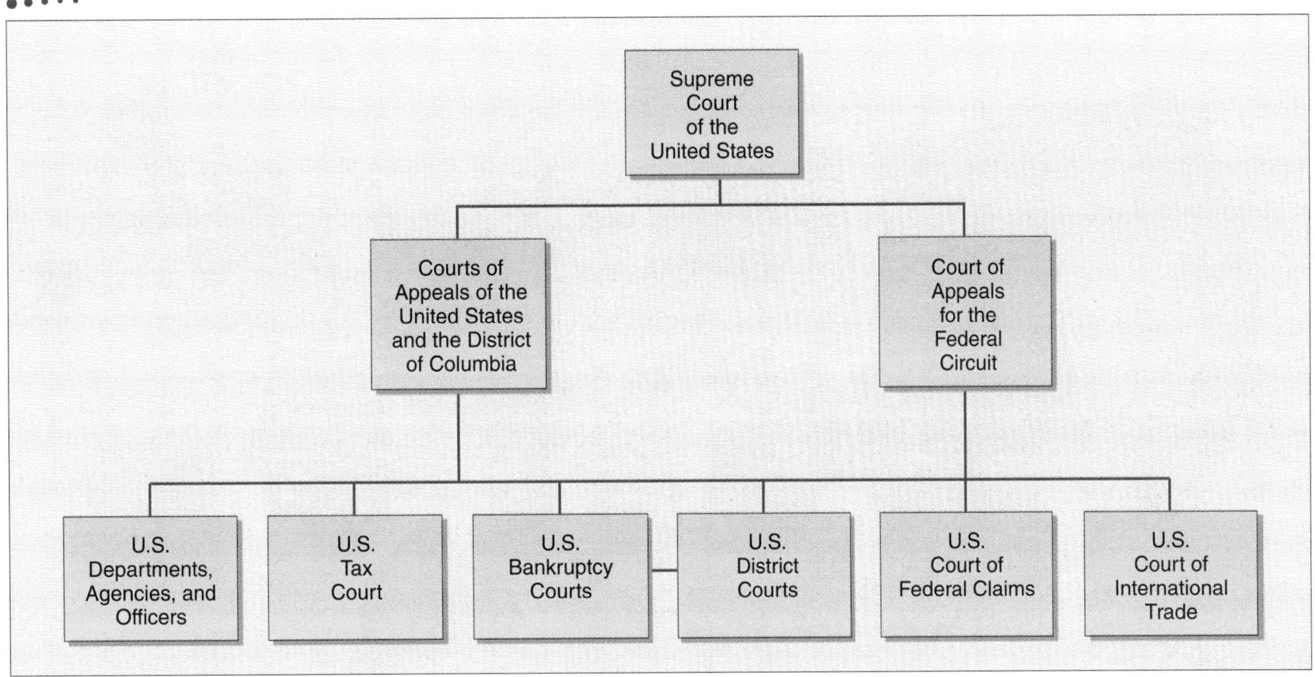

U.S. Courts of Appeals

In the federal court system, there are thirteen U.S. courts of appeals—also referred to as U.S. circuit courts of appeals. The federal courts of appeals for twelve of the circuits hear appeals from the federal district courts located within their respective judicial circuits. The court of appeals for the thirteenth circuit, called the federal circuit, has national appellate jurisdiction over certain types of cases, such as cases involving patent law and cases in which the U.S. government is a defendant.

A party who is dissatisfied with a federal district court's decision on an issue may appeal that decision to a federal circuit court of appeals. As in state courts of appeals, the decisions of the circuit courts are made by a panel of three or more justices. The justices review decisions made by trial courts to see if any errors of law were made, and the justices generally defer to a district court's findings of fact. The decisions of the circuit courts of appeals are final in most cases, but appeal to the United States Supreme Court is possible. Exhibit 7.4 on the following page shows the geographical boundaries of U.S. circuit courts of appeals and the boundaries of the U.S. district courts within each circuit.

The United States Supreme Court

The United States Supreme Court consists of nine justices. These justices, like all federal judges, are nominated by the president of the United States and confirmed by the Senate.

EXHIBIT 7.4

U.S. Courts of Appeals and U.S. District Courts

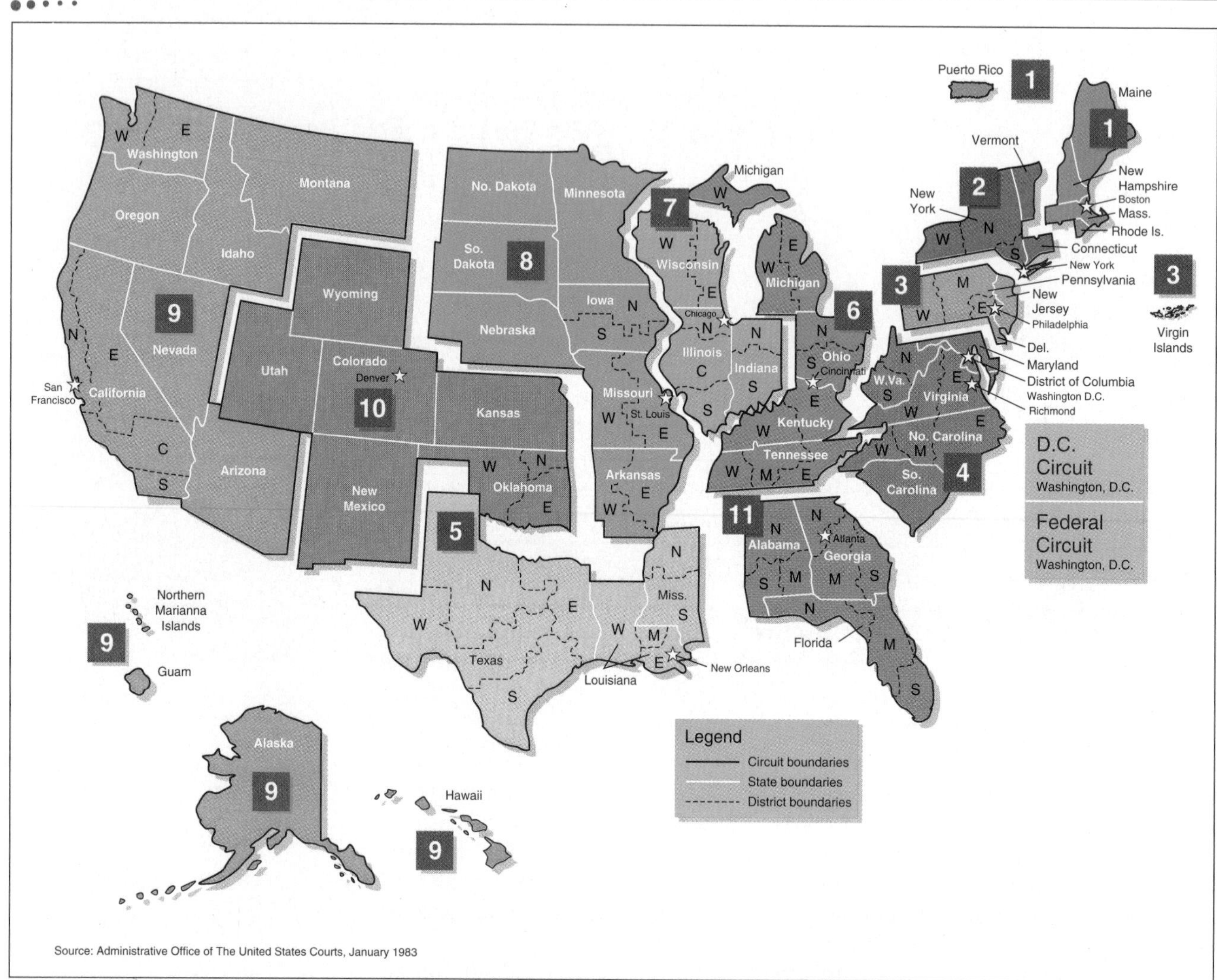

Source: Administrative Office of The United States Courts, January 1983

The Supreme Court is given original, or trial court, jurisdiction in a small number of situations. Under Article III, Section 2, of the U.S. Constitution, the Supreme Court can exercise original jurisdiction in all cases "affecting Ambassadors, other public Ministers and Consuls, and those in which a State shall be a Party." In all other cases, the Supreme Court may exercise only appellate jurisdiction "with such Exceptions, and under such Regulations as the Congress shall make." Most of the Supreme Court's work is as an appellate court. The Supreme Court can review any case decided by any of the federal courts of appeals, and it also has appellate authority over some cases decided in the state courts.

How Cases Reach the Supreme Court. Many people are surprised to learn that there is no absolute right of appeal to the United States Supreme Court.

Thousands of cases are filed with the Supreme Court each year, yet it hears, on average, fewer than 150 of these cases.

To bring a case before the Supreme Court, a party requests the Court to issue a writ of *certiorari.* A **writ of *certiorari***[6] is an order issued by the Supreme Court to a lower court requiring the latter to send it the record of the case for review. Parties can petition the Supreme Court to issue a writ of *certiorari,* but whether the Court will issue one is entirely within its discretion. The Court will not issue a writ unless at least four of the nine justices approve of it. This is called the **rule of four**. The Court is not required to issue a writ of *certiorari,* and most petitions for writs are denied. A denial is not a decision on the merits of a case, nor does it indicate agreement with the lower court's opinion. It simply means that the Supreme Court declines to grant the request (petition) for appeal. Furthermore, denial of the writ has no value as a precedent.

WRIT OF *CERTIORARI*
A writ from a higher court asking the lower court for the record of a case.

RULE OF FOUR
A rule of the United States Supreme Court under which the Court will not issue a writ of *certiorari* unless at least four justices approve of the decision to issue the writ.

Types of Cases Reviewed by the Supreme Court. Typically, the petitions granted by the Court involve cases that raise important constitutional questions or that conflict with other state or federal court decisions. Similarly, if federal appellate courts are rendering inconsistent opinions on an important issue, the Supreme Court may review a case involving that issue and generate a decision to define the law on the matter.

For example, suppose that an employer fires an employee who refuses to work on Saturdays, which is forbidden by the employee's religion. The fired employee applies for unemployment benefits from the state unemployment agency, and the agency, concluding that the employer had good reason to fire the employee, denies unemployment benefits. The fired employee sues the state unemployment agency on the ground that the employee's right to freely exercise her religion—a constitutional right—was violated. The case is ultimately appealed to a state supreme court, which decides the issue in a way that is contrary to several recent federal appellate courts' interpretations of freedom of religion in the employment context. If the losing party petitions the Supreme Court for a writ of *certiorari,* the Court may grant the petition and review the case.

The Federal Court System and the Paralegal

In your work as a paralegal, you will probably be dealing occasionally with the federal court system. As discussed above, certain cases involving diversity of citizenship may be brought in either a state or a federal court. Many litigants who could sue in a state court will opt for a federal court if diversity of citizenship exists for the reasons mentioned earlier.

You may also be working on behalf of plaintiffs whose claims involve a federal question. An increasing number of cases in federal courts are brought by plaintiffs who allege employment discrimination in violation of federal laws, such as Title VII of the Civil Rights Act of 1964, which prohibits employment discrimination based on race, color, national origin, gender, or

6. Pronounced sur-shee-uh-*rah*-ree.

PROCEDURAL LAW CONCEPT SUMMARY

The Federal Court System

U.S. District Courts	The federal district court is the equivalent of the state trial court. The district court exercises general jurisdiction over claims arising under federal law or based on diversity of citizenship. Federal courts of limited jurisdiction include the bankruptcy courts and other courts listed on the lowest tier of Exhibit 7.3.
U.S. Courts of Appeals	There are thirteen intermediate courts of appeals (or circuit courts of appeals) in the federal court system. Of those circuits, twelve hear appeals from the district courts within their circuits. The thirteenth circuit has national appellate jurisdiction over certain types of cases, such as cases involving patent law (see Chapter 9) and cases in which the U.S. government is a defendant.
United States Supreme Court	The United States Supreme Court is the highest court in the federal court system and the final arbiter of the Constitution and federal law. Although the Supreme Court has original jurisdiction in some cases, it functions primarily as an appellate court. If the Supreme Court decides to review a case, it will issue a writ of *certiorari,* an order to a lower court requiring the latter to send it the record of the case for review.
Federal Court Judges and Justices	Judges and justices in the federal court system are appointed by the president of the United States and confirmed by the Senate. Federal court judges and justices receive lifetime appointments.

religion. Other federal laws prohibit discrimination based on age or disability. Sexual harassment and pregnancy discrimination are considered by the courts to fall under the protective umbrella of Title VII's prohibition against gender discrimination, and such cases frequently come before federal courts.

As indicated in Exhibit 7.1, federal courts exercise exclusive jurisdiction over cases relating to bankruptcy, patents, copyrights, trademarks, federal crimes, and certain other claims. If you work on such cases, you will be dealing with the federal court system and the court procedures set forth in the Federal Rules of Civil Procedure. As with state courts, you should make sure that you know the specific requirements of the particular federal court in which a client's lawsuit is to be filed, because each federal court has some discretionary authority over its procedural rules. You will read in detail about the procedural rules governing litigation proceedings in federal courts in Chapters 10 and 11.

ALTERNATIVE DISPUTE RESOLUTION

Litigation in court is generally a last resort because of the high costs associated with litigating even the simplest complaint. In addition, because of the growing backlog of cases pending in the courts, it may sometimes be several years before a case is actually tried. Finally, the legal process is beset with uncertainties. One cannot know in advance how effectively the opposing side will argue its case or how the personal views and perceptions of judges and jurors may affect the outcome of the trial.

For these reasons, more and more individuals and business firms are turning to **alternative dispute resolution (ADR)** instead of resolving their disputes in court. Approximately 95 percent of all civil lawsuits are settled without a trial. Sometimes, a claim is settled before a lawsuit has been initiated. Most frequently, a settlement is achieved after the lawsuit is filed but before a trial takes place. In such situations, pretrial investigations give the parties and their attorneys an opportunity to assess the plaintiff's damages realistically and determine the relative strengths and weaknesses of the disputants' cases. Because so many cases are settled before they reach trial, attorneys and paralegals usually devote as much attention to these possibilities as to trial preparations. We now look at the various methods employed for settling disputes outside the court system.

ALTERNATIVE DISPUTE RESOLUTION (ADR)
The resolution of disputes in ways other than those involved in the traditional judicial process. Mediation and arbitration are forms of ADR.

Negotiation

Negotiation is one alternative means of resolving disputes. Attorneys frequently advise their clients to negotiate a settlement of their disputes voluntarily before they proceed to trial. During pretrial negotiation, the parties and/or their attorneys may meet informally one or more times to see if a mutually satisfactory agreement can be reached.

NEGOTIATION
A method of alternative dispute resolution in which disputing parties, with or without the assistance of their attorneys, meet informally to resolve the dispute out of court.

For example, assume that Katherine Baranski is suing Tony Peretto for damages. Peretto ran a stop sign, and as a result, his van crashed into Baranski's car, causing her to sustain numerous injuries and damages exceeding $100,000. After pretrial investigations into the matter, both plaintiff Baranski and defendant Peretto realize that Baranski has a good chance of winning the suit. At this point, Peretto's attorney may make a settlement offer on behalf of Peretto. Baranski may be willing to accept a settlement offer for a lower amount than the amount of damages she claimed in her complaint simply to avoid the time, trouble, and expense involved in taking the case to trial.

To facilitate an out-of-court settlement, Baranski's attorney may ask his paralegal to draft a letter to Baranski pointing out the strengths and weaknesses of her case against Peretto, the ADR options for settling the case before trial, and the advantages and disadvantages associated with each ADR option. Additionally, the paralegal may be asked to draft a letter to Peretto's attorney indicating the strengths of Baranski's case against him and the advantages to Peretto of settling the dispute out of court.

As a result of these pretrial negotiations, a **settlement agreement**, such as that shown in Exhibit 7.5 on the next page, may be reached between Baranski and Peretto. Baranski would give up her right to continue the litigation in return for Peretto's payment to her of a designated, agreed-on sum of money.

SETTLEMENT AGREEMENT
An out-of-court resolution to a legal dispute, which is agreed to by the parties in writing. A settlement agreement may be reached at any time prior to or during a trial.

Mediation

MEDIATION
A method of settling disputes outside of court by using the services of a neutral third party, who acts as a communicating agent between the parties; a method of dispute settlement that is less formal than arbitration.

Another alternative method of resolving disputes is to enlist the aid of a mediator. A mediator is expected to propose solutions, but he or she does not *impose* any solution or decision on the parties. In the **mediation** process, the parties themselves must reach agreement; the role of the mediator is to help

EXHIBIT 7.5
A Sample Settlement Agreement

SETTLEMENT AGREEMENT

THIS AGREEMENT is entered into this twelfth day of May, 1996, between Katherine Baranski and Tony Peretto.

WITNESSETH

WHEREAS, there is now pending in the U.S. District Court for the District of Nita* an action entitled Baranski v. Peretto, hereinafter referred to as "action."

WHEREAS, the parties hereto desire to record their agreement to settle all matters relating to said action without the necessity of further litigation.

NOW, THEREFORE, in consideration of the covenants and agreements contained herein, the sufficiency of which is hereby mutually acknowledged, and intending to be legally bound hereby, the parties agree as follows:

1. Katherine Baranski agrees to accept the sum of seventy-five thousand dollars ($75,000) in full satisfaction of all claims against Tony Peretto as set forth in the complaint filed in this action.

2. Tony Peretto agrees to pay Katherine Baranski the above-stated amount, in a lump-sum cash payment, on or before the first day of July, 1996.

3. Upon execution of this agreement and payment of the sum required under this agreement, the parties shall cause the action to be dismissed with prejudice.

4. When the sum required under this agreement is paid in full, Katherine Baranski will execute and deliver to Tony Peretto a release of all claims set forth in the complaint filed in the said action.

Katherine Baranski
Katherine Baranski

Tony Peretto
Tony Peretto

Sworn and subscribed before me this twelfth day of May, 1996.

Leela M. Shay
Leela M. Shay
Notary Public
State of Nita

*A hypothetical state.

THE LEGAL TEAM AT WORK

ADR versus Adversarial Justice

As a member of a litigation team, you will be involved in the seemingly impossible task of working simultaneously toward two mutually exclusive goals. On the one hand, you will be assisting your supervising attorney in working toward an out-of-court settlement of the dispute. On the other hand, you will be assisting in trial preparations so that, if no settlement agreement is reached, your client's case will be ready by the trial date.

Working toward these two goals simultaneously means that you will need to switch back and forth between two different approaches to the case. Preparing to litigate a case in court requires your team to view the opponent as an adversary. Implicitly, this view emphasizes the points of *disagreement* between the parties and reflects the win-lose philosophy that has traditionally characterized the adversarial system of justice. Settlement negotiations, in contrast, involve a totally different approach, one that is geared toward finding grounds for *agreement* between the parties.

The success of settlement negotiations or other method of ADR often depends on the negotiation and communication skills of the members of the legal team. There is every indication that the trend toward ADR will continue to grow and that the legal team will devote even more time in the future toward helping clients solve their problems through voluntary out-of-court settlements rather than adversarial proceedings. In preparing to work as a paralegal and legal teammate, you will thus want to improve and fine-tune your communication skills so that you will be a valuable ally in working toward settlements.

the parties view their dispute more objectively and find common grounds for agreement.

The parties may select a mediator on the basis of his or her expertise in a particular field or reputation for fairness and impartiality. The mediator may not need to be a lawyer. The mediator may be one person, such as a paralegal, an attorney, or a volunteer from the community, or a panel of mediators may be used. Usually, a mediator charges a fee, which can be split between the parties. As mentioned previously, many state and federal courts require that parties mediate their disputes before being allowed to resolve the disputes through trials. When mediation is required by a court before the parties can have the court hear their dispute, the mediators may be appointed by the court.

Mediation usually results in the quick settlement of disputes. Initial meetings between the parties and the mediator often occur within several weeks after a voluntary request to mediate has been made by one or both parties. (See this chapter's featured-guest article entitled "Mediation and the Paralegal" for further details on the functions performed by mediators and the role played by paralegals in the mediation process.)

Arbitration

A more formal method of alternative dispute resolution is **arbitration**. The key difference between arbitration and the forms of ADR just discussed,

ARBITRATION
The settling of a dispute by submitting it to a disinterested third party (other than a court), who renders a legally binding decision.

FEATURED GUEST: ANDREA NAGER CHASEN

Mediation and the Paralegal

Biographical Note

Andrea Nager Chasen received her master's degree in public administration, specializing in the theory and practice of decision-making processes, from New York University. Four years later, she earned her law degree at the American University School of Law. Following graduation from law school, through her work as a litigator, she became interested in alternative methods of dispute resolution. Her interest led her to an in-depth exploration of mediation as one method of resolving disputes out of court. As a consequence, she has developed and taught courses in mediation and has served as a mediator. Currently, she mediates and arbitrates disputes on a full-time basis in her private practice.

With all of the attention on alternative dispute resolution (ADR) methods as tools for conflict resolution, how is the traditional law firm to respond? Will the availability of ADR result in the end of the trial as we know it and the exhaustive amount of work that goes into preparing for trial? Rest assured, there is still work (and lots of it) to be done. But the type of work will differ from what the average attorney and paralegal are used to doing. This feature focuses on just one method of ADR—mediation—and the paralegal's role in this process.[a]

WHAT DOES A MEDIATOR DO?

Before considering the paralegal's role in the mediation process, it is important to know how mediators help parties in settling their conflicts. Generally, the mediator undertakes to do the following:

1. Learn what the parties' real interests are (as opposed to the positions that the parties have put forward).
2. Assess realistically the alternative ways in which the dispute might be resolved.
3. Deal with the differences between the parties' perceptions of the issues involved in the dispute.
4. Learn (in private sessions with each party) what information the parties are unwilling to disclose to each other.
5. Devise options and solutions that meet the interests of all parties involved in the dispute.

Throughout the proceedings, the mediator maintains a neutral position and focuses on the parties' feelings and statements that can be used productively. The mediator never imposes a judgment but acts as a facilitator to help the parties reach their own agreement.

THE PARALEGAL'S ROLE IN THE MEDIATION PROCESS

What tasks does the paralegal perform in relation to the mediation process? Perhaps the best way to answer this question is to divide the mediation process into various stages and examine the role of the paralegal during each stage. Generally, as with cases that go to trial, a good deal of the paralegal's efforts will be involved in overall case management.

Stage One: Premediation. The first stage of the mediation process consists of finding out the facts about a client's claim against another party and determining whether mediation might be appropriate at this point. In divorce or custody matters, if the couple has retained attorneys but negotiations appear to be failing, then an attempt to mediate the dispute may be useful. Sometimes, the client's case will already be in the initial stages of litigation, and pretrial investigations will be underway. Mediation may also be forced

a. EDITOR'S NOTE: The author of this article describes some of the general features of the mediation process and the paralegal's role in mediation. Realize, however, that the mediation process may be voluntary or mandated by a court, and different states (and different courts within a state) may have different mediation procedures.

FEATURED GUEST, Continued

upon the parties by a court or other authority at almost the "eleventh hour" prior to trial—after both parties are fully prepared to present their respective cases to the court.

Paralegals play an important role during the premediation stage by investigating the factual background of the dispute, organizing the results of all preliminary investigations and other data relevant to the dispute, contacting the parties, and generally managing the case.

Stage Two: Selecting Mediation. Certain factors should be considered in reviewing the available tools (including litigation) for conflict resolution. If the disputing parties have a continuing relationship—as business partners, for example—court-imposed decisions may alienate the parties and intensify the conflict. Also, having the conflict resolved by a court can be costly and time consuming.

Generally, mediation can be arranged to meet the scheduling demands of the parties and is far less costly than litigation. Furthermore, because the mediator does not impose the decision, the parties control how the agreement is shaped. Unlike litigation, mediation is not adversarial in nature; rather, it seeks to find common grounds on which an agreement can be based. Therefore, the process tends to reduce the antagonism between the disputants and to allow them to resume their former relationship more easily.

The paralegal's role during this preliminary stage is to develop a clear understanding of the client's needs and interests so that the attorney can better assess whether mediation would be a desirable alternative for resolving the dispute. The paralegal can also provide the attorney with a list of prescreened, qualified mediators. (Such lists can be obtained from numerous organizations, including the American Arbitration Association, the federal Mediation and Conciliation Service, local courts, and chambers of commerce.) The parties can then select the appropriate mediator for their dispute from this list. Depending on what person or organization will be mediating the dispute, the paralegal may wish to obtain information on what kinds of procedures will be involved and secure any necessary forms.

Stage Three: Mediation Sessions. During the mediation sessions, the mediator allows both sides to present their views and spends time with the parties, either jointly or in private meetings with each party, to uncover the real interests and needs of the disputants. Sometimes, the parties may reach agreement after just one mediation session, but commonly several sessions are held so that the parties have the time and opportunity to obtain information on issues that need to be addressed. It may be necessary, for example, to obtain financial data relating to one or both of the parties. And, of course, several sessions may be required simply to reach a satisfactory agreement.

The paralegal can play a crucial role during this stage of the mediation process by helping to provide additional information for the sessions as they progress. The paralegal can also help in the drafting of any preliminary responses that are required during the course of the mediation. The paralegal may also draft the final agreement—unless that duty is assumed by the mediator.

"THE MEDIATOR NEVER IMPOSES A JUDGMENT BUT ACTS AS A FACILITATOR TO HELP THE PARTIES REACH THEIR OWN AGREEMENT."

CONCLUSION

Mediation can be useful at many stages of a dispute between parties. Mediation may help to resolve the entire dispute or just one aspect of it. Case management within the legal office is as important for the cases that are to be mediated as it is for the cases that will be tried in court. The paralegal can play a significant role in overall case management by doing the following:

1. Maintaining good methods of tracking and organizing data during the premediation stage.
2. Assisting the parties in selecting an appropriate mediator.
3. Providing necessary data and information during mediation sessions.

negotiation and mediation, is that in those forms of ADR, the parties themselves settle their dispute—although a third party may assist them in doing so. In arbitration, the third party hearing the dispute normally makes the decision for the parties. In a sense, the arbitrator becomes a private judge, even though the arbitrator does not have to be a lawyer. Frequently, a panel of experts arbitrates the dispute.

Depending on the parties' circumstances and preferences, the arbitrator's decision may be legally binding or nonbinding on the parties. In nonbinding arbitration, the parties submit their dispute to a third party but remain free to reject the third party's decision. Nonbinding arbitration is more similar to mediation than to binding arbitration. As will be discussed in the final section of this chapter, arbitration that is mandated by the courts is often not binding on the parties. If, after mandatory arbitration, the parties are not satisfied with the results of arbitration, they may then ignore the arbitrator's decision and have the dispute litigated in court. Even if the arbitrator's decision is legally binding, a party can appeal the decision to a court for judicial review—as will be discussed below.

Arbitration Clauses and Statutes. Virtually any commercial matter can be submitted to arbitration. When a dispute arises, parties can agree to settle their differences through arbitration rather than through the court system. Frequently, however, disputes are arbitrated because of an arbitration clause in a contract entered into before the dispute arose. An **arbitration clause** provides that any disputes arising under the contract will be resolved by arbitration. For example, an arbitration clause in a contract for the sale of goods might provide that "any controversy or claim arising under this contract will be referred to arbitration before the American Arbitration Association."[7]

ARBITRATION CLAUSE
A clause in a contract that provides that, in case of a dispute, the parties will determine their rights by arbitration rather than through the judicial system.

It is important to note that if parties enter into a contract containing an arbitration clause, it is likely that either a state or a federal statute will compel them to arbitrate any dispute arising under the contract. Most states have statutes under which arbitration clauses are enforced, and some state statutes compel arbitration of certain types of disputes, such as those involving public employees. At the federal level, the Federal Arbitration Act (FAA) of 1925 enforces arbitration clauses in contracts relating to certain types of activities, such as those involving interstate commerce (commerce between two or more states). Even business activities that have only remote or minimal effects on commerce between two or more states are regarded as interstate commerce. Thus, arbitration agreements involving transactions only slightly connected to the flow of interstate commerce may fall under the FAA.

The FAA does not establish a set arbitration procedure. The parties themselves must agree on the manner of resolving their disputes. The FAA only provides that if the parties have agreed to arbitrate disputes arising in relation to their contract, through an arbitration clause, the arbitration clause will be enforced. In other words, arbitration must take place before a party can take a dispute to the courts.

7. As will be discussed shortly, the American Arbitration Association is a leading provider of arbitration services in the United States.

Arbitration Services. Arbitration services are provided by both government agencies and private organizations. The primary provider of arbitration services is the **American Arbitration Association (AAA).** Most of the largest law firms in the nation are members of this association. Founded in 1926, the AAA now settles more than fifty thousand disputes a year in its numerous offices around the country. Settlements usually are effected quickly and, at times, in informal settings, such as a conference room or even a hotel room, depending on the preferences of the parties.

Cases brought before the AAA are heard by an expert or a panel of experts in the area relating to the dispute. Generally, about half of the panel members are lawyers. To cover its costs, the nonprofit organization charges a fee, paid by the party filing the claim. In addition, each party to the dispute pays a specified amount for each hearing day, as well as a special additional fee in cases involving personal injuries or property loss.

The Arbitration Process. The first step in the arbitration process is the **submission agreement**, which occurs when the parties agree to submit their dispute for arbitration. (If an arbitration clause is included in a contract, the clause itself is the submission to arbitrate.) Most states require that an agreement to submit a dispute to arbitration must be in writing. The submission agreement typically identifies the parties, the nature of the dispute to be resolved, the monetary amounts involved in the dispute, the place of arbitration, and the powers that the arbitrator will exercise. Frequently, the agreement includes a signed statement that the parties intend to be bound by the arbitrator's decision. A sample submission form—that used by the American Arbitration Association—is shown in Exhibit 7.6 on the next page.

The next step in the process is the *hearing*. Normally, the parties agree prior to arbitration—in an arbitration clause or in a submission-to-arbitrate agreement, for example—on what procedural rules will govern the proceedings. In a typical hearing, the parties begin as they would at a trial by presenting opening arguments to the arbitrator and stating what remedies should or should not be granted. After the opening statements have been made, evidence is presented. Witnesses may be called and examined by both sides. After all evidence has been presented, the parties give their closing arguments. Although arbitration is in some ways similar to a trial, the rules (such as rules regarding what kinds of evidence may be introduced) are usually much less restrictive than those involved in formal litigation.

After each side has had an opportunity to present evidence and to argue its case, the arbitrator reaches a decision. The final decision of the arbitrator is called an **award**, even if no money is conferred on a party as a result of the proceedings. Under most arbitration statutes, the arbitrator must render an award within thirty days of the close of the hearing.

A paralegal may become extensively involved in preparations for arbitration, just as he or she would in preparing for a trial. The paralegal will assist in obtaining and organizing all evidence relating to the dispute, may interview witnesses and prepare them for the hearing, and generally will assist in other tasks commonly undertaken prior to a trial (see Chapter 10).

The Role of the Courts in the Arbitration Process. The role of the courts in the arbitration process is limited. One important role is played at the prearbitration stage. When a dispute arises as to whether the parties have agreed

ETHICAL CONCERN

Potential Arbitration Problems

Many individuals and business firms prefer to arbitrate disputes rather than take them to court. For that reason, they often include arbitration clauses in their contracts. These clauses normally specify who or what organization will arbitrate the dispute and where the arbitration will take place. To safeguard a client's interests, when drafting and reviewing arbitration clauses in contracts, the careful paralegal will be alert to the possibility that those who arbitrate the dispute might not be totally neutral or that the designated place of arbitration is so geographically distant from the client's location that it may pose a great inconvenience and expense for the client should a dispute arise that needs to be arbitrated. The paralegal should call any such problems to his or her supervising attorney's attention. The attorney can then discuss the problem with the client and help the client negotiate an arbitration clause that is more favorable to the client's position.

AMERICAN ARBITRATION ASSOCIATION (AAA)
The major organization offering arbitration services in the United States.

SUBMISSION AGREEMENT
A written agreement to submit a legal dispute to an arbitrator or arbitrating panel for resolution.

AWARD
In the context of ADR, the decision rendered by an arbitrator.

EXHIBIT 7.6
A Sample Submission Form

American Arbitration Association
SUBMISSION TO DISPUTE RESOLUTION

Date:________________

The named parties hereby submit the following dispute for resolution under the____________ ______________________ Rules* of the American Arbitration Association:

Procedure Selected: ☐ Binding arbitration ☐ Mediation settlement
☐ Other______________________
(Describe)

For Insurance Cases Only:
__________ __________to__________ __________
Policy Number Effective Dates Applicable Policy Limits
______________________ ______________________
Date of Incident Location
Insured______________________ Claim Number:__________

Name(s) of Claimant(s)	Check if a Minor	Amount Claimed
______________	☐	__________
______________	☐	__________

Nature of Dispute and/or Injuries Alleged (attach additional sheets if necessary):

Place of Hearing:______________________________

We agree that, if binding arbitration is selected, we will abide by and perform any award rendered hereunder and that a judgment may be entered on the award.

To be Completed by the Claimant	To be Completed by the Respondent
Name of Party	Name of Party
Address	Address
City, State, and ZIP Code	City, State, and ZIP Code
Telephone Fax	Telephone Fax
Signature†	Signature†
Name of Party's Attorney or Representative	Name of Party's Attorney or Representative
Address	Address
City, State, and ZIP Code	City, State, and ZIP Code
Telephone Fax	Telephone Fax
Signature†	Signature†

Please file three copies with the AAA.

* If you have any questions as to which rules apply, please contact the AAA.
†Signatures of all parties are required for arbitration.

Form G1-7/90

in an arbitration clause to submit a particular matter to arbitration, one party may file suit to compel arbitration. The court before which the suit is brought will not decide the basic controversy but must decide whether the dispute is *arbitrable*—that is, whether the matter is one that can be resolved through arbitration. For example, if the dispute involves a claim of employment discrimination on the basis of age, the court will have to decide whether the Age Discrimination in Employment Act of 1967 (which protects persons forty years of age and older against employment discrimination on the basis of age) permits claims brought under this act to be arbitrated. As for any other court trial, the attorney's legal team will gather all the evidence and facts relating to the dispute, research the relevant arbitration statute and previous case law, and so on, as necessary to support the client's position.

Courts also may play an important role at the postarbitration stage. If the arbitration has produced an award, one of the parties may appeal the award or may seek a court order compelling the other party to comply with the award. In determining whether an award should be enforced, a court conducts a review that is much more restricted in scope than an appellate court's review of a trial court decision. The general view is that because the parties were free to frame the issues and set the powers of the arbitrator at the outset, they cannot complain about the result.

An arbitration award may be set aside, however, in certain circumstances. An arbitrator's award may be set aside if the award resulted from the arbitrator's misconduct or "bad faith." For example, if the arbitrator exhibited bias or corruption, refused to hear pertinent evidence, or acted in any way that substantially prejudiced the rights of one of the parties, the award may be set aside. Another basis for setting aside an award exists if the arbitrator exceeded his or her powers in arbitrating the dispute. An arbitrator is permitted to resolve only those issues that are covered by the agreement to submit to arbitration. As already mentioned, if the arbitrability of a dispute is in question, the courts must decide that issue, not the arbitrator.

Summary Jury Trials and Mini-trials

A relatively new form of ADR that has been successfully employed in the federal court system is the **summary jury trial (SJT).** In an SJT, the parties present their arguments and supporting evidence (other than witness testimony—witnesses are not called in an SJT), and the jury then renders a verdict. Unlike in an actual trial, the jury's verdict is not binding. The verdict does, however, act as a guide to both sides in reaching an agreement during the mandatory negotiations that immediately follow the SJT. Because no witnesses are called, the SJT is much speedier than a regular trial, and frequently the parties are able to settle their dispute without resorting to an actual trial. If no settlement is reached, both sides have the right to a full trial later. Because they have proved to be a cost-effective and efficient way to settle disputes, SJTs are now held in numerous federal courts.

SUMMARY JURY TRIAL (SJT)
A relatively recent method of settling disputes in which a trial is held but the jury's verdict is not binding. The verdict only acts as a guide to both sides in reaching an agreement during the mandatory negotiations that immediately follow the trial. If a settlement is not reached, both sides have the right to a full trial later.

Another fairly recent development in the area of ADR is the use of mini-trials. Unlike court-sponsored SJTs, **mini-trials** are private proceedings. Typically, mini-trials are undertaken by business firms involved in contractual or other types of disputes to resolve disputes outside the court system. In a mini-trial, each party's attorney briefly argues the party's case before representatives of each firm who have the authority to settle the dispute. Often, a neutral third party, such as a retired judge, presides over the proceedings and acts as an adviser. If the parties fail to reach an agreement, the adviser renders an opinion as to how a court would likely decide the issue. The advantage of the mini-trial is similar to that of the SJT: it allows the parties to assess the relative strengths and weaknesses of their cases before an actual trial is held.

MINI-TRIAL
A private proceeding that assists disputing parties in determining whether to take their case to court. During the proceeding, each party's attorney briefly argues the party's case before the other party and (usually) a neutral third party, who acts as an adviser. If the parties fail to reach an agreement, the adviser renders an opinion as to how a court would likely decide the issue.

ETHICAL CONCERN

Rent-a-judge Courts

The use of private rent-a-judge courts has been controversial. Critics raise the ethical question as to whether it is fair to put a "price tag" on justice by making dispute-settlement forums more available to those who can afford them than to those who cannot. Supporters of private courts maintain that any alternative that can help reduce the heavy caseload of the courts ultimately helps everybody. As a concerned citizen, you may have strong views on the matter. In your capacity as a paralegal, however, you should not let your personal ethical standards prevent you from implementing whatever (legal) course of action the client, in consultation with your supervising attorney, chooses to undertake.

"Rent-a-judge" Courts

Other private alternatives to traditional court proceedings include private "rent-a-judge" courts. This option first became available in 1976 in California, when that state's legislature enacted a statute that allowed disputing parties to bypass the formal court system by hiring former judges of the California courts to hear their disputes. The California statute provided that jurors could be selected from the public jury roll, and verdicts could be appealed to a state appellate court.

The system of "private justice" spread quickly, and now hundreds of firms throughout the country offer dispute-resolution services by hired judges. Two of the leading firms in this legal industry, Endispute of Washington, D.C., and Judicial Arbitration and Mediation Services of California, have recently merged and now offer dispute-resolution services throughout the country. Private courts are a boon to those who do not wish to wait for years to go to trial. In Los Angeles County, for example, parties to lawsuits must wait from three to eight years (the national average is twenty-two months) to be heard in a public court.

Procedures in these private courts are fashioned to meet the desires of the clients seeking their services. For example, the parties usually can decide on the date of the hearing, the presiding judge, whether the judge's decision will be legally binding, and the site of the hearing—which could be a conference room, a law-school office, or a leased courtroom. The judges follow procedures similar to those of the federal courts and use similar rules. Normally, each party to the dispute pays a filing fee and a designated fee for a hearing session or conference. Although rent-a-judge courts first became popular in settling contract and employment disputes, in recent years they have been frequently used to settle disputes relating to family law and personal injuries as well.

Mandatory ADR

Up to this point, we have been discussing ADR that is undertaken by the parties *voluntarily*. Increasingly, the courts are *requiring* that parties attempt to settle their differences through some form of ADR before proceeding to trial. Usually, the claims involved must fall under a certain threshold amount. Since 1984, federal courts in several districts have been experimenting with court-sponsored, nonbinding arbitration for cases involving up to $100,000. Because of the success of this program (less than 10 percent of the cases referred for arbitration go to trial), federal courts continue to use this method. State courts are also increasingly turning to ADR programs as a means of relieving their burgeoning caseloads. Many states now require that certain types of disputes, such as child-custody disputes, be mediated.

In the federal courts and in many state courts, when cases are referred for arbitration, the arbitrator's decision is not binding. If either party rejects the award, the case proceeds to trial, and the court reconsiders all of the evidence and legal questions pertaining to the dispute. To encourage parties to accept decisions reached through ADR as final, courts frequently make those who resort to litigation following ADR pay for the costs of the court proceedings.

PROCEDURAL LAW CONCEPT SUMMARY

Alternative Dispute Resolution

Negotiation	A method of ADR in which the parties come together, with or without attorneys to represent them, and try to reach a settlement without the involvement of a third party.
Mediation	A method of ADR in which the parties themselves try to reach an agreement, but with the help of a third party, called a mediator, who proposes solutions.
Arbitration	A more formal method of ADR in which the parties submit their dispute to a neutral third party, the arbitrator (or panel of arbitrators), who renders a decision. The decision may or may not be legally binding, depending on the circumstances. Court-mandated arbitration, for example, is normally nonbinding. In arbitration proceedings voluntarily entered into by parties, such as through an arbitration clause in a contract voluntarily agreed on by the parties, the arbitrator's decision is usually binding. Arbitrators' decisions, even in binding arbitration, may be appealed to the courts for review if a party claims that the award should be set aside because the arbitrator exceeded his or her authority or for some other reason.
Summary Jury Trial (SJT)	A kind of trial employed by some federal courts in which litigants present their evidence and arguments to a jury, which renders a nonbinding verdict. The jury's verdict acts as a guide to both parties in reaching an agreement during the mandatory negotiations that immediately follow the SJT.
Mini-trial	A private proceeding in which each party's attorney argues the party's case before a panel of representatives from both sides. A neutral third party often acts as an adviser and renders an opinion on how a court would likely decide the issue.
Rent-a-judge Courts	The parties rent (hire) a judge to hear their case and render a verdict to which the parties agree to be bound. Several firms now provide for this kind of private justice.
Mandatory ADR	Many federal and state courts today require parties to lawsuits to undergo some form of ADR (mediation or arbitration, for example) before the parties will be entitled to bring their lawsuits before the courts.

ADR and the Paralegal

The time and money costs associated with litigating disputes in court continue to rise, and, as a result, disputing parties are increasingly turning to ADR as a means of settling their disputes. As a way to reduce their caseloads, state and federal courts are also increasingly requiring litigants to undergo arbitration prior to bringing their suits before the courts. Although paralegals have always assisted attorneys in work relating to the negotiation of out-of-court settlements for clients, they may play an even greater role in the future. Some paralegals are qualified mediators and directly assist parties in reaching a mutually satisfactory agreement. Some paralegals serve as arbitrators. As more and more parties utilize ADR, paralegals will have increasing opportunities in this area of legal work.

TODAY'S PROFESSIONAL PARALEGAL

Arbitrating Commercial Contracts

Julia Lorenz has worked as a legal assistant for International Airlines (IA) for ten years. She works in the legal department on the staff of the general counsel. Her job has been to work with Jim Manning, senior attorney. This attorney is responsible for all of the corporation's contracts, including the following: major contracts with jet manufacturers for the purchase of aircraft, contracts with catering companies to supply food during flights, fuel contracts, employment and labor contracts, and many small contracts for the purchase and lease of equipment and supplies for the many airline offices and ticket counters.

REVIEWING PROPOSED CONTRACTS

Julia's job is to review the provisions of proposed major contracts, such as the contracts to purchase jet aircraft, and to provide Jim with an article-by-article summary of the contracts' provisions. Jim then negotiates these contracts to obtain the most favorable terms possible for the airline. Once he has negotiated a contract, Julia makes the final changes and forwards it to the appropriate IA corporate official to review and sign.

ATTENDING ARBITRATION PROCEEDINGS

All of the airline's major contracts contain arbitration clauses that require all contract disputes to be resolved through binding arbitration services provided by the American Arbitration Association (AAA). On numerous occasions, Julia has attended arbitration proceedings with Jim. In preparing for arbitration, Julia obtains affidavits, prepares subpoenas, and arranges for witnesses to be present to testify. During the arbitration proceedings, she assists in presenting material into evidence. She and Jim have developed a good rapport with several arbitrators at the local AAA office, and they usually request these arbitrators when they have a case that must be arbitrated.

BECOMING AN ARBITRATOR

Julia's knowledge of arbitration procedures and her outstanding work in preparing for arbitration, as well as during the proceedings, won her significant recognition from this group of arbitrators. One of the arbitrators eventually approached Julia and suggested that she apply for approval as an arbitrator. She said that she would consider it.

Julia later mentioned the arbitrator's suggestion to Jim. He thought that Julia had been paid quite a compliment. He encouraged her to contact the AAA to inquire about the possibility of being approved as an arbitrator. When Julia called the AAA, she learned that arbitrators in the area of commercial arbitration are not required to be attorneys. She would need eight years of experience in her field and would have to meet certain educational requirements. When Julia realized that she had the necessary qualifications, she submitted an application. About two months later, she was approved as an arbitrator.

KEY TERMS AND CONCEPTS

CHAPTER SUMMARY

1. Before a court can hear a case, the court must have jurisdiction over the person against whom the suit is brought or over the property involved in the suit. It must also have jurisdiction over the subject matter of the dispute. Courts of general jurisdiction can hear most types of disputes. Courts of limited jurisdiction are restricted in the types of actions they can decide. Courts having original jurisdiction are courts in which the trial of a case begins. Courts having appellate jurisdiction are reviewing courts. They do not try cases anew but review the decisions of trial courts.

2. Federal courts have limited jurisdiction. They can exercise jurisdiction over claims involving (1) a federal question, which arises when the plaintiff's claim is based at least in part on the U.S. Constitution, a treaty, or a federal law; or (2) diversity of citizenship, which arises when the case involves citizens of different states, a foreign country and citizens of a state or different states, or citizens of a state and citizens or subjects of a foreign country. The amount in controversy must exceed $50,000 for jurisdiction based on diversity of citizenship to arise.

3. Venue has to do with the appropriate geographical area in which a case should be brought. The concept of venue reflects the policy that a court trying a suit should be in the geographic neighborhood (usually the county) in which the incident leading to the suit occurred or in which the parties involved in the suit reside.

4. Before a plaintiff can bring a lawsuit, he or she must have standing to sue. To have standing, a plaintiff must have a sufficient stake in a controversy to justify taking the issue before a court. Additionally the controversy must be justiciable—that is, it must be actual and real, not hypothetical or academic.

5. Paralegals should become familiar with the procedural rules of the specific court in which a case is filed. Federal court procedures are set forth in the Federal Rules of Civil Procedure. States rules vary from state to state—and even from court to court within a given state. Also, court procedural rules are different for civil cases than for criminal cases.

6. The structure of state court systems varies from state to state. A typical state court system may consist of several tiers. On the bottom tier are courts of limited jurisdiction. On the next tier are usually the trial courts of general jurisdiction. Trial courts are courts of original jurisdiction—in other words, courts in which lawsuits are initiated, trials are held, and evidence is presented. The upper tier consists of appellate courts, to which trial court decisions can be appealed. Appellate courts are reviewing courts; their function is to review the trial court's decision in cases that are appealed. The highest state appellate court is typically called the state supreme court, although there are exceptions. Cases can be appealed from state supreme courts to the United States Supreme Court only if a federal question is involved.

7. The federal court system consists of U.S. district courts (trial courts), U.S. courts of appeals (intermediate appellate courts), and the United States Supreme Court. Decisions from a district court can be appealed to the court of appeals of the circuit (geographical area) in which the district court is located. There are thirteen circuit courts of appeals. Decisions rendered by these circuit courts may be appealed to the United States Supreme Court.

8. The United States Supreme Court is the highest court in the land. There is no absolute right of appeal to the Supreme Court, and the Court hears only a fraction of the cases that are filed with it each year. If the Court decides to review a case, it will issue a writ of *certiorari*, which is an order by the Supreme Court to a lower court requiring the latter to send it the record of the case for review. Generally, only those petitions that raise the possibility of important constitutional questions are granted.

9. The costs and time-consuming character of litigation, as well as the public nature of court proceedings, have caused many to turn to various forms of alternative dispute resolution (ADR) for settling their disputes. Out-of-court settlements are reached in the majority of lawsuits, usually before the trial begins.

10. Negotiation, the simplest method of ADR, may or may not involve a third party; the parties to the dispute simply try to work out their problems to avoid going to court. Mediation is a form of ADR in which the parties attempt to reach agreement with the help of a neutral third party, called a mediator (or a panel of mediators), who helps the disputants explore alternative possibilities for settling their differences as amicably as possible. The mediator proposes various solutions for the parties to consider.

11. Arbitration is the most formal method of ADR. In arbitration, a neutral third party (a lawyer, expert, panel of specialists, or other party) renders a decision after the parties present their cases and evidence in a hearing. Normally, in voluntary arbitration (as opposed to court-mandated ADR), the parties agree at the outset to be legally bound by the arbitrator's decision, which is called an award. Increasingly, parties are including in their contracts arbitration clauses—provisions by which the parties agree to arbitrate any disputes that may arise under the contract. Arbitration clauses will likely be enforced under a federal or state arbitration statute.

12. Other forms of ADR include summary jury trials and mini-trials. In a summary jury trial, the parties present their arguments and evidence to a jury, and the jury renders a verdict. The verdict is not legally binding but serves to guide the parties in reaching an agreement on the disputed matter. Mini-trials are private proceedings in which each party's attorney briefly argues the party's case before the other party. Often, a neutral third party, who acts as an adviser, is also present. If the parties fail to reach an agreement, the adviser renders an opinion as to how a court would likely decide the issue.

13. "Rent-a-judge" courts have also become an attractive ADR option for many people. In these private courts, former judges are hired to hear disputes and render decisions. The rent-a-judge option began in California in 1976, and now hundreds of firms throughout the country offer such dispute-resolution services.

14. To ease their heavy caseloads, numerous state and federal courts today require that certain disputes (under a certain dollar threshold, for example) be mediated or arbitrated before they can be heard in court. If a party is not satisfied with the results of mediation or arbitration, however, that party can take the issue to court.

QUESTIONS FOR REVIEW

1. Define *jurisdiction* and explain why jurisdiction it is important.

2. What is the difference between personal jurisdiction and subject-matter jurisdiction? What is a long-arm statute?

3. Define *original jurisdiction*. Define *appellate jurisdiction*. What is the difference between the two?

4. Over what types of cases may federal courts exercise jurisdiction?

5. What is the relationship between state and federal jurisdiction?

6. What is venue? What is the difference between venue and jurisdiction?

7. Describe the functions of a trial court. How do they differ from the functions of an appellate court?

8. What are the typical courts in a state court system? What are the three basic tiers, or levels, of courts in the federal court system?

9. How do cases reach the United States Supreme Court?

10. List and explain the various methods of alternative dispute resolution.

ETHICAL QUESTIONS

1. Larry Simpson is working on a lawsuit that was recently filed in a federal district court on the basis of diversity-of-citizenship jurisdiction. Larry, a legal assistant, just received the plaintiff's answers to interrogatories (attorneys' written questions to the parties in a lawsuit), which he is summarizing. Larry discovers that the plaintiff's damages are nowhere near the $50,000 required for diversity jurisdiction. What should Larry do?

2. Diane Post, a paralegal, is working on the defense team in a civil lawsuit that has just been filed in the county court, which has limited jurisdiction over civil lawsuits. The plaintiff is seeking an injunction and $3,000 in damages. (Recall from Chapter 6 that an injunction is an equitable remedy in which a court orders a person to do or refrain from doing a particular act.) The superior court is the only court with jurisdiction over equitable remedies. No one but Diane has noticed that the plaintiff is seeking a remedy that the county court does not have the jurisdictional authority to grant. What should Diane do?

3. Suzanne Andersen's supervising attorney, Amy Lynch, works occasionally as a mediator for family-law cases in the local courts. Amy has mediated a case today involving custody and visitation rights for a wealthy businessperson, who happens also to be a defendant in another lawsuit in which Amy represents the plaintiff. As a result of her mediation today, Amy has learned some confidential financial information about this man. She now has come to Suzanne, her paralegal, and asked her to use this information to his disadvantage in the lawsuit. How should Suzanne handle this situation?

PRACTICE QUESTIONS AND ASSIGNMENTS

1. Look at Exhibit 7.4. In which federal circuit is your state located? How many federal judicial districts are located in your state?

2. Based on the information provided in this chapter, including the exhibits, determine which federal court (or courts) could hear the following cases and on what jurisdictional grounds:

a. A case in which the Internal Revenue Service sues a taxpayer for back taxes.
b. A case involving an automobile accident between a citizen of Chicago, Illinois, and a citizen of St. Louis, Missouri, seeking damages of $100,000.
c. A bankruptcy case.
d. A lawsuit claiming sexual harassment in violation of Title VII of the federal Civil Rights Act of 1964.
e. A lawsuit claiming that the defendant violated the federal statute prohibiting racketeering crimes.

3. Using Exhibit 7.5 as a model, draft a settlement agreement for a lawsuit involving the following facts:

> Harry Jones is suing Burt Gaston in the U.S. District Court for the Western District of Kentucky, docket number 95-123456. On June 12, 1996, Harry agrees to accept $100,000 in settlement of the lawsuit. Harry's attorney will prepare a settlement agreement for their signatures on June 30. Harry will be paid in one lump-sum cash payment upon the execution of the settlement agreement, and he will give up his right to all claims against Burt and release Burt from all future liability for all claims arising out of this occurrence.

QUESTIONS FOR CRITICAL ANALYSIS

1. Why are Americans increasingly turning to ADR as a way of settling their disputes? What are the implications of ADR, including the increased use of "private justice," for the American system of justice generally?

2. Suppose that you are a plaintiff in a case brought against the defendant for damages in the amount of $250,000. The case arose as a result of injuries and property damage that you incurred in a car accident caused by the defendant's reckless driving. You know that you have a good chance of winning that amount of damages if the case goes to trial. The defendant offers to settle the case for $175,000. Assume that it would take three years before the court could hear the case. What factors would you consider in deciding this question? What would your decision be?

3. Some individuals have claimed that mandatory ADR infringes on a person's constitutional right to a jury trial. Do you agree with this view? Why or why not?

ROLE-PLAYING EXERCISES

1. Review this chapter's *Developing Paralegal Skills* entitled "Choice of Courts: State or Federal?" Working in pairs, one student should assume the role of Joan Dunbar, the legal assistant, and the other the role of Susan Radtke, Joan's supervising attorney. The student playing the roal of Joan should ask Susan several questions about the pros and cons of filing the client's case in a state court versus a federal court. The student playing the role of Susan, when responding to Joan's questions, should keep in mind the client's situation as described in the feature. If time permits, reverse roles.

2. Jenny Morey, a paralegal, has just taken a job with a mid-sized law firm. Another paralegal, Bridget Johnson, is orienting Jenny to the work. Working in pairs, one student should assume the role of Jenny and the other Bridget. The person playing the role of Jenny should ask Bridget questions about one or more concepts covered in this chapter, such as diversity-of-citizenship jurisdiction, concurrent jurisdiction, state court systems, and the federal court system. The person playing the role of Bridget should answer Jenny's question or questions carefully and thoroughly. If time permits, reverse roles.

PROJECTS

1. Contact a local trial court and request a copy of a chart, pamphlet, or other publication that lists the courts in your state and describes the jurisdiction of each.

2. Contact the American Arbitration Association and ask what kind of disputes (contract disputes, employment disputes, and so on) they arbitrate. Request a copy of its procedural rules for the arbitration of disputes in one of the areas it handles. Review the rules and summarize the procedures involved.

3. Review the table of contents of the court rules of your state courts or the federal courts. What subjects are covered? How do these relate to the topics discussed in this chapter? You should be able to locate these rules in your school's library or in a law-school library.

ANNOTATED SELECTED READINGS

BRODSKY, DAVID M. *ADR Discovery Techniques.* New York: American Law Institute and American Bar Association, 1990. A discussion of the methods for limiting discovery that can be undertaken during alternative dispute resolution, specifically in mini-trials and arbitration. (Discovery consists of attorneys' formal investigations of claims prior to lawsuits or other legal proceedings—see Chapter 10.) The book provides a good overview of what takes place in a mini-trial and in arbitration.

BRYAN, PENELOPE E. "Killing Us Softly: Divorce Mediation and the Politics of Power." *Buffalo Law Review,* Spring 1992. An eye-opening look at the role divorce mediation plays in the divorce process. It challenges the effectiveness of mediation as a tool for women, claiming that mediation "empowers the already more powerful husband."

CHERMERINSKY, EDWIN, AND LARRY KRAMER. "Defining the Role of the Federal Courts." *Brigham Young University Law Review,* 1990. A look at the direction in which the federal courts are going. The article raises the question of whether the role of the federal courts should be expanded or diminished and examines the potential impact of each option.

FIEDMAN, BARRY. "A Different Dialogue: The Supreme Court, Congress and Federal Jurisdiction." *Northwestern University Law Review,* Fall 1990. An article that explains and challenges the checks and balances in our system and their impact on the jurisdiction exercised by the federal courts. The author questions the perception that Congress should have the authority to determine federal court jurisdiction.

HARALAMBE, ANN M. *Mediation and Negotiation: Alternatives to Litigation.* Tucson, Ariz.: Sun Family Advocacy, 1990. A good overview of the mediation and negotiation processes used in the family-law context.

MILLER, ROGER LEROY, AND GAYLORD A. JENTZ. *Fundamentals of Business Law.* 2d ed. St. Paul: West Publishing Co., 1993. (3d ed. to be published in 1996.) A highly readable and succinct presentation of the major principles of American law. Chapter 3 of the book examines the federal and state court systems and related concepts.

PANKEN, PETER M. *Avoiding Employment Litigation: Alternative Dispute Resolution of Employment Disputes in the '90s.* New York: American Law Institute and American Bar Association, 1991. An interesting discussion of arbitration versus litigation in resolving employment disputes.

WIEGAND, SHIRLEY A. "A New Light Bulb or the Work of the Devil? A Current Assessment of Summary Jury Trials." *Oregon Law Review*, 1990. The article provides a good description of the procedure involved in a summary jury trial, as well as a critical analysis of the pros and cons of this method of ADR.

8

FUNDAMENTAL LEGAL CONCEPTS

CHAPTER OBJECTIVES

After completing this chapter, you will know:

- **What kinds of promises are contractual promises—that is, promises that will be enforced by a court.**
- **The elements of a valid contract and defenses to contract formation and enforceability.**
- **The law governing contracts for the sale of goods (sales contracts).**
- **What kinds of wrongful actions are called *torts* and the difference between a tort and a crime.**
- **The difference between real property and personal property.**
- **How one acquires, holds, and transfers ownership rights in property.**
- **The meaning of intellectual property, including patents, copyrights, trademarks, and trade secrets, and how the law protects ownership rights in intellectual property.**

CHAPTER OUTLINE

INTRODUCTION

The law regulates virtually every transaction or activity engaged in by individuals across the nation. Simple, everyday transactions—such as purchasing a carton of milk from your corner grocer or loaning a friend your paralegal textbook—are subject to specific laws that define the rights and duties of the parties involved in the transaction.

As a paralegal, you will be directly involved in the process of applying legal concepts and principles to specific situations that arise in the everyday world around you. Your activities, including making sure that required procedures and deadlines are met, are essential to the legal process. After all, our rights under the law would be of little value if there were no established procedures for enforcing those rights. Some of your work may also involve legal research and analysis. You may be asked, for example, to find cases on point (cases in which the facts and legal issues are similar to those in a case that your supervising attorney is litigating). A basic understanding of the legal principles involved in the case will help direct your research efforts.

In the pages that follow, you will read about some of the fundamental concepts of American law. Some of these principles and concepts originated centuries ago, in the common law of medieval England. Others are of more recent origin; they have been formed by the courts or enacted by legislatures to solve problems unique to twentieth-century America.

CONTRACTS

The noted legal scholar Roscoe Pound once said that "[t]he social order rests upon the stability and predictability of conduct, of which keeping promises is a large item."[1] Contract law deals with, among other things, the keeping of promises. A *promise* is a declaration that something either will or will not happen in the future. A **contract** is an exchange of promises that can be enforced in court. It is an agreement (made orally or in writing) formed by two or more parties who promise to perform or refrain from performing some act now or in the future. If the contractual promise is not fulfilled, the party who made it is subject to the sanctions of a court for **breach of contract** (failure to perform what was promised in the contract). The breaching party may be required to pay money damages to compensate the other party for losses caused by the breach or, in some situations, may be ordered to perform the contract as promised.

CONTRACT
An agreement or bargain struck between parties, in which each party assumes a legal duty to the other party. The requirements for a valid contract are agreement, consideration, contractual capacity, and legality.

BREACH OF CONTRACT
The failure of a contractual party to perform the obligations assumed in a contract.

Like other types of law, contract law reflects our social values, interests, and expectations at a given point in time. It shows, for example, the kinds of promises or commitments that society has decided should be legally binding (enforceable by the courts). It also shows what excuses our society will or will not accept for breaking such promises.

In your work as a paralegal, you may deal extensively with contract formation or breach-of-contract claims. A basic understanding of contract law

1. R. Pound, *Jurisprudence,* Vol. 3 (St. Paul: West Publishing Co., 1959), p. 162.

will help guide your understanding and serve as a point of departure for all work that you do involving contracts. This section will explain the required elements of a valid contract, the defenses that can be asserted against a claim that a contract was breached, and the remedies available to the nonbreaching party. These principles apply to all contracts unless statutory law has modified the common law—as it has in the area of contracts for the sale of goods, for example, which are discussed in the next section.

Requirements of a Valid Contract

If a client alleges that a party has breached a contract, the first issue to be decided is whether a *valid contract* (a contract that will be enforced by a court) was ever formed. In determining this issue, an attorney investigates (or asks a paralegal to investigate) the circumstances to see if the following four requirements for a valid contract have been met:

- Agreement (offer and acceptance).
- Consideration.
- Contractual capacity.
- Legality.

Agreement. A contract is, in essence, an **agreement** between two or more parties. Therefore, if the parties failed to reach an agreement, no contract exists. Agreement becomes an issue when a dispute arises and one party alleges that he or she never intended to form a contract. To determine the intention of the parties, the courts separate contractual agreement into two events—one party's offer to form a contract and the other party's acceptance of that offer.

AGREEMENT
A meeting of two or more minds, and a requirement for a valid contract. In contract law, the process of agreement is separated into two distinct events: an offer to form a contract and the acceptance of that offer.

Offer. A contractual **offer** is a promise to do something (such as sell your car) in return for something of value (such as money). To be legally effective, an offer must reflect a serious and objective intention on the part of the *offeror* (the person making the offer) to enter into a contract with the *offeree* (the person to whom the offer is made). Offers made in jest, in undue excitement, or in obvious anger do not meet the intent requirement, and an offeree's acceptance of such an offer does not create a contractual agreement.

OFFER
A proposal to form a contract with another person or entity (the offeree). The offeree's acceptance of an effective offer creates a legally binding contract, providing all other requirements for a valid contract have been met.

For example, suppose that Al and Sue ride to work together each day in Sue's car, which has a market value of $15,000. One cold morning, Al and Sue get into the car, but Sue cannot get it started. She yells in anger, "I'll sell this car to anyone for $200!" Al drops $200 in Sue's lap. Has a contract to sell the car been formed? If Al consults with your supervising attorney, claiming that Sue breached a contract because she refused to give him the car, would your supervising attorney take Al's claim seriously? Probably not. The attorney would probably advise Al that a reasonable person, taking into consideration Sue's frustration and the obvious difference in value between the car's market price and the purchase price, would declare that Sue's offer was not made with serious and objective intent and that no contract was formed.

The terms of an offer must also be sufficiently definite—so that if the offer is accepted, the specific terms of the resulting contract will be clear to a court if a dispute arises. For example, suppose that Kim wants to sell her set of legal encyclopedias but has not mentioned any price. James says to Kim, "I'll buy the encyclopedias and pay you some money for them next week." In this situation, no valid contract will result because "some" money is not a definite term. If James paid Kim $50 and then sued her for breach of contract when Kim refused to part with her encyclopedias, the court would declare that the contract failed for lack of definite terms.

ACCEPTANCE
In contract law, the offeree's notification to the offeror that the offeree agrees to be bound by the terms of the offeror's offer, or proposal to form a contract.

Acceptance. Once an offer is made, the offeree can accept or reject it. **Acceptance** occurs when the offeree indicates, by words or actions, that he or she agrees to the terms of the offer. Upon acceptance, a contract is formed. If the offeree wants to modify the terms of the offer, he or she can make a *counteroffer*, thus assuming the role of an offeror. For example, assume that Kirk offers to sell Christina his van for $3,000. Christina responds that she will not pay that much for the car, but she is willing to buy it for $2,500. Christina has both rejected Kirk's offer and created another offer—a counteroffer. Now Christina is the offeror, and if Kirk (the offeree in this situation) accepts Christina's offer, a contract normally will result.

Note that for a valid contract to exist, acceptance must be made by the offeree (rather than a third party—that is, someone to whom the offer was *not* made). If, for example, Christina's friend John overheard the offer and tells Kirk that he will accept the offer, no contract will be formed because John was not the offeree. Christina was—and only if Christina accepts the offer will a contract be formed.

An acceptance must also be timely. If the offeror states that the offer will be open for ten days, acceptance must normally occur within that period of time for a contract to result. If the offeror does not indicate how long the offer will remain open, then acceptance must occur within a reasonable period of time. (What constitutes a reasonable period of time in the eyes of a court varies, depending on the circumstances.) Normally, an offeror can *revoke* (take back) an offer at any time before it is accepted, although there are some exceptions to this rule.

CONSIDERATION
Something of value, such as money or the performance of an action not otherwise required, that motivates the formation of a contract. Each party must give consideration for the contract to be binding.

Consideration. Another requirement of a valid contract is that consideration be exchanged. **Consideration** in contract law is normally defined as "something of value"—which may be money or the performance of certain actions that are not otherwise required. Consideration lies at the heart of a contract because the reason people enter into contracts is to obtain something they desire—something of value to them. For example, you presumably would not enter into a contract to buy a car unless you *wanted* the car. Similarly, a car dealer would not be motivated to part with a car unless he or she received something of value (money) in exchange.

The requirement of consideration distinguishes contracts from gifts. For example, if you promise to give your friend a thousand dollars as a gift and she promises to accept your gift, no contract results, because your friend has given no consideration for the contract. Although you might feel that you have a moral obligation to fulfill your promise, the law will not require you to do so. If, however, you give your friend a thousand dollars in exchange for her promise to take care of your house and garden for six months, the promise normally will be enforceable, because consideration has been given.

Your consideration is the thousand dollars; your friend's consideration is the assumption of an obligation that she otherwise would not assume.

Contractual Capacity. The third element required for the formation of a valid contract is contractual capacity. **Contractual capacity** exists when a person has the mental competence to enter into a contract. A person adjudged by a court to be mentally incompetent, for example, cannot form a legally binding contract with another party. A contract entered into by an intoxicated person who did not comprehend the legal consequences of his or her actions is not binding on that person.

CONTRACTUAL CAPACITY
The threshold mental capacity required by law for a party who enters into a contract to be bound by that contract.

In other situations, a person may have the capacity to enter into a valid contract but may also have the right to avoid liability under it. For example, minors usually are not legally bound by the contracts into which they enter. In most states, the age of majority (the age when a person is no longer a minor) for contractual purposes is eighteen years. If a minor enters into a contract (such as a contract to purchase a car) and then changes his or her mind, the minor can return whatever consideration (such as the car) that he or she received from the other party and *disaffirm* (in effect, cancel) the contract and legally avoid responsibilities under the contract. An adult entering into a contract with a minor, however, does not have the same option—the contract is *voidable* (capable of being canceled, or nullified) only at the option of the minor.

Legality. The fourth requirement for a valid contract is legality. A contract to do something that is prohibited by federal or state legislation is illegal and, as such, void at the outset (that is, no contract exists). For example, a contract to purchase cocaine from a drug dealer is void because it is illegal. No court would enforce the contract if a lawsuit was brought for breach of the contract.

Defenses to Contract Formation or Enforceability

If the attorney you work for is defending a client against a breach-of-contract claim, you may be asked to do research to establish whether the defendant can successfully raise one or more defenses to the claim. A **defense** is a legally acceptable reason, raised by a defendant in a lawsuit, why the court should not grant what the plaintiff is seeking. One defense that your client might assert is that the contract was not in writing when, by law, it was required to be in writing. We look at this defense and other defenses to contract formation or enforceability below.

DEFENSE
That which a defendant offers and alleges in an action or suit as a reason why the plaintiff should not be granted whatever it is the plaintiff is seeking.

The Statute of Frauds. Each state has a **Statute of Frauds** specifying that certain types of contracts must be in writing to be enforceable. These laws are the American counterparts of the original Statute of Frauds, which was passed by the English Parliament in the seventeenth century. The primary purpose of the English statute was to ensure that contracts relating to important transactions were evidenced in writing and to prevent fraud (specifically, the all-too-frequent practice, in seventeenth-century England, of "hiring" witnesses to an oral contract that never existed). Today, state laws likewise provide that certain types of contracts, because of their importance, must be in writing.

STATUTE OF FRAUDS
A state statute that requires certain types of contracts to be in writing to be enforceable.

Under the Statute of Frauds, the following types of contracts must be in writing to be enforceable:

- Contracts for the sale of land.
- Contracts that are impossible to perform within one year.
- Contracts made in consideration of marriage—such as prenuptial agreements (sometimes called antenuptial agreements), which specify how marital property will be divided if the marriage ends.
- Contracts in which one party agrees to be responsible for another's debts or obligations.
- Contracts for the sale of goods priced at $500 or more.

- **If any of these types of contracts is made orally, the contract is generally not enforceable.**

Genuineness of Assent. Another defense that a defendant can raise is that he or she did not genuinely assent (or agree) to the contract. Genuineness of assent may be lacking because of a mistake. For example, if Kevin agrees to purchase his friend's Macintosh computer and his friend assumes that she is selling Kevin her IBM, Kevin can defend against performing his obligations under the agreement (that is, having to pay his friend for the IBM) by asserting that a mutual mistake occurred.

FRAUD
Any misrepresentation, either by misstatement or by the omission of a material fact, knowingly made with the intention of deceiving another and on which a reasonable person would rely and on which an actual person has relied to his or her detriment.

A defendant might also assert the defense of **fraud**. A defendant might allege, for example, that (1) the plaintiff mispresented certain facts or failed to disclose certain information, (2) the defendant relied on the plaintiff's misrepresentation in consenting to the contract, and (3) therefore the contract should not be enforced. For example, suppose that Kevin goes to a computer store and purchases a new Power Macintosh computer, paying for it with his MasterCard. The salesperson retrieves from the back of the store an already-opened box that contains a used Power Macintosh. The salesperson, even though he knows that the computer has been used, nonetheless tells Kevin that the computer is brand new. When Keven unpacks the computer at his home, he notices that the computer is stained and dirty and that it has obviously been used for some time. If Kevin decides not to pay for the computer and the computer dealer sues him for breach of contract, Kevin can assert fraud as a defense.

Genuineness of assent may also be lacking if a contract is formed under duress or undue influence. *Duress* involves being forced to agree to a contract. *Undue influence* exists when someone uses his or her influence over another (especially someone of diminished mental capacity) to induce that person to enter into a contract that benefits the inducing party. For example, suppose that an elderly person who is completely dependent on others for basic bodily care has a nurse-companion whom he likes. The nurse keeps telling the elderly person how difficult it is for her to run errands for him without a car and how, if she only had car, she could do a much better job of caring for his needs. She stresses also how his car remains unused in the garage. After the nurse has cared for the elderly person for three weeks, he consents to form a contract to sell her his Rolls Royce, which is in excellent condition, for only $500. The children of the elderly person might assert that the contract resulted from undue influence on the part of the nurse and therefore should not be enforced.

Unconscionability. Some contracts are not enforceable because of the negative impact they would have on society. Such contracts are said to be contrary to public policy, or to what are considered by the courts to be the interests of society as a whole. An example of a contract contrary to public policy is an **unconscionable contract**, which is a contract or clause in a contract that is so oppressive, one sided, or unfair that it "shocks the conscience" of the court. Although courts usually will not interfere with contracts between private parties—even though the parties may have formed an unwise or foolish bargain—if a contract is deemed unconscionable, the court will relieve the innocent party of part or all of his or her duties under the contract.

UNCONSCIONABLE CONTRACT
A contract that is void on the basis of public policy because it is so oppressive, one sided, or unfair that it "shocks the conscience" of the court.

As an example of an unconscionable contract, consider a situation in which a salesperson persuades an uneducated and economically disadvantaged customer to buy a refrigerator on the installment plan. The customer signs an agreement promising to pay $50 a month for five years. The customer does not realize that, by signing the agreement, she has obligated herself to pay $3,000 for a refrigerator worth $500. If the customer failed to make the payments and the seller sued her for the balance due, a court could refuse to enforce such a one-sided, unfair contract on the ground that it is unconscionable.

Impossibility of Performance. Another defense against a breach-of-contract claim is the assertion that the contract cannot be performed because it is objectively impossible to perform it. If the subject matter of the contract (such as the Macintosh computer in the above example) is destroyed, for example, the contract cannot be performed because the computer cannot be delivered to the buyer—it no longer exists. Similarly, if one of the parties to the contract dies or becomes incapacitated, or if a law enacted after the contract was made makes the contract illegal, performance will normally be deemed impossible.

Remedies for Breach of Contract

Any client alleging breach of contract is primarily interested in obtaining a remedy for any harm suffered as a result of the breach. Recall from Chapter 6 that there are two basic types of remedies: remedies at law (money damages) and remedies in equity (remedies that are granted when money damages are inadequate).

In breach-of-contract cases, plaintiffs often claim *compensatory damages*—compensation (in the form of money) for the expenses they had to incur as a result of the breach of contract. For example, suppose that a raisin grower breached a contract to deliver a certain amount of raisins to a cereal maker. As a result of the breach, the cereal maker had to purchase at the last minute the same amount of raisins for twice the price. The extra costs (the difference between the contract price and the price that the cereal maker actually had to pay to obtain the raisins) could be claimed as compensatory damages.

A plaintiff might also claim *consequential damages*—foreseeable damages that result from a party's breach of contract. For example, if the cereal maker was unable to obtain any raisins after the raisin seller breached the

SUBSTANTIVE LAW CONCEPT SUMMARY

The Common Law of Contracts

Requirements of a Valid Contract	A contract is an exchange of promises that can be enforced in court. For a contract to be valid, the following four requirements must be met: **1.** *Agreement*—The making of an offer (a promise to do something in return for something else) and the acceptance of that offer by the one to whom the offer was made. **2.** *Consideration*—Something of value (such as money or an action one would not otherwise be required to undertake) given in exchange for performance or a promise of performance. **3.** *Contractual capacity*—The required level of mental competence to enter into a legally binding contract. **4.** *Legality*—The contract must be for a legal purpose.
Defenses to Contract Formation or Enforceability	**1.** *Failure to comply with the Statute of Frauds*—The following types of contracts fall under the Statute of Frauds and must be in writing to be enforceable: a. Contracts involving interests in land. b. Contracts whose terms cannot be performed within one year. c. Contracts made in consideration of marriage. d. Contracts in which one party agrees to be responsible for the debts or obligations of another. e. Contracts for the sale of goods priced at $500 or more. **2.** *Lack of genuineness of consent*—If a defendant can prove that he or she did not genuinely assent to the terms of the contract (because of mistake, fraud, duress, or undue influence, for example), the contract normally will not be enforceable. **3.** *Unconscionable contract*—A contract that is so oppressive, one sided, or unfair to the defendant that it "shocks the conscience" of the court is not enforceable. **4.** *Impossibility of performance*—A court will not enforce a contractual obligation that is objectively impossible to perform, as when the subject matter of the contract has been destroyed.

contract, the cereal maker would be unable to sell its usual amount of raisin-containing cereals and would consequently lose profits. These lost profits could be claimed as consequential damages.

In certain situations, such as contracts for the sale of unique goods or items, money damages may be an inadequate remedy. In such a situation, a plaintiff might ask the court to grant an equitable remedy, such as *specific performance* (the performance of what was promised in the contract) or *rescission* (cancellation) of the contract. These equitable remedies were both described in Chapter 6. Note, though, that when rescission is granted as a remedy and the contract is rescinded (or canceled), each party must make **restitution** to the other by returning goods, property, or money previously conveyed. An equitable remedy that was not mentioned in Chapter 6 is **reformation**. In breach-of-contract cases, this remedy occurs when the court revises a contract to reflect the true intention of the parties—if a mutual mistake occurred, for example.

RESTITUTION
An equitable remedy under which a person is restored to his or her original position prior to loss or injury, or placed in the position that he or she would have been in had the breach not occurred.

REFORMATION
An equitable remedy granted by a court to correct, or "reform," a written contract so that it reflects the true intentions of the parties.

SUBSTANTIVE LAW CONCEPT SUMMARY, Continued

Remedies for Breach of Contract	When a contract is breached, the remedies available to the nonbreaching party include remedies at law (money damages) and remedies in equity (normally not granted unless the remedy at law is inadequate): **1.** *Money damages*— a. Compensatory damages—Expenses incurred by the nonbreaching party as a result of the breach (such as the additional price that had to be paid to purchase goods from another seller). b. Consequential damages—Foreseeable damages resulting from a breach of contract (such as lost profits). **2.** *Equitable remedies*— a. Specific performance—The breaching party is ordered by the court to perform the promised contractual obligation. Normally, specific performance is only available in special situations—such as those involving contracts for the sale of unique goods or land. b. Rescission—An action to cancel the contract and return the parties to the positions that they occupied prior to the transaction. Available when fraud, mistake, duress, or failure of consideration is present. c. Restitution—When a contract is rescinded, or canceled, both parties must make restitution to each other by returning the goods, property, or money previously exchanged under the contract. Restitution prevents the unjust enrichment of the defendant. d. Reformation—The court revises the contract to reflect the true intention of the parties.

Contract Law and the Paralegal

Regardless of where you work (for a large or small law firm, for a corporation, or for the government) and regardless of your area of specialty as a paralegal, you may be asked to handle matters that require an understanding of the basic principles of contract law. This is because contracts are so pervasive in our society. Business firms and government agencies routinely form contracts. Individuals in all walks of life commonly make contracts with others for goods or services.

Each of us has a personal interest in contract law because our individual agreements may be subject to that law. When you agree to work for a law firm or other organization as a paralegal, for example, your agreement with the employer is an employment contract. As an employee, you will thus be subject to contract law. You will want to understand the law of contracts when facing such questions as the following: If your employment agreement is oral, does it nonetheless constitute a valid contract? Do the promises made in an employment manual issued by your employer constitute contractual promises? Of course, many aspects of the employment relationship are now governed by statutes, such as those prohibiting discrimination in employment (discussed in Chapter 9).

As a legal professional, it is vital that you have some knowledge of contract law because, as mentioned, legal work frequently involves contracts. If you work for a law firm, you may be asked to assist clients who need help with the formation of contracts or with breach-of-contract claims. If you work for a corporation, part of your duties may involve drafting or reviewing the corporation's contracts to make sure that the terms are accurate and protect the corporation's interests. If the corporation sues another firm (or is sued by another firm) for breach of contract, you may be asked to assist in the settlement or litigation of the suit. As a government employee, you might also be involved with contracts, such as those formed between the agency for which you work and private contractors.

Many of the specialty areas of practice discussed in Chapter 2 involve contracts. Paralegals specializing in employment and labor law, corporate law, and intellectual-property law, for example, often assist in legal work relating to contracts. Even areas such as probate law and bankruptcy law may involve contracts. For example, if you work in the area of probate administration, you may be asked to determine if a contract made by the decedent before his or her death is legally binding on the decedent's heirs. Just as litigation may arise in any area of the law, so may claims relating to contracts.

Here are just a few of the tasks you might perform, in any workplace and in any capacity, that involve contracts:

- Interview a client or other person (such as the appropriate corporate manager, if you work for a corporation) to obtain information about a contract to be drafted or a breach-of-contract claim.
- Review a contract to make sure that its terms are sufficiently definite, that it has met all of the requirements (agreement, consideration, capacity, and legality) for a valid contract, and that its terms do not affect the client's interests adversely.
- Research previous cases decided by courts in your jurisdiction to determine whether a defense raised against a breach-of-contract claim will likely succeed or to determine how the courts have interpreted a certain type of contract provision.
- Gather and read through relevant documents and other evidence to determine the amount of damages sustained as a result of a breach of contract, including possible consequential damages.
- Assist in litigating a breach-of-contract claim.
- Draft a settlement letter to settle a contract dispute.
- Assist in arbitration or other dispute-settlement proceedings held for the purpose of settling a contract dispute.
- Contact representatives of business firms (perhaps in foreign countries) for the purpose of contract negotiations or the settlement of contract disputes.

SALES LAW

Millions of **sales contracts**—contracts for the sale of goods—are formed each day. If you buy a tube of toothpaste at your corner drug store, you implicitly enter into a contract, and the law governing sales contracts applies to the transaction. If you purchase a new VCR, the law of sales comes into play. Businesses form sales contracts for goods ranging in value from a few dollars to millions of dollars. Just as paralegals commonly deal with contract law regardless of where they work, so, too, do paralegals frequently assist in work involving sales contracts. For that reason, you will benefit by a basic understanding of the law governing sales contracts.

SALES CONTRACT
A contract for the sale of goods, as opposed to a contract for the sale of services, real property, or intangible property. Sales contracts are governed by Article 2 of the Uniform Commercial Code.

Sales contracts are governed by state statutes that are based on Article 2 of the **Uniform Commercial Code (UCC).** The UCC is one of the many—and one of the most significant—of the uniform laws created by the American Law Institute and the National Conference of Commissioners on Uniform State Laws. The UCC was first issued in 1952 and has since been revised to reflect the changing customs and needs of business and society. The UCC has been adopted, in whole or in part, by all of the states. State statutory codes are not necessarily called the Uniform Commercial Code, however. In Ohio, for example, UCC provisions are incorporated into the Ohio Commercial Code.

UNIFORM COMMERCIAL CODE (UCC)
A uniform code of laws governing commercial transactions that has been adopted in part or in its entirety by all of the states. Article 2 of the UCC governs contracts for the sale of goods.

The Scope of Article 2

In regard to Article 2 of the UCC, two things should be kept in mind. First, Article 2 deals with the sale of *goods,* not real property (real estate), services, or intangible property—property that cannot be seen or touched, such as the rights represented by stock certificates. Second, the rules may vary quite a bit, depending on whether the buyer or seller is a merchant. You should always note the subject matter of a dispute and the kind of people (merchants or consumers) involved when you are dealing with cases involving contractual disputes. If the subject is goods, then the UCC will govern. If it is real estate or services, then the common law principles discussed earlier will apply.

The UCC and the Common Law of Contracts

The UCC does not *replace* the common law of contracts—the body of law discussed in the previous section on contract law. A contract for the sale of goods is also subject to the common law requirements of agreement, consideration, contractual capacity, and legality. Similarly, the common law defenses against contract formation or enforceability also apply to sales contracts. If the UCC *has not modified* a common law principle, then the common law governs. The general rule is thus as follows:

- **When the UCC speaks, its principles apply; when the UCC is silent on a particular matter, then the common law of contracts applies.**

If the UCC *has modified* a common law requirement, then the UCC provision will govern. For example, in regard to the requirement of agreement, the UCC defines acceptance somewhat differently. Under the UCC, an acceptance may contain additional terms and still be considered an acceptance instead of a counteroffer, depending on the significance of the additional terms. Under the common law, however, an acceptance of an offer must mirror exactly the terms of the offer. If it does not, then it is not an acceptance but a counteroffer.

The UCC modified this "mirror image" rule of the common law because variations in terms between the offer and the acceptance can cause considerable problems in commercial transactions. This is particularly true in contracts involving the sale of goods when different standardized purchase forms of the seller and buyer are exchanged in the process of offer and acceptance. Seldom do the terms of the purchase forms match each other exactly, but often this fact goes unnoticed until problems arise. Say, for example, that a buyer contracts with a seller over the phone to purchase a certain piece of equipment. The parties agree to all of the terms of the sale. The buyer then enters the terms of the agreement on the appropriate form and sends it to the seller. The seller does likewise. Because the parties presume that they have reached an oral agreement on the telephone, discrepancies on their respective forms may go unnoticed. The buyer, for example, may not notice that the seller's form says nothing about a warranty—which is a condition of purchase on the buyer's form.

Performance of a Sales Contract

The overall performance of a sales contract is controlled by the the agreement reached between the buyer and the seller. If the parties have specifically agreed to certain rights and duties under a contract, the UCC will not intervene. The phrase "unless otherwise agreed" appears again and again in the UCC. The UCC normally comes into play only if a dispute arises over a matter not covered by the contract (such as the date or place of delivery) or if the parties disagree on the meaning of a given contractual term.

Remedies for Breach of a Sales Contract

Remedies for breach of a contract for the sale of goods are designed to put the aggrieved party in as good a position as if the other party had fully performed. The seller's remedies for breach include the right to stop or withhold delivery of the goods and the right to recover damages or the purchase price of the goods from the buyer. The buyer's remedies include (1) the right to reject *nonconforming goods* (goods that do not conform to those specifically agreed upon in the contract) or improperly delivered goods; (2) the right to *cover* (to buy the goods elsewhere and recover from the seller the extra cost of obtaining the substitute goods); (3) the right to recover damages; and (4) in certain circumstances, the right to obtain specific performance of the sales contract.

WARRANTY
An express or implied promise by a seller that specific goods to be sold meet certain criteria, or standards of performance, upon which the buyer may rely.

Warranties under the UCC

The UCC provides that a **warranty** of title arises in any sale of goods—that is, a seller automatically warrants (promises) to a buyer that the seller has good title to (legitimate ownership rights in) the goods being sold and can transfer that good title to the buyer. If the goods turn out to be stolen, for example, and the buyer has to return the goods to the real owner, the seller will be liable to the buyer for the value of the goods. The UCC also has provisions regarding express warranties and implied warranties.

Express Warranties. An *express warranty* is an oral or written promise made by a seller concerning the nature of the goods being sold. For example, the statement "This is a new Power Macintosh 8100 computer" is an express warranty, or promise, that the computer is indeed a Power Macintosh 8100 and that is it new. If you purchase the computer and learn that it is not new but used, the seller has breached an express warranty.

Implied Warranties. Implied warranties also arise in sales transactions. For example, the UCC provides that every merchant makes an *implied warranty of merchantability* when goods are sold. The goods must be merchantable—that is, they must be "reasonably fit for the ordinary purposes for which such goods are used." Some examples of unmerchantable goods are a light bulb that explodes when switched on, a hamburger that contains fragments of glass in the ground meat, and a new boat that leaks.

The UCC also provides that goods sold by merchants must be fit for the particular purpose for which they are sold. For this *implied warranty of fitness for a particular purpose* to arise, the buyer must rely on the seller's skill or judgment in selecting suitable goods. For example, assume that you need a gallon of paint to match the color of your living room walls—a light shade of peach. You take a sample of the color to your local hardware store and request a gallon of paint of that color. Instead, you are given a gallon of bright blue paint. Here, the salesperson has not breached any warranty of implied merchantability (the bright blue paint is of high quality and suitable for interior walls), but he or she has breached an implied warranty of fitness for a particular purpose.

Warranty Disclaimers. The UCC permits express warranties to be disclaimed or limited by specific and unambiguous language, provided that this is done in a manner that protects the buyer from surprise. For example, a written disclaimer in language that is clear and conspicuous, and called to a buyer's attention, could negate all oral express warranties not included in the written sales contract. This allows the seller to avoid false allegations that oral warranties were made, and it ensures that only representations made by properly authorized individuals are included in the bargain. Note, though, that a buyer must be made aware of any warranty disclaimers or modifications *at the time the sales contract is formed.* In other words, any oral or written warranties—or disclaimers—made during the bargaining process cannot be modified at a later time by the seller.

The UCC also permits a seller to disclaim implied warranties. To disclaim an implied warranty of fitness for a particular purpose, the disclaimer *must* be in writing and be conspicuous (printed in larger or contrasting type or in a different color, for example). A merchantability disclaimer must mention the word *merchantability,* but it need not be in writing. If it is made in

DEVELOPING PARALEGAL SKILLS

Contract Review

Samantha Thompson works as a paralegal for a corporation. She prepares and reviews contracts that her company receives from *vendors* (companies that want to sell their products to her company). Today, Samantha is reviewing a vendor contract for the sale of fifteen personal computers. The contract is a preprinted contract that the vendor sends to all of its customers. It is a two-sided document with approximately thirty paragraphs of "fine print." It also has blanks to be filled in with the specific quantity of items being sold, the price, and the delivery and payment terms. Samantha has just read a paragraph that states, in large, boldfaced letters, the following:

ALL WARRANTIES, EXPRESS AND IMPLIED, INCLUDING WARRANTIES OF MERCHANTABILITY AND FITNESS FOR A PARTICULAR PURPOSE, ARE DISCLAIMED.

Samantha is not certain what this language means, but she remembers that warranties for the sale of goods are governed by the Uniform Commercial Code (UCC) in her state. Samantha leaves her office, walks down the hall to the firm's library, and locates a copy of the UCC. She finds a provision stating that implied warranties may be disclaimed by the seller. The statutory provision also specifies that any written disclaimer of implied warranties must be "conspicuous." Samantha concludes that the disclaimer appearing in the contract that she was just reviewing, because it was set off from the surrounding text in large, boldfaced letters, was conspicuous and therefore a valid disclaimer.

Samantha reads through the contract provision again. She realizes that if the disclaimer of express warranties is also valid, there will be no warranties for the new computers. "Management should definitely know about this disclaimer," thinks Samantha. "I'd better prepare a memo for my supervising attorney to review and sign, informing management of this provision."

writing, the writing must be conspicuous. Generally speaking, unless circumstances indicate otherwise, the implied warranties of merchantability and fitness are disclaimed by the expression "as is," "with all faults," and other similar language that in common understanding for *both* parties call the buyer's attention to the fact that there are no implied warranties.

Sales Contracts and the Paralegal

All of the comments made earlier in the section entitled "Contract Law and the Paralegal" could be made here as well. As mentioned, the UCC does not replace the common law of contracts but modifies it to facilitate commercial transactions. In other words, as a paralegal, you would undertake the same types of tasks in relation to sales contract formation or claims of breached sales contracts as you would for contracts that fall under the common law of contracts, such as contracts for services.

In addition to these tasks, however, you may be involved in legal work that arises only in relation to sales contracts. You may need to determine, for example, whether one of the parties to a contract qualifies as a "merchant" as defined by Article 2 of the UCC. If so, different rules may apply to the contract. You may be asked to investigate a breach-of-warranty claim to determine whether a warranty was made and whether the seller's actions (or failure to act) constituted a breach of warranty.

Many paralegals assist in work relating to product-liability lawsuits. **Product liability** is the term given to the legal liability of manufacturers and sellers to buyers, users, and bystanders for injuries or damages suffered because of defects in goods. Liability arises when a product has a defective condition that makes it unreasonably dangerous and the product causes damage or injury to a person using the product. Product liability may be based on warranty theory or on the tort theories of negligence, misrepresentation, or strict liability—theories that we examine in the next section.

PRODUCT LIABILITY
The legal liability of manufacturers and sellers to buyers, users, and sometimes bystanders for injuries or damages suffered because of defects in goods purchased. Liability arises when a product has a defective condition that makes it unreasonably dangerous to the user or consumer.

TORTS

The word **tort** is French for "wrong." Tort lawsuits are frequent occurrences in the American legal arena, and many attorneys and paralegals devote a substantial amount of their time to serving clients who either want to bring or need to defend against tort lawsuits. Of course, a tort is not the only type of wrongful action that exists; crimes also involve wrongs. A crime, however, is an act so reprehensible that it is considered to be a wrong against the state or against society as a whole, as well as against the individual victim. Therefore, the state (the district attorney, county attorney, or other official representing the state's interest) prosecutes a person who has been accused of committing a criminal act (see Chapter 12). A tort action, in contrast, is a civil action in which one party brings a personal lawsuit against another to recover damages. Note that in some cases, such as assault and battery, a basis could exist for a criminal prosecution as well as a tort action (as will be discussed below).

TORT
A civil (as opposed to criminal) wrong not arising from a breach of contract. A breach of a legal duty, owed by the defendant to the plaintiff, that caused the plaintiff to suffer harm.

One of the primary reasons for the existence of tort law is to compensate individuals for losses that they have suffered because of either the actions of others or the failure of others to act when they should have. Generally, compensation takes the form of compensatory damages. Occasionally, an injured person is given extra compensation in the form of what are called punitive damages. **Punitive damages**—also called *exemplary damages*—are designed to punish the wrongdoer and deter other members of society from engaging in similar actions.

PUNITIVE DAMAGES
Damages that are awarded in a civil lawsuit to punish the wrongdoer. Punitive damages are usually awarded only in cases involving willful or malicious misconduct.

This section will discuss two basic categories of torts: intentional torts and torts resulting from negligence. It will also examine the concept of *strict liability*, a tort doctrine under which a defendant may be liable for harm or injury to another regardless of intention or fault.

Intentional Torts

An **intentional tort** is an intended action, whose consequences interfere with the personal or business interests of another in a way not permitted by law.

INTENTIONAL TORT
A wrongful act knowingly committed that interferes with the interests of another in a way not permitted by law.

SUBSTANTIVE LAW CONCEPT SUMMARY

Sales Contracts

The Scope of Article 2 of the UCC	Contracts for the sale of *goods* (tangible, movable property) are governed by Article 2 of the Uniform Commercial Code. Buyers and sellers are free to fashion their own contracts. The UCC normally comes into play if a dispute arises over ambiguous or absent contractual terms.
The UCC and the Common Law of Contracts	The UCC does not displace the common law of contracts but modifies common law doctrines as necessary to facilitate commercial transactions. If the UCC *has* modified a common law principle, then the UCC will govern. If the UCC *has not* modified a common law principle, then the common law will govern.
Performance of a Sales Contract	The overall performance of a sales contract is controlled by the agreement reached by the parties. If the parties have specifically agreed to certain rights and duties under a contract, the UCC will not intervene.
Remedies for Breach of a Sales Contract	**1.** *Seller's remedies—* a. Nondelivery—The right to stop or withhold delivery of the goods. b. Damages—The right to recover damages or the purchase price of the goods from the buyer. **2.** *Buyer's remedies—* a. Rejection—The right to reject nonconforming goods or improperly delivered goods. b. Cover—The right to buy the goods elsewhere and recover from the seller the extra cost of obtaining the substitute goods. c. Damages—The right to obtain compensation for expenses incurred as a result of the breach (may include consequential damages). d. Specific performance—In rare situations, the court will order the seller to undertake the specific performance promised in the contract.
Warranties under the UCC	**1.** *Types of warranties—* a. Warranty of title—Arises in any sale of goods. The seller automatically warrants (promises) to the buyer that the seller has good title to the goods being sold. b. Express warranty—The seller's oral or written promise concerning the nature of the goods being sold. c. Implied warranty of merchantability—An implied warranty that the goods sold are reasonably fit for the ordinary purposes for which such goods are sold. d. Implied warranty of fitness for a particular purpose—An implied warranty that the goods sold are fit for the particular purpose for which they are sold. The buyer must have relied on the seller's skill or judgment in selecting suitable goods. **2.** *Warranty disclaimers*—Express and implied warranties may be disclaimed, but the buyer must be made aware of any warranty disclaimers or modifications *at the time the sales contract is formed.*

In tort law, intent means that the actor intended the consequences of his or her act or knew with substantial certainty that certain consequences would result from the act. Note that the intent requirement does not necessarily mean that the actor intended to harm someone; only that he or she intended to commit the act and, implicitly, intended the act's consequences.

- **The law generally assumes that individuals intend the normal consequences of their actions.**

Thus, forcefully pushing another—even if done in jest and without any wish to harm the person—is an intentional tort (if injury results) because someone who is forcefully pushed can ordinarily be expected to fall down and possibly be injured.

Some intentional torts are similar to acts prohibited by state criminal laws. For example, both state criminal codes and tort law provide for a legal action in cases of assault and battery. An **assault** is an intentional, unexcused act that causes another to reasonably fear immediate harmful or offensive contact. A **battery** is the completion of the fear-inducing act or any actual contact with another that is offensive to the other person (a person does not have to be afraid, or fear immediate harm, for an act to constitute a battery). For example, if Chris threatens to hit Cynthia with his fist, Chris's action constitutes assault. If Chris actually hits Cynthia with his fist, Chris's action constitutes a battery.

ASSAULT
Any word or action intended to make another person fearful of immediate physical harm; a reasonably believable threat.

BATTERY
The unprivileged, intentional touching of another.

Defamation. Harming another's good reputation by making false statements is known as the tort of **defamation** of character. The law imposes a general duty on all persons to refrain from making false, defamatory statements about others. Breaching this duty orally involves the tort of *slander;* breaching it in writing or in any permanent form (such as a film strip shown on a television news show, a videotape, or an audiocassette) involves the tort of *libel.*

DEFAMATION
Anything published or publicly spoken that causes injury to another's good name, reputation, or character.

The basis of the tort is the publication of statements that hold an individual up to contempt, ridicule, or hatred. The term *publication* as used here means that the defamatory statements are communicated to third parties—persons other than the defamed party. If Karla writes Angelo a private letter accusing him of theft, the action does not constitute libel, because the message was not communicated to a third party. If Karla calls Angelo dishonest, unattractive, and incompetent when no one else is around, the action does not constitute slander. In neither case is the message communicated to a third party.

Privileged Speech. Some statements do not qualify as defamatory because a privilege is involved. For example, statements made by attorneys and judges during a trial are privileged and therefore cannot be the basis for a defamation charge. Statements made by members of Congress on the floor of Congress are privileged. Legislators have complete immunity from liability for false statements made in debate, even if they make such statements maliciously—that is, knowing them to be untrue.

Public Figures. In general, false and defamatory statements about public figures (public officials, rock stars, film stars, and generally anyone who is in the public limelight) that are published in the press or other media are privileged. The reason for this rule is that public figures have greater resources, including access to the media, than most others and are better able to tell their side of the story. The rule only applies, however, if the statements are made without actual malice. *Actual malice* is defined as the making of a statement with either a knowledge of its falsity or with a reckless disregard for the truth.

For example, assume that a news reporter hears rumors that a film star has AIDS (acquired immune-deficiency syndrome) and publishes those rumors knowing the rumors are false or not bothering to verify whether they are true. In this situation, if the film star sues the reporter for libel, the news reporter will normally be held liable for defamation.

Fraudulent Misrepresentation. Another tort frequently alleged by plaintiffs is fraud, or fraudulent misrepresentation. Fraud occurs when one person intentionally causes another to believe in a condition that is different from the one that actually exists. For example, if the seller of a breeding stallion tells the buyer that the stallion is in excellent physical condition, when the seller knows that the stallion is suffering from a disease that prevents him from breeding, the seller has fraudulently misrepresented a condition. To succeed in a tort action for fraud, the plaintiff must prove that the following events occurred:

- The defendant misrepresented facts with knowledge that they were false or with reckless disregard for the truth.
- The defendant intended to induce the plaintiff to rely on the misrepresentation.
- The plaintiff justifiably relied on the misrepresentation and suffered damages as a result of the reliance.
- The defendant's misrepresentation caused the plaintiff's injury.

Intentional Infliction of Emotional Distress. The tort of intentional infliction of emotional distress can be defined as an intentional act that amounts to extreme and outrageous conduct resulting in severe emotional distress to another. For example, a prankster telephones an individual and says that the individual's spouse has just been in a horrible accident. As a result, the individual suffers intense emotional anxiety. The caller's behavior is deemed to be extreme and outrageous conduct that exceeds the bounds of decency accepted by society and therefore constitutes a ground for a tort lawsuit. Because it is difficult to prove the existence of emotional distress, a few states require that the mental or emotional disturbance be evidenced by some physical illness.

False Imprisonment. The tort of false imprisonment occurs when one person intentionally confines or restrains another person's activities without justification. If a merchant delays a suspected shoplifter without sufficient reason and for an unreasonable period of time, for example, the merchant might face a lawsuit for false imprisonment.

Invasion of Privacy. The tort of invasion of privacy occurs when one person's actions intrude upon the privacy or seclusion of another. Wiretapping a person's phone line without legal authorization to do so may constitute an invasion of privacy. Taking unwanted photographs of another and using another's name or picture for commercial purposes without permission are both acts that invade the privacy of others. Informing the public of private facts or of the private affairs of a person may qualify as an invasion of privacy. Publishing information that places a person in a false light also is an invasion of privacy (publishing such a story could also involve the tort of defamation).

Trespass to Land. If someone enters onto another's land without permission, the landowner may have a cause of action under tort law for trespass to land. Tort law seeks to protect the right of a landowner to the exclusive possession of his or her property. Common types of trespass include walking or driving on land that belongs to someone else, cutting trees on another's property, throwing rocks or spraying water on a building owned by another, shooting a gun over the land, and placing part of one's building on an adjoining landowner's property.

Trespass to land involves wrongful interference with another person's property rights. But if it can be shown that the trespass was warranted, as when a trespasser enters onto another's property to assist someone in danger, a complete defense exists.

Negligence

NEGLIGENCE
The failure to exercise the standard of care that a reasonable person would exercise in similar circumstances.

The tort of **negligence** occurs when someone suffers injury because of another's failure to live up to a required *duty of care* (this duty will be discussed shortly). In negligence actions, the actor neither intends to bring about the consequences of the act nor believes that they will occur. This distinguishes negligence from intentional torts. Many of the actions discussed in the section on intentional torts would constitute negligence if the element of intent were missing. For example, if Sarah intentionally shoves Tony, who falls and breaks an arm as a result, Sarah has committed an intentional tort—battery. In contrast, if Sarah carelessly bumps into Tony, and Tony falls and breaks an arm as a result, Sarah's action constitutes negligence. In either situation, Sarah has committed a tort.

Not just any careless act results in a negligence action. Certain elements must be present for a plaintiff to recover damages under negligence theory. Even if these elements are proved, a defendant may not be liable if he or she successfully asserts one of the defenses to negligence.

The Elements of Negligence. As just mentioned, the tort of negligence occurs when someone breaches a duty of care and that breach causes injury or harm to another. This definition of negligence encompasses four distinct elements, listed below in the form of questions:

- Did the defendant owe a duty of care to the plaintiff?
- Did the defendant breach this duty?
- Did the plaintiff suffer a legally recognizable injury?
- Did the defendant's breach of the duty of care cause the plaintiff's injury?

Duty of Care. When evaluating a negligence claim, the first question you need to ask is whether the defendant owed a duty of care to the plaintiff. The concept of a duty of care arises from the notion that if we are to live in society with other people, some actions can be tolerated and some cannot, some actions are right and some are wrong, and some actions are reasonable and some are not. The basic principle underlying the duty of care is as follows:

- **People are free to act as they please so long as their actions do not infringe on the interests of others.**

The required standard of care varies from person to person, depending on the person's circumstances. Generally, everyone in society has a duty not to harm the interests of others, but some people are expected to exercise a higher standard of care. For example, if an individual has knowledge or skills superior to that of an ordinary person, the individual's conduct must be consistent with that status—that is, that individual has a higher standard of care. Professionals—attorneys, physicians, dentists, architects, accountants, and others—are required to have a *minimum level* of special knowledge and ability. An attorney, for example, is expected to know when and in which court a certain type of claim should be filed. If the attorney fails to file the claim within the required time period and with the correct court, he or she may be sued for malpractice (the name given to negligence actions against professionals).

ETHICAL CONCERN

Malpractice Suits

Attorneys and paralegals are not perfect and occasionally fail to perform a required duty. But the law will not "look the other way" if a client is harmed as the result of an attorney's negligence and then brings a malpractice suit against the attorney. It will not matter that the attorney specifically requested his or her paralegal to send a settlement letter to a defendant's attorney by a certain date. Nor will it matter that the attorney was under the impression that the letter had actually been sent by that date. The attorney, as the person responsible for the paralegal's work, will bear the legal consequences of the paralegal's negligent action if the client is harmed as a result and brings suit. The paralegal might also be held liable. As a paralegal, you should always make sure that you carry out instructions to the letter and perform your tasks accurately and in a timely manner, so that you do not expose your supervising attorney or yourself to liability for malpractice.

Breach of the Duty of Care. Generally, the duty of care is measured under a **reasonable-person standard,** which reflects society's judgment as to how a reasonably prudent person would act in a specific set of circumstances. (This hypothetical "reasonable person" appears again and again in the law.) When determining whether a duty of care has been breached, a court will compare the defendant's actions against those that would have been taken (or not taken) by a reasonably prudent person *in the defendant's position.* A reasonably prudent person would not drive carelessly and create the risk of harming others. A reasonably prudent attorney would not miss a filing deadline and thus harm his or her client's interests. A reasonably prudent seller would not market a product that had not been sufficiently tested for safety. And a reasonably prudent retail business owner would ensure that his or her customers were safe while on the owner's business premises.

REASONABLE-PERSON STANDARD
The standard of behavior expected of a hypothetical "reasonable person." The standard against which negligence is measured and that must be observed to avoid liability for negligence.

The Injury Requirement. As mentioned earlier, the primary purpose of tort law is to compensate persons who suffer harm or injuries as a result of the wrongful acts of others. This means that a compensable harm or injury must occur. If no harm or injury results from a given negligent action, there is nothing to compensate—and no tort exists. For example, if you carelessly bump into a passerby, who stumbles and falls as a result, you may be liable in tort if the passerby is injured in the fall. If the person is unharmed, however, there generally can be no lawsuit for damages, because no injury was suffered.

Causation. The final element necessary for a tort action is causation—that is, the wrongful activity must have caused the plaintiff's harm or injury. Causation can be a difficult element to prove. Generally, if a plaintiff can show that the injury would not have occurred "but for" the defendant's action, *causation in fact* will be established.

But what if the defendant's action unleashed a chain of events that ultimately resulted in the plaintiff's injury? For example, what if the defendant carelessly left a campfire burning? The fire not only burned down the forest but also set off an explosion in a nearby chemical plant that spilled chemicals into a river, killing all the fish for one hundred miles downstream and ruining the economy of a tourist resort. Should the defendant be liable to the resort owners? To the tourists whose vacations were ruined? These are questions of **proximate cause** (sometimes called *legal cause*).

PROXIMATE CAUSE
The "next" or "substantial" cause; in tort law, a concept used to determine whether a plaintiff's injury was the natural and continuous result of a defendant's negligent act.

In determining proximate cause, courts evaluate whether the connection between the defendant's act and the plaintiff's injury is strong enough to justify imposing liability. Generally, the courts have used foreseeability as the test for proximate cause: a plaintiff can only recover damages if the defendant could reasonably have foreseen that the consequences of his or her actions would create a risk of injury to the plaintiff.

Defenses to Negligence. The basic defenses in negligence cases are the following:

- Assumption of risk.
- Contributory negligence.
- Comparative negligence.
- The "last-clear-chance" doctrine.

Assumption of Risk. The defense of assumption of risk may be raised if the plaintiff (1) voluntarily entered into a risky situation and (2) was fully aware of the risk involved. The risk can be assumed by express agreement or can be implied by the plaintiff's knowledge of the risk and subsequent conduct. For example, a driver entering a race knows that there is a risk of being injured or killed if another vehicle in the race crashes into his. The driver thus assumes the risk of injury.

Contributory and Comparative Negligence. In some jurisdictions, if a plaintiff's own negligence contributed to his or her injury, the defense of *contributory negligence* can be raised. In these jurisdictions, if a defendant can demonstrate that the plaintiff was also negligent, the plaintiff will be barred from any recovery. In a majority of states, however, courts have now adopted a *comparative negligence* standard. Instead of allowing a plaintiff's negligence to negate a cause of action completely, the court determines the degree to which each party was negligent, and the liability for damages is distributed accordingly.

For example, assume that a pedestrian crosses a street, in the middle of the block, and is hit and injured by a bicyclist. The injured pedestrian sues the bicyclist for negligence. The pedestrian alleges that the bicyclist was not watching where he was going and produces witnesses who testify that the bicyclist was looking over his shoulder at another bicyclist just behind him at the time of the accident. The bicyclist claims that the pedestrian was also negligent and produces witnesses who testify that the pedestrian was not only crossing the street in the middle of the block but also reading a newspaper when she walked out into the street. In this situation, a court might conclude that the parties were equally liable and that the plaintiff-pedestrian can

SUBSTANTIVE LAW CONCEPT SUMMARY **Torts**	
Intentional Torts	An intentional tort is an intended act whose consequences interfere with the personal or business interests of another in a way not permitted by law. The actor must intend the act and know with substantial certainty that certain consequences will result from the act. (The law assumes that persons intend the normal consequences of their actions.) Intentional torts include the following: 1. *Assault and battery*—An *assault* is an unexcused and intentional act that causes another person reasonably to fear immediate harmful or offensive contact. A *battery* is the completion of the fear-inducing act or any actual contact with another that is offensive to the other person. 2. *Defamation*—A false statement of fact, not made under privilege, that is communicated to a third person and that causes damage to a person's reputation. Defamation is called *slander* when defamatory statements are made orally and *libel* when defamatory statements are made in writing or in any permanent form. Statements made about public figures are not defamatory unless they are made with *actual malice* (with knowledge that the statements are untrue or with reckless disregard for the truth). Certain statements are privileged (such as those made in Congress) and thus cannot serve as the basis of a legal action for defamation. 3. *Fraud/misrepresentation*—A false representation made by one party through misstatement of facts or through conduct, with the intention of deceiving another and on which the other reasonably relies to his or her detriment. 4. *Intentional infliction of emotional distress*—An intentional act that amounts to extreme and outrageous conduct resulting in severe emotional distress to another. 5. *False imprisonment*—Intentional confinement or restraint of another person's movement without justification. 6. *Invasion of privacy*—An action that intrudes upon the privacy or seclusion of another person without that person's permission or approval. 7. *Trespass to land*—Invasion of another's real property without consent or privilege.

thus only recover 50 percent of the damages she suffered. If the jury finds that the plaintiff incurred damages of $30,000 in medical expenses and lost wages, for instance, this amount would be reduced to $15,000.

Last-clear-chance Doctrine. Another defense to negligence is known as the *last-clear-chance doctrine.* This doctrine operates when the plaintiff or the plaintiff's property, through the plaintiff's own negligence, is endangered by a defendant who missed an opportunity to avoid causing damage. For example, if Callahan walks across the street against the light and Riggs, a motorist, sees her in time to avoid hitting her but hits her anyway, Riggs normally is not permitted to use Callahan's prior negligence as a defense. (Note that the adoption of the comparative negligence rule has effectively abolished the last-clear-chance doctrine in most jurisdictions.)

Strict Liability

Intentional torts and torts of negligence are based on fault. They involve acts that depart from a reasonable standard of care and cause injuries. Under the

SUBSTANTIVE LAW CONCEPT SUMMARY, Continued	
Negligence	1. *Definition of negligence*—The careless performance of a legally required duty or the failure to perform a legally required act. More generally, the failure to exercise a reasonable standard of care. 2. *Elements required for negligence*—To succeed in a negligence action, the plaintiff must prove the following: a. That the defendant owed a duty of care to the plaintiff. b. That the defendant breached the duty of care. c. That the plaintiff sustained a legally recognizable injury. d. That the plaintiff's injury was caused by the defendant's breach of the duty of care. 3. *Defenses to negligence*— a. Assumption of risk—The plaintiff was fully aware of the risk of injury attending a certain action or event and voluntarily assumed that risk. b. Contributory negligence—The plaintiff's own negligence contributed to his or her injury. In a few states, contributory negligence on the part of the plaintiff is a complete defense against liability for the plaintiff's injury. c. Comparative negligence—If the plaintiff was also negligent, the degree of negligence on the part of both the plaintiff and defendant is computed, and the liability for damages is distributed accordingly. d. Last clear chance—If the defendant missed the last opportunity to avoid causing harm to the plaintiff or the plaintiff's property, the defendant may not raise the plaintiff's contributory negligence as a defense. The last-clear-chance doctrine has been effectively abolished in those states that have adopted a comparative-negligence standard.
Strict Liability	Liability for injury imposed for reasons other than fault because of the inherent danger of an activity (such as blasting with dynamite) or situation (such as the possession of dangerous animals). Strict liability may also be imposed for reasons of public policy, as when strict product liability is imposed on manufacturers and sellers of products that are unreasonably dangerous when used as intended and that harm consumers as a result.

doctrine of **strict liability**, liability for injury is imposed without considering fault. Strict liability for damages proximately caused by abnormally dangerous or exceptional activities is one application of this doctrine. Strict liability is applied in such cases because of the extreme risk of the activities. For example, even if blasting with dynamite is performed with all reasonable care, there is still a risk of injury. Because of the potential for harm, the courts have deemed it fair to ask the person who engaged in the activity to pay for any injuries caused by that activity. Although there may be no fault, there is still responsibility because of the dangerous nature of the undertaking.

STRICT LIABILITY
Liability regardless of fault. In tort law, strict liability may be imposed on those who engage in abnormally dangerous activities that cause harm to others, on merchants who introduce into commerce goods that are unreasonably dangerous, and in certain other situations.

There are other applications of the strict liability principle. Persons who keep dangerous animals, for example, are strictly liable for any harm inflicted by the animals. A significant application of strict liability is in the area of product liability. As mentioned earlier, product liability may be based on warranty theory or on the tort theories of misrepresentation or negligence. It may also be based on strict liability. Strict product liability may be imposed on a manufacturer when a defect in the manufacturer's product causes the product to be unreasonably dangerous when used as intended—and harms a consumer as a result—regardless of whether the manufacturer did or did not exercise reasonable care.

Strict product liability is a matter of social policy and is based on two considerations: (1) the manufacturing company is making a profit from its activities and therefore should bear the cost of injury as an operating expense, and (2) the manufacturing company can better bear the cost of injury because it can spread the cost throughout society by increasing prices of goods and services.

Tort Law and the Paralegal

Many paralegals become involved in tasks relating to tort lawsuits. If you work for a litigation firm, chances are that you will handle numerous assignments involving tort claims. Many law firms specialize in personal-injury litigation and represent plaintiffs who have been injured in car accidents or other incidents resulting from the defendants' alleged negligence. Many law firms or departments of law firms also specialize in other areas of tort litigation, such as medical malpractice and product liability.

If you work for a corporation, your responsibilities might include assisting attorneys in work relating to tort lawsuits brought by or against the corporation. A consumer who was injured by one of the corporation's products, for example, might initiate a product-liability suit against the firm. A person who was injured in an accident caused by one of the company's truck drivers might sue the corporation for damages under negligence theory.

Specific types of tasks that paralegals perform in personal-injury cases are listed in Chapter 2, in the section describing personal-injury law. When working on medical-malpractice or product-liability cases, as well as on personal-injury cases, you might be asked to undertake any of the tasks typically performed by litigation paralegals, including those listed in Chapter 2 in the section on the litigation paralegal (and described at length in Chapters 10 and 11). You will find that in any tort litigation, you will profit from a knowledge of the fundamental concepts of tort law discussed in this section.

PROPERTY LAW

From an early period, the law has divided property into two classifications: real property and personal property. **Real property**, or *real estate,* is land and all things attached to the land (such as trees and buildings), as well as the minerals below the surface of the land and the air above the land. **Personal property** is all other property. Personal property can be either tangible or intangible. Tangible personal property, such as a television set or a car, has physical substance. Intangible personal property represents a set of rights and interests but has no real physical existence. Stocks and bonds are examples of intangible personal property. You will read about other forms of intangible personal property later, in the section on intellectual property.

REAL PROPERTY
Immovable property consisting of land, and the buildings and plant life thereon.

PERSONAL PROPERTY
Any property that is not real property. Generally, any property that is movable or intangible is classified as personal property.

FEE SIMPLE
A form of property ownership entitling the owner to use, possess, or dispose of the property as he or she chooses during his or her lifetime. Upon death, the interest in the property descends to the owner's heirs.

Ownership Rights in Property

Property ownership is often viewed as a "bundle of rights." One who owns the entire bundle of rights—ownership rights to the greatest degree possible—is said to own the property in **fee simple**.

- **An owner in fee simple is entitled to use, possess, or dispose of the real or personal property (by sale, gift, or other means) however he or she chooses during his or her lifetime. Upon the owner's death, the interests in the property descend to the owner's heirs.**

Of course, those who own real property even in fee simple may be subject to certain restrictions on their right to use the property absolutely as they choose. For example, zoning laws may prohibit an owner of property in a given area from conducting certain types of activities (such as running a business) on the property. Also, under its power of **eminent domain**, the government has a right to take private property for public use (for a highway, for example), as long as the government compensates the owner for the value of the land taken.

EMINENT DOMAIN
The power of a government to take land for public use from private citizens for just compensation.

Property owned in fee simple may also be subject to an *easement,* which is the right of another to use the owner's land for a limited purpose—a neighbor's right to use the land to reach a roadway, for example, or a utility company's right to erect and maintain power lines and poles or gas lines on the land.

In contrast to ownership in fee simple, other forms of ownership, including those discussed below, involve limited ownership rights.

Concurrent Ownership. Persons who share the bundle of ownership rights to either real or personal property are said to be concurrent owners. There are two principal types of concurrent ownership: tenancy in common and joint tenancy.

A **tenancy in common** is a form of co-ownership in which two or more persons own undivided interests in certain property. If a tenant in common dies, the tenant's ownership rights pass to his or her heirs.

TENANCY IN COMMON
Co-ownership of property in which each party owns an undivided interest that passes to his or her heirs at death.

A **joint tenancy** is also a form of co-ownership in which two or more persons own undivided interests in property. The key feature of a joint tenancy is the "right of survivorship." When a joint tenant dies, that tenant's interest passes to the surviving joint tenant or tenants and not to the deceased tenant's heirs, as it would with a tenancy in common. If a joint tenant transfers his or her interest in the property while he or she is living, the joint tenancy terminates. The new co-owner (the one to whom the rights were transferred) and the other tenant or tenants become tenants in common.

JOINT TENANCY
Co-ownership of property in which each party owns an undivided interest in the property. On the death of one of the joint tenants, his or her interest automatically passes to the other joint tenant or tenants and cannot be transferred by the will of the deceased.

Two other types of concurrent ownership take the form of a tenancy by the entirety and community property. A *tenancy by the entirety* is a form of co-ownership by husbands and wives that is similar to a joint tenancy, except that the spouses cannot separately transfer their interests in the property during their lifetime. In a few states, husbands and wives can hold property as community property. In those states, *community property* is all property acquired during the marriage; each spouse technically owns an undivided one-half interest of the property.

Life Estates. A *life estate* is an interest in real property that is transferred to another for the life of that individual. A conveyance "to Allison for her life" creates a life estate. In a life estate, the life tenant cannot injure the land in a manner that would adversely affect its value for the owner of the future interest in it.

FEATURED GUEST: JOHN D. DELEO

The Paralegal's Relationship to the Law

Biographical Note

John D. DeLeo received his bachelor of arts degree in political science from Pennsylvania State University. He received his paralegal certificate from Long Island University and was a practicing paralegal for two years before starting law school. He earned a J.D. degree from Loyola University School of Law, New Orleans, in 1984 and has been licensed to practice law in Louisiana and Pennsylvania. After practicing law for a time, DeLeo joined the faculty of Central Pennsylvania Business School in Summerdale, Pennsylvania. DeLeo teaches a variety of courses in the legal-assistant program at that school, including courses on torts, constitutional law, evidence, and civil procedure. He was named faculty member of the year in 1990 and 1993.

Working in the legal field can be a daunting and sometimes mystifying experience. "The law" is so vast that no matter how long you study, you can never completely master it. Here are some suggestions on how you, as a paralegal, can start to find your way through this potential quagmire.

WHAT IS THE PURPOSE OF YOUR TASK?

Whenever you receive an assignment, you should ask yourself why you are being asked to do it. What is the legal purpose of the task? The answer to this question will aid you in your work and bring things into focus.

DOES THE ISSUE RELATE TO PROCEDURAL OR SUBSTANTIVE LAW?

Also ask yourself whether the issue relates to procedural or substantive law. Procedural law concerns how legal rights are enforced. Substantive law defines what those rights are. Examples of substantive law are contract law, tort law, and property law. Procedural law involves knowing the appropriate court in which to file a case, the appropriate time for filing various documents relating to litigation, and other rules. With the procedural and substantive distinction in mind, you can better separate and analyze the issues of the case. It is also impor-

Future Interests. When someone who owns real property in fee simple conveys the property conditionally to another or for a limited period of time (such as with a life estate), the original owner still retains an interest in the land. This interest is called a *future interest* because it will only arise in the future. The holder of a future interest may transfer it to another during his or her lifetime; if the interest is not transferred, it will pass to the owner's heirs on his or her death.

The Transfer and Sale of Property

Property can be transferred in numerous ways. Property can be given to another as a gift, willed or transferred to another by inheritance, leased to another, or sold. Most commonly, property is transferred by sale. The sale of tangible personal property (goods) is covered by the common law of contracts, as modified by Article 2 of the Uniform Commercial Code, which we have already discussed in the section on sales law. Rights in certain types of intangible property (such as checks, money orders, and other documents) are covered by other articles of the UCC. The purchase and sale of securities

FEATURED GUEST, Continued

tant to know that when you do legal research, you will use different references for procedural issues than for substantive issues.

BE AWARE OF THE LARGER PICTURE

A key factor in paralegal work is the ability to be aware of the overarching situation in any case on which you are assigned to work. Different rules and procedures apply, depending on the facts of the case before you. When working on a file, you should know, for example, whether this is a civil or a criminal case, whether it has been filed in a federal court or a state court, and what general area of law governs the claims being made. The answers to these questions will direct your actions and work on the case.

For example, assume that your supervising attorney is defending a client who has been sued for negligence. The plaintiff claims that the defendant ran a red light, that the defendant's car crashed into hers as a result, and that the defendant therefore should be liable for the plaintiff's injuries from the accident.

The plaintiff has filed suit in a federal court, alleging diversity-of-citizenship jurisdiction. You have been asked to gather medical records, physicians' reports, medical bills, and other information relating to the plaintiff's claim.

If you are aware that in order for federal courts to take jurisdiction based on diversity of citizenship the amount in controversy must be more than $50,000, you will have a better understanding of what you should be looking for during your investigation. For example, if it appears that the plaintiff's damages are less than $50,000, you should advise your supervising attorney of your findings. Your attorney could then file with the federal court a *motion to dismiss* the case for lack of subject matter jurisdiction.

Generally, a paralegal who can keep in mind the larger framework of an issue while still doing a particular assignment can be a valuable asset to a law firm. When you receive an assignment and you know why this task is important as well as what the legal basis of the lawsuit is, you will be able to do your job in a more effective way.

"A KEY FACTOR IN PARALEGAL WORK IS THE ABILITY TO BE AWARE OF THE OVERARCHING SITUATION."

(stocks, bonds, and so on), which are also forms of intangible property, are governed by federal acts, as will be discussed in Chapter 9. The sale of real property is governed by both the common law of contracts as well as state (and, to a limited extent, federal) statutory law.

This section focuses on real-estate sales, in which paralegals frequently play a significant role. As a paralegal, you may be asked to assist your supervising attorney's clients or others (such as a corporate employer) in the purchase or sale of real property. You might even specialize in real-estate law. Recall from Chapter 3 that in at least one state (the state of Washington), paralegals are licensed to provide assistance directly to the public in real-estate transactions.

For most individuals, the purchase of real property is their most expensive purchase. Typically, individuals who buy or sell real estate are unfamiliar with the legal requirements and consequences of real-property transactions. As a paralegal, if you work in the area of real estate, you need to take great care to make sure that the client's legal interests are protected in every respect. You will thus want to become familiar with your state's requirements relating to real-estate transactions. Here we look at some of the basic steps and procedures involved in the sale of real estate. These steps and procedures are summarized in Exhibit 8.1.

Offer and Acceptance. The common law contractual requirements of agreement (offer and acceptance), consideration, contractual capacity, and legality all apply to real-estate contracts. When a buyer wishes to purchase real estate, he or she submits an offer to the seller. The offer specifies all of the terms of the proposed contract—a description of the property, the price, and any other conditions that the buyer wishes to include. Often, a buyer conditions the offer on the buyer's ability to obtain financing. The offer might also specify which party will bear the cost of any repairs that need to be made. The purchase and sale agreement presented in Exhibit 8.2 beginning on page 294 illustrates the terms and conditions that might be included in an offer to purchase real estate, which, when signed by the buyer and the seller, constitutes a contract for the sale of land that is binding on the parties.

The buyer normally tenders a sum of money, called *earnest money,* along with the offer. By paying earnest money, the buyer indicates that he or she is making a serious offer. Normally, the offer will provide that if the seller accepts the offer (and forms a contract with the buyer), the buyer will forfeit this money if he or she breaches the contract. Other damages for breach might also be specified in the agreement. If the deal goes through, the earnest money is usually applied to the purchase price of the real estate.

Once the offer is submitted to the seller, the seller has three options: he or she can accept the offer, reject it, or modify its terms—thus creating a counteroffer. The buyer, in turn, can then accept, reject, or modify the terms of the counteroffer—thus creating yet another counteroffer for the seller to consider. In real-estate transactions, bargaining over price and other conditions of the sale frequently involves the exchange of one or more counteroffers. Once one of the parties accepts an offer or counteroffer, a contract is formed by which both parties normally must abide.

The Role of the Escrow Agent. The sale of real property normally involves three parties: the seller, the buyer, and the escrow agent. Frequently, both the buyer and the seller are assisted by realtors, attorneys, and paralegals. The escrow agent, which may be a title company, bank, or special escrow company, acts as a neutral party in the transaction and facilitates the sale by allowing the buyer and the seller to complete the transaction without having to exchange documents and funds directly with each other.

To understand the vital role played by the escrow agent, consider the problems that might arise otherwise. Essentially, in the sale of property, the buyer gives the seller money, and the seller conveys (transfers) to the buyer a deed, representing ownership rights in the property (deeds will be discussed shortly). Neither the buyer nor the seller wishes to part with the money or the deed until all conditions of the sale and purchase have been met.

The solution is the use of an escrow agent. The escrow agent holds the deed until the buyer pays the seller for the property at the closing. The escrow agent also holds any money paid by the buyer, including the earnest money mentioned above, until the sale is completed. At the *closing* (the final step in the sale of real estate), the escrow agent receives money from the buyer, the buyer is given the deed, and the seller is given the money. The tri-

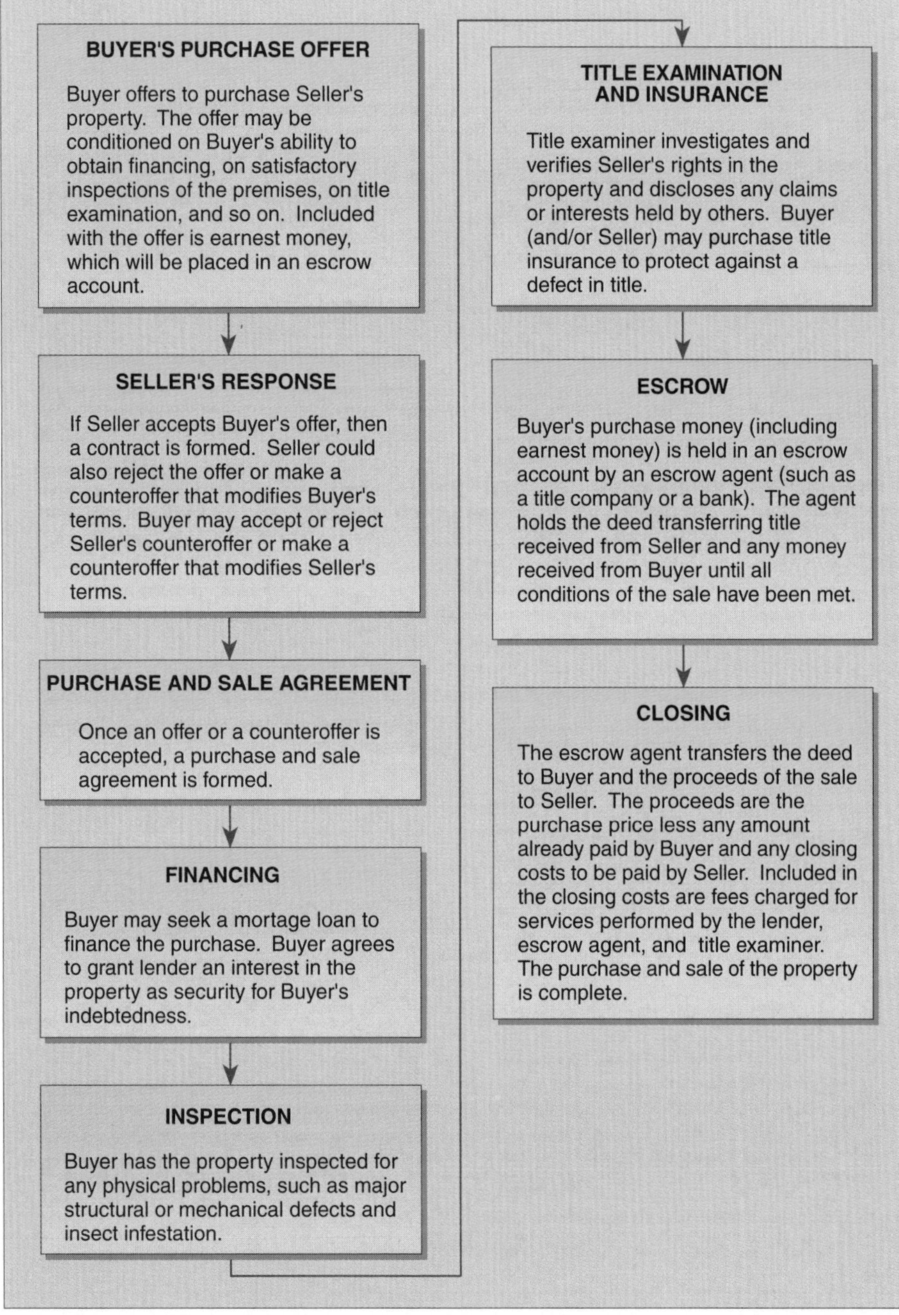

EXHIBIT 8.1
Steps Involved in the Sale of Real Estate

angular relationship that exists among the buyer, the seller, and the escrow agent is depicted in Exhibit 8.3 on page 298.

Financing. Because few buyers can or want to pay cash for real property, buyers generally need to secure financing. Commonly, a buyer of real property finances the purchase by obtaining a loan—called a **mortgage**—from a bank, a mortgage company, or some other party. When a buyer obtains a

MORTGAGE
A written instrument giving a creditor an interest in the debtor's property as security for a debt.

EXHIBIT 8.2
A Sample Purchase and Sale Agreement

BUY AND SELL AGREEMENT

THIS IS A LEGALLY BINDING CONTRACT, READ ALL PARTS CAREFULLY BEFORE SIGNING.
Buyers & Sellers are advised to seek legal counsel. Buyer and Seller acknowledge that agency relationship has been disclosed.

REALTOR® EQUAL HOUSING OPPORTUNITY

DATE: ____________, 19 ___, __________ A.M./P.M.

SELLING OFFICE ____________________, REALTOR ____________________, AGENT FOR: Seller/Buyer
LISTING OFFICE ____________________, REALTOR ____________________, AGENT FOR: Seller/Buyer

1. BUYER'S OFFER
The undersigned ____________________, hereinafter called the Buyer hereby, offers to buy the following property commonly known as (Address) ____________________ located in the City/Twp. of ____________________, County of ____________________ Michigan, Legally described as: ____________________

____________________ and/or tax ID # ____________________ subject to any existing building and use restrictions, zoning ordinances and easements, for the sum of ____________________ Dollars ($ ____________________)

2. TERMS OF PURCHASE as indicated by "X" below: (other unmarked terms of purchase do not apply). Payment of such money shall be made in cash, certified check, or bank money order.

CASH ❑ The full purchase price upon execution and delivery of Warranty Deed.

NEW MORTGAGE ❑ The full purchase price upon the execution and delivery of Warranty Deed, contingent upon Buyer's ability to obtain a ______________ Mortgage for no less than ________ years, for no less than ________ % of purchase price at no more than ________ % interest per annum which Buyer agrees to apply for within ________ calendar days after acceptance and secure and accept commitment on or before ____________________ (date).

CONTRACT ❑ $ ______________ upon execution and delivery of Land Contract, wherein the balance of $ ______________ shall be payable in monthly installments of $ ______________ or more including interest at ________ % per annum, interest to start on date of closing and the first such payment to become due one month after closing date. This contract shall be payable in full ________ months/years from date of closing.

EQUITY ❑ Upon execution and delivery of: ( ) Assignment of vendee interest in land contract ( ) Warranty Deed subject to existing mortgage. Buyer to pay the difference (Approximately $ ____________) between the purchase price and balance of said Mortgage or Land Contract which Buyer ❑ formally ❑ informally assumes and/or agrees to pay. Buyer agrees to reimburse Seller for any funds held in escrow for payment of future taxes and insurance premiums.

3. CREDIT REPORT ❑ Buyer hereby agrees to provide a credit report satisfactory to seller and/or lender and release necessary information. ____________________

4. OTHER PROVISIONS: ____________________

5. PROPERTY TAXES: For purposes of this agreement, taxes are to be prorated in arrears, on a calendar year basis, the amount to be based on the latest assessment and millage figures. The seller is responsible for taxes through ____________________ and the buyer is responsible for taxes thereafter. Exceptions: ____________________.

6. ASSESSMENTS: Perpetual assessments shall be assumed and paid by the buyer. All other assessments which become a lien on the property at time of closing shall be:
❑ Assumed by the buyer. Any current year's installments shall be prorated on a calendar year basis with the seller paying the prorated amount through closing.
❑ Paid in full by seller. ❑ ____________________

7. TITLE: Seller shall:
❑ Furnish an owner's policy of title insurance covering the foregoing described property in the amount of the purchase price.
❑ Pay $ ______________ toward owner's title insurance costs for the buyer. ❑ ____________________
IT IS RECOMMENDED THAT ANY EVIDENCE OF TITLE AND SUPPORTING DOCUMENTS BE EXAMINED BY AN ATTORNEY.

8. SALE IS TO BE CLOSED by ____________________, subject to paragraph 4 above. An additional period of up to thirty (30) days shall be allowed for closing to accommodate delays in title work or the correction of title defects which can be readily corrected, delays in obtaining any required inspections, surveys, or repairs, or if the terms of purchase require participation of a lender and the lender has issued a commitment consistent with the requirement but is unable to participate in a closing on the agreed date. Any further extension shall be by written mutual agreement.

9. THE SELLER SHALL DELIVER and the purchaser shall accept possession of said property subject to the rights of the following tenants ____________________.
If the Seller occupies the property, it shall be vacated ____________________ closing. From the date after closing until the date of vacating the property as agreed, Seller shall pay a the sum of $ ______________ per day.

mortgage, the bank or mortgage company takes a security interest in the property. That is, the bank or mortgage company secures the right to claim ownership of the property if the buyer fails to make the scheduled payments.

Inspection of the Premises. In addition to obtaining financing, buyers may have the premises inspected to see if there are any major electrical or plumbing problems, structural defects, termite or insect infestation, or other prob-

EXHIBIT 8.2
Continued

10. For valuable consideration Buyer gives seller ____________ calendar day(s) for written acceptance of this offer. This offer, when signed, will constitute a binding agreement between Buyer and Seller. Buyer herewith deposits $ ____________ evidencing Buyer's good faith, said deposit to be held by said REALTOR®/Broker, and to apply as part of the purchase price. If this sale is not consummated, the deposit made herein shall be subject to the provisions of Paragraph 106 on the reverse side of this Agreement.

11. INSPECTIONS: This agreement is contingent upon buyer's satisfaction of the following (check box) indicated inspections:

a) Buyer to pay for ❑ water; ❑ well; ❑ septic; ❑ mechanical; ❑ structural; ❑ plumbing; ❑ heating; ❑ electrical; ❑ pest; ❑ environmental; ❑ Lender Req.; ❑ other

b) Seller to pay for ❑ water; ❑ well; ❑ septic; ❑ mechanical; ❑ structural; ❑ plumbing; ❑ heating; ❑ electrical; ❑ pest; ❑ environmental; ❑ Lender Req.; ❑ other

c) ❑ Inspections shall be deemed acceptable to buyer unless written notice of objection is delivered to seller, or seller's agent by ____________. Failure to submit written notice of said objection shall be deemed a waiver of buyer's inspection and repair rights and buyer agrees to accept the property in its present condition. In the event of any claim or demand to remedy or repair any item, The Seller shall have the option of: 1) making said items operational provided the Seller agrees to the expense in writing, 2) Giving the Buyers a credit for the items, providing the expense has been approved by the Seller, or 3) Cancelling the contract of sale and refunding the Buyer any earnest money deposit held by Broker less any expenses incurred on Buyers behalf.

d) ❑ Buyer(s) waive all inspections without benefit of an opinion by a licensed contractor.

12. Buyer hereby acknowledges receipt of a copy of this agreement.

13. NOTE: GENERAL CONDITIONS OF SALE PRINTED ON REVERSE SIDE NUMBERED 101 THROUGH 119 HAVE BEEN REVIEWED AND ARE INCORPORATED HEREIN AND MADE A PART OF THIS AGREEMENT.

____________ Initial ____________ Initial

14. Witness ____________ X ____________ Buyer

Buyer's Address ____________ X ____________ Buyer

____________ Zip ____________ Buyer's Phone: (Res.) ____________ (Bus.) ____________

Received from above named buyer deposit monies in the form of ____________ by ____________ Realtor/Broker

15. SELLER'S ACCEPTANCE Date: ____________, 19 ______, ____________ AM/PM

The above agreement is hereby accepted ____________

NOTE: GENERAL CONDITIONS OF SALE PRINTED ON REVERSE SIDE NUMBERED 101 THROUGH 119 HAVE BEEN REVIEWED AND ARE INCORPORATED HEREIN AND MADE A PART OF THIS AGREEMENT.

Seller Has Read This Agreement And Acknowledges Receipt Of A Copy. ____________ Initial ____________ Initial

Witness ____________ X ____________ Seller

Buyer's Address ____________ X ____________ Seller

____________ Zip ____________ Seller's Phone: (Res.) ____________ (Bus.) ____________

BUYER'S RECEIPT OF SELLER'S ACCEPTANCE Date: ____________, 19 ______, ____________ AM/PM

16. Receipt is Hereby Acknowledged by Buyer of Seller's acceptance of Buyer's offer. In the event the acceptance was subject to certain changes from Buyer's offer, Buyer agrees to accept said changes, ALL OTHER TERMS AND CONDITIONS REMAINING UNCHANGED, EXCEPT: ____________

Witness ____________ X ____________ Buyer

X ____________ Buyer

SELLER'S RECEIPT OF ACCEPTANCE Date: ____________, 19 ______, ____________ AM/PM

17. Seller's Receipt of Acceptance: Seller hereby Acknowledges receipt of a copy of Buyer's acceptance of his counter offer (in the event Seller has made a counter offer).

Witness ____________ X ____________ Seller

Revised and approved 4/94 Gratiot-Isabella Board of Realtors® X ____________ Seller

lems. Often, the contract of sale is conditioned on the outcome of these inspections. If problems surface during the inspections, the buyer and seller may negotiate (or may have included in the contract) arrangements specifying which party will pay what portion of the costs of any necessary repairs.

Title Examination and Insurance. Whenever title to property is transferred from one party to another, that transfer is recorded by the county recording

EXHIBIT 8.2
Continued

101. THE PROPERTY INCLUDES ANY OF THE FOLLOWING PRESENTLY ON THE PREMISES: All buildings; TV antenna and controls; satellite dish and controls; garage door opener and transmitter(s); carpet; light fixtures and shades; drapery and curtain hardware; window shades and blinds; screens; storm windows and doors; stationary laundry tubs; water softener (unless rented); water heater; incinerator; sump pump; heating and air conditioning equipment, (window units excluded); water pump and pressure tank; built-in kitchen appliances including garbage disposal; awnings; mail box; all plantings; fence(s); attached fireplace screens, doors, and equipment; attached supplemental heating units; all attached mirrors and all bathroom mirrors; smoke, heat, and fire detectors; burglar alarms; and any gas, oil, and mineral rights owned by the seller. ADDITIONS OR EXCEPTIONS SHOULD BE NOTED IN # 4.

102. Seller shall be responsible for fire and extended coverage insurance until sale is closed, and buyer is responsible thereafter.

103. Prorations: Rent; casualty insurance, if assigned; fuel; interest on any existing land contract, mortgage, or other lien assumed and/or to be paid by the Buyer shall be adjusted to the date of closing of the sale. Security deposits and lease agreements shall be assigned to Buyer at closing.

104. It is agreed by the REALTOR®/Broker and Seller or Lessor, parties to this agreement, that as required by law, discrimination because of race, creed, color, national origin, sex, marital status, height, weight, age or handicap by said parties with respect to the sale or lease of the subject property is prohibited.

105. The convenants herein shall bind and insure to the benefit of the executors, administrators, successors, personal representatives and assigns of the parties hereto. SELLER ALSO AGREES to pay Listing REALTOR®/Broker named on the face hereof a commission as stated in the Listing Agreement corresponding to the property described herein for negotiating this sale. All deposits are to be held by Selling REALTOR®/Broker in accordance with the terms hereof and in accordance with the Occupational Code and the rules of the Bureau of Occupational and Professional Regulation of the Michigan Department of Commerce.

106. DEFAULT: If Seller refuses to complete the sale, the full commission shall be due and payable upon such refusal. If a Buyer refuses to complete the sale, the Buyer's earnest money deposit shall be forfeited. The deposit shall be first applied to reimburse the Broker for all expenses incurred by the Listing Broker on Seller's behalf including, but not limited to, abstracting charges, counsel, and fees of public officers. One-half of the remainder of such deposit (but not in excess of the amount of the full commission) shall be retained by the Listing Broker in full payment for services rendered and the balance of the deposit shall be paid over to the Seller. If this transaction is subject to any contingencies which cannot be met, Buyer's earnest money deposit shall be first applied to reimburse the Broker for all expenses incurred by the Broker on Buyer's behalf. The balance of the deposit shall be paid over to the Buyer.

107. SELLER understands that consummation of the sale or transfer of the property described in this agreement shall not relieve the Seller of any liability that Seller may have under the mortgage(s) to which the property is subject unless otherwise agreed to by the lender or required by law or regulation.

108. INFORMATION DISCLOSURE: The purchase price and terms of this sale shall be disclosed to the Gratiot-Isabella Board of REALTORS® in the ordinary conduct of business.

109. MERGER: This agreement supersedes any and all representations and agreements and constitutes the entire agreement between the parties, and no prior representations or agreements, oral or written, shall be considered a part hereof.

110. TIME shall be deemed as of the very essence of this agreement.

111. TO SELLERS BEST KNOWLEDGE:

A. No other person or persons have any right, title, or interest in said real estate (except as Seller discloses herein or shown by title insurance commitment); that said owners have made no deeds of conveyance or deeds to change title, that they have not entered into any contracts to convey said real estate or any agreements for the sale of said real estate, or any mineral, oil, gravel, rental or other leases affecting said real estate except under this Purchase Agreement.

B. The title to the premises has never been disputed, questioned, or rejected to the sellers knowledge: that there is no suit or proceeding pending affecting the premises; that all bills and charges for work, labor and services rendered and materials furnished in the improvement of the premises or nay part thereof have been paid, and that no person or corporation has filed or has a right to file a mechanic's lien thereon; that no financing statement has been filed against any fixtures or chattels attached to or used in the operation of the premises; that the premises upon closing will be free and clear of all encumbrances, liens or charges of every nature or description, save and except: (TO BE SET FORTH UNDER PARAGRAPH 4 REVERSE SIDE)

C. There are no judgements or tax liens against them unsatisfied of records in the courts of the State or the United States, and that no proceedings in bankruptcy have been instituted by or against them.

112. THE BUYER ACKNOWLEDGES that the REALTOR® cannot warrant the condition of any fixtures, equipment, or personal property being purchased by Buyer from Seller.

113. THE SELLER ACKNOWLEDGES THE FOLLOWING:

A. That a credit report on the Buyer has been recommended by REALTOR®; and that if a credit report is not obtained, the Seller is accepting Buyer on Buyer's own merit trust.

office. A *title examination* involves checking these records carefully to make sure that the seller is actually the owner of the property described in the purchase offer and to determine whether claims (such as a tax lien for overdue taxes) on the property exist that were not disclosed by the seller. The title examination is an important task to be accomplished prior to the purchase of real estate. The title examination may be undertaken by the buyer or the

EXHIBIT 8.2
Continued

B. That REALTOR® cannot warrant that the Buyer will be able to obtain financing at the time of any balloon payment specified in this agreement.

114. TYPICAL SELLERS COST:
Transfer tax on deed;
All costs required and necessary to clear title;
Accumulated interest on any existing indebtedness;
Updated abstract or Owner's Title, Insurance Policy;
Preparation of Deed, Land Contract, Bill of Sale and/or other documents necessary to convey clear title, if required.

TYPICAL BUYERS COST:
Preparation of Mortgage, Note, or any other security instruments except Land Contract
Mortgage Title Insurance Policy;
Mortgage Inspection Survey Report, if required;
Recording of Deed and/or Security Instruments;
Attorney's Opinion and/or services on behalf of the Buyer;
Mortgage closing cost as required by mortgagee including appraisal and closing fees (except V.A.)
Transfer fee on Mortgage Assumption;
Closing Fee

115. EXAMINATION OF TITLE: In addition to any encumbrances referred to herein, Purchaser shall take title to the property subject to: 1) Real Estate Taxes not yet due, and 2) Covenants, Conditions, Restrictions, Rights of Way, and Easements of record, if any, which do not materially affect the value or intended use of the property.

116. CONTINGENCIES SATISFIED IN WRITING: Each contingency contained herein shall be satisfied according to its terms or waived in writing by the party responsible within the time specified for any extension thereof agreed to by the parties in writing. This paragraph contemplates that each party shall diligently pursue the completion of this transaction.

117. NO TAX ADVICE: Purchaser and Seller acknowledge that they have not received or relied upon any statements or representations by the REALTOR®, regarding the effect of this transaction upon their tax liability.

118. FAX TRANSMISSION: The facsimile transmission of a signed copy hereof or any counter offer to the other party or his/her agent, followed by faxed acknowledgment of receipt, shall constitute delivery of said signed document. The parties agree to confirm such delivery by mailing or personally delivering a signed copy to the other party or agent.

119. CONDITION OF PREMISES: Buyer has personally inspected the property and agrees to accept it in "as is" condition except as otherwise provided in this agreement. Buyer acknowledges that it has been recommended the buyer seek and secure inspections of the property not limited to matters of survey, use permits, easements, rights of way, water, well, septic systems, municipal systems, structural, plumbing, heating, electrical, pest, environmental concerns, subdivision restrictions, zoning, soil borings, franchising, use permits, ADA requirements, etc.

Purchaser acknowledges that he/she has not relied upon any representations either expressed or implied, by brokers and/or agents as to the condition of the premises or contents thereof and that they are not relying on any such warranty or representation as a condition to purchase except as specifically set forth in writing, fully executed by all parties and attached hereto.

ALL BUYERS AND SELLERS OF REAL ESTATE ARE ADVISED TO SEEK LEGAL COUNSEL.

DISCLAIMER: This form is provided as a service of the Gratiot-Isabella Board of REALTORS®. Please review both the form and details of the particular transaction to ensure that each section is appropriate for the transaction. The Gratiot-Isabella Board of REALTORS® is not responsible for use or misuse of the form, for misrepresentation, or for warranties made in connection with the form.

buyer's attorney (paralegals frequently assume this responsibility), or by the lending institution, a title insurance company, or another party.

Normally, the history of past ownership and transfers of the property is already summarized in a document called an *abstract,* which may be in the possession of the seller (or the holder of the seller's mortgage or other company or institution). After examining the abstract, the title examiner gives an opinion as to the validity of the title. Title examinations are not foolproof,

EXHIBIT 8.3
The Concept of Escrow

This exhibit illustrates the triangular relationship among the escrow agent, the seller, and the buyer in a transfer of real estate. As the exhibit indicates, the seller gives the escrow agent the deed, the buyer gives the escrow agent the money, and at the time of the closing, the escrow agent gives the seller the money and the buyer the deed—simultaneously.

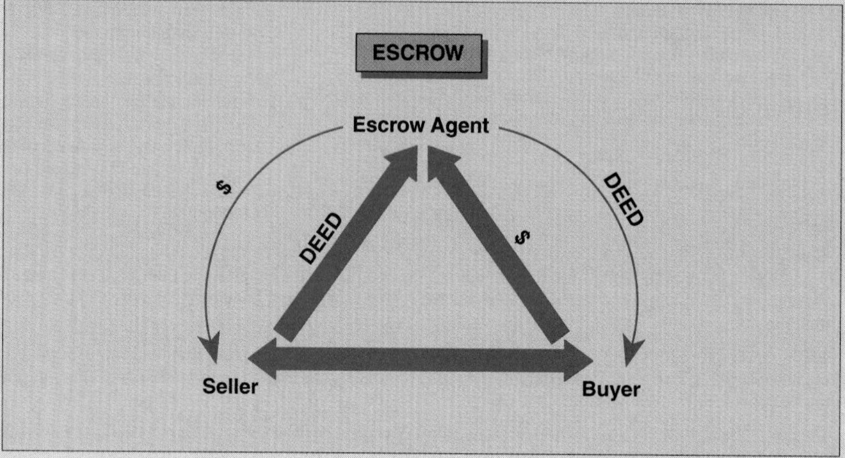

though, and buyers of real property generally purchase title insurance to protect their interests in the event that some defect in the title was not discovered during the examination.

The Closing. One of the terms specified in the contract is when the closing will take place. The closing—also called the settlement or the closing of escrow—is coordinated by the escrow agent. At the closing, several events happen nearly simultaneously: the buyer signs the mortgage note (if the purchase was financed by a mortgage), title insurance is obtained, the seller receives the proceeds of the sale (the purchase price less the amount previously paid by the buyer and less closing costs), and the deed to the property is delivered to the buyer.

DEED
A document by which title to property is transferred from one party to another.

A **deed** is the instrument of conveyance (transfer) of real property. As indicated on the sample deed in Exhibit 8.4, a deed gives the names of the seller (grantor) and buyer (grantee), describes the property being transferred, evidences the seller's intent to convey (for example, "I hereby bargain, sell, grant, or give") the property, and contains the seller's signature.

Closing costs comprise fees for services, including those performed by the lender, escrow agent, and title company. These costs can range from several hundred to several thousand dollars, depending on the amount of the mortgage loan and other conditions of sale, and must be paid, in cash, at the closing. Usually, the buyer and seller can learn in advance, by checking (or having their attorneys or realtors check) with the escrow agent handling the closing what the closing costs will be. Also, under the federal Real Estate Settlement Procedures Act of 1976, lending institutions must notify—within a specified time period—each applicant for a mortgage loan of the specific costs that must be paid at the closing.

EXHIBIT 8.4
A Sample Deed

Date: May 31, 1996

Grantor: RAYMOND A. GRANT AND WIFE, JOANN H. GRANT

Grantor's Mailing Address (including county):
4106 North Loop Drive
Austin, Travis County, Texas

Grantee: DAVID F. FRIEND AND WIFE, JOAN E. FRIEND, AS JOINT TENANTS WITH RIGHT OF SURVIVORSHIP

Grantee's Mailing Address (including county):
5929 Fuller Drive
Austin, Travis County, Texas

Consideration:
For and in consideration of the sum of Ten and No/100 Dollars ($10.00) and other valuable consideration to the undersigned paid by the grantees herein named, the receipt of which is hereby acknowledged, and for which no lien is retained, either express or implied.

Property (including any improvements):
Lot 23, Block "A", Northwest Hills, Green Acres Addition, Phase 4, Travis County, Texas, according to the map or plat of record in volume 22, pages 331-336, of the Plat Records of Travis County, Texas.

Reservations from and Exceptions to Conveyance and Warranty:

This conveyance with its warranty is expressly made subject to the following: Easements and restrictions of record in volume 7863, page 53, volume 8430, page 35, volume 8133, page 152, of the Real Property Records of Travis County, Texas; and to any other restrictions and easements affecting said property which are of record in Travis County, Texas.

Grantor, for the consideration and subject to the reservations from and exceptions to conveyance and warranty, grants, sells, and conveys to Grantee the property, together with all and singular the rights and appurtenances thereto in any wise belonging, to have and hold it to Grantee, Grantee's heirs, executors, administrators, successors, or assigns forever. Grantor binds Grantor and Grantor's heirs, executors, administrators, and successors to warrant and forever defend all and singular the property to Grantee and Grantee's heirs, executors, administrators, successors, and assigns against every person whomsoever lawfully claiming or to claim the same or any part thereof, except as to the reservations from and exceptions to conveyance and warranty.

When the context requires, singular nouns and pronouns include the plural.

BY: Raymond A Grant
Raymond A. Grant

BY: JoAnn H Grant
JoAnn H. Grant

STATE OF TEXAS
COUNTY OF TRAVIS

This instrument was acknowledged before me on the 31st day of May 1996 by Raymond A. and JoAnn H. Grant

Rosemary Potter
Notary Public, State of Texas
Notary's name (printed): ROSEMARY POTTER

Notary Seal

Notary's commission expires: 1/31/1999

Leases

LEASE
A transfer by the landlord/lessor of real or personal property to the tenant/lessee for a period of time for consideration (usually the payment of rent). Upon termination of the lease, the property reverts to the lessor.

An owner of either personal or real property can lease, or rent, the property to another person or business firm. A **lease** is a contractual agreement under which a property owner (the lessor) agrees to rent his or her property to

PARALEGAL PROFILE

Real-estate Paralegal and Office Manager

SUSAN TRUMPOWER received her bachelor of arts degree in business administration in 1977 from the University of Georgia. After working at a variety of jobs, mainly in retail, Trumpower accepted a position as a deputy clerk at the Madison County courthouse, where she met an attorney from Graham & Graham, the law firm for which she now works. She initially worked as a secretary for the firm during the day, and at night she pursued her paralegal certificate at the Athens Technical Institute. Trumpower admits that even though it took her five years to receive her certificate, it has been well worth it. She currently works as a real-estate paralegal as well as an office manager for the firm.

What do you like best about your work?

"The thing I like most about title work is piecing the puzzle together, because there's always an answer I'll like if I dig deep enough. I also like title work because it is not repetitive, and because in a small office I'm able to follow it all the way through. I also enjoy my role as office manager and see it as a challenge. Every day I am faced with a different problem, and so I'm always finding new ways to deal with problems efficiently and effectively."

What is the greatest challenge that you face in your area of work?

"The greatest challenge of working in a small law firm is being able to prioritize the work that has to be done. A typical day involves balancing my paralegal work with my managerial duties. Combining a wide variety of managerial duties with real-estate paralegal duties makes it necessary to list the tasks that need to be completed and to assign a priority to each task. Also, one of the big challenges is establishing and maintaining the office filing system. With a large client base and seven employees accessing the files, it is quite a challenge to try to develop methods to keep the files orderly, know who has which file, and so on."

"TIPS FOR REAL-ESTATE PARALEGALS INCLUDE ONE MAIN THING: BE THOROUGH!"

What advice do you have for would-be paralegals in your area of work?

"My advice to paralegal students involves two things. First, they should find out what area of the law piques their interest and look for a job in that particular area of law. Second, I recommend that they evaluate their personalities and determine whether they want a job that involves extensive contact with the public. Paralegals are afforded the opportunity of working closely with the public or of having very little public contact, depending on the area of law in which they choose to work."

What are some tips for success as a paralegal in your area of work?

"Tips for real-estate paralegals include one main thing: be thorough! Don't try to rush through anything. If you miss something in deed records, it could be a terrible error, and you can't take it lightly. It could cost you your job."

another (the lessee) for a specified period of time. Leases of personal property (cars or equipment) are covered by the Uniform Commercial Code, which spells out the rights and duties of lessors and lessees.

Leases of real property are governed in part by the common law of contracts and in part (and to an increasing extent) by state statutory law. Although under the common law, an oral lease is valid, a party who seeks to enforce an oral lease may have difficulty proving its existence. In most states, statutes mandate that leases exceeding one year's duration must be in writing. When real property is leased, the lessor (landlord) retains ownership rights to the property, but the lessee (tenant) obtains the right to the exclusive possession of the property. Most leases, however, give the landlord the right to come onto the property for certain purposes—to make repairs, for example.

Paralegals frequently draft or review lease agreements for clients (or for corporate employers), and you should be familiar with the types of terms that are typically included in a lease agreement, or contract. Normally, a lease contract will specify the names of the lessor and lessee, the location of the premises being leased, the amount of rent to be paid by the lessee, the duration of the lease, and the respective rights and duties of the parties in regard to the use and maintenance of the leased premises. Exhibit 8.5 on page 304 illustrates the kinds of provisions that are commonly included in lease agreements.

Property Law and the Paralegal

Paralegals frequently undertake tasks that require an understanding of real-property law. If you work for a small legal practice, some of your work may involve assisting your supervising attorney in handling real-estate transactions. If you work for a law firm (or a department within a law firm) that specializes in real-estate transactions, you will have extensive contact with buyers and sellers of real property, as well as with real-estate agents, title companies, banking institutions that finance real-estate purchases, and the attorneys and paralegals who represent the other parties in real-estate sales.

If a real-estate agent is involved, the agent will assist the seller or the buyer in drawing up a purchase contract, in arranging for inspections, in having the title examined and title insurance procured, and in preparing the closing papers. In this situation, your job will be to assist the attorney in verifying, on behalf of your client, that all of the documents needed have been prepared and that the documents contain the correct purchase price, mortgage amount, property description, and other terms. Generally, you will be responsible for making sure that the documents are in order and that the client's interests are fully protected.

Here are just some of the types of tasks that you might perform as a real-estate paralegal working for a law firm, many of which were also mentioned in Chapter 2 as tasks of the paralegal who specializes in real-estate law:

- Interview a client who wants to buy or sell property.
- Assist the client with the preliminary negotiations (offers and counteroffers) leading up to the purchase contract.
- Draft the offers and counteroffers, as well as other documents necessary to the sale.
- Conduct a title examination—by going to the county courthouse and examining previous property transfers.
- Obtain or create a title abstract.
- Contact the title company to arrange for the closing.
- Handle the escrow account.
- Attend the closing. (In some states, paralegals are allowed to represent clients at closings.)

ETHICAL CONCERN

Accurate Paperwork and the Sale of Real Estate

Art Guthrie, a paralegal, was drafting a real-estate offer for one of the firm's corporate clients. Instead of keying in $90,000 as the amount being offered for the property, Art accidentally entered $900,000. No one detected the error. The seller accepted the offer, and only when Art was reviewing the closing package did he notice the mistake and tell his supervising attorney about it. The seller agreed to cancel the contract (because in the meantime she had received an offer of $110,000 for the property). Eventually the client paid $115,000—$25,000 more than it otherwise would have had to pay—for the desired property. The client sued the attorney for negligence, alleging that the attorney had breached the duty of competence and seeking the extra $25,000 in damages. The picture emerging from this hypothetical scenario is clear: when handling paperwork relating to real-estate transactions, as with all legal documents, the paralegal must make absolutely sure that the documents are accurate.

DEVELOPING PARALEGAL SKILLS

Reviewing the Closing Package

Ann Cannon works as a legal assistant for a sole practitioner. The attorney handles a number of real-estate closings. Ann's job is to request a copy of the closing package from the title company and review it before the closing takes place, to make sure that there are no mistakes. The package consists of the purchaser's requirements, closing statement, settlement statement, deed, bill of sale, mortgage documents, and title insurance policy.

Last Monday, Ann called the title company to request the closing package for a closing scheduled for Thursday at 2 P.M. She received the package Tuesday at 5 P.M., just as she was leaving the office. She came in early today, Wednesday morning, to review the package before the phones start ringing. If changes are needed, they will have to be made today so that they are ready for the closing on Thursday.

THE PURCHASER'S REQUIREMENTS SHEET

Ann begins by reviewing the purchaser's requirements sheet. She reads down the column, which starts with the address of the property being purchased and the date, location, and time of the closing. Following the closing information is the amount of money that the purchasers are to bring to the closing, $20,000. The sheet states that the purchasers are required to bring a certified or cashier's check for that amount.

THE CLOSING STATEMENT

The next document in the package is the closing statement, which contains several columns of numbers. It starts with a column entitled "Credits to the Seller." That column lists the sale price of the home, $250,000, and then adds to that amount $3,802 for city and county taxes, which are prorated from the beginning of the year to the date of closing. The total under this column is therefore $253,802. The next column is entitled "Credits to the

Corporations also purchase and sell property, and some larger corporations have real-estate groups within their legal departments. If you work for a corporation that buys and sells a significant amount of property, your employer will be the "client," and you will perform similar tasks on the corporation's behalf.

The law governing real property also comes into play in other contexts than real-estate purchases or sales. If you work in the area of probate administration, for example, you will need to have an understanding of how ownership rights in property may be acquired and transferred.

INTELLECTUAL PROPERTY
Property resulting from intellectual, creative processes—the products of an individual's mind. Examples of intellectual property are literary and artistic works, computer software, trade names and trademarks, inventions, and trade secrets.

INTELLECTUAL PROPERTY

As mentioned in the previous section, intangible personal property is property that cannot be seen, touched, or otherwise perceived by the senses. A form of intangible personal property not yet discussed is **intellectual property**, which

DEVELOPING PARALEGAL SKILLS, Continued

Purchaser," and it lists first the purchaser's cash deposit of $5,000 and then the amount of the mortgage, which is $228,802. At the bottom of the column entitled "Credits Due from Purchaser" is the net amount due from the purchasers, $20,000 ($253,802 – $233,802). There is also a column entitled "Additional Costs to Purchaser." This column lists recording fees of $16. These are the fees for having the deed recorded with the county recording office, or register of deeds. Ann checks to make sure that all the numbers add up correctly.

THE SETTLEMENT STATEMENT

Ann also reviews the numbers in the settlement statement, which shows how much the sellers will receive at the closing. The statement also shows the commissions that the brokers will receive at the closing. In addition, it shows other costs, such as title insurance, revenue stamps on the deed, and miscellaneous expenses that are paid out of the mortgage to cover the closing costs and other fees. These numbers add up correctly, too. Next, Ann reads through the mortgage documents. She verifies that the names and property description are correct and that the amount of the mortgage is stated correctly. She also carefully checks the deed and the bill of sale to make sure that the clients' names are on them and that the names are spelled correctly. She knows that the clients intend to hold the property as joint tenants, but the deed indicates that they will own the property as tenants in common. Ann makes a note of this important error and continues reading through the documents.

FINAL PREPARATIONS FOR THE CLOSING

All of the documents are in order, except the deed, so she talks to her supervising attorney about the error. The attorney tells her to call the bank and ask to have the changes made before the closing takes place. The attorney also asks her to call the clients and review with them the items that they will need to bring to the closing.

consists of the products of one's mind—products that result from intellectual creative processes. We acquire rights in intellectual property whenever we invent something.

The need to protect individuals' rights in creative works was voiced by the framers of the U.S. Constitution over two hundred years ago. Article I, Section 8, of the Constitution authorized Congress "[t]o promote the Progress of Science and useful Arts, by securing for limited Times to Authors and Inventors the exclusive Right to their respective Writings and Discoveries." The patent, trademark, copyright, and other laws discussed below are explicitly designed to protect and reward inventive and artistic creativity.

Patents

A **patent** is a grant from the federal government that allows an inventor to have the exclusive right to make, use, and sell his or her invention for a period of seventeen years. To secure a patent, an inventor must demonstrate

PATENT
A government grant that gives an inventor the exclusive right or privilege to make, use, or sell his or her invention for a limited time period.

EXHIBIT 8.5
Typical Lease Terms

Term of lease: Indicates the duration of the lease, including the beginning and ending dates.

Rental: Indicates the amount of the rent payments and the intervals (monthly, yearly, etc.) at which rent will be paid.

Maintenence and use of leased premises: Describes which areas will be repaired and maintained by the landlord and which by the tenant.

Utilities: Stipulates whether and which utilities (electricity, water, etc.) will be paid by the landlord and by the tenant.

Alterations: Normally states that no structural alterations to the property will be made by the tenant without the landlord's consent.

Assignment: States whether the tenant's rights in the lease can be assigned (transferred) by the tenant to a third party.

Insurance: Indicates whether the landlord or the tenant will insure the premises against damage. (Normally, the landlord secures insurance coverage for the building, and the tenant obtains a "renter's policy" for his or her own personal property—furniture and other possessions—that will be housed in the building.)

Taxes: Designates which party will be liable for taxes or special assessments on the property. (Normally, the landlord assumes this responsibility, but in some commercial leases, the tenant agrees to take on this responsibility.)

Destruction: States what will happen in the event that the premises are totally destroyed by fire or other casualty.

Quiet enjoyment: A covenant (promise) by the landlord that the tenant shall possess and enjoy the premises without interference by any third party.

Termination: Usually specifies that the tenant's right to possession of the premises ends when the lease expires.

Renewal: Indicates that the tenant has an option to renew the lease if the landlord is notified of the intent to renew within a certain period of time (such as one month or three months) before the lease expires.

to the satisfaction of the U.S. Patent and Trademark Office that the invention is genuine, useful, and not obvious in light of the technology of the time. Anyone who makes, uses, or sells another's patented product or process without the patent holder's permission commits the tort of patent infringement.

TRADEMARK
A distinctive mark or motto that a manufacturer affixes to the goods it produces to distinguish the goods from goods produced by other manufacturers.

Trademarks and Related Property

A **trademark** is a distinctive mark or motto that a manufacturer stamps, prints, or otherwise affixes to the goods it produces so that those goods can be distinguished from the goods of other manufacturers and merchants.

SUBSTANTIVE LAW CONCEPT SUMMARY

Property Law

Property Classifications	**1.** *Real property*—Immovable property, including the land and all things attached to it, the minerals below the surface of the land, and the air above the surface of the land. **2.** *Personal property*—All property that is not real property (movable property, intangible property).
Ownership Rights in Property	**1.** *Fee simple*—The most complete form of ownership. **2.** *Concurrent ownership*—An interest in property held jointly with others. Types of concurrent ownership include the following: a. Tenancy in common—A form of co-ownership of property in which two or more persons own an undivided interest in the property. Upon one tenant's death, the property passes to his or her heirs. b. Joint tenancy—A form of co-ownership in which two or more persons own an undivided interest in property. Upon the death of a joint tenant, the property interest transfers to the remaining tenant(s), not to the heirs of the deceased tenant. c. Tenancy by the entirety—A form of co-ownership between a husband and wife that is similar to a joint tenancy, except that a spouse cannot transfer separately his or her interest during his or her lifetime. d. Community property—A form of co-ownership between a husband and wife in which each spouse owns one-half of the property acquired during the marriage (exists in only a few states). **3.** *Life estate*—An estate that lasts for the life of a specified individual. **4.** *Future interest*—A residuary interest (such as the interest of an owner who transfers property to another as a life estate) in existing property that arises only in the future (such as when the holder of the life estate dies).
The Transfer and Sale of Property	Property may be transferred by gift, by will or inheritance, by lease, or by sale. Commonly, property is transferred by sale. **1.** *The sale of personal property*— a. Goods (movable and tangible personal property)—The sale of goods is governed by Article 2 of the Uniform Commercial Code. b. Intangible property (stocks, bonds, rights to payment evidenced by checks or other documents)—The sale of intangible personal property is governed by other articles of the UCC or by other laws, such as the securities laws discussed in Chapter 9. **2.** *The sale of real property*— a. Governing law—The sale of real property is governed by the common law of contracts as well as by state (and, to a limited extent, federal) statutory law. b. Procedures—For a summary of the basic steps and procedures involved in the sale of real estate, see Exhibit 8.1.
Leases	A lease is a contractual agreement under which a property owner (the lessor) agrees to rent his or her property to another (the lessee) for a specified period of time. Both personal and real property can be leased. **1.** *Personal property*—Leases of personal property (cars or equipment) are covered by the Uniform Commercial Code, which spells out the rights and duties of lessors and lessees. **2.** *Real property*—Leases of real property are governed in part by the common law of contracts and in part (and to an increasing extent) by state statutory law.

Examples of trademarks are brand-name labels on jeans, luggage, and other products. Generally, to be protected under trademark law, a mark must be distinctive. A distinctive mark might consist of uncommon words (such as *Kodak* or *Xerox*) or words that are used in an uncommon or fanciful way (such as *English Leather* for an after-shave lotion instead of for leather processed in England).

Trademark law gives the originator of the mark the exclusive right to use that mark. Someone who uses the same mark without permission commits the tort of trademark infringement. Trademark rights provide an incentive for merchants to invest in product development and improvement. Laws protecting trademarks also assist consumers, because trademarks allow consumers to distinguish easily one manufacturer's goods from another.

TRADE NAME
A name used in commercial activity to designate a particular business, a place at which a business is located, or a class of goods. Trade names can be exclusive or nonexclusive. Examples of trade names are Sears, Safeway, and Firestone.

Trademarks apply to *products.* The term **trade name** is used to indicate part or all of a business's name, such as McDonald's. Unless the trade name is also used as a trademark (as with Kodak, Xerox, and Coca-Cola, for example), the name is not protected under federal trademark law. Trade names are protected under the common law, however. Holiday Inns, Inc., for example, could sue a motel owner who used that name or a portion of it (such as "Holiday Motels") without permission for infringing on its trade name. As with trademarks, words must be unusual or fancifully used if they are to be protected as trade names. The word *Safeway,* for example, was considered by a court to be sufficiently fanciful to obtain protection as a trade name for a chain of food stores.

Copyrights

COPYRIGHT
The exclusive right of an author to publish, print, or sell a literary work, an artistic work, or other work of authorship (such as a computer program) for a statutory period of time.

Literary or artistic productions (including computer software) are protected under copyright law. A **copyright** gives the creator of a work the right to the exclusive use of that work for a given period of time. Works created after January 1, 1978, are automatically given statutory copyright protection for the life of the author plus fifty years. For copyrights owned by publishing houses, the copyright expires seventy-five years from the date of publication or one hundred years from the date of creation, whichever is first. For works by more than one author, the copyright expires fifty years after the death of the last surviving author.

Note that it is not possible to copyright an *idea.* The underlying ideas embodied in a work may be freely used by others. What is copyrightable is the particular way in which an idea is *expressed.* Whenever an idea and an expression are inseparable, the expression cannot be copyrighted. Generally, anything that is not an original expression of an idea does not qualify for copyright protection. Facts widely known to the public are not copyrightable. Page numbers are normally not copyrightable because they follow a sequence known to everyone.

A literary or artistic work is protected under copyright law regardless of whether its creator applied to the U.S. Copyright Office for a copyright on the work. If another person uses a significant portion of the work without the author's permission, the author can sue that person for copyright infringement. All the author has to do is demonstrate that he or she produced the work prior to the publication of the copied version. An exception to this rule is allowed under the so-called "fair use" provision of the federal

Copyright Act. This provision allows certain persons or organizations (such as nonprofit educational institutions) to reproduce copyrighted material for certain purposes without the copyright holder's permission. The provision's guidelines on what constitutes a fair use of copyrighted material are very broad, and the courts decide whether a particular use is fair on a case-by-case basis.[2] Thus, anyone reproducing copyrighted material, even if for educational purposes, may still be violating another's copyright.

TRADE SECRET
Information or a process that gives a business an advantage over competitors who do not know the information or process.

Trade Secrets

Some business processes and information that are not (or cannot be) patented, copyrighted, or trademarked are nevertheless protected under the common law as **trade secrets**. Customer lists, plans, research and development, pricing information, marketing techniques, and generally anything that makes a particular company unique and that would have value to a competitor constitute trade secrets.

Intellectual Property and the Paralegal

Many lawsuits involve the alleged infringement of intellectual-property rights. If you work for a general law practice, one of the firm's clients may seek legal assistance when the client discovers that someone has used, without permission, something that he or she created—such as a software program, the words or music to a song, a novel, a patented invention, or a trademark.

Many law firms specialize in such areas as patent law or have special departments dealing with patent cases. Paralegals who work in such firms or departments may face the challenge of managing voluminous materials and paperwork for just one case. A lawsuit for the alleged infringement of patent rights in a sophisticated product, such as a genetically engineered drug for treating leukemia, can result in thousands of exhibits and other documents that must be organized, safeguarded, and retrievable at the right moment. A paralegal who can meet this challenge successfully will be a great asset to his or her firm.

An increasing number of paralegals are now working in the corporate environment. Many of today's corporations invest heavily in the development of new products. A major concern of such companies—and their legal departments—is to protect their investment in research and development by obtaining patents, trademarks, or copyrights. If you work for a corporation, you might be responsible for much of the document preparation and control necessary to securing such protection and to litigating cases involving the infringment of intellectual property. The U.S. Patent and Trademark Office and the U.S. Copyright Office also employ paralegals. If you work for either of these offices, you would be handling exclusively applications and other records relating to patents and trademarks or copyrights.

ETHICAL CONCERN

Meeting Federal Court Deadlines

As yet another example of the consequences of missing a court procedural deadline, suppose that a client of your firm has been sued in tort for the conversion of intellectual property. *Conversion* is the wrongful taking of another's property—the civil counterpart of theft. The plaintiff, an author, has filed suit against the client in a state court, alleging that the defendant has used portions of a textbook written by the plaintiff without permission. You are asked to prepare a "notice of removal" so that the case can be removed (transferred) from the state court to a federal court—because the claim is essentially a copyright claim, over which federal courts exercise jurisdiction. If the notice is not filed with the federal court within thirty days of the defendant's receipt of the complaint and summons (and nothing is filed with the state court), the defendant may lose the right to defend against the suit and may end up having to pay whatever damages the plaintiff is seeking. If this happened, the client, in turn, could then sue the attorney, and possibly the paralegal, to recover the damages that the defendant had to pay the plaintiff due to the attorney's breach of the duty of competence.

2. For more details on the "fair use" provision of the Copyright Act, see the sample court case presented in Chapter 18, in the fold-out exhibit (Exhibit 18.1). In that case, the United States Supreme Court had to determine whether the rap group 2 Live Crew's parody version of "Oh, Pretty Woman" constituted a "fair use" of the original, copyrighted version of the song.

Here are some specific types of tasks that you might undertake in the area of intellectual-property law (many of which were also mentioned in Chapter 2):

- Interview a client (or a manager of a corporation for which you work) to obtain information regarding intellectual property to be registered.
- Call the U.S. Patent and Trademark Office to find out if someone has applied for patent or trademark protection for a certain type of product that your firm's client (or your corporate employer) wants to develop and register.
- Draft the documents that are necessary to apply for patent, trademark, or copyright protection.
- Draft contracts that provide for another's authorized use of a copyrighted, patented, or trademarked product in return for *royalties* (a percentage of the proceeds received as a result of the authorized use of the intellectual property).
- Review marketing data and sales statements to verify royalties due for another's authorized use of your employer's trademarked, patented, or copyrighted product.
- Assist in litigation resulting from the infringement of rights in intellectual property.

The Growth in Statutory Law

The legal concepts and principles discussed in this chapter provide the foundation for much of today's law—the law at a given point in time. As a para-

Substantive Law Concept Summary

Intellectual Property

Patents	A patent is a grant from the federal government that gives an inventor the exclusive right to make, use, and sell his or her invention for a period of seventeen years. The inventor must demonstrate that the invention is genuine, useful, and not obvious in light of current technology.
Trademarks	A trademark is a distinctive mark or motto that a manufacturer stamps, prints, or affixes to goods so that its products are distinguishable from those of others. The owner of a trademark has the exclusive right to use that mark.
Copyrights	The right of an author or creator of a literary work, artistic creation, or other production (such as a computer program) to have the exclusive use of that work for a given period of time. Only the *expression* of an idea (and not the idea itself) can be protected by copyright.
Trade Secrets	A trade secret is a valuable business secret that makes a particular company or product unique and that would be of value to a competitor. Trade secrets include customer lists, plans, research and development, and pricing information. Trade secrets are protected under the common law.

TODAY'S PROFESSIONAL PARALEGAL

Relocation Assistance

Paralegal Marla Mann works in the real-estate group in the legal department of a large corporation that has offices throughout the United States. Marla works for the attorney who handles employee relocations. Whenever an employee is transferred, the company takes care of all of the arrangements for selling the house that the employee is vacating. Marla works extensively with realtors, attorneys for the purchasers, title companies, and banks and other institutions that provide mortgage financing.

MEETING WITH A REALTOR

Marla's telephone rings. It is Lou Holt, a realtor. He has an offer on a transferred employee's house. He will drop it off in about an hour. Marla continues to review the closing documents for the sale of another transferred employee's home. An hour later, the receptionist announces that Lou Holt is in the lobby. Marla walks to the lobby, meets Lou, and takes the offer. Lou tells Marla that he will be out of the office tomorrow and to call his partner, John Stoff, if Marla or her supervising attorney has any questions or if they want to negotiate any of the terms of the offer.

DEALING WITH APPRAISALS

Marla's telephone rings again. This time it is June Sember, a loan officer at the National Bank. She has some questions about an appraisal on another house. Marla answers June's questions. June's call reminds Marla that she was going to call Bob Redding, a real-estate appraiser, to set up an appraisal for another house. She calls Bob, and he tells Marla that this afternoon would be the best time for him to appraise the property. They agree to meet at the property at 2 P.M. Marla notes it on her calendar. Marla continues to review the closing package until lunch time.

After lunch, Marla leaves to meet Bob Redding for the appraisal. They walk through the house. Bob looks at every room, takes measurements, and makes notes. He walks around the outside of the house, inspects it, and takes some more measurements. He looks at a book containing the prices for which comparable houses have been sold in the neighborhood. He agrees that this house is worth the price that was offered for it, based on the prices at which other, similar homes have been sold. Bob tells Marla that he will prepare a written appraisal and forward it to the bank, with a copy to her. She thanks him and returns to her office to continue her other work.

legal, you need to be aware that the law is constantly changing. A statute or common law rule or doctrine that was current three years ago may not be current today. One aspect of the American legal tradition, however, seems to remain fairly constant: the increasing enactment of common law doctrines into statutory law or the replacement of common law doctrines by statutory law or administrative law.

For example, although the common law of contracts remains a significant body of law, contracts for the sale of goods are now governed by statutory law (each state's equivalent of the Uniform Commercial Code, or UCC). If a dispute over the terms of a sales contract arises, the UCC governs the issue. Although the UCC incorporates many principles of the common law of contracts, modified as necessary to meet the needs of sellers and buyers in today's marketplace, it is nonetheless statutory law. Property ownership and transfers are also regulated by state statute to a significant extent. In the following chapter, you will read about other ways in which the common law has been replaced by federal or state statutes or administrative agency regulations in the interest of protecting employees, consumers, and competition in the marketplace.

KEY TERMS AND CONCEPTS

acceptance 268
agreement 267
assault 281
battery 281
breach of contract 266
consideration 268
contract 266
contractual capacity 269
copyright 308
deed 298
defamation 281
defense 269
eminent domain 289
fee simple 288
fraud 270
intellectual property 302
intentional tort 279
joint tenancy 289
lease 299
mortgage 293
negligence 283
offer 267
patent 303
personal property 288
product liability 279
proximate cause 285
punitive damages 279
real property 288
reasonable-person standard 284
reformation 272
restitution 272
sales contract 275
Statute of Frauds 269
strict liability 287
tenancy in common 289
tort 279
trade name 306
trade secret 307
trademark 304
unconscionable contract 271
Uniform Commercial Code (UCC) 275
warranty 276

CHAPTER SUMMARY

1. An understanding of basic legal concepts and principles helps the paralegal by providing a framework for the specific tasks that he or she performs.

2. A contract is an exchange of promises, either oral or in writing, that can be enforced in court. Four elements must exist for a valid contract to be formed: there must be an agreement (through an offer and an acceptance of that offer) to form a contract; the contract must be supported by consideration (that is, the parties must promise to exchange something of value); the parties must have contractual capacity; and the contract must have a legal purpose.

3. Each state has a Statute of Frauds that requires certain types of contracts to be in writing to be enforceable. Defenses against contract formation or enforceability include the Statute of Frauds, as well as the claim that the defendant did not genuinely assent to the terms of the contract. Additionally, contracts that are deemed unconscionable (so grossly one sided or unfair as to "shock the conscience" of the court) and contracts that are objectively impossible to perform (due to destruction of the subject matter, for example) will not be enforced.

4. If one party breaches the contract (fails to do what was promised in the contract), the other can sue in court to obtain a remedy for the breach. Plaintiffs frequently seek compensatory and perhaps consequential damages to compensate them for losses caused by the breach. The equitable remedies of specific performance, rescission and restitution, and reformation will normally be granted only when the remedy at law (money damages) is inadequate.

5. Contracts for the sale of goods are covered by the Uniform Commercial Code (UCC), the provisions of which have been adopted (partially or totally) as law in every state. The UCC, which particularly applies when certain terms of a contract are absent or unclear, has significantly modifed some common law contract doctrines. The UCC spells out the remedies that are available to the buyer and seller when a sales contract is breached. The UCC also has provisions on the types of warranties that can arise when a sales contract is formed.

6. A tort is a wrongful act that harms another or another's property. The purpose of tort law is to compensate victims who are harmed by the actions of others, not to punish the wrongdoers; but punitive damages may be awarded to deter certain types of acts. Intentional torts require intention—that is, the wrongdoer must intend to undertake an act and intend the normal consequences of the act, although the intent to harm another is not required. Intentional torts include defamation of character, fraudulent misrepresentation, intentional infliction of emotional distress, false imprisonment, invasion of privacy, and trespass to land.

7. The tort of neglience occurs when an individual's breach of a duty of care causes another to suffer a legally recognized injury. To prove negligence, a plaintiff must show that the defendant had a duty of care, the defendant breached that duty of care, the plaintiff suffered a legally recognizable injury, and the defendant's breach of the duty of care caused that injury. Defenses to negligence include assumption of risk, contributory or comparative negligence, and the "last-clear-chance" doctrine.

8. Under the tort doctrine of strict liability, a party may be held liable for a tort even though he or she exercised reasonable care and was not at fault for the harm caused. Examples of the application of strict liability include liability for dangerous animals and product liability.

9. Real property is land and all things permanently affixed to the land. Personal property includes all other property, as well as intangible property (property—such as ownership rights in stock—that cannot be perceived by the senses). The most complete form of property ownership is the fee simple. One can also own property concurrently with others (as in a joint tenancy and a tenancy in common) or conditionally, as when property is held as a life estate (for the duration of the life of the holder).

10. Ownership rights in property are commonly transferred by sale. The sale of personal property (goods) is governed by the Uniform Commercial Code and other statutes. When real property is sold, the parties form a contract specifying the terms and conditions of the sale. Frequently, the contract is conditioned on the buyer's ability to obtain financing. Buyers normally have the premises inspected to learn of any defects, have the title examined, and (often) obtain title insurance. At the closing, which is the final step in the sales transaction, the deed is transferred to the buyer, the seller receives the proceeds of the sale, and all other accounts are settled, including the payment of closing costs by the buyer and the seller. Ownership rights in property can also be transferred in other ways, including by lease (renting the property temporarily to another) or by gift, will, or inheritance.

11. Intellectual property consists of the products of one's mind—creative works such as inventions, artistic works, and literary works. To encourage creativity, federal statutory law (patent, copyright, and trademark law) grants to individuals the exclusive right (for a limited period of time) to use or sell their intellectual property. Trade secrets, another form of intellectual property, are protected under the common law.

QUESTIONS FOR REVIEW

1. What two events must occur for a contractual agreement to be formed? What is consideration? Besides agreement and consideration, what other requirements must be met for a valid contract to be formed?

2. What defenses can be raised against a breach-of-contract claim? What remedies are available to the nonbreaching party when a contract is breached?

3. How do contracts for the sale of goods differ from other contracts? What is the Uniform Commercial Code (UCC)? What is the relationship between the UCC and the common law of contracts?

4. What is a warranty? How and when do warranties arise under the UCC? Can a seller disclaim or limit warranties?

5. What does the French word *tort* mean? How are torts different from crimes? List and define four intentional torts. How do intentional torts differ from torts arising from negligence?

6. What elements are required for a negligence claim? Explain the concept of the duty of care and how it can be breached. Does everyone have the same duty of care toward others in all circumstances?

7. How does the tort doctrine of strict liability differ from the law governing intentional torts? How does it differ from negligence theory?

8. What are the two main classifications of property? What is a fee simple? What are some other ways in which ownership rights in property can be held? What basic steps are involved in the sale of real property?

9. What is a lease? Describe some of the provisions typically included in lease contracts when real property is leased.

10. What is intellectual property? List and define the four categories of intellectual property covered in the chapter. What laws permit and protect ownership rights in intellectual property?

ETHICAL QUESTIONS

1. Douglas Coleman works as a paralegal for an oil company. The attorney he works for is responsible for negotiating franchise deals with people who want to purchase gas-station franchises. Most of those applying for franchises have lawyers who negotiate for them. Bob Little is applying for a franchise without a lawyer to represent him. It is apparent from talking to Little that he does not have much education, and he has indicated that he has never owned a gas station before. He has, however, recently inherited some money, and he wants to achieve his life-long dream of owning his own gas station.

He has been sent a copy of the standard-form franchise agreement. The standard-form agreement is very one sided and unfair to the franchisee (the person purchasing the franchise). Little calls and says that he is ready to negotiate his franchise agreement with the oil company and asks Coleman to set up a telephone conference for that purpose. Coleman would like to tell Little that he really should have a lawyer represent his interests during the negotiations. Can he recommend to Little that he retain a lawyer? Should he give Little any tips about how to negotiate a franchising arrangement with the oil company? What might happen if Coleman does either of these things? What might happen if he does nothing?

2. Jeffrey Singleman is an experienced legal assistant in a personal-injury practice. He is given a great deal of responsibility and has minimal supervision. One day, Georgia Wellington, an associate with the firm, has two court appearances scheduled at the same time. One appearance is in federal court, which is on one side of town, and the other is in the county circuit court, which is on the other side of town. Georgia asks Jeffrey to handle the hearing in the county circuit court for her. What should Jeffrey do?

3. Melinda Park has been asked to review an offer to purchase real estate. The offer was made by a client who is a first-time buyer and who has no experience in real-estate transactions. The client wants to understand what the legal obligations of the buyer and the seller are before he signs the offer. Park is a new paralegal with the law firm for which she is working, and her supervising attorney, Chad Abraham, gives her the offer to review because he thinks it would be good experience for her. She is to go through the offer, summarize each provision, and note the legal effect of each provision on both the buyer and the seller.

Park begins to read the offer, and she sees a paragraph that states that the premises are being sold "as is." Park thinks that she understands what this provision means, so she doesn't check on its actual meaning. Instead, she writes, "The house is sold as it appears, and there is no legal effect on the buyer." (The "as is" clause in fact means that there is no warranty on the house; and if there is anything wrong with it, such as a leaking roof, the seller is not obligated to cover repair costs. The buyer must pay for the repairs himself or herself.) What has Park done? How could she have better handled the situation?

4. Using the facts from the situation in Ethical Question 3 above, assume that Park's supervising attorney did not have time to review her work before giving it to the client. Has the attorney violated any ethical or legal obligation? What effect might Park's explanation of the legal effect of the "as is" clause have on the client? On Park? On the attorney?

PRACTICE QUESTIONS AND ASSIGNMENTS

1. Using the information on intentional torts and negligence presented in this chapter, identify the following torts:

a. Mary receives a telephone call at 5:25 P.M. while she is making dinner for her husband, who will be home shortly. The caller says, "I've got your husband and his money, and I'm taking him to Brazil. You'll never see him again." In a panic, Mary, knowing that her husband has just received a large bonus from his employer, suffers a heart attack. The call was actually made by her husband's friend, Joe. Joe frequently plays practical jokes on Mary and her husband, and the call was another one of his pranks.

b. A picture appears in the newspaper showing the governor of Arkansas at a county fair, holding a cute little boy and feeding the boy a hot dog. The words "Deli-Dog," printed on the hot dog's paper wrapper, appear clearly in the picture. The Deli-Dog company takes the picture out of the newspaper and uses it, without obtaining the governor's permission, to promote its hot dogs.

c. The *Local Inquirer* publishes an article that claims that the sister of a famous movie star, whose name it mentions, is dying from AIDS. The article is false and is published without having been investigated by the reporter.

d. Jennifer is driving her children home from school. The two oldest children are fighting in the back seat. She turns to scold them, taking her eyes off the road temporarily. When she turns back, there is a child on a bike crossing the street in front of her. Jennifer tries but is unable to swerve to avoid hitting the boy.

2. Using the material on ownership rights in property presented in this chapter, identify the types of ownership rights described in the following statements.

a. John and Linda, a brother and a sister, jointly own a cottage that they inherited from their mother. They have rights of survivorship.

b. Jeannette conveys her beachfront property to her mother for as long as her mother lives. On her mother's death, the property is to go to Jeanette's daughter.

c. Louise Winter owns her home, and she may use, possess, or dispose of it as she pleases.

d. John Tully and Sam Marsh jointly own a large farm in Iowa. If either of them dies, the heirs of the deceased owner will inherit that owner's share of the farm.

3. Using the material on intellectual property presented in this chapter, identify the type of legal protection that is given to each form of intellectual property described below.

a. Karen Wilson designs book bags for students. Her logo is a small schoolhouse stamped on the book bag. Karen's logo distinguishes her book bags from those of other manufacturers.

b. Mike Pierson starts a pizza business that he calls Pizza Express. After several years of successfully operating the business, he begins to expand and eventually owns a chain of Pizza Express shops in five states.

c. Mike Pierson has developed a highly successful strategy for marketing his pizza and for locating his pizza shops. This strategy has made his company, Pizza Express, unique and prosperous.

d. Carol Garcia writes a textbook, which is published. The publisher's payments to Carol are in the form of royalties.

e. Dr. Alston invents a unique type of windshield wipers. He wants the right to sell his invention.

QUESTIONS FOR CRITICAL ANALYSIS

1. Many people claim that the Statute of Frauds, which requires certain types of contracts to be in writing, results in more injustice than justice because it can be used by parties to avoid contractual obligations that they freely assumed under an oral contract. Do you agree with this contention? Do you think that the Statute of Frauds should be abolished, as it has been in England (where it originated)?

2. Review this chapter's discussion of intellectual property. What are the advantages of granting patent, copyright, and trademark protection to the creators of intellectual property? Can you think of any disadvantages? What would result if rights to intellectual property were not protected by law?

ROLE-PLAYING EXERCISES

1. Using the facts presented in Ethical Question 3, assume that Melinda Park's supervising attorney, Chad Abraham, did not review her work before it went out to the client but looked at it several days later. He noticed her incorrect definition of the "as is" provision and is upset that there is an error in the memo that was sent to the client. Role-play the discussion between Abraham and Park in which the attorney points out the error to the paralegal and the impact that the error will have on the client. Attorney Abraham should be understanding about the error, but he should also impress upon paralegal Park the seriousness of her error and the possibility of a malpractice suit against the firm.

2. Paralegal Mike Fassen works in a law firm that specializes in intellectual-property law. His supervising attorney, Margaret Gorman, is attending an out-of-town hearing today, and the receptionist has transferred a call from a client to Mike. The client states that he heard a song that he composed (and copyrighted) being performed on the radio by a famous rock band. The client is very upset because the band recorded the song without his permission. The client demands to speak to Margaret. When Mike tells the client that Margaret is not available, the client demands that Mike answer his legal questions. Role-play the conversation between Mike and the client. Mike should inform the client that he cannot give legal advice, but he should also try to appease the client.

PROJECTS

1. Call or write the U.S. Copyright Office, which is located in the Library of Congress in Washington, D.C. Ask for information on copyright law and for copyright registration forms.

2. Find out what defenses against negligence are used in your state. Do the courts in your state allow the defense of contributory negligence, or have they adopted the comparative-negligence doctrine?

3. Visit the register of deeds office for your county. Ask to see how and where they record deeds. Find out what the term *liber* means.

ANNOTATED SELECTED READINGS

BUTTERWORTH-HEINENMANN, RISA, AND ALF ERLING. "Preference Revelation in Strict Liability Product Safety Markets." *International Review of Law and Economics*, March 1994. An interesting discussion of the reasons and justifications for applying strict liability theory to product-liability cases.

CALAMARI, JOHN D., AND JOSEPH M. PERILLO. *Contracts.* 3d ed. St. Paul: West Publishing Co., 1987. A book that provides supplemental reading on contract law.

GREGORY, DONALD A., CHARLES W. SABER, AND JON D. GROSSMAN. *Introduction to Intellectual Property Law.* Washington, D.C.: Bureau of National Affairs, Inc., 1994. A thorough yet readable introduction to the law governing intellectual property. The authors clearly define and describe the various types of intellectual property and the underlying reasons why owners' rights in intellectual property are protected by law. The book also is filled with practical advice for legal professionals who practice in this area, including tips on how to draft contracts relating to intellectual property, how to transfer rights in such property, and how to apply for patent, trademark, or copyright protection.

LLOYD, ROSS. "Deeds: Grantor under General Warranty Deed May Not Dispute Title Conveyed to Grantee." *Real Estate Law Report*, April, 1991. An article that contains an enlightening explanation of a fundamental concept in real-estate law: the difference between a quitclaim deed and a warranty deed.

MILLER, ROGER LEROY, AND GAYLORD A. JENTZ. *Business Law Today: The Essentials.* 3d ed. St. Paul: West Publishing Co., 1994. An informative and readable textbook that offers detailed coverage of each topic dealt with in this chapter. Chapter 4 of Miller and Jentz's book focuses on torts and intellectual property; Chapters 6, 7, and 8 cover the common law of contracts; Chapters 9 and 10 look at sales law; and Chapters 20 and 21 explore the basic concepts relating to real and personal property.

MOYNIHAN, CORNELIUS. *Introduction to Real Property.* St. Paul: West Publishing Co., 1987. A good reference for reviewing property-law concepts.

PROCTOR, STEPHEN M., AND LAURIE A. PEARD. "Confronting Common Sales Contract Problems." *Illinois Bar Journal*, October 1993. An excellent article with many practice tips and pointers on how to review a contract for the sale of goods under Article 2 of the Uniform Commercial Code.

PROSSER, WILLIAM L., PAGE W. KEETON, DAN B. DOBBS, ROBERT E. KEETON, AND DAVID G. OWEN. *The Law of Torts.* 5th ed. St. Paul: West Publishing Co., 1984. A treatise that is regarded as the "Bible" of tort law. It provides solid supplemental reading for anyone interested in this field of law.

9

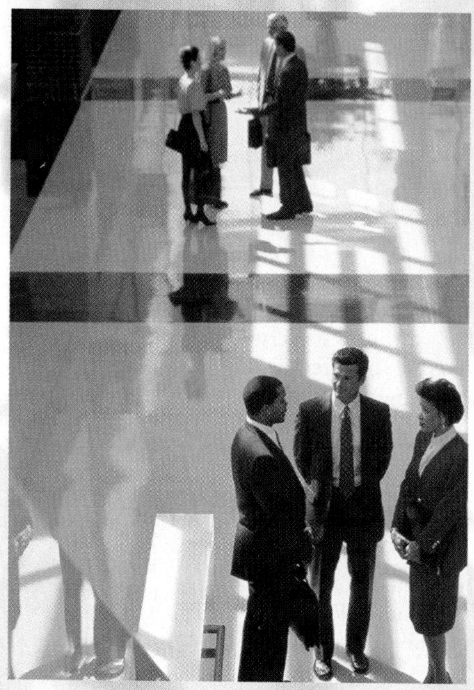

Corporate Law and Government Regulation

Chapter Objectives

After completing this chapter, you will know:

- The basic concepts of agency law and how they affect business operations and employment relationships.
- The most common forms of businesses and how they are created, operated, and terminated.
- How the profits, losses, risks, and liabilities associated with the different types of business organizations are distributed.
- How the government regulates employer-employee relationships through laws governing labor-union activities and employment discrimination.
- Some of the ways in which the government protects consumers against unfair business practices and harmful products.

Chapter Outline

INTRODUCTION

Recall from Chapter 5 that there are three basic forms of business organization: the sole proprietorship, the partnership, and the corporation. In that chapter, we briefly discussed the major characteristics of each of these forms, focusing mostly on how each form affects the working environment of the paralegal. In this chapter, we explore the topic of business organizational forms in greater detail. No matter where you work as a paralegal or what kind of work you perform, you will benefit from having a basic understanding of business forms and how they are created, operated, and terminated.

As you will see, each type of business form creates certain rights and responsibilities for the owners of the business. In your work as a paralegal, you will want to have some idea of what these rights and duties are when you work on behalf of business clients. Additionally, you should know how the laws discussed later in this chapter—laws governing employment relationships and consumer law—establish further rights and duties for business owners. Indeed, much of the work undertaken by attorneys and paralegals today touches, either directly or indirectly, on the topics examined in the following pages.

Before we discuss these topics, however, we first need to examine another body of law—the law of agency. This is because agency law shapes, to a great extent, the rights and duties of both business owners and those who work for them or on their behalf.

THE LAW OF AGENCY

AGENCY
A relationship between two persons in which, by agreement or otherwise, one person (the principal) is bound by the words and acts of another (the agent).

AGENT
A person who is authorized to act for or in the place of another person (the principal).

PRINCIPAL
In agency law, a person who, by agreement or otherwise, authorizes another person (the agent) to act on the principal's behalf in such a way that the acts of the agent become binding on the principal.

An **agency** relationship exists when one party, called the **agent**, agrees to represent or act for another party, called the **principal**. An agency agreement can take the form of an express written contract, as when an attorney and a client agree, in a written retainer agreement, that the attorney will represent the client. An agency agreement can also be formed orally, as when a paralegal orally agrees to work for a firm and there is no written employment contract. In some situations, an agency agreement may be implied by conduct.

The law of agency applies to all forms of business organization. Indeed the agency relationship is one of the most common, important, and pervasive legal relationships. By using agents, a principal (such as a corporation) can conduct multiple business operations simultaneously in various locations. A business world without agents is hard to imagine. Picture Henry Ford trying to sell all of the cars that Ford Motor Company manufactured. Obviously, other people must be appointed to fill in—act as agents—for the owner of a large company—the principal.

Types of Agency Relationships

Agency relationships commonly exist between employers and employees and sometimes between employers and independent contractors who are hired to perform special tasks or services.

Employer-employee Relationships. An **employee** is defined as one whose physical conduct is controlled by or subject to the control of the employer. Normally, all employees who deal with third parties are deemed to be agents. As a paralegal employee, for example, you will be an agent of your employer.

EMPLOYEE
In agency law, one whose physical conduct is controlled by or subject to the control of the employer.

State and federal employment laws apply only to the employer-employee relationship. Statutes governing Social Security, withholding taxes, workers' compensation, unemployment compensation, and workplace safety, for example, are applicable only if there is an employer-employee relationship. In contrast, these laws do not apply to the independent contractor.

Independent Contractors. An **independent contractor** is defined as a person who contracts with another party to do something for that party but who is neither controlled by nor subject to the control of the other party in respect to the physical performance of the undertaking. Because those who hire independent contractors have no control over the details of their job performance, independent contractors are not deemed to be employees. Building contractors and subcontractors are independent contractors, for example, and a property owner does not control the acts of either of these professionals. Truck drivers who own their equipment and hire out on a per-job basis are independent contractors; but truck drivers who drive company trucks on a regular basis are usually employees. A collection agent and a real-estate broker are other examples of independent contractors.

INDEPENDENT CONTRACTOR
One who works for, and receives payment from, an employer but whose working conditions and methods are not controlled by the employer. An independent contractor is not an employee but may be an agent.

The relationship between a principal and an independent contractor may or may not involve an agency relationship. To illustrate: An owner of real estate who hires a real-estate broker to negotiate the sale of his or her property has not only contracted with an independent contractor (the real-estate broker) but also established an agency relationship for the specific purpose of assisting in the sale of the property. Another example is an insurance agent, who is both an independent contractor and an agent of the insurance company whose policies he or she sells.

A question frequently faced by the courts in determining liability under agency law is whether a person hired by another to do a job is an employee or an independent contractor. Because employers are normally held liable as principals for the actions of their employee-agents within the scope of employment (as will be discussed shortly), the court's decision on this question can be significant for the parties. Generally, the greater the employer's control over the work, the more likely it is that the worker will be considered an employee. Another key factor is whether the employer withholds taxes from payments made to the worker and pays unemployment and Social Security taxes covering the worker.

Rights and Duties of Agents and Principals

An agency relationship is a fiduciary relationship. The term **fiduciary** is at the heart of agency law. The term can be used either as a noun or as an adjective. When used as a noun, it refers to a person who has a duty created by his or her undertaking to act primarily for another's benefit in matters connected with the undertaking. When used as an adjective, as in "fiduciary relationship" or

FIDUCIARY
As a noun, a person having a duty created by his or her undertaking to act primarily for another's benefit in matters connected with the undertaking. As an adjective, a relationship founded upon trust and confidence.

"fiduciary duties," it refers to a relationship involving trust and confidence or duties stemming from such a relationship.

Because agency is a fiduciary relationship, certain rights and duties arise whenever an agency relationship comes into existence. In general, the principal has a right corresponding to every duty owed by the agent, and vice versa. The principal's duties to the agent include the following:

- The duty to cooperate with the agent.
- The duty to provide safe working conditions for the agent.
- The duty to reimburse the agent for expenses incurred while working on the principal's behalf.
- The duty to compensate the agent for work performed.

The agent, in turn, has certain duties to the principal. These duties include the following:

- The duty to perform his or her tasks competently.
- The duty to obey and be loyal to the principal.
- The duty to notify the principal of knowledge or events significant to the agency.
- The duty to render an accounting to the principal of how, when, and for what purpose the principal's funds were used.

The Duty of Loyalty. Loyalty is one of the most fundamental duties in a fiduciary relationship. Basically stated, the agent has the duty to act solely for the benefit of his or her principal and not in the interest of the agent or a third party. For example, an agent cannot represent two principals in the same transaction unless both know of the dual capacity and consent to it. The duty of loyalty also means that any information or knowledge acquired through the agency relationship is considered confidential. It would be a breach of loyalty to disclose such information either during the agency relationship or after its termination. Attorneys, as agents, have a duty of loyalty to their clients; and as the ethical rules governing the legal profession specify, this loyalty cannot be divided. An attorney cannot represent both parties in a lawsuit, for example (see Chapter 4).

ETHICAL CONCERN

The Paralegal as Subagent

As an agent of your attorney, you have fiduciary duties to that attorney (your principal). As a subagent of the attorney's client, you have fiduciary duties to that client (the attorney's principal). The attorney is delegated certain authority through the client. As a subagent, you are delegated certain authority through your attorney and can bind the client by your acts. This is because the client is bound by the acts of the attorney, who is carrying out his or her fiduciary responsibilities through the use of a paralegal (the subagent). As a general rule, you should always treat both your attorney and the client as principals and serve their interests with the utmost care.

The Duties of Subagents. Whenever an attorney agrees to represent a client, the attorney becomes an agent of the client. But what is the status of the paralegal who works for the attorney-agent on the client's behalf? In this situation, the paralegal becomes both an agent (of the attorney) and a subagent (of the client). Subagents also owe fiduciary duties to the principal. A paralegal who works for a law firm thus has a duty of loyalty (as an agent) to the firm and (as a subagent) to the client.

Agency Relationships and Third Parties

Agents frequently form contracts with third parties on behalf of the principal, and sometimes an agent's action may, intentionally or unintentionally, cause a third party to suffer harm. In such situations, the following question arises: Who is liable under the contract or for the harm caused—the agent, the principal, or both?

Liability for Agent's Contracts. In a principal-agent relationship, the parties have agreed that the agent will act *on behalf and instead of* the principal in negotiating and transacting business with third persons. An agent is empowered to perform legal acts that are binding on the principal and can bind a principal in a contract with a third person.

For example, Elena Lopez works as a paralegal for the law firm of Jeffers, Gilmore & Dunn. Lopez has been asked to make sure that a VCR and other equipment are rented and available in the courtroom on the day of an upcoming trial. Lopez makes arrangements (forms a contract) with a rental agency to rent the equipment and have it delivered to the courtroom on the day of the trial. Lopez asks the rental agency to bill the law firm. The law firm is bound by this contract because it was formed by its agent, Elena Lopez.

Agent's Authorized Actions. Generally, a principal is liable only for the *authorized* actions of his or her agent. An agent may be expressly authorized, either orally or in writing, to undertake certain actions; or the agent's authority may be implied by custom—that is, an agent normally has the authority to do whatever is customary or necessary to fulfill the purpose of the agency. A paralegal office manager, for example, has the implied authority to enter into a contract to purchase office supplies on behalf of the firm because the office manager needs to have the authority to purchase supplies to fulfill his or her duties.

Agent's Unauthorized Actions. If an agent is *not authorized* to enter into a contract on behalf of the principal, then normally, the principal will not be bound by the contract unless he or she voluntarily accepts (ratifies) it. On rare occasions, though, in the interests of fairness, courts enforce contracts formed by agents acting beyond the scope of their authority (or by nonagents who are perceived by third parties to be agents) to protect third parties who have relied on such contracts.

Liability for Agent's Torts. Under the doctrine of ***respondeat superior***,[1] the principal-employer is liable for any harm caused to a third party by an agent-employee in the scope of employment. The doctrine imposes **vicarious liability** on the employer—that is, liability without regard to the personal fault of the employer—for torts committed by an employee in the course or scope of employment. The theory of *respondeat superior* is similar in this respect to the theory of strict liability covered in Chapter 8.

RESPONDEAT SUPERIOR
In Latin, "Let the master respond." A doctrine in agency law under which a principal or an employer may be held liable for the wrongful acts committed by agents or employees while acting within the scope of their agency or employment.

VICARIOUS LIABILITY
Legal responsibility placed on one person for the acts of another.

Rationale for the Doctrine. At early common law, an employer-employee relationship was referred to as a master-servant relationship. The servant (employee) was viewed as the employer's (master's) property. The master was deemed to have absolute control over the servant's acts and was held strictly liable for them no matter how carefully the master supervised

1. Pronounced ree-*spahn*-dee-uht soo-*peer*-ee-your. The doctrine of *respondeat superior* applies not only to employer-employee relationships but also to principal-agent relationships as long as the principal has the right of control over the agent.

the servant. The rationale for the doctrine of *respondeat superior* was based on the principle that every person has a duty to manage his or her affairs, whether accomplished by the person or through agents or servants, in such a way so as not to injure another. Today the doctrine continues. Liability is imposed on employers because they are deemed to be in a better financial position to bear the loss. The superior financial position carries with it the duty to be responsible for damages.

Scope of Employment. Third persons injured as a result of an employee's negligence or intentional tort can sue either the employee who was negligent or the employer. As mentioned above, there is an important condition that must be met before an employer will be held liable for an agent's tort:

- **For the employer to be liable under the doctrine of *respondeat superior*, the act causing injury must have occurred within the scope of the employee's employment.**

Traveling to and from work or to and from meals is usually considered outside the scope of employment. Traveling for a job-related purpose, however, is usually considered within the scope of employment. A paralegal employee sent to the county courthouse to file a document with the court on a client's behalf, for example, is acting within the scope of his or her employment. A person employed by a pizza company to deliver pizzas is acting within the scope of employment when delivering the pizzas. All travel time of a traveling salesperson is normally considered within the scope of employment for the duration of the business trip, including the return trip home.

Is the employer liable for an act that occurs when an employee goes off on his or her own—that is, departs from the employer's business to take care of personal affairs? It depends. If the employee's activity is a substantial departure, then the employer normally is not liable. For example, suppose that a paralegal delivers documents to the courthouse (within the scope of employment) but then, before returning to work, drives to a town thirty-five miles away to visit a relative who is ill. Travel to and from the relative's home would probably not be considered within the scope of employment.

Termination of an Agency Relationship

An agency may be terminated either voluntarily by agreement of the parties or by the occurrence of certain events that make it impossible for the relationship to continue.

Termination by the Parties. An agency relationship can be terminated through mutual agreement—that is, the agent and principal can simply agree to end the agency. With some exceptions, an agency can be ended by just one of the parties, as well. For example, suppose that a paralegal has agreed to work for an attorney, and neither the paralegal nor the attorney has promised to continue the agency for any specific period of time. In this situation, either party may terminate the agency at any time, although usually a reasonable amount of notice is required. (Of course, the attorney-employer cannot fire the paralegal-employee if doing so would violate any laws governing employment relationships, such as laws prohibiting discrimination.)

Events That Automatically Terminate an Agency. Certain occurrences or events automatically terminate an agency relationship. For example, if either the principal or the agent dies or becomes mentally incompetent, generally the agency is automatically terminated. An agency is also terminated when the specific subject matter of the agency is destroyed or lost. For example, suppose that your supervising attorney has been retained by a client to assist the client in the sale of the client's business premises. Shortly after this agency relationship is established, the premises burn to the ground. In this situation, the agency relationship is automatically terminated because the subject matter of the agency—the business premises—has been destroyed.

Other events that may automatically terminate an agency include significantly changed circumstances, bankruptcy of the principal or the agent, and war between the principal's country and the agent's country.

SUBSTANTIVE LAW CONCEPT SUMMARY

The Law of Agency

Agency Relationships	An agency relationship arises when one person (called the *agent*) agrees to act for or in the place of another person (called the *principal*). Types of agency relationships include the following: **1.** *Employer-employee relationships*—Employees who deal with third parties are normally considered to be agents of their employers. **2.** *Employer–independent contractor relationships*—Independent contractors may or may not be agents, depending on a number of factors. An important factor is the degree to which the actions of the independent contractor are subject to the control of the employer.
Rights and Duties of Agents and Principals	**1.** *The agent's duties to the principal—* a. Competent performance—The agent must perform his or her tasks competently. b. Notification—The agent is required to notify the principal of all matters that come to his or her attention concerning the subject matter of the agency. c. Obedience and loyalty—The agent must follow all lawful and clearly stated instructions of the principal. The agent has a duty to act solely for the benefit of his or her principal and not in the interest of the agent or a third party. d. Accounting—The agent has a duty to make available to the principal records of all property and money received and paid out on behalf of the principal. **2.** *The principal's duties to the agent—* a Cooperation—A principal must cooperate with and assist an agent in performing his or her duties. b. Safe working conditions—A principal must provide safe working conditions for the agent-employee. c. Reimbursement—The principal must reimburse the agent for all sums of money disbursed at the request of the principal and for all sums of money the agent paid for necessary expenses in the course of reasonable performance of his or her agency duties. d. Compensation—The principal must pay the agent the agreed-on value of the work performed by the agent on the principal's behalf.

SUBSTANTIVE LAW CONCEPT SUMMARY, Continued	
Agency Relationships and Third Parties	**1.** *Liability for an agent's contracts*—In an agency relationship, the principal normally is bound by all contracts formed by the agent on behalf of the principal, as long as the action was authorized. If the action was not authorized, the principal will not be liable unless he or she voluntarily agrees to be bound by (ratifies) the contract. **2.** *Liability for an agent's torts*—Agents are personally liable for the torts that they commit. If an agent commits a tort within the scope of his or her employment as an agent, the principal may also be held liable under the doctrine of *respondeat superior.*
Agency Termination	An agency may be terminated in the following ways: **1.** *By actions of the parties*—The parties may agree to terminate the agency on a certain date or on the occurrence of a certain event, such as the achievement of the purpose of the agency. The agency will also terminate if one party chooses to end the agency relationship. **2.** *Automatically*—Certain events or occurrences automatically terminate an agency relationship. These events or occurrences may include the following: a. The death or mental incompetence of either the principal or the agent. b. The destruction of the subject matter of the agency. c. Significantly changed circumstances. d. Bankruptcy of the principal or the agent. e. War between the principal's country and the agent's country.

Agency Law and the Paralegal

A knowledge of agency law is important for the paralegal for several reasons. As a paralegal employee, you will be directly involved in an agency relationship, and it is to your advantage to know what kinds of rights and duties are involved in that relationship. A knowledge of agency law also helps you understand the ethical rules of the legal profession, many of which are derived from the common law of agency.

Furthermore, in your work as a paralegal, you will often be dealing with agents. Each partner in a partnership, for example, is considered an agent of every other partner in the firm—as you will learn shortly. Corporate officers (such as corporate presidents and vice presidents) are agents of the corporation and, as such, assume the fiduciary duties discussed above. Paralegals who work on behalf of corporate clients or who specialize in the area of corporate law will find that agency law permeates the corporate environment.

FORMS OF BUSINESS ORGANIZATION

As mentioned, the three most common forms of business organization are the sole proprietorship, the partnership, and the corporation. Each form involves different relationships, rights, obligations, and regulatory schemes. We look at each of these forms below, as well as some important new options for business owners who seek to maximize their tax advantages and minimize their personal liability for business debts and obligations.

Sole Proprietorships

The sole proprietorship is the simplest form of business. As discussed in Chapter 5, a sole proprietorship is a business owned by one person. The owner is entitled to all of the business's profits and bears personal responsibility for all the business's debts and other obligations.

Sole proprietorships are very common. In fact, they constitute over two-thirds of all American businesses. They are also usually small enterprises—fewer than 1 percent of the sole proprietorships in the United States earn over $1 million per year. Sole proprietors can own and manage any type of business, from an informal, home-office undertaking to a large restaurant or construction firm.

Paralegals often work on behalf of clients who run their businesses as sole proprietors. Also, as mentioned in earlier chapters, many paralegals work for attorneys who are sole practitioners, or sole proprietors. If you go to work for such an attorney, and there are few employees on his or her staff, you may be asked to help keep records of the firm's income and expenses for tax purposes or to help the attorney secure or maintain liability insurance (to protect against claims of malpractice). Whether you work on behalf of or for a sole proprietor, you will benefit by having an understanding of the sole proprietor's legal rights and liabilities.

Formation of a Sole Proprietorship. The sole proprietorship is usually easier and less costly to start than any other kind of business, as few legal forms are involved. No partnership agreement need be formed, because there are no partners. No papers need be filed with the state (as when a corporation is formed) to establish the business. At most, there will be only minor paperwork involved, depending on the law of the city in which the business is located. Because it is the simplest business form to create, persons just starting up a business, such as an attorney setting up a law practice, often choose to operate as sole proprietors. Generally, anyone who does business without creating a separate business entity, such as a partnership or corporation, has a sole proprietorship.

Advantages and Disadvantages of Sole Proprietorships. A major advantage of the sole proprietorship is that the sole proprietor is entitled to all the profits made by the firm (because he or she takes all the risk). The sole proprietor is also free to make any decision he or she wishes concerning the business—whom to hire, when to take a vacation, what kind of business to pursue, and so on. Additionally, sole proprietors are allowed to establish tax-exempt retirement accounts, such as Keogh plans. (A **Keogh plan** is a retirement program designed for self-employed persons by which such persons can shelter a certain percentage of their income from taxation. The principal and interest earnings are not taxed until funds are withdrawn from the plan.)

KEOGH PLAN
A tax-deferred pension or retirement plan for self-employed taxpayers. The taxpayer funds the plan each year with tax-deductible contributions, which are capped at a certain amount.

A major disadvantage of the sole proprietorship is that the proprietor alone, as the firm's sole owner, bears the burden of any losses or liabilities incurred by the business enterprise. In other words, the sole proprietor has unlimited liability, or legal responsibility, for all obligations incurred in doing business. This unlimited personal liability means that the owner's personal assets (such as a car, a home, or an investment account) may have to be sacrificed to cover business debts if the business fails.

As a paralegal, if you are asked to do a preliminary investigation of a client's claim against a business entity, one of the first things you should check is the form of the business. For example, suppose that your firm's client wants to sue a business firm for damages. If you learn that the firm is a sole proprietorship, then you will know that if the firm itself has insufficient assets to pay damages to the client (should the client win in court), the firm's owner will personally be liable for the damages. Depending on what you learn about the firm's financial condition, you may want to investigate the owner's personal financial position also.

Taxation and Sole Proprietorships. A sole proprietor must pay income taxes on business profits, but he or she does not have to file a separate tax return for the business. Rather, the profits are reported on the sole proprietor's personal tax return and taxed as personal income.

Termination of the Sole Proprietorship. In a sole proprietorship, the owner *is* the business. For that reason, when the owner dies, so does the business—it is automatically dissolved. If the business is to be transferred to family members or other heirs, a new proprietorship is created. Similarly, if the proprietor sells the business, whoever purchases it must establish either a new sole proprietorship or some other business form, such as a partnership or a corporation.

Partnerships

As a paralegal you may find yourself working for a law partnership or assisting in legal work on behalf of partnership clients. In either situation, you will find it helpful to understand how partnerships are formed, what rights and responsibilities exist among partners, and how partnerships are terminated.

The Uniform Partnership Act (UPA) governs the operation of partnerships *in the absence of express agreement* and has done much to reduce controversies in the law relating to partnerships. Except for Louisiana, the UPA has been adopted in all of the states, as well as in the District of Columbia. In the discussion that follows, we will refer to the UPA's provisions as they relate to partnership creation, the rights and duties of partners, and partnership termination. Keep in mind, however, that these provisions govern a partnership only if the partners have not expressly agreed otherwise, as just mentioned. A revised version of the UPA, known as the Revised Uniform Partnership Act (RUPA), was formally adopted by the National Conference of Commissioners on Uniform State Laws in 1993. The RUPA has already been adopted in at least two states (Montana and Wyoming), and other states are considering its adoption.

Partnership Formation. Under the UPA, a *partnership* is defined as "an association of two or more persons to carry on as co-owners a business for profit."[2] To create a partnership, two or more persons interested in establishing a profit-making business simply agree to do so, as partners. The partnership agreement can be expressed orally or in writing, or it can be implied by conduct. If the partnership must continue for over a year, then the agreement must be in writing to satisfy the Statute of Frauds, a state statute that specifies what types of contracts must be in writing to be enforceable (discussed in Chapter 8).

Rights and Duties of Partners. When two or more persons agree to do business as partners, they enter into a special relationship with one another. To an extent, their relationship is similar to an agency relationship because each partner is deemed the agent of the other partners and of the partnership. Agency concepts thus apply—specifically, the imputation of knowledge of, and responsibility for, acts done within the scope of the partnership relationship. Note also that the following rule applies to partners:

- **In their relationship to one another, partners are bound by the fiduciary ties that bind an agent and principal under agency law.**

Partnership law is distinct from agency law in one significant way, however. A partnership is based on a voluntary contract between two or more competent persons who agree to place some or all of their money or other assets, labor, and skill in a business, with the understanding that profits and losses will be proportionately shared. In a nonpartnership agency relationship, the agent usually does not have an ownership interest in the business, nor is he or she obligated to bear a portion of the ordinary business losses.

The rights of partners are often written into the partnership agreement. If the agreement does not specify these rights, then the UPA comes into play (the state's version of the UPA, as adopted). Some of the important rights of partners are listed in Exhibit 9.1 on the following page.

Liability of Partners. Historically, a partnership could not be sued or initiate a lawsuit in its own name. This traditional rule treated all partnerships as aggregates of individuals. Under this rule, which is still followed in some states, only the individual partners—not the partnership—can be sued. Because this approach is so cumbersome, most states today recognize the partnership as an entity that may sue or be sued and collect judgments in the partnership's name.

Joint Liability. A distinguishing feature of the partnership, and one that is often regarded as a disadvantage of this form of business, is the potentially extensive personal liability faced by partners for partnership obligations and for the actions of the other partners. Partners have **joint liability**, or shared liability. In other words, partners may be held personally liable not only for their own actions and those of the partnership as an entity but also for the actions of other partners.

2. UPA 6(1).

ETHICAL CONCERN

The Paralegal as an Apparent Partner

If you work as a paralegal for a law partnership, you need to be especially careful to ensure that clients do not mistakenly conclude that you are an attorney-partner of the firm. For example, assume that you and your supervising attorney are waiting for a client to arrive for an intake interview. You are sitting in the attorney's office talking about another matter when the client arrives. During the course of the interview, the attorney asks you about an ordinance just passed by the city that might affect the client's planned renovations of an office building. Your answer indicates that you are knowledgeable in the law. The client leaves the office assuming that you are an attorney, even though you were introduced as the attorney's legal assistant. Because of the client's assumption, you will need to be very careful to avoid saying anything that the client may conclude is legal advice on the matter. The client might rely to his or her detriment on something you say and later sue you and the firm for damages. In that case, you could be liable for the unauthorized practice of law if the client convinces the court that you "held yourself out as an attorney."

JOINT LIABILITY
Shared liability. In partnership law, partners incur joint liability for partnership obligations and debts.

EXHIBIT 9.1
Rights of Partners

PARTNERS HAVE THE RIGHT:

- To hold an ownership interest in the firm and to receive a share of the profits.
- To inspect partnership books and records.
- To an accounting of partnership assets and profits (for example, to determine the value of each partner's share in the partnership). An accounting can be performed voluntarily or compelled by a court order. Formal accounting occurs by right in connection with partnership dissolution proceedings.
- To participate in the management of the business operation unless the partnership agreement specifies otherwise.

JOINT AND SEVERAL LIABILITY
In partnership law, joint and several liability means that a third party may sue one or more of the partners separately or all of them together. This is true even if one of the partners sued did not participate or know about whatever it was that gave rise to the cause of action.

Joint and Several Liability. Partners may also be subject to **joint and several liability**—that is, joint or individual liability. Joint and several liability allows a plaintiff to sue and seek judgment against any one—or all—of the jointly liable defendants. Fault is not an issue. In a partnership, joint and several liability gives a third party the option of suing any one or more of the partners without suing all of them or the partnership itself. The third party may even sue a partner who had no knowledge of the circumstances that gave rise to the cause of action.

For example, suppose that a plaintiff wants to recover for damages allegedly caused by a physician's negligence (medical malpractice). The physician is one of four partners who own a partnership. The plaintiff could sue the physician who allegedly caused the harm, the partnership, one of the other physicians (even if that physician had nothing to do with the plaintiff's treatment), or all of the physicians to recover damages. The liability faced by partners is a major reason for the rapid growth of a new form of partnership, the *limited-liability partnership,* which will be discussed later.

Taxation of Partnerships. The partnership itself, as an entity, does not pay federal income taxes. The partnership as an entity files an *information return* with the Internal Revenue Service in which the income received by the partnership is reported. The partners declare their shares of the partnership's profits on their personal income tax returns.

Partnership Termination. The partnership agreement may specify the duration of the partnership by indicating that the partnership will end on a certain date or on the occurrence of a certain event. It would be a breach of the partnership agreement for one partner to withdraw from the partnership before the specified date arrived or the specified event occurred. The withdrawing partner would be liable to the remaining partners for any related losses.

When an agreement does not specify the duration of the partnership, the partners are free to withdraw at any time without incurring liability to the remaining partners. Under the UPA, withdrawal by a partner results in the **dissolution** (the formal disbanding) of the partnership (although a new partnership may arise among those who stay with the enterprise). Under the revised UPA, or RUPA, however, the withdrawal of a partner causes a partnership to be dissolved only if the withdrawal results in the breakup of the

DISSOLUTION
The formal disbanding of a partnership or a corporation.

partnership itself and the business cannot continue. The occurrence of certain events also results in partnership termination. The death or bankruptcy of a partner, for example, terminates the partnership.

Partnership termination is a two-step process. Dissolution is the first step in the process. The second step is the **winding up** of partnership affairs. Once the firm is dissolved, it continues to exist legally until the process of winding up all business affairs (collecting and distributing the firm's assets) is complete.

WINDING UP
The process of winding up all business affairs (collecting and distributing the firm's assets) after a partnership or corporation has been dissolved.

Limited Partnerships. Ordinary partnerships, such as those just discussed, are often referred to as *general partnerships.* The **limited partnership**, in contrast, is a special form of partnership involving two different types of partners—general partners and limited partners. The *general partners* manage the business and have the rights and liabilities of partners in a general partnership. The *limited partners* are, for the most part, simply investors in the business. A limited partnership may be formed, for example, to purchase and develop real estate. The limited partners play a passive role. Their funds help to finance the venture, and they receive a share of the profits in return.

LIMITED PARTNERSHIP
A partnership consisting of one or more general partners (who manage the business and are liable to the full extent of their personal assets for debts of the partnership) and of one or more limited partners (who contribute only assets and are liable only up to the amount contributed by them).

The limited partner does not participate in the management of the partnership and, in return, enjoys limited-liability status. Unlike general partners, who are personally liable for partnership obligations, limited partners are liable only up to the amount that they have invested. In other words, if the partnership goes bankrupt, they will lose their investment but cannot be held liable for partnership debts beyond that amount.

In contrast to the informal, private, and voluntary agreement that usually suffices to create a general partnership, the formation of a limited partnership is a public and formal proceeding that must follow state statutory requirements. The partners must sign a *certificate of limited partnership,* which requires information similar to that found in a corporate charter. The certificate must be filed with the designated state official—usually, the secretary of state. In this respect, the limited partnership resembles the corporation—another creature of statute.

Corporations

Paralegals frequently work on behalf of corporate clients or on legal matters involving corporations. A small but increasing number of paralegals are working for corporate enterprises. As a paralegal, you should thus have a basic knowledge of how corporations are formed and operated. You should also be familiar with the basic rights and responsibilities of corporate personnel. Corporate personnel include the **shareholders** (the owners of the business, called shareholders because they purchase corporate **shares**, or stock), the **directors** (persons elected by the shareholders to direct corporate affairs), and the **officers** (persons hired by the directors to manage the day-to-day operations of the corporation).

Although it is owned by individuals, the corporation is a separate legal entity, which is created and recognized by state law. In the eyes of the law, a corporation is a legal "person" that enjoys many of the rights and privileges that U.S. citizens enjoy, such as the right of access to the courts as an entity that can sue or be sued. It also has, among other rights, the right to due

SHAREHOLDER
Any person or entity that purchases one or more shares of corporate stock, thus giving that person or entity an ownership interest in the corporation.

SHARE
A unit of stock; a measure of ownership interest in a corporation.

DIRECTOR
A person elected by the shareholders to direct corporate affairs.

OFFICER
A person hired by corporate directors to assist in the management of the day-to-day operations of the corporation. Corporate officers include the corporate president, vice president, secretary, treasurer, and possibly others, such as a chief financial officer and chief executive officer. Corporate officers are employees of the corporation and subject to employment contracts.

THE LEGAL TEAM AT WORK

Prohibition on Fee Sharing—A Boon for the Paralegal Profession

Recall from Chapter 3 that the ethical rules governing attorneys prohibit lawyers from splitting fees with nonattorneys. This means that you, as a paralegal, will never become a partner in a firm or share legal fees in any way with the lawyers for whom you work. Should you ever think that this is disadvantageous to you or the paralegal profession, think again. One of the reasons that lawyers hire paralegals instead of associate attorneys is precisely because paralegals cannot become partners. If a firm hires an associate attorney, the associate will likely aspire to become a partner in the firm. After all, one of the factors that motivates individuals to undergo the difficulty and expense of acquiring a law-school education is the future income that the educational investment will reap.

But what happens if a partnership does not want to expand in size but needs additional staff members who are legally trained to assist in the work? If the firm hires an associate attorney but cannot offer him or her the possibility of future partnership status (the one thing the associate attorney most desires), how can the firm make sure that the associate will remain loyal to the firm and be satisfied with his or her job? Such a situation can adversely affect the ability of the partners and the associate to work together effectively as a legal team. Some firms have solved this problem by hiring attorneys with the understanding that they may *never* be partners with the firm. Other firms have solved the problem by hiring paralegals, who are trained to do some of the tasks that attorneys would otherwise perform. The paralegal's goal is not to become a partner but to assist the attorney in whatever tasks need to be done in rendering legal services to clients. The paralegal is, by training and vocational aspiration, a team player.

---

process of law and the right to freedom from unreasonable searches and seizures.

The Model Business Corporation Act (MBCA) is a codification of modern corporation law that has been influential in the codification of corporation statutes. Today, the majority of state statutes are guided by a revision of the MBCA known as the Revised Model Business Corporation Act (RMBCA). There is, however, considerable variation among the statutes of the states that have based their statutes on the MBCA or the RMBCA, and several states do not follow either act. Because of this, as a paralegal you will need to rely on individual state corporation laws rather than the MBCA or RMBCA.

We look next at corporate formation; various classifications of corporations; rights and responsibilities of corporate personnel; corporate mergers, consolidations, and termination; and corporate financing.

Corporate Formation. Generally, forming a corporation involves two steps. The first step consists of preliminary organizational and promotional undertakings—particularly, obtaining capital for the future corporation. Before a corporation becomes a reality, people invest in the proposed corporation as subscribers. The subscribers become the shareholder-owners of the corporation when the corporation becomes a legal entity. Contracts to purchase shares of the corporation are frequently made by *promoters* on behalf of the future corporation. Promoters are those who, for themselves or others, take the preliminary steps in organizing a corporation. One of the tasks of the promoter is to issue a prospectus. A **prospectus** is a document that describes the corporation and its operations so that those who wish to purchase stock (invest) in the corporation have the basis for making an informed decision.

PROSPECTUS
A document that discloses relevant facts about a company and its operations so that those who wish to purchase stock (invest) in the corporation have the basis for making an informed decision.

The second step in forming a corporation is the process of incorporation. Exact procedures for incorporation differ among states, but the basic requirements are similar. The primary document needed to begin the incorporation process is called the **articles of incorporation** (see Exhibit 9.2 on the next page for sample articles of incorporation for a small corporation). The articles include basic information about the corporation and serve as a primary source of authority for its future organization and business functions. Once they have been filed in the appropriate state office, the articles of incorporation will become a public record.

ARTICLES OF INCORPORATION
The document filed with the appropriate governmental agency, usually the secretary of state's office, when a business is incorporated. State statutes usually prescribe what kind of information must be contained in the articles of incorporation.

Paralegals frequently assist their supervising attorneys in preparing incorporation papers and filing the papers with the appropriate state office. Also, as a paralegal, you may need to obtain information about a corporation, such as when you are conducting an investigation. For both of these reasons, you should know what information is generally included in the articles of incorporation. Exhibit 9.3 on page 333 lists and describes this kind of information.

After the articles of incorporation have been prepared, signed, and authenticated by the incorporators, they are sent to the appropriate state official, usually the secretary of state, along with the appropriate filing fee. In many states, the secretary of state then issues a **certificate of incorporation** representing the state's authorization for the corporation to conduct business. (This may be called the **corporate charter**.) The certificate and a copy of the articles are returned to the incorporators, who then hold the initial organizational meeting that completes the details of incorporation.

CERTIFICATE OF INCORPORATION (CORPORATE CHARTER)
The document issued by a state official (usually the secretary of state) granting a corporation legal existence and the right to function.

Classifications of Corporations. Corporations are classified in several ways. How a corporation is classified depends on its purpose, ownership characteristics, and location. A *private* corporation is, as the term indicates, a corporation that is privately owned. A *public* corporation is formed by the government for a political or governmental purpose, as when a town incorporates. Note that a public corporation is not the same as a *publicly held* corporation. A publicly held corporation is any corporation whose shares are publicly traded in securities markets, such as the New York Stock Exchange.

Corporations may also be classified as either *for-profit* corporations or *not-for-profit* (or *nonprofit*) corporations. Not-for-profit corporations may be formed by a group—such as a charitable group, a hospital, or a religious organization—to conduct its business without exposing the individual owners to personal liability.

Corporations owned by a small group of shareholders, such as family members, are called *close*, or *closely held*, corporations. Unlike large corporations, close corporations cannot sell their shares on public securities markets and usually place restrictions on the transfer of corporate shares—to

EXHIBIT 9.2
Articles of Incorporation

Filed with Secretary of State
_______________, 19_______

SHORT FORM
ARTICLES OF INCORPORATION
OF
Hiram, Inc.

ARTICLE I

The name of this corporation Hiram, Inc.

ARTICLE II

The purpose of this corporation is to engage in any lawful act or activity for which a corporation may be organized under the General Corporation Law of New Pacum other than the banking business, the trust company business, or the practice of a profession permitted to be incorporated by the New Pacum Corporation Code.

ARTICLE III

The name and address in the State of New Pacum of this corporation's initial agent for service of process is: Hiram Galliard, 8934 Rathburn Avenue, North Bend, New Pacum 98754

ARTICLE IV

The corporation is authorized to issue only one class of shares of stock; and the total number of shares that this corporation is authorized to issue is 10,000.

ARTICLE V

The corporation is a close corporation. All the corporation's issued shares of stock shall be held of record by not more than ten (10) persons.

DATED: June 3, 1996

Hiram Galliard   Martha Bonnell

[Signature(s) of Incorporator/ Directors(s)]

I (we) hereby declare that I (we) am (are) the person(s) who executed the foregoing Acticles of Incorporation, which execution is my (our) act and deed.

Hiram Galliard   Martha Bonnell

keep the business in the family, for example, or for some other reason. State laws may provide more flexibility for close corporations, in terms of statutory formalities that must be observed, than for other corporations. Also, certain close corporations are permitted to elect a special corporate tax status under Subchapter S of the Internal Revenue Code. These corporations are called *S corporations.*

EXHIBIT 9.3
Information Generally Included in Articles of Incorporation

THE NAME OF THE CORPORATION

The choice of a corporate name is subject to state approval to ensure against duplication or deception. State statutes usually require that the secretary of state run a check on the proposed name in the state of incorporation. Once cleared, a name can be reserved for a short time, for a fee, pending the completion of the articles of incorporation.

THE NATURE AND PURPOSE OF THE CORPORATION

The intended business activities of the corporation must be specified in the articles, and, naturally, they must be lawful. Stating a general corporate purpose (for example, "to engage in the production and sale of agricultural products") is usually sufficient to give rise to all of the powers necessary or convenient to the purpose of the organization.

THE DURATION OF THE CORPORATION

A corporation can have perpetual existence under most state corporate statutes. A few states, however, prescribe a maximum duration after which the corporation must formally renew its existence.

THE CAPITAL STRUCTURE OF THE CORPORATION

The capital structure of the corporation is generally set forth in the articles. A few state statutes require a relatively small capital investment (for example, $1,000) for ordinary business corporations but a greater capital investment for those engaged in insurance or banking. The number of shares of stock authorized for issuance, their valuation, the various types or classes of stock authorized for issuance, and other relevant information concerning equity, capital, and credit must be outlined in the articles.

THE INTERNAL ORGANIZATION OF THE CORPORATION

Whatever the internal management structure of the corporation, it should be described in the articles, although it can be included in bylaws adopted after the corporation is formed.

THE REGISTERED OFFICE AND AGENT OF THE CORPORATION

The corporation must indicate the location and address of its registered office within the state. Usually, the registered office is also the principal office of the corporation. The corporation must give the name and address of a specific person who has been designated as an agent and who can receive legal documents (including service of process) on behalf of the corporation.

THE NAMES AND ADDRESSES OF THE INCORPORATORS

Each incorporator must be listed by name and must indicate an address. An incorporator is a person—often, the corporate promoter—who applies to the state on behalf of the corporation to obtain its corporate charter. The incorporator need not be a shareholder and need not have any interest at all in the corporation. Many states do not impose residency or age requirements for incorporators. States vary on the required number of incorporators; it can be as few as one or as many as three. Incorporators are required to sign the articles of incorporation when they are submitted to the state; often this is their only duty. In some states, they participate at the first organizational meeting of the corporation.

As discussed in Chapter 5, lawyers, physicians, accountants, architects, engineers, and other professionals frequently incorporate as *professional corporations*. Such corporations may be designated as professional corporations (PCs), service corporations (SCs), or professional associations (PAs).

DEVELOPING PARALEGAL SKILLS

Reserving a Corporate Name

Jon Thomas is a paralegal in a law firm that specializes in corporate law. Jon and the attorney for whom he works, Sara Black, have just concluded a meeting with some new clients. The clients, Nathan Lansberry and Dan Jenkins, own a construction business. They have operated the business as a partnership for years, under the name of L&J Building Construction, and now want to incorporate their business. They want the corporate name to be L&J Building Construction, Inc.

After the clients leave the office, Sara says, "Jon, the first thing we need to find out is whether the corporate name that the clients want is available. Call the secretary of state's office and check to see if it's available. If it is, reserve it immediately."

CONTACTING THE SECRETARY OF STATE'S OFFICE

Jon goes to his office and looks up the number for the corporate division of the secretary of state's office. There is a 900 number to call to find out about the availability of corporate names. Jon dials it and gets a busy signal. He dials it several more times before he succeeds in reaching the corporate division.

"Hello. Yes, I'd like to check to see if a corporate name is available. The name is L&J Building Construction, Inc. Yes, I'll hold while you check the computer." Jon holds for about three minutes. Finally, a voice returns to the phone. "There is no other business with that name," the voice says. "Thank you. I'll send the Reservation of Corporate Name form to you by express mail," replies Jon. "Would you please reserve the name until you receive the form?" Jon then explains that Sara Black is the attorney handling the incorporation process, and he gives Sara's name and address. He hangs up the telephone and turns to his computer.

FILLING OUT THE NAME-RESERVATION FORM

Jon retrieves the Reservation of Corporate Name form from his computer files and fills in the name to be reserved—L&J Building Construction, Inc. He checks the appropriate box to indicate that the name will be used for a for-profit corporation and fills in the information in the "Notice of Transfer" section of the form. This will allow him to transfer the right to use the name to the clients. Jon then proofreads the document and prints it out. He also prints a standard transmittal letter to the corporate division of the secretary of state's office. Jon must also obtain a check payable to the secretary of state, in the amount of $20, for the filing fee. He prepares a check-request form and takes it to the office manager for processing. Once Jon obtains the check, he puts together the package, makes copies of its contents, and takes it to Sara for review.

Sara approves Jon's work and signs the form and the letter, and Jon gives the packet to his secretary to send out. Sara also asks Jon to prepare a letter to the clients notifying them that the name was available and that she has reserved it. Jon prepares the letter and encloses a copy of the materials sent to the secretary of state's office.

Directors and Officers. The articles of incorporation name the initial board of directors, which is appointed by the incorporators. Thereafter, the board of directors is elected by a majority vote of the shareholders. The board holds formal meetings and records the minutes. Each director has one vote, and generally, the majority rules. The directors' rights include the right to participate in board meetings and the right to inspect corporate books and records. The director's responsibilities to the corporation and its shareholders include the following: declaring and paying **dividends** (payments to shareholders representing their share of corporate profits), appointing and removing officers, and making significant policy decisions.

DIVIDEND
A distribution to corporate shareholders, disbursed in proportion to the number of shares held.

The board of directors appoints the corporate officers, who manage the day-to-day operations of the firm. They include the president, vice president, secretary, treasurer, chief financial officer, and chief executive officer. The officers are employees of the corporation and are subject to employment contracts. As employees, they are also agents of the corporation.

Directors and officers have fiduciary duties to the corporation and its shareholder-owners, including the duty of loyalty and the duty to exercise reasonable care when conducting corporate business. The duty of loyalty is breached when an officer or director uses corporate funds or confidences for personal gain, as when an officer discloses company secrets (such as a proposed merger) to an outsider. The duty of care is breached when a director's or officer's negligence—failure to exercise reasonable care in corporate operations or decision making—results in harmful consequences for the corporate entity.

Shareholders. Any person who purchases a share in a corporation becomes an owner of the corporation. Through shareholders' meetings, the shareholders play an important role in the corporate entity—they elect the directors who control the corporation, and they have a right to vote (one vote per share) on decisions that significantly affect the corporation. They also have a right to a share in corporate profits proportionate to the number of shares they hold. Shareholders do not manage the daily affairs of the corporation, nor are they liable for corporate debts or other obligations beyond the amount of their investments. Corporate owners, or shareholders, thus have limited liability—a key advantage of the corporate form of business.

Corporate Taxation. The corporation as an entity pays income taxes on corporate profits. Then, when the profits are distributed to the shareholders in the form of dividends, the shareholders pay personal income taxes on the income they receive. This double-taxation feature of the corporate form of business is one of its major disadvantages. Some small (close) corporations are permitted to avoid the double taxation of corporate profits by electing S-corporation status under Subchapter S of the Internal Revenue Code. An S corporation, like a partnership, is a "pass-through" entity for tax purposes. The S corporation itself does not pay taxes (it files an information return only), and the only taxes on the corporation's profits are paid by the shareholders.

MERGER
A process in which one corporation (the surviving corporation) acquires all the assets and liabilities of another corporation (the merged corporation).

CONSOLIDATION
A process in which two or more corporations join to become a completely new corporation. The original corporations cease to exist, and the new corporation acquires all their assets and liabilities.

Corporate Merger and Consolidation. As a paralegal, you may be asked to help a corporate client in procedures relating to major corporate changes, such as a merger or a consolidation. A **merger** is a process through which one corporation (the surviving corporation) acquires all the assets and liabilities of another corporation (the merged corporation). The shareholders of the merged corporation receive payment for their shares, either in cash or in shares in the surviving corporation. A **consolidation** is a similar process. The difference is that in a consolidation, both existing corporate entities disappear and a completely new corporation is formed. The differences between a merger and a consolidation are illustrated graphically in Exhibit 9.4.

State laws vary somewhat as to the procedures that must be undertaken to accomplish a merger or a consolidation. As a paralegal, you will need to find out what the specific requirements are in your state. Generally, the following requirements must be met:

- The boards of directors and the shareholders of each corporation involved must approve the merger or consolidation.
- Once the merger or consolidation is approved by these groups, *articles of merger* or *articles of consolidation* must be filed with the state, usually with the secretary of state's office.
- When state formalities have been satisfied, the state issues a *certificate of merger* to the surviving corporation or a *certificate of consolidation* to the newly consolidated corporation.

EXHIBIT 9.4
Merger and Consolidation

A merger involves the legal combination of two or more corporations in such a way that only one of the corporations continues to exist. For example, Corporation A and Corporation B decide to merge. It is agreed that A will absorb B, so upon merger, B ceases to exist as a separate entity and A continues as the surviving corporation. Consolidation occurs when two or more corporations combine in such a way that both corporations cease to exist and a new one emerges. For example, Corporation A and Corporation B consolidate to form an entirely new organization, Corporation C. In the process, A and B both are terminated as legal entities, and C comes into existence as an entirely new entity.

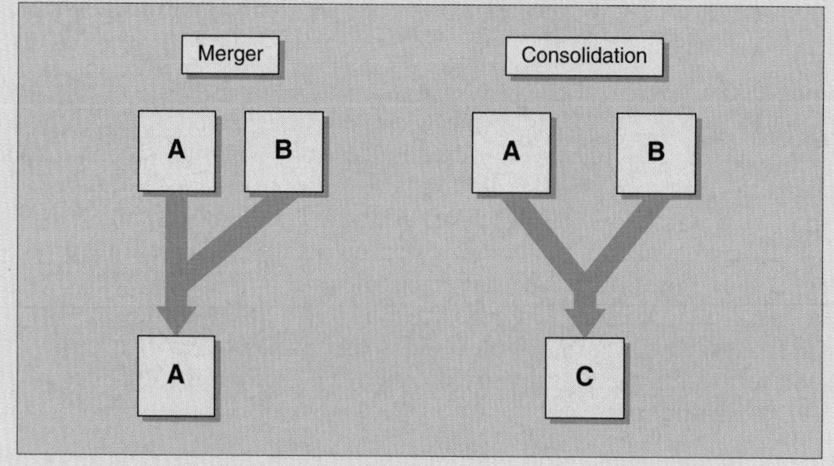

As a paralegal, you should realize the difference in legal effect between a merger or consolidation and an *acquisition,* which occurs when one corporation acquires or purchases all or almost all of the assets of another company. As noted above, in a merger or a consolidation, the surviving corporation or the newly consolidated corporation assumes not only the assets but also the *liabilities* of the previously existing entities. If a person has a valid claim against one of those entities, this claim is a liability that will be assumed by the surviving or newly consolidated corporation. A person injured by a defective product manufactured by one of the previously existing corporations, for example, could sue the surviving or new corporation and recover damages. In contrast, if an acquisition has occurred, the acquiring corporation has acquired the assets of the other corporations but normally has not assumed responsibility for the liabilities of that corporation.

Corporate Termination. As with partnership termination, the process of corporate termination involves two steps. The first step, dissolution, extinguishes the legal existence of the corporation. The second step, **liquidation**, involves the winding up of the corporation's business affairs. After creditors have been paid, all remaining assets are distributed to the shareholders.

LIQUIDATION
The process by which corporate assets are converted into cash and distributed among creditors and shareholders.

Corporations can be terminated at a time specified in the articles of incorporation or by the agreement of the shareholders and the board of directors. In certain circumstances, a court may dissolve a corporation. For example, if the directors are deadlocked and cannot agree on the management of the corporation, a court may grant a shareholder's petition to dissolve the corporation. A corporation may also be terminated by law if it fails to meet certain statutory requirements, such as the payment of taxes or annual fees.

SECURITY
A stock certificate, bond, or other document or certificate that evidences an ownership interest in a corporation or a promise of repayment by a corporation.

Corporate Financing. Corporations are financed by the issuance and sale of **securities**, which include stocks (shares) and bonds. **Stocks** represent ownership in the corporation as measured in units of shares. The stockholder, or shareholder, has a right to a share of the corporation's profits or assets when they are distributed. **Bonds**, in contrast, represent funds borrowed from investors. The bondholder has a right to repayment of the borrowed amount at an agreed-upon rate of interest. Significant attributes of and differences between stocks and bonds are listed in Exhibit 9.5 on the following page.

STOCK
In corporation law, an equity or ownership interest in a corporation, measured in units of shares.

BOND
A certificate that evidences a corporate debt. It is a security that involves no ownership interest in the issuing corporation.

As a paralegal, you may be involved in researching and drafting documents to be filed on behalf of a large corporate client that intends to sell securities. Alternatively, a client charged with violating securities laws may seek legal assistance from the attorney for whom you work. In these and similar situations, you will benefit from a knowledge of the most important laws regulating the purchase and sale of securities.

Federal Securities Acts. Two very important federal statutes regulate and control securities in the United States: the Securities Act of 1933 and the Securities Exchange Act of 1934. The 1933 law was enacted to address some of the problems that led to the stock-market crash of 1929. The act prohibits fraud and seeks to stabilize the securities industry by requiring corporations to disclose pertinent information to purchasers of corporate securities. In 1934, the Securities and Exchange Commission (SEC) was created to enforce and administer the act. In general, unless a security is specifically exempted

EXHIBIT 9.5
How Do Stocks and Bonds Differ?

STOCKS	BONDS
1. Stocks represent ownership.	1. Bonds represent debt.
2. Stocks (common) do not have a fixed dividend rate.	2. Interest on bonds must always be paid, whether or not any profit is earned.
3. Stockholders can elect a board of directors, which controls the corporation.	3. Bondholders usually have no voice in or control over the management of the corporation.
4. Stocks do not have a maturity date; the corporation does not usually repay the stockholder.	4. Bonds have a maturity date on which the bondholder is to be repaid the value stated on the face of the bond.
5. All corporations issue or offer to sell stocks. This is the usual definition of a corporation.	5. Corporations do not necessarily issue bonds.
6. Stockholders' claims against the property and income of a corporation cannot be met until all creditors' claims have been met.	6. Bondholders' claims against the property and income of a corporation must be met before the claims of stockholders.

from the requirements of the act, it must be registered with the SEC. A corporation must provide specific information about the corporation—including how it is managed and its financial condition—in a *registration statement.* The information in the registration statement makes it possible for the inexperienced investor to evaluate intelligently the risks associated with that stock purchase.

The Securities Exchange Act of 1934 attempts to protect investors by requiring that public securities exchanges (such as the New York Stock Exchange), brokers, dealers, and dealer associations register with the SEC. The 1934 act also protects against fraud and insider trading. **Insider trading** occurs when someone uses "inside information"—corporate information that has not yet been made available to the public—for personal gain. Insider-trading laws are based on the assumption that it is unfair to give to a few individuals an advantage over the rest of the market. Laws prohibiting insider trading are designed to level the playing field for all traders.

INSIDER TRADING
Purchasing or selling securities on the basis of information that has not been made available to the public.

For example, assume that a corporation is about to market a new product that will generate a substantial increase in corporate profits. Directors or officers and other corporate employees are prohibited from purchasing stock in the corporation based on their knowledge of this new product until the knowledge becomes public. Similarly, suppose a paralegal learns through his or her work that a particular corporation's stock will likely increase in value in the near future and this information is not known to the public. The paralegal will be liable for insider trading if he or she buys the corporation's stock as a result of this knowledge. Both federal and state laws impose penalties for insider trading.

BLUE SKY LAWS
State laws that regulate the offer and sale of securities.

State Securities Laws. The states also have their own securities regulations, called **blue sky laws**, which are designed to protect investors from "speculative schemes which have no more basis than so many feet of blue sky." State blue sky laws work together with the federal regulatory scheme. Like their federal counterparts, the state laws have antifraud, registration, and qualification provisions for securities issued or traded within the state.

Limited-liability Organizations

In recent years, two new forms of limited-liability business organizations have emerged, the limited-liability partnership and the limited-liability company. The use of these new forms is spreading quickly because of the advantages they offer to businesspersons in regard to business taxation and liability—advantages not available through the partnership or corporate forms of business.

For example, one of the major tax advantages of a partnership is that the partnership's income passes through to the partners as personal income. Consequently, partners avoid the double-taxation feature of the corporate form of business. But there is a price to pay for this tax advantage: partners face unlimited personal liability. The partners can avoid unlimited personal liability by incorporating their business, because corporate owners (shareholders) have limited liability. But again, there is a price to pay for this limited liability: the double taxation of profits characteristic of the corporate form of business.

As mentioned, one way to achieve both goals—limited liability and single taxation of profits—is to elect S-corporation status. Certain requirements must be met, however, before a corporation can qualify for S-corporation status. One requirement is that the corporation have thirty-five or fewer shareholders—thus excluding larger firms. Another requirement is that shareholders must be U.S. citizens—thus excluding foreign participants.

Limited-liability Partnerships. In 1991, the state of Texas enacted a statute permitting the use of **limited-liability partnerships (LLPs)** in that state. Delaware, Louisiana, North Carolina, and Washington, D.C., quickly followed suit. By 1994, similar LLP bills were pending in Illinois, Massachusetts, Mississippi, New Mexico, Pennsylvania, and South Carolina. It is predicted that the majority of states will enact similar statutes in the near future.

The LLP can be used by all professionals and allows them to enjoy the tax benefits of a partnership while avoiding the personal liability of partners for partnership obligations and the malpractice of other partners. In essence, each state LLP statute limits in some way the normal joint and several liability of partners. For example, Delaware law protects innocent partners from the "debts and obligations of the partnership arising from negligence, wrongful acts, or misconduct." In North Carolina, Texas, and Washington, D.C., the LLP statutes protect innocent partners from obligations arising from "errors, omissions, negligence, incompetence, or malfeasance."

Limited-liability Companies. Another new form of limited-liability business organization is the **limited-liability company (LLC)**. The first statute authorizing the creation of a limited-liability company was enacted by the state of Wyoming in 1977. The LLC is a hybrid form of business enterprise that combines the pass-through tax benefits of S corporations and partnerships with the

ETHICAL CONCERN

Insider Trading and the Paralegal

As a paralegal, you may be handling sensitive information relating to securities trading. For example, assume that one of your firm's corporate clients, a leading pharmaceutical company, has successfully cloned the genetic structure of a natural hormone found only in monkeys. The company can now create a synthetic drug that promises to be a breakthrough in the treatment of leukemia. You know that when the company announces this breakthrough, the value of the company's stock is sure to increase dramatically. If you purchase stock in the company, however, you are in essence engaging in insider trading in violation of securities laws. Even if you advise someone else—for example, your spouse, a sister, or a friend—to invest in the company's stock, you are violating insider-trading laws if that other person invests in the company's stock on the basis of your inside information.

LIMITED-LIABILITY PARTNERSHIP (LLP)
A hybrid form of business organization authorized by a state that allows professionals to enjoy the tax benefits of a partnership while limiting in some way the normal joint and several liability of partners.

LIMITED-LIABILITY COMPANY (LLC)
A hybrid form of business organization authorized by a state in which the owners of the business have limited liability and taxes on profits are passed through the business entity to the owners.

SUBSTANTIVE LAW CONCEPT SUMMARY

Forms of Business Organization

Sole Proprietorships	**1.** *Creation*—The simplest form of business; used by anyone who does business without creating an organization. **2.** *Operation*—The owner is the business. The owner can conduct all business operations himself or herself (such as in a small home office) or hire employees to run the business. **3.** *Taxation*—The owner pays personal income taxes on all profits. **4.** *Liability*—The owner is personally liable for all business debts and obligations. **5.** *Termination*—A sole proprietorship terminates on the owner's death or whenever the owner ceases doing business.
Partnerships	**1.** *Creation*—Created by the written or oral agreement of the parties to do business jointly as partners. (The creation of a limited partnership is a formal proceeding that must comply with state statutory requirements.) **2.** *Operation*—Each partner has an equal voice in management, unless otherwise provided for in the partnership agreement. The partners may hire employees to assist them in running the business. (In a limited partnership, only the general partners may participate in management.) **3.** *Taxation*—The partnership as an entity does not pay income taxes, but files an informational tax return with the Internal Revenue Service each year. Each partner pays personal income taxes on his or her share of the profits of the partnership, whether or not they are distributed. **4.** *Liability*—Partners are personally liable for partnership debts and obligations. (In a limited partnership, only the general partners have unlimited personal liability; the liability of limited partners is limited to the amount of their investment in the enterprise.)

limited liability of limited partners and corporate shareholders. Interest in LLCs mushroomed after 1988, when the Internal Revenue Service ruled that Wyoming LLCs would be taxed as partnerships instead of as corporations. Before that ruling, the only other state to enact a statute authorizing LLCs was Florida, in 1982. After the ruling, however, numerous states adopted LLC statutes. By 1994, at least thirty-six states had enacted laws authorizing LLCs, and legislatures in many of the remaining states were considering the adoption of such statutes.

Although LLCs and LLPs offer significant advantages for businesspersons, there are also some disadvantages. The major disadvantage is that there are no uniform laws (laws accepted by all of the states) concerning these organizations. Furthermore, because these forms are relatively new, there is very little existing case law. This makes it difficult to predict whether an LLC or LLP formed in one state will have unlimited liability in a different state.

Business Organizations and the Paralegal

We have already mentioned many of the ways in which paralegals benefit from a knowledge of business organizations. Because so much legal work has

SUBSTANTIVE LAW CONCEPT SUMMARY, Continued	
Partnerships (continued)	5. *Termination*—A partnership may be terminated by the agreement of the partners or by the occurrence of certain events, such as the death or bankruptcy of a partner.
Corporations	1. *Creation*—A corporation is created by a state-issued charter. 2. *Operation*—The shareholders elect directors, who set policy and appoint officers to manage the day-to-day corporate affairs. 3. *Taxation*—The corporation pays income tax on net profits; shareholders again pay income tax on profits distributed as dividends. 4. *Liability*—Shareholders have limited liability and are not personally liable for the debts of the corporation (beyond the amount of their investment). 5. *Termination*—A corporation may be terminated at a time specified in the articles of incorporation, by the agreement of the shareholders and the board of directors, or by court decree. 6. *Corporate financing*—Corporations are financed through the issuance of shares of stock (which, when purchased by shareholders, represent ownership interests in the corporation) or bonds (which represent funds borrowed by the corporation from investors). 7. *Securities laws*—The purchase and sale of corporate securities over public securities exchanges, such as the New York Stock Exchange, are governed by both federal and state securities law. Two important federal statutes regulating securities markets are the Securities Act of 1933 and the Securities Exchange Act of 1934. These and other federal securities laws and regulations are implemented by the federal Securities and Exchange Commission.
Limited-liability Organizations	Two relatively new forms of business organization are the limited-liability partnership (LLP) and the limited-liability company (LLC). Generally, these organizations allow business owners to combine the tax advantages of the partnership with the limited liability of limited partners or corporate shareholders.

to do with business clients, it is impossible to summarize the many tasks involving business organizations that paralegals perform. The following list, however, will give you an idea of some of the types of work that paralegals frequently perform in this area:

- Research state laws governing partnerships, corporations, and limited-liability organizations.
- Assist in litigation relating to a corporate employer or a corporate client.
- Prepare applications for licenses, certificates, and permits on behalf of a corporation.
- Draft incorporation papers and bylaws.
- File incorporation papers with the state office.
- Maintain corporate stock-transfer records on the sale or purchase of stocks.
- Reserve a corporate name for an incorporator.
- Draft stock-option agreements for use by corporate clients. (A *stock option* is an option to purchase the corporation's stock at a specified price, ordinarily below the market value.)
- Schedule shareholders' meetings.

PARALEGAL PROFILE Environmental-law Specialist

ERIN KREIS received her associate's degree in the legal-assistant program at Henry Ford Community College, Dearborn, Michigan, in 1979. She then enrolled in a bachelor's-degree program at Madonna University, Livonia, Michigan, majoring in legal assistance and administration. While attending school, she worked as a legal assistant on workers' compensation claims and investigations, as well as defense litigation. After she graduated in 1982, she worked for a firm whose major area of practice is transportation law and related labor and corporate matters. In 1988, she was hired as a legal assistant by General Motors Corporation. Her area of specialty at General Motors is environmental law, particularly regulations pertaining to air quality.

What do you like best about your work?

"There are six legal assistants in the environmental-practice area. We all work rather independently on our projects and in specific environmental disciplines. I perform a lot of document-retrieval work and have designed databases for managing the extensive number of documents generated in my area of work. Research on state and federal environmental regulations and their application also plays a large role in my position. I enjoy the independence and the high level of responsibility. The attorneys with whom we work all show a great deal of confidence in the legal assistants."

What is the greatest challenge that you face in your area of work?

"When a majority of your assignments are in one particular area, it can be frustrating to receive an assignment in another area—one with which you are not so familiar. As a result, it is very challenging to get 'up to speed' in a short amount of time in order to complete the assignment successfully. Likewise, keeping up with the basic regulations in other areas, as well as changes in all environmental regulations, can be very challenging."

"GENERALLY, IN YOUR ROLE AS A LEGAL ASSISTANT, IT IS IMPORTANT TO BE VERY AWARE OF ETHICAL CONSIDERATIONS."

What advice do you have for would-be paralegals in your area of work?

"Generally, in your role as a legal assistant, it is important to be very aware of ethical considerations. I believe that this area should be discussed more in school because many entry-level paralegals do not have a realistic view of what constitutes unethical behavior—what constitutes giving legal advice, for example. With respect to an environmental practice, a basic understanding of environmental law, document management, and computer databases would be very helpful."

What are some tips for success as a paralegal in your area of work?

"I recommend that students or paralegals who are interested in environmental work take a basic environmental-science class in order to get a feel for the subject and the terminology. I also think that math classes can be very helpful. Even though we rely on engineers to run and analyze data, legal assistants are often required to read, verify, and apply the calculations and the results."

- Maintain corporate records, including minutes of directors' and shareholders' meetings.
- Draft partnership agreements.
- Draft articles of merger or consolidation.
- Assist in the dissolution of a partnership or corporation.
- Draft a corporate prospectus.

EMPLOYMENT RELATIONSHIPS

Whenever a business organization hires an employee, an employment relationship is established. Both the employer and the employee acquire legal rights and duties as a result of the relationship. These rights and duties have changed over time to meet changing economic and social conditions that affect the workplace. A century ago, employers had numerous rights but few duties. Conversely, employees had numerous duties but few rights. Today, federal and state statutes have dramatically altered the character of the traditional workplace and employer-employee relationships.

Because attorneys and paralegals are frequently involved in legal work relating to employment relationships, you should have a basic understanding of employment law. In this section, after a brief discussion of the common law doctrine governing employment relationships, we look at some of the ways in which the government regulates today's workplace.

Employment at Will

Prior to the 1930s, employment relationships between employers and employees were dominated by the common law doctrine of **employment at will**. According to this doctrine, an employment relationship could be terminated at any time by either the employee or the employer—for any reason or for no reason at all. Since the 1930s, however, numerous federal and state statutes have been enacted to regulate employment relationships. Therefore, even though at-will employment is still the law in some states, statutes governing the workplace have significantly curbed the right of employers to hire and fire employees at will.

EMPLOYMENT AT WILL
A common law doctrine under which employment is considered to be "at will"—that is, either party may terminate the employment relationship at any time and for any reason, unless the contract specifies otherwise.

Labor Laws

In the early decades of the twentieth century, employees began to organize to protect their interests. They formed associations called *labor unions* and elected union representatives to bargain with employers for improved wages and working conditions. The ultimate weapon of the labor union was, of course, the *strike*. By their organized refusal to work, employees could bring their employer's operations to a halt—to the financial detriment of the employer.

In 1932, Congress established the legal right of employees to organize labor unions with the passage of the Norris-LaGuardia Act. The act protected peaceful strikes, picketing, and boycotts and restricted the power of the federal courts to *enjoin* (stop or prohibit) labor unions from engaging in peaceful strikes. Other acts, including those discussed below, granted further protections to workers.

National Labor Relations Act. The Norris-LaGuardia Act was strengthened by the enactment of the National Labor Relations Act (NLRA) of 1935. The twin goals of the NLRA were to protect workers' efforts to organize into unions and to promote *collective bargaining* (bargaining between union representatives and employers) as a peaceful method of dispute resolution. The

NLRA sought to curb activities that would discourage or prevent collective-bargaining efforts conducted on behalf of the workers. The NLRA also created the National Labor Relations Board (NLRB) to oversee the enforcement of the statute. Congress gave the NLRB the power to investigate alleged NLRA violations and to prevent continued violations by particular employers.

Fair Labor Standards Act. The Fair Labor Standards Act (FLSA) of 1938, among other things, prohibited the oppression or exploitation of children by regulating the employment of minors. For example, under the act, children under the age of sixteen cannot be employed on a full-time basis except under very limited circumstances. The FLSA also established guidelines regulating overtime pay and minimum hourly wages. The act provided that if in any week an employee works more than forty hours, the hours in excess of the first forty must be compensated at one-and-a-half times the employee's regular hourly rate. As for the minimum hourly wage, it represents the absolute minimum amount that an employer can pay an employee per hour. The minimum wage rate, which is set by Congress, is changed periodically to reflect inflation.[3]

The FLSA exempts certain employees (including administrative and professional employees) from its provisions. Recall from Chapter 2 that one of the issues facing paralegals today is whether they should be classified as professional employees who are exempt from the act's requirements regarding overtime pay.

Employment Discrimination

The early 1960s marked a period in our history in which we, as a nation, focused our attention on the civil rights of all Americans, regardless of race, color, national origin, gender, or religion. Out of this movement to end racial and other forms of discrimination grew a body of law protecting workers against discrimination in employment. Although our discussion focuses on the federal laws prohibiting discrimination in the workplace, state laws also prohibit employment discrimination.

Title VII of the Civil Rights Act of 1964. The Civil Rights Act of 1964 was enacted to protect certain groups from the discriminatory practices of business owners, educational institutions, employers, and other groups. One section of the act, known as Title VII, pertains to employment practices. Title VII prohibits employers from discriminating against employees or potential employees on the basis of race, color, national origin, religion, or gender.

The Pregnancy Discrimination Act of 1978 amended Title VII to expand the definition of gender-based discrimination to include discrimination based on pregnancy. A pregnant employee cannot be fired or even disciplined when her pregnancy limits or alters her ability to work. The pregnant worker is entitled to sick leave, unpaid leave, and any other benefit normally made available by the employer to workers who are temporarily affected by a health condition that interferes with their working abilities.

3. As of the beginning of 1995, the minimum hourly wage rate was $4.25.

The courts have also extended Title VII protection to those who are subject to **sexual harassment** in the workplace. There are two types of sexual harassment. *Quid-pro-quo harassment* occurs when a superior doles out awards (promotions, raises, benefits, or other advantages) to a subordinate in exchange for sexual favors. (*Quid pro quo* means in Latin "this for that" or "something for something.") In contrast, *hostile-environment harassment* occurs when an employee is subjected to offensive sexual comments, jokes, or physical contact in the workplace that makes it difficult (or impossible) for the employee to perform a job satisfactorily.

SEXUAL HARASSMENT
In the employment context, the hiring or granting of job promotions or other benefits in return for sexual favors (*quid-pro-quo* harassment) or language or conduct that is so sexually offensive that it creates a hostile working environment (hostile-environment harassment).

Intentional and Unintentional Discrimination. Title VII has been interpreted by the courts to prohibit both intentional and unintentional discrimination. Intentional discrimination is referred to as **disparate-treatment discrimination**. Because intent to discriminate can be difficult to prove, the courts have established certain procedures for resolving disparate-treatment cases.

DISPARATE-TREATMENT DISCRIMINATION
In an employment context, intentional discrimination against individuals on the basis of race, color, gender, national origin, or religion.

Suppose, for example, that a Hispanic woman applies for employment as a paralegal with a law firm and is rejected. If the paralegal sues on a theory of disparate-treatment discrimination in hiring, she will be required to establish that (1) she is a member of a protected class (a group protected by Title VII), (2) she has applied and is qualified for the position, (3) her application was rejected by the employer, and (4) the employer continued to seek other applicants for the same position or filled the position with an individual who was not within a protected class under Title VII. The burden then shifts to the employer-defendant, who must articulate a legal reason for not hiring the plaintiff. For example, the employer might say that the plaintiff was not hired because she lacked sufficient experience or training. The plaintiff must then show that the employer's reason is a *pretext* (not the true reason) and that discriminatory intent actually motivated the employer's decision.

Unintentional discrimination, called **disparate-impact discrimination**, occurs when certain employer practices or procedures have a discriminatory impact, or effect, even though they were not intended to be discriminatory. For example, suppose that a city requires all of its firefighters to be at least six feet tall. In effect, that job requirement discriminates against women—because few women are that tall. The effect of the rule is discriminatory, even though the intent in adopting the rule might have been merely to ensure an able-bodied firefighting crew. If an employee can show that an employment practice has a discriminatory impact in violation of Title VII, the burden then shifts to the employer to prove why the practice is necessary. In the hypothetical example just given, for example, the city (the employer) would have to demonstrate to the court's satisfaction that the height requirement was a **bona fide occupational qualification**. In other words, the employer would have to show a definite connection between the height requirement and ability to perform the job adequately.

DISPARATE-IMPACT DISCRIMINATION
In the employment context, discrimination that results from certain employer practices or procedures that, although not discriminatory on their face, have a discriminatory effect. For example, a requirement that all employees have high school diplomas is not necessarily discriminatory, but it may have the effect of discriminating against certain groups.

BONA FIDE OCCUPATIONAL QUALIFICATION
Under Title VII of the Civil Rights Act of 1964, characteristics (such as education, training, and physical strength) that are reasonably necessary to adequate job performance.

Enforcement of Title VII. The Equal Employment Opportunity Commission (EEOC) is a federal agency that administers and enforces Title VII. Claims of Title VII violations must first be filed with the EEOC, which investigates the facts and attempts to bring the employer and employee together to settle the dispute voluntarily. If the EEOC is

FEATURED GUEST: JUDY A. LONG

Paralegal Positions in Government

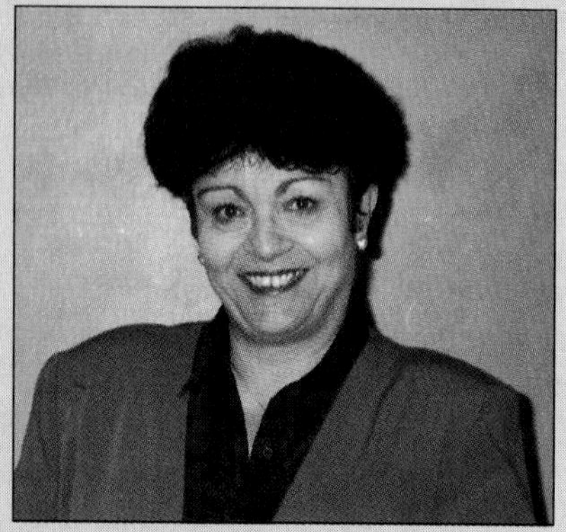

Biographical Note

Judy A. Long received her bachelor's degree and master's degree in business administration from California State University in Long Beach. She received her J.D. with honors from Western State University College of Law and is a member of the California State Bar Association. She developed the ABA-approved paralegal program at Rio Hondo College in Whittier, California., and is presently the paralegal coordinator at Rio Hondo College, where she also teaches classes in the program. Long has been involved in the legal profession for many years as a paralegal, an attorney, and a professor. She has coauthored a textbook on basic business law.

The federal government and state, county, and local governments all offer positions for paralegals. Duties and responsibilities are as varied as the different government departments and agencies.

Unlike paralegals who work for private law firms, who often work long hours, paralegals who work for the government usually work a standard thirty-five or forty hours a week. There are many other advantages to working for the government. These advantages include good salaries, excellent benefits (such as medical and dental insurance), and time off work for vacations, government holidays, and sick leave. Paralegals receive regularly scheduled performance reviews and are usually given annual salary increases. In some cases, however, they must take tests to receive promotions.

The working environment is generally more structured in government offices than in private law firms, corporations, or other organizations. Depending on your preferences, this may also be perceived as an advantage.

THE FEDERAL GOVERNMENT

Paralegals are employed by the federal government in several different departments. To obtain a position with the federal government, you must contact the Office of Personnel Management (OPM), which has thirty-nine branch offices in various areas of the country. You can learn the location of these offices by writing the OPM at 1900 E Street N.W., Washington, DC 20415-0001, or contacting the OPM by phone at (202) 606-1800. The OPM administers examinations to all entry-level paralegal applicants. After the results have been obtained, the applicants' names are placed on a register from which federal agencies select job candidates.

When applying for a federal position, you need to complete Form 171. This form, which can obtained from the OPM, is similar to an employment application. You must complete a separate form for each position for which you apply. It is therefore a good idea to fill out the form, leaving the specific position blank, and make several copies. Then, as you apply for different positions, all you have to do is type in the position. You should also keep a copy of each form that you submit. Before completing the form, read through the booklet entitled *Hiring Standards for Paralegals,* which can also be obtained from the OPM, so that your application will be geared to the qualifications required for the open position.

The largest employer of paralegals in the federal government is the Department of Justice (DOJ), which has branches in many cities throughout the country. Paralegals who work for the DOJ may be involved in investigating criminal cases, conducting legal research, interviewing witnesses, and gathering and documenting exhibits and other evidence needed for prosecuting criminal violations. Subagencies within the DOJ include the Drug Enforcement Administration (DEA), the Office of the Solicitor General, and the Immigration and Naturalization Service. Other government departments and agencies that employ paralegals include the military, the Civil Rights Commission, the Equal Employment Opportunity Commission (EEOC),

FEATURED GUEST, Continued

the Department of Transportation, the United States Postal Service, the Federal Deposit Insurance Corporation, the Department of Commerce, the Department of Labor, and the Securities and Exchange Commission (SEC).

In general, paralegals who work for the federal government may be involved in examining case files, preparing documents, conducting legal research and analysis, interviewing witnesses, and preparing material for trials. The kinds of cases the paralegal might work on vary depending on the agency and could range from prosecuting drug dealers (DEA) to employment discrimination (EEOC) to securities fraud (SEC), along with numerous other possibilities.

STATE AND COUNTY GOVERNMENTS

Many state and county departments employ paralegals in the criminal-justice area. Paralegals in these areas assist in preparing cases for trial, undertaking legal research, finding and preparing witnesses for trial, and investigating cases. If they work for the public defender's office, they may spend time interviewing accused persons and investigating their backgrounds. The state attorney general's office employs paralegals for investigation, legal research, document preparation, and assistance with litigation.

County governments also employ paralegals in various capacities. For instance, some of my former paralegal students are employed as consumer counselors and investigators for the Los Angeles County Department of Consumer Affairs. Their duties and responsibilities include handling and investigating consumer complaints against businesses.

"GETTING YOUR FOOT IN THE DOOR"

Spending time as a student intern in a government office prepares you for a government position after graduation. With our economy in its present state, many government offices are facing layoffs and cutbacks. Volunteer assistance from student interns is often welcomed. When these interns graduate, they have an inside track to a permanent position with a government office.

Our paralegal program also includes an internship class in which students work for unit credits but are not paid. Some of the students work in government offices.

If there is a particular government office in which you are interested, invite a guest speaker from that office to speak to your class (with your instructor's permission, of course). Not only will this enable you to learn more about what paralegals do in that office, but you will have made a contact that may prove valuable when you graduate and are looking for a job.

Visiting government offices is an excellent way to learn about different areas of government. If you would like to know more about the state attorney general's office, for instance, call that office and set up an appointment to interview an attorney or paralegal in the office to see what this person does. Again, you will establish a contact that you may be able to use after graduation.

In our paralegal program, a fieldwork class has been established in conjunction with the Los Angeles County Department of Consumer Affairs. Students learn consumer law in the classroom and then work as volunteers doing consumer counseling in the Department of Consumer Affairs. They also assist litigants in Small Claims Court. Several of the students have obtained positions as a direct result of this experience.

If you are interested in a position that has regular hours, good benefits, and a competitive salary, then you should consider working for the government. Start your investigation today by contacting the departments in which you are interested, or call the nearest branch of the federal Office of Personnel Management to obtain more information about positions in the federal government. You may find that the steady, secure government position suits you better than the stress and long hours associated with working for a private law firm. It is never too early to start your job search! Every contact you make while you are a student is a potential employer when you graduate.

"SPENDING TIME AS A STUDENT INTERN IN A GOVERNMENT OFFICE PREPARES YOU FOR A GOVERNMENT POSITION AFTER GRADUATION."

unable to achieve a voluntary settlement, or conciliation, it may sue the employer under Title VII. If the EEOC decides not to sue the employer—for example, if the EEOC thinks the employee is not truthful or does not have sufficient evidence to support the claim—the injured employee is entitled to file a civil suit against the employer.

An employer's liability under Title VII can be extensive. In general, the court can order injunctive relief against the employer (a judicial order to prevent future discrimination), retroactive promotions that were wrongfully withheld from the employee, and past wages to compensate the employee for the time he or she was wrongfully unemployed. Damages are also available in cases involving *intentional* (disparate-treatment) discrimination.

Discrimination Based on Age. The Age Discrimination in Employment Act of 1967 prevents employers from discriminating against workers between the ages of forty and seventy on the basis of their age. The act was passed, in part, in response to an increasing tendency on the part of employers to reduce costs by excluding older workers from their work forces and hiring younger workers (at lower salaries) instead.

Discrimination Based on Disability. Congress enacted the Americans with Disabilities Act (ADA) in 1990 to strengthen existing laws prohibiting discrimination in the workplace against individuals with disabilities. At the time of the ADA's enactment, employers with twenty-five or more workers fell within the scope of the statute. As of 1994, however, employers with as few as fifteen employees were also obliged to satisfy the requirements of the ADA.

As defined by the 1990 statute, disabilities include heart disease, cancer, blindness, paralysis, acquired immune-deficiency syndrome (AIDS), emotional illnesses, and learning disabilities. Under the ADA, an employer is not permitted to discriminate against a person with a disability if *reasonable accommodations* can be provided to assist the worker in satisfactorily performing the job. An employer is not required to accommodate a worker with a disability if the accommodation would constitute an *undue hardship* for the employer, however. For example, if the cost of accommodating the employee is extremely high, that high cost might constitute an undue hardship for the employer. Although enforcement of the ADA falls within the jurisdiction of the EEOC, the paralegal should note that the worker alleging discrimination in violation of the ADA may also file a civil lawsuit against the employer for violation of the act.

Employment Relationships and the Paralegal

Employment relationships necessarily affect the paralegal. As an employee, you will be subject to the laws governing employment relationships. As a legal professional, depending on the firm or organization for which you work, you may be extensively involved in work relating to labor and employment laws. You may work in the corporate counsel's office of a large corporate enterprise, for example. If the corporation's employees belong to a labor union, the corporate counsel's office will handle matters governed by labor

SUBSTANTIVE LAW CONCEPT SUMMARY

Employment Relationships

Employment at Will	Traditionally, the employment relationship has been "at will"—that is, the relationship can be terminated at any time for any reason by either the employer or the employee. Statutes and court decisions have limited the at-will doctrine in certain circumstances.
Labor Laws	1. *Norris-LaGuardia Act (1932)*—Permitted employees to organize into unions and to engage in peaceful strikes. 2. *National Labor Relations Act (1935)*—Established the right of the employees to engage in collective bargaining and to strike. The act also created the National Labor Relations Board (NLRB) to oversee elections and to prevent employers from engaging in unfair and illegal union-labor activities and unfair labor practices. 3. *Fair Labor Standards Act (1938)*—Established guidelines regulating overtime pay and minimum hourly wages. Prohibited the exploitation of children by regulating their employment.
Employment Discrimination	1. *Title VII of the Civil Rights Act (1964)*—Prohibits employment discrimination against job applicants and employees on the basis of race, color, national origin, gender, or religion. Title VII has been interpreted by the courts to prohibit both disparate-treatment (intentional) discrimination and disparate-impact (unintentional) discrimination. 2. *Age Discrimination in Employment Act (1967)*—Prohibits employment discrimination on the basis of age (against employees or job applicants aged forty or older). 3. *Americans with Disabilities Act (1990)*—Prohibits discrimination on the basis of disability against individuals qualified for a given job. Employers must reasonably accommodate the needs of persons with disabilities.

laws, such as collective-bargaining agreements and labor-management disputes. As a paralegal in a law firm or a government agency, you might assist in work relating to claims of employment discrimination, which may require you to interact with the Equal Employment Opportunity Commission. Here are just a few tasks that paralegals commonly undertake in the area of labor and employment law:

- Draft employment contracts for an employer.
- Assist with contract negotiations between labor and management.
- Research and analyze trends in labor law.
- Prepare for arbitration proceedings before the NLRB.
- Respond to inquiries from the NLRB regarding a client's alleged unfair labor practices.
- Prepare for and attend administrative hearings before the EEOC.
- Gather factual information to counter or support a claim of employment discrimination.
- Prepare reports and furnish documentation in response to an EEOC investigation into an employee's claim of employment discrimination.
- Draft a policy manual for a business client concerning what actions constitute discriminatory employment practices.
- Prepare notices regarding a firm's employment policies, important changes in employment laws, and so on.

DEVELOPING PARALEGAL SKILLS

EEOC Practice

Fred Cashen works as a paralegal in a corporation's legal department. Today, his supervising attorney has assigned to him the task of drafting a letter to the Equal Employment Opportunity Commission (EEOC) in response to a claim of discrimination filed with the EEOC by a woman who was denied a job by the corporation. The woman, Bridget Nelson, was a few weeks pregnant when she was offered a job with the company. She accepted the job offer and then told the corporate personnel manager that she would need to take a six-week maternity leave beginning in late November. The company then retracted its offer to hire the woman, because the end of the year—from the middle of November to December 31—is the company's busiest season. The primary reason for hiring someone was to help relieve the workload during the peak season.

THE NATURE OF THE CLAIM

When the woman was denied the job, she filed a claim with the EEOC, stating that the corporation had discriminated against her because she was pregnant. The company has to respond to the claim. Before drafting the response letter to the EEOC, Fred needs to talk to the personnel manager, Lisa Moore, who made the job offer. Fred faxes Lisa the claimant's statement, and Lisa and Fred arrange to discuss the claim on the phone at 1 P.M. At 12:55 P.M., Fred pulls out his file and a legal pad to take notes during the call.

INVESTIGATING THE CLAIM

Fred calls Lisa at 1 P.M., and they begin to discuss the incident. Lisa agrees with most of the facts in Nelson's statement, but she tells Fred that she did not discriminate against Nelson on the basis of pregnancy. "I just needed to hire someone who could work during the busy season, and she could not," says Lisa. "I told her that I was sorry that it wouldn't work out but that we needed someone to help out when she would be on leave. I never said that I was refusing to hire her because she was pregnant."

"Okay," says Fred. "I needed to verify what happened and what you said to her. I'll call you if I have any more questions. Thanks for your time."

DEFENDING AGAINST THE CLAIM

Well, thinks Fred, it sounds like there was a legitimate business justification for refusing to hire the woman. The law allows businesses to discriminate when there is a valid business need for discriminating. There was such a need here—the woman would be on maternity leave during the precise time when she was needed. Fred reviews the matter with his supervising attorney, who agrees with Fred's assessment. Fred then sits down at his computer and begins to draft a letter responding to the EEOC, in which he will explain that the discrimination was based on a business necessity.

CONSUMER LAW

CONSUMER
An individual who purchases (or is given) products and services for personal or household use.

Paralleling the movement for greater protection of employees in the workplace was the consumer movement that began in the 1960s. A **consumer** is a person who purchases, for private use, goods or services from business firms. Some have labeled the period following the 1960s "the age of the consumer" because so much legislation was passed in an attempt to protect consumers against unfair practices and unsafe products. During the 1980s and early 1990s, the impetus driving the consumer movement lessened, to a great extent because so many of its goals had been achieved. Both state and federal legislation now regulates how businesses may advertise, engage in mail-order transactions, package and label their products, and so on. In addition, numerous local, state, and federal agencies now exist to help consumers settle their grievances with sellers and producers. **Consumer law** consists of all statutes, agency rules, and common law judicial rulings that protect the interests of consumers.

CONSUMER LAW
Statutes, agency rules, and judicial decisions protecting consumers of goods and services from dangerous manufacturing techniques, mislabeling, unfair credit practices, deceptive advertising, and so on. Consumer laws provide remedies and protections that are not ordinarily available to merchants or to businesses.

Attorneys and paralegals frequently handle claims brought by consumers against sellers of goods and services. As a paralegal, you may be asked to investigate or do research relating to such a claim. Your task will be simpler if you understand some of the ways in which the government regulates the marketplace to protect consumers. In this section, you will read about how the government regulates advertising practices, the labeling and packaging of products, certain types of sales transactions, consumer health and safety, and credit transactions.

Deceptive Advertising

Over the past three decades, consumers have received increased protection against **deceptive advertising**. The protection has come more from statutes and government agency rules than from the common law. Under the common law, if a seller misrepresented the quality, price, or availability of a certain product, the consumer's only recourse was to sue the seller for fraud. Fraud requires proof of *intent* to misrepresent the product's usefulness to the buyer. Frequently, the burden of having to prove intent was too great, and consumers were left with little or no legal recourse against such deceptive practices.

DECEPTIVE ADVERTISING
Advertising that misleads consumers, either by unjustified claims concerning a product's performance or by the failure to disclose relevant information concerning the product's composition or performance.

Today, numerous government agencies, both federal and state, are empowered to protect consumers from deceptive advertising. At the federal level, the most important agency regulating advertising is the Federal Trade Commission (FTC). The Federal Trade Commission Act of 1914 authorizes the FTC to determine what constitutes a deceptive practice within the meaning of the act.

Deceptive advertising comes in many forms. Deception may arise from a false statement or claim about a company's own products or a competitor's products. Some advertisements contain "half-truths," meaning that the presented information is true but incomplete, leading consumers to a false conclusion. For example, the makers of Campbell's soups advertised that most Campbell's soups were low in fat and cholesterol and thus were helpful in fighting heart disease. What the ad did not say was that Campbell's soups are high in sodium and that high-sodium diets may increase the risk of heart disease. The FTC ruled that Campbell's claims were thus deceptive. Generally, the test for whether an ad is deceptive is *whether a reasonable consumer would be deceived by the ad.*

If a sufficient number of consumers complain to the FTC about the deceptive practices of a given retailer, the FTC has the power to investigate the problem and take action. If, after its investigation, the FTC believes that a given advertisement is unfair or deceptive, it drafts a formal complaint and sends it to the alleged offender. The company may agree to settle the complaint without further proceedings. If the company does not agree to a settlement, the FTC can conduct a hearing—which is similar to a trial—in which the company can present its defense. (See Chapter 13 for a detailed discussion of hearings and other proceedings conducted by government agencies.) If the FTC succeeds in proving that an advertisement is deceptive, it usually issues a *cease-and-desist order* requiring that the challenged advertising be stopped. It might also impose a sanction known as *counteradvertising* by requiring the company to supply new advertising—in print, on radio, and on television—to inform the public about the earlier misinformation.

Labeling and Packaging Laws

A number of federal and state laws now require manufacturers and sellers to provide labels that give consumers accurate information or warnings about products or their possible misuse. In general, labels must be accurate, which means that they must use words as they are ordinarily understood by consumers. For example, a regular-size box of cereal cannot be labeled "giant" if that word would exaggerate the amount of cereal contained in the box. Labels often must specify the raw materials used in the product, such as the percentage of cotton, nylon, or other fibers in a shirt.

An important federal law in this area is the Fair Packaging and Labeling Act of 1966. This act requires that consumer goods have labels that identify the product, the manufacturer, the packer or distributor and its place of business, the net quantity of the contents, and the quantity of each serving if the number of servings is stated. This statute also governs product descriptions and savings claims, disclosure of ingredients of nonfood products, and the partial filling of packages.

Food labeling acts are implemented by the federal Food and Drug Administration (FDA). The FDA recently developed new guidelines to standardize nutritional information on packaged foods. These regulations require, among other things, that producers of similar products use the same portion size to designate the products' nutritional content, such as the amount of saturated fat, sodium, and calories they contain. The guidelines specify that, for example, businesses that manufacture and market food products cannot label a salad dressing as " low calorie" or "light" when in fact its caloric value is the same as that of regular salad dressing but the recommended serving size is smaller. The FDA also defined some popular terms used to promote products, such as *healthy*, *light*, and *low-fat.* These laws and guidelines are designed to reduce consumer confusion over the contents of packaged foods.

Sales Transactions

As discussed in Chapter 8, Article 2 of the Uniform Commercial Code (UCC), which has been adopted by virtually all of the states, is the law that governs the purchase and sale of goods in the marketplace. Numerous UCC provisions protect consumers from unfair or deceptive sales practices. Particularly important are the provisions relating to unconscionable contracts (contracts that are so one-sided and unfair to the buyer that they "shock the conscience" of the court) and warranties. Product-liability laws—which are based on tort theories of negligence and strict liability, as well as warranty law—also afford consumers a degree of protection by allowing them to sue manufacturers and sellers for compensation when they are harmed or injured by faulty products.

Federal and state statutes and regulations also protect consumers who purchase specific types of goods or services. For example, the Federal Trade Commission has issued rules requiring sellers of certain types of goods or services (such as used cars and funeral services) to disclose pertinent information to consumers. Other laws protecting consumers include those discussed below.

Door-to-door Sales. Door-to-door sales are singled out for special treatment under both federal and state law. A number of states have passed what are known as *cooling-off laws*, which permit the buyers of goods sold door to door to cancel their contracts within a specified period of time after the sale, usually two to three days. At the federal level, a Federal Trade Commission regulation also requires sellers to give consumers three days to cancel any door-to-door sale, so that even in those states without such laws, consumers are protected against the consequences of succumbing to high-pressure, door-to-door sales representatives and purchasing products they may not want or need.

Goods Purchased by Telephone, Fax, or Mail. Consumers who purchase goods by telephone, fax, or mail are protected against sellers' deceptive or fraudulent practices by an FTC rule, by the federal statute prohibiting the use of the mails to defraud individuals, by state statutes governing solicitation by mail, and by the Postal Reorganization Act of 1970. The latter provides that individuals who receive unsolicited merchandise through the U.S. mail may do as they wish with the goods without incurring any obligation to the senders.

Real-estate Transactions. Various federal and state laws also apply to consumer transactions involving real estate. The disclosure requirements of the Truth-in-Lending Act, which will be discussed shortly, apply to a number of real-estate transactions. For example, in certain real-estate transactions, consumers have the right to rescind (cancel) their purchase contracts if a lender fails to make certain disclosures to them or fails in any way to comply with the act's requirements.

Consumer Health and Safety

In 1906, Congress passed the Pure Food and Drug Act, which was the first step toward protecting consumers against adulterated and misbranded food and drug products. In 1938, the Federal Food, Drug and Cosmetic Act was passed to strengthen the 1906 legislation. These acts and subsequent amendments established standards for foods, specified safe levels of potentially dangerous food additives, and created classifications of foods and food advertising. They also required that drugs must be proved effective as well as safe before they are marketed. Also in 1906, Congress passed the Meat Inspection Act, the first of a series of laws that established inspection requirements for all meat and poultry sold for human consumption. Most of the statutes involving food and drugs are monitored and enforced by the Food and Drug Administration.

Congress has enacted a number of statutes in an attempt to protect individuals from harmful products as well. In response to public concern over the dangers of cigarette smoking, for example, Congress required that warnings be placed on cigarette and little-cigar packages, as well as on containers of smokeless tobacco. Statutes categorized as product-safety acts protect consumers by carefully regulating the distribution of hazardous or defective products. One example is the Flammable Fabrics Act of 1953, which prohibits the sale of highly flammable fabrics and clothing. Another example is the Consumer Product Safety Act of 1972, which was enacted to protect consumers from unreasonably dangerous products. The Consumer Product Safety Commission, which was created by the act to implement its provisions, sets standards of product safety, is empowered to ban the production of unreasonably hazardous products, and keeps the public informed about unsafe products.

Consumer Credit Protection

Because of the extensive use of credit by American consumers, credit protection has become an important area regulated by consumer-protection legislation. One of the most significant statutes regulating the credit and credit-card industry is the Truth-in-Lending Act (TILA), the name commonly given to Title 1 of the Consumer Credit Protection Act, which was passed by Congress in 1974.

The Truth-in-Lending Act. The TILA requires sellers and lenders to disclose credit terms or loan terms so that individuals can more effectively shop around for the best financing arrangements. TILA requirements apply to any transaction involving an installment sales contract by which payment is to be made in more than four installments. These transactions typically include installment loans, retail and installment sales, car loans, home-improvement loans, and certain real-estate loans if the amount of financing is less than $25,000. Under the provisions of the TILA, all of the terms of a credit instrument must be fully disclosed. The TILA provides that a consumer can cancel the contract if a creditor fails to follow *exactly* the procedures required by the act.

In 1974, Congress enacted the Equal Credit Opportunity Act (ECOA) as part of the earlier-enacted TILA. The ECOA prohibits the denial of credit solely on the basis of race, religion, national origin, color, gender, marital status, or age. The act also prohibits credit discrimination on the basis of whether an individual receives certain forms of income, such as public-assistance benefits. Creditors are prohibited from requesting any information from a credit applicant that could be used for the type of discrimination covered by the act and its amendments. Under the ECOA, a creditor may not require the signature of an applicant's spouse, other than as a joint applicant, on a credit instrument if the applicant qualifies under the creditor's standards of creditworthiness for the amount and terms of the credit requested.

The TILA also contains provisions regarding credit cards. One provision limits the liability of a cardholder to $50 per card for unauthorized charges made before the creditor is notified that the card has been lost. Another provision prohibits a credit-card company from billing a consumer for any unauthorized charges on a credit card that was improperly issued by the company. For example, if a consumer receives an unsolicited credit card in the mail and the card is later stolen and used by the thief to make purchases, the consumer to whom the card was sent is not liable for the unauthorized charges. Further provisions of the act concern billing disputes related to credit-card purchases. A debtor may think that an error has occurred in billing or may wish to withhold payment for a faulty product purchased by credit card. The act outlines specific procedures for both the consumer and the credit-card company to follow in settling such a dispute.

Fair Credit Reporting. To ensure that consumers can find and alter any inaccurate information about their credit records, Congress passed the Fair Credit Reporting Act (FCRA) in 1970. The FCRA covers all credit bureaus, investigative reporting companies, detective and collection agencies, and computerized information-reporting companies. Under the act, the consumer has the right to be notified of reporting activities, to have access to information contained in reports, and to demand correction of any erroneous information on which a denial of credit, employment, or insurance might have been based.

Upon request and proper identification, any consumer is entitled to know what information about him or her is contained in the agency's file, as well as the sources of the information and the identity of those who have received a consumer credit report, such as businesses that may wish to extend credit to the consumer. Under the act, no investigative report can be prepared on an individual consumer unless that person is notified and given the right to request information on the nature and scope of the pending investigation.

Fair Debt-collection Practices. In 1977, Congress passed the Fair Debt Collection Practices Act in an attempt to curb what were perceived to be abuses by collection agencies. The act applies only to debt-collection agencies that, usually for a percentage of the amount owed, regularly attempt to collect debts on behalf of someone else. Creditors who attempt to collect debts are not covered by the act unless, by misrepresenting themselves to the debtor, they cause the debtor to believe that they are collection agencies.

The act prohibits such debt-collection practices as contacting the consumer at his or her place of employment if the employer objects, contacting the consumer at inconvenient or unusual times, and contacting the consumer if he or she is represented by an attorney. The act also prohibits debt-collection agencies from contacting third parties (other than parents, spouses, or financial advisers) about the payment of a debt unless authorized to do so by a court, using harassment and intimidation (such as abusive language),

DEVELOPING PARALEGAL SKILLS

Discharged for Garnishment

Eva White works as a paralegal for a firm that specializes in labor law. A business client has called Eva's supervising attorney to ask for advice concerning a garnishment proceeding. Basically, the client wants to know if he can fire an employee so that he can avoid having to comply with garnishment proceedings that have been initiated against the employee. The attorney, Melinda Jenks, has asked Eva to research recent case law on the question of whether an employer may fire an employee for such a reason.

Eva goes to the firm's law library, which is down the hall from her office. She begins her research by looking in the digests (summaries of case law, described in Chapter 17) under the topic of garnishment. Eva comes across a case in which an employee was fired two days after his employer received a notice of garnishment. The case discusses a federal statute that prohibits employers from discharging an employee "by reason of the fact that his earnings have been subjected to garnishment for any one indebtedness." The issue in the case turns on whether the employer had notice that garnishment proceedings had already been initiated against the employee. The case gives the citation for the federal statute—in other words, it indicates where the statute can be located in the *United States Code* (in which all federal statutes are published). Eva's next step is to check the statute itself. She checks the annotated version of the *United States Code,* which refers to court cases interpreting the statute, to ensure that she has up-to-date knowledge of how the statute is being applied.

using false or misleading information (such as posing as a police officer), and communicating with the consumer after receipt of a notice that the consumer is refusing to pay the debt (except to advise the consumer of further action to be taken by the collection agency).

GARNISHMENT
A proceeding in which a creditor legally seizes a portion of a debtor's property (such as wages) that is in the possession of a third party (such as an employer).

Garnishment Proceedings. Creditors have numerous remedies available to them when consumers fail to pay their debts. Among these remedies is garnishment. **Garnishment** occurs when a creditor, after complying with procedures mandated by state law, legally seizes a portion of a debtor's property (such as wages) in the possession of a third party (such as an employer). The creditor must first obtain an *order of garnishment* from the court, which allows the creditor to have access to the debtor's wages while they are still in the control of the employer. State laws governing garnishment vary from state to state, and some states (for example, Texas) do not permit garnishment of wages by private parties except under a child-support order.

Garnishment can create a hardship for the consumer-debtor if he or she is relying on wages for support. To protect consumers, both federal and state laws limit the amount of income that can be taken from a debtor's weekly take-home pay. The federal Consumer Credit Protection Act of 1968 provides that a debtor can keep either 75 percent of the net earnings per week or a sum equivalent to the pay for thirty hours of work at federal minimum

TODAY'S PROFESSIONAL PARALEGAL

Developing a Policy on Sexual Harassment

Erika Delong, a legal assistant, works in the office of the general counsel at ABC Manufacturing Corporation. She works closely with the personnel department. Today, she is attending a meeting with her supervisor, Gene Tompkins, who is the general counsel, to discuss the company's policy on sexual harassment with the vice president of personnel, the president of the corporation, and the vice presidents of several of the corporation's divisions. Erika has been asked to attend the meeting because her supervisor will ultimately be responsible for preparing the policy and he wants her to draft it. Erika has already obtained copies of other companies' policies to use as samples in the meeting.

The meeting is held in a large conference room. The president opens the meeting by explaining its purpose—to develop a policy on sexual harassment. "We want to discourage it and to have a written policy that includes reporting and investigation procedures. Erika and Gene have several samples that we can review," says the president.

SETTING POLICY GOALS AND DEFINING SEXUAL HARASSMENT

Erika passes out the sample policies. The group then reviews the various policies, with Gene explaining the legal ramifications of each one. The president remarks that he thinks the policy should begin with a statement that the corporation wants to promote an atmosphere in which authority and power are not abused and in which sexual harassment is not condoned. He points out some language that he likes in one of the samples. Erika highlights it so that she will have an idea of how to draft the introduction.

Gene then states, "After an introduction and general statement of the corporation's policy, we should give the legal definition of what constitutes sexual harassment. The definition in sample three is very good from both a legal and a practical point of view because it also gives examples." Erika highlights the definition paragraph in sample three and puts a number 2 next to it, so that she knows it should come second. She flips back to the sample the president referred to and she puts a number 1 next to it.

DEVELOPING PROCEDURES

As the discussion continues, the vice president of personnel comments on the procedure for filing a complaint, the investigation that will take place, and the disciplinary measures that will be imposed for sexual harassment. The vice president does not like any of the samples, and the group spends quite a bit of time working through specific language to pin down what he wants. When the meeting is over, the group goes to lunch in the executive dining room. After lunch, Gene informs the others that Erika will prepare a draft of the policy and will circulate it among them for review and comment. Once all of their comments have been reviewed, the group will meet again to decide on the final provisions. Erika will then prepare and circulate a final draft of the policy. Erika returns to her office to begin work on the initial draft.

wage rates, whichever is greater. State laws also provide dollar exemptions, and these amounts are often larger than those provided by federal law. State and federal statutes can be applied together to create a pool of funds to enable a debtor to continue to provide for family needs while reducing the amount of the debt in a reasonable way.

Understandably, employers dislike garnishment proceedings. After all, such proceedings impose time costs on employers (appearance at court hearings, record-keeping costs, and so on). To protect the job security of employees whose wages are subject to garnishment, federal law provides that garnishment of an employee's wages for any one indebtedness cannot be grounds for that employee's dismissal.

SUBSTANTIVE LAW CONCEPT SUMMARY

Consumer Law

Deceptive Advertising	Advertising that misleads consumers or that is based on false claims is prohibited by the Federal Trade Commission (FTC). Generally, the test for whether an ad is deceptive is whether a reasonable consumer would be deceived by the ad.
Labeling and Packaging Laws	Manufacturers must comply with labeling or packaging requirements for their specific products. In general, all labels must be accurate and not misleading.
Sales Transactions	**1.** *Door-to-door sales*—The FTC requires all door-to-door sellers to give consumers three days to cancel any sale. **2.** *Sales by telephone, fax, or mail*—Regulated by an FTC rule governing sales by telephone, fax, or mail; by federal and state statutes that prohibit certain practices of sellers who solicit through the mails and that prohibit the use of the mails to defraud individuals; and by a federal statute that provides that any unsolicited merchandise sent by U.S. mail may be disposed of in any manner without incurring liability to the sender. **3.** *Real-estate sales*—Various federal and state laws apply to consumer transactions involving real estate, including the federal Truth-in-Lending Act.
Consumer Health and Safety	Laws protecting the health and safety of consumers include laws governing the processing and distribution of meat and poultry, poisonous substances, and drugs and cosmetics; laws requiring warnings of health hazards associated with certain products, such as cigarettes; and the Consumer Product Safety Act of 1972, which created the Consumer Product Safety Commission to inspect consumer products, ban the manufacture of hazardous products, and remove from the market products that are deemed to be imminently hazardous.
Consumer Credit Protection	**1.** *Truth-in-Lending Act (TILA) (1974)*—A disclosure law requiring sellers and lenders to disclose credit terms or loan terms. Transactions covered by the act typically include retail and installment sales and loans, car loans, home-improvement loans, and certain real-estate loans. The TILA also provides for the following: a. *Equal credit opportunity*—Prohibits creditors from discriminating on the basis of race, religion, marital status, gender, national origin, color, or age. b. *Credit-card protection*—Limits liability of cardholders for unauthorized charges and protects consumers from liability for unauthorized charges made on unsolicited credit cards. c. *Credit-card rules*—Allows credit-card users to withhold payment for faulty products purchased by credit cards and to withhold payment for charges billed in error until disputes are resolved. **2.** *Fair Credit Reporting Act (1970)*—Entitles consumers to be informed when credit-reporting agencies send credit reports to third parties, to request verification of the accuracy of the reports, and to have unverified information removed from their files. **3.** *Fair Debt Collection Practices Act (1977)*—Prohibits debt-collecting agencies from using unfair collection practices (such as calling at unreasonable times, contacting certain third parties about the debt, harassment, and intimidation).
Garnishment Proceedings	Garnishment occurs when a creditor legally seizes a portion of a debtor's property (such as wages) in the possession of a third party (such as an employer). Both state and federal laws regulate garnishment proceedings to protect individuals from unfair procedures or from being deprived of too much of their income. Federal law also prohibits an employer from firing an employee because of a single garnishment proceeding.

Consumer Law and the Paralegal

Because consumer laws protect all individuals, as a paralegal you will undoubtedly encounter a client with a claim that falls under a federal or state consumer-protection law. You might even find yourself working for a consumer group. In the area of consumer law, paralegals may be asked to perform the following types of tasks:

- Investigate a client's complaint alleging deceptive advertising.
- Assist in work relating to a business client who has been charged with violating Federal Trade Commission rules governing deceptive trade practices.
- Develop acceptable standards for a food producer to ensure compliance with the labeling laws implemented by the Food and Drug Administration.
- Investigate a client's use of hazardous products to ensure compliance with Consumer Product Safety Commission standards.
- Draft a letter to a credit-reporting agency to rectify an error on a client's credit report.
- Assist a client in collecting a debt through garnishment proceedings.
- Maintain and keep current the law firm's consumer-law library.

KEY TERMS AND CONCEPTS

agency 318
agent 318
articles of incorporation 331
blue sky law 338
bona fide occupational qualification 345
bond 337
certificate of incorporation 331
consolidation 336
consumer 350
consumer law 351
corporate charter 331
deceptive advertising 351
director 329
disparate-impact discrimination 345
disparate-treatment discrimination 345
dissolution 328
dividend 335
employee 319
employment at will 343
fiduciary 319
garnishment 356
independent contractor 319
insider trading 338
joint and several liability 328
joint liability 327
Keogh plan 325
limited-liability company (LLC) 339
limited-liability partnership (LLP) 339
limited partnership 329
liquidation 337
merger 336
officer 329
principal 318
prospectus 331
respondeat superior 321
security 337
sexual harassment 345
share 329
shareholder 329
stock 337
vicarious liability 321
winding up 329

CHAPTER SUMMARY

1. Under the common law, employment in the United States has traditionally been "at will"—both the employer and employee could terminate the employment relationship at any time for any

reason. State and federal statutes regulating employment now govern employment relationships to a significant extent. Since the 1930s, a number of laws have been enacted to allow employees to form labor unions, strike peacefully, and bargain collectively with management for improved working conditions and benefits. Labor laws generally regulate union-management relations and prohibit both employers and unions from engaging in certain types of activities.

2. In an agency relationship, one party (the agent) agrees to represent or act for another party (the principal). Employees who deal with third parties (customers, for example) are normally considered to be agents of their employers. Independent contractors may or may not be agents.

3. An agency relationship is a fiduciary relationship, one that involves trust and gives rise to certain duties. The principal has a duty to cooperate with, provide safe working conditions for, reimburse, and compensate the agent. The agent has a duty to perform work competently, obey and be loyal to the principal, notify the principal of knowledge or events significant to the agency, and render an accounting to the principal of how the principal's funds were used.

4. Under agency law, the principal is bound by an agent's authorized actions and may be held liable, under the doctrine of *respondeat superior,* for the agent's torts committed within the scope of the agency. An agency may be terminated by agreement of the parties or through the occurrence of certain events, such as the death or mental incompetence of the principal or the agent.

5. The three major forms of business organization are the sole proprietorship, the partnership, and the corporation. The simplest form of business is the sole proprietorship. Anyone who does business without creating an organization is a sole proprietor. The owner is entitled to enjoy the firm's profits, assumes full responsibility for the firm's operations and obligations, and pays personal income taxes on all profits. If the owner dies or ceases doing business, the sole proprietorship terminates.

6. A partnership is created when two or more persons, orally or in writing, agree to undertake business jointly for a profit. Agency concepts apply to partners: each partner is deemed the agent of the other partners and, as a result, assumes certain rights and fiduciary duties. The partnership as an entity does not pay income taxes; rather, each partner pays personal income taxes on his or her share of the profits. Partners assume personal liability for business obligations, and, depending on state law, their liability may be joint and several. A partnership may be terminated by the agreement of the partners, when the goal of the partnership has been achieved, when a certain time period lapses, or by certain events, such as the death or bankruptcy of a partner.

7. The formation of a limited partnership is a formal undertaking involving compliance with specific state-imposed requirements. In a limited partnership, the general partners manage the business operations and assume personal responsibility for the firm's obligations. The limited partners are investors only—they do not participate in management, and their liability for business obligations is limited to the amount of their investment in the enterprise.

8. A corporation is formed with the state's permission (by a state-issued charter) and governed by state corporation laws. Corporate personnel include the shareholders (who purchase shares in the corporation's stock and thus become the owners of the business), the directors (who are elected by the shareholders to establish corporate policy and oversee the firm's operations), and the officers (who are appointed by the directors to manage the day-to-day affairs of the corporation).

9. Corporate income is subject to "double taxation"—the corporation as an entity pays income taxes on its profits, and the shareholders again pay personal taxes on the profits when they are distributed in the form of dividends. Unlike sole proprietors and partners, corporate shareholders have limited liability and are not personally liable (beyond the amount of their investment in the business) for corporate obligations. A corporation may be terminated at a time specified in the articles of incorporation or by the agreement of the directors and shareholders. Corporations are financed through the issuance of corporate securities—stocks and bonds. The purchase and sale of corporate securities over public securities exchanges, such as the New York Stock Exchange, are governed by federal and state securities laws.

10. Two relatively new forms of business organization are the limited-liability company (LLC) and the limited-liability partnership (LLP). These organizations combine the tax benefits of the partnership form of business (the business entity does not pay income taxes) with the limited personal liability of the corporate form of business.

11. Title VII of the Civil Rights Act of 1964 prohibits employment discrimination against job applicants and employees on the basis of race, color, national origin, gender, and religion. The courts have interpreted Title VII to prohibit not only intentional (disparate-treatment) discrimination but also unintentional (disparate-impact) discrimination. The Age Discrimination in Employment Act of 1967 prohibits employment discrimination based on age, and other statutes, including the Americans with Disabilities Act of 1990, prohibit employment discrimination against persons with disabilities. Employees with disabilities must be reasonably accommodated by employers. Laws prohibiting employment discrimination are enforced by the Equal Employment Opportunity Commission.

12. Numerous federal and state statutes have been enacted to protect consumers from harmful products or unfair practices on the part of sellers. The Federal Trade Commission prohibits deceptive advertising, which is usually defined as any advertising that would deceive a reasonable consumer. Packaging and labeling laws protect consumers by requiring producers to label their products accurately and truthfully and to disclose certain information on product labels. In addition to the Uniform Commercial Code's provisions that protect consumers (the provisions on warranties and unconscionability, for example), federal and state statutes and regulations also regulate certain types of sales transactions (door-to-door sales, telephone and mail-order sales, real-estate sales, and so on) in the interest of protecting consumers.

13. Consumers are also protected by federal laws and regulations governing the sale of foods and drugs, which establish standards relating to health and safety that must be met by producers of foods and drugs before their products can be marketed. Federal laws also provide protection for consumers in credit transactions by imposing specific requirements on institutions that extend credit to consumers, credit-card companies, credit-reporting agencies, and credit-collection agencies. Federal and state laws also regulate garnishment proceedings against debtors.

QUESTIONS FOR REVIEW

1. What is an agency relationship? How is an agency relationship formed? What is the difference between an employee and an independent contractor?

2. What are the rights and duties of principals and agents? What is the rationale for the doctrine that a principal-employer can be held liable for an agent-employee's torts? What is this doctrine called?

3. How does the law of agency affect the rights and duties of employers and employees? How does it affect the rights and duties of partners and corporate personnel?

4. What are the three most common forms of business organization? How is each form created and terminated?

5. How are the profits distributed in each of the three major forms of business organization? How do the three forms compare in terms of the liability of the owners for business debts and obligations?

6. What are limited-liability partnerships and limited-liability companies? What advantages do these relatively new business forms offer to businesspersons?

7. What is meant by employment at will? What are some of the major employment statutes that govern employer-employee relationships today?

8. What federal statutes prohibit employment discrimination? What kinds of discrimination are prohibited under these statutes?

9. What is the difference between disparate-impact discrimination and disparate-treatment discrimination? What federal agency handles claims of employment discrimination?

10. What are some of the ways in which the law attempts to protect consumers? Name some of the most important consumer-protection statutes.

ETHICAL QUESTIONS

1. Mark Anderson has been the operations manager of Division B of the Widget Company for fifteen years. The Widget Company is now undergoing a reorganization and is combining the management of Division B with that of Division A. The operations manager of Division A, a younger man who has been with the firm for only three years, has been asked to take over Mark's responsibilities. The net result for Mark is that he has been given the choice of retiring earlier than planned (with a special retirement bonus) or taking another job with the company with less pay and little job security. Mark has always received favorable performance evaluations and does not want to retire. He concludes that he is being discriminated against on the basis of age and calls to make an appointment with an attorney to seek legal advice. His main question is whether the company would have a legitimate reason to fire him if he discusses the matter with the Equal Employment Opportunity Commission. The attorney is out of town, and the attorney's paralegal, June Carter, takes the call. How should June respond to Mark's question?

2. Allison Palermo has worked as a paralegal for years with a major law firm in her community. The firm specializes in corporate law, and one of the firm's clients, Acumen, Inc., has just consulted with her supervising attorney about a corporate acquisition that will enhance the value of Acumen's stock enormously. Allison realizes that she could make a small fortune if she purchased stock in Acumen before the merger becomes public (and the price of the stock rises). She and her husband have been facing severe financial problems lately, and the profits she could realize through the purchase and later sale of Acumen's stock would solve their financial problems. Allison buys several shares of stock and also passes the information about the corporate acquisition on to her good friend, Sarah Dorman. Sarah also purchases stock in the corporation. Has Allison violated any of the ethical rules governing the legal profession? Has Sarah violated any law?

PRACTICE QUESTIONS AND ASSIGNMENTS

1. Determine whether each of the business firms described below is a sole proprietorship, a partnership, or a corporation and why:

   a. Terence and Lars have owned a business together for three months. Terence contributed 60 percent of the capital needed to start the business, and Lars contributed the other 40 percent. Each is responsible for a proportionate share of the profits and the losses of the business, and each participates in managing the business.

   b. Four wealthy individuals create a business that will fund and build a new commerce center to revitalize the downtown business district in their city. Each individual contributes 25 percent of the funds needed. All the individuals share equally in the firm's profits and losses. They all sign an agreement.

   c. Anne Hall, Joe Richie, and Mike Wenner are all certified public accountants. They decide to do business together. By the end of its first year, the firm has become very profitable. As a result, the firm has to pay a substantial amount in income taxes.

   d. Dr. Menendez practices medicine on his own; he has not incorporated.

   e. The Pear Company is a for-profit business that has a charter issued by the state and provides limited liability to its owners.

2. Identify what type of employment discrimination, if any, is being practiced in each of the following hypothetical situations:

   a. Lana Lonsky, a legal assistant in an all-male law firm, is the subject of constant sexual jokes, comments, and occasional uninvited touching—all of which are offensive to her and make it difficult for her to do her job.

b. Monica Pierson, a partner in a large law firm, interviews seven potential legal assistants, including an Asian American. Although the Asian American is the best qualified for the job in terms of education and training, Monica does not hire him because he speaks English with an accent, which might offend some of the firm's clients.

c. Diana Bekins, the manager of an insurance agency, makes it clear to Mack McBride, a new sales representative, that she will promote him only if he provides sexual favors in return.

d. The Small Town Post Office has a rule that all mail carriers must be able to bench-press two hundred pounds, because the mail bags are so heavy.

QUESTIONS FOR CRITICAL ANALYSIS

1. Assume that you have the option of assisting an attorney either as an independent contractor (that is, on a freelance basis) or as the attorney's employee. What are the pros and cons of working as an independent contractor versus working as an employee?

2. Attorneys are agents of their clients and thus are governed by the principles of agency law discussed in this chapter. Do you see any similarities between the duties of agents to their principals and the ethical rules governing attorneys (discussed in Chapters 3 and 4)? If so, what are the similiarities? In other words, which duties of agents, if any, correspond to specific ethical rules?

ROLE-PLAYING EXERCISES

1. Susie Jamison works as a payroll clerk for a small logging company. She is the only female employee of the firm, and the loggers frequently make jokes about her "sexy" body, give her unwelcome hugs, and generally act in ways that she finds offensive. The company's owner has not responded to her complaints about the loggers' behavior. In fact, the owner is as offensive, if not more so, than the others. Recently, the owner has made it clear to Susie that if she isn't more cooperative and pleasant, she will lose her job. Susie calls the law offices of Donahue & Ward and talks with Carol March, a paralegal. Carol explains that both of the firm's attorneys are out of town for the rest of the week but that she can set up an appointment for Susie to see one of them on the following Tuesday. Susie tells Carol that before she comes into the office, she just wants to know whether she has any legal recourse. She presses Carol for answers to the following kinds of questions:

a. Aren't there laws prohibiting sexual harassment?

b. Is there any way that I can keep my job without having to put up with the loggers' offensive behavior?

c. What if I'm fired? Do I have any right to force the owner to take me back?

d. Can I sue the owner for sexual harassment?

e. How do the lawyers in your firm charge their clients? By the hour? How much do you think it would cost to have them help me with this problem?

f. What would you do in this kind of situation?

Working in pairs, act out the roles of Carol March and Susie Jamison. The student playing the role of Susie should aggressively seek answers to her questions. The student playing the role of Carol should be tactful and sympathetic to Susie's plight but avoid giving legal advice.

2. Review Ethical Question 1 above. Working in pairs, act out the roles of Mark Anderson, who thinks he is a victim of age discrimination, and the paralegal who takes his call. The student playing the role of Mark should be the type of person who wants advice and wants it now. The student playing the role of the paralegal should show concern for Mark's situation yet avoid giving legal advice (engaging in the unauthorized practice of law). If time permits, reverse roles.

PROJECTS

1. Find out if your state's corporation statute is based on the Model Business Corporation Act or the Revised Model Business Corporation Act.

2. Call the appropriate department in your state for information about a company located in your area. See how much information you can acquire about that company from the government office.

3. Do some research on cases within your state relating to employment. Find out whether the courts in your state adhere to the employment-at-will doctrine. Also find out if, and in what circumstances, they make exceptions to this doctrine.

ANNOTATED SELECTED READINGS

COVINGTON, J. S., AND SUSANNE W. EVANS. *The Law of Business Organizations for Undergraduate and Paralegal Studies.* Houston: John Marshall Publishing Co., 1991. A text that provides a thorough review of the major forms of business organizations, corporate finance, and public corporations. It contains numerous hypothetical examples to illustrate the topics covered.

LUBELL, ADELE. "Mergers and Acquisitions: The Paralegal's Role." *Legal Assistant Today,* November/December 1991. An interesting description of the paralegal's role in relation to mergers and acquisitions.

MILLER, ROGER LEROY, AND GAYLORD A. JENTZ. *Business Law Today: Text, Summarized Cases, Legal, Ethical, Regulatory and International Environment.* 3d ed. St. Paul: West Publishing Co., 1994. A thorough yet readable text on business law. Chapters on partnerships and corporations describe in detail how these forms of business are created, operated, and terminated. The book also covers numerous other topics, including agency law, employment and labor law, and consumer law.

MOYE, JOHN E. *The Law of Business Organizations.* 4th ed. St. Paul: West Publishing Co., 1994. An outstanding textbook that reviews all of the forms of business organization and the requirements for setting up each form. It reviews the Model Business Corporation Act and the Revised Model Business Corporation Act, as well as the various requirements for corporate meetings, shareholders, boards of directors, and so on.

NEILSON, MARTHA G. "Dusting the Cobwebs Off the Neglected Corporations." *Legal Assistant Today,* November/December 1993. An interesting article on corporate law. The article contains a very helpful checklist for corporate record keeping and indicates generally what is involved in working as a paralegal in the field of corporate law.

WHITESIDE, FRANCIS B. "Forming and Maintaining a Corporation." *Legal Assistant Today,* November/December 1991. An article that explains, in practical terms, how a corporation is formed. It also provides a good practical review of what paralegals do who work in this area.

PART THREE

LEGAL PROCEDURES AND PARALEGAL SKILLS

10

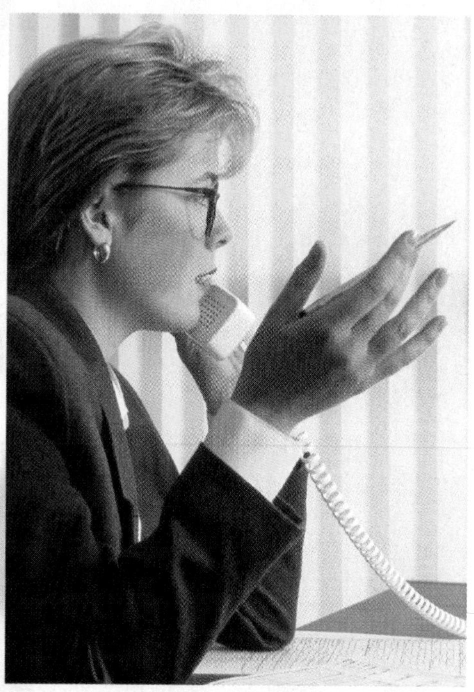

Civil Litigation—Before the Trial

Chapter Objectives

After completing this chapter, you will know:

- The basic steps involved in the civil litigation process and the types of tasks that may be required of paralegals during each step of the pretrial phase.
- What a litigation file is, what it contains, and how it is organized, maintained, and reviewed.
- How a lawsuit is initiated and what documents are filed during the pleadings stage of the civil litigation process.
- What a motion is and how certain pretrial motions, if granted by the court, will end the litigation before the trial begins.
- What discovery is and the kind of information that attorneys and their paralegals obtain from parties to the lawsuit and witnesses when preparing for trial.

Chapter Outline

INTRODUCTION

The paralegal plays a particularly important role in helping the trial attorney prepare for and conduct a civil trial. Popular television shows and movies tend to glamorize courtroom trials as semantic battles between quick-witted litigators, but the success of any trial depends primarily on how well the attorney and the paralegal have prepared for it.

Preparation for trial involves a variety of tasks. The law relating to the client's case must be carefully researched. Evidence must be gathered and documented. The litigation file must be created and carefully organized. Procedural requirements and deadlines for filing certain documents with the court must be met. **Witnesses**—persons who are asked to testify at trial—must be prepared in advance and must be available to testify at the appropriate time during the trial. Any exhibits, such as charts, photographs, or videotapes, to be used at the trial must be properly prepared, mounted, or filmed. Arrangements must be made to have any necessary equipment, such as a VCR, videodisc, or CD-ROM player and projector, available for use at the trial. The paralegal's efforts are of critical importance in preparing for trial, and attorneys usually rely on paralegals to ensure that nothing has been overlooked during trial preparation.

WITNESS
A person who is asked to testify under oath at a trial.

Attorneys may request that their paralegals assist them during the trial also. In the courtroom, the paralegal can perform numerous tasks. For example, the paralegal can locate documents or exhibits as they are needed. The paralegal can also observe jurors' reactions to statements made by attorneys or witnesses, check to see if a witness's testimony is consistent with sworn statements made by the witness before the trial, and perhaps give witnesses some last-minute instructions outside the courtroom before they are called to testify.

The complexity of even the simplest civil trial requires that the paralegal have some familiarity with the litigation process and the applicable courtroom procedures. Much of this expertise, of course, can only be acquired through hands-on experience. Yet every paralegal should be acquainted with the basic phases of civil litigation and the forms and terminology commonly used in the process. In this chapter, you will learn about the pretrial stages of a civil lawsuit, from the initial attorney-client meeting to the time of trial. In the next chapter, you will read about trial and posttrial procedures.

CIVIL LITIGATION—A BIRD'S EYE VIEW

Although civil trials may vary greatly in terms of complexity, cost, and detail, they all share similar structural characteristics. They begin with an event that gives rise to the legal action, and (provided the case is not settled by the parties at some point during the litigation process—as most cases are) they end with the issuance of a **judgment**, the court's decision on the matter. In the interim, the litigation itself may involve all sorts of twists and turns. Even though each case has its own "story line," most civil lawsuits follow some version of the course charted in Exhibit 10.1.

JUDGMENT
The court's final decision regarding the rights and claims of the parties to a lawsuit.

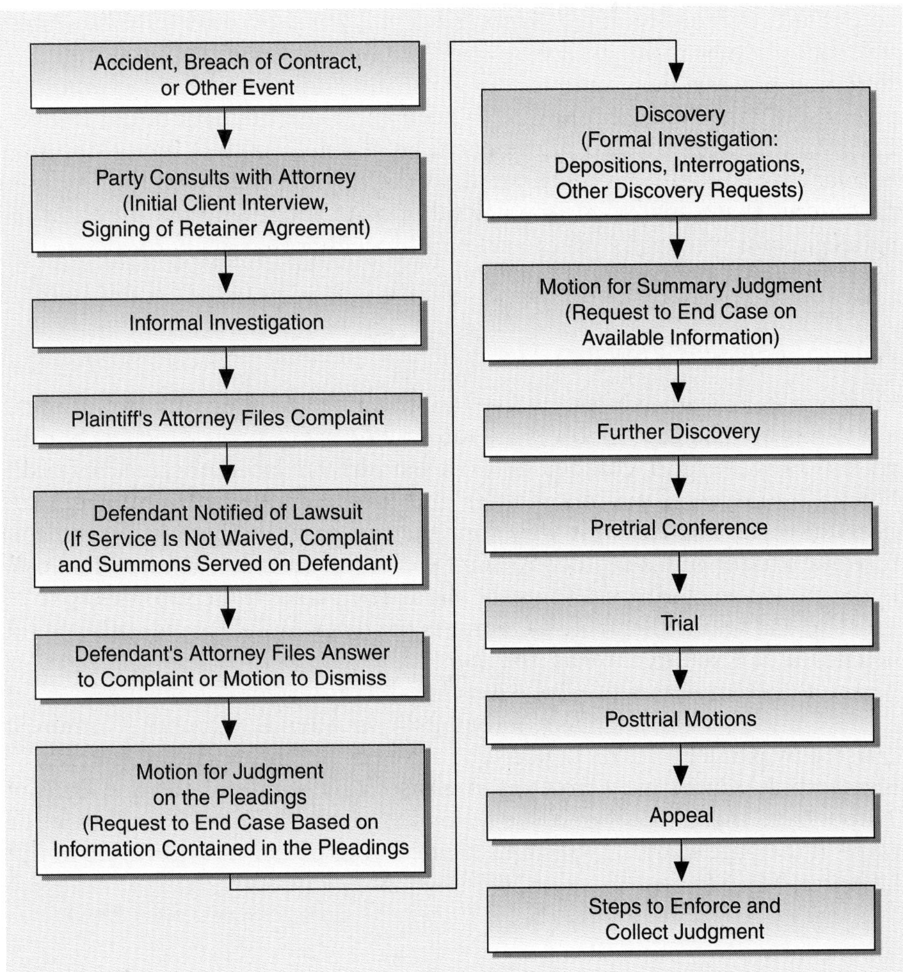

EXHIBIT 10.1
A Typical Case Flow Chart

Pretrial Settlements

As just mentioned, in most cases, the parties reach a *settlement*—an out-of-court resolution of the dispute—before the case goes to trial. Lawsuits are costly in terms of both time and money, and it is usually in the interest of both parties to settle the case out of court. Throughout the pretrial stage of litigation, the attorney will therefore attempt to help the parties reach a settlement. At the same time, though, the attorney and the paralegal will operate under the assumption that the case will go to trial because if it does, all pretrial preparation must be completed prior to the trial date.

Procedural Requirements

Understanding and meeting procedural requirements is essential in the litigation process. These requirements are spelled out in the procedural rules of the court in which a lawsuit is brought. All civil trials held in federal district

FEDERAL RULES OF CIVIL PROCEDURE (FRCP)
The rules controlling all procedural matters in civil trials brought before the federal district courts.

courts are governed by the **Federal Rules of Civil Procedure (FRCP).**[1] These rules specify what must be done during the various stages of the federal civil litigation process. For example, FRCP 4 (Rule 4 of the FRCP) describes the procedures that must be followed in notifying the defendant of the lawsuit. Each state also has its own rules of civil procedure (which in many states are similar to the FRCP).[2] In addition, many courts have their own local rules of procedures that supplement the federal or state rules. The attorney and the paralegal must comply with the rules of procedure that apply to the specific court in which the trial will take place.

A Hypothetical Lawsuit

To illustrate the procedures involved in litigation, we present a hypothetical civil lawsuit. The case involves an automobile accident in which a car driven by Tony Peretto collided with a car driven by Katherine Baranski. Baranski suffered numerous injuries and incurred substantial medical and hospital costs. She also lost wages for the five months that she was unable to work. Baranski has decided to sue Peretto for damages. Because Baranski is the person initiating the lawsuit, she is the plaintiff. Peretto, because he must defend against Baranski's claims, is the defendant. The plaintiff and the defendant are referred to as the *parties* to the lawsuit, as discussed in Chapter 6. (Some cases involve several plaintiffs and/or defendants.)

The attorney for the plaintiff (Baranski) is Allen P. Gilmore. Gilmore is assisted by paralegal Elena Lopez. The attorney for the defendant (Peretto) is Elizabeth A. Cameron. Cameron is assisted by paralegal Gordon McVay. Throughout this chapter and the following chapter, *Case at a Glance* features in the page margins will remind you of the names of the players in this lawsuit.

CASE AT A GLANCE

The Plaintiff—
Plaintiff: Katherine Baranski
Attorney: Allen P. Gilmore
Paralegal: Elena Lopez

The Defendant—
Defendant: Tony Peretto
Attorney: Elizabeth A. Cameron
Paralegal: Gordon McVay

THE PRELIMINARIES

Katherine Baranski arranges to meet with Allen P. Gilmore, an attorney with the law firm of Jeffers, Gilmore & Dunn, to see if Gilmore will represent her in the lawsuit. Gilmore asks paralegal Elena Lopez to prepare the usual forms and information sheets, including a retainer agreement and a statement of the firm's billing procedures, and to bring them with her to the initial interview with Baranski.

The Initial Client Interview

As discussed in Chapter 5, most often an initial client interview is conducted by the attorney—for several reasons. First, if attorney Gilmore is inter-

1. Some practitioners use the abbreviation FRCivP to distinguish the Federal Rules of Civil Procedure from the Federal Rules of Criminal Procedure.
2. The 1993 revision of the FRCP substantially changed the rules governing some of the topics discussed in this chapter, and it is uncertain at this time whether state courts will adopt similar changes in their procedural rules. In the meantime, the revised FRCP may vary significantly from state rules, as will be discussed later in this chapter.

ested in taking on a new client, he will want to explain to the client the value of his services and those of his firm. Second, only an attorney can agree to represent a client. Third, only an attorney can set fees, and if Gilmore decides to take Baranski on as a client, fee arrangements will be discussed, and possibly agreed on, during the initial client interview. Finally, only an attorney can give legal advice, and the initial client interview may involve advising Baranski of her legal rights and options. In short, what transpires during the initial client interview normally falls under the umbrella of "the practice of law," and, as you read in Chapter 3, only attorneys are permitted to practice law.

Because attorney Gilmore and paralegal Lopez will be working together on the case, however, Gilmore will ask Lopez to sit in on the interview. Gilmore will want Lopez to meet Baranski, become familiar with Baranski's claim, and perhaps make arrangements for follow-up interviews with Baranski should Gilmore decide to take the case.

When a paralegal conducts an initial client interview, the paralegal must be constantly aware of the ethical pitfalls inherent in these situations. Suppose that attorney Gilmore is out of town but wants to obtain information about Baranski's legal matter as soon as possible. In this situation, he might ask Lopez to conduct an initial interview solely for the purposes of gaining information from Baranski about her claim. To avoid potential liability for the unauthorized practice of law, Lopez must be careful not to advise Baranski in regard to fees or her legal rights and obligations.

During the initial client interview, Katherine Baranski explains to attorney Gilmore and paralegal Lopez the facts of her case as she perceives them. Baranski tells them that Tony Peretto, who was driving a Dodge van, ran a stop sign and crashed into the driver's side of her Ford Tempo as she was driving through the intersection of Mattis Avenue and Thirty-eighth Street in Nita City, Nita. The accident occurred at 7:45 A.M. on August 4, 1995. Baranski has misplaced Peretto's address, but she knows that he lives in another state, the state of Zero.[3] Baranski claims that as a result of the accident, she has been unable to work for five months and has lost approximately $15,000 in wages. Her medical and hospital expenses total $85,000, and the property damage to her car is estimated to be $10,000.

Gilmore agrees to represent Baranski in the lawsuit against Peretto. He explains the fee structure to Baranski, and she signs the retainer agreement.[4] He also has Baranski sign forms authorizing Gilmore to obtain relevant medical, employment, and other records relating to the claim. (These forms, which are called *release forms,* will be discussed in Chapter 15.) At the end of the interview, Gilmore also asks Lopez to schedule a follow-up interview with Baranski. Lopez will conduct the follow-up interview and obtain more details from Baranski about the accident and its consequences.

ETHICAL CONCERN

The Unauthorized Practice of Law

If you know the answer to a question that a client, a friend, or some other person asks you, it is only natural to answer the question. Paralegals must be especially careful in this respect. Assume that attorney Gilmore is delayed in court and is late for the initial client interview with Baranski. While waiting for Gilmore, Baranski asks Gilmore's paralegal, Lopez, whether she thinks Baranski has a valid claim and what the likelihood is that Baranski will win in court. Based on what Baranski had told her earlier on the phone, Lopez tells Baranski that it sounds like she has a valid claim and very likely might win in court. Although Lopez has the best of intentions, she has engaged in the unauthorized practice of law because she has essentially given "legal advice"—advice pertaining to Baranski's legal rights or options. Although paralegals may give clients certain kinds of information, such as the date for an upcoming court hearing, they cannot give legal advice, as Lopez did in this instance.

Preliminary Investigation

After Baranski leaves the office, attorney Gilmore asks his paralegal, Lopez, to undertake a preliminary investigation to glean as much information as

3. Nita and Zero, are fictitious states invented for the purpose of this hypothetical.
4. See Chapter 5 for a discussion of legal fees and the form and function of the retainer agreement.

THE LEGAL TEAM AT WORK

Holding the Client's Many Hands

Although attorneys and paralegals may deal daily with legal procedures, clients often do not know what to expect when initiating a lawsuit or other legal proceeding. Also, many legal matters involve an emotional element for the client. Bankruptcy petitions, divorce actions, and probate procedures (dealing with the transfer of property upon death) may be particularly upsetting emotionally. To ease a client's frustrations and anxieties, legal practitioners have traditionally engaged in what is known as "hand-holding," or gently guiding the client through the various steps involved in litigation or other legal procedures. Unfortunately, as one attorney put it, "the client has eight hands, and I only have two." Teamwork provides a solution to this problem. The attorney's hands are joined by those of paralegals (and others on the project), and each team member can observe and respond to the client's needs for information, guidance, and support.

possible concerning the factual circumstances of Baranski's accident. Sources of this information will include the police report of the accident, medical records, employment data, and eyewitness accounts of the accident.

You will read in Chapter 15 about the steps that a paralegal, such as Lopez, can take when investigating the facts of a client's case, and therefore we will not discuss investigation here. Bear in mind, though, that at this point in the pretrial process, the paralegal may engage in extensive investigation. Legal investigation is an important part of pretrial work, and facts discovered (or not discovered) by the legal investigator may play an important role in determining the outcome of the lawsuit.

Creating the Litigation File

Attorney Gilmore also asks his paralegal, Lopez, to create a litigation file for the case. Lopez will ask the legal secretary to create the file, and Lopez will check it to make sure that such things as correspondence, bills, research and investigation results, and all documents and exhibits relating to the litigation are in the file and segregated in an organized manner.

Each law firm or legal department has its own specific organizational scheme to follow when creating and maintaining client files. Recall from Chapter 5 that the goal of any law-office filing system is threefold: to preserve confidentiality, to safeguard legal documents, and to ensure that the file contents can be easily and quickly retrieved when needed. Usually, it is the paralegal's responsibility to make sure that the litigation file is properly created and maintained. Lopez, for example, will periodically check the file to see that its contents are in order.

As a case progresses through the litigation process, subfiles may be created for documents relating to the various stages. For example, at this point in the Baranski case, the litigation file will contain notes taken during the initial client interview, the signed retainer agreement, and information and documents gathered by paralegal Lopez during her preliminary investigation

EXHIBIT 10.2
Types of Pleadings

Initial Pleadings

Complaint—Filed by the plaintiff to initiate the lawsuit.
Answer—Filed by the defendant in response to the plaintiff's complaint.

Counterclaim and Reply

Counterclaim—Filed by the defendant against the plaintiff, asserting a claim for an injury arising from the same incident that forms the basis for the plaintiff's claim. There are two types of counterclaims:

1. A *compulsory* counterclaim must be asserted if it arises out of the same transaction or event that gave rise to the plaintiff's complaint or the right to assert the claim will be waived (forgone). Example: Defendant Peretto claims that plaintiff Baranski's negligence caused him to suffer injuries for which he should be compensated.

2. A *permissive* counterclaim arises from a separate transaction than the one forming the basis for the original lawsuit. Example: Defendant Peretto claims that plaintiff Baranski, prior to the accident, had purchased a used Rolls-Royce from him, and Baranski's check bounced. If Peretto chooses not to raise this counterclaim, he would not be precluded from filing a separate suit against Baranski in the future to recover that debt because it arose from a completely separate incident.

Reply—Filed by the plaintiff in response to the defendant's counterclaim.

Cross-claim and Answer

Cross-claim—Filed by a defendant against another defendant or a plaintiff against another plaintiff. When cross-claims are made, the defendants are suing one another (or the plaintiffs are suing one another). Example: Assume that plaintiff Baranski had been struck by two vehicles, one belonging to defendant Peretto and one belonging to Leon Balfour. If Peretto and Balfour had been named as co-defendants in Baranski's complaint, then Peretto's attorney could also file a cross-claim on behalf of Peretto against Balfour.

Answer—Filed by the party against whom a cross-claim is brought.

Third Party Complaint and Answer

Third Party Complaint—Filed by the defendant (in response to the plaintiff's complaint) or by the plaintiff (in response to the defendant's counterclaim) to bring into the litigation a third party who could be liable. Example: Defendant Peretto files a third party complaint against the manufacturer of the van that he was driving. Peretto asserts that the manufacturer should be liable for Baranski's injuries because the van's brakes were defective and therefore Peretto was unable to stop at the stop sign.

Answer—Filed by the third party in response to the third party complaint.

The rules also differ from state to state and even from court to court within the same state. Lopez could obtain pleading forms, either from "form books" available in the law firm's files or library (or on computer) or from pleadings drafted previously in similar cases litigated by the firm in the court in which the Baranski case will be filed.

The Caption. All documents submitted to the court or other parties during the litigation process begin with a caption. The caption of the complaint

EXHIBIT 10.3
The Complaint

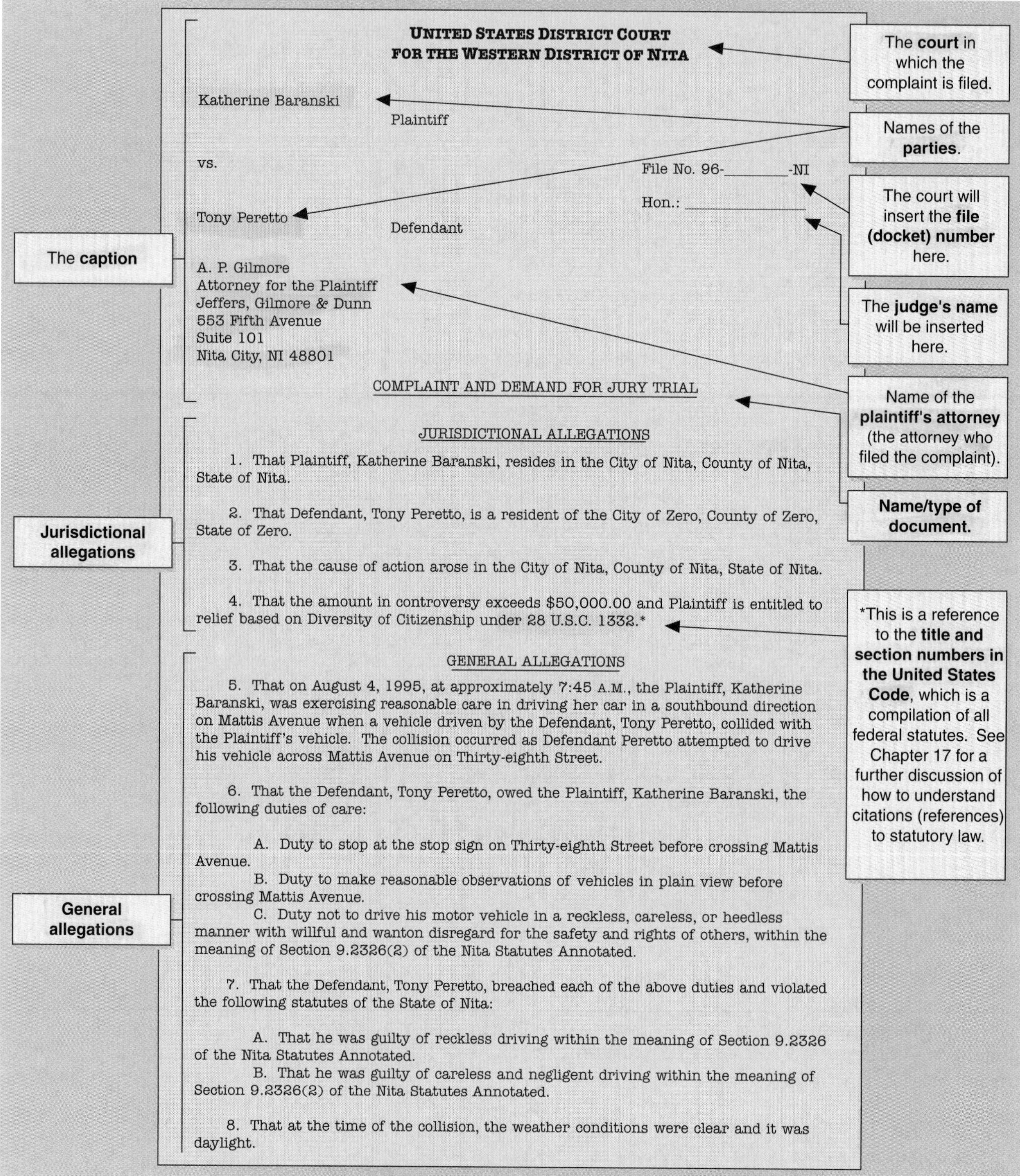

UNITED STATES DISTRICT COURT
FOR THE WESTERN DISTRICT OF NITA

Katherine Baranski
Plaintiff

vs.

File No. 96-________-NI

Hon.: ____________

Tony Peretto
Defendant

A. P. Gilmore
Attorney for the Plaintiff
Jeffers, Gilmore & Dunn
553 Fifth Avenue
Suite 101
Nita City, NI 48801

COMPLAINT AND DEMAND FOR JURY TRIAL

JURISDICTIONAL ALLEGATIONS

1. That Plaintiff, Katherine Baranski, resides in the City of Nita, County of Nita, State of Nita.

2. That Defendant, Tony Peretto, is a resident of the City of Zero, County of Zero, State of Zero.

3. That the cause of action arose in the City of Nita, County of Nita, State of Nita.

4. That the amount in controversy exceeds $50,000.00 and Plaintiff is entitled to relief based on Diversity of Citizenship under 28 U.S.C. 1332.*

GENERAL ALLEGATIONS

5. That on August 4, 1995, at approximately 7:45 A.M., the Plaintiff, Katherine Baranski, was exercising reasonable care in driving her car in a southbound direction on Mattis Avenue when a vehicle driven by the Defendant, Tony Peretto, collided with the Plaintiff's vehicle. The collision occurred as Defendant Peretto attempted to drive his vehicle across Mattis Avenue on Thirty-eighth Street.

6. That the Defendant, Tony Peretto, owed the Plaintiff, Katherine Baranski, the following duties of care:

A. Duty to stop at the stop sign on Thirty-eighth Street before crossing Mattis Avenue.
B. Duty to make reasonable observations of vehicles in plain view before crossing Mattis Avenue.
C. Duty not to drive his motor vehicle in a reckless, careless, or heedless manner with willful and wanton disregard for the safety and rights of others, within the meaning of Section 9.2326(2) of the Nita Statutes Annotated.

7. That the Defendant, Tony Peretto, breached each of the above duties and violated the following statutes of the State of Nita:

A. That he was guilty of reckless driving within the meaning of Section 9.2326 of the Nita Statutes Annotated.
B. That he was guilty of careless and negligent driving within the meaning of Section 9.2326(2) of the Nita Statutes Annotated.

8. That at the time of the collision, the weather conditions were clear and it was daylight.

The court in which the complaint is filed.
Names of the parties.
The court will insert the file (docket) number here.
The judge's name will be inserted here.
Name of the plaintiff's attorney (the attorney who filed the complaint).
Name/type of document.
*This is a reference to the title and section numbers in the United States Code, which is a compilation of all federal statutes. See Chapter 17 for a further discussion of how to understand citations (references) to statutory law.
The caption
Jurisdictional allegations
General allegations

9. That at the time of the collision, the Plaintiff, Katherine Baranski, was a generally healthy female, twenty-five years of age.

10. That as a result of the collision, the Plaintiff, Katherine Baranski, suffered severe physical injuries, which prevented her from working for five months, and property damage to her vehicle. The costs that the Plaintiff, Katherine Baranski, incurred as a result of the collision included $85,000 in medical bills, $15,000 in lost wages, and $10,000 in automobile-repair costs.

11. That the injuries sustained by the Plaintiff as a result of the collision were solely caused by the negligence of the Defendant, Tony Peretto.

The **prayer for relief**.

WHEREFORE, the Plaintiff prays for the following relief:

A. That the Plaintiff be awarded appropriate compensatory damages;

B. That the Plaintiff be awarded an amount deemed fair and just by a Jury to compensate the Plaintiff for damages sustained as presented by the evidence in this case;

C. That the Plaintiff be awarded such other further relief as the Court deems proper. Plaintiff Katherine Baranski claims judgment against the Defendant in an amount in excess of $50,000 in actual, compensatory, and exemplary damages together with attorneys' fees, court costs, and other costs as provided by law.

The **signature** of the plaintiff's attorney.

Date: 2/10/96

Jeffers, Gilmore & Dunn
Allen P. Gilmore
Allen P. Gilmore
Attorney for Plaintiff
553 Fifth Avenue
Suite 101
Nita City, NI 48801

Affidavit (and plaintiff's signature).

Katherine Baranski, being first duly sworn, states that she has read the foregoing Complaint by her subscribed and that she knows the contents thereof, and the same is true, except those matters therein stated to be upon information and belief, and as to those matters, she believes to be true.

Katherine Baranski
Plaintiff

Sworn and subscribed before me this 10th day of February, 1996.

Leela M Shay
Notary Public, Nita County,
State of Nita

My Commission Expires:
March 10, 1999

Demand for a jury trial.

DEMAND FOR A JURY TRIAL

The Plaintiff demands a trial by jury.

Date: 2/10/96

Jeffers, Gilmore & Dunn
Allen P. Gilmore
Allen P. Gilmore
Attorney for the Plaintiff
553 Fifth Avenue
Suite 101
Nita City, Nita 48801

identifies the court in which the action is being filed, the names of the parties, and the designation of the document as a "Complaint." The caption leaves a space for the court to insert the name of the judge who will be hearing the case. The caption also leaves a space for the court to insert the file number, or case number, that it assigns to the case. (The court's file number may also be referred to as the *docket number.* A **docket** is the list of cases entered on a court's calendar and thus scheduled to be heard.) Exhibit 10.3 shows how the caption will read in the case of *Baranski v. Peretto.*

DOCKET
The list of cases entered on a court's calendar and thus scheduled to be heard by the court.

Jurisdictional Allegations. Because attorney Gilmore is filing the lawsuit in a federal district court, he will have to include in the complaint an allegation that the federal court has jurisdiction to hear the dispute. (An **allegation** is an assertion, claim, or statement made by one party in a pleading that sets out what the party expects to prove to the court.) Recall from Chapter 7 that federal courts can exercise jurisdiction over disputes involving either a *federal question* or *diversity of citizenship.* A federal question arises whenever a claim in a civil lawsuit relates to a federal law, the U.S. Constitution, or a treaty executed by the U.S. government. Diversity of citizenship exists when the parties involved in the lawsuit are citizens of different states and the amount in controversy exceeds $50,000. Because Baranski and Peretto are citizens of different states (Nita and Zero, respectively) and because the amount in controversy exceeds $50,000, the case meets the requirements for diversity-of-citizenship jurisdiction. Gilmore thus asserts that the federal court has jurisdiction on this basis, as illustrated in Exhibit 10.3.

ALLEGATION
A party's statement, claim, or assertion made in a pleading to the court. The allegation sets forth the issue that the party expects to prove.

As explained in Chapter 7, certain matters—such as those involving patent or copyright disputes, the Internal Revenue Service, or bankruptcy—can *only* be brought in federal courts. Certain cases, however, including those involving diversity of citizenship, may be brought in either a state court or a federal court. Thus, an attorney in Gilmore's position can advise the client that he or she has a choice. Gilmore probably considered several factors when advising Baranski on which court would be preferable for her lawsuit. An important consideration is how long it would take to get the case to trial. Many courts are overburdened by their caseloads, and sometimes it can take years before a court will be able to hear a case. If Gilmore knows that the case could be heard two years earlier in the federal court than in the state court, that will be an important factor to consider.

General Allegations (the Body of the Complaint). The body of the complaint contains a series of allegations, stated in numbered paragraphs. In plaintiff Baranski's complaint, the allegations outline the factual events that gave rise to Baranski's claims.[6] The events are described in a series of chronologically arranged, numbered allegations so that the reader can understand

6. The body of the complaint described in this section is a *fact pleading,* in which sufficient factual circumstances must be alleged to convince the court that the plaintiff has a cause of action. State courts often require fact pleadings, whereas federal courts only require *notice pleading.* FRCP 8(a) requires only that the complaint have "a short and plain statement of the claim showing that the pleader is entitled to relief." Fact pleading and notice pleading are not totally different—that is, the same allegation of facts could be in the body of a complaint submitted to either a federal or a state court. Federal courts simply have fewer requirements in this respect, and therefore they are often more attractive to litigants.

them easily. As Exhibit 10.3 shows, the numbers of the paragraphs in the body of the complaint continue the sequence begun in the section on jurisdictional allegations.

When drafting the complaint, paralegal Lopez will play the role of advocate. She must present the facts forcefully and in a way that supports and strengthens the client's claim. The recitation of the facts should demonstrate that defendant Peretto had engaged in conduct that entitles plaintiff Baranski to relief. Even though she will want to present the facts in a light most favorable to Baranski, Lopez must be careful not to exaggerate the facts or make false statements. Rather, she must present the facts in such a way that the reader could reasonably infer that defendant Peretto was negligent and that his negligence caused Baranski's injuries and losses.

What if her research into the case had given Lopez reason to believe that a fact was probably true even though she could not be certain as to its validity? She could still include the statement in the complaint by prefacing it with the phrase, "On information and belief. . . ." This language would indicate to the court that the plaintiff, Baranski, had good reason to believe the truth of the statement but that the evidence for it either had not yet been obtained or might not hold up under close scrutiny.

The most effective complaints are those that are clear and concise. Moreover, brevity and simplicity are required under FRCP 8(a). As in all legal writing, Lopez should strive for clarity. When drafting the complaint, Lopez should use clear language and favor simple and direct statements over more complex sentences. This is because the court may, at the request of opposing counsel, strike (delete) from the complaint ambiguous phrases—phrases whose meaning is unclear or that may be interpreted in more than one way. Lopez should also resist the temptation to include facts that are not absolutely necessary for the complaint. By reducing the body of the complaint to the simplest possible terms, Lopez will not only achieve greater clarity but also minimize the possibility of divulging attorney Gilmore's trial strategies or hinting at a possible defense that the opponent might use to defeat the claim.

After telling plaintiff Baranski's story, paralegal Lopez will add one or more paragraphs outlining the harms suffered by the plaintiff and the remedy (in money damages) that the plaintiff seeks. In general, it is preferable that all allegations of damages—such as hospital costs, lost wages, and auto-repair expenses—be included in a single paragraph, as in Exhibit 10.3. Lopez should check the relevant court rules, however, to see whether the court requires that certain types of damages (Baranski's lost wages, for example) must be alleged in a separate paragraph.

Prayer for Relief. Paralegal Lopez will include at the end of the complaint a paragraph, similar to that shown in Exhibit 10.3, asking that judgment be entered for the plaintiff and appropriate relief be granted. This **prayer for relief** will indicate that plaintiff Baranski is seeking money damages to compensate her for the harms that she suffered.

Prayer for Relief
A statement at the end of the complaint requesting that the court grant relief to the plaintiff.

Signature. In federal practice, the signature following the prayer for relief certifies that the plaintiff's attorney (or the plaintiff, if he or she is not represented by an attorney) has read the complaint and that the facts alleged are true to the best of his or her knowledge. In addition to the attorney's signature, some courts require an affidavit signed by the plaintiff verifying that the complaint is true to the best of the plaintiff's knowledge. **Affidavits** are sworn statements attesting to the existence of certain facts. They are acknowledged by a notary public or another official authorized to administer such oaths or affirmations. Exhibit 10.3 illustrates an affidavit for the Baranski complaint.

AFFIDAVIT
A written statement of facts, confirmed by the oath or affirmation of the party making it and made before a person having the authority to administer the oath or affirmation.

Demand for a Jury Trial. A trial can be held with or without a jury. If there is no jury, the judge determines the truth of the facts alleged in the case. The Seventh Amendment to the U.S. Constitution guarantees the right to a jury trial in federal courts in all "suits at common law" when the amount in controversy exceeds $20. Most states have similar guarantees in their own constitutions, although many states put a higher minimum dollar restriction on the guarantee (for example, in Iowa the minimum amount is $1,000). If this threshold requirement is met, either party may request a jury trial.

The right to a trial by jury does not have to be exercised, and many cases are tried without one. In most states and in federal courts, one of the parties must request a jury or the right is presumed to be waived (that is, the court will presume that neither party wanted a jury trial). The decision to exercise the right to a jury trial usually depends on what legal theory the party is using and which judge is assigned to the trial. In the Baranski case, plaintiff Baranski's attorney, Gilmore, may advise Baranski to demand a jury trial if he believes that a jury would be sympathetic to Baranski's position. If plaintiff Baranski wants a jury trial, Gilmore will ask his paralegal, Lopez, to include a demand for jury trial (similar to the one illustrated in Exhibit 10.3) with the complaint.

Filing the Complaint

Once the complaint has been prepared, carefully checked for accuracy, and signed by attorney Gilmore, paralegal Lopez will file the complaint with the court in which the action is being brought. To file the complaint, Lopez will deliver it to the clerk of the court, together with a check payable to the court in the amount of the required filing fee. (If Lopez is not aware of the court's specific procedures for filing the complaint, she should call the court clerk to verify the amount of the filing fee and how many copies of the complaint need to be filed.) The court clerk files the complaint by stamping the date on the document; assigning the case a file number, or docket number; and assigning the case to a particular judge. (In state courts, the file number may not be assigned until later.)

Although the complaint is normally delivered personally to the court clerk, the 1993 revision of Rule 5(a) of the FRCP provides that federal courts may permit filing by fax (facsimile) or "other electronic means." In the future, filing court documents electronically will likely become a more common method of filing.

SCHEDULING CONFERENCE
A meeting (conducted shortly after a plaintiff's complaint is filed) attended by the judge and the attorneys for both parties to the lawsuit. Following the conference, the judge issues a scheduling order for the pretrial events and the trial date.

After the complaint has been filed, the court will consult with the attorneys for both sides, often through a **scheduling conference**. Following this meeting, the judge will enter a *scheduling order* that sets out the time limits

DEVELOPING PARALEGAL SKILLS

Federal Court Rules—Creating a Complaint Checklist

Ann Marsdon, a paralegal, has been assigned the task of preparing a checklist for drafting complaints to be filed in federal court. The checklist will be used by the other paralegals and lawyers in her medium-sized law firm. She will base her checklist on Rules 8, 10, and 11 of the Federal Rules of Civil Procedure (FRCP), which specify the kind of information that should be included in complaints filed in federal courts.

COMPLAINT CHECKLIST

Ann begins her task by making a list of all the things that she does before she sits down to draft a complaint:

- Get the file and review my notes and memos from the client interview or use whatever notes are in the file.
- Check the date on which the injury or other action that harmed the plaintiff occurred and find out when the statute of limitations expires.
- Review any reports—such as police reports, insurance investigators' reports, or other similar documents—in the file. This information is necessary to describe how and when the injury occurred.
- Find out the plaintiff's and the defendant's correct legal names. Contact the secretary of state to obtain the legal name of a defendant corporation.
- Look for notes that may indicate in which court the complaint will be filed. If that information is not included, discuss the issue with the attorney.
- Obtain the appropriate complaint form for the type of case involved from either the forms file or a forms book.
- Review the court rules of the court in which the complaint will be filed to ensure that we comply with that court's requirements for the complaint.

REVIEWING THE RULES

Ann pulls a copy of the FRCP off her bookshelf to review the complaint requirements. She reads through Rule 8, which tells her that a complaint has to contain a statement showing that the court has jurisdiction over the case, another statement showing that the plaintiff is entitled to the damages or other relief for which he or she is asking, and a demand for a judgment for that relief. Ann then looks at Rule 10, which outlines the format for a complaint.

Rule 11 says that the complaint must be signed by an attorney, if the plaintiff is represented by one. This is interesting, thinks Ann. It says here that the attorney's signature means that the attorney has read the complaint and that to the best of the attorney's "knowledge, information and belief, formed after an inquiry reasonable under the circumstances," the allegations (claims, or contentions) of fact can be supported by evidence, are warranted by existing law, and are not being used for an improper purpose, such as to harass or delay. If a complaint is signed in violation of these rules, sanctions may be imposed. After reading through Rule 11, Ann continues drafting her checklist and includes in it the requirements for a complaint under the FRCP.

within which pretrial events (such as the pleadings, discovery, and the final pretrial conference) must be completed and the date of the trial. Under FRCP 16(b), the scheduling order should be entered "as soon as practicable and in no event more than 120 days after the complaint is filed."

Service of Process

SERVICE OF PROCESS
The delivery of the summons and the complaint to a defendant.

SUMMONS
A document served on a defendant in a lawsuit informing a defendant that a legal action has been commenced against the defendant and that the defendant must appear in court on a certain date to answer the plaintiff's complaint.

Before the court can exercise jurisdiction over the defendant—in effect, before the lawsuit can begin—the court must have proof that the defendant was notified of the lawsuit. If defendant Peretto did not agree to *waive* service of process (waiver of service will be discussed below) or if the case against Peretto had been filed in a state court, Peretto would be served with a summons. Serving the summons and complaint—that is, the delivery of these documents to the defendant in a lawsuit—is referred to as **service of process**.

The Summons. The **summons** identifies the parties to the lawsuit, as well as the court in which the case will be heard, and directs the defendant to respond to the complaint within a specified period of time. In the Baranski case, paralegal Lopez, will prepare a summons by filling out a form similar to that shown in Exhibit 10.4. Lopez will also prepare a cover sheet for the case, which is required in the federal courts and in most state courts. A sample cover sheet is shown in Exhibit 10.5 on page 384.

If the case were being brought in a state court, paralegal Lopez would deliver the summons to the court clerk at the same time she delivered the complaint. (In federal court cases, as will be discussed below, the complaint may already have been filed under the new FRCP provisions relating to waiver of notice.) After the clerk files the complaint and signs, seals, and issues the summons, attorney Gilmore will be responsible for making sure that the documents are served on defendant Peretto. The service of the complaint and summons must be effected within a specified time—120 days under FRCP 4(m)—after the complaint has been filed.

Serving the Complaint and Summons. How service of process occurs depends on the rules of the court or jurisdiction in which the lawsuit is brought. Under FRCP 4(c)(2), service of process in federal court cases may be effected "by any person who is not a party and who is at least 18 years of age." Paralegal Lopez, for example, could serve the summons by personally delivering it to defendant Peretto or leaving it at his home or with someone living in his home. Alternatively, she could make arrangements for someone else to do so, subject to the approval of attorney Gilmore. In some types of cases, Gilmore might request that the court have a U.S. marshal or other federal official serve the summons.

Under FRCP 4(e)(1), service of process in federal court cases may also be effected "pursuant to the law of the state in which the district court is located." Many state courts require that the complaint and summons be served by a public officer, such as a sheriff.

Regardless of how the summons is served, attorney Gilmore will need some kind of proof that defendant Peretto actually received the summons. In federal court cases, unless service is made by a U.S. marshal or other official,

EXHIBIT 10.4
A Summons in a Civil Action

United States District Court

WESTERN DISTRICT OF NITA

Katherine Baranski

V.

Tony Peretto

SUMMONS IN A CIVIL ACTION

CASE NUMBER:

TO:

Tony Peretto
1708 Johnston Drive
Zero City, ZE 59806

YOU ARE HEREBY SUMMONED and required to file with the Clerk of this Court and serve upon

PLAINTIFF'S ATTORNEY
Allen P. Gilmore
Jeffers, Gilmore & Dunn
553 Fifth Avenue
Suite 101
Nita City, NI 48801

an answer to the complaint which is herewith served upon you, within 20 days after service of this summons upon you, exclusive of the day of service. If you fail to do so, judgment by default will be taken against you for the relief demanded in the complaint.

C. H. Hynek
CLERK

February 10, 1996
DATE

John Dolan
BY DEPUTY CLERK

proof of service can be established by having the process server fill out and sign a form similar to the **return-of-service form** shown in Exhibit 10.6 on page 385. This form can then be submitted to the court as evidence that service has been effected.

RETURN-OF-SERVICE FORM
A document signed by a process server and submitted to the court to prove that a defendant received a summons.

Paralegal Lopez must be very careful to comply with the service requirements of the court in which plaintiff Baranski's suit has been filed. If service is not properly made, defendant Peretto will have a legal ground (basis) for asking the court to dismiss the case against him, thus delaying the litigation. As mentioned earlier, the court will not be able to exercise jurisdiction over Peretto until he has been properly notified of the lawsuit being brought against him.

EXHIBIT 10.5
A Federal Civil Cover Sheet

JS 44
(Rev. 07/86)

CIVIL COVER SHEET

The JS 44 civil cover sheet and the information contained herein neither replace nor supplement the filing and service of pleadings or other papers as required by law, except as provided by local rules of court. This form, approved by the Judicial Conference of the United States in September 1974, is required for the use of the Clerk of Court for the purpose of initiating the civil docket sheet. (SEE INSTRUCTIONS ON THE REVERSE OF THE FORM.)

I. (a) PLAINTIFFS
Katherine Baranski

(b) COUNTY OF RESIDENCE OF FIRST LISTED PLAINTIFF Nita
(EXCEPT IN U.S. PLAINTIFF CASES)

DEFENDANTS
Tony Peretto

COUNTY OF RESIDENCE OF FIRST LISTED DEFENDANT Zero
(IN U.S. PLAINTIFF CASES ONLY)
NOTE: IN LAND CONDEMNATION CASES, USE THE LOCATION OF THE TRACT OF LAND INVOLVED

(c) ATTORNEYS (FIRM NAME, ADDRESS, AND TELEPHONE NUMBER)
Allen P. Gilmore
Jeffers, Gilmore & Dunn
553 Fifth Avenue, Suite 101
Nita City, NI 48801

ATTORNEYS (IF KNOWN)

II. BASIS OF JURISDICTION (PLACE AN X IN ONE BOX ONLY)

☐ **1 U.S. Government Plaintiff**
☐ **3 Federal Question** (U.S. Government Not a Party)
☐ **2 U.S. Government Defendant**
☒ **4 Diversity** (Includes Citizenship of Parties in Item III)

III. CITIZENSHIP OF PRINCIPAL PARTIES (For Diversity Cases Only) (PLACE AN X IN ONE BOX FOR PLAINTIFF AND ONE BOX FOR DEFENDANT)

	PTF	DEF		PTF	DEF
Citizen of This State	☒ 1	☐ 1	**Incorporated *or* Principal Place of Business in This State**	☐ 4	☐ 4
Citizen of Another State	☐ 2	☒ 2	**Incorporated *and* Principal Place of Business in Another State**	☐ 5	☐ 5
Citizen of Subject of a Foreign Country	☐ 3	☐ 3	**Foreign Nation**	☐ 6	☐ 6

IV. CAUSE OF ACTION (CITE THE U.S. CIVIL STATUTE UNDER WHICH YOU ARE FILING AND WRITE A BRIEF STATEMENT OF CAUSE. DO NOT CITE JURISDICTIONAL STATUTES UNLESS DIVERSITY.)
28 U.S.C. 1332. Action for damages caused by negligent operation of motor vehicle.

V. NATURE OF SUIT *(PLACE AN X IN ONE BOX ONLY)*

CONTRACT
❑ **110** Insurance
❑ **120** Marine
❑ **130** Miller Act
❑ **140** Negotiable Instrument
❑ **150** Recovery of Overpayment & Enforcement of Judgment
❑ **151** Medicare Act
❑ **152** Recovery of Defaulted Student Loans
❑ **153** Recovery of Overpayment of Veteran's Benefits
❑ **160** Stockholders' Suits
❑ **190** Other Contract
❑ **195** Contract Product Liability

REAL PROPERTY
❑ **210** Land Condemnation
❑ **220** Foreclosure
❑ **230** Rent Lease & Ejectment
❑ **240** Torts to Land
❑ **245** Tort Product Liability
❑ **290** All Other Real Property

TORTS

PERSONAL INJURY
❑ **310** Insurance
❑ **315** Airplane Product Liability
❑ **320** Assault, Libel & Slander
❑ **330** Federal Employers' Liability
❑ **340** Marine
❑ **345** Marine Product Liability
❑ **350** Motor Vehicle
☒ **355** Motor Vehicle Product Liability
❑ **360** Other Personal Injury

PERSONAL INJURY
❑ **362** Personal Injury -- Med Malpractice
❑ **365** Personal Injury-- Product Liability
❑ **368** Asbestos Personal Injury Product Liability

PERSONAL PROPERTY
❑ **370** Other Fraud
❑ **371** Truth in Lending
❑ **380** Other Personal Property Damage
❑ **385** Property Damage Product Liability

CIVIL RIGHTS
❑ **441** Voting
❑ **442** Employment
❑ **443** Housing/ Accommodations
❑ **444** Welfare
❑ **440** Other Civil Rights

PRISONER PETITIONS
❑ **510** Motions to Vacate Sentence
❑ **530** Habeas Corpus
❑ **540** Mandamus & Other
❑ **550** Civil Rights

FORFEITURE/PENALTY
❑ **610** Agriculture
❑ **620** Food & Drug
❑ **630** Liquor Laws
❑ **640** R.R. & Truck
❑ **650** Airline Regs
❑ **660** Occupational Safety/Health
❑ **690** Other

LABOR
❑ **710** Fair Labor Standards Act
❑ **720** Labor/Mgmt. Relations
❑ **730** Labor/Mgmt. Reporting & Disclosure Act
❑ **740** Railway Labor Act
❑ **790** Other Labor Litigation
❑ **791** Empl. Ret. Inc. Security Act

BANKRUPTCY
❑ **422** Appeal 28 USC 158
❑ **423** Withdrawal 28 USC 157

PROPERTY RIGHTS
❑ **820** Copyrights
❑ **830** Patent
❑ **840** Trademark

SOCIAL SECURITY
❑ **861** HIA (1395ff)
❑ **862** Black Lung (923)
❑ **863** DIWC (405(g))
❑ **863** DIWW (405(g))
❑ **864** SSID Title XVI
❑ **865** RSI (405(g))

FEDERAL TAX SUITS
❑ **870** Taxes (U.S. Plaintiff or Defendant)
❑ **871** IRS - Third party 26 USC 7609

OTHER STATUTES
❑ **400** State Reapportionment
❑ **410** Antitrust
❑ **430** Banks and Banking
❑ **450** Commerce/ICC Rates/etc.
❑ **460** Deportation
❑ **470** Racketeer Influenced and Corrupt Organizations
❑ **810** Selective Service
❑ **850** Securities/Commodities/ Exchange
❑ **875** Customer Challenge 12 USC 3410
❑ **891** Agricultural Acts
❑ **892** Economic Stabilization
❑ **893** Environmental Matters
❑ **894** Energy Allocation Act
❑ **895** Freedom of Information Act
❑ **900** Appeal of Fee Determination Under Equal Access to Justice
❑ **950** Constitutionality of State Statutes
❑ **890** Other Statutory Actions

VI. ORIGIN *(PLACE AN X IN ONE BOX ONLY)*

☒ 1 Original Proceeding ☐ 2 Removed from State Court ☐ 3 Remanded from Appellate Court ☐ 4 Reinstated or Reopened ☐ 5 Transferred from another district (specify) ☐ 6 Multidistrict Litigation ☐ 7 Appeal to District Judge from Magistrate Judgment

VII. REQUESTED IN COMPLAINT: ☐ CHECK IF THIS IS A **CLASS ACTION** UNDER F.R.C.P. 23
DEMAND $ Excess of $50,000
Check YES only if demanded in complaint:
JURY DEMAND: ☒ YES ☐ NO

VII. RELATED CASE(S) (See Instructions) **IF ANY**
JUDGE________ DOCKET NUMBER________

DATE 2/10/96
SIGNATURE OF ATTORNEY OF RECORD Allen P. Gilmore

UNITED STATES DISTRICT COURT

EXHIBIT 10.6
A Return-of-Service Form

AO 440 (Rev. 5/85) Summons in a Civil Action

RETURN OF SERVICE

Service of the Summons and Complaint was made by me[1]	DATE 2/11/96
NAME OF SERVER Elena Lopez	TITLE Paralegal

Check one box below to indicate appropriate method of service

☒ Served personally upon the defendant. Place where served: Defendant Peretto's Home: 1708 Johnston Drive, Zero City, Zero 59806

☐ Left copies thereof at the defendant's dwelling house or usual place of abode with a person of suitable age and discretion then residing therein.
Name of person with whom the summons and complaint were left: ______

☐ Returned unexecuted: ______

☐ Other (specify): ______

STATEMENT OF SERVICE FEES

TRAVEL	SERVICES	TOTAL
40 miles @ 25¢/mile	1 hour @ $25/hour	$35.00

DECLARATION OF SERVER

I declare under penalty of perjury under the laws of the United States of America that the foregoing information contained in the Return of Service and Statement of Service Fees is true and correct.

Executed on 2/11/96 (*Date*) — Elena Lopez (*Signature of Server*)

308 University Avenue, Nita City, Nita 48804
Address of Server

1) As to who may serve a summons see Rule 4 of the Federal Rules of Civil Procedure.

Serving Corporate Defendants. In cases involving corporate defendants, the summons and complaint may be served on an officer or *registered agent* (representative) of the corporation. The name of a corporation's registered agent is usually obtainable from the secretary of state's office in the state in which the company incorporated its business (and, usually, the secretary of state's office in any state in which the corporation does business).

Finding the Defendant. Because some defendants may be difficult to locate, paralegals sometimes have to investigate and attempt to locate a defendant so that process may be served. Information sources that may be consulted to help locate a defendant include telephone directories, banks, former business partners or fellow workers, credit bureaus, Social Security offices, insurance companies, landlords, state and county tax rolls, utility companies, automobile-registration bureaus, bureaus of vital statistics, and the post office. (Chapter 15 discusses these and other possible sources that the paralegal might consult when trying to locate parties or witnesses involved in lawsuits.)

Notice and Waiver of Service—FRCP 4(d)

The 1993 revision of the FRCP added Rule 4(d), which allows for a simpler and less costly alternative to service of process. Under this rule, a plaintiff's attorney is permitted to notify the defendant directly, through the mails or "other reliable means," of the lawsuit. After the complaint has been filed, attorney Gilmore will thus probably ask paralegal Lopez to follow the procedures outlined in FRCP 4(d).

To comply with FRCP 4(d), Lopez will need to fill out two forms. Form 1A, which is shown in Exhibit 10.7, is entitled "Notice of Lawsuit and Request for Waiver of Service of Summons." This form, which must be signed by attorney Gilmore, requests defendant Peretto to waive the requirement that he be notified of the lawsuit by having a summons served on him. Next, Lopez will fill out Form 1B, entitled "Waiver of Service of Summons." Exhibit 10.8 on page 388 indicates the information that must be included in this form. Once these forms are filled out and attorney Gilmore has reviewed and signed them, paralegal Lopez will send to defendant Peretto a packet containing the following contents:

- Two copies each of Form 1A and Form 1B.
- A copy of the complaint.
- An addressed, stamped envelope for defendant Peretto to use when returning Form 1B.

If defendant Peretto agrees to waive service of process, he will need to sign and return the waiver to attorney Gilmore within thirty days after the waiver form was sent by Gilmore. (For defendants located in a foreign country, the time period is extended to sixty days.)

The aim of FRCP 4(d) is to eliminate the costs associated with service of process and to foster cooperation among adversaries. To encourage defendants to agree to the waiver of service, FRCP 4(d)(3) provides that defendants

EXHIBIT 10.7
Form 1A—Notice of Lawsuit and Request for Waiver of Service of Summons

TO: ______________(A)______________
[as ____(B)____ of ____(C)____]

A lawsuit has been commenced against you (or the entity on whose behalf you are addressed). A copy of the complaint is attached to this notice. It has been filed in the United States District Court for the ____(D)____ and has been assigned docket number____(E)____.

This is not a formal summons or notification from the court, but rather my request that you sign and return the enclosed waiver of service in order to save the cost of serving you with a judicial summons and an additional copy of the complaint. The cost of service will be avoided if I receive a signed copy of the waiver within____(F)____days after the date designated below as the date on which this Notice and Request is sent. I enclose a stamped and addressed envelope (or other means of cost-free return) for your use. An extra copy of the waiver is also attached for your records.

If you comply with this request and return the signed waiver, it will be filed with the court and no summons will be served on you. The action will then proceed as if you had been served on the date the waiver is filed, except that you will not be obligated to answer the complaint before 60 days from the date designated below as the date on which this notice is sent (or before 90 days from that date if your address is not in any judicial district of the United States).

If you do not return the signed waiver within the time indicated, I will take appropriate steps to effect formal service in a manner authorized by the Federal Rules of Civil Procedure and will then, to the extent authorized by those Rules, ask the court to require you (or the party on whose behalf you are addressed) to pay the full costs of such service. In that connection please read the statement concerning the duty of parties to waive the service of the summons, which is set forth on the reverse side (or at the foot) of the waiver form.

I affirm that this request is being sent to you on behalf of the plaintiff, this__________day of____ ,___.

____
Signature of Plaintiff's Attorney or
Unrepresented Plaintiff

Notes:
A-Name of individual (or name of officer or agent of corporate defendant)
B-Title, or other relationship of individual to corporate defendant
C-Name of corporate defendant, if any
D-District
E-Docket number of action
F-Addressee must be given at least 30 days (60 days if located in foreign country) in which to return waiver

who return the required waiver are not required to respond to the complaint for sixty days (ninety days for defendants outside the United States) after the date on which the request for waiver of service was sent. In contrast, if a defendant does not agree to waive service and a complaint and summons must be served, then (under FRCP 12) the defendant must respond to the complaint within twenty days after process is served.

The Defendant's Response

Once a defendant receives the plaintiff's complaint, either via mail or through service of process, the defendant must respond to the complaint within a specified time period (in federal cases, within the time periods specified above). If the defendant fails to respond within that time period, the

EXHIBIT 10.8
Form 1B—Waiver of Service of Summons

TO: (name of plaintiff's attorney or unrepresented plaintiff)

I acknowledge receipt of your request that I waive service of a summons in the action of (caption of action), which is case number (docket number) in the United States District Court for the (district). I have also received a copy of the complaint in the action, two copies of this instrument, and a means by which I can return the signed waiver to you without cost to me.

I agree to save the cost of service of a summons and an additional copy of the complaint in this lawsuit by not requiring that I (or the entity on whose behalf I am acting) be served with judicial process in the manner provided by Rule 4.

I (or the entity on whose behalf I am acting) will retain all defenses or objections to the lawsuit or to the jurisdiction or venue of the court except for objections based on a defect in the summons or in the service of the summons.

I understand that a judgment may be entered against me (or the party on whose behalf I am acting) if an answer or motion under Rule 12 is not served upon you within 60 days after (date request was sent), or within 90 days after that date if the request was sent outside the United States.

Date

Signature ____________
Printed/typed name: ____________
[as ____________]
[of ____________]

To be printed on foot of or on reverse side of form:

DUTY TO AVOID UNNECESSARY COSTS OF SERVICE OF SUMMONS

Rule 4 of the Federal Rules of Civil Procedure requires parties to cooperate in saving unnecessary costs of service of the summons and complaint. A defendant located in the United States, who, after being notified of an action and asked by a plaintiff located in the United States to waive service of a summons, fails to do so will be required to bear the cost of such service unless good cause be shown for its failure to sign and return the waiver.

It is not good cause for a failure to waive service that a party believes that the complaint is unfounded, or that the action has been brought in an improper place or in a court that lacks jurisdiction over the subject matter of the action or over its person or property. A party who waives service of the summons retains all defenses and objections (except any relating to the summons or to the service of the summons), and may later object to the jurisdiction of the court or to the place where the action has been brought.

A defendant who waives service must within the time specified on the waiver form serve on the plaintiff's attorney (or unrepresented plaintiff) a response to the complaint and must also file a signed copy of the response with the court. If the answer or motion is not served within this time, a default judgment may be taken against that defendant. By waiving service, a defendant is allowed more time to answer than if the summons had been actually served when the request for waiver of service was received.

DEFAULT JUDGMENT
A judgment entered by a clerk or court against a party who has failed to appear in court to answer or defend against a claim that has been brought against him or her by another party.

court, on the plaintiff's motion, will enter a **default judgment** against the defendant. The defendant will then be liable for the entire amount of damages that the plaintiff is claiming and will lose the opportunity to either defend against the claim in court or settle the issue with the plaintiff out of court.

In the Baranski case, assume that defendant Peretto consults with an attorney, Elizabeth A. Cameron, to decide on a course of action. Before Cameron advises Peretto on the matter, she will want to investigate plaintiff Baranski's claim and obtain evidence of what happened at the time of the accident. She may ask her paralegal, Gordon McVay, to call anyone who may have witnessed the accident and any police officers who were at the scene. Attorney Cameron will also ask McVay to gather relevant documents, including the traffic ticket that Peretto received at the time of the accident and any reports that might have been filed by the police. If all goes well, attorney Cameron and paralegal McVay will complete their investigation in a few days and then meet to assess the results.

As mentioned earlier, most cases are settled out of court before they go to trial. But even if Peretto's attorney suspects that an out-of-court settlement might be financially preferable to a trial, she will still draft a response to plaintiff Baranski's claim. She knows that if defendant Peretto does not respond to the plaintiff's complaint within the proper time period, the court will enter a default judgment against Peretto. In deciding how best to respond to the complaint, Peretto's attorney, Cameron, must consider whether to file an answer or a motion to dismiss the case.

CASE AT A GLANCE

The Plaintiff—
Plaintiff: Katherine Baranski
Attorney: Allen P. Gilmore
Paralegal: Elena Lopez

The Defendant—
Defendant: Tony Peretto
Attorney: Elizabeth A. Cameron
Paralegal: Gordon McVay

The Answer. A defendant's **answer** must respond to each allegation in the plaintiff's complaint. FRCP 8(b) permits the defendant to admit or deny the truth of each allegation. Defendant Peretto's attorney may advise Peretto to admit to some of the allegations in plaintiff Baranski's complaint, because doing so narrows the number of issues in dispute.

ANSWER
A defendant's response to a plaintiff's complaint.

- **Any allegations that are not denied by the defendant will be deemed to have been admitted.**

If defendant Peretto has no knowledge as to whether a particular allegation is true or false, then his attorney, Cameron, may indicate that in the answer. This puts the burden of proving the allegation on plaintiff Baranski, just as if it were an outright denial. It is not necessary for Peretto's attorney to include in the answer any of the reasons for the denial of particular allegations in Baranski's complaint. These reasons may be revealed during the discovery phase of the litigation process (discussed later in this chapter).

Exhibit 10.9 on pages 390 and 391 illustrates the types of responses that defendant Peretto might make in his answer. Like the complaint, the answer begins with a caption and ends with the attorney's signature. It may also include, following the attorney's signature, an affidavit signed by the defendant, as well as a demand for a jury trial, as in Exhibit 10.9.

Answer and Affirmative Defenses. A defendant may assert, in the answer, a reason why he or she should not be held liable for the plaintiff's injuries even if the facts, as alleged by the plaintiff, are true. This is called raising an **affirmative defense**.

AFFIRMATIVE DEFENSE
A response to a plaintiff's claim that does not deny the plaintiff's facts but attacks the plaintiff's legal right to bring an action.

For example, Peretto might claim that someome else was driving his Dodge van when it crashed into Baranski's car. Peretto's attorney might also raise the defense of **contributory negligence**. That is, she could argue that even though defendant Peretto's car collided with Baranski's, plaintiff Baranski was also negligent because she was exceeding the speed limit when the accident occurred and was thus unable to avoid being hit by Peretto's car. In a few states, if it can be shown that the plaintiff was contributorily negligent, the plaintiff will be completely barred from recovery, and the judge would likely grant a defendant's motion to dismiss the case on this basis. Most

CONTRIBUTORY NEGLIGENCE
A theory in tort law under which a complaining party's own negligence, if it contributed to or caused the injuries complained of, is an absolute bar to recovery. Only a minority of jurisdictions adhere to the doctrine of contributory negligence.

EXHIBIT 10.9
The Answer

UNITED STATES DISTRICT COURT
FOR THE WESTERN DISTRICT OF NITA

Katherine Baranski
Plaintiff

vs.

Tony Peretto
Defendant

File No. 96-14335-NI

Hon. Harley M. LaRue

Elizabeth A. Cameron
Attorney for the Defendant
Cameron & Strauss, P.C.
310 Lake Drive
Zero City, ZE 59802

ANSWER AND DEMAND FOR JURY TRIAL

JURISDICTIONAL ALLEGATIONS

1. Defendant lacks sufficient information to form a belief as to the truth of the allegations contained in paragraph 1 of Plaintiff's Complaint.

2. Defendant admits the allegations contained in paragraph 2 of Plaintiff's Complaint.

3. Defendant admits the allegations contained in paragraph 3 of Plaintiff's Complaint.

4. Defendant lacks sufficient information to form a belief as to the truth of the allegations contained in paragraph 4 of Plaintiff's Complaint.

GENERAL ALLEGATIONS

5. Defendant admits the allegations contained in paragraph 5 of Plaintiff's Complaint.

6. Defendant admits the allegations contained in paragraph 6 of Plaintiff's Complaint.

7. Defendant contends that he was operating his vehicle properly and denies the allegations contained in paragraph 7 of Plaintiff's Complaint for the reason that the allegations are untrue.

8. Defendant admits the allegation contained in paragraph 8 of Plaintiff's Complaint.

9. Defendant lacks sufficient information to form a belief as to the truth of the allegation contained in paragraph 9 of Plaintiff's Complaint.

10. Defendant lacks sufficient information on the proximate cause of Plaintiff's injuries to form a belief as to the truth of the averments contained in paragraph 10 of Plaintiff's Complaint.

11. Defendant denies the allegation of negligence contained in paragraph 11 of Plaintiff's Complaint.

EXHIBIT 10.9
Continued

NEW MATTER AND AFFIRMATIVE DEFENSES

Although denying that the Plaintiff is entitled to the relief prayed for in the Plaintiff's Complaint, Defendant further states that the Plaintiff is barred from recovery hereunder by reason of the following:

1. That the Plaintiff's injuries were proximately caused by her own contributory negligence and want of due care under the circumstances prevailing at the time of the accident.

2. That the Plaintiff was exceeding the posted speed limit at the time and place of the accident and therefore was guilty of careless and negligent driving within the meaning of Section 9.2325(1) of the Nita Statutes Annotated.

3. That the Plaintiff failed to exercise that standard of care that a reasonably prudent person would have exercised under the same or similar conditions for her own safety and that her own negligence, contributory negligence, and/or comparative negligence caused or was a contributing factor to the incident out of which the Plaintiff's cause of action arises.

4. The Defendant reserves the right, by an appropriate Motion, to move the Court to amend the Defendant's Answer to the Plaintiff's Complaint, to allege other New Matters and Affirmative Defenses as may be revealed by discovery yet to be had and completed in this case.

WHEREFORE, the Defendant prays for a judgment of no cause of action with costs and attorneys' fees to be paid by the Plaintiff.

Cameron & Strauss, P.C.
Elizabeth A. Cameron
Date: 2/25/96
Elizabeth A. Cameron
Attorney for the Defendant

310 Lake Drive
Zero City, ZE 59802

Tony Peretto, being first duly sworn, states that he has read the foregoing Answer by him subscribed and that he knows the contents thereof, and the same is true, except those matters therein stated to be upon information and belief, and as to those matters, he believes to be true.

Tony Peretto
Defendant

Sworn and subscribed before me this 25th day of February, 1996.

Laura Curtis
Notary Public, Zero County,
State of Zero

My Commission Expires:
December 8, 1998

DEMAND FOR A JURY TRIAL

The Defendant demands a trial by jury.

Cameron & Strauss, P.C.
Elizabeth A. Cameron
Date: 2/25/96
Elizabeth A. Cameron
Attorney for the Defendant
310 Lake Drive
Zero City, Zero 59802

states, however, have abandoned the doctrine of contributory negligence in favor of a **comparative negligence** standard. In these states, a plaintiff whose own negligence contributed to an injury can still recover damages, but the damages are reduced by a percentage that represents the degree of the plaintiff's negligence. Although affirmative defenses are directed toward the plaintiff, the plaintiff is not required to file additional pleadings in response to these defenses.

COMPARATIVE NEGLIGENCE
A theory in tort law under which the liability for injuries resulting from negligent acts is shared by all persons who were guilty of negligence (including the injured party), on the basis of each person's proportionate carelessness.

COUNTERCLAIM
A claim made by a defendant in a civil lawsuit against the plaintiff; in effect, a counterclaiming defendant is suing the plaintiff.

Answer and Counterclaim. Peretto's attorney may follow the answers to the plaintiff's allegations with one or more *counterclaims.* A **counterclaim** is like a reverse lawsuit in which the defendant asserts a claim against the plaintiff for injuries that the defendant suffered from the same incident. For example, defendant Peretto might contend that plaintiff Baranski lost control of her car and skidded into Peretto's car, causing Peretto to be injured. This allegation would be a counterclaim. The plaintiff is required to reply to any counterclaims made by the defendant.

MOTION
A procedural request or application presented by an attorney to the court on behalf of a client.

MOTION TO DISMISS
A pleading in which a defendant admits the facts as alleged by the plaintiff but asserts that the plaintiff's claim fails to state a cause of action (that is, has no basis in law) or that there are other grounds on which a suit should be dismissed.

Motion to Dismiss. A **motion** is a procedural request submitted to the court by an attorney on behalf of his or her client. When one party files a motion with the court, they must also send to, or serve on, the opposing party a *notice of motion.* The notice of motion informs the opposing party that the motion has been filed and indicates when the court will hear the motion. The notice of motion gives the opposing party an opportunity to prepare for the hearing and argue before the court why the motion should not be granted.

The **motion to dismiss**, as the phrase implies, requests the court to dismiss the case for reasons provided in the motion. Defendant Peretto's attorney, for example, could file a motion to dismiss if she believed that Peretto had not been properly served, that the complaint had been filed in the wrong court, that the statute of limitations for that type of lawsuit had expired, or that the complaint did not state a claim for which relief (a remedy) could be granted. See Exhibit 10.10 for an example of a motion to dismiss.

SUPPORTING AFFIDAVIT
An affidavit accompanying a motion that is filed by an attorney on behalf of his or her client. The sworn statements in the affidavit provide a factual basis for the motion.

MEMORANDUM OF LAW
A document (known as a *brief* in some states) that delineates the legal theories, statutes, and cases on which a motion is based.

If defendant Peretto's attorney decides to file a motion to dismiss plaintiff Baranski's claim, she may want to attach one or more **supporting affidavits**—sworn statements as to certain facts that may contradict the allegations made in the complaint. Peretto's attorney may also have her paralegal draft a **memorandum of law** (which is called a *brief* in some states) to be submitted along with the motion to dismiss and the accompanying affidavits. The memorandum of law will present the legal basis for the motion, citing any statutes and cases that support it. A supporting affidavit gives factual support to the motion to dismiss, while the memorandum of law provides the court with the legal grounds for the dismissal of the claim.[7]

7. The memorandum of law described here should not be confused with the legal memorandum discussed in Chapter 18. The latter is an internal memorandum (that is, a memo submitted—usually by the paralegal—to his or her supervising attorney).

EXHIBIT 10.10
A Motion to Dismiss

UNITED STATES DISTRICT COURT
FOR THE WESTERN DISTRICT OF NITA

Katherine Baranski
Plaintiff
File No. 96-14335-NI

vs.

Hon. Harley M. LaRue

Tony Peretto
Defendant

Elizabeth A. Cameron
Attorney for the Defendant
Cameron & Strauss, P.C.
310 Lake Drive
Zero City, ZE 59802

MOTION TO DISMISS

The Defendant, Tony Peretto, by his attorney, moves the court to dismiss the above-named action because the statute of limitations governing the Plaintiff's claim has expired, as demonstrated in the memorandum of law that is being submitted with this motion. The Plaintiff therefore has no cause of action against the Defendant.

Cameron & Strauss, P.C.
Elizabeth A. Cameron

Date: 2/20/96

Elizabeth A. Cameron
Attorney for the Defendant
310 Lake Drive
Zero City, ZE 59802

ETHICAL CONCERN

Deadlines and the Duty of Competence

Experienced paralegals often stress how easy it is to miss deadlines. A very important deadline that the paralegal should always check is when the statute of limitations expires for the type of claim being made. For example, suppose that the state of Nita's statute of limitations requires Baranski to file her complaint against Peretto within two years or forever forgo the right to sue him. Also suppose that Baranski did not realize that she would always have a limp until a year or so after the accident. Baranski consults with attorney Gilmore about the matter a month before the two-year statute of limitations expires. Gilmore and his paralegal, Lopez, should immediately check the statute of limitations to make sure that they do not waste any time. Otherwise, by the time Lopez completes her initial investigation into the matter, has further consultations with Baranski, and completes other preliminaries—including the drafting of the complaint—the statute might expire before the complaint is filed. All attorneys (and their paralegals) are charged with a duty of competence, and a breach of this duty (such as failing to notice and advise a client on the date a statute of limitations expires) may subject the attorney to a lawsuit for professional negligence (malpractice).

Amending the Pleadings

An attorney may be called upon by a client to file a complaint or an answer without having much time to become familiar with the facts of the case. Because no attorney can anticipate how a case will evolve over time, the complaint or answer may have to be amended to account for newly discovered facts or evidence. Amendments may also be desirable when circumstances dictate that a different legal theory or defense be put forward.

PRETRIAL MOTIONS

Many motions may be made during the pretrial litigation process, including those listed and described in Exhibit 10.11. Some pretrial motions, if granted by the court, will end a case before trial. These motions include the

PARALEGAL PROFILE Litigation Paralegal

AL SANCHEZ received an associate's degree in design and drafting in 1971 from Don Bosco Technical Institute. He then worked for sixteen years as an engineering drafter for the aerospace industry. Sanchez decided to become a paralegal in 1987. In 1992, he received his paralegal degree from Rio Hondo College. He now works for an attorney who practices personal-injury law.

What do you like best about your work?

"The best aspect of my job is having people appreciate the work that I've done for them. I feel like I go the extra mile, and it's nice to be appreciated."

What is the greatest challenge that you face in your area of work?

"The greatest challenge is dealing with and balancing the volume of work involved in my caseload and still giving clients personal attention. I do everything from the initial client interview to settlement or litigation support. I have a lot of contact with clients, insurance companies, and doctors. I also do some office management. It is also a challenge to keep up with changes in both substantive law and procedural law."

"...TRY TO REMEMBER THAT YOUR CLIENTS ARE PEOPLE, NOT JUST CASE NUMBERS."

What advice do you have for would-be paralegals in your area of work?

"My advice is to gain computer skills and take psychology classes to help you better understand clients and their problems. Organizational skills and the ability to prioritize are also very important. I feel that my job is a 'good fit' because I am a 'people person,' and my job allows me to deal more with the public. It is also important to learn more about the law and attend continuing-education seminars to keep current with the law."

What are some tips for success as a paralegal in your area of work?

"I feel it is important to spend some time in the courthouse observing various proceedings. Also, try to remember that your clients are people, not just case numbers. Finally, keep in mind that quality work takes time and attention to detail. Therefore, paralegals need to put in a lot of hours."

CASE AT A GLANCE

The Plaintiff—
Plaintiff: Katherine Baranski
Attorney: Allen P. Gilmore
Paralegal: Elena Lopez

The Defendant—
Defendant: Tony Peretto
Attorney: Elizabeth A. Cameron
Paralegal: Gordon McVay

motion to dismiss (which has already been discussed), the motion for judgment on the pleadings, and the motion for summary judgment. Here we examine the latter two motions.

Motion for Judgment on the Pleadings

Once the two attorneys in the Baranski case, Gilmore and Cameron, have finished filing their respective pleadings and amendments, either one of them may file a **motion for judgment on the pleadings**. Motions for judgment on the pleadings are often filed when it appears from the pleadings that the plaintiff has failed to state a cause of action for which relief may be granted. They

EXHIBIT 10.11
Pretrial Motions

MOTION TO DISMISS

A motion filed by the defendant in which the defendant asks the court to dismiss the case for a specified reason, such as improper service, lack of personal jurisdiction, or the plaintiff's failure to state a claim for which relief can be granted.

MOTION TO STRIKE

A motion filed by the defendant in which the defendant asks the court to strike (delete from) the complaint certain of the paragraphs contained in the complaint. Motions to strike help to clarify the underlying issues that form the basis for the complaint by removing paragraphs that are redundant or irrelevant to the action.

MOTION TO MAKE MORE DEFINITE AND CERTAIN

A motion filed by the defendant to compel the plaintiff to clarify the basis of the plaintiff's cause of action. The motion is filed when the defendant believes that the complaint is too vague or ambiguous for the defendant to respond to it in a meaningful way.

MOTION FOR JUDGMENT ON THE PLEADINGS

A motion that may be filed by either party in which the party asks the court to enter a judgment in its favor based on information contained in the pleadings. A judgment on the pleadings will only be made if there are no facts in dispute and the only question is how the law applies to a set of undisputed facts.

MOTION TO COMPEL DISCOVERY

A motion that may be filed by either party in which the party asks the court to compel the other party to comply with a discovery request. If a party refuses to allow the opponent to inspect and copy certain documents, for example, the party requesting the documents may make a motion to compel production of documents.

MOTION FOR SUMMARY JUDGMENT

A motion that may be filed by either party in which the party asks the court to enter judgment in its favor without a trial. Unlike a motion for judgment on the pleadings, a motion for summary judgment can be supported by evidence outside the pleadings, such as witnesses' affidavits, answers to interrogatories, or other evidence obtained prior to or during discovery.

may also be filed when the pleadings indicate that no facts are in dispute and the only question is how the law applies to a set of undisputed facts. For example, assume for a moment that in the Baranski case, defendant Peretto admitted to all of plaintiff Baranski's allegations in his answer and raised no affirmative defenses. In this situation, Baranski's attorney, Gilmore, would file a motion for judgment on the pleadings in Baranski's favor.

MOTION FOR JUDGMENT ON THE PLEADINGS
A motion, which can be brought by either party to a lawsuit after the pleadings are closed, for the court to decide the issue without proceeding to trial. The motion will be granted only if no facts are in dispute and the only issue concerns how the law applies to a set of undisputed facts.

Motion for Summary Judgment

MOTION FOR SUMMARY JUDGMENT
A motion requesting the court to enter a judgment without proceeding to trial. The motion can be based on evidence outside the pleadings and will be granted only if no facts are in dispute and the only issue concerns how the law applies to a set of undisputed facts.

A **motion for summary judgment** is similar to a motion for judgment on the pleadings in that the party filing the motion is asking the court to grant a judgment in its favor without a trial. As with a motion for judgment on the pleadings, a court will only grant a motion for summary judgment if it determines that no facts are in dispute and the only question is how the law applies to a set of facts agreed on by both parties.

When the court considers a motion for summary judgment, it can take into account *evidence outside the pleadings.* This distinguishes the motion for summary judgment from the motion to dismiss and the motion for judgment on the pleadings. To support a motion for summary judgment, one party can submit evidence obtained at any point prior to trial (including during the discovery stage of litigation—to be discussed shortly) that refutes the other party's factual claim. In the Baranski case, for example, suppose that Peretto was in another state at the time of the accident. Defendant Peretto's attorney could make a motion for summary judgment in Peretto's favor and attach to the motion a witness's sworn statement that Peretto was in the other state at the time of the accident. Unless plaintiff Baranski's attorney could bring in sworn statements by other witnesses that Peretto was at the scene of the accident, Peretto would normally be granted his motion for summary judgment.

A motion for summary judgment would be particularly appropriate if plaintiff Baranski had previously signed a release waiving her right to sue defendant Peretto on the claim. In that situation, Peretto's attorney, Cameron, would attach a copy of the release to the motion before filing the motion with the court. Cameron would also prepare and attach a memorandum of law in support of the motion. When the motion is heard by the court, Cameron would argue that the execution of the waiver barred plaintiff Baranski from pursuing her claim against defendant Peretto.

The burden would then shift to plaintiff Baranski's attorney, Gilmore, to demonstrate that the release was invalid or otherwise not binding on Baranski. If the judge believes that the release had been voluntarily signed by plaintiff Baranski, then the judge might grant the motion for summary judgment in Peretto's favor. If attorney Gilmore is able to convince the judge that the release signed by Baranski had been procured by coercive or fraudulent practices, however, then the judge would deny the motion for summary judgment and permit the case to go to trial.

TRADITIONAL DISCOVERY TOOLS

DISCOVERY
Formal investigation prior to trial. During discovery, opposing parties use various methods, such as interrogatories and depositions, to obtain information from each other to prepare for trial.

Before a trial begins, the parties can use a number of procedural devices to obtain information and gather evidence about the case. Plaintiff Baranski's attorney, for example, will want to know how fast defendant Peretto was driving, whether he had been drinking, whether he saw the stop sign, and so on. The process of obtaining information from the opposing party or from other witnesses is known as **discovery**.

Discovery serves several purposes. It preserves evidence from witnesses who might not be available at the time of the trial or whose memories will fade as time passes. It can pave the way for summary judgment if both parties agree on all of the facts. It can lead to an out-of-court settlement if one party decides that the opponent's case is too strong to challenge. Even if the case does go to trial, discovery prevents surprises by giving parties access to evidence that might otherwise be hidden. This allows both parties to learn as much as they can about what to expect at a trial before they reach the courtroom. It also serves to narrow the issues so that trial time is spent on the main questions in the case.

The FRCP and similar rules in the states set forth the guidelines for discovery activity. Discovery includes gaining access to witnesses, documents, records, and other types of evidence. The rules governing discovery are designed to make sure that a witness or a party is not unduly harassed, that **privileged information** (communications that may not be disclosed in court) is safeguarded, and that only matters relevant to the case at hand are discoverable. Currently, the trend is toward allowing more discovery and thus fewer surprises. The 1993 revision of the FRCP significantly changed the rules governing discovery in federal court cases. To the extent that state courts decide to follow the new federal rules, discovery in such cases will also be affected. You will learn how the revised rules affect the traditional discovery process in the next section.

Traditional discovery devices include interrogatories, depositions, requests for documents, requests for admissions, and requests for examinations. Each of these discovery tools is examined below.

PRIVILEGED INFORMATION
Confidential communications between certain individuals, such as an attorney and his or her client, that are protected from disclosure except under court order.

INTERROGATORIES
A series of written questions for which written answers are prepared and then signed under oath by a party to a lawsuit (the plaintiff or the defendant).

Interrogatories

Interrogatories are written questions that must be answered, in writing, by the parties to the lawsuit and then signed by the parties under oath. Typically, the paralegal drafts the interrogatories for the attorney's review and approval. In the Baranski case, for example, attorney Gilmore will probably ask paralegal Lopez to draft interrogatories to be sent to defendant Peretto.

Drafting Interrogatories. All discovery documents, including interrogatories, normally begin with a caption similar to the complaint caption illustrated earlier in this chapter. Following the caption, Lopez will add the name of the party who must answer the interrogatories, instructions to be followed by the party, and definitions of certain terms that are used in the interrogatories. The body of the document consists of the interrogatories themselves—that is, the questions that the opposing party must answer. The interrogatories should end with a signature line for the attorney below which appears the attorney's name and address.

Before drafting the questions, Lopez will want to review carefully the contents of the case file (including the pleadings and the evidence and other information that she obtained during her preliminary investigation into plaintiff Baranski's claim) and consult with attorney Gilmore on what litigation strategy should be pursued. For further guidance, she might consult form books containing sample interrogatories as well as interrogatories used in similar cases previously handled by the firm. For a discussion of how to

ETHICAL CONCERN

Keeping Client Information Confidential

As it happens, attorney Gilmore's legal assistant, Lopez, is a good friend of plaintiff Baranski's daughter. Lopez learns from the results of Baranski's medical examination that Baranski has a terminal illness. Lopez is sure that the daughter, who quarreled with her mother two months ago and hasn't spoken to her since, is unaware of the illness and would probably be very hurt if she learned that Lopez knew of it and didn't tell her. Should Lopez tell her friend about the illness? No. This is confidential information at this point, which Lopez only became aware of by virtue of her job. Should the information be revealed publicly during the course of the trial, then Lopez would be free to disclose it to her friend if the friend still remained unaware of it. In the meantime, Lopez is ethically (and legally) obligated not to disclose the information to anyone who is not working on the case, including her friend.

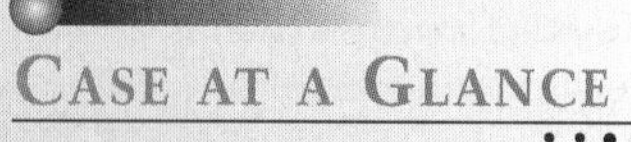

CASE AT A GLANCE

The Plaintiff—
Plaintiff: Katherine Baranski
Attorney: Allen P. Gilmore
Paralegal: Elena Lopez

The Defendant—
Defendant: Tony Peretto
Attorney: Elizabeth A. Cameron
Paralegal: Gordon McVay

draft effective interrogatories, see this chapter's featured-guest article entitled "Ten Tips for Drafting Interrogatories."

Depending on the complexity of the case, interrogatories may be few in number, or they may run into the hundreds. Exhibit 10.12, which begins on page 400, illustrates the types of interrogatories that have traditionally been used in cases similar to the Baranski-Peretto case. Depending on the rules of the court in which the Baranski case is being filed, paralegal Lopez might draft similar interrogatories for defendant Peretto to answer. Realize that some state courts now limit the number of interrogatories that can be used, and the 1993 revision of FRCP 33 limits the number of interrogatories in federal court cases to twenty-five (unless a greater number is allowed by stipulation of the parties or by court order). Therefore:

- **Before drafting interrogatories, the paralegal should always check the rules of the court in which an action is being filed to find out if that court limits the number of interrogatories that can be used.**

Answering Interrogatories. Upon receiving the interrogatories, defendant Peretto would have to answer them within a specified time period (thirty days under FRCP 33) in writing and under oath, as mentioned above. Very likely, he will have substantial guidance from his attorney and his attorney's paralegal in forming his answers. Peretto must answer each question truthfully, of course, because he is under oath. His attorney and her paralegal would counsel him, though, on how to phrase his answers so that they are both truthful and strategically sound. For example, they would advise Peretto on how to limit his answers to prevent disclosing more information than is necessary.

Depositions

DEPOSITION
A pretrial question-and-answer proceeding, usually conducted orally, in which an a party or witness answers an attorney's questions. The answers are given under oath, and the session is recorded.

Like interrogatories, **depositions** are given under oath. Unlike interrogatories, however, depositions are usually conducted orally (except in certain circumstances, such as when the party being deposed is at a great distance and cannot be deposed via telephone). Furthermore, they may be taken from witnesses. As indicated earlier, interrogatories can only be taken from the parties to the lawsuit.

The attorney wishing to depose a party must give that party's attorney reasonable notice in writing by serving the attorney with a notice similar to that shown in Exhibit 10.13 on page 404. Typically, the notice will be accompanied by a cover letter to the attorney.

Normally, the defendant's attorney deposes the plaintiff first, and then the plaintiff's attorney deposes the defendant. Following these depositions, the attorneys may depose witnesses and other parties to obtain information about the event leading to the lawsuit. When both the defendant and the plaintiff are located in the same jurisdiction, the site of the deposition will usually be the offices of the attorney requesting the deposition. When the parties are located in different jurisdictions, other arrangements may be made. In the Baranski case, attorney Gilmore will travel to defendant Peretto's city, which is located in another state, and depose Peretto in the office of Peretto's attorney, Cameron.

When an attorney takes the deposition of a party or witness, the attorney is able to question the person being deposed (the **deponent**) in person and then follow up with any other questions that come to mind. Even though the deposition is usually taken at the offices of one of the party's attorneys, the fact that the deponent has sworn to tell the truth necessitates that both the attorney and the deponent treat the deposition proceedings as seriously as they would if the deponent were on the witness stand in court.

DEPONENT
A party or witness who testifies under oath during a deposition.

FRCP 30, as revised in 1993, prohibits the taking of any depositions in federal court cases before the parties have made the disclosures required under revised Rule 26 and discussed in the next section. Revised Rule 30 also states that the court's approval is required if, without written agreement by the parties, either attorney wants to take more than one deposition from the same party or witness, or more than a total of ten depositions.

Drafting Deposition Questions. Depositions are conducted by attorneys. Although paralegals may attend depositions, they do not ask questions during the deposition. Deposition questions are often drafted by paralegals, however. In the Baranski case, for example, attorney Gilmore might ask paralegal Lopez to draft questions for a deposition of defendant Peretto or someone else, such as an eyewitness to the accident. For Peretto's deposition, Lopez might draft questions similar to those presented in Exhibit 10.14 on page 405. Attorney Gilmore can then use Lopez's list as a kind of checklist during the deposition. Note, though, that Gilmore's questions will not be limited to the questions included in the list. Other, unforeseen questions may arise as Gilmore learns new information during the deposition. Also, the deponent's answer to one question may reveal the answer to another, so that not all questions will need to be asked.

Preparing the Client for a Deposition. No attorney can predict a deponent's answers beforehand. Spontaneous and perhaps even contradictory statements can seriously damage the deponent's case. For this reason, the deposed party and his or her lawyer will want to prepare for the deposition by formulating mock answers to anticipated questions. For example, if defendant Peretto's attorney plans to depose plaintiff Baranski, attorney Gilmore and paralegal Lopez might have Baranski come into their office for a run-through of possible questions that Peretto's attorney might ask her during the deposition. This kind of preparation does not mean that the lawyer tells the deponent what to say. Instead, the lawyer offers suggestions as to how the answers to certain questions should be phrased. The answers must be truthful, but the truth can be presented in many ways.

The Role of the Deponent's Attorney. The deponent's attorney will attend the deposition, but the attorney's role will be limited. The attorney may make occasional objections to the opposing attorney's questions if the questions appear to be irrelevant to the case or ask for privileged information. If plaintiff Baranski were to be deposed by defendant Peretto's attorney, Cameron, then Baranski's attorney, Gilmore, would object to any of Cameron's questions that were misleading or ambiguous or that wandered too far from the issues relating to the claim.

EXHIBIT 10.12
Sample Interrogatories

UNITED STATES DISTRICT COURT
FOR THE WESTERN DISTRICT OF NITA

Katherine Baranski
Plaintiff

File No. 96-14335-NI

vs.

Hon. Harley M. LaRue

Tony Peretto
Defendant

A. P. Gilmore
Attorney for the Plaintiff
Jeffers, Gilmore & Dunn
553 Fifth Avenue
Suite 101
Nita City, NI 48801

PLAINTIFF'S FIRST INTERROGATORIES TO DEFENDANT

PLEASE TAKE NOTICE that the following Interrogatories are directed to you under the provisions of Rule 26(a)(5) and Rule 33 of the Federal Rules of Civil Procedure. You are requested to answer these Interrogatories and to furnish such information in answer to the Interrogatories as is available to you.

You are required to serve integrated Interrogatories and Answers to these Interrogatories under oath, within thirty (30) days after service of them upon you. The original answers are to be retained in your attorney's possession and a copy of the answers are to be served upon Plaintiff's counsel.

The answers should be signed and sworn to by the person making answer to the Interrogatories.

When used in these Interrogatories the term "Defendant," or any synonym thereof, is intended to and shall embrace and include, in addition to said Defendant, all agents, servants and employees, representatives, attorneys, private investigators, or others who are in possession or who may have obtained information for or on behalf of the Defendant.

These Interrogatories shall be deemed continuing and supplemental answers shall be required immediately upon receipt thereof if Defendant, directly or indirectly, obtains further or different information from the time answers are served until the time of trial.

1. Were you the driver of an automobile involved in an accident with plaintiff on the ______________ day of ______________, 19 ___, at about _____ o'clock ______ A.M. at the intersection of __________ and ____________, in the city of __________ in the county of __________, state of__________? If so, please state the following:

   (a) Whether your name is correctly spelled in the complaint in this cause of action;
   (b) Any other names by which you have been known, including the dates during which you have used those names;
   (c) Your Social Security number and place and date of birth;
   (d) Your height, weight, and eye and hair color;
   (e) Your address at the time of the accident;
   (f) The names, addresses, and phone numbers of your present and former spouses (if any) and all of your children, whether natural or adopted, who were residing with you at the time of the accident (if any).

2. Please list your places of residence for the last five years prior to your current residence, including complete addresses and dates of residence as well as the names of owners or managers.

EXHIBIT 10.12
Continued

3. Please indicate where you have worked during the five years prior to and including your present employment. When so doing, please indicate the following:

(a) The names, addresses, and telephone numbers of each employer or place of business, including the dates during which you worked there;
(b) How many hours you worked, on average, per week;
(c) The names, addresses, and telephone numbers of your supervisors (or owners of the business);
(d) The nature of the work that you performed.

4. Please give all relevant information with respect to your driver's license that you had on the date of the accident, including the following:

(a) The state of issuance and the number of your license;
(b) The type and date of issuance as well as its expiration date;
(c) Any violations, offenses, or restrictions that were recorded against your license.

5. Indicate whether you have ever had your driver's license suspended, revoked, or canceled, and whether you have ever been denied the issuance of a driver's license for mental or physical reasons. If you have, please indicate the date and state of such an occurrence as well as the reasons for it.

6. Do you have normal vision without the use of glasses or contact lenses? If your answer is in the negative, please indicate the following:

(a) The date on which glasses or contact lenses were prescribed and the name and address of the prescriber;
(b) The date and complete address of the business from which they were purchased;
(c) The present location of the glasses or contact lenses;
(d) Whether or not you were wearing the glasses or contact lenses at the time of the accident.

7. Do you have normal hearing without the use of a hearing aid? If your answer is in the negative, please indicate the following:

(a) The date on which the hearing aid was prescribed and the name and address of the prescriber;
(b) The date and complete address of the business from which it was purchased;
(c) The present location of the hearing aid;
(d) Whether or not you were wearing the hearing aid at the time of the accident.

8. When is the last time you had your vision checked within the last five years?

9. If you have had your vision checked, please indicate the following:

(a) The date and reason for the vision examination;
(b) The name, address, and telephone number of the examiner;
(c) The results and/or actions taken.

10. When is the last time you had your hearing checked within the last five years?

11. If you have had your hearing checked, please indicate the following:

(a) The date and reason for the hearing examination;
(b) The name, address, and telephone number of the examiner;
(c) The results and/or actions taken.

EXHIBIT 10.12
Sample Interrogatories, Continued

12. Have you ever suffered from any form of fits or convulsions, fainting spells, epilepsy, mental illness, nervous breakdowns, alcoholism, or drug addiction? If your answer is yes, for each such occurrence or reoccurrence within one year prior to this accident, please indicate the following:

(a) The date of onset;
(b) The actual condition;
(c) Your address at the time of onset;
(d) The names and addresses of those qualified persons who treated you for the condition, including the dates of such treatment;
(e) The names and addresses of hospitals or other institutions in which you were treated for such condition, including the dates of treatment;
(f) The date of termination or present status of the condition.

* * * *

[Now would come various interrogatories about whether the defendant in the automobile accident owned the automobile, and, if not, who the owner was and the relationship between the owner and the defendant. There might also be questions relating to the defendant's military service record.]

* * * *

30. When the accident occurred, did you have full use of all of your limbs and extremities? If you answer is in the negative, please state the following:

(a) The limbs or extremities affected;
(b) The dates and causes of any impairments;
(c) The details of any impairments.

31. Within the twenty-four hours preceding the accident, did you ingest any narcotic, tranquilizer, drug, sedative, or other form of medication? If so, please state the following:

(a) The identity of the drug or medication and the reason for taking it;
(b) The dosage and the number of times taken;
(c) The date and address where the medication was purchased;
(d) The name, address, and phone number of the person who prescribed the medication;
(e) The prescription number.

32. Within twenty-four hours prior to the accident, were you in a residence or an establishment in which liquor was served? If so, for each occasion, please state the following:

(a) The name and address of the residence or establishment;
(b) The time during which you were at such residence or establishment;
(c) The names and addresses of the persons accompanying you;
(d) The name, type, and quantity of each alcoholic beverage consumed;
(e) The time of consumption of each drink.

33. After the accident, did any authority request that you undergo a sobriety test? If so, please indicate the following:

(a) The type of test;
(b) How long after the accident the test was given;
(c) The name and address of the person and place where the test was given;
(d) The results of the test;

EXHIBIT 10.12
Continued

(e) The name and address of the person currently having custody of the records indicating the test results;
(f) If you were requested to take such a test and refused, the name, address, and telephone number of each person whom you refused.

34. For the twenty-four hours preceding the accident, please describe in hourly detail your general activities, including your hours of employment and what you did during each of those hours.

35. Please answer the following questions with respect to the trip you were taking by automobile at the time of the accident:

(a) From what point did you start and where were you going?
(b) What time was it when you started and what time were you scheduled to arrive at your destination?
(c) What was the purpose of your trip?
(d) What was the address of each place where you stopped during the trip?
(e) What were the exact routes that you took, by street and by compass direction?
(f) What is the name, address, phone number, and present whereabouts of each passenger who accompanied you at any time during you the trip?

36. At the time of the accident, please state the following to the best of your recollection:

(a) The time, day of the week, and date;
(b) The direction in which you were traveling prior to impact;
(c) The visibility and light conditions;
(d) The weather, including the temperature, wind, rain, fog, etc.;
(e) The speed at which you were traveling just prior to the point of impact;
(f) The speed at which you were traveling 50 feet before the impact;
(g) The speed at which you were traveling 250 feet before the impact;
(h) The speed at which you were traveling one-quarter mile before the impact;
(i) The speed at which you were traveling one-half mile before the impact;
(j) The speed at which you were traveling one mile before the impact.

37. The general character of the neighborhood.

* * * *

[Additional interrogatories would probably be asked. Some interrogatories would relate to the scene of the accident, including road surface, coloring, posted speed limits, shoulders and curbs on the side of the road, whether the surface was wet, etc. There would be further interrogatories about whether the defendant's attention was diverted from traffic just prior to the accident and whether there were traffic controls at or near the accident scene. The defendant would be asked to indicate when he or she noticed the plaintiff's vehicle and where it was located. There would be further questions about the plaintiff's speed, whether the plaintiff braked, whether the plaintiff remained in the defendant's line of vision, whether there were other vehicles between the defendant's and plaintiff's vehicles, etc. Other interrogatories would include information about the defendant's car, lighting, etc. and whether the defendant applied his or her brakes prior to impact, whether he or she blew the horn, and so on. Information about the extent of damages to the parties involved and to the vehicles would then be asked.]

Dated: March 15, 1996

Jeffers, Gilmore & Dunn
Allen P. Gilmore
Allen P. Gilmore
Attorney for Plaintiff
553 Fifth Avenue
Suite 101
Nita City, NI 48801
(618) 555-1212

EXHIBIT 10.13
Notice of Taking Deposition

UNITED STATES DISTRICT COURT
FOR THE WESTERN DISTRICT OF NITA

Katherine Baranski
Plaintiff

vs.

File No. 96-14335-NI

Hon. Harley M. LaRue

Tony Peretto
Defendant

Allen P. Gilmore
Attorney for the Plaintiff
Jeffers, Gilmore & Dunn

553 Fifth Avenue
Suite 101
Nita City, NI 48801

Elizabeth A. Cameron
Attorney for the Defendant
Cameron & Strauss, P.C.
310 Lake Drive
Zero City, ZE 59802

TO: Elizabeth A. Cameron
Cameron & Strauss, P.C.
310 Lake Drive
Zero City, ZE 59802

NOTICE OF TAKING DEPOSITION

PLEASE TAKE NOTICE that Katherine Baranski, by and through her attorneys, Jeffers, Gilmore & Dunn, will take the deposition of Tony Peretto on Wednesday, April 15, 1996, at 1:30 P.M., at the law offices of Cameron & Strauss, P.C., 310 Lake Drive, Zero City, ZE 59802, pursuant to the Federal Rules of Civil Procedure, before a duly authorized and qualified notary and stenographer.

Dated: March 20, 1996

Jeffers, Gilmore & Dunn
Allen P. Gilmore
Allen P. Gilmore
Attorney for Katherine Baranski
553 Fifth Avenue, Suite 101
Nita City, NI 48801

Gilmore would also caution Baranski to limit her responses to the questions and not to engage in speculative answers that might prejudice her claim. If plaintiff Baranski was asked whether she had ever been involved in an automobile accident before, for example, Gilmore would probably caution her to use a simple (but truthful) "yes" or "no" answer. Attorney Gilmore normally would permit Baranski to volunteer additional information only in response to precisely phrased questions.

DEPOSITION QUESTIONS

1. Please state your full name and address for the record.
2. What is your age, birth date, and Social Security number?
3. What is your educational level and what employment position do you hold?
4. Do you have a criminal record and if so, for what?
5. Have you ever been involved in previous automobile accidents? What driving violations have you had? Has your driver's license ever been suspended?
6. What is your medical history? Have you ever had health problems? Are you in perfect health? Were you in perfect health at the time of the accident?
7. Do you wear glasses or contact lenses? If so, for what condition? Were you wearing your glasses or contacts at the time the accident occurred?
8. Do you take medication of any kind?
9. Do you have any similar lawsuits or any claims pending against you?
10. Who is your automobile insurer? What are your policy limits?
11. Were there any passengers in your vehicle at the time of the accident?
12. Describe your vehicle. What was the mechanical condition of your vehicle at the time of the accident? Do you do your own mechanical work? What training do you have in maintaining and repairing automobiles? Had you taken your vehicle to a professional mechanic's shop prior to the accident?
13. State the date the accident occurred.
14. Where were you prior to the accident, at least for the six hours preceding the accident?
15. Where were you going when the accident occurred, and for what purpose?
16. What were you doing during the last few moments before the accident? Were you smoking, eating, drinking, or chewing gum?
17. What were you thinking about just before the accident occurred?
18. What route did you take to reach your destination, and why did you take this particular route?
19. Describe the weather conditions at the time of the accident.
20. Please recite the facts of how the accident occurred.
21. Please describe the area in which the accident occurred. Were there many cars and pedestrians on the streets? Were there traffic controls, obstructions, or the like?
22. What was your location and in what direction were you going?
23. When did you see the Plaintiff's automobile approaching?
24. How far away were you when you first saw the auto? What was your rate of speed?
25. Did your vehicle move forward or was it pushed backward by the impact?
26. When did you first apply your brakes? Were your brakes functioning properly?
27. Did you attempt to avoid the accident? If so, how?
28. Did you receive a traffic ticket as a result of the accident?
29. Do you own the vehicle that you were driving at the time of the accident?
30. Were you acting within the scope of your employment when the accident occurred?
31. What were the conditions of the parties affected by the accident just after the accident occurred?
32. Did you attempt to provide first aid to any party?
33. How did the Plaintiff leave the scene and what was her physical condition?
34. What was the damage to your vehicle, and has it been repaired?

EXHIBIT 10.14
Deposition Questions

As will be discussed below, deposition proceedings are recorded. If both attorneys agree to do so, however, they can go "off the record" to clarify a point or discuss a disputed issue. Depositions are stressful events, and tempers often flare. In the event that the deposition can no longer be pursued in an orderly fashion, the attorney conducting the deposition may have to terminate it.

The above description of the role of the deponent's attorney at a deposition is typical for cases filed in state courts and, until the 1993 revision of the FRCP, in federal courts as well. The revised FRCP, however, imposes strict limitations on an attorney's right to object to questions asked of his or her client during a deposition. Rule 30(d)(1) now requires that an attorney may instruct a deponent not to answer only "when necessary to preserve a privilege, to enforce a limitation on evidence directed by the court, or to present a motion [to terminate the deposition]." The revised rule also states that all objections during a deposition must be stated concisely and in a nonargumentative, nonsuggestive manner. This rule is consistent with the revised FRCP 26, which imposes an ongoing duty on each party to disclose relevant information to the other party in the lawsuit.

DEPOSITION TRANSCRIPT
The official transcription of the recording taken during a deposition.

The Deposition Transcript. Every utterance made during a deposition is recorded. A court reporter will usually record the deposition proceedings and create an official **deposition transcript.** Methods of recording a deposition include stenographic recording (a traditional method that involves the use of a shorthand machine), tape recording, videotape recording, or some combination of these methods. Revised Rule 30(b)(2) of the FRCP states that unless the court orders otherwise, a deposition "may be recorded by sound, sound-and-visual, or stenographic means."

IMPEACH
To call into question the credibility of a witness by challenging the truth or accuracy of his or her trial statement.

The deposition transcript may be used by either party during the trial to prove a particular point or to **impeach** (call into question) the credibility of a witness who says something during the trial that is different from what he or she stated during the deposition. For example, a witness in the Baranski case might state during the deposition that defendant Peretto *did not* stop at the stop sign before proceeding to cross Mattis Avenue. If at trial, the witness states that Peretto *did* stop at the stop sign before crossing Mattis Avenue, plaintiff Baranski's attorney (Gilmore) could challenge the witness's credibility on the basis of the deposition transcript. Exhibit 10.15 shows a

DEVELOPING PARALEGAL SKILLS
Deposition Summaries

After a deposition is taken, each attorney orders a copy of the deposition transcript. Copies may be obtained in printed form or on a computer disk. When the transcript is received, the legal assistant's job is to prepare a summary of the testimony that was given. The summary is typically only a few pages in length.

The legal assistant must be very familiar with the lawsuit and the legal theories that are being pursued so that he or she can point out inconsistencies in the testimony and how the testimony varies from the pleadings. The paralegal might also give special emphasis to any testimony given by deponents that will help to prove the client's case in court.

After the deposition summary has been created, the paralegal places the summary in the litigation file, usually in a special discovery folder or binder within the larger file. The deposition summary will be used to prepare for future depositions, to prepare pretrial motions, and to impeach witnesses at the trial, should they give contradictory testimony.

Q: Where were you at the time of the accident?
A: I was on the southwest corner of the intersection.
Q: Are you referring to the intersection where Thirty-eighth Street crosses Mattis Avenue?
A: Yes.
Q: Why were you there at the time of the accident?
A: Well, I was on my way to work. I usually walk down Mattis Avenue to the hospital.
Q: So you were walking to work down Mattis Avenue and you saw the accident?
A: Yes.
Q: What did you see?
A: Well, as I was about to cross the street, a dark green van passed within three feet of me and ran the stop sign and crashed into another car.
Q: Can you remember if the driver of the van was a male or a female?
A: Yes. It was a man.
Q: I am showing you a picture. Can you identify the man in the picture?
A: Yes. That is the man who was driving the van.
Q: Do you wear glasses?
A: I need glasses only for reading. I have excellent distance vision.
Q: How long has it been since your last eye exam with a doctor?
A: Oh, just a month ago, with Dr. Sullivan.

page 4

EXHIBIT 10.15
A Deposition Transcript (Excerpt)

page from a transcript of a deposition conducted by attorney Gilmore in the Baranski case. The deponent was Julia Williams, an eyewitness to the accident. On the transcript, the letter "Q" precedes each question asked by Gilmore, and the letter "A" precedes each of Williams's answers.

Summarizing and Indexing the Deposition Transcript. Typically, the paralegal will summarize the deposition transcript. The summary, which along with the transcript will become part of the litigation file, allows the members of the litigation team to review quickly the information obtained from the deponent during the deposition.

In the Baranski case, assume that paralegal Lopez is asked to summarize the deposition transcript of Julia Williams. A commonly used format for deposition summaries is to summarize the information sequentially—that is, in the order that it was given during the deposition—as shown in Exhibit 10.16 on page 408. Notice that the summary includes the page and line numbers in the deposition transcript where the full text of the information can be found.

EXHIBIT 10.16
A Deposition Summary (Excerpt)

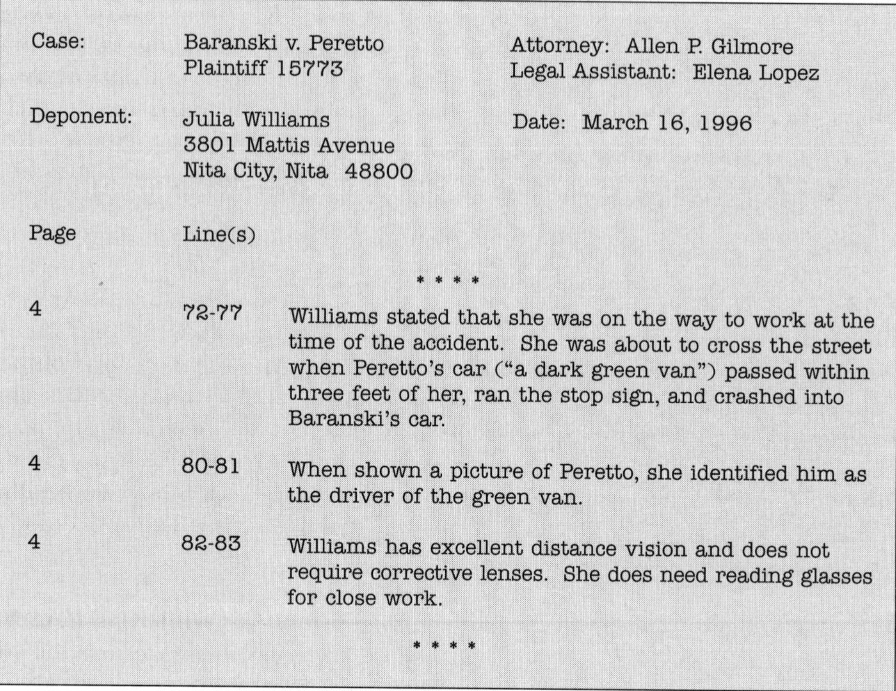

Case:	Baranski v. Peretto Plaintiff 15773	Attorney: Allen P. Gilmore Legal Assistant: Elena Lopez
Deponent:	Julia Williams 3801 Mattis Avenue Nita City, Nita 48800	Date: March 16, 1996

Page	Line(s)	
		* * * *
4	72-77	Williams stated that she was on the way to work at the time of the accident. She was about to cross the street when Peretto's car ("a dark green van") passed within three feet of her, ran the stop sign, and crashed into Baranski's car.
4	80-81	When shown a picture of Peretto, she identified him as the driver of the green van.
4	82-83	Williams has excellent distance vision and does not require corrective lenses. She does need reading glasses for close work.
		* * * *

Often, in addition to summarizing the transcript, the paralegal provides an index to the document. The index consists of a list of topics (such as education, employment status, injuries, medical costs, and so on) followed by the relevant page and line numbers of the deposition transcript. Together, the summary and the index allow anyone involved in the case to locate information quickly.

Other Discovery Requests

During the discovery phase of litigation, attorneys often request documents so that they may familiarize themselves with specific facts or events that were earlier disclosed by the parties or learned on investigation. In federal court cases, the revised FRCP 34 authorizes each party to request documents and other forms of evidence held by other parties and witnesses, but such requests cannot be made until after the initial prediscovery meeting of the parties (discussed below) has taken place. In most state courts, and depending on the nature of the case, the inspection of documents may be the first step in the discovery process if document inspection will facilitate the widest possible scope of discovery.

During discovery, a party can also request that the opposing party admit the truth of matters relating to the case. For example, plaintiff Baranski's attorney can request that defendant Peretto admit that he did not stop at the stop sign before crossing Mattis Avenue at Thirty-eighth Street. Such admissions save time at trial because the parties will not have to spend time proving facts on which they already agree. Any matter admitted under such a request is conclusively established as true for the trial. FRCP 36 permits requests for admission, but the 1993 revision of this rule stipulates that a request for admission cannot be made, without the court's permission, prior to the prediscovery meeting of the attorneys. In view of the limitations on the number of interrogatories under the revised FRCP (and under some state procedural rules that impose similar limitations), requests for admissions are a particularly useful discovery tool.

During discovery, the defendant's attorney may also want to verify the nature and extent of any injuries alleged by the plaintiff. If a defendant has genuine doubts as to the nature of the injuries suffered by the plaintiff, then the defendant may petition the court to order that the plaintiff submit to a medical examination. Although a medical examination may appear to be overly intrusive, FRCP 35(a) permits such an examination when the existence of the plaintiff's claimed injuries is in dispute. The examination, however, must be preceded by a court order. Because plaintiff Baranski is suing defendant Peretto for injuries arising from the accident, the existence, nature, and extent of her injuries is vitally important in calculating the damages that she might be able to recover from Peretto. Consequently, Baranski will probably be ordered by the court to undergo a physical examination if Peretto's attorney submits a request for a medical examination.

CASE AT A GLANCE

The Plaintiff—
Plaintiff: Katherine Baranski
Attorney: Allen P. Gilmore
Paralegal: Elena Lopez

The Defendant—
Defendant: Tony Peretto
Attorney: Elizabeth A. Cameron
Paralegal: Gordon McVay

REVISED DISCOVERY PROCEDURES UNDER FRCP 26

The 1993 amendments to the FRCP significantly changed discovery procedures in the federal courts. Under the revised rules, each party to a lawsuit has a duty to disclose to the other party specified types of information prior to the discovery stage of litigation. Under revised Rule 26(f), once a lawsuit is brought, the parties (the plaintiff and defendant and/or their attorneys, if the parties are represented by counsel) must schedule a prediscovery meeting to discuss the nature of the lawsuit, any defenses that may be raised against the claims being brought, and possibilities for promptly settling or otherwise resolving the dispute. The meeting should take place as soon as practicable but at least fourteen days before a scheduling conference is held or a scheduling order issued. Either at this meeting or within ten days after it, the parties must also make the initial disclosures described below and submit to the court a plan for discovery. As the trial date approaches, the attorneys must make subsequent disclosures relating to witnesses, documents, and other information that is relevant to the case.

The new discovery rules do not replace the traditional methods of discovery discussed in the preceding section. Rather, the revised rules impose a duty on attorneys to disclose automatically specified information to opposing counsel early in the litigation process so that the time and costs of traditional discovery methods can be reduced. Under the revised rules, attorneys may still use the traditional discovery tools (depositions, interrogatories, and so on) to obtain information, but they cannot use these methods until the prediscovery meeting has been held and initial disclosures have been made. Also, to save the court's time, the revised rules give attorneys a freer hand in crafting

FEATURED GUEST: JAMES W. H. MCCORD

Ten Tips for Drafting Interrogatories

Biographical Note

Since 1978, James McCord has been active in paralegal education as the director of paralegal programs at Eastern Kentucky University. He has served as president of the American Association for Paralegal Education, is a member of the American Bar Association Legal Assistant Program Approval Commission, and chairs the Kentucky Bar Association Committee on Paralegals. He received his law degree from the University of Wisconsin and practiced law before taking the position at Eastern Kentucky University. McCord is the author of *The Litigation Paralegal: A Systems Approach,* which is now in its second edition; *ABA Approval: An Educator's Guide;* and (as co-author) *Criminal Law and Procedure for the Paralegal.* He lives in Richmond, Kentucky, with his wife and son.

Interrogatories that are well thought out and carefully phrased can help to clarify the factual circumstances of the case, the types of evidence that can be obtained, and the issues in dispute. Because they help to define and shape a lawsuit, your ability to draft good interrogatories will make you a valued member of the litigation team. Here are some tips that you might find useful when you are asked to draft interrogatories.

1 Know the Limits of Interrogatories. Interrogatories have limits. The questions must seek information that is relevant to the issues or that will lead to relevant facts. The number of questions may be limited by the relevant rules or by the judge. Ethical standards explicitly forbid using interrogatories to harass a party or for the primary purpose of swamping the opponent with paperwork. Objections to interrogatories cause unwanted delay and possible loss of valuable information. Opponents usually object to questions that are irrelevant, vague or ambiguous, unduly burdensome, too numerous, or too broad in scope (covering too great a time span, for example). An attorney will also object to questions that seek protected information (such as the privileged communication between spouses or between an attorney and his or her client) or the ideas and strategies that make up the attorney's work product.

2 Develop Objectives for the Interrogatories. Review the case file to familiarize yourself with its contents. Meet with your supervising attorney to discuss the attorney's approach to the case. Identification of the key issues in the case, as well as the strategies and directions the attorney intends to pursue at trial, will help you streamline your work. With your attention focused on only the pertinent matters, reread the complaint, answer, and any other pleadings. Identify the elements to be proved and the defenses to be asserted, then list possible evidence that would support or disprove those elements or defenses. Divide the list into three parts: the information you already possess, information you have that needs to be clarified, and information that you need but do not yet possess. For items in the last two groups, indicate likely persons, files, documents, or other sources that will provide the information or give you leads to the information.

3 Refer to Forms Books or Previous Interrogatories. Collections of commonly used interrogatories can be found in the firm's library, a law library, or practice manuals. These are frequently categorized by the type of case—personal injury, contract, antitrust, and so on. Check interrogatories from similar cases in the firm's files to locate pertinent questions. Local examples keyed to local practice are especially helpful. Use the gathered examples as a guide only, then shape your questions to the unique needs of your case. Input useful examples into your computer and edit them to your satisfaction. Add your own questions to fully address the elements of the case at hand.

4 Use Preliminary Sections to Define and Instruct. Following the desired case caption, draft an introductory paragraph stating the name of the person to whom the questions are directed, that answers to the questions are requested, the date answers are due, and the applicable rule or rules of procedure. A subsequent section should define any terms or identify any acronyms that will be repeated in the questions. This promotes clarity and avoids repetitious language. It

FEATURED GUEST, Continued

reduces evasiveness by giving you the power to define the terms as broadly or as narrowly as needed. Interrogatories from previous cases define commonly repeated terms, such as *document, identify, you,* and *corporate officer,* and thus are good sources for the definitions section. Review your proposed definitions in light of your case to make sure that they do not exclude a particularly valuable area of information. The definition and instruction sections should not be so long that they are difficult to read.

5 Cover the "Who, What, Why, When, Where, and How." When planning your interrogatories, try to cover the "who, what, why, when, where, and how." Focus on the pleadings. Include in the interrogatories questions that will elicit the basis for each allegation and each denial made in the pleadings. Also include questions that will help you locate evidence that go beyond the allegations and denials in the pleadings. You might draft questions that ask, for example, for the address and custodian of certain documents, physical evidence, exhibits and witnesses to be relied on, and other items. (Under the revised FRCP, much of the information will already have been disclosed by the parties.)

6 Phrase Your Questions Simply, Concisely, and Accurately. The questions should be written simply and concisely. Try to eliminate all unnecessary adjectives and adverbs. Break complex questions into shorter and simpler components. Avoid giving the defendant options that allow the defendant to select the easiest and least informative answer. Be reasonable in the scope of your requests. For example, you should limit the time span for which records or other kinds of information are sought.

Also, make sure that no words are misspelled. Misspellings create an impression of incompetence and may allow respondents to answer legitimately that they have no knowledge of the whereabouts of "Mr. Fones" when you need information about "Mr. Jones."

7 Avoid Questions Calling for a "Yes" or "No" Answer. Questions that permit a "yes" or "no" response are of little value unless you include follow-up questions. Questions should determine if the person's statement is based on personal observation or secondhand knowledge. "Why" questions are easily circumvented with such responses as "That is what he wanted to do," or "He believed he should."

8 Make Effective Use of Opinion and Contention Questions. Opinion and contention questions are permitted by federal and most state rules. They identify where the opponent stands on key factual questions. For example, "Do you contend that the intersection light was red before the defendant entered the intersection? If so, on what do you base your contention? What persons have knowledge of these facts?" and so forth. The answers to these types of questions identify the facts in contention and the evidence on which the contention is based. This is extremely useful because other discovery devices do not get at the reasons or evidence that forms the basis for a contention or opinion. It is best to reserve this kind of question for a time later in the discovery process when previous discovery has revealed the contentions and most of the investigation in the case is completed. Otherwise, "I do not know yet" is a likely response.

"YOUR ABILITY TO DRAFT GOOD INTERROGATORIES WILL MAKE YOU A VALUED MEMBER OF THE LITIGATION TEAM."

9 Add Concluding or Summary Interrogatories. Include one or more questions to provide some protection for anything you forgot to address. This may prevent the opponent from using evidence at trial that you should have learned about earlier. A concluding request might be, "Identify any additional information pertinent to this lawsuit but not set out in your previous answers."

10 Employ the Evasiveness Test and Submit the Document to Your Supervising Attorney. Proofread the drafted interrogatories. Test your questions by placing yourself in the position of the other party and seeing if you can weasel your way around and out of providing such information. Redraft questions if necessary. Once this is done, give the document to your supervising attorney for any final review and signature. Have the interrogatories served on defendant.

a discovery plan that is appropriate to the nature of the claim, the parties' needs, and so on.[8]

Initial Disclosures

FRCP 26(a)(1) requires each party to disclose the following information to the other party either at an initial meeting of the parties or within ten days following the meeting:

- The name, address, and telephone number of any person who is likely to have "discoverable information" and the nature of that information.
- A copy or "description by category and location" of all documents, data, and other "things in the possession, custody, or control of the party" that are relevant to the dispute.
- A computation of the damages being claimed by the disclosing party. The party must make available to the other party, for inspection and copying, documents or other materials on which the computation of damages is based, "including materials bearing on the nature and extent of injuries suffered."
- Copies of any insurance policies that cover the injuries or harms alleged in the lawsuit and that may pay part or all of a judgment (damages, for example) resulting from the dispute.

In the Baranski case, following the new requirements under revised Rule 26 would mean that attorney Gilmore and paralegal Lopez would have to work quickly to assemble all relevant information, documents, and other evidence that Lopez had gathered during client interviews and during her preliminary investigation into the case. Lopez would have to prepare copies of the documents or other information—or a description of them—for attorney Gilmore's review and signature. The copies or descriptions would then have to be filed with the court and delivered to defendant Peretto's attorney.

Note that in the information disclosed to defendant Peretto's attorney, paralegal Lopez would have to include even information that might be damaging to the Baranski's position. Lopez would not need to disclose *privileged information,* however. If defendant Peretto's attorney seeks information that attorney Gilmore claims is privileged, Peretto's attorney will be able to obtain that information only through a court order.

A party will not be excused from disclosing relevant information simply because the party has not yet completed an investigation into the case or because the other party has not yet disclosed the required information. Revised FRCP 37(c) makes it clear that the failure to make these initial disclosures can result in serious sanctions. That rule states that if a party fails

8. The 1993 revision of the FRCP, including the revision of Rule 26 governing discovery requirements, has created substantial controversy. Revised Rule 26(a)(1) allows federal district courts to modify, or opt not to follow, these rules requiring early disclosures. As of mid-1994, of the ninety-six federal districts in the United States, thirty-two districts had adopted the early-disclosure rule, thirty-one districts had adopted a modified version of the rule, and twenty-three districts had opted out of the rule. See Mark Hansen, "Early Disclosure Hits Snag," *ABA Journal,* May 1994, p. 35.

to disclose certain relevant information, that party will not be able to use the information as evidence at trial. In addition, the court may impose other sanctions, such as ordering the party to pay reasonable expenses, including attorneys' fees, created by the failure to disclose. In sum, attorney Gilmore and paralegal Lopez would need to make sure that all relevant information (that is not privileged) was disclosed, or Gilmore would not be able to use it in court (and may face other sanctions as well).

Discovery Plan

As mentioned above, at the initial meeting of the parties, the attorneys must also work out a **discovery plan** and submit a report describing the plan to the court within ten days of the meeting. The type of information to be included in the discovery plan is illustrated in Exhibit 10.17 on page 414, which shows the new Form 35 that has been generated for this purpose. As indicated by that form, the revised Rule 26(f) allows the attorneys substantial room to negotiate the details of discovery, including the time schedules to be followed.

DISCOVERY PLAN
A plan formed by the attorneys litigating a lawsuit, on behalf of their clients, that indicates the types of information that will be disclosed by each party to the other prior to trial, the testimony and evidence that each party will or may introduce at trial, and the general schedule for pretrial disclosures and events.

In the Baranski case, paralegal Lopez will make sure that attorney Gilmore takes a copy of Form 35 with him to the initial prediscovery meeting of the parties to use as a checklist. After the attorneys decide on the details of the plan to be proposed to the court, attorney Gilmore will probably have paralegal Lopez draft a final version of the plan for his review and signature.

Subsequent Disclosures

In addition to the initial disclosures just discussed, each party must make other disclosures prior to trial. All subsequent disclosures must also be made in writing, signed by the attorneys, and filed with the court. Subsequent disclosures include information relating to expert witnesses and other witnesses and exhibits that will or may be used at trial.

Expert Witnesses. Under FRCP 26(a)(2), each party must disclose to the other party the names of any expert witnesses who may be called to testify during the trial. Additionally, the following information about each expert witness must be disclosed in a report signed by the expert witness:

- A statement by the expert witness indicating the opinions that will be expressed, the basis for the opinions, and the data or information considered by the witness when forming the opinions.
- Any exhibits that will be used to summarize or support the opinions.
- The qualifications of the expert witness, including a list of all publications authored by the witness within the preceding ten years.
- The compensation to be paid to the expert witness.
- A list of any other cases in which the witness has testified as an expert at trial or by deposition within the preceding four years.

These disclosures must be made either at times set by the court or, if the court does not indicate any times, at least ninety days prior to the trial date.

[Caption and Names of Parties]

1. Pursuant to Fed. R. Civ. P. 26(f), a meeting was held on ___(date)___ at ___(place)___ and was attended by:

___(name)___ for plaintiff(s) ___(party name)___
___(name)___ for defendant(s) ___(party name)___
___(name)___ for defendant(s) ___(party name)___

2. Pre-Discovery Disclosures. The parties [have exchanged] [will exchange by ___(date)___] the information required by [Fed. R. Civ. P. 26(a)(1)] [(local rule ______)].

3. Discovery Plan. The parties jointly propose to the court the following discovery plan: [Use separate paragraphs or subparagraphs as necessary if parties disagree.]

Discovery will be needed on the following subjects: ___(brief description of subjects on which discovery will be needed)___
All discovery commenced in time to be completed by ___(date)___. [Discovery on ___(issue for early discovery)___ to be completed by ___(date)___.]
Maximum of ____ interrogatories by each party to any other party. [Responses due ____ days after service.]
Maximum of ____ requests for admission by each party to any other party. [Responses due ____ days after service.]
Maximum of ____ depositions by plaintiff(s) and ____ by defendant(s).
Each deposition [other than of ______] limited to maximum of ____ hours unless extended by agreement of parties.
Reports from retained experts under Rule 26(a) (2) due:
from plaintiff(s) by ___(date)___
from defendant(s) by ___(date)___
Supplementations under Rule 26(e) due ___[time(s) or intervals(s)]___.

4. Other Items. [Use separate paragraphs or subparagraphs as necessary if parties disagree.]

The parties [request] [do not request] a conference with the court before entry of the scheduling order.
The parties request a pretrial conference in ___(month and year)___.
Plaintiff(s) should be allowed until ___(date)___ to join additional parties and until ___(date)___ to amend the pleadings.
Defendant(s) should be allowed until ___(date)___ to join additional parties and until ___(date)___ to amend the pleadings.
All potentially dispositive motions should be filed by ___(date)___.
Settlement [is likely] [is unlikely] [cannot be evaluated prior to ___(date)___] [may be enhanced by use of the following alternative dispute resolution procedure: ______].
Final lists of witnesses and exhibits under Rule 26(a) (3) should be due
from plaintiff(s) by ___(date)___.
from defendant(s) by ___(date)___.
Parties should have ____ days after service of final lists of witnesses and exhibits to list objections under Rule 26(a)(3).
The case should be ready for trial by ___(date)___ [and at the time is expected to take approximately ___(length of time)___].
[Other matters.]

Date: ______________

EXHIBIT 10.17
Form 35—Report of Parties' Planning Meeting

Other Pretrial Disclosures. Under revised FRCP 26(a)(3), each party must also disclose to the other party the following information about other witnesses that will testify at trial or any exhibits that will or may be used:

- A list containing the names, addresses, and telephone numbers of other witnesses that may or will be called during the trial to give testimony. The witness list must indicate whether the witness "will be called" or "may be called."

TODAY'S PROFESSIONAL PARALEGAL

Confidentiality—The Duty Continues

Laura Lowe has just been hired as a paralegal by a Chicago law firm, Chase & Chase. It is a firm with three hundred lawyers, ninety paralegals, and a large support staff. The firm's specialty is corporate law, and Laura works in the antitrust section. She works as part of a legal team that includes herself, another paralegal, a legal secretary, and three attorneys. One of the attorneys, Melanie Mintz, is an associate attorney for the firm, while the other two attorneys are partners.

LAURA'S ASSIGNMENT

Melanie assigns Laura to work on a case, *Video Land, Inc. v. Worldwide Studios, Inc.* Chase & Chase is representing the plaintiff, Video Land, which is suing Worldwide Studios for price-fixing in violation of federal antitrust law. Melanie tells Laura that she is preparing to take the deposition of Worldwide's chief financial officer (CFO). Melanie casually says to Laura, "As I expected, Worldwide is claiming that their pricing policy is confidential business information and that it would hurt them to disclose it. Too bad I don't have time to file a motion compelling discovery. That way, the judge could decide what they had to disclose. It would really help me to get to the bottom of this case."

AN ETHICAL DILEMMA

Laura is worried about working on the case because at her former firm, Howe & Johnson, she worked on the same case, only Howe & Johnson represented the defendant, Worldwide Studios. Laura expresses her concerns about a conflict of interest to Melanie, but she is told not to worry about it. Laura is fairly certain that Melanie's lack of concern over Laura's participation in the case is a breach of professional ethical standards. For the next two days, Laura considers her options. She could just keep quiet about the conflict and continue to work on the case, or she could discuss the situation with one of the partners on the team, Jeremy Chase. She decides to take the latter course, but before she can do so, Melanie asks Laura to come down to her office and to bring the interrogatory file with her.

Melanie says, "Laura, you know how important this case is to the firm. I really need something solid to go on to help me pin down Worldwide's pricing policy. Is there anything you know that could help me?" Laura recalls a confidential conversation between the CFO and her former supervising attorney about the pricing policy in regard to the videos. The CFO called her supervising attorney to ask him if it was illegal to require dealers to purchase certain unpopular videos if they wanted to sell the popular ones. Her supervising attorney advised the CFO that it was illegal. Laura knows that it is unethical to disclose this information to Melanie because it would breach Worldwide's right to confidentiality—which she must continue to respect even though she has left the firm that represents Worldwide. Because she does not want to breach her duty to keep client information confidential, Laura does not tell Melanie about this conversation. Instead, Laura answers that anything she knows from her previous work on the case is confidential and that she is sorry, but she cannot tell Melanie anything.

DEALING WITH THE ISSUE

Shortly after her conversation with Melanie, Laura is able to see Jeremy Chase. Laura explains her situation to him. He agrees with Laura that she has an ethical obligation to keep confidential everything she learned about the Worldwide case while working for her former employer, Howe & Johnson. He also tells her that depending on what she knows, Chase & Chase might have to be disqualified from handling the case. He tells her that she is off the case, effective immediately, and that he will have to disclose to Worldwide the fact that she was assigned to work on the case. He also tells her that he will be talking to Melanie about the matter shortly.

Laura knows that, as a result of discussing the situation with the senior partner, she may have jeopardized her working relationship with Melanie—and even perhaps Melanie's chances of becoming a partner in the firm. But she also knows that she had no other choice and is satisfied that she has done the right thing in this awkward situation.

- A list of any witnesses whose deposition testimony may be offered during the trial and, if not taken stenographically, a transcript of the relevant sections of the deposition testimony.
- A list of exhibits that indicates which exhibits will be offered and which exhibits may be offered if the need arises.

These disclosures must be made at least thirty days before trial, unless the court orders otherwise. Once the disclosures have been made, the opposing party has fourteen days within which to file with the court any objections to the use of any deposition or exhibit. If objections are not made, they are deemed to be waived (unless a party can show good cause why he or she failed to object to the disclosures within the fourteen-day time period).

An attorney's duty to disclose relevant information is ongoing throughout the pretrial stage. Any time an attorney learns about relevant supplemental information concerning statements or responses made earlier, that information must be disclosed to the other party.

KEY TERMS AND CONCEPTS

affidavit 380
affirmative defense 389
allegation 378
answer 389
complaint 374
comparative negligence 392
contributory negligence 389
counterclaim 392
default judgment 388
deponent 399
deposition 398
deposition transcript 406
discovery 396
discovery plan 413
docket 378
Federal Rules of Civil Procedure (FRCP) 370
impeach 406
interrogatories 397
judgment 368
memorandum of law 392
motion 392
motion for judgment on the pleadings 395
motion for summary judgment 396
motion to dismiss 392
pleadings 374
prayer for relief 379
privileged information 397
return-of-service form 383
scheduling conference 380
service of process 382
summons 382
supporting affidavit 392
witness 368

CHAPTER SUMMARY

1. The paralegal assists the attorney in a variety of tasks in the pretrial civil litigation process. The paralegal's efforts are of critical importance because attorneys rely on paralegals to make sure that nothing has been overlooked in preparing for the trial.

2. Although civil lawsuits vary from case to case in terms of their complexity, cost, and detail, all civil litigation involves similar procedural steps, as described in Exhibit 10.1.

3. The first step in the civil litigation process occurs when the attorney initially meets with a client who wishes to bring a lawsuit against another party or parties. The attorney normally conducts this initial client interview, although the paralegal often attends the interview, meets the client, and may make arrangements with the client for subsequent interviews.

4. Once the attorney agrees to represent the client in the lawsuit and the client has signed the retainer agreement, the attorney and the paralegal undertake a preliminary investigation into the matter to ascertain the facts alleged by the client and gain other factual information relating to the case.

5. A litigation file is also created for the case. All documents and records pertaining to the lawsuit will be kept in the litigation file. Each law firm or department usually has specific procedures for organizing and maintaining litigation files. Generally, the litigation file will expand, as the case progresses, to include subfiles for the pleadings, discovery, and other documents and information relating to the litigation.

6. The pleadings—which consist of the plaintiff's complaint, the defendant's answer, and any counterclaim or other pleadings listed in Exhibit 10.2—inform each party of the claims of the other and delineate the details of the dispute.

7. A lawsuit in a federal or state court normally is initiated by the filing of a complaint with the clerk of the appropriate court. The complaint includes a caption, jurisdictional allegations, general allegations (the body of the complaint) detailing the cause of action, a prayer for relief, a signature, and, if appropriate, a demand for a jury trial.

8. Typically, the defendant is notified of a lawsuit by the delivery of the complaint and a summons (service of process). The summons identifies the parties to the lawsuit, identifies the court in which the case will be heard, and directs the defendant to respond to the complaint within a specified time period. In federal court cases, revised FRCP 4 permits the plaintiff's attorney to notify the defendant, by first-class mail or other reliable means, of the lawsuit and enclose with the notice a form that the defendant can sign to waive the requirement of service of process. If the defendant does not sign and return the form, then the plaintiff's attorney will arrange to have the defendant served with the complaint and summons.

9. On receiving the complaint (and summons, if process is served), the defendant has several options. The defendant may submit an answer. The answer may deny any wrongdoing, or it might assert an affirmative defense against the plaintiff's claim, such as the plaintiff's contributory negligence. The answer may be followed by a counterclaim, in which the defendant asserts a claim against the plaintiff arising from the event giving rise to the lawsuit. Both the complaint and the answer may be amended as the case evolves and more evidence is discovered, subject to procedural rules. Alternatively or simultaneously, the defendant might make a motion to dismiss the case, perhaps on the ground that the relevant statute of limitations has expired.

10. A motion for judgment on the pleadings is a pretrial motion that may be filed by either party after all pleadings and amendments have been filed. The motion may be granted if it can be shown that no factual dispute exists. A motion for summary judgment may be filed by either party during or after the discovery stage of litigation. The latter motion is distinguished from a motion for judgment on the pleadings by the fact that the judge, in determining whether to grant the motion, can consider evidence apart from the pleadings—such as evidence contained in affidavits, depositions, and interrogatories. The motion for summary judgment will not be granted if any facts are in dispute.

11. In preparing for trial, the attorney for each party undertakes a formal investigative process called discovery to obtain evidence helpful to his or her client's case. Traditional discovery tools include interrogatories and depositions. Interrogatories are written questions that the parties to the lawsuit must answer, in writing and under oath. Depositions, like interrogatories, are given under oath, but unlike interrogatories, depositions may also be taken from witnesses. Furthermore, the attorney is able to question the deponent (the person being deposed) in person. Usually, a court reporter records the official transcript of the deposition. During discovery, the attorney for either side may also submit various requests, including a request for documents in the possession of the other party or opposing counsel (or a third party), a request for admission (of the truth of certain statements) by the opposing party, and a request for examination (to establish the truth of claimed injuries or health status).

12. In federal court cases, revised FRCP 26 requires that the attorneys cooperate in forming a discovery plan early in the litigation process. The rule also requires attorneys to automatically disclose relevant information. Under FRCP 26, only after initial disclosures have been made can attorneys resort to the use of traditional discovery tools.

QUESTIONS FOR REVIEW

1. What happens during the initial client interview? Who normally conducts this interview, the attorney or the paralegal? Why?

2. What are the basic steps in the litigation process prior to the trial? How does the paralegal assist the attorney in each of these steps?

3. What kinds of documents are contained in a litigation file? How might these documents be classified, or organized, within the file?

4. What documents constitute the pleadings in a civil lawsuit? What is the effect of each type of document on the litigation?

5. How are defendants notified of lawsuits that have been brought against them? What new procedures are required under revised FRCP 4 for notifying the defendant of a lawsuit?

6. What is service of process. Why is it important?

7. Name three pretrial motions and state the purpose of each motion.

8. What is a counterclaim? What is an affirmative defense? What is the effect of each of these on the litigation?

9. What is discovery? When does it take place? List three discovery devices that can be used to obtain information prior to trial.

10. How have the 1993 amendments to the FRCP affected the discovery process in federal court cases?

ETHICAL QUESTIONS

1. Pamela Hodges has just started working as a paralegal for Lawyers, Inc., a high-volume, low-overhead law firm that handles mostly simple and routine legal matters. Her supervising attorney, Carol Levine, has two initial client meetings scheduled at the same time. Carol tells Pam to handle one, and she (Carol) will come in to sign the retainer agreement. After one and a half hours, Carol is still tied up, and the client is demanding that Pam sign the retainer agreement or he will find another attorney. Should Pam let the client leave and risk losing his business, or should Pam sign the retainer agreement? Does she have other options?

2. Your next-door neighbor's son was beaten up while at school. The boy's mother is facing over $1,000 in medical and dental expenses as a result of his injuries, which she cannot afford to pay. She knows that you work in a law firm as a paralegal, so she asks you if you will help her. She wants you to write a letter threatening legal action, which she will then sign, and she also wants to know whether she can sue the parents of the boys who beat up her son. Should you write the letter? Should you advise her on what action she might take against the other boys' parents? What are your ethical obligations in this situation? How could you help her without violating professional ethical standards?

3. Bruce Miller, a paralegal, is meeting with Callie Nelson, a client, to prepare answers to interrogatories. In the course of preparing the answers, Callie asks Bruce if he thinks that she has a good case, if there are better legal theories that she should pursue to win her case, and what her options are if she loses. How should Bruce answer these questions?

4. Scott Emerson takes a job as a paralegal with a large law firm that specializes in defending clients against product-liability claims. The firm's clients are some of the largest manufacturing companies in the country. Mark Jones, an associate attorney, assigns Scott the job of drafting and sending out interrogatories to the plaintiff in a case brought against one of the firm's clients. Specifically, Scott is told to send out a standard set of one hundred interrogatories, each with five parts. Scott eventually learns that one of the favorite discovery tactics of the firm is to inundate plaintiffs with discovery requests, interrogatories, and depositions to cause continuous delays and to outspend the plaintiffs. Scott knows that the relevant state court rules do not limit the number of interrogatories that can be used, but he suspects that the firm's tactics are ethically questionable. Are they? What should Scott do?

PRACTICE QUESTIONS AND ASSIGNMENTS

1. Assume that you work for attorney Tara Jolans of Adams & Tate, 1000 Town Center, Suite 500, White Tower, Michigan. Jolans has decided to represent Sandra Nelson in her lawsuit against David Namisch. Based on the following information, draft a complaint to be filed in the U.S. District Court for the Eastern District of Michigan.

> Sandra Nelson is a plaintiff in a lawsuit resulting from an automobile accident. Sandra was turning left at a traffic light at the intersection of Jefferson and Mack Streets, while the left-turn arrow was green, when she was hit from the side by a car driven by David Namisch, who failed to stop at the light. The accident occurred on Friday, June 3, 1995, at 11:30 P.M. David lived in New York, was visiting his family in Michigan, and just prior to the accident had been out drinking with his brothers. Several witnesses saw the accident. One of the witnesses called the police.
>
> Sandra was not wearing her seat belt at the time of the accident, and she was thrown against the windshield, sustaining massive head injuries. When the police and ambulance arrived, they did not think that she would make it to the hospital alive, but she survived. She wants to claim damages of $500,000 for medical expenses, $65,000 for lost wages, and $35,000 for property damage to her Rolls Royce. The accident was reported in the local newspaper, complete with photographs.

2. Draft the first ten questions for a set of interrogatories to be directed to the plaintiff, Sandra Nelson, based on the facts given in Question 1 above.

QUESTIONS FOR CRITICAL ANALYSIS

1. As indicated in footnote 8, the revised federal rules governing discovery have caused substantial controversy, and many federal courts have opted not to adopt them. If you were a federal court judge and the decision were up to you, would you adopt the revised discovery rules? Why or why not?

2. Anatol Fedorovich is a famous Russian violinist. While shopping at the Corner Drugstore, which is owned by Joe Rossini, he slipped and fell, breaking his right arm. His arm healed, but its use is severely impaired. Having only recently immigrated to the United States, Anatol is unaware of his right to sue. Nearly two years later, because he is now unable to earn a living by playing the violin, he consults a lawyer. You are working for the lawyer as paralegal, and after the consultation, the lawyer asks you to do some preliminary checking into Anatol's claim. What would you check first, and why?

ROLE-PLAYING EXERCISES

1. Review the hypothetical scenario presented in Practice Question 1 above. Assume that Sandra Nelson's attorney is scheduled to depose David Namisch, and David's attorney is preparing David for the questions that David should anticipate and how David should handle them. Assume that David had drunk at least eight cans of beer during the three hours prior to the accident and that this is his second accident resulting from drunk driving. The last time, David lost his license for three months. Working in pairs, one student should assume the role of David and the other the role of the attorney. If time allows, reverse the roles.

2. For this role-playing exercise, you will need to work in pairs. One student should assume the role of the attorney and the other that of the paralegal in the scenario described below. You will need to discuss how the paralegal is to solve her problem. If time allows, reverse the roles.

> Anne Hall, a paralegal at Klein & Long, P.C., is instructed by her boss to take a complaint and file it in person in federal court because

the statute of limitations expires at midnight tonight. Anne makes the necessary copies, checks the office copy of the filing-fee schedule for the fee, and obtains a check in the amount of the fee. She drives three hours to the federal courthouse, arriving at 11:30 A.M., and presents the complaint to the court clerk for filing. The clerk will not accept it because today a new filing fee goes into effect and Anne's check is not in the correct amount.

Anne does not have time to drive back to the office to get another check because the clerk's office closes at 4 P.M. She cannot file the complaint tomorrow because the statute of limitations will have run. Anne calls her boss and explains the situation to him. They discuss how to handle the situation.

PROJECTS

1. Visit the county court clerk's office (or the clerk's office of a local court) and obtain the following: local court rules, summons and return-of-service forms, and a filing-fee schedule.

2. Review your state's court rules to determine if counterclaims and the other types of pleadings listed in Exhibit 10.2 are permissible. If so, when are they permitted?

3. Review your state's court rules to determine which, if any, of the pretrial motions covered in this chapter are used in the courts in your state. Are the rules the same for all courts in your state? If not, how are they different?

4. Find out when a local court's "motion day" is and attend court for two to three hours on that day. Observe as many motions for summary judgment as possible. Write a one-page summary of what you observed. Be sure to include the name of the court you visited, the date, and the judge's name.

ANNOTATED SELECTED READINGS

FRIEDENTHAL, JACK H., MARY KAY KANE, AND ARTHUR R. MILLER. *Civil Procedure.* 2d ed. St. Paul: West Publishing Co., 1993. A hornbook providing detailed guidance on the Federal Rules of Civil Procedure. A good reference for those new to federal practice.

GREENE, CHRISTINE B. *Litigation and Administrative Practice Handbook Series—Summarizing Depositions: Old Techniques and New Techniques.* New York: Practising Law Institute, 1991. A handbook that presents a good discussion of how to summarize a deposition. The text also discusses alternatives to summarizing the deposition transcript.

QUARLES, SANDRA L. "Litigation Support: Using WordPerfect with Style." *Legal Assistant Today,* March/April 1993. An article containing tips for using the WordPerfect styles library to set up standard forms. Reading it is a must for the novice at word processing.

TOKUMITSU, CYNTHIA. "Ten Secrets of Efficient Litigation Paralegals." *Legal Assistant Today,* September/October 1992. An article offering some valuable tips for the litigation paralegal, such as learning how to anticipate the paths that a case might take and taking advantage of technology to save time. The article also gives insights into the types of tasks undertaken by litigation paralegals in their daily work.

VAUGHN TUPIS, CYNTHIA. "Tips for Compelling and Limiting Discovery." *Legal Assistant Today,* May/June 1992. An article that is full of discovery tips. Good reading for the more experienced litigation paralegal.

WRIGHT, CHARLES ALAN. *Wright's Law of Federal Courts.* 5th ed. St. Paul: West Publishing Co., 1994. A hornbook detailing the federal court system; federal jurisdiction, venue, and procedure; and the law applied by federal courts. The book contains a good explanation of the relationships between state and federal courts and is a basic resource for those involved in federal practice.

11

TRIAL PROCEDURES

Chapter Objectives

After completing this chapter, you will know:

- How attorneys prepare for trial and the ways in which paralegals assist in this task.
- How jurors are selected and the role of attorneys and their legal assistants in the selection process.
- The various phases of a trial and the kinds of trial-related tasks that paralegals often perform.
- The options available to the losing party after the verdict is in.
- How a case is appealed to a higher court for review.

Chapter Outline

INTRODUCTION

Trials are costly in terms of both time and money. For this reason, parties to lawsuits often try to avoid the necessity of going to trial. Pretrial negotiations between the parties and their respective attorneys may lead to an out-of-court settlement. Using the pretrial motions discussed in Chapter 10, the parties may attempt to end the litigation after the pleadings are filed or while discovery takes place. In many cases, parties opt for alternative methods of dispute resolution, such as mediation or arbitration, to avoid the time, expense, and publicity of courtroom trials. Recall from Chapter 7 that alternative dispute resolution is not always an option—many state and federal courts *mandate* that a dispute be mediated or arbitrated by the parties before they are permitted to bring the dispute before a court. If the parties fail to settle their dispute through any of these means, the case will go to trial.

To illustrate how attorneys and paralegals prepare for trial, we will continue using the hypothetical scenario developed in Chapter 10, in which Katherine Baranski (the plaintiff) was suing Tony Peretto (the defendant) for negligence. In the Baranski-Peretto case, Allen P. Gilmore is the attorney for plaintiff Baranski, and Gilmore's legal assistant is Elena Lopez. Defendant Peretto's attorney is Elizabeth A. Cameron, and Cameron's legal assistant is Gordon McVay.

CASE AT A GLANCE

The Plaintiff—
Plaintiff: Katherine Baranski
Attorney: Allen P. Gilmore
Paralegal: Elena Lopez

The Defendant—
Defendant: Tony Peretto
Attorney: Elizabeth A. Cameron
Paralegal: Gordon McVay

PREPARING FOR TRIAL

As the trial date approaches, the attorneys for the plaintiff and the defendant and their respective paralegals complete their preparations for the trial. The paralegals collect and organize all of the documents and other evidence relating to the dispute. They may find it useful to create a trial-preparation checklist similar to the one in Exhibit 11.1. Even though settlement negotiations may continue throughout the trial, both sides assume, for planning purposes, that the trial court will have to decide the issue.

At this point in the litigation process, plaintiff Baranski's attorney, Gilmore, will focus on legal strategy and how he can best use the information learned during the pleadings and discovery stages when presenting Baranski's case to the court. He will meet with his client and with his key witnesses to make last-minute preparations for trial. He might also meet with defendant Peretto's attorney to try once more to settle the dispute. Gilmore's legal assistant, Elena Lopez, will be notifying witnesses of the trial date and helping Gilmore prepare for trial. For example, she will make sure that all exhibits to be used during the trial are ready and verify that the trial notebook (discussed below) is in order.

Contacting and Preparing Witnesses

Typically, the paralegal is responsible for ensuring that witnesses are available and in court on the day of the trial. As mentioned in Chapter 10, a witness is any person asked to testify at trial. The person may be an eyewitness (that is, someone who saw the accident or event leading to a lawsuit), a per-

EXHIBIT 11.1
Trial-preparation Checklist

TWO MONTHS BEFORE THE TRIAL

—— Review the status of the case and inform the attorney of any depositions, interrogatories, or other discovery procedures that need to be undertaken prior to trial.
—— Interview witnesses and prepare witness statements.
—— Review deposition transcripts/summaries, answers to interrogatories, witness statements, and other information obtained about the case. Inform the attorney of any further discovery procedures that should be undertaken prior to trial.
—— Begin preparing the trial notebook.

ONE MONTH BEFORE THE TRIAL

—— Make a list of the witnesses who will testify at the trial for the trial notebook.
—— Prepare a subpoena for each witness, and arrange to have the subpoenas served.
—— Prepare any exhibits that will be used at trial, and reserve any special equipment (such as a VCR) that will be needed at the trial.
—— Draft *voir dire* questions and perhaps prepare a jury profile.
—— Prepare motions and memoranda.
—— Continue assembling the trial notebook.

ONE WEEK BEFORE THE TRIAL

—— Check the calendar and call the court clerk to confirm the trial date.
—— Complete the trial notebook.
—— Make sure that all subpoenas have been served.
—— Prepare the client and witnesses for trial.
—— Make the final arrangements (housing, transportation, etc.) for the client or witnesses, as necessary.
—— Check with the attorney to verify how witnesses should be paid (for lost wages, travel expenses, etc.).
—— Make final arrangements to have all equipment, documents, and other items in the courtroom on the trial date.

ONE DAY BEFORE THE TRIAL

—— Meet with others on the trial team to coordinate last-minute efforts.
—— Have a final pretrial meeting with the client.

son who has knowledge that is relevant to the lawsuit (such as an ambulance driver who assisted the accident victims or anyone who can testify to the truth of a claim being made by one of the parties), an official witness (such as a police officer), or an expert witness.

Several types of negligence lawsuits require expert witnesses. As discussed in Chapter 10, an expert witness is one who has specialized knowledge in a particular field. Such witnesses are often called to testify in negligence cases, because one element to be proved in a negligence case is the reasonableness of the defendant's actions. In medical-malpractice cases, for example, it takes someone with specialized knowledge in the defendant physician's area of practice to establish the reasonableness of the defendant's actions. A layperson does not know what is reasonably required in diagnosing or treating a specific illness or injury.

DEVELOPING PARALEGAL SKILLS

Locating Expert Witnesses

Patricia Wolff is a paralegal in a law firm that specializes in defending physicians in medical-malpractice cases. When expert witnesses may be needed, Patricia lines them up early. This ensures that they will be available on the date that they are needed in court. It also allows the attorney to interview the expert in advance to determine more precisely what legal theories or defenses should be used in court to prove the case.

Patricia's role is to locate expert witnesses. She often finds it helpful to look in the law firm's files of similar medical-malpractice cases to find out which witnesses were used in those cases and to obtain these witnesses' addresses and telephone numbers. Another way that Patricia locates expert witnesses is by consulting the firm's expert-witness file or resource person. In Patricia's firm, as in other firms that specialize in medical-malpractice cases, a resource person is kept on the staff to provide this information.

If there are no resources within the firm for Patricia to consult, she may contact professional associations for assistance. Patricia has occasionally consulted the American Medical Association to obtain lists of experts in particular medical fields. She has also consulted expert-witness directories, such as Philo, Robb, and Goodman's *Directory of Expert Witnesses in Technology* or Best's *Expert Witness Directory. Expertnet,* an expert-witness database, is available on WESTLAW (see Chapter 16 for a discussion of how to conduct research using WESTLAW).

After obtaining a list of several experts, Patricia reviews the names and credentials of the experts to be contacted. She then prepares a letter to each expert describing the type of case and why the expert is needed. The letter will also indicate that Patricia's firm would like to retain the expert and that the expert, if interested, should contact Patricia. If the expert responds that he or she is interested in testifying in the case, then arrangements will be made for the expert to meet with Patricia and her supervising attorney.

Contacting Witnesses and Issuing Subpoenas. In the Baranski case, attorney Gilmore and paralegal Lopez will have lined up witnesses to testify on behalf of their client, plaintiff Baranski. In preparing for the trial, Lopez will inform each of the witnesses that the trial date has been set and that they will be expected to appear at the trial to testify. A **subpoena**—an order issued by the court clerk directing a person to appear in court—will be served on each of the witnesses to ensure their presence in court. A subpoena to appear in a federal court is shown in Exhibit 11.2. (Although not shown in the exhibit, a return-of-service form, similar to the one illustrated in Chapter 10, will be attached to the subpoena to verify that the witness received it.)

SUBPOENA
A document commanding a person to appear at a certain time and place to give testimony concerning a certain matter.

Unless she is already familiar with the court's requirements, paralegal Lopez will want to check with the court clerk to find out about what fees and documents she needs to take to the court to obtain the subpoena. The subpoena will then be served on the witness. Most subpoenas to appear in federal court can be served by anyone who is eighteen years of age or older,

EXHIBIT 11.2
A Subpoena

United States District Court

Katherine Baranski

v.

Tony Peretto

DISTRICT Nita

DOCKET NO. 96-14335-NI

TYPE OF CASE ☒ CIVIL ☐ CRIMINAL

SUBPOENA FOR ☒ PERSON ☐ DOCUMENT(S) or OBJECT(S)

TO: Julia Williams
3765 Mattis Avenue
Nita City, NI 48803

YOU ARE HEREBY COMMANDED to appear in the United States District Court at the place, date, and time specified below to testify in the above-entitled case.

PLACE	COURTROOM
4th and Main Nita City, NI	B
	DATE AND TIME 8/4/96 10:00 A.M.

YOU ARE ALSO COMMANDED to bring with you the following document(s) or Object(s): (1)

☐ *See additional information on reverse*

This subpoena shall remain in effect until you are granted leave to depart by the court or by an officer acting on behalf of the court.

U.S. MAGISTRATE (2) OR CLERK OF COURT
C. H. Hynek

DATE
July 13, 1996

(BY) DEPUTY CLERK
John Dolan

This subpoena is issued upon application of the:

☒ Plaintiff ☐ Defendant ☐ U.S. Attorney

ATTORNEY'S NAME AND ADDRESS
Allen P. Gilmore
Jeffers, Gilmore & Dunn
553 Fifth Avenue, Suite 101
Nita City, NI 48801

(1) If not applicable, enter "none"
(2) A subpoena shall be issued by a magistrate in a proceeding before him, but need note be under the seal of the court. (Rule 17(a). Federal Rules of Criminal Procedure.)

including paralegals, who often serve subpoenas. Subpoenas to appear in state court are often served by the sheriff or other process server.

When contacting *friendly witnesses* (those favorable to Baranski's position), Lopez should take care to explain that all witnesses are served with subpoenas, as a precaution, and to tell each witness when he or she can expect to receive the subpoena. Otherwise, a friendly witness might assume that Gilmore and Lopez did not trust the witness to keep his or her promise to appear in court.

Preparing Witnesses for Trial. No prudent attorney ever puts a party or a witness on the stand unless the attorney has discussed the testimony beforehand with the party or witness. Prior to the trial, attorney Gilmore and paralegal Lopez will meet with each witness and prepare the witness for trial.

Ethical Concern

Why Subpoena Friendly Witnesses?

The beginning paralegal might logically ask why it is necessary to subpoena friendly witnesses. The answer to this question is twofold. First, subpoena's make it easier for witnesses to be excused from their jobs and any other obligations on the date that they are to appear in court. Second, attorneys must take reasonable steps (and serving witnesses with subpoenas is a reasonable measure) to ensure that the clients' interests are best served. If a witness had not been subpoenaed and for some reason failed to appear at trial, the lack of his or her crucial testimony could jeopardize the client's chances of winning the case. By serving the witness with a subpoena, the attorney has proof that he or she has not breached the duty of competence to the client.

Gilmore will prepare the witness for the types of questions to expect from himself and from opposing counsel during the trial. He might do some role playing with the witness to help the witness understand how the questioning will proceed during the trial and to prepare the witness for the opposing attorney's questions. Gilmore will also review with the witness any sworn statements made during discovery—during a deposition, for example. Additionally, Gilmore will review the substantive legal issues involved in the case and how the witness's testimony will affect the outcome of those issues.

Lopez will handle other aspects of witness preparation. She will advise the witness on trial procedures, when and where the witness will testify, and so on. Lopez might take the witness to the courtroom in which the trial will take place (if the courtroom is not in use) and familiarize the witness with the courtroom environment. She will show the witness where he or she will sit while giving testimony, where the judge and jurors will be, and where the attorneys will be seated. If necessary, Lopez might also do some role playing, acting out the roles of the attorneys and asking the kinds of questions that they might ask the witness during the trial.

Additionally, Lopez will advise witnesses on other details involved in trial preparation. For example, she might recommend appropriate clothing and grooming or tell them where to look when giving testimony and how to remain calm and poised when speaking to the court. After going over the trial procedures and the witness's role during the trial, Lopez may follow up on the discussion with a letter to the witness. Familiarity with the trial setting and what will be expected of him or her at trial will help to reduce a witness's discomfort in facing a new situation and allow the witness to control better his or her responses when called to testify.

Exhibits and Displays

Paralegals are frequently asked to prepare exhibits or displays that will be presented at trial. Attorney Gilmore may wish to present to the court a photograph of plaintiff Baranski's car taken after the accident occurred, a diagram of the intersection, an enlarged document (such as a police report), or other evidence. Paralegal Lopez will be responsible for making sure that all exhibits are properly prepared and ready to introduce at trial. If any exhibits require special equipment, such as an easel or a VCR, Lopez must also make sure that these will be available in the courtroom and properly set up when they are needed.

The Trial Notebook

Trial Notebook
A binder that contains copies of all of the documents and information that an attorney will need to have at hand during the trial.

To present plaintiff Baranski's case effectively, attorney Gilmore will need to have in the courtroom all of the relevant documents; he will also need to be able to locate them quickly. To accomplish both of these ends, Lopez will prepare a **trial notebook**. The notebook will contain copies of the pleadings, interrogatories, deposition transcripts and summaries, pretrial motions, a list of exhibits and when they will be used, a witness list and the order in which the witnesses will testify, relevant cases or statutes that Gilmore

DEVELOPING PARALEGAL SKILLS

Trial Support

Scott Greer, a paralegal with the firm of Dewey & Stone, is assisting an attorney, Sue Jefferson, in a personal-injury lawsuit. The lawsuit was brought by a client who was injured in an automobile accident. Scott has received a memo from attorney Jefferson requesting him to prepare a diagram of the accident and to arrange to have a "day-in-the-life" videotape created for presentation in court. The videotape will show what a typical day in the life of the plaintiff is like as a result of injuries sustained in the accident.

Scott begins his tasks by contacting Trial Support Services, Inc., a firm that specializes in litigation support services. Included in these services are investigations, photographic services, and the preparation of videotapes and other demonstrative evidence, such as graphs, charts, and scale drawings. Scott explains that he needs a day-in-the-life tape made that details the day-to-day living experiences of the plaintiff, who is now a paraplegic as a result of the accident. This video will be shown to the jury to make them aware of the kind of life the plaintiff now leads as a result of the defendant's negligence. Scott arranges to meet with an employee of Trial Support Services at the plaintiff's home on the following day so that the videotape can be made.

Because Scott has so many other responsibilities in preparing for this trial, he does not have time to prepare the graphs and charts on his computer at the office, as he often does. Scott arranges to have Trial Support Services enlarge the diagram of the accident site so that it can be viewed clearly by the jury. The diagram will help the jury understand how the accident occurred. Scott delivers the diagram, which measures 8½ by 11 inches, to Trial Support Services that afternoon and asks them to enlarge it to 2½ by 4½ feet. Scott further requests that the enlarged diagram be done in color and placed on an easel, which Trial Support Services can also provide.

Trial Support Services agrees to deliver a VCR, a television set, the enlarged diagram, copies of the diagram for the jurors, and the easel to the courtroom prior to the trial. Scott makes a deposit on the equipment, and Trial Support Services agrees to bill the firm for the balance. Scott will have to contact the judge's clerk to arrange for a convenient time for the delivery of these items. He will also have to meet with an employee of Trial Support Services in the courtroom prior to the trial so that the employee can show Scott how to work the video equipment and set up the easel.

Now that Scott has performed the work assigned to him, he prepares a memo detailing the arrangements that he has made and puts it in the file. He sends a copy of the memo to his supervising attorney so that she knows that he has completed the assignment.

plans to cite, and generally any document or information that will be important to have close at hand during the trial.

- **Unless the paralegal knows from prior experience what his or her supervising attorney wants to include in the trial notebook and how it should be organized, the paralegal should discuss these matters with the attorney.**

CASE AT A GLANCE

The Plaintiff—
Plaintiff: Katherine Baranski
Attorney: Allen P. Gilmore
Paralegal: Elena Lopez

The Defendant—
Defendant: Tony Peretto
Attorney: Elizabeth A. Cameron
Paralegal: Gordon McVay

Typically, the trial notebook is a three-ring binder (or several binders, depending on the complexity of the case). The contents of the notebook are separated by divider sheets with tabs on them. Paralegal Lopez will create a general index to the notebook's contents and place this index at the front of the notebook. She may also create an index for each section of the binder and place those indexes at the beginnings of the sections. Some paralegals use a computer notebook and a software retrieval system to help them quickly locate documents, especially in complicated cases involving thousands of documents.

When preparing the trial notebook, always remember the following:

- **The documents in the trial notebook should not be the original documents but rather copies of them.**

The original documents (unless they are needed as evidence at trial) should always remain in the firm's files, both for reasons of security (should the trial notebook be misplaced) and to ensure that Lopez or others in the office will have access to the documents while the notebook is in court with the attorney.

Paralegal Lopez will not wait until the last minute to prepare the trial notebook. Rather, at the outset of the lawsuit, she will make copies of the pleadings and other documents as they are generated to include in the notebook. That way, she will not have to spend valuable time just before the trial, when other needs are pressing, to do work that could have been done earlier. For further suggestions on how to prepare a trial notebook, see this chapter's featured-guest article entitled "Ten Tips for Preparing a Trial Notebook."

PRETRIAL CONFERENCE

PRETRIAL CONFERENCE
A conference prior to trial in which the judge and the attorneys litigating the suit discuss settlement possibilities, clarify the issues in dispute, and schedule forthcoming trial-related events.

MOTION *IN LIMINE*
A motion requesting that certain evidence not be brought out at the trial, such as prejudicial, irrelevant, or legally inadmissible evidence.

Before the trial begins, the attorneys usually meet with the trial judge in a **pretrial conference** to explore the possibility of resolving the case and, if a settlement is not possible, at least agree on the manner in which the trial will be conducted. In particular, the parties may attempt to clarify the issues in dispute and establish ground rules to restrict such things as the admissibility of certain types of evidence. For example, attorney Gilmore might have paralegal Lopez draft a **motion *in limine***[1] (a motion to limit evidence) to submit to the judge at this time. The motion will request the judge to order that certain types of evidence not be brought out at trial.

For example, suppose that plaintiff Baranski had been arrested in the past for illegal drug possession. Gilmore knows that evidence of the arrest, if introduced by the defense at trial, might prejudice the jury against Baranski. In this situation, Gilmore might submit a motion *in limine* to keep the defense from presenting the evidence. Exhibit 11.3 presents a sample motion *in limine.* Note that Gilmore would include with the motion affidavits and/or a memorandum of law (brief)—these documents were discussed in Chapter 10—to convince the judge that the motion should be granted.

Once the pretrial conference has concluded, both parties will turn their attention to the trial itself. Assuming that the trial will be heard by a jury,

1. Pronounced in *leem*-in-ay.

EXHIBIT 11.3
Motion *in Limine*

UNITED STATES DISTRICT COURT
FOR THE WESTERN DISTRICT OF NITA

Katherine Baranski
Plaintiff

vs. File No. 96-14335-NI

Hon. Harley M. LaRue

Tony Peretto
Defendant

A. P. Gilmore
Attorney for the Plaintiff
Jeffers, Gilmore & Dunn
553 Fifth Avenue
Suite 101
Nita City, NI 48801

MOTION IN LIMINE

The Plaintiff respectfully moves the Court to prohibit counsel for the Defendant from directly or indirectly introducing or making any reference during the trial to the Plaintiff's arrest in 1984 for the possession of illegal drugs.

The grounds on which this motion is based are stated in the accompanying affidavits and memorandum.

Date: 6/18/96

Allen P. Gilmore
Allen P. Gilmore
Attorney for the Plaintiff
Jeffers, GIlmore & Dunn
553 Fifth Avenue
Suite 101
Nita City, NI 48801

however, one more step is necessary before the trial begins: selecting the jurors who will hear the trial and render a verdict on the dispute.

JURY SELECTION

Before the trial gets under way, a panel of jurors must be assembled. The clerk of the court usually notifies local residents by mail that they have been selected for jury duty. The process of selecting the names of these prospective jurors varies, depending on the court, but often they are randomly selected by the court clerk from lists of registered voters or those within a state to whom driver's licenses have been issued. The persons selected then report to the courthouse on the date specified in the notice. At the courthouse, they are gathered into a single pool of jurors, and the process of selecting those jurors who will actually hear the case begins. Although some types of trials require twelve-person juries, most civil matters can be heard by a jury of six persons.

FEATURED GUEST: VITONIO F. SAN JUAN

Ten Tips for Preparing a Trial Notebook

Biographical Note

Vitonio F. San Juan is a graduate of the University of the Philippines College of Law. He has a master of law degree (an advanced law degree) from the University of California School of Law in Los Angeles. He is also a J.S.D. (doctor of the science of law) candidate at the University of California School of Law in Berkeley (Boalt Hall). He practiced corporate and securities law before devoting his time to legal education and to the law governing international trade and investments. At present, he is the director of paralegal studies at the University of La Verne in La Verne, California. The program offers a paralegal certificate, an associate's degree, and a bachelor of science degree in paralegal studies at two campus sites. San Juan also teaches in the program and in the College of Law.

The trial notebook compiles all the essential case information for the ready reference of the trial attorney. Prepared by the paralegal, the notebook reorganizes the central office file in such a way that the trial attorney has quick access to the information he or she needs during the trial. In preparing the notebook, the paralegal might find it helpful to follow the tips given below.

1 Check with the Attorney before Creating the Notebook. The one hard-and-fast rule for organizing the trial notebook is that it must be organized so that it assists the attorney during the trial. To learn the attorney's preferences, the legal assistant should check with the attorney. The trial attorney will be the one presenting the evidence during trial, anticipating the opposition's moves, and ultimately summarizing the client's case in the closing argument. As a member of the trial team, you must communicate closely with the attorney during the pretrial stages to make sure that the trial notebook is organized efficiently for the attorney's use during the trial.

2 Prepare the Notebook Early. The paralegal must keep track of many things while helping prepare for a trial. With the increasing number of jobs to be done and the accompanying details, it is very easy to forget something. To avoid this possibility, start preparing the notebook once you learn what the trial attorney wants to have included in it. Having the notebook not only makes you feel more confident and in control, but it could also help the attorney in the settlement stage. During that stage, the notebook will send a message to opposing counsel that your side is prepared and that you have a strong case. In any event, even if the case goes to trial, the notebook will show the client just how well your firm works.

3 Think "Easy Access." In preparing the notebook you should try to make every document easily retrievable. The attorney who can easily locate the document that he or she needs, at the moment that it is needed, projects a positive image to the jury. If it takes more than a few seconds to get the document or to access prior testimony, the jury can easily lose confidence in the attorney and brand him or her as a fumbler. Normally, a three-ring binder is used. This will make the notebook flexible; it can be expanded and updated as needed. If there will be a large number of pages, a large-size binder might be used. The color of the binder should be coordinated with the colors of any other binders. A unique color will assist you in finding a specific item in a hurry and can again create the impression in court that the case has been carefully thought out and organized.

4 Create a Notebook That Works. Once you've talked to the trial attorney and determined his or her preferences, you can start creat-

FEATURED GUEST, Continued

ing the notebook. Most notebooks have a table of contents and are divided into sections. There could be sections for the pleadings and pretrial motions; the opening statement and the discovery plan; jury research notes, proposed *voir dire* questions, and notes on the accepted jurors; witnesses (subdivided into friendly, hostile, and expert); and notes regarding closing arguments. Various indexes may also be included (such as a deposition index, a key-document index, an exhibit index, and a demonstrative-evidence index).

Each section should be tabbed. Consider using color tabs that match a predetermined color code (for example, red for exhibits, yellow for witnesses, blue for documents, and so on).

Use notebook dividers and be sure to have extra ones handy. You can put extra tabs and dividers in a prepunched pocket envelope. The pocket envelope can also contain extra yellow pads of paper. Attorneys often need to make notes during the trial, and the yellow paper can be easily distinguished from the rest of the white paper in the notebook.

Finally, cases vary in complexity and length. If you can't fit all the information into one notebook, use more.

5 Have a Section for Contact Information. This section of the trial notebook should include the names, addresses, and phone and fax numbers of all the parties and attorneys involved in the case. It is also a good idea to include a section for your vendors (suppliers), including your graphics vendors, photocopying vendors, and couriers.

6 Create a Back-up Trial Notebook. Keep a duplicate copy of the main trial notebook so that a copy will be available if the original is lost or, more likely, a portion of its contents is misplaced.

7 Create Your Own Paralegal Notebook. This notebook should contain key information for your use. While the trial notebook is assembled to meet the trial needs of the attorney, this notebook will enable you to have key information at your fingertips. It should contain some of the information found in the trial notebook and checklists to help you remember all the various deadlines and details. You may also include a section for adding notes during the trial. For example, you could jot down jury responses to the behavior of certain witnesses—information that may be helpful to you when you are preparing witnesses for trial in the future.

8 Consult with Co-workers. If you have questions, consult with other, more experienced paralegals when preparing your trial notebook. Some of their ideas and experiences may help you avoid mistakes.

9 Review the Contents Periodically. Check and recheck the contents of the trial notebook periodically. Make sure that the sections are complete and that all information is current. If the attorney removes a section from the notebook, make sure before the trial begins that the section is in its proper place.

"THE ATTORNEY WHO CAN EASILY LOCATE THE DOCUMENT THAT HE OR SHE NEEDS, AT THE MOMENT THAT IT IS NEEDED, PROJECTS A POSITIVE IMAGE TO THE JURY."

10 Check with the Attorney Again. Once you've put together the trial notebook, make sure that it contains everything that is needed. Schedule some convenient time with the trial attorney to go over the notebook. He or she may want to include other sections or indexes. Try to anticipate any problems, and take care of them before they occur. Remember that you must be flexible and take every new problem in stride. The trial notebook is an essential tool for the attorney trying a case. A very personalized tool, it contains information that must be readily accessible. Remember: when in doubt, check with the attorney.

Voir Dire

VOIR DIRE
A French phrase meaning "to speak the truth." The phrase is used to describe the preliminary questions that attorneys for the plaintiff and the defendant ask prospective jurors to determine whether potential jury members are biased or have any connection with a party to the action or with a prospective witness.

Both the plaintiff's attorney and the defendant's attorney have some input into the ultimate make-up of the jury. Each attorney will question prospective juror's in a proceeding known as ***voir dire***.[2] Legal assistants often work with their attorneys to write up the questions that will be asked of jurors during *voir dire.* Because all of the jurors will have previously filled out forms giving basic information about themselves, the attorneys and their paralegals can tailor their questions accordingly. They fashion the questions in such a way as to uncover any biases on the part of prospective jurors and to find persons who might identify with the plights of their respective clients. When large numbers of jurors are involved, during the *voir dire* process, the attorneys may direct their questions to groups of jurors, as opposed to individual jurors, to minimize the amount of time needed to choose the jurors who will sit on the jury. Note that in some courts, judges may question the jurors, using questions prepared by the attorneys.

Challenges during *Voir Dire*

CHALLENGE
An attorney's objection, during *voir dire,* to the inclusion of a particular person on the jury.

During *voir dire,* the attorney for each side may exercise a certain number of **challenges** to prevent particular persons from being allowed to serve on the jury. As plaintiff Baranski's attorney, Gilmore will want to exclude jurors who may already have formed an unfavorable impression about the validity of Baranski's claim. To uncover any underlying hostility toward Baranski, Gilmore might ask a juror whether he or she has ever been sued. Defendant Peretto's attorney, in contrast, will want to ferret out jurors who might be inclined to render a verdict against Tony Peretto, perhaps because they have been injured in a car accident caused by another person's negligent driving. Experienced litigators try to conserve their challenges so that they may eliminate the prospective jurors who are the most hostile.

During the jury-selection process, attorney Gilmore may have paralegal Lopez observe the prospective jurors carefully as they respond to the attorneys' questions. Lopez, because she is not participating in the questioning process, is free to observe the jurors more closely than Gilmore. As a result, she may uncover a verbal or nonverbal response that Gilmore might not notice.

CASE AT A GLANCE

The Plaintiff—
Plaintiff: Katherine Baranski
Attorney: Allen P. Gilmore
Paralegal: Elena Lopez

The Defendant—
Defendant: Tony Peretto
Attorney: Elizabeth A. Cameron
Paralegal: Gordon McVay

Types of Challenges. Both attorneys can exercise two types of challenges: challenges "for cause" and peremptory challenges. If attorney Gilmore concludes that a particular prospective juror is biased against Baranski for some reason, Gilmore may exercise a **challenge for cause** and request that the prospective juror not be included in the jury. Each attorney may also exercise a limited number of **peremptory challenges**. Attorneys may exercise peremptory challenges without giving any reason for their desire to exclude a particular juror. Peremptory challenges based on racial criteria or gender, however, are illegal.[3]

CHALLENGE FOR CAUSE
A *voir dire* challenge for which an attorney states the reason why a prospective juror should not be included in the jury.

PEREMPTORY CHALLENGE
A *voir dire* challenge to exclude a potential juror from serving on the jury without any supporting reason or cause. Peremptory challenges based on racial or gender criteria are illegal.

2. A French phrase meaning "to speak the truth." Pronounced vwahr *deehr.*
3. Discriminating against prospective jurors on the basis of race was prohibited by the United States Supreme Court in *Batson v. Kentucky,* 476 U.S. 79, 106 S.Ct. 1712, 90 L.Ed.2d 69 (1986). Discriminating against prospective jurors on the basis of gender was prohibited by the Supreme Court in *J.E.B. v. Alabama ex rel. T.B.,* ____U.S.____, 114 S. Ct. 1419, 128 L.Ed.2d 89 (1994). See Chapter 17 for an explanation of how to read court citations.

After both sides have completed their challenges, those jurors who have been excused are permitted to leave. The remaining jurors, those found to be acceptable by both attorneys, will be seated in the jury box.

Alternate Jurors. Because unforeseeable circumstances or illness may necessitate that one or more of the sitting jurors be dismissed, the court also seats several *alternate jurors* who will also hear the entire trial. Depending on the rules of the particular jurisdiction, a court might have two or three alternate jurors present throughout the trial. If a juror has to be excused in the middle of the trial, then an alternate may take his or her place without disrupting the proceedings. Once the jury members are seated, the judge swears in the jury and the trial itself can begin.

The Trial

During the trial, the attorneys, Allen Gilmore and Elizabeth Cameron, will present their cases to the jury. Because the attorneys will be concentrating on the trial, it will fall to their paralegals to coordinate the logistical aspects of the trial and observe as closely as possible the trial proceedings. Because paralegal Lopez is thoroughly familiar with the case and Gilmore's legal strategy, she will be a valuable ally during the trial. She will be able to anticipate Gilmore's needs and provide appropriate reminders or documents as Gilmore needs them.

At the end of each trial day, for example, Lopez will assemble the documents and materials that will be needed in court the next day. During the court proceedings, Lopez will make sure that attorney Gilmore has within reach any documents or exhibits that he will need to have at hand for questioning parties or witnesses. When attorney Gilmore no longer needs the documents or exhibits, Lopez will put them aside in an appropriate place. At the end of the day, she will again organize the documents and materials, decide what will be needed for the next day, and file the documents that can remain in the office.

Paralegal Lopez must also monitor each witness's testimony to ensure that it is consistent with previous statements made by the witness. Lopez will have the relevant deposition transcript (and summary) at hand when a witness takes the stand. She will follow the deposition transcript (or summary) of each witness as that witness testifies. This way, she can pass a note to Gilmore if he misses any inconsistencies in the witness's testimony.

Lopez will also act as a second pair of eyes and ears during the trial. She will observe how the jury is responding to various witnesses and their testimony or to the attorneys' demeanor and questions. She will take notes during the trial on these observations as well as on the points being stressed and the types of evidence introduced by the opposing counsel, Cameron. At the end of the day, Lopez and Gilmore may review the day's events, and Lopez's "trial journal" will provide a ready reference to the major events that transpired in the courtroom.

Ethical Concern

Should You Tell Your Supervising Attorney What You Know about a Prospective Juror?

During *voir dire,* paralegal Lopez notices one of her neighbors among the prospective jurors. Lopez knows that her neighbor is strongly biased against foreigners and will probably not be an impartial juror in the case against Tony Peretto, who has a slight foreign accent. Lopez also knows that she and attorney Gilmore want their client, plaintiff Baranski, to win the case, and a juror biased against Peretto would definitely help them achieve this goal. Should Lopez tell Gilmore what she knows about this prospective juror? Yes. It is to Gilmore's—and his client's—advantage to know all he can about the prospective jurors, and it is up to Gilmore to decide how to use whatever information he obtains. Furthermore, Lopez has no duty to keep confidential any information that she has learned about her neighbor.

Case at a Glance

The Plaintiff—
Plaintiff: Katherine Baranski
Attorney: Allen P. Gilmore
Paralegal: Elena Lopez

The Defendant—
Defendant: Tony Peretto
Attorney: Elizabeth A. Cameron
Paralegal: Gordon McVay

THE LEGAL TEAM AT WORK
In the Courtroom

Many paralegals, like Elena Lopez, attend trials with their attorneys. And many attorneys say that they do not know how they could manage the many things that need to be done during the trial without such assistance. Suppose, for example, that an attorney wants to check on the contents of a document that was not included in the trial notebook. There is no way that the attorney can leave the courtroom while the court is in session. His paralegal, however, can. If the paralegal brought a cellular phone with him or her, as many paralegals who attend trials do, the paralegal can simply step out into the hallway, dial a number, and get the information from the office over the phone or arrange to have documents brought to the courthouse immediately. (The legal assistant must take care when using a cellular phone to preserve confidentiality. For example, he or she must not reveal the client's name or any other information that could identify the client because conversations over cellular phones may be tapped. As with any phone call, paralegals must also be careful to make sure that the conversation is not overheard by any third party, such as someone in the hallway of the courthouse.)

The paralegal can also assist at trial by comparing statements made in court by a witness for the opponent to statements made earlier by that witness during his or her deposition. If the witness gives testimony that is inconsistent with earlier statements, the attorney will want to prove this inconsistency to the court by pointing to the relevant page of the deposition transcript. The paralegal, if he or she was checking the testimony against the deposition transcript, will have the relevant page numbers of the transcript at hand and can quickly direct the attorney's attention to those pages.

The old adage "Two heads are better than one" is certainly true in the context of trial work. Although their duties and functions differ, the lawyer and the paralegal both play essential roles in representing the client's best interests in the courtroom.

Opening Statements

OPENING STATEMENT
An attorney's statement to the jury at the beginning of the trial. The attorney briefly outlines the evidence that will be offered during the trial and the legal theory that will be pursued.

The trial both opens and closes with attorneys' statements to the jury. In their **opening statements**, the attorneys will give a brief version of the facts and the supporting evidence that they will use during the trial. Because some trials can drag on for weeks or even months, it is extremely helpful for jurors to hear a summary of the story that will unfold during the trial. Otherwise, they may be left wondering how a particular piece of evidence fits into the dispute.

In short, the opening statement is a kind of "road map" that describes the destination that each attorney hopes to reach and outlines how he or she plans to reach it. Plaintiff Baranski's attorney, Gilmore, will focus on such things as his client's lack of fault and the injuries that she sustained when she was hit by defendant Peretto's car. Peretto's attorney, Cameron, will highlight the points that weaken plaintiff Baranski's claim (for example, Cameron might point out that Baranski was speeding) or otherwise suggest that defendant Peretto had not committed any wrongful act.

The Plaintiff's Case

Once the opening statements have been made, Gilmore will present the plaintiff's case first. Because he is the plaintiff's attorney, he has the burden of proving that defendant Peretto was negligent.

Direct Examination. Attorney Gilmore will call several eyewitnesses to the stand and ask them to tell the court about the sequence of events that led to the accident. This form of questioning is known as **direct examination**. For example, Gilmore will call Julia Williams, an eyewitness who saw the accident occur, and ask her questions such as those presented in Exhibit 11.4 on page 438. He will also call other witnesses, including the police officer who was called to the accident scene and the ambulance driver. Gilmore will try to elicit responses from these witnesses that strengthen plaintiff Baranski's case—or at least that do not visibly weaken the claim.

DIRECT EXAMINATION
The examination of a witness by the attorney who calls the witness to the stand to testify on behalf of the attorney's client.

During direct examination, attorney Gilmore will not usually be permitted to ask **leading questions**, which are questions that lead the witness to a particular desired response. A leading question might be something like the following: "So, Mrs. Williams, you noticed that the defendant ran the stop sign, right?" If Mrs. Williams says "yes" to this question, she has, in effect, been "led" to this conclusion by Gilmore's leading question. The fundamental purpose behind a trial is to establish what actually happened, not to tell witnesses what to say.

LEADING QUESTION
A question that suggests, or "leads to," a desired answer. Generally, leading questions may be asked only of hostile witnesses.

- **Leading questions may distort the testimony by discouraging witnesses from telling their stories in their own words.**

When Gilmore is dealing with *hostile witnesses* (uncooperative witnesses or those who are testifying on behalf of the other party), however, he is normally permitted to ask leading questions. This is because hostile witnesses may be uncommunicative and unwilling to describe the events they witnessed. If Gilmore asked a hostile witness what he or she observed on the morning of August 4 at 7:45 A.M., for example, the witness might respond, "I saw two trucks driving down Mattis Avenue." That answer is true, but it has nothing to do with the Baranski-Peretto accident. Therefore, to elicit information from this witness, Gilmore would be permitted to use leading questions, which would force the witness to respond to the question at issue.

CROSS-EXAMINATION
The questioning of an opposing witness during the trial.

Cross-examination. After attorney Gilmore has finished questioning a witness on direct examination, defendant Peretto's attorney, Cameron, will begin her **cross-examination** of that witness. During her cross-examination, Cameron will be primarily concerned with reducing the witness's credibility in the eyes of the jury and the judge. Cameron's questions for Gilmore's witnesses will be based on their answers to interrogatories and depositions submitted during discovery. Consequently, Cameron will have a fairly good idea as to what areas of questioning may prove fruitful. Moreover, she can attack the credibility of these witnesses if their answers on the witness stand vary considerably from answers they gave in response to the same questions during discovery or if other evidence obtained during discovery contradicts their testimony.

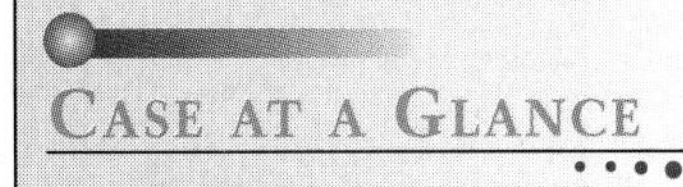

The Plaintiff—
Plaintiff: Katherine Baranski
Attorney: Allen P. Gilmore
Paralegal: Elena Lopez

The Defendant—
Defendant: Tony Peretto
Attorney: Elizabeth A. Cameron
Paralegal: Gordon McVay

EXHIBIT 11.4
Direct Examination—Sample Questions

ATTORNEY:	Mrs. Williams, please explain how you came to be at the scene of the accident.
WITNESS:	Well, I was walking north on Mattis Avenue toward Nita City Hospital, where I work as a nurse.
ATTORNEY:	Please describe for the court, in your own words, exactly what you observed when you reached the intersection of Mattis Avenue and Thirty-eighth Street.
WITNESS:	I was approaching the intersection when I saw the defendant run the stop sign on Thirty-eighth Street and crash into the plaintiff's car.
ATTORNEY:	Did you notice any change in the speed at which the defendant was driving as he approached the stop sign?
WITNESS:	No. He didn't slow down at all.
ATTORNEY:	Mrs. Williams, are you generally in good health?
WITNESS:	Yes.
ATTORNEY:	Have you ever had any problems with your vision?
WITNESS:	No. I wear reading glasses for close work, but I see well in the distance.
ATTORNEY:	And how long has it been since your last eye examination?
WITNESS:	About a month or so ago, I went to Dr. Sullivan for an examination. He told me that I needed reading glasses but that my distance vision was excellent.

The defendant's attorney, Cameron, must confine her cross-examination to matters brought up during direct examination and matters that relate to a witness's credibility. She normally may not introduce evidence that a witness for the plaintiff is a smoker or dislikes children, for example, unless she can demonstrate that such matters are relevant to the case. In general, Cameron will try to uncover relevant physical infirmities of the plaintiff's witnesses (such as poor eyesight or hearing) as well as any evidence of bias (such as a witness's habit of playing a friendly round of golf with plaintiff Baranski every Saturday). When cross-examining Gilmore's witnesses for the plaintiff, Cameron is permitted to ask leading questions, because Gilmore's witnesses will be hostile witnesses in respect to Peretto's defense. Some questions that Cameron might ask Julia Williams, Gilmore's eyewitness, are presented in Exhibit 11.5.

Redirect and Recross. After defendant Peretto's attorney, Cameron, has finished cross-examining each witness, plaintiff Baranski's attorney, Gilmore, will need to repair any damage done to the credibility of the witness's testimony—or, indeed, to the case itself. Gilmore will do this by again questioning the witness and allowing the witness to explain his or her answer. This process is known as **redirect examination**.

REDIRECT EXAMINATION
The questioning of a witness following the adverse party's cross-examination.

If Cameron's cross-examination revealed that one of Gilmore's eyewitnesses to the accident had vision problems, for example, Gilmore could ask

EXHIBIT 11.5
Cross-examination—Sample Questions

ATTORNEY:	You have just testified that you were approaching the intersection when the accident occurred. Isn't it true that you stated earlier, under oath, that you were at the intersection at the time of the accident?
WITNESS:	Well, I might have, but I think I said that I was close to the intersection.
ATTORNEY:	In fact, you said that you were at the intersection. Now, you say that you were approaching it. Which is it?
WITNESS:	I was approaching it, I suppose.
ATTORNEY:	Okay. Exactly where were you when the accident occurred?
WITNESS:	I think that I was just in front of the Dairy Queen when the accident happened.
ATTORNEY:	Mrs. Williams, the Dairy Queen on Mattis Avenue is at least seventy-five yards from the intersection of Mattis Avenue and Thirty-eighth Street. Were you watching the defendant's car as it proceeded north on Mattis Avenue toward the intersection?
WITNESS:	Well, not at first, I guess.
ATTORNEY:	When did you start observing the defendant's car?
WITNESS:	I believe it was when the defendant ran the stop sign.
ATTORNEY:	Mrs. Williams, I suggest that you did not really look at the defendant's car until after the collision focused your attention on it. Isn't that true?

the witness whether he or she was wearing corrective lenses at the time of the accident. Gilmore might also have the witness demonstrate to the court that he or she has good vision by having the witness identify a letter or object at the far end of the courtroom. Because redirect examination is primarily used to improve the credibility of cross-examined witnesses, it is limited to matters raised during cross-examination. (If attorney Cameron chooses not to cross-examine a particular witness, then, of course, there can be no redirect examination by Gilmore.)

Following Gilmore's redirect examination, defendant Peretto's attorney, Cameron, will be given an opportunity for **recross-examination**. When both attorneys have finished with the first witness, Gilmore will call the succeeding witnesses in plaintiff Baranski's case, each of whom will be subject to cross-examination (and redirect and recross, if necessary).

RECROSS-EXAMINATION
The questioning of an opposing witness following the adverse party's redirect examination.

Motion for a Directed Verdict (Motion for Judgment as a Matter of Law)

After attorney Gilmore has presented his case for plaintiff Baranski, then Cameron, as counsel for defendant Peretto, may decide to make a **motion for a directed verdict** (now also known as a **motion for judgment as a matter of law** in federal courts). Through this motion, attorney Cameron will be saying to the court that the plaintiff's attorney, Gilmore, has not offered enough evidence to support a claim against defendant Peretto. If the judge agrees to grant the motion, then a judgment will be entered for defendant

MOTION FOR A DIRECTED VERDICT (MOTION FOR JUDGMENT AS A MATTER OF LAW)
A motion requesting that the court grant judgment in favor of the party making the motion on the ground that the other party has not produced sufficient evidence to support his or her claim.

EXHIBIT 11.6
Motion for Judgment as a Matter of Law

UNITED STATES DISTRICT COURT
FOR THE WESTERN DISTRICT OF NITA

Katherine Baranski
Plaintiff
File No. 96-14335-NI

vs.

Hon. Harley M. LaRue

Tony Peretto
Defendant

Elizabeth A. Cameron
Attorney for the Defendant
Cameron & Strauss, P.C.
310 Lake Drive
Zero City, ZE 59802

MOTION FOR JUDGMENT AS A MATTER OF LAW

The Defendant, Tony Peretto, at the close of the Plaintiff's case, moves the court to withdraw the evidence from the consideration of the jury and to find the Defendant not liable.

As grounds for this motion, Defendant Peretto states that:

(1) No evidence has been offered or received during the trial of the above-entitled cause of action to sustain the allegations of negligence contained in Plaintiff Baranski's complaint.

(2) No evidence has been offered or received during the trial proving or tending to prove that Defendant Peretto was guilty of any negligence.

(3) The proximate cause of Plaintiff Baranski's injuries was not due to any negligence on the part of Defendant Peretto.

(4) By the uncontroverted evidence, Plaintiff Baranski was guilty of contributory negligence, which was the sole cause of the Plaintiff's injuries.

Date: 7/21/96

Elizabeth A. Cameron
Elizabeth A. Cameron
Attorney for the Defendant
Cameron & Strauss, P.C.
310 Lake Drive
Zero City, ZE 59802

Peretto, plaintiff Baranski's case against him will be dismissed, and the trial will be over. A sample motion for judgment as a matter of law is shown in Exhibit 11.6 above.

The motion for a directed verdict (judgment as a matter of law) is seldom granted because only those cases that involve genuine factual dispute's are permitted to proceed to trial in the first place. If the judge had believed that Baranski's case was that weak before the trial started, then the judge would probably have granted a pretrial motion to dismiss the case, thereby avoiding the expense of a trial. Occasionally, however, the occurrence of certain events—such as the death of a key witness—might mean that the plaintiff has no evidence at all to support his or her allegations. In that event, the court may grant the defendant's motion for a directed verdict, or judgment as a matter of law.

The Defendant's Case

Assuming that the motion for directed verdict (motion for judgment as a matter of law) is denied by the court, the two attorneys, Gilmore and Cameron, will now reverse their roles. Attorney Cameron will now begin to present evidence demonstrating the weaknesses of plaintiff Baranski's claims against defendant Peretto. She will essentially follow the same procedure used by Gilmore when he presented plaintiff Baranski's side of the story. Cameron will call witnesses to the stand and question them. After Cameron's direct examination of each witness, that witness will be subject to possible cross-examination by Gilmore, redirect examination by Cameron, and recross-examination by Gilmore.

In her presentation of the defendant's case, attorney Cameron will attempt to counter the points made by attorney Gilmore during his presentation of plaintiff Baranski's side of the story. To that end, Cameron and her paralegal, Gordon McVay, may have to prepare exhibits and assorted memoranda of law in addition to those originally prepared. The need to prepare additional exhibits and memoranda sometimes arises when the plaintiff's attorney pursues a different strategy from the one anticipated by the defense team. Depending on Cameron's preference or strategy, she may choose to begin by exposing the weaknesses in the plaintiff's case (by asserting that the plaintiff was speeding, for example) or by presenting defendant Peretto's version of the accident. Regardless of the procedure taken, however, paralegal McVay, like paralegal Lopez, will have to keep track of the materials brought to court each day to faciliate Cameron's presentation.

Once Cameron has finished presenting her case on behalf of defendant Peretto, Gilmore will be permitted to offer evidence to *rebut* (refute) evidence introduced by Cameron in Peretto's behalf. After Gilmore's rebuttal, if any, both attorneys will make their closing arguments to the jury.

ETHICAL CONCERN

Communicating with Jurors

Suppose that you are the paralegal working on the Baranski case with attorney Allen Gilmore, and one of your neighbors is a juror in the case. One evening, while you are gardening in your back yard, your neighbor approaches you and says, "You know, I didn't really understand what that witness, Williams, was saying. Did she really see the accident? Also, is it true that Mrs. Baranski will never be able to walk normally again?" You know the answers to these questions, and you would like the juror to know the truth. You also know that it would enhance Baranski's chances of winning the case if this juror were as familiar with the factual background as you are. What should you do? First, you should inform your neighbor that as a paralegal, you have a ethical duty to abide by the professional rules of conduct governing the legal profession. One of these rules prohibits *ex parte* (private) communications with jurors about a case being tried. Second, you should remind your neighbor that jurors are not permitted to discuss a case they are hearing with anyone.

Closing Arguments

In their **closing arguments**, the attorneys summarize their presentations and argue in their clients' favor. A closing argument should include all of the major points that support the client's case. It should also emphasize the shortcomings of the opposing party's case. Jurors will view a closing argument with some skepticism if it merely recites the central points of a party's claim or defense without also responding to the unfavorable facts or issues raised by the other side. Of course, neither attorney wants to focus too much on the other side's position, but the elements of the opposing position do need to be acknowledged and their flaws highlighted.

CLOSING ARGUMENT
An argument made by each side's attorney after the cases for the plaintiff and defendant have been presented. Closing arguments are made prior to the jury charge.

PARALEGAL PROFILE Litigation Paralegal

DENISE WRIGHT attended the legal-assistant program at the University of Toledo Community and Technical College and received her associate's degree in 1979. She interned in a law firm and was hired by the firm after graduation. Wright stayed with the firm for over eight years, first working in the area of probate administration and then in litigation.

In 1988, Wright moved to her position at Dana Risk Management, which is a part of Dana Corporation. Dana Corporation manufactures vehicle and industrial components, such as transmissions and axles. While working at Dana, she continued her education, and in 1993, she received her bachelor of arts degree from the University of Toledo.

Wright coordinates Dana Corporation's product-liability lawsuits and claims. Her group consists of one lawyer, two legal assistants, and one secretary. Wright manages cases and deals with case strategies, budgeting and reviewing bills from outside counsel, discovery requests, interrogatories, and settlement decisions.

What do you like best about your work?

"The thing I like best about my job is that I think it is what every paralegal would want to do. In handling cases, I do everything from assigning counsel, introducing outside counsel to Dana Corporation's technical people, talking with outside counsel, being involved in strategic decisions (such as whether to settle a case or to file a motions for summary judgment), and analyzing the most cost-effective way to handle the case. I feel that I do a lot of what lawyers are doing without crossing the line between the authorized and unauthorized practice of law. I have had outside counsel comment on how amazed they are at the level of responsibility that I and my co-workers assume. I feel that my level of responsibility is the highest that a paralegal can achieve without a law degree. I also enjoy the fact that my work is a real coordinated team effort. Our group acts as the contact point between outside counsel and in-house technical experts. There are a lot of conference calls when preparing for discovery, for example."

What is the greatest challenge that you face in your area of work?

"The most challenging thing about my work is prioritizing my workload. There is a lot of work to be done in a short amount of time. Dana Corporation has twenty-eight divisions, and another paralegal and I split the work. I am continually reprioritizing, sometimes every hour, to make sure that the most important tasks get done. If I find that I am having trouble with a deadline, I call the people that it affects to see if there is any flexibility or any compromise that can be worked out so that everybody is satisfied."

"A COMPUTER IS LIKE YOUR RIGHT HAND."

What advice do you have for would-be paralegals in your area of work?

"If I were to do anything different in my education, I would have taken more computer classes. A computer is like your right hand, especially in corporate work. If you are able to go into an office environment with some basic training with the common software programs, then you are a step ahead. I also feel that communication skills are critical qualities for any paralegal. In my job, there are demands from in-house technical people and from outside counsel, and I need to work with both of them to try to find ways to get the needed result within the allotted time frame. I often have to convince each side to give a little so that a satisfactory result can be obtained."

What are some tips for success as a paralegal in your area of work?

"My advice for success as a paralegal is to always find ways to streamline the handling of a case. The paralegal should read everything regarding a case and not skip over even the smallest bit of information because it can be significant. The paralegal should also take the initiative and demonstrate how his or her skills can be utilized more effectively. For example, if you are asked to review pleadings that are just thrown in a file, recommend placing them in a notebook in chronological order to improve efficiency."

Both attorneys will want to organize their presentations so that they can explain to the jury their respective arguments and show how their arguments are supported by the evidence. Once both attorneys have completed their remarks, the case will be submitted to the jury and the attorneys' role in the trial will be finished.

Jury Instructions

Before the jurors begin their deliberations, the judge gives the jury a **charge**, in which the judge sums up the case and instructs the jurors on the rules of law that apply to the issues involved in the case. Because the jury's role is to serve as the fact finder, the factual account contained in the charge is not binding upon them. Indeed, the jurors may disregard the facts as noted in the charge. They are *not* free to ignore the statements of law, however. The charge contains a request for findings of fact, which is typically phrased in an "if, then" format. For example, in the charge presented in Exhibit 11.7 on page 444, the jury is first asked to decide if the defendant was negligent. The next question states that *if* the jury decides that the defendant was negligent, *then* the jury must decide whether the defendant's negligence caused the plaintiff's injuries. This format helps to channel the jurors' deliberations.

CHARGE
The judge's instruction to the jury following the attorneys' closing arguments setting forth the rules of law that the jury must apply in reaching its decision, or verdict.

Charges, which are also called jury instructions, are usually drafted by the attorneys before the trial begins, and an attorney's trial strategy will likely be linked to the charges. Often, the paralegal drafts the charges for the attorney's review. The judge, however, has the final decision as to what charge will be submitted to the jury.

The Verdict

Following its receipt of the charge, the jury begins its deliberations. Once it has reached a decision, the jury issues a **verdict** in favor of one of the parties. If the verdict is in favor of the plaintiff, the jury will specify the amount of damages to be paid by the defendant. Following the announcement of the verdict, the jurors are discharged. Usually, immediately after the verdict has been announced and the jurors discharged, the party in whose favor the verdict was issued makes a motion asking the judge to issue a *judgment*—which is that court's final word on the matter—consistent with the jury's verdict. For example, if the jury in the Baranski case finds that defendant Peretto was negligent and awards plaintiff Baranski damages in the amount of $75,000, the judge will order defendant Peretto to pay the plaintiff that amount.

VERDICT
A formal decision made by a jury.

POSTTRIAL MOTIONS AND PROCEDURES

Every trial must have a winner and a loser. Although civil litigation is an expensive and cumbersome process, the losing party may wish to pursue the matter further after the verdict has been rendered. Assume that plaintiff Baranski wins at trial and is awarded $75,000 in damages. Cameron, as defendant Peretto's attorney, may wish to file a posttrial motion, such as one of those discussed below, or appeal the decision to a higher court. Note that

CASE AT A GLANCE

The Plaintiff—
Plaintiff: Katherine Baranski
Attorney: Allen P. Gilmore
Paralegal: Elena Lopez

The Defendant—
Defendant: Tony Peretto
Attorney: Elizabeth A. Cameron
Paralegal: Gordon McVay

EXHIBIT 11.7
Jury Charge—Request for Findings of Fact

The jury is requested to answer the following questions:

(1) Was the defendant negligent?

Answer: (yes or no) __________

(2) If your answer to question (1) is "yes," then you must answer this question: Was the defendant's negligence a proximate (direct) cause of the plaintiff's injuries?

Answer: (yes or no) __________

(3) Was the plaintiff negligent?

Answer: (yes or no) __________

(4) If your answer to question (3) is "yes," then you must answer this question: Was the plaintiff's negligence a proximate (direct) cause of the accident and injuries that she suffered?

Answer: (yes or no) __________

(5) If your answer to either question (1) or question (3) is "yes," then answer the following:

Taking 100% as the total fault causing the accident and injuries, what percentage of the total fault causing the accident and injuries do you attribute to:

____________________ the defendant

____________________ the plaintiff

(If you find that a party has no fault in causing the accident, then attribute 0 percentage of the fault to that party.)

(6) Regardless of how you answered the previous questions, answer this question:

Disregarding any negligence or fault on the part of the plaintiff, what sum of money would reasonably compensate the plaintiff for her claimed injury and damage?

Answer: $ __________

plaintiff Baranski, even though she won the case, could also appeal the judgment. For example, she might appeal the case on the ground that she should have received $110,000 in damages instead of $75,000, arguing that the latter amount inadequately compensates her for the harms that she suffered as a result of defendant Peretto's negligence.

MOTION FOR JUDGMENT NOTWITHSTANDING THE VERDICT
A motion (also referred to as a motion for judgment as a matter of law in federal courts) requesting that the court grant judgment in favor of the party making the motion on the ground that the jury verdict against him or her was unreasonable and erroneous.

Posttrial Motions

Assume that defendant Peretto's attorney, Cameron, believes that the verdict for plaintiff Baranski is not supported by the evidence. In this situation, she may file a **motion for judgment notwithstanding the verdict** (also known as a *motion for judgment as a matter of law* in the federal courts).[4] By filing this motion, attorney Cameron asks the judge to enter a judgment in favor of defendant Peretto on the ground (basis) that the jury verdict in favor of plaintiff Baranski was unreasonable and erroneous. Cameron may file this motion only if she previously filed a motion for a directed verdict (or judgment as a matter of law) during the trial and the motion was denied at that time. If she decides to file this motion, she must file it within ten days of the date that the judgment is entered against defendant Peretto following the conclusion of the trial.

Like virtually all motions in federal court, this motion must be accompanied by a supporting affidavit or a memorandum of law, or brief (discussed in Chapter 10). Assuming that attorney Cameron files the motion, then it will fall upon the judge to determine whether the jury's verdict was reasonable in view of the evidence presented at trial. If the judge concludes that the verdict was reasonable, then he will deny Cameron's motion. If he agrees with Cameron, however, then he will set the jury's verdict aside and enter a judgment in favor of defendant Peretto.

Rule 50 of the Federal Rules of Civil Procedure permits either party to file a **motion for a new trial**. Such a motion may be submitted along with a motion for a judgment notwithstanding the verdict. A motion for a new trial is a far more drastic tactic because it asserts that the trial was so pervaded by error or otherwise fundamentally flawed that a new trial should be held. Because such a motion reflects adversely on the way in which the judge conducted the trial, it should only be filed if the attorney truly believes that a miscarriage of justice will otherwise result.

MOTION FOR A NEW TRIAL
A motion asserting that the trial was so fundamentally flawed (because of error, newly discovered evidence, prejudice, or other reason) that a new trial is needed to prevent a miscarriage of justice.

For a motion for a new trial to have a reasonable chance of being granted, the motion must allege such serious problems as jury misconduct, prejudicial jury instructions, excessive or inadequate damages, or the existence of newly discovered evidence (but not if the evidence could have been discovered earlier through the use of reasonable care). As with other posttrial motions in federal courts, the motion for a new trial must be filed within ten days following the entry of the judgment. Exhibit 11.8 on page 446 illustrates a motion for judgment as a matter of law or, in the alternative, for a new trial.

Appealing the Verdict

If attorney Cameron's posttrial motions are unsuccessful or if she decides not to file them, she may still file an **appeal**. The purpose of an appeal is to have the trial court's decision either reversed or modified by an appellate court (court of appeals). As discussed in Chapter 7, appellate courts, which usually consist of a panel of three or more judges, are *reviewing* courts, not

APPEAL
The process of seeking a higher court's review of a lower court's decision for the purpose of correcting or changing the lower court's judgment or decision.

4. Amendments to the FRCP in 1991 designated both the motion for a directed verdict and the motion for judgment notwithstanding the verdict as motions for judgment as a matter of law. One of the reasons for the change was to allow both the preverdict and postverdict motions to be referred to with a terminology that does not conceal their common identity (both motions claim, at different times during the proceedings, that there is insufficient evidence against the defendant to justify a claim—or a verdict—against the defendant). Many judges and attorneys continue to use the former names of these motions, however, so we include them in our discussion.

EXHIBIT 11.8
Motion for Judgment as a Matter of Law or for a New Trial

UNITED STATES DISTRICT COURT
FOR THE WESTERN DISTRICT OF NITA

Katherine Baranski
Plaintiff
vs.
Tony Peretto
Defendant

File No. 96-14335-NI

Hon. Harley M. LaRue

Elizabeth A. Cameron
Attorney for the Defendant
Cameron & Strauss, P.C.
310 Lake Drive
Zero City, ZE 59802

MOTION FOR JUDGMENT AS A MATTER OF
LAW OR, IN THE ALTERNATIVE,
MOTION FOR A NEW TRIAL

The Defendant, Tony Peretto, moves this Court, pursuant to Rule 50(b) of the Federal Rules of Civil Procedure, to set aside the verdict and judgment entered on August 15, 1996, and to enter instead a judgment for the Defendant as a matter of law. In the alternative, and in the event the Defendant's motion for judgment as a matter of law is denied, the Defendant moves the Court to order a new trial.

The grounds for this motion are set forth in the attached memorandum.

Date: 8/16/96

Elizabeth A. Cameron
Elizabeth A. Cameron
Attorney for the Defendant
Cameron & Strauss, P.C.
310 Lake Drive
Zero City, ZE 59802

trial courts. In other words, no new evidence will be presented to the appellate court, and there is no jury. The appellate court will review the trial court's proceedings to decide whether the trial court erred in applying the law to the facts of the case, in instructing the jury, or in administering the trial generally. Appellate courts rarely tamper with a trial court's findings of fact because the judge and jury were in a better position than the appellate court to evaluate the credibility of witnesses, the nature of the evidence, and so on.

As grounds for the appeal, defendant Peretto's attorney, Cameron, might argue that the trial court erred in one of the ways mentioned in the preceding paragraph. Unless she believes that a reversal of the judgment is likely, however, she will probably advise Peretto not to appeal the case, as an appeal will simply add to the costs and expenses already incurred by Peretto in defending against plaintiff Baranski's claim.

Notice of Appeal. When the appeal involves a federal district court decision, as in the Baranski case, the **appellant** (the party appealing the decision) must file a notice of appeal with the district court that rendered the judgment. The clerk of the court then notifies the **appellee** (the party against whom the appeal is taken) as well as the court of appeals. The clerk then forwards a transcript of the trial court proceedings along with any related pleadings and exhibits; these materials together constitute the **record on appeal**.

APPELLANT
The party who takes an appeal from one court to another; sometimes referred to as the petitioner.

APPELLEE
The party against whom an appeal is taken—that is, the party who opposes setting aside or reversing the judgment; sometimes referred to as the respondent.

RECORD ON APPEAL
The items submitted during the trial (pleadings, motions, briefs, and exhibits) and the transcript of the trial proceedings that are forwarded to the appellate court for review when a case is appealed.

The Appellate Brief and Oral Arguments. When a case is appealed, the attorneys for both parties submit written *briefs* that present their positions regarding the issues to be reviewed by the appellate court. The briefs outline each party's view of the proper application of the law to the facts. (Appellate briefs will be discussed further in Chapter 18.)

After the appellate court has had an opportunity to review the briefs, the court sets aside a time for both attorneys to argue their positions before the panel of judges. The attorneys will then present their arguments and answer any questions that the judges might have. Generally, the attorneys' arguments before an appellate court are limited in terms of both the time allowed for argument and the scope of the argument. Following the oral arguments, the judges will decide the issue and then issue a formal written opinion, which normally will be published in the relevant reporter (see Chapter 17 for a detailed discussion of how court opinions are published).

The Appellate Court's Options. Once they have reviewed the record and heard oral arguments, the judges have several options. For example, in the Baranski case, if the appellate court decided to uphold the trial court's decision, then the judgment for plaintiff Baranski would be **affirmed**. If the judges decided to **reverse** the trial court's decision, however, then Peretto would no longer be obligated to pay the damages awarded to Baranski by the trial court. The court might also affirm or reverse a decision *in part.* For example, the judges might affirm the jury's finding that Peretto was negligent but **remand** the case—that is, send it back to the trial court—for further proceedings on another issue (such as the extent of Baranski's damages). An appellate court can also *modify* a lower court's decision. If, for example, the appellate court decided that the jury awarded an excessive amount in damages, the appellate court might reduce the award to a more appropriate, or fairer, amount.

AFFIRM
An appellate court's decision to uphold the trial court's judgment in a case.

REVERSE
An appellate court's decision that is contrary to the trial court's judgment.

REMAND
An appellate court's decision to send a case back to the trial court for further proceedings.

The decision of the appellate court may sometimes be appealed further. A state appellate court's decision, for example, may be appealed to the state supreme court. A federal appellate court's decision may be appealed to the United States Supreme Court. It will be up to these higher courts to decide whether they will review the case. In other words, these courts are not normally *required* to review cases. Recall from Chapter 7 that although thousands of cases are submitted to the United States Supreme Court each year, it hears less than 150. (An action decided in a state court, however, has a somewhat greater chance of being reviewed by the state supreme court.)

DEVELOPING PARALEGAL SKILLS

Locating Assets

Paralegal Myra Cullen works for a law firm that represented Jennifer Roth in a lawsuit brought by Roth against Best Eatery, a local restaurant. Roth sued the restaurant to obtain compensation for injuries that she incurred on the restaurant's premises. Roth had walked into the dimly lit lobby of the restaurant on a rainy morning, had stepped into a puddle of water that had gathered near the door, and had fallen, breaking her left ankle in the process. Roth won at trial, and the jury awarded her $100,000 in damages. Myra has now been assigned the task of investigating Best Eatery's assets to determine whether and how the judgment can be collected. Myra already knows from reviewing the pretrial interrogatories that the owner of the restaurant, John Dobman, carries a very small liability insurance policy that will only pay $25,000 of the judgment.

Dobman owns the restaurant as a sole proprietor. In a sole proprietorship, the owner is personally liable for all the debts and obligations of the business, including court judgments against the business. If Dobman refuses to pay the judgment, the court can order the sheriff or other authority to seize (take ownership of) and sell the restaurant and other assets that Dobman owns to satisfy the judgment. Myra will therefore want to learn what assets are owned by Best Eatery as well as what assets are owned personally by Dobman.

Because Best Eatery is locally owned and operated, Myra goes to the county Register of Deeds office and looks under the names of both Best Eatery and John Dobman. The Register of Deeds has records indicating who owns real property (land and things permanently attached to the land) in the county, whether any mortgages on the property have been recorded, and other information. Myra learns that Dobman owns both the land on which Best Eatery is located and the building housing the restaurant. She also learns that Dobman paid $80,000 for the property last year and that there is a mortgage on the property for $50,000. Myra also finds out that Dobman owns a home for which he paid $100,000 ten years ago. The home is also mortgaged, with $40,000 still owing on the mortgage loan.

With this information, Myra knows that Dobman has equity in real property worth at least $90,000 ($30,000 in the restaurant and $60,000 in his home). Given the fact that both properties have probably appreciated in value since Dobman purchased them, his equity in the properties would probably be closer to $115,000. In any event, it is clear that if Dobman does not have enough money to pay the judgment, he would probably qualify for a loan of $75,000 (the amount of the judgment that the insurance company will not pay) to cover the obligation. If he refuses to pay the judgment, the plaintiff can petition the court to issue a writ of execution so that Dobman's nonexempt assets can be seized and sold, if necessary, to cover at least some of the amount of the judgment.

TODAY'S PROFESSIONAL PARALEGAL

Drafting *Voir Dire* Questions Like a Pro

Andrea Leed, a legal assistant, is preparing for trial. Her boss is a famous trial attorney, Mary Marshall. Mary rarely loses a case. One of her many secrets to success is that she always draws up a jury profile and prepares carefully for *voir dire.*

Mary is defending a corporation in an environmental liability case. The case has many complex engineering and scientific issues that the jury will need to understand in order to reach its verdict. It is a common practice in these types of cases to select a "blue ribbon" jury—a jury consisting of persons who are very well educated. Mary has suggested that Andrea hire a psychologist to prepare a jury profile.

CONSULTING WITH AN EXPERT WITNESS

Andrea contacts TrialPsych, Inc., a consulting firm headed by Dr. Linda Robertson, who specializes in jury selection. Dr. Robertson would be delighted to work on the case, but her services are very expensive, and Andrea must find out whether the client is willing to pay Dr. Robertson's fee. The client agrees to pay the fee, so Andrea meets with Dr. Robertson to discuss the case. Andrea explains that the client is a corporation and that the case involves complex scientific and engineering issues. Dr. Robertson consults her files for statistical information on these types of cases. She finds that the ideal jury would be made up of white-collar professionals holding advanced degrees in engineering or another applied science. Also, the prospective jurors would ideally be against extensive government regulation of the corporate world.

DRAFTING *VOIR DIRE* QUESTIONS

Andrea returns to the office and conveys this information to Mary in a meeting. Mary asks Andrea to draft some questions for *voir dire.* Andrea then drafts a list of about twenty questions, including such questions as the following:

1. Please state your name and address.
2. Where are you employed, and how long have you been employed there?
3. What is the highest level of education that you have attained: high school diploma, some college but no degree, college degree, advanced degree (please specify)?
4. If you have attended college or received a college degree, what was your field of study?
5. Have you ever been fired by a corporate employer in a way that you believed was unfair?
4. Have you ever worked for a government regulatory agency, and if so, what were your responsibilities in that position?
5. Have you, or persons or business firms with whom you are or have been associated, ever been sued for violating environmental statutes or regulations? If so, what were the violations?
6. In your opinion, what should be the government's role in regulating a company's operations?

REVIEWING THE *VOIR DIRE* QUESTIONS

Andrea faxes the list of questions to Dr. Robertson, who reviews them and faxes back some suggested changes, which Andrea incorporates. When the final list of questions is drawn up, Andrea presents it to Mary and places a copy of the list in the trial notebook. Mary asks Andrea to call Dr. Robertson and ask her if she is available to sit in on the actual *voir dire* process to ensure that jury selection goes smoothly.

ENFORCING THE JUDGMENT

The uncertainties of the litigation process are compounded by the lack of guarantees that any judgment will be enforceable. It is one thing to have a court enter a judgment in your favor; it is quite another to collect the money to which you are entitled from the opposing party. Even if the jury awarded Baranski the full amount of damages requested ($110,000), for example, she might not, in fact, "win" anything at all. Peretto's auto insurance coverage might have lapsed, in which event the company would not cover any of the

WRIT OF EXECUTION
A writ that puts in force a court's decree or judgment.

JUDGMENT CREDITOR
A creditor who is legally entitled, by a court's judgment, to collect the amount of the judgment from a debtor.

CASE AT A GLANCE

The Plaintiff—
Plaintiff: Katherine Baranski
Attorney: Allen P. Gilmore
Paralegal: Elena Lopez

The Defendant—
Defendant: Tony Peretto
Attorney: Elizabeth A. Cameron
Paralegal: Gordon McVay

damages. Alternatively, Peretto's insurance coverage may be limited to $20,000, meaning that Peretto would have to pay personally the remaining $90,000. If Peretto personally did not have that amount of money available, then Baranski would need to go back to court and request that the court issue a **writ of execution**—an order, usually issued by the clerk of the court, directing the sheriff to seize (take temporary ownership of) and sell Peretto's assets. The proceeds of the sale would then be used to pay the damages owed to Baranski. Any excess proceeds of the sale would be returned to Peretto.

Even as a **judgment creditor** (one who has obtained a court judgment against his or her debtor), Baranski may not be able to obtain the full amount of the judgment from Peretto. Laws protecting debtors provide that certain property (such as a debtor's home up to a certain value, tools used by the debtor in his or her trade, and so on) is *exempt.* Exempt property cannot be seized and sold to pay debts owed to judgment creditors. Similar exemptions would apply if Peretto declared bankruptcy. Thus, even though Baranski won at trial, she, like many others who are awarded damages, might not be able to collect them.

The difficulty of enforcing court judgments, coupled with the high costs accompanying any litigation (including attorneys' fees, court costs, and the litigants' time costs), is a major reason why most disputes are settled out of court, either before or during the trial.

KEY TERMS AND CONCEPTS

affirm 447
appeal 445
appellant 447
appellee 447
challenge 434
challenge for cause 434
charge 443
closing argument 441
cross-examination 437
direct examination 437
judgment creditor 450
leading question 437
motion for a directed verdict 439
motion for a new trial 445
motion for judgment as a matter of law 439
motion for judgment notwithstanding the verdict 444
motion *in limine* 430
opening statement 436
peremptory challenge 434
pretrial conference 430
record on appeal 447
recross-examination 439
redirect examination 438
remand 447
reverse 447
subpoena 426
trial notebook 428
verdict 443
voir dire 434
writ of execution 450

CHAPTER SUMMARY

1. Before the trial begins, attorneys for both sides and their paralegals gather and organize all evidence, documents, and other materials relating to the case. It is helpful to create a trial-preparation checklist to ensure that nothing is overlooked during this stage. Paralegals often assist in contacting and issuing subpoenas to witnesses, as well as in preparing witnesses for trial. Paralegals also assume responsibility for making sure that all exhibits and displays are ready by the trial date and that the trial notebook is prepared.

2. Prior to the trial, the attorneys for both sides meet with the trial judge in a pretrial conference to decide whether a settlement is possible or, if not, to decide how the trial will be conducted and what types of evidence will be admissible. A motion *in limine* (to limit evidence) may be made by one or both of the attorneys at this time.

3. The jury-selection process is called *voir dire.* During this process, attorneys for both sides may question individual jurors or groups of jurors to determine if bias exists or if for other reasons certain jurors should not be included in the jury. The attorneys can exclude certain persons in the jury pool from sitting on the jury through the exercise of challenges for cause and a limited number of peremptory challenges.

4. Once the jury has been selected and seated, the trial begins. The paralegal, if he or she attends the trial, coordinates witnesses' appearances, tracks the testimony of witnesses and compares it with sworn statements that the witnesses made prior to the trial, and provides the attorney with appropriate reminders or documents when necessary. The paralegal generally acts as a second set of eyes and ears for the attorney during the trial.

5. The trial begins with opening statements in which both attorneys briefly give their versions of the facts of the case and the evidence supporting their views.

6. Following the attorneys' opening statements, the plaintiff's attorney presents evidence supporting the plaintiff's claim, including the testimony of witnesses. The attorney's questioning of the witnesses whom he or she calls is referred to as direct examination. The defendant's attorney may then cross-examine the witness, after which the plaintiff's attorney may question the witness on redirect examination, followed by possible recross-examination by the defendant's attorney.

7. After the plaintiff's attorney has presented his or her client's case, the defendant's attorney may make a motion for a directed verdict, also called a motion for judgment as a matter of law. This motion asserts that the plaintiff has not offered enough evidence to support the validity of the plaintiff's claim against the defendant. If the judge grants the motion, the case will be dismissed.

8. The attorneys then reverse their roles, and the defendant's attorney presents evidence and testimony to refute the plaintiff's claims. Any witnesses called to the stand by the defendant's attorney will be subject to direct examination by that attorney, cross-examination by the plaintiff's attorney, and possibly redirect examination and recross-examination.

9. After the defendant's attorney has finished his or her presentation, both attorneys give their closing arguments. Each attorney summarizes the major points that he or she made during the trial and attempts to show how the evidence presented favors a verdict in his or her client's favor.

10. Following the attorneys' closing arguments, the judge instructs the jury in a charge—a document that includes statements of the applicable law and a review of the facts as they were presented during the trial. The jury must not disregard the judge's instructions as to what the applicable law is and how it should be applied to the facts of the case as interpreted by the jury. The jury then begins its deliberations. When the jury has reached a decision, it issues a verdict in favor of one party or the other.

11. After the verdict has been pronounced and the trial concluded, the losing party's attorney may do any of the following: He or she may file a motion for judgment notwithstanding the verdict (now also called a motion for judgment as a matter of law in federal courts), alleging that the judge should enter a judgment in favor of the losing party in spite of the verdict because the verdict was not supported by the evidence or was otherwise erroneous. In conjunction with the motion, or in the alternative, the attorney may also file a motion for a new trial, asserting that the trial was so flawed—by judge or juror misconduct or by other pervasive errors—that a new trial should be held. Finally, the attorney may, depending on the client's wishes, appeal the decision to an appellate court for further review and decision.

12. Even though a plaintiff wins a lawsuit for damages, it may be difficult to enforce the judgment against the defendant, particularly if the defendant has few assets.

QUESTIONS FOR REVIEW

1. What is involved in preparing witnesses, exhibits, and displays for trial? What role does the paralegal play? How can the paralegal assist the attorney in preparing the trial notebook?

2. What is a pretrial conference? What issues are likely to be raised and decided at a pretrial conference?

3. How are jurors selected? What role does the attorney play in the selection process? Does the paralegal play a role in the process?

4. What is the difference between a peremptory challenge and a challenge for cause?

5. What role does the paralegal play during a trial? What types of trial-related tasks may the paralegal perform?

6. What are leading questions? When are they used?

7. What is a jury charge? Can the jury decide matters of law?

8. Name the posttrial motions that are available. In what situation is each of them used?

9. Describe the procedure for filing an appeal. What factors are considered by an attorney when deciding whether a case should be appealed?

10. Why do appellate courts defer to trial courts' findings of fact? What options might an appellate court pursue after it has completed its review of a case?

ETHICAL QUESTIONS

1. Anthony Paletti, a paralegal, is attending a trial with his supervising attorney. Anthony leaves the courtroom to go meet a witness. On his way down the hall, he runs into the defendant in the case. The defendant says to Anthony, "You work for the plaintiff's attorney, don't you? I have a question for you about that contract that your attorney offered into evidence." Should Anthony answer the defendant's question? Why or why not?

2. A client claiming to have severely injured his back at work comes into the office of a law firm. The client, in a wheelchair, seeks legal advice about filing a lawsuit, and the attorney decides to take the case. Two days later, Alvin Kerrigan, the attorney's paralegal, sees the new client on the roof of a building installing shingles. What should Alvin do?

3. During a lunch break in the course of a trial, Louise Lanham, a paralegal, was washing her hands in the restroom. One of the members of the trial jury came up to her and said, "I don't understand what negligence is. Can you explain it to me?" How should Louise answer this question?

PRACTICE QUESTIONS AND ASSIGNMENTS

1. Draft a series of questions for the plaintiff's attorney and for the two defendants' attorneys (the attorneys representing the doctor and the pharmaceutical company, respectively) to use during *voir dire* in a case involving the following facts:

> The plaintiff's daughter died five days after starting on a regimen of taking weight-control pills. The daughter died because the pills were incompatible with her blood type. Prior to taking the pills, she was a perfectly healthy, twenty-five-year-old law student. The mother is bringing a medical-malpractice suit against the doctor for prescribing the wrong type of pill. The mother is also suing the pharmaceutical company that manufactured the pill on the ground that it failed to warn of the dangers of its pill for those persons, including her daughter, whose blood types were incompatible with the pill.

DATA DISK

2. Draft a subpoena for a friendly witness using the following facts:

> Simon Kolstad of 100 Schoolcraft Road, Del Mar, California, is a witness to be subpoenaed in *Sumner v. Hayes,* a civil lawsuit filed in the U.S. District court for the Eastern District of Michigan, docket number 123492–96. He is being subpoenaed by the plaintiff's attorney, Marvin W. Green, whose office is located at 300 Penobscot Building, Detroit, Michigan. Kolstad is to appear in room number 6 of the courthouse, which is located at 231 Lafayette Boulevard, Detroit, Michigan, at 2:30 P.M. on January 10, 1996. Kolstad is to bring with him a letter from the defendant to Kolstad dated February 9, 1993.

QUESTIONS FOR CRITICAL ANALYSIS

1. Some judges and legal scholars feel that peremptory challenges, which have a long history in our legal system, should be banned entirely because of their discriminatory potential. This view was urged by the Supreme Court Justice Thurgood Marshall in *Batson v. Kentucky* (see footnote 3 in this chapter), in which the Court held that peremptory challenges could not be motivated by racial considerations. Do you agree with Marshall's view? Why or why not?

2. Why would an attorney ever recommend to a client that a nonjury trial would be preferable to a jury trial?

ROLE-PLAYING EXERCISES

1. This exercise will involve the entire class or groups of sixteen students. It will involve the selection of a jury for a trial. You will need to select a paralegal and an attorney for both the plaintiff and each of the two defendants. The remaining twelve students in the group will be the prospective jurors who will be questioned during *voir dire.* You will need to use the *voir dire* questions that you drafted in Practice Question 1 above.

Using the scenario of the law student who died after taking weight-control pills that were incompatible with her blood type, each side is to select the jurors who would be the most favorable to their respective clients' positions. Additional factual information relating to the two defendants includes the following:

a. The doctor has prescribed this pill on numerous occasions and has never had a patient die as a result of taking it. The doctor did not take a thorough medical history of the plaintiff, nor did he note her blood type.

b. The pharmaceutical company did include a package insert to warn doctors of the dangers involved in taking the drug and instructing them as to the types of tests that should be undertaken before the pill was prescribed.

DATA DISK

2. You are a paralegal in a litigation firm. Because you are new on the job, the attorney for whom you work is meeting with you to teach you how to draft questions to be used on direct examination in an upcoming trial. Assume the following facts:

> Your client, a surgeon, is suing a lawyer for slander (a tort arising when someone makes a verbal statement that harms another's good name or reputation—see Chapter 8). The lawyer was representing the surgeon in a malpractice case. In the presence of several other physicians, the lawyer told the surgeon that she "ought to have her head examined" and that she was so "incompetent at her job" that he had decided not to defend her against the malpractice claim. The surgeon is suing the lawyer for slander because, as a result of his comments, her staff privileges at a major hospital have been suspended and she can no longer perform surgery there.

Work in pairs. One of you should assume the role of the legal assistant and the other the role of the attorney. Draft questions to ask your client, the surgeon, during the trial. If time allows, draft questions to ask the defendant lawyer on cross-examination also.

PROJECTS

1. Call a local court clerk or administrator (not a judge) to obtain a list of the cases on the court's trial docket. Arrange to attend a trial that is not expected to last longer than a few days. Attend the trial for as many days as you can and observe carefully the following proceedings: *voir dire,* opening statements, the presentation of evidence, and closing arguments. Also note how paralegals are used. Prepare a three-page summary of your observations, making sure to include the name and docket number of the case, the name of the court, and the name of the judge.

2. Look up your state's court rules and find out how many challenges for cause are allowed during *voir dire*. How many peremptory challenges are permitted during *voir dire*?

ANNOTATED SELECTED READINGS

ALBERT, BARBARA L. *Litigation and Administrative Practice Course Handbook Series: The Role of the Litigation Paralegal at Trial.* New York: Practising Law Institute, 1992. An excellent discussion of how a paralegal can assist an attorney in putting together a well-organized trial presentation.

CLARK, LANA J. "Federal vs. State Court Trial Preparation." *Legal Assistant Today,* May/June 1993. A good overview of the federal courts, from the appointment of federal judges by the president of the United States to procedural rules to advice on how not to be intimidated by them. Good reading for any paralegal new to federal court practice.

HALL, JANICE E. "Building Trial Notebooks." *Legal Assistant Today,* January/February 1991. A helpful article that discusses everything about the trial notebook, including when to start the notebook, its contents, and the type of notebook to use. Recommended reading for any legal assistant interested in trial work.

KLIGERMAN, SUSAN D. *Litigation and Administrative Practice Course Handbook Series—Investigating the Medical Malpractice Case.* New York: Practising Law Institute, 1992. A good anatomy of a medical-malpractice case. The book walks the reader through the steps of the litigation.

SHIMPOCK-VIEWEG, KATHY. "How to Find a Few Good Expert Witnesses." *Legal Assistant Today,* May/June 1993. A helpful article on the criteria for selecting expert witnesses and the sources to consult to find them. Helpful reading for both the experienced and not-so-experienced paralegal.

12

CRIMINAL LAW AND PROCEDURES

Chapter Objectives

After completing this chapter, you will know:

- The difference between crimes and other wrongful acts.
- The elements that are required for criminal liability and some of the more common defenses that are raised when defending against criminal charges.
- The constitutional rights of persons accused of crimes.
- The basic steps involved in criminal procedure from the time a crime is reported to the resolution of the case.
- Why a criminal suspect may be released and the case dismissed prior to trial.
- How and why criminal litigation procedures differ from civil litigation procedures.

Chapter Outline

INTRODUCTION

More than one million people are arrested for crimes and enter the criminal justice system each year. As the crime rate continues to increase, so does the work of the attorneys and legal assistants involved in criminal-law cases. Criminal cases are prosecuted by **public prosecutors,** who are employed by the government. The public prosecutor in federal criminal cases is called a U.S. attorney. In cases tried in state or local courts, the public prosecutor may be referred to as a *prosecuting attorney, state prosecutor, district attorney, county attorney,* or *city attorney.*

PUBLIC PROSECUTOR
An individual, acting as a trial lawyer, who initiates and conducts criminal cases in the government's name and on behalf of the people.

Defendants in criminal cases may hire private attorneys to defend them. If a defendant cannot afford to hire an attorney, the court will appoint one for him or her. Everyone accused of a crime that may involve a jail sentence has a right to counsel, and this right is ensured by court-appointed attorneys, called **public defenders**, who are paid by the state.

PUBLIC DEFENDER
A court-appointed attorney who is paid by the state to represent a criminal defendant who is unable to hire private counsel.

Some legal assistants and paralegals work for state prosecutors; others work for public defenders; still others work for private attorneys who specialize in criminal defense. Paralegals may also come into contact with criminal defendants in the course of their work in a general law practice or in a corporate legal department. A client may be arrested for driving while intoxicated or for the possession of illegal drugs, for example, or a corporation might need legal assistance in defending against alleged criminal violations of federal environmental laws.

This chapter begins by explaining the legal nature of crime, the elements of criminal liability, and the constitutional protections that come into play when a person is accused of a crime. The rest of the chapter focuses on criminal procedures. Because many of the procedures involved in criminal litigation are similar to those discussed in Chapters 10 and 11, details of these procedures will not be repeated here. Rather, in this chapter, we offer an overview of criminal law and procedure and the ways in which criminal litigation differs from civil litigation.

WHAT IS A CRIME?

A **crime** can be distinguished from other wrongful acts, such as torts, in that a crime is an *offense against society as a whole.* Criminal defendants are prosecuted by public officials on behalf of the state, as mentioned above, not by their victims or other private parties. In addition, those who have committed crimes are subject to penalties, including fines, imprisonment, and in some cases, death. As discussed in Chapter 8, tort remedies—remedies for civil wrongs—are generally intended to compensate the injured party (by awarding money damages, for example). Criminal law, however, is concerned with punishing the wrongdoer in an attempt to deter others from similar actions.

CRIME
A broad term for violations of law that are punishable by the state and are codified by legislatures. The objective of criminal law is to protect the public.

Another factor distinguishing criminal law from tort law is that criminal law is primarily statutory law. Essentially, a crime is whatever a legislature has declared to be a crime. Although federal crimes are defined by the U.S. Congress, most crimes are defined by state legislatures. As mentioned in

Chapter 6, at one time criminal law was governed primarily by the common law. Over time, common law doctrines and principles were codified, expanded on, and enacted in statutory form. Although many crimes were defined originally by the common law, the statutory definitions of those crimes may differ significantly from the common law definitions.

For example, under the common law, the crime of *burglary* was defined as the breaking and entering of another's dwelling at night with the intent to commit a felony. Originally, the definition was aimed at protecting an individual's home and its occupants. Most state statutes have eliminated some of the requirements found in the common law definition. Thus, the time at which the breaking and entering occurs is usually immaterial, and many state statutes do not require that the building that is entered need be a person's dwelling or home.

There are also significant differences between civil and criminal procedural law, as will be discussed in this chapter. Note that it is possible for the same act to constitute both a crime and a tort. For example, if Jackson intentionally shot and killed Avery, the state could prosecute Jackson for the crime of murder. Avery's wife could also bring a civil lawsuit in tort law against Jackson to obtain compensation (in the form of money damages) for the losses she suffered as a result of Avery's death.

A criminal act does not necessarily involve a victim, in the sense that the act directly and physically harms another. If Jeffers grows marijuana in her backyard for her personal use, she may not be physically or directly harming another's interests, but she is nonetheless commiting a crime. Why? Because she is violating a rule of society that has been enacted into law by duly elected representatives of the people. She has committed an offense against society's values, safety, and welfare.

Classifications of Crimes

Crimes are generally divided into two broad classifications, felonies and misdemeanors.

Felonies. A **felony** is a serious crime that may be punished by imprisonment for more than one year or (in some states) death. Examples of felonies include *murder*, *rape*, *robbery* (theft involving the use of force or fear), *arson* (the intentional burning of another's building or structure), and *grand larceny*. Larceny is the nonviolent theft of another's money or property. Larceny is referred to as grand larceny when the theft involves more than a threshold amount defined by state law. Threshold amounts range from $50 to $2,000.

FELONY
A crime—such as arson, murder, rape, or robbery—that carries the most severe sanctions. Sanctions range from one year in a state or federal prison to life imprisonment or (in some states) the death penalty.

Felonies are commonly classified by degree. The Model Penal Code,[1] for example, provides for four degrees of felony: capital offenses for which the

1. The American Law Institute (discussed in Chapter 6) issued the Official Draft of the Model Penal Code in 1962. The Model Penal Code is a rational and integrated body of material drafted for the purpose of assisting state legislatures in reexamining and recodifying state criminal laws. Uniformity among the states is not as important in criminal law as in other areas of the law. Crime varies with local circumstances, and it is appropriate that punishments vary accordingly.

maximum penalty is death, first-degree felonies punishable by a maximum penalty of life imprisonment, second-degree felonies punishable by a maximum of ten years' imprisonment, and third-degree felonies punishable by up to five years' imprisonment.

MISDEMEANOR
A less serious crime than a felony, punishable by a fine or imprisonment for up to one year in other than a state or federal penitentiary.

Misdemeanors. A **misdemeanor** is a crime that may be punished by imprisonment for not more than one year. A misdemeanor, by definition, is a less serious crime. Under federal law and in most states, a misdemeanor is any crime that is not defined by law as a felony. State legislatures specify what crimes are classified as felonies or misdemeanors and what the potential punishment for each type of criminal act may be. Examples of misdemeanors include *petty larceny* (the nonviolent theft of another's property worth less than the threshold amount required for grand larceny), *prostitution*, *disturbing the peace,* and *public intoxication.*

PETTY OFFENSE
In criminal law, the least serious kind of wrong, such as a traffic or building-code violation.

Petty Offenses. Certain types of criminal or quasi-criminal actions, such as violations of building codes, are termed **petty offenses**, or *infractions.* In most jurisdictions, such actions are considered to be a subset of misdemeanors. Some states, however, consider them a separate classification of crimes.

The Variety of Criminal Acts

The number of actions classified as criminal is nearly endless. Besides variations on the crimes mentioned above, criminal acts also include writing bad checks, credit-card violations, resisting arrest, disorderly conduct, obstruction of highways and public places, vagrancy, loitering, and numerous other actions.

Federal jurisdiction is limited to certain types of crimes. If a federal law or a federal government agency (such as the U.S. Department of Justice or the federal Environmental Protection Agency) defines a certain type of action as a crime, federal jurisdiction exists. Generally, federal criminal jurisdiction is limited to crimes that occur outside the jurisdiction of any state, crimes involving interstate commerce or communications, crimes that interfere with the operation of the federal government or its agents, and crimes directed at citizens or property located outside the United States.

ELEMENTS OF CRIMINAL LIABILITY

For a person to be convicted of a crime, two elements must exist simultaneously: (1) the performance of a criminal act and (2) a specified state of mind, or intent. This section describes these two elements of criminal liability and some of the defenses that can be used to avoid liability for crimes.

The Criminal Act

ACTUS REUS
A guilty (prohibited) act. The commission of a prohibited act is one of the two essential elements required for criminal liability, the other element being the intent to commit a crime.

A criminal act is known as the ***actus reus***,[2] or guilty act. Most crimes require an act of *commission;* that is, a person must *do* something in order to be

2. Pronounced *ak*-tuhs *ray*-uhs.

accused of a crime. In some cases, an act of *omission* can be a crime, but only when a person has a legal duty to perform the omitted act. Failure to file a tax return is an example of an omission (failure to act) that is a crime.

The guilty-act requirement is based on one of the premises of criminal law—that a person is punished for *harm done* to society. As in tort law, which deals with civil wrongs, a criminal wrong will not exist unless the act or failure to act caused another (or society generally) to suffer an injury, or harm. Thinking about killing someone or about stealing a car may be wrong, but the thoughts do no harm until they are translated into action. Of course, a person can be punished for *attempting* murder or robbery, but normally only if substantial steps toward the criminal objective have been taken.

State of Mind

Even a completed act that harms society is not legally a crime unless the court finds that the second element—the required state of mind—was present. A wrongful mental state, or ***mens rea***,[3] normally is as necessary as a wrongful act in establishing criminal liability. What constitutes such a mental state varies according to the wrongful action. For murder, the criminal act is the taking of a life, and the mental state is the intent to take life. For theft, the guilty act is the taking of another person's property, and the mental state involves both the knowledge that the property belongs to another and the intent to steal that property. Without the mental state required by law for a particular crime, there is no crime.

MENS REA
A wrongful mental state, or intent. A wrongful mental state is a requirement for criminal liability. What constitutes a wrongful mental state varies according to the nature of the crime. For the crime of murder to exist, for example, the required *mens rea* is the intent to take another person's life.

Degree of Wrongfulness of the Defendant's State of Mind. The same criminal act can result from varying mental states, and how a crime is defined and punished depends on the degree of "wrongfulness" of the defendant's state of mind. For example, taking another's life is *homicide*, a criminal act. The act can be committed coldly, after premeditation, as in *murder in the first degree*, which carries the most severe criminal penalty. The act can be committed in the heat of passion, as in *voluntary manslaughter*, which carries a less severe penalty than murder. Or the act can be committed as a result of criminal negligence (reckless driving or driving while intoxicated, for example), as in *involuntary manslaughter*. In each of these situations, the law recognizes a different degree of wrongfulness, and the harshness of the punishment depends on the degree to which the act of killing another was an *intentional* act.

Proving Lack of Required Mental State. Proving that a defendant did or did not possess the required mental state for a given crime is difficult because a person's state of mind is, by nature, a subjective attribute. For example, assume that Jackson shot and killed Avery. Jackson is arrested and charged with the crime of murder. Jackson contends that he did not commit murder because he was too drunk to know what he was doing and thus lacked the required mental state for murder—intent to kill. Jackson may have committed a criminal act (homicide). In view of his mental state, however, he committed not the crime of murder but (probably) the crime of involuntary

3. Pronounced mehns *ray*-uh.

manslaughter. Of course, there will probably have to be some facts in evidence tending to show that Jackson was indeed so drunk that he could not have intended to kill Avery.

Criminal defendants may assert that they lacked the required degree of criminal intent for other reasons, including *insanity* (the inability to distinguish between right and wrong due to diminished mental capacity), *duress* (which exists when one is forced to commit a specific act), or *mistake* (for example, taking someone else's property, such as a briefcase, thinking that it is one's own).

Defenses to Criminal Liability

Asserting that a defendant lacks the required degree of criminal intent for a specific crime is, of course, one way of defending against criminal liability. Other defenses include those discussed below.

SELF-DEFENSE
The legally recognized privilege to protect oneself or one's property against injury by another. The privilege of self-defense only protects acts that are reasonably necessary to protect oneself or one's property.

Protection of Persons or Property. We all have the right to protect ourselves from physical attacks by others; this is the right of **self-defense**. The force we use to protect ourselves must be reasonable under the circumstances, though. The force used must be justified by the degree of threat posed in a given situation. If someone is about to take your life, the use of *deadly force* (shooting that person with a gun, for example) might be deemed reasonable, depending on the circumstances. If, however, someone in a shopping mall tries to pick your pocket to steal your wallet, you normally do not have a right to shoot him or her, because there was no physical threat to your person.

DEFENSE OF OTHERS
The use of reasonable force to protect others from harm.

Similarly, we have the right to use force in **defense of others** if they are threatened with imminent harm. If you and a friend are walking down a city street one night and someone attacks and threatens to kill your friend, you are justified in using whatever force is reasonable under the circumstances to protect your friend. As with self-defense, it must be shown that the force used was reasonable in view of the nature of the threat.

DEFENSE OF PROPERTY
The use of reasonable force to protect one's property from the harm threatened by another. The use of deadly force in defending one's property is seldom justified.

We also have the right to use reasonable force in the **defense of property**. In particular, if someone is illegally trespassing on our property or is stealing our property, we have the right to use force to stop the trespassing or prevent the theft; but again, the amount of force used must be reasonable. Because human life has a higher value than property, deadly force is normally not allowed in the protection of property unless the thief or trespasser poses a threat to human life.

Statutes of Limitations. With some exceptions, such as for the crime of murder, statutes of limitations apply to crimes just as they do to civil wrongs. In other words, criminal cases must be prosecuted within a certain number of years. If a criminal action is brought after the statutory time period has expired, the accused person can raise the statute of limitations as a defense.

Other Defenses. Further defenses include *mistaken identity* and other reasons why the criminal charges might not be valid. For example, a defendant may offer an *alibi* (proof that the defendant was somewhere else at the time of the crime, for example) as a defense. Still other defenses to criminal liability have to do with violations of procedural law. For example, the police officer or officers who arrested the defendant must have had the proper authority to do so, and the court in which the action is brought must have jurisdiction over the subject matter of the case and over the person brought before the court.

Because criminal law brings the force of the state, with all its resources, to bear against the individual, law-enforcement authorities must make sure that they abide by the letter of procedural law when arresting and prosecuting a person accused of a crime. If they do not, the defendant may be able to use procedural violations as a defense against criminal liability, depending on the nature of the defendant's right that was violated and the degree of violation.

CONSTITUTIONAL SAFEGUARDS

From the very moment a crime is reported until the trial concludes, law-enforcement officers and prosecutors must be careful to abide by the specific criminal procedures that have been established to protect an accused person's constitutional rights. Before allowing a case to go to trial, the prosecutor and legal assistants assigned to the case review all pretrial events very closely to make sure that all requirements were properly observed. Defense attorneys and their legal assistants also investigate and review closely the actions of arresting and investigating police officers in an attempt to obtain grounds for dismissal of the charges against their clients.

The U.S. Constitution provides specific procedural safeguards to protect persons accused of crimes against the potentially arbitrary or unjust use of government power. These safeguards are stated in the first ten amendments to the Constitution, which constitute the Bill of Rights. As you will see in the following pages, criminal procedure is rooted in the constitutional rights and protections spelled out in the Fourth, Fifth, Sixth, and Eighth Amendments. These rights and protections are summarized below. The full text of the U.S. Constitution, including the Bill of Rights, is presented in Appendix L.

1. The Fourth Amendment requirement that no warrants for a search or an arrest may be issued without probable cause (to be discussed shortly).
2. The Fifth Amendment requirement that no one shall be deprived of "life, liberty, or property without due process of law." **Due process of law** means that the government must follow a set of reasonable, fair, and standard procedures (that is, criminal procedural law) in any action against a citizen.
3. The Fifth Amendment prohibition against **double jeopardy** (trying someone twice for the same criminal offense).
4. The Fifth Amendment guarantee that no person shall be "compelled in any criminal case to be a witness against himself."
5. The Sixth Amendment guarantees of a speedy and public trial, a trial by jury, the right to confront witnesses, and the right to a lawyer at various stages in some proceedings.
6. The Eighth Amendment prohibitions against excessive bail and fines and cruel and unusual punishment.

DUE PROCESS OF LAW
The Fifth Amendment to the U.S. Constitution prohibits the deprivation of "life, liberty, or property without due process of law," meaning that fair, reasonable, and standard procedures must be used by the government in any legal action against a citizen.

DOUBLE JEOPARDY
To place at risk (jeopardize) a person's life or liberty at risk twice. The Fifth Amendment to the U.S. Constitution prohibits a second prosecution for the same criminal offense in all but a few circumstances.

The *Miranda* Rule

In regard to criminal procedure, one of the questions that had been facing many courts in the 1950s and 1960s was not whether suspects had constitutional rights—that was not in doubt—but how and when those rights could

DEVELOPING PARALEGAL SKILLS

Year-and-a-day Defense

Jennifer Wall and Ed Roper are paralegals in a criminal defense firm. The firm is defending Robert Baines who has been charged with murder. Baines got into a fight in a bar with Gerald Litton, on January 1, 1995. Litton was beaten so severely by Baines that Litton went into a coma and never regained consciousness. He died on January 4, 1996.

The senior attorney handling the case has assigned Jennifer and Ed the task of looking at the rules governing murder to see if they can come up with a defense. The attorney said that he remembered a rule from law school requiring that, for a person to be prosecuted for murder, the victim has to die within a certain time period after the injury was incurred. If the victim does not die within that time period, then the perpetrator cannot be prosecuted for the crime of murder. Jennifer and Ed go to the law library to research criminal law.

LOCATING THE RULE

Jennifer begins by looking under the topic of murder in a digest (a book that provides an index to case law—see Chapter 17). Ed starts with a legal encyclopedia that summarizes the law. He turns to the section that discusses time limits in murder cases. "Look at this," he says. Ed shows Jennifer a discussion of a rule stating that the victim must die within a year and a day from the defendant's conduct, or the defendant cannot be prosecuted for murder. The encyclopedia explains that this is "an old rule originating when the quality of medical care was not so advanced as it is today, and people's life expectancies were so short that if the victim lived for more than a year and a day after the attack, it could not be said with reasonable certainty that intervening causes, such as illness or physical infirmities, were not to blame for the victim's death. Thus, the requirement of probable cause was not met where the victim died more than a year and a day from the date of the attack."

Ed and Jennifer apply the rule to Baines's case and conclude that under the rule, Baines should not be subject to prosecution for murder because his victim died more than a year and a day from the date of his attack.

CHECKING STATE LAW

"That rule will help our client," agrees Ed. "But we took it from the encyclopedia, which only summarizes the law and does not indicate what the law is in our state. We had better check our state cases and statutes." Jennifer and Ed research their state's laws and find that the rule in their state requires that the victim must live for at least three years from the date of the attack for the defendant to evade prosecution. Clearly, the rule cannot be used as a defense in Baines's case. Disappointed, they returned to the office to inform their supervising attorney of their research results.

SELF-INCRIMINATION
The act of giving testimony that implicates one's own guilt or participation in criminal wrongdoing. The Fifth Amendment to the U.S. Constitution states that no person "shall be compelled in any criminal case to be a witness against himself."

be exercised. For example, the Fifth Amendment to the Constitution guarantees the privilege against compulsory **self-incrimination**. As indicated in the list presented above, that amendment states, among other things, that no person "shall be compelled in any criminal case to be a witness against himself." But could this right be exercised during pretrial interrogation proceedings or only during the trial? Were confessions obtained from suspects admissible in court if the suspects had not been advised of their right to remain silent and other constitutional rights?

To clarify these issues, in 1966 the United States Supreme Court issued a landmark decision, *Miranda v. Arizona*.[4] The *Miranda* decision established the rule that individuals who are arrested and taken into custody must be informed of certain constitutional rights, which have come to be called the ***Miranda* rights**, before any statements they make can be admissible in court. These rights, which include the right to remain silent and the right to counsel, are listed in Exhibit 12.1.

MIRANDA RIGHTS
The constitutional rights of accused persons taken into custody by law-enforcement officials. Following the United States Supreme Court's decision in *Miranda v. Arizona*, on taking an accused person into custody, the arresting officer must inform the person of certain constitutional rights, such as the suspect's right to remain silent or right to counsel.

Under what is known as the **exclusionary rule**, all evidence obtained in violation of the constitutional rights of the defendant must normally be excluded, as well as all evidence derived from the evidence obtained illegally. For example, if a police officer or a private investigator breaks into a suspect's home (that is, enters the home illegally with neither the suspect's permission nor a search warrant) and obtains evidence that the suspect committed a crime, that evidence normally will not be admissible in court.

EXCLUSIONARY RULE
In criminal procedure, a rule under which any evidence that is obtained in violation of the accused's constitutional rights guaranteed by the Fourth, Fifth, and Sixth Amendments, as well as any evidence derived from illegally obtained evidence, will not be admissible in court.

The Erosion of the *Miranda* Rule

Although the Supreme Court and lower courts have enforced the rules discussed above hundreds of times since the *Miranda* decision, the *Miranda* rights of defendants have been gradually eroded. Congress in 1968 passed the Omnibus Crime Control and Safe Streets Act, which provided—among other things—that in cases involving federal crimes a voluntary confession could be used as evidence even if the accused was not informed of his or her rights.

Several subsequent decisions by the United States Supreme Court also eroded the rule. In 1984, for example, the Court recognized a "public safety"

4. 384 U.S. 436, 86 S.Ct. 1602, 16 L.Ed.2d 694 (1966). How to read case citations is discussed in Chapter 17.

EXHIBIT 12.1
The *Miranda* Rights

Upon taking a criminal suspect into custody and before any interrogation takes place, law-enforcement officers are required to communicate the following rights and facts to the suspect:

1. **The right to remain silent.**
2. **That any statements made may be used against the person in a court of law.**
3. **The right to talk to a lawyer and have a lawyer present while being questioned.**
4. **If the person cannot afford to hire a lawyer, the right to have a lawyer provided at no cost.**

In addition to being advised of these rights, the suspect must be asked if he or she understands the rights and whether he or she wishes to exercise the rights or waive (not exercise) the rights.

exception to the *Miranda* rule.[5] The need to protect the public warranted the admissibility of statements made by the defendant (in this case indicating where he placed the gun) as evidence in a trial, even when the defendant was not informed of his *Miranda* rights. In 1990, the Court recognized a "routine booking questions" exception to *Miranda*.[6] The statements made by the defendant to the police in answer to questions regarding "biographical data necessary to complete booking or pretrial services" were exempted from *Miranda*. Today, juries are permitted to accept confessions without being convinced of their voluntariness. Even in cases that are not tried in federal court, confessions made by criminal suspects who have not been completely informed of their legal rights may be taken into consideration. In *Minnick v. Mississippi*,[7] however, a 1990 case heard by the Supreme Court, the Court held that once a defendant has requested counsel, the defendant cannot be questioned by police unless the defendant's attorney is present.

CRIMINAL PROCEDURES PRIOR TO PROSECUTION

In most matters, the police (or other persons or agencies authorized by the state to do so) control the criminal justice process up to the time a case is turned over for prosecution. Although lawyers and legal assistants are usually not extensively involved in this initial stage of the criminal process, events that take place at this stage may affect the final outcome of the case. Therefore, paralegals—and especially those working with criminal defense attorneys—need to be familiar with the basic steps that occur in this phase of the criminal process.

We offer in this section (and illustrate graphically in Exhibit 12.2) a general version of the procedural steps involved in the criminal process. Bear in mind, however, that procedural details vary significantly, depending on the locality and jurisdiction in which an accused person is arrested and prosecuted and depending on the nature of the crime. Realistically, there is no way that an introductory paralegal text such as this one can describe the many procedural variations involved in the criminal process. As a paralegal, if you work in the area of criminal law or on a case involving criminal law, you therefore must do the following:

- **Check with your supervising attorney or the court hearing the case to learn the specific procedural requirements that apply to the case.**

Arrest

ARREST
To take into custody a person suspected of criminal activity.

In a lawful **arrest**, the suspect is taken into custody by the police, may be searched for weapons or evidence, and is taken to the police station to be formally charged with the crime. Most arrests are for misdemeanors, and in such situations, the arresting officers often release the suspects with cita-

5. *New York v. Quarles*, 467 U.S. 649, 104 S.Ct. 2626, 81 L.Ed.2d 550 (1984).
6. *Pennsylvania v. Muniz*, 496 U.S. 582, 110 S.Ct. 2638, 110 L.Ed.2d 528 (1990).
7. 498 U.S. 146, 111 S.Ct. 486, 112 L.Ed.2d 489 (1990).

EXHIBIT 12.2
Major Procedural Steps in a Criminal Case

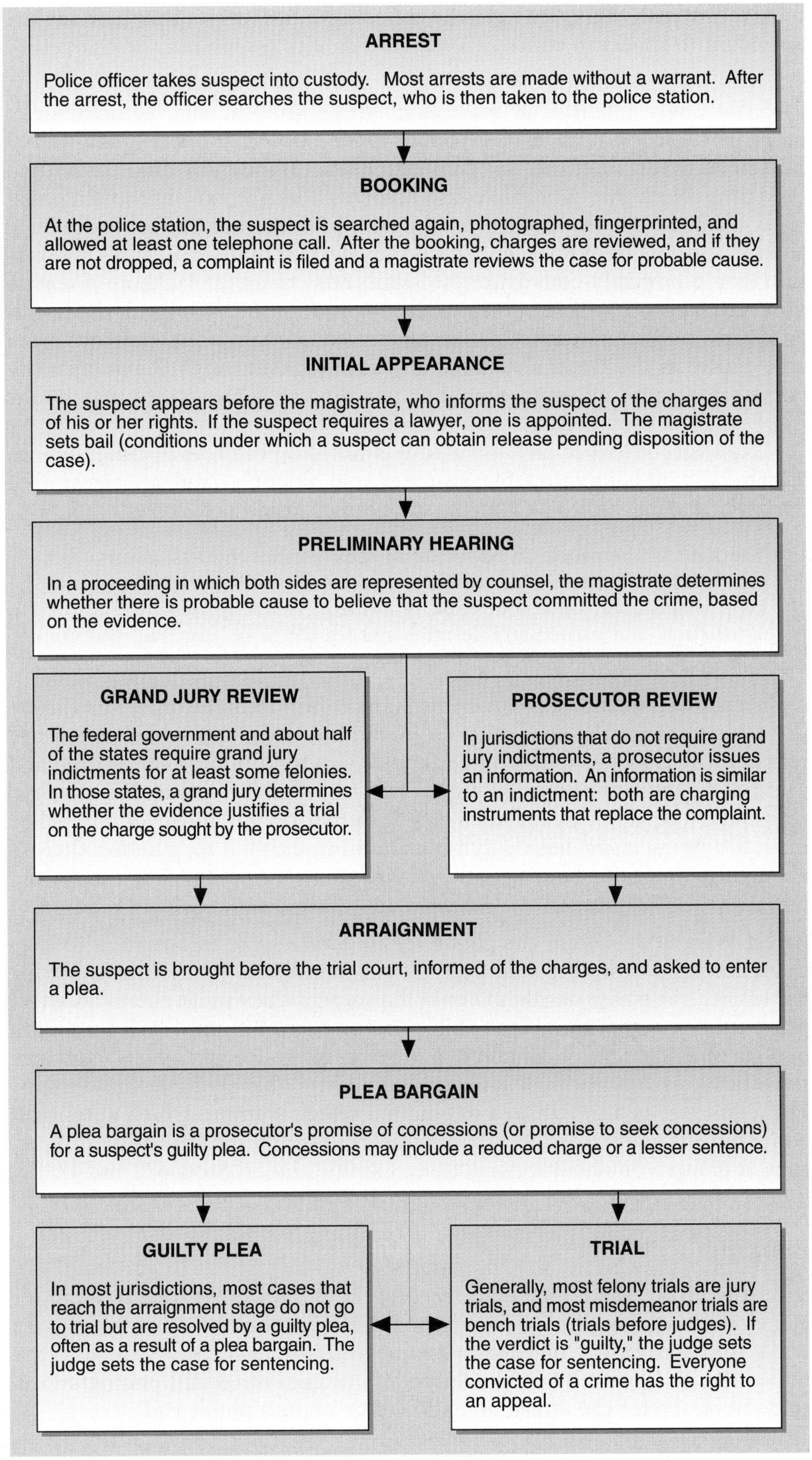

ARREST

Police officer takes suspect into custody. Most arrests are made without a warrant. After the arrest, the officer searches the suspect, who is then taken to the police station.

BOOKING

At the police station, the suspect is searched again, photographed, fingerprinted, and allowed at least one telephone call. After the booking, charges are reviewed, and if they are not dropped, a complaint is filed and a magistrate reviews the case for probable cause.

INITIAL APPEARANCE

The suspect appears before the magistrate, who informs the suspect of the charges and of his or her rights. If the suspect requires a lawyer, one is appointed. The magistrate sets bail (conditions under which a suspect can obtain release pending disposition of the case).

PRELIMINARY HEARING

In a proceeding in which both sides are represented by counsel, the magistrate determines whether there is probable cause to believe that the suspect committed the crime, based on the evidence.

GRAND JURY REVIEW

The federal government and about half of the states require grand jury indictments for at least some felonies. In those states, a grand jury determines whether the evidence justifies a trial on the charge sought by the prosecutor.

PROSECUTOR REVIEW

In jurisdictions that do not require grand jury indictments, a prosecutor issues an information. An information is similar to an indictment: both are charging instruments that replace the complaint.

ARRAIGNMENT

The suspect is brought before the trial court, informed of the charges, and asked to enter a plea.

PLEA BARGAIN

A plea bargain is a prosecutor's promise of concessions (or promise to seek concessions) for a suspect's guilty plea. Concessions may include a reduced charge or a lesser sentence.

GUILTY PLEA

In most jurisdictions, most cases that reach the arraignment stage do not go to trial but are resolved by a guilty plea, often as a result of a plea bargain. The judge sets the case for sentencing.

TRIAL

Generally, most felony trials are jury trials, and most misdemeanor trials are bench trials (trials before judges). If the verdict is "guilty," the judge sets the case for sentencing. Everyone convicted of a crime has the right to an appeal.

CITATION
In criminal procedure, an order for a defendant to appear in court or indicating that a person has violated a legal rule.

PROBABLE CAUSE
Reasonable grounds to believe the existence of facts warranting certain actions, such as the search or arrest of a person.

tions rather than taking them to the police station. The **citation** instructs the defendant to appear in court at some later date to respond to the charges.

Probable Cause. Before an individual can be arrested, the requirement of probable cause must be met. **Probable cause** exists if there is a substantial likelihood that (1) a crime was committed and (2) the individual committed the crime. Note that probable cause involves a *likelihood*—not just a possibility—that the suspect committed the crime. For example, if Castle observed Jackson running from the scene of a homicide, gun in hand, Castle's observation would probably constitute probable cause to arrest Jackson. If Castle observed Jackson walking unhurriedly away from the vicinity of the homicide, with no gun in hand, Castle's observation would not constitute probable cause. In the latter situation, although Jackson might have been the perpetrator, more evidence would be required to demonstrate that it was *likely* that Jackson committed the crime.

The requirement of probable cause is based on the Fourth Amendment, which prohibits unreasonable searches and seizures (and an arrest is a "seizure" of a person). The Fourth Amendment reads as follows:

> The right of the people to be secure in their persons, houses, papers, and effects, against unreasonable searches and seizures, shall not be violated, and no Warrants shall issue, but upon probable cause, supported by Oath or affirmation, and particularly describing the place to be searched, and the persons or things to be seized.

If a police officer observes a crime being committed, the officer can arrest the wrongdoer on the spot without a warrant, because the probable-cause requirement is satisfied (the officer knows that a crime was committed and that the person being arrested did, in fact, commit the crime). If a crime is reported to the police by a victim or some other person, however, the police must decide if a crime has really been committed and, if so, whether there is enough information about the alleged wrongdoer's guilt to justify an arrest.

ARREST WARRANT
A written order, based on probable cause and issued by a judge or public official (magistrate), commanding that the person named on the warrant be arrested by the police.

SEARCH WARRANT
A written order, based on probable cause and issued by a judge or public official (magistrate), commanding that police officers or criminal investigators search a specific person, place, or property to obtain evidence.

Arrest Warrants. Often, the police try to gather more information to help them determine whether a suspect should be arrested. If, after investigating the matter, the police decide to arrest the suspect, they must obtain an **arrest warrant**, such as that shown in Exhibit 12.3 on pages 470 and 471, from a judge or other public official. To obtain this warrant, the police will have to convince the official, usually through supporting affidavits, that probable cause exists. Probable cause is also required to obtain a **search warrant**, which authorizes police officers or other criminal investigators to search specifically named persons or property to obtain evidence (see Exhibit 12.4 on pages 472 and 473).

Booking

BOOKING
The process of entering a suspect's name, offense, and arrival time into the police log (blotter) following his or her arrest.

After the arrest, the police take the suspect to the police station, a jail, or some other *holding facility* where the booking occurs. **Booking** takes place when an officer enters the suspect's name, offense, and time of arrival on the police log, or *blotter.* Then the suspect is fingerprinted and photographed, told the reason for the arrest, and allowed to make a phone call.

For most lesser offenses, after booking the suspect may be released on his or her promise to appear at some later date before a **magistrate** (a civil official or officer who has limited judicial authority, such as a justice of the peace). Sometimes, the suspect is required to deposit a small amount of cash, or bail (discussed below), as security for his or her later appearance before the magistrate. For more serious offenses (and for some minor offenses), the suspect will be incarcerated (locked up in a jail cell) until the date of his or her appearance before a magistrate. Before being incarcerated, the suspect is thoroughly searched to make sure that no weapons get into the jail. Personal effects are listed and stored.

MAGISTRATE
A public civil officer or official with limited judicial authority, such as the authority to issue an arrest warrant.

Investigation after the Arrest

As already mentioned, when a suspect is caught "red-handed," the police may arrest the suspect without an arrest warrant and may not have to undertake much of an investigation of the alleged offense after the arrest. In other cases, however, the police must find and interview witnesses and conduct searches—of the suspect's home or car, for example—to collect evidence. Witnesses may view the suspect individually in a *line-up,* in which the suspect appears with a group of several others. In more serious cases, detectives may take charge of the investigation.

As the police review the evidence at hand, they may conclude that there is insufficient evidence to justify recommending the case for prosecution. If they reach this conclusion, the suspect may be released and the case may be closed. Alternatively, the police may decide to change the charge that was initially brought against the suspect, usually reducing the charge to a lesser offense. The police may also decide to release the suspect with a warning or a referral to a social service agency. Unless the suspect is released, at this point in the criminal process, control over the case moves from the police to the public prosecutor.

THE PROSECUTION BEGINS

The prosecution of a criminal case begins when the police inform the public prosecutor of the alleged crime, provide the reports written by the arresting and investigating officers, and turn over evidence relating to the matter. The prosecutor has the discretion to investigate the case further by personally interviewing the suspect, the arresting and investigating officers, and witnesses and gathering other evidence. The prosecutor's legal assistants often participate in these tasks. Based on a review of the police file or an investigation, the prosecutor decides whether to take the case to trial or drop the case and allow the suspect to be released. Major reasons for releasing the suspect include insufficient evidence and unreliable witnesses.

Because prosecutions are expensive and resources are limited, most prosecutors do not go forward with cases unless they think that they have a strong chance of proving the charges against the suspect in court. In many jurisdictions, at least half of all felony suspects are released or offered the alternative of participating in a diversion program to avoid being prosecuted and to clear their records. **Diversion programs** attempt to deter the suspect

DIVERSION PROGRAM
In some jurisdictions, an alternative to prosecution that is offered to certain felony suspects to deter them from future unlawful acts.

EXHIBIT 12.3
An Arrest Warrant

United States District Court

_____________ DISTRICT OF _____________

UNITED STATES OF AMERICA
V.

WARRANT FOR ARREST

CASE NUMBER:

To: The United States Marshal
and any Authorized United States Officer

YOU ARE HEREBY COMMANDED to arrest _____________
Name

and bring him or her forthwith to the nearest magistrate to answer a(n)

☐ Indictment ☐ Information ☐ Complaint ☐ Order of court ☐ Violation Notice ☐ Probation Violation Petition

charging him or her with (brief description of offense)

in violation of Title _______ United States Code, Section(s) _______

Name of Issuing Officer | Title of Issuing Officer

Signature of Issuing Officer | Date and Location

Bail fixed at $ _____________ by _____________
Name of Judicial Officer

RETURN		
This warrant was received and executed with the arrest of the above-named defendant at _____________		
DATE RECEIVED	NAME AND TITLE OF ARRESTING OFFICER	SIGNATURE OF ARRESTING OFFICER
DATE OF ARREST		

[G13861]

from further wrongdoing by, for example, requiring the suspect to stay employed, to attend special classes (perhaps on drug education), or to perform special community services. In some cases, the suspects may be required to make restitution (by returning or paying for stolen property, for example) to the victims of their crimes to avoid prosecution.

If the decision is to prosecute the case, then a complaint is filed and other procedures undertaken. The procedures discussed below (and summarized earlier in Exhibit 12.2) assure that the accused person's Fifth Amendment right to due process of law is not jeopardized.

EXHIBIT 12.3
Continued

THE FOLLOWING IS FURNISHED FOR INFORMATION ONLY:

DEFENDANT'S NAME: ____________________

ALIAS: ____________________

LAST KNOWN RESIDENCE: ____________________

LAST KNOWN EMPLOYMENT: ____________________

PLACE OF BIRTH: ____________________

DATE OF BIRTH: ____________________

SOCIAL SECURITY NUMBER: ____________________

HEIGHT: __________ WEIGHT: __________

SEX: __________ RACE: __________

HAIR: __________ EYES: __________

SCARS, TATTOOS, OTHER DISTINGUISHING MARKS: ____________________

FBI NUMBER: ____________________

COMPLETE DESCRIPTION OF AUTO: ____________________

INVESTIGATIVE AGENCY AND ADDRESS: ____________________

[G13862]

Filing the Complaint

The criminal litigation process may begin with the filing of a *complaint* (see Exhibit 12.5 on page 476). Once the decision to prosecute the case is made, then the prosecutor files a complaint against the suspect, usually with the magistrate's court. (In some cases, however, a grand jury is called at this point to determine probable cause, as will be discussed below.) The complaint includes a statement of the charges that are being brought against the suspect. The suspect now becomes a criminal defendant. Because the defendant is in the court system, prosecutors must show that they have legal grounds to proceed. They must show probable cause that a crime was committed and that the defendant committed the crime. Note that the Fourth Amendment requirement of probable cause comes under scrutiny several times during the prosecution of a criminal offense.

Initial Appearance

In most jurisdictions, defendants are taken before a magistrate within hours of arrest, usually within twenty-four hours. During this *initial appearance*, a brief proceeding takes place. The magistrate makes sure that the person presented is the person named in the complaint, informs the defendant of the charge or charges made in the complaint, and explains to the defendant

EXHIBIT 12.4
A Search Warrant

Ch. 89 SEARCH AND SEIZURE § 7942
Rule 41

§ 7942. Search Warrant

AO 93 (Rev. 5/85) Search Warrant

United States District Court

________ DISTRICT OF ________

In the Matter of the Search of
(Name, address or brief description of person or property to be searched)

SEARCH WARRANT

CASE NUMBER:

TO: ________ and any Authorized Officer of the United States

Affidavit(s) having been made before me by ________ (Affiant) who has reason to believe that ☐ on the person of or ☐ on the premises known as (name, description and/or location)

in the ________ District of ________ there is now concealed a certain person or property, namely (describe the person or property)

I am satisfied that the affidavit(s) and any recorded testimony establish probable cause to believe that the person or property so described is now concealed on the person or premises above-described and establish grounds for the issuance of this warrant.

YOU ARE HEREBY COMMANDED to search on or before ________ (Date)

(not to exceed 10 days) the person or place named above for the person or property specified, serving this warrant and making the search (in the daytime — 6:00 A.M. to 10:00 P.M.) (at any time in the day or night as I find reasonable cause has been established) and if the person or property be found there to seize same, leaving a copy of this warrant and receipt for the person or property taken, and prepare a written inventory of the person or property seized and promptly return this warrant to ________ (U.S. Judge or Magistrate) as required by law.

________ Date and Time Issued at ________ City and State

BAIL
The amount or conditions set by the court to assure that an individual accused of a crime will appear for further criminal proceedings. If the accused person provides bail, whether in cash or by means of a bail bond, then the person is released from jail.

his or her constitutional rights—particularly, the right to remain silent (under the Fifth Amendment) and the right to be represented by counsel (under the Sixth Amendment). If the defendant cannot afford to hire a private attorney, a public defender may be appointed, or private counsel may be hired by the state to represent the defendant.

The magistrate may release the defendant from jail pending further legal proceedings on certain conditions. Defendants who have been arrested for misdemeanors, for example, may be released on their own recognizance (on their promise to return at a later date for further proceedings). For more serious crimes, the defendant will be released only if he or she posts **bail**—an

EXHIBIT 12.4
Continued

§ 7942 SPECIAL PROCEEDINGS Ch. 89
Rule 41

AO 93 (Rev. 5/85) Search Warrant

RETURN

DATE WARRANT RECEIVED	DATE AND TIME WARRANT EXECUTED	COPY OF WARRANT AND RECEIPT FOR ITEMS LEFT WITH

INVENTORY MADE IN THE PRESENCE OF

INVENTORY OF PERSON OR PROPERTY TAKEN PURSUANT TO THE WARRANT

CERTIFICATION

I swear that this inventory is a true and detailed account of the person or property taken by me on the warrant.

Subscribed, sworn to, and returned before me this date.

U.S. Judge or Magistrate Date

[G13951]

amount of money paid by the defendant to the court and retained by the court until the defendant returns for further proceedings. For some serious crimes, bail may be denied.

Often, defendants are unable to pay the amount of bail set by the court. In such a situation, the defendant may make arrangements with a *bail bondsperson* to post a bail bond on behalf of the defendant. The bondsperson, in effect, promises the court that he or she will turn over to the court

DEVELOPING PARALEGAL SKILLS

The Prosecutor's Office—Warrant Division

Kathy Perello works as a legal assistant in the county prosecutor's office, which is located in a major metropolitan area. She works in the division that is responsible for issuing arrest and search warrants. Kathy works specifically on arrest warrants.

Ryan McCarthy, a police officer, is in her office with a police report of a burglary. The police have a suspect whom they want to arrest. McCarthy has the paperwork from the prosecutor that authorizes the arrest. Kathy asks McCarthy for the defendant's criminal history, which is a history of the individual and any crimes that he or she has committed in the past. McCarthy gives Kathy the history. Kathy gives the paperwork to her secretary so that the secretary may type the warrant. Kathy continues to review other files while she waits for the warrant on the burglary case.

When Kathy receives the typed warrant from her secretary, she reviews it to ensure that it contains certain items, such as a statement that there will be no plea bargaining once the suspect is being prosecuted. This is a county policy in felony cases. The prosecutor has established this unusual requirement because he wants people to know that they won't get off easily if they commit felonies in his county. Kathy also reviews the warrant to make sure that it contains a criminal history and that the criminal history matches the individual who is named in the warrant. She finds that the warrant is in order in every respect.

Kathy phones the officer and informs him that his warrant is ready. McCarthy comes over to pick it up. He will take it to court and swear to the truth of its contents. If the judge agrees that there is sufficient probable cause to arrest the suspect, the judge will sign the warrant and McCarthy can make the arrest.

the full amount of the bail if the defendant fails to return for the further proceedings. The defendant usually must give the bondsperson a certain percentage of the bail (often 10 percent) in cash. This amount, which is often not returned to the defendant later, is considered as payment for the bondsperson's assistance and assumption of risk. Depending on the amount of the bail bond, the defendant may also be required to sign over to the bondsperson rights to certain property (such as a car, a valuable watch, or other asset) as security for the bond.

MOTION TO REDUCE THE AMOUNT OF BAIL
A motion requesting that the bail needed to release the defendant be lowered because it is unreasonably high under the circumstances and may violate the Eighth Amendment's prohibition against excessive bail.

Normally, the defendant's attorney (or the attorney's paralegal) makes arrangements for bail with the court or a bail bondsperson. A paralegal working on a criminal case may also be asked to draft a **motion to reduce the amount of bail** if the defendant's attorney deems that the amount of bail set by the judge is unreasonably high. Under the Eighth Amendment to the Constitution, "Excessive bail shall not be required." In a motion to reduce the amount of bail, the attorney may argue that the bail set by the court is "excessive" in view of the nature of the crime or the circumstances in which the crime was committed.

PARALEGAL PROFILE

Public Defender for the Penobscot Indian Nation

JOHN M. TROTT received his associate's degree, with a paralegal major, from Beal College in Bangor, Maine. He then worked as an independent paralegal from his own office. Trott later attended the University of Maine, where he received his bachelor of arts degree in psychology and philosophy. When a job opened up with the Penobscot Indian Nation for a public defender, he applied for the position. Trott also received training in divorce mediation through the Academy of Family Mediators in Eugene, Oregon, and Divorce Mediation Training Associates in Boston. He is a member of the National Federation for Paralegal Associations and hopes to start an affiliated group in Maine. We asked Trott to give us some thoughts on his area of paralegal work.

What do you like best about your work?

"One thing I enjoy is the variety of work that I do. In my capacity as public defender for the Penobscot Nation, I defend, in tribal court, persons accused of certain classes of misdemeanors.* I also act as a mediator in divorce proceedings and volunteer as an arbitrator with the Better Business Bureau. I also enjoy being right on top of the latest cases. Additionally, I enjoy the process of sifting through recent cases and information, not only to determine what might pertain to state law, but also sifting through and interpreting whether it applies to the Indian Civil Rights Act. I find these tasks to be mentally stimulating."

What is the greatest challenge that you face in your area of work?

"One of the greatest challenges is simply getting the work done. I do all the work myself, including research and typing, without the aid of a secretary."

What advice do you have for would-be paralegals in your area of work?

"My recommendation for students is to study everything and anything that can prepare them for their jobs, and to study hard. I am a great advocate of paralegals working to their greatest capacity, and I feel we can often be a great asset in the practice of law. If I could go back and do it again, I would have started my legal education when I was eighteen instead of forty-eight, because I truly love my work."

What are some tips for success as a paralegal in your area of work?

"Even though my position as public defender for the Penobscot Indian Nation is treated as a paralegal role and I have a supervising attorney, the judge holds me to the same standards that an attorney would be expected to meet. My first few times in court were difficult for me because I wasn't as familiar with evidentiary rules as an attorney would be. To overcome that unfamiliarity, I would study as much as I could, and I would also go to court about once a week to observe different attorneys. So I would suggest that a student study anything and everything that will expose him or her to a variety of areas of paralegal work."

"ONE THING I ENJOY IS THE VARIETY OF WORK THAT I DO."

* Indian nations are allowed to create and implement tribal laws to govern activities within their reservations. A tribal court may authorize nonattorneys, such as John Trott, to represent parties in court.

Preliminary Hearing

The defendant again appears before a magistrate or judge at a **preliminary hearing**. During this hearing, the magistrate or judge determines whether the

PRELIMINARY HEARING
An initial hearing in which a magistrate decides if there is probable cause to believe that the defendant committed the crime for which he or she is charged.

EXHIBIT 12.5
A Complaint

United States District Court

_______________ DISTRICT OF _______________

UNITED STATES OF AMERICA
V.

CRIMINAL COMPLAINT

CASE NUMBER:

(Name and Address of Defendant)

I, the undersigned complainant being duly sworn state the following is true and correct to the best of my knowledge and belief. On or about _______________ in _______________ county, in the _______________ District of _______________ defendant(s) did, (Track Statutory Language of Offense)

in violation of Title _______ United States Code, Section(s) _______________.

I further state that I am a(n) _______________ (Official Title) and that this complaint is based on the following facts:

Continued on the attached sheet and made a part hereof: ☐ Yes ☐ No

____
Signature of Complainant

Sworn to before me and subscribed in my presence,

_______________ at _______________
Date City and State

evidence presented is sufficient to establish probable cause to believe that the defendant committed the crime for which he or she is charged. This may be the first adversarial proceeding in which both sides are represented by counsel. Paralegals may become extensively involved in the process at this point by assisting in the preparation for the hearing. The prosecutor may present witnesses, who may be cross-examined by defense counsel (the defense rarely presents its witnesses prior to trial). If the defendant intends to plead guilty, he or she usually waives the right to a preliminary hearing to help move things along more quickly. In many jurisdictions, however, the preliminary hearing is required in certain felony cases.

If the magistrate finds that the evidence is insufficient to establish probable cause, either the charge is reduced to a lesser charge, or charges are dropped altogether and the defendant is released. If the magistrate believes that there is sufficient evidence to establish probable cause, the prosecutor issues an information. The **information** replaces the complaint as the formal charge against the defendant and binds over the defendant to further proceedings, which usually means that the case proceeds to trial.

INFORMATION
A formal accusation or complaint, usually issued by a prosecuting attorney, against a criminal suspect. The information initiates the criminal litigation process.

Grand Jury Review

The federal government and about half of the states require a grand jury, and not the prosecutor, to make the decision as to whether a case should go to trial. In other words, a grand jury's indictment (see below) is an alternative to a prosecutor's information as the formal complaint that initiates the criminal litigation process.

A **grand jury** is a group of citizens called to decide whether probable cause exists—that is, whether it is likely that the defendant committed the crime for which he or she is charged and therefore whether the case should go to trial. Even in those courts in which grand-jury review is not required, the prosecutor may call a grand jury to evaluate the evidence against a suspect, which will indicate to the prosecutor the relative strength or weakness of the case.

GRAND JURY
The group of citizens called to decide whether probable cause exists to believe that a suspect committed the crime with which he or she has been charged.

The grand jury sits in closed session and only hears evidence presented by the prosecutor—the defendant cannot present evidence at this hearing. The prosecutor presents to the grand jury whatever evidence the state has against the defendant, including photographs, documents, tangible objects, test results, the testimony of witnesses, and other items. If the grand jury finds that probable cause exists, it issues an **indictment** against the defendant called a *true bill.* The indictment is filed with the trial court and becomes the formal charge against the defendant. An example of an indictment is shown in Exhibit 12.6 on page 480.

INDICTMENT
A charge or written accusation, issued by a grand jury, that probable cause exists to believe that a named person has committed a crime.

Arraignment

Based on the information or the indictment filed, the prosecutor submits a motion to the court, similar to that shown in Exhibit 12.7 on page 481, to order the defendant to appear before the trial court for an **arraignment**. Due process of law, which is guaranteed by the Fifth Amendment, requires that a criminal defendant be informed of the charges brought against him or her and be offered an opportunity to respond to those charges. The arraignment is one of the ways in which due process requirements are satisfied by criminal procedural law.

ARRAIGNMENT
A court proceeding in which the suspect is formally charged with the criminal offense stated in the indictment. The suspect then enters a plea (guilty, not guilty, or *nolo contendere*) in response.

At the arraignment, the defendant is informed of the charges against him or her, and the defendant must respond to the charges by pleading not guilty or guilty. The defendant may also enter a plea of ***nolo contendere***, which is Latin for "I will not contest it." The plea of *nolo contendere* is neither an admission of guilt nor a denial of guilt.

NOLO CONTENDERE
Latin for "I will not contest it." A criminal defendant's plea in which he or she chooses not to challenge, or contest, the charges brought by the government. Although the defendant may still be sentenced or fined, the plea neither admits nor denies guilt.

At the arraignment, the defendant can move to have the charges dismissed, which happens in a fair number of cases for a variety of reasons. The

FEATURED GUEST: PAMELA POOLE WEBER

Paralegals and Criminal Litigation

Biographical Note

Pamela Poole Weber graduated from Stetson University College of Law and is licensed to practice law in Florida. In 1989, after working in both the corporate and public sectors as a litigator, she joined Seminole Community College in Central Florida. There she developed a two-year legal-assistant program and is currently the director of that program. Weber remains active in various legal areas, teaching police recruits in the area of juvenile law and lecturing to seniors on issues relating to the rights of elderly persons.

The gavel strikes, the trial is over, and the jury is escorted to the jury room to deliberate. Your pulse begins to pound, and the gravity of the situation overwhelms you. This is the first time that you, as a paralegal, have assisted your supervising attorney in a criminal case. Now comes the most difficult time—waiting for the decision. But you take satisfaction in knowing that you have done the best job you can.

* * * * *

Criminal litigation is a very fast-paced area of law that is continually undergoing change. Many people do not understand what is involved in defending or prosecuting someone accused of a crime. First and foremost, both sides must be familiar with current laws and especially with changes or new interpretations of those laws. Attorneys do not always have the time required to keep up with these changes. Paralegals can be a valuable asset to a law office by keeping informed on current developments—by reading current court decisions, by reviewing summaries of new laws or modifications to existing laws, by being alert for emerging trends reported in the media, and by generally keeping their eyes and ears open. This behind-the-scenes work is in many ways just as interesting as the spectacular trial scenes on television, and a paralegal's input with respect to current law may well determine the outcome of a case.

Both the defense and the prosecution must review every aspect of the case. This requires combining legal research with critical analysis. Attorneys and paralegals work together in planning a course of action for each case, regardless of whether the case is simple or highly complex. This team approach is becoming more widely accepted because of the results it generates. As the old saying goes, "Two minds are better than one."

OPPORTUNITIES FOR PARALEGALS

Criminal litigation may present paralegals with a variety of opportunities, although paralegals are not utilized as extensively in criminal litigation as they are in civil litigation. Some attorneys do not use paralegals to their fullest capabilities because they do not know how to maximize paralegal services. Often, paralegals must suggest tasks that they can perform or, if appropriate, must simply go ahead and perform the tasks on their own. Remember, though, that paralegals cannot engage in any actions that only attorneys are licensed to perform.

What are some of the services that paralegals can provide? Obviously, legal research is critical to successful criminal litigation, and paralegals can perform this research for attorneys. Such research may involve a review and analysis of the law or laws that allegedly have been violated by the defendant, various defense strategies, procedural problems, and evidentiary problems—just to name a few. Sometimes, research is very detailed, requiring days and even weeks to complete. At other times, research may have to be done at the last minute within only an hour or two.

Paralegals who want more contact with people can involve themselves in the evidentiary side of the case. Both the defense attorney and the prosecuting attorney in a criminal case have some sort of evidence—physical evidence, witnesses' testimony, or confessions, for

FEATURED GUEST, Continued

example—with which to work. The paralegal may interview witnesses, prepare deposition questions, review police and laboratory reports, or identify photographs that may be useful at trial.

Many paralegals enjoy the challenge of critical analysis and strategic thinking. The criminal-litigation paralegal is continually provided with challenges in this respect. In this area, the paralegal can assist in actually preparing the case for trial. The paralegal may be asked to draft pretrial motions, review the available research and documents, draft responses to the opposing side's motions, prepare questions for jury selection, and prepare jury instructions for the conclusion of the case.

HOW CAN I ASSIST IN THE DEFENSE OF A CRIMINAL?

This question, long asked by attorneys, is now being asked by paralegals. Many people look at this area of law and say that they could never represent such defendants as Ted Bundy or Jeffrey Dahmer (convicted serial killers). Perhaps these people believe that by representing such defendants, the attorneys are somehow condoning their criminal actions. Or perhaps they detest those defendants so much that they want them convicted and punished without the benefit of due process. But attorneys and their legal assistants must remind themselves that until the verdict is in, the defendants are only *accused* of committing the criminal acts. They are guilty of no crime until the jury decides they are guilty *beyond a reasonable doubt.* Our country's criminal justice system is founded on the principle that a person is "innocent until proven guilty." The paralegal must remember that his or her job is not to decide the guilt or innocence of an accused person. Rather, it is to ensure that *justice* is being served.

A paralegal working for the prosecutor will strive to ensure that the people of a particular city, county, or state, or even the United States, are having their interests protected. The prosecution does not represent the victim of a criminal act but rather the citizens of a community.

The defense paralegal will work to ensure the protection of the rights of the accused. The U.S. Constitution guarantees that all persons have certain rights, including the right to a trial in which they may confront their accusers and the right to be represented by legal counsel during that trial. These rights apply to *everyone*—including those who actually commit the crimes with which they are charged. It is up to the defense team to make sure that the defendant has not been deprived of any of his or her constitutional rights.

The defense attorney and his or her legal assistants will examine closely all the circumstances, procedures, and evidence involving the defendant to make sure that the defendant has been allowed to exercise these rights. It may be the task of the paralegal to determine if evidence, including a confession, was properly obtained. If it was not, the paralegal may assist in drafting motions to bring this to the attention of the court. The defense team will also explore various defenses that may be available to the accused.

Paralegals who wish to work in the area of criminal justice must be prepared to be highly objective about criminal proceedings. They must be able to separate their personal and emotional responses to a particular defendant's alleged criminal acts from their professional goal of serving that defendant's best interests by doing all they can to ensure that his or her rights have been observed.

"THE DEFENSE PARALEGAL WILL WORK TO ENSURE THE PROJECTION OF THE RIGHTS OF THE ACCUSED."

CONCLUSION

Criminal litigation offers numerous opportunities for legal assistants, but it is important to remember that in some cases it may be difficult to achieve the necessary personal and emotional distance from a case to deal with it objectively and professionally.

* * * * *

The bailiff returns and announces that the jury has reached a verdict. Your heart leaps into your throat. You take a deep breath and wait. The jury returns a verdict for your side, and you realize that you have just experienced a first victory as a paralegal. After all, you say to yourself, your efforts were crucial to the success of your attorney's case. You know that not all future cases will be "won," but you experience the rewarding feeling of being an integral part of the system seeking justice for all Americans.

EXHIBIT 12.6
An Indictment

[*Title of Court and Cause*]

The Grand Jury charges that:

On or about ______, 19__, at ______, ______, in the ______ District of ______, ______ having been convicted of knowingly acquiring and possessing food stamp coupons in a manner not authorized by the provisions of Chapter 51, Title 7, United States Code, and the regulations issued pursuant to said chapter, a felony conviction, in the federal district court for the ______ District of ______, and sentenced on ______, 19__, did knowingly possess a firearm that had been transported in and affecting commerce, to-wit: an OMC Pistol, Back Up 380 Caliber, serial number ______; all in violation of Section 1202(a)(1) of Title 18, United States Code, Appendix.

A True Bill

______________________,
Foreperson.

______________________,
United States Attorney.

ETHICAL CONCERN

The Ethics of Plea Bargaining

Paralegals who work on criminal cases may be ethically troubled by plea bargaining. In such situations, it may be helpful to view the issues in the larger context of the American justice system and American society. American courts are overburdened with cases, and it is in the public interest to reduce their caseloads. American jails are overcrowded, and reducing prison sentences is one way to deal with this issue. In the larger context, then, the ethical issue is whether you believe that it is fair to balance society's interest in obtaining strict justice against society's interest in lowering the social costs (more prisons, more courts, more judges, and so on) of that justice. Also, and more directly to the point, your job as a paralegal is to serve the client's best interests—and it may be in the client's best interests to plea bargain. In such a situation, you will need to set your personal feelings aside.

defendant may claim, for example, that the case should be dismissed because the statute of limitations for the crime in question has lapsed. Most frequently, however, the defendant pleads guilty to the charge or to a lesser charge that has been agreed on through **plea bargaining** between the prosecutor and defendant. If the defendant pleads guilty, no trial is necessary, and the defendant is sentenced based on the plea. If the defendant pleads not guilty, the case will go to trial.

PLEA BARGAINING
The process by which the accused and the prosecutor in a criminal case work out a mutually satisfactory disposition of the case, subject to court approval. Usually, plea bargaining involves the defendant's pleading guilty to a lesser offense in return for a lighter sentence.

Pretrial Motions

Defense attorneys and their paralegals will search for and be alert to any violation of the defendant's constitutional rights. Many pretrial motions are based on possible violations of the defendant's rights as provided by the Constitution and criminal procedural law. The motion to reduce the amount of bail, for example, which has already been discussed, is rooted in the Eighth Amendment's prohibition against excessive bail. A motion to dismiss the case (see Chapter 10) is usually based on an assertion that a constitutional right—or a criminal procedure stemming from that right—has been violated. For example, a motion to dismiss might assert that the evidence against the defendant was obtained illegally (without a search warrant, for instance, if in the circumstances a search warrant should have been

The United States of America by ______, United States Attorney for the ______ District of ______, by direction of the Attorney General, requests the Court to issue an order directing the defendant herein, ______, to be and appear before the United States District Court for the ______ District of ______ at ______, in person, on ______, 19__, at 10:00 A.M. for arraignment. This request is made in compliance with the order for warrant of removal issued on the ______ day of ______, 19__, by United States District Judge ______ in the United States District Court for the District of ______.

____
United States Attorney.

EXHIBIT 12.7
Motion for Order Directing Defendant to Appear for Arraignment

obtained). Alternatively, the attorney may ask the paralegal to draft a **motion to suppress evidence**. Exhibit 12.8 on the following pages illustrates a motion to suppress evidence seized illegally (without a search warrant).

Other pretrial motions that may be made prior to trial include a **motion challenging the sufficiency of the indictment** (claiming that there was insufficient evidence to establish probable cause), a motion *in limine* (to limit evidence that may be submitted—see Chapter 11), and a **motion for a change of venue** (to a more convenient venue, for example, or to ensure the defendant's right to a fair and impartial trial).

Various other motions—including motions to reduce the charges against the defendant, to obtain evidence (during discovery), or to extend the trial date—may also be made prior to the trial. As with motions made during the civil litigation process, each motion must be accompanied by supporting affidavits and/or legal memoranda.

MOTION TO SUPPRESS EVIDENCE
A motion requesting that certain evidence be excluded, or suppressed, from consideration during the trial.

MOTION CHALLENGING THE SUFFICIENCY OF THE INDICTMENT
A motion claiming that the evidence submitted by the prosecutor was insufficient to establish probable cause that the defendant committed the crime with which he or she has been charged.

MOTION FOR A CHANGE OF VENUE
A motion requesting that a trial be moved to a different location to ensure a fair and impartial proceeding, for the convenience of the parties, or for some other acceptable reason.

Discovery

In preparing for trial, public prosecutors, defense attorneys, and paralegals engage in discovery proceedings (including depositions and interrogatories), interview and subpoena witnesses, prepare exhibits and a trial notebook, examine relevant documents and evidence, and do other tasks necessary to prosecute or defend the defendant most effectively. Although similar to civil litigation in these respects, criminal discovery is generally more limited than civil discovery, and the time limits relating to discovery also are different in criminal cases.

During discovery, defendants are generally entitled to obtain any evidence in the possession of the prosecutor relating to the case, including statements previously made by the defendant, objects, documents, and

EXHIBIT 12.8
Motion to Suppress Evidence

[*Title of Court and Cause*]

MOTION TO SUPPRESS

The Defendant, ______, by and through his/her attorney of record, moves this Court for an order pursuant to the Federal Rules of Criminal Procedure suppressing the use or any reference at any stage of the legal proceedings, to evidence taken from the person, property, or the premises of the Defendant, ______, under the following grounds.

1. The search and seizure were made without lawful authority or justification.

2. The arrest and detention was illegal, unconstitutional and unreasonable, in that at the time the arrest was made, no offense was being committed in the officers' presence, the arrest was made without probable cause, the detention was without legal justification, and the arrest came after the search and seizure.

3. There were no circumstances justifying or authorizing the search and seizure.

4. The search and seizure were the fruits of a previous illegal, unconstitutional and unreasonable search, arrest, detention, intrusion, and/or statement.

5. The search and seizure violated the defendant's rights granted him by the Fourth, Fifth and Fourteenth amendments of the United States Constitution.

6. Any statements given were given without legal counsel and without the defendant's waiver of his/her rights to counsel.

7. All such statements, whether oral or written, were obtained from defendant in violation of his/her rights under the Fifth, Sixth, and Fourteenth Amendments to the United States

reports of tests and examinations. Defendants are given this right to offset the fact that the prosecution (the state) has more resources at its disposal than the defendant (an individual citizen).

MOTION FOR DISCOVERY AND INSPECTION
A motion requesting permission from the court to obtain evidence in the adversary's possession.

To obtain evidence from the prosecutor's office, the defense attorney asks his or her legal assistant to draft a **motion for discovery and inspection** similar to that shown in Exhibit 12.9 on page 484. The motion must be submitted to the court within a specified period of time (for a case being tried in a federal court, the motion must be submitted within ten days following the arraignment). The legal assistant will also draft an affidavit in support of the motion. The affidavit contains the sworn testimony of the defendant as to the defendant's knowledge of papers, documents, and other evidence in the possession of the prosecutor.

EXHIBIT 12.8
Continued

Constitution, and Article I, Sections 19, 18(a), and 10 of the Constitution.

8. All such statements, whether oral or written, were made before the defendant was offered an opportunity to consult with counsel, without counsel present, and without warning to the defendant of his constitutional rights.

9. All such statements, whether oral or written, were involuntary in that defendant was induced and coerced to make such statements by threats, promises, and actions of the investigative officers.

10. All such statements, whether oral or written, were obtained in violation of defendant's rights under Miranda v. Arizona, 384 U.S. 436 (1966), in that defendant did not make a knowing, voluntary and intelligent waiver of his/her Miranda rights because interrogating officers misrepresented the nature, character, and sufficiency of the evidence against him/her. See Woods v. Clusen, 794 F.2d 293, 297 (7th Cir.1986).

The items sought to be suppressed are as follows:

a. Any and all clothes, baggage, papers, books, documents, records, notes, correspondence, currency, financial statements, photographs, furnishings, narcotics, narcotics paraphernalia, or weapons seized during or in relation to a search and arrest that occurred on or about ______, 19__, at approximately ______ and ______.

b. Any and all pre and post arrest statements made by the defendant in relation to the above named incident.

c. Any and all clothes, baggage, papers, books, documents, records, notes, correspondence, currency, financial statements, photographs, furnishings, narcotics, narcotics paraphernalia, or weapons seized during or in relation to a search and arrest that occurred on or about ______, 19__, at or near ______.

d. Any and all pre and post arrest statements made by the defendant in relation to the above named incident.

WHEREFORE, Defendant, ______, moves this Court for an Order consistent with the relief requested herein.

Respectfully submitted,

____

EXHIBIT 12.9
Motion for Discovery and Inspection

[*Title of Court and Cause*]

MOTION OF DEFENDANT FOR DISCOVERY AND INSPECTION

The above-named defendant moves this Honorable Court, pursuant to the provisions of Rule 16(a), Title 18, United States Code, to permit the defendant to inspect and copy or photograph the following items:

1. All written or recorded statements made by the defendant, or copies thereof, within the possession, custody or control of the government, the existence of which is known, or by the exercise of due diligence may become known, to the attorney for the government;

2. The substance of any oral statement which the government intends to offer in evidence at the trial made by the defendant whether before or after arrest in response to interrogation by any person then known to the defendant to be a government agent;

3. The recorded testimony of the defendant, if any, before a grand jury which relates to the offense charged herein;

4. The defendant's prior criminal record, if any, as is within the possession, custody or control of the government, the existence of which is known, or by the exercise of due diligence may become known, to the attorney for the government;

5. All books, papers, documents, photographs, tangible objects, buildings or places, or copies or portions thereof, which are within the possession, custody or control of the government, and which are material to the preparation of the defendant's defense, or are intended for use by the government as evidence in chief at the trial, or were obtained from or belong to the defendant;

6. The results or reports of physical or mental examinations, and of scientific tests or experiments, if any, or copies thereof, which are within the possession, custody, or control of the government, the existence of which are known, or by the exercise of due diligence may become known, to the attorney for the government, and which are material to the preparation of the defense or are intended for use by the government as evidence in chief at trial.

Respectfully submitted,

____

THE TRIAL

You have already seen that after arrest, in most cases, either (1) the suspect is released or the charges are dropped for lack of probable cause or some other reason, or (2) the suspect pleads guilty to the crime (or to a lesser crime as a

DEVELOPING PARALEGAL SKILLS

Discovery in the Criminal Case

The law firm of McCoy & Warner is defending Taylor Rogers in a case of attempted murder. Taylor allegedly shot a person in a drive-by shooting on the expressway. Lee Salomone, a paralegal, is working on the case. Today, Lee has received from the prosecutor's office a copy of all of the evidence that the prosecutor has in her files on this case. Lee had previously prepared a motion for discovery and inspection. His supervising attorney had argued his motion in court, and the court granted it.

Now that McCoy & Warner has received copies of the prosecutor's evidence, Lee's first task is to organize the discovery materials in the file. He creates and labels sections for the defendant's statements, witnesses' statements, police reports, and tests. He then reviews the evidence obtained from the prosecutor and summarizes it in a memo, which he also places in the file. After lunch, he will meet with his supervising attorney to review the prosecutor's evidence.

During the meeting, attorney Warner asks Lee to contact an eyewitness for an interview. The witness, Melanie Kuhn, claims to have witnessed the shooting incident and called the police. She described a car different from that of the defendant as the one from which the shots were fired. The attorney also wants Lee to interview the police officers to see if their explanations of the events that occurred are consistent with witness Kuhn's account.

Lee calls witness Kuhn to arrange for an interview. Kuhn is reluctant to talk to Lee, but he explains to her that the descriptions of the cars do not match and that they do not want an innocent person convicted. In view of these circumstances, Kuhn agrees to talk to Lee, and he arranges for her to come to the office the following day. Next, he calls the police station and arranges to talk to the police officers about the shooting. They can see him shortly, so he leaves his current project and goes to the police station for the meeting. By the end of the day, Lee has completed all of his assigned tasks. In the morning, he will consult with his supervising attorney about what further discovery should be undertaken.

result of plea bargaining) prior to trial, usually at the arraignment, in which case sentencing occurs and no trial takes place. As a result, only a small fraction of all criminal cases actually go to trial.

Very few misdemeanor cases go to trial, and when they do, the trials are usually quite short. Most criminal trials involve felonies. Although some criminal trials are spectacular trials that go on for weeks and become newsworthy, most are over very quickly, usually within two days.

There are many procedural similarities between a civil trial and a criminal trial. As in a civil trial, the prosecutor and the defendant's attorney make their opening statements to the court, examine and cross-examine witnesses, and summarize their positions in closing arguments. The jury is charged (instructed), and when the jury renders its verdict, the trial comes to an end. Despite these similarities, there are some significant procedural differences between civil litigation and criminal litigation, including those discussed below.

Special Features of Criminal Trials

As mentioned earlier, criminal procedures are designed to protect the individual from the state. Criminal trial procedures reflect this greater need for protection of the criminal defendant. Many of the significant rights of the criminal defendant, including his or her right to a "speedy and public trial" and the right to a jury trial, are spelled out in the Sixth Amendment. That amendment reads, in part, as follows:

> In all criminal prosecutions, the accused shall enjoy the right to a speedy and public trial, by an impartial jury of the State and district wherein the crime shall have been committed, . . . and to be informed of the nature and cause of the accusation; to be confronted with the witnesses against him; to have compulsory process for obtaining witnesses in his favor; and to have the Assistance of Counsel for his defence.

A "Speedy and Public Trial." The right to a jury trial in civil cases is stated in the Seventh Amendment, but that amendment mentions nothing about a "speedy and public" trial. In contrast, the Sixth Amendment requires a speedy and public trial for criminal prosecutions. The reason for this requirement is obvious: depending on the seriousness of the crime with which a defendant is charged, the defendant may lose his or her right to move freely (and may remain incarcerated prior to trial). Also, the accusation that a person has committed a crime jeopardizes that person's reputation in the community. If the defendant is innocent, the sooner the trial is held, the sooner the defendant can establish his or her innocence in the eyes of the court (and of the public).

The Sixth Amendment does not specify what is meant by the term *speedy.* Generally, in determining whether a defendant's right to a speedy trial has been violated, courts will examine several factors, including the reason for the delay and how the delay affects the defendant's position.

The criminal defendant's right to a *public* trial is an important constitutional protection. It helps to ensure that the prosecution of the defendant will be undertaken fairly and honestly.

The Role of the Jury. In all felony cases, the defendant is entitled to a jury trial. In some states, juries may also be requested for misdemeanor cases. If the defendant waives his or her right to trial by jury, the waiver must be documented by a form such as that shown in Exhibit 12.10 or otherwise be made on the record in court. Of the criminal cases that go to trial, a majority are tried by a jury. If the right to a jury trial is waived, the case will be decided by the judge.

While the jury is traditionally composed of twelve persons, many states have reduced the size of juries to six persons for lesser offenses. In most jurisdictions, jury verdicts in criminal cases must be *unanimous* for **acquittal** or conviction. If the jury cannot obtain unanimous agreement on whether to acquit or convict the defendant, the result is a **hung jury**, and the judge may order a new trial.

ACQUITTAL
A certification or declaration following a trial that the individual accused of a crime is innocent, or free from guilt, in the eyes of the law and is thus absolved of the charges.

HUNG JURY
A jury whose members are so irreconcilably divided in their opinions that they cannot reach a verdict. The judge in this situation may order a new trial.

The Presumption of a Defendant's Innocence. A presumption in criminal law is that a defendant is innocent until proved guilty. The burden of prov-

EXHIBIT 12.10
Waiver of Trial by Jury

[*Title of Court and Cause*]

Waiver of Jury Trial

______, the defendant herein having been furnished a copy of the ______ [*insert indictment or/and information*] and informed of his rights waives trial by jury and requests that he be tried by the court.

______________________,
Defendant.

The government consents.

______________________,
United States Attorney.

Approved by the Court.

____

ing guilt falls on the state (the public prosecutor). Even if a defendant in fact committed the crime, he or she will be "innocent" in the eyes of the law unless the prosecutor can substantiate the charge with sufficient evidence to convince a jury (or judge in a nonjury trial) of the defendant's guilt.

Beyond a Reasonable Doubt
The standard used to determine the guilt or innocence of a person charged with a crime. To be guilty of a crime, a suspect must be proved guilty "beyond and to the exclusion of every reasonable doubt."

A Strict Standard of Proof. In a criminal trial, the defendant has no burden of proof. As mentioned, the burden of proving the defendant's guilt lies entirely with the state. In other words, it is up to the state to prove that the defendant committed the crime with which the defendant is charged. Furthermore, the state must prove the defendant's guilt **beyond a reasonable doubt**. The prosecution must show that, based on all the evidence, the defendant's guilt is clear and unquestionable. This strict standard of proof is higher than in civil proceedings, in which the case is usually decided on a preponderance of the evidence. A "preponderance of the evidence" means that the evidence offered in support of a certain claim outweighs the evidence offered to negate the claim.

The higher standard of proof in criminal cases reflects a fundamental social value—a belief that it is worse to convict an innocent individual than to let a guilty person go free. The consequences to the life, liberty, and reputation of an accused person from an erroneous conviction for a crime are usually more serious than the effects of an erroneous judgment in a civil case. Placing a high burden of proof on the prosecution reduces the margin of error in criminal cases.

The Privilege against Self-incrimination. The Fifth Amendment to the U.S. Constitution states that no person can be forced to give testimony that might be self-incriminating. Therefore, a defendant does not have to testify at trial. Witnesses may also refuse to testify on this ground. For example, if a witness, while testifying, is asked a question and answering the question would reveal his or her own criminal wrongdoing, the witness may "take the

Ethical Concern

Preparing Exhibits for Trial

In preparing exhibits for trial, especially when creating an exhibit from raw data, it is important that the paralegal ensure that the exhibit is accurate and not misleading. An attorney has a duty not to falsify evidence, and if erroneous evidence is introduced in court and challenged by opposing counsel, your supervising attorney may face serious consequences. By preparing an inaccurate exhibit (for example, by miscalculating a column of figures), the paralegal may be jeopardizing the attorney's professional reputation by causing the attorney to breach a professional duty.

ETHICAL CONCERN

The Benefits of Good Record Keeping

One of your jobs as a paralegal is to make sure that witnesses are in court at the proper time. This job relates to the attorney's duty of competence, which, if breached, could expose the attorney to potential liability for malpractice. For all your efforts, however, a key witness fails to appear in court. Your supervising attorney is understandably upset about the fact and asks you how this could have happened. You show the attorney the memorandum of your interview with the client, in which you noted that the witness was willing to testify; the receipt from the certified letter that you sent to the witness, which contained the subpoena, indicating that the witness had received it; and a telephone memo of a call that you made to the witness a week prior to the trial in which the witness agreed to be in court on the date of the trial. Although your documentation is not a cure for the problem presented by the missing witness, it does provide evidence—should it be necessary—that neither you nor the attorney was negligent.

Fifth" and refuse to testify on the ground that the testimony may incriminate him or her.

Rules of Evidence. Courts have complex rules about what types of evidence may be presented and how the evidence may be brought out in criminal cases, especially in jury trials. These rules, are designed to ensure that evidence presented to the judge and jury is relevant, reliable, and not unfairly prejudicial to the defendant. Often, one of the tasks of the defense attorney is to challenge evidence presented by the prosecution and the prosecution's witnesses to establish that the evidence is not reliable. Of course, the prosecutor also tries to demonstrate the irrelevance or unreliability of exhibits or testimony brought forward by the defense.

Rules of evidence will be discussed further in Chapter 15, which deals with legal investigation. Paralegals who undertake legal investigations must be especially careful to collect and preserve evidence properly. Otherwise, it may not be admissible in court.

Sentencing

When a defendant is found guilty by a trial court (or pleads guilty to a crime and no trial takes place), the judge will pronounce a **sentence**, which is the penalty imposed on anyone convicted of a crime. According to the punishment prescribed by law for the crime involved, which frequently involves minimum and maximum penalties, the judge may sentence the defendant to one or more of the following:

1. Imprisonment in a jail (for less serious crimes involving short sentences) or in a state or federal penitentiary (for serious crimes involving long sentences).
2. Death (in some states).
3. Probation, house arrest, or other form of supervised release.
4. Financial penalties—including fines, restitution to victims, and payment of litigation costs.

Although juries decide whether a criminal defendant is guilty or innocent and often make recommendations concerning sentencing, the judge has the final authority in regard to sentencing. In federal criminal cases, judges must follow mandatory sentencing guidelines that have been established by the U.S. government. The guidelines specify a range of penalties that are to be imposed for different types of crimes. The judge is free to select an appropriate penalty within the range, however, as long as it is at least the minimum mandatory sentence. In deciding which penalty should be imposed, a judge may be guided by his or her personal evaluation of the defendant's actions, by recommendations from the prosecuting attorney and other court aides, by recommendations from social-service administrators, and by state laws.

SENTENCE
The punishment, or penalty, ordered by the court to be inflicted on a person convicted of a crime.

Appeal

Persons convicted of crimes have a right of appeal. (The prosecution may appeal certain types of decisions, but it may not appeal a *not-guilty* verdict.) Most felony convictions are appealed to an intermediate court of appeal,

TODAY'S PROFESSIONAL PARALEGAL

Working for the District Court

Amanda Bowin is a legal assistant who is assigned to work for six of the twelve judges who serve the district court. Today is "criminal call," and she is in the courtroom observing an arraignment. She has in front of her a docket sheet for the defendant. She listens while the judge explains the criminal charges. The defendant pleads not guilty, and the date for the pretrial hearing is set. (If the defendant had pled guilty, then a sentencing date and probation interview would have been scheduled.) Amanda notes the plea and the pretrial hearing date on the docket sheet. She then observes five more arraignments and notes the defendants' pleas on their respective docket sheets.

"SHOW CAUSE" MOTIONS

Several attorneys enter the courtroom. They are present for "show cause" motions. A "show cause" motion is made when a defendant has violated the terms of his or her probation or sentence. The first motion is made by an assistant prosecutor against a defendant who was stopped on the highway for speeding and was found to be carrying a handgun. The judge evaluates the evidence and gives the defendant the option of either pleading guilty to the violation of probation or going to trial on the issue. The defendant chooses to plead guilty and is sentenced by the judge. Amanda notes all of the information on her docket sheet for this case. She listens to the remaining "show cause" motions and makes notes on the pleas and sentences.

SENTENCING HEARINGS

Next, the sentencing hearings begin. Amanda listens and notes the sentences on the relevant docket sheets. The last item up this morning is the sentencing of a woman who has been convicted for criminal neglect—she had abandoned her two-year-old child at a gas station. The child has been placed in a foster home. The defense attorney is allowed to call a witness to testify as to the defendant's character and how well she cared for her daughter. This is an attempt to convince the judge to impose the lightest possible sentence allowable for this crime.

The attorney calls a social worker to the stand. The social worker testifies that the defendant-mother had previously had a drug problem for which she had sought treatment. There had been no place for her to go for treatment where she could take her baby, and she had no one with whom she could leave her baby. For those reasons, she had opted for an outpatient program, a less effective form of treatment. She had tried hard to fight her addiction to "crack" cocaine and had been doing well, but sometimes it takes more than one attempt at treatment to succeed. The social worker continues by telling the court that unfortunately, the defendant mother had strayed from her treatment and was under the influence of cocaine at the time that her friend talked her into abandoning her child.

The mother is very remorseful and regrets her actions. She truly loves her daughter and does not want to lose custody of her permanently. If the judge gives her a long jail sentence, she is afraid that she will ultimately lose custody of her child. After this testimony, the social worker steps down from the stand.

The judge considers the testimony. He knows that if he puts the defendant-mother in jail, she will not receive the treatment that she needs. This will not help either the defendant or her daughter. He sentences her to one year of drug rehabilitation in a live-in facility. This means that her child will remain in foster care for that time. The decision regarding her daughter's custody after that time will be left up to the agency that placed the daughter in the foster home. If the mother's treatment is successful, the agency might consider returning the child to the mother's custody. The defendant is to appear before the court every three months and give a progress report.

CRIMINAL CALL ENDS

Amanda notes this sentence on her docket sheet. She leaves the courtroom, now that the criminal call is over. She takes the files containing the docket sheets and her notes for the cases to the Records Department. There the information will be entered into the county's computer system to update the status of these cases.

although in some states there is no intermediate court of appeal, so the appeal goes directly to the state's highest appellate court, usually called the supreme court of the state. Most convictions that result in supervised release or fines are not appealed, but a high percentage of the convictions that result in prison sentences are appealed. About 10 to 20 percent of such convictions are reversed on appeal. The most common reason for reversal is that the trial court admitted improper evidence, such as evidence obtained by a search that did not meet constitutional requirements.

If a conviction is overturned on appeal, the defendant may or may not be tried again, depending on the reason for the reversal and on whether or not the case was reversed with or without prejudice. A decision reversed "with prejudice" means that no further action can be taken on the claim or cause. A decision reversed "without prejudice" means that the defendant may be prosecuted again for the crime.

KEY TERMS AND CONCEPTS

acquittal 487
***actus reus* 460**
arraignment 477
arrest 466
arrest warrant 468
bail 472
beyond a reasonable doubt 487
booking 468
citation 468
crime 458
defense of others 462
defense of property 462
diversion program 469
double jeopardy 463
due process of law 463
exclusionary rule 465
felony 459
grand jury 477
hung jury 487
indictment 477
information 477
magistrate 469
***mens rea* 461**
***Miranda* rights 465**
misdemeanor 460
motion challenging the sufficiency of the indictment 481
motion for a change of venue 481
motion for discovery and inspection 482
motion to reduce the amount of bail 474
motion to suppress evidence 481
***nolo contendere* 477**
petty offense 460
plea bargaining 480
preliminary hearing 476
probable cause 468
public defender 458
public prosecutor 458
search warrant 468
self-defense 462
self-incrimination 464
sentence 488

CHAPTER SUMMARY

1. Crimes are defined as such by state legislatures or the federal government. A crime is distinguished from other types of wrongs, such as torts, by the fact that crimes are deemed to be offenses against society as a whole. Whereas tort litigation involves private parties suing each other, criminal litigation involves the state prosecuting a wrongdoer.

2. Crimes fall into two basic classifications—felonies and misdemeanors. Felonies are more serious crimes (such as murder, rape, and robbery) for which the penalty may include imprisonment for a year or longer or (in some states) death. Misdemeanors are less serious crimes (such as prostitution, disturbing the peace, and public intoxication) for which the penalty may include imprisonment for up to a year. A seemingly endless variety of acts have been defined as crimes by either state or federal statutes.

3. Two elements are required for criminal liability to exist: a wrongful act *(actus reus)* and a specified state of mind *(mens rea)*. Criminal liability may be avoided if the state of mind required for the crime was lacking or some other defense against liability can be raised. Defenses against criminal liability include self-defense, defense of others, defense of property, the running of a statute of limitations, and others (procedural violations, alibi, and so on).

4. Because criminal law involves bringing the substantial resources of the state against an individual, specific procedures must be followed in arresting and prosecuting a criminal suspect to safeguard the suspect's constitutional rights. The U.S. Constitution guarantees that every person accused of a crime has specific rights, including the right to due process of law, the right to an attorney, the privilege against self-incrimination (the right to remain silent), and the right to a speedy trial. At the time of the arrest and taking into custody of a criminal suspect, the arresting officers must inform the suspect of his or her rights by reading the *Miranda* warnings. Any evidence or confession obtained in violation of the suspect's rights will normally not be admissible in court.

5. The initial procedures undertaken by the police after a crime is reported include arrest, booking, and investigation after arrest. Criminal litigation against a suspect begins when the prosecutor decides to prosecute the case and files a complaint. See Exhibit 12.2 for a graphical illustration and summary description of the major steps in the criminal justice process.

6. Prior to the trial, the defendant's attorney may file pretrial motions requesting the court to dismiss the case for various reasons. A pretrial motion may challenge the sufficiency of the evidence, may assert that certain key evidence was obtained illegally, or may argue that for some other reason the case should be dismissed.

7. Prior to the trial of a criminal case, discovery takes place. The defendant in a criminal case is entitled to obtain any evidence relating to the case possessed by the prosecution, including documents, statements previously made by the defendant, objects, reports of tests or examinations, and other evidence.

8. Most trials involving felonies are tried by a jury; most trials involving misdemeanors are decided in a bench trial (by the judge). Criminal trials differ from civil trials in a number of ways. Special features of criminal trials include the right to a speedy and public trial, unanimous agreement by the jury on the verdict, a presumption of the defendant's innocence, a higher standard of proof (the defendant must be found guilty "beyond a reasonable doubt"), the privilege against self-incrimination, and complex rules covering what types of evidence can be introduced at trial and how the evidence is introduced.

9. At the conclusion of a trial, a defendant who has been found guilty is sentenced by the judge. The sentence may involve fines, imprisonment, or (in some states) death. Alternatively, the defendant may be sentenced to probation or some other type of supervised release.

10. If the defendant loses at trial, he or she may appeal the case to a higher court. Only a minority of decisions are reversed on appeal, however.

QUESTIONS FOR REVIEW

1. How does a crime differ from a tort? What are the major classifications of crimes?

2. What elements are required for criminal liability? What defenses can be raised against criminal liability?

3. What are the constitutional rights of a person accused of a crime? Which constitutional amendments provide these rights?

4. What are the basic steps involved in criminal procedure from the time a crime is reported to the resolution of the case?

5. How is probable cause defined? Who determines whether probable cause exists?

6. What is the difference between an indictment and an information? When is each used?

7. What different pleas may a defendant enter during an arraignment? What is plea bargaining, and when does it typically occur?

8. When may a criminal suspect be released and the case dismissed prior to trial?

9. What pretrial motions may be filed in a criminal case?

10. What are the major procedural differences between civil litigation and criminal litigation? What are the reasons for these differences?

ETHICAL QUESTIONS

1. Linda Lore is an experienced paralegal who works for a criminal defense firm. The lawyers trust her implicitly and feel that she is as knowledgeable as they are. One Monday morning, John Dodds, an attorney with the firm, is scheduled to be in court for a motion and, at the same time, at a deposition. John calls Linda into his office and asks her to take the deposition. Should Linda take it? Why or why not?

2. Janice Henley is a legal assistant to a criminal defense attorney. They are defending a notorious drug dealer who was arrested in a huge drug bust. The drug bust was videotaped by the agents of the Drug Enforcement Administration who carried it out. The videotape is their best evidence against the client.

In the hall outside the courtroom, Janice observes the girlfriend of the defendant approach the federal prosecutor and talk to him. He happens to be holding the videotape, along with some papers, in his hand. The girlfriend pulls what appears to be a large magnet from her oversized purse and leans toward the videotape. If the magnet makes contact with the tape, it will erase it. What should Janice do?

3. Larry Dow works as a paralegal for the criminal defense firm of Rice & Rowen. He and his boss have just met with Joe Dollan, an attorney from another well-known law firm. Joe has been arrested for embezzling (stealing) funds from an estate that he was managing for a client and needs a criminal defense attorney to handle the case. Embezzlement is a felony, and if convicted, Joe will lose his license to practice law. Larry knows that a good friend of his recently retained Joe to handle the estate of her uncle. Should Larry tell his friend that Joe has been charged with embezzlement? Is there anything that Larry can do to help his friend?

PRACTICE QUESTIONS AND ASSIGNMENTS

1. Using the following information, draft a motion for an order directing the defendant to appear in your local district court for an arraignment.

> Paul M. James, the U.S. attorney for your district, requests the defendant, Patrick C. Duffy, to appear for his arraignment on June 3, 1995, at 10:00 A.M., pursuant to a warrant issued on March 12, 1995, by Judge William T. Richardson of the district court in your district.

2. Review your state's court rules to see how the rules for criminal cases differ from those for civil cases. List and describe the major differences.

QUESTIONS FOR CRITICAL ANALYSIS

1. Look at the U.S. Constitution in Appendix L. Is there anything in the Bill of Rights that requires the police to give criminal suspects the *Miranda* warnings upon arrest?

2. Why do you think that so many procedural safeguards were included in the Constitution for the protection of criminal defendants?

ROLE-PLAYING EXERCISES

1. You are a legal assistant in a criminal defense law firm. Your firm has a new client. He has been accused of being a serial killer. From the news reports, it appears very likely that he killed the people he is accused of killing; he was caught red-handed carrying a box of human remains into his apartment, and there were many other body parts in his freezer. You are upset at the prospect of having to work with this client, but your supervising attorney says that she wants you to come with her to interview the client at the county jail. She wants you to meet the client, ask him some questions, and give her your impressions of the client and his mental state.

Working in pairs, one of you should assume the role of the legal assistant and the other the role of the client. The legal assistant should interview the client regarding the crimes with which he has been charged, focusing particularly on the information reported in the news media. The legal assistant must not show disdain toward the client. If time allows, reverse the roles.

2. Using the facts given in Role-playing Exercise 1, assume that you have decided that you cannot work on this case because you are convinced that the client committed the crimes and you know that your feelings will prejudice your work and perhaps even the work of the attorney. Play the role of the legal assistant telling the attorney about his or her feelings and asking to be excused from working on the case.

PROJECTS

1. Call the state court in your city that handles pretrial criminal procedures, such as the initial hearings, arraignments, and other procedures. Arrange to be in court when these matters are being heard.

2. Call the state court in your city that handles more serious crimes (for example, felonies and/or serious misdemeanors) and obtain a list of the criminal trials that are on the docket. Arrange to attend one of the trials for as long as possible. Observe how legal assistants are used by the trial attorneys.

3. Call the county prosecutor's office in your area and ask if it gives tours to students. If so, arrange to go on a tour of the prosecutor's office and try to learn how warrants are issued and how the prosecutor prepares for trial. Also observe how paralegals are utilized in the office.

4. Contact your local police department and ask if it gives tours to students. If so, arrange to take a tour of the department and learn, to the extent possible, what procedures are followed in regard to booking and investigation.

ANNOTATED SELECTED READINGS

COFFEE, JOHN C. "Does 'Unlawful' Mean 'Criminal'?: Reflection on the Disappearing Tort/Crime Distinction in America." *Boston University Law Review*, March 1991. A look at how the line between crimes and torts has become blurred over the past decade. The author believes that this blurring will weaken the criminal justice system.

EDWARDS, IVANA. "The General Practice Paralegal." *Legal Assistant Today*, March/April 1991. An article containing an interesting interview with a paralegal in a general-practice law firm located in Vermont. The firm specializes in criminal defense litigation. Good reading for those interested in or curious about this particular type of practice.

MANN, KENNETH. "Punitive Civil Sanctions: The Middle Ground between Criminal and Civil Law." *Yale Law Journal*, June 1992. A provocative look at white-collar crime (nonviolent crime committed by businesspersons and others) and the sanctions used.

MARKEY, DANIEL J., AND MARY Q. DONNELLEY. *Criminal Law for Paralegals.* Cincinnati, Ohio: South-Western Publishing Co., 1994. A text designed for paralegals that contains detailed coverage of criminal law and procedure. Good outside reading for those interested in knowing more about the topic.

MCCORD, JAMES W. H., AND SANDRA L. MCCORD. *Criminal Law and Procedure for the Paralegal: A Systems Approach.* St. Paul: West Publishing Co., 1995. A text that offers comprehensive coverage of the paralegal's role in the criminal law office. The authors emphasize practical skills as well as ethics.

SAFRAN, VERNA. "When the Law Breaks Down: The L.A. Riots." *Legal Assistant Today,* September/October 1992. A revealing look at Los Angeles during and after the 1992 riots and what the legal community and paralegals did to help in the aftermath.

13

Administrative Law and Procedures

Chapter Objectives

After completing this chapter, you will know:

- How and why administrative agencies are created.
- The powers exercised by administrative agencies and some limitations on those powers.
- The government functions performed by administrative agencies.
- How administrative agencies establish and enforce rules.
- The opportunities for paralegals in the area of administrative law.
- What to anticipate as a paralegal when working with administrative agencies.

Chapter Outline

INTRODUCTION

Recall from Chapter 6 that *administrative law* consists of the rules, orders, and decisions of administrative agencies at all levels of government.[1] Also recall that *administrative agencies* were defined in that chapter as government bodies that are charged with administering and implementing legislation. Paralegals often deal with administrative agencies in their work. A client may need assistance in obtaining benefits under the Medicare program, which is administered by the federal Social Security Administration. A corporate client or employer may need legal advice on how to comply properly with environmental regulations created and enforced by the federal Environmental Protection Agency (or a state environmental agency). In these and numerous other similar situations, you would need to contact and work with agency representatives.

You may even represent the client at an agency hearing (a trial-like proceeding conducted by the agency). Although paralegals cannot practice law, some administrative agencies, including the Social Security Administration, allow nonlawyers to represent clients at agency hearings. Some paralegals also work for administrative agencies.

In this chapter, you will learn how and why administrative agencies are created, how they establish rules, and how they investigate and enforce those rules. You will also read about how an agency's decision can be challenged both formally and informally through a pathway of administrative proceedings (and ultimately through the court system). Although our discussion focuses on federal administrative agencies, we will also examine the relationship between state and federal agencies. The chapter concludes with a hypothetical example to illustrate how agency procedures apply to real-life settings.

AGENCY CREATION AND POWERS

Federal administrative agencies are created by Congress. Because Congress cannot possibly oversee the actual implementation of all the laws it enacts, it must delegate such tasks to others, particularly when the issues relate to highly technical areas, such as air and water pollution. By delegating some of its authority to make and implement laws, Congress is able to monitor indirectly a particular area in which it has passed legislation without becoming bogged down in the many details relating to enforcement—details that are often best left to specialists.

Enabling Legislation

ENABLING LEGISLATION
Statutes enacted by Congress that authorize the creation of an administrative agency and specify the name, purpose, composition, and powers of the agency being created.

To create a federal administrative agency, the U.S. Congress passes **enabling legislation**, which specifies the name, purpose, function, and powers of the

1. Administrative law is variously defined. Some scholars define administrative law as the law that governs the authority, powers, and functions of administrative agencies.

agency being created. Note that administrative agencies may exercise only those powers delegated to them by Congress in enabling legislation. State agencies are created by state legislatures through similar enabling acts.

Enabling acts are important information sources for paralegals who are researching legal matters involving administrative agencies. Suppose, for example, that you are employed by a law firm and that a client is being investigated by the Federal Trade Commission (FTC) for deceptive advertising practices. In your research, you would learn that the FTC was created by the Federal Trade Commission Act of 1914, which prohibits unfair and deceptive trade practices. You would learn what procedures the agency must follow to charge persons or organizations with a violation and whether the act provides for judicial review of agency orders. You would also discover that the act grants to the FTC the power to do the following:

- Create "rules and regulations for the purpose of carrying out the Act."
- Conduct investigations of business practices.
- Obtain reports from interstate corporations concerning their business practices.
- Investigate possible violations of federal antitrust statutes (laws prohibiting certain kinds of anticompetitive business behavior).
- Publish the findings of its investigations.
- Recommend new legislation.
- Hold trial-like hearings to resolve certain kinds of trade disputes that involve FTC regulations or federal antitrust laws.

Types of Administrative Agencies

There are two basic types of administrative agencies, executive agencies and independent regulatory agencies. Federal **executive agencies** include the cabinet departments of the executive branch, which were formed to assist the president in carrying out executive functions, and the subagencies within the cabinet departments. The Occupational Safety and Health Administration, for example, is a subagency within the Department of Labor. Exhibit 13.1 lists the cabinet departments and illustrates how administrative agencies fit into the organizational structure of the U.S. government.

EXECUTIVE AGENCY
A type of adminsitrative agency that is either a cabinet department or a subagency within a cabinet department. Executive agencies fall under the authority of the president, who has the power to appoint and remove federal officers.

Although all administrative agencies are part of the executive branch of government, **independent regulatory agencies** are outside the major executive departments, as you can see in Exhibit 13.1. The Federal Trade Commission and the Securities and Exchange Commission are examples of independent regulatory agencies.

INDEPENDENT REGULATORY AGENCY
A type of administrative agency that is more independent of presidential control than an executive agency. Officials of independent regulatory agencies cannot be removed without cause.

The significant difference between the two types of agencies lies in the accountability of the regulators. Agencies that are considered part of the executive branch are subject to the authority of the president, who has the power to appoint and remove federal officers. In theory, this power is less pronounced in regard to independent agencies, whose officers serve for fixed terms and cannot be removed without just cause. In practice, however, the president's power to exert influence over independent agencies is often considerable.

EXHIBIT 13.1
The Government of the United States

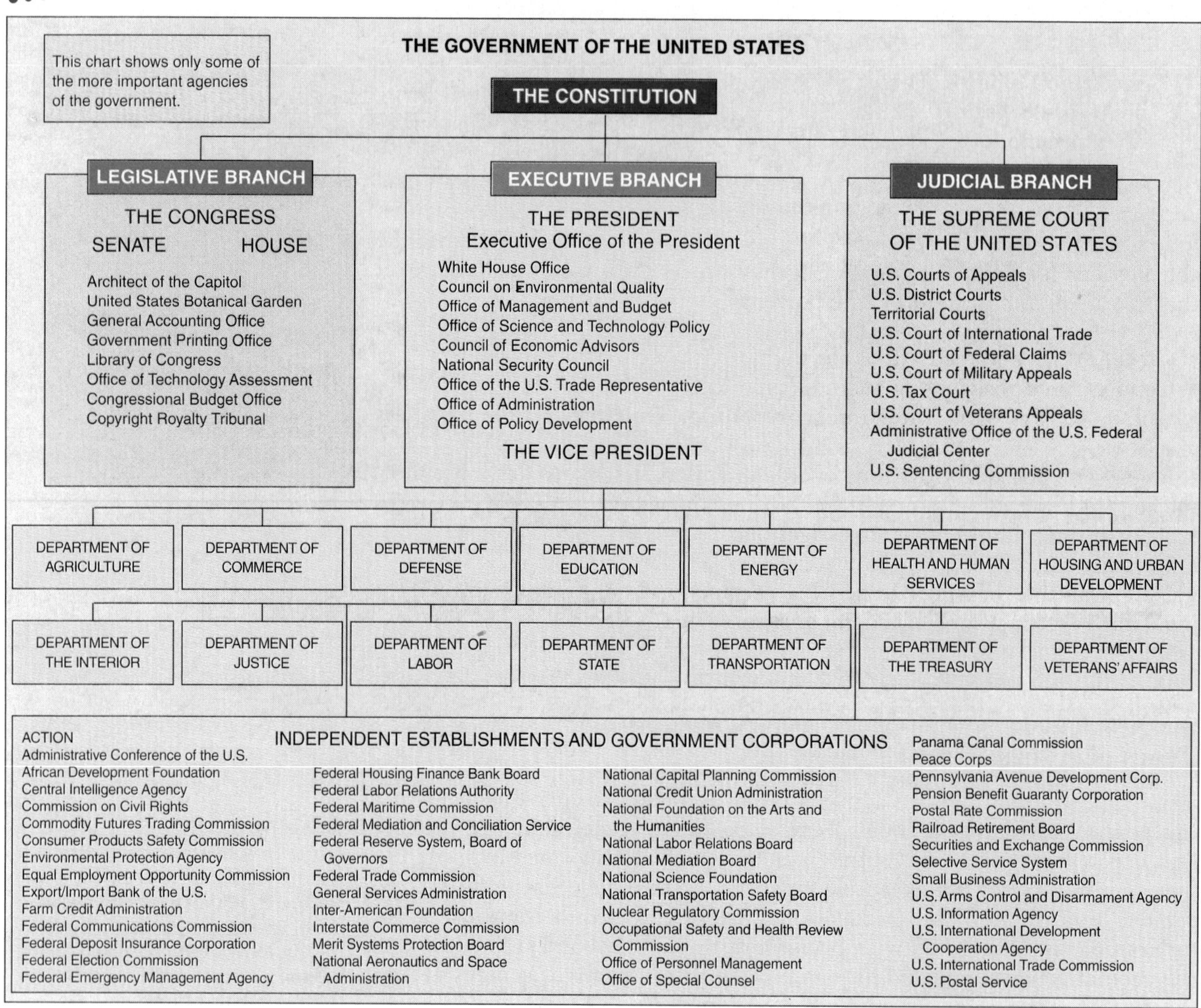

SOURCE: *U.S. Government Manual, 1993–1994.*

Agency Powers and the Constitution

Administrative agencies occupy an unusual niche in the American legal system because they exercise powers that are normally divided among the three branches of government. Notice that in the FTC's enabling legislation discussed above, the FTC's grant of power incorporates functions associated with the legislature (rulemaking), the executive branch (enforcement of the laws), and the courts (**adjudication**, or the formal resolution of disputes).

ADJUDICATION
The act of resolving a controversy and rendering an order or decision based on a review of the evidence presented.

The constitutional principle of *checks and balances* allows each branch of government to act as a check on the actions of the other two branches.

Furthermore, under the Constitution, only the legislative branch is authorized to create laws. Yet administrative agencies, which are not specifically referred to in the Constitution, make **legislative rules**, or *substantive rules,* that are as legally binding as laws passed by Congress.

LEGISLATIVE RULE
A rule created by an administrative agency that is as legally binding as a law enacted by a legislature.

The constitutional authority for delegating such powers to administrative agencies—and the basis of all administrative law—is generally held to be implied by Article I of the U.S. Constitution. Section 1 of that article grants all legislative powers to Congress and requires Congress to oversee the implementation of all laws. Article I, Section 8, gives Congress the power to make all laws necessary for executing its specified powers. These passages have been interpreted by the courts, under what is known as the **delegation doctrine**, as granting to Congress the power to establish administrative agencies that can create rules for implementing those laws. The expansive interpretation given to this grant of authority has been dictated by the practical considerations mentioned previously.

DELEGATION DOCTRINE
A doctrine that authorizes Congress to delegate some of its lawmaking authority to administrative agencies. The doctrine is implied by Article I of the U.S. Constitution, which grants specific powers to Congress to enact and oversee the implementation of laws.

Although the three branches of government exercise certain controls over agency powers and functions, as will be discussed shortly, in many ways administrative agencies function independently. For this reason, administrative agencies, which constitute the **bureaucracy**, are sometimes referred to as the "fourth branch" of the American government.

BUREAUCRACY
The organizational structure, consisting of government bureaus and agencies, through which the government at all levels implements and enforces laws.

Limitations on Agency Powers

Combining the functions normally divided among the three branches of government into a single governmental entity, such as the FTC mentioned above, concentrates considerable power in the agency. Because of this concentration of authority, one of the major policy objectives of the government is to control the risks of arbitrariness and overreaching by the agency without hindering the effective use of agency power to deal with a particular problem area, as Congress had intended.

An important check on agency authority is, of course, the agency's enabling legislation. An agency may not exceed the powers delegated to it through its enabling legislation. Agency authority is also held in check by executive and legislative controls. The executive branch of government exercises control over agencies both through the president's powers to appoint federal officers and through the president's veto powers. The president may veto enabling legislation presented by Congress or congressional attempts to modify an existing agency's authority.

Congress also exercises authority over agency powers. Legislative authority is required to fund an agency, and the enabling legislation usually sets certain time and monetary limits relating to the funding of particular programs. Congress can always revise these limits. In addition to its power to create and fund agencies, Congress also has the authority to investigate the implementation of its laws and the agencies that it has created. Individual legislators may also affect agency policy through their "casework" activities, which involve attempts to help their constituents deal with agencies.

Controls over agency powers are also exercised by the judicial branch, as will be discussed later in this chapter in the section on judicial review. The Administrative Procedure Act, discussed in the next section, also acts as a check on agency actions.

ADMINISTRATIVE PROCESS

ADMINISTRATIVE PROCESS
The procedure used by administrative agencies in the administration of law.

JUDICIAL PROCESS
The procedures relating to the administration of justice through the courts.

The three functions mentioned previously—rulemaking, enforcement, and adjudication—make up what has been termed administrative process. **Administrative process** involves the administration of law by administrative agencies, in contrast to **judicial process**, which involves the administration of law by the courts.

The Administrative Procedure Act (APA) of 1946 imposes detailed procedural requirements that all federal agencies must follow in their rulemaking, adjudication, and other functions. The APA is such an integral part of the administrative process that its application will be examined as we go through the basic functions carried out by administrative agencies.

Rulemaking

RULEMAKING
The actions undertaken by administrative agencies when formally adopting new regulations or amending old ones. Under the Administrative Procedure Act, rulemaking includes notifying the public of proposed rules or changes and receiving and considering the public's comments.

A major function of an administrative agency is **rulemaking**—the formulation of new regulations. An agency's power to make rules is conferred on it by Congress in its enabling legislation. For example, the Occupational Safety and Health Administration (OSHA) was authorized by the Occupational Safety and Health Act of 1970 to develop and issue rules governing safety in the workplace. In 1991, OSHA deemed it in the public interest to issue a new rule regulating the health-care industry to prevent the spread of such diseases as acquired immune-deficiency syndrome (AIDS). OSHA created a rule specifying various standards—on how contaminated instruments should be handled, for example—with which employers in that industry must comply.

NOTICE-AND-COMMENT RULEMAKING
A three-step administrative rulemaking procedure that involves the publication of a notice of a proposed rulemaking in the *Federal Register*, a comment period for interested parties to express their views on the proposed rule, and the publication of the agency's final rule in the *Federal Register*.

In formulating its rule, OSHA had to follow specific rulemaking procedures required under the APA. We look here at the most common rulemaking procedure, called **notice-and-comment rulemaking**. This procedure involves three basic steps: notice of the proposed rulemaking, a comment period, and the final rule.

Notice of the Proposed Rulemaking. When a federal agency decides to create a new rule, the agency publishes a notice of the proposed rulemaking proceedings in the *Federal Register*, a daily publication of the executive branch that prints government orders, rules, and regulations. The notice states where and when the proceedings will be held, the agency's legal authority for making the rule (usually, its enabling legislation), and the terms or subject matter of the proposed rule.

Comment Period. Following the publication of the notice of proposed rulemaking proceedings, the agency must allow ample time for persons to comment in writing on the proposed rule. The purpose of this comment period is to give interested parties the opportunity to express their views on the proposed rule in an effort to influence agency policy. The comments may be in writing or, if a hearing is held, may be given orally. The agency need not respond to all comments, but it must respond to any significant comments that bear directly on the proposed rule. The agency responds by either modifying its final rule or explaining, in a statement accompanying the final rule, why it did not.

Final Rule. After the comments have been received and reviewed, the agency drafts the final rule and publishes it in the *Federal Register*. Exhibit 13.2 on the following page shows a page from the *Federal Register* (the first page of OSHA's final rule setting forth the standards for the health-care industry mentioned above). Rules and regulations adopted by federal administrative agencies are later compiled in the *Code of Federal Regulations*. This code, which is an important source for paralegals researching administrative law, will be discussed further in Chapter 17. A final rule has binding legal effect unless overturned later by the courts.

Enforcement—Investigation

Administrative agencies conduct investigations of regulated entities to monitor compliance with agency rules. Agencies investigate a wide range of activities, such as coal mining, automobile manufacturing, and the industrial discharge of pollutants into the environment. Procedures vary among the different agencies. A typical agency investigation might begin when a paralegal on the agency's staff takes a statement from someone who wants to report a violation of an agency rule. Alternatively, an investigation may begin when an agency determines that it needs to gather information about a certain individual, firm, or industry.

Many agencies gather information through on-site inspections. Sometimes, searching an office, a factory, or some other business facility is the only way to obtain information or the evidence needed to prove a regulatory violation. At other times, physical inspection or testing is used in place of a formal hearing to correct or prevent an undesirable condition. Inspection and testing cover a wide range of activities, including safety inspections of underground coal mines, safety tests of commercial equipment and automobiles, and environmental monitoring of factory emissions. An agency may also gather information by requesting that a firm or individual submit certain documents and records to the agency for examination.

Normally, business firms comply with agency requests to inspect facilities or business records because it is in any firm's interest to maintain a good relationship with regulatory bodies. In some instances, though, such as when a firm thinks an agency request is unreasonable and may be detrimental to the firm's interest, the firm may refuse to comply with the request. In such situations, an agency may need to resort to the use of a subpoena or a search warrant.

Subpoenas. There are two basic types of subpoenas. The subpoena *ad testificandum* ("to testify") is the technical term for the ordinary subpoena. It is a writ, or order, compelling a witness to appear before an agency hearing. The subpoena *duces tecum* ("bring it with you") compels an individual or organization to hand over specified books, papers, records, or documents to the agency. Administrative agencies may use either type of subpoena in obtaining needed testimony or documents.

Search Warrants. The Fourth Amendment protects against *unreasonable* searches and seizures by specifying that in many instances a physical search for evidence must be conducted under the authority of a search warrant. As

ETHICAL CONCERN

Advocacy and Administrative Process

Paralegals dealing with an administrative agency know how frustrating it can sometimes be. You are told what the requirements are, comply with those requirements exactly, and then learn that yet another requirement must be met. Or the person you need to contact is unavailable or doesn't return your calls. If you, as a paralegal, are working with a particular agency for the first time, your patience may be tested by these or other obstacles to communication efficiency. As an advocate of a clients' interests, you should always try to avoid letting your frustration interfere with your goal, which is to enlist the agency staff members' cooperation in settling your client's claim as soon as possible. A good way to learn about agency requirements and personnel is to talk to co-workers who have dealt with the agency. Once you become familiar with agency procedures and personnel, either through your co-workers' assistance or through your own experience, you can develop strategies for dealing efficiently with the agency.

EXHIBIT 13.2 A Page from the *Federal Register*

64004 **Federal Register** / Vol. 56, No. 235 / Friday, December 6, 1991 / Rules and Regulations

DEPARTMENT OF LABOR

Occupational Safety and Health Administration

29 CFR Part 1910.1030

[Docket No. H-370]

Occupational Exposure to Bloodborne Pathogens

AGENCY: Occupational Safety and Health Administration (OSHA), Labor

ACTION: Final rule.

SUMMARY: The Occupational Safety and Health Administration hereby promulgates a standard under section 6(b) of the Occupational Safety and Health Act of 1970 (the Act), 29 U.S.C. 655 to eliminate or minimize occupational exposure to Hepatitis B Virus (HBV), Human Immunodeficiency Virus (HIV) and other bloodborne pathogens. Based on a review of the information in the rulemaking record, OSHA has made a determination that employees face a significant health risk as the result of occupational exposure to blood and other potentially infectious materials because they may contain bloodborne pathogens, including hepatitis B virus which causes Hepatitis B, a serious liver disease, and human immunodeficiency virus, which causes Acquired Immunodeficiency Syndrome (AIDS). The Agency further concludes that this exposure can be minimized or eliminated using a combination of engineering and work practice controls, personal protective clothing and equipment, training, medical surveillance, Hepatitis B vaccination, signs and labels, and other provisions.

DATES: This standard shall become effective on March 6, 1992.

Any petitions for review must be filed not later than the 59th day following the promulgation of the standard. See Section 6(f) of the OSH Act; 29 CFR 1911.18(d) and *United Mine Workers of America* v. *Mine Safety and Health Administration*, 900 F.2d 384 (D.C. Cir. 1990).

ADDRESSES: For additional copies of this standard, contact: OSHA Office of Publications; U.S. Department of Labor, room N3101, 200 Constitution Ave., NW., Washington, DC 20210, Telephone (202) 523–9667.

For copies of materials in the docket, contact: OSHA Docket Office, Docket No. H–370, room N2625, U.S. Department of Labor, 200 Constitution Ave, NW., Washington, DC 20210, Telephone (202) 523–7894. The hours of operation of the Docket Office are 10 a.m. until 4 p.m.

In compliance with 28 U.S.C. 2112(a), the Agency designates for receipt of petitions for review of the standard, the Associate Solicitor for Occupational Safety and Health, Office of the Solicitor, room S–4004, U.S. Department of Labor, 200 Constitution Avenue, NW., Washington, DC 20210.

FOR FURTHER INFORMATION CONTACT: Mr. James F. Foster, OSHA, U.S. Department of Labor, Office of Public Affairs, Room N3647, 200 Constitution Avenue, NW., Washington, DC 20210, telephone (202) 523–8151.

SUPPLEMENTARY INFORMATION:

Table of Contents

References to the rulemaking record are in the text of the preamble. References are given as "Ex." followed by a number to designate the reference in the docket. For example, "Ex. 1" means exhibit 1 in the Docket H–370. This document is a copy of the Advance Notice of Proposed Rulemaking for Bloodborne Pathogens that was published in the Federal Register on November 27, 1987 (52 FR 45438). References to the transcripts of the public hearings are given as "Tr." followed by the date and page. For example, "Mr. Clyde R. Bragdon, Jr. Tr. 9/14/89, p. 100" refers to the first page of the testimony of Mr. Clyde A. Bragdon, Jr., Administrator of the U.S. Fire Administration, given at the public hearing on September 14, 1989. A list of the exhibits, copies of the exhibits, and copies of the transcripts are available in the OSHA Docket Office.

I. Introduction

The preamble to the Final Standard for Occupational Exposure to Bloodborne Pathogens discusses the events leading to the promulgation of final standard, health effects of exposure, degree and significance of the risk, an analysis of the technological and economic feasibility of the standard's implementation, regulatory impact and regulatory flexibility analysis, and the rationale behind the specific provisions of the standard.

The public was invited to comment on these matters following publication of the Advance Notice of Proposed Rulemaking on November 27, 1987 (52 FR 45436) and following publication of the Proposed Standard on May 30, 1989 (54 FR 23042).

The Agency recognizes the unique nature of both the healthcare industry and other operations covered by this standard. The Agency concludes the employee protection can be provided in a manner consistent with a high standard of patient care.

Hazardous Waste Operations and Emergency Response Standard

The Hazardous Waste Operations and Emergency Response (HAZWOPER) Standard (29 CFR 1910.120) covers three groups of employees: workers at uncontrolled hazardous waste remediation sites; workers at Resource Conservation Recovery Act (RCRA) permitted hazardous waste treatment, storage, and disposal facilities; and those workers expected to respond to emergencies caused by the uncontrolled release of hazardous substances.

The definition of hazardous substance includes any biological agent or infectious material which may cause disease or death. There are three potential scenarios where the bloodborne and hazardous waste operations and emergency response standard may interface. These scenarios include: workers involved in cleanup operations at hazardous waste sites involving regulated waste; workers at RCRA permitted incinerators that burn infectious waste; and workers responding to an emergency caused by the uncontrolled release of regulated waste (e.g., a transportation accident).

Employers of employees engaged in these three activities must comply with the requirements in 29 CFR 1910.120 as well as the Bloodborne Pathogens Standard. If there is a conflict or overlap, the provision that is more protective of employee health and safety applies.

Information Collection Requirements

5 CFR part 1320 sets forth procedures for agencies to follow in obtaining OMB clearance for information collection requirements under the Paperwork Reduction Act of 1980, 44 U.S.C. 3501 et seq. The final bloodborne pathogen standard requires the employer to allow OSHA access to the exposure control plan, medical and training records. In accordance with the provisions of the Paperwork Reduction Act and the regulations issued pursuant thereto, OSHA certifies that it has submitted the information collection to OMB for review under section 3504(h) of that Act.

Public reporting burden for this collection of information is estimated to average five minutes per response to

DEVELOPING PARALEGAL SKILLS

Monitoring the *Federal Register*

Robin Hayes is a legal assistant for CARCO, Inc., a large company that manufactures automobile parts. She works in the environmental-law group, which is part of the corporation's legal department. One of her job responsibilities is to monitor the *Federal Register* for newly proposed environmental regulations and for changes to existing rules. When she comes across a proposed change or new regulation, she summarizes it in a memo and circulates the memo to the attorneys in her firm who need to know of the proposed change or new regulation.

REVIEWING THE *FEDERAL REGISTER*

Robin begins her day, as usual, by reviewing today's copy of the *Federal Register.* She first looks in the table of contents for topics relating to environmental law. There she sees the topic "Environmental Protection Agency." She reviews the subtopics, which include notices, rules, and proposed rules. She stops when she sees "RCRA; Notice of Change to Hazardous Waste Manifest; Certification Statement Required, 58761."

Robin turns to page 58761 and begins to read the notice. The proposed change would require all business firms or other entities that create over 1,000 kilograms per month of hazardous waste to certify their efforts to reduce the amount of hazardous waste they generate. The certification would appear on the manifest form, which is a document that travels with the hazardous waste from the business firm's site to the disposal facility.

NOTIFYING THE ATTORNEYS OF THE NEW RULE

Hazardous-waste generators (those who create hazardous waste) are already required to file regular reports detailing their attempts to reduce the amount of hazardous waste they create. The proposed rule modification—requiring certification of such attempts on manifest forms—would, in effect, serve as a reminder to business firms that they must try to reduce the amount of hazardous waste that they generate. The proposed change should not have a major impact on CARCO's business, but the attorneys will want to be informed of it. They will have to notify management of the changes that will need to be made on the manifest form and advise management about the legal effect of signing the modified form.

Robin turns to her computer and begins a memo to the attorneys in the environmental-law group. The memo summarizes the proposed rule modification and its effect on the company. She attaches a copy of the announcement in the *Federal Register*. She gives the memo and the attachment to the group's secretary to copy and circulate to the attorneys.

discussed in Chapter 12, a search warrant is a court order directing law-enforcement officials to search a specific place for a specific thing and present it to the court. Although it was once thought that administrative inspections were exempt from the warrant requirement, the United States Supreme Court held in *Marshall v. Barlow's, Inc.,*[2] that the requirement does apply to the administrative process.

2. 436 U.S. 307, 98 S.Ct. 1816, 56 L.Ed.2d 305 (1978). (See Chapter 17 for a discussion of how to read case citations.)

DEVELOPING PARALEGAL SKILLS

Working for a Pollution-control Agency

Judy Barron is a paralegal at the state pollution-control agency, in the enforcement division. She works for a team of attorneys who prosecute violations of the environmental laws.

LEARNING OF A VIOLATION

One Friday afternoon, while three of the attorneys are in court, the telephone rings. Judy picks up the phone, and on the other end is someone calling from a car phone. There is a lot of static, and Judy has trouble understanding what the other person is saying, although she can tell that some kind of dumping is going on. "I'm sorry, I can't hear you, there's so much static. Can you please repeat what you said?" she asks. "I'm on [static interference] street, behind the old Carcom Plant. There is a truck [static interference] with [static interference] valve open and [static interference] liquid is pouring out of the truck. It looks like it's going [static interference] sewer. I wanted to report it," says the caller.

"I still didn't get all of what you said, because of the static," responds Judy. "Can you repeat your location to me?" The caller begins to speak but this time is disconnected by a burst of static. A few minutes later, the phone rings again. It is the same caller, only this time the reception is better. Judy is able to take down the information about where the reported dumping is taking place. She also takes down the caller's name, address, and telephone number. She thanks him for calling to report what he saw.

REPORTING THE VIOLATION

Judy then calls the district office that covers the location where the dumping is taking place. She speaks with Ned Hirsch, the district director. "Not again!" Ned responds. "We've had so many problems in that area. It's on the list of sites scheduled to be cleaned up in the spring. It seems like everyone with something to get rid of thinks that it's okay to dump it behind the old Carcom plant, because someone else is already picking up the tab. Did you happen to get a description of the truck or a license plate number?"

Judy responds, "Yes, the license plate number is MMC-3457, and it was a Petro Tanker, according to the report I received." Ned exclaims, "I can't believe they'd try it again! We've had trouble with them before. Thanks for calling. I'm going to call the state police and have them meet me over there."

Judy is glad that she called when she did. If she had not known whom to call, or had waited, it would have been too late to catch this repeat offender. She types a memo reporting the incident to her supervising attorney and returns to her other work.

Agencies are permitted to conduct warrantless inspections, or searches, in several situations. Firms that sell firearms or liquor, for example, are automatically subject to inspections without warrants. Sometimes, a statute permits warrantless searches of certain types of hazardous operations, such as coal mines. Also, a warrantless inspection in an emergency situation is normally considered reasonable.

Enforcement—Adjudication

Once its investigation is concluded, an agency may begin an administrative action against an individual or organization. The majority of such actions are resolved through negotiated settlements at their initial stages, without the need for formal adjudication. Depending on the agency, negotiations may take the form of a casual conversation or a series of special conferences. Whatever form the negotiations take, their purpose is to rectify the problem to the agency's satisfaction and eliminate the need for additional proceedings.

Settlement is an appealing option to firms for two reasons. First, regulated industries often do not want to appear uncooperative with the regulating agency. Second, litigation can be very expensive. To conserve their own resources and avoid formal actions, administrative agencies devote a great deal of effort to giving advice and negotiating problems.

If a settlement cannot be reached, the agency may exercise its prosecutorial powers and issue a formal *complaint* against the offending party. If the Environmental Protection Agency (EPA), for example, finds that a factory is responsible for polluting the groundwater in violation of federal pollution laws, the EPA will issue a complaint against the violator in an effort to bring the factory into compliance with the federal regulations. This complaint is a public document and may even be accompanied by a press release. The factory charged in the complaint will respond by filing an *answer* to the EPA's allegations. If the factory and the agency cannot effect an informal settlement, the case is then heard in a trial-like setting before an **administrative law judge** (**ALJ**). The adjudication process is described below and illustrated graphically in Exhibit 13.3 on the following page.

Administrative Law Judge (ALJ)
One who presides over an administrative agency hearing and who has the power to administer oaths, take testimony, rule on questions of evidence, and make determinations of fact.

The Role of the Administrative Law Judge. The ALJ presides over the hearing and has the power to administer oaths, take testimony, rule on questions of evidence, and make determinations of fact. Although formally, the ALJ works for the agency prosecuting the case (in our example, the EPA), he or she is required by law to be an unbiased adjudicator (judge).

Certain safeguards promote fairness and prevent bias from entering the proceedings through the agency's ALJ. For example, the Administrative Procedure Act (APA) requires that the ALJ be separate from the EPA's investigative and prosecutorial staff. The APA also prohibits *ex parte* (private) communications between the ALJ and any party to an agency proceeding, such as the EPA or the factory. Finally, provisions of the APA protect the ALJ from agency disciplinary actions unless the agency can clearly show good cause for such an action.

Hearing Procedures. Hearing procedures vary widely from agency to agency. Administrative agencies generally can exercise substantial discretion over the type of hearing procedures that will be used. Frequently, disputes are resolved through rather informal adjudication proceedings. For example, the parties, their counsel, and the ALJ may simply meet at a table in a conference room for the dispute-settlement proceedings. A formal adjudicatory hearing, in contrast, resembles a trial in many respects. Prior to the hearing, the parties are permitted to undertake extensive discovery proceedings (involving depositions, interrogatories, and requests for documents or

EXHIBIT 13.3
The Process of Administrative Adjudication

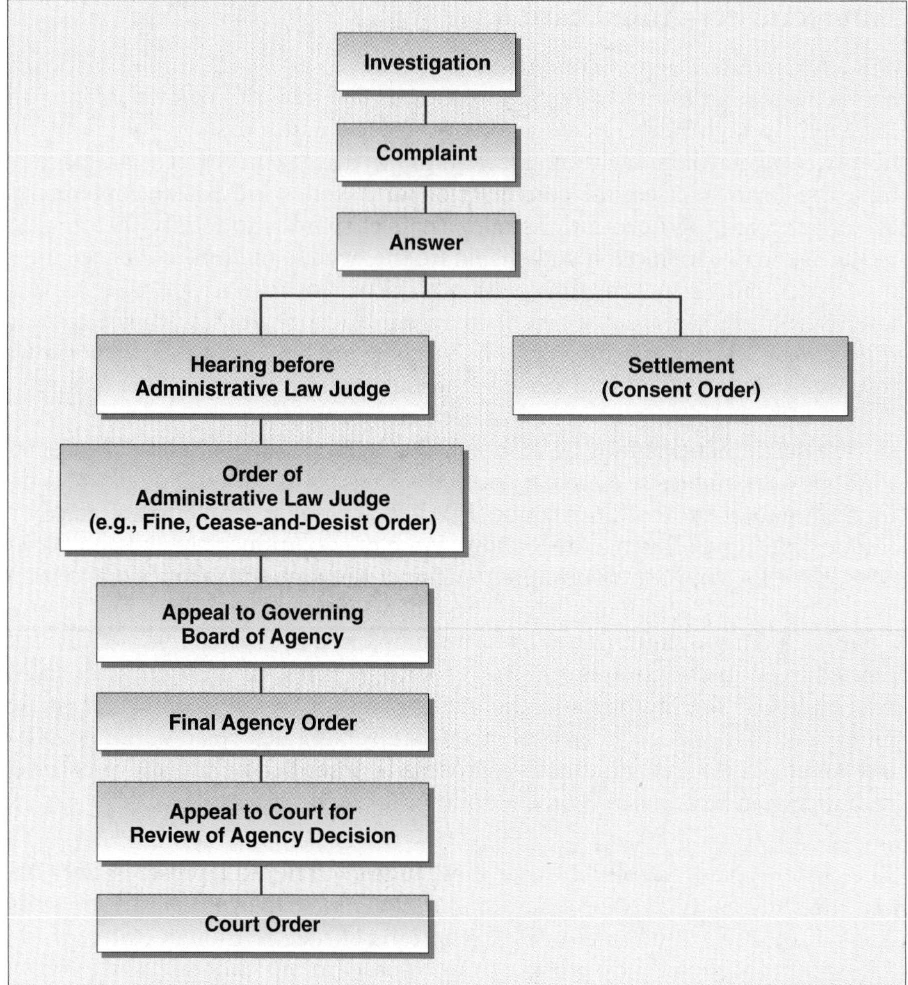

other information, as described in Chapter 10). During the hearing, the parties may give testimony, present other evidence, and cross-examine adverse witnesses.

A significant difference between a trial and an administrative agency hearing, though, is that normally, much more information, including hearsay (secondhand information, discussed in Chapter 15), can be introduced as evidence during an administrative hearing.

INITIAL ORDER
The decision rendered by an administrative law judge following an administrative hearing. The initial order becomes final unless it is appealed.

FINAL ORDER
The final decision of an administrative agency on an issue. If no appeal is taken, or if the case is not reviewed by the agency commission, the administrative law judge's initial order becomes the final order of the agency.

Agency Orders. Following the hearing, the ALJ renders an **initial order**, or decision, on the case. Either party may appeal the ALJ's decision to the commission or board that governs the agency. If the factory is dissatisfied with the ALJ's decision, for example, it may appeal the decision to the appropriate EPA commission. If the factory is dissatisfied with the commission's decision, it may appeal the decision to a federal court of appeals. If no appeal is taken, the ALJ's decision becomes the **final order** of the agency. If the case is appealed, the final order must come from the commission's decision or that of the reviewing court.

JUDICIAL REVIEW

The APA provides for judicial review of most agency decisions. If the factory in the above example was dissatisfied with the agency's order, it could appeal the decision to a federal appeals court. Agency actions are not *automatically* subject to judicial review however. Parties seeking review must first demonstrate that they meet certain requirements, including those listed here:

- The action must be *reviewable* by the court. The APA creates a presumption that agency actions are reviewable, making this requirement relatively easy to satisfy.
- The party must have *standing to sue* the agency (the party must have a direct stake in the outcome of the judicial proceeding).
- The party must have *exhausted all possible administrative remedies.* (Each agency has its "chain of review," and the challenger must follow agency appeal procedures before a court will deem that administrative remedies have been exhausted.)
- There must be an *actual controversy* at issue (the court will not review cases before it is necessary to decide them).

Recall from Chapter 7 that appellate courts normally defer to the decisions of trial courts on questions of fact. In reviewing administrative actions, the courts are similarly reluctant to review the factual findings of agencies. In most cases, the courts accept the facts as found in the initial agency proceedings. Normally, when a court reviews an administrative agency decision, the court considers the following types of issues:

- Whether the agency has exceeded its authority under the enabling legislation.
- Whether the agency has properly interpreted laws applicable to the agency action under review.
- Whether the agency has violated any constitutional provisions.
- Whether the agency has acted in accordance with procedural requirements of the law.
- Whether the agency's actions were arbitrary, capricious, or an abuse of discretion.
- Whether any conclusions drawn by the agency were not supported by substantial evidence.

STATE ADMINISTRATIVE AGENCIES

Although most of this chapter deals with federal administrative agencies, state agencies also play a significant role in regulating activities within the states. The growing presence of state agencies has been fostered by many of the same factors that have encouraged the proliferation of federal agencies, particularly the inability of the state legislatures to oversee the implementation of their laws and the need for greater technical competence in the implementation of these laws.

ETHICAL CONCERN

Decorum before Agency Hearings

What do you do when an administrative law judge (ALJ) is obviously biased against you or your client? Suppose that you are representing a client who is suffering from alcoholism and related medical problems. The client is trying to obtain disability benefits from a state agency. The ALJ makes it clear that he does not believe that those who voluntarily abuse alcohol should be entitled to state disability or medical assistance for alcohol-related problems. Throughout the hearing, your patience and poise are put to the test by the judge's perceptibly hostile attitude and intimidating words. In situations such as these, you need to remember that you are not at the hearing to serve your own interests but those of the client. Angry responses to the ALJ will only worsen your client's chances for a favorable decision, and if the decision is appealed, your heated responses will be on the record for review. As Rule 3.5 of the Model Rules of Professional Conduct points out, no matter what judges may do, the advocate must "protect the record for subsequent review and preserve professional integrity by patient firmness."

FEATURED GUEST: DEBORAH A. HOWARD, J.D.

Paralegal Job Opportunities in Administrative Law

Biographical Note

Deborah A. Howard graduated from the University of Louisville School of Law in Louisville, Kentucky, and is licensed to practice in the state of Indiana. She was named to *Who's Who in American Law* in 1991 and 1992, *Who's Who of Emerging Leaders in America* in 1992, and *2000 Notable American Women* in 1993. She practiced law as a litigator in employment-discrimination cases and as a staff attorney for Legal Services Organization of Indiana, Inc. Currently, Howard is the director of the legal studies program and associate professor of law at the University of Evansville (UE) in Evansville, Indiana. Howard teaches in the program and also teaches business law in the School of Business Administration at UE.

The number of administrative agencies has grown dramatically since the 1960s. Along with that growth have come job opportunities for paralegals in government agencies, both directly and indirectly. The duties of Congress have simply become so vast that Congress continues to delegate many of its functions to administrative bodies. Administrative agencies are here to stay.

THE SOCIAL SECURITY SYSTEM AND HEALTH-CARE BENEFITS

One area of administrative law that has continued to grow is the Social Security system. As the baby-boomer generation reaches retirement age, more and more claims will be made for Social Security payments. Medicare is a part of the Social Security system. The area of retirement and health-care benefits is a legal area that will be growing quickly in the next two decades. That growth will no doubt provide job opportunities for paralegals interested in practicing in administrative law.

THE LEGAL SERVICES ORGANIZATION (LSO)

One federal organization that already makes wide use of paralegals is the Legal Services Organization (LSO).

As a paralegal, you may find yourself working with a state agency, a federal agency, or perhaps both simultaneously. Unlike federal agencies, whose rules are eventually published in the *Code of Federal Regulations,* state agencies do not always publish their regulations in a compiled form. This makes the paralegal's job of researching state regulations more difficult, at least until he or she has become familiar with the workings of a particular agency.

Parallel Agencies

Commonly, a state agency is created as a parallel to a federal agency to provide similar services on a more localized basis. Such parallel agencies include the federal Social Security Administration and the state welfare agency, the Internal Revenue Service and the state revenue agency, and the Environmental Protection Agency and the state pollution-control agency. Not all federal agencies have parallel state agencies, however. The U.S. Postal Service, the Federal Bureau of Investigation, and the Nuclear Regulatory Commission have no parallel state agencies.

FEATURED GUEST, Continued

LSO offices provide legal assistance for needy persons in civil matters. The idea of providing legal services to the less privileged came out of President Lyndon Johnson's "War on Poverty" during the 1960s. The Legal Services Corporation (LSC) was created, and the president was given the power to appoint LSC board members. Congress provides funds to the LSC to be distributed throughout the country to local LSO programs (grantees) that aid the underprivileged by providing legal representation for them in civil cases.

STATE AND LOCAL LSOs

LSO funds are distributed to approximately three hundred local grantees throughout the country. Each year the local programs are reviewed by the LSC, and funding is established for the following year based on the review. LSO grantees are nonprofit organizations, so they may seek additional funding from other government or private sources.

All states have LSO programs, and using paralegals has helped LSO offices stretch their funding to serve as many people as possible.

Indiana has four LSO grantees. All of those programs use paralegals. The paralegals work as advocates before the Social Security Administration and at Medicaid hearings. They help attorneys investigate cases such as those involving child custody. They act as the go-between for the LSO programs and *pro bono* panels of local bar associations. They help prepare cases for trial and help investigate when clients are denied benefits, lose their jobs, have their utilities cut off, or are evicted from their apartments. LSO grantees train their paralegals to handle as many kinds of cases as the paralegals can learn to handle.

"THE AREA OF RETIREMENT AND HEALTH-CARE BENEFITS IS A LEGAL AREA THAT WILL BE GROWING QUICKLY IN THE NEXT TWO DECADES."

A REWARDING CAREER

Working in LSO offices allows paralegals to develop experience in the field of administrative law while developing expertise in the other areas of law that affect the poor. The legal needs of underprivileged Americans seem to grow every year. Paralegals interested in serving the needy in their community might find working in an LSO office to be a most rewarding career.

Conflicts between Parallel Agencies

In the event that the actions of parallel state and federal agencies come into conflict, the actions of the federal agency will prevail. For example, if the Federal Aviation Administration specifies the hours during which airplanes may land at and depart from airports, a state or local government is prohibited from issuing inconsistent laws or regulations governing the same activity. The priority of federal law over conflicting state laws is based on the **supremacy clause** of the U.S. Constitution. This clause, which is found in Article VI of the Constitution, states that the U.S. Constitution and "the Laws of the United States which shall be made in Pursuance thereof . . . shall be the supreme Law of the Land."

SUPREMACY CLAUSE
The clause in Article VI of the U.S. Constitution that provides that the Constitution, laws, and treaties of the United States are "the supreme Law of the Land." Under this clause, a state law that directly conflicts with a federal law will be rendered invalid.

ADMINISTRATIVE AGENCIES AND PARALEGAL PRACTICE

Paralegals, as well as other qualified nonlawyers, are permitted to practice administrative law in some situations under the Section 555 of the APA, which reads, in part, as follows:

PARALEGAL PROFILE LSO Paralegal

MARVALINE PRINCE is a paralegal with the Evansville Office of Legal Services Organization of Indiana, Inc. (LSOI). Prince has worked with LSOI since May 1978. She received her training directly through LSOI at its Midwest Resource Training Center. In addition to her training, Prince attended courses on advocacy, Social Security, and Medicaid. She states, however, that most of her training was acquired "on the job." The Evansville office serves ten counties. Its priority is helping underprivileged persons determine their eligibility for government benefits. Prince's area of work involves representing clients before the Social Security Administration.

What do you like best about your work?

"I find my job very challenging and rewarding. Although there are ups and downs to the job, I can't imagine not doing the work I do. I believe my job is fairly unique. Paralegals can do research and case preparation with a private firm, but they will not work as directly with the clients and the courts in most jobs as I do in mine. I also am able to go with clients to hearings and to present evidence. If a case is unusual or difficult, I consult with my supervising attorney at LSOI."

What is the greatest challenge that you face in your area of work?

"My greatest challenge is helping people with their claims for benefits. Ninety percent of my cases are SSI (Supplemental Security Income) cases, and the other 10 percent are Medicaid and food-stamp cases. I have a reputation for aggressive advocacy before the Social Security Administration, and some clients call LSOI asking that I take their case, even though they are aware that I am a paralegal and not an attorney."

"ANY PARALEGAL WHO RESISTS USING COMPUTER TECHNOLOGY IS TRULY AT A DISADVANTAGE."

What advice do you have for would-be paralegals in your area of work?

"My advice to any would-be paralegal is to obtain the best education possible. A large part of my job is assessing whether or not a client qualifies for SSI benefits, which I am able to do by determining their educational background, areas of skill, and medical history. It is important for paralegals in my area of work to have an extensive knowledge of many areas when trying to determine eligibility for a client."

What are some tips for success as a paralegal in your area of work?

"Regardless of whether a paralegal works for a private law firm or with a legal services organization, it is essential that paralegals become familiar with computers. My own desk-top computer allows me to draft memoranda in half the time that it would take me to draft them manually. Any paralegal who resists using computer technology is truly at a disadvantage. Paralegals should insist that their employers invest in computers for all staff members to use, and not just support staff."

> A person compelled to appear in person before an agency or representative thereof is entitled to be accompanied, represented, and advised by counsel or, if permitted by the agency, by other qualified representative.

By allowing "other qualified representative[s]" to practice administrative law, an agency increases efficiency while reducing the costs involved—the client is not required to hire an attorney to pursue an administrative claim (unless, of course, court action is required). Federal agencies that allow representation by nonlawyers include the Social Security Administration, the Wage and Appeals Board (Department of Labor), and the Interstate Commerce Commission, to name only a few.

One agency, the Federal Maritime Commission, requires nonlawyer representatives to register, pay a small fee, and satisfy certain educational requirements. To represent someone before the Social Security Administration, in contrast, one need only obtain from the agency the "Appointment of Representative" form shown in Exhibit 13.4 on pages 514 and 515 and have the client sign it. Other agencies that allow nonlawyers to represent clients may require the nonlawyer to pass an examination or to meet specific educational requirements.

Although only federal agencies must follow the APA, state agency procedures are usually similar to those required by the APA, and both federal and state agencies may allow paralegals to represent clients. If you, as a paralegal, want to practice in a certain area of administrative law, you should do the following:

- **Contact the relevant agency and ask about its specific representation requirements and procedures.**

A list of selected federal agencies, including their addresses and telephone numbers, is presented in Exhibit 13.5 on page 516.

AGENCY PROCEDURES—A HYPOTHETICAL EXAMPLE

The following pages present a hypothetical example to clarify what the paralegal should anticipate, procedurally, when entering the administrative law arena. The hypothetical example involves Calvin Novak, an experienced paralegal who performs freelance services for attorneys, always under their supervision. The law in Novak's state allows paralegals to do freelance work as long as the attorneys for whom they work supervise the work and assume responsibility for the final work product.[3]

Before becoming a freelancer, Novak had worked for a large law firm and participated occasionally in the firm's *pro bono* work. Recall from Chapter 3 that attorneys commonly perform legal services *pro bono publico* ("for the benefit of the public") at a free or reduced rate, usually for a certain number of hours each month. Paralegals also assist in *pro bono* work. In our hypothetical example, Novak has decided to work *pro bono* on behalf of a friend's mother, Kim Lee Barker. Barker is trying, with little success, to obtain needed medical and disability benefits from the state social services agency. Through his work for attorneys, Novak has acquired substantial experience with administrative agencies and knows that nonattorneys, including paralegals, can represent clients before both the state social services agency and the parallel agency at the federal level, the Social Security Administration (SSA).[4] The SSA manages and operates the federal disability programs that help elderly, disabled, and needy people pay for medical care. The federal Supplemental Security Income

3. Unlike independent paralegals (or legal technicians), who deliver services directly to the public, freelance paralegals work under the supervision of attorneys. As long as attorneys supervise their work, freelance paralegals are not engaging in the unauthorized practice of law.
4. Note that when paralegals are authorized by an administrative agency to represent clients before the agency, the problem of unauthorized practice of law does not arise—as long as the paralegal complies with the agency's specific requirements.

EXHIBIT 13.4
Appointment of Representative Form, Social Security Administration

DEPARTMENT OF
HEALTH AND HUMAN SERVICES
SOCIAL SECURITY ADMINISTRATION

NAME (Claimant) (Print or Type) Kim Lee Barker	SOCIAL SECURITY NUMBER 368 - 90 - 0914
WAGE EARNER (if different)	SOCIAL SECURITY NUMBER

Section I APPOINTMENT OF REPRESENTATIVE

I appoint this individual Calvin Novak, 1616 Norton, Tucson, AZ 85710

to act as my representative in connection with my claim or asserted right under:

☐ Title II (RSDI) ☒ Title XVI (SSI) ☐ Title IV FMSHA (Black Lung) ☐ Title XVIII (Medicare Coverage)

I authorize this individual to make or give any request or notice; to present or elicit evidence; to obtain information; and to receive any notice in connection with my pending claim or asserted right wholly in my stead.

SIGNATURE (Claimant) Kim Lee Barker	ADDRESS 703 N. Easterbrook Ln. Tucson, AZ 85711
TELEPHONE NUMBER 602-555-2011	DATE 9/5/95

Section II ACCEPTANCE OF THE APPOINTMENT

I, Calvin Novak, hereby accept the above appointment. I certify that I have not been suspended or prohibited from practice before the Social Security Administration; that I am not, as a current or former officer or employee of the United States, disqualified from acting as the claimant's representative; and that I will not charge or receive any fee for the representation unless it has been authorized in accordance with the laws and regulations referred to on the reverse side hereof. In the event that I decide not to charge or collect a fee for the representation, I will notify the Social Security Administration. (Completion of Section III satisfies this requirement.)

I am a/an Paralegal
(Attorney, union representative, relative, law student, etc.)

SIGNATURE (Representative) Calvin Novak	ADDRESS 1616 Norton, AZ 85710
TELEPHONE NUMBER 602-555-0202	DATE 9/5/95

Section III (Optional) WAIVER OF FEE

I waive my right to charge and collect a fee under Section 206 of the Social Security Act, and I release my client (the claimant) from any obligations, contractual or otherwise, which may be owed to me for services I have performed in connection with my client's claim or asserted right.

SIGNATURE (Representative) Calvin Novak	DATE 9/5/95

WAIVER OF DIRECT PAYMENT

I ONLY waive my right to a direct certification of a fee from the withheld past-due benefits of my client (the claimant). I do NOT, however, waive my right to petition for and be authorized to charge and collect a fee directly from my client.

SIGNATURE (Representative) Calvin Novak	DATE 9/5/95

(See Important Information on Reverse)

(SSI) program provides supplemental income to persons who are elderly, blind, or disabled and to others who need assistance.

State Medicaid Programs

Under the Social Security Act's Medicaid provisions, the states may create and expand, with matching federal funds, their public assistance to persons,

EXHIBIT 13.4
Continued

HOW TO COMPLETE THIS FORM

Print or type your full name and your Social Security number.

Section 1 – APPOINTMENT OF REPRESENTATIVE

You may appoint as your representative an attorney or any other qualified individual. You may appoint more than one person, but see "The Fee You Owe The Representative(s)." You may NOT appoint as your representative an organization, the law firm, a group. etc. Example, you go to a law firm or legal aid group for help with your claim, you may appoint any attorney or other qualified individual from that firm or group, but NOT the firm or group itself.

Check the block(s) for the program in which you have a claim. Title II, check if your claim concerns disability or retirement benefits, etc. Title XVI, check if the claim concerns Supplemental Security Income (SSI) payments. Title IV FMSHA (Federal Mine Safety and Health Act), check if the claim is for black lung benefits. Title XVIII, check only in connection with a proceeding before the Social Security Administration involving entitlement to medicare coverage or enrollment in the supplementary medical insurance plan (SMIP). More than one block may be checked.

Section II – ACCEPTANCE OF APPOINTMENT

The individual whom you appoint in Section I above, completes this part. Completion of this section is desirable in all cases, but it is mandatory only if the appointed individual is not an attorney.

Section III (Optional) – WAIVER OF FEE

This section may be completed by your representative if he/she will not charge any fee for services performed in this claim. If you had appointed a co-counsel (second representative) in Section I and he/she will also not charge you a fee, then the co-counsel should also sign this section or give a separate waiver statement.

GENERAL INFORMATION

1. When you have a representative:

   We will deal directly with your representative on all matters that affect your claim. Occasionally, with the permission of your representative, we may deal directly with you on specific issues. We will rely on your representative to keep you informed on the status of your claim, but you may contact us directly for any information about your claim.

2. The authority of your representative:

   Your representative has the authority to act totally on your behalf. This means he/she can (1) obtain information about your claim the same as you; (2) submit evidence; (3) make statements about facts and provisions of the law; and (4) make any request (including a fee request). It is important, therefore, that you are represented by a qualified individual.

3. When will the representation stop:

   We will stop recognizing or dealing with your representative when (1) you tell us that he/she is no longer your representative; (2) your representative does any one of the following: (a) submits a fee petition, or (b) tells us that he/she is withdrawing from the claim, or (c) he/she violates any of our rules and regulations, and a hearing is held before an administrative law judge (designated as hearing officer) who orders your representative disqualified or suspended as a representative of any Social Security claimant.

4. The fee you owe the representative(s):

   Every representative you appoint has a right to petition for a fee. To charge you a fee, a representative must first file a fee petition with us. Irrespective of your fee agreement, you never owe more than the fee we have authorized in a written notice to you and your representative(s). (Out of pocket expenses are not included). If your claim went to court, you may owe an additional fee for your representative's services before the court.

5. How we determine the fee:

   We use the criteria on the back of the fee petition (Form SSA 1560-U4), a copy of which your representative must send you.

6. Review of the fee authorization:

   If you or your representative disagrees with the fee authorization, either of you may request a review. Instructions for filing this review are on the fee authorization notice.

7. Payment of fees:

   If past-due benefits are payable in your claim, we generally withhold 25 percent of the past-due benefits toward possible attorney fees. If no past-due benefits are payable or this is an SSI claim, then payment of the fee we have authorized is your responsibility.

8. Penalty for charging an unauthorized fee:

   If your representative wants to charge and collect from you a fee that is greater than what we had authorized, then he/she is in violation of the law and regulations. Promptly report this to your nearest Social Security office.

regardless of age, whose income is insufficient to pay for health care. Because Medicaid is state administered, the particulars vary from one state to another. Some state Medicaid programs, such as California's MediCal program, are generously funded, while others are less so. To receive federal Medicaid funds the state agency must comply with federal regulations and guidelines.

EXHIBIT 13.5
Selected Federal Agencies

Board of Immigration Appeals (BIA)
Executive Officer
Department of Justice
Falls Church, VA 22041
(703) 756-6171

Bureau of Reclamation (BOR)
Department of the Interior
Washington, DC 20240-0001
(202) 208-4662

Department of Transportation Maritime Administration (MA)
400 Seventh Street, SW
Washington, DC 20590
(202) 366-5807

Equal Employment Opportunity Commission (EEOC)
1801 L Street, NW
Washington, DC 20507
(202) 663-4900
(1-800-USA-EEOC)

Federal Bureau of Investigation (FBI)
Ninth Street & Pennsylvania Avenue, NW
Washington, DC 20535
(202) 324-3000

Federal Mediation and Conciliation Service (FMCS)
2100 K Street, NW
Washington, DC 20427
(202) 653-5290

Internal Revenue Service (IRS)
111 Constitution Avenue, NW
Washington, DC 20224
(202) 566-5000

National Transportation Safety Board (NTSB)
490 L'Enfant Plaza, SW
Washington, DC 20594
(202) 382-6600

Small Business Administration (SBA)
409 Third Street, SW
Washington, DC 20416
(202) 205-6600
(1-800-U-Ask-SBA)

Bureau of Indian Affairs (BIA)
1951 Constitution Avenue, NW
Washington, DC 20245
(202) 208-7315

Consumer Product Safety Commission (CPSD)
5401 Westbard Avenue
Bethesda, MD 20207
(301) 492-6580

Drug Enforcement Administration (DEA)
600-700 Army Navy Drive
Arlington, VA 22202
(202) 307-10000

Farm Credit Administration (FCA)
1501 Farm Credit Drive
McLean, VA 22102-5090
(703) 883-4000

Federal Energy Regulatory Commission (FERCO)
Department of Energy
1000 Independence Avenue, SW
Washington, DC 20591
(202) 208-0300

Federal Trade Commission (FTC)
Pennsylvania Avenue at Sixth Street, NW
Washington, DC 20580
(202) 326-2222

Interstate Commerce Commission (ICC)
Twelfth Street and Constitution Avenue, NW
Washington, DC 20423
(202) 927-7119

Occupational Safety and Health Administration (OSHA)
Department of Labor
200 Constitution Avenue, NW
Washington, DC 20210
(202) 523-8151

Social Security Administration (SSA)
6401 Security Boulevard
Baltimore, MD 21235
(410) 965-7700

Bureau of Land Management (BLM)
Department of the Interior
Washington, DC 20240
(202) 208-3435

Department of Commerce
Office of Public Affairs
Patent and Trademark Office (PTO)
2011 Crystal Drive
Arlington, VA 22202
(703) 305-8341

Environmental Protection Agency (EPA)
401 M Street, SW
Washington, DC 20460
(202) 260-2090

Federal Aviation Administration (FAA)
800 Independence Avenue, SW
Washington, DC 20591
(202) 267-3484

Federal Housing Authority (FHA)
Department of Housing and Urban Development
451 7th Street, SW
Washington, DC 20416
(202) 755-6422

Food and Drug Administration (FDA)
5600 Fishers Lane
Rockville, MD 20857
(301) 443-1544

National Labor Relations Board (NLRB)
1717 Pennsylvania Avenue
Washington, DC 20570
(202) 254-8064

Securities and Exchange Commission (SEC)
450 Fifth Street, NW
Washington, DC 20549
(202) 272-3100

Veterans Administration (VA)
Department of Veterans Affairs
810 Vermont Avenue, NW
Washington, DC 20420
(202) 535-8300

DEVELOPING PARALEGAL SKILLS

Approval to Practice before the IRS

Damian Forsythe has an associate's degree in accounting. He is also interested in law and has completed his first semester in a legal-assistant program. In one of his courses, Law 100 ("Introduction to Law"), he learned that some administrative agencies allow non-lawyers to practice before them. One of those agencies is the Internal Revenue Service (IRS).

CONTACTING THE IRS

Damian thinks he might be interested in representing clients before the IRS. He also remembers that his instructor told the class members to contact the agency if they wished to find out more about the agency's requirements for nonlawyer representation. Damian decides to investigate these requirements.

Damian finds the telephone number for the IRS in his telephone directory, calls the agency, and asks for information on admission to practice before the IRS. He is referred to the Office of the Director of Practice, in Washington, D.C., and is transferred to that department.

IRS REQUIREMENTS FOR PARALEGAL PRACTICE

The administrative assistant who answers the telephone explains that the IRS does allow nonlawyers, including noncertified accountants, to practice before it. Nonlawyers and noncertified accountants have to pass the "Enrolled Agents Exam," however. If they pass the exam, they would be sent an application to become an enrolled agent. There are no educational requirements other than those required to pass the exam. The exam is very difficult, however, and requires a knowledge of accounting and tax laws and regulations. It is only given once a year. Damian will have to request a copy of Publication 1470, "Special Enrollment Exam," to learn more about the exam and enrolled-agent status. The publication becomes available in June, a few months before the exam is given.

Once a person is an enrolled agent, he or she is allowed to represent clients before the IRS and to advise clients on tax matters. Damian asks the administrative assistant if advising clients constitutes the unauthorized practice of law, and the answer is "No." Damian is pleased with the information that he has obtained from the IRS. He writes a reminder on his calendar to request a copy of Publication 1470 in June so that he can learn more about the exam.

Medicaid eligibility determinations made by state agencies are normally subject to review by the federal SSA.

MedSafe—A Hypothetical Medicaid Program

Our hypothetical state has a Department of Human Services and Welfare (DHSW, or "the department") that parallels the federal Social Security Administration. The DHSW administers the state's Medicaid program, "MedSafe." Applicants who qualify for MedSafe disability benefits may also qualify for federal disability benefits, as will be discussed in greater detail later.

- **In the real world, each state handles its medical-benefit programs differently. The forms, department procedures, and agency rules discussed in this hypothetical scenario are fictional; they are used only to illustrate typical agency rules and procedures.**

The Client—Kim Lee Barker

Kim Lee Barker is a fifty-four-year-old American citizen who was born in Korea. She speaks Korean fluently, but she reads it only at an eighth-grade level. As a teenager, she married an American soldier stationed in Korea. Shortly thereafter, during the mid-1950s, she arrived in the United States with her new husband and began raising an American family. She cannot read English well, but orally she can communicate her basic needs to others.

After her third child was born, her husband filed for divorce. To support herself and her family, Kim Lee worked at three part-time jobs simultaneously. She worked as a hairdresser's assistant (she was provided with an interpreter while being trained for this work), a restaurant dishwasher, and a house cleaner for several working couples in her community. An energetic woman, Kim Lee worked at all three jobs until she became ill.

Kim Lee's Disability

Kim Lee's hair-salon employer had noticed that Kim Lee was coughing excessively over a period of several weeks and that the condition appeared to be worsening. The employer was concerned for the health of her customers as well as for Kim Lee. Kim Lee agreed to see her family physician about the problem. On June 8, 1995, however, before Kim Lee met with the physician, her oldest son, Ted Barker, found her alone in her home, unconscious. Ted rushed her to the county hospital, where she remained for twenty-two days, eight of which were spent in the intensive care unit.

Because Kim Lee had no money and no medical insurance, the hospital insisted that she complete a DHSW application for MedSafe medical benefits to repay the hospital for the medical costs incurred for her care. The DHSW application requested personal information, details on income and assets, medical history, and a list of household expenses. Jessica Su Barker, Kim Lee's youngest daughter, filled out the twenty-nine page application as best she could with the information she knew. Parts of the application are shown in Exhibits 13.6 and 13.7 on the following pages.

The hospital undertook numerous diagnostic procedures, including complete blood tests and X-rays. The attending physician, Dr. Prentice, suspected that Kim Lee had tuberculosis (TB), but the tests were inconclusive. Even her chest X-rays did not confirm a diagnosis of TB. Dr. Prentice eventually diagnosed her condition as chronic obstructive pulmonary disease (COPD) of unknown origin, which was complicated by allergies to dust, pollen, and chemicals, as well as fatigue. Antibiotics were prescribed for Kim Lee, and she was scheduled for monthly medical exams with Dr. Prentice and sent home. In the meantime, the application for DHSW MedSafe was submitted to the county DHSW extension office.

As the weeks went by, Kim Lee's condition worsened substantially. She quit the restaurant and cleaning jobs because the work was too strenuous for

EXHIBIT 13.6
Application for State Social Services—Page 1

MEDSAFE

FOR OFFICE USE ONLY

Case Name

Case Number

County	District	Unit	Worker

INSTRUCTIONS: Please read each item carefully before you answer it. The answers you give will be used to determine if you are eligible to receive assistance. Complete this page by printing the answer or checking the box(es).

PLEASE PRINT **DO NOT USE THE SHADED AREAS**

1. Your First Name: KIM Middle Name: LEE Last Name: BARKER

2. Birthdate Month: 2 Day: 21 Year: 41

3. Does anyone in your home use a teletype for the deaf? If yes, enter the TDD or TTY number: NO

4. Address where you live Number, Street, Rural Route: 703 N. Easterbrook Ln. Apartment Number:
City: Tucson State: AZ Zip Code: 85711 County: Bent Arrow

5. Your Phone Number (602) 555-2011

6. Name of person and phone number where you may be reached
Name: Ted Barker (son)
Phone number: (602) 555-6148

CHECK AS MANY OF THE FOLLOWING STATEMENTS AS APPLY TO YOUR SITUATION

7. ☒ I need help paying my rent, heat, utilities and/or other daily living expenses (Aid to Dependent Children/ State Disability Assistance/State Family Assistance).

8. ☒ I need help paying medical bills such as doctor bills, hospital bills, nursing home bills, or prescriptions (Medicaid/State Medical Program).

9. ☐ I have a utility shut-off, eviction notice or some other emergency situation (State Emergency Relief). Describe the situation:

10. ☒ I need help paying for food (Food Stamps).

YOU MAY BE ELIGIBLE FOR EXPEDITED FOOD STAMPS. TO HELP US DECIDE IF YOU QUALIFY FOR THIS FASTER FOOD STAMP SERVICE, PLEASE ANSWER THE FOLLOWING QUESTIONS.

a. What is the total amount of CASH ASSETS belonging to your household (include only cash, savings or checking accounts, saving bonds, etc.)? $ 105.00

b. What is the total INCOME your household will receive this month (include money from earnings, child support, unemployment compensation benefits, Social Security benefits, etc.)? $ 220.00

c. What is the amount of your monthly rent or mortgage payment? If none enter zero. $ 275.00

d. If you pay your own heat and/or utility bills, what do you estimate will be the total cost of your heat and utilities this month? If none, enter zero. $ 30.00

e. Is anyone in your household a migrant or seasonal farm worker? ☐ Yes ☒ No
If yes, answer the next 3 questions:
(1) Has anyone in your household received any income this month? ☐ Yes ☐ No
If yes, how much? $
(2) Did your household recently lose its only source of income? ☐ Yes ☐ No
(3) Does anyone in your household expect to receive income later this month? ☐ Yes ☐ No
If yes, how much? $

f. Do any of the following describe your current home? If yes, check the box to the left.
☐ No regular night-time place to sleep.
☐ A supervised public or private emergency shelter for homeless people.
☐ A half-way house for temporary shelter until you find your own home.
☐ Temporary emergency shelter in the home of a friend, acquaintance, or relative.
☐ A place not usually used as a home, such as a public hallway, a bus station, a park, a building entrance, etc.

I HAVE READ AND UNDERSTAND THE INFORMATION ON THE BACK OF THIS PAGE

11. To File Today for Aid Sign Here (Client or Authorized Representative): Jessica Su Barker Date: 6/10/95

her—she was fatigued and simply could not catch her breath. She was dismissed from her job with the hair salon because she was "putting off" the customers with her incessant coughing. Her deteriorating condition forced her to stay home and remain indoors most of the time. She lost her ability to clean her own home, go to the grocery store, and exercise proper hygiene.

EXHIBIT 13.7
Application for State Social Services—Page 28

RELEASES

14. Social Security Information. I will allow the Social Security Administration to give the Department of Human Services and Welfare all information to determine my right to benefits under the Aid to Dependent Children, Medicaid, Food Stamps, State Disability Assistance, State Family Assistance or State Medical Program until the second month following the expiration of my elegibility based on the current application.
15. Eligibility Information. I understand that the information I have provided will be used to make sure my household is eligible for Food Stamps, other federally assisted state programs such as school lunch, ADC, and Medicaid. Fraudulent participation in the Food Stamp Program may result in criminal or civil action or administrative claims.

AFFIDAVIT

16. I certifiy, under penalty of perjury, that all the information that I have written on this form or told to a caseworker is true. I understand that I can be prosecuted for perjury if I have intentionally given false information. I also know that I may be asked to give proof of any information I have given. I also know that if I have intentionally left out any information or if I have given false information, which causes me to receive assistance I am not entitled to or more assistance than I am entitled to, I can be prosecuted for fraud.

IF YOU HAVE ANY QUESTIONS BE SURE TO ASK YOUR WORKER BEFORE SIGNING THE APPLICATION.

CLIENT OR AUTHORIZED REPRESENTATIVE SIGNATURES	DATE	AGENCY WITNESS	DATE
Jessica S. Barker ID Daughter	6/10/95	**SIGNATURE:** **PRINT NAME AND LOAD #:**	
ID		**SIGNATURE:** **PRINT NAME AND LOAD #:**	
ID		**SIGNATURE:** **PRINT NAME AND LOAD #:**	
ID		**SIGNATURE:** **PRINT NAME AND LOAD #:**	
Two witness signatures if X is used above: 1. 2.	DATE	Signature of person who helped complete this application	DATE

If you signed this application as an authorized representative on behalf of someone else, print your name and phone number where you can be reached.

Name Jessica S. Barker **Phone Number** (602) 555 - 2557
(First, Middle Initial, Last)

She had to sleep in an upright position on the couch to breathe effectively. Kim Lee was relying heavily on the financial assistance and caregiving of her children. It was now August 1, 1995.

The First Denial—Failure to Provide Verifications

On August 2, Kim Lee received written notice from the DHSW that she was not eligible for medical and disability benefits under the MedSafe program.

Kim Lee's son, Ted Barker, read the notice later that evening. He explained to his mother that the DHSW had denied her MedSafe application because she had failed to provide appropriate verification of her income. Exhibit 13.8 on the next page presents the essential provisions of this notice.

Ted discovered that his mother had received, on July 9, the notice referred to by the DHSW caseworker in the denial. The notice was called "Required Verifications—Form No. 2314," and it required the recipient to respond in fourteen days, which meant that a response was long past due. Kim Lee had not understood the importance of this form when it arrived but had dutifully placed it in her "special drawer" containing bills and other items that her children would handle at the end of the month.

While reading the verification request, Ted noted that the caseworker, Morey Denton, had successfully contacted Kim Lee's restaurant and hair-salon employers based on the information provided in Kim Lee's MedSafe application. Denton, however, had been unable to acquire employment information regarding the house-cleaning services that Kim Lee had provided to local families—because her daughter had not listed the names and addresses of those employers on the application.

Establishing Authorized Representation

Ted had met Calvin Novak at a local softball tournament earlier in the summer. He knew that Calvin was a paralegal and telephoned him to find out what, if anything, could be done about MedSafe's denial of benefits to his mother. Calvin discussed the matter briefly with Ted over the telephone and arranged a meeting for the next evening at Kim Lee's home. At the meeting, Calvin explained to both Kim Lee and Ted what procedures were involved in appealing the denial. Calvin agreed to act as Kim Lee's *agent* (a person who acts on behalf of another, as explained in Chapter 9) and to represent her in an appeal of the MedSafe denial.

Calvin had Kim Lee sign and date an "Authorization of Representation" form (provided by the DHSW on request), as well as an "Information Release and Authorization of Representation" form that Calvin had drafted himself. This second form would be necessary to obtain medical information held by Kim Lee's doctors and the county hospital in which Kim Lee was treated. These forms are shown in Exhibits 13.9 and 13.10 on pages 523 and 524.

Informal Settlement of the Dispute

Calvin copied all documents, lab reports, progress notes, and correspondence from the DHSW regarding Kim Lee's illness. At the initial conference, he took as much relevant information from Ted and Kim Lee as possible, including her prescriptions; the names and addresses of her doctors, children, and employers; and the activities she was still able to perform for herself. Calvin later filed both "Authorization of Representation" forms with the DHSW and directed the department to send him copies of all correspondence and records involving Kim Lee. He wanted to know exactly what the DHSW knew about Kim Lee and her case, including what kind of medical information it had and what verifications it had received from Kim Lee's employers.

Calvin's efforts were primarily focused on gaining the department's cooperation. If he could convince the caseworker that Kim Lee's application for

EXHIBIT 13.8
Notice of Denial of MedSafe Benefits

Case Name: Kim Lee Barker
Case No.: f11906687-14MS
Program: MedSafe
Caseworker: Morey Denton

You were issued a Required Verifications checklist on July 5, 1995, with which you failed to comply. You have been denied eligibility for MedSafe medical benefits due to your failure to provide proper income verifications as required under DHSW Rule 310, Item 16, page 21, of the State Eligibility Manual (SEM), which provides:

> Medical assistance applicants must provide the department with income verification for both earned and unearned income. Such verifications may be in the form of documents (e.g., pay stubs or award notice) or written statements from persons with knowledge of the applicant's income (e.g., employer or agency issuing benefits). Failure to provide this information is grounds for denial of MedSafe medical benefits.

A hearing request, if filed, must be submitted within thirty (30) days from the date of this denial notice.

Morey Denton — Caseworker
July 30, 1995 — Date

MedSafe benefits should not have been denied, the DHSW might agree to settle the issue and continue processing Kim Lee's application for MedSafe.

Contacting the Caseworker. Calvin telephoned the caseworker, Morey Denton. It became apparent that Denton did not have the authority to settle the problem. Calvin would have to contact Denton's supervisor, Ann Skinner. After a bit of friendly small-talk about sports and "the big game last night," Calvin wrote down the supervisor's name and telephone number.

Agency Contacts Notebook
A reference guide with names, telephone numbers, and other generalized information about individual contacts working within a particular administrative agency.

In his work as a paralegal, Calvin frequently contacted representatives of the DHSW. To save himself valuable time, he had created an **agency contacts notebook** as a quick reference guide to the DHSW. The notebook listed the names of employees, their job titles, their telephone and/or fax numbers, and general comments to refresh his memory. (See Exhibit 13.11 on page 525 for a page from the notebook.) Now, he pulled that same notebook from his bookshelf and paged through to the heading "Bent Arrow County," the county in which Kim Lee's disability claim was filed. He entered Morey Denton's telephone number, along with the following comment: "Very nice, plays racquetball at the YMCA, supervisor is Ann Skinner, 555-4893."

Contacting the Supervisor. Calvin telephoned Denton's supervisor, Ann Skinner, and explained to her that Kim Lee was functionally illiterate in the

EXHIBIT 13.9
DHSW Authorization of Representation

STATE DEPARTMENT
of
HUMAN SERVICES AND WELFARE
Bureau of Administrative Hearings

Authorization of Representation

In the matter of: Case # f11906687-14MS

Kim Lee Barker
Claimant

APPOINTMENT OF AUTHORIZED REPRESENTATIVE

The undersigned hereby authorizes Calvin Novak
of 1616 Norton, Tuscon, AZ 85710
(Address)
to act as my representative in all proceedings arising from my requested hearing dated 8/5/95 and to receive documents, medical reports, etc. to be used at my hearing.

Dated: 8/5/95 Signature: Kim Lee Barker
Claimant

APPEARANCE OF ATTORNEY OR AUTHORIZED REPRESENTATIVE

My appearance as ☐ Legal aid, etc. representative for claimant in the
☐ Law student
(check one) ☐ Private attorney
☒ Non-lawyer

above-entitled cause is hereby filed.

Dated: 9/5/95 Signature: Calvin Novak
Attorney/Authorized Representative

Address: 1616 Norton
Tucson, AZ
85710

English language and could not have read the verification notice sent to her. The supervisor agreed that the failure of Kim Lee to submit the requested verifications was understandable under the circumstances and agreed to rectify the situation by extending the due date for the submission of verifications for another five days.

Calvin had Ted ask the people who had employed Kim Lee as a house cleaner to sign the verification forms. Two days later, Calvin faxed copies of these forms to Morey Denton, the caseworker, and sent duplicate copies to

EXHIBIT 13.10
Information Release and Authorization of Representation

INFORMATION RELEASE and AUTHORIZATION of REPRESENTATION

Department of Human Services and Welfare
Print Name

The individual or entity named above is authorized to release the following types of information from my personal files:

- •Information in my file at the Department of Human Services and Welfare or in the files of the agencies or organizations listed above.
- •Medical records (admitting histories, physical examinations, discharge summaries, laboratory reports, test results, clinical evaluations, treatment for alcohol and drug abuse, psychiatric and psychological reports, and information on communicable diseases, sexually transmitted diseases, and tuberculosis).
- •Financial, employment, earned income, and unearned income information.
- •Any education or rehabilitation records.
- •Also release : any other pertinent information.

I hereby authorize Calvin Novak to act on my behalf as my representative in any proceedings necessary to establish Medicaid or Social Security eligibility for the coverage of medical expenses. I understand that there is no guarantee that coverage can be established and that I am ultimately responsible for my medical bills if coverage is not established.

This release expires six (6) months from the date of my signature below and may be revoked by me at any time before that. The release shall cover any information existing at the time of this signing and any information generated during the following (6) months.

A COPY OF THIS DOCUMENT HAS THE SAME EFFECT AS THE ORIGINAL.

Kim Lee Barker	8/5/95
Signature of Patient/Guardian	Date
Kim Lee Barker	2/21/41
Patient's Name	Birthdate
703 N. Easterbrook	602-555-2011
Address	Telephone
Tucson, AZ 85711	368-90-0914
City, State, Zip Code	Soc. Sec. No.
Ted Barker	8/5/95
Witness Signature	Date

Denton by certified mail, return receipt requested.[5] Denton informed Calvin, as Kim Lee's agent, that the verifications had been received and that Kim Lee's application was being processed for medical eligibility.

The Second Denial—Failure to Satisfy the Durational Requirements

One month later, Calvin received another denial notice from the DHSW. The denial stated that Kim Lee was ineligible for medical benefits because she failed to satisfy "the durational requirements necessary for MedSafe eligibility." The problem, this time, was that the department's medical reviewers—after having reviewed Kim Lee's medical records—did not believe that Kim Lee would be disabled for twelve continuous months.

As discussed earlier, the supremacy clause of the Constitution requires that the federal law be given priority over any inconsistent state

5. If you send a letter by certified mail and check the box on the mail form indicating your desire for a return receipt, then the recipient must sign for the mail. The post office then mails the signed card back to you. By sending duplicates to Morey Denton via certified mail, Calvin acquires proof that the DHSW received the documents within the agreed-on time period.

BENT ARROW COUNTY
3393 W. Main
Tucson, AZ 85705

Name	Date	Phone/Fax	Comments
Sarah Bender (caseworker)	5/2/93	555-4888	Two daughters: Kate is 10; Jewel is 7.
Mel Campbell (client advocate)	5/20/93	555-4810	Used to work at the old Kilmer Plant before they closed it two years ago.
Allen Fenkle (caseworker)	6/1/93	555-4857	Supervisor is Bill Cochran. 555-4886
Morey Denton (caseworker)	8/19/95	555-4890 555-4629 Fx	Very nice, plays racquetball at the YMCA, supervisor is Ann Skinner. 555-4893

EXHIBIT 13.11
Agency Contacts Notebook (Excerpt)

law. For Calvin's purposes, this meant that if the federal Social Security Administration (SSA) determined that Kim Lee was "disabled," the state's finding of "not disabled" would be inconsistent with the federal law. The state agency's finding would therefore have to be reversed, and as a result, Kim Lee would be eligible for both state (MedSafe) and federal Supplemental Security Income (SSI) disability benefits.

Calvin quickly mapped out his strategy and then informed Ted and Kim Lee of his plans. First, he would file an administrative appeal with the DHSW, challenging the department's denial. Then, he would apply to the SSA for disability benefits for Kim Lee under the SSI program. The procedures would be similar to those used with the DHSW. He would file an application and "Appointment of Representative" form with the SSA (this form was shown in Exhibit 13.4), along with a complete medical packet duplicating most of the information accumulated by the DHSW, a letter of introduction, and a chronology of relevant events.

To be successful against the DHSW, Calvin knew that he would need more convincing medical evidence. He had to establish that Kim Lee's condition would be disabling from approximately June 1995 through June 1996. He would ask Kim Lee to undergo additional testing, hoping for a more precise diagnosis of her condition to supplement the evidence he would present at the formal hearing before the DHSW. This new medical information, assuming that it was beneficial to the case, would be provided both to the administrative law judge at the DHSW hearing and to the SSA. Kim Lee was scheduled for a pulmonary (respiratory) function test (PFT) and a medical examination with Dr. Colman at the Pulmonary Testing Center. Calvin hoped to obtain clinical evidence, such as test results, or a doctor's diagnosis and opinion indicating that Kim Lee's disabling condition would last a full year.

ETHICAL CONCERN

Confidentiality and Administrative Practice

One of the challenges facing paralegals who deal with administrative agencies is remembering at all times the duty to keep client information confidential. Suppose, for example, that you are working on behalf of a client who is trying to obtain disability benefits. In pursuing the client's claim, you deal with a number of employees of the relevant state agency. One day, you receive a phone call from a person who states that he is working for the agency. He asks you to send him information on your client's financial position (income, property holdings, and other assets) and gives you his fax number. Without thinking twice about it, you fax him this confidential information and then continue with your work on another case. What if the person who requested the information is not an employee of the agency after all but someone who, for any number of reasons, wants to learn of the client's financial condition? This can and does happen. To avoid breaching the duty of confidentiality, you should always verify that anyone requesting information has a right to obtain it. Generally, you should not transmit confidential information by fax.

Administrative Appeal of the Denial

Calvin filed a "Hearing Request" form with the DHSW on behalf of Kim Lee, using the department's simplified form. He indicated on Kim Lee's behalf, as the ground for the hearing request, "because I believe that I am disabled." On the form, he stated that he would represent the client at the prehearing medical conference and hearing, and he included a copy of the "Authorization of Representation" form. Morey Denton, Kim Lee's caseworker, contacted Calvin a week later, acknowledging the hearing request and setting the date for a prehearing conference.

The Prehearing Conference. The prehearing conference is an intermediate step before the formal hearing to determine if new medical evidence or some other reason warrants a reevaluation of the record by the DHSW medical experts. Ted, Kim Lee, and Calvin were greeted by Morey Denton and his supervisor at the DHSW extension office before the prehearing. They were escorted to a small conference room on the third floor. The agency's medical expert, who was at the state capital some 215 miles away, telephoned the conference room and connected with everyone via the speakerphone.

The medical expert discussed in detail the evidence already in the record and her reasons for finding that the evidence was insufficient to establish a long-term disability. Calvin said that if the department would hold off on the formal hearing, he would produce the results of a pulmonary function test along with additional medical evidence in about a week. The expert stated that she would neither change her decision nor delay the scheduling of a formal administrative hearing before an administrative law judge (ALJ).

Preparing for the Hearing. By the time Calvin received notice of the hearing schedule, he had possession of the PFT results, a detailed medical report (see Exhibit 13.12 on page 528) from Dr. Colman, and the medical progress reports from Dr. Prentice—the doctor's own notes covering every appointment with Kim Lee since her hospitalization in June. Calvin sent duplicate copies of the new medical evidence to the SSA. He also prepared the exhibits for the DSHW hearing, scheduled for January 16, 1996. Calvin believed that he had a compelling argument and sufficient evidence to support his client's disability claim. He looked forward to the hearing with quiet anticipation.

The exhibit packet that Calvin compiled included documents in support of Kim Lee's position, as well as documents that he intended to discredit. Calvin did not prepare a written brief (a persuasive document that describes the facts, states the issues, and analyzes the application of law to those issues and facts) for submission to the ALJ. He had attended hearings with this ALJ before and knew that the judge did not like to have written briefs submitted. "All it does is delay the process," Judge Powers would say. Calvin rehearsed his oral argument, and when the hearing date arrived, he was well prepared.

The Administrative Hearing. The DHSW hearing was held in the third-floor conference room at the DHSW extension offices in the county in which Kim Lee resided. The participants included Judge Powers, Calvin, Kim Lee, Ted, Morey Denton, and Morey's supervisor, Ann Skinner. The judge sat at the head of the table, with the DHSW employees at his left and Calvin, Kim Lee, and Ted to his right.

While gathering his thoughts prior to the hearing, Judge Powers noted the evidence packets, one provided by the DHSW and one provided by Calvin. Then he opened the hearing.

> Judge Powers: *Mr. Novak, are you an attorney?*
>
> Calvin: *No, your honor. I am a paralegal authorized to represent Ms. Barker.*
>
> Judge Powers: *That's fine. You should know that this hearing will be recorded on tape. If you need to listen to this tape at a later date, you are free to come to the department and do so. If you need a written transcript, however, you must pay the cost of having it transcribed. Understand?* [Heads nod in affirmation.] *Good. We're ready, so let us begin with the hearing.*
>
> *Starting with the department, please state your name and your reason for being here for the record.* [The DHSW employees, followed by Kim Lee, Ted, and Calvin, stated for the record their names and reasons for being at the hearing.]
>
> *This case is brought before me pursuant to State Administrative Rule 599.09 upon a timely request for a hearing filed by the claimant, Ms. Kim Lee Barker, who disagrees with the department's denial of MedSafe benefits. Again, we'll begin with the department. Please state your basis for the denial of Ms. Barker's application.*
>
> Ann Skinner: *"Your honor, Ms. Barker failed to establish that her medical condition would last for the twelve-month period required under the Social Security laws for her to be disabled. Please refer to Exhibit DHSW-33 . . .* [Ann Skinner pointed out the medical exhibits on which the department's decision was based.]

Judge Powers questioned the department on its decision in some detail. He then turned his attention to Calvin.

> Judge Powers: *Mr. Novak, why do you think your client satisfied the duration requirement when the department does not?*

Calvin launched into his oral argument. He discussed the new evidence, the pulmonary function test, and how it proved that his client's condition would continue to be disabling at least for the remainder of the twelve-month period and possibly for the rest of her life. Calvin questioned Kim Lee, bringing out testimony establishing her dependence on others for her care and the extent to which her medical condition affected her daily activities. He closed his argument with a final statement summing up the law as it applied to the facts of this case. Once the hearing was over, there was nothing to do but wait for the ALJ's decision.

The Initial Order and Further Appeal. One month later, Judge Powers's decision and order arrived. The ALJ affirmed the department's decision:

> Based on the evidence in the record, MedSafe benefits were properly denied, and the department's order is hereby affirmed. Claimant failed to satisfy the twelve-month duration requirement to establish a disability. The law provides that within thirty (30) days of receipt of this Decision and Order the claimant may appeal it to the circuit court for the county in which he or she lives.

ETHICAL CONCERN

Loyalty to Your Client

Paralegals representing clients seeking medical or disability benefits under a state or federal program frequently work closely with spouses or relatives of the client. This can present a problem when a spouse or relative wants one thing and the client another. For example, suppose that in this chapter's hypothetical example, both the state agency and the federal Social Security Administration deny Kim Lee's claim for disability benefits. Kim Lee's only recourse is to appeal the decision to the courts. Kim Lee wants to drop the matter, but her son insists that Calvin turn over all of the relevant documents to an attorney to begin the judicial appeal process. What should Calvin do in this situation? While it may be true that Kim Lee does not fully understand the matter, recall from the discussion of agency law in Chapter 9 that Calvin has a duty, as Kim Lee's agent, to obey her instructions. Perhaps the best thing for him to do in this circumstance is to end the agency relationship and turn over the case file to Kim Lee.

EXHIBIT 13.12
Medical Examination Report

MEDICAL EXAMINATION REPORT
Department of Human Services and Welfare

Case Name: KIM LEE BARKER
Case Number: FII906687-14 MS 9-5-95
County: 0 | District: 1 | Unit: 0 | Worker: A | Other ID (If required):

SECTION 1 – (To be completed by worker)

1. Name of Client: KIM LEE BARKER
2. Social Security No.: 368-90-0914
3. Date of Birth: 2/21/41
4. Client Address (Number, Street, City, Zip Code): 703 N EASTERBROOK LN, TUCSON, AZ, 85701
5. Sex: ☐ Male ☒ Female
6. Description of Last Job (Duration, When Discontinued, Why): House Cleaner, Hair Salon Assistant, Dsh
7. Usual Occupation: SAME
8. Client States That He/ She Has the Following Disabilities (Date of onset of each): COPD 5/95
9. Worker's Signature: Kim Lee Barker

SECTION 2 – (To be completed by client)

TO EXAMINING PHYSICIAN: You are hereby authorized to release the information requested below to the Department of Human Services and Welfare

10. Signature of Client/ Patient: Kim Lee Barker — Date: 9-5-95

SECTION 3 – (To be completed by examining physician)

DOCTOR, PLEASE NOTE: This limited diagnostic examination is to assist the Department to determine the extent of this client's DISABILITY as related to EMPLOYABILITY. We would, therefore, appreciate your careful description of abnormal objective clinical findings that substantiate the symptoms and/ or your diagnoses. This includes any information relative to the diagnosis or treatment of HIV, ARC or AIDS, if applicable.
This examination is at the client's expense unless accompanied by form DHSW–95, Medical Services Authorization, Invoice and Payment Voucher. Extensive clinical procedures and tests will not be reimbursed by the Department unless prior authorization is given. Return completed Medical Examination Report and Form DHSW–95 promptly to the Department of Human Services and Welfare in the pre-addressed, stamped envelope.

11. HISTORY OF DISABLING CONDITIONS (Including date of onset of illness, injury and/ or date of surgery)

(see attached hospital records)

COPD

12. PHSYICAL EXAMINATION (Vital signs plus pertinent abnormal findings)

Height	Weight	Pulse Rate	Blood Pressure	Respiratory Rate
5´ 0"	92 lbs	92	138/90	20

shortness of breath, fatigue, expectoration

(see attached progress notes)

13. LABORATORY DATA (Pertinent abnormal findings or lab, radiologic and other diagnostic procedures). Attach copies if available.

(see attached lab results) Positive PFT

Once again, Calvin met with Ted and Kim Lee to determine what to do next. They decided to request a rehearing directly from the State Hearing Review Board (SHRB). If the SHRB refused a rehearing, nothing more would be done. Although Kim Lee could appeal the ALJ's decision to a state court, she could not afford to hire an attorney—and Calvin, as a paralegal, could not represent her in court. She made the decision not to pursue the claim beyond the SHRB level. Calvin prepared a "Request for Rehearing" and a brief and forwarded it to the SHRB. Two weeks later, the SHRB denied the request.

EXHIBIT 13.12
Continued

14. DIAGNOSIS

COPD— Chronic obstructive pulmonary disease.

15. CHARACTERISTICS OF IMPAIRMENTS (Check appropriate terms)

STATUS: ☐ Improving ☐ Stable ☒ Deteriorating

PROGNOSIS: ☐ Remediable by Treatment ☐ Improvement by Treatment ☒ Not Remediable ☐ Terminal

16. PHYSICAL LIMITATIONS ☐ No Limitations ☒ Limited (Indicate on chart below)

A. LIFTING/CARRYING

Up to 5 lbs.	☐	☒	☐
6-10 lbs.	☒	☐	☐
11-20 lbs.	☒	☐	☐
21-25 lbs.	☒	☐	☐
26-50 lbs.	☒	☐	☐
51-100 lbs.	☒	☐	☐

STANDING/ WALKING & SITTING

Based on an 8 hour work day how many hours, in your estimation, can the following activities be tolerated by this client?

Standing 1 hours/day

Walking .5 hours/day

Sitting 6.5 hours/day

B. Additional functional limitations (i.e. driving, bending, climbing, exposure to dust, fumes etc.)

allergy to pollutants restricts environment;

patient cannot exert herself, cannot walk upstairs or more than two city blocks

17. EMPLOYABILITY ☐ Employable ☐ No limitations ☐ Limitations as noted above

☒ Unemployable: ☐ 60 days or less, ☒ More than 60 days forever

18. MEDICATION (Please specify type, dosage and schedule and potential side effects)

(See attached prescription list)

19. RECOMMENDATIONS (Please indicate what additional diagnostic studies or treatment is needed. If referral to specialist is advisable, please specify type.)

Continue on medications permanently;

another PFT is scheduled for 90 days from last appointment;

regular monthly visits to primary care physician

20. Can the client meet his/ her needs in the home? ☐ Yes ☒ No

If no, what assistance is needed? bathing, house cleaning, and shopping

21. Will you be treating this client? ☒ Yes ☐ No | Number Visits Per Month 1 | Number of Months of Treatment indefinite

REMARKS: Please use addditional sheet for remarks and expansion of any of the above items. Thank you.

22. Physician's Signature C. Colman, M.D.	23. Printed name of Physician J. COLMAN,M.D.	24. M.D. or D.O. (Specialty, if any) M.D./Pulmonary
25. Address 6000 Fourth Avenue, Tucson, AZ 85701		26. Date of Examination 9/15/95

The SSA's Decision. One month later, the SSA notified Kim Lee and Calvin of its determination. The SSA found Kim Lee to be disabled. As Calvin explained to Ted and Kim Lee the following day, all that was left to do was notify the DHSW of the SSA's finding that Kim Lee was disabled under the federal law. The DHSW would have to accept the SSA's finding. Calvin may not have been able to persuade the department and the ALJ that Kim Lee's disability would last a year, but he had persuaded the federal government—and that, in the end, is all that mattered.

TODAY'S PROFESSIONAL PARALEGAL

Working for an Administrative Agency

TODAY'S Professional PARALEGAL

The Environmental Protection Agency (EPA) employs several paralegals. One of them is Mary Ulrich, who works for the Freedom of Information Act (FOIA) officer. The Freedom of Information Act of 1966 requires federal government agencies to disclose certain records to any person on request. Some types of records, however, such as those containing information relating to trade secrets, are exempt from this requirement. Anyone who wishes to obtain information from a government agency must submit a written request to the agency. Mary Ulrich's job involves responding to FOIA requests on behalf of the EPA. FOIA requests must be made in writing, but often legal assistants or attorneys from law firms or corporations call before they submit written requests.

RECEIVING AN INFORMATION REQUEST

Mary's telephone rings. It is Scott Webb, a paralegal with Sims and Howard in Chicago. He wants to talk to Mary about the EPA's file on the Black Hole landfill, a toxic-waste site to which one of Sims and Howard's clients has allegedly contributed hazardous waste. Scott wants to know the size of the file on the landfill and the type of information that it contains. If the EPA's file is small enough, Scott will request copies of most of its relevant contents. He will request the copies over the phone and will also follow up on the conversation with a letter. Mary will be able to tell Scott if there are documents in the file that might have to be reviewed by an agency attorney before they can be reproduced.

Mary pulls the file and finds that it contains at least ten thousand pages of documents. She informs Scott of this. Because the agency charges for copying costs, including the time that Mary spends copying the records, Scott asks for specific types of documents. One type of record that he wants is a list of the types and quantities of hazardous waste that other parties have allegedly contributed to the site.

DEALING WITH FOIA EXEMPTIONS

Mary looks for this information in the file. She finds it but also sees that information on several of the alleged contributors is exempt from FOIA disclosure requirements under trade-secrets exemptions. Mary informs Scott of this fact. Scott also wants information on why the agency decided to include his firm's client in the list of contributors to the toxic-waste site. Mary reminds Scott that interagency memos are usually privileged and that his request will have to be reviewed by agency counsel to determine if the agency could disclose this information.

Mary and Scott finish their conversation. Mary decides to wait for Scott's formal FOIA letter before starting to work on the request because so many of the documents will have to be reviewed by counsel before they can be sent out. Maybe Scott and the attorney for whom he works will rethink their strategy or make a different request now that they know they will have to wait for a decision from the agency's counsel office, especially when a good part of their request might be denied.

THE PERVASIVENESS OF ADMINISTRATIVE LAW

The functions of administrative agencies permeate almost every area of legal practice. No matter where you work, you should anticipate that sooner or later you will be interacting with a government agency. Suppose that you work for a small law firm (or sole practitioner) that specializes in personal-injury claims. You may communicate directly with an investigator for the Occupational Safety and Health Administration when the firm handles a personal-injury claim involving an employer's violation of workplace safety standards.

If you work for a large law firm, you may be required to deal with several agencies simultaneously. The firm's environmental-law department may ask you to obtain the new list of pollution-control guidelines from the

Environmental Protection Agency on behalf of a client planning to build a factory near a wetland. The firm's department that handles legal issues involving the elderly may ask you to request blank forms from the Social Security Administration to keep on file. The firm's antitrust department (which deals with anticompetitive business practices) may require that you send exhibits to the Federal Trade Commission. The firm's employment-law department may request that you contact the Equal Employment Opportunity Commission to reschedule a hearing date.

Of course, you may work as an employee of an administrative agency. If you do, you will become especially knowledgeable in that agency's procedures and requirements. Generally, the paralegal specializing in an area of administrative law will find that the opportunities for paralegals in this area continue to expand.

KEY TERMS AND CONCEPTS

adjudication 500
administrative law judge (ALJ) 507
administrative process 502
agency contacts notebook 522
bureaucracy 501
delegation doctrine 501
enabling legislation 498
executive agency 499
final order 508
independent regulatory agency 499
initial order 508
judicial process 502
legislative rule 501
notice-and-comment rulemaking 502
rulemaking 502
supremacy clause 511

CHAPTER SUMMARY

1. The study of administrative law is important to the paralegal because paralegals are routinely involved with administrative agencies. Paralegals in any area of paralegal work should have an understanding of the basic functions and procedures of administrative agencies.

2. The federal Congress and state legislatures create administrative agencies to help implement the many laws enacted by the legislatures and to issue rules and regulations governing a certain area. Federal administrative agencies are created by Congress through enabling legislation. An enabling act specifies the name, purpose, function, and powers of the agency being created. State administrative agencies are created by enabling legislation enacted by state legislatures.

3. There are two types of federal administrative agencies. Executive agencies comprise the cabinet departments and the subagencies within those departments. Executive agencies are subject to the authority of the president, who has the power to appoint or remove federal officers. Independent regulatory agencies are outside the major executive departments and are more independent of presidential control, because their officers serve for fixed terms and cannot be removed without just cause.

4. Administrative agencies combine functions normally associated with the three branches of government—the executive, legislative, and judicial branches. The constitutional authority for delegating such powers to administrative agencies is generally held to be implied by sections in Article I of the U.S. Constitution that grant all legislative powers to Congress, require Congress to oversee the implementation of all laws, and give Congress the power to make all laws necessary for executing its specified powers.

5. Limitations on agency powers include enabling legislation (which defines the scope of an agency's authority), executive controls (including the presidential power to appoint federal officers and to veto enabling legislation), and legislative controls (including the power to reduce or withhold funding for agencies). Agency powers are further checked by the Administrative Procedure Act of 1946 (which sets forth procedural requirements that all federal administrative agencies must follow) and by the courts through the process of judicial review.

6. The administrative process includes rulemaking, enforcement, and judicial functions. Agency rulemaking typically involves a three-step process: notifying the public of a proposed rule, receiving and reviewing comments from interested parties on the proposed rule, and publishing the final rule in the *Federal Register,* a daily government publication.

7. The agency's enforcement function involves investigation (including on-site inspections—if necessary to obtain information, the agency can issue subpoenas or search warrants) and adjudication. Most agency actions against violators are settled prior to adjudication. When an agency action is not settled to the satisfaction of both parties, the dispute will be adjudicated at a hearing conducted by an administrative law judge (ALJ). Hearing procedures vary from agency to agency and may be informal or formal. Following the hearing, the ALJ renders an initial order, which becomes the final order if it is not appealed. A party may request that an agency decision be reviewed by the commission or board that heads the agency (or other internal agency authority, depending on the agency's procedural requirements).

8. Ultimately, if a party has made every possible effort to obtain a remedy from an administrative agency and is still dissatisfied, the party normally may appeal the agency's decision to a court. Usually, a reviewing court defers to an agency's findings of fact, and the scope of judicial review is limited. A party challenging an agency decision must meet certain requirements before a court will review the case: the case must be one that is reviewable, and the party must have standing to sue the agency, must have exhausted all available administrative remedies, and must show that there is an actual controversy at issue.

9. Administrative agencies exist at all levels of American government—federal, state, and local. Many federal agencies have parallel state agencies, requiring that the paralegal be familiar with the administrative rules and procedures of both agencies. If a conflict of law arises between a federal and a state agency, the supremacy clause of the U.S. Constitution requires that the federal agency's decisions or rules take priority over those of the state agency.

10. Some agencies permit qualified paralegals to represent and advise clients during administrative proceedings. The appointment of a paralegal as a representative ordinarily requires a signed writing from the client that authorizes the paralegal to act as the client's agent, and the paralegal must meet agency requirements for nonlawyer representation.

QUESTIONS FOR REVIEW

1. Why are administrative agencies created? How are they created? By what government bodies are they created?

2. Why is it said that administrative agencies play a unique role in the American system of government? What is the source of an agency's powers?

3. How are agency powers constitutionally justified? How are agency powers held in check?

4. What steps are involved in the rulemaking process? How is the public informed of agency rules and proposed rules? Do people or interest groups outside the agency have any input in the rulemaking process?

5. How does an administrative agency investigate violations? Are there any limits on an agency's investigatory powers? If so, what are they?

6. How do agencies prosecute violations of their regulations? What is adjudication? Are all disputes involving administrative agency rules formally adjudicated?

7. How are agency hearings conducted? What is the role of the administrative law judge (ALJ)? What is the ALJ's decision called?

8. What requirements must be met before a party may appeal a federal administrative agency decision to a federal court?

9. How do the parallel state and federal agencies interrelate? If there is a conflict between a federal agency and a parallel state agency, which agency's decision takes priority, and why?

10. Under what authority are paralegals allowed to practice before administrative agencies? Name two agencies that allow nonlawyers to represent clients before them.

ETHICAL QUESTIONS

1. Trevor Holland is an independent paralegal who is interested in working in the area of workers' compensation. He contacts the state workers' compensation board to request information on whether a nonlawyer may represent clients who have workers' compensation claims. He is told that nonlawyers are not allowed to practice before the agency. What would happen if he began practicing in this area anyway?

2. Janet Koons is a legal assistant working for the state unemployment office. A young woman comes into the office to file a claim for unemployment compensation. The woman states that she was fired from her job while on maternity leave, although the duration of the leave did not exceed the leave time allotted by the company. The woman asks Janet if her job termination constitutes sex discrimination. Should Janet answer her question? What should she say?

PRACTICE QUESTIONS AND ASSIGNMENTS

1. Using the material on the rulemaking process discussed in this chapter, discuss the steps that an agency would follow if it wanted to create the following rule:

> Every legal assistant shall be entitled to have the day off on his or her birthday. If the birthday falls on a weekend or a holiday, the paralegal shall be given a day off during the week to celebrate his or her birthday.

2. Rhonda Raines works as a legal assistant for a busy attorney. While the attorney is taking a deposition in the firm's conference room, a client calls. The client owns a restaurant and has just returned from out of town to find an inspector from the Department of Health at the restaurant's door. The client has not inspected the kitchen yet, and he wants to look it over himself before the inspector sees it. If the restaurant gets another citation for violating the health code, the agency could put the restaurant out of business permanently. The client wants to know if there is any way that he can prevent the inspector from coming in and inspecting the restaurant. Rhonda tells him that the attorney is tied up, but that she can slip into the conference room and hand him a note asking what the client can do to put off the inspection. On the basis of what you have learned in this chapter, write a note from the attorney to Rhonda instructing the client on how to keep the inspector out of his kitchen.

3. Review the Kim Lee Barker hypothetical in this chapter. If the Social Security Administration (SSA) had found her not to be disabled, would Kim Lee have met the requirements necessary to have a federal court review the SSA's decision? Explain.

QUESTIONS FOR CRITICAL ANALYSIS

1. Do you think that Congress delegates too much of its authority to make and implement laws to administrative agencies?

2. The U.S. Constitution provides for a separation of powers among the executive, legislative, and judicial branches of government. Why, then, are administrative agencies allowed to exercise executive, legislative, and judicial powers? What would result if agencies could not exercise this combination of powers?

3. Some administrative agencies allow nonlawyers, such as paralegals, to represent clients in their dealings with the agencies. Can you think of any reasons why paralegals should not also be allowed to represent clients in court?

ROLE-PLAYING EXERCISES

1. Role-play the situation described in Practice Question 2, in which Rhonda Raines goes into the conference room, presents her supervising attorney with the note, and returns to the phone to relay the attorney's instructions to the client. The client should ask Rhonda some legal questions, such as the following: "What will happen if I insist that the inspector obtain a warrant?" "What do I do if he won't leave?" "How can I tell what a warrant looks like, if he returns with a paper that he calls a warrant?" Rhonda should be careful that her responses do not constitute the unauthorized practice of law.

2. Using the Kim Lee Barker hypothetical, role-play the DHSW hearing before Judge Powers, the ALJ. One person will need to play the role of Judge Powers, one the role of Calvin Novak, one the role of Ann Skinner, one the role of Morey Denton, and others the roles of Ted and Kim Lee Barker. The person playing the role of Calvin will need to spend some advance time preparing his oral argument based on the facts, evidence, and law presented in this chapter.

PROJECTS

1. Visit a local law library to determine if your state has an administrative code similar to the federal government's *Code of Federal Regulations*. If your state has such a code, what is it called? Does your state also have a publication similar to the *Federal Register*? If so, what is it called? How often is it published?

2. Using a telephone book or a state directory, make a list of five state administrative agencies that you would be interested in working for, along with the phone number of each agency. Call each agency and ask if nonlawyers are allowed to practice before that agency. Record your results and report them to the class. Discuss with others in the class which agency they would prefer to work for. Using the phone numbers listed in Exhibit 13.5, contact some federal agencies and see what their policies are in regard to nonlawyer representation.

3. Contact one of the state agencies listed in your answer to Project 2. Arrange to visit the agency to observe what kind of work paralegals perform at that agency.

ANNOTATED SELECTED READINGS

CONGRESSIONAL QUARTERLY, INC. *Federal Regulatory Directory.* 6th ed. Washington, D.C.: Congressional Quarterly, Inc., 1990. A nine-hundred-page guide to federal agencies. It is more agency specific than the *Washington Information Directory* (discussed below).

CONGRESSIONAL QUARTERLY, INC. *Washington Information Directory 1993–94.* Washington, D.C.: Congressional Quarterly, Inc., 1993. A one-thousand-page directory that will help you find "the right person, office, or organization" quickly and easily.

ENVIRONMENTAL PROTECTION AGENCY. *Access EPA.* Washington, D.C.: Government Printing Office, 1993. A helpful book that describes the various services provided by the EPA and that serves as a pathfinder to clearing-houses, hotlines, records, databases, models, and documents.

GELLHORN, ERNEST, AND RONALD M. LEVIN. *Administrative Law in a Nutshell.* St. Paul.: West Publishing Co., 1990. A book—part of the "Nutshell" series—that provides a detailed review of administrative law.

HADERS, WILLIAM D. *The Paralegal's Guide to Administrative Law.* Cincinnati: Anderson Publishing Co., 1994. A good overview of the principles of administrative law, agency activities, and several statutes, including workers' compensation statutes, the Social Security Act, and the Administrative Procedure Act.

Knight, Lynn C. "Paralegals in Federal Government." *National Paralegal Reporter,* Winter 1993. A useful look at paralegal jobs in federal government agencies. The article states that the federal government is one of the largest employers of paralegals, with over 300,000 law-related jobs for which paralegals may qualify. It gives the advantages and disadvantages of working for the government, describes the hiring process, and gives a close-up view of the job of paralegal specialist.

Parisi, Alice T. "Paralegal Opportunities in Environmental Law." *Legal Assistant Today,* January/February 1991. An article that provides insights into the variety of tasks involved in environmental law (and, by extension, in administrative law generally).

Sutherland, Linda, and Richard Herman. *The Paralegal's Guide to U.S. Government Jobs: How to Land a Job in 70 Law-Related Careers.* 6th ed. Washington, D.C.: Federal Law Reports, Inc., 1993. A useful book that, among other things, provides advice on how to obtain employment in administrative agencies.

14

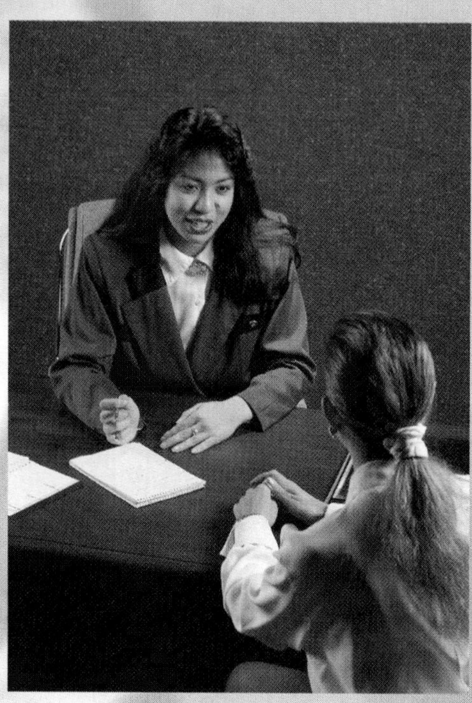

Conducting Interviews

Chapter Objectives

After completing this chapter, you will know:

- **What kinds of skills are employed during the interviewing process.**
- **What kinds of questions are most effective in eliciting responses from different types of clients or witnesses in different situations.**
- **Various types of listening strategies and how to use listening techniques in the interviewing context.**
- **How to prepare for an interview with a client or witness.**
- **The common types of client interviews.**
- **How to deal with different types of witnesses in the interviewing context.**

Chapter Outline

INTRODUCTION

Paralegals frequently interview clients. After the initial client interview (which is usually conducted by the supervising attorney), the paralegal may conduct one or more subsequent interviews to obtain detailed information from the client. How the paralegal relates to the client has an important effect on the client's attitude toward the firm and toward the attorney or legal team handling the case. Paralegals also often interview witnesses. As part of a preliminary investigation into a client's claim, for example, the paralegal may interview one or more witnesses to gain as much information as possible.

Learning how to conduct interviews is thus an important part of preparing for your career as a paralegal. In this chapter, you will read about the basic skills and concepts that you can apply when interviewing clients or witnesses.

INTERVIEWING SKILLS

INTERVIEWEE
The person who is being interviewed.

The primary goal of any interview is to obtain factual information from the **interviewee**—the person being interviewed. Interviewing skills are essentially any skills—particularly interpersonal and communication skills—that help you to attain this goal. In this section, you will learn how the use of interpersonal and communication skills can help you establish a comfortable relationship with the interviewee. Then, you will read about specific questioning and listening techniques that can help you control the interview and elicit various types of information.

Interpersonal Skills

At the outset of any interview, remember that your primary goal is to obtain information from the client or witness being interviewed. Although some people communicate information and ideas readily and effectively, others may need considerable coaching and encouragement. If they feel comfortable in your presence and in the interviewing environment, they will generally be more willing to disclose information. Here we look at some techniques that you can employ to put the interviewee at ease and establish a good working relationship with that person.

Put the Interviewee at Ease. As you begin an interview, you should remember that the interviewee may be very nervous or at least uncomfortable. Because the time you have to talk with a client or witness will be limited, you should put that individual at ease as quickly as possible. A minute or two spent chatting casually with the client or witness is time well spent. Also, saying or doing something that shows your concern for the interviewee's physical comfort helps to make the interviewee feel more relaxed. For example, you might offer the individual a cup of coffee or other beverage.

Use Language that Communicates. Using language that the interviewee will understand is essential in establishing a good working relationship with that person. If you are interviewing a client with only a grade-school education, for example, do not use the phrase "facial lacerations" when talking about "cuts on the face." If you are interviewing a witness who does not speak English very well, arrange to have an interpreter present unless you are fluent in the witness's native language.

When conducting interviews, you should be particularly attentive to the following fact:

- **Most clients and witnesses are not familiar with legal terminology. You should generally avoid using legal terms that will not be clearly understood by the interviewee.**

If you must use a specific legal term to express an idea, be sure that you define the term and that it is clearly understood.

Instill a Sense of Confidence and Trust. When you conduct an interview, you represent the firm for which you work—you are a member of a professional team. From the outset, you should try to instill in the client or witness a sense of confidence in your professional ability to deal with the matter at hand. You can do several things to accomplish this goal, including the following:

- Confidently greet the interviewee and give him or her your full attention.
- Make sure that the interviewee is aware of the relationship between specific questions and the general topic being explored during the interview. If you do not, the interviewee might assume that he or she is being placed in a subservient position and may be less willing to communicate. Also, by understanding the context, the interviewee can respond to the questions more appropriately.
- Use appropriate verbal language (avoid using slang and legalese, speak clearly, use grammatically correct sentences, and so on).
- Use appropriate nonverbal language (body language and facial gestures that show you are interested in what the interviewee is saying).
- Prevent unnecessary interruptions—hold all phone calls, for example—so that you can give your full attention to the interviewee.

In deciding what actions you might take to gain the interviewee's trust and confidence, you should also use common sense. Place yourself in the interviewee's position. What would cause you to trust or have confidence in an interviewer in a similar situation?

Questioning Skills

When questioning witnesses or clients, you should remember to remain objective at all times and gather as much relevant factual information as possible. Sometimes, you may have difficulty remaining objective when questioning witnesses because you sympathize with the client and may not want to hear about facts that are contrary to the client's position. But relevant factual information includes those details that adversely affect the client's case as well as those that support the client's position. Indeed, your supervising attorney must know *all* of the facts, especially any that might damage the client's case in court.

ETHICAL CONCERN

Confidentiality and Interviews

When you interview a client or a witness, a major concern on your part is to make sure that you fulfill the duty of confidentiality. If possible, arrange for the interview to be held in a conference room so that the interview will not be overheard by third parties. If a conference room is not available and you interview someone in your office, make sure that your desk and office are cleared of any confidential materials relating to other clients, and avoid taking phone calls in the presence of the interviewee. Also, escort the interviewee from the reception area to your office or to the conference room (and back to the reception area when the interview is over). Greeting a client or witness in the reception area and escorting him or her to the interviewing site is not only a courteous act but also helps to prevent the interviewee from overhearing or seeing confidential information.

The experienced legal interviewer uses certain questioning techniques to prompt the interviewees to communicate the information needed. There are several types of questions, including open-ended, closed-ended, hypothetical, pressure, and leading questions. Several of these question formats were discussed and illustrated in Chapter 2 in the context of employment interviews. Here, we look at how you can apply these formats when you interview clients or witnesses.

OPEN-ENDED QUESTION
A question that is phrased in such a way that it elicits a relatively detailed discussion of an experience or event.

Open-ended Questions. The **open-ended question** is a broad, exploratory question that invites any number of possible responses. The open-ended question can be used when you want to give the interviewee an opportunity to talk at some length about a given subject. "What happened on the night of October 28—the night of the murder?" is an open-ended question. Other examples of open-ended questions are "And what happened next?" and "What did you see as you approached the intersection?" When you ask a question of this kind, be prepared for a lengthy response. If a witness has difficulty in narrating the events that he or she observed or if a lull develops during the explanation, you will need to encourage the witness to continue through the use of various prompting responses (which will be discussed shortly in the context of listening skills).

Open-ended questions are useful in interviewing clients or friendly witnesses (witnesses who favor the client's position). This is because these kinds of interviewees are usually forthcoming, and you will be able to gain information from them by indicating in broad terms what you want them to describe.

CLOSED-ENDED QUESTION
A question that is phrased in such a way that it elicits a simple "yes" or "no" answer.

Closed-ended Questions. The **closed-ended question**, in contrast, is intended to elicit a "yes" or "no" response from the interviewee. "Did you see the murder weapon?" is an example of a closed-ended question. Although closed-ended questions tend to curb communication, they are useful in some situations. For example, if an interviewee tends to digress frequently from the topic being discussed, using closed-ended questions can help keep him or her on track. Closed-ended questions, because they invite specific answers, also may be useful in relaxing the interviewee in preparation for more difficult questions that may follow later in the interview. In addition, closed-ended questions may help to elicit information from adverse witnesses (those who are not favorable to the client's position) who may be reluctant to volunteer information.

HYPOTHETICAL QUESTION
A question based on hypothesis, conjecture, or fiction.

Hypothetical Questions. As a paralegal, you may be asked to interview an expert witness either to gather information about a case or to evaluate whether that person would be an effective expert witness at trial (expert witnesses will be discussed later in this chapter). The **hypothetical question** is frequently used with expert witnesses. Hypothetical questions allow you to obtain an answer to an important question without giving away the facts (and confidences) of a client's case. For example, you might invent a hypothetical situation involving a certain type of knee injury (the same kind of injury as that sustained by a client) and then ask an orthopedic surgeon what kind of follow-up care would ordinarily be undertaken for that type of injury.

Pressure Questions. Sometimes, interviewers use a type of question known as a pressure question. **Pressure questions** are intended to make the interviewee feel uncomfortable and to induce the interviewee to respond emotionally. The pressure question may be useful in eliciting a response from an interviewee who is reluctant to discuss a matter with you. If an eyewitness, for example, refuses to state whether he or she saw the murderer, an interviewer might pressure him or her into responding by asking a question such as the following: "The murder weapon—a heavy board—was found a mile from the victim's body. Did you know that the board was traced to the construction site right next door to your store?"

PRESSURE QUESTION
A question intended to make the interviewee feel uncomfortable and respond emotionally. Pressure questions are sometimes used by interviewers to elicit answers from interviewees who may otherwise be unresponsive.

Note that pressure questions should be used only as a last resort and then used very carefully. As an interviewer, you want to enlist the interviewee's cooperation, not alienate him or her.

Leading Questions. The **leading question** is one that suggests to the listener the answer to the question. "Isn't it true that you were only ten feet away from where the murder took place?" is a leading question. This question, of course, invites a "yes" answer. Leading questions are very effective for drawing information out of eyewitnesses or clients, particularly when they are reluctant to disclose information. They are also useful when interviewing adverse witnesses who are reluctant to communicate information that may be helpful to the client's position. When used with clients and friendly witnesses, however, leading questions have a major drawback:

LEADING QUESTION
A question that suggests, or "leads to," a desired answer. Interviewers may use leading questions to elicit responses from witnesses who otherwise would not be forthcoming.

- **Leading questions may lead to distorted answers because the client or witness may tailor the answer to fit his or her perception of what the interviewer wants to know.**

For this reason, in the interviewing context, leading questions should be used cautiously and only when the interviewer is fully aware of the possible distortions that might result. For additional examples of leading questions, see Exhibit 14.1.

Listening Skills

The interviewer's ability to listen is perhaps the most important communication skill used during the interviewing process. Whenever you conduct an

EXHIBIT 14.1
Leading Questions

Q. You were drinking beer in the parking lot during lunch and then got behind the wheel to drive anyway, didn't you?

A. Yes.

Q. You saw the driver of the green van run the stop sign, right?

A. Yes.

Q. Isn't it true that you were so intoxicated at the time of the accident that you can't remember what happened?

A. Yes.

interview, you will want to absorb fully the interviewee's verbal answers as well as his or her nonverbal messages. Prior to the interview, you should make sure that the room in which the interview is to be held will be free of noises, phone calls, visitors, and other interruptions or distractions. Recall from Chapter 5 that noises and other distractions impede the communication process because they make attentive listening difficult. During the interview itself, you can use several listening techniques to maximize communication and guide the interviewee toward the fullest disclosure of needed information.

ACTIVE LISTENING
The act of listening attentively to the speaker's verbal or nonverbal messages and responding to those messages by giving appropriate feedback.

Active Listening. Communication is an interactive process that requires the listener to engage in active listening. **Active listening** requires the listener to pay close attention to what the speaker is saying. Paying attention to every detail of the discussion is critical to a productive interview. Lack of attention means that important details may be missed, and ultimately, the client will suffer.

- **If you ever find your attention wandering during an interview, have the interviewee repeat what he or she just said to make sure that you have not missed anything.**

You do not have to admit that your attention was wandering, of course. Simply say that you want to make sure that your impression of what the interviewee said is accurate.

Active listening also involves feedback. As a listener, you can give feedback, in the form of both verbal and nonverbal cues, to encourage the speaker to continue discussing a topic. An example of a verbal cue is "I'm listening, please go on." A nonverbal cue can be any facial expression or body language that shows you are interested in what is being said. Nodding positively, for example, is an effective way to convey, nonverbally, your interest.

Finally, active listening involves the ability to analyze on the spot the interviewee's comments in the context of the larger picture. Often, something that the interviewee says opens a door to another area that should be explored. When this happens, you need to decide whether to explore that area now or later—perhaps at a subsequent interview.

- **In general, you need to be constantly analyzing your interviewee's responses and deciding how those responses should direct your further questioning.**

RETENTIVE LISTENING
The act of listening attentively to what the speaker is saying for the purpose of remembering, or retaining, the information communicated.

Retentive Listening. Whenever your primary goal in listening is to remember what somebody is saying, you are engaging in **retentive listening**. Retentive listening requires, first of all, that you understand exactly what was said. We often assume that we understand messages only to learn later, when we act on them or try to relay them to another person, that we are not really clear on what was said. A good way to test your understanding of a message is to rephrase it in your own words. If you are not sure of what an interviewee means by a certain statement or phrase, for example, rephrase it in your own words and ask the interviewee if that is what he or she meant by the statement. For example, if a witness says, "I saw him do it," you might clarify the meaning of that statement by saying, "Do you mean that you saw the person throw the heavy board into the pond?"

Once a message is clarified, you will want to retain it. Taking notes during the interview facilitates the retention of important information. How extensively you take notes and what information you include in your notes will depend, to some extent, on whether the interview is being tape-recorded. (The use of tape recorders for interviews will be discussed later.)

Supportive Listening. There may be times during an interview when you must show support for the interviewee. For example, suppose that you are conducting a preliminary investigation on behalf of a client who was seriously injured in a car accident. You are interviewing an eyewitness to the accident, who happens to be a good friend of the client. Although your primary interest is in the information being disclosed, you must also show that you are concerned for the witness's feelings and that you understand how difficult it is for the witness to describe the crash. This kind of listening is sometimes referred to as **supportive listening**.

SUPPORTIVE LISTENING
The act of providing comments, utterances, or gestures that convey to the speaker an interest in what the speaker is saying and that encourage the speaker to continue speaking.

In the interviewing context, supportive listening may be employed effectively to encourage a client or witness to continue speaking about his or her perceptions or feelings in regard to a certain matter. Let the speaker know that you are listening attentively by giving appropriate feedback. Maintaining eye contact and murmuring an "uh huh" here or a "hmm" there may suffice. Alternatively, you might give supportive feedback in the form of a question or two, such as "And then what happened?" Asking questions not only provides feedback but it also allows the speaker to elaborate on the message being sent.

Reading Body Language. In the courtroom, the credibility, or believability, of a witness giving testimony is strongly affected by body language. The ability to read body language is also an important skill for the interviewer. As experienced interviewers know, some of the most informative communication is transmitted nonverbally through facial expressions, other body movements, and general demeanor (how one sits, stands, moves, and so on). By carefully observing body language, you can, in effect, "listen between the lines." The paralegal interviewing a witness may ask the question, "Why were you in the store at the time of the murder?" The witness's response, "To buy a few groceries," may seem insincere if she shifts around in her seat, crosses and uncrosses her legs, and clears her throat before answering the question.

Learning how to read nonverbal communication may help you not only to interpret an interviewee's responses more accurately but also to determine whether a client or potential witness will be able to testify effectively on the client's behalf. (This topic will be discussed further in Chapter 15.)

PLANNING THE INTERVIEW

Planning an interview involves organizing many details. As a paralegal, you may be responsible for locating a witness (see Chapter 15), scheduling the interview, determining where the interview should take place, arranging for

DEVELOPING PARALEGAL SKILLS

The Importance of Body Language

Robin Lewis, a paralegal in a law firm, is interviewing witnesses in a negligence case involving an automobile accident. Joe Carrega, a witness to the accident, is shown into her office. He sits down in the chair next to her desk. He folds his arms across his chest and looks down toward the floor. Robin begins by asking him his name. Without looking at her, he mumbles, "Joe Carrega."

Robin begins to ask him questions regarding the accident. She begins with the question, "What did you observe at the time of the accident?" Joe continues to look at the floor as he responds, "The red car struck the brown van, which was in the intersection, because it ran the red light. The red car was driving very fast, too fast for a business area, and it seemed to be weaving back and forth between lanes. The brown van rolled over twice after being struck by the red car and stopped when it hit a snow bank." Joe speaks very rapidly and does not pause between sentences or change his tone of voice. After making these statements, his eyes flash up, he glances quickly at Robin, and then he looks downward again toward the floor.

Robin asks Joe several more questions about the accident. He never looks at her while answering and continues to speak rapidly. Robin asks Joe if he remembers if there were other people who witnessed the accident. He again fires off a rapid answer, "Yeah," Joe responds. "Another guy named Tony stopped and went over to the brown van to see if he could help the driver." Robin asks Joe for Tony's full name and address. Joe tells her he does not know that information.

When Robin has finished questioning Joe, she excuses him. Joe gets up and leaves, without ever looking at Robin. She makes a note on her pad that reads, "Joe Carrega's body language indicated that he was very nervous. He glanced at me only once, looking at the floor during the rest of the interview. He always spoke very rapidly, and he sat with his arms and legs crossed. He would not make a good impression on a jury."

the use of one of the firm's conference rooms or other office space for the interview, and other related details. The following discussion will help prepare you to plan either client or witness interviews.

Scheduling the Interview

When scheduling an interview, you should make sure that sufficient time is set aside for the interview session. When the session will be attended by other members of the law firm, such as an attorney or another paralegal specialist, their schedules must also be coordinated. The time required for an interview varies depending on the purpose of the interview. An initial client interview may require forty-five minutes or more. A subsequent interview with the client may require fifteen minutes or an hour or more, depending on how much information must be gathered.

Whenever possible, you should schedule interviews for a time of day when you will be relatively free of distractions—perhaps at the beginning or end of the workday. You should also consider such factors as the interviewee's schedule and the time of day during which people are normally more alert and attentive—such as mid-morning or sometime before lunch.

With experience, the paralegal interviewer becomes adept at judging how long a given interview will take, when to schedule it, and which members of the firm or legal team should attend the interview.

Preparing the Interviewee

You should give the client or witness ample notice of the upcoming interview. You should also indicate what items or documents the interviewee should bring to the interview. At times, the request may be very general ("Bring any information you have relating to the problem"); at other times, the request will be more specific ("Bring in your bank statements for the months of June and July"). When a client petitioning for bankruptcy is to be interviewed, you may want to ask him or her to bring in numerous financial documents. If an expert witness, such as a handwriting expert, is to be interviewed, you may ask the witness to bring credentials sufficient to verify his or her expertise.

Once an interview is scheduled and the interviewee is notified (usually by phone), you might want to send the interviewee a follow-up, confirming letter as a reminder. The letter will state the time and place of the interview and list the documents or items that the interviewee should bring to the interview.

Preparing Questions

Prior to any interview, you should have clearly in mind the kind of information you want to obtain from the client or witness. You should know what questions you want to ask and have them prepared in advance. Crucial to the success of any interview is how well you are prepared for it. Advance preparation for an interview depends, of course, on the type of interview being conducted.

Preprinted or Computerized Forms. In many situations, the paralegal (or the firm) will already have created specific preprinted or computerized forms indicating what kind of information should be gathered during client interviews relating to particular types of claims. Using preprinted forms ensures that all essential information will be obtained.

If you are interviewing a client who is petitioning for bankruptcy, for example, you will need to obtain from the client the types of information that must be included in the bankruptcy forms to be submitted to the court. The bankruptcy forms will serve as a checklist for you to follow during the client interview. Similarly, if your firm frequently handles personal-injury cases, you will probably have available a preprinted or computerized personal-injury intake sheet, such as that shown in Exhibit 14.2 on the following pages, to use as a guide when obtaining client information during the initial client interview.

Preparing Your Own Checklist. At times, you will need to devise your own checklist of questions to ask during an interview. For example, suppose

ETHICAL CONCERN

Handling Client Documents

Clients frequently give paralegals important documents relating to their cases during interviews. As stressed in Chapter 3, state codes of ethics impose strict requirements on attorneys in regard to the safekeeping of clients' funds and other property, including documents. Suppose, for example, that a client gives you, during an interview, the only copy she has of her divorce agreement. You should never rely on memory when it comes to client documents. Instead, immediately after the conclusion of the interview, you should record the receipt of any documents or other items received from the client. The information may be recorded in an evidence log (discussed in Chapter 15) or otherwise, depending on the procedures established by your firm to govern the receipt and storage of such property. An evidence log or other method of recording documents and items received from clients provides you with evidence—should it be necessary—of what you did (or did not) receive from a client.

EXHIBIT 14.2
Personal-injury Intake Sheet

PERSONAL-INJURY INTAKE SHEET

Prepared for Clients of
Jeffers, Gilmore & Dunn

1. Client Information:

Name: Katherine Baranski

Address: 335 Natural Blvd.
Nita City, NI 48802

Social Security No.: 206-15-9858

Marital Status: Married Years Married: 3

Spouse's Name: Peter Baranski

Children: None

Phone Numbers: Home (473) 555-2211 Work (473) 555-4849

Employer: Nita State University
Mathematics Department

Position: Instructor of Mathematics

Responsibilities: Teaching

Salary: $ 36,000

2. Related Information:

Client at Scene: Yes

Lost Work Time: 5 months

Client's Habits: Normally drives south on Mattis avenue on way to university each morning at about the same time.

that a client of your firm was injured in an automobile accident and is bringing a lawsuit against the driver of the other car for negligence. You are conducting a preliminary investigation into the case and have scheduled an interview with an eyewitness to the accident. In this situation, you may not have a prepared form to guide you. The kinds of questions that you will need to ask the witness will be determined by a number of factors, including the factual background of the case already known to you and your supervising attorney, the law governing the client's claim, and your supervising attor-

EXHIBIT 14.2
Continued

3. Incident/Accident:

Date: August 4, 1995 Time: 7:45 A.M.

Place: Mattis Avenue and 38th street, Nita City, Nita

Description: Mrs. Baranski was driving south on Mattis avenue when a car driven by Tony Peretto, who was attempting to cross Mattis at 38th Street, collided with Mrs. Baranski's vehicle.

Witnesses: None known by Mrs. Baranski

Defendant: Tony Peretto

Police: Nita City

Action Taken: Mrs. Baranski was taken to City Hospital by ambulance (Nita City Ambulance Co.).

4. Injuries Sustained:

Nature: Multiple fractures to left hip and leg; lacerations to left eye and left side of face; multiple contusions and abrasions

Medical History: No significant medical problems prior to the accident

Treating Hospital: Nita City Hospital

Treating Physician: Dr. Swanson

Hospital Stay: August 4, 1995 to November 20, 1995

Insurance: Southwestern Insurance Co. of America

Policy No: 00631150962 -B

Interview Conducted by:

Allen P. Gilmore — January 30, 1996
Attorney — Date

Elena Lopez — January 30, 1996
Paralegal/Witness — Date

ney's legal strategy. In Chapter 15, you will read in further detail about the kinds of information that are obtained from witnesses during preliminary investigations.

Whether you use a prepared form or a checklist that you create yourself, you should always abide by the following rule:

- **Never let the form or checklist become a substitute for human interaction.**

In other words, do not let a printed form or checklist constrain a client's comments on a legal matter or concern—so long as the client does not stray too far from relevant topics, of course. Part of your value as a team member lies in your ability to relate to clients on a personal, human level. Also, as will be discussed later in this chapter, much valuable information may be learned through casual or unanticipated comments made by a client during an interview.

Preparing the Interview Environment

Usually, clients are interviewed at the law firm's offices. Witnesses may be interviewed in their homes or at some other place convenient to them. When you are deciding where an interview should take place within your firm's offices, a foremost concern is confidentiality, as mentioned earlier. Also, you should prevent potential distractions and interruptions by making sure that the environment is quiet and that you will not be interrupted by phone calls or by other employees entering or leaving the area during the interview.

A large table may be useful if the interviewee will be bringing documents to be examined. Prepare the room by setting out anything you might want to have at hand during the interview, such as pencils, note pads, or any special documents to which you might want to refer (or show to the client). If you plan to tape-record the session (to be discussed shortly), have the equipment set up, tested, and ready to operate before the interview begins

You might also give some thought to seating arrangements. Where you seat the client or witness during the interview may help to make the person feel more at ease and comfortable. If you seat someone across a desk or table

---

The Legal Team at Work
Humanizing Legal Practice

Clients know that attorneys often face busy schedules and that an attorney's time is costly. For both of these reasons, clients are often reluctant to talk to their attorneys about matters that do not seem essential to the legal representation. The team approach opens the door to improved attorney-client communications by involving paralegals and support staff in the legal work for the client. Some firms that use the teamwork approach advise clients at the outset that whenever they want to contact the office, it is to their advantage to contact the paralegal first because the paralegal's time is less costly. If the paralegal can handle a client's question or problem, the client will not have to bear the greater expense involved in a consultation with the attorney. Clients tend to communicate more frequently—and more freely—with paralegals and support staff than they do with the attorneys because of the lower cost involved. Details that the client might have been reluctant to discuss with the attorney, but that may be critical to a successful resolution of the client's case, may thus emerge in the course of a casual conversation with the paralegal. As many attorneys have realized, the team approach not only increases communication possibilities but also adds a more personal, human touch to legal practice.

from you, for example, that person may sense that this meeting will be confrontational because of the barrier between you. Placing someone at a right angle to your desk or sitting side-by-side may convey a more collaborative spirit. Exhibit 14.3 illustrates some possible seating arrangements that are conducive to good communication.

Recording the Interview

Some interviewers tape-record their interviews. Before you tape-record an interview, you should always do the following:

- **Obtain permission to tape-record the interview from both your supervising attorney and the person being interviewed.**

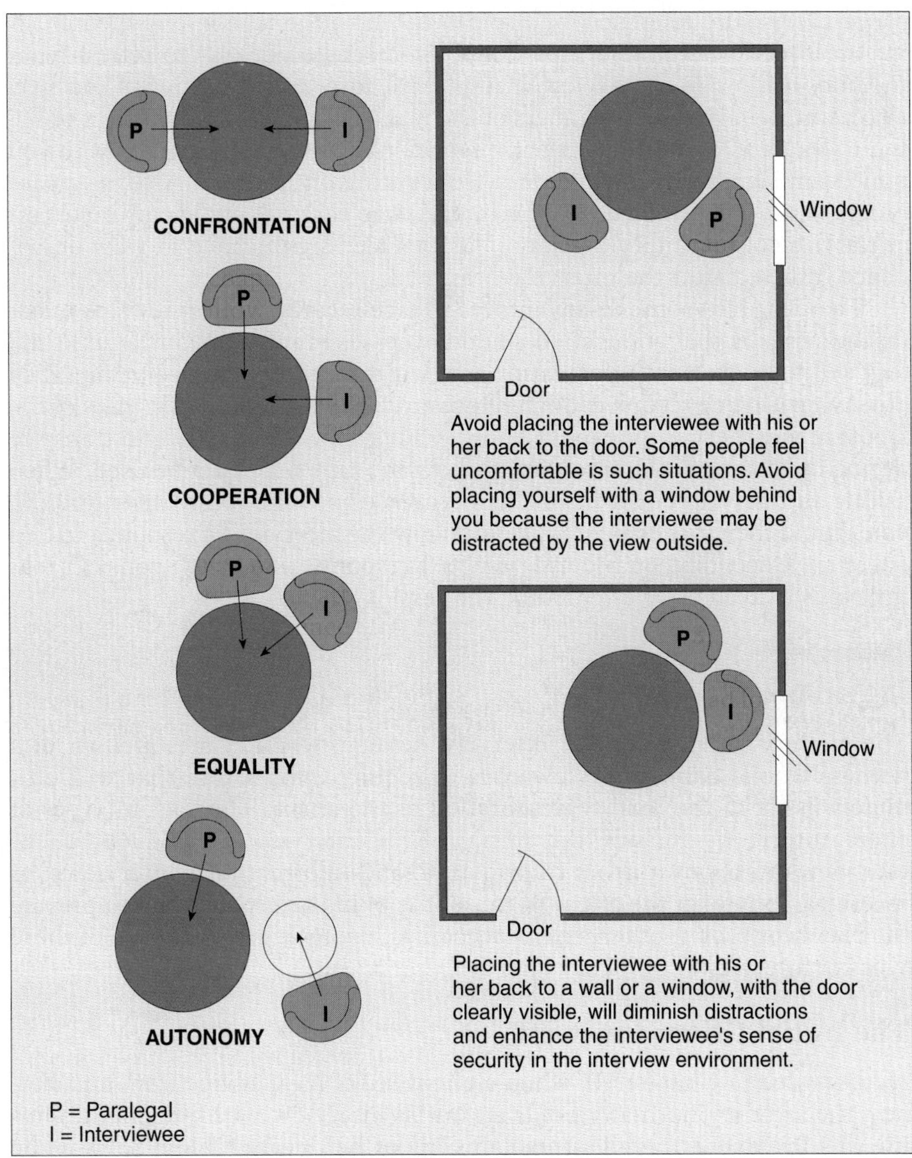
P
I
CONFRONTATION
P
I
COOPERATION
P
I
EQUALITY
P
I
AUTONOMY
P = Paralegal
I = Interviewee
I
P
Window
Door
Avoid placing the interviewee with his or her back to the door. Some people feel uncomfortable is such situations. Avoid placing yourself with a window behind you because the interviewee may be distracted by the view outside.
P
I
Window
Door
Placing the interviewee with his or her back to a wall or a window, with the door clearly visible, will diminish distractions and enhance the interviewee's sense of security in the interview environment.

EXHIBIT 14.3
Seating Arrangements

When you are using a tape recorder, you should state at the beginning of the tape the following identifying information:

- The name of the person being interviewed and any other information about the interviewee that is relevant.
- The name of the person conducting the interview.
- The names of other persons present at the interview, if any.
- The date, time, and place of the interview.

If more than one tape is used, you should indicate at the end of each tape that the interview will be continued on the next tape in the series, and each subsequent tape should contain identifying information.

There are several advantages to tape-recording an interview. For one thing, having a record of the interview on tape reduces the need to take extensive notes during the interview. You can either have the tape transcribed for future reference, or you can listen to the tape later (when creating an interview summary, for example—discussed below) to refresh your memory of how the interviewee responded to certain questions. You may also want to have other members of the legal team read the transcript or listen to the tape. Sometimes, what might not have seemed significant to you may seem significant to someone else working on the case. Also, as a case progresses, a remark made by the interviewee that did not seem important at the time of the interview may take on added significance in view of evidence gathered after the interview was held.

There are also some disadvantages to tape-recording interviews. A major disadvantage is that some clients and witnesses may be uncomfortable and less willing to disclose information freely if they know that everything they are saying is being recorded. Such reluctance is understandable in view of the fact that the interviewee cannot know in advance what exactly will transpire during the course of the interview or how the tape may later be used. When asking an interviewee for his or her permission to tape-record an interview, you should therefore evaluate carefully how the interviewee responds to this question. Depending on the interviewee's response, you might consider taking notes instead of tape-recording the session.

ETHICAL CONCERN

Telephone Interviews and Confidentiality

When you must interview a witness or a client over the phone, you should take special care that your conversation will not be overheard by other persons who are not dealing directly with the client's case. For example, suppose that you are about to begin a telephone conference with a client. You are sitting in your office, alone, and there is no one in the reception area outside your office door. Just as you connect via phone with the client, an attorney from an office in the same building enters the reception area and overhears you saying, "Hello, Mr. Palermo? This is Elena Lopez in Mr. Gilmore's office. Are you ready to start our interview about your malpractice action against Dr. Sloan?" At this point, you notice the other attorney and realize the consequences of having left your door open. The attorney now knows not only that Mr. Palermo is your client but also that he is suing Dr. Sloan, a well-known heart surgeon. To avoid breaching the duty of confidentiality when conducting telephone interviews, you should always make sure that you close your office door (or the door to whatever room you are using) before beginning the telephone conversation.

INTERVIEWING CLIENTS

The primary objective of any interview session, whether it is a client or a witness who is being interviewed, is to acquire information that will ultimately assist in the legal representation of the client. The various types of client interviews include the initial client interview, subsequent client interviews to obtain further information, and informational interviews, or meetings, to inform the client of the status of his or her case and to prepare the client for trial or other legal proceedings. We look below at each of these types of interviews.

The Initial Client Interview

As discussed in Chapter 10, when a client seeks legal advice from an attorney, the attorney normally holds an initial interview with the client. During this interview, the client explains his or her legal problem so that the

DEVELOPING PARALEGAL SKILLS

The Tape-recorded Interview

Justin Hooper, a paralegal, is preparing for an interview that will be tape-recorded. Justin has already received permission to tape-record the interview from his supervising attorney and from the witness to be interviewed. The first step is to set up the tape recorder in the conference room in which the interview will take place. After Justin sets it up, he inserts a new, blank tape into the recorder and tests it to make sure that the tape and the recorder work.

The witness arrives and is shown into the conference room by the receptionist. From a file folder, Justin removes a prepared statement containing the introductory remarks typically used in a tape-recorded interview. He reads it into the tape recorder: "My name is Justin Hooper, a paralegal at the law firm of Smith & Howard, representing Mr. Barry Buckner, the defendant in *Jones v. Buckner.* What follows is a taped interview with Ms. Jennifer Tompkins, a witness to the accident that is the subject of the *Jones v. Buckner* litigation. This tape-recorded interview is taking place in the law offices of Smith & Howard on January 6, 1996. The time is two o'clock P.M."

Justin then turns to the witness and asks, "Ms. Tompkins, will you please state and spell your first and last name for the record?" Ms. Tompkins responds accordingly. Next, Justin asks, "Ms. Tompkins, may we record the interview that we are about to conduct?" Ms. Tompkins answers, "Yes, you have my permission to record today's interview." Justin then begins the interview.

attorney can advise the client on possible legal options and the legal fees that may be involved. Either then or at a later time, the client and the attorney will agree on the terms of the representation, if the attorney decides to take the case.

Paralegals often attend initial client interviews. Although the attorney normally conducts this first interview, the paralegal plays an important role. Usually, you will observe the client, take notes on what the client is saying, and provide the client with forms, statements explaining the firm's fees, and other prepared information that is normally given to new clients. Following the interview, you and the attorney may compare your impressions of the client and of what the client said during the interview.

All of the law-firm personnel present at the interview should be introduced to the client, their titles given, and the reason for their presence at the interview made known to the client. In introducing you, the paralegal, to the potential client, the attorney will probably stress that you are not a lawyer.

- **If your supervising attorney does not indicate your nonattorney status to the client, you must do so.**

If a firm decides to take a client's case, the client should be introduced to every member of the legal team who will be working on the case.

A follow-up letter, such as the one shown in Exhibit 14.4 on the next page, will be sent to the client after the interview. The letter will state whether or not the attorney has decided to accept the case or, if the attorney

EXHIBIT 14.4
A Sample Follow-up Letter to a Client

Jeffers, Gilmore & Dunn
553 Fifth Avenue
Suite 101
Nita City, NI 48801

Telephone: (616) 555-9690
Fax: (616) 555-9679

February 2, 1996

Ms. Katherine Baranski
335 Natural Boulevard
Nita City, Nita 48802

Dear Ms. Baranski:

It was a pleasure to meet and talk with you on January 30. Jeffers, Gilmore & Dunn will be pleased to act as your representative in your action against Tony Peretto to obtain compensation for your injuries.

I am enclosing a fee agreement for your review. If you wish this firm to act as your legal counsel, please sign and date the agreement and return it to me as soon as possible. A self-addressed, stamped enveloped is enclosed for your convenience. As soon as I receive the completed agreement, we will begin investigating your case.

As I advised during our meeting, to protect your rights, please refrain from speaking with the driver of the vehicle, his lawyer, or his insurance company. If they attempt to contact you, simply tell them that you have retained counsel and refer them directly to me. I will handle any questions that they may have.

If you have any questions, please do not hesitate to call me or my paralegal, Ms. Elena Lopez.

Sincerely,

Allen P. Gilmore

Allen P. Gilmore
Attorney at Law

APG/db

Encs.

orally agreed during the initial client interview to represent the client, will confirm the oral agreement in writing.

Subsequent Client Interviews

Paralegals are often asked to conduct additional interviews with clients whose cases have been accepted. For example, assume that a client wants to obtain a divorce. After the initial interview, your supervising attorney may ask you to arrange for a subsequent interview with the client to obtain all the information necessary to prepare the divorce pleadings. When scheduling the interview, you should tell the client what kinds of documents or other data the client should bring to the interview. During the interview, you will fill out the form that the firm uses to record client information in divorce cases. Paralegals often assume responsibility for gathering most of the information needed to file for a divorce or to begin child-custody proceedings.

When conducting a client interview, the paralegal should always disclose his or her nonlawyer status if this fact was not made clear at an earlier session. Remember, even if you had been introduced to the client as a "legal assistant," the client may not realize that a legal assistant is not an attorney. To protect yourself against potential claims that you have engaged in the unauthorized practice of law, you should clearly state to the client that you are "not an attorney."

The Informational Interview

The informational interview, or meeting, is an interview in which the client is brought in to discuss upcoming legal proceedings. Most clients know very little about the procedures involved in litigation, and firms often have their paralegals explain these procedures to clients and prepare clients for the trial experience. For example, the paralegal can describe to clients what will take place during the trial, how to groom themselves appropriately for trial, where to look when they testify, and so on. The informational interview helps the client understand why certain proceedings are taking place and his or her role in those proceedings.

Summarizing the Interview

The interviewing process does not end with the close of the interview. A final and crucial step in the process involves summarizing the results of the interview for the legal team working on the case. As a paralegal, you will create an intake memorandum following each initial client interview. If the firm has a prepared intake form for particular types of cases, such as the personal-injury intake sheet referred to earlier and illustrated in Exhibit 14.2, the completed form might constitute the interview summary. Information obtained during any subsequent interviews with a client should be analyzed and summarized in a memo for your supervising attorney or other team members to review and for later inclusion in the client's file.

Your interview summary should be created immediately after the interview, while the session is still fresh in your mind. When summarizing the results of a client interview, you should carefully review your notes and, if the session was tape-recorded, review the tape. You should never rely totally on your memory of the statements made during the interview. It is very easy to forget the client's exact words, and it may be very important later to know exactly how the client phrased a certain comment or response. Relying on memory is also risky because, as mentioned earlier, sometimes a statement that seemed irrelevant at the time of the interview may turn out to be very important to the case. You should thus make sure that the facts are accurately recorded and are as reliable as possible.

ETHICAL CONCERN

Interviewing Clients and the Unauthorized Practice of Law

Paralegals must be especially careful not to give legal advice when interviewing clients. Suppose that you are conducting a follow-up interview of a client, Sue Collins. Collins was injured in a car accident and is suing the driver of the other car involved in the accident for negligence. During the initial client interview, Collins told you and your supervising attorney that the accident was totally the result of the other driver's negligence. During the course of your follow-up interview, however, Collins presents you with an interesting hypothetical. She says to you, "What would happen, in a lawsuit such as mine, if the plaintiff was not watching the road when the accident occurred? What if the plaintiff was looking in the back seat to see why her baby was crying? Could the plaintiff still expect to win in court?" You know that under the laws of your state, contributory negligence on the part of the plaintiff (discussed in Chapter 8) is an absolute bar to the recovery of damages. Should you explain this to Collins? No. Even though the question is phrased as a hypothetical, it is possible that your answer could affect Collins's future actions. Your best option is tell Collins that you are not permitted to give legal advice but that you will relay the "hypothetical" question to your supervising attorney.

FEATURED GUEST: ANNA DURHAM BOLING

Ten Tips for More Effective Interviewing

Biographical Note

Anna Durham Boling graduated from the University of Georgia School of Law in 1984 and is licensed to practice law in the state of Georgia. Following graduation from law school, Boling practiced real-estate law for four years. She then accepted a position as an instructor in the paralegal studies program at Athens Area Technical Institute in Athens, Georgia. She was named director of the program in July 1989. Under her direction, the program was approved by the American Bar Association in February 1992. Boling currently works for the Institute of Government at the University of Georgia.

Interviewing clients and witnesses is a learned skill. Interviewers, whether they are lawyers, legal assistants, or others, become more effective over time as they acquire more interviewing experience. There are many interviewing "tips" that can enhance the abilities of even the novice interviewer, however. The following suggestions are the ones that I have found to be particularly helpful. As you develop your interviewing skills, you may find that the tips that serve you best are the ones you develop yourself. In the meantime, you can learn from the experiences of others.

1 Verify Information. When interviewing clients and witnesses, realize that every bit of information obtained must be verified. I do not mean to suggest that all clients or all witnesses lie (although, unfortunately, some do). On the contrary, each individual client or witness will describe his or her perception of what happened, and you will find that no two people ever perceive the same factual occurrence in exactly the same way. A good way to verify information is therefore to interview several people about the event or issue under investigation. Another way to verify information is to use additional sources, such as documentary evidence.

2 Let the Interviewee Vent His or Her Emotions. Sometimes, clients or witnesses come to interviews with heightened emotions regarding the matters about which they are to be questioned. In such situations, they may need an opportunity to vent their feelings before they can relax enough to discuss a subject that is painful or bothersome to them. When this happens, it is often helpful to put the time clock aside and interact with the interviewee on a personal level. Showing compassion for the interviewee's emotional needs will help you establish a rapport with that person, which will enhance the possibility of effective communication.

3 Keep an Open Mind. Be careful not to categorize a client's problem. Both the interviewer and the person being interviewed can fall prey to this trap, particularly during the initial interview. For example, a client in financial distress might say that he wants to declare bankruptcy. All he knows is that his financial situation is worsening and that he wants to obtain some relief. He thinks that bankruptcy is the only answer, but there may be other answers to the client's dilemma, and other legal issues may be involved. Explore the client's entire situation. In this example, find out what caused the financial distress so that you can better understand the client's specific circumstances. In this way, the legal team will be better able to offer the best and most complete service possible.

4 Listen Carefully. Listen carefully to the person being inter-

FEATURED GUEST, Continued

viewed. Do not make assumptions about the interviewee or anticipate a particular answer before asking the question. An interviewer taking this approach may miss important or even critical information. Learn to listen to the interviewee's answers and "digest" the information objectively—without letting any assumptions interfere with the listening process. In this way, you may discern valuable pieces of information that could significantly affect the outcome of the case.

5 Record Information. Write down everything that is learned in the course of an interview. Recording the information on paper, on a computer, or with a tape recorder is especially important for the beginner because of the level of detail that must be reported. You may think, "I could never forget that piece of information." But in a busy practice full of distractions, you may have forgotten that information by the end of the interview.

6 Engage in Interactive Communication. Interviewing should be interactive. It should involve a meaningful exchange between the interviewer and the interviewee. When listening to the answers to your questions, ask yourself, "In light of this response, what else would I like to know?" By posing this question to yourself, you will be able to carry each line of questioning to its logical extreme and, in doing so, arrive at the most complete picture possible.

7 Be Prepared for the Interview. Be thoroughly prepared for your interview. Preparation is particularly important for the inexperienced interviewer. Reviewing closed files in your law firm that are similar to the case at hand is often very helpful. Determine what information in those files is significant. Notice which questions recur from file to file. This will enable you to construct a line of questioning that will elicit the desired information. Interview preparation is time consuming, but the benefits can be enormous. As your interviewing skills develop, the preparation time for subsequent interviews will decrease significantly.

8 Learn the Chronology of the Factual Circumstances. If possible, have the person being interviewed relate what he or she knows about the subject matter of your investigation in the order in which the events occurred. If the interviewee can relay his or her story in this manner, then the risk of omitting important facts is lessened substantially. Encourage your interviewee to supply as complete a description as possible and to avoid omitting any details. Although this request may elicit some useless information, it is better to have too much, rather than too little, information. You will be able to weed out unimportant or irrelevant information after the interview.

9 Remain Objective. It is important to have an objective understanding of the client's problem. When assisting in the representation of a client, it is quite natural to feel sympathy for that person, particularly if he or she has suffered a substantial hardship. But too much sympathy may prevent you from objectively evaluating the factual circumstances of the client's case. Remember that your supervising attorney will be in a better position to defend the client's interests if the attorney is aware of all information relating to the case, including information that appears to be unfavorable to the client's interests.

10 Evaluate the Results. Just as it is important to prepare for interviews, it is important to review your work once the case has been resolved. In retrospect, you can determine whether any information that turned out to be important to the case was missed and if so, how or why it was missed. You can also learn how important information was successfully obtained. This evaluation exercise will enhance your effectiveness as an interviewer and help you prepare for interviews in future cases.

"INTERVIEWING CLIENTS AND WITNESSES IS A LEARNED SKILL."

INTERVIEWING WITNESSES

Interviewing witnesses is in many ways similar to interviewing clients. A major difference between clients and witnesses, however, is that the latter may not always be friendly to the client's position.

Types of Witnesses

Witnesses include expert witnesses, lay witnesses, eyewitnesses, friendly witnesses, and adverse (or hostile) witnesses.

EXPERT WITNESS
A witness with professional training or substantial experience qualifying him or her to testify on a particular subject.

Expert Witnesses. An **expert witness** is an individual who has professional training, advanced knowledge, or substantial experience in a specialized area, such as medicine, computer technology, ballistics, or construction techniques. Paralegals often arrange to hire expert witnesses either to testify in court or to render an opinion on some matter relating to the client's case. Expert witnesses are often used in cases involving medical malpractice and product liability to establish the duty, or standard of care, that the defendant owed to the plaintiff. For example, if a client of your firm is suing a physician for malpractice, your supervising attorney might arrange to have another physician testify as to the standard of care owed by a physician to a patient in similar circumstances.

LAY WITNESS
A witness who can truthfully and accurately testify on a fact in question without having specialized training or knowledge; an ordinary witness.

Lay Witnesses. Most witnesses in court are lay witnesses. In contrast to expert witnesses, **lay witnesses** do not possess any particular skill or expertise relating to the matter before the court. They are people who happened to observe or otherwise have factual knowledge about an event. A professional or expert in one field may be a lay witness in regard to another field about which he or she does not have expert knowledge. A physician involved in a fraud claim, for example, might give testimony about the fraud as a lay witness but not as an expert witness.

EYEWITNESS
A witness who testifies about an event that he or she observed or has experienced first hand.

Eyewitnesses. In attempting to gain more information about an event relating to a client's legal claim, paralegals may be required to interview eyewitnesses. **Eyewitnesses** are lay witnesses who have witnessed an event and may testify in a court of law as to what they observed. The term *eyewitness* is deceiving. An eyewitness may have firsthand knowledge of an event, but this knowledge need not have been derived from the sense of sight—that is, from actually *seeing* the event. An eyewitness may be someone who listened in on a telephone conversation between an accused murderer and his or her accomplice. A blind man may have been an eyewitness to a car crash, because he heard it.

In interviews, eyewitnesses are ordinarily asked to describe an event, in their own words and as they recall it, that relates to the client's case. Eyewitness accounts may be lengthy, and the paralegal may want to tape-record the interview session to ensure accuracy. The experienced paralegal may also find that different eyewitnesses to the same event have contradictory views on what actually took place. People's perceptions of reality differ, as paralegals often find when comparing eyewitness reports.

Friendly Witnesses. Some witnesses to an event may be the client's family, friends, co-workers, neighbors, or other persons who know the client and who want to be helpful in volunteering information. These witnesses are regarded as **friendly witnesses**. You may think that friendly witnesses are the best kind to interview, and they often are. They may also be biased in the client's favor, however, so the paralegal should look closely for the actual facts (and not the witness's interpretation of the facts) when interviewing friendly witnesses.

FRIENDLY WITNESS
A witness who gives voluntary testimony at an attorney's request on behalf of the attorney's client; a witness who is prejudiced against the client's adversary.

Adverse Witnesses. Witnesses who may be prejudiced against your client or friendly to your client's adversary are regarded as **adverse witnesses** (often referred to as **hostile witnesses**). Interviewing adverse witnesses can be challenging. Sometimes the witness has an interest in the outcome of the case and would stand in a better position if your client lost in court. For example, if the client is a tenant who refuses to pay rent until the landlord makes a structural repair to the roof, then the paralegal interviewing the landlord's manager should be prepared to deal with that person as a potentially hostile witness. You will learn more about how to deal with hostile witnesses in Chapter 15, in the context of legal investigations.

ADVERSE (HOSTILE) WITNESS
A witness for the opposing side in a lawsuit or other legal proceeding; a hostile witness.

Witness Statements

The witness statement is a *written statement* that documents what the witness said during an interview. This statement identifies the witness, the incident, and the details and facts discovered during the interview. The statement also includes an *attestation clause.* An attestation clause, which is ordinarily located at the end of the statement, indicates that the witness affirms the statement as his or her own words. The statement is signed by the witness.

Because witness statements are made out of court and are not made under oath, they are considered somewhat unreliable by the courts and are generally not admissible as evidence. They are, however, useful for other purposes, such as calling into question the truthfulness or accuracy of a witness who makes a statement in court that contradicts what was said in the interview earlier. In this situation, the written statement may be used to impeach (challenge the credibility of) the witness. Witness statements are discussed in further detail in Chapter 15; that chapter also includes an exhibit showing a sample witness statement.

SPONTANEITY AND FLEXIBILITY

Earlier in this chapter, we mentioned that you should not let a prepared form or checklist of questions totally control the direction an interview may take. You should always allow for spontaneity and flexibility in the interviewing process, both when preparing questions and when conducting the interview. Although you should have a clear agenda in mind when the interview starts, the agenda should not be totally controlling. Experienced interviewers know that, in the course of a conversation, a client or witness may offhandedly

DEVELOPING PARALEGAL SKILLS

Interviewing a Witness by Telephone

Adam Haskell, a legal assistant for a sole practitioner, is going to conduct a telephone interview of a witness to a car accident. The witness lives in a distant state but happened to be visiting the area when the accident occurred. For economic reasons, the initial interview will be conducted over the telephone, with a follow-up interview to be done in person if Adam's supervising attorney wants to have the witness, Sam Toole, testify at trial.

Adam had previously arranged with the witness to conduct the phone interview today at 10:30 A.M. Adam prepared a list of questions yesterday and is now making final preparations for the interview. First, he gathers all of the materials that he will need for the interview: the client file, the list of prepared questions, a note pad, and a couple of pens. Next, he takes his tape recorder from his desk. He takes a blank tape from the drawer and inserts it into the recorder. If Sam Toole consents, Adam will hook up the recorder to the telephone and tape-record the interview.

Adam then walks to the secretary's desk and asks for the portable fax machine. There is an extra phone jack for a fax machine in the conference room, which was installed for this purpose. Having the fax machine available will allow the witness to fax any relevant documents or other items, such as a drawing of the accident. Adam checks the fax machine to make sure that it has enough paper in it. Then he takes all of the materials that he has gathered to the conference room. He sets up the tape recorder and the fax machine, turns them on, and tests them to make certain that they are in operating condition before the interview begins.

Adam's final step in preparing for his phone interview is to make sure that he will not be interrupted. He returns to the secretary's desk and tells her that he will be involved in a telephone interview and that he does not want to be interrupted. He asks her to hold all of his calls and not to come in with any messages or let anyone else in the conference room. Adam walks back into the conference room and dials Sam's telephone number. The interview begins.

communicate crucial factual information—information that the interviewer would not otherwise have sought out.

When you conduct an interview, the interviewee may lead you into an area of discussion that was not anticipated when the questions (or forms) were prepared. You should remain open-minded and refrain from letting the prepared questions or forms limit the interview's potential. Unanticipated comments or observations made during the interview may be of utmost importance to the case. Because of this, it is crucial that you allow room for spontaneity and flexibility at all times in the interviewing process. A good rule is the following:

- **Do not force the flow of the interview. Instead, gently guide the discussion and explore unanticipated but relevant avenues as they arise.**

PARALEGAL PROFILE

Administrative Paralegal

DAVID L. HAY has an associate's degree from the legal-assistant program at El Centro Community College in Dallas, Texas. While working as an administrative assistant for a Wisconsin company, Hay had taken some classes in the legal-assistant program at an area technical college and discovered his interest in the legal field. He also worked as a legal secretary for a time.

Hay currently works for the general counsel for the Dallas County Community College. Communication and interviewing skills are important in Hay's work. His responsibilities include contributing to the policy manual used by the college, researching and interpreting federal law, preparing memos, and often providing the first contact to students who call with a legal question.

What do you like best about your work?

"I like the variety. In my job there is never a dull moment. I also like the freedom to set my own priorities. I'm often involved in investigations to locate people, and I enjoy my contact with students."

What is the greatest challenge that you face in your area of work?

"My greatest challenge is working with administrators to communicate what needs to be done. When new laws require a change, it is my responsibility to make the administrators understand what changes need to be put into effect. I also have the challenge of educating people as to what a paralegal is, because many persons assume that I am a lawyer. I clarify immediately that I am not a lawyer and remind them that I cannot give legal advice."

What advice do you have for would-be paralegals in your area of work?

"My advice is to take advantage of the informational interview process, internships, and community-service programs to learn more about different types of paralegal work and the kinds of jobs available. The informational interview allows the paralegal to interview the firm: it's a learning process. The paralegal can find out what the firm looks for in a paralegal in terms of qualifications or credentials and can learn about the type of work that is available. Internships and community-service programs also provide opportunities for paralegals to 'test the waters.' Often, such programs lead to full-time positions. It's much better to find out by trial and error which areas of law you want to work in than to go into the work force as unprepared and uninformed employees. By getting involved with information interviews, internships, and community-service programs, you will know which direction to pursue as a paralegal."

"IN MY JOB THERE IS NEVER A DULL MOMENT."

What are some tips for success as a paralegal in your area of work?

"One important tip is to follow up and not delay if someone is waiting for a response from you. I also recommend interviewing and checking several sources for a more complete picture. Don't be afraid to probe and schedule other interviews for further information—a second or third interview might reveal information the first interview did not."

If you are faced with new and surprising information, you may wish to explore it on the spot. Making a note to get back to that discussion may work just as well, depending on the circumstances. If the interview is running late, for example, you may need to wrap up the discussion quickly. You should make a note in your interview summary about the unexpected lead or information so that it can be explored during the next interview.

TODAY'S PROFESSIONAL PARALEGAL

Interviewing a Client

TODAY'S Professional PARALEGAL

Amanda Blake, a paralegal, works for John Kerrigan, a sole practitioner. A new client, Joel Sontag, calls for an appointment to make his will. The attorney has to go out of town for a court hearing. Because Sontag seems to be anxious to get the will done, the attorney asks Amanda to meet with Sontag and interview him to obtain some basic information. The attorney will review the information when he returns from his trip and then call Sontag to advise him on the will and other estate-planning possibilities.

Amanda reserves the conference room. On the day of Sontag's visit, she has it set up for the interview. She has already made a copy of the estate-planning checklist that she will use to ensure that she obtains all of the essential information from Sontag. The secretary shows Sontag into the conference room when he arrives.

MEETING THE CLIENT

Amanda introduces herself, saying, "Hello, Mr. Sontag, I'm Amanda Blake, John Kerrigan's legal assistant. I'll be meeting with you today to obtain the estate-planning information that Mr. Kerrigan needs if he is to advise you." Sontag responds, "Mr. Kerrigan told me that we would be meeting today. He also told me how capable you are." Amanda smiles and says, "Thanks. And did Mr. Kerrigan explain to you that I'm not an attorney?" Sontag responds, "Yes, he did." Amanda offers Sontag a cup of coffee, which he accepts. Then he says, "By the way, Amanda, please call me Joel." Amanda says, "All right. And please call me Amanda." She then leaves the conference room and asks her secretary to bring them each a cup of coffee. She returns to the conference room and removes her checklist and note pad from her file.

OBTAINING INFORMATION FROM THE CLIENT

"I'll be reviewing this checklist to make sure that we obtain all of the information that we need for your will," Amanda informs Joel. "First, I need you to fill out the client-information form," instructs Amanda. "As you can see, it requires you to give us personal information, such as your name, legal residence, date of birth, and other data." Joel takes the form and fills it out. When he is finished, he hands it to Amanda.

"Now I need some other information. First, I need to know if you're married," states Amanda. "Yes, I am," responds Joel. "Your wife's name is?" asks Amanda. "Nicole Lynn Sontag," answers Joel. "And your wife resides with you at the address that you've given on the client-information form?" asks Amanda. "Yes, she does," Joel states. "When was she born, and what's her Social Security number?" asks Amanda. "She was born on January 17, 1958, and her Social Security number is 363-46-2350," says Joel.

"Now, Joel, do you have any children?" asks Amanda. "Yes, we have one son, Joel, Jr., age four," answers Joel. "Do you want to provide for both of them in your will?" asks Amanda. "Yes," responds Joel. "Do you have any other relatives that you want to provide for?" asks Amanda. "Yes, I have a brother, Alfred Sontag, who lives in a home for autistic people," answers Joel. "I'll need the address of the home," responds Amanda. Joel takes an address book out of his briefcase and gives her the address. "Is there anyone else whom you want to provide for in your will?" asks Amanda. "No," responds Joel.

"Now we need to discuss property," Amanda informs Joel. "Do you own a home?" she asks. "Yes," he answers. Amanda says, "I need to know if the home is located at the address you gave on the form, when you bought it, what it cost, what its present approximate market value is, whether you own it jointly with your wife, and the balance on your mortgage." Joel gives her all of the requested information. Amanda continues questioning Joel about his property holdings until she has covered all the items on her checklist.

CONCLUDING THE INTERVIEW

"Well," says Amanda, "we've covered everything on the checklist. Now we need to set up a time for you to meet with Mr. Kerrigan to discuss estate-planning procedures and your will. Because you jointly own property with your wife, Mr. Kerrigan may want both of you to meet with him. Would two o'clock next Tuesday afternoon be a good time for you both to come in to meet with Mr. Kerrigan?" Joel tells Amanda that he thinks that both he and his wife could arrange to meet with the attorney at that time. They schedule an appointment for that date. Joel gets up to leave the office, saying that he'll probably see her again next Tuesday. "I'll look forward to that," says Amanda. Amanda then begins to prepare a detailed summary of the interview.

KEY TERMS AND CONCEPTS

active listening 542
adverse witness 557
closed-ended question 540
expert witness 556
eyewitness 556
friendly witness 557
hostile witness 557
hypothetical question 540
interviewee 538
lay witness 556
leading question 541
open-ended question 540
pressure question 541
retentive listening 542
supportive listening 543

CHAPTER SUMMARY

1. Paralegals often interview clients and witnesses. The paralegal may interview an individual alone on behalf of the firm or as part of a legal team that includes an attorney. Becoming a successful interviewer takes practice, dedication, and good interviewing skills.

2. Interviewing skills include interpersonal skills, questioning skills, and communication skills, particularly listening skills. Interpersonal skills are helpful in establishing a comfortable and productive relationship with the interviewee. Establishing a rapport with the client or witness and putting him or her at ease is the cornerstone of an effective interview. To communicate effectively with the interviewee, the interviewer should use language that is familiar to that person. Particularly, the paralegal should avoid using legal terminology unless the terms are defined clearly for the interviewee (or the interviewee is familiar with legal terms).

3. Paralegals can use several types of questions during the interviewing process, including open-ended, closed-ended, hypothetical, pressure, and leading questions. Understanding how these questions function and what types of responses they elicit helps the paralegal control the interview and maximize the amount of information obtained from the interviewee.

4. Good listening skills are essential for the interviewer. Interruptions and distractions should be kept to a minimum so that both the interviewer and the interviewee can concentrate on the subject being discussed. The paralegal should be an active participant in the communication process even while listening. Active listening involves paying careful attention to what is being said, giving appropriate feedback to the speaker, and analyzing what is being said in light of the larger picture. Retentive listening—listening to retain information—is particularly important in the interviewing context. At times, the paralegal needs to engage in supportive listening, in which the listener responds to the emotional needs of the speaker.

5. Successful interviews require careful preparation. Prior to the interview, the paralegal schedules the session, notifies the interviewee of what (if any) documents or items should be brought to the interview, and prepares a list of questions for the client or witness to answer. The paralegal also prepares the interview environment to ensure that interruptions and delays will be minimized, that the client will be comfortable, and that any necessary supplies and equipment are at hand. If an interview is to be tape-recorded, the paralegal must obtain permission from both his or her supervising attorney and the interviewee to tape the session.

6. There are basically three types of client interviews: the initial interview, the subsequent interview, and the informational interview (or meeting). The initial interview is usually conducted by the attorney but often is attended by the paralegal (and possibly other members of the legal team). The paralegal is ordinarily responsible for documenting and summarizing the results of the initial session. Preprinted or computerized forms are often used to obtain initial information about a client and the client's legal problem. If the firm accepts the case, a subsequent interview may be scheduled to gather additional information. This session is often conducted by the paralegal alone. The informational interview, or meeting, is also handled by the paralegal. In this interview, the client is updated on case progress, procedures, trial dates, and other information that the paralegal is authorized to convey to clients. As soon as possible after an interview is concluded, the paralegal should summarize in a written memorandum the information gathered in the interview.

7. Witnesses interviewed by paralegals include expert witnesses, lay witnesses, eyewitnesses, friendly witnesses, and adverse (hostile) witnesses. Expert witnesses have specialized training in a given area, making their educated opinions helpful when certain facts and issues related to a given case are difficult to understand. Lay witnesses are ordinary witnesses who have factual information about the matter before the court but who are not experts in that area. Eyewitnesses are those who have observed or have firsthand knowledge about an incident. Friendly witnesses are often relatives or friends of the client and are generally supportive of the client's position. Adverse, or hostile, witnesses are prejudiced against the client and often have an interest in the outcome of the case that is adverse to the client's interests.

8. For whichever type of witness is interviewed, the paralegal creates a witness statement. This statement identifies the witness, discloses what was discovered during the interview, and is signed by the witness, who attests that the written statement is a fair representation of his or her own words.

9. Although having a prepared agenda is crucial to a successful interview, flexibility is also important. Often, unanticipated responses lead to opportunities to gather more factual information about a case. The interviewer should be alert for these opportunities and should not let his or her agenda totally control the interview.

QUESTIONS FOR REVIEW

1. What kinds of skills do interviewers employ during interviews?

2. What are interpersonal skills, and why are they important to the interviewing process?

3. What are the different types of questions that can be used in an interview? When would you use each type?

4. What are the different types of listening techniques that are used in interviewing? When would you use each type? What is body language, and why is it important in the interviewing context?

5. What are the steps involved in preparing for an interview? Why is each step important?

6. What takes place during the initial client interview? What is the paralegal's role at this interview?

7. What other types of client interviews are commonly conducted by paralegals? What is the purpose of each type?

8. What is the difference between an expert witness and a lay witness? In what kinds of situations might each of these types of witnesses be used?

9. What is the difference between a friendly witness and an adverse (or hostile) witness?

10. What is a witness statement? How is it used?

ETHICAL QUESTIONS

1. Leah Fox, a legal assistant, has been asked by the attorney for whom she works to contact several potential witnesses to see what they know about an event. The first witness that Leah calls says, "I don't know if I should get involved. I don't want to get in trouble. You see, I was supposed to be at work, but I called in sick. If I get involved and my employer finds about where I really was, I might get fired. You're a lawyer, what do you think?" How should Leah respond?

2. Leah Fox, a legal assistant, is conducting a follow-up interview with a new client, who is seeking a divorce. Leah is asking the client about the couple's marital property. According to the client, the couple wants to divide the property evenly on their divorce. When Leah asks the client about checking or savings accounts, the client says to Leah, "You know, Leah, I have this 'secret' savings account, but I don't want anybody to know about it. Please don't tell Mr. Harcourt [Leah's supervising attorney] what I've just told you." What should Leah do in this situation?

PRACTICE QUESTIONS AND ASSIGNMENTS

1. Review the Baranski-Peretto hypothetical case discussed earlier in this text (see Chapter 10). Then write sample questions that you would ask the interviewee when interviewing eyewitnesses to the accident. Phrase at least one question in each of the question formats discussed in this chapter.

2. Using the information in this chapter on questioning skills, identify the following types of questions:

a. "From January 10, 1995, until January 17, 1995, you were on a cruise in the Bahamas, Mr. Johnson. Your credit-card records, which were subpoenaed, indicate that you purchased two tickets. If your wife did not accompany you on that cruise, who did?"

b. "Did you go on a cruise in the Bahamas with another woman, Mr. Johnson?"

c. "Isn't it true, Mr. Johnson, that someone other than your wife accompanied you on a cruise in the Bahamas?"

d. "Mr. Johnson, will you please describe your whereabouts between January 10, 1995, and January 17, 1995?"

QUESTIONS FOR CRITICAL ANALYSIS

1. Expert witnesses give testimony relating to incidents that they have not observed or people whom they may never have met. What, then, is the value of expert testimony? Why do courts allow expert witnesses to testify?

2. The ability to "think on your feet"—that is, to analyze what the interviewee is saying and ask for further details during the course of an interview—is an important skill for you to have as an interviewer. Why is this skill important? What would happen if the interviewer did not do this?

ROLE-PLAYING EXERCISES

1. Elena Lopez is a legal assistant at the law firm of Jeffers, Gilmore & Dunn. Elena has been assigned the task of calling Katherine Baranski, a potential new client, to prepare Baranski for an interview that Elena has scheduled for January 30, 1996, at 8:30 A.M. She will be asking Baranski to bring specific documents, if she has them in her possession, to the interview. Role-play the telephone call between Elena Lopez and Katherine Baranski. Elena should ask Baranski if she has certain items and, if so, should ask her to bring them to the interview. Baranski should be cooperative and should have most, if not all, of the documents that Elena requests.

You will need to work in pairs, with one of you playing the role of Elena Lopez and the other the role of Katherine Baranski. Reverse roles if time allows.

2. Working in pairs, role-play the estate-planning interview between Amanda Blake and Joel Sontag that was discussed in this chapter's *Today's Professional Paralegal.* Begin the interview informally, with some social conversation, the offer of a cup of coffee, and so on. Next, move to the client information form. Reverse roles if time allows.

3. Working in groups of three, role-play the initial client interview described in Chapter 10 between Katharine Baranski and the legal team—attorney Allen Gilmore and paralegal Elena Lopez. Attorney Gilmore will need to prepare a list of questions and will ask most of the questions during the interview. Paralegal Lopez will take notes during the interview, provide the retainer-agreement and release forms, and schedule the follow-up interview. Change roles if time allows.

PROJECTS

1. Go to a library and do research on listening skills. Write a one-page (double-spaced) paper giving additional information on the listening techniques discussed in this chapter.

2. Watch an interview on television. Write a two-page, double-spaced paper describing the interview. Include in your description the following information:

a. The names of the interviewer and the interviewee.
b. The subject of the interview.
c. The date and time of the interview and the television channel over which it was broadcast.
d. The different types of questions (open-ended, closed-ended, and so on) used by the interviewer and the types of responses elicited by the different kinds of questions.
e. The ways in which the interviewer and interviewee communicated nonverbally.
f. Your overall evaluation of the interviewer's skill at interviewing this particular interviewee.

ANNOTATED SELECTED READINGS

CLARK, LANA J. "Understanding Evidence." *Legal Assistant Today,* November/December 1992. An article that places the purpose of interviewing witnesses into perspective by considering how witness statements are used at trial. It gives good examples of different types of questions, such as leading questions, and their uses.

DANIELSON, STEPHANIE. "The Value of Expert Opinion." *Legal Assistant Today,* September/October 1993. An interesting and informative description of several types of experts used in personal-injury cases. The article discusses medical experts, accident reconstructionists, vocational and rehabilitation experts, and economics experts and gives suggestions on how to locate such experts. The article stresses that an expert's credentials should always be checked because credibility is the "name of the game" in using expert witnesses.

KOERSELMAN, VIRGINIA, and the NATIONAL ASSOCIATION OF LEGAL ASSISTANTS, INC. "Human Relations and Interviewing." Chapter 6 of *CLA Review Manual.* St. Paul: West Publishing Co., 1993. A detailed description of the interviewing process. The section entitled "Preparing for the Interview" provides good tips on this topic.

NATIONAL ASSOCIATION OF LEGAL ASSISTANTS, INC. "Interviewing Techniques." Chapter 6 of *NALA Manual for Legal Assistants.* 2d ed. St. Paul: West Publishing Co., 1992. Twenty pages of informative and helpful additional reading on interviewing techniques.

READE, KATHLEEN M. "Conducting Effective Client Conferences." *Legal Assistant Today,* May/June 1994. An article full of helpful tips for paralegals on how they can conduct effective interviews with clients, including disabled clients.

SOBELSON, ROY M. "Interviewing Clients Ethically." *Practicing Law Journal,* January 1991. An article that provides tips for lawyers on how to interview their clients without violating ethical professional codes. The article explains why lawyers do or do not ask certain types of questions and how ethical responsibilities affect the interviewing process.

15

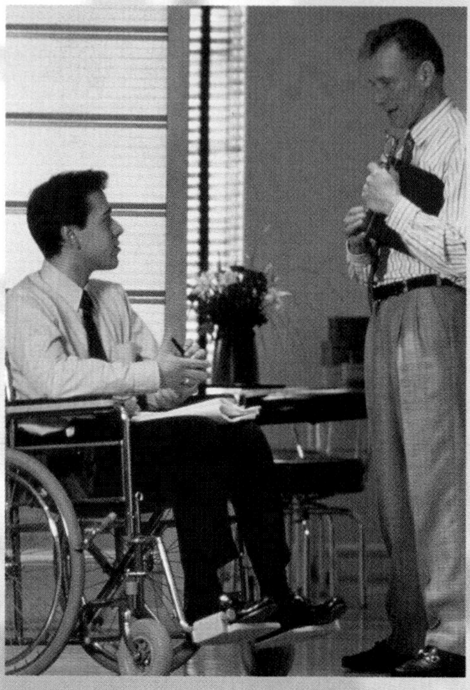

Conducting Investigations

Chapter Objectives

After completing this chapter, you will know:

- **How to create an investigation plan.**
- **Some basic principles that guide legal investigators.**
- **Rules governing what types of evidence are admissible in court.**
- **The variety of sources that you can use when trying to locate information or witnesses.**
- **Some useful techniques for interviewing witnesses and how to prepare witness statements.**
- **How to summarize your investigation results.**

Chapter Outline

INTRODUCTION

Attorneys are interested in facts. A fact is a "thing done"; it may be an event, a circumstance, or any other happening that actually occurred. The more factual evidence that can be gathered in support of a client's claim, the better the client's chances in court—or in any other dispute-settlement proceeding. If a client alleges that she was injured by a negligent driver, the attorney's first action will be to investigate the circumstances surrounding the accident to verify that the client's allegations are supported by factual evidence.

Because factual evidence is crucial to the outcome of a legal problem, investigation is necessarily an important part of legal work. Attorneys often rely on paralegals to conduct investigations, and you should be prepared to accept the responsibility for making sure that an investigation is conducted thoroughly and professionally. In this chapter, you will read about the basics of legal investigation—how to plan and undertake an investigation, how the rules of evidence shape the investigative process, and the importance of carefully documenting the results of your investigation.

Based on the results of your investigation, the attorney with whom you work will be in a better position to advise the client as to his or her chances of winning in court or of obtaining a favorable settlement out of court. If a lawsuit is brought, further investigation will be possible during the discovery stage of pretrial litigation (discussed in Chapter 10). This chapter focuses on pre-discovery investigation.

PLANNING YOUR INVESTIGATION

Assume that you work for Allen Gilmore, the attorney who represented the plaintiff in the hypothetical case discussed in Chapters 10 and 11. Recall that the plaintiff in that case, Katherine Baranski, sued Tony Peretto for negligence. Peretto had run a stop sign at an intersection and as a result, his car collided with Baranski's. Further assume that the case is still in its initial stages. Attorney Gilmore has just met with Katherine Baranski for the initial client interview. You sat in on the interview, listened carefully to Baranski's description of the accident and of the damages she sustained as a result (medical expenses, lost wages, and so on), and took thorough notes.

After the interview, Gilmore asks you to do a preliminary investigation into Baranski's claim. It is now your responsibility to find the answers to a number of questions. Did the accident really occur in the way perceived by the client, Katherine Baranski? Exactly where and when did it happen? How does the police report describe the accident? Were there any witnesses? Was Tony Peretto insured and, if so, by what insurance company? What other circumstances (such as weather) are relevant? Your supervising attorney will want to know the answers to these and other questions before advising Baranski as to what legal action should be pursued.

Where Do You Start?

In undertaking any legal investigation, your logical point of departure is the information you have already acquired about the legal claim or problem. In

CASE AT A GLANCE

The Plaintiff—
Plaintiff: Katherine Baranski
Attorney: Allen P. Gilmore
Paralegal: Elena Lopez

The Defendant—
Defendant: Tony Peretto
Attorney: Elizabeth A. Cameron
Paralegal: Gordon McVay

the Baranski case, this information consists of the statements made by Baranski during the initial client interview and summarized in your notes. Baranski had described what she remembered about the accident, including the date and time it occurred. She said she thought that the police investigator had the names of some persons who had witnessed the accident. She also stated that she was employed as an assistant professor in the math department at Nita State University, earning approximately $36,000 a year. By using common sense and a little imagination, you can map out a fairly thorough investigation plan based on this information.

Creating an Investigation Plan

An **investigation plan** is simply a step-by-step list of the tasks that you plan to take to verify or obtain factual information relating to a legal problem. The order in which the steps are listed should follow a logical pattern. In other words, if you need to get information from source A (such as a police report of an accident) before you can contact source B (such as an eyewitness whose name and address are in the police report), source A should precede source B on your list. For each step, you should indicate what kind of information you plan to request or obtain and how you plan to obtain it. When creating your plan, you can add columns for "date requested" and "date received" beside each item; this way, your plan will also serve as a checklist on the status of your investigation.

In the Baranski case, the steps in your investigation plan would include those summarized in Exhibit 15.1 on the next page and discussed below.

Contacting the Police Department. The initial step in your plan should be to contact the police department. You will want to look at a copy of the police report of the accident, view any photographs that were taken at the scene, obtain the names of persons who may have witnessed the accident, and, if possible, talk to the investigating officer.

Contacting and Interviewing Witnesses. Next, you will want to contact and interview any known witnesses and document their descriptions of what took place at the time of the accident.

- **Remember, when you introduce yourself to a witness, you should inform him or her that you are not an attorney.**

Known witnesses include the driver (Tony Peretto) of the vehicle that hit Katherine Baranski, the police officer at the scene, and the other witnesses noted in the police investigation report. Keep in mind that if Tony Peretto is aware of Baranski's intention to sue him, he will probably have retained an attorney. If he has, then you are not permitted to contact him directly—all communications with him will have to be through his attorney.

Obtaining Medical and Employment Records. To justify a claim for damages, you will need to ascertain the nature of the injuries sustained by Baranski as a result of the accident, the medical expenses that she incurred, and her annual or monthly income (to determine the amount of wages she lost as a result of the accident). To obtain this information, you will need copies of her medical and employment records.

ETHICAL CONCERN

Confidentiality and Spousal Relationships

Wanting to share information about your daily work activities with your spouse is natural. As a paralegal, though, you need to guard against the temptation to share—even with your spouse—information relating to the work you do on behalf of clients. For example, assume that you are the paralegal investigating the Baranski case. Your husband, Tony, is a history professor at Nita State University and knows Katherine Baranski, who teaches in the math department. Tony has talked to you in the past about Baranski's accident, and you are tempted to tell Tony about the lawsuit. Should you? No, you should not. Even though Tony is your husband and even if he swears to keep the information secret, you should not say anything about the case—even in general terms—that may lead him to conclude that your firm has anything to do with Katherine Baranski. Keeping client information confidential can sometimes be difficult, but it is a requirement of the profession.

INVESTIGATION PLAN
A plan that lists each step involved in obtaining and verifying the facts and information that are relevant to the legal problem being investigated.

EXHIBIT 15.1
An Investigation Plan

INVESTIGATION PLAN
File No. 15773

	Date Requested	Date Received
1. Contact Police Department		
—To obtain police report	____	____
—To ask for photographs of accident scene	____	____
—To talk with investigating officer	____	____
—SOURCE: Nita City Police Dept.		
—METHOD: Request in person or by mail		
2. Contact Known Witnesses		
—Tony Peretto, van driver		
—Michael Young, police officer at accident scene	____	____
—Julia Williams, witness at accident scene	____	____
—Dwight Kelly, witness at accident scene	____	____
—SOURCE: Police report		
—METHOD: Contact witnesses by initial phone call and personal interview when possible		
3. Obtain Employment Records		
—To learn employment status and income of Mrs. Baranski	____	____
—SOURCE: Nita State University		
—METHOD: Written request by mail with Mrs. Baranski's release enclosed		
4. Obtain Hospital Records		
—To learn necessary information about Mrs. Baranski's medical treatment and costs	____	____
—SOURCE: Nita City Hospital		
—METHOD: Written request by mail with Mrs. Baranski's release enclosed		

Note that the institutions holding these records will not release them to you unless Katherine Baranski authorizes them to do so. Therefore, you will also need to arrange with Baranski to sign release forms to include with your requests for copies. A sample authorization form to release medical records is shown in Exhibit 15.2. You should make sure that Baranski signs these forms before she leaves the office after the initial interview. Otherwise, waiting for her to return the signed forms may delay your investigation.

Contacting the National Weather Service. Weather conditions at the time of the accident may have an important bearing on the case. If it was snowing heavily at the time of the Baranski-Peretto accident, for example, Peretto's attorney may argue that Peretto did not see the stop sign or that ice on the road prevented him from stopping. You will therefore want to ascertain what the weather conditions were at the time of the accident by

EXHIBIT 15.1
Continued

	Date Requested	Date Received
5. Contact National Weather Service		
—To learn what the weather conditions were on the day of the accident	______	______
—SOURCE: National Weather Service or newspaper		
—METHOD: Phone call or written request		
6. Obtain Title and Registration Records		
—To verify Tony Peretto's ownership of the vehicle	______	______
—SOURCE: Department of Motor Vehicles		
—METHOD: Order by mail		
7. Contact Tony Peretto's Insurance Co.		
—To find out about insurance coverage	______	______
—To check liability limits	______	______
—SOURCE: Insurance Company		
—METHOD: Written request by mail		
8. Use a Professional Investigator		
—To contact such witnesses as –ambulance attendants –doctors –residents in neighborhood of accident scene	______	______
—To inspect vehicle	______	______
—To take photos of accident site	______	______
—To investigate accident scene, etc.	______	______
—SOURCE: Regular law-firm investigator		
—METHOD: In person		

contacting the National Weather Service. Also, when you interview eyewitnesses, you should ask them about weather conditions at the place and time of the accident.

Obtaining Vehicle Title and Registration Records. To verify that Tony Peretto owns the vehicle that he was driving at the time of the accident, you will need to obtain title and registration records. Usually, these can be obtained from the state department of motor vehicles, although in some states, the secretary of state's office handles such records. The requirements for obtaining such information vary from state to state and may include the submission of special forms and fees. Therefore, you should call the relevant state department or office in advance to find out what procedures should be followed.

Contacting the Insurance Company. If you learned the name of Peretto's insurance company from Baranski or from the police report, you will want to

EXHIBIT 15.2
Authorization to Release Medical Records

TO: Nita City Hospital & Clinic
Nita City, NI 48803

PATIENT: Katherine Baranski
335 Natural Boulevard
Nita City, NI 48802

You are hereby authorized to furnish and release to my attorney, Allen P. Gilmore of Jeffers, Gilmore & Dunn, all information and records relating to my treatment for injuries incurred on August 4, 1995. Please do not disclose information to insurance adjusters or to other persons without written authority from me. The foregoing authority shall continue in force until revoked by me in writing, but for no longer than one year following the date given below.

Date: January 30, 1996.

Katherine Baranski
Katherine Baranski

Please attach your invoice for any fee or photostatic costs and send it with the information requested above to my office.

Thank you,

Allen P. Gilmore

Allen P. Gilmore
Jeffers, Gilmore & Dunn
Attorneys at Law
553 Fifth Avenue
Suite 101
Nita City, NI 48801

Helena Moritz
Helena Moritz
Notary Public State of Nita
Nita County
My Commission Expires November 12, 2000

contact that company to find out what kind of insurance coverage Peretto has and the limits of his liability under the insurance policy. Insurance companies usually are reluctant give this information to anyone other than the policyholder. They sometimes cooperate with such requests, however, because they know that if they do not, the information can be obtained during discovery, should a lawsuit be initiated.

Using a Professional Investigator's Services. Some law firms routinely use the services of professional investigators. Depending on the circumstances, your supervising attorney may decide to use a professional investigator for certain tasks, including those described above. You might be responsible for working with the investigator. For example, you might arrange for the investigator to inspect and take photographs of the accident scene.

Locating certain witnesses (witnesses who have moved, for example) may be difficult and time consuming. This is another task that your supervising attorney may prefer the professional investigator to handle, particularly if the attorney needs your assistance in the office. The investigator might also be asked to locate other witnesses, such as the ambulance driver or attendants, physicians who treated Baranski, or residents in the area who might have observed the accident.

Consulting with Your Supervising Attorney

In planning and conducting your preliminary investigation, you will want to work closely with your supervising attorney. Primarily, this is because you will need to learn what legal theories the attorney wants to pursue and in what order of priority. The attorney may also know of additional sources that you should investigate or may indicate that there is no need to investigate a certain area of a client's claim. Also, for strategic reasons, the attorney might want you to concentrate more on some areas than others.

Once you have formed your investigation plan, you should submit it, with a cover memo, to your supervising attorney for review and evaluation. If you anticipate any problem areas or have have specific questions about how to proceed, you can point these out in your cover memo. A sample cover memo for the investigation plan in the Baranski case is shown in Exhibit 15.3 on the following page.

Investigation during Discovery

Investigators should be familiar with the pretrial discovery procedures discussed in Chapter 10. If a lawsuit is initiated, further investigation can be conducted during the discovery phase of the litigation. As a paralegal, you will be able to use discovery tools—such as depositions, interrogatories, requests for admissions or documents, as well as subpoenas—to obtain evidence that might not be made available to you during your preliminary investigation.

In planning and pursuing your investigation, you should make notes of any documents or information that you are unable to obtain now and that you will want to obtain during discovery. In the Baranski case, for example, you may have to wait until discovery to obtain information from Peretto's insurance company about Peretto's insurance coverage and liability limits, because the company may not release this information without a subpoena. (Note that under the revised Federal Rules of Civil Procedure, this information will be automatically disclosed—see Chapter 10.)

CONDUCTING YOUR INVESTIGATION—BASIC PRINCIPLES

There is no one correct way to conduct a legal investigation. This is because each person has unique attributes and personality characteristics. While a

---

ETHICAL CONCERN

Telephone Calls and Confidentiality

In a busy legal office, it is very easy to breach the duty of confidentiality unintentionally and without even being aware that you have done so. For example, assume that you are investigating the Baranski case and have left a message at the police department for a police detective to call you back. He returns your call, and just then a client walks into the office area in which you are working. You say on the telephone, "Oh, hello, Detective Proust. I'd like to talk with you about some of the details of a case you worked on last fall—the accident on Mattis Avenue and Thirty-eighth Street in which Katherine Baranski was injured. Allen Gilmore, an attorney in our law firm, has been retained by Mrs. Baranski, and we are looking into the matter." You arrange with the detective for an appointment the following day, hang up the phone, and then ask the client if you can help her (the receptionist is on his lunch break). Without meaning to, you have divulged to a third party the name of a client and (by implication) the nature of the client's claim. To guard against breaching confidentiality, you should always make sure that no one will overhear your end of the conversation whenever you talk on the phone about any matter relating to a client.

EXHIBIT 15.3
Cover Memo for Investigation Plan

TO: Allen P. Gilmore
Partner

FROM: Elena Lopez
Paralegal

DATE: February 13, 1996

RE: Investigation plan for Katherine Baranski's personal-injury claim. File #15773.

Attached is a proposed checklist of the information I plan to obtain during the investigation of Mrs. Baranski's claim. The plan is based on the information given by Mrs. Baranski during the initial client interview on January 30, 1996. The information needed and the probable sources of the information are indicated within the investigation plan. Please let me know if you have any suggestions for additions to this checklist.

Once the preliminary investigation is completed, I will let you know the types and sources of information that we can only obtain during discovery.

low-key, methodical style might work for one person, it might not be appropriate for a more aggressive person who likes to have several things happening at once. Over time and with practice, you will learn what approach works best for you and will acquire your own particular style of investigation. Generally, you will find that your greatest allies in investigatory work are common sense, good organizational skills, and creative thinking.

Although investigative approaches vary from person to person, all legal investigators can use the basic principles discussed below to help them achieve their goal of uncovering and verifying relevant facts.

Focus on the Who, What, and Where

Before undertaking any step on your investigation plan, you should know which people you need to contact, what information you want to uncover or verify, and where information sources can be found. For example, if you want to obtain information from a large organization, such as a government agency, make sure that you contact the appropriate person—that is, the person who has the expertise and authority to answer your questions or fulfill your request. Your firm may have directories of various federal, state, and local agencies that will give you this information. If not, you may have to contact several people within an agency before you learn which employee is authorized to handle your request.

If you need to visit a geographical area with which you are unfamiliar, do some preliminary investigation to find out what the area is like. If the neighborhood is a high-crime area, you may want to conduct your investigation with a partner and during the day, when you will be less at risk, or hire a private investigator to handle that aspect of the investigatory work.

Develop and Maintain Personal Contacts

Experienced investigators rely to a great extent on contacts they have established during previous investigations. By knowing the right people in the right places, investigators are able to obtain reports or other information quickly and efficiently. Whenever you conduct an investigation, keep an eye toward your future needs as an investigator and cultivate good relationships with people whose cooperation might be helpful to you at a later time. For example, you may need to obtain documents and reports from the county clerk on a regular basis. If you establish a good relationship with that person, he or she may be more willing to respond quickly to your requests and thus make your task easier. Similarly, if during an investigation you need to contact an employee at the police department, take time to cultivate the employee's goodwill. You never know when you might need that person's assistance again.

You should create a special notebook or file in which you keep a record of the information you learned about each person you contact. You can refer to the information when you contact that person again. A three-ring binder is useful for this purpose, because you can use dividers to create sections for different categories of contacts. For example, you might have a section for police-department personnel, one for court personnel, and so on.

During the course of your investigation, you will find that some people are more cooperative, perceptive, or pleasant than others. Regardless of these differences, you should always follow this cardinal rule of investigation:

- **Treat all of the individuals you meet with respect and courtesy.**

A sure way to make your investigation less productive and more difficult is to disregard this rule. You also may make future investigations more difficult if you alienate a person whose assistance would be valuable to you. Also remember that as a paralegal, you represent the firm for which you work. Even if someone is stubborn and difficult, you should remain professional and courteous at all times because how you conduct yourself is a reflection on your firm.

Be Flexible

In many ways, conducting an investigation is similar to interviewing a client or witness. Before an interview begins, you normally prepare for that interview by creating a checklist of the topics you wish to discuss and the kind of information you want to obtain from the client or witness. But you do not let that checklist constrain you. Similarly, when conducting a legal investigation, you form an investigation plan, but you should also allow room for some unexpected twists. One source of information may lead you to other sources of which you were unaware.

For example, assume that you are interviewing Julia Williams, an eyewitness to the Baranski-Peretto auto accident. Williams mentions that a local furniture company's delivery truck was just behind Peretto's van and

ETHICAL CONCERN

Keeping the Client Informed

Attorneys have a duty to keep their clients reasonably informed about their cases or claims, and paralegals are instrumental in making sure that attorneys do not breach this duty. Periodic notes or phone calls to the client not only keep the client informed about progress on the case but also keep you in touch with the case status—and you and your supervising attorney will be less likely to miss important deadlines relating to the litigation. Frequent communications with clients also cultivate goodwill. Clients generally welcome any news from their attorneys' offices. Even a letter saying that "nothing is happening" is usually appreciated. To make sure that the client is kept informed, you will want to have some kind of a tickler system to remind you to contact the client at periodic intervals.

FEATURED GUEST: MELANIE A. P. ROWAND

Ten Tips for Pre-discovery Investigation

Biographical Note

Melanie A. Pirozzolo Rowand serves as litigation counsel for American Protective Services, Inc. (APS), which is headquartered in Oakland, California. The legal department of APS provides legal services to over seventy offices across the United States. Rowand obtained her bachelor of arts degree in education and her master of arts degree in communication. Before becoming an attorney, Rowand was a legal assistant for approximately ten years. As a legal assistant, she worked as a supervisor for several large San Francisco law firms that specialized in litigation. She has also worked in Hawaii as an aide in that state's legislature, as well as a court clerk. Rowand currently teaches introductory law courses at California State University, Hayward, at San Francisco State University, and at the University of California, Berkeley.

The basic rule to follow when conducting an investigation is that of the news reporter—learn the "who, what, when, where, and why" of your case. What was done? Who did it? When was it done? Where did it occur? Why was it done? To these "five Ws" of the journalist, the legal investigator should add "how": How did the event or action occur? Listed below are ten tips for paralegals undertaking legal investigations. Each tip indicates a source to which you can turn for factual information. By identifying significant facts during the pre-discovery stage, paralegals will gain an early insight into strategies to be pursued during discovery. Uncovering critical information before the discovery process begins may also result in an early settlement of the claim.

1 Personally Interview Witnesses, Including Your Client. Remember, your firm's client is your key witness. If after the initial client interview you find you need more information, arrange for another interview with the client. Instruct him or her to produce all documents that relate to the incident, and indicate which types of documents may be relevant. These documents might include tax statements, photographs of the incident, police reports, personnel files, insurance company reports, workers' compensation reports, repair estimates, and others. Personally interview witnesses to determine courtroom appeal. Try to determine beforehand if the individual to be interviewed will be a friendly or a hostile witness. Look to your supervising attorney for guidance on this and on the type of information you should gather during each interview.

2 Obtain the Police Report. Most police departments will provide you with a copy of a police report for a nominal fee. Some departments, however, require a written explanation as to why the report is being requested. This can take the form of a letter that simply states that the issues raised in the police report are currently being litigated. Specific identification of the case name, case number, and court will add credibility to your request. Be aware that issues involving juvenile matters will usually require a subpoena.

3 Check for Newspaper and Magazine Accounts. Public libraries are wonderful resources for the legal investigator. Generally, larger libraries keep back issues of newspapers and magazines on microfilm. Some libraries maintain newspaper microfilm files for issues dated as far back as fifty years. Computerized research services, such as WESTLAW and LEXIS, also offer access to printed publications from around the country. Check with your supervising attorney about these services.

4 Photograph the Scene of the Incident. Photograph the scene of the incident, any property that was damaged, and any injury that was sustained by the harmed individual. Arrange to photograph the scene and visit the area at the time of day the incident occurred. This will give you a more accurate picture of how the scene may have appeared at the time of the incident—how busy the intersection was, for example, or how well lighted the area was. A photograph will "preserve the scene" for the record. If the claim is litigated, it may be two or three years before it reaches trial,

FEATURED GUEST, Continued

and photographic documentation may be crucial evidence. Even if the location has changed since the date of the incident, take photographs anyway. Talk with residents in the neighborhood to learn why the changes occurred.

5 Obtain an Accurate Map of the Location of the Incident. A map of the locale in which the incident took place, as well as of the surrounding area, could make or break your case. Maps can shed light on a variety of claims, particularly those involving real property. Don't forget to obtain this commonly overlooked necessity.

6 Check Census Publications. The population of the area in which the incident occurred could be a critical factor. Census publications provide key information to those working on certain types of cases, such as cases relating to real property or business development. Contact your local census bureau for more information.

7 Request Reports from Government Agencies. In addition to census reports, other information compiled by government agencies may sometimes provide key information concerning an incident that you are investigating. If a claim involves an alleged violation of an environmental law or regulation, for example, a report prepared by the federal Environmental Protection Agency or your state's environmental agency or department may provide important information relating to the incident.

8 For Claims Involving Corporations, Contact the Secretary of State's Office in Your State. Corporations must register with the state secretary of state's office for incorporation purposes.[a] To gain information about a corporation, a paralegal can phone the secretary of state's office. Most offices allow two inquiries per call. Information available from this office includes the names of the officers and directors of a corporation, the corporation's principal place of business, and the name of the individual who has been designated to receive service of process on behalf of the corporation. Computer databases, such as Information America, provide direct access to the secretary of state's office in most states.

9 Obtain All Relevant Records. To obtain nonpublic records relating to your client, such as medical records, have your client sign a written authorization to release those records. Medical, business, and other records relating to an opposing party normally must be subpoenaed. Deeds and titles to property can be obtained from the county recorder's office.[b] Such information will enable you to prepare a property profile of a potential litigant. Records relating to previous litigation by a party can be obtained from the county court or the courts in surrounding counties. Such information will indicate to the investigator whether an individual is litigious (has a history of bringing lawsuits), is legally sophisticated, or has a history of litigating issues similar to the issue being investigated.

"UNCOVERING CRITICAL INFORMATION BEFORE THE DISCOVERY PROCESS BEGINS MAY ALSO RESULT IN AN EARLY SETTLEMENT OF THE CLAIM."

10 Obtain Publications of Local and Special-interest Organizations. These types of publications may provide additional insight into the standards of an industry and may eventually assist in the selection of expert witnesses. For example, if you are investigating a car accident, you might check with *Consumer Reports* and other consumer publications to find out if the make and model of the car involved in the incident has a history of malfunctioning.

a. While this is true in most states, a few states require incorporation papers to be filed with a different state department, such as the department of commerce.

b. Called the register of deeds office in many counties.

CASE AT A GLANCE

The Plaintiff—
Plaintiff: Katherine Baranski
Attorney: Allen P. Gilmore
Paralegal: Elena Lopez

The Defendant—
Defendant: Tony Peretto
Attorney: Elizabeth A. Cameron
Paralegal: Gordon McVay

probably had a good view of the accident. The witness had not remembered to tell the police about the truck when they questioned her at the time of the accident. The driver of that truck, though, would be a valuable witness, so you make a note to call the furniture company and make some inquiries to see if you can find out who the driver was.

Generally, you will want to be able to adjust your schedule to follow up on any new leads that surface during the course of your investigation. For example, even though you had not planned to interview yet another witness and want to conclude your investigation quickly, you realize that the testimony of the furniture company's truck driver may be valuable. You therefore contact the truck driver and set up an appointment to interview him.

Be Open Minded and Objective

Even though your goal is to uncover or verify information helpful to your client, you should not let that goal close your mind to facts that may adversely affect the client. Remember that as an investigator, you play a neutral role and not that of a judge or jury member. Your job is to gather factual information as objectively as possible, regardless of how it may affect your client's interests.

For example, in the Baranski case, it might be important to know whether Katherine Baranski was exercising reasonable care when she was driving down Mattis Avenue just before the accident occurred. You might therefore ask a witness whether the witness had observed Baranski's car immediately before the accident—to find out if she was speeding, for example, or looking away from the road at the time the accident occurred. Even though the witness's answers to these questions might be detrimental to your client's interests, your supervising attorney will want to know these and any other facts that might have a bearing on the case so that the attorney can prepare in advance for opposing counsel's arguments.

As another example, suppose that the following developments take place. You interview the furniture company's truck driver and are surprised to learn that his perception of what happened just prior to the accident is quite different from that of another eyewitness, Julia Williams. Williams had told you that she saw Peretto's green van run the stop sign and crash into Baranski's car. Now, the furniture company's truck driver states that he is quite sure that the green van ahead of him stopped at the stop sign before proceeding across Mattis Avenue.

Realize that if you were able to learn about and locate this witness (the furniture truck driver), defendant Peretto's attorney and paralegal will probably also be able to do so should Baranski bring suit against Peretto. Therefore, you need to find out as much as possible about the truck driver's perceptions of the accident. In view of his statements, your supervising attorney, Gilmore, may decide not to take Baranski's case. If Gilmore does accept the case, he will need to determine how to deal with the truck driver's testimony if opposing counsel offers it in court.

Be Imaginative

The creative investigator keeps the goal of the investigation in mind at all times. In the Baranski case, for example, one of Baranski's goals is to obtain damages from Tony Peretto, the potential defendant. To achieve that goal, your supervising attorney must have evidence that (1) Peretto was indeed negligent (driving carelessly or recklessly, in breach of a duty and in violation of the law)[1] and (2) Peretto has sufficient assets or insurance coverage to pay the amount of damages Baranski seeks to obtain. In determining how to find the necessary evidence, give your imagination free rein.

In addition to investigating the police report of the accident and interviewing police officers and other witnesses, try to think of other possible information that might be helpful in establishing that Peretto was negligent. Did Peretto have a record of careless driving and traffic violations? If so, his driving record (if allowed in court) would help convince a jury that he might have been negligent in the Baranski case. Did Peretto have a medical condition that required the use of medication that might have affected his driving? Did he have any vision problems that required corrective lenses for driving? If so, was he wearing corrective lenses at the time of the accident?

In regard to Peretto's assets, you have already included in your investigation plan a note to find out from Peretto's insurance carrier the limits of his liability coverage (although you may not be able to obtain this information until discovery, as mentioned earlier). It will also be useful to know of any assets that can be reached to satisfy a judgment for Baranski. (See Chapter 11 for a discussion of how assets can be located and used to satisfy court judgments.)

Focusing on the desired outcome of the case—and the kind of evidence that will help to bring about that outcome—gives direction to your imaginative and creative efforts. Inevitably, there will be times during an investigation when you think you have reached a dead end or exhausted all possible sources. Whether you are trying to locate witnesses or other types of information, you will find that your imagination is always a great resource in identifying further potential sources.

INVESTIGATION AND THE RULES OF EVIDENCE

Because an investigation is conducted to obtain information and verify facts that may eventually be introduced as evidence at trial, you should know what kind of evidence will be admissible in court before undertaking your investigation.

Evidence is anything that is used to prove the existence or nonexistence of a fact. Whether evidence will be admitted in court is determined by the **rules of evidence**—rules that have been created by the courts to ensure that any evidence presented in court is fair and reliable. The Federal Rules of Evidence govern the admissibility of evidence in federal courts. For cases brought in state courts, state rules of evidence apply. (Many states have adopted evidence rules patterned on the federal rules.) Of course, you will not need to become an expert in evidentiary rules, but a basic knowledge of how evidence is classified and what types of evidence are admissible in court will greatly assist your investigative efforts.

EVIDENCE
Anything that is used to prove the existence or nonexistence of a fact.

RULES OF EVIDENCE
Rules governing the admissibility of evidence in trial courts.

1. See Chapter 8 for a discussion of what elements constitute the tort of negligence.

DEVELOPING PARALEGAL SKILLS

Creative Investigating

Larry Bork, an attorney, and his legal assistant, Jennifer Smith, are reviewing several witness statements for a case involving their client, B&O Railroad. The case involved a car/train accident in which a woman, Lisa Schrader, while driving across the train tracks at a railroad crossing, was hit by an oncoming train. Now her family is suing B&O for negligence, claiming that B&O was responsible for the loss of Lisa Schrader's life. Larry and Jennifer are trying to put together a defense for the railroad.

THE WITNESSES' TESTIMONY

The witness statements indicated that there were no gates to bar automobile traffic from the crossing, but there were flashing lights and bells that warned that a train was coming. The first witness stated that the lights had, in fact, been flashing and the bells ringing. The second witness agreed and stated that there had also been a clear line of sight for about fifty to seventy yards. These two witnesses and a third witness all stated that the woman had had her window open as she approached and crossed the tracks.

"I just can't imagine it. How could someone drive up to railroad tracks with the window open and cross them when there were bells ringing and lights flashing? Do you think that she was driving under the influence of drugs or alcohol?" asked Jennifer. "That's a good question," commented Larry. "We need to get a copy of the autopsy report to see what, if any, drugs or alcohol were in her system."

THE AUTOPSY REPORT

When the autopsy report arrived in the mail, the report indicated that the deceased had had a blood alcohol level of .18. "Well, that's it!" thought Jennifer. "A blood alcohol level of .10 is considered driving under the influence in our state. She was driving under the influence of alcohol. Her mental abilities were impaired."

Jennifer told Larry what she had learned. "I think you're probably right," he agreed. "Now I want you to find out if she had a history of alcoholism. If she didn't, I want you to try to find out why she would have been drinking at six o'clock on a Tuesday evening."

A DEFENSE FOR B&O

Jennifer completed the investigation and learned that Schrader had not had a history of alcoholism. Apparently, the reason Schrader had been drinking was that she had been told earlier that day that she was going to be laid off work. One of Schrader's co-workers said that Schrader had left work early to go "drown her sorrows" at Hal's Bar down the street. Jennifer discussed what she had learned with Larry, and Larry said to her, "Good work, Jennifer! It looks like we've got our defense! We can claim that it was Schrader's own negligence, and not that of B&O, that caused the accident."

Direct versus Circumstantial Evidence

Two types of evidence may be brought into court—direct evidence and circumstantial evidence. **Direct evidence** is any evidence that, if believed, establishes the truth of the fact in question. For example, bullets found in the body of a shooting victim provide direct evidence of the type of gun that fired them. **Circumstantial evidence** is indirect evidence that, even if believed, does not establish the fact in question but only the degree of likelihood of the fact. In other words, circumstantial evidence can create an inference that a fact exists.

DIRECT EVIDENCE
Evidence establishing the existence of a fact that is in question without relying on inferences.

CIRCUMSTANTIAL EVIDENCE
Indirect evidence that is offered to establish, by inference, the likelihood of a fact that is in question.

For example, suppose that your firm's client owns the type of gun that shot the bullets found in the victim's body. This circumstantial evidence does not establish that the client committed the crime. Combined with other circumstantial evidence, however, it is possible that a jury could be convinced that the client committed the crime. For instance, if other circumstantial evidence indicates that your firm's client had a motive for harming the victim and that the client was at the scene of the crime at the time the crime was committed, a jury might conclude that the client committed the crime.

Relevance

Evidence will not be admitted in court unless it is relevant to the matter in question. **Relevant evidence** is evidence that tends to prove or disprove the fact in question. For example, evidence that the gun belonging to your firm's client was in the home of another person when the victim was shot would be relevant, because it would tend to prove that the client did not shoot the victim.

RELEVANT EVIDENCE
Evidence tending to make a fact in question more or less probable than it would be without the evidence. Only relevant evidence is admissible in court.

Even relevant evidence may not be admitted in court if its probative (proving) value is substantially outweighed by other important considerations. For example, even though evidence is relevant, it may not be necessary—the fact at issue may already have been sufficiently proved or disproved by previous evidence. In that situation, the introduction of further evidence would be a waste of time and would cause undue delay in the trial proceedings. Relevant evidence may also be excluded if it would tend to distract the jury from the main issues of the case, mislead the jury, or cause the jury to decide the issue on an emotional basis.

Authentication of Evidence

At trial, an attorney must lay the proper foundation for the introduction of certain evidence, such as documents, exhibits, and other objects, and must demonstrate to the court that the evidence is what the attorney claims. The process by which this is accomplished is referred to as **authentication.** The authentication requirement relates to relevance, because something offered in evidence becomes relevant to the case only if it is authentic, or genuine.

AUTHENTICATION
Establishing the genuineness of an item that is to be introduced as evidence in a trial.

- **As a legal investigator, you therefore need to make sure that the evidence you obtain is not only relevant but also capable of being authenticated if introduced at trial.**

Commonly, evidence is authenticated by the testimony of witnesses. For example, if an attorney wants to introduce an autopsy report as evidence in a case, he or she can have the report authenticated by the testimony of the medical examiner who signed it. Generally, an attorney must offer enough proof of authenticity to convince the court that the evidence is in fact what it is purported to be.

The rules of evidence require authentication because certain types of evidence, such as exhibits and objects, cannot be cross-examined by opposing counsel, as witnesses can, yet such evidence may have a significant effect on the jury. The authentication requirement provides a safeguard against the introduction of nonverified evidence that may strongly influence the outcome of the case.

The Federal Rules of Evidence provide for the self-authentication of certain types of evidence. In other words, certain documents or records need not be authenticated by testimony. Certified copies of public records, for example, are automatically deemed authentic. Other self-authenticating evidentiary documents include official publications (such as a report issued by the federal Environmental Protection Agency), documents containing a notary public's seal or the seal of a public official, newspaper or magazine articles, and manufacturers' trademarks or labels.

Hearsay

HEARSAY
An oral or written statement made by an out-of-court declarant that is later offered in court by a witness (not the declarant) concerning a matter before the court. Hearsay is generally not admissible as evidence.

When interviewing witnesses, you need to make sure that a witness's statements are based on the witness's own knowledge and not hearsay. **Hearsay** is defined as any testimony given in court about a statement made by someone else. Literally, it is what someone heard someone else say. For example, if a witness in the Baranski case testified in court as to what he or she heard another observer say about the accident, that testimony would be hearsay. Generally, hearsay is not admissible as evidence. To a great extent, this is because the listener may have misunderstood what another person said, and without the opportunity of cross-examining the originator of the statement, the misperception cannot be challenged.

Exceptions to the hearsay rule are made in certain circumstances. Generally, these exceptions allow for hearsay to be considered as evidence when the hearsay consists of statements that are highly reliable or believable. For example, under the Federal Rules of Evidence, hearsay that consists of a dying person's statement on the cause or circumstances of his or her impending death may be admissible. Statements made by persons in a moment of excitement caused by a startling event or condition may be admissible. These and some other exceptions to the hearsay rule are listed and described in Exhibit 15.4.

Competence and Reliability of Witnesses

The rules of evidence include certain restrictions and qualifications pertaining to witnesses. Witnesses must have sufficient mental competence to understand the significance of testifying under oath. As will be discussed shortly, witnesses must also be competent in the sense that they have the necessary knowledge or skill to testify about certain matters.

EXHIBIT 15.4
Some Exceptions to the Hearsay Rule

Present Sense Impression—A statement describing an event or condition made at the time the declarer perceived the event or condition or immediately thereafter [FRE 803(1)].* Example: "I smell smoke."

Excited Utterance—A statement relating to a startling event or condition made while the declarer was under the stress or excitement caused by the startling event or condition [FRE 803(2)]. Example: "Oh no! The brakes aren't working!"

State of Mind—A statement of the declarer's then existing state of mind, emotion, sensation, or physical condition (such as intent, plan, motive, design, mental feeling, pain, or bodily health). Such statements are considered trustworthy because of their spontaneity [FRE 803(3)]. Example: "My leg is bleeding and hurts terribly."

Recorded Recollection—A memorandum or record indicating a witness's previous statements concerning a matter that the witness cannot now remember with sufficient accuracy to testify fully about the matter. If admitted in court, the memorandum or record may be read into evidence but may not itself be received as an exhibit unless offered by an adverse party [FRE 803(5)]. Example: An employer's memo to one of his or her employees in which the employer responds to the employee's complaint about safety violations in the workplace.

Former Testimony—Testimony that was given at another hearing or deposition by a witness who is now unavailable, if the party against whom the testimony is now offered was a predecessor in interest and had an opportunity to examine the witness in court during the previous hearing or deposition [FRE 804(b)(1)]. Example: An employee's testimony about his or her employer that was introduced at a trial brought by the employee's co-worker against that employer for sexual harassment. The employer is now being sued by another employee for sexual harassment, and the employee who testified in the previous trial is out of the country. The employee's testimony in the previous trial may be admissible.

Business Records—A document or compilation of data made in the course of a regularly conducted business activity, unless the source of the information or the method or circumstances of the document's preparation indicates that it is not trustworthy as evidence. The source of information must be from a person with first-hand knowledge, although this person need not be the person who actually made the entry or created the document [FRE 803(6)]. Example: Financial statements of a business firm.

Dying Declarations—In a prosecution for homicide or in a civil action or proceeding, a statement made by a person who believes that his or her death is impending about the cause or circumstances of his or her impending death [FRE 804(b)(2)]. Example: Derek said just before he died, "Jethro stabbed me."

Statement against Interest—A statement that was made by someone who is now unavailable and that was, at the time of its making, so far contrary to the declarer's financial, legal, or other interests that a reasonable person in the declarer's position would not have made the statement unless he or she believed it to be true [FRE 804(b)(3)]. Example: Peretto says that Jackson, who is now missing, made the following statement to Peretto just before leaving town: "I committed the perfect crime!"

Miscellaneous Exceptions—Miscellaneous exceptions include records of vital statistics [FRE 803(9)]; records of religious organizations [FRE 803(11)]; marriage, baptismal, or similar certificates [FRE 803(12)]; family records (including charts, engravings on rings, inscriptions on family portraits, and engravings on tombstones) [FRE 803(13)]; and statements offered as evidence of a material fact that are trustworthy because of the circumstances in which they were uttered [FRE 804(b)(5) and FRE 803(24)].

*Federal Rules of Evidence.

When interviewing a potential witness during a legal investigation, you will also want to ascertain whether that witness is reliable. For example, if you are interviewing an eyewitness in the Baranski case—that is, someone who actually saw the accident occur—you will want to find out whether the witness has good vision and was capable of clearly seeing the accident from his or her vantage point. You will also want to evaluate how certain the witness is about what he or she saw. Although a witness may be competent to

DEVELOPING PARALEGAL SKILLS

Keeping an Evidence Log

Steve Fessler works as a paralegal for Marty Melman, a sole practitioner. Marty is representing June Linden, the plaintiff in a personal-injury case. Marty has asked Steve to obtain the X-rays of the plaintiff's fractured ankle. The fracture occurred as a result of an auto accident.

Steve receives a phone call from the hospital indicating that the X-rays are ready to be picked up. He drives to the hospital, picks up the X-rays, and brings them back to the office. He places them in a special folder and applies an exhibit label to the folder, which contains a thorough description of the X-rays for purposes of identification. The special folder will preserve the X-rays. Next, he places the folder in the evidence cabinet, which is kept locked so that access to its contents is controlled. He takes out a notebook entitled "Evidence Log" and places a clean log sheet in it. He fills in the blanks on the log sheet as follows:

- NAME OF CASE: *Linden v. Thompson*
- EVIDENCE: X-rays of June Linden's left-ankle fracture
- DATE ACQUIRED: January 17, 1996
- ACQUIRED BY: Steve Fessler
- HOW ACQUIRED: By Steve Fessler from St. Paul's Hospital
- IDENTIFYING MARKS: Exhibit 14
- LOCATION OF EVIDENCE: Evidence cabinet of the law offices of Marty Melman
- EVIDENCE CUSTODIAN: Steve Fessler

The rest of the form contains columns for recording the chain of custody of the evidence. There is a column for the name of each person to whom the evidence was released, a column for the date on which it was released, and a column for the purpose of the release. This way, if the evidence needs to be reviewed by someone, such as an expert witness, there will be a record of the evidence and who has or had custody of it. Maintaining an evidence log also helps to protect against claims that the evidence is not authentic or has been altered in any way while in the law firm's possession.

testify, that does not necessarily mean the witness will be a reliable witness in court.

Expert Witnesses. As discussed in earlier chapters, opinions of expert witnesses may be admissible if scientific, technical, or other specialized knowledge will assist the court in understanding the evidence or determining a fact in question. In the Baranski case, for example, suppose that Katherine Baranski suffered brain damage as a result of the accident and could no longer work as a math instructor. In this situation, a qualified economist might be called as an expert witness to give an expert opinion on Katherine Baranski's potential lifetime earnings as a math professor (that had to be forgone as a result of the accident and thus were being claimed as damages).

Lay Witnesses. Lay witnesses (discussed in Chapter 14) are competent to testify on factual matters that are normally perceived accurately by the average person. For example, in the Baranski case, a lay witness who saw the accident (an eyewitness) would be competent to testify as to the color and type of vehicle that hit Baranski's car, whether the vehicle did or did not stop at the stop sign, and so on. A lay witness's *opinion,* however, unlike that of an expert, is not admissible. For example, a lay witness could not competently testify as to the nature and extent of the injuries sustained by Baranski in the accident. The relationship between the accident and the injuries complained of would have to be established by a medical expert.

For this reason, you should also be careful to differentiate statements of fact from statements of opinion when you interview witnesses. Suppose that in the Baranski case, a witness testified that she saw a green van run through a stop sign and crash into a car. That statement is based on the witness's perception of a factual event. But if the witness states that the driver was driving recklessly, the witness is stating an opinion, because the statement is based on the witness's interpretation of the facts. This opinion will normally not be admissible because no person, merely by observing the accident, could have determined whether the driver of the van was driving recklessly. The driver might have run the stop sign for reasons that could not be perceived by an observer—because the van's brakes failed to work properly, for example, or because the driver had a fainting spell and lost control of the vehicle momentarily.

Privileges

Testimony that is reliable and relevant may be excluded if it is protected by a privilege. A witness who is called to testify may have a legal duty not to disclose certain types of information because it is privileged. When conducting an investigation, you should thus be aware of the fact that certain information may not be admissible in court because it is privileged.

Recall from Chapter 4 that written and oral communications between an attorney and a client are privileged if they concern the client's legal rights or problems. The client, not the attorney, holds the privilege, and the client may, if he or she so chooses, *waive* (forgo the right to exercise) the privilege. Communications between a physician and his or her patient are also normally protected by privilege, as are communications between an individual and his or her priest or other clergy member and communications between spouses.

There are, of course, times when privileged information may (or should) be disclosed. In regard to the attorney-client privilege, as discussed previously in Chapter 4, if a client sues an attorney, the attorney is permitted to disclose confidential information when he or she must do so to defend against the lawsuit. Another exception to the attorney-client privilege is made when an attorney knows that a client is about to commit a serious crime (such as killing or seriously injuring another person).

The Fifth Amendment of the U.S. Constitution states that no person "shall be compelled in any criminal case to be a witness against himself." This means that a witness cannot be forced to answer questions that would tend to incriminate him or her. A person may also claim his or her Fifth Amendment privilege in any number of noncriminal proceedings. Whether at a divorce proceeding, a congressional hearing, or a disciplinary meeting before a local school board, a person normally need not provide evidence that is potentially self-incriminating. The courts, not the individuals who claim it, decide when the Fifth Amendment applies.

Settlement Negotiations

Evidence that the parties to a lawsuit were involved in settlement negotiations is not normally admissible to prove liability. For example, if in the Baranski case, defendant Peretto offered to settle the claim for $75,000, that settlement offer could not be admitted as evidence of Peretto's liability for the accident. Similarly, evidence of conduct or statements made during negotiations is not normally admissible. If such evidence were admissible in court, parties to lawsuits would be reluctant to make settlement offers. In the Baranski case, for example, Peretto would be reluctant to offer to settle the claim if he thought that his offer might be used in court as evidence that he assumed responsibility for the accident.

Evidence otherwise subject to pretrial discovery must not be excluded simply because it was presented in the course of settlement negotiations, however. For example, suppose that Katherine Baranski's medical records established that she had suffered a broken hip as a result of the accident. If Baranski's attorney presented a copy of those records to Peretto during the course of settlement negotiations, the records could still be introduced as evidence later, during the trial.

- **The rule that evidence of settlement negotiations is inadmissible applies only to information relating to the negotiations that could not otherwise be obtained through discovery.**

LOCATING WITNESSES

Perhaps one of the most challenging tasks for the legal investigator is locating a witness whose address is unknown or who has moved from a previous, known address. Suppose, for example, that in the Baranski case, the police investigation report lists the name, address, and telephone number of Edna Ball, a witness to the accident. When you call her number, a recording informs you that the phone has been disconnected. You go to her address, and the house appears to be vacant. What is your next step?

At this point, many paralegals suggest to their supervising attorneys that a professional investigator take over the search. But if you alone must locate the witness, there are several sources to which you can turn. A good starting point is to visit other homes in the neighborhood. Perhaps someone living nearby knows Edna Ball and can give you at least some leads as to where she is or what happened to her. Other sources are discussed below.

Telephone and City Directories

The telephone directory can sometimes be a valuable source of information for the investigator. In trying to locate Edna Ball, for example, you might

PARALEGAL PROFILE Legal Investigator

JUDY SHOLL received her bachelor of arts degree from the University of Pittsburgh in 1963 and then received a degree in education from Oxford University in England. She taught high school for about four years in Massachusetts and then took about thirteen years off to raise her children. Before reentering the work force, Sholl did some research and discovered that there were good job prospects in the paralegal field. After receiving her paralegal certificate from Arapahoe Community College, in Littleton, Colorado, she did an internship with the Colorado State Public Defender's Office, where she worked as an investigator. She currently works as an investigator with the Federal Public Defender's Office in Colorado.

What do you like best about your work?

"My job is not a desk job. I have a wide variety of responsibilities, which include being part of the trial team, responding to investigation requests, being accurate and attentive to detail, and writing reports in a professional and timely manner. I investigate only federal criminal cases, including cases that involve military bases and Indian reservations. My position requires some travel, but travel requirements vary from case to case. I enjoy the tremendous amount of 'people contact.' I interact with witnesses, experts, and attorneys. What makes my job enjoyable is the changing scene from week to week."

"VOLUNTEERING IN ANY CAPACITY IS THE BEST INVESTMENT YOU WILL EVER MAKE."

What is the greatest challenge that you face in your area of work?

"I have many challenges in my job, but probably the greatest challenge is finding out what other information is available to support our case or a client's position. I am given information from the government about each case, but it is up to me to find and check sources or locate people. I have to be very resourceful."

What advice do you have for would-be paralegals in your area of work?

"I feel that it is important to do an internship if the prospective paralegal is interested in criminal law. Volunteering in any capacity is the best investment you will ever make. Volunteer work lets you see if a particular area of law is for you. It also allows others to see your capabilities, and it therefore may open some doors to job possibilities."

What are some tips for success as a paralegal in your area of work?

"Any paralegal working in my area must be willing to work hard and long hours. This particular work can also be very emotionally and personally exhausting. It requires common sense and determination. A good paralegal in this area should be goal oriented and have highly developed investigative skills.

check to see if her name is still listed in the current directory and, if so, whether it is listed jointly with someone, such as her husband. Your local telephone information service might have a new number listed for her. If the information-service operator indicates that the number is unlisted, you can explain the nature of your concern and request that the operator phone Edna Ball at that number to see if she is willing to call you.

City directories are also good potential sources of information. Such directories may be available in the local library or the law firm's library. A city directory generally contains more information than a phone book. For example, some city directories list places of employment and spouses' names in addition to addresses and telephone numbers. Typically, city directories provide a listing of names and phone numbers by street address. In the Baranski case, if you wanted to obtain the telephone numbers of persons who live in the area of the Baranski-Peretto accident, you could consult a city directory for addresses near the intersection where the accident occurred.

Other Information Sources

Other sources of information are media reports (newspaper and magazine articles and television videos covering the event being investigated); court records (probate proceedings, lawsuits, etc.); deeds to property (usually located in the county courthouse); birth, marriage, and death certificates; voter registration lists; the post office (to see if the witness left a forwarding address); credit bureaus; the tax assessor's office; and city utilities, such as the local electric or water company.

Professional organizations may be useful sources as well. For example, if you have learned from one of Edna Ball's neighbors that she is a paralegal, you can check with state and local paralegal associations to see if they have current information on her. You might also check with federal, state, or local governmental agencies or bureaus (discussed in the following section) to see if the information contained in public records will be helpful in locating Edna Ball.

ACCESSING GOVERNMENT INFORMATION

Records and files acquired and stored by government offices and agencies can be a tremendous resource for the legal investigator. Public records available at local government buildings or offices (such as the county courthouse or post office) were mentioned above. Additionally, it is possible to obtain information from federal agencies, such as the Social Security Administration, and from state departments or agencies, such as the state revenue department or the secretary of state's office. If you wish to obtain information from any government files or records, you should check with the specific agency or department to see what rules apply. Exhibit 15.5 describes the kinds of information collected by selected federal government agencies.

The Freedom of Information Act (FOIA), which was enacted by Congress in 1966, requires the federal government to disclose certain "records" to "any person" on request. A request that complies with the FOIA procedures need only contain a reasonable description of the information sought. Exhibit 15.6 on page 590 illustrates the proper format for a letter requesting information under the FOIA. Note that the FOIA exempts some types of information from the disclosure requirement, including classified information (information concerning national security), confidential material dealing with trade secrets, government personnel rules, and personal medical files.

EXHIBIT 15.5
Data Collected by Selected Federal Government Agencies

Bureau of the Census, Department of Commerce, Washington, DC 20233. (301) 763-4040—The U.S. Bureau of the Census collects data every ten years on the U.S. population. Information collected includes the age, address, sex, ethnic origin or race, marital status, income, and place of employment of every person living in every household.

Department of Defense (DOD), Office of the Secretary, The Pentagon, Washington, DC 20301-1155. (703) 545-6700—The DOD has information on anyone who has sought a security clearance.

Federal Bureau of Investigation (FBI), Ninth Street & Pennsylvania Avenue N.W., Washington, DC 20535 (202) 324-3000—The FBI has a file on anyone who has ever been employed by the federal government, been in the military, or attempted to obtain a security clearance. The FBI also keeps files on some other individuals—for example, those who may be involved in activities counter to the interests the U.S. government.

Federal Housing Authority (FHA), Department of Housing and Urban Development, 451 7th Street S.W., Washington, DC 20233. (202) 755-6422—The FHA has information on all persons who have applied for federal housing assistance.

Internal Revenue Service (IRS), 1111 Constitution Avenue N.W., Washington, DC 20224. (202) 566-5000—The IRS has information concerning the age, sex, and marital status of taxpayers, as well as all their sources of income—jobs, checking and savings accounts, investments, and so on.

Securities and Exchange Commission (SEC), 450 Fifth Street N.W., Washington, DC 20549. (202) 272-3100—The SEC has information on anyone involved in the sale of securities (such as corporate stocks and bonds).

Selective Service System (SSS), National Headquarters, Washington, DC 20435. (202) 724-0820—The SSS has information on draft registration.

Social Security Administration (SSA), 6401 Security Boulevard, Baltimore, MD 21235. (410) 965-7700—The SSA has a record of every person who has ever been an employee and collected wages. Additionally, the SSA has information concerning the income, indebtedness, marital status, medical history, and household arrangements of anyone who has applied for Social Security benefits, Medicare, Medicaid, or Aid to Families with Dependent Children.

Veterans Administration (VA), Department of Veterans Affairs, 810 Vermont Avenue, N.W., Washington, DC 20420. (202) 535-8300—The VA has information in its files concerning all persons who have served in the military. This includes not only military records but also information relating to jobs held, medical histories, education, and residences prior to entry into the service. Additional information will be entered if a veteran is receiving service-related benefits, such as a VA mortgage loan, educational assistance, or medical care.

INTERVIEWING WITNESSES

Witnesses play a key role in establishing the facts of an event. As a legal investigator, your goal is to elicit as much relevant and reliable information as possible from each witness about the event that you are investigating. How you approach witnesses, what kinds of questions you ask, how you ask those questions, and how you respond to the witnesses' answers—all of

EXHIBIT 15.6
Freedom of Information Act Request Form

Agency Head or FOIA Officer
Title
Name of Agency
Address of Agency
City, State, Zip

Re: Freedom of Information Act Request.

Dear________________:

Under the provisions of the Freedom of Information Act, 5 U.S.C. 552, I am requesting access to (identify the records as clearly and specifically as possible).

If there are any fees for searching for, or copying, the records I have requested, please inform me before you fill the request. (Or:...please supply the records without informing me if the fees do not exceed $____________.)

[Optional] I am requesting this information (state the reason for your request if you think it will assist you in obtaining the information).

[Optional] As you know, the act permits you to reduce or waive fees when the release of the information is considered as "primarily benefiting the public." I believe that this request fits that category and I therefore ask that you waive any fees.

If all or any part of this request is denied, please cite the specific exemption(s) that you think justifies your refusal to release the information, and inform me of the appeal procedures available to me under the law.

I would appreciate your handling this request as quickly as possible, and I look foward to hearing from you within 10 days, as the law stipulates.

Sincerely,

Signature
Name
Address
City, State, Zip

Source: U.S. Congress, House Committee on Government Operations, *A Citizen's Guide on How to Use the Freedom of Information Act and the Privacy Act Requesting Government Documents*, 95th Congress, 1st Session (1977).

these factors affect your chances of achieving that goal. Many of the interviewing skills discussed in Chapter 14 apply, of course, to all interviews. This section describes some basic skills and principles that are particularly relevant to investigative interviews. As mentioned earlier, each investigator uses whatever approach works best for him or her. Similarly, when interviewing witnesses, you will ultimately discover what tactics or strategies work best for you in different situations with different types of witnesses.

Questioning Witnesses

When you are asking questions as a legal investigator, you should follow this rule of thumb:

- **Phrase your questions so that they lead to the most complete answer possible.**

Investigative questions should be open ended. Compare, for example, the following two questions:

1. "Did you see the driver of the green van run the stop sign?"
2. "What did you see at the time of the accident?"

The first question calls for a "yes" or "no" answer. The second question, in contrast, invites the witness to explain fully what he or she actually saw. Something else that the witness saw could be important to the case—but unless you allow room for the witness's full description, you will not learn about this information.

Notice that the first question also assumes a fact—that the driver of the green van ran the stop sign. The second question, however, makes no assumptions and conveys no information to the witness that may influence his or her answer. Generally, the less the witness knows about other witnesses' descriptions, the better, because those other descriptions could influence the witness's perception of the event. You want to find out exactly what the witness observed, in his or her own words.

Listening Carefully and Responsively

As discussed in Chapter 14, in any interview, your primary role is that of a listener. A certain amount of casual conversation, or small talk, is necessary as the interview begins because it helps in establishing a rapport with the witness and putting the witness at ease. Once the interview is under way, however, you want the witness to do the talking. Follow the person's answers carefully. Indicate to the witness, using both verbal and nonverbal cues, that you are listening. Various prompting questions (such as, "And then what happened?" and "What did you do then?") indicate to the witness that you are listening closely. They can also help to keep the witness on track or allow the witness to tell you more about what he or she observed. Be careful to keep your prompting questions open ended, though. After all, you do not want your questions to limit the witness's description.

If you are not clear about the meaning of something the witness is saying, respond with a question that invites clarification of the statement. For example, if a witness to the Baranski accident states, "I don't think that the driver of the green van saw the stop sign," you might ask, "Why is that?"

When conducting investigations, you often will need to discuss sensitive and uncomfortable matters with those whom you interview. It is not necessarily unprofessional to show that you care and are concerned. If you are interviewing someone who has to describe a painful experience, such as the loss of a loved one in a car accident, respond naturally to the situation by extending your sympathy and condolences, briefly and with sensitivity.

Checking the Witness's Qualifications

When you are interviewing a witness during the course of an investigation, you often will not know whether the testimony of that witness will be needed in court or even whether the claim you are investigating will be litigated.

DEVELOPING PARALEGAL SKILLS

Accessing Government Information

Ellen Simons has started a new job as a paralegal for Smith & Case, a firm that handles federal Superfund cases. The federal Superfund law requires responsible parties to pay for the clean-up of hazardous-waste sites that, due to leakage or other emissions, pose a threat to the environment. (Responsible parties include owners and operators of the sites, as well as parties who created or transported the hazardous waste.) If the responsibile parties do not undertake clean-up operations, the law authorizes the Environmental Protection Agency (EPA) to clean up the sites with funds set aside for that purpose (hence the name "Superfund"). The EPA then recovers the costs of the clean-up operations from the responsible parties.

There are often many defendants in these cases because for any one toxic-waste site, there may be many responsible parties. The EPA has numerous documents in its files relating to the types of pollution present at the site and the potentially responsible parties.

Ellen is about to request copies of EPA documents pertaining to a case on which she is working, which involves the Suburban Landfill Superfund site. Her supervisor has given her the standard FOIA (Freedom of Information Act) form to submit to the EPA. Ellen reads through it and sees that several different types of requests may be made. The first is a request for all information that the EPA has in its files pertaining to the site. The second is a request for specific documents. Ellen decides to review the file and see what kinds of information she needs to obtain from the EPA. After all, there is no reason to request all of the documents if they are not necessary.

CONTACTING THE EPA'S REGIONAL OFFICE

Ellen's review of the file indicates that all she needs from the EPA is the "waste in–waste out" report, a document that gives the total volume of hazardous

Nonetheless, you should operate under the assumption that each witness is a potential court witness. Thus, you should make sure that the witness is competent to testify and reliable. Is there any indication that the witness has a physical or mental disability that might interfere with the accuracy of his or her perception of the witnessed event? Has the witness ever been convicted of a crime? Does he or she abuse drugs or have a reputation in the community as a troublemaker? As discussed earlier, if it can be shown that a witness is unreliable or incompetent to testify, the witness's testimony normally will not be admitted in court.

Also investigate the witness's possible biases. Does the witness have an interest in the claim being investigated that would tend to make his or her testimony prejudicial? Is the witness a relative or close friend of one of the parties involved in the claim? Does the witness hold a grudge against one of the parties? If the answer to any of these questions is yes, the witness's testimony may be discredited in court. In any event, it will probably not be as convincing as testimony given by a neutral, unbiased witness.

DEVELOPING PARALEGAL SKILLS, Continued

waste at the site and lists the parties that may be potentially responsible. Ellen decides to call the regional office of the EPA in the area in which the site is located to ask if it has this information, and, if so, what would be involved in copying it.

Ellen calls and speaks to Christopher Peters, a paralegal who processes FOIA requests for the EPA. Ellen identifies herself as a paralegal from the law firm of Smith & Case, which is representing a client involved with the Suburban Landfill Superfund site. She is greeted with an icy silence. Ellen, wondering what she might have said to offend him, asks him if the EPA has the waste in–waste out document.

CULTIVATING A GOOD RELATIONSHIP WITH AN AGENCY EMPLOYEE

Christopher responds, in a surprised voice, that they do have the documents. "Is that all that you want?" he asks. "Yes, that's all that we need now, until we determine our client's involvement at the site," responds Ellen. "Are you new?" asks Christopher. "Is it that obvious?" jokes Ellen. "No, not really," replied Christopher. "It's just that the paralegal before you always just sent in a FOIA request for everything that we had in our files, and it took weeks to respond to a request from your firm. Believe me, your firm has quite a reputation around here."

Ellen knows that she has handled things the right way. She smiles to herself and tells Christopher that she would submit the FOIA request for only the item that she has mentioned over the phone. "No one will believe that this request is from Smith & Case," laughs Christopher. Ellen knows that she is off to a good start in her new job and with an important legal assistant at the EPA.

Dealing with Hostile Witnesses

Witnesses may be friendly, neutral, or hostile (or adverse) witnesses. As discussed in Chapter 14, friendly witnesses are those who are friendly to your client's interests, and hostile witnesses are those who support the adversary's position or for some other reason do not wish to cooperate. Generally, anyone who resents being interviewed qualifies as a hostile witness as far as the investigator is concerned. Neutral witnesses are, as the phrase suggests, neither friendly nor hostile. They are parties who have no interest in the outcome of the case and who are not partial to either side in the legal controversy.

Friendly and neutral witnesses rarely present any problems in terms of cooperation or willingness to part with information. Sometimes, hostile witnesses refuse to be interviewed. On learning that the alternative might be a subpoena, however, a hostile witness may consent to at least a limited interview. If you plan to interview hostile witnesses, keep in mind the following rule of thumb:

- **Contact and interview hostile witnesses in the early stages of your investigation. The longer you wait, the greater the chance that they may be influenced by the opposing party's attorney or the opinions of persons sympathetic to the opposing party.**

When interviewing hostile witnesses, you need to be especially careful to be objective, fair, and unbiased in your approach. This does not mean that you have to ignore your client's interests. On the contrary, you will best serve those interests by doing all you can to keep from further alienating a witness whose information might ultimately help your client's case.

WITNESS STATEMENTS

WITNESS STATEMENT
The written transcription of a statement made by the witness during an interview and signed by the witness.

Whenever you interview a witness, you should take notes and prepare a memorandum of the interview. Depending on the procedures followed by your firm, you may want to have the witness—particularly if he or she is a hostile witness—sign a statement. A **witness statement** is a written statement setting forth what the witness said during the interview. Statutes and court rules vary as to the value of witness statements as evidence. Usually, statements made by witnesses during interviews cannot be introduced as evidence in court, but they can be used for other purposes. For example, if a hostile witness's testimony in court contradicts something that he or she said during your interview, the witness statement may be used to impeach the witness—that is, to call into question the witness's testimony or demonstrate that the witness is unreliable. Witness statements also can be used to refresh a witness's memory.

The Content of a Witness Statement

Exhibit 15.7 shows the type of information that is normally contained in a witness statement. The statement should begin by identifying the witness, the interviewer, the time and place of the interview, and the event that was witnessed. In some circumstances—if you suspect that a witness might change his or her mind about what was said during the interview, for example—you may want to create a handwritten statement for the witness to sign immediately. In other situations, you may want to return to the office and type up a statement for the witness to sign later.

When writing or typing a witness statement, you should—to the extent possible or feasible—include the witness's own words. The statement should conclude with an attestation clause, which is a sentence indicating that the witness has read the statement and attests to its accuracy or truth. Some investigators have the witness initial each page of the statement; others simply add to the final attestation clause the number of pages—for example, "I affirm that the information given in the three pages of this statement are accurate and true to the best of my knowledge." Exhibit 15.8 on page 596 presents a portion of a sample witness statement.

Recording Interviews

Some investigators tape-record their interviews as an alternative to writing up statements—providing, of course, that the witness agrees to have the

EXHIBIT 15.7
Information Contained in a Witness Statement

1. **Information about the Witness**
   —Name, address, and phone number
   —Name, address, and phone number of the witness's employer or place of business
   —Interest, if any, in the outcome of the claim being investigated

2. **Information about the Interview**
   —Name of the interviewer
   —Name of the attorney or law firm for which the claim is being investigated
   —Date, time, and place of interview

3. **Identification of the Event Witnessed**
   —Nature of the action or event observed by the witness
   —Date of the action or event

4. **Witness's Description of the Event**

5. **Attestation Clause**
   —Provision or clause at the end of the statement affirming the truth of the witness's description as written in the statement.

[Witness's Signature]

interview tape-recorded. As pointed out in Chapter 14, if you are using a tape recorder, you need to state at the beginning of the tape the name of the witness; other relevant witness information; the name of the person who conducted the interview; the date, time, and place of the interview; and other information that would normally appear in a written statement. If more than one tape is used, you should indicate at the end of each tape that the interview will be continued on the next tape in the series, and each subsequent tape should contain identifying information.

Some of the advantages and disadvantages of tape-recording interviews were discussed in Chapter 14. In regard to tape-recorded witness statements, you should check with your supervising attorney to learn the firm's preferences with respect to tape-recorded versus written witness statements.

SUMMARIZING YOUR RESULTS

The final step in any investigation is summarizing the results. How you organize your summary depends to a large extent on your own organizational preferences and the scope of the investigation. Generally, though, your investigation report should provide the following:

- An overall summary of your findings.
- A summary of the facts and information gathered from each source that you investigated.
- Your general conclusions and recommendations based on the information obtained during the investigation.

EXHIBIT 15.8
A Sample Witness Statement (Excerpt)

STATEMENT OF JULIA WILLIAMS

I, Julia Williams, am a thirty-five-year-old female. I reside at 3801 Mattis Avenue, Nita City, Nita 48800, and my home telephone number is (408) 555-8989. I work as a nurse at the Nita City Hospital & Clinic, 412 Hospital Way, Nita City, Nita 48802. My work telephone number is (408) 555-9898. I am making this statement in my home on the afternoon of February 8, 1996. The statement is being made to Elena Lopez, a paralegal with the law firm of Jeffers, Gilmore & Dunn.

In regard to the accident on the corner of Mattis Avenue and Thirty-eighth Street on August 4, 1995, at approximately 7:45 A.M. on that date, I was standing at the southwest corner of that intersection, waiting to cross the street, when I observed . . .

* * * *

I affirm that the information given in this statement is accurate and true to the best of my knowledge.

Julia Williams
Julia Williams

Overall Summary

The overall summary of the investigation should thoroughly describe for the reader all of the facts that you have gathered about the case. This section should be written in such a way that someone not familiar with the case could read it and become adequately informed of the factual background.

Source-by-source Summaries

A second step is to create a list of your information sources, including witnesses, and summarize the facts gleaned from each of these sources. Each "source section" should contain all of the information gathered from that source, including direct quotes from witnesses. Each source section should also contain a subsection giving your personal comments on that particular source. You might comment on a witness's demeanor, for example, or on whether the witness's version of the facts was consistent or inconsistent with that of other witnesses. Your impressions of the witness's competence or reliability could be noted. If the witness provided you with further leads to be explored, this information could also be included.

General Conclusions and Recommendations

In the final section, you will present your overall conclusions about the investigation, as well as any suggestions that you have on the development of the case. Attorneys rely heavily on their investigators' impressions of witnesses and evaluations of investigative results because the investigators have firsthand knowledge of the sources. Your impression of a potentially important witness, for example, may help the attorney decide whether to arrange for a follow-up interview with the witness. Usually, the attorney will want

TODAY'S PROFESSIONAL PARALEGAL

Locating a Witness

Darin Styles, a legal assistant in a litigation firm, is trying to locate a missing witness in a product-liability case. The witness, Bob Morey, saw the plaintiff's hand being crushed by a press in the factory where both he and the plaintiff worked. Morey helped the plaintiff remove his hand from the press and obtain medical treatment.

LOCATING THE WITNESS

Darin has tried to contact Morey by telephoning him and by going to his listed address, but Morey has apparently moved. He also no longer works at the factory where the accident occurred. When Darin was unable to find Morey at his home, he asked some of the neighbors if they knew where Morey now lived, but he had no success in finding a forwarding address.

Darin has now decided to go to the post office. He approaches the counter and asks if there is a forwarding address for Bob Morey of 1234 Grove Street, Appleton, Michigan. The clerk gives Darin a form to fill out. The clerk then checks the records and finds a forwarding address for Bob Morey. Darin copies it down, thanks her, and leaves. He drives to the address. It appears that someone is living in the house. Darin gets out of the car, goes to the door, and knocks.

INTERVIEWING THE WITNESS

A man answers the door. Darin introduces himself and explains the reason for his visit. The man is Bob Morey. Morey tells Darin that he is concerned about giving a statement because he lost his job as a result of complaining about the working conditions after the accident happened. He is afraid that if he gets involved in a lawsuit, he will have an even harder time finding another job.

Darin tries to persuade Morey to cooperate. He tells Morey to think about the serious injury that his friend suffered and about how his friend may never work again because of his crushed hand. Darin also tells Morey that his testimony might help others and prevent this type of accident from happening again in the future. "If we win this case and others like it, the manufacturers of presses are going to have to change the design of their presses so they won't have to pay huge sums of money to people who are injured by their apparently negligent design," explains Darin.

Morey thinks about this. "Well, maybe if it will help others," he murmurs. "I don't know. I'll have to think about it. I'll let you know." Darin has not wanted to threaten Morey with a subpoena and turn him into a hostile witness, but he senses that if he does not mention the possibility of one now, he may have to use a subpoena to make Morey testify.

Darin says, "You know, Mr. Morey, you're a very important witness in this case. We need your testimony, and we'd like to get it voluntarily. But you're so important that we can get a court order—a subpoena—to require you to testify, if we have to." "You mean you can make me testify, even if I don't want to?" asks Morey. "Yes," answers Darin. "Well, in that case, I might as well tell you everything and help you as much as I can," responds Morey. Darin takes out his note pad and begins to interview Morey.

to interview only the most promising witnesses, and your impressions and comments will serve as a screening device. Based on your findings during the investigation, you might also suggest to the attorney what further information can be obtained during discovery, if necessary, and what additional research needs to be done.

KEY TERMS AND CONCEPTS

authentication 581
circumstantial evidence 581
direct evidence 581
evidence 579
hearsay 582
investigation plan 569
relevant evidence 581
rules of evidence 579
witness statement 594

CHAPTER SUMMARY

1. Investigation of the facts and circumstances of a legal matter is an important part of legal work because factual evidence is crucial to the outcome of a legal claim or case. Attorneys frequently rely on their paralegals to conduct or oversee legal investigations.

2. Before starting the investigation, the paralegal should create an investigation plan. The plan should be a step-by-step list of what sources will be investigated to obtain specific types of information. The paralegal should discuss the plan with his or her supervising attorney before embarking on the investigation.

3. Each person develops his or her own unique style of investigation—what works for one person may not work for another. As a general rule, however, all investigators benefit from abiding by certain basic principles. These principles include (a) focusing on the who, what, and where at all times; (b) maximizing the use of personal contacts; (c) maintaining flexibility; (d) being open minded and objective; and (e) being imaginative and creative in searching out relevant information and potential information sources.

4. Evidence is anything that is used to prove the existence or nonexistence of a fact. Direct evidence is any evidence that, if believed, establishes the truth of the fact in question. Circumstantial evidence is evidence that does not directly establish the fact in question but that indicates the degree of likelihood of the fact's existence. Because an investigation is undertaken to verify or uncover factual information that may eventually be used at trial, the paralegal should be familiar with what kind of evidence is admissible in court. Rules of evidence established by the federal and state courts spell out what types of evidence may or may not be admitted in court.

5. To be admissible in court, evidence must be relevant. Evidence must also be authenticated by a demonstration (usually by the testimony of a witness) that the evidence is what the attorney claims it to be. Some forms of evidence, such as certified copies of public records, are automatically deemed to be authentic and need not be authenticated by testimony. Hearsay (secondhand knowledge) is generally not admissible, although there are certain exceptions to this rule.

6. Witnesses must be competent and reliable. The opinions of expert witnesses are normally admissible. Lay witnesses are competent to testify on matters that are normally perceived accurately by the average person. Evidence protected by privilege (such as the attorney-client privilege) may be excluded, and evidence of settlement negotiations that would be unobtainable during discovery is not admissible to prove liability.

7. There are several information sources available to paralegals who wish to locate factual information regarding witnesses or other persons involved in a lawsuit. These sources include telephone and city directories, media reports, court records, utility companies, professional organizations, and information recorded, compiled, or prepared by federal, state, and local government entities. The Freedom of Information Act of 1966 requires that federal agencies disclose certain of their records to any person on request, providing that the form of the request complies with the procedure mandated by the act.

8. Witnesses play a key role in establishing the facts of a case, and an important part of the legal investigator's job is to interview witnesses. The paralegal should exercise good listening skills while interviewing witnesses and should ask open-ended questions to learn as much as possible from witnesses about what they know or observed. During an interview, the paralegal should evaluate the competence and reliability of the witness and whether the witness would be convincing in court. Depending on the wishes of the attorney, a witness statement may be prepared for the witness's signature, either at the time of the interview or shortly thereafter. As an alternative (again, depending on the attorney's wishes), an interview can be tape-recorded, if the witness agrees, and this recording can serve as documentation for what the witness said during the interview.

9. When the investigation is complete, the paralegal should summarize the results. The summary should include an overall summary, a source-by-source summary, and a final section giving the paralegal's conclusions and recommendations.

QUESTIONS FOR REVIEW

1. How do you create an investigation plan? Why might investigation plans differ for different cases?

2. What are the basic principles for conducting an investigation?

3. What is evidence? How are the rules of evidence used?

4. What is the difference between direct evidence and circumstantial evidence? What is relevant evidence? Why must evidence be relevant? Will relevant evidence always be admitted?

5. Why must evidence be authenticated? How is this accomplished?

6. What is hearsay? List and describe at least two exceptions to the hearsay rule and give examples of when they are used. What are privileges? How are they used in relation to evidence?

7. List five sources that you would consult in attempting to locate a witness. Which would be the most useful? The least useful? Why?

8. What techniques are used in interviewing witnesses? Rank the techniques in order from the most important to the least important.

9. What information should be contained in a witness statement?

10. What is included in an investigation summary? Why should one be prepared?

ETHICAL QUESTIONS

1. Thomas Lent is a new legal assistant with a law firm that specializes in personal-injury cases. He is reviewing a "Request to Produce Documents" that was recently received in a case that his supervising attorney is handling for the plaintiff. The document requests the plaintiff's medical records, but it does not state specifically which records or for what injuries. Thomas's supervising attorney instructs Thomas to obtain copies of all of the plaintiff's medical records. The plaintiff's medical-records file is several inches thick because of the plaintiff's age and various medical problems. Thomas is instructed to bury the relevant medical records in the stack and not to make them obvious to the defendant's attorney. If she wants these records, she will have to sort through the file, says the attorney. What should Thomas do? Can the attorney be disciplined for this kind of behavior?

2. In response to a discovery request, Lynnette Banks, a paralegal in a corporate law firm, receives a package of documents in the mail. She opens the package and begins to read through the documents. As she reads, she discovers documents with the words "Privileged and Confidential" stamped on them. She scans a document and realizes that it is a letter from the opposing counsel to his client. The letter reveals the opposing attorney's legal strategy in the case on which Lynnette is now working. What should Lynnette do?

PRACTICE QUESTIONS AND ASSIGNMENTS

1. Using the factual background presented in Practice Question 2 below, draft an "Authorization to Release Medical Information" letter for Lena Phillips to sign. Her full name and address are Lena A. Phillips, 150 North Street, Northville, New Hampshire, 12345.

2. Lena Phillips, a fifty-two-year-old self-employed seamstress, fell down the three steps in front of her house and fractured her right wrist. She was treated in the emergency room at the Neighborhood Hospital by Dr. Ralph Dean on the day that she fell, January 10, 1995, and released.

On January 17, January 25, and February 11, 1995, she visited Dr. Dean's office for follow-up care to make sure that the wrist was healing properly. It appeared that the wrist was healing properly during the month in which she was treated by Dr. Dean. She noticed, however, that even though she had a full range of motion in her wrist, the wrist angled inward somewhat. When she queried Dr. Dean about this, he told her that some angling of the wrist was inevitable.

Over the course of the following year, her wrist became increasingly crooked and bent inward. She went to an orthopedist, Dr. Alicia Byerly, on March 30, 1996. Dr. Byerly tried a splint, but without success. She eventually performed surgery on the wrist at the Neighborhood Hospital on May 3, 1996, but was unable to correct the problem. Dr. Byerly told Ms. Phillips that she should have had surgery on the wrist during the first three weeks after it was broken to correct the angling problem.

Lena Phillips has come to the firm for which you work, the law firm of Samson & Goren, 5000 West Avenue, Northville, New Hampshire 12345, because she wants to sue Dr. Dean for medical malpractice. On May 15, 1996, you are asked to investigate her case. Draft an investigation plan.

3. Assume that a witness is being questioned about statements that she heard a third party make. Determine which of the following statements would qualify as exceptions to the hearsay rule:

a. The third party exclaimed, "Watch out, he's not stopping at the red light!"
b. The third party apologized, "Are you all right? I am so sorry. I didn't mean to hurt you."
c. The third party uttered just before he died, "Make sure you find Joe. He is the one who shot me. Tom didn't have anything to do with this."
d. The third party exclaimed, "I smell gas fumes!"
e. The third party, who was the defendant's mistress, said, "He couldn't have killed Bob. He was with me last night."

QUESTIONS FOR CRITICAL ANLYSIS

1. During the course of a murder trial, a prosecuting attorney paraded through the courtroom carrying a hand that had been unearthed the day before and widely publicized as belonging to the murder victim. The defense attorney strenuously objected on the ground that the hand was not relevant. Should the judge sustain the objection?

2. Determine whether each statement below is a statement of fact or a statement of opinion, and explain why.

a. I am sure that the suspect took the money because when I saw him near the cash register, he looked around suspiciously and then tried to sneak away without being seen.
b. The man who took the money from the cash register was wearing a green trench coat, brown pants, and black boots and was carrying a large tan briefcase.

ROLE-PLAYING EXERCISES

DATA DISK

1. Using the facts from the Baranski-Peretto hypothetical presented in Chapter 10, role-play paralegal Elena Lopez and attorney Allen Gilmore. The paralegal and the attorney should discuss the investigation plan described in this chapter. The legal assistant should point out problem areas, and the attorney should suggest additional sources to investigate or indicate that there is no need to investigate certain areas. The attorney should also try to focus the investigation on certain areas.

2. Using the facts from this chapter's *Developing Paralegal Skills* on the car/train accident, act out an interview in which Jennifer Smith, the legal assistant, interviews one of the eyewitnesses to the accident, whose name is Louise Raymond. One student should play the role of the legal assistant and the other the role of the witness. Reverse roles if time allows.

The interviewer should meet Mrs. Raymond at her home and begin the interview with casual conversation and small talk. The interviewer should use open-ended questions and listen responsively and sensitively. During the interview, the interviewer should check the witness's qualifications, in the event that she has to testify.

Mrs. Raymond should start out as a hostile witness in the sense that she resents being interviewed, but she should be fairly easily won over by being persuaded that her testimony is important. Once the Mrs. Raymond decides to cooperate, she should be a friendly witness.

PROJECTS

1. Locate some law libraries in your city or county that are open to the public. What resources does each library have that would help you locate expert witnesses?

2. Call the county offices for your county and ask if they give tours. If they do, arrange to go on a tour of the offices. Find out what information is kept there, such as data on birth, death, marriage, and property. Also find out what information is available to the public and what procedures must be followed to obtain this information.

3. Using *public records only,* find out either of the following:

a. The name of the spouse of the person sitting next to you in class (if he or she is married). If he or she is not married, find out the name of at least one of his or her siblings or another relative. Start by making a list of the public sources that you could search.
b. The name of at least one of the parents of the person sitting next to you. Start by making a list of the public sources that you could search.

ANNOTATED SELECTED READINGS

CLARK, LANA J. "Developing a Strategy for Witness Interviews." *Legal Assistant Today,* January/February 1993. An article providing useful strategies that can be applied in interviewing witnesses.

DANIELSON, STEPHANIE A. "Dealing with the Personal Injury Client." *Legal Assistant Today,* January/February 1993. An article that discusses the types of demands that the personal-injury client is likely to place on the legal assistant and/or the lawyer. It includes some interesting hypothetical situations and how to respond to the client in each situation.

DANIELSON, STEPHANIE A. "Making Sense of Medical Records." *Legal Assistant Today,* May/June 1992. A remarkably clear explanation of medical records and their components, as well as medical prefixes and suffixes, symbols, and abbreviations commonly found in medical records.

LEITHER, RICHARD A., AND KATHLEEN MILLER. "Medical Research: And You Thought Legalese Was Hard to Understand?" *Legal Assistant Today,* July/August 1993. A helpful guide on how to conduct medical research. It provides references to basic research tools, including relevant periodicals and computer databases.

MYERS, REBECCA. "Strategies for Managing Discovery." *Legal Assistant Today,* November/December 1991. An article that discusses interviewing and investigation in a plaintiff's personal-injury case prior to discovery. It also discusses the point at which formal discovery begins and what it involves.

TALLEY, MARY. "How to Find the Government Official Who Knows." *Legal Assistant Today,* May/June 1992. A helpful article on how to focus your search when contacting a government agency for information. The article provides references to numerous federal and state government directories that will help you pinpoint your research.

TALLEY, MARY. "Using a Paper Trail to Verify or Discredit Expert Witnesses." *Legal Assistant Today,* November/December 1991. An interesting article on how to locate written documents that can be used to evaluate an expert witness's credibility. The article includes references to directories, databases, specialized sources, jury-trial information, and other sources.

16

Computers and the Legal Profession

Chapter Objectives

After completing this chapter, you will know:

- The effect of computers on law-office operations and on the nature of the work performed by paralegals.
- The types of computers in use, the types of components used in computer systems, and the types of external devices on which computer data and files can be stored.
- The difference between operating-system software and application software.
- How networking and electronic-mail systems can be used to share data and software or transmit communications via computer.
- The three basic types of application software and some of the specific types of application programs used in law offices.

Chapter Outline

SOFTWARE
Computer programs that instruct and control the computer's hardware and operations.

HARDWARE
The physical components (mechanical, magnetic, electronic, and so on) of the computer, including the computer itself, the keyboard, the monitor, and other peripheral devices attached to the computer.

ETHICAL CONCERN

Accuracy in Data Entry

Paralegals are ethically obligated to abide by the ethical duties imposed on attorneys, including the duty of competence. When working on computers, paralegals must, among other things, take special care in checking and double-checking the accuracy of data entered into computers. This is because, once entered, the data may appear on numerous future drafts, as well as in other related documents. Assume, for example, that you work as a paralegal specializing in real estate. Your work is made simpler by a computer program specifically designed for real-estate transactions. One day, you mistakenly key in the buyer's deposit as $9,800 instead of $8,900. The erroneous amount is replicated on a number of other forms produced by the program that relate to the same transaction, and the mistake is not detected until an audit at the end of the month reveals a $900 discrepancy in the buyer's account. You have just learned the hard way how important it is to ensure that initial entries of data are accurate.

INTRODUCTION

Computers have simplified the tasks of paralegals enormously. They have changed the pace of document preparation and have made law-office operations more efficient. They have also made it possible for paralegals to spend more time performing substantive legal work and less time engaging in mechanical tasks, such as retyping documents to incorporate revisions. In the area of legal research, computerized legal-research services such as WESTLAW and LEXIS (discussed later in this chapter) have made it possible for attorneys and paralegals to access court cases, statutes, regulations, articles in law journals, and numerous other information sources and data without leaving the law office.

Because of the widespread use of computers in today's law offices, computer literacy is a must for paralegals. No one textbook chapter can cover all of the various ways in which computers are used by the firms and other organizations that hire paralegals or all of the computer programs used in law offices. Even if it could, you would not benefit by learning about *all* computer systems and programs for two reasons. First, much of what you need to know will be determined to a great extent by where you work. Each law firm, corporation, government agency, or other organization that hires paralegals has its own computer system and software applications with which you will need to become familiar. (**Software** consists of computer programs that instruct the computer to perform certain functions or tasks.) Second, specific features of computer systems and specific software applications become outdated very quickly—because newer and better computer programs are produced regularly. Although we mention some specific computer programs in this chapter, bear in mind that by the time you read this book, other improved programs will probably be available for law-office use.

We present in this chapter an overview of computer technology and how computers are used in legal practice. The information contained in the following pages will furnish you with a basic knowledge of computer systems, computer networks, the basic types of application software commonly used in law offices, and some of the benefits and costs involved in computerized legal research. You can consider this chapter a stepping stone on the way to computer literacy. Once you begin working as a paralegal, you can take the further step of learning how to operate the specific computer system and software used in your workplace—or, if little computer technology is used, how it might be applied to the tasks performed in your office.

COMPUTER HARDWARE

The term **hardware** is used to describe the physical components of a computer system. Computer hardware varies with the type of system in use. Here we look at the types of computers and computer components frequently used in legal offices.

Types of Computers

Computers range in size and capacity from large mainframe computers to small personal, or desktop, computers.

The Mainframe Computer. At one time, all computers were mainframe computers. A **mainframe computer** is a centralized, large computer processing unit that can handle and store vast amounts of data. Because of the expense of purchasing and maintaining mainframe computers, typically they are used only by very large organizations and government agencies. For example, databases provided by computerized legal-research services, such as WESTLAW and LEXIS, are stored and processed by mainframe computers. Airline companies track their reservation and scheduling systems through mainframes. The Internal Revenue Service and state government tax bureaus use mainframes to handle tax returns. The college or university that you are attending probably uses a mainframe computer. Only a few of the largest law firms, or megafirms, own mainframes.

MAINFRAME COMPUTER
A large, centralized computer processing unit that can service multiple terminals simultaneously and that is capable of storing, handling, and retrieving vast amounts of data (used by large organizations, such as megafirms, government agencies, and universities).

Multiple *terminals* can be connected to a mainframe so that its computing ability and data can be accessed by a number of users. Access to databases in mainframe computers is typically restricted to authorized users. Paralegals who access mainframe computers therefore normally will be assigned a **security code**, or **password**.

SECURITY CODE (PASSWORD)
A predetermined series of numbers and/or letter characters that an authorized user keys in to gain access to a computer system or data contained in computer files.

Minicomputers and Servers. Today, computer technology has made it possible for law offices to obtain, at a significantly lower cost, smaller computer systems with sufficient memory and computing ability to serve their needs. The **minicomputer** is a computer with more power and capabilities than most individual users need, but its capabilities are not as great as those of a mainframe computer. The minicomputer is frequently found in large departments or in middle-sized businesses or law firms. Typically, as with a mainframe, the minicomputer is connected to a number of terminals so that it can be used simultaneously by a number of users. Often, the term *server*

MINICOMPUTER
A computer with more power and capacity than a microcomputer but less than a mainframe computer. Like the mainframe, the minicomputer (server) can be connected to a number of terminals (clients) simultaneously.

EXHIBIT 16.1
An IBM ES/9000 Mainframe

EXHIBIT 16.2
A DEC Microvax Minicomputer System

is used for a minicomputer, and the terminals that are connected to it are called *clients*. A law firm might use a server/client system to permit numerous users to have access to the data in the minicomputer.

The Personal Computer. Often, a paralegal is assigned an individual processing unit and monitor, commonly referred to as a **personal computer (PC)**, a desktop computer, or a microcomputer. This unit will be used for applications tailored to the individual's assignments. Personal computers normally contain **hard drives** (or hard disk drives). The hard drive allows the computer to store, in its permanent memory, software and data files that are tailored to the paralegal's needs and work assignments. Without the hard drive, the software and data would have to be "loaded" from diskettes each time the user turned on the computer. Legal professionals can use personal computers and modems (discussed below) to access the data contained in the mainframes of service bureaus such as WESTLAW and LEXIS.

PERSONAL COMPUTER (PC)
A desktop computer, or microcomputer, with its own central processing unit, which is ordinarily used for applications that are tailored to the user's employment, domestic, or educational needs.

HARD DRIVE
A unit that enables a personal computer to store software programs and data files in permanent memory. The hard drive contains a hard disk.

Components

Every computer, whether it is a large mainframe unit or a personal computer, is composed of several parts, which we discuss below. We also describe other components of a computer system, including optical scanners, printers, and modems.

The Central Processing Unit. The **central processing unit (CPU)** is the component of a computer system that controls the interpretation and execution of instructions. In a sense, it is the "brain" of the computer. The CPU controls the functions of the other computer components. It temporarily stores the information contained in the computer programs, or software, and executes the operator's commands as they are input through the keyboard. Each personal computer has its own CPU. In a mainframe system, in contrast, only the mainframe computer itself has a CPU. Each terminal normally contains only a monitor and a keyboard with which the user can access the central CPU, or mainframe.

CENTRAL PROCESSING UNIT (CPU)
The part of a computer that controls the function of the other computer components, stores the information contained in software programs, and executes the operator's keyboard commands.

The Monitor. The **monitor** is a screen, like a television screen, that displays the current activities of the computer. The technology of monitors varies, and different software programs require different levels of technology. Monitors also come in different sizes. Additionally, some monitors display data or information only in shades of black and white, while others offer full-color displays.

MONITOR
A black-and-white or multicolor display screen that displays the current activities of the computer.

The Keyboard. The **keyboard** is used to send information to the computer's processing unit; in turn, this information is displayed on the monitor. The keyboard looks much like a typewriter keyboard but differs from a typewriter keyboard in several ways. In addition to containing the letters of the alphabet and numbers, the computer keyboard usually has specialized *function keys* designed for communicating with the computer's processing unit. The keyboard usually also contains a separate numeric keypad to speed the input of arithmetic data.

KEYBOARD
A computer input device with alphanumeric characters (arranged similarly to the traditional typewriter) and function keys.

Computers, because they allows paralegals to "cut and paste" part or all of the contents of one document to another, reduce to some extent the need for "perfect" typing skills. Nonetheless, the ability to type quickly and accurately is an essential paralegal skill. Experienced paralegals find that the better they are at keyboarding, the more efficiently and accurately they can produce necessary documents.

EXHIBIT 16.3
An IBM Performance Spacesaver Personal Computer with Monitor, Internal Hard Drive, Keyboard, and Mouse

The Mouse. Many computers use a **mouse**, which is a pointing device that lets the user give commands without using the keyboard. The mouse, which is usually no larger than a person's hand, contains a rotating ball inside it. Moving the mouse across the desk rotates the ball and creates corresponding movements in the *cursor,* a symbol indicating where the next character—if keyed in—will appear on the monitor. An alternative to a mouse is a *trackball,* in which the rotating ball is mounted in a fixed base.

Optical Scanners. Law firms are increasingly utilizing optical-imaging technology for data-input purposes. An *optical scanner* is a device that, when moved over a document, "scans" and copies the contents of the document in a form readable by the computer. Optical scanning is thus an alternative input device to a keyboard. You will read more about the benefits of optical imaging for the law office in the *Today's Professional Paralegal* feature at the end of this chapter.

MOUSE
A device that lets a computer user move the cursor's position on the monitor and give commands to the computer without using a keyboard.

MODEM
A device that converts the computer's digital signals into analog sound waves and vice versa so that messages can be transmitted and received over a telephone line. Using a modem and communications software, a user can transfer information from one computer to another via a phone line.

Printers. A printer transfers data that you see on your computer screen and from computer files to a permanent, readable form. In some offices, each CPU is linked to an individual printer; in other offices, computers are linked to a shared printer. The computer document transferred to paper is referred to as a *hard copy*. There are a variety of types of printers. Law firms typically use *laser printers* because of their speed and the high quality of the printed results.

Modems. A **modem** is a device that, when connected to a computer and a telephone line, allows computer users to transmit and receive information and documents directly from other computers. The modem converts outgoing data from the digital signals used by the computer to analog sound waves that can be transmitted over a telephone line. The receiving computer's modem then translates the incoming data from analog form to digital form so that the information can be displayed by the receiving computer's screen. Specialized *communications software* is needed to convert data to a form that can be communicated via modem over telephone lines.

EXHIBIT 16.4
An Optical Scanner

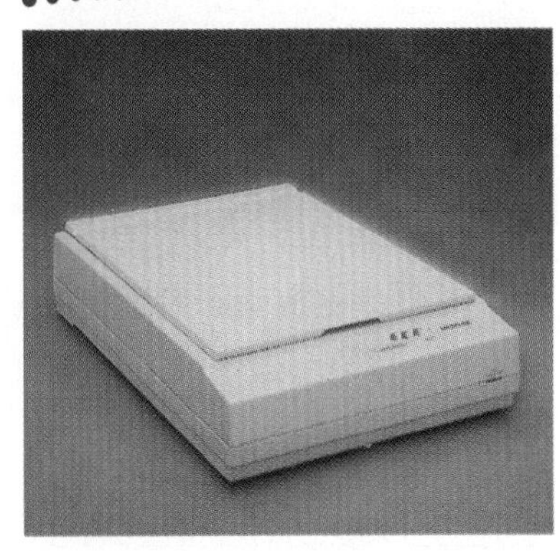

Storage Devices

Storage devices are used to store programs, data, and work performed on the computer. Personal computers generally contain internal hard drives (or hard disk drives), as mentioned earlier. The internal hard drive is built into the computer unit. The computer user can store software and work files on the computer's hard drive, where they are accessible whenever the computer is switched on.

EXHIBIT 16.5
HP LaserJet 4MV Printer

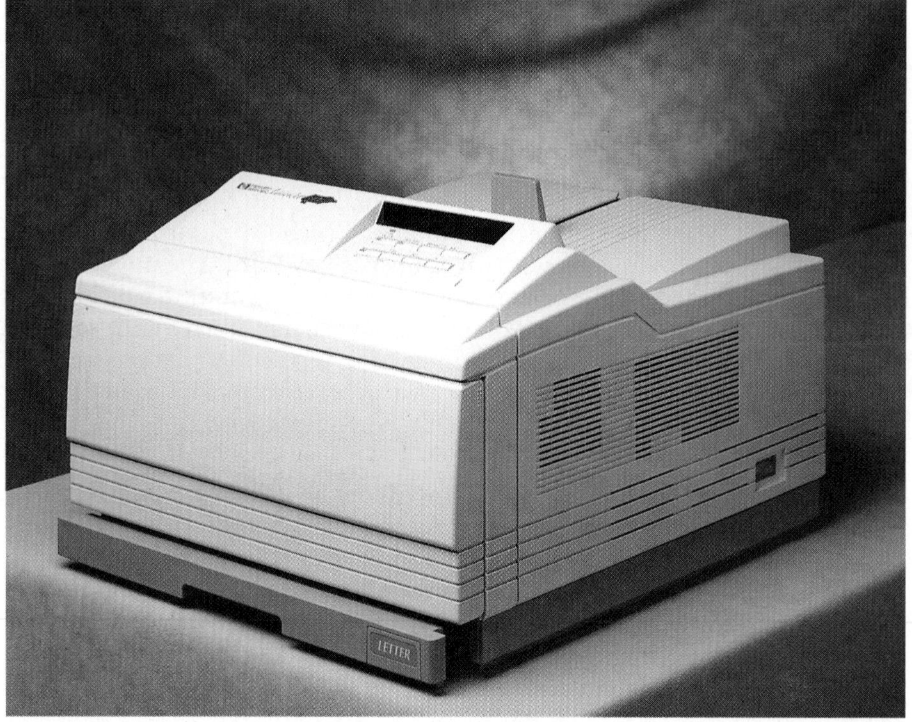

Many users store work on their computer hard drives. The amount of data that can be stored on hard drives varies, depending on the computer. Internal hard drives are sold with various storage capacities ranging from as little as forty megabytes up to several thousand megabytes. Note that computer memory is measured in units called *bytes*. A byte may represent a character, such as a letter or numeral, or a character space. A *kilobyte* is a thousand bytes; a *megabyte* is a million bytes.

Most computer users also "back up" their work on external storage devices. For one thing, users commonly need extra storage space. For another, users usually wish to create back-up copies of their work so that the documents or files are not lost if the computer system fails. We will look shortly at the importance of "saving" computer-generated work to an internal hard drive and of backing up work on an external storage device. Here we look at some of the external storage devices currently in use.

EXHIBIT 16.6
Diskettes

External Hard Drives. An external hard drive (which is similar to the internal hard drive discussed above) can be connected to a computer to provide ongoing storage opportunities. In other words, while using the computer, you can periodically transfer documents and data to the external hard drive for storage without having to insert a diskette or other storage device into the computer.

Diskettes. Removable diskettes are commonly used to back up and store computer files and data. A diskette can be inserted into the disk drive of the computer, and data from the computer can be transferred, or backed up on,

THE LEGAL TEAM AT WORK
Communications Systems and Teamwork

We have stressed earlier in this text how important communication is to effective teamwork. To ensure that nothing crucial is overlooked in preparing for a trial or other legal proceeding, each team member must be kept informed of what the other team members are doing and the current status of each member's work. Communicating with team members would not be difficult if all of the attorneys and paralegals working on a case were at all times in close physical proximity to each other. But that is not always the situation. Attorneys frequently have to attend meetings, conferences, or other proceedings outside their offices—sometimes in distant cities or even other countries. Similarly, paralegals sometimes need to leave their offices for significant time periods, as when traveling to other cities to interview witnesses, obtain evidence, or perhaps do legal research.

Being physically distant from one another no longer poses the communication problems for team members that it once did. Today, using modems and communications software, an attorney or paralegal can transfer documents and other information from a home computer to the office computer or, while traveling within the United States or even in other countries, from a hotel room or other site (using a notebook computer with a built-in modem) to the home office. Increasingly, judges are permitting attorneys to use computer equipment in the courtroom. In some trials, paralegals and attorneys no longer have to leave the courtroom to call their offices on the phone. Instead, they can send and receive E-mail messages while in the courtroom. If necessary, they can transmit documents via modem back and forth between their offices and the courtroom, as well as access legal-research databases, such as WESTLAW and LEXIS, from the courtroom to conduct research.

the diskette for storage and safekeeping. Most computers accept 3½-inch diskettes, but others use 5¼-inch diskettes (the latter are almost never used anymore, however). Although diskettes provide a convenient way to store data, their storage capacity is usually limited to two megabytes or less.

Optical Disks. Law firms can now purchase recordable optical disk drives and optical disks to record and store data. Each 3½-inch optical disk can store 230 megabytes of data—the equivalent of a typical hard drive. To store data on an optical disk, you insert the disk into the optical disk drive, which (usually) is an external device connected to the computer.

CD-ROMs. A more recent technological breakthrough allows vast amounts of data to be accessed through a *compact disk, read-only memory (CD-ROM).* CD-ROM technology allows the legal researcher to access a variety of legal data on a small, compact laser disk, much like the compact disks that have revolutionized the world of music. CD-ROM libraries combine the power of personal computers with traditional legal-research techniques. A CD-ROM holds the equivalent of over 600 megabytes of data. This means that one CD-ROM can store approximately 300,000 pages, or over one hundred volumes of legal reference material. CD-ROMs thus can contain material that, in printed form, would fill many shelves in a library. For example, the entire 215-volume *United States Code Annotated* (discussed

EXHIBIT 16.7
An Optical Disk

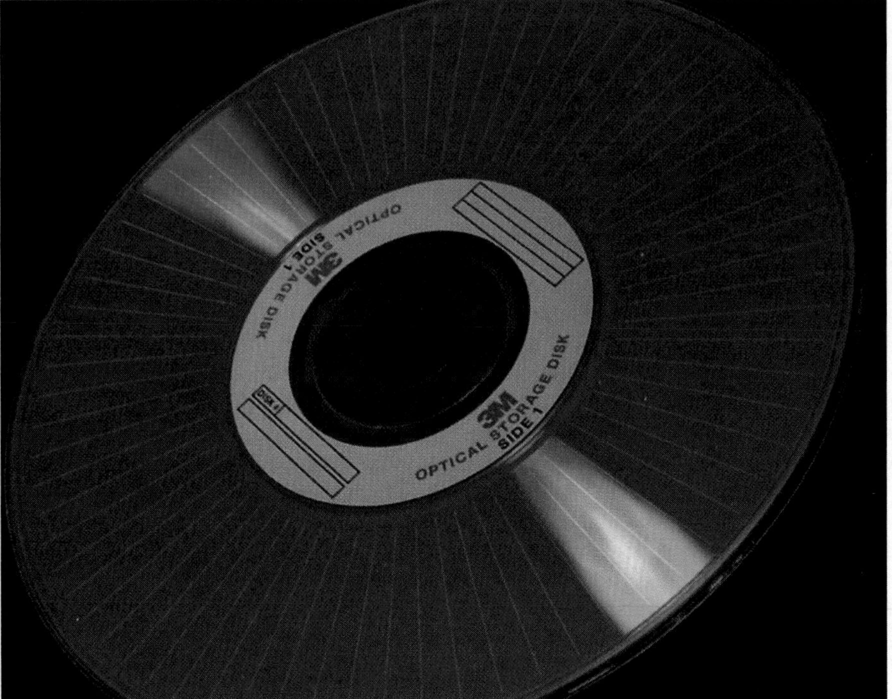

in Chapter 17) is contained on only two CD-ROMs. Federal government publications and other research sources will be increasingly available in CD-ROM format.

CD-ROMs are accessed through a CD-ROM reader, which is similar to a disk drive. The CD-ROM reader is designed to read and display the contents of the CD-ROM inserted into the reader. Depending on the computer system, the CD-ROM reader, or drive, can either be an internal drive or be attached through cables and appear as a separate, external part of the computer system. The software program, which allows the computer operating system to communicate with the CD-ROM, will be installed when the CD-ROM reader is installed.

As technology improves, more and more law firms will also be purchasing CD-ROM recording machines to record their own CD-ROMs. A recordable CD-ROM is basically the same as a diskette and can be used instead of a diskette to store data.

Magnetic Tape. Another type of storage device for high volumes of information is a *magnetic-tape system.* Unlike most CD-ROM devices, magnetic tape systems can both read *and write* data. In other words, in addition to accessing information contained on a magnetic tape, a computer user can transfer data from a hard drive to a magnetic tape for back-up storage.

The magnetic tape can be used in two formats, either small cartridges of magnetic tape or larger reels of tape. Magnetic-tape systems are typically used to make back-up copies of large quantities of data. There is now a *digital audiotape* (DAT) that has even greater storage capability. A DAT is typically smaller than a regular cassette and can hold as much data as a CD-ROM.

EXHIBIT 16.8
A Magnetic Tape in a Magnetic Tape Drive

Saving and Backing Up Your Work

An important aspect of proficiency in computer use involves two processes—saving your work and backing it up on an external storage device.

Saving Your Work. Whenever you perform work on a computer, you should save your work at frequent intervals. *Saving* refers to the process in which the work you are currently performing on the computer is transferred to, or saved on, the internal hard drive of your computer. For example, suppose that you are revising a document on a personal computer that has an internal hard drive. While you are performing this work, your changes or additions to the document are stored in the computer's temporary memory. Should a power failure cause your computer to shut down, all work stored in temporary memory will be lost.

To store work in permanent memory, you need to use the "Save" command on your computer. Computer users today install special software that automatically saves your work to the computer's hard drive at frequent intervals, such as every two minutes. Many such "auto-save" programs are available. Because it is difficult to remember to save your work periodically, to protect yourself against the possibility of losing valuable work time, you should take special note of the following advice:

- **Whatever program you are using, make sure that you have an automatic-save system in place that transfers your current work to the computer's hard drive every two minutes.**

Backing Up Your Work. Another important aspect of computer proficiency is remembering to *back up* your work on a diskette or another external storage device at the end of each project (or at the end of each day). If work is not backed up on an external storage device, it can easily be lost. For example, if your computer system "crashes," you may not be able to retrieve the data that have been saved on your hard drive. In this situation, you will lose valuable documents or data that may have taken hours (or days) to create and that may not be replaceable.

OPERATING-SYSTEM SOFTWARE

Computers work according to certain *operating systems*. **Operating-system software** controls the communication between the computer system and application software. **Application software** is the term used to describe computer programs that instruct the CPU how to perform specific tasks, such as word processing or arithmetic computations. Application software designed for one operating system will not usually function on a computer that uses a different operating system. We look below at disk operating systems and the problem of compatibility in regard to application software.

OPERATING-SYSTEM SOFTWARE
A program allowing the computer to control the sequencing and processing of application software programs so that the computer responds correctly to the operator's commands.

APPLICATION SOFTWARE
Computer programs designed to instruct the central processing unit on the operation and performance of certain tasks.

Disk Operating System (DOS) and Alternatives

One of the most common operating systems is the *disk operating system (DOS)* developed by Microsoft Corporation. Because Microsoft (MS) developed this system, it is often referred to as *MS-DOS.* IBM and IBM-compatible computers typically operate using the DOS system. An alternative for these computers is *System 2,* offered by IBM.

The primary alternative to IBM and IBM-compatible computers in law offices is Apple's *Macintosh* computer. Macintosh computers have used some version of an operating system called *System 7* for a few years. New versions are available regularly, the latest of which is *Mac OS.* Newspapers and magazines often contain advertisements for various new operating systems and for updates to existing operating systems.

ETHICAL CONCERN

Back It All Up

Even a person who uses computers on a routine basis can easily forget—while the computer system is working—that a power failure or other problem can occur at any time. If a power failure occurs while you are working, you will lose all current work that has not been saved to your hard disk. You should also remember to back up your work product frequently on a diskette or other external storage device. Storing your work this way can "save the day" if the computer system crashes, or fails to the extent that data on the hard drive cannot be retrieved. If you routinely back up documents, you may save yourself the hours of valuable time that could be required to recreate a document or file. You will also save yourself and the firm from the problem of deciding who will pay—the client or the law firm—for the extra time you had to spend to complete the work. Moreover, with back-up copies available, your employer will never have to be without a crucial document when it's needed.

Compatibility

As mentioned, application software is typically manufactured for use with a particular operating system. New technology, however, is allowing both operating-system and application-software manufacturers to claim that their operating-system or application software is *compatible* (workable) with other systems or software. An expert computer user should be consulted about all questions related to the compatibility of one system with another.

Traditionally, personal computer systems used in law offices have been either IBM (or IBM-compatible) systems or Macintosh systems. Each has had its own typical operating system and applications programs. Thus, work done on an IBM system using DOS could be transferred only to another IBM or IBM-compatible computer. Today, however, special software programs allow users to translate data created on DOS systems to Macintosh computers and vice versa.

User Interfaces

USER INTERFACE
The computer connection, or link, between the software and the hardware that controls the image that an operator views on the monitor and the method of accomplishing a given task.

One of the major differences between operating systems has traditionally been something called the **user interface**. The user interface controls what the user sees on the computer screen. For DOS, the user must learn—or consult the user's manual for—commands and codes to communicate with the computer. Macintosh users do not have to learn as many codes and keyboard commands, because the Macintosh system provides icons, or pictures (such as a picture of a file), to illustrate various functions. To open a computer file using a Macintosh computer, for example, you use the mouse to direct the cursor on the screen to a particular file, double-click on the mouse, and the file opens.

The user interface called *Windows* was developed for use with DOS. The most recent version of this user interface is *Windows 95,* which became available in the spring of 1995. The Windows program provides an interface involving icons. For Windows to work, however, the computer system must meet certain requirements related to processing speed and specific kinds of internal memory.

Another aspect of the user interface is the appearance of the screen when the computer is turned on, before any software program has been loaded. The operating system also controls this aspect of the interface. With a computer using DOS, for example, the computer screen usually shows C:—which is known as the *C-prompt.* The C-prompt indicates that the computer is ready to accept user commands. The most typical command is for the computer to *load* a software system of the user's choice. Some law offices use an interface or menu program with DOS. Such a program may provide an introductory screen featuring icons (as with Windows) or a *menu*—a list of the software programs available to the user. Computers can also be set up so that a preferred software program is automatically loaded into the system when the power is turned on.

OFFICE NETWORK SYSTEMS

While individual computer users can share files or information through the use of modems, law firms may want to have individual computers share information on a more consistent and routine basis. Networks serve this purpose.

Local and Wide Area Networks

A **local area network (LAN)** connects personal computers or minicomputers in a local area, such as a room or a building, so that they can communicate with each other and share software or data. The network also allows the linked computer units to use the same printer, hard drive, or other *peripheral* (support) devices. Using a LAN also allows one user on the network to view on his or her computer screen a document created by another user. For example, suppose that you have finished drafting a complaint that needs to be filed very soon with the court. Your supervising attorney's office is at the other end of the building. Using a LAN, your supervising attorney could review the complaint on his or her computer screen. If revisions need to be made, you could make them and print out the final draft of the document.

LOCAL AREA NETWORK (LAN)
A system of physically dispersed computers that are interconnected, via telecommunications, within a local area, such as an office building. Users at each connected computer can share information and software with other computers connected to the network.

A **wide area network (WAN)** allows multiple computer users located across a large geographical area to enjoy the benefits of direct communication. National and international law firms can take advantage of WANs to share a common pool of data and office or operations information.

WIDE AREA NETWORK (WAN)
A system of computers, physically dispersed over a large geographical area, in which the users are able to communicate directly with each other via computer.

Network Design

Firms use two basic models of network design. The first, the *client/server* model, was discussed earlier in the section on minicomputers. This model requires a powerful server computer to act as an information manager for client personal computers in the network. The server contains master software, files, and data. The client computers can access the wealth of tools and information available on the server and can also use the server as an electronic "post office" to send and receive electronic-mail **(E-mail)** messages. Users of client computers cannot communicate directly with each other unless they communicate through the server. Creating a client/server network usually requires professional assistance, both to *configure,* or set up, the hardware system and to select and install software to support the network.

E-MAIL
An abbreviation for electronic mail; an electronic message sent over a computer network from one computer terminal to another or others.

PARALEGAL PROFILE

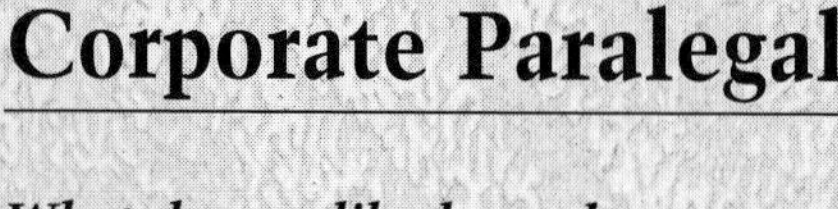

Corporate Paralegal

ARIE MARIE BAGGETT started her career as a legal secretary in a Chicago law firm with thirteen attorneys, who worked in various areas of the law. In 1983, she received her paralegal certificate from Roosevelt University, in Chicago. After receiving her certificate, she continued to work for the same firm, mainly performing research in the areas of bankruptcy, litigation, and securities law. In 1986, when the firm moved to Texas, she was hired by Information Resources, Inc., a marketing research corporation. The company creates and sells software that assists retailers and manufacturers in researching and analyzing their sales of consumer products. Baggett's responsibilities at Information Resources include trademark searches, some patent applications, records automation, and general records management.

What do you like best about your work?

"The thing that I like best about my job is the variety. I am always working on a little bit of everything and am continually learning new things. I also like the fact that the variety of work I do allows me to utilize all of my skills and educational training. I had experience in records automation at my previous job, so I took the initiative and started automating the files. So far, I've automated about half of them. Other departments in the corporation, including the accounting and engineering departments, now can call for data and get results much faster due to the automation. I also enjoy the contacts I have with a variety of people, including department heads and people in foreign countries, as well as the fact that I am able to work to a great extent on my own and at my own pace."

"COMPUTER TECHNOLOGY CAN HELP ATTORNEYS AND PARALEGALS BE MORE PRODUCTIVE"

What is the greatest challenge that you face in your area of work?

"The most challenging aspect of my job is taking on new responsibilities. When I first take on an area of responsibility, it is challenging until I master it. For example, at first I thought that dealing with document discovery was very challenging, especially if it involved a major litigation case. But now I feel much more comfortable with this area of work. Another challenging area at first was how to treat plaintiffs' attorneys when they want to look at documents. It is a sensitive position. Often, the plaintiff's attorney is waiting downstairs while I am going through the files to see what documents might be privileged. I never make decisions on what is privileged myself and always present the documents to the attorneys so that they can make that decision."

What advice do you have for would-be paralegals in your area of work?

"If I were a student now, I would be more attentive to everything, especially to topics (such as securities, bankruptcy, and intellectual property) that I thought were boring when I was in school. Now I work in corporate law and deal with matters relating to these topics on a daily basis. You never know what you're going to be using when you get out into the field, and it is important to realize that everything you study may be of critical importance on the job."

What are some tips for success as a paralegal in your area of work?

"The most important attributes for a paralegal to have in the area of corporate law are dependability, initiative, and self-motivation. I also feel that it is very important to continue to take classes and educate yourself. Additionally, I recommend circulating new or updated information to the attorneys. Many attorneys may be hesitant to take advantage of computer technology that goes beyond simple word processing or other basic functions. I have been able to show how computer technology can help attorneys and paralegals be more productive."

The second model for designing a network is a file-sharing system, in which every personal computer acts as both a client and a server. The individual computer user determines which files and programs to make available to the network. The file-sharing (or "peer-to-peer") network is easier to set up and operate than the client/server network. The file-sharing model cannot be used effectively, however, for more than twenty or thirty computers.

Both network systems require certain expertise that is not normally associated with the use of the stand-alone personal computer. Network users must learn to transmit and receive information. They must also be aware of security procedures, so that unauthorized users cannot gain access to files.

Electronic Mail

Law offices frequently take advantage of the ability of computers to communicate with each other by establishing an electronic-mail bulletin board, or E-mail system. E-mail allows people in offices to send messages directly to one another's computer screens. Interoffice communications and even client-attorney communications can be speeded up through the use of E-mail. To ensure the privacy and confidentiality of E-mail communications, many people today invest in software programs, called *encryption programs,* that encode, or encrypt, data transmitted or received via E-mail.

Millions of individuals today send E-mail messages over the Internet, an international network connecting over thirty-five thousand educational, corporate, and research computer networks around the world. Internet can be accessed through colleges and universities, most of which are directly connected to the Internet, and through commercial on-line services such as Delphi, CompuServe, Prodigy, and others. Clearly, because of the vast number of individuals using the Internet, confidential E-mail messages should be encoded for transmission via the Internet. You will read more about using the Internet in Appendix B at the end of this text.

APPLICATION SOFTWARE

Application software, as indicated earlier, creates a dialogue between the computer user and the central processing unit and determines the kinds of tasks that the computer will perform. The same CPU can run different software programs at different times. This section describes the law-office activities that benefit from computer assistance and the types of application software that are frequently used to perform these activities.

Generally, application software falls into three categories: word-processing software, database management systems, and spreadsheet software. We look at each of these types of software in the following sections.

Word-processing Software

Virtually all law firms now use word-processing programs on their computer systems to prepare documents. **Word-processing software** is a term used to describe computer programs that allow the user to create the text of documents and save, edit, or otherwise change the content and the appearance of those documents.

WORD-PROCESSING SOFTWARE
Specialized application software that allows a computer user to create, edit, revise, save, and generally manipulate textual material and document formatting.

DEVELOPING PARALEGAL SKILLS

Out-of-town Hearing

Barbara Holmes, a corporate legal assistant, is attending a regulatory hearing in Washington, D.C., along with three attorneys from her corporation. The corporation, TexMex Transmission, Inc., is a natural gas pipeline company. The Federal Energy Regulatory Commission (FERC) is holding the hearing to determine whether to grant permission to the pipeline industry to vastly expand current lines to provide much-needed additional service to the northeastern states. The hearing is expected to last almost a year, so Barbara and the attorneys from her department—along with representatives of the marketing, rates, engineering, and public relations departments—have rented the top five floors of a Washington hotel for their use during the hearing. The top floor contains their offices. They have brought along their secretaries and computer equipment to supply word-processing, electronic-mail, and fax capabilities.

WITNESS SCHEDULES AND TESTIMONY

Barbara's duties include coordinating witnesses' schedules, assisting in their travel arrangements when necessary, and summarizing each day the transcripts of the witnesses' testimony. These summaries are then circulated for use by the witnesses and attorneys. They are also forwarded to the general corporate counsel at the home office in Dallas, Texas, so that the boss can monitor the hearing without having to be present for the entire procedure.

HEARING SCHEDULES

The commission is hearing testimony from the last of the local gas utility companies in Boston, Massachusetts, and has issued the schedule of New York companies, whose testimony will be heard next. The testimony of the New York companies will help the commission determine if there is enough demand to justify expanding the pipelines. Barbara, using the wide area network (WAN) established prior to the hearing, has finished keying in the schedule for the New York companies on her computer and has just transmitted the schedule to the general counsel in Dallas.

COMMUNICATING WITH THE HOME OFFICE

While waiting for a response from Dallas, Barbara accesses her E-mail and reads through the messages that she has received today. There are some interesting memos from the personnel department concerning some changes in health insurance, but otherwise things are quiet on the Dallas front. She then begins to read through the transcripts of yesterday's hearing so that she can summarize them, distribute them to the attorneys present, and then forward them to the general counsel for his review. The general counsel will have the transcripts edited and distributed to others in the corporation.

Form Documents. Recall from Chapter 5 that law offices and legal practitioners in other environments frequently maintain a forms file for routinely created documents, such as wills and contracts. For example, in each state, a will must meet specific requirements established by state law. If your forms file contains a sample copy of a will that addresses all of these requirements, you can use that form as a model and modify it as necessary when you are drafting a will for a client.

In the past, preprinted forms were routinely used. Now, software programs, such as *West's Desktop Practice Systems,* supply those same preprinted forms on disk. The user can choose forms from a table of contents or search the entire contents of the disk automatically. Once a form is chosen, the user can fill in the blanks using the software and move the form into a word processor for editing and printing. A customized document—instead of a form with the blanks filled in—is the result. It is no longer easy to tell from the face of the document which language or provisions are **boilerplate** (terms and clauses used in all such documents) and which have been specially prepared for the individual client. Also, document revision is much simpler when using computerized forms.

Document Revision. Documents must frequently be revised—that is, phrases, paragraphs, or sections must be added, deleted, or otherwise modified. Word-processing software allows such changes to be made simply and speedily. Page length, margins, and other formatting features can be changed by simple commands, and some word-processing software even allows for automatic paragraph renumbering.

For example, suppose that you have been asked to create a last will and testament for a client, Anne Lampher. You locate the diskette containing sample forms for wills and find a form for a will that is similar to the one you want to create for Lampher. You insert the diskette into the computer's disk drive, copy the selected form to your hard drive, and ask the computer to save the document as "LAMPHER1." Then you open the form document and modify it as necessary to meet Lampher's specific wishes, periodically commanding the computer to save the revised document to your hard drive (unless you have special software on your computer that automatically saves your work at specified intervals).

Once you have prepared a first draft of the will, you can print out the document for your supervising attorney to review. Assuming that some modifications are necessary, you will again open the document and make the necessary changes. Once the changes are made, you may want either to replace the first document with the revised document or to retitle the revised document "LAMPHER2."

Naming Documents. The name you assign to a document or file must be unique—that is, one that is not already entered for another document that is stored on your hard drive. If there is already a document on your hard drive named "LAMPHER1" (as there would be in the above hypothetical scenario), you may be asked whether you would like to replace the existing document under the same name. If you say yes, the preexisting file will be erased, or destroyed—just as if you had taken the only paper copy of a document and run it through a shredder. Generally, you should abide by the following rule when naming computer files:

- **Before you replace any existing document on a computer, you need to know what the existing document is and whether you or another employee of your firm will want to keep it.**

ETHICAL CONCERN

Software Piracy

Computer software can be very costly to create and to purchase. If you own a personal computer, you could avoid having to pay for computer software already purchased by your employer for the office computer system. It would be simple—just make a back-up copy (or use the original copy) of the software, take it home, load it onto your hard disk, and return it to the office the next morning. It is relatively easy to convince yourself that because no one is being deprived of anything in a situation such as this, no theft has occurred. But remember that the company that produced that software has ownership rights in the intellectual property (see Chapter 8). By using the software company's property without authorization, you are engaging in an unethical (and probably illegal) action.

BOILERPLATE
Certain terms or clauses that are normally included in specific types of legal documents.

If you are at all uncertain, the safest step is to assign your new work product a new file name and leave the existing document as it is.

Law offices have different policies as to the retention of various versions of a document or file. Because attorneys and paralegals often bill their clients based on the hours spent performing the client's work, firms may wish to keep a record of the various steps they have taken in order to reach the end results desired by the clients. You should determine, therefore, whether your office would like you to give each revision of a document a separate name and retain it on your computer. If so, you will call the revision of Lampher's will "LAMPHER2," and the original draft ("LAMPHER1") will be retained in the computer's memory. Your office may instead prefer that you keep a paper copy, or hard copy, of the first version on file to avoid cluttering the computer's hard drive. In any event, you will need to be familiar with the document-retention policy of your firm before you can be certain that you are performing this function correctly.

Commonly Used Word-processing Features and Terms. Although many different types of word-processing systems are used in law offices, certain features and terms are typically used in all systems. Exhibit 16.9 shows some of the more commonly used terms and features used in word-processing software.

Database Management Systems

DATABASE MANAGEMENT SYSTEM
Software that makes it possible to store information in fields, records, and files for easy retrieval and manipulation by the operator.

Attorneys and paralegals typically deal with large collections of information. A law firm may want to send a mailing to each of its clients to announce the opening of a new office, track discovery documents in a complex trial, or maintain a list of expert witnesses in different specialty areas. A **database management system** allows users to organize data in specific ways, create reports, and print out information in a variety of formats. Exhibit 16.10 on page 620, for example, shows part of a specialized expert-witness database. Like word-processing software, database software uses a specialized vocabulary to describe its features. Exhibit 16.11 on page 620 lists and defines some basic terms commonly used in database software.

Law offices and legal practitioners in other environments use database management systems to perform certain functions with the data, or information, that the systems contain. For these functions to be performed effectively, information about the intended use of the database should be carefully gathered. The database should then be planned according to its intended use. A first step in creating a database is, of course, deciding what information it must contain. The information is then organized logically into fields, records, and files (see Exhibit 16.11 for definitions of these terms). Exhibit 16.12 on page 621 presents some basic rules for planning a database.

An important consideration in planning and creating a database is the ability to *search* the database. When the database is organized so that each key item is placed in its own field, the user can locate the item easily by commanding the database to perform a search of the fields. For example, to find a dentist in the expert-witness database shown in Exhibit 16.10, the user could have the program search for the term *dentistry.* This greatly speeds the process of finding needed information.

EXHIBIT 16.9
Terms Commonly Used in Word Processing

CURSOR: The symbol on the computer screen indicating the position at which the user's changes or additions will appear. The cursor can appear as a blinking hyphen, as a shaded line, or in some other fashion. The cursor must be positioned at the place at which changes, additions, or deletions should be made. The user moves around a document by changing the position of the cursor.

EDITING: The word processor's ability to allow changes, additions, deletions, and formatting changes without the necessity of retyping or recreating the entire document.

FONT: The kind of typeface selected for a document. Most word processors offer a variety of sizes and types of font. For example, *ten-point italic will look like this*, *and eight-point italic will look like this*. Many word processors allow the user to go back and change the font selected for the document after the document has already been prepared. Word processors also allow multiple fonts to be used in the same document.

FOOTNOTES: Legal documents frequently require citations (see Chapter 17) for cases, articles, and other sources used as authority for the author's statement. These citations are indicated by placing a footnote number immediately following the statement, with the corresponding number placed at the bottom of the page together with the associated information as to the name of the source being cited and in what publication the source can be found. Word processors allow footnotes to be inserted, edited, and deleted as an editing feature. Word processors also place the footnote at the bottom of the correct text page or at the end of the document—depending on the user's preference.

FORMATTING: The same text can vary in appearance, depending on whether it is single or double spaced, the font used, the location of page numbers, the size of the margins, and whether the margins are ragged or justified (see below, under margins). The word processor gives the user many formatting options. A document can be reformatted (after it has been created) as well.

INSERT: A method of editing in which new text or information is added at the place in the document where the cursor is positioned.

MARGINS: The amount of space between the top, bottom, right edge, or left edge of a page and the text printed on the page. Word-processing software allows you to change the margins of a document after the document has been created. Word processors also give you the option of creating a justified, or smooth, right margin.

MOVE AND BLOCK (or cut and paste): A word-processing editing capability that allows you to move text from one section of a document to another.

SEARCH AND REPLACE: A word-processing editing capability that allows you to find each occurrence of a certain word or symbol in a document and replace the word or symbol with a new choice. If, for example, a client of your firm proposed to lease Suite 1420, which is mentioned twenty-three times in the lease agreement, but later decided to lease Suite 1755, you could substitute 1755 for 1420 automatically with the search-and-replace function. The search-and-replace function is often used in revising a document originally prepared for a previous client by changing the previous client's name with that of the present client for whom the document is being prepared.

SPELL CHECKER: A feature that allows you to check the spelling of each word in a document by comparing it against a dictionary that is part of the word processor. The spell checker highlights words that are either misspelled or not contained in the dictionary. (For example, a spell checker might highlight a client's name if it does not find the name in its dictionary.) Note that the spell checker cannot find user errors that involve incorrect word use rather than incorrect spelling. If, for example, you use *there* instead of *their*, the spell checker will not highlight the word *there*, because it is spelled correctly.

GRAMMAR CHECKER: A feature that allows you to check your document to see if it contains any grammatical errors, such as errors in subject-verb agreement (as in "The clients wants a will prepared"), and make suggestions for correcting any errors that are found. The grammar checker may also point out the sentences in which the passive voice has been used (see Chapter 18), how many words the documents contains, and the line length of the document.

WORD WRAP: On typewriters, a person must press the "return" key at the end of every line. With word-processing systems, the typist can continue from line to line without interruption because of word wrap. The lines automatically wrap, or move from one line to the beginning of the next line.

EXHIBIT 16.10
An Expert-witness Database (Excerpt)

Last Name	First Name	Address	City	State	Zip Code	Telephone Number	Specialty	Fee
Allen	Fred	34 Cedar Street	Miami	FL	33156	(503) 555-1908	Construction	$400
Dobbs	Susan	55 Spruce Drive	Portland	ME	04112	(207) 555-9320	Pediatrics	$350
Menkin	Gerald	320 Park Avenue	New York	NY	10166	(212) 555-9690	Psychiatry	$550
Olin	Barbara	Four Square Drive	Chicago	IL	60690	(312) 555-6641	Internal Medicine	$800
Payne	Daniel	214 Illinois Street	Austin	TX	78711	(512) 555-3823	Dentistry	$650

As mentioned, database systems allow users to create reports and print information in a variety of formats. The user can ask the database to sort, or organize, information in various ways. The sort function allows you to create a variety of end products using the same data.

Database Software for Tracking Litigation Documents. The discovery and trial phases of litigation involve preparing, distributing, and receiving numerous documents. Database systems are useful in managing and tracking the flow of documents and evidence, as well as in locating particular information when needed. Specialized database software, such as *FoxPro* and *Paradox*, allows attorneys and paralegals to consolidate and manage documents involved in complex litigation, such as litigation involving multiple plaintiffs and defendants. For example, a case involving liability for cleaning up a site contaminated by toxic waste may involve hundreds of potentially responsible parties as litigants and thousands of exhibits and documents. Storing and retrieving such data through automated systems can allow the

EXHIBIT 16.11
Terms Commonly Used in Database Software

FIELD: An individual item of data is a field. If a database is to contain client records, for example, a field might be established for each client's last name. Another field would contain the client's telephone number. Information is added to a database field by field. Determining what fields will be included in the database is an important function when planning and creating a database.

RECORD: Fields exist in logical relation to one another. A group of fields treated as a unit is referred to as a record. For example, a particular name, address, city, state, zip code, telephone number, and case number would together be referred to as a record.

FILE: A collection of records intended to be used as a unit is referred to as a file. For example, the entire list of client names, addresses, and telephone numbers would be stored in the database as the client file. If the firm also had a collection of records for prospective clients, these would be kept in a separate file. Some database management systems refer to files by other names, such as *tables* or *databases*.

EXHIBIT 16.12
Rules for Planning a Database

RULES FOR PLANNING A DATABASE

Keep the following rules in mind when planning a database.

1. **Get Started:** Many times, a computerized database's design is based on a manual system. Start the process by enumerating what you like and dislike about the manual system. For example, suppose that you are designing a client database. If your law firm previously used a manual card system for keeping track of clients, this would be a good starting point for designing the computerized version.

2. **Plan Ahead:** Plan ahead for the future. If you think you might need an extra field later, add it now for safety. For example, in the client database, if you think you might eventually want a field for a work phone number, go ahead and include it now even though you may not use it right away. Try to anticipate your future needs.

3. **Keep Fields in Logical Order:** When you create the database or design an entry screen (the screen that you see to enter additional records), make sure the fields are put in a logical order that flows well. For example, in the client database, you would not want the Last Name field followed by the Zip Code field. Design the entry screen so that it is easy for additional records to be entered.

4. **Allow Plenty of Space for Each Field:** If you have to enter a maximum field length, leave plenty of space. If you have plenty of space available on your hard disk or other storage device, a good rule is to estimate how many characters you think you will need and then double it for safety. For instance, if you only allowed for five digits for a Zip Code field, you would have a problem, since some Zip Codes today are nine digits.

5. **Separate Data into Small Fields:** It is almost always better to separate data into small fields, rather than having multiple kinds of information in large fields. Instead of using one name field (Name), for example, use two smaller name fields (Last Name and First Name). Also, always separate city, state, and zip code instead of combining them. Sometime in the future you may want to sort or search using these specified fields.

6. **Make Field Names as Small as Possible:** When you are naming the fields for your database, make the names as small as possible. When you print the data, large field names get in the way, especially when the data they contain have only a few characters.

7. **Anticipate How the Database Will Be Used:** Before you make the design, think about how the information will be searched, how it will be sorted, and what format your reports and printouts will take. Most databases that fail do so because this rule was not followed.

8. **Always Test the Design:** No matter how good you think a design is, always test it before you put in hundreds of records, only to find out it is faulty.

SOURCE: Adapted from Brent D. Roper, *Computers in the Law: Concepts and Applications* (St. Paul: West Publishing Co., 1992), pp. 145-146.

legal team to access critical information in seconds—versus the minutes or hours that might otherwise be required to find the information.

Docket-control Software. As mentioned in previous chapters, a docket is a schedule, or calendaring system, used by courts to list the cases that it will hear on certain dates. Law firms also use a docketing, or calendaring, system

DEVELOPING PARALEGAL SKILLS

Efficiently Organizing Deposition Transcripts

Eric Hawk is an experienced litigation paralegal. Part of his job is to summarize deposition transcripts. Thanks to the computer software that has been developed over the past decade, such as *Discovery ZX* and *Summation II,* his job is much easier than it used to be. Before these programs existed, he used to have to read and reread deposition transcripts several times to find and mark critical testimony. Then he had to photocopy each page containing this testimony, highlight what he needed on each page, and dictate a summary of the transcript.

With these programs, Eric's job is much easier because he can receive the deposition transcript on a diskette, which can be inserted into his computer. Using *Discovery ZX* or *Summation II,* Eric only needs to read the deposition transcript once. He can locate the critical testimony through word searches and use the software to organize the summary in any order he chooses—by page or by line, chronologically, or by category—and then print out his finished summary. Let's see how he does it.

REVIEWING AND ANNOTATING THE TRANSCRIPT

Eric begins reading a 265-page transcript of a physician's deposition. The physician will serve as an expert witness in a medical-malpractice case. He receives the transcript on both hard copy and diskette. Because Eric attended this deposition with the attorney, he is very familiar with the testimony, so he chooses to review it on the disk. When he is unfamiliar with the testimony, he uses the hard copy because it is easier to read. Eric needs to include the physician's credentials, which are included at the beginning of the transcript. He highlights this information on the computer. If Eric had not known the location of this information, he would have done a word search for the term "credentials," and it would have been located for him by the computer. He makes a note next to the credentials section.

He also needs to include the physician's exact testimony regarding the standard of care in the case. He decides to perform a search for the words "reasonable" (because standard of care is closely linked to reasonable care under the circumstances), "standard," and "care." He locates several pages of testimony on this topic. He makes more margin notes and highlights this portion of the testimony as well. Then he continues to look through the transcript. He comes across a reference to some medical records with which he is not familiar. He highlights the reference and makes another margin note to himself to request a copy of these records.

PREPARING THE DEPOSITION SUMMARY

When Eric finishes reviewing the transcript, he is ready to prepare his summary. He wants to summarize the important testimony by the pages and lines on which it appears. He chooses the page/line summary format. All of the lines that he highlighted begin to appear on the screen. Next, he uses the *sort* function to organize the information in the order in which he wants it to appear. When he prints it, it will appear with his notes first, followed by any excerpted testimony that he has highlighted.

to make sure that they comply with the multiple deadlines and requirements involved in the cases on which they are working. To assist them in this effort, they use specialized software, called *docket-control software.* Docket-control software helps track important dates and deadlines, such as court appearances and the dates by which certain documents must be filed with the court. A built-in reminder—or "tickler"—system gives advance notice of an approaching deadline so that the needed work can be completed at the appropriate time. Typical calendar display screens for docket-control software are shown in Exhibit 16.13.

Legal professionals also use docket-control software to help them monitor deadlines in other areas. For example, if you are assisting an attorney who is involved in a complex acquisition or financing transaction, docket-control software makes it easier for you to monitor the various deadlines set forth in the contract or loan documents. Docket-control software is also useful in scheduling routine firm meetings. Suppose that you have been asked to schedule a meeting of the partners and paralegals who are working on a particular case. The software will typically advise you of the dates and times when members of the team will be free to meet and enter your suggested meeting time and date on each team member's calendar.

A docket-control program typically includes a perpetual calendar. Unlike paper calendars, it will not become obsolete at the end of a year. In addition,

EXHIBIT 16.13
Typical Calendar Display Screens

January 1995 DOCKET for RSS

SUN	MON	TUE	WED	THU	FRI	SAT
1	2	3	4	5	6	7
8	9 4 1 1	10 2 1 1	11 1	12 1 1	13 1 2	14
15	16 1	17 1 1	18 1 1 1	19	20 1 1 1	21
22	23 1 1 1	24	25 1	26	27 1	28
29	30 1	31				
				APPOINT-MENTS	CRITICAL DEADLINES	SELF-IMPSD DEADLINES

Enter day to display, ← for last month, → for next month: _

Summary for RSS on Wednesday January 18, 1995

ITEM	TIME	ACCOUNT/CLIENT	SERVICE/INFO.
1	A 10:30 AM	00010000 Joseph Trimble	Discuss Tax Evasion Charges
2	* C 02:00 PM	00011537 Hilltop Auto Sales	Trial - Hilltop v. Triple K Judge Berry, Room 306
3	S	00011024 Avery International	Amend Complaint Add Defendants

Press ← for yesterday, press → for tomorrow.

Enter ITEM no., PgDn for more items, Home to start over, or Ins to add:

FEATURED GUEST: JAN RICHMOND

Keeping Current on Computer Technology

Biographical Note

Jan Richmond is currently pursuing her master of arts degree in legal studies at Webster University in St. Louis, Missouri. As an undergraduate, she specialized in systems and data processing. She received her undergraduate degree from Washington University. Richmond has been an adjunct faculty member in the legal-assisting program at St. Louis Community College since 1989. Her teaching schedule includes courses in Computers and the Law, Advanced Computer Utilization, and Legal Administration, in addition to classes in WordPerfect 5.1 and 6.0, and Windows, Excel, Lotus, and numerous other software applications. Richmond has been a consultant in law-office training for nine years. For the past four summers, she has offered computer classes for the Missouri Bar Association.

Computer technology is developing at such a rapid pace that you can almost rest assured that what's here today will be changed or gone tomorrow. That means that paralegals must learn to tackle the tremendous problem of keeping their computer systems up to date.

There are several ways that you can learn about current developments in the area of computer technology and software. One way is to read computer magazines, such as those listed and described below. Other ways include attending computer workshops and seminars, participating in user groups, and attending software demonstrations or obtaining demonstration software diskettes, or "demos."

COMPUTER MAGAZINES

There are a number of monthly or bimonthly publications to which you or your firm can subscribe. By routinely scanning through some or all of these publications, you can keep abreast of what's happening in the computer world in regard to technology or software relating to law offices and legal research.

The Lawyer's PC (published by Shepard's/McGraw-Hill, P. O. Box 35300, Colorado Springs, CO 80935-3530) is a monthly publication for lawyers who use personal computers. Each month, a different topic is addressed. One issue, for example, featured an article entitled "Changing the Way We Work: Where Are Computers Taking Us?" The topic was right on target for attorneys and paralegals who wish to assess the impact of computer technology on their work habits. Each November, the entire issue is devoted to a list of software applications for the law office. The list is particularly helpful because it groups the software according to specific legal fields (such as bankruptcy) or specific functions in the law office (such as calendar and docket control). Information on vendors (sellers), prices, and software capabilities is also included. *The Perfect Lawyer,* a similar type of monthly publication also published by Shepard's/McGraw-Hill, deals with WordPerfect word-processing software and legal applications specific to that software.

Law Office Technology is a bimonthly publication that covers a wide variety of topics and deals with all aspects of law and computing. Topics covered range from the most commonly used WordPerfect macros to automating the job of estate management. To obtain information on this magazine, write to *Law Office Technology,* 3520 Cadillac Avenue, Suite E, Costa Mesa, CA 92626.

Computer Counsel is similar to *The Lawyer's PC* in that it discusses different types of software applications specifically designed for the law office. For information, contact *Computer Counsel,* 641 West Lake Street, Suite 403, Chicago, IL 60661.

Legal Assistant Today (3520 Cadillac Avenue, Suite E, Costa Mesa, CA 92626) and *Legal Professional* (6060 North Central Expressway, Suite 670, Dallas, TX 75206-9947) are less oriented toward computer technology but do contain computing articles of interest and offer differing points of view on particular topics.

Last but not least are *PC Week* (P. O. Box 1769, Riverton, NJ 08077-7369) and other similar computing magazines. These publications differ from those just discussed because they deal with computer hardware and software that are not directly related to the legal area. They are very informative, though, in regard to new developments in computer technology, current prices, and new versions of software that can be used to

FEATURED GUEST, Continued

upgrade your current system. The material in these magazines is usually easy to read and understand.

WORKSHOPS AND SEMINARS

Every professional organization offers workshops and seminars dealing with computers. If you are a member of an association for paralegals, you will have an opportunity to meet and exchange ideas with others doing similar work. Check with your state, city, or county organization—or with the American Bar Association—to find out when seminars or workshops will be offered and on what specific topics. Computer workshops and seminars are not just for the technologically astute; even the novice can benefit from this type of meeting.

Seminars may be attended by attorneys, legal assistants, systems administrators, technical support personnel, and general support staff. If you attend a seminar dealing with computers, you can find out how computers are currently being used in other offices as well as gain ideas on how your office can maximize the computing capabilities available. You can learn how a particular software package can automate a task, and you benefit from candid information on the problems that attend almost every product. You can also exchange ideas and establish connections with others in your profession during these meetings.

USER GROUPS

User groups come in two varieties: specific and generic. Specific groups deal with one particular product, such as WordPerfect. I have attended meetings of WordPerfect users in several cities and have found that those attending these meetings have the same common goal: to get the most out of the product. You can gain invaluable information from both knowledgeable members attending these meetings and WordPerfect personnel. You will pick up tips from both groups that can help make your tasks easier.

Generic groups include groups formed by IBM-computer users, Macintosh users, and others. Such groups often meet on a monthly basis and discuss different software application packages that operate on personal computers. Usually, vendors attend these meetings and give away software to the groups for their use. Although the group's interests may not be the same as yours, you will not know until you attend a meeting or two.

Bar associations are beginning to sponsor special-interest groups that exchange information. In addition, a number of state bar association meetings now address special topics at the end of each meeting. These topics may include vendor displays of new computer products and programs relating to law-office management, litigation, and so on.

SOFTWARE DEMONSTRATIONS

When a new software product piques your interest, you will not want to purchase it without having first had an opportunity to explore its capabilities and how it can be applied to your firm's needs. One way of evaluating new software is by contacting the vendor and requesting a demonstration by a local dealer. You might also request from the vendor the names of some other firms in your area using the product. Then make some telephone calls to those firms to see if they might be willing to discuss with you the advantages and disadvantages of the product. Usually, people are anxious to tell you about the problems they have experienced—which would be most helpful for you.

"PARALEGALS MUST LEARN TO TACKLE THE TREMENDOUS PROBLEM OF KEEPING THEIR COMPUTER SYSTEMS UP TO DATE."

You can also ask the vendor for a demonstration diskette with supporting literature. Demonstration diskettes are usually very simple to use and very informative. Others in your firm can also view them and help in the evaluating process. Literature is always helpful because it will give you the hardware requirements of the program, such as how much space will be needed on the hard drive and how much internal memory is required for the program to run smoothly. The down side of demonstration diskettes is that you may receive an abbreviated version of the software and thus may not be able to see its full capabilities.

CONCLUSION

Computer technology is an ever-changing field. New kinds of hardware and software seem to appear every day. Keeping current in regard to computer technology can be frustrating, but it is also exciting. Generally, the best way to keep current is by reading computer literature and by communicating with others who share your needs and concerns.

a "recurring entry"—an event that will take place periodically at set intervals—need only be entered once. Also, a docket-control program can adjust related dates to correspond to a change in one of the dates. For example, court procedures may require that certain actions be taken at certain predetermined intervals. If a scheduled date for one of the actions is changed, the docket-control program can automatically adjust subsequent dates to correspond to the required time interval.

Docket programs can also be used to generate reports and personal schedules. A paralegal may want to know what events and deadlines have been scheduled over the next thirty days. A managing partner may want to know all activities or appearances scheduled in a client's behalf. Docket-control software allows the rapid and painless acquisition and analysis of such scheduling information.

Spreadsheet Programs and Accounting Software

SPREADSHEET PROGRAM
A computer program that completes calculations, does numerical tracking, and allows the operator to manipulate numeric data for statistical and reporting purposes (such as budget reporting).

Law offices use **spreadsheet programs** to expedite and automate functions requiring numerical tracking, calculation, and manipulation. If, for example, a firm is preparing a budget report on its income and expenses, all expenses and income can be entered on a spreadsheet, and calculations will be performed automatically. If one attorney's salary was omitted or incorrectly entered the first time, the correct data can be entered, and the spreadsheet will automatically adjust related computations. Spreadsheet entries for a law firm's budget are shown in Exhibit 16.14.

Spreadsheets have many uses. For example, assume that you are a litigation paralegal. Your firm has been retained by a large insurance company, which is a defendant in a malpractice suit against a brain surgeon. The plaintiff is one of the surgeon's patients, who is now disabled, allegedly because of the surgeon's negligence. The plaintiff's attorney is trying to prove that the plaintiff will suffer a loss of earnings over his lifetime of $4 million. You are preparing a series of projections—based on different hypothetical recovery periods and different future wage rates—to show that even if the physician was negligent, the loss of earnings would be no more than $500,000. Instead of having to recalculate, retype, and then proofread each projection as you change one of the variables (recovery period or wage rate), you will use a spreadsheet program. When one number changes, appropriate calculations are made automatically by the program, based on formulas that you have entered.

A spreadsheet is organized in a grid of vertical *columns* and horizontal *rows,* which create individual cells. (You can see these elements in Exhibit 16.14.) Spreadsheet software, like word-processing software, has a cursor that points to your present location within the spreadsheet. The cursor needs to be at the cell in which you wish to make an entry (or a change). You can enter either data (words or numbers) or formulas in the cells.

In addition to general-purpose software such as *Lotus 1-2-3, Excel,* and *Quattro Pro,* law firms use specialized spreadsheet programs. For example, one specialized program makes calculations for loan amortizations. The user can enter the loan amount, the interest rate, and the number of payments to be made, and the spreadsheet will calculate the monthly payment. Additional specialized programs are discussed below.

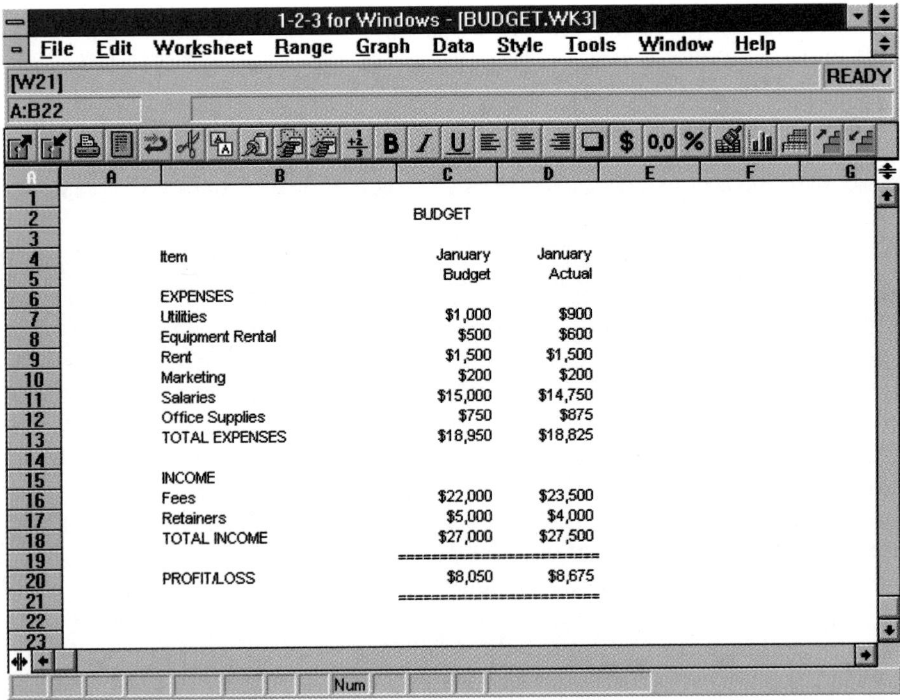

BUDGET

Item	January Budget	January Actual
EXPENSES		
Utilities	$1,000	$900
Equipment Rental	$500	$600
Rent	$1,500	$1,500
Marketing	$200	$200
Salaries	$15,000	$14,750
Office Supplies	$750	$875
TOTAL EXPENSES	$18,950	$18,825
INCOME		
Fees	$22,000	$23,500
Retainers	$5,000	$4,000
TOTAL INCOME	$27,000	$27,500
PROFIT/LOSS	$8,050	$8,675

EXHIBIT 16.14
A Law Firm's Budget

Client Trust Accounts. Spreadsheet programs also exist to handle client trust accounts. As discussed in Chapter 5, law firms typically have a trust account in which they place funds being held for clients—advance funds for costs that the firm may incur, funds received through the settlement of a legal claim, and so on. Some firms have more than one trust account, but often, the trust account contains funds held for numerous clients. The firm is ethically and legally obligated to keep a strict record of the amount of funds deposited into and disbursed from the trust account on behalf of each client, as well as the current balance of funds being held for each client. Using a spreadsheet program, the paralegal or attorney can enter an amount deposited or disbursed on behalf of a particular client, and the program will make the appropriate calculations and create a new balance.

Tax-return Software. Federal, state, and local taxation requires accurate record keeping and complicated analyses of income, expenses, and other data to determine tax liabilities. Specialized *tax-return software* allows tax attorneys to view more easily client financial information, analyze tax liabilities, and prepare corresponding tax returns. Many programs generate not only the information to be inserted in the form but also the form itself. Computerized preparation of tax returns offers a major advantage when changes or corrections are required after the form has already been prepared. Tax software often automatically recalculates tax liabilities and then produces a revised and corrected form.

Time-and-billing Software. One way that law offices have adapted the concept of spreadsheet software to their particular needs is through *time-and-billing software,* which integrates features of database programs with the accounting capabilities of spreadsheet software. Some programs in widespread use include *Verdict, TABS II, Juris, Timeslips, Profit$ource,* and *AccountMate.* The programs differ not only in their operating features but also in the amount and complexity of information that they support. Thus, some of the programs are better suited for small or medium-sized firms, while others are most effectively used in large national or international firms.

Tracking Time and Expenses. As discussed in Chapter 5, the cost of the law firm's services is often measured by the amount of time spent by attorneys, paralegals, and legal secretaries on the client's legal matter. The procedure used to track and bill the number of hours that firm professionals devote to each client's business is thus critical. In addition to timekeeping, the firm needs to track its expenses on behalf of the client so that it can be reimbursed by the client for these expenses. Furthermore, it is not sufficient for the firm to know merely that one attorney or one paralegal spent one hour on a client's business; the firm will typically tell the client the particular nature of the work that was done.

For example, a statement produced for client Thomas Jones, M.D., will not simply indicate that paralegal Elena Lopez spent 1.5 hours on "work relating to the Jones case" but will specifically indicate what work was performed during the 1.5 hours. The statement may read "Interview: Susan Mathews (nurse): 1.5 hours." Even if the more specific information is not presented on the billing statement, the firm will want easy access to more detailed information so that it can respond to any questions that the client may have about the bill.

The time-and-billing program does not relieve the firm's employees from the important responsibility of keeping track of their time. Often, this first tracking stage is performed manually, when the timekeeper fills out a paper time slip (discussed and illustrated in Chapter 5). The time slip is then entered into the computer by someone on the firm's staff who understands the importance of accuracy at this key step. The firm also enters into the computer information about the billing arrangement with the client. The computer program can then merge the billable hours with the billing rate and calculate the sum to be billed to the client.

Reviewing and Finalizing the Client's Bill. Once the bill has been calculated, the attorney in charge of the client's work will review a "prebilling report"—a draft version of the bill. The attorney reviews the bill for accuracy and may also determine that the amount calculated from the time slips should be modified.

Once the billing statement is adjusted to reflect any changes made by the responsible attorney, the program generates a final bill to be mailed to the client. The program should also generate management reports, which indicate the total amount of time billed by each attorney or paralegal for the month and possibly for the year to date. The report also indicates the amount billed, client by client, for the firm as a whole. Many programs allow the firm to track payments as they are made by the clients; management reports can then also indicate the status of the firm's collections for the amounts billed.

Integrated, Special-use Programs

Most software programs can be described as word-processing software, database programs, or spreadsheet programs. Many law-office tasks require a combination of these processing tools, however. Law offices frequently take advantage of specially integrated programs—software that has been developed to assist in the practice of a particular area of the law.

For example, an area of practice in which the integration of word-processing, database, and financial spreadsheet capabilities is useful is bankruptcy law. A paralegal assisting a bankruptcy attorney may be asked to handle pleadings and court documents, advise creditors of the status of the proceedings, and produce financial reports. An integrated program keyed to the requirements of federal bankruptcy practice can simplify, expedite, and even improve the quality of legal work in this area.

COMPUTER-ASSISTED LEGAL RESEARCH (CALR)

One of the great benefits of computer technology for legal practitioners is *computer-assisted legal research (CALR).* As you will read in Chapter 17, thorough and up-to-date legal research requires access to voluminous source materials, including cases decided by state and federal courts and state and federal statutory law. Additionally, the legal researcher often needs to refer to publications, such as legal encyclopedias, law books, and articles in legal periodicals, that provide background information on a particular legal issue.

CALR has made it possible to access databases containing many of the most important legal resources. By accessing databases provided through computerized legal-research services, such as WESTLAW and LEXIS, legal professionals can obtain within seconds or minutes, without leaving their offices, case law or statutory law governing a particular issue. Although not all printed legal sources are contained on these databases, many of them are. See, for example, Exhibit 16.15 on page 632, which shows the directory of research sources available through WESTLAW.

Advantages of CALR

An obvious advantage of CALR is that you can locate and print out court cases, statutory provisions, and other legal documents within a matter of minutes without leaving your work station. Of course, if the firm for which you work has an extensive law library and the case or statute you need to find is contained in that library, it would make sense to refer to the printed source. But many small law offices have neither the money nor space available to acquire a very extensive law library. For attorneys and paralegals working in such environments, it may be cost-effective to access needed information using CALR instead of traveling to the nearest law library to obtain it—especially if the nearest law library is over a hundred miles away.

As you will read in Chapter 17, a key advantage of CALR is that new case decisions and changes in statutory law are entered almost immediately into the database. In other words, legal sources on databases accessed through WESTLAW or LEXIS are more current than printed sources.

DEVELOPING PARALEGAL SKILLS

Computerized Legal Research

Kathleen Connors has been assigned the task of researching an issue on WESTLAW. John Ralstrom, one of the firm's clients, has been sued by a friend who attended Ralstrom's annual Christmas party. The friend, David Wheeler, was drunk when he left the party and got into a car accident in which he severely injured his left leg. As a result of the accident, Wheeler lost 70 percent of his use of the leg. Because he is a high school gym teacher, Wheeler's leg injury has greatly impaired his ability to work. Wheeler wants to obtain compensatory damages, including lost wages, from Ralstrom in the lawsuit.

THE PRELIMINARIES

Kathleen will be researching state statutes and case law to determine whether Ralstrom can be held liable for Wheeler's injury. She begins by familiarizing herself with the issue. She consults a legal encyclopedia to find background information on the topic, which will help her define the issue. After some preliminary research, Kathleen decides what the central issue is and writes it down: What is the liability of a social host with respect to serving intoxicating beverages?

Now Kathleen needs to choose the specific WESTLAW database that she will be using. She knows that she wants Illinois cases, because the lawsuit is being brought in an Illinois state court, so she chooses the Illinois Courts database, *IL-CS.* She will also be researching in the Illinois Statutes Annotated database, *IL-ST.* She enters the names of these databases on the form.

DRAFTING THE QUERY

The next step is to draft a query, which creates an index of terms for the computer to search. Kathleen selects the important terms relating to her issue: *social, host, liability,* and *alcohol.* Because the computer will only retrieve cases containing the terms that the user gives it, she chooses some

If your supervising attorney is preparing for trial, for example, the attorney will want to base his or her legal argument on current legal authorities. A precedential case that may have been "good law" three months ago may be "bad law" today. The case may have been overturned by a higher court since then, and the only way you would know this would be through CALR (because the case would not yet be included in printed sources).

- **Making sure that your research results reflect current law is a crucial step in legal research.**

Charges for Legal-research Services

To use a computerized legal-research service, such as WESTLAW or LEXIS, a law firm or other user signs a contract with the provider of the service. Charges for the service are typically based on either on-line time (WESTLAW) or the number of database searches performed (LEXIS). Although the com-

DEVELOPING PARALEGAL SKILLS, Continued

alternative terms as well. She chooses *guest* as an alternative to *host* because these types of cases often discuss liability to social guests. She chooses *responsibility, culpability,* and *negligence* as alternatives to *liability*. For *alcohol,* she uses *intoxicating, inebriating, liquor,* and *drunk.*

Then she has to decide if she needs to use the root expander (!) or the universal character (*) in her query. If she places the root expander at the end of the root, the program will give her all forms of a term. For example, *liab!* will give her *liable, liability,* and so on. The universal character is a variable character that may be placed in the middle or at the end of a term to retrieve various forms of the term. For example, *dr*nk* retrieves *drank* and *drunk.* Kathleen uses both the root expander and the universal character for the term *drunk: dr*nk!* She uses the root expander for all of the terms describing liability and alcohol.

The last step is to decide how to connect the terms. She connects *social* and *host!* with *A/S,* which means that they should appear within the same sentence. All of the the terms are connected with *A/P* to indicate that they should appear within the same paragraph.

ACCESSING WESTLAW

Now that her query is drafted, Kathleen accesses WESTLAW on her computer and signs on, using her password. When she sees the *Welcome to WESTLAW* screen, she enters the client file number. At the *WESTLAW Directory* screen, she types *IL-CS* for the Illinois Courts database. The next screen that she sees is the *Enter Query* screen. The screen says that she may enter a query in Natural Language—a search method on WESTLAW that lets you type your search request in plain English. For this research session, however, Kathleen decides to use the traditional terms-and-connectors search method, as she had planned, because she is familiar with this traditional method of searching. For someone less familiar with the terms-and-connectors method, using natural language would be an attractive alternative.

puter terminal gains access to the service through a modem over a telephone line, the cost of the long-distance connection is built into the price of using the service. In other words, the entity paying for the service generally does not pay long-distance charges as well.

Using Legal-research Services

There are several ways to access cases, statutes, and other sources provided by legal-research services, such as WESTLAW and LEXIS. When you know the citation[1] to a case or statute, it may be entered using one of several commands. The service will then display the case or statute requested. When the researcher wants to retrieve a group of cases or statutes relating to a certain

ETHICAL CONCERN

Cutting the Cost of Legal Research

As a paralegal, you have an ethical duty to the client to minimize costs, including the cost of computerized research—which, after all, is paid for by the client. One way you can reduce research costs is to plan your inquiries carefully before accessing a service such as LEXIS or WESTLAW. This way, you do not have to spend on-line time making such decisions.

1. As will be explained in Chapter 17, a citation indicates the abbreviated name and volume number of the publication in which a case, statute, or regulation can be found, as well as the page number within that volume on which the case, statute, or regulation begins.

EXHIBIT 16.15
Directory of Research Sources Available through WESTLAW

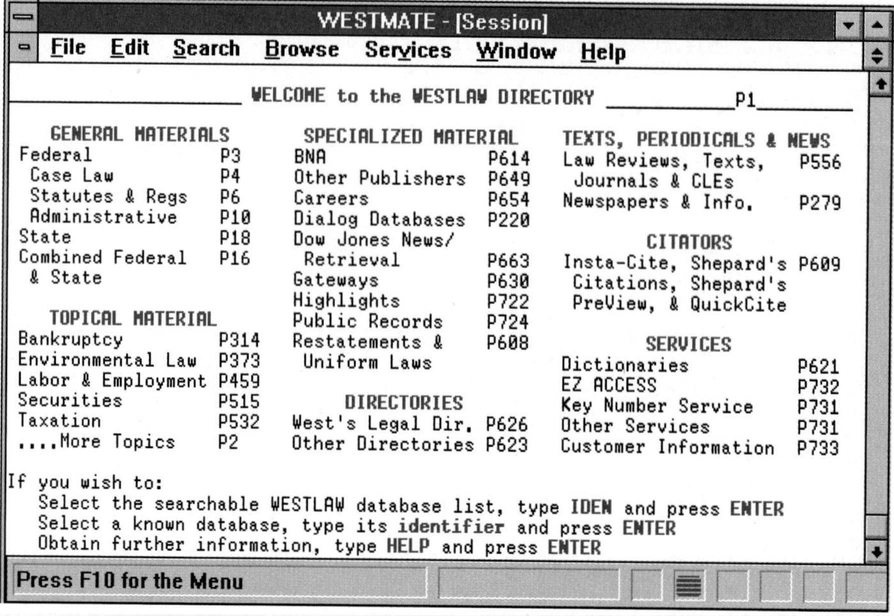

issue, a word search can be performed. This requires the researcher to input a group of the most important terms from the legal issue, called a *query.*

Drafting Queries. To best utilize computerized legal-research services, you should make sure that you draft your queries effectively. For example, suppose that one of your firm's clients is suing a restaurant for serving her "tainted oysters." Apparently, the oysters were tainted by bacteria that caused the client to become critically ill after eating them and to sustain permanent nerve damage. You have been asked to research case law to find similar cases. You want to make sure that your query is not too broad (as it would be if you entered just the term *restaurant*). Your search will be futile because so many thousands of documents contain that term.

Similarly, if your query is to narrow (as it would be if you entered the terms *restaurant* and *tainted oysters*), you might not retrieve any documents. Over time, you will learn how to phrase queries in such a way that the documents you retrieve from the computerized database are relevant to your research goal. For further information on how to draft a query using the traditional "terms-and-connectors" approach, see this chapter's *Developing Paralegal Skills* features entitled "Computerized Legal Research." Exhibit 16.16 shows how the query on the legal issue discussed in that feature would appear on the WESTLAW query screen.

Both WESTLAW and LEXIS have made it easier for legal professionals to search their databases by allowing for "natural-language" (WESTLAW) or "associative-language" (LEXIS) searching. WESTLAW's system is called WIN (Westlaw is Natural), while LEXIS's system is called FREESTYLE. Using the WIN or FREESTYLE method of searching, you can draft a query using ordinary language. For example, in researching the tainted-oyster case, you might draft a natural-language query on WESTLAW as follows: "What is the liability of a restaurant owner to a customer who suffers injury from food

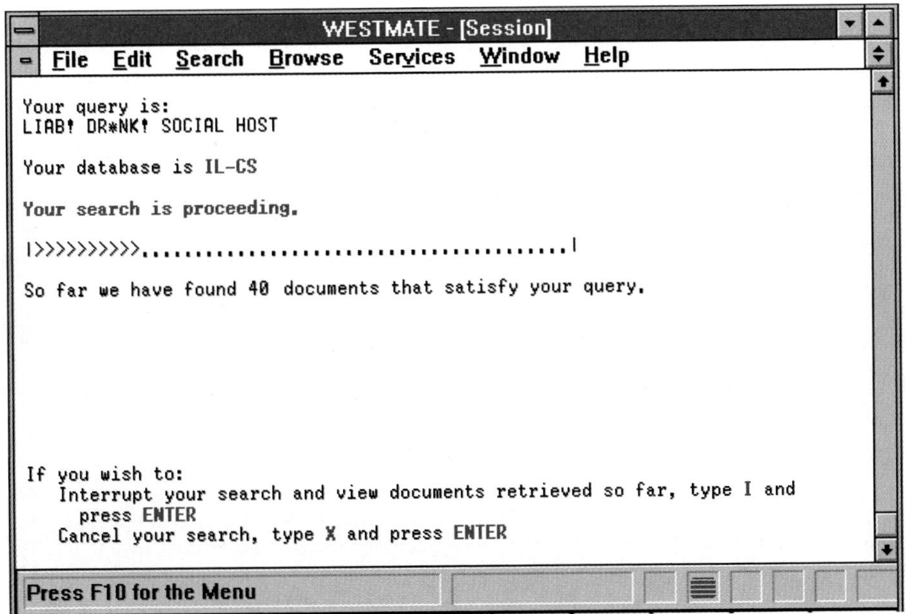

WESTMATE - [Session]
File Edit Search Browse Services Window Help
Your query is:
LIAB! DR*NK! SOCIAL HOST
Your database is IL-CS
Your search is proceeding.
So far we have found 40 documents that satisfy your query.
If you wish to:
Interrupt your search and view documents retrieved so far, type I and press ENTER
Cancel your search, type X and press ENTER
Press F10 for the Menu

EXHIBIT 16.16
A WESTLAW Query Screen

prepared and served by the restaurant?" WESTLAW will then retrieve a maximum of twenty cases that most closely match your description.

West Publishing Company has developed a voice-recognition system, called *LawTalk,* that can be integrated into the WIN system. If you have LawTalk available for CALR, you can simply give voice commands to the computer, rather than keying in your queries. Note that LawTalk is an add-on product—that is, it does not come with WESTLAW and WIN. Special software, as well as a significant amount of computer power, is required.

Passwords and File Names. Because users are billed for using the database, the user needs a password to access the service. In some firms, each paralegal using legal-research services will be assigned a separate access code; in other firms, each department, practice group, or attorney is assigned a code.

Charges for CALR constitute an expense that ultimately will be paid for by the client. Therefore, a separate research file should be opened for each client. WESTLAW assists this function by asking the user to enter the file name each time the system is accessed. The paralegal should remember to enter a separate file name for each client if several research projects are undertaken for different clients during the same WESTLAW session. This can be done by typing CLIENT when you wish to open a new file.

A WORD OF CAUTION

We have seen how the computer in the law-office setting has revolutionized the way that legal work is done. By eliminating duplicative, routine tasks, computers have allowed law offices to increase their productivity and often the quality of their work. But computers have also placed a premium on the careful planning of projects and on the painstaking review of entries that will

TODAY'S PROFESSIONAL PARALEGAL

Dedicated Imaging Systems

Ashley Wagner is a legal assistant in an environmental-law practice. Her firm's client is responding to an Environmental Protection Agency (EPA) information request. The client, a manufacturing company, is being investigated by the EPA for potential violations of its requirements relating to air permits. These permits are required for the company to emit into the air the wastes that result from its production process. Ashley is responsible for organizing the ten thousand documents needed to respond to the information request.

Ashley is used to managing documents because environmental cases usually involve a tremendous number of them. She uses a computer to summarize each document and to index and code all of the documents so that they can be located. In this case, she needs to be able to access and retrieve, quickly and easily, any document when requested.

FINDING A SOLUTION TO STORAGE AND RETRIEVAL PROBLEMS

Ashley needs to find a reliable way to access and retrieve all of the documents. She begins by calling a computer consulting firm, CompuLaw, Inc., whose services she and others in her law firm often use. She speaks with Sandra Bossin, a consultant. Ashley describes the situation to Sandra and asks Sandra if she has anything that could help the storage and retrieval problems presented by this case. Sandra tells Ashley that imaging technology might provide a solution for Ashley's problem and offers to demonstrate the technology for Ashley. They agree to meet at Ashley's office the following day.

DEDICATED IMAGING SYSTEMS

The next day, Sandra arrives with some equipment that resembles a personal computer. She calls it a dedicated imaging system and explains that it contains an optical scanner that allows it to scan a document and copy it, much as a photocopy machine does. Images of all of the documents that are copied are then stored on either disks or tapes. The documents on the disks or tapes can be indexed so that the user can view them on a PC. The firm would still have to assign an employee to scan all of the documents.

Ashley is impressed. The imaging systems could save much time and office space. She excuses herself and walks across the hall to the office of her supervising attorney, Nate Wenger. She had arranged previously for Nate to attend the demonstration if she thought that Sandra had a solution to their problem. He had agreed and said that he would be in his office at the time of Ashley's meeting with Sandra.

Ashley returns to her office with Nate. She asks Sandra to demonstrate how the optical scanner works. Ashley gives Sandra a form from a forms file, and Sandra runs the scanner over it. Sandra then shows Nate the image that was created and stored on the disk. She explains all of the system's benefits to Nate.

AN ALTERNATIVE—CONTRACTING FOR IMAGING SERVICES

Sandra also tells Nate and Ashley that there are companies that provide imaging services. "You submit your documents, and they return either the disks or tapes to you. They create the indexes and do all of the scanning so that you don't have to," explains Sandra. Nate says that he thinks optical scanning is a great idea and asks Sandra if she has some literature on the system that she had just demonstrated, as well as the names of the companies that provide imaging services and the approximate costs.

After Sandra leaves the office, Ashley meets with Nate. They discuss how useful this system would be and how much time it would save. Nate tells Ashley that he thinks it might be better to start with an outside service, because the firm does not have a full-time employee available to scan the documents. He makes it clear that her job cannot include that task because it is too time consuming. Ashley agrees with the idea of starting with a scanning service. Nate then asks Ashley to "shop around" and find out what rates the different companies charge for the service. "Once I have the cost data," explains Nate, "I can discuss the issue with the other partners at the next partnership meeting."

be automatically replicated at many stages of a project. Detailed planning and review require a significant amount of time. While outside consultants may be retained to minimize the time spent on planning, consultants are expensive. Also, a carefully devised system for backing up computer data on external storage devices is essential. If a system fails and data are not backed up, crucial information may be lost. If back-up copies are made but are difficult to locate, much valuable time may be required to find the back-up copies. In sum, computers have simplified law-office work, but they have not replaced the human management skills that are required to use the technology as productively as possible.

KEY TERMS AND CONCEPTS

application software 611
boilerplate 617
central processing unit (CPU) 606
database management system 618
E-mail 613
hard drive 606
hardware 604
keyboard 606
local area network (LAN) 613
mainframe computer 605
minicomputer 605
modem 607
monitor 606
mouse 607
operating-system software 611
password 605
personal computer (PC) 606
security code 605
software 604
spreadsheet program 626
user interface 612
wide area network (WAN) 613
word-processing software 615

CHAPTER SUMMARY

1. Computers have made it possible for paralegals to spend less time on mechanical tasks (such as retyping entire documents to incorporate revisions) and more time exercising their professional skills and abilities.

2. Hardware consists of the physical components of a computer system. Computers range in size and capacity from large mainframe computers to minicomputers to personal, or desktop, computers. Because of the expense involved in purchasing and maintaining mainframes, they are normally used only by very large organizations and firms. Minicomputers are less powerful than mainframes and are typically used by middle-sized firms—law firms with fifty or so lawyers, for example. Most law firms today use personal computers, often linked to other computers in the same office.

3. Components of a computer system include the central processing unit (CPU), which controls the functions of the computer components; the monitor, which displays the current activities of the computer; the keyboard, which sends input to the computer's CPU, which in turn displays the information on the monitor; and the mouse, which directs the cursor on the monitor. In addition to the keyboard, there are other input devices, including optical scanners, which "scan" and copy the contents of documents in a form readable by computers. Output devices, such as printers, transfer data from the computer to permanent, readable forms (on hard copy, for example). Modems, when used with specialized communications software, allow the user to transfer data from one computer to another.

4. Storage devices include internal hard disk drives, external hard disk drives, removable diskettes, optical disks, CD-ROMs, and magnetic-tape systems (which can be used in two formats, cartridges and reels).

5. Operating-system software controls the communication between the computer system and the application software used by the computer. IBM and IBM-compatible computers have typically used the disk operating system (DOS). Traditionally, computer operating systems have been manufactured to operate with either IBM and IBM-compatible computers or the Apple Macintosh family of computers. Translation programs allow data created on one operating system to be translated into a format compatible with a different operating system. Each operating system has a special user interface, which controls what the computer user sees on the screen and how the user gives commands to the computer.

6. Office network systems link personal computers together so that data and software can be shared. These systems include local area networks (LANs), which link computers in an office or building, and wide area networks (WANs), which link multiple computers over a wide geographical area. Networking can also be done via electronic-mail (E-mail) systems, by which users can send messages from one computer to another.

7. Application software consists of computer programs that instruct the computer on how to perform specific tasks. Three basic types of application software are word-processing software, database management systems, and spreadsheet software.

8. Word-processing software allows users to create documents and save, edit, and otherwise change the content and appearance of those documents. Form documents can be customized using word-processing software.

9. Database management systems offer an alternative to manual indexing or filing systems. Database systems allow users to organize data in specific ways, create reports, and print out information in a variety of formats. Database software also allows legal professionals to track litigation documents, and docket-control software can help track important deadlines, such as court appearances and the dates by which certain documents must be filed with the court.

10. Spreadsheet programs automate functions requiring numerical tracking, calculation, and manipulation. Spreadsheets are computerized grids of vertical columns and horizontal rows. The user can enter data or formulas to instruct the computer to perform certain calculations, such as totaling a column of figures. Software utilizing spreadsheets includes time-and-billing software and tax-return software.

11. Integrated, special-use programs combine various features of word-processing, database, and spreadsheet programs. Integrated, special-use programs are generally developed for a particular legal area, such as bankruptcy.

12. Computer-assisted legal research (CALR) has revolutionized the way in which many paralegals and attorneys conduct legal research. Widely used in the legal arena are computerized legal-research services, such as WESTLAW and LEXIS. These services provide access to databases that contain comprehensive law libraries. For a fee, which is normally based on either on-line time or the number of searches performed, legal professionals can access relevant case law, statutory law, or other legal authorities on particular legal issues within minutes without leaving their offices. A key advantage of CALR is that legal professionals can obtain the most current law, because new court decisions, statutory law, and other legal documents are available through computerized legal-research services shortly after the decisions or changes in the law have been made.

QUESTIONS FOR REVIEW

1. What kinds of work do legal assistants perform on computers?

2. List the various types of computers that are in use. What are their components?

3. What are some of the external storage devices currently in use? Why are saving and backing up computer work essential to computer proficiency?

4. What is the difference between operating-system software and application software? What is DOS? On what types of computers has it traditionally been used?

5. What are the two primary types of networks? What is electronic mail? How are networks used to share data and software or transmit communications via the computer?

6. How is word-processing software used? List and define five terms that are commonly used in word processing.

7. What is a database? What is the difference between a field and a record? How can the use of database software enhance the efficiency of legal work?

8. What are spreadsheet programs? How are they used by legal professionals?

9. What are integrated, special-use programs? Give an example of one.

10. What are some of the benefits for legal professionals of computer-assisted legal research? Who pays for the cost of using computerized legal-research services?

ETHICAL QUESTIONS

1. Tom Malcomb works as a paralegal in a large law firm. The firm recently hired two attorneys and a paralegal from another firm. Before they were hired, the attorneys and the paralegal had worked as a team on the opposite side of a major case Tom's firm is handling, *Black v. Walker Manufacturing Co.* As a result, Tom's firm faced a potential conflict of interest. Under the code of ethics adopted in Tom's state, the firm could continue to represent its client in the case but only if it erected an "ethical wall" to prevent the new team from participating in the case in any way. As part of the ethical wall, Tom's firm created a special password. This password was required to access any computerized files relating to this case.

Tom has just printed out a research memo concerning an important issue in the case. Because the copier on his floor is not working, he takes the elevator up to the next floor to the copier there. Tom accidentally drops the card that contains the *Black v. Walker Manufacturing Co.* password. Tom makes his copy and returns to his office. Susan Hines, the paralegal on the newly hired team, finds the card on the floor next to the copier that Tom used. What ethical obligation does Susan have?

2. Amelia and Richard are paralegals in the same law firm, and they have both been working on the same brief, the written argument that will be submitted to the appellate court in support of a client's position. Each of them has researched and written sections on specific issues. Amelia, however, has a great deal of expertise on one of Richard's issues. Amelia does not agree with the way he has prepared the brief on that issue, and she is unable to persuade him to follow her suggestions on how it should be written. While Richard is at lunch, Amelia accesses his portion of the brief on the firm's computer network and changes it. Richard does not notice the changes until after the brief is reviewed by the supervising attorney and filed with the court. He can look at the directory and tell that Amelia accessed the brief and changed it. What should Richard do?

3. Judy Harris works as a paralegal for a small law firm. She has worked for the last three hours on a legal memorandum summarizing her research results on a case being litigated by her supervising attorney. Normally, whenever Judy creates or modifies documents on the personal computer she uses, she periodically enters the *Save* command so that her work will be saved on the computer's hard disk. Today, however, she has been so engrossed in her task that she has forgotten to take this precaution. Suddenly, her computer screen "freezes," and she realizes that there is no way that she can save her memo. She will have to shut down and restart her system, and she will have to recreate everything she had written in the last three hours. She spends another three hours redoing the previous work and spends an additional two hours to complete the memo—all the time saving her work at frequent intervals. When the memo is finished, she enters on a time slip the name of the client and the nature of the work performed on the client's behalf. She looks at the space where she needs to enter the number of hours spent on the task and is faced with a dilemma. Should she bill the client for five hours (the time it would have taken to complete the job had the computer failure not occurred) or eight hours (the actual time she had to spend creating the memorandum)? What would you do if you were in Judy's position?

PRACTICE QUESTIONS AND ASSIGNMENTS

1. What types of software would do the following?

a. Prevent you from missing deadlines.

b. Manage documents in complex litigation.

c. Perform legal research.

d. Find quickly and summarize in a report all scheduled appearances for a particular client.
e. Store and organize information on expert witnesses.

2. What type of computer would you select for the following offices?

a. A small law firm in which the legal assistant also serves as the legal secretary.
b. A medium-sized law firm in which there is a large number of legal assistants who frequently draft documents.
c. A large law firm with 350 attorneys, 90 legal assistants, and 190 secretaries, all of whom need or want computers on their desks for drafting documents, creating tables and graphs, performing financial projections and analyses, and the like.
d. A megafirm of 900 attorneys.

3. Your supervising attorney is the chairperson of the state bar association's probate and estate section, which has 275 members. The attorney wants you to create a database for the section members. The database should include the members' names and bar (license) numbers (for those members who are attorneys), as well as their law firms' names, addresses, and telephone numbers. The database should also include the names of the committees—such as the estate-planning committee, trust committee, or tax committee—on which the the members serve. What fields and records would you create in generating your database?

QUESTIONS FOR CRITICAL ANALYSIS

1. Included in the *Selected Annotated Readings*, on page 640, is an article entitled "Five Ways to Commit Malpractice with Your Computer." If you have not read the article, try to describe how a computer-related problem or event could lead to a malpractice suit on the part of a client. If you have read the article, can you think of any other ethical pitfalls (besides those mentioned in the article) that attorneys and paralegals must guard against in the computerized legal workplace?

2. Should paralegals assume responsibility for keeping up to date on new computer technology for the law office? Why or why not?

ROLE-PLAYING EXERCISES

1. Paralegal Janet Rowe has worked for attorney Carl Benton, a sole practitioner, for several years. Janet spends nearly half of her time doing accounting and administrative work. For example, it is her responsibility to keep a record of the amount of time spent on each client's work and the costs incurred on each client's behalf. She also prepares the monthly bills that are sent to clients at the end of each month. In addition, she maintains the firm's checking account and the client trust account, records all expenses paid and income received by the firm in the appropriate ledgers, and prepares routine quarterly tax returns. Carl's practice is very successful, and he and Janet are finding it increasingly difficult to perform all the necessary legal work. Janet has read, in paralegal magazines and other legal publications, about how certain types of software designed specifically for law offices could simplify her bookkeeping and administrative tasks and thus free up much of her time for legal assistance. She mentions this possibility to Carl, and they discuss the matter.

Working in pairs, role-play the discussion between Janet and her supervising attorney in which Janet describes to the attorney how investing in computer technology could be a solution to their problem of work overload. The student playing the role of Janet should be enthusiastic about computerizing the workplace and the benefits, in terms of time saving, that computer technology offers. She should also mention how computerized research—using CD-ROM libraries and legal-research services such as WESTLAW and LEXIS—would benefit the attorney. The student playing the role of Carl should be concerned mostly about cost. He should also be rather intimidated by (and somewhat skeptical about) technology generally. He should ask questions such as, "What happens, though, if there is a computer failure?" If time permits, reverse roles.

2. Susan MacNamara works as a paralegal for a relatively small law firm, Marks & Jefferson. Susan and Kim Painter, a paralegal who works five mornings a week for the firm, have become close friends over the year that they have worked together. Susan has learned that Kim spends her afternoons doing freelance work for other attorneys. Kim performs much of her freelance work in her home office and often transmits legal memoranda and other documents to her employers via modem. One day, Susan was asking Kim about the costs of running a home office, including the cost of application software. Kim told Susan that much of her software was "free"—she simply "borrowed" the software from Marks & Jefferson's diskette library. She would take a diskette home, load the software onto her computer, and return the diskette the next day. Kim goes on to explain to Susan how using the firm's software has really simplified her billing procedures, tax returns, and other record keeping.

Working in pairs, role-play a scene in which Susan and Kim debate the ethical and legal implications raised by Kim's "software piracy." The student playing the role of Susan should raise the issues of copyright infringement (review the section on intellectual property in Chapter 8), property theft, and generally the ethical aspects of Kim's unauthorized use of her employer's software. The person playing the role of Kim should assume that she has done nothing wrong because she has not deprived her employer of anything—she merely took advantage of an opportunity to save money by using the employer's software. If time permits, reverse roles.

PROJECTS

1. Try to visit a computer consulting firm that works with law firms. Learn as much as you can about the types of computers or computer systems used by firms of different sizes and different legal specialties. Find out what kinds of software are being used for word processing and for database management. Ask for a demonstration.

2. If you are unfamiliar with the components of a computer, visit a local computer store and look at the computers that it is selling. Ask a salesperson to show you the various computer components.

3. Locate and read an article relating to software used in the law office, and create a one-page summary of the article (refer to the discussion of computer magazines in this chapter's featured-guest article).

ANNOTATED SELECTED READINGS

BALDWIN-LECLAIR, JACK. "Love Techno-American Style: The Laptop and Laplink." *Legal Assistant Today*, March/April 1993. An informative review of laptop, notebook, palmtop, and portable computers. The article also discusses *Laplink*, a program used to transfer information between laptops and PCs, and reviews some of the products that have recently come on the market.

BERGMAN, RENEE M. "The Paperless Trial." *Legal Assistant Today*, September/October 1992. A fascinating account of a trial in a class-action suit. The suit involved hundreds of thousands of documents, but no paper documents were used at the trial. A computer-imaging system was used instead to transmit images of the documents by computer for courtroom viewing.

JARCHOW, DAVID J. "The Legal Assistant Role at the High-tech, Multi-media Trial." *National Paralegal Reporter*, Fall 1994. An insightful glimpse at a litigation team's use of computer technology in the courtroom during an actual trial. During the trial, attorneys and paralegals used computer technology to access databases (in-house databases as well as those available through WESTLAW and LEXIS), communicate with team members in their offices, telecommunicate documents to and from the courtroom, print out documents, and present evidence.

LEITER, RICHARD D. "Computer-Assisted Legal Research (CALR), Naturally!" *Legal Assistant Today*, May/June 1994. An informative comparison of the natural-language systems—FREESTYLE (available on LEXIS) and WIN (available on WESTLAW). The article also includes an analysis of the pitfalls involved in using these systems.

MOORE, LINDA S. "Managing Deposition Testimony." *Legal Assistant Today,* May/June 1993. A review of *Summation II,* a program for managing depositions, including summarizing deposition testimony and creating case chronologies.

ROPER, BRENT D. "Desktop Programs to Organize Your Work and Time." *Legal Assistant Today,* May/June 1993. A review of a desktop program called a personal information manager (PIM). The article discusses the functions of a PIM, which include scheduling, note taking, to-do lists, and creating telephone and address lists. It gives students an understanding of how desktop software is used and refers the reader to available programs.

ROPER, BRENT D. "The 10 Best Features in WordPerfect 6.0." *Legal Assistant Today,* May/June 1994. An informative article on the newest version of WordPerfect word-processing software. The article describes the top ten features of WordPerfect 6.0 and how to convert from WordPerfect 5.1 to WordPerfect 6.0.

VANDAGRIFF, DAVID P. "Five Ways to Commit Malpractice with Your Computer." *National Paralegal Reporter,* Fall 1994. A helpful article warning legal professionals about the potential pitfalls of relying too extensively on computers. The article indicates some steps that legal professionals should take—including backing up data—to prevent errors and to avoid losing valuable information.

17

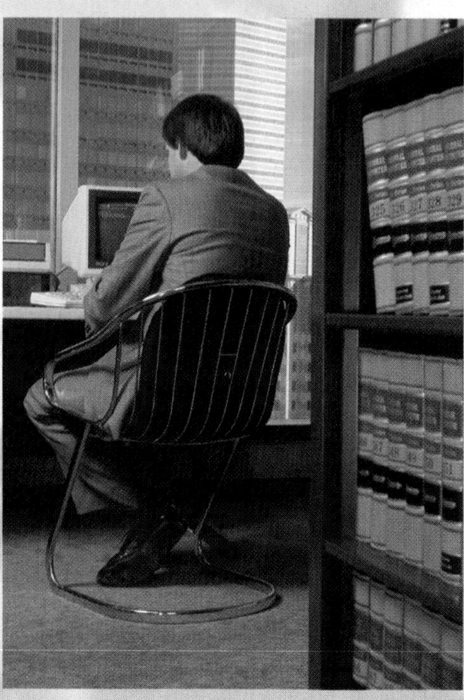

LEGAL RESEARCH

Chapter Objectives

After completing this chapter, you will know:

- How primary and secondary sources of law differ and how to use each of these types of sources in the research process.
- How to use legal encyclopedias and other secondary sources to find case law relevant to your research topic.
- How court decisions are published and how to read case citations.
- How federal statutes and regulations are published and the major sources of statutory and administrative law.
- What kinds of resources are available for researching the legislative history of a statute.
- Why finding current law is important and how to verify that your research results are up to date.
- How CD-ROMs are providing an alternative to printed research materials.

Chapter Outline

INTRODUCTION

For many paralegals, legal research is a fascinating part of their jobs. They find it intrinsically interesting to read the actual words of a court's opinion on a legal question or the text of a statute. Additionally, they acquire a first-hand knowledge of the law and how the law applies to actual people and events. Research is also a crucial part of the paralegal's job, and the ability to conduct research thoroughly yet efficiently enhances a paralegal's value to the legal team.

As a paralegal, you may be asked to perform a variety of research tasks. Some research tasks will be simple. You may be asked to locate and copy a court case, for example. Other research tasks may take days or even weeks to complete. In almost all but the simplest of research tasks, legal research overlaps extensively with legal analysis, which is covered in the following chapter. To find relevant case law, for example, you need to be able to analyze the cases that you find to ensure that they are indeed relevant. Although we discuss research and analysis separately, keep in mind that the two processes are closely related.

As discussed in the preceding chapter, computers have greatly simplified the task of legal research. Many paralegals now conduct research without even entering a law library. Computerized legal services such as WESTLAW and LEXIS allow legal professionals to find the text of cases, statutes, and other legal documents without leaving their desks. An increasing number of law firms today are also purchasing reference materials on CD-ROMs, as will be discussed later in this chapter. To a great extent, how you do your research—that is, whether you conduct research via a computer or in a law library—will depend on your employer and the computer facilities available to you. In some workplaces, paralegals are expected to conduct much of their research using computerized legal services. In other workplaces, paralegals may be asked to do the bulk of their legal research using printed legal sources in law libraries.

Regardless of whether legal research is conducted via computer or in a law library, it is essential to know what sources to consult for different types of information. You will learn about these sources in this chapter. You will also learn how to make sure that the law you find is up to date and still "good law."

PRIMARY SOURCE
In legal research, a document that establishes the law on a particular issue, such as a case decision, legislative act, administrative rule, or presidential order.

SECONDARY SOURCE
In legal research, any publication that indexes, summarizes, or interprets the law, such as a legal encyclopedia, a treatise, or an article in a law review.

PRIMARY AND SECONDARY SOURCES

Generally, research sources fall into two broad categories—primary sources and secondary sources. Printed decisions of the various courts in the United States, statutes enacted by legislative bodies, rules and regulations created by administrative agencies, presidential orders, and generally any documents that *establish* the law are **primary sources** of law. **Secondary sources** of law consist of books and articles that summarize, systematize, compile, or otherwise interpret the law. Legal encyclopedias, which summarize the law, are secondary sources of law.

Normally, researchers in any field or profession begin their research with secondary sources. Secondary sources are often referred to as *finding tools,* because they help the researcher to find primary sources on the topics they are researching and to learn how those sources have been interpreted by others. If you are asked to research case law on a certain issue, you should do likewise. You should first refer to secondary sources to learn about the issue and find relevant primary sources concerning it. Then, you can go to the primary sources themselves (such as statutes or court cases) to research the established law on the issue.

In the following sections, you will read about the primary and secondary sources that are most frequently used in researching case law, statutory law and legislative history, administrative law, and constitutional law.

RESEARCHING CASE LAW—THE PRELIMINARY STEPS

Any research project normally involves the following five steps:

- Defining the issue(s) to be researched.
- Determining the goal of the research project.
- Consulting relevant secondary sources.
- Researching relevant primary sources.
- Synthesizing and summarizing research results.[1]

To illustrate how you would follow the first two steps when researching case law, we present a hypothetical case. The case involves one of your firm's clients, Trent Hoffman, who is suing Better Homes Store for negligence. During the initial client interview, Hoffman explained to you and your supervising attorney that he had gone to the store to purchase a large mirror. As he was leaving the store through the store's side entrance, carrying the bulky mirror, he ran into a large pole just outside the door. He did not see the pole because the mirror blocked his view. Upon hitting the pole, the mirror broke, and a piece of glass entered Hoffman's left eye, causing permanent loss of eyesight in that eye. Hoffman claims that the store was negligent in placing a pole so close to the exit and is suing the store for $3 million in damages.

You have already undertaken a preliminary investigation into the matter and obtained evidence supporting Hoffman's account of the facts. Your supervising attorney now asks you to do some research. Your job now is to research case law to find other cases with similar fact patterns and see how the courts decided the issue in those cases.

Defining the Issue

Before you consult any source, primary or secondary, you must know the legal issue that needs to be researched. Your first task will be to examine closely the facts of Hoffman's case to determine the nature of the legal issue

1. This final step—because it involves legal analysis and writing—is covered in the next chapter.

ETHICAL CONCERN

Efficiency in Research

Attorneys have a duty to charge their clients reasonable fees. As a paralegal, you help your attorney fulfill this duty by working efficiently—to minimize the number of hours you spend on work relating to the client's matter. Legal research can be extremely time consuming, as every paralegal knows. To reduce the time spent in researching a particular legal issue, start out on your quest with a clear idea of your research task. After all, your time is expensive not only for the client (who pays for it) but also for your supervising attorney (who may need your assistance on other cases as well). By knowing as precisely as possible what the goal of your research is, you can reach that goal more quickly and thus better serve the interests of both the client and your supervising attorney.

involved. Based on Hoffman's description of the factual circumstances (verified through your preliminary investigation) and on his allegation that Better Homes Store should not have placed a pole just outside one of the store's entrances, you know that the legal issue relates to the tort of negligence. As a starting point, you should therefore review what you know about negligence theory.

Recall from Chapter 8 that the tort of negligence is defined as the failure to exercise reasonable care, and to succeed in a negligence action, a plaintiff must establish that (1) the defendant had a duty of care to the defendant, (2) the defendant breached that duty, (3) the plaintiff suffered a legally recognizable injury, and (4) the injury was caused by the defendant's breach of the duty of care. A knowledge of these elements will help you determine the issue that needs to be researched in Hoffman's case. There is little doubt that the third requirement has been met—Hoffman's loss of sight in his left eye is a legally recognizable injury for which he can be compensated—*if* he succeeds in proving the other three elements of negligence. The fourth element, causation, is largely dependent on proving the first two elements. In your research, you will therefore want to focus on the first two elements. Specifically, you need to find answers to the following questions:

- Did Better Homes Store owe a duty of care to its customer, Hoffman? You might phrase this question in more general terms: Do business owners owe a duty of care to **business invitees**, customers and others whom they invite onto their premises?
- If so, what is the extent of that duty, and how is it measured? In other words, are business owners always liable, in all circumstances, when customers are injured on their premises? Or must some condition be met before store owners will be liable? For example, must a customer's injury be a *foreseeable* consequence of a condition on the premises, such as the pole outside the store's door, for the store owner to be liable for the injury?
- If the injury must be a foreseeable consequence of a condition, would a court find that Hoffman's injury in this case was a foreseeable consequence of the pole's placement just outside the store's door?

These, then, are the issues that you need to research. Notice how the term *issue* has become plural. You will find that this is a common occurrence in legal research—only rarely will you be researching a single legal issue.

BUSINESS INVITEE
A person, such as a customer or client, who is invited onto business premises by the owner of those premises for business purposes.

Determining Your Research Goals

Once you have defined the issue or issues to be researched, you will be in a better position to determine your research goals. Remember that you are working on behalf of a client, who is paying for your services. Your overall goal is thus to find legal support for Hoffman's claim. To achieve this goal, you will want to do two things: find cases on point and cases that are mandatory authorities. Depending on what you find, you may also need to look for persuasive authorities.

CASE ON POINT
A case involving factual circumstances and issues that are similar to the case at bar (before the court).

Cases on Point. One of your research goals is to find a case (or cases) on point in which the court held for the plaintiff. A **case on point** is a previous

DEVELOPING PARALEGAL SKILLS

Defining the Issues to Be Researched

Bernie Berriman was observed by federal government agents in his parked car talking on his car phone. Later, other cars were seen driving up to Bernie's car and stopping. The drivers received brown bags in exchange for money. Bernie was questioned, and his car was searched. Cocaine was found in the car. He was arrested for transporting and distributing cocaine, and his car and phone were taken by the police. Natalie Martin, a legal assistant with the U.S. attorney's office, has been assigned the task of researching federal statutes and cases to determine if the government had the authority to require Bernie to forfeit his car and car phone.

Before Natalie can begin her research project, she must thoroughly review the facts of the case to determine what specific issues need to be researched. Using a method described in *Sample Pages,* a West Publishing Company publication that she used in school, she breaks the facts down into five categories: parties, places and things, basis of action or issue, defenses, and relief sought. On a sheet of paper, she writes down these categories to use as headings and inserts the appropriate information for this case under each heading.

Natalie begins by identifying the *parties.* What people are involved in the action? Under this heading, she writes "U.S. attorney and drug-enforcement officers" and "Bernie Berriman and drug dealer." She then turns to the next category, *places and things.* Under this heading, she lists "car," "car phone," and "cocaine." Under the third heading, *basis of action or issue,* Natalie writes that the reason for the action is the transportation and distribution of a controlled substance (cocaine).

The fourth category is *defenses.* Natalie thinks for a time and then decides that Berriman, the defendant, will probably argue that his constitutional rights were violated because the agents did not have probable cause to search the vehicle. She writes this down as a defense. The defendant might also argue that the government did not have the authority to require him to forfeit his car and car phone, so Natalie also includes this argument as a defense. The last category is *relief sought,* which is the legal remedy sought in a civil case by the plaintiff. Because this is a criminal case, Natalie crosses out the word *relief* and inserts *penalty* instead, so that the heading reads *penalty sought.* Under this heading, Natalie writes that the government is seeking the forfeiture of the vehicle and the car phone. Now Natalie is ready to go to the library to begin her research.

case involving fact patterns and legal issues that are similar to a case that has not yet been decided by a court. In regard to Hoffman's negligence claim, a case on point would be one in which the plaintiff alleged that he or she was injured while on a store's premises because of a dangerous condition on those premises.

The ideal case on point, of course, would be a case in which all four elements of a case (the parties, the circumstances, the legal issues involved, and the remedies sought by the plaintiff) are very similar. Such a case is called a

CASE ON "ALL FOURS"
A case in which all four elements of a case (the parties, the circumstances, the legal issues involved, and the remedies sought by the plaintiff) are very similar.

case on "all fours."[2] In regard to Hoffman's claim, a case on "all fours" would be a case on point, such as just described, in which the plaintiff-customer did not expect a condition (such as an obstacle in his or her path) to exist and was prevented from seeing the obstacle by some action that a customer would reasonably undertake (such as carrying a large box out of a store). The parties and the circumstances of the case would thus be very similar to those in Hoffman's case. If the plaintiff also sustained a permanent injury, as Hoffman did, and sought damages for negligence, then the case would be, relative to Hoffman's case, a case on "all fours."

MANDATORY AUTHORITY
Any source of law that a court must follow when deciding a case. Mandatory authorities include constitutions, statutes, and regulations that govern the issue at bar and court decisions made by a superior court in the jurisdiction.

Mandatory Authorities. In researching Hoffman's case, another goal is to find cases (on point or on "all fours") that are also mandatory authorities. A **mandatory authority** is any authority that the court *must* rely on in its determination of the issue. A mandatory authority may be a statute, regulation, or constitution that governs the issue, or it may be a previously decided court case that is controlling in your jurisdiction.

For a case to serve as mandatory authority, it must be on point and decided by a superior court. A superior court, in the sense that it is used here, is any court that is on a higher tier in the court system. Recall from Chapter 7 that both the federal and state court systems consist of several levels, or tiers, of courts. *Trial courts,* in which evidence is presented and testimony given, are on the bottom tier (which also includes lower courts handling specialized issues). Decisions from a trial court can be appealed to a higher court, which commonly is an intermediate *court of appeals,* or *appellate court.* Decisions from these intermediate courts of appeals may be appealed to an even higher court, such as a state supreme court or, if a federal question is involved, the United States Supreme Court.

A lower court is bound to follow the decisions set forth by a higher court in the same jurisdiction. An appellate court's decision in a case involving facts and issues similar to a case brought in a trial court in the same jurisdiction would thus be a mandatory authority—the trial court would be bound to follow the appellate court's decision on the issue. A higher court is never required to follow an opinion written by a lower court in the same jurisdiction, however. For example, if a California court of intermediate appeal is deciding a case, it does not have to abide by decisions previously made by California trial courts on the issue, although it might take these decisions into consideration. But the court of intermediate appeal is obligated to abide by a decision on the issue rendered by the California Supreme Court.

State courts have the final say on state law, and federal courts have the final say on federal law. Thus, except in deciding an issue that involves federal law, state courts do not have to follow the decisions of federal courts. In deciding issues that involve federal law, however, state courts must abide by the decisions of the United States Supreme Court.

- **When you are performing research, look for cases on point decided by the highest court in your jurisdiction, because those cases carry the most weight.**

2. Some scholars maintain that this phrase originated from the Latin adage that "nothing similar is identical unless it runs on all four feet."

Persuasive Authorities. A **persuasive authority** is not binding on a court. In other words, the court is not required to follow that authority in making its decision. Examples of persuasive authorities are (1) prior court opinions of other jurisdictions, which, although they are not binding, may be suggestive as to how a particular case should be decided; (2) legal periodicals, such as those published in law reviews, in which the issue at hand is discussed by legal scholars; (3) encyclopedias summarizing legal principles or concepts relating to a particular issue; and (4) legal dictionaries that describe how the law has been applied in the past.

PERSUASIVE AUTHORITY
Any legal authority, or source of law, that a court may look to for guidance but on which it need not rely in making its decision. Persuasive authorities include cases from other jurisdictions and secondary sources of law, such as scholarly treatises.

Often, a court refers to persuasive authorities when deciding a *case of first impression*, which, as discussed in Chapter 7, is a case involving an issue that has never been addressed by that court before. For example, if in your research of Hoffman's claim you find that no similar cases have ever reached a higher court in your jurisdiction, you would look for similar cases decided by courts in other jurisdictions. If courts in other jurisdictions have faced a similar issue, the court may be guided by those other courts' decisions when deciding Hoffman's case. Your supervising attorney will want to know about these persuasive authorities so that he can present them to the court for consideration.

SECONDARY SOURCES OF CASE LAW

Finding cases that are both on point and mandatory legal authorities is not always easy. The body of American case law consists of about five million decisions. Each year, more than forty thousand new cases are added to this collection. Because the decisions of the courts are published in chronological order, finding relevant precedents would be a Herculean task if it were not for secondary sources of law that classify decisions according to subject. A logical place to begin your research is thus with secondary sources of case law. In researching Hoffman's claim, you might look first at a legal encyclopedia to learn more about the topic of negligence and the duty of care of business owners to business invitees. Generally, to help you find topics that shed light on your subject, you should make a list of all relevant legal terms and phrases, as well as their synonyms, before beginning the research process.

Legal Encyclopedias

Legal encyclopedias provide detailed summaries of legal rules and concepts. Legal encyclopedias also arrange topics alphabetically and refer readers to leading cases in that area of law.

Encyclopedias are helpful resources for the student who is new to legal research or for an experienced legal professional who is researching an unfamiliar area of law. By referring to an encyclopedia, you can obtain background information on the topic that will help you direct your research more effectively. Two popular legal encyclopedias are *American Jurisprudence*, Second Edition, and *Corpus Juris Secundum*. Another popular legal resource is *Words and Phrases*. We discuss each of these works here. (Note that there are also state-specific encyclopedias—that is, encyclopedias that refer readers to state cases or statutes relating to a specific topic. You can check with

EXHIBIT 17.1
American Jurisprudence 2d

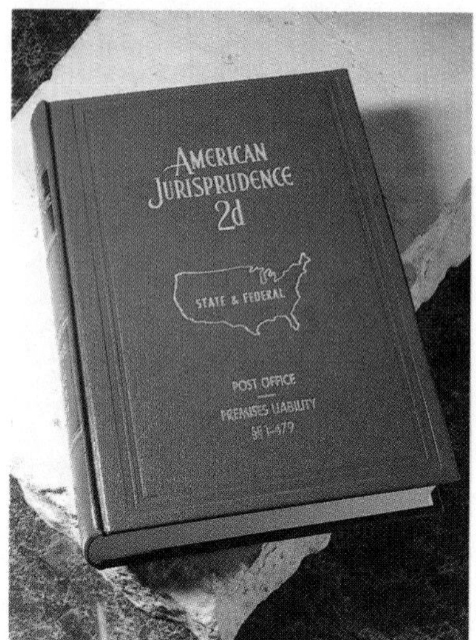

the reference librarian in your local law library to find a state-specific encyclopedia, if your state has one.)

***American Jurisprudence,* Second Edition.** *American Jurisprudence,* Second Edition, is commonly referred to as *American Jurisprudence 2d* or, more briefly, as *Am. Jur. 2d.* (A photograph of one of the volumes of this encyclopedia is shown in Exhibit 17.1.) This encyclopedia, which is published by the Lawyers Cooperative Publishing Company, offers a detailed discussion of virtually every area of American law. The encyclopedia covers more than 440 topics in 58 volumes. Each topic is further divided into various subtopics containing narrative descriptions of the general rules of law that have emerged from generations of court decisions. If there are conflicting decisions on an issue or topic, the encyclopedia indicates this and offers explanations for the differing opinions. The encyclopedia also provides various cross-references to specific court cases, annotations in *American Law Reports* (to be discussed shortly), law reviews, and other relevant sections of *American Jurisprudence.* The volumes are kept current through supplements called **pocket parts** (because they slip into a pocket in the back of the volume), which contain additions to the various topics and subtopics.

As with any encyclopedia, topics in *American Jurisprudence 2d* are presented alphabetically. Each general topic is organized to allow a researcher to find quickly the specific area of interest. Each volume of the encyclopedia also contains an index, located at the back of the volume. A separate index is also provided for the entire encyclopedia once a series, or edition, is completed. The indexes can be very helpful to the researcher. For example, in researching the issue in Hoffman's lawsuit against Better Homes Store for negligence, you could look in the index for such terms as *premises liability, business invitees, duty of care, landowners,* or some other term or phrase. Exhibit 17.2 shows the first page of the discussion of premises liability. Although not shown in the exhibit, an outline of the major topics of the section follows, complete with descriptive subsections. The outline allows the researcher to locate easily any relevant areas within the general subject matter.

POCKET PART
A separate pamphlet containing recent cases or changes in the law that is used to update hornbooks, legal encyclopedias, and other legal authorities. It is called a "pocket part" because it slips into a sleeve, or pocket, in the back binder of the volume.

Corpus Juris Secundum. Another enclopedia helpful to the legal researcher is *Corpus Juris Secundum,* or *C.J.S.,* which is published by West Publishing Company. This encyclopedia, like *American Jurisprudence 2d,* provides detailed information on almost every area of the law. *C.J.S.* consists of 101 volumes and covers 433 topics, each of which is further divided into subtopics. One of the volumes of this set is depicted in Exhibit 17.3 on page 652.

The approaches of *C.J.S.* and *American Jurisprudence 2d* are very similar. *C.J.S.* offers an explanation of contradictory court decisions on an issue, if there are any, and provides the names of these cases and of the published sources in which they can be found. *C.J.S.* also contains alphabetical entries as well as indexes for locating relevant legal information. The indexes are located at the end of each volume and in a multivolume index at the end of a set. To keep its information up to date, *C.J.S.* also provides supplements (pocket parts) containing current materials. In regard to Hoffman's claim, if you looked up the word *business* in the *C.J.S.,* you would find a discussion

EXHIBIT 17.2
Excerpt from *American Jurisprudence 2d*

PREMISES LIABILITY

by

Irwin J. Schiffres, J.D. and Sheila A. Skojec, J.D.

Scope of topic: This article discusses the principles and rules of law applicable to and governing the liability of owners or occupants of real property for negligence causing injury to persons or property by reason of defects therein or hazards created by the activities of such owners or occupants or their agents and employees. Treated in detail are the classification of persons injured as invitees, licensees, or trespassers, and the duty owed them, as well as the rules applicable in those jurisdictions where such status distinctions are no longer determinative of the duty owed the entrant; the effect of "recreational use" statutes on the duty owed persons using the property for such purposes; the greater measure of duty owed by the owner to children as compared to adult licensees and trespassers, including the attractive nuisance doctrine; and the specific duties and liabilities of owners and occupants of premises used for business or residential purposes. Also considered is the effect of the injured person's negligence on the plaintiff's right to recover under principles of contributory or comparative negligence.

Federal aspects: One injured on premises owned or operated by the United States may seek to recover under general principles of premises liability discussed in this article. Insofar as recovery is sought under the Federal Torts Claims Act, see 35 Am Jur 2d, FEDERAL TORTS CLAIMS ACT § 73.

Treated elsewhere:

Mutual obligations and liabilities of adjoining landowners with respect to injuries arising from their acts or omissions, see 1 Am Jur 2d, ADJOINING LANDOWNERS AND PROPERTIES §§ 10, 11, 28 et seq., 37 et seq.

Liability for the acts or omissions of the owners or occupants of premises abutting on a street or highway which cause injury to those using the way, see 39 Am Jur 2d, HIGHWAYS, STREETS, AND BRIDGES §§ 517 et seq.

Liability for violation of building regulations, see 13 Am Jur 2d, BUILDINGS §§ 32 et seq.

Liability of employer for injuries caused employees on the employer's premises, see 53 Am Jur 2d, MASTER AND SERVANT §§ 139 et seq.

Liability for injuries caused by defective products on the premises, see 63 Am Jur 2d, PRODUCTS LIABILITY

Respective rights and liabilities of a landlord and tenant where one is responsible for an injury suffered by the other, or by a third person, on leased premises or on premises provided for the common use of tenants, see 49 Am Jur 2d, LANDLORD AND TENANT §§ 761 et seq.

Liability of a receiver placed in charge of property for an injury sustained thereby or thereon by someone other than the persons directly interested in the estate, see 66 Am Jur 2d, RECEIVERS § 364

Duties and liabilities of occupiers of premises used for various particular types of businesses or activities, see 4 Am Jur 2d, AMUSEMENTS AND EXHIBITIONS §§ 51 et seq.; 14 Am Jur 2d, CARRIERS §§ 964 et seq.; 38 Am Jur 2d, GARAGES, AND FILLING AND PARKING STATIONS §§ 81 et seq.; 40 Am Jur 2d, HOSPITALS AND ASYLUMS § 31; 40 Am Jur 2d, HOTELS, MOTELS, AND RESTAURANTS §§ 81 et seq.; 50 Am Jur 2d, LAUNDRIES, DYERS, AND DRY CLEANERS §§ 21, 22; 54 Am Jur 2d, MOBILE HOMES, TRAILER PARKS, AND TOURIST CAMPS § 17; 57 Am Jur 2d, MUNICIPAL, COUNTY, SCHOOL, AND STATE TORT LIABILITY; AND 59 AM JUR 2D, PARKS, SQUARES, AND PLAYGROUNDS §§ 43 et seq.

Duties and liabilities with respect to injuries caused by particular agencies, such as

317

of that topic, including a reference to business invitees (as shown on the page from the *C.J.S.* presented in Exhibit 17.4 on page 653).

Words and Phrases. *Words and Phrases* is a forty-six-volume encyclopedia of definitions and interpretations of legal terms and phrases published by West Publishing Company. It is a useful tool for learning how the courts

EXHIBIT 17.3
Corpus Juris Secundum

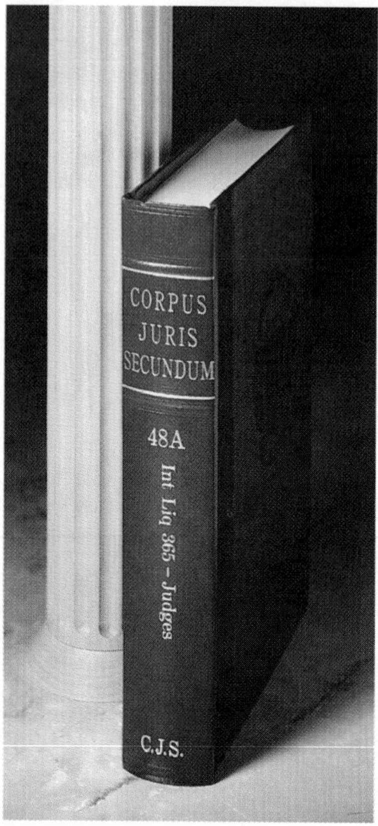

have interpreted a particular term or phrase. The words and phrases covered are arranged in alphabetical order. Each is followed by abstracts (brief summary statements) from federal or state court decisions in which the word or phrase has been interpreted or defined. The abstract also indicates the names of the cases and the reporters in which they can be located. **Reporters** are publications containing the actual texts of court cases, as will be discussed later in this section. When researching Hoffman's claim, you could find out how various courts have defined *negligence* by looking up that term in *Words and Phrases.* Part of the entry for this term is shown in Exhibit 17.5 on page 654. *Words and Phrases* is updated by annual supplementary pocket parts.

REPORTER
A publication in which court cases are published, or reported.

DIGEST
A compilation in which brief summaries of court cases are arranged by subject and subdivided by jurisdiction and courts.

ANNOTATION
A brief comment, an explanation of a legal point, or a case summary found in a case digest or other legal source.

KEY NUMBER
A number (accompanied by the symbol of a key) corresponding to a specific topic within the West Publishing Company's key-number system to facilitate legal research of case law.

HEADNOTE
A note near the beginning of a reported case summarizing the court's ruling on an issue.

Case Digests

In researching the issue in Hoffman's case against Better Homes Store, you might want to check a case digest as well as a legal encyclopedia for references to relevant case law. **Digests**, which are produced by various publishers, are helpful research tools because they provide indexes to case law—from the earliest recorded cases through the most current opinions. Case digests arrange topics alphabetically and provide information to help you locate referenced cases, but they do not offer the detail found in legal encyclopedias. Collected under each topic heading in a case digest are annotations. **Annotations** are comments, explanatory notes, or case summaries. In case digests, annotations consist of very short statements of relevant points of law in reported cases.

The digests published by West Publishing Company offer the most comprehensive system for locating cases by subject matter. West publishes digests of both federal court opinions and state court opinions, as well as regional digests, and digests that correspond with its reporters covering specialized areas, such as bankruptcy.

The West Key-number System. In the late nineteenth century, West Publishing Company developed its key-number system of classification. This system, which has simplified the task of researching case law, divides all areas of American law into specific categories, or topics, arranged in alphabetical order. The topics are further divided into many specific subtopics, each designated by a **key number**, which is accompanied by the West key symbol: 🔑 Exhibit 17.6 on page 655 shows some of the key numbers used for subtopics under the topic of negligence.

West editors provide abstracts, or **headnotes**, for every area of the law discussed within each decision appearing in the West reporters. Every headnote is described by its topic name, which is followed by a key number indicating the specific subject discussed. This system of arranging legal and factual issues by subject matter allows West to gather all headnotes under the same topic and key number into one published work—the digest. If you consulted a West digest when researching Hoffman's case, the digest would indicate the names of cases relating to the topic as well as the reporters in which the texts of those cases can be found.

EXHIBIT 17.4
Excerpt from *Corpus Juris Secundum*

BUSINESS 12A C. J. S.

Business time. The term "business time" has been held to mean the ability to engage in a sustained effort of a character sufficiently substantial to negative the idea that there was not a total loss of power reasonably to continue a business or profession.[18]

Business use. The phrase "business use" may have different meanings in different statutes, ordinances, and other writings.[19] The generally accepted meaning of the term necessarily implies employment of one or more persons for the purpose of earning a livelihood, activities of persons to improve their economic conditions and desires, and generally relates to commercial and industrial engagements.[20]

Business visitor. "Business visitors" are deemed to fall into two classes, first, those who enter upon the premises of another for a purpose connected with the business which the possessor conducts thereon, and, second, those who come upon the premises for a purpose connected with their own business which is connected with any purpose, business or otherwise, for which the possessor uses the premises.[21]

The phrase "business visitor" has been held equivalent to "invitee,"[22] and has been compared or contrasted with "licensee"[23] and "gratuitous licensee."[24]

Other phrases employing the word "business," as an adjective, are set out in the note.[25]

Iowa.—Crane Co. v. City Council of Des Moines, 225 N.W. 344, 345, 208 Iowa 164.

N.J.—Duke Power Co. v. Hillsborough Tp., Somerset County, 26 A.2d 713, 729, 20 N.J.Misc. 240.

N.C.—Mecklenburg County v. Sterchi Bros. Stores, 185 S.E. 454, 457, 459, 210 N.C. 79.

Okl.—State v. Atlantic Oil Producing Co., 49 P.2d 534, 538, 174 Okl. 61—Grieves v. State ex rel. County Attorney, 35 P.2d 454, 456, 168 Okl. 642.

Or.—Endicott, Johnson & Co. v. Multnomah County, 190 P. 1109, 1111, 96 Or. 679.

18. Ark.—Pacific Mut. Life Ins. Co. v. Riffel, 149 S.W.2d 57, 59, 202 Ark. 94.

19. Ga.—Snow v. Johnston, 28 S.E.2d 270, 277, 197 Ga. 146.

Test

Definite test of business use would usually be whether or not profit was being made, directly or indirectly, by owner, on particular occasion.

N.Y.—Juskiewicz v. New Jersey Fidelity & Plate Glass Ins. Co., 206 N.Y.S. 566, 568, 210 App.Div. 675.

20. Ga.—Snow v. Johnston, 28 S.E.2d 270, 277, 197 Ga. 146.

21. Kan.—Bessette v. Ernsting, 127 P.2d 438, 440, 155 Kan. 540—Kurre v. Graham Ship by Truck Co., 15 P.2d 463, 465, 136 Kan. 356.

See generally C.J.S. Negligence §§ 63(41)–63(56).

What constitutes

Cal.—Crane v. Smith, 144 P.2d 356, 361, 362, 23 Cal.2d 288.

Held "business visitors"

Cal.—Turnipseed v. Hoffman, 144 P.2d 797, 798, 23 Cal.2d 532—Hill v. Eaton & Smith, 149 P.2d 762, 763, 65 Cal.App.2d 11.

Mass.—Fortier v. Hibernian Bldg. Ass'n of Boston Highlands, 53 N.E.2d 110, 113, 315 Mass. 446.

N.Y.—Haefeli v. Woodrich Engineering Co., 175 N.E. 123, 125, 255 N.Y. 442.

Vt.—Rheaume v. Goodro, 34 A.2d 315, 316, 113 Vt. 370.

22. U.S.—Robey v. Keller, C.C.A.Va., 114 F.2d 790, 794—McCann v. Anchor Line, C.C.A.N.Y., 79 F.2d 338, 339.

Conn.—Knapp v. Connecticut Theatrical Corporation, 190 A. 291, 292, 122 Conn. 413.

Kan.—Kurre v. Graham Ship by Truck Co., 15 P.2d 463, 465, 136 Kan. 356.

Mo.—Stevenson v. Kansas City Southern Ry. Co., 159 S.W.2d 260, 263, 348 Mo. 1216.

Pa.—Hartman v. Miller, Super., 17 A.2d 652, 653, 143 Pa.Super. 143.

R.I.—Royer v. Najarian, 198 A. 562, 564, 60 R.I. 368.

23. U.S.—McCann v. Anchor Line, C.C.A.N.Y., 79 F.2d 338, 339.

Cal.—Oettinger v. Stewart, 148 P.2d 19, 20, 21, 24 Cal.2d 133, 156 A.L.R. 1221.

24. Cal.—Oettinger v. Stewart, 148 P.2d 19, 20, 21, 24 Cal.2d 133, 156 A.L.R. 1221.

N.H.—Sandwell v. Elliott Hospital, 24 A.2d 273, 274, 92 N.H. 41.

N.Y.—Haefeli v. Woodrich Engineering Co., 175 N.E. 123, 125, 255 N.Y. 442.

Petluck v. McGolrick Realty Co., 268 N.Y.S. 782, 786, 240 App.Div. 61.

25. Particular terms

(1) "Business compulsion" as analogous to "duress."

Cal.—Sistrom v. Anderson, 124 P.2d 372, 376, 51 C.A.2d 213.

(2) "Business assets" distinguished from "personal asset."

Cal.—In re Friedrichs' Estate, 290 P. 54, 55, 107 Cal.App. 142.

(3) "Business compulsion" contrasted with "duress."

Wash.—Ramp Buildings Corporation v. Northwest Bldg. Co., 4 P.2d 507, 509, 164 Wash. 603, 79 A.L.R. 651.

(4) "Business district" defined in statute and contrasted with "residential district."

N.C.—Mitchell v. Melts, 18 S.E.2d 406, 410, 220 N.C. 793.

(5) "Business enterprise" requires investment of capital, labor, and management.

U.S.—Helvering v. Jewel Mining Co., C.C.A.8, 126 F.2d 1011, 1015.

(6) One's home is not a "business enterprise."

Minn.—State v. Cooper, 285 N.W. 903, 905, 205 Minn. 333, 122 A.L.R. 727.

(7) Renting rooms in dwelling house is not engaging in a "business enterprise."

Tex.—Austin v. Richardson, Com.App., 288 S.W. 180, 181.

(8) "Business establishment" held to be a statutory phrase restricted to one resembling a mill, workshop, or other manufacturing establishment.

N.Y.—O'Connor v. Webber, 147 N.Y.S. 1053, 163 App.Div. 175, 178.

(9) "Business loss (or losses)" contrasted with "damage to property."

490

West's Federal Digests. West's federal digests cover cases from the United States Supreme Court, the U.S. courts of appeals, the U.S. district courts, and various specialized federal courts, such as bankruptcy courts. Cases from all of these courts are organized according to the West key-number system. Headnotes from the United States Supreme Court are listed first, followed by appellate court and district court cases.

There are five separate federal digests, providing coverage from 1754 to the present. The *Federal Digest* covers the years 1754 through 1939. The

EXHIBIT 17.5
Excerpt from *Words and Phrases*

NEGLIGENCE

Estoppel by Negligence
Fault
General Negligence
Gross Negligence
Hazardous Negligence
Heedlessness
High Degree of Negligence
Homicide by Negligence
Imputed Contributory Negligence
Imputed Negligence
Incurred Without Fault or Negligence
Independent Act of Negligence
Independent Negligence
Injury Resulting from Negligence
Insulated Negligence
Intentional Negligence
Joint Negligence
Legal Negligence
Liability Created by Law
Marine Cause
Mistake, Error or Negligence
Mutual Contributory Negligence
Negligent
Notice of Negligence
Nuisance
Nuisance Dependent Upon Negligence
Ordinary Care
Ordinary Negligence
Otherwise
Persistent Negligence
Preponderance
Presumption of Negligence
Prima Facie Case of Negligence
Prima Facie Negligence
Prior Negligence
Proof of Negligence
Proximate Contributory Negligence
Reckless; Recklessly; Recklessness
Separate Negligence
Simple Negligence
Situation Created by Actor's Negligence
Slight Negligence
Specific Negligence
Subsequent Negligence
Supervening Negligence
Trespass
Wanton Negligence
Wantonness
Willful and Intentional Negligence
Willful Negligence
Willfulness
Without Negligence

In general

"Negligence", in absence of statute, is defined as the doing of that thing which a reasonably prudent person would not have

In general—Cont'd

done, or the failure to do that thing which a reasonably prudent person would have done, in like or similar circumstances. Biddle v. Mazzocco, Or., 284 P.2d 364, 368.

"Negligence" is a departure from the normal or what should be the normal, and is a failure to conform to standard of what a reasonably prudent man would ordinarily have done under the circumstances, or is doing what such man would not have done under the circumstances. Moran v. Pittsburgh-Des Moines Steel Co., D.C.Pa., 86 F. Supp. 255, 266.

"Negligence" being failure to do that which ordinarily prudent man would do or doing of that which such a man would not do under same circumstances, an ordinary custom, while relevant and admissible in evidence of negligence, is not conclusive thereof, especially where it is clearly a careless or dangerous custom. Tite v. Omaha Coliseum Corp., 12 N.W.2d 90, 94, 144 Neb. 22, 149 A.L.R. 1164.

Whether or not an act or omission is "negligence" seems to be determined by what under like circumstances would men of ordinary prudence have done. Cleveland, C., C. & St. L. R. Co. v. Ivins, Ohio, 12 O.C.D. 570.

"Negligence" means simply the want of ordinary care under the circumstances surrounding that particular case and the transaction in question, and "negligently" simply means doing an act in such a manner that it lacks the care which men of ordinary prudence and foresight use in their everyday affairs of life under the same or similar circumstances. Smillie v. Cleveland Ry., Ohio, 31 O.C.D. 323, 325, 20 Cir.Ct.R.,N.S., 302.

"Negligence" is the failure to do what a reasonable and prudent man would ordinarily have done under circumstances of situation or doing what such a person, under existing circumstances, would not have done. Judt v. Reinhardt Transfer Co., 17 Ohio Supp. 105, 107, 32 O.O. 161.

By "negligence" is meant negligence of such character that in the discretion of the court, the defendant should have inflicted upon him the punative penalties of having his license suspended and that the public required such protection. Com. v. Galley, 17 Som. 54.

"Negligence" is a failure to use ordinary care, that is, such care as persons of ordinary prudence are accustomed to exercise

524

EXHIBIT 17.6
Subtopics and Key Numbers in a West Digest

NEGLIGENCE.

Scope-Note.

INCLUDES failure to use due care, either in respect of acts or of omissions, in performance or observance of a duty not founded on contract, which failure is the proximate cause of unintended injury to the person to whom such duty is owing; nature and extent of liability for such injuries in general; nature and effect of negligence or other fault on the part of the person injured contributing to his injury; comparison of negligence of the parties; imputation to the person injured of others' negligence; civil remedies for such injuries; and criminal responsibility for such negligence in general, and prosecution and punishment thereof as a public offense.

Matters not in this topic, treated elsewhere, see Descriptive-Word Index.

Analysis.

I. ACTS OR OMISSIONS CONSTITUTING NEGLIGENCE, 🔑1–55.
- A. PERSONAL CONDUCT IN GENERAL, 🔑1–15.
- B. DANGEROUS SUBSTANCES, MACHINERY, AND OTHER INSTRUMENTALITIES, 🔑16–27.
- C. CONDITION AND USE OF LAND, BUILDINGS, AND OTHER STRUCTURES, 🔑28–55.

II. PROXIMATE CAUSE OF INJURY, 🔑56–64.

III. CONTRIBUTORY NEGLIGENCE, 🔑65–101.
- A. PERSONS INJURED IN GENERAL, 🔑65–83.
- B. CHILDREN AND OTHERS UNDER DISABILITY, 🔑84–88.
- C. IMPUTED NEGLIGENCE, 🔑89–96.
- D. COMPARATIVE NEGLIGENCE, 🔑97–101.

IV. ACTIONS, 🔑102–143.
- A. RIGHT OF ACTION, PARTIES, PRELIMINARY PROCEEDINGS, AND PLEADING, 🔑102–119.
- B. EVIDENCE, 🔑120–135.
- C. TRIAL, JUDGMENT, AND REVIEW, 🔑136–143.

V. CRIMINAL RESPONSIBILITY, 🔑144.

I. ACTS OR OMISSIONS CONSTITUTING NEGLIGENCE.

A. Personal Conduct in General.

🔑1. Nature and elements of negligence in general.
2. Duty to use care.
3. Degrees of care in general.
4. Ordinary or reasonable care.
5. Customary methods and acts.
6. Requirements of statutes or ordinances.
7. Care as to children.
8. Care as to infirm or helpless persons.

48 F.D.—1

Modern Federal Digest begins coverage in 1939 and ends with the year 1961. The *Federal Practice Digest 2d* covers the time period from 1961 to 1975, and the *Federal Practice Digest 3d* covers 1975 through 1991. The *Federal Practice Digest 4th,* the current edition, begins with 1991. Exhibit 17.7 on

PARALEGAL PROFILE

Medical-malpractice Paralegal

DONNA SCHOEBEL has a degree in nursing (R.N.) as well as a master's degree in business. After working as a nurse for several years, she was looking for a career change and enrolled in the paralegal program at the University of Cincinnati. Schoebel completed an internship at the Cincinnati law firm of Kohnen & Patton and accepted a position with the firm. She specializes in the area of medical malpractice and focuses mostly on defense litigation. Schoebel feels that her nursing background is a significant asset in her work. Schoebel enjoys her work and considers paralegal practice to be an exciting field with many changes on the horizon. She is active in the Cincinnati Paralegal Association and teaches courses in the paralegal program at the University of Cincinnati.

What do you like best about your work?

"I find that my work is very appealing. It is a new, fresh, and exciting field for me, and my job will stay this way because I will always be working on different cases. I most enjoy wading through all of the records and finding things that will help or damage our case. I enjoy the challenge of fitting these puzzle pieces together. I also enjoy working closely with the attorney from the beginning to the end of the case. Another reason I like my job is that it allows me to work directly with nurses and physicians."

"BASICALLY, COMPUTER LITERACY IS CRITICAL."

What is the greatest challenge that you face in your area of work?

"My greatest challenge is to meet all of the deadlines when I am working on many projects simultaneously. I find it a challenge to time things and determine what is moving along and what isn't. I am dealing with many cases at once, and they are all at different stages. Legal work is much different from nursing. In nursing, everything happens in minutes or seconds, whereas litigation extends over weeks and months. As a litigation paralegal, I have to have excellent organizational skills and an efficient planning and tracking system."

What advice do you have for would-be paralegals in your area of work?

"My advice to paralegal students is to get a good handle on computerized legal research while they're in school. I can't emphasize enough how important this background is. In my office, we use computerized legal research systems and databases extensively, particularly Medline. Basically, computer literacy is critical."

What are some tips for success as a paralegal in your area of work?

"My tips for success as a medical-malpractice paralegal doing defense work (basically, litigation) include being extremely familiar with the court system and the ins and outs of due dates and procedures. I also feel that it is very important to have good personal and communication skills. These skills help to build good working relationships with the attorneys and are especially important in litigation because so much depends on working as a team. Writing skills are also very important to being a successful medical-malpractice paralegal."

the next page shows excerpts from West's *Federal Practice Digest 4th* on the topic of negligence. As shown in the exhibit, the section begins with a general topical outline (shown in the lower, right-hand portion of the exhibit). You can scan through the outline to find the specific subtopic covering the issue you are researching. Then, you can turn to the pages covering that subtopic (the beginning page of one of the subtopics is shown in the upper left-hand side of the exhibit) to find references to relevant case law.

EXHIBIT 17.7
West's *Federal Practice Digest 4th* on Negligence

⚷26 NEGLIGENCE 77 F P D 4th—530

For later cases see same Topic and Key Number in Pocket Part

imposition of strict liability under Louisiana law; contractor had no scheduling authority and performed repairs only in accordance with specific directions from premises owner. LSA-C.C. art. 2317.

In re Shell Oil Refinery, 765 F.Supp. 324.

⚷27.

See PRODUCTS LIABILITY.

(C) CONDITION AND USE OF LAND, BUILDINGS, AND OTHER STRUCTURES.

⚷28. Care required in general.

Library references

C.J.S. Negligence §§ 63(1), 63(57) et seq., 74.

C.A.7 (Ind.) 1990. Person may not use his land in such way as unreasonably to injure interests of persons not on his land—including owners of adjacent lands, as well as other landowners and users of public ways.

Justice v. CSX Transp., Inc., 908 F.2d 119, rehearing denied.

C.A.1 (Mass.) 1990. Under traditional Massachusetts landowner liability principles, there must be a defect, apart from natural accumulation of water, ice, or snow, in order to hold landowner liable in slip-and-fall action for negligence.

Athas v. U.S., 904 F.2d 79.

C.A.9 (Mont.) 1986. Under Montana law, duty of care owed by a landowner does not depend on whether the injured party was a trespasser, licensee or invitee.

Berge v. Boyne USA, Inc., 779 F.2d 1445.

D.D.C. 1990. In slip and fall case, burden was on plaintiff to prove that defendant was negligent either in creating a dangerous condition or in allowing one to continue without correction and that such negligence was proximate cause of the injuries, and to make out prima facie case of liability predicated on existence of dangerous condition, it was necessary to show that defendant had actual notice of dangerous condition or that condition existed for such length of time that, in the exercise of reasonable care, its existence should have become known and corrected.

Thomas v. Grand Hyatt Hotel, 749 F.Supp. 313.

N.D.Ill. 1990. Liability of owners and occupiers of land is evaluated under principles of ordinary negligence, under Illinois law. Ill. S.H.A. ch. 80, ¶ 302.

O'Clair v. Dumelle, 735 F.Supp. 1344, affirmed 919 F.2d 143.

D.Kan. 1991. Under Kansas law, person is entitled to use their own premises for any lawful purpose; however, landowner's freedom to use his premises is not absolute, but is subject to important qualification that such use be ordinary and usual, conforming to standard of care expected of reasonably prudent person, and failure to conform to this standard may constitute negligence.

Reese Exploration, Inc. v. Williams Natural Gas Co., 768 F.Supp. 1416.

D.Mass. 1990. Under Massachusetts law, landowner is not under legal duty to remove natural accumulations of ice or snow.

Swann v. Flatley, 749 F.Supp. 338.

For cited U.S.C.A. sections and legislative h

NEGLIGENCE

SUBJECTS INCLUDED

Failure to use due care, either in respect of acts or of omissions, in performance or observance of a duty not founded on contract, which failure is the proximate cause of unintended injury to the person to whom such duty is owing

Nature and extent of liability for such injuries in general

Nature and effect of negligence or other fault on the part of the person injured contributing to his injury

Comparison of negligence of the parties

Imputation to the person injured of others' negligence

Civil remedies for such injuries

Criminal responsibility for such negligence in general, and prosecution and punishment thereof as a public offense

SUBJECTS EXCLUDED AND COVERED BY OTHER TOPICS

Death, actions for damages for, see DEATH

Manslaughter by negligence, see AUTOMOBILES, HOMICIDE

Particular kinds of property, negligence in care and use of, see MINES AND MINERALS, WATERS AND WATER COURSES, ANIMALS, SHIPPING, COLLISION, and other specific topics

Particular kinds of works, public improvements, etc., negligence in construction and use of, see RAILROADS, BRIDGES, HIGHWAYS, MUNICIPAL CORPORATIONS, and other specific topics

Particular personal relations, occupations, employments, contracts, etc., negligence in respect of duties incident to, see ATTORNEY AND CLIENT, EMPLOYERS' LIABILITY, PHYSICIANS AND SURGEONS, CARRIERS, LANDLORD AND TENANT, BAILMENT and other specific topics

For detailed references to other topics, see Descriptive-Word Index

Analysis

I. ACTS OR OMISSIONS CONSTITUTING NEGLIGENCE, ⚷1–55.

(A) PERSONAL CONDUCT IN GENERAL, ⚷1–15.

(B) DANGEROUS SUBSTANCES, MACHINERY, AND OTHER INSTRUMENTALITIES, ⚷16–27.

(C) CONDITION AND USE OF LAND, BUILDINGS, AND OTHER STRUCTURES, ⚷28–55.

Each of these federal digests provides headnotes of cases appearing in the *Supreme Court Reporter* (which reports cases decided by the United States Supreme Court), the *Federal Reporter* (which reports cases from the federal courts of appeals), the *Federal Supplement* (which reports cases from the federal district courts), and the *Federal Rules Decisions* (which covers federal rules of procedure). As mentioned, West also publishes specialized digests corresponding to its special federal reporters. Examples of these digests are *West's Bankruptcy Digest, Military Justice Digest, Education Law Digest, Reporting Services Digest,* and *United States Claims Digest*. West also provides exclusive digest coverage of the decisions of the United States Supreme Court in the *United States Supreme Court Digest*.

West's State and Regional Digests. West's digest system also provides state digests for the cases of all states except Utah, Nevada, and Delaware. State digests include references to decisions issued by federal courts located within the state. Some state court decisions are also represented in West's regional digests. West currently publishes four regional digests, corresponding to four of its seven regional reporters (the names and coverage of West's regional reporters will be discussed later in this chapter).

West's Comprehensive *American Digest System*. West's *American Digest System* is a comprehensive set of volumes incorporating case abstracts from West's state, federal, and regional digests. Most of the cases catalogued are from appellate courts, although some trial court decisions are included. The *American Digest System* is particularly helpful when you are looking for persuasive authorities. To find persuasive authorities, you will want to consider cases from all jurisdictions. The *American Digest System* will help you locate them efficiently.

EXHIBIT 17.8
West's *General Digest*, Eighth Series

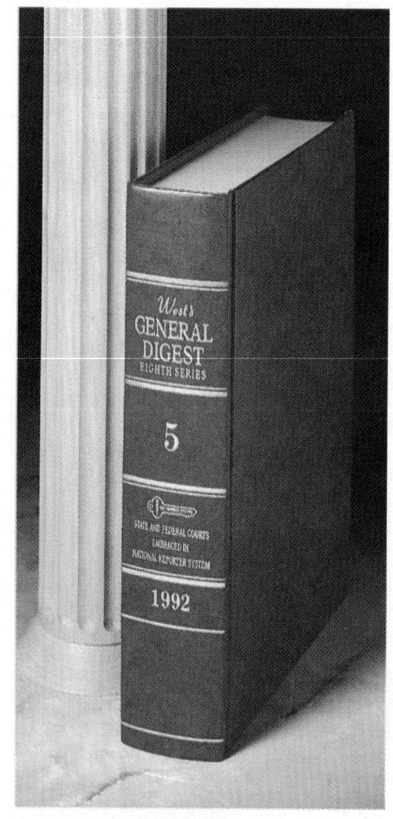

Sequential Sets. The *American Digest System* is divided into three different sets, each covering a specific period of time. The *American Digest Century Edition* provides coverage of all cases from 1658 through 1896. The *Decennial Digest* includes all cases issued from 1896 to the present. Each volume in the set covers a ten-year period; for example, the *Eighth Decennial Digest* covers cases reported between 1966 and 1976. West has slightly changed the decennial digest publication schedule because of the increased number of reported cases. Today, "decennial" digests are issued every five years, rather than every ten years. The most recently published cases can be found in West's *General Digest,* which is an annual publication. One of these digests is shown in Exhibit 17.8.

Advantages of the American Digest System. The advantage of the *American Digest System* is its vast coverage of cases from different courts. The digests cover almost every topic, and most key numbers are represented, even though they may relate to only a few cases. Some of the more common areas of the law contain hundreds of different case abstracts, offering the researcher a wide variety of resources to consider. Under each key number, cases are listed by type of court. Federal court cases appear first, starting with a listing of decisions issued by the United States Supreme Court. This listing is followed by listings of appellate court decisions and, finally, district court cases. State court cases follow the federal court listings and are arranged in alphabetical order by state.

Each of West's decennial digests also offers the researcher many helpful finding tools. The **table of cases** lists all of the cases included in the digest, in alphabetical order. This listing usually appears in the last volume of the set. The decennial digests also have topical outlines that list various subtopics. If you know the specific topic on which you want to focus, all you need to do is locate the digest containing that topic and review the outline for specific subtopics. Exhibit 17.9 shows outlines for the topic and subtopics relating to negligence, as well as key-numbered annotations. Each volume of the digest system lists the various topics that it contains.

TABLE OF CASES
An alphabetical list of the cases that have been cited or reproduced in a legal text, case digest, or other legal source.

Other Digests. Although West is the only publisher of comprehensive digests, other publishers offer digests for specific jurisdictions and specialized interest areas. The *Lawyers' Edition of the Digest of the Supreme Court Reports* corresponds to decisions listed in the *Lawyers' Edition of the*

EXHIBIT 17.9
Outlines for Topics and Subtopics in a West Decennial Digest

29 10th D Pt 1—1117

NEGLIGENCE

SUBJECTS INCLUDED

Failure to use due care, either in respect of acts or of omissions, in performance or observance of a duty not founded on contract, which failure is the proximate cause of unintended injury to the person to whom such duty is owing
Nature and extent of liability for such injuries in general
Nature and effect of negligence or other fault on the part of the person injured contributing to his injury
Comparison of negligence of the parties
Imputation to the person injured of others' negligence
Civil remedies for such injuries
Criminal responsibility for such negligence in general, and prosecution and punishment thereof as a public offense

SUBJECTS EXCLUDED AND COVERED BY OTHER TOPICS

Death, actions for damages for, see DEATH
Manslaughter by negligence, see AUTOMOBILES, HOMICIDE
Particular kinds of property, negligence in care and use of, see MINES AND MINERALS, WATERS AND WATER COURSES, ANIMALS, SHIPPING, COLLISION, and other specific topics
Particular kinds of works, public improvements, etc., negligence in construction and use of, see RAILROADS, BRIDGES, HIGHWAYS, MUNICIPAL CORPORATIONS, and other specific topics
Particular personal relations, occupations, employments, contracts, etc., negligence in respect of duties incident to, see ATTORNEY AND CLIENT, EMPLOYERS' LIABILITY, PHYSICIANS AND SURGEONS, CARRIERS, LANDLORD AND TENANT, BAILMENT and other specific topics

For detailed references to other topics, see Descriptive-Word Index

Analysis

I. ACTS OR OMISSIONS CONSTITUTING NEGLIGENCE, 🔑1–55.
(A) PERSONAL CONDUCT IN GENERAL, 🔑1–15.
(B) DANGEROUS SUBSTANCES, MACHINERY, AND OTHER INSTRUMENTALITIES, 🔑16–27.
(C) CONDITION AND USE OF LAND, BUILDINGS, AND OTHER STRUCTURES, 🔑28–55.

II. PROXIMATE CAUSE OF INJURY, 🔑56–64.

III. CONTRIBUTORY NEGLIGENCE, 🔑65–101.
(A) PERSONS INJURED IN GENERAL, 🔑65–83.11.
(B) CHILDREN AND OTHERS UNDER DISABILITY, 🔑84–88.
(C) IMPUTED NEGLIGENCE, 🔑89–96.
(D) COMPARATIVE NEGLIGENCE, 🔑97–101.

IV. ACTIONS, 🔑102–143.
(A) RIGHT OF ACTION, PARTIES, PRELIMINARY PROCEEDINGS, AND PLEADING, 🔑102–119.
(B) EVIDENCE, 🔑120–135.

NEGLIGENCE 29 10th D Pt 1—1118

IV. ACTIONS, 🔑102–143—Cont'd
(B) EVIDENCE, 🔑120–135.—Cont'd
1. PRESUMPTIONS AND BURDEN OF PROOF, 121–123.
2. ADMISSIBILITY, 124–133.
3. WEIGHT AND SUFFICIENCY, 🔑134–135.
(C) TRIAL, JUDGMENT, AND REVIEW, 🔑136–143.

V. CRIMINAL RESPONSIBILITY, 🔑144.

I. ACTS OR OMISSIONS CONSTITUTING NEGLIGENCE.

(A) PERSONAL CONDUCT IN GENERAL.

🔑1. Nature and elements of negligence in general.
2. Duty to use care.
3. Degrees of care in general.
4. Ordinary or reasonable care.
5. Customary methods and acts.
6. Requirements of statutes or ordinances.
7. Care as to children.
8. Care as to infirm or helpless persons.
9. Inadvertent acts or omissions.
10. Unintended consequences.
11. Willful, wanton, or reckless acts or conduct.
12. Acts in emergencies.
13. Degrees of negligence.
14. Persons liable.
15. Joint and several liability.

(B) DANGEROUS SUBSTANCES, MACHINERY, AND OTHER INSTRUMENTALITIES.

🔑16. Care required in general.
17. Customary methods and acts.
18. Requirements of statutes or ordinances.
19. Injurious substances and articles.
20. Defective and dangerous machinery, tools, and appliances.
21. Fires.
22. Dangerous instrumentalities and operations.
22½. Private vehicles.
23. Machinery and other things as attractions to children.
(1). In general.
(2). Railroad turntables and cars.
24. Knowledge of defect or danger.
25. Precautions against injury.
26. Persons liable in general.

(C) CONDITION AND USE OF LAND, BUILDINGS, AND OTHER STRUCTURES.

🔑28. Care required in general.
29. Duty to use care.
30. Customary methods and acts.
31. Requirements of statutes or ordinances.
32. Care as to licensees or persons invited.
(1). In general.
(2). Who are licensees, and status of person going on land of another in general.
(2.1). Classes of licensees, and distinction between them in general.
(2.2). Bare licensees.
(2.3). Invitees in general.
(2.4). Implied invitation in general.
(2.5). Automobile service stations and parking service.
(2.6). Bill collectors.
(2.7). Buildings in process of construction, alteration, or demolition.
(2.8). Business visitors, and store and restaurant patrons.
(2.9). Deliverymen and haulers.
(2.10). Employees and contractors.
(2.11). Frequenters.
(2.12). Gratuitous licensees.
(2.13). Guests in private homes.
(2.14). Meter readers.
(2.15). Persons accompanying invitees.
(2.16). Postmen.
(2.17). Public officials in general.
(2.18). Firemen and policemen.
(3). Exceeding or abusing license or invitation.
(4). Children and others under disability.
33. Care as to trespassers.
(1). In general.
(2). Who are trespassers.
(3). Children.
34. Care as to persons on adjacent premises.
35. Care as to persons on adjacent highway.
36. Private grounds in general.
37. Places open to public; recreational use.
38. Places abutting on or near highways.
39. Places attractive to children.
41. Streams, ponds, and wells.
42. Excavations.
43. Embankments and piling of materials.
44. Buildings and other structures.
45. Elevators, hoistways, and shafts.
46. Use of property.
47. Traps, pitfalls, and harmful devices.
48. Knowledge of defect or danger.
49. Precautions against injury.
50. —— In general.
51. —— Barriers, or covering or guarding dangerous places.
52. —— Notices and warnings.
53. Persons liable.
54. —— In general.
55. —— Acts or omissions of independent contractors.

EXHIBIT 17.10
American Law Reports

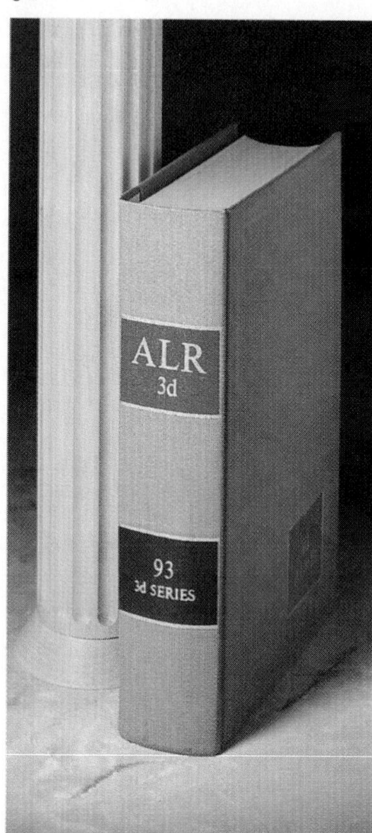

Supreme Court Reports. Both are published by the Lawyers Cooperative Publishing Company and are similar in organizational style to the West digests. Each topic begins with an outline of contents and arranges headnotes according to section number. The classification system is limited to United States Supreme Court cases and is not applicable to similar cases found in lower federal courts or state courts. The digest provides cross-references to the *American Law Reports* and other legal publications of the Lawyers Cooperative Publishing Company. Some publishers also publish state-specific digests, such as Callahan's *Michigan Digest.*

Annotations: *American Law Reports*

The *American Law Reports (A.L.R.)* and *American Law Reports Federal (A.L.R. Federal),* published by the Lawyers Cooperative Publishing Company, are also useful resources for the legal researcher. An *A.L.R.* volume is shown in Exhibit 17.10. These reports are multivolume sets that present the full text of selected cases in numerous areas of the law. They are helpful in finding cases from jurisdictions throughout the country with similar factual and legal issues.

There are five different series of *American Law Reports,* covering case law since 1919. The fourth series *(A.L.R.4th),* the current edition, began in 1980. *A.L.R. Federal,* the current edition for coverage of federal decisions, began in 1969. The *A.L.R.1st* and *A.L.R.2d* series contain separate digests that provide references to cases and also have word indexes to assist the researcher in locating specific areas.

Quick Indexes. *A.L.R.3d, A.L.R.4th,* and *A.L.R. Federal* use a new method of accessing information through the *Quick Index* approach (see Exhibit 17.11), which is a combination of the topical approach and the factual-word approach in an alphabetical listing. This approach is now the standard means used to access annotations throughout all of the series. The *A.L.R. Federal's Quick Index* covers the annotations in *A.L.R. Federal,* as well as the annotations in the *Lawyers' Edition of the Supreme Court Reports* (mentioned previously) and other federal law research tools.

Annotations. The cases presented in these reporters are followed by annotations. In the *A.L.R.,* annotations consist of articles that focus on specific issues; these reports can therefore be an excellent source to turn to in researching case law. The annotations also present an overview of the specific area of law addressed by the case, indicate current trends in that area, and refer to other case law relating to the specific issue or issues.

As shown in Exhibit 17.12 on page 662, an annotation begins with an outline of the subject matter or topic discussed and is followed by a detailed index of subtopics. This is followed by a table of the jurisdictions represented in the discussions of the topic. The annotations contain cross-references to other publications of the Lawyers Cooperative Publishing Company, such as *American Jurisprudence 2d.*

Updating Supplements. *A.L.R.* annotations are periodically updated by the addition of relevant recent cases. The annotations in *A.L.R.1st* are supple-

ALR 3d QUICK INDEX

ABANDONMENT

Contracts (this index)

Criminal enterprise: withdrawal from or abandonment of criminal enterprise, 8 Am Jur POF 2d, pp 231–266

Disclosure of trade secret in court proceedings as abandonment of secrecy, 58 ALR3d 1318

Easement: abandonment of easement, 3 Am Jur POF 2d, pp 647–674

Eminent domain: what constitutes abandonment of eminent domain proceeding so as to charge condemnor with liability for condemnee's expenses or the like, 68 ALR3d 610

Felony-murder: what constitutes termination of felony for purpose of felony-murder rule, 58 ALR3d 851

Fire insurance: obtaining new property insurance as cancellation of existing insurance, 3 ALR3d 1072

Harassment or other mistreatment by employer or supervisor as "good cause" justifying abandonment of employment, 76 ALR3d 1089, 9 Am Jur POF2d, pp 697–728

Home, abandonment of: what voluntary acts of child, other than marriage or entry into military service, terminate parent's obligation to support, 32 ALR3d 1055

Infestation of leased dwelling or apartment with vermin as entitling tenant to abandon premises or as constructive eviction by landlord in absence of express covenant of habitability, 27 ALR3d 924

Mechanics' lien: abandonment of construction or of contract as affecting time for filing mechanics' liens or time for giving notice to owner, 52 ALR3d 797

Mines and Minerals (this index)

Mitigation: landlord's duty, on tenant's failure to occupy, or abandonment of, premises, to mitigate damages by accepting or procuring another tenant, 21 ALR3d 534

Nonconforming use: zoning-abandonment of lawful nonconforming use, 18 Am Jur POF 2d, pp 731–777

Oil or gas: duty and liability as to plugging oil or gas well abandoned or taken out of production, 50 ALR3d 240

Physician's abandonment of patient, 3 Am Jur POF 2d, pp 117–165

Principal and agent: insurance agent's statement or conduct indicating that insurer's cancellation of policy shall not take effect as binding on insurer, 3 ALR3d 1135

Proofs: abandonment, 1 Am Jur POF, pp 1–10

Real estate contract: purchaser's abandonment of land sales contract, 5 Am Jur POF 2d, pp 165–188

Trade Secrets (this index)

Unemployment Compensation (this index)

Withdrawal, after provocation of conflict, as reviving right of self-defense, 55 ALR3d 1000

Zoning (this index)

ABANDONMENT OF CASE

Condemnation of rural property for highway purposes, abandonment of action involving, 8 Am Jur Trials, pp 57–102

ABANDONMENT-OF-SHIP DRILL

Liability for injury to or death of passenger in connection with a fire drill or abandonment-of-ship drill aboard a vessel, 8 ALR3d 650

ABANDONMENT OF SPOUSE OR CHILD

Desertion (this index)

ABATEMENT

Action.

Consult POCKET PART for later annotations 1

EXHIBIT 17.11
Excerpt from the *A.L.R. Federal Quick Index*

mented by a six-volume set called *A.L.R.1st Blue Book of Supplemental Decisions* (see Exhibit 17.13 on page 663). *A.L.R.2d* is updated by the *A.L.R. Later Case Service* (see Exhibit 17.14 on page 664). *A.L.R.3d*, *A.L.R.4th*, and *A.L.R. Federal* are made current by pocket-part supplements located in the front of each volume. An additional updating tool for *A.L.R.2d*, *A.L.R.3d*, *A.L.R.4th*, and *A.L.R. Federal* is the Annotation History Tables located at the end of the Quick Indexes for *A.L.R.3d* and *A.L.R.4th* and at the end of

EXHIBIT 17.12
Annotation from *American Law Reports*

ANNOTATION

VALIDITY AND CONSTRUCTION, AS TO CLAIM ALLEGING DESIGN DEFECTS, OF STATUTE IMPOSING TIME LIMITATIONS UPON ACTION AGAINST ARCHITECT OR ENGINEER FOR INJURY OR DEATH ARISING OUT OF DEFECTIVE OR UNSAFE CONDITION OF IMPROVEMENT TO REAL PROPERTY

by

Jane Massey Draper, B.C.L.

I. PRELIMINARY MATTERS

§ 1. Introduction:
[a] Scope
[b] Related matters

TOTAL CLIENT-SERVICE LIBRARY® REFERENCES

5 Am Jur 2d, Architects § 25; 51 Am Jur 2d, Limitation of Actions §§ 27–30, 136

2 Am Jur Pl & Pr Forms (Rev), Architects, Form 33; 17 Am Jur Pl & Pr Forms (Rev), Limitation of Action, Forms 121–151

2 Am Jur Legal Forms 2d, Architects, Engineers, and Surveyors §§ 24:62, 24:65, 24:111; 12 Am Jur Legal Forms 2d, Limitation of Actions §§ 167:14, 167:20, 167:53

24 Am Jur Proof of Facts 285, Architect's Negligence

USCS Constitution, Amendment 14

US L Ed Digest, Constitutional Law §§ 496, 780, 784; Limitation of Actions §§ 5, 6, 121, 179

ALR Digests, Architect § 2; Limitation of Actions §§ 2, 133, 134, 141, 195, 196, 200

L Ed Index to Annos, Architects; Limitation of Actions

ALR Quick Index, Architects; Death; Defects and Irregularities; Engineers; Improvement; Limitation of Actions; Plans and Specifications; Property Damage

Federal Quick Index, Architects; Death; Engineers; Limitation of Actions; Property Damage

Consult POCKET PART in this volume for later cases

1242

93 ALR3d TIME LIMITATION—ACTION AGAINST ARCHITECT
93 ALR3d 1242

§ 2. Background, summary, and comment:
[a] Generally
[b] Practice pointers

II. VALIDITY

§ 3. Generally:
[a] Statute held valid
[b] Statute held invalid

III. CONSTRUCTION

§ 4. Effect of statute, generally:
[a] Commencement of limitation period
[b] Duration of limitation period
§ 5. Effect on other statutes of limitation
§ 6. Applicability to particular types of actions:
[a] Breach of contract or warranty; negligence
[b] Indemnity
§ 7. Infancy as tolling statute
§ 8. Construction of particular terms:
[a] "Improvement to real property"
[b] "Owners, tenants, or otherwise"
[c] "Limitation shall not apply"

INDEX

Air conditioning machinery, negligent design of rooms housing, § 3
Alumni building, design and construction of, §§ 4[b], 6[b]
Apartment house, unsafe condition of, § 4[b, c]
Asphyxiation of city employees by sewer gas, § 8[c]
Automobile manufacturer, action against, § 8[a]
Background, summary, and comment, § 2
Bank complex, design and construction of, § 5
Breach of contract or warranty, § 6[a]
Bridge, negligent design, construction, maintenance and control of, § 8[a]
Ceiling, sagging of suspended ceiling resulting in building becoming untenantable, § 4[a]
Commencement of limitation period, § 4[a]
Construction of statute, generally, §§ 4-8
Contract, breach of, § 6[a]
Conveyor system, negligence in design of alterations of, § 3
Courthouse building, negligent construction of, § 6[a]
Drainage system for townhouse complex, faulty design of, § 3
Duration of limitation period, § 4[b]
Effect of statute, § 4
Heater, building burning as result of installation of, § 3
Hospital building, negligent design in construction of, § 6[a]
"Improvement to real property", construction of, § 8[a]
Indemnity, § 6[b]
Infancy as tolling statute, § 7
Introduction, § 1
"Limitation shall not apply", construction of, § 8[c]
Minor injured as result of running through glass side light, action by, §§ 5, 7
Municipal building, action involving preparation of plans and specifications for, § 4[b]
Negligence, § 6[a]
Other statutes of limitation, effect on, § 5

1243

each pocket-part supplement. *A.L.R.1st* contains annotations of supplementing and superseding (overruling or modifying) cases in the last volume of the *A.L.R.1st Blue Book*. The history tables allow the researcher to see if any new annotations supplement or supersede an earlier annotation.

Treatises

TREATISE
In legal research, a text that provides a systematic, detailed, and scholarly review of a particular legal subject.

A **treatise** is a formal scholarly work that treats a given subject systematically and in detail. Treatises are written by individuals such as law professors, legal scholars, and practicing attorneys. Law treatises are commentaries that summarize, interpret, or evaluate different areas of substantive and procedural law. Some treatises are published in multivolume sets, and others are contained in a single book. The organization of the text of a treatise is

EXHIBIT 17.13
A Page from the *A.L.R.1st Blue Book of Supplemental Decisions*

Seventh Permanent Volume OF SUPPLEMENTAL DECISIONS FOR ANNOTATIONS IN THE AMERICAN LAW REPORTS

Vols. 1–175

1 ALR 39-136
U.S.—Davis v F. (ND Ill) 717 F Supp 614
Mass.—Ogden Suffolk Downs, Inc. v B., 18 Mass App 101, 463 NE2d 575
Tex.—Stafford v J. (App Houston (14th Dist)) 687 SW2d 784

1 ALR 143-145
Supplemented 38 ALR 229 and 89 ALR 966◆

1 ALR 148-149
Superseded 74 ALR2d 828◆

1 ALR 156-162
Supplemented 99 ALR 938◆

1 ALR 203-218
Supplemented 2 ALR 767 and 41 ALR 405◆

1 ALR 222-264
Supplemented 102 ALR 174 and 116 ALR 1064◆
Subdiv VIII superseded 71 ALR2d 1140◆

1 ALR 272-274
Supplemented 18 ALR 87◆

1 ALR 276-297
R.I.—Celona v R. I. E. C., 544 A2d 582

1 ALR 329-331
Superseded 36 ALR2d 861◆

1 ALR 336-338
Supplemented 20 ALR 1535 and 73 ALR 1494◆

1 ALR 343-349
Superseded 51 ALR2d 1404◆

1 ALR 362-365
La.—Ursin v N. O. A. B. (App 5th Cir) 506 So 2d 947

1 ALR 374-380
Supplemented 101 ALR 1282 and 104 ALR 1352◆

1 ALR 383-392
Superseded 13 ALR4th 1153◆

1 ALR 394-400
U.S.—Dunavant Enterprises, Inc. v S. S. Co. (CA11 Ala) 730 F2d 665
F.—Re Tinnell Traffic Services, Inc. (BC MD Tenn) 43 BR 277
Re STN Enterprises, Inc. (BC DC Vt) 45 BR 955
Re Windsor Communications Group, Inc. (BC ED Pa) 80 BR 712
Re Hawkins Co. (BC DC Idaho) 104 BR 317, 10 UCCRS2d 468
Ill.—Mueller v S. (5th Dist) 160 Ill App 3d 699, 112 Ill Dec 589, 513 NE2d 1198
Mont.—Interstate Brands Corp. v C., 708 P2d 573
Ohio.—Konicki v S., Inc., 16 Ohio App 3d 40, 16 Ohio BR 43, 474 NE2d 347, 41 UCCRS 103
Va.—Noland Co. v N.-R. Corp., 234 Va 266, 360 SE2d 852

1 ALR 403-405
Mo.—Stegman v S. E. Co. (App) 678 SW2d 416

1 ALR 436-439
Supplemented 46 ALR 1192 at p 1194◆

1 ALR 449-450
Superseded 28 ALR2d 662◆

1 ALR 459-470
Supplemented 160 ALR 295◆

1 ALR 483-486
Supplemented 46 ALR 814◆

1 ALR 498-502
Supplemented 72 ALR 278◆

1 ALR 528-532
N.Y.—Blackmore v W. L. Corp. (3d Dept) 97 App Div 2d 889, 470 NYS2d 713
Agency, Broad & Cornelia Street, Inc. v L. (3d Dept) 97 App Div 2d 934, 470 NYS2d 729
Trenga Realty v W. H., Inc. (3d Dept) 138 App Div 2d 875, 526 NYS2d 251
O'Connor Realty Services, Inc. v H. (2d Dept) 149 App Div 2d 492, 539 NYS2d 975

1 ALR 546-547
Superseded 50 ALR2d 1324◆

1 ALR 564-568
Supplemented 8 ALR 493◆

1 ALR 598-593
Ga.—Georgia Insurers Insolvency Pool v M., 175 Ga App 430, 333 SE2d 383

◆When Supplemented see later Note and Blue Book under caption of later Note

3

easy to follow. Each text contains a table of contents and an index or indexes for efficient reference, and most contain a table of cases referred to within the text. Although treatises are secondary materials and have no binding effect on courts, they may merit particular judicial respect and recognition when written by leading scholars in the field. Many of these scholarly works

EXHIBIT 17.14
A Page from the *A.L.R. Later Case Service*

LATER CASE SERVICE **81 ALR2d 750–787**

salary before and after accident was sufficient to establish comparative salary range and, accordingly, award for lost earning capacity was not speculative or contrary to weight of evidence. Turner v Chicago Transit Authority (1984, 1st Dist) 122 **Ill** App 3d 419, 77 Ill Dec 928, 461 NE2d 551.

It was not error to admit testimony regarding plaintiff's wages from last period of employment, even though plaintiff was unemployed at time of accident, where wages were probative of earning capacity at time of injury since plaintiff had held same job for ten years and wages were earned only seven months prior to accident. Cantara v Massachusetts Bay Transp. Authority, 3 **Mass** App 81, 323 NE2d 759 (citing annotation).

Evidence of wages earned by plaintiff during regular employment for five-year period ending two months before she was injured in automobile accident was not too remote on issue of impairment of earning capacity. Matthews v Porter, 239 **SC** 620, 124 SE2d 321 (quoting annotation).

[b] Change in employment; temporary or permanent nature of work.

Evidence as to deceased's past earnings as self-employed trucker-broker was admissible notwithstanding deceased was not employed in such business at time of death where other evidence indicated that deceased intended to return to such business in very short time. Blackburn v Aetna Freight Lines, Inc. (CA3 Pa) 368 **F2d** 345.

81 ALR2d 750–787

Liability of proprietor of business premises for injury from fall on exterior walk, ramp, or passageway connected with the building in which the business is conducted.

New sections and subsections added:

§ 9.1. Comparative negligence.

---

§ 1. Scope and related matters, p. 753.

Status of one who enters a store or other place of public resort solely for purpose of using facilities accessible to public, such as telephone, mailbox, lavatory, or the like. 93 ALR2d 784.

Duty of proprietor toward visitor upon premises on private business with or errand or work for employee. 94 ALR2d 6.

Liability of owner or operator of shopping center to patrons for injuries from defects or conditions in sidewalks, walks, or pedestrian passageways. 95 ALR2d 1341.

Liability of owner or operator of garage or gasoline filling station for bodily injury to nonemployees on premises. 8 ALR3d 6.

Liability for injury to patron, of owner or operator of retail store failing to provide carry-out service. 21 ALR3d 931.

Liability of owner or occupant of premises for injuries sustained by mail carrier. 21 ALR3d 1099.

Premises liability: proceeding in the dark along outside path or walkway as contributory negligence. 22 ALR3d 599.

Liability of owner or operator of self-service laundry for personal injury or damages to patron or frequenter of premises from defect in premises or appliances. 23 ALR3d 1246.

Liability of owner or occupant of premises to building or construction inspector coming upon premises in discharge of duty. 28 ALR3d 891.

Liability of owner or operator of premises for injury to meter reader or similar employee of public service corporation coming to premises in course of duties. 28 ALR3d 1344.

Liability of owner or operator of premises for injury to person coming to premises in course of delivery or pickup of merchandise or similar products. 32 ALR3d 9.

Liability of owner or operator of parking lot for personal injuries allegedly resulting from condition of premises. 38 ALR3d 10.

Liability of owner or operator of parking lot for personal injuries caused by movement of vehicles. 38 ALR3d 138.

Liability of lessee of particular premises in shopping center for injury to patron from condition on portion of premises not included in his leasehold. 48 ALR3d 1163.

Liability of landlord for personal injury or death due to inadequacy or lack of lighting on portion of premises used in common by tenants. 66 ALR3d 202.

Store or business premises slip-and-fall: Modern status of rules requiring showing of notice of proprietor of transitory interior condition allegedly causing plaintiff's fall. 85 ALR3d 1000.

Liability for injuries in connection with allegedly dangerous or defective doormat on nonresidential premises. 94 ALR3d 389.

Liability of operator of grocery store to invitee slipping on spilled liquid or semiliquid substance. 24 ALR4th 696.

Liability of operator of store, office, or similar place of business to invitee slipping on spilled liquid or semiliquid substance. 26 ALR4th 481.

81

HORNBOOK
A secondary source presented as a single-volume scholarly discussion, or treatise, on a particular legal subject (such as property law).

are classics and serve as a valuable source of information many years after publication.

Hornbooks are single-volume treatises that synthesize the basic principles of an area of the law. Paralegals who seek to familiarize themselves with a particular area of the law, such as torts or contracts, should review one of the many available hornbooks. For example, in researching the issue in Trent Hoffman's negligence case, you might want to locate the learned treatise *Prosser and Keeton on the Law of Torts,* Fifth Edition, which is included in West's Hornbook Series, and read the sections on negligence in that volume. (Exhibit 17.15 shows the page of this book that opens the chapter on negligence.) This text was written by distinguished lawyers from leading law schools. In addition to providing a clear and organized discussion of the subject matter, hornbooks present many examples of case law and references to cases that may be helpful in searching for cases with similar facts and issues.

Treatises are usually organized by section numbers rather than by page numbers. And, as is characteristic of other legal sources, they are divided into topics and subtopics. Most treatises are updated by supplementary loose-leaf pages or pocket-part additions.

EXHIBIT 17.15
A Page from the Hornbook on the Law of Torts

Chapter 11

NEGLIGENCE: DEFENSES

Table of Sections

§ 65. Contributory Negligence

The two most common defenses in a negligence action are contributory negligence and assumption of risk. Since both developed at a comparatively late date in the development of the common law,[1] and since both clearly operate to the advantage of the defendant, they are commonly regarded as defenses to a tort which would otherwise be established. All courts now hold that the burden of pleading and proof of the contributory negligence of the plaintiff is on the defendant.[2]

Contributory negligence is conduct on the part of the plaintiff, contributing as a legal cause to the harm he has suffered, which falls below the standard to which he is required to conform for his own protection.[3] Unlike assumption of risk, the defense does not rest upon the idea that the defendant is relieved of any duty toward the plaintiff. Rather, although the defendant has violated his duty, has been negligent, and would oth-

§ 65

1. The earliest contributory negligence case is Butterfield v. Forrester, 1809, 11 East 60, 103 Eng.Rep. 926. The first American case appears to have been Smith v. Smith, 1824, 19 Mass. (2 Pick.) 621. Assumption of risk first appears in a negligence case in 1799. See infra, § 68 n. 1.

2. E.g., Wilkinson v. Hartford Accident & Indemnity Co., La.1982, 411 So.2d 22; Moodie v. Santoni, 1982, 292 Md. 582, 441 A.2d 323; Addair v. Bryant, 1981, ___ W.Va. ___, 284 S.E.2d 374; Pickett v. Parks, 1981, 208 Neb. 310, 303 N.W.2d 296; Hatton v. Chem-Haulers, Inc., Ala.1980, 393 So.2d 950; Sampson v. W. F. Enterprises, Inc., Mo.App.1980, 611 S.W.2d 333; Howard v. Howard, Ky.App.1980, 607 S.W.2d 119; cf. Reuter v. United States, W.D.Pa.1982, 534 F.Supp. 731 (presumption that person killed or suffering loss of memory was acting with due care). Illinois and certain other jurisdictions held to the contrary for some time. See West Chicago Street Railroad Co. v. Liderman, 1900, 187 Ill. 463, 58 N.E. 367; Kotler v. Lalley, 1930, 112 Conn. 86, 151 A. 433; Dreier v. McDermott, 1913, 157 Iowa 726, 141 N.W. 315. See Green, Illinois Negligence Law II, 1944, 39 Ill.L.Rev. 116, 125–130.

3. Second Restatement of Torts, § 463. See generally, Malone, The Formative Era of Contributory Negligence, 1946, 41 Ill.L.Rev. 151; James, Contributory Negligence, 1953, 62 Yale L.J. 691; Bohlen, Contributory Negligence, 1908, 21 Harv.L.Rev. 233; Lowndes, Contributory Negligence, 1934, 22 Geo.L.J. 674; Malone, Some Ruminations on Contributory Negligence, 1981, 65 Utah L.Rev. 91; Schwartz, Contributory and Comparative Negligence: A Reappraisal, 1978, 87 Yale L.J. 697; Note, 1979, 39 La.L.Rev. 637.

451

FEATURED GUEST: E. J. YERA

Ten Tips for Effective Legal Research

Biographical Note

E. J. Yera graduated from the University of Miami School of Law in 1987 and served as a research instructor at the school until 1989. He then clerked in the U.S. District Court for the Southern District of Florida until 1993. He has lectured and taught in paralegal programs, including the programs at Miami Dade Community College in Miami, Florida, and Barry University in Miami Shores, Florida. He has twice been named to *Who's Who in American Law* and has authored and published works on intellectual property. Yera is licensed to practice law in Florida and Washington, D.C. He is currently the assistant corporate counsel at Holmes Regional Medical Center in Melbourne, Florida.

If you perform legal research frequently, you will develop a routine. The purpose of this article is not to give you ironclad rules but to set out ten guidelines that will help you find the routine that is most comfortable for you. You may come back to this article and reread it over time. Now, however, as you read it for the first time, think about how you can use the tips in your future research tasks.

1 Before You Start, Make Sure That You Know Exactly What Legal Issue Is to Be Researched. You would be surprised at how many students, paralegals, and lawyers research a question for hours only to find that the reason they are getting nowhere is because they do not know what the question is. Before you start your research, you should determine what the legal question, or issue, is that needs to be researched. You might learn this from reviewing information you already have available, such as a summary of a client interview. If you have an opportunity to ask questions of the attorney giving you a research assignment, do so. What counts, in the end, is coming back with the correct answers, not impressing the attorney by appearing to understand the research task completely when you first hear about it. It will take you twice as long to finish the assignment if you research the wrong issue or if you are unsure what the issue is.

2 Understand the Language of the Issue. Often, the researcher finds that he or she cannot find the answer because the legal terms used in defining the problem are unfamiliar to him or her. Legal terms, or "terms of art," as they are often called, are as unfamiliar to many people as a foreign language. If you are uncertain about the meaning of any term or phrase, look it up in a law dictionary or encyclopedia to get a basic idea of its meaning. Depending on how broad the term is, you may want to read a hornbook on the topic to give you a basic understanding. For example, assume that you are researching an issue relating to securities law. If you do not have a clear understanding of what securities are, there is no way in the world that you can conduct effective research on this issue. You will need to acquire some background knowledge before you focus on the particular research topic.

3 Be Aware of the Circular Nature of Legal Research and Use It to Your Advantage. Students often ask whether primary or secondary sources should be researched first. The answer is that it does not matter, as long as you always research both types of sources. By researching both primary and secondary sources on a topic, you can be assured that you are almost always double-checking your own work. For example, in a case (a primary source of law) on a particular issue, the judge writing the opinion will discuss any pertinent statutes on the issue. Similarly, most annotated versions of a statute (the annotations are secondary sources of law) give a listing, following the text of the statute, of cases applying the statute and the context in which the statute was applied. The reason that you check both sources is to make sure that you have found all of the relevant materials.

4 Until You Hand in the Assignment, Always Assume That There are Additional Relevant Materials to Find. You need to keep on your toes until you complete your research task. Always assuming that further relevant materials

FEATURED GUEST, Continued

must be located will help you do this. Of course, there comes a point when you have to assume that you *have* covered the research territory, and knowing when to stop doing research is perhaps one of the hardest things to learn. Certain legal issues can be researched for months and even years. The intention of this tip, though, is to encourage you not to cut corners when conducting research.

5 Keep a List of What Sources You Have Found and to What Sources They Have Led You. You do not want to spend valuable time wondering if you have already checked certain sources. Therefore, it is important to construct a "road map" of where you have been and where you are going.

6 Take the Time to Become Familiar with the Sources That You Are Using. It probably seems obvious that you need to become familiar with your sources, yet this requirement is sometimes overlooked. For example, a case digest (a volume summarizing cases) may indicate on its spine that the digest covers the years "1961 to Date." "To Date," however, does not mean that it is the most current digest; it only means that the digest covers cases up to the date of publication of the new digest replacing it. You should take the time to read the first few pages of the digest to verify its contents. This is true generally for any source you are using—look it over carefully before assuming that it contains the sources you need to find.

7 Always Be Aware of the Jurisdiction and the Time Frame That You Are Researching. If you are researching an issue that will be resolved by a Florida state court, then your emphasis should be on Florida cases. Of course, there are times when no case law is available, and you must then find cases on point from other states to use as persuasive authorities. You must also be aware of the time frame covered by the source you are using (as mentioned in Tip 6). Be aware when researching any area of the law that very often there is either a loose-leaf service or a pamphlet or pocket part (the latter is a small booklet that slips into a pocket of the bound volume) containing newer information. Always ask yourself the following question: Where can the most up-to-date material be found? If you don't know, ask a law librarian who does.

8 Always Use *Shepard's* to Make Sure That the Cases You Are Using Are Up to Date. *Shepard's Citations* is a set of volumes that helps the researcher of case law in two ways. First, it tells you what other cases have cited the cases that you have found. This information is helpful because if another case has cited a case you have found, that other case may also be relevant to your issue, and thus you may be able to use it. Also, cases that cite your case are more recent, and using one or more of those cases may thus be advantageous. Second, *Shepard's* tells you, among other things, whether the cases that you have found are still "good law"—that is, whether the cases have been overruled, reversed, or the like. Knowing this information is crucial—because presenting a case to your attorney that no longer represents good law could well be a short cut to the unemployment line.

"WHAT COUNTS, IN THE END, IS COMING BACK WITH THE CORRECT ANSWERS."

9 Use Computerized Legal Research Services to Update Your Research Results. Computerized legal databases such as WESTLAW and LEXIS allow you to update your research results by "Shepardizing" cases by computer. Also, these services allow you to search the available case law for words or phrases. By doing so, you can actually create your own indexing system.

10 Twice a Year, Take Three or Four Hours and Browse through Your Local Law Library. You cannot use sources effectively if you do not know that they exist. You should periodically—say, twice a year—spend an afternoon in the law library browsing through the shelves. Read the first few pages of each new source, and then make a note of what the source contains. Ask the librarian for new sources in your area. The time you save later will more than compensate for an afternoon's time spent in the library. You will be surprised at how quickly the new sources you discovered or were told about at the law library come quickly to mind when you receive a new research assignment, and they may figure significantly in your research.

ETHICAL CONCERN

Avoiding Plagiarism

Plagiarism—copying the exact, or nearly exact, words of another without acknowledging the author of those words—may constitute a violation of federal copyright law (discussed in Chapter 8). You should realize, though, that it is possible to plagiarize another's words *unintentionally.* Suppose, for example, that you are taking notes from a legal treatise, such as a hornbook on the law of torts, and you copy several paragraphs word for word for your future reference. You don't enclose the paragraphs in quotation marks because you know you will remember that those are not your words but the words of the authors of the hornbook. A week or so later, you are preparing a brief and, referring to your notes, you include those paragraphs, assuming that they are your own version of what the authors said in the hornbook. In short, you have plagiarized a substantial portion of another's copyrighted work without even being aware of that fact. To ensure that your employer will not face a lawsuit for copyright infringement, always remember to include quotation marks (and the exact source of the quoted material) when copying another's words.

Restatements of the Law

Another source of general background information is the Restatements of the Law, produced by the American Law Institute, an organization established in 1923 by a group of prominent judges, law professors, and practicing attorneys. The Restatements present an overview of the basic principles of the common law in ten specific fields: agency law, conflict of laws, contracts, foreign relations law, judgments, property, restitution, security, torts, and trusts. Most of the Restatements have been updated by the issuance of second or third editions. The *Restatement of the Law of Torts,* for example, a photograph of which is shown in Exhibit 17.16, is now in its second edition.[3] The Restatements are often abbreviated when referred to by legal professionals. The *Restatement of the Law of Torts,* Second Edition, is often referred to as the *Restatement (Second) of the Law of Torts,* or, more simply, as the *Restatement (Second) of Torts.*

Restatements are helpful resources when researching issues involving common law doctrines, such as negligence. Each section in the Restatements contains a statement of the principles of law that are generally accepted by the courts and/or embodied in statutes on the topic, followed by a discussion of these principles. The Restatements are useful research tools because they present particular cases as examples and also discuss variations on the general propositions of the law. The overall organization of the texts is easy to follow. There is a general index for the Restatements in the first series, in addition to the separate indexes available for the individual Restatements. Later editions contain appendices, including notes of decisions citing the first series, Reporter's Notes, and cross-references to *A.L.R.* annotations.

The Restatements are *not* primary sources of law and therefore are not binding on the courts. But they are highly respected secondary sources of law and are often referred to by the courts as the basis for their decisions.

Legal Periodicals

Legal periodicals are another source of secondary authority and as such are not binding. Legal periodicals, such as law reviews, contain thoroughly researched information on a specific area of the law. The authors are usually law professors, attorneys prominent in their field, judges, legal scholars, or law students. The periodicals discuss and evaluate specific laws and their implications. Additionally, they may advocate changes in the law.

Articles in legal periodicals can be extremely helpful to paralegals. For example, many law-review articles present well-written and informative overviews of areas of the law with which paralegals may be unfamiliar. Legal periodicals may be a helpful case-finding aid as well. Many articles contain numerous footnotes citing relevant cases and statutes or offering factual background. Legal periodicals often contain references to other secondary sources of authority, such as treatises, other law-review articles, and legal texts as well. Additionally, articles in legal periodicals can be a good source

3. Plans are in progress to publish a third edition of the *Restatement of the Law of Torts.*

of information on recent developments and trends in the law. As with all legal sources, articles in legal periodicals can become outdated, and it is important to remember to find up-to-date articles that discuss current law.

Paralegals can locate articles relevant to a particular issue by looking at various periodical guides in the law library. The two most popular guides are the *Index to Legal Periodicals*, covering publications beginning in 1908, and the *Current Legal Index*, which began coverage in 1980. Most law libraries contain at least one of these publications. The *Index to Legal Periodicals* (see Exhibit 17.17) indexes articles appearing in approximately five hundred periodicals, and the *Current Legal Index* covers over seven hundred legal periodicals. Both indexes are published twelve times a year, with cumulative issues quarterly and a cumulative bound volume at the end of the year. These publications have both a subject index and an index of authors and titles. Exhibit 17.18 on the following page illustrates how entries are listed in the *Index to Legal Periodicals.*

EXHIBIT 17.16
Restatement (Second) of the Law of Torts

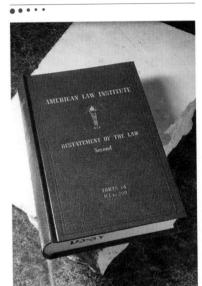

THE CASE REPORTING SYSTEM

The primary sources of case law are, of course, the cases themselves. Once you have learned what cases are relevant to the issue that you are researching, you need to find the cases and examine the exact words of the court opinions. Assume, for example, that in researching the issue in Hoffman's case, you learn that your state's supreme court, a few years ago, issued a decision on a case with a very similar fact pattern. In that case, the state supreme court upheld a lower court's judgment that a retail business owner had to pay extensive damages to a customer who was injured on the store's premises. You know that the state supreme court's decision is a mandatory authority, and to your knowledge, the decision has not been overruled or modified. Therefore, the case will likely provide weighty support to your attorney's arguments in support of Hoffman's claim.

At this point, however, you have only read *about* the case in secondary sources. To locate the case itself and make sure that it is applicable, you need to understand the case reporting system and the legal "shorthand" employed in referencing court cases.

EXHIBIT 17.17
Index to Legal Periodicals

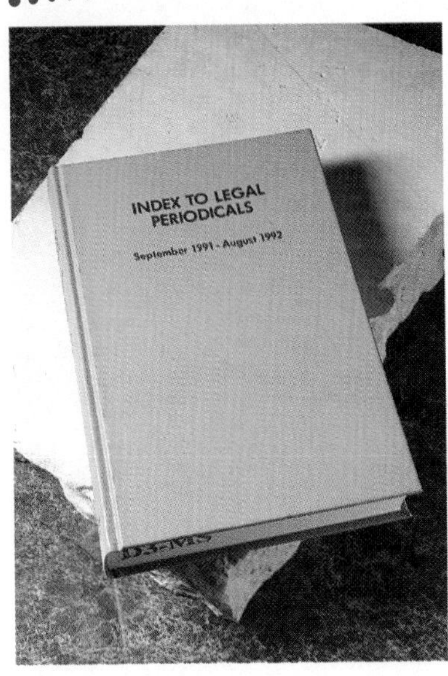

State Court Decisions

New York and a few other states publish selected opinions of their trial courts, but most state trial court decisions are not published. Decisions from the state trial courts are usually just filed in the office of the clerk of the court, where they are available for public inspection.

State Reporters. Written decisions of the appellate courts, however, are usually published and distributed. The reported appellate decisions are published—in chronological order by date of decision—in volumes called *reports*, which are numbered consecutively. State appellate court decisions are found in the reports of that particular state. State court decisions are usually published in both official and unofficial reporters. The official reports are designated as such by the state legislature, are issued by the individual courts, and

EXHIBIT 17.18
Entries in the *Index to Legal Periodicals*

PERIODICALS INDEXED

All data as of latest issue received

A

ABA Journal. See American Bar Association Journal
Adelaide Law Review. $40. semi-ann (ISSN 0065-1915) University of Adelaide Law School, GPO Box 498, Adelaide, S.A. 5001, Australia
North American distribution rights: William S. Hein & Co. Inc., 1285 Main St., Buffalo, NY 14209
The Adelphia Law Journal. $10. ann (ISSN 8756-3630) Sigma Nu Phi National Headquarters, Suite 1500, 625 Fourth Ave. South, Minneapolis, MN 55415
Administrative Law Journal. $20. q (ISSN 1052-2913) Washington College of Law, American University, 4400 Massachusetts Ave., NW, Washington, DC 20016
Name changed to Administrative Law Journal of the American University with Vol. 6, 1992
Administrative Law Journal of the American University. $20. q (ISSN 1052-2913) Washington College of Law, American University, 4400 Massachusetts Ave., NW, Washington, DC 20016
Formerly Administrative Law Journal; name changed with Vol. 6, 1992
Administrative Law Review. $35. q (ISSN 0001-8368) American Bar Association, Section of Administrative Law, 750 N. Lake Shore Dr., Chicago, IL 60611
The Advocates' Quarterly. $65. q (ISSN 0704-0288) Canada Law Book Inc., 240 Edward St., Aurora, Ont. L4G 3S9, Canada
AIPLA Quarterly Journal. $45. q (ISSN 0883-6078) AIPLA Headquarters, Suite 203, 2001 Jefferson Davis Highway, Arlington, VA 22202
The Air Force Law Review. $12. semi-ann (ISSN 0094-8381) Superintendent of Documents, U.S. Government Printing Office, Washington, DC 20402
Akron Law Review. $20. q (ISSN 0002-371X) University of Akron School of Law, Akron, OH 44325
Akron Tax Journal. ann (ISSN 1044-4130) University of Akron School of Law, Akron, OH 44325
Alabama Law Review. $24. tri-ann (ISSN 0002-4279) University of Alabama School of Law, Box 870382, Tuscaloosa, AL 35487-0382
The Alabama Lawyer. $20. 7 times a yr (ISSN 0002-4287) Alabama State Bar, 415 Dexter Ave., Montgomery, AL 36104
Alaska Law Review. $20. semi-ann (ISSN 0883-0568) Duke University School of Law, Room 006, Durham, NC 27706
Albany Law Review. $25. q (ISSN 0002-4678) Albany Law School of Union University, 80 New Scotland Ave., Albany, NY 12208
Alberta Law Review. $30. tri-ann (ISSN 0002-4821) Faculty of Law, University of Alberta, Edmonton, Alta. T6G 2H5, Canada
The American Bankruptcy Law Journal. $50. q (ISSN 0027-9048) The American Bankruptcy Law Journal, P.O. Box 983, Lexington, KY 40588
American Bar Association Journal. $66. m (ISSN 0747-0088) American Bar Association Journal, 750 N. Lake Shore Dr., Chicago, IL 60611
American Bar Association Section of Administrative Law. See Administrative Law Review
American Bar Association Section of Antitrust Law. See Antitrust Law Journal
American Bar Association Section of Business Law. See The Business Lawyer
American Bar Association Section of Criminal Justice. See American Criminal Law Review
American Bar Association Section of Family Law. See Family Law Quarterly
American Bar Association Section of International & Comparative Law. See The International Lawyer
American Bar Association Section of Labor and Employment Law. See The Labor Lawyer
American Bar Association Section of Natural Resources Law. See Natural Resources & Environment
American Bar Association Section of Public Contract Law. See Public Contract Law Journal
American Bar Association Section of Real Property, Probate & Trust Law. See Real Property, Probate and Trust Journal
American Bar Association Section of Taxation. See The Tax Lawyer
American Bar Association Section of Tort and Insurance Practice. See Tort & Insurance Law Journal
American Bar Association Section of Urban, State and Local Government Law. See The Urban Lawyer
American Business Law Journal. $23. q (ISSN 0002-7766) Abilene Christian University, c/o Prof. Brad Reid, Subscription Mgr., Box 8335, Abilene, TX 79699
American Criminal Law Review. $33. q (ISSN 0164-0364) American Criminal Law Review, Georgetown University Law Center, 600 New Jersey Ave., N.W., Washington, DC 20001
American Indian Law Review. $10. semi-ann (ISSN 0094-002X) College of Law, University of Oklahoma, 300 Timberdell Rd., Norman, OK 73019
American Intellectual Property Law Association Quarterly Journal. See AIPLA Quarterly Journal
The American Journal of Comparative Law. $20. q (ISSN 0002-919X) Boalt Hall, University of California, Berkeley, CA 94720
American Journal of Criminal Law. $20. tri-ann (ISSN 0092-2315) University of Texas School of Law, 727 E. 26th St., Austin, TX 78705
American Journal of Family Law. $120. q (ISSN 0891-6330) Professional Education Systems, 200 Spring St., P.O. Box 1428, Eau Claire, WI 54702
American Journal of International Law. $100. q (ISSN 0002-9300) American Journal of International Law, 2223 Massachusetts Ave., N.W., Washington, DC 20008-2864
The American Journal of Jurisprudence. $19. ann (ISSN 0065-8995) American Journal of Jurisprudence, Law Bldg., Notre Dame, IN 46556
American Journal of Law & Medicine. $70. q (ISSN 0098-8588) American Society of Law & Medicine, 765 Commonwealth Ave., Boston, MA 02215
The American Journal of Legal History. $20. q (ISSN 0002-9319) Temple University School of Law, 1719 N. Broad St., Philadelphia, PA 19122
The American Journal of Tax Policy. $22. semi-ann (ISSN 0739-7569) The American Journal of Tax Policy, P.O. Box 870382, Tuscaloosa, AL 35487
The American Journal of Trial Advocacy. $24. tri-ann (ISSN 0160-0281) Cumberland School of Law, Samford University, Box 2263, Birmingham, AL 35229
American Society of International Law Proceedings. $15. ann (ISSN 0272-5037) American Society of International Law Proceedings, 2223 Massachusetts Ave., N.W., Washington, DC 20008
The American University Journal of International Law and Policy. $22. q (ISSN 0888-630X) Washington College of Law, The American University, 4400 Massachusetts Ave., NW, Washington, DC 20016
The American University Law Review. $30. q (ISSN 0003-1453) Washington College of Law, American University, 4400 Massachusetts Ave., NW, Washington, DC 20016
The Anglo-American Law Review. £70. q (ISSN 0308-6569) Barry Rose Law Periodicals Ltd., Little London, Chichester, West Sussex, PO19 1PG England
Annals of Air and Space Law. $31.50. ann (ISSN 0701-158X) Institute and Centre of Air and Space Law, McGill University, 3690 Peel St., Montreal, Que. H3A 1W9, Canada
Annuaire canadien de droit international. See The Canadian Yearbook of International Law
Annual Conference on Intellectual Property. ann Albany Law School of Union University, 80 New Scotland Ave., Albany, NY 12208
Annual Review of Banking Law. $64. ann (ISSN 0739-2451) Warren, Gorham & Lamont, Inc., 210 South St., Boston, MA 02111

serve as the authoritative text of the decision. Any cases on point appearing in an official report must be cited in briefs or research memoranda.

A few of the states, including New York and California, publish more than one official state reporter. These states usually have a large volume of litigation and require greater reporter coverage. For example, New York publishes three official reporters: the *New York Reports* (providing coverage of the Court of Appeals—that state's highest court), the *Appellate Division Reports* (covering decisions of the Appellate Division of the Supreme Court—the latter is the name of a trial court in New York), and *Miscellaneous Decisions,* offering coverage of selected lower court decisions. In addition to this extensive state coverage, West Publishing Company publishes the *New York Supplement* series, which combines the cases from all three official publications.

West's National Reporter System. Additionally, state court opinions appear in regional units of the *National Reporter System,* published by West Publishing Company. Most libraries have the West reporters because they report cases more quickly and are distributed more widely than the state-published reports. In fact, many states have eliminated their own reporters in favor of West's National Reporter System.

The National Reporter System divides the states into the following geographical areas: *Atlantic* (A. or A.2d), *South Eastern* (S.E. or S.E.2d), *South Western* (S.W. or S.W.2d), *North Western* (N.W. or N.W.2d), *North Eastern* (N.E. or N.E.2d), *Southern* (So. or So.2d), and *Pacific* (P. or P.2d). Note that the *2d* in the preceding abbreviations refers to *Second Series.* The states included in each of these regional divisions are indicated in Exhibit 17.19 on the next page, which illustrates West's National Reporter System.

Citation Format. After an appellate decision has been published, it is normally referred to *(cited)* by the name of the case (often called the *style* of the case) and the volume number, abbreviated name, and page number of each reporter in which the case has been published. This information is included in what is called the **citation**. When more than one reporter contains the text of the same case, a reference to the other reporter or reporters in which the case can be found—called a **parallel citation**—is also included. The first citation will be to the state's official reporter (if different from West's National Reporter System). Note that in every citation to a reporter, the number preceding the abbreviated name of the reporter will be the volume number, and the first number following it will be the page number of the first page of the case.

CITATION
In case law, a reference to the volume number, name, and page number of the reporter in which a case can be found. In statutory and administrative law, a reference to the title number, name, and section of the code in which a statute or regulation can be found.

PARALLEL CITATION
A second (or third) citation to another case reporter in which a case has been published. When a case is published in more than one reporter, each citation is a parallel citation to the other(s).

To illustrate how to find case law from citations, suppose that you want to find the following case: *Ward v. K-Mart Corp,* 136 Ill.2d 132, 554 N.E.2d 223 (1990). You can see that the opinion in this case may be found in volume 136 of the official *Illinois Reports, Second Series,* on page 132. The parallel citation is to volume 554 of West's *North Eastern Reporter, Second Series,* page 223. Exhibit 17.20 on pages 674 and 675 further illustrates how to read citations to state court decisions.

When conducting legal research, you need to include in your research notes the citations to the cases or other legal sources that you have consulted, quoted, or want to refer to in a written summary of your research results. Several guides have been published on how to cite legal sources. The most widely used guide is a book entitled *A Uniform System of Citation,* which is published by the Harvard Law Review Association. The Bluebook, as this book is often called (because of its blue cover), explains the proper format for citing cases, statutes, constitutions, regulations, and other legal sources. It is

EXHIBIT 17.19
National Reporter System—Regional and Federal

Regional Reporters	**Coverage Beginning**	**Coverage**
Atlantic Reporter (A. or A.2d)	1885	Connecticut, Delaware, Maine, Maryland, New Hampshire, New Jersey, Pennsylvania, Rhode Island, Vermont, and District of Columbia.
North Eastern Reporter (N.E. or N.E.2d)	1885	Illinois, Indiana, Massachusetts, New York, and Ohio.
North Western Reporter (N.W. or N.W.2d)	1879	Iowa, Michigan, Minnesota, Nebraska, North Dakota, South Dakota, and Wisconsin.
Pacific Reporter (P. or P.2d)	1883	Alaska, Arizona, California, Colorado, Hawaii, Idaho, Kansas, Montana, Nevada, New Mexico, Oklahoma, Oregon, Utah, Washington, and Wyoming.
South Eastern Reporter (S.E. or S.E.2d)	1887	Georgia, North Carolina, South Carolina, Virginia, and West Virginia.
South Western Reporter (S.W. or S.W.2d)	1886	Arkansas, Kentucky, Missouri, Tennessee, and Texas.
Southern Reporter (So. or So.2d)	1887	Alabama, Florida, Louisiana, and Mississippi.
Federal Reporters		
Federal Reporter (F., F.2d, or F. 3d)	1880	U.S. Circuit Court from 1880 to 1912; U.S. Commerce Court from 1911 to 1913; U.S. District Courts from 1880 to 1932; U.S. Court of Claims (now called U.S. Court of Federal Claims) from 1929 to 1932 and since 1960; U.S. Court of Appeals since 1891; U.S. Court of Customs and Patent Appeals since 1929; and U.S. Emergency Court of Appeals since 1943.
Federal Supplement (F.Supp.)	1932	U.S. Court of Claims from 1932 to 1960; U.S. District Courts since 1932; and U.S. Customs Court since 1956.
Federal Rules Decisions (F.R.D.)	1939	U.S. District Courts involving the Federal Rules of Civil Procedure since 1939 and Federal Rules of Criminal Procedure since 1946.
Supreme Court Reporter (S.Ct.)	1882	U.S. Supreme Court since the October term of 1882.
Bankruptcy Reporter (Bankr.)	1980	Bankruptcy decisions of U.S. Bankruptcy Courts, U.S. District Courts, U.S. Courts of Appeals, and U.S. Supreme Court.
Military Justice Reporter (M.J.)	1978	U.S. Court of Military Appeals and Courts of Military Review for the Army, Navy, Air Force, and Coast Guard.

NATIONAL REPORTER SYSTEM MAP

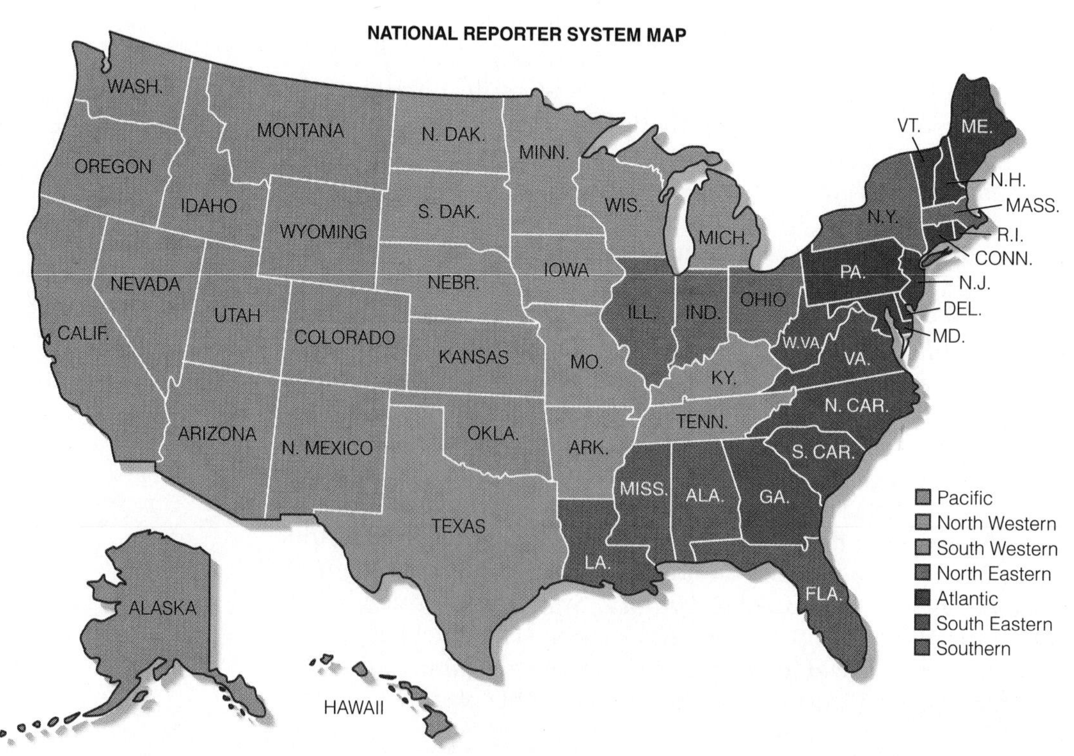

a good idea to memorize the basic format for citations to cases and statutory law because these legal sources are frequently cited in legal writing.[4] Another popular guide is a small booklet entitled *The Unversity of Chicago Manual of Legal Citation,* which is often referred to as the Maroon Book (because of its maroon cover).

Federal Court Decisions

As mentioned earlier, court decisions from the U.S. district courts (federal trial courts) are published in West's *Federal Supplement* (F.Supp.), and opinions from the circuit courts of appeals are reported in West's *Federal Reporter* (F., F.2d, or F.3d). These are both unofficial reporters (there are no official reporters for these courts). Both the *Federal Reporter* and the *Federal Supplement* incorporate decisions from specialized federal courts. West also publishes separate reporters, such as its *Bankruptcy Reporter,* that contain decisions in certain specialized fields under federal law. Sample citations for federal court decisions are also listed and explained in Exhibit 17.20.

United States Supreme Court Decisions

Opinions from the United States Supreme Court are published in several reporters, including the *United States Reports,* West's *Supreme Court Reporter,* and the *Lawyers' Edition of the Supreme Court Reports,* each of which we discuss below.

The *United States Reports.* The *United States Reports* (U.S.) is the official edition of all decisions of the United States Supreme Court for which there are written opinions. Published by the federal government, the series includes reports of Supreme Court cases dating from the August term of 1791. Approximately two to four weeks after the Supreme Court issues a decision, the official slip opinion is published by the U.S. Government Printing Office. The **slip opinion** is the first authoritative text of the opinion and is printed as an individual pamphlet. After a number of slip opinions have been issued, the advance sheets of the official *United States Reports* appear. These are issued in pamphlet form to provide a temporary resource until the official bound volume is finally published.

SLIP OPINION
A judicial opinion published shortly after the decision is made and not yet included in a case reporter or advance sheets.

Virtually all Supreme Court decisions, as well as the text of many treaties and statutes, are now available in electronic format on the Internet. Supreme Court opinions are available on the Internet within minutes after their release. Thus, if you have access to the Internet and want to read the text of a Supreme Court decision made yesterday or even just hours ago, you may be able to view it on your computer screen. (The Internet is discussed in detail in Appendix B.)

4. Because the rules presented in the Bluebook may be difficult to understand, you might want to refer to Alan L. Dworsky, *User's Guide to the Bluebook* (Littleton, Colo.: F. B. Rothman, 1988).

EXHIBIT 17.20
How to Read Case Citations

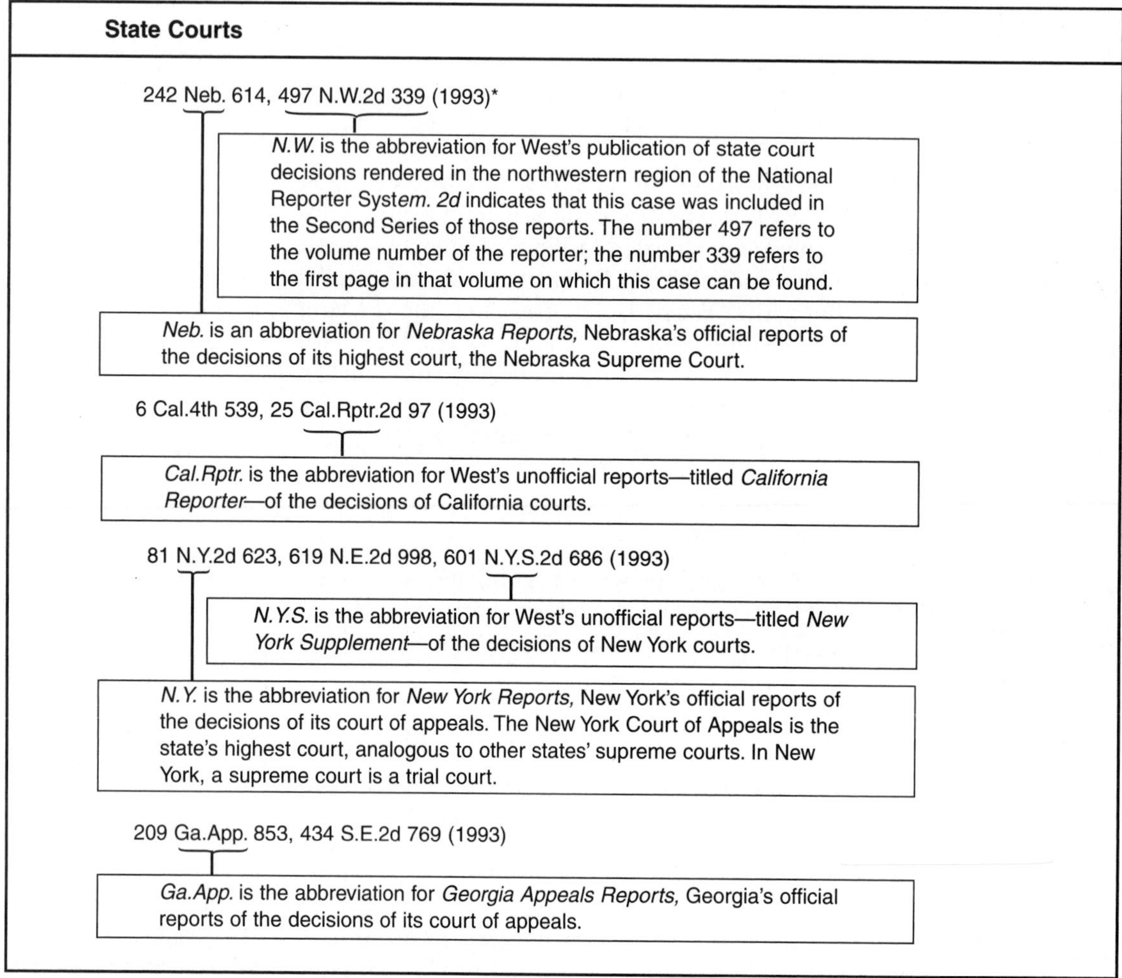

State Courts
242 Neb. 614, 497 N.W.2d 339 (1993)*
N.W. is the abbreviation for West's publication of state court decisions rendered in the northwestern region of the National Reporter System. 2d indicates that this case was included in the Second Series of those reports. The number 497 refers to the volume number of the reporter; the number 339 refers to the first page in that volume on which this case can be found.
Neb. is an abbreviation for Nebraska Reports, Nebraska's official reports of the decisions of its highest court, the Nebraska Supreme Court.
6 Cal.4th 539, 25 Cal.Rptr.2d 97 (1993)
Cal.Rptr. is the abbreviation for West's unofficial reports—titled California Reporter—of the decisions of California courts.
81 N.Y.2d 623, 619 N.E.2d 998, 601 N.Y.S.2d 686 (1993)
N.Y.S. is the abbreviation for West's unofficial reports—titled New York Supplement—of the decisions of New York courts.
N.Y. is the abbreviation for New York Reports, New York's official reports of the decisions of its court of appeals. The New York Court of Appeals is the state's highest court, analogous to other states' supreme courts. In New York, a supreme court is a trial court.
209 Ga.App. 853, 434 S.E.2d 769 (1993)
Ga.App. is the abbreviation for Georgia Appeals Reports, Georgia's official reports of the decisions of its court of appeals.

* The case names have been deleted from these citations to emphasize the publications. It should be kept in mind, however, that the name of a case is as important as the specific page numbers in the volumes in which it is found. If a citation is incorrect, the correct citation may be found in a publication's index of case names. The date of a case is also important because, in addition to providing a check on error in citations, the value of a recent case as an authority is likely to be greater than that of earlier cases.

SYLLABUS
A brief summary of the holding and legal principles involved in a reported case, which is followed by the court's official opinion.

The *Supreme Court Reporter.* Supreme Court cases are also published in West Publishing Company's *Supreme Court Reporter* (S.Ct.). West's *Supreme Court Reporter* is an unofficial edition of Supreme Court opinions dating from the Court's term in October 1882. In this reporter, the case report—the formal court opinion—is preceded by a brief **syllabus** (summary of the case) and headnotes with key numbers (used throughout the West reporters and digests) prepared by West editors.

The *Lawyers' Edition of the Supreme Court Reports.* The Lawyers Cooperative Publishing Company of Rochester, New York, publishes the *Lawyers' Edition of the Supreme Court Reports.* This unofficial edition of

EXHIBIT 17.20
Continued

Federal Courts

___ U.S. ___, 114 S.Ct. 1164, 127 L.Ed.2d 500 (1994)

L.Ed. is an abbreviation for *Lawyers' Edition of the Supreme Court Reports,* an unofficial edition of decisions of the United States Supreme Court.

S.Ct. is the abbreviation for West's unofficial reports—titled *Supreme Court Reporter*—of United States Supreme Court decisions.

U.S. is the abbreviation for *United States Reports,* the official edition of the decisions of the United States Supreme Court. Volume and page numbers are not included in this citation because they have not yet been assigned.

Statutory and Other Citations

15 U.S.C. Section 1262(e)

U.S.C. denotes *United States Code,* the codification of *United States Statutes at Large.* The number 15 refers to the statute's U.S.C. title number and 1262 to its section number within that title. The letter e refers to a subsection within the section.

UCC 2-206(1)(a)

UCC is an abbreviation for *Uniform Commercial Code.* The first number 2 is a reference to an article of the UCC and 206 to a section within that article. The number 1 refers to a subsection within the section and the letter a to a subdivision within the subsection.

Restatement (Second) of Torts, Section 568

Restatement (Second) of Torts refers to the second edition of the American Law Institute's *Restatement of the Law of Torts.* The number 568 refers to a specific section.

16 C.F.R. Section 453.2

C.F.R. is an abbreviation for *Code of Federal Regulations,* a compilation of federal administrative regulations. The number 16 is a reference to the regulation's title number and 453.2 to a specific section within that title.

the entire series of the Supreme Court reports contains many decisions not reported in early official volumes. The advantage offered to the legal researcher by the *Lawyers' Edition* is its research tools. In its second series, it precedes each case report with a full summary of the case and discusses in detail selected cases of special interest to the legal profession. Also, the

DEVELOPING PARALEGAL SKILLS

Understanding Case Citations

Wendy Morgan is a legal secretary studying to become a paralegal. She has just read a chapter in her text on legal research and is studying the section on case citations. She shows a citation to Janet Honner, a legal assistant at the office, and asks Janet to go over the case citation with her. The name of the case is *O'Driscoll v. Hercules, Inc.*, and its citation is 12 F.3d 176 (10th Cir. 1994). Janet tells Wendy that the names in the case title are the names of the parties to the lawsuit. Next is the volume number, which is 12. This number is imprinted on the outside binding of the book, or reporter, in which the case is contained. The name of the reporter is indicated by F.3d, which is the abbreviation for West's *Federal Reporter, Third Series.* The next number, 176, indicates that the case begins on page 176 of volume 12. The information in parentheses shows that the case was decided by the U.S. Court of Appeals for the Tenth Circuit in 1994.

Next, Wendy wants to check her understanding by explaining a citation to Janet. She finds a citation to *Gypsy Moth v. Rose,* 652 F.Supp. 1109 (S.D.N.Y. 1975) and says, "This case appears in volume 652 of the *Federal Supplement* on page 1109. The information in parentheses is the name of the court. I know that this case is from a federal district court because the reporter is the *Federal Supplement,* which is the unofficial reporter for the federal district courts. So the S.D.N.Y. must mean a district in New York. Is it the southern district?" "Yes," responds Janet. Finally, Wendy determines that the case was decided in 1975.

Lawyers' Edition is the only reporter of Supreme Court opinions that provides summaries of the briefs presented by counsel.

Unofficial Loose-leaf Services. Unofficial loose-leaf services publish Supreme Court decisions the day after a decision is announced. Two loose-leaf services cover Supreme Court opinions: *United States Law Week,* which is published by the Bureau of National Affairs, and the *Supreme Court Bulletin,* which is published by the Commerce Clearing House.

RESEARCHING STATUTORY LAW

The case law that we have been discussing up to this point is often referred to as *judge-made law* because it is made by the judges and justices of the American court system. Other primary sources of American law are the statutes and ordinances passed by legislative bodies, such as the U.S. Congress, state legislatures, and town governments. Collectively, the law created by these bodies is referred to as *statutory law.*

Statutes enacted by legislative bodies are generally intended to govern the conduct of a broad group of persons and activities. Some statutes serve to supplement the common law, and other statutes replace it. The legislature has broad power to establish laws, and if a common law principle conflicts with a statutory provision, the statute will normally take precedence. Additionally, the legislature may create statutes that deal with areas not covered by the common law, such as age discrimination in employment, workers' compensation benefits, and other employment-related issues.

The process of enacting a statute is similar at the state and federal levels. The process begins when legislation is proposed and presented to the legislature for debate. The proposed legislation is usually called a *bill.* If the bill is passed, it is sent to the president or governor, who has the authority to sign it into law. Once legislation is signed into law, it is published.

To find the relevant statutory law governing a particular legal issue or area, you will need to know, first of all, the names of the various publications in which statutory law can be found. In this section, we look first at how federal statutes are published and how you can find, within these publications, statutes governing the issue you are researching. A more difficult task in researching statutory law is deciding whether a statute you have found is really applicable to the issue being researched. This determination requires a careful reading of the statute and may require further research. You may need to analyze what the legislature intended when it passed the bill and how the courts have interpreted the statute.

ETHICAL CONCERN

Citing Sources

Before returning a legal source to the library shelf (or signing off a computerized legal research service), you should make sure that you have included in your research notes the proper reference or citation for that authority. If you forget to cite your source, you will have to spend additional time relocating the source once again to obtain the citation. As has been stressed elsewhere, your time is a valuable resource for your attorney and a costly one for your client. If you have to spend another hour's time going to and from a library to obtain a citation that you should have included in your notes in the first place, the client may not consider charges for that hour to be "reasonable"—and attorneys have a duty to charge their clients reasonable fees.

The Publication of Federal Statutes

Federal statutes in the United States are published in three forms. The first official publication of a statute's text is the slip law. **Slip laws** present the text of statutes in the form of pamphlets or single sheets. These pamphlets or sheets are not indexed, but they can be identified by their **public law number**, or P.L. number—a number assigned to each statute upon completion of the legislative process. Slip laws are available through the *United States Code Service (U.S.C.S.)* advance service and the *United States Code Congressional and Administrative News (U.S.C.C.A.N.)* advance service. They are published in pamphlet form by the U.S. Government Depository Library. (The *U.S.C.S.* and the *U.S.C.C.A.N.* will be discussed in greater detail shortly.)

The second form in which statutes are officially published is the session law. **Session laws** are collections of statutes contained in volumes and arranged by the year or legislative session during which they were enacted. Each volume contains an index. The session laws of the U.S. Congress appear in the *United States Statutes at Large,* which is published by the U.S. government. *Statutes at Large* volumes contain the language of the legislation as it appeared at the time of passage. They also include references to the House or Senate bill number, which can be helpful in directing the researcher to legislative sources, such as committee hearings and reports. These sources are valuable to the researcher trying to determine the intended meaning of a particular statute. Each state issues its own official session laws. Some states have both an official and an unofficial version. The titles of the volumes vary by state.

Finally, statutory material is published in compilations referred to as **codes**. Unlike the sources just discussed, codes arrange statutory provisions by topic, thus facilitating legal research. Most statutory codes are updated through the issuance of supplemental pocket parts or by loose-leaf services. Paralegals conducting research on statutory law should begin by reviewing the index provided for the relevant statutory code.

SLIP LAW
The first official publication of a statute that comes out shortly after the legislation is passed (presented as a single sheet or pamphlet).

PUBLIC LAW NUMBER
An identification number that has been assigned to a specific statute, or public law, following the legislative process.

SESSION LAW
A law passed by legislators and officially published chronologically by order of legislative session in a multivolume set.

CODE
A systematic and logical presentation of laws, rules, or regulations.

The *United States Code*

The *United States Code,* or *U.S.C.,* is published by the U.S. government every six years and is updated annually. The *U.S.C.* is divided into fifty topic classifications. As shown in Exhibit 17.21, each of these topics, called *titles* of the code, carries a descriptive title and a number. For example, laws relating to commerce and trade are collected in Title 15. Laws concerning the courts or judicial procedures are collected in Title 28. Titles are subdivided into chapters (sections) and subchapters. A citation to the U.S.C. includes title and section numbers. Thus, a reference to "28 U.S.C. Section 1346" means that the statute can be found in Section 1346 of Title 28. "Section" may also be designated by the symbol §, and "Sections" by §§.

EXHIBIT 17.21
Titles in the *United States Code*

TITLES OF UNITED STATES CODE

*1. General Provisions.
2. The Congress.
*3. The President.
*4. Flag and Seal, Seat of Government, and the States.
*5. Government Organization and Employees; and Appendix.
†6. [Surety Bonds.]
7. Agriculture.
8. Aliens and Nationality.
*9. Arbitration.
*10. Armed Forces; and Appendix.
*11. Bankruptcy; and Appendix.
12. Banks and Banking.
*13. Census.
*14. Coast Guard.
15. Commerce and Trade.
16. Conservation.
*17. Copyrights.
*18. Crimes and Criminal Procedure; and Appendix.
19. Customs Duties.
20. Education.
21. Food and Drugs.
22. Foreign Relations and Intercourse.
*23. Highways.
24. Hospitals and Asylums.
25. Indians.
26. Internal Revenue Code.
27. Intoxicating Liquors.
*28. Judiciary and Judicial Procedure; and Appendix.
29. Labor.
30. Mineral Lands and Mining.
*31. Money and Finance.
*32. National Guard.
33. Navigation and Navigable Waters.
‡34. [Navy.]
*35. Patents.
36. Patriotic Societies and Observances.
*37. Pay and Allowances of the Uniformed Services.
*38. Veterans' Benefits.
*39. Postal Service.
40. Public Buildings, Property, and Works.
41. Public Contracts.
42. The Public Health and Welfare.
43. Public Lands.
*44. Public Printing and Documents.
45. Railroads.
*46. Shipping; and Appendix.
47. Telegraphs, Telephones, and Radiotelegraphs.
48. Territories and Insular Possessions.
*49. Transportation; and Appendix.
50. War and National Defense; and Appendix.

*This title has been enacted as law. However, any Appendix to this title has not been enacted as law.
†This title was enacted as law and has been repealed by the enactment of Title 31.
‡This title has been eliminated by the enactment of Title 10.

Page III

One approach to finding statutory law in the *U.S.C.* is simply to refer to the title descriptions listed in the front of each volume. This approach is most beneficial for researchers who can quickly find the applicable title for the statute they are researching. Alternatively, the researcher can consult the index to the *U.S.C.* The index provides an alphabetical listing of all federal statutes by subject matter and by the name of the act. The researcher should consider the various ways in which the statute could be listed and then review the index for the appropriate description. The more descriptive words the researcher can think of, the more likely it is that he or she will be able to locate a particular statute. The index provides the exact location of the statute, by title and section.

Sometimes a researcher may know the popular name of a legislative act but not its official name. In this situation, the researcher can consult the *U.S.C.* volume entitled *Popular Name Table,* which lists statutes by their popular names. Many legislative bills enacted into law are commonly known by a popular name. Some have descriptive titles reflecting their purpose; others are named after their sponsors. The Labor-Management Reporting and Disclosure Act of 1959, for example, is also known as the Landrum-Griffin Act. Searching by popular name will allow the researcher to find the title and section of the statute and therefore locate the statute in the *U.S.C.*

The *U.S.C.* also lists, after the text of the statute, citations to the *United States Statutes at Large.* These citations are helpful for paralegals who wish to examine previous versions of the statute in the *Statutes at Large.*

Unofficial Versions of the Federal Code

There are two unofficial versions of the federal code that are similar to the *U.S.C.*, but they contain some important differences. They provide annotations describing cases and other sources that have applied or interpreted a given statute. Additionally, they contain more cross-references to related sections of the code than does the *U.S.C.* These two unofficial federal codes are discussed below.

The *United States Code Annotated.* One of the unofficial versions of the *U.S.C.* is the *United States Code Annotated (U.S.C.A.),* published by West Publishing Company. The *U.S.C.A.* contains the full text of the *U.S.C.*, the U.S. Constitution, the Federal Rules of Evidence, and various other rules, including the Rules of Civil Procedure and the Rules of Criminal Procedure. This useful set of approximately two hundred volumes offers historical notes relating to the text of each statute and any amendments to the act. As shown in Exhibit 17.22 on the next page, cross-references to other titles and sections within the *U.S.C.A.* are also given. Annotations, referred to as "Notes of Decisions," offer additional research assistance by listing cases that have analyzed, discussed, or interpreted the particular statute.

The *U.S.C.A.* is more current than the *U.S.C.* The supplements updating the *U.S.C.* often lag behind current statutory law by more than a year (or sometimes, two years), whereas the *U.S.C.A.* provides updated statutory information through supplemental pocket parts and pamphlets many times a year.

EXHIBIT 17.22
Excerpt from the *United States Code Annotated*

Ch. 11 PEACETIME DISABILITY 38 § 1131

CROSS REFERENCES

Rates of peacetime death compensation same as specified under this section, see 38 USCA § 1142.

LIBRARY REFERENCES

American Digest System
Veterans' benefits; rights and disabilities in general, see Armed Services ⇐101.
Encyclopedias
Veterans' benefits; compensation for dependents and survivors, see C.J.S. Armed Services § 254.
Veterans' benefits; general considerations, see C.J.S. Armed Services § 251.
Veterans' benefits; payment of benefits, see C.J.S. Armed Services § 265.
Law Reviews
Making intramilitary tort law more civil: A proposed reform of the Feres Doctrine. David Schwartz, 95 Yale L.J. 992 (1986).

WESTLAW ELECTRONIC RESEARCH

Armed services cases: 34k[add key number].
See, also, WESTLAW guide following the Explanation pages of this volume.

NOTES OF DECISIONS

Death of claimant 1
Withdrawal of claim 2

1. Death of claimant
Where the widow filed a claim but died before decision was made in her favor, awards were made as if there had been no surviving widow. 1943, A.D.V.A. 524.

2. Withdrawal of claim
Where the stepfather's claim for death compensation had not yet been favorably considered, a withdrawal of his claim had the effect of entitling the mother to be considered as the only person who had established a right to the benefit under former § 472b of this title, and she was accordingly entitled to the $45 rate therein provided for one parent. 1940, A.D.V.A. 458.

SUBCHAPTER IV—PEACETIME DISABILITY COMPENSATION

CROSS REFERENCES

Amounts payable under this subchapter exempt from tax levy, see 26 USCA § 6334.

§ 1131. Basic entitlement

For disability resulting from personal injury suffered or disease contracted in line of duty, or for aggravation of a preexisting injury suffered or disease contracted in line of duty, in the active military, naval, or air service, during other than a period of war, the United States will pay to any veteran thus disabled and who was discharged or released under conditions other than dishonorable from the period of service in which said injury or disease was incurred, or preexisting injury or disease was aggravated, compensation as provided in this subchapter, but no compensation shall be paid if

237

38 § 1131 DISABILITY, ETC., COMPENSATION Ch. 11

the disability is a result of the veteran's own willful misconduct or abuse of alcohol or drugs.

(Pub.L. 85–857, Sept. 2, 1958, 72 Stat. 1122, § 331; Pub.L. 101–508, Title VIII, § 8052(a)(3), Nov. 5, 1990, 104 Stat. 1388–351; renumbered Pub.L. 102–83, § 5(a), Aug. 6, 1991, 105 Stat. 406.)

HISTORICAL AND STATUTORY NOTES

Revision Notes and Legislative Reports
1958 Act. Senate Report No. 2259 and House Report No. 1298, see 1958 U.S. Code Cong. and Adm.News, p. 4352.
1990 Act. House Report No. 101–881 and House Conference Report No. 101–964, see 1990 U.S.Code Cong. and Adm.News, p. 2017.

Amendments
1990 Amendment. Pub.L. 101–508 substituted "a result of the veteran's own willful misconduct or abuse of alcohol or drugs" for "the result of the veteran's own willful misconduct".

Effective Dates
1990 Act. Amendment by Pub.L. 101–508 effective with respect to claims filed after Oct. 31, 1990, see section 8052(b) of Pub.L. 101–508, set out as a note under section 105 of this title.

LIBRARY REFERENCES

American Digest System
Veterans' benefits; compensation for disability, see Armed Services ⇐104.
Veterans' benefits; rights and benefits in general, see Armed Services ⇐101.
Encyclopedias
Veterans' benefits; disability compensation, see C.J.S. Armed Services § 255.
Veterans' benefits; general considerations, see C.J.S. Armed Services § 251.
Law Reviews
Federal Tort Claims Act—Feres Doctrine. (1985) 24 Duquesne L.Rev. 309.

WESTLAW ELECTRONIC RESEARCH

Armed services cases: 34k[add key number].
See, also, WESTLAW guide following the Explanation pages of this volume.

NOTES OF DECISIONS

Action against government contractor 4
Civilian 2
Indemnity 3
Law governing 1

1. Law governing
The Veterans' Benefits Act did not preempt Navy enlisted man's action under state law against private corporation which operated government-owned nuclear reactor facility, to recover for injuries sustained while enlisted man was on duty and a deck on which he was standing collapsed, despite provision in contract between corporation and the Government that Government would reimburse corporation for all judgments incurred in connection with the contract; such clause apparently was added by the parties without specific statutory or regulatory direction and, even if indemnification would frustrate the Act, preemption would operate against corporation's indemnity claim and not against the enlisted man's claim against the corporation. Chapman v. Westinghouse Elec. Corp., C.A.9 (Idaho) 1990, 911 F.2d 267.

2. Civilian
A civilian is ineligible under this section for any injuries resulting from improper activation into military service. Valn v. U.S., C.A.Del.1983, 708 F.2d 116.

3. Indemnity
Where this chapter is present, it is sole or exclusive remedy for claims which involve service-related injuries, irrespective of who sues United States; thus, in a case growing out of service-connected injury, there cannot be a recovery of indemnity for payments to serviceman

238

Locating statutory law in the *U.S.C.A.* is similar to locating statutes in the *U.S.C.* Researchers can use the topical or index approach and, if necessary, look through the *Popular Name Table.*

The *United States Code Service.* The second unofficial version of the federal code is the *United States Code Service (U.S.C.S.),* published by the Lawyers Cooperative Publishing Company. The *U.S.C.S.* offers some of the same features offered by the *U.S.C.A.,* such as annotations. The *U.S.C.S.* and the *U.S.C.A.* are distinguishable by the research tools they provide. The research section of the *U.S.C.S.* provides references and citations to some sources that are not contained in the *U.S.C.A.*, including non-West publications such as *American Law Reports*, legal periodicals, and *American Jurisprudence.*

Like the *U.S.C.A.*, the *U.S.C.S.* offers an effective updating service in the form of replacement volumes and pocket parts. The *U.S.C.S.* issues softbound updated volumes called *Cumulative Later Case and Statutory Service*, which compile cases—including annotations—that have been published since the last printed pocket-part supplement. Another *U.S.C.S.* updating service is the advance service, a monthly compilation of slip laws and other legislative decrees.

Paralegals can begin statutory research in the *U.S.C.S.* by reviewing the *Subject Index* or the *Popular Name Table.* Both annotated codes also have conversion charts listing all public acts by public law number, *Statutes at Large* references, and *U.S.C.* title and section numbers.

Interpreting Statutory Law

Paralegals should understand that often the key to successful statutory research is determining whether a statute is applicable to the legal issue being researched. This can prove to be a difficult task. In your analysis of a statute's applicability to a research problem, it is crucial that you read the language of the statute carefully. As will be discussed in the next chapter, there are several approaches to interpreting statutory law. One approach involves researching case law on the subject and determining how other courts—in particular, higher courts within your jurisdiction, whose decisions create binding precedents—have interpreted a given statute. Another approach, which we discuss below, involves determining what the legislature intended when it enacted the statute.

Researching Legislative History

Prior to the enactment of any statute, the U.S. Congress or a state legislature analyzes carefully the wording and the implications of the statute. Federal statutes pass through committees in both the House of Representatives and the Senate before being voted on by the legislature and signed by the president. The statutes may be debated extensively on the floor of each chamber of Congress, and a congressional hearing may be held to clarify certain issues relating to the proposed law. Committee reports and transcripts of congressional debates and hearings can shed much light on why the statute was passed, why it was worded in a certain way, what the goals of the act were, and so on. These sources are described in fuller detail below.

Before you can study these sources, however, you need to know how to find them. The easiest way to locate them is to refer to the unofficial, annotated versions of the federal code, such as the *U.S.C.A.* and the *U.S.C.S.* These codes often contain information regarding the legislative history of a statute. For example, the statute's public law number and date of passage is included in these annotated codes, as are cross-references to sources that will provide you with more detailed information on a statute's legislative history. Each source that you discover will likely lead you to other useful sources.

DEVELOPING PARALEGAL SKILLS

Researching the *U.S.C.A.*

Natalie Martin has completed her factual analysis of the case involving Bernie Berriman (see the *Developing Paralegal Skills* feature entitled "Defining the Issues to Be Researched") and begins her research. The issue she is researching is whether the government, which arrested Bernie for the transportation and distribution of cocaine, had the authority to confiscate Bernie's car and car phone. Natalie's supervising attorney has told her to start her research by looking at the relevant federal statutes.

USING *U.S.C.A.* INDEXES

Natalie goes to the firm's library and selects the general index to the *United States Code Annotated (U.S.C.A.)*. The general index is the best place to start, unless the specific *U.S.C.A.* title (topic) is known. (If the specific *U.S.C.A.* title is known, then the research should begin in the title index, which is a detailed index in the volume where the title appears.) Natalie decides that she could look under several topics in the general index, including *drugs, controlled substances, distribution of controlled substances,* and *forfeiture.* She selects the topic "Drugs" and removes from the shelf the general index volume labeled "Di–F." She turns to "Drugs" and finds several entries under that general heading. She scans the column until she comes to the entry "Fines, penalties, and forfeitures." Below that subtopic is another subtopic, "Property subject to forfeiture to U.S." Still another subtopic under that entry is "Enumeration, 21 sec. 881." Natalie concludes that the term *enumerated* must mean *listed.* Therefore, the entry must mean that the property subject to forfeiture is listed in Section 881 of Title 21. Natalie copies down the citation.

She continues to peruse the pages under the topic "Drugs" until she comes to the subtopic "Process." Under that subtopic is another subtopic, "Forfeiture, property subject to, issuance, 21 sec. 881." "This is the same citation I just found," Natalie says to herself. Continuing to scan the columns, Natalie comes to the subtopic "Vehicle" and notices under this entry the subtopic "Used for illegal conveyance of controlled substances, 21 sec. 881." The same section again. Natalie decides to take a look at it.

Natalie returns the index to the shelf and takes down the volume containing "Title 21—Food and Drugs." She opens it up to Section 881 and reads through the section. It says that vehicles are subject to forfeiture if they are used or intended to be used to transport controlled substances. "That gives

Committee Reports. Committee reports provide the most important source of legislative history. Congressional committees produce reports for each bill, and these reports often contain the full text of the bill, a description of its purpose, and the committee's recommendations. Several tables are also included to set out dates for certain actions. The dates can help the researcher locate floor debates and committee testimony in the *Congressional Record* (described below) and various other publications. Committee reports are published according to a numerical series and are available through the U.S. Government Printing Office.

DEVELOPING PARALEGAL SKILLS, Continued

the prosecutor the right to confiscate the car," thinks Natalie. "I had better check the pocket part to see if this statute has been amended, though." She finds that the relevant part of the statute that she was reading has not been changed. She makes a note to check on the statute using the firm's legal-research service. The computer database will include recent modifications to the law that might not yet be available in printed research materials.

FINDING RELEVANT CASE LAW

So the government has the authority to confiscate the car, but what about the car phone? She turns several pages until she comes to the case annotations following Section 881. She does not find any annotations in the main volume, so she turns to the pocket part. There she finds a case entitled *U.S. v. One 1978 Mercedes Benz,* 711 F.2d 1297 (5th Cir. 1983). The annotation states as follows:

> Although automobile was properly forfeited to government on basis of its use in violation of drug control laws, automobile telephone attached to automobile, which was easily removable, had identity and use separate from automobile, and was separately insured, was not subject to forfeiture with automobile itself, especially where there was no evidence that the telephone was used in furtherance of the underlying crime.

"Well," thinks Natalie, "this case verifies that a car may be properly forfeited to the government, but it limits the forfeiture of the car phone to very specific circumstances. The government is not permitted to confiscate the car phone if the car phone is easily removable, is separately insured, and has not been shown to have been used in furtherance of the crime. I'll have to go back to the file and find out if there are any more facts regarding Bernie's car phone. If the file doesn't contain the information, I'll have to go to the impoundment lot and take a look at it."

Natalie takes the case reporter—the *Federal Reporter, Second Series*—from the shelf and locates the case. She makes a copy of it to read closely later, to see if there are any additional factors that were not contained in the annotation but that could affect the interpretation of the rule regarding car phones. She also makes a note to verify the recent history of this case by using the firm's computerized legal-research service, just to make sure that the case hasn't been recently reversed or modified by a subsequent court decision. She then returns to the office to continue her factual research.

The *Congressional Record.* The *Congressional Record,* which is published daily while Congress is in session, contains *verbatim* (word-for-word) transcripts of congressional debates and proceedings. The transcripts include remarks made by various members of Congress, proposed amendments, votes, and occasionally the text of the bill under discussion.

Legislative hearings, another important source of legislative research, can be found in the transcripts of testimony before the House and Senate committees considering the proposed legislation. The purpose of conducting hearings is to determine if such legislation is needed. As a result, many types

EXHIBIT 17.23
United States Code Congressional and Administrative News

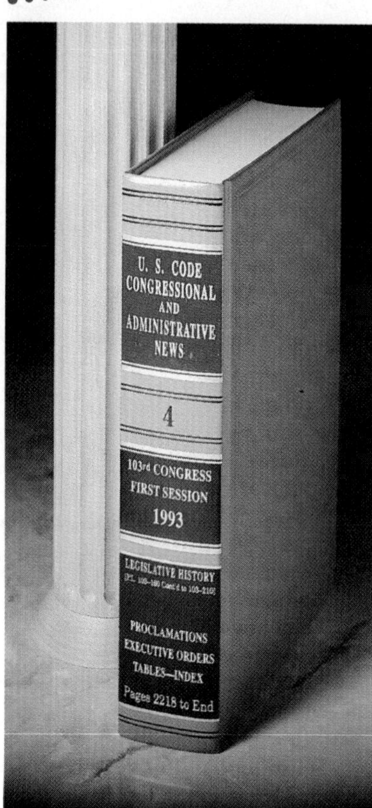

of testimony are presented. The researcher may find some helpful testimony in these sources, yet it is important to remember that much of it may be biased, because of the interested positions of the parties presenting the information. Hearings may be informative but are not as authoritative as committee reports in determining legislative intent.

Other Sources of Legislative History. The two tools most frequently used in conducting research on legislative history are the *United States Code Congressional and Administrative News (U.S.C.C.A.N.)* and the *Congressional Information Service (C.I.S.)*. The *U.S.C.C.A.N.*, a West publication shown in Exhibit 17.23, contains reprints of statutes as published in the *Statutes at Large* and sections describing the statutes' legislative history, including committee reports. Statutes in the *U.S.C.A.* are followed by notations directing the researcher to the corresponding legislative history in the *U.S.C.C.A.N.* The *C.I.S.*, a U.S. government publication, contains information from committee reports, hearing reports, documents from both houses, and special publications. Both the *C.I.S.* and the *U.S.C.C.A.N.* provide a system of indexing and abstracting that allows quick access to information.

State Codes

State codes follow the *U.S.C.* pattern of arranging statutes by subject. They may be called codes, revisions, compilations, consolidations, general statutes, or statutes, depending on the preference of the states. In some codes, subjects are designated by number. In others, they are designated by name. For example, "13 Pennsylvania Consolidated Statutes Section 1101" means that the statute can be found in Section 1101 of Title 13 of the Pennsylvania code. "California Commercial Code Section 1101" means that the statute can be found in Section 1101 under the heading "Commercial" in the California Code. Abbreviations may be used. For example, "13 Pennsylvania Consolidated Statutes Section 1101" may be abbreviated to "13 Pa.C.S. § 1101," and "California Commercial Code Section 1101" may be abbreviated to "Cal. Com. Code § 1101."

In many states, official codes are supplemented by annotated codes published by private publishers. Annotated codes follow the numbering scheme set forth in the official state code but provide outlines and indexes to assist in locating information. These codes also provide references to case law, legislative history sources, and other documents in which the statute has been considered or discussed. Like their federal counterparts, the annotated codes at the state level are kept current with pocket parts and other supplementary materials.

RESEARCHING ADMINISTRATIVE LAW

Administrative rules and regulations constitute a growing source of American law. As discussed in Chapter 13, Congress frequently delegates authority to administrative agencies through enabling legislation. For example, in 1914, Congress passed the Federal Trade Commission Act, which established the Federal Trade Commission, or FTC. The act gave the FTC the authority to issue and enforce rules and regulations relating to unfair trade practices in the United States. Other federal administrative agencies include the Occupational Safety and Health Administration, the Consumer Product Safety Commission, and the Securities and Exchange Commission. The orders, regulations, and decisions of such agencies are legally binding and, as such, are primary sources of law.

EXHIBIT 17.24
Code of Federal Regulations

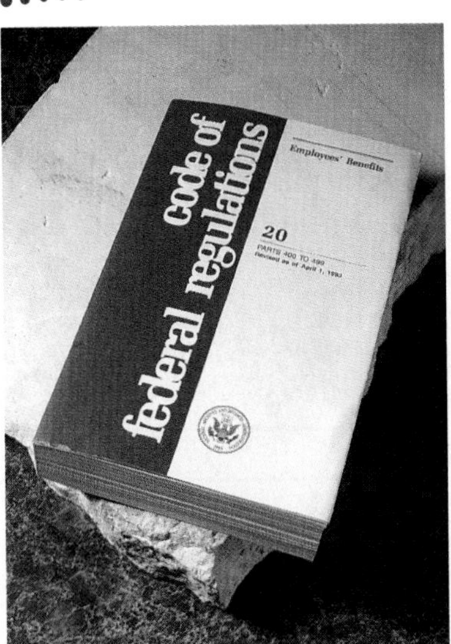

The *Code of Federal Regulations*

The *Code of Federal Regulations (C.F.R.)* is a government publication containing all federal administrative agency regulations (see Exhibit 17.24). The regulations are compiled from the *Federal Register*, a daily government publication consisting of executive orders and administrative regulations and in which administrative regulations are first published. (See Chapter 13 for a discussion of administrative rule-making procedure and a sample page from the *Federal Register.*)

The *C.F.R.* uses the same titles as the *United States Code* (shown previously in Exhibit 17.21). This subject matter organization allows the researcher to determine the section in the *C.F.R.* in which a regulation will appear. Each title of the *C.F.R.* is divided into chapters, subchapters, parts, and sections. Exhibit 17.25 on the next page shows some pages from *C.F.R.* Title 20 (Chapter III, Part 416) that relate to the Social Security Administration. (In the hypothetical scenario presented in Chapter 13, the paralegal, Calvin Novak, relied on these provisions as the basis of his client's disability claim.)

Publication of the *C.F.R.*

The *C.F.R.* is revised and republished four times a year. Recent regulations appear in the *Federal Register* until they are later incorporated into the *C.F.R.* If, as a paralegal, you are searching for administrative regulations in the *C.F.R.*, you should begin with the index section of the *Index and Finding Aids* volume. This index will allow you to locate the relevant title and the section of the *C.F.R.* that pertains to the problem. The next step is locating the regulation in the most recent volume of that title in the *C.F.R.* You should also review the *List of C.F.R. Sections Affected*, issued in monthly pamphlets, to determine if any changes have been made to the section since the last revision. A page from this publication is shown in Exhibit 17.26 on page 687. You can find updates to these monthly pamphlets by looking at the *Federal Register*'s cumulative publication, *List of C.F.R. Parts Affected*, which reflects changes made during the current month.

Finding Tools for Administrative Law

The *Congressional Information Service (C.I.S.)* also provides an index to the *C.F.R.* The *C.I.S.* index is helpful in locating *C.F.R.* regulations by subject matter and also in determining the geographical areas affected by the regulation. The *American Digest System* can be of additional help to the paralegal, because it provides coverage of court cases dealing with administrative questions. The digests, however, do not contain any agency rulings. Additionally, certain loose-leaf services provide administrative decisions for

EXHIBIT 17.25
Subdivisions of Titles and Provisions from the *Code of Federal Regulations*

CHAPTER III—SOCIAL SECURITY ADMINISTRATION, DEPARTMENT OF HEALTH AND HUMAN SERVICES

rity Administration, HHS

the Secretary of Labor. If nt, upon notification by the urity Administration of his right to review (see)) requests that the claim filed with the Social Security tration be forwarded to the Workers' Compensation Program review, or if more than one been filed with the Secretary of Labor by the same claimant, s shall be merged and processed with the first claim filed with the Office of Workers' Compensation

Security Administration of entitle- BLBRA of entitlement ty Administration G is binding Compensation determina-

ls. termination ty Administration his subpart of Workers' f the Social oes not ap- its review aim will be f Worker's and the nsation Program review the rkers' Compensation provide an aimant to ce if it is claim. See part. If the tration applicant dis- e Social Security determination, e Office of Programs to Administra- e § 410.704

Pt. 416

PART 416—SUPPLEMENTAL SECURITY INCOME FOR THE AGED, BLIND, AND DISABLED

Subpart A—Introduction, General Provisions and Definitions

Social Security Administration, HHS **§ 416.204**

Public institution means an institution that is operated by or controlled by the Federal government, a State, or a political subdivision of a State such as a city or county. The term *public institution* does not include a publicly operated community residence which serves 16 or fewer residents.

Resident of a public institution means a person who can receive substantially all of his or her food and shelter while living in a public institution. The person need not be receiving treatment and services available in the institution and is a resident regardless of whether the resident or anyone else pays for all food, shelter, and other services in the institution. A person is not a resident of a public institution if he or she is living in a public educational institution for the primary purpose of receiving educational or vocational training as defined in this section. A *resident* of a public institution means the same thing as an *inmate* of a public institution as used in section 1611(e)(1)(A) of the Social Security Act. (See § 416.211(b), (c), and (d) of this subpart for exceptions to the general limitation on the eligibility for Supplemental Security Income benefits of individuals who are residents of a public institution.)

SSI means supplemental security income.

State assistance means payments made by a State to an aged, blind, or disabled person under a State plan approved under title I, X, XIV, or XVI (AABD) of the Social Security Act which was in effect before the SSI Program.

We or *Us* means the Social Security Administration.

You or *Your* means the person who applies for or receives SSI benefits or the person for whom an application is filed.

[47 FR 3103, Jan. 22, 1982, as amended at 49 FR 19639, May 19, 1984; 50 FR 48570, Nov. 26, 1985; 50 FR 51517, Dec. 18, 1985; 54 FR 19164, May 4, 1989]

§ 416.202 Who may get SSI benefits.

You are eligible for SSI benefits if you meet all of the following requirements:

(a) You are—

(1) Aged 65 or older (subpart H);

(2) Blind (subpart I); or

(3) Disabled (subpart I).

(b) You are a resident of the United States (§ 416.1603), and—

(1) A citizen or a national of the United States (§ 416.1610);

(2) An alien lawfully admitted for permanent residence in the United States (§ 416.1615);

(3) An alien permanently residing in the United States under color of law (§ 416.1618); or

(4) A child of armed forces personnel living overseas as described in § 416.215.

(c) You do not have more income than is permitted (subparts K and D).

(d) You do not have more resources than are permitted (subpart L).

(e) You file an application for SSI benefits (subpart C).

[47 FR 3103, Jan. 22, 1982, as amended at 58 FR 4897, Jan. 19, 1993]

§ 416.203 Initial determinations of SSI eligibility.

(a) *What happens when you apply for SSI benefits.* When you apply for SSI benefits we will ask you for documents and any other information we need to make sure you meet all the requirements. We will ask for information about your income and resources and about other eligibility requirements and you must answer completely. We will help you get any documents you need but do not have.

(b) *How we determine your eligibility for SSI benefits.* We determine that you are eligible for SSI benefits for a given month if you meet the requirements in § 416.202 in that month. However, we usually determine the amount of your SSI benefits for that month based on your income in an earlier month (see § 416.420). Thus, it is possible for you to meet the eligibility requirements in the given month but receive no benefit payment for that month.

[47 FR 3103, Jan. 22, 1982, as amended at 50 FR 48570, Nov. 26, 1985]

§ 416.204 Redeterminations of SSI eligibility.

(a) *Redeterminations defined.* A redetermination is a review of your eligibility to make sure that you are still

EXHIBIT 17.26
A Page from the *List of C.F.R. Sections Affected*

List of CFR Sections Affected

All changes in this volume of the Code of Federal Regulations which were made by documents published in the FEDERAL REGISTER since January 1, 1986, are enumerated in the following list. Entries indicate the nature of the changes effected. Page numbers refer to FEDERAL REGISTER pages. The user should consult the entries for chapters and parts as well as sections for revisions.

For the period before January 1, 1986, see the "List of CFR Sections Affected, 1949-1963, 1964-1972, and 1973-1985" published in seven separate volumes.

1986

20 CFR 51 FR Page

Chapter III
404 Technical correction... 5989, 15883
SSA representation project........21156
404.1—404.3 (Subpart A) Heading and authority citation revised..........11718
404.1 Introductory text, (c), (j), (l), (p), and (q) revised; (r) through (v) added..........11718
404.2 (a) introductory text, (a)(1), (b) introductory text, and (b)(1) revised; (a) (2) through (13) and (b)(3) removed; (a) (14) through (19) and (b) (4) and (5) redesignated as (a) (2) through (7) and (b) (3) and (4); new (b) (3) and (4) revised.......... 11718
404.3 (c) amended.......... 11718
404.201—404.290 (Subpart C) Authority citation revised...4482, 12603
404.211 (d)(1) revised; (d)(4) added.......... 4482
404.212 (b)(1) amended; authority citation removed.......... 4482
404.270 Amended.......... 12603
404.271 (a) and (c) amended.......... 12603
404.272 Revised.......... 12603
404.273 Revised.......... 12603
404.274 Revised.......... 12603
404.275 Revised; authority citation removed.......... 12604
404.277 (b) nomenclature change.......... 12604
404.278 Added.......... 12604

20 CFR—Continued 51 FR Page

Chapter III—Continued
404.301—404.395 (Subpart D) Authority citation revised...4482, 10615, 12603, 17617
404.310 (b) amended.......... 10616
404.312 (b) amended.......... 12604
404.313 Added.......... 12605
404.315 (c) amended.......... 10616, 16166
404.316 (c)(1)(iv) and (v) removed; (c)(1)(vi) redesignated as (c)(1)(iv); (c)(1)(iii) amended; new (c)(1)(iv) *Example* revised; interim.......... 17617
404.320 (b)(1) amended.......... 10616
404.331 Introductory text revised; (f) added; authority citation removed.......... 11911
404.332 (a) and (b)(3) revised; (b)(8) added; authority citation removed.......... 11911
404.333 Revised.......... 11912
404.335 (e) revised; authority citation removed.......... 4482
(a)(2)(ii) and (c) amended.......... 10616
404.336 (e) revised; authority citation removed.......... 4482
404.337 (b)(1) removed; (b)(2), (3), (4), and (5) redesignated as (b)(1), (2), (3), and (4).......... 4482
(c)(1)(iv) and (v) removed; (c)(1)(vi) redesignated as (c)(1)(iv); (c)(1)(iii) amended; interim.......... 17617
404.338 Amended.......... 4482
404.352 (c)(1)(iv) and (v) removed; (c)(1)(vi) redesignated as (c)(1)(iv); (c)(1)(iii) amended; interim.......... 17617

925

particular specialty fields, such as taxation. If available, they are a useful research tool.

Whenever you need to research administrative law, remember that the most efficient way to find what you are looking for may be simply to call the agency and ask agency personnel how to access information relevant to your research topic.

FINDING CONSTITUTIONAL LAW

The federal government and all fifty states have their own constitutions describing the powers, responsibilities, and limitations of the various branches of government. Constitutions can be replaced or amended, and it is important that researchers have access to both current versions and older ones.

The text of the U.S. Constitution can be found in a number of publications. A useful source of federal constitutional law is *The Constitution of the United States of America*, published under the authority of the U.S. Senate and available through the Library of Congress. It includes the full text of the U.S. Constitution, corresponding United States Supreme Court annotations, and a discussion of each provision, including background information on its history and interpretation. Additional constitutional sources are found in the *U.S.C.A.* and the *U.S.C.S.*, both of which contain the entire text of the Constitution and its amendments as well as citations to cases discussing particular constitutional provisions. Annotated state codes provide a similar service for their state constitutions. Constitutional annotations are updated through supplementary pocket parts. State constitutions are usually included in the publications containing state statutes.

UPDATING THE LAW—LEARNING TO USE CITATORS

Almost every day, new court decisions are made, new regulations are issued, and new statutes are enacted or existing statutes amended. Because the law is ever changing, a critical factor to consider when researching a topic or point of law is whether a given court opinion, statute, or regulation is still valid. A case decided six months ago may prove to be "bad law" today (if it has been reversed or significantly modified on appeal, for example). Similarly, statutes are frequently amended and new statutes enacted. This means that statutory law, too, is constantly changing. The careful researcher will avoid assuming that the case law or statutory law on a specific issue is the same today as it was last month or last year. This section will show you how to make sure that a law or court interpretation of the law is up to date and still "good law"—that is, currently valid law.

Case Law

Shepard's Citations, which is published by Shepard's/McGraw-Hill, Inc., is a research tool with which all paralegals should become familiar. *Shepard's* contains the most comprehensive system of case citators in the United States. A **citator** provides a list of legal references that have cited or interpreted the case or law. A *case citator* provides, in addition, a history of the particular case. *Shepard's* lists every case published in an official or unofficial reporter by its citation.

CITATOR
A book or on-line service that provides the subsequent history and interpretation of a statute, regulation, or court decision and a list of the cases, statutes, and regulations that have interpreted, applied, or modified a statute or regulation.

Shepard's citators are available for many different jurisdictions. *Shepard's United States Citations* covers the decisions of the United States Supreme Court as reported in *United States Reports, Supreme Court Reporter,* and *Lawyers' Edition of the Supreme Court Reports. Shepard's Federal Reporter Citations* provides coverage of the various federal courts of appeal and district courts. *Shepard's* citators also exist for the reports of every state, the District of Columbia, and Puerto Rico. Every region of the National Reporter System is covered by *Shepard's*. Exhibit 17.27 shows a *Shepard's* case citator.

One of the most valuable functions of *Shepard's* is that it provides the researcher with a means to verify the history of a case. For example, if a paralegal wants to know whether a certain court decision has been reversed by a higher court, *Shepard's* provides that information. Note, though, that it takes some time before the printed versions of *Shepard's* citators are updated. As will be discussed later in this section, to make absolutely sure that your research is truly up to date, you will want to use one of the on-line citators provided by computerized legal-research services.

EXHIBIT 17.27
Shepard's Citations

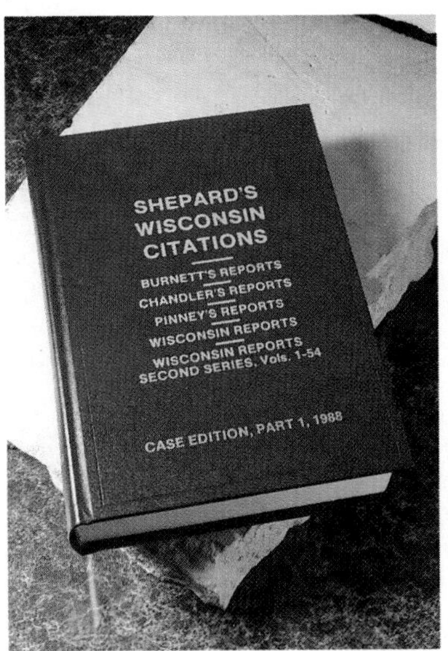

The Organization of *Shepard's Citations.* At first glance, the unique organizational structure and language of *Shepard's* can appear confusing. The researcher begins by finding the appropriate citator, the one that corresponds with the researched case's citation. For example, if the citation for the main case indicates that it is from the *Atlantic Reporter,* the citator to locate is *Shepard's Atlantic Citations.* Then, to locate the case in this publication, the researcher finds the pages covering the relevant volume of the *Atlantic Reporter.* The volume numbers are printed in the upper left-hand corner of each page for easy reference. Once the correct pages are found, the researcher reviews the listings to locate the page on which the case begins. Parallel citations to other reporters are listed in parentheses with the case. Following this is a listing of citations identifying any higher courts that have reviewed the case. Then comes a listing of cases that have cited the main case.

Types of Information Provided by *Shepard's Citations.* Paralegals can use *Shepard's* citators to accomplish several research objectives. First, *Shepard's* provides parallel citations for the cited case, allowing the paralegal to locate the case in other official or unofficial reporters.

Second, *Shepard's* lists other cases ("citing cases") that have cited the main case (the "cited case"). For example, suppose that in researching Hoffman's claim you have found a case on point. You can check *Shepard's Citations* to find out what other cases have dealt with one or more issues in your case (the cited case). Also, *Shepard's* listing of citing cases may include other cases on point that you will want to check. *Shepard's* has an elaborate abbreviation system to provide information on how the cited case has been used in the citing case. For example, if the ruling in the cited case has been followed by a citing case, the symbol *F* (for "followed") will appear after the name of the citing case. Exhibit 17.28 on the next page explains other symbols used in *Shepard's.*

Third, if you are researching a case on point, *Shepard's* provides further research tips by referring to helpful periodical articles and annotations in the *American Law Reports.*

Finally, as mentioned earlier, *Shepard's* provides a history of the cited case. If the decision in your case on point has been overturned on appeal, *Shepard's* will indicate this—or any other further history of the cited case.

Statutory and Constitutional Law

Shepard's citators for constitutions and statutes are similar to the case citators. The cited constitutional or statutory sources are listed by section number on each page and appear in boldfaced print for quick reference. *Shepard's*

EXHIBIT 17.28
Abbreviations Used in *Shepard's*

ABBREVIATIONS—ANALYSIS

History of Case

a	(affirmed)	Same case affirmed on rehearing.
cc	(connected case)	Different case from case cited but arising out of same subject matter or intimately connected therewith.
m	(modified	Same case modified on rehearing.
r	(reversed)	Same case reversed on rehearing.
s	(same case)	Same case as case cited.
S	(superseded)	Substitution for former opinion.
v	(vacated)	Same case vacated.
US	cert den	Certiorari denied by U.S. Supreme Court.
US	cert dis	Certiorari dismissed by U.S. Supreme Court.
US	reh den	Rehearing denied by U.S. Supreme Court.
US	reh dis	Rehearing dismissed by U.S. Supreme Court.

Treatment of Case

c	(criticised)	Soundness of decision or reasoning in cited case criticised for reasons given.
d	(distinguished)	Case at bar different either in law or fact from case cited for reasons given.
e	(explained)	Statement of import of decision in cited case. Not merely a restatement of the facts.
f	(followed)	Cited as controlling.
h	(harmonized)	Apparent inconsistency explained and shown not to exist.
j	(dissenting opinion)	Citation in dissenting opinion.
L	(limited)	Refusal to extend decision of cited case beyond precise issues involved.
o	(overruled)	Ruling in cited case expressly overruled.
p	(parallel)	Citing case substantially alike or on all fours with cited case in its law or facts.
q	(questioned)	Soundness of decision or reasoning in cited case questioned.

ABBREVIATIONS—COURTS

Cir. Fed. - U.S. Court of Appeals, Federal Circuit
Cir (number) - U.S. Court of Appeals Circuit (number)
CIT - United States Court of International Trade
CCPA - Court of Customs and Patent Appeals
Cl Ct - Claims Court (U.S.)
Ct Cl - Court of Claims Reports (U.S.)
Cu Ct - Customs Court Decisions
DC - District of Columbia
EC or ECA - Temporary Emergency Court of Appeals
ML - Judicial Panel on Multidistrict Litigation
RRR - Special Court Regional Rail Reorganization Act of 1973

can serve as a valuable tool in constitutional and statutory research by identifying other sources that have discussed the researched provision and by providing information on the status of the provision.

On the federal level, the *Statutes Edition of Shepard's United States Citations* contains listings of the following publications:

- The U.S. Constitution.
- The *U.S.C., U.S.C.A., and U.S.C.S.*
- The *United States Statutes at Large* provisions that have not yet been incorporated into the *U.S.C.*
- Federal reporter citations.
- Annotations from the *American Law Reports* and the *Lawyers' Edition of the Supreme Court Reports.*

Shepard's also cites publications for all state constitutions and statutes, including a listing of federal statutory and constitutional provisions that have been cited in state sources.

Administrative Regulations

Shepard's Code of Federal Regulations Citations provides citations to decisions of federal and state courts relating to administrative law, articles in legal periodicals discussing sections of the *C.F.R.*, and other reference sources. The citation lists in *C.F.R. Shepard's* are organized by title and *C.F.R.* section. To acknowledge the frequent republication of the *C.F.R.*, each citation is followed by either the date of the publication of the *C.F.R.* edition cited or the date of the citing reference. *Shepard's* uses a system of abbreviations, including those listed below, to indicate the impact that a court decision has had on the cited regulation.

- **C** (constitutional).
- **U** (unconstitutional).
- **Up** (unconstitutional in part).
- **V** (void).
- **Va** (valid).

Shepard's also publishes a variety of topical citators covering the regulations of federal agencies in specific areas. Examples include *Occupational Safety and Health Citations, Federal Energy Law Citations,* and *Bankruptcy Citations.*

Legal Periodicals

Shepard's Law Review Citations includes citations to approximately two hundred legal periodicals and law reviews. Researchers can use it to locate references to law-review articles mentioned in court decisions and other legal services. The researcher finds the cited source by looking for the name of the legal periodical and then locating the volume and page number. Once the specific article has been found, the researcher reviews the list of citing sources that have referred to the article. *Shepard's* provides coverage of local law reviews and twenty national law reviews in each of its state citators. At the federal level, *Shepard's* publishes *Federal Law Citations in Selected Law Reviews*, providing indexes of law review citations to federal court cases and other statutory information.

ETHICAL CONCERN

The Importance of Finding Current Law

It is easy to forget that the law is continually changing and, in certain areas, changing very quickly. Even though you might have researched a certain legal issue as recently as three months ago—and for a case very similar to the one your supervising attorney is now litigating—it is a mistake to assume that the earlier research results are still valid. Between then and now, a leading case on the issue might have been overruled or a statute amended or a regulatory guideline changed. Even though you may have checked the relevant printed volume of *Shepard's Citations,* you need to realize that the most recent changes in the law will not be included in printed legal reference materials. To make absolutely certain that your research results are still valid, you should use an on-line citator to see if recent cases or modifications to statutes or regulations affect your research. Failure to update your research results may seriously harm your attorney's chances at success in arguing a client's case. In sum, if your attorney trusts you to do legal research, never rely on yesterday's law.

On-line Citators

Several computerized legal research services provide on-line citators. On-line citators are extremely useful to legal researchers because they are more up to date than *Shepard's* printed citators. Computerized legal-research services, such as WESTLAW and LEXIS, provide access to several types of citators, including the following:

- *Shepard's Citator Services*—Provides information not yet included in *Shepard's* printed citations (available through both WESTLAW and LEXIS).
- *Shepard's PreView*—Updates *Shepard's* citators with the most recent cases reported in West reporters (available through WESTLAW).
- *QuickCite*—Provides a list of all cases citing a case, including the most recent cases (available through WESTLAW).
- *LexCite*—Provides a listing of the most recent cases citing a case (available through LEXIS).
- *Insta-Cite*—Summarizes the prior and subsequent history of the cited case, and includes references to the cited case made in the *Corpus Juris Secundum* (available through WESTLAW).
- *Auto-Cite*—Summarizes the prior and subsequent history of the cited case, and includes references to the cited case made in *American Law Reports* annotations (available through LEXIS).

These and other on-line citators allow you to update the law within seconds. If you want to learn the direct history of a case, you can go to *Insta-Cite* (on WESTLAW) or *Auto-Cite* (on LEXIS) and immediately find the information you need. For example, suppose that you want to learn if there has been any subsequent history in relation to the case *Ward v. K-Mart Corp,* 136 Ill.2d 132, 554 N.E.2d 223 (1990). If you were using WESTLAW, you would first call up the case by entering *FI* (for "find") and then one of the parallel citations. Within a second or two, the beginning page of the case would appear on the screen. Then you would enter the command to call up *Insta-Cite.* A second or two later, you would view the screen presented in Exhibit 17.29.

If you want more information on the case, such as a list of other cases that have cited it, you could access *Shepard's* citators—or "Shepardize" the case—using either LEXIS or WESTLAW. Again, you would call up the case in question and enter the appropriate command to call up *Shepard's.* Exhibit 17.30 shows a sample page from the citator for the *North Eastern Reporter* as it appears on the WESTLAW screen.

CD-ROMs AND LEGAL RESEARCH

Most firms have law libraries containing legal encyclopedias, case digests, statutory compilations, and other research materials that are frequently used by the firms' attorneys and paralegals. Law libraries and the physical space required to house them are expensive items for any law firm. Increasingly, today's law firms are turning to a new medium for storing research materials: the CD-ROM. (Exhibit 17.31 on page 695 shows a photograph of a CD-ROM legal library.) As discussed in Chapter 16, a CD-ROM can store over 600 megabytes of data, which is the equivalent of the entire *Encyclopedia*

```
                              INSTA-CITE                        Only Page
CITATION: 554 N.E.2d 223
                            Direct History

    1  Ward v. K Mart Corp., 185 Ill.App.3d 153, 540 N.E.2d 1036,
         133 Ill.Dec. 170 (Ill.App. 4 Dist., Jun 21, 1989) (NO. 4-88-0844)
       Appeal Allowed by
    2  Ward v. K-Mart Corp., 127 Ill.2d 643, 545 N.E.2d 134, 136 Ill.Dec. 610
         (Ill., Oct 05, 1989) (TABLE, NO. 68962)
       AND Judgment Reversed by
=>  3  Ward v. K Mart Corp., 136 Ill.2d 132, 554 N.E.2d 223, 143 Ill.Dec. 288
         (Ill., Apr 18, 1990) (NO. 68962)

                       Negative Indirect History

 Declined to Extend by
    4  Anglin v. Oros, 257 Ill.App.3d 213, 628 N.E.2d 873, 195 Ill.Dec. 409
         (Ill.App. 1 Dist., Dec 23, 1993) (NO. 1-92-2257)

   ▸ Shepard's  ▸ Shepard's PreView  ▸ QuickCite  ▸ Commands  ▸ SCOPE
(C) Copyright West Publishing Company 1994

Press F10 for Menu WESTLAW
```

EXHIBIT 17.29
A Sample *Insta-Cite* Screen Format

Britannica. That means that in a few inches of physical space, the law firm can store hundreds of volumes of legal reference materials.

State case law, state statutes, the *United States Code Annotated,* and numerous other legal reference materials are now available on CD-ROM (and more will be available in the future). A paralegal using CD-ROMs for

SHEPARD'S (Rank 1 of 2) Page 2 of 13

CITATIONS TO: 554 N.E.2d 223
CITATOR: NORTHEASTERN REPORTER CITATIONS
DIVISION: North Eastern Reporter 2nd

Retrieval No.	Analysis		Citation	Headnote No.
1	F	Followed	563 N.E.2d 1228, 1229	5
2			565 N.E.2d 687, 689	3
3	F	Followed	566 N.E.2d 239, 241	
4			566 N.E.2d 239, 243	4
5			567 N.E.2d 423, 426	
6	F	Followed	567 N.E.2d 423, 427	9
7			569 N.E.2d 214, 215	
8	D	Distinguished	569 N.E.2d at 216	7
9	D	Distinguished	569 N.E.2d at 216	9
10			569 N.E.2d 579, 583	2
11			569 N.E.2d 579, 583	3
12			570 N.E.2d 1218, 1222	3
13	E	Explained	571 N.E.2d 479, 481	4
14			571 N.E.2d 815, 817	

▸ Insta-Cite ▸ Shepard's PreView ▸ QuickCite ▸ Commands ▸ SCOPE
Copyright (C) 1994 McGraw-Hill, Inc.; Copyright (C) 1994 West Publishing Co.
Press F10 for Menu WESTLAW

EXHIBIT 17.30
A *Shepard's* Screen Format on WESTLAW

TODAY'S PROFESSIONAL PARALEGAL

Mapping Out a Research Strategy

Bill Cather is a paralegal in a criminal defense firm located in a major metropolitan area. Bill has been assigned a research project on a case involving one of the firm's clients, who was arrested for drug dealing. The police had seen the client making phone calls from a public telephone booth and suspected that he was engaged in drug trafficking. The police placed an electronic device into the phone booth—without a warrant—and learned that what they suspected was true. Bill is now going to map out his research strategy before he undertakes the project.

STEP ONE: IDENTIFYING THE ISSUE

Bill's first step is to analyze the facts and identify the issue involved. He knows that the police may search certain areas without a warrant. The courts determine which areas are entitled to the protection of a warrant by considering whether a person has a reasonable expectation of privacy in the area. Bill wonders whether a person has a reasonable expectation of privacy in a public phone booth. Do people customarily expect others to hear what they are saying on the phone when they are in a phone booth with the door closed? Bill will have to research the issue. If a person using a phone booth is entitled to a reasonable expectation of privacy, then probably the police would have to obtain a search warrant before using an electronic device to listen to—and record—any telephone conversation within a public phone booth.

STEP TWO: IDENTIFYING SECONDARY SOURCES

Because he is not familiar with the topic that he is going to research, Bill will use a research method that is helpful to new researchers. He will begin by doing some background research. He can choose from a variety of secondary sources, such as legal encyclopedias and treatises. He prefers legal encyclopedias because they are easy to read and understand. He particularly prefers the *Corpus Juris Secundum (C.J.S.)* because it provides numerous citations to cases. He writes "*C.J.S.*" on his list as the first source to consult.

STEP THREE: IDENTIFYING PRIMARY SOURCES

Next he will want to consult the various primary sources of law. He will want to look at the Fourth Amendment to the U.S. Constitution to find the exact wording of the amendment in regard to freedom from unreasonable searches and seizures and the warrant requirement. He can find the Constitution in the *U.S.C.A.* He writes "Constitution" on his list as a primary source to consult. He will also want to consult state and federal statutory codes to find out whether the police's action violated a wiretapping statute, if one exists, so he writes "federal and state statutory codes" on his list. To find cases on point—in addition to those cited in the *C.J.S.*—relating to the topic, Bill can consult case digests.

STEP FOUR: UPDATING AND VERIFYING RESEARCH RESULTS

After Bill finds and reads through relevant cases, he will have to Shepardize them to verify that they are still good law. *Shepard's* will also provide an additional source of case law because it includes every subsequent case that cited the case being Shepardized. He writes "*Shepard's*" on his list.

Bill will also want to either run a computer search or return to the secondary sources, such as an encyclopedia, to make certain that he has not overlooked any case law. As a final measure, he will want to use an online citator to verify that his research results are as up to date as possible. Bill writes "*C.J.S.* and citators—WESTLAW or LEXIS" as the final item on his list. Once Bill is comfortable with the results of his research, he will return to his office and prepare a memorandum of law to inform his supervisor of his findings.

legal research would find the CD-ROM containing the relevant reference materials—a legal encyclopedia, for example—and use the CD-ROM's index to locate quickly a given topic or subtopic.

CD-ROMs offer many advantages to legal researchers. For example, if you are researching a state statute, you can search through the statute for certain words or section numbers using the search command, which saves

EXHIBIT 17.31
A CD-ROM from a West CD-ROM Library

valuable research time. You can also copy segments of the statute directly to your computer, which reduces the amount of time you spend in document preparation as well as the risk of error. West's CD-ROM libraries offer the advantage of the key-number system, which simplifies research by allowing you to search key numbers to find relevant case law or other legal sources.

KEY TERMS AND CONCEPTS

annotation 652
business invitee 646
case on "all fours" 648
case on point 646
citation 671
citator 688
code 677
digest 652
headnote 652
hornbook 664
key number 652
mandatory authority 648
parallel citation 671
persuasive authority 649
pocket part 650
primary source 644
public law number 677
reporter 652
secondary source 644
session law 677
slip law 677
slip opinion 673
syllabus 674
table of cases 659
treatise 662

CHAPTER SUMMARY

1. Primary sources of law consist of all documents that establish the law, including court decisions, statutes, regulations, constitutions, and presidential orders. Secondary sources of law are sources written about the law, such as legal encyclopedias, digests, treatises, and periodicals.

2. The first step in the legal-research process is to identify the legal question, or issue, to be researched (often, more than one issue will be involved). The next step is to determine the goal of the research project. In researching case law, the researcher's goal is to find cases that are on point (ideally, cases on "all fours") and that are mandatory authorities. Mandatory authorities are all legal authorities (statutes, regulations, constitutions, or cases) that courts must follow in making their decisions. In contrast, courts are not bound to follow persuasive authorities (such as cases decided in other jurisdictions).

3. Legal encyclopedias and case digests are helpful secondary sources of case law for researchers who want to find background information on the issue being researched. These sources present legal topics alphabetically and contain citations to cases and statutes relating to the topic. Two popular legal encyclopedias are *American Jurisprudence,* Second Edition, and *Corpus Juris Secundum.* Both encyclopedias contain a wealth of information on the topics presented. A third encyclopedia, *Words and Phrases,* covers legal terms and phrases and cites cases in which the terms or phrases appear. The case digests published by West Publishing Company are major secondary sources of law. These digests, which use the West system of topic classification and key numbers, provide cross-references to topics contained in other West publications.

4. Other important secondary resources of case law include the *American Law Reports,* which contain leading cases, each of which is followed by an annotation that discusses the key issues in the case and that refers the researcher to other sources on the issues; law treatises, which are scholarly publications discussing specific legal topics or areas; the Restatements of the Law, which are highly respected scholarly compilations of the common law; and legal periodicals, such as law reviews.

5. Primary sources of case law are the cases themselves. Most state trial court decisions are not published in printed volumes. State appellate court opinions, including those of state supreme courts, are normally published in state reporters, although many states have eliminated their own reporters in favor of West's National Reporter System. Federal trial court opinions are published unofficially in West's *Federal Supplement,* and opinions from the federal circuit courts of appeals are published unofficially in West's *Federal Reporter.* United States Supreme Court opinions are published officially in the *United States Reports,* published by the federal government, and unofficially in West's *Supreme Court Reporter* and the *Lawyers' Edition of the Supreme Court Reports.* The latter is published by the Lawyers Cooperative Publishing Company.

6. Federal statutes are published officially in the *United States Code (U.S.C.).* The *U.S.C.* organizes statutes into fifty subjects, or titles, and further subdivides each title into chapters (sections) and subchapters. The researcher can find a statute in the *U.S.C.* by searching through the topical outlines, by looking in the index, or by looking under the act's popular name in the volume entitled *Popular Name Table.* The *United States Code Annotated* and the *United States Code Service* are unofficial publications of federal statutes. Both of these sources are useful to researchers because they provide annotations and citations to other resources.

7. In researching statutory law, it is important to make sure that a given statute is really relevant to the issue being researched. In determining the intent of the statute, the researcher may want to investigate its legislative history. Important sources for researching legislative history include transcripts of committee reports and hearings, transcripts of congressional proceedings, and the wording of statutes as first published in the *United States Statutes at Large.* Helpful resources in this area include the *Congressional Record,* the *United States Code Congressional and Administrative News,* and the *Congressional Information Service.*

8. Regulations issued by federal administrative agencies are primary sources of law. Agency regulations are published in the *Code of Federal Regulations (C.F.R.).* The *C.F.R.* follows a format similar to that of the *United States Code (U.S.C.),* and the subject classifications (titles) of the *C.F.R.* correspond to the titles in the *U.S.C.* To locate recently published regulations, the researcher should refer to the *Federal Register's* cumulative *List of C.F.R. Sections Affected,* which reflects changes made during the current month. Constitutions are also primary sources of law. The U.S. Constitution can be found in a number of publications, including the extensively annotated official publication, which is available through the Library of

Congress. Annotated versions of state constitutions are also available.

9. Crucial in legal research is making sure that the research results are still valid. The various volumes of *Shepard's Citations* allow the researcher to verify whether a case has been overruled or reversed, a statute repealed or amended, an agency regulation voided or superseded, and the like. Online citators, including *Auto-Cite* (LEXIS) and *Insta-Cite* (WESTLAW) enable the researcher to access recent cases, statutes, or regulations (or amendments or modifications to existing statutes or regulations) and thus ensure that research results are as up to date as possible.

10. Many legal research materials are now available on CD-ROMs, a relatively new form of storage medium that can store hundreds of volumes of legal sources in just a few inches of space.

QUESTIONS FOR REVIEW

1. What are the differences between primary and secondary sources of law? How are each of these types of sources used in legal research?

2. What is a case on point? What is a case on "all fours"? Why is finding such a case important when researching case law?

3. What is the difference between mandatory authority and persuasive authority? Which type of authority should you strive to find when conducting legal research?

4. How are legal encyclopedias and other secondary sources used to find case law relevant to a research topic?

5. What is a case digest? How do case digests help legal researchers find case law? What is the West key-number system, and how does it simplify the legal-research process?

6. Describe the forms in which court decisions are published, from their initial publication to their final published form.

7. Identify the various parts of a case citation. How do they help you locate a case?

8. Describe the forms in which statutes are published, from their original issuance to their final published form. Do the same for regulations. What are the major sources for statutes and regulations?

9. What is meant by the term *legislative history*? What resources are available for researching the legislative history of a statute?

10. Why is it important to find the most current law? How can you verify that your research results are up to date?

ETHICAL QUESTIONS

1. Kristine Connolly, a paralegal in a litigation firm, has finished reading a brief that the opposing side submitted to the court in support of a motion for summary judgment. In the brief, she notices a citation to a state supreme court case of which she is unaware. She is experienced in the field and keeps current with new cases as they are decided. She wants to look at the case because it gives the other side a winning edge. She checks in the advance sheets, digests, and state encyclopedias, as well as on WESTLAW. She finally calls the state supreme court clerk's office and asks about the case. The office has no record of such a case. She asks the legal assistant for the opposing counsel to give her a copy of the case. When she does not receive it, she decides that the case is probably fictional. What should Kristine do?

2. Barbara Coltiers is a legal assistant in a very busy litigation practice. She gets a call from a nervous attorney in her firm thirty minutes before the attorney is to appear in court. He wants her to do some research before he goes to court. He has just heard about a case that might help him win and gives her the citation. Because he is in a hurry, he gives her the wrong volume number. She has a hard time finding the case, but after about fifteen minutes of searching turns to the table of cases and locates the citation. She quickly copies the case and runs to his office with it so that he can hurry across the street to the court for his appearance. She is in such a hurry that she forgets to use *Insta-Cite* to check the subsequent history of the case.

It turns out that the case had been overruled by the state supreme court and was therefore no longer controlling in the jurisdiction. The attorney is chastised by the judge for citing it. In fact, the judge is so annoyed with the attorney for making an argument that was not based on existing law that he denies the attorney's motion and makes the attorney pay the other side's court costs. When the client finds out why the motion was denied, she is irate. Does the client have any remedy against the attorney? Against Barbara?

3. John Hernandez is studying at a local college to be a legal assistant. The college has WESTLAW for its students to use. The software license specifically prohibits the faculty or students of the college from using the program for personal work. John knows that Kathy has a part-time job with a law firm, and he becomes aware that Kathy is using WESTLAW regularly to do research for her supervising attorney in that firm. What should John do?

PRACTICE QUESTIONS AND ASSIGNMENTS

1. Mr. John D. Consumer bought a new car eight months ago. The car frequently stalls. The problem began the first week after he purchased the vehicle. It stalled late at night on an expressway while he was returning home from a business trip. It has stalled at least monthly since then, often in potentially dangerous areas. Not only has he taken the car to the dealer, who has repeatedly attempted to repair the problem without success, but he has also notified the manufacturer in writing of the problem. Most states have a lemon law that requires manufacturers to replace vehicles that cannot be repaired, even if the warranty has expired. Does your state have a lemon law? If so, would the lemon law help Mr. Consumer?

Research this question and try to find the answer to Mr. Consumer's problem. Begin by analyzing the facts. Then make a list of relevant legal and relevant terms to look up in an index.

Select a legal encyclopedia—either *American Jurisprudence* or *Corpus Juris Secundum*—to use in your research. Write down the name of the encyclopedia. Consult the general index volumes.

a. Write down the index topics under which you found relevant information. (If you have difficulty locating relevant information, try checking the topic indexes in the individual volumes.)

b. Write down the citations to encyclopedia sections containing relevant information.

c. Look up these citations in the appropriate volumes of the encyclopedia to find an answer to Mr. Consumer's problem. Be sure to check the pocket part for more current citations. According to the encyclopedia, what is the answer to Mr. Consumer's problem?

2. After analyzing the facts of Mr. Consumer's problem and making a list of legally and factually relevant terms, as described in Practice Question 1, do the following:

a. Locate the index to the annotated version of your state statutes. Using your list of terms, look in the index for citations to relevant statute sections. Write down the citations.

b. If you did Practice Question 1 above, compare how you found the citations in the index to your state statutes with how you found them in the legal encyclopedia. Under what topics did you look in each situation?

c. Now that you have found relevant citations, go to the volume of the statute containing the cited sections and read those sections. (Be sure to check the pocket part of the volume.) What answer does the statute in your state give to Mr. Consumer's problem? If you answered Practice Question 1 above, is the answer given by your state statute similar to that given in the encyclopedia? If not, how do the answers differ?

3. Using the annotated version of your state statutes, look for relevant case law on Mr. Consumer's problem. If no annotated version of your state statute exists or if no cases appear in the annotated version—or if you want to learn to use another source—locate a state digest. Find the relevant section(s) and locate case law that interprets the statute and that is as similar to Mr. Consumer's problem as possible.

a. Write down the citations to no more than three relevant cases. Now look up those cases in the case reporters.

b. Read through the summary and headnotes of each case. Do the cases still appear to be relevant? If not, go back to the annotated statute or digest and look for more relevant cases.

c. What did you find? Did the courts' application of the statute change in any way your answer to Mr. Consumer's problem?

QUESTIONS FOR CRITICAL ANALYSIS

1. What is a parallel citation? Why are parallel citations used?

2. The written opinions of judges sitting on state and federal appellate courts are usually published in reporters. Why is it that trial court decisions are not routinely published in reporters?

ROLE-PLAYING EXERCISES

1. Review the hypothetical case discussed in this chapter in which Trent Hoffman is suing Better Homes Store for negligence. Working in pairs, role-play a scene in which a paralegal is asking the reference librarian at a law library for advice on what secondary sources she should consult to find background information and case law relevant to the issue. The librarian should describe each of the secondary sources of law discussed in this chapter. The paralegal should ask for details on how to use each source and generally be very inquisitive. If time permits, reverse roles.

2. If you did not participate in the role-playing exercise above, review the hypothetical case discussed in this chapter in which Trent Hoffman is suing Better Homes Store for negligence. Working in pairs, role-play the scene in which the attorney asks the paralegal to do some research on the issue. The paralegal should ask the attorney for advice on what issue the attorney wants her to research and what her research goals should be. The attorney should answer each of the paralegal's questions as fully as possible. If time permits, reverse roles.

PROJECTS

1. Using a state bar directory or other type of legal directory, find out which law libraries in your area are open to the public. Make arrangements to visit a law library. If tours of the library are offered, try to be present for a tour.

2. Make arrangements through your professor, a local bar association, or your personal contacts to visit the law library of a law firm or a legal department of a corporation or government office. If you also participated in Project 1 above, compare the materials available in the libraries of firms or government agencies with those available in law libraries. Why is it necessary for legal professionals to use law libraries other than those located in their offices?

3. Find out if your state has an official reporter for its appellate courts. If it does, find out where the reporter is printed and how often the advance sheets are compiled into a hardbound volume and distributed.

4. Obtain a copy of *A Uniform System of Citation* (the Bluebook) and look up the citation formats for your state court reporters and statutes.

5. Using information from Chapter 7, make a diagram of the federal court system. List the reporters for each court in the system, using the information given in this chapter.

Annotated Selected Readings

Cohen Morris L., and Kent C. Olson. *Legal Research in a Nutshell.* St. Paul: West Publishing Co., 1991. A compact yet thorough guide to the various sources of law.

Dworsky, Alan L. *User's Guide to the Bluebook.* Littleton, Colo.: F. B. Rothman, 1991. An excellent resource for helping the novice researcher to understand how to use the Bluebook.

Griffith, Cary. "Cite Checking Made Painless." *Legal Assistant Today,* May/June 1994. A discussion of the numerous on-line citators that can help the legal researcher quickly find relevant legal sources and update research results.

Jacobstein, J. Myron, and Roy M. Mersky. *Legal Research Illustrated.* 5th ed. Westbury, N.Y.: Foundation Press, 1990. An exhaustive text explaining in great detail the primary and secondary sources of law. A good reference item for one's personal library.

Leiter, Richard A. "Researching State Statutes: Easier Said Than Done." *Legal Assistant Today,* November/December 1993. An informative discussion of state statutory codes that contains some tips for the legal professional on how to research state statutory law.

Leiter, Richard A. "The Theory and Practice of Using Looseleaf Services." *Legal Assistant Today,* March/April 1994. A discussion of loose-leaf services and their value to the legal researcher who either is new to an area of law or wants to find a detailed analysis of a particular issue.

Morgan, Barbara C. "Ten Ways the Law Library Can Work for You." *Legal Assistant Today,* January/February 1991. Ten tips on additional ways (beyond basic legal research) that the law library can be of help to legal assistants. The article includes numerous tips for finding information and provides a good look at on-the-job realities facing the paralegal.

Reichard, David A. "How to Develop Facts and Legal Issues: Suggestions for a Legal Research Strategy." *Legal Assistant Today*, November/December 1991. A helpful article that explains how to evaluate facts; identify issues; map out, use, and update legal sources; record information; and communicate research results.

18

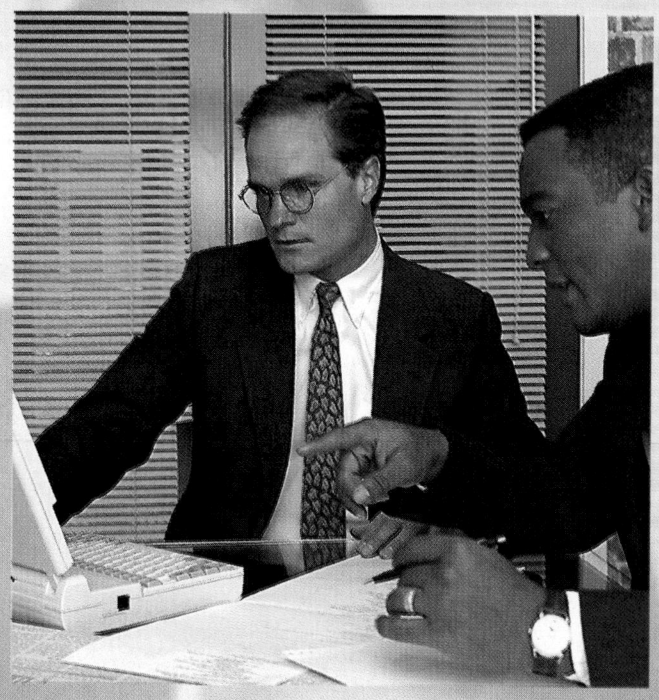

Legal Analysis and Writing

Chapter Objectives

After completing this chapter, you will know:

- How to read and analyze case law.
- Some techniques for reading statutory law and guidelines traditionally used for interpreting statutory law.
- What factors you should consider before undertaking a legal-writing assignment.
- What factors you should consider when drafting a legal document.
- The purpose and format of the most common types of legal letters.
- How to prepare a legal memorandum.

Chapter Outline

INTRODUCTION

To a certain extent, legal research, analysis, and writing are all part of the same process. In Chapter 17, we looked primarily at the various types of resources available to the legal researcher and how to locate them. This chapter focuses on how to analyze those resources and communicate the research results in writing. Much legal writing, however, is not directly related to the research process. As a paralegal, your typical day will involve other types of writing responsibilities as well. You will be expected to know how to draft letters to clients or opposing counsel, internal memos, documents to be submitted to court clerks or judges in regard to pending lawsuits, and a variety of other documents.

This chapter opens with some guidelines on how to analyze legal sources, including case law, statutory law, and administrative law. The remainder of the chapter, which deals with legal writing, includes suggestions on how you can learn to write effectively and a description of the types and formats of legal documents that are commonly prepared by paralegals. When a case is appealed to a higher court, attorneys for both parties submit appellate briefs to the court. An *appellate brief* is an attorney's written argument setting forth the legal reasons why the court should rule in favor of the attorney's client. For those paralegals who are interested in learning how to draft appellate briefs, we present a special appendix on that topic at the end of this chapter.

ANALYZING CASE LAW

As mentioned, *case law* is that body of law created by the decisions of court judges. Attorneys may rely heavily on case law to support a given position or argument. If you can find a *case on point* or a *case on "all fours,"*[1] that case may serve as a mandatory authority to support your supervising attorney's argument in a case now being litigated.

One of the difficulties that all legal professionals face in analyzing case law is the sheer length and complexity of some court opinions. While certain court opinions may be only two or three pages in length, others can occupy hundreds of pages. Understanding the components of a case—that is, the basic format in which cases are presented—can simplify your task of reading and analyzing case law. You will find that over time, as you acquire experience, case analysis becomes easier.

The Components of a Case

Reported cases contain much more than just the court's decision. Cases have many different parts, and you should understand why each part is there and

1. Recall from Chapter 17 that a case on point is a previous case having fact patterns and issues that are similar to the case being litigated. A case on "all fours" has nearly identical fact patterns and issues.

what information it communicates. The annotations on the sample court case shown in fold-out Exhibit 18.1 (following page 708) indicate the various components of a case.

The case presented in fold-out Exhibit 18.1 is an actual case that was decided by the United States Supreme Court in 1994. The lawsuit was initiated by Acuff-Rose Music, Inc., which held the copyright to a popular song entitled "Oh, Pretty Woman." The rap group 2 Live Crew authored and profited from a parody (satiric rendition) of the song. As discussed in Chapter 8, federal copyright law allows writers, artists, and other authors of creative works to have the exclusive right to reproduce those works. Copyright infringement occurs when someone reproduces a copyrighted work without the author's permission to do so.

Important sections, terms, and phrases in the case are defined or discussed in the margins. You will note also that triple asterisks (* * *) and quadruple asterisks (* * * *) frequently appear in the exhibit. The triple asterisks indicate that we have deleted a few words or sentences from the opinion for the sake of readability or brevity. Quadruple asterisks mean that an entire paragraph (or more) has been omitted. Also, when the opinion cites another case or legal source, the citation to the referenced case or source has been omitted to save space and to improve readability.

We discuss below the various components of a case. As you read through the descriptions of these components, refer to fold-out Exhibit 18.1, which illustrates most of the components discussed below.

Citation and Case Title. Typically, the case citation is found just above or below the case title (or *style*). As discussed in Chapter 17, the *citation* indicates the name, volume number, and page number of the reporter series in which the case appears. The case presented in fold-out Exhibit 18.1 is a printout of the WESTLAW[2] version of the case, and the parallel citations are to West's *Supreme Court Reporter* and the *Lawyers' Edition of the Supreme Court Reports.* When the parallel citation to the *United States Reports* becomes available, it will be added by WESTLAW as well. (Recall from Chapter 17 that West's *Supreme Court Reporter* and the *Lawyers' Edition of the Supreme Court Reports* are unofficial reporters; the official reporter for cases decided by the United States Supreme Court is the *United States Reports.*) In fold-out Exhibit 18.1, the case title immediately follows the citation.

Docket Number. The docket number immediately follows the case title. Recall from Chapter 10 that a docket number is assigned by the court clerk when a case is initially filed. The number serves as an identifier for all papers submitted in connection with the case. A case published in a reporter should not be cited by its docket number, but the docket number may serve as a valuable tool in obtaining background information on the case. Cases appearing in slip-opinion form (cases that have been decided but that are not yet published in a reporter—see Chapter 17) are usually identified, filed, and

2. Recall from previous chapters that WESTLAW is one of the computerized legal services through which legal professionals and others can access court cases, statutes, regulations, articles in law journals, and numerous other types of information.

cited by docket number. After publication of the decision, the docket number may continue to serve as an identifier for appellate records and briefs (see the appendix at the end of this chapter for a discussion of appellate briefs).

Dates Argued and Decided. An important component of a case is the date on which it was decided by the court. Usually, the date of the decision immediately follows the docket number. In addition to the date of the court's decision on the matter, the date on which the case was argued before the court (in appellate court cases) may also be included here, as in fold-out Exhibit 18.1.

Syllabus. Following the docket number is the *syllabus.* As discussed in Chapter 17, a syllabus is a brief synopsis of the facts of the case, the issues analyzed by the court, and the court's conclusion. In official reporters, the courts usually prepare the syllabi; in unofficial reporters, the publishers of the reporters usually prepare them. The syllabus is often a helpful research tool. It provides a clear overview of the case and points out various legal issues discussed by the court. But always keep in mind the following caution:

- **Reading the syllabus is not a substitute for reading the case.**

Headnotes. Often, unofficial reporters, such as those published by West Publishing Company, make extensive use of case *headnotes*. As discussed in Chapter 17, headnotes are short paragraphs following the general syllabus. They serve to highlight and summarize specific rules of law mentioned in the case. In reporters published by West Publishing Company, they are correlated to the comprehensive West key-number system. In the case presented in fold-out Exhibit 18.1, the nineteen headnotes were deleted for reasons of space, as were the names of counsel.

Names of Counsel. The published report of the case usually contains the names of the lawyers (counsel) representing the parties. The attorneys' names are usually found just following the syllabus (and headnotes, if any).

Name of Judge or Justice Authoring the Opinion. The name of the judge or justice who authored the opinion in the case will also be included in the published report of the case, just before the court's opinion (discussed below). In the case presented in fold-out Exhibit 18.1, Justice Souter of the United States Supreme Court authored the opinion.

In some cases, instead of the name of a judge or justice, the decision will be authored *per curiam* (Latin for "by the court"), which means that the opinion is that of the whole court and not the opinion of any one judge or justice. Sometimes the phrase is used to indicate that the chief justice or presiding judge wrote the opinion. The phrase also may be used for an announcement of a court's disposition of a case that is not accompanied by a written opinion.

Opinion. As you may have noted in previous chapters, the term *opinion* is often used loosely to refer to a court case or decision. In fact, the term has a precise meaning. The formal opinion of the court contains the analysis and decision of the judge or judges that heard and decided the case. Most opinions contain a brief statement of the facts of the case, a summary of the legal issues raised by the facts, and the remedies sought by the parties. In appellate court cases, the court summarizes the errors of the lower court, if any, and the impact of these errors on the case's outcome. The main body of the court's opinion is the application of the law to the particular facts. The court often mentions case precedents, relevant statutes, and administrative rules and regulations to support its reasoning. Additionally, court opinions often contain discussions of policy and other factors that clarify the underlying reason for the court's decision.

When all of the judges unanimously agree in their legal reasoning and their decision, the opinion is deemed a *unanimous* opinion. When the opinion is not unanimous, a *majority* opinion is written, outlining the views of the majority of the judges deciding the case. There may also be a *concurring* opinion or a *dissenting* opinion. (See Chapter 6 for an explanation of these different types of opinions.)

The Court's Conclusion. In the opinion, the judges will indicate their conclusion, or decision, on the issue or issues before the court. If several issues are involved, as often happens, there may be a conclusion at the end of the discussion of each issue. Often, at the end of the opinion, the conclusions presented within the opinion will be briefly reiterated and summarized, or, if no conclusions were yet presented, they will be presented in the concluding section of the opinion.

An appellate court also specifies what the *disposition* of a case should be. As discussed in Chapter 11, if the appellate court agrees with a lower court's decision, it will *affirm* that decision, which means that the decision of the lower court remains unchanged. If the appellate court concludes that the lower court erred in its interpretation of the law, the court may *reverse* the lower court's ruling. Sometimes, if an appellate court concludes that further factual findings are necessary or that a case should be retried and a decision made that is consistent with the appellate court's conclusions of law, the appellate court will *remand* the case to the lower court for further proceedings consistent with its opinion. In the sample case presented in fold-out Exhibit 18.1, the United States Supreme Court reversed the lower court's decision and remanded the case.

Analyzing Cases

When you are researching case law, you should identify the components of the case. The syllabus and headnotes are often helpful in giving you an overview of the issues involved. Your main focus, though, should be on the opinion—the words of the court itself.

You will inevitably find that some opinions are easier to understand than others. Some judges write more clearly and logically than others. You may need to reread a case (or a portion of a case) to understand what is being said, why it is being said at that point in the case, and what the judge's underlying legal reasoning is. Some cases contain several pages describing facts and issues of previous cases and how those cases relate to the one being decided by the court. You might want to reread these discussions several times to distinguish between comments made in the previous case and comments that are being made about the case at bar (before the court).

Often, the judge writing the opinion provides some guideposts, perhaps by indicating sections and subsections within the opinion by numbers, letters, or subtitles. Note that in fold-out Exhibit 18.1, Roman numerals are used to divide the opinion into basic sections. Scanning through the opinion for these types of indicators can help orient you to the opinion's format.

In cases that involve dissenting or concurring opinions, you need to make sure that you identify these opinions so that you do not mistake one of them for the majority opinion. Generally, you should scan through the case a time or two to identify its various components and sections and then read the case (or sections of the case) until you understand the facts and procedural history of the case, the issues involved, the applicable law, the legal reasoning of the court, and how the reasoning leads to the court's conclusion on the issue or issues.

HOLDING
The binding legal principle, or precedent, that is drawn from the court's decision in a case.

DICTA
A Latin term referring to nonbinding (nonprecedential) judicial statements that are not directly related to the facts or issues presented in the case and thus not essential to the holding.

In reading and analyzing cases, you should also be able to determine which statements of the court are legally binding and which are not. Only the **holding** (the legal principle to be drawn from the court's decision) is binding. Other views expressed in the opinion are referred to as ***dicta*** and are not binding in subsequent cases. *Dicta* is the plural of *dictum.* As used here, *dictum* is an abbreviated form of the Latin *obitur dictum,* which means "a remark by the way." *Dicta* are any statements made by a judge that go beyond the facts of the case or that do not directly relate to the facts of the case or to the resolution of the issue being addressed. *Dicta* include comments used by the court to illustrate an example and statements concerning a rule of law that is not essential to the case at hand. You can probably assume that statements are *dicta* if they begin with "If the facts were different" or "If the plaintiff had . . ." or some other "if/then" phrase.

Summarizing and Briefing Cases

IRAC METHOD
IRAC is a mnemonic for issue, rule, application, and conclusion. The IRAC method helps legal researchers and writers focus on the four critical elements of a case.

A method that is commonly used by legal researchers, including paralegals, to summarize a case is the **IRAC method**. IRAC stands for Issue, Rule, Application, and Conclusion. The IRAC approach helps to focus your attention on the essential aspects of the case in both the prewriting and writing stages of a research project. The format for IRAC method is shown in Exhibit 18.2. Note that in cases involving more than one issue, you will use IRAC to analyze each separate issue.

BRIEFING A CASE
Summarizing a case. A typical case brief will indicate the case title and citation and then briefly state the factual background and procedural history of the case, the issue or issues raised in the case, the court's decision, the applicable rule of law and the legal reasoning upon which the decision is based, and conclusions or notes concerning the case made by the one who is briefing it.

After you have read and analyzed a case, you may decide that it is on point and that you want to include a reference to it in your legal writing. If so, you will want to summarize in your notes the important facts in the case, as well as information that you summarized using the IRAC method. This is called **briefing a case**.[3]

There is a fairly standard format that you can use when you brief any court case. Although the format may vary, typically it will present the essentials of the case under headings such as those illustrated and described in Exhibit 18.3 on page 710. As you can see in the exhibit, the headings used in a case brief are similar to those used in the IRAC method. The difference is that in a case

3. Note that a *case brief* is not the same as a *legal brief* that an attorney submits to a court. (Legal briefs are discussed in this chapter's appendix.)

ISSUE: What issue is being addressed by the court?
RULE: What rule of law applies to the issue? The rule of law may be a rule stated by the courts in previous decisions, a state or federal statute, or a state or federal administrative-agency regulation.
APPLICATION: How does the court apply the rule of law to the facts involved in this particular case?
CONCLUSION: What is the court's conclusion?

Exhibit 18.2
The IRAC Method

brief, the background and facts leading up to the lawsuit are included. Also, when more than one issue is involved in a case, the issues are combined in the *Issue* section, the decisions regarding each issue may be combined under the *Decision* section, and so on. See Exhibit 18.4 on page 711 for a briefed version of the sample court case presented in fold-out Exhibit 18.1. Depending on the issue you were researching, you would add a conclusion to the brief indicating how the Supreme Court's ruling affected that issue.

Synthesizing Your Research Results

Once you have analyzed and briefed the cases that you want to use in support of a legal argument, you will need to synthesize your research results. In synthesizing your results, you extract the most important rules of law, issues, and defenses from the cases that you have read and analyzed and combine them in such a way that they can be effectively incorporated into whatever legal document you need to draft. You can synthesize your results in three different ways:

- By grouping cases according to their *rules of law.*
- By grouping cases according to their *issues.*
- By grouping cases according to the *defenses* that were raised by the defendants.

For example, assume that you have found several cases in which the court enunciated the following rule of law: an owner of business premises is liable to a customer who sustained an injury as a result of the store's failure to warn the customer of a dangerous condition on the premises, if the store owner knew or should have known of the condition. You might group the cases you have found under the heading "Liability of Retail Business Owners to Customers."

Similarly, you could group cases under a heading relating more specifically to the issue with which you are directly concerned. You might have a heading such as "slip-and-fall cases" and include the cases that involve such issues under this heading.

Finally, you might arrange the cases under the various defenses that store owners can raise against liability claims. One defense that business owners sometimes raise, for example, is that a dangerous condition was so open and obvious that there was no need to warn customers of it. Another defense might be that the customer knew of a particular risk and deliberately

Exhibit 18.3
Format for Briefing a Case

1. NAME (TITLE, OR STYLE) OF CASE. Give the full name of the case.
2. CASE CITATION. Give the full citation for the case, including all parallel citations, the date the case was decided, and the name of the court deciding the case.
3. FACTS. Briefly indicate (a) the reasons for the lawsuit; (b) the identity and arguments of the plaintiff(s) and defendant(s); and (c) if the case was decided by an appellate court, the lower court's opinion on the issues.
4. ISSUE. Concisely phrase the essential legal issue(s) before the court.
5. DECISION (RULING, HOLDING). Indicate here the court's decision on the issue(s).
6. REASON. Summarize as briefly as possible the legal reasoning on which the court based its decision.

assumed that risk. If you work for the firm representing the defendant store in a slip-and-fall case brought by one of the store's customers, grouping cases in terms of the defenses raised might be a logical organizational strategy to use when synthesizing your research results.

ANALYZING STATUTORY LAW

Because of the tremendous growth in statutory and regulatory law in the last century, the legal issues dealt with by attorneys are frequently governed by statutes and administrative agency regulations. Legal assistants must understand how to interpret and analyze this body of law. Although we use the terms *statute* and *statutory law* in this section, the following discussion applies equally well to the regulations issued by administrative agencies.

If a statute applies to the legal issues in your case, you must understand the statute thoroughly before evaluating how it does or does not apply to the issue that you are researching. The first step in statutory analysis is therefore to read the language of the statute very carefully. The next step is to interpret the meaning of the statute.

Reading Statutory Law

As with court cases, some statutes are more difficult to read than others. Some are extremely wordy or lengthy or difficult to understand for some other reason. By carefully reading and rereading a statute, however, you can usually determine the reasons for the statute's enactment, the class of people to which the statute applies, the kind of conduct being regulated by the statute, and the circumstances in which that conduct is prohibited, required, or permitted. You can also learn whether the statute allows for any exceptions and, if so, in what circumstances. When reading a statute, you can do several things to simplify your task, including those discussed below.

Coverage and Effective Date. When researching statutory law on behalf of a client, one of the first things you should find out is whether the statute is

EXHIBIT 18.4
Briefed Version of Sample Court Case

NAME OF CASE Campbell v. Acuff-Rose Music, Inc.
CITATION __ U.S. __, 114 S.Ct. 1164, 127 L.Ed.2d 500 (1994).

FACTS The song "Oh, Pretty Woman" was written in 1964 by Roy Orbison and William Dees. Their ownership rights in the song were transferred to Acuff-Rose Music, Inc.—the current copyright owner and the respondent in this appeal. In 1989, the rap group 2 Live Crew parodied the song without Acuff-Rose's permission. In 1990, after about 250,000 copies of the parody version had been sold, Acuff-Rose sued 2 Live Crew and its record company, alleging copyright infringement. 2 Live Crew claimed that their parodic use of the original song fell within the "fair use" exception to the Copyright Act of 1976. 2 Live Crew contended that the parody commented on and satirized the original work, which is considered a fair use under the act in some circumstances. The district court found for 2 Live Crew, holding that the parody version was a fair use. Acuff-Rose appealed. The court of appeals reversed, holding that 2 Live Crew's parody carried with it a presumption of unfair use because of its intrinsically commercial nature. 2 Live Crew appealed to the United States Supreme Court.

ISSUE Could 2 Live Crew's parody version of "Oh, Pretty Woman" be considered a fair use of the original copyrighted song under the Copyright Act of 1976?

DECISION Yes. The Supreme Court reversed the appellate court's decision and remanded the case.

REASON Section 107 of the Copyright Act sets forth a four-factor test to be used when determining whether the unauthorized use of another's copyrighted work is a "fair use." In regard to the first factor (the "purpose and character of the use, including whether such use is of a commercial nature"), the appellate court held that the commercial nature of 2 Live Crew's parody rendered the group's use presumptively unfair. The Supreme Court disagreed, holding that the transformative value of parody must also be considered. On the second factor (the "nature of the copyrighted work"), the Supreme Court affirmed the lower courts' decision that the original version of "Oh, Pretty Woman" warranted copyright protection under the act. On the third factor (the "amount and substantiality of the portion used in relation to the copyrighted work as a whole"), the appellate court held that 2 Live Crew's parody copied the heart, or essence, of the original work and therefore borrowed too much. The Supreme Court stated that a parody must necessarily "conjure up" enough of the original work for the audience to recognize the "critical wit" intended, and this may require copying the heart of the original version. Whether 2 Live Crew copied musical elements to a greater extent than necessary to accomplish this was an issue to be decided on remand. On the final factor (the "effect of the use upon the potential market for or value of the copyrighted work"), the Supreme Court held that because the original and parodic versions served different market functions, the parodic version would probably not affect the market for the original.

applicable to the client's case. Suppose that your firm's client is a small corporation with ten employees. Your firm is defending the client against a lawsuit for employment discrimination based on disability in violation of the Americans with Disabilities Act (ADA) of 1990. In researching this statute, the first thing you will want to check is what firms are subject to the statute. (You will find that the ADA applies only to employers who have fifteen or more employees, and thus the client is not subject to the act's provisions.)

Each statute also indicates the date on which it will become legally effective. This is something that you will want to verify at the outset of your inquiry. Note that the effective date may be a year or two later than the date on which the statute was enacted into law. For example, the provisions relating to employment in the Americans with Disabilities Act of 1990 did not become legally effective until July 26, 1992. Questions also arise in regard to whether the provisions of the act will apply *retroactively*—that is, to lawsuits filed before the effective date of the statute. If the statute is unclear on its applicability in this respect, you will want to research relevant case law to find out how the courts have decided this issue.

Definitions. Usually, near the beginning of a statute or the beginning of each major section within the statute, you can find a list of terms followed by their definitions. In the hypothetical case mentioned above, which involves a lawsuit based on discrimination against a person with a disability, you will want to read carefully the statutory definition of *disability*. You will also want to learn how the ADA defines other terms or phrases that may be important in determining the defendant firm's liability. For example, the ADA requires employers reasonably to accommodate persons with disabilities. You will want to find out how the act defines *reasonable accommodation.*

Subdivisions. Another helpful tactic in reading statutory law is to identify the various sections and subsections in the statute. Often, statutes indicate subsections by letters or numbers, but it is easy to lose sight of the relationship between one subsection and another. Consider the excerpt from the ADA shown in Exhibit 18.5. You will find that there are several levels of subsections within this section of the statute and that each subsection is preceded by a number or letter. You may also find that you have to scan through the section more than once to identify the relationship between the subsections. Statutes frequently contain even more levels of subsections, and at times, you may want to diagram the structure of the text to discern the interrelationship of various subsections.

And* versus *Or. When reading a statute, you should also pay careful attention to the words *and* and *or* in the text. For example, suppose that a section of a statute begins with the words "A contract which does not satisfy the requirements of subsection (1) but which is valid in other respects is enforceable if . . ." Following these words, two conditions are listed. A crucial factor in interpreting the section is whether the conditions are connected by *and* or *or.* If *and* is used, then both conditions must be met before the contract is enforceable. If *or* is used, then only one of the conditions must be met. Consciously looking for these *connectors* in positions such as the one just described can help to clarify the meaning of a statutory provision.

Interpreting Statutory Law

Generally, when trying to understand the meaning of statutes, you should do as the courts do. We therefore now look at some of the typical techniques

§ 12112. Discrimination

(a) General rule
No covered entity shall discriminate against a qualified individual with a disability because of the disability of such individual in regard to job application procedures, the hiring, advancement, or discharge of employees, employee compensation, job training, and other terms, conditions, and privileges of employment.
(b) Construction
As used in subsection (a) of this section, the term "discriminate" includes—
(1) limiting, segregating, or classifying a job applicant or employee in a way that adversely affects the opportunities or status of such applicant or employee because of the disability of such applicant or employee;
(2) participating in a contractual or other arrangement or relationship that has the effect of subjecting a covered entity's qualified applicant or employee with a disability to the discrimination prohibited by this subchapter (such relationship includes a relationship with an employment or referral agency, labor union, an organization providing fringe benefits to an employee of the covered entity, or an organization providing training and apprenticeship programs);
(3) utilizing standards, criteria, or methods of administration—
(A) that have the effect of discrimination on the basis of disability; or
(B) that perpetuate the discrimination of others who are subject to common administrative control;
(4) excluding or otherwise denying equal jobs or benefits to a qualified individual because of the known disability of an individual with whom the qualified individual is known to have a relationship or association;
(5)(A) not making reasonable accommodations to the known physical or mental limitations of an otherwise qualified individual with a disability who is an applicant or employee, unless such covered entity can demonstrate that the accommodation would impose an undue hardship on the operation of the business of such covered entity; or
(B) denying employment opportunities to a job applicant or employee who is an otherwise qualified individual with a disability, if such denial is based on the need of such covered entity to make reasonable accommodation to the physical or mental impairments of the employee or applicant;
(6) using qualification standards, employment tests or other selection criteria that screen out or tend to screen out an individual with a disability or a class of individuals with disabilities unless the standard, test or other selection criteria, as used by the covered entity, is shown to be job-related for the position in question and is consistent with business necessity; and
(7) failing to select and administer tests concerning employment in the most effective manner * * * .

EXHIBIT 18.5
Excerpt from the Americans with Disabilities Act of 1990

used by courts when they are faced with the task of interpreting the meaning of a given statute or statutory provision.

Rules of Construction. Certain statutory rules of interpretation, called **rules of construction**, may prove helpful in your analysis of the statute's language and intent. Examples of statutory rules of interpretation used in many jurisdictions are the following:

RULES OF CONSTRUCTION
The rules that control the judicial interpretation of statutes.

- Specific provisions are given greater weight than general provisions when there is a conflict between the two.
- Recent provisions are given greater weight than earlier provisions when there is a conflict between the two.
- Masculine pronouns refer to both males and females.
- Singular nouns also include the plural forms of the nouns.

PLAIN-MEANING RULE
A rule of statutory interpretation. If the meaning of a statute is clear on its face, then that is the interpretation the court will give to it; inquiry into the legislative history of the statute will not be undertaken.

The Plain-Meaning Rule. In interpreting statutory language, courts also apply the **plain-meaning rule.** Under this rule, the words chosen by the legislature must be understood according to their common meaning. If the statute is clear and unambiguous *on its face* (in its apparent and obvious meaning), and therefore capable of only one interpretation, that interpretation must be given to it. No additional inquiries, such as inquiries into legislative intent or history, are permitted when the meaning of the statute is clear on its face.

The plain-meaning rule, although seemingly simple, is usually not so simple to apply. For one thing, the plain meaning of a statute is rarely totally clear, because legal language, especially in statutes, is difficult to understand and often inherently ambiguous. Also, each word or phrase in a statute takes on meaning only in context—as it relates to the surrounding text. Thus, the interpretation of the meaning of a statutory word, phrase, or provision remains ultimately subjective.

Furthermore, laws, by their very nature, cannot be too specific. When enacting a statute, the legislators often state a broad principle of law and then leave it up to the courts to apply this principle to specific circumstances—which vary from case to case. For example, consider the final two lines of the excerpt from the ADA presented in Exhibit 18.5. What exactly does the clause "failing to select and administer tests concerning employment in the most effective manner" mean? In interpreting this provision, you would need to research case law to see how the courts have interpreted the provision or study the legislative history of the act to understand the legislators' intent in wording the clause in that particular way.

Previous Judicial Interpretation. Paralegals often find that researching statutory law also involves researching case law—to see how the courts have interpreted and applied statutory provisions. As discussed in Chapter 17, courts are obligated to follow the precedents set by higher courts in their jurisdictions. A statutory interpretation made by a higher court therefore must be accepted as binding by lower courts in the same jurisdiction. You can find citations to court cases relating to specific statutes by referring to annotated versions of state or federal statutory codes, as discussed in Chapter 17.

Legislative Intent. Another common technique employed in statutory interpretation is learning the intent of the legislature. A court relying on this method determines the meaning of the statute by attempting to find out why the legislators chose to phrase the statute in the particular language they used or, more generally, what the legislators sought to accomplish by enacting the statute. To discern the intent of the legislators who drafted a particular law, it is often necessary to investigate the legislative history of

DEVELOPING PARALEGAL SKILLS

Interpreting Statutes

Ralph Winter, a paralegal, works for an attorney who is representing the plaintiff in a negligence case. The plaintiff stepped on a broken stair step in her apartment building, fell, and broke her hip. She is suing the owner of the building for negligence. The attorney has successfully opposed the owner-defendant's motion for summary judgment in the case, but the defense is now trying a new tactic. The defense wants to get the venue of the case changed to a county in which the landlord owns and operates a restaurant and owns a significant amount of other commercial property—on the assumption that a jury in that area might be more inclined to favor the defendant. The defense has filed a motion for change of venue, and Ralph is once again researching the law.

He has located a statute entitled "Venue in County Designated." It reads:

> Notwithstanding any provision of this article, the place of trial of an action shall be in the county designated by the plaintiff, unless the place of trial is changed to another county by order, upon motion, or by consent as provided in subdivision (b) of Rule 511. N.Y. Civil Practice Sec. 509 (McKinney 1976).

"This statute is pretty clear and should apply to all civil cases," thinks Ralph. "I'd better check the case annotations and make sure that the courts have applied it to cases similar to that of our client." He turns to the annotations following section 509. Under note 5, he finds the title "Motion for Change of Venue." He begins to read through the annotations and finds a case involving an injured tenant. The annotation states that the court held that proper venue in that case was in the county in which the plaintiff resided, the accident occurred, the plaintiff was treated, and the building's superintendant resided, rather than in the county in which the owner of the apartment building's residence and principal place of business were located.

"This helps our case," thinks Ralph. "We are the plaintiffs, and we filed in the county where the plaintiff resided, the accident occurred, and the plaintiff was treated. The only other county involved is the county in which the defendant does business and owns a significant amount of commercial property. The defense shouldn't be able to change venue to that county. I'd better locate this case and read it carefully to make sure it says what the annotation indicates."

the statute. This can be done by researching committee reports, records of congressional hearings or other proceedings, and other relevant documents. (Refer to Chapter 17 for a discussion of how to research the legislative history of a statute.)

LEGAL WRITING—THE PRELIMINARIES

Part of legal research involves summarizing your results in writing. As a paralegal, you will find that in addition to drafting research summaries, you will be expected to draft numerous other types of materials. In fact, much of your work as a paralegal will involve writing assignments. We will look at writing skills and the kinds of legal materials that paralegals create in subsequent sections. Here, you will read about some of the more general requirements involved in legal writing.

Whenever you receive a writing assignment, you need to understand at the outset (1) the nature of your writing assignment, (2) when it must be completed, and (3) what type of writing approach is appropriate to the assignment. We examine each of these basic requirements here.

Understanding the Assignment

The practice of law is often hectic, and frequently paralegals are requested to research, analyze, and report their results on particular issues within a short time period. When you receive a writing assignment, you should always make sure that you understand the exact nature of the writing request so that you can execute your task as efficiently as possible. The writing style, format, and methodological approach used in legal writing vary, depending on the specific objectives of the document that you are supposed to create. If you need to ask questions, do so. You should never equate asking questions with incompetence. As the adage states, the only "dumb question" is the one that is not asked.

Time Constraints and Flexibility

The time factor is an important consideration in legal writing. When you receive a writing assignment, you need to understand clearly when the assignment must be completed. In some situations, you will be required to submit writings to a court by a certain date, which is inflexible. Additionally, clients usually demand quick responses to questions. And frequently, during the course of litigation or other legal activities, crucial new issues arise that must be addressed immediately, often overnight or within two or three days. As a paralegal, you will need to assess such situations realistically. If little time is given for the completion of a project, you have to make informed judgment calls, deciding what information is crucial to the writing and what can be omitted.

In addition to time constraints, other circumstances may influence the way a paralegal handles an assignment. For example, external circumstances, such as newly enacted laws, may affect the legal treatment of an issue. Additionally, a client may unexpectedly demand a change in the course of action. These situations require flexibility. Whenever you undertake a writing task, you should be prepared for the possibility that you may have to make quick changes and go in new directions before your assignment is completed.

Writing Approaches

Another thing you should determine when you receive a writing assignment is what type of writing is required. Many of your writing assignments will require *objective analysis,* which either focuses on facts or discusses fairly both sides of a legal matter. Other types of assignments will require advocacy, which involves presenting the facts and issues in a light most favorable to your client.

For example, assume that your attorney hands you two lease agreements and asks you to compare them and note whether the differences in the wording of the agreements lead to different obligations. Your concern will not be to point out which agreement is better but to analyze and compare the documents objectively and point out which clauses lead to what kinds of obligations. Objective analysis may also be required when an attorney seeks assistance in providing clients with information regarding a particular legal matter. Clients often seek the advice of an attorney to determine whether or not they have a claim that merits the filing of a lawsuit. In this situation, an attorney may request the paralegal to investigate the issues thoroughly and provide a memorandum containing an accurate and unbiased analysis of the issue.

If the writing assignment is intended to advocate a position, the style of writing will be somewhat different from the style in an objective discussion of the law. In advocating a position, you are primarily concerned with convincing the reader that the argument proposed is stronger than the opposing party's position. You will need to develop supportive legal arguments and present the matter in the light most favorable to the client. (Remember, though, that attorneys have a duty of candor. This duty requires an attorney to disclose mandatory authorities to the court even if those authorities are adverse to the client's position.)

THE IMPORTANCE OF GOOD WRITING SKILLS

As mentioned in Chapter 5, the legal profession is primarily a communications profession. Effective written communications are particularly crucial in the legal arena. For paralegals, good writing skills therefore go hand in hand with successful job performance. The more competent a writer you are, the more likely it is that your finished products will be satisfactory to the attorney with whom you are working. You should also keep in mind that some of your written work, such as correspondence, represents the firm for which you work. A well-written document is a positive reflection on the firm and upholds the firm's reputation for good work.

Each writing assignment that you receive will give you an opportunity to improve and perfect your writing skills. In the following sections, we offer some guidelines that you can follow as you strive to improve your writing. Paralegals who are seriously interested in improving their writing skills also will have close at hand a good dictionary, a thesaurus, a style manual (such as Strunk and White's *Elements of Style* or the *Chicago Manual of Style*), and perhaps a book or two on basic English grammar.

Organize and Outline Your Presentation

Once you know what it is you want to demonstrate, discuss, or prove to your reader, you need to decide how best to organize your ideas to achieve this end. Because organization is essential to effective legal writing, you should have your organizational framework in mind before you begin writing. Most people find that an outline—whether it is a simple sketch in pencil on a scrap of paper or a detailed outline created by a specialized computer program—makes writing easier. It not only saves time but also produces a more organized result.

When creating an outline, you decide the sequence in which topics should be discussed. Some issues will need to be discussed before others, either for logical reasons or for purposes of clarity and readability. Similar issues should be grouped together, either in the same section or under the same topic heading. Some other factors that you will want to consider when organizing your presentation are format and structural devices.

Choice of Format. An important requirement in legal writing is selecting the appropriate format. The format of a document has to do with such things as how wide or narrow the margins should be, how many spaces paragraphs should be indented, how many line spaces should be between paragraphs or other sections, and so on. Documents to be filed with a court must conform to the procedural rules of the particular jurisdiction. Most law firms also adopt special formats for other types of documents, such as correspondence sent to clients and opposing counsel and internal legal memoranda. When writing these types of documents, you need to know what format your firm prefers to use.

Structural Devices. If you are writing about a complex legal research project involving numerous issues, you may want to divide your presentation into several sections, with each section dealing with one issue. You can make it easier for the reader to follow the discussion by including a "road map" to the document. For example, you might preface the writing with an introduction that highlights the points that will be discussed and the conclusion that will be reached, thus orienting the reader to the document's contents. Also, try to "walk" your reader through the analysis and discussion by including descriptive headings and subheadings in the body of the document so that the reader never gets lost.

CHRONOLOGICALLY
In a time sequence; naming or listing events in the time order in which they occurred.

Arranging events **chronologically**—that is, in a time sequence—can also serve as a structural device. A chronologically structured discussion can sometimes be easier for the reader to follow. This is particularly true when you are describing the factual background leading to a lawsuit. Presenting the facts and events in chronological order helps to orient the reader. Even if you are discussing legal issues instead of facts, you might want to use a chronological structure for at least part of your discussion. For example, if you are writing about the historical development of a particular rule of law, you will want to structure that part of the discussion chronologically.

Write to Your Audience

Paralegals prepare legal documents and correspondence for a wide range of people. Whenever you draft legal correspondence or legal documents of any kind, you should keep in mind that legal documents are not ends in themselves. They are created for someone (a judge, an attorney, a client, a witness, or some other person) to read. The ultimate goal of legal writing is to *com-*

municate information or ideas to your reader. It is therefore important to tailor the writing to the intended audience. For example, a letter directed to an attorney may include legal terms and concepts that would be inappropriate in a letter to a layperson, who probably would not understand those terms and concepts. You must therefore consider to whom the legal writing is directed and what legal understanding they possess.

In addition to the reader's legal knowledge, paralegals should consider how well the reader understands the subject matter. You cannot presume, especially in cases dealing with technical and scientific matters, that your reader knows as much as the attorney or yourself. Indeed, you should normally assume the contrary—that the reader has had neither the time nor the background to gain a comprehensive understanding of every legal or factual matter presented. Both in consideration of your reader's needs and in the interests of effective communication, you should present your information or analysis clearly, carefully leading the reader from point A to point B, from point B to point C, and so on.

Avoid Legalese

As a paralegal, writing to your audience often requires you to minimize or eliminate legal jargon, or legalese. As discussed earlier in this text, legalese consists of terms that are used by legal professionals but that are unknown to most people outside the legal profession. Therefore, if you are writing a letter to a client, either avoid using legal terms that the client may not understand or define such terms for your reader. For example, if you are advising a client of the date on which *voir dire* will take place, consider saying "jury selection"—or perhaps "*voir dire* (jury selection)"—instead. Although a certain amount of legal terminology in legal writing is unavoidable, you should minimize the use of language that may confuse the reader.

Lawyers have traditionally used certain terms in legal documents—words such as *hereof, therein,* and *thereto,* for example—that you should avoid whenever possible in your writing. These and similar words sound strange and excessively formal to the ordinary person. Legal documents are also often filled with redundancies. Consider, for example, the following sentence from an agreement to finance a business:

> If Borrower shall have made any representation or warranty herein . . . which shall be in any material respect false and/or erroneous and/or incorrect . . .

What is the difference between *false, erroneous,* and *incorrect*? Often, these terms are used synonymously, and it is hard to imagine that something could be erroneous and still be correct—so why should it be necessary to add *incorrect* to the clause?

Other commonly used legal phrases containing obvious redundancies include *all the rest, residue, and remainder; null and void; full and complete;* and *cease and desist.* In the first phrase, the words *rest, residue,* and *remainder* mean essentially the same thing. In the second phrase, the words *null* and *void* are synonymous, as are the coupled terms in the other phrases. Yet these types of phrases are commonplace in legal documents, largely because they have been traditionally used in the legal profession and because of the natural inclination of lawyers to want to make sure that all aspects of a given subject are covered.

As a paralegal, you should strive to minimize the use of legalese, including redundancies, in your own writing—but be cautious:

- **When translating legalese into plain English, you need to make sure that you correctly understand the intent of the legal phrase. If you have any doubts, always ask your supervising attorney.**

Be Brief and to the Point

Just as the use of legalese can hinder communication, so, too, can the use of too many words. Writing effectively requires efficiency in word usage. Unnecessary words can become stumbling blocks for your reader and prevent a clear understanding of the point that you want to make. When you are proofreading your document, take time to make sure that your statements are brief and to the point. Exhibit 18.6 offers some examples of how efficient word usage can enhance clarity.

Generally, you should only use words that are essential to the point that you are making; unnecessary words will only distract or confuse your reader. Similarly, you should include in your writing only concepts or factual information that are directly relevant to your topic.

Writing Basics: Sentences

A good writer uses a high proportion of short, concrete sentences because they are easier to understand. Additionally, forceful sentences include active, dynamic verbs rather than nominalizations (which are verbs transformed into nouns). For example, it is simpler and more effective to say "the plaintiff decided to settle the case" than "the plaintiff made a decision to settle the case." In the first example, the verb *decide* is direct and forceful. In the second example, the conversion of *decided* into *made a decision* detracts from the forcefulness of the verb.

Writing in the active voice also makes sentences easier to understand. The active voice sets up a subject-verb-object sentence structure, whereas the passive voice uses an object-verb-subject format. For example, "The defendant stole the diamond" uses the active voice. Contrast the simplicity and strength of this statement with its passive equivalent: "The diamond was stolen by the defendant." The use of the active voice puts people, actors, movers, and doers into your writing and thus makes your writing more reflective of reality. Sometimes, however, you may want to maintain the facelessness of the actor or doer. For example, if your firm is defending a plaintiff who has been accused of stealing a diamond, considering writing "the diamond that was stolen" instead of "the diamond that the plaintiff allegedly stole." In this situation, the passive voice effectively removes the plaintiff from the action.

You should also make sure that you use correct grammar when writing legal documents. Grammatical and punctuation errors, such as those in the following sentences, distract your reader and may reflect poorly on your (and your firm's) professional reputation and status.

21

EMPLOYMENT LAW

EXHIBIT 18.6
Using Words Efficiently

Do not write:
Ms. Carpenter never drives at night due to the fact that she has poor night vision.

Write instead:
Ms. Carpenter does not drive at night because she has poor night vision.

Do not write:
The new client who brought his business to our attention yesterday has a number of issues pertaining to his legal problems that he needs to discuss with us as soon as possible.

Write instead:
The client who hired us yesterday needs to discuss his legal problems immediately.

Do not write:
The defendant worked for one of the members of an organized crime ring for a period of seven years. During that seven-year period of time, the defendant witnessed crimes numbering in the hundreds.

Write instead:
During the seven years that the defendant worked for a member of an organized crime ring, he witnessed hundreds of crimes.

- *Incorrect:* The plaintiff should *of* consulted with the defendant.
  Correct: The plaintiff should *have* consulted with the defendant.
- *Incorrect:* The defendant could not possibly have *did* what the plaintiff alleged.
  Correct: The defendant could not possibly have *done* what the plaintiff alleged.
- *Incorrect:* The *plaintiffs* allegations were vague and ambiguous.
  Correct: The *plaintiff's* allegations were vague and ambiguous.

When proofreading your documents, you should make sure that they are free of any errors involving subject-verb agreement, punctuation, spelling, the use of apostrophes, and other elements.

Writing Basics: Paragraphs and Transitions

A paragraph is a group of sentences that develops a particular idea. A paragraph should have unity and coherence. Each paragraph should begin with a *topic sentence* that indicates what the paragraph is about. Each subsequent sentence in the paragraph should contribute to the development of the topic; if it does not, consider placing the sentence elsewhere or simply deleting it. When you write, be conscious of why you begin a new paragraph—or why you do not. When you proofread, watch carefully for how you are using paragraphs. You should create a new paragraph whenever you start discussing another idea. Paragraphs that are not logically constructed are often confusing and pointless for the reader.

Take your reader with you as you move from one paragraph to another. Although the connection between paragraphs may be clear to you, the writer, it may not be clear to your reader. You need to show, by including transitional sentences or phrases, how a topic discussed in one paragraph relates to the subsequent paragraph. Exhibit 18.7 on the next page lists some of the terms and phrases that writers commonly use to effect smooth transitions.

EXHIBIT 18.7
Transitional Terms and Phrases

1. **Words that indicate a conceptual or causal sequence or relationship. Examples:**

   The *third* element required for a cause of action under negligence theory is that the plaintiff must have suffered a legally recognizable injury.

   As a result of the fall, the plaintiff was injured.

2. **Words that indicate a chronological sequence of events. Examples:**

   After the fall, the plaintiff was taken to Nita City Hospital & Clinic.

   Before the plaintiff's accident, she was in excellent health.

3. **Words that refer back to the subject discussed in the previous paragraph. Examples:**

   Courts make exceptions to *this rule* in certain situations, however.

   The act does not apply to employers who have fewer than fifteen employees, however.

   If the *above-mentioned conditions* are not met, the injured party cannot recover damages.

   In contrast to negligence actions, actions in strict liability do not require the plaintiff to prove that the defendant breached a duty of care.

   If the *plaintiff* had not been *injured in the fall*, then she would have no cause of action against the store owner.

4. **Words that introduce summaries. Examples:**

   In short, the plaintiff has a valid claim against the defendant.

   In summary, the plaintiff met all four conditions for a negligence action against the defendant.

   To conclude, the plaintiff established the element of causation by demonstrating that she would not have been injured if it had not been for the defendant's actions.

Be Alert for Sexist Language

The language of the law has traditionally used masculine pronouns inclusively—that is, to refer to both males and females. Jurists, legal scholars, and others in the legal profession are consciously moving away from this tradition. As a paralegal, you should take special care to become aware of and avoid sexist language in your own writing. For example, if you see a word with "man" or "men" in it (such as *policeman, fireman,* or *workmen's compensation*) use a gender-neutral substitute for it (such as *police officer, fire fighter,* or *workers' compensation*). In the past decade or so, writers have devised various ways to avoid using masculine pronouns when the gender of the referent is unknown. Some of these ways are as follows:

- Use *he or she* rather than *he.*
- Alternate between the use of masculine and feminine pronouns.
- Make the noun plural so that a gender-neutral plural pronoun (*they, their,* or *them*) can be used.
- Repeat the noun rather than using a pronoun.

Proofread and Revise Your Document

A crucial part of legal writing involves proofreading and revising your document. When you receive a writing assignment, you should always allow time to proofread and revise whatever it is that you are writing. Virtually no writer can turn out an error-free document on the first try, and as a paralegal, you will be especially concerned with accuracy. Proofreading your document allows you to discover and correct typographical errors, to see whether your document reflects a logical progression of thought from one topic to another, and to verify whether you have covered all of the relevant facts or issues. You should use the spell checker in your computer, and perhaps the grammar checker as well, to assist you in proofreading.

When you write your first draft, you have much to think about, and you may overlook many things. When proofreading your document, you can pay more attention to organizational coherence, transitions, paragraph construction, sentence formation, word choice, sexist language, and the like. You might find it helpful to develop a "writing checklist" to remind you of certain things you want to avoid or achieve in your writing—particularly if there is a required format for the particular type of document on which you are working. When you are writing legal documents, always keep the following advice in mind:

- **Creating a polished document takes time, and a good portion of that time should be spent in proofreading and revising your written work product.**

ETHICAL CONCERN

Ethics and Time Management

Many paralegals learn the hard way—through trial and error—that the ability to manage their time effectively is an essential part of doing a good job. One of the easiest things to overlook when engaging in research and writing is that good writing takes time—you may need to revise a document several times before you are satisfied with its quality. Whenever you are given a writing assignment, you should make sure that you allow yourself enough time to revise and polish your final document. As a paralegal, you have an ethical duty to your supervising attorney, the firm, and the client to serve their best interests. In regard to legal writing, their interests are served by the production of clear and convincing legal documents—and by your ability to manage time so that this goal can be achieved.

PLEADINGS AND DISCOVERY

Many writing tasks undertaken by paralegals involve forms that must be submitted to the court or to opposing counsel before a trial begins or after the trial has commenced. These documents were covered in detail earlier in this text, in Chapters 10 and 11. You can review those chapters for explanations and illustrations of the forms required for pretrial procedures (pleadings, discovery procedures, and pretrial motions) and for motions made during the trial.

It is especially important that such documents contain the required information and be presented in the appropriate format. Form books and computerized forms offer guidelines, but you should always become familiar with the rules of the court in which the documents are being filed to ensure that you use the proper format.

GENERAL LEGAL CORRESPONDENCE

Paralegals are often asked to draft letters to clients, witnesses, opposing counsel, and others. Even when a message may already have been conveyed orally (in person or by phone) to one of these parties, the paralegal may be asked to write a letter confirming in writing what was discussed orally. Lawyers are extremely conscious of the need to document communications so as to avoid future problems. The existence of the written

FEATURED GUEST: RICHARD M. TERRY

Ten Tips for Effective Legal Writing

Biographical Note

Richard M. Terry received his bachelor's degree and master's degree from the University of Baltimore. He worked as a legal assistant for ten years. During that time, he was a supervisor in the Office of the Public Defender for Baltimore City. Currently, he is an assistant professor and the coordinator of the legal-assistant program at Baltimore City Community College.

Writing is one of the major forms of communication. As a paralegal, you will be asked to write every day throughout your career. Writing in this profession can take many forms, depending on your specialty and on your employer. You may be asked to prepare letters to clients, reports on client interviews and investigations, and responses to legal questions that you have researched. And make no mistake—every document you prepare will be important. The tips for effective legal writing given below are not cast in stone. They are general guidelines that will make you a better legal writer, not only while you are in school but also when you enter the profession.

1 Plan before You Write. In this age of computerized word processing, there is a tremendous temptation just to sit down at the keyboard and begin to type, creating as you go along. Avoid this temptation. Instead, prepare a plan of action before you put the first word on paper. Your plan of action will consist of a few simple steps. First, if your supervising attorney has asked you to write the document, make sure that he or she has spelled out clearly what is needed. Second, if you are drafting a particular type of document (such as a pleading or memorandum) for the first time, ask for or find a sample to use, perhaps in your firm's files. Third, outline the document before you begin writing. Making an outline is the key to producing a well-organized document. Fourth, just before printing out the final copy of the document, check with the attorney again, just to make sure that you have not missed any key points.

2 Write with a Purpose. Writing with a purpose means writing with an identifiable goal in mind. The document that you produce must reflect that purpose. Generally, the purpose for any legal document is either objective or adversarial. A document with an objective purpose simply passes on information, without any appearance of bias. A document with an adversarial purpose emphasizes the strong points of one position versus the weak points of another. Adversarial writing reflects a definite bias.

3 Write Clearly. Remember that simple is usually better. Try to say exactly what you mean, and use standard vocabulary and terms that are clear and concrete. It is not necessary to show that you have a mastery of legal language. Identify your audience, and write to the people who will ultimately read your document. The style and tone of your writing should change with the document's intended audience, as well as with the purpose of the document. When you write to a client, for example, try to avoid the use of technical or legal terms. Your tone should be explanatory, and you should define legal terms and describe the consequences of legal actions. In contrast, when you are writing to the court or to attorneys, you will not need to explain legal terms or concepts. Remember, too, that readers normally do not have

document clarifies any ambiguities that might arise in connection with the oral conversation and confirms that the conversation took place.

Law firms normally have an official letterhead and stationery. The letterhead contains certain information about the firm. Most letterheads

FEATURED GUEST, Continued

time to figure out what you are trying to say. Structure what you write, get to the point, and stick to it.

4 Use Proper Grammar and Sentence Structure. Legal documents once were routinely written in highly formal, complex language, but over the past few years, writing in plain English has become the rule. As a result, legal documents are no longer as long and complicated as they once were. No matter which style you use, however, you must observe the rules of basic grammar and punctuation that you learned in junior and senior high school. Make sure, for example, that you write in complete sentences and punctuate long sentences correctly.

5 Use an Appropriate Writing Style. Style is a broad term. In a general sense, it refers to how you express what you have to say, as opposed to the content of your writing. For example, a piece of writing can have a formal or an informal style. More narrowly, style can refer to specific forms, such as the form of a legal citation or of the names of particular courts. A good style manual can assist in determining what is an appropriate style. Style manuals give many basic rules and explain how the rules apply in different contexts. Well-known style manuals include *The Elements of Style* by William Strunk, Jr., and E. B. White, and the *Chicago Manual of Style,* currently in its fourteenth edition. For the proper format for legal citations, a good source to consult is *A Uniform System of Citation* (known as the Bluebook).

6 Edit Your Work. The first draft of a document is not necessarily correct in every detail. Always go back and review objectively what you have written. If possible, have someone else read it for you. If that is not possible, try reading the document backwards—that is, from the last line to the first line. More often than not, you will catch at least some spelling and punctuation errors this way.

7 Use Computers Effectively. The computer has come of age in the law office of the 1990s. Using computers saves time and reduces the potential for errors in legal writing. There is no excuse for sending out any document containing spelling and grammatical mistakes if the document was produced on a computer. Use the spell-checker and grammar-checker functions to ensure that the document has no spelling or grammatical errors before you print it. Because today's law office relies heavily on computers for both research and writing, legal assistants who wish to succeed on the job should become knowledgeable in the use of computers and legal software.

8 Keep Copies. Whenever you create a document, keep a copy for your files. For one thing, this will help you to create a "forms file." Legal writing is somewhat repetitive. The form stays the same, and only the names and facts are changed. Creating a forms file will, in the long run, save you time and effort.

"IDENTIFY YOUR AUDIENCE, AND WRITE TO THE PEOPLE WHO WILL ULTIMATELY READ YOUR DOCUMENT."

9 Consider New Writing Methods and Styles. Keeping abreast of what others in the field are doing and how they write may affect the format and style of your writing. Read as many trade publications as possible. Papers such as the *National Law Journal* are great sources of information, and magazines such as *Legal Assistant Today* often give interesting writing tips. Another way of keeping up with current information is to network with others in the profession. Maybe another legal assistant has a method or style of writing that is suited to your situation. Don't close your mind to it.

10 Practice, Practice, Practice. Good, effective writing is an art that requires a great deal of practice. The more you write, the better you become.

include the firm's name, address, and phone number. Some firms have more descriptive letterheads that include the names of partners in the firm or the various geographical locations in which the firm has offices. You should always use your firm's letterhead when writing a letter on behalf of one of

the firm's attorneys or when writing as a representative of the firm. The first page of any correspondence from the firm should be composed on letterhead paper. Any additional pages can be printed on numbered continuing sheets (plain, matching stationery).

In this section, you will read about some typical requirements relating to legal correspondence. Keep in mind, though, that the particular law firm, corporate legal department, or government agency for which you work will probably have its own specific procedures and requirements that you will need to follow.

General Format for Legal Correspondence

Although there are many types of legal correspondence, the general format of a legal letter includes the components discussed below and illustrated in Exhibit 18.8.

Date. Legal correspondence must be *dated.* The date appears below the official letterhead of the firm. You should make sure that the date is correctly keyed in. Be especially careful after the turn of a year. Many people continue to use the preceding year on correspondence, checks, and other documents simply out of habit. In a legal document, however, entering the wrong year could have important legal consequences.

As explained earlier, dates serve an important function in legal matters. The date of a letter may be important in matters involving legal notice of a particular event. Additionally, legal correspondence normally is filed chronologically. Without any indication of when the letter was written, accurate filing of the letter would be difficult, if not impossible. As a general rule, you should always place a date on every written item that you create, including telephone messages, memos to file, and personal reminders to yourself.

ADDRESS BLOCK
That part of a letter that indicates to whom the letter is addressed. The address block is placed in the upper left-hand portion of the letter, above the salutation (or reference line, if one is included).

Method of Delivery and Address Block. Below the date is a line indicating the method of delivery, or how the letter was sent (if other than by U.S. mail), which is followed by the **address block**, which indicates to whom the letter is addressed. If the letter was sent by Federal Express, the line before the recipient's name and address will read VIA FEDERAL EXPRESS. If the letter is hand delivered, the line will read BY HAND DELIVERY. Communication by facsimile can be described by the words BY FAX or BY FACSIMILE. The address block should contain the name of the person to whom the letter is written, the person's title, and the name and address of the person's firm or place of business.

REFERENCE LINE
The portion of the letter that indicates the matter to be discussed in the letter, such as "RE: Summary of Cases Applying the Family and Medical Leave Act of 1993." The reference line is placed just below the address block and above the salutation.

Reference Line and Salutation. Following the address block, the writer may include a **reference line** identifying the matter discussed in the letter. In a letter regarding a pending lawsuit, the reference line may contain the name of the case, its case file (or docket) number, and a brief notation of the nature of the legal dispute. Many attorneys also include the firm's file number for the case. In an informative letter (to be discussed shortly), the reference line may take the form of a title. For example, a letter concerning the closing procedures for a financing transaction may be entitled "RE: Closing Procedures for ABC Company's $4,000,000 Financing Package."

EXHIBIT 18.8
Components of a Legal Letter

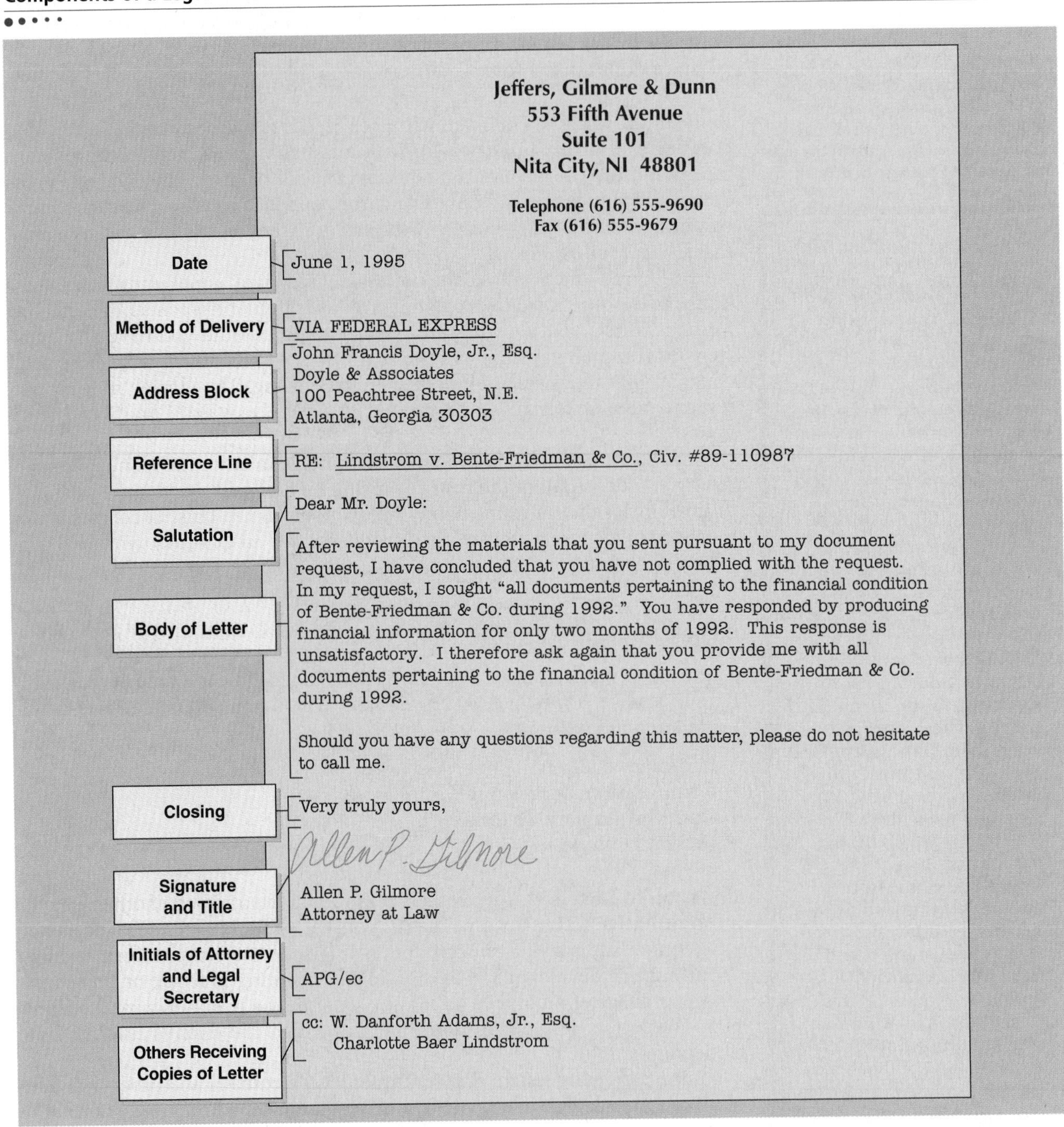
Jeffers, Gilmore & Dunn
553 Fifth Avenue
Suite 101
Nita City, NI 48801

Telephone (616) 555-9690
Fax (616) 555-9679

June 1, 1995

VIA FEDERAL EXPRESS

John Francis Doyle, Jr., Esq.
Doyle & Associates
100 Peachtree Street, N.E.
Atlanta, Georgia 30303

RE: Lindstrom v. Bente-Friedman & Co., Civ. #89-110987

Dear Mr. Doyle:

After reviewing the materials that you sent pursuant to my document request, I have concluded that you have not complied with the request. In my request, I sought "all documents pertaining to the financial condition of Bente-Friedman & Co. during 1992." You have responded by producing financial information for only two months of 1992. This response is unsatisfactory. I therefore ask again that you provide me with all documents pertaining to the financial condition of Bente-Friedman & Co. during 1992.

Should you have any questions regarding this matter, please do not hesitate to call me.

Very truly yours,

Allen P. Gilmore

Allen P. Gilmore
Attorney at Law

APG/ec

cc: W. Danforth Adams, Jr., Esq.
Charlotte Baer Lindstrom

The **salutation**, which appears just below the reference line, is a greeting to the addressee. Because legal correspondence is a professional means of communication, the salutation, as well as the body of the letter, should be formal in tone. There are, of course, circumstances in which a formal

SALUTATION
The formal greeting to the addressee of the letter. The salutation is placed just below the reference line.

Closing
A final comment to a letter that is placed above the signature, such as "Very truly yours."

Informative Letter
A letter that conveys certain information to a client, a witness, an adversary's counsel, or other person regarding some legal matter (such as the date, time, place, and purpose of a meeting).

greeting may not be necessary. For example, if the addressee is someone you know quite well, it may be appropriate to address the person by his or her first name, rather than by "Mr." or "Ms." In these situations, you must use your discretion to determine the appropriate level of formality. Generally, when in doubt, use a formal salutation.

Body and Closing. The main part of the letter is the body of the letter. The body of the letter should be formal and should effectively communicate information to the reader. As a representative of the firm, the paralegal must be careful to proofread all outgoing correspondence to ensure that the letter contains accurate information, is clearly written, and is free of any grammatical or spelling errors.

Following the body of the letter are standard concluding sentences. These final sentences are usually courteous statements such as "Thank you for your time and attention to this matter," or "Should you have any questions or comments, please call me at the above-listed number." These brief concluding statements are followed by the **closing**. The closing in legal correspondence is formal—for example, "Sincerely yours" or "Very truly yours."

Finally, you should always include your title in any correspondence written by you on behalf of the firm. Your title ("Paralegal" or "Legal Assistant" or other title) should immediately follow your name. This, of course, is not a concern when you prepare correspondence for an attorney who will provide a signature.

Ethical Concern

"Confidential" Correspondence

As a paralegal, you may be faced with the question of whether you should open letters to the attorney for whom you work when the letters are marked "Confidential." For example, suppose that you work for an attorney who is out of the country for two weeks. Because she will be hard to reach during this time, she has instructed you to open all of her mail for her and respond appropriately to certain matters. She has explicitly told you to call her only if an emergency arises. While she is gone, you receive a letter to the attorney that is marked "Confidential." You recognize the sender's name (an attorney who is defending against a lawsuit brought by one of your supervising attorney's clients) and suspect that the letter pertains to the lawsuit. Should you open the letter? Should you hold it until your attorney returns? Or should you try to contact your attorney for advice? To avoid this kind of situation, ask your employer in advance how you should handle confidential mail. Some attorneys routinely have their paralegals open this type of mail; others do not.

Types of Legal Letters

There are several types of legal correspondence, and each type serves a different purpose. Types of legal letters with which you should become familiar include the following:

- Informative letters.
- Confirmation letters.
- Opinion (advisory) letters.
- Demand letters.

Informative Letters. A letter that conveys information to another party is an **informative letter**. As a paralegal, you will write many such letters—to clients, for example. Informative letters might be written to inform a client about current developments in a case, an upcoming meeting or procedure, the general background on a legal issue, or simply a breakdown of the firm's bill. The letters you write should be tailored to the client's level of legal understanding.

Informative letters are also sent to opposing counsel and other individuals. For example, law firms often send litigation-scheduling information to opposing counsel, witnesses, and other persons who may be involved in a trial. Informative letters may also be used as transmittal (cover) letters when documents or other materials are sent to a client, a court, opposing counsel, or some other person. Exhibit 18.9 shows a sample letter written to an individual who will testify during an arbitration procedure.

EXHIBIT 18.9
A Sample Informative Letter

Jeffers, Gilmore & Dunn
553 Fifth Avenue
Suite 101
Nita City, NI 48801

Telephone (616) 555-9690
Fax (616) 555-9679

June 24, 1995

Bernadette P. Williams
149 Snowflake Drive
Irving, TX 75062

RE: Kempf/Joseph Arbitration Proceedings

Dear Ms. Williams:

The arbitration will resume on Monday, August 1, 1995. Please arrive at the offices of the American Arbitration Association (the AAA) before 8:30 A.M. The offices of the AAA are located at 400 West Ferry Boulevard in Dallas. You will be called as a witness some time before 12:00 noon.

Should you have any questions or concerns regarding your responsibilities as a witness, please do not hesitate to contact me.

Sincerely,

Elena Lopez

Elena Lopez
Legal Assistant

Confirmation Letters. Another type of letter frequently written by paralegals is the confirmation letter. **Confirmation letters** are similar to informative letters in that they communicate certain information to the reader. Confirmation letters put into written form the contents of an oral discussion. In addition to providing attorneys with a permanent record of earlier conversations, confirmation letters also safeguard against any misinterpretation or misunderstanding of what was communicated orally. See Exhibit 18.10 on page 731 for an example of a confirmation letter.

CONFIRMATION LETTER
A letter that states the substance of a previously conducted verbal discussion to provide a permanent record of the oral conversation.

Opinion Letters. The function of an **opinion letter**, or **advisory letter**, is to provide not only information but also advice. In contrast to informative letters, opinion letters actually give a legal opinion about the matter discussed. Attorneys providing opinion letters are required to provide a detailed analysis of the law and to bring the analysis to a definite conclusion, setting forth the firm's opinion on the matter.

OPINION (ADVISORY) LETTER
A letter from an attorney to a client that contains a legal opinion on an issue raised by the client's question or legal claim. The opinion is based on a detailed analysis of the law.

In addition to rendering the law firm's legal opinion, opinion letters may also be used to inform a client of the legal validity of a specific action. For example, a company seeking to establish operations in a foreign country may

DEVELOPING PARALEGAL SKILLS

Writing to Clients

Leslie Linden works as a paralegal for Sandra O'Connell, a sole practitioner who owns a small family-law practice. Sandra asks Leslie to draft a letter to a client, Karen Young, explaining that her divorce hearing is scheduled for June 3, 1995, and informing her that she needs to be present in court on that date. Leslie is also supposed to tell the client what the procedure will be and ask her to call the office to make an appointment to discuss the proceeding before June 3.

Leslie sits down at her word processor and begins to draft the letter to the client. First, she types the date, the method of delivery, the address block, and the salutation. Because it is a formal letter, she uses "Dear Mrs. Young" in the salutation. Next, she begins the body of the letter:

> The hearing for your divorce is scheduled to take place on Monday, June 3, 1995, at 10 A.M. The hearing will be conducted in Room 2B of the Jefferson County Courthouse in Jefferson City. Please arrive at the courthouse by 9:30 A.M.
>
> Because this is a no-fault divorce state, your divorce is not contested, and we have worked out your property settlement in advance, the hearing will be brief. We expect you to be on the stand for only fifteen minutes at the most. You will be asked to make a statement concerning your reasons for wanting a divorce, and the judge will ask you a few questions.
>
> Ms. O'Connell would like you to call the office and schedule an appointment, at your convenience, to prepare you for the hearing. She will discuss with you at that time what you will say on the stand and the kinds of questions that the judge will probably ask you. Please contact the office at your earliest convenience.

Leslie then inserts the closing, leaves four lines, and types her name and just below it her title, Legal Assistant. She prints the letter on the firm's stationery, proofreads it carefully, and sends it to Mrs. Young.

seek a lawyer's opinion on whether a certain action it plans to undertake is legally permissible. The attorney (or a paralegal) will research the issue and then draft an advisory letter to the client. Opinion letters are commonly quite long and include detailed explanations of how the law applies to the client's factual situation. Sometimes, the attorney just summarizes his or her conclusion in the opinion letter (as in the opinion letter shown in Exhibit 18.11 on page 732) and attaches a legal memorandum to the letter explaining the legal sources and reasoning used in forming that conclusion.

Opinion letters issued by a firm reflect legal expertise and advice on which a client can rely. Note the following rule:

- **Opinion letters must be signed by attorneys.**

Should doubts about the legal validity of an opinion letter surface at a later date, the client may bring a malpractice suit against the firm. The signature

EXHIBIT 18.10
A Sample Confirmation Letter

Jeffers, Gilmore & Dunn
553 Fifth Avenue
Suite 101
Nita City, NI 48801

Telephone (616) 555-9690
Fax (616) 555-9679

August 3, 1995

Pauline C. Dunbar
President
Minute-Magic Corporation
7689 Industrial Boulevard
San Francisco, CA 80021

RE: Purchase of real estate from C. C. Barnes, Inc.

Dear Ms. Dunbar:

The following information describes the current status of the negotiations between C. C. Barnes, Inc., and Minute-Magic Corporation:

Selling Price: $400,000
Financing Agreement: Citywide Bank
Interest Rate: 8.5%

This information confirms what I told you on the phone today. I look forward to seeing you next week. Should you have any questions or comments in the meantime, please give me a call.

Very truly yours,

Allen P. Gilmore

Allen P. Gilmore
Attorney at Law

APG/ec

of an attorney represents the attorney's acceptance of responsibility for what is stated in the document and can serve as the basis for liability.

Demand Letters. Another basic type of letter is the demand letter. **Demand letters** are adversarial in nature and seek to advance the interests of a client. Usually, a demand letter attempts to persuade the reader to accept the position most favorable to the client. For example, your supervising attorney may ask you to draft a letter to a client's debtor, demanding payment for an amount owed. Whatever the content of a demand letter, its purpose is to demand something of the recipient on behalf of the client.

DEMAND LETTER
An adversarial letter that attempts to persuade the reader that he or she should accept a position that is favorable to the writer's client—that is, demanding that the reader do or not do a certain thing.

The demand letter should adopt a serious and persuasive tone, and the client's demand must not be frivolous. Although the letter should be insistent and adversarial, it should not come across as unreasonable or harassing. After all, demand letters seek to accomplish something rather than foreclose

EXHIBIT 18.11
A Sample Opinion Letter

Jeffers, Gilmore & Dunn
553 Fifth Avenue
Suite 101
Nita City, NI 48801

Telephone (616) 555-9690
Fax (616) 555-9679

December 9, 1995

J. D. Joslyn
President and Chief Executive Officer
Joslyn Footwear, Inc.
700 Kings Avenue, Suite 4000
New City, NI 48023

Dear Ms. Joslyn:

After careful consideration of your plans to expand Joslyn Footwear, Inc., into Latin American markets, I have concluded that to implement the current plans would subject you to potentially significant liability.

The most serious flaw in the current plans concerns your construction of massive shoe-producing industrial plants. Unfortunately, the plans fail to conform to the minimum legal and industrial regulations in Mexico, Uruguay, and Argentina.

The enclosed legal memorandum explains in detail how the law applies to your situation and the reasons for my conclusion. Please call me if you have any questions.

Very truly yours,

Allen P. Gilmore

Allen P. Gilmore
Attorney at Law

APG/ec

Enclosure

ETHICAL CONCERN

Letters and the Unauthorized Practice of Law

As has been stressed in other areas of this text, engaging in the unauthorized practice of law is one of the most serious potential ethical and legal problems facing paralegals. To avoid liability for the unauthorized practice of law, you should never sign opinion (advisory) letters with your own name, and when you sign other types of letters, you should always indicate your status as a paralegal. Even if the person to whom you are sending the letter knows you quite well and knows that you are a paralegal, you should indicate your status on the letter itself. By doing so, you will prevent potential confusion as well as potential legal liability. Even if your name and status is included in the letterhead (as is permitted under some state laws), as a precaution, you should type your title below your name at the end of the letter as well.

opportunities. A common form of demand letter in litigation firms is a letter in which an attorney requests a response from an adversarial party in a lawsuit to an offer to settle the case. Exhibit 18.12 illustrates this type of demand letter.

THE INTERNAL MEMORANDUM

The internal legal memorandum, as the term implies, is prepared for internal use within a law firm, legal department, or other organization or agency. As a paralegal, you may be asked to draft a legal memorandum for your

EXHIBIT 18.12
A Sample Demand Letter

Jeffers, Gilmore & Dunn
553 Fifth Avenue
Suite 101
Nita City, NI 48801

Telephone (616) 555-9690
Fax (616) 555-9679

June 15, 1996

Christopher P. Nelson, Esq.
Nelson, Johnson, Callan & Sietz
200 Way Bridge
Philadelphia, PA 40022

RE: Furman v. Thompson

Dear Mr. Nelson:

This morning, I met with my clients, Mark and Andrea Furman, the plaintiffs in the lawsuit against your client, Laura Thompson. Both Mark and Andrea expressed a desire to withdraw their complaint and settle with Ms. Thompson. The Furmans' settlement demand is $20,000, payable by certified check no later than July 7, 1996. Considering the strength of the plaintiffs' claims against Ms. Thompson and the possibility of a jury award exceeding $100,000, the Furmans and I think that you and your client will find this demand quite reasonable.

Please contact me by Friday, June 25, 1996, if you plan to take advantage of the Furmans' demand. If we do not hear from you by that date, we will interpret your inaction as a rejection of the Furmans' settlement offer.

Very truly yours,

Allen P. Gilmore

Allen P. Gilmore
Attorney at Law

APG/ec

supervising attorney. Generally, the legal memo presents a thorough summary and analysis of a particular legal problem.

The attorney for whom the document is prepared may be relying on the memo for a number of reasons. For example, the attorney may be preparing a brief on behalf of a client or an opinion letter regarding a client's claim. Thus, if you are asked to draft the memo, you will want it to be extremely thorough and clearly written. Because the legal memo is directed to attorneys who are knowledgeable in the law, there is no need to avoid sophisticated legal terminology or to define basic legal theories or procedures.

The purpose of the memo is to provide an attorney with all relevant information regarding the case, so the document is written objectively. It is

PARALEGAL PROFILE Administrative-law Paralegal

DIANE SOROKO has a bachelor of arts degree from Georgia State University and received her paralegal certificate, with honors, from the National Center of Paralegal Training in Atlanta. Soroko has worked for about four years in the area of administrative law, which deals mainly with industries regulated by the federal and state governments.

What do you like best about your work?

"What I like most about my job is the client contact. I work primarily with immigration and naturalization, telecommunications, and health care. A typical day for me involves monitoring meetings and assisting clients. I enjoy working with people and building relationships to achieve goals. The failure or success of our efforts in such areas as immigration can dramatically affect clients' lives."

"THE GREATEST CHALLENGE FOR ME IS THE CROSS-CULTURAL DIMENSION OF MY JOB."

What is the greatest challenge that you face in your area of work?

"The greatest challenge for me is the cross-cultural dimension of my job. I deal with many international clients, and cultural differences can be challenging. I have to be sensitive to other perspectives, viewpoints, and customs."

What advice do you have for would-be paralegals in your area of work?

"I recommend a focus on both communication and writing skills. Organizational skills are also critical for all paralegal work and especially in the area of administrative law."

What are some tips for success as a paralegal in your area of work?

"Tips for success as an administrative-law paralegal include having excellent writing, communication, and computer skills. People skills are also an important asset. Don't be afraid to carve out a niche for yourself and aggressively seek what you want to do."

an explanatory memo informing the attorney of all sides of the issues presented, including both the strengths and weaknesses of the client's claim or defense. You should keep the following in mind:

- **Your goal in drafting a legal memorandum is to inform, explain, and evaluate the client's claim or defense.**

A legal memorandum is organized in a logical manner. Although there is no one way to structure the legal memo, most are divided into sections that perform distinct functions. Of course, if the law firm or the attorney for whom you are working prefers a particular format, that format should be followed. Generally, legal memos contain the following sections:

- Heading.
- Statement of the facts.
- Questions presented.
- Brief conclusion to questions presented.

- Discussion and analysis of the facts and the applicable law.
- Conclusion.

Heading

The *heading* of a legal memorandum contains four pieces of information:

- The date on which the memo is submitted.
- The name of the person submitting the memo.
- The name of the person for whom the memo was prepared.
- A brief description of the matter, usually in the form of a reference line.

Exhibit 18.13 illustrates a sample heading for a legal memorandum.

Statement of the Facts

The *statement of the facts* introduces the legal issues by describing the factual elements of the dispute. Only the relevant facts are included in this section. Thus, a key requirement of paralegals is that they learn which facts are legally significant. In other words, as a paralegal, you will need to determine which facts have a bearing on the legal issues in the case and which facts are irrelevant.

Facts presented in a legal memo must not be slanted in favor of the client. The legal memo is not an adversarial argument on the client's behalf. Rather, it is an objective presentation of both the facts and the legal issues. Therefore, you should never omit facts that are unfavorable to the client's claim or defense. The attorney for whom you work needs to know all of the facts that will influence the outcome of the case.

The statement of the facts should contain a logical and concise description of the events surrounding the conflict. Presenting events chronologically often helps to clarify the factual pattern in a case. Alternatively, facts relating to the same issue can be grouped together. The latter organizational technique is especially useful when the facts are complicated and numerous legal issues are presented.

Exhibit 18.14 on the following page indicates what kinds of information are typically included in a statement of the facts. It also shows what writing style is generally used.

EXHIBIT 18.13
Legal Memorandum—Heading

MEMORANDUM

DATE: August 6, 1995

TO: Allen P. Gilmore, Partner

FROM: Elena Lopez, Paralegal

RE: Neely, Rachel: Emotional Distress—File No. 95-2146
Neely, Rachel, and Melanie: Emotional Distress—File No. 95-2147

EXHIBIT 18.14
Legal Memorandum—Statement of the Facts

STATEMENT OF THE FACTS

Ms. Rachel Neely ("Neely") and Ms. Melanie Neely ("Melanie"), our clients, seek advice in connection with possible emotional distress claims against Mr. Miles Thompson ("Thompson"). The claims arose as a result of (1) Neely's distress at hearing a car crash, caused by Thompson and involving her eleven-year-old daughter, Melanie, and subsequently viewing Melanie's injuries; and (2) Melanie's distress related to statements made by Thompson.

In February 1993, Neely and Melanie moved to Union City from San Francisco. Neely immediately began working for an investment firm in downtown Union City. At that firm, she became acquainted with the defendant, Thompson. Thompson was Neely's boss. At first, the two had a friendly, professional relationship. During this time, Thompson and Neely spent much time together socially and learned much about each other. Thompson, for example, knew that Neely had left San Francisco after her marriage ended. Neely had confided in Thompson that the divorce and the events preceding it were extremely traumatic for herself and for Melanie. Melanie knew Thompson and was comfortable with him. Thompson had spent time with Melanie and knew that Melanie had suffered emotionally because of her parents' bitter divorce.

The relationship between Thompson and Neely became strained approximately six months after Neely began working with Thompson. Tension between the parties arose as a result of Thompson's expression of romantic interest in Neely. Neely, who was dating someone else, had no romantic interest in Thompson and communicated to him her lack of interest in pursuing that type of relationship with him.

On April 2, 1995, Thompson visited the Neely home. Melanie was not fully aware of the problem her mother was having with Thompson. Thompson came to the door, and Melanie, who was alone in the house, let him in. Thompson invited Melanie for a ride in his Corvette. Melanie willingly went with him. Meanwhile, Neely, who had gone to the grocery store to buy some milk, returned to the house to find Melanie missing. She panicked, called the neighbors, and then called the police.

Thompson, who claims that he took Melanie for a ride so that she could be informed about her mother's "bad behavior," drove around Union City with Melanie for approximately thirty minutes. During this ride, Thompson told Melanie that her mother was a "wicked, selfish, woman, who could care less about Melanie." Thompson also told Melanie that her mother was a "no good, sex-crazed woman who would leave Melanie once the right man came along." Upon returning to the Neely home, Thompson made a left turn from Oak Street onto Maple Road, and his car was hit by an oncoming vehicle. According to the police report of the accident, Thompson's blood-alcohol level indicated that he was intoxicated.

The Neely home is located on the corner of the intersection of Maple Road and Oak Street. Neely heard the crash and ran outside. Seeing the accident and recognizing Thompson's car, she approached the site of the accident. There she saw Melanie bleeding profusely from head injuries. As a result of the accident, Melanie spent two days at Union City Memorial Hospital, where she was kept under observation for possible internal injuries. Melanie continues to be severely depressed and emotionally unstable as a result of Thompson's comments. Additionally, she has frequent nightmares and finds it difficult to speak without stuttering. Since the time of the accident, she has been under psychiatric therapy for these problems. Neely, who fainted after viewing her daughter's injuries, spent one day in Union City Memorial Hospital for extreme anxiety and trauma.

Questions Presented

The *questions presented* address the legal issues presented by the factual circumstances described in the statement of the facts. The questions should be specific and straightforward. They should refer to the parties by name, suc-

cinctly set out the legal problem, and specifically indicate the important and relevant events. The questions-presented section may involve just one simple issue or a number of complex issues. Regardless of the complexity of the matter, this section helps bring the main points of the conflict into focus. See Exhibit 18.15 for an example of how the questions presented might be phrased.

Brief Conclusion

The *brief conclusion* (or *short answer* or *brief answer)* sets forth succinct responses to the questions presented in the previous section. The responses may vary in length. For example, as indicated in Exhibit 18.16 on the following page, certain questions can be answered simply by a "yes," "no," "probably so," or "probably not," followed by a brief sentence summarizing the reason for that answer. For complicated legal questions, a more detailed statement might be appropriate. Even so, each conclusion should be limited to a maximum of one paragraph. The discussion of the legal analysis, which is the main part of the memo, provides ample opportunity for supporting details.

Discussion and Analysis

The *discussion and analysis* section of the legal memorandum, as the phrase implies, contains a discussion and legal analysis of each issue to be resolved. If the facts of the dispute concern only one legal issue, the entire discussion will revolve around that. Legal memoranda usually address multiple issues, however. When multiple issues are involved, the paralegal should organize the discussion into separate parts so that each legal issue can be analyzed separately. For example, if the dispute involves two potential legal claims, the discussion should be divided into two sections with a descriptive heading for each section. The headings of the two sections might read as follows:

I. Negligent Infliction of Emotional Distress.
II. Intentional Infliction of Emotional Distress.

The legal analysis presented in the memo should answer the following questions:

- What options are available to the client?
- Which of the options are favorable?
- Will these options offer a reasonable resolution of the issues?

EXHIBIT 18.15
Legal Memorandum—Questions Presented

QUESTIONS PRESENTED

1. Does Neely have a claim for the negligent infliction of emotional distress as a result of viewing the injuries sustained by her daughter in a car accident caused by Thompson's negligence?

2. Does Melanie have a claim for the intentional infliction of emotional distress arising out of Thompson's statements to her on April 2, 1995?

EXHIBIT 18.16
Legal Memorandum—Brief Conclusion

BRIEF CONCLUSION

1. Probably not. Neely cannot recover under the rule that is currently applied in this jurisdiction. This rule requires that the plaintiff be present at the scene when the accident occurs.

2. Most likely, yes. Thompson's conduct toward Melanie appears to have been (1) reckless, (2) outrageous and extreme, and (3) the direct cause of Melanie's severe emotional distress.

ETHICAL CONCERN

Objectivity and the Legal Memorandum

Assume that you are conducting research on behalf of a client who is bringing a lawsuit against a restaurant for negligence. The client's wife choked to death on a piece of meat, and none of the restaurant's employees offered to help. As a member of the legal team representing the client's interests, your goal is to maximize the client's chances of winning in court. During your research, you discover that although no precedential cases involving a similar fact pattern have been decided in your jurisdiction, another state's supreme court has recently held for the defendant restaurant in a very similar case. Because the courts in your state are not obligated to follow this ruling, you might be tempted to downplay the case's significance in your legal memorandum. Do not do this. In deciding whether the client should sue, the attorney needs to make an informed judgment—and he or she will be relying on you to supply objective information. It is in the best interests of the client to point out to your attorney the potential arguments of opposing counsel.

- What law supports the strongest position?
- Is it case law or statutory law?
- What law goes against the client's claim or defense?
- Are there any constitutional issues involved?
- On what law would the other side rely to support its position?
- How can the attorney respond to the other side's strongest arguments?

The discussion is the core of the legal memo. This section provides an opportunity for paralegals to demonstrate good research and writing skills. After the research is completed, you must relate the legal findings to the facts of the matter. The reader expects to find a thorough analysis of the law. Points of law should be identified and supported with proper citations. Occasionally, legal sources will directly address a point that applies to the case at hand. In these situations, it is effective to quote directly from the text or the case, statute, or other legal source. You should not rely too heavily on quoted material, however. Although quotations from a case or other legal authority can lend extremely helpful support, you should always keep the following fact in mind:

- **The attorney for whom the memo is prepared wants to see your analysis, not a reiteration of a court's opinion.**

Exhibit 18.17 presents a portion of a discussion section in a legal memorandum.

When discussing how other cases have addressed certain issues, you need to include citations to the cases. As mentioned in Chapter 17, there are various guides to citation formats, including the book entitled *A Uniform System of Citation,* which is published by the Harvard Law Review Association.

Conclusion

The *conclusion* is the culmination of the legal memo. Many issues have been analyzed, and both the strengths and weaknesses of the client's matter have been evaluated. Now you should conclude the analysis by taking a position. The conclusion is your opinion of how the issues discussed may be resolved. Exhibit 18.18 shows an example of a conclusion to a legal memorandum.

The concluding section may acknowledge the fact that research into a particular area bore little fruit. For example, there may be no cases on point

EXHIBIT 18.17
Legal Memorandum—Discussion (Excerpt)

DISCUSSION (excerpt)

I. Negligent Infliction of Emotional Distress

Recovery Restriction

An individual's right to emotional tranquility is recognized by the law protecting persons against the negligent infliction of emotional distress. The method for determining whether protection should be afforded for emotional distress caused by the knowledge of a third person's injury as a result of a defendant's negligent action is clear in this jurisdiction. The rule adopted in this jurisdiction is the "impact rule."

The impact rule requires that a plaintiff alleging emotional distress must also suffer an impact (directly and physically) from the same force that injured the victim. Saechao v. Matsakoun, 717 P.2d 165, 168 (Or.App. 1986). This test provides the courts with a "bright line" from which they can easily determine the relationship between compensability and the defendant's breach of a duty owed to the victim. Id. at 169. The impact rule, which evolved as a result of the law's early reluctance to acknowledge the authenticity of emotional distress claims, avoids the problems of floodgate litigation. Id. at 169. It strictly limits a victim's recovery.

Some strong arguments can be made against the application of the impact rule. Although the rule limits a defendant's liability and offers an easy decision-making criterion for the courts, it also lends itself to arbitrary and often unjust results. The impact rule makes an after-the-fact determination of duty, protecting those suffering from emotional distress only if they also suffered harm directly and physically as a result of the defendant's negligence. Id. at 171.

The impact rule has been applied by the Union County courts. The rule's bright line immediately eliminates Neely's possibility of recovery. She was in her house when the accident occurred and witnessed the accident scene after the crash had occurred. Thompson would not owe a duty to protect Neely from negligently inflicted emotional distress under the impact rule.

EXHIBIT 18.18
Legal Memorandum—Conclusion

CONCLUSION

It is unlikely that Neely has a cause of action against Thompson for the emotional distress that she allegedly suffered due to Thompson's negligence.

It is likely that Melanie has a cause of action for the intentional infliction of emotional distress based on Thompson's outrageous comments to her about her mother.

Note that Neely might pursue, on her own behalf, a claim for the intentional infliction of emotional distress against Thompson for Thompson's reckless behavior in taking Melanie from her home and telling Melanie outrageous things. I recommend that we speak with Neely about the effect on her of Thompson's statements to Melanie. This, in my opinion, is a strong claim. I believe that we could argue successfully that Thompson intended to injure Neely through this egregious act.

TODAY'S PROFESSIONAL PARALEGAL

Preparing the Internal Memorandum

Ken Lawson, a legal assistant, works for Rhonda Mulhaven. Rhonda is representing the defendant, the Gourmet House Restaurant, in a slip-and-fall case. Ken is surprised that the plaintiff filed suit, because the plaintiff admitted that she saw water on the floor but walked through it anyway, apparently so that she could get to the telephone. Ken knows that there are several defenses available, including contributory or comparative negligence and assumption of risk.

RESEARCHING AND ANALYZING CASE LAW

Ken looks in a legal encyclopedia, which defines assumption of risk as follows:

> The plaintiff knew that the situation was dangerous and, despite her knowledge of the danger involved, voluntarily subjected herself to the danger or risk. When a plaintiff has assumed the risk of danger, then the plaintiff cannot recover from the defendant for her injuries.

Ken often uses the IRAC method to analyze legal problems. First, he states the issue. Second, he states the rule of law. Third, he applies the rule to the client's facts. And fourth, he reaches a conclusion. Ken has found this method useful because it helps him to think through all aspects of the problem and to apply the law to the facts to reach a conclusion. He decides to apply the IRAC method to the case on which he is working to determine whether the defense of assumption of risk could be successfully applied.

APPLYING THE IRAC METHOD

First, Ken identifies the issue in the case: Did the plaintiff assume the risk of falling when she walked across the wet floor? Next, Ken notes the applicable rule of law, as stated in the encyclopedia: a plaintiff who knows of a dangerous condition and voluntarily subjects himself or herself to it has assumed the risk and cannot hold a defendant liable. Ken then applies the rule of law to the facts of the case: the plaintiff knew of the dangerous condition, because she knew that the floor was wet. She voluntarily subjected herself to the danger by walking across the wet floor to get to the telephone. Ken then forms a conclusion: because the plaintiff knew of the dangerous condition and voluntarily subjected herself to it, she assumed the risk involved in walking across the wet floor instead of walking around the puddle. She normally cannot hold the defendant liable when she assumed the risk and was injured as a result.

Ken believes that the defense of assumption of risk might be appropriate in the client's case. He decides to continue researching case law and looks through a state digest. There he finds several cases that contain a definition of assumption of risk similar to the one he read in the encyclopedia. He reviews the cases and then Shepardizes each case on WESTLAW to make sure that it is still current law.

CREATING THE LEGAL MEMORANDUM

Ken sits down at his computer and prepares the following outline for a memorandum to Rhonda:

I. Statement of the Facts—A chronological statement of the events that led to the injury.
II. Question Presented—Did the plaintiff assume the risk of falling when she walked across the wet floor?
III. Brief Conclusion—Yes.
IV. Discussion
  A. Did the plaintiff assume the risk of falling when she walked across the wet floor?
  B. Encyclopedia's definition of assumption-of-risk defense and state case law supporting this definition.
  C. Apply the rules in B above to the facts in this case.
V. Conclusion—Based on the results of C above.

Having outlined the memo, Ken writes a first draft, edits and revises it, proofreads it carefully, and delivers it to Rhonda. The next day, she comes into his office and tells him that she is impressed with the quality and organization of his memo and with his analytical skills. She says that based on his research and the memorandum, she has been able to settle the case by convincing the plaintiff's attorney that his client has a weak case.

to support one of the issues. The conclusion also may inform the attorney that more information is needed or may demonstrate that a certain issue needs to be evaluated further. Finally, this section presents you with an opportunity to make strategical suggestions. Paralegals should feel comfortable—especially after a careful legal analysis—in recommending a course of action. Not only do your recommendations reflect thorough analysis, but they also indicate that you are willing to exercise initiative and make a mature judgment, which will be helpful to your supervising attorney.

KEY TERMS AND CONCEPTS

address block 726
advisory letter 729
briefing a case 708
chronologically 718
closing 728
confirmation letter 729
demand letter 731
dicta 708
holding 708
informative letter 728
IRAC method 708
opinion letter 729
plain-meaning rule 714
reference line 726
rules of construction 713
salutation 727

CHAPTER SUMMARY

1. Paralegals who undertake legal research and writing need to be able to analyze the applicable case law, which they will find in reporters. Reporters use somewhat different formats in presenting cases. Typically, though, case formats include the following components: the title (name, or style), citation, and docket number of the case; the dates on which the case was argued and decided, and the name of the court deciding the case; a syllabus and headnotes; the names of counsel; the names of the judge or justice who authored the opinion; the opinion (the court's own words on the matter being litigated); and the court's decision (ruling, or holding) on the matter.

2. In analyzing case law, it is essential to understand the significance of the various components of a case. The IRAC (Issue, Rule, Application, and Conclusion) method is a helpful tool in understanding and organizing a written summary of case law. Legal professionals often use a technique called case briefing to reduce the content of the case to its essentials. The case brief is similar to an IRAC summary, but it also includes background and facts. Knowing how to read, analyze, and summarize cases makes it easier to compare and synthesize research results accurately and efficiently.

3. Reading and analyzing statutory language is often difficult. In reading statutory law, you should first note the statute's provisions concerning its coverage and effective date to ensure that it applies to the case or claim being researched. You should also note the definitions given in the statute and determine the relationships among subsections within the statute. In interpreting statutory law, the paralegal can turn to several helpful guidelines: the statutory rules of construction; the plain-meaning rule; previous judicial interpretations of the statute, if any exist; and the legislative history of the statute.

4. On receiving a writing assignment, the paralegal should make sure that he or she clearly understands the nature of the assignment, when the assignment should be completed, and what approach (objective versus adversarial, for example) should be used.

5. Good writing skills are essential for creating legal documents. The writing should be well organized and aimed at the intended audience. It should avoid legalese, when possible, be brief and to the point, present well-constructed sentences and paragraphs, use effective transitions, use gender-neutral language, and be free of typographical errors, misspelled words, and other flaws.

6. Much legal writing consists of documents relating to litigation procedures, such as pleadings and discovery documents. These important forms of legal writing were discussed in Chapters 10 and 11.

7. Paralegals frequently are responsible for maintaining correspondence files and writing legal letters. Most firms have a preferred format for legal correspondence, and the paralegal should become familiar with it. Paralegals commonly draft the following types of letters: informative letters (to notify clients or others of some action or procedure or to transmit documents), confirmation letters (to confirm an oral transaction or agreement), opinion letters (to convey to a client or other party a formal legal opinion or advice on an issue), and demand letters (to advance the client's cause by demanding something from an adversarial party on the client's behalf).

8. The internal legal memorandum is a thoroughly researched and objectively written summation of the facts, issues, and applicable law relating to a particular legal claim. The purpose of the memo is to inform the attorney for whom the document is written of the strengths and weaknesses of the client's position. Generally, the legal memo is presented in a format that includes the following sections: heading, statement of the facts, questions presented, brief conclusion, discussion and analysis of the facts and the applicable law, and conclusion.

QUESTIONS FOR REVIEW

1. List and briefly describe the components of a reported case. What is the syllabus, and how is it helpful to the legal researcher?
2. What is the IRAC method?
3. How do you brief a case? What is the purpose of briefing a case?
4. What are some points to consider when reading and interpreting statutory law?
5. List and describe some of the traditional guidelines used by the courts in interpreting statutory law.
6. What factors should you consider before undertaking a legal-writing assignment?
7. List and describe each of the guidelines for effective writing. What is meant by the statement "You should write to your audience"?
8. List the component parts of a typical legal letter. What is the function of each type of letter discussed in this chapter?
9. How is an internal memorandum organized? List and describe its components.
10. What must you know and understand before you begin to prepare a legal memorandum?

ETHICAL QUESTIONS

1. Lynette Bennett, a paralegal, works as a clerk for a judge in the county circuit court. She has just finished reviewing the plaintiff's and defendant's briefs in an auto-accident case. The plaintiff's brief described the injury as follows:

> The plaintiff was struck by the defendant's car as she crossed Lincoln Avenue at the crosswalk. She sustained serious injuries to her left knee, for which she had surgery. She also experiences pain and discomfort in her back and neck.

The defendant's brief described the injury as follows:

> The plaintiff was struck when she suddenly stepped in front of the defendant's vehicle. In her lawsuit against the defendant, the plaintiff claims that she sustained significant injuries from this minor accident.

Lynette is disturbed by the disparity in the two descriptions of the plaintiff's injuries. It sounds to Lynette as if someone is lying. What do you think? What, if anything, should Lynette do?

2. Bill Richardson, a legal assistant, has been asked by his supervising attorney to prepare an internal memorandum analyzing a client's claim. When Bill reviews the facts, he realizes that the client has a very weak case and will probably lose. But Bill thinks that the client was taken advantage of and that she should be given a chance to try to recover at least something.

He knows that his supervisor will not take a losing case to court, so he writes the memo in such a way as to favor the client's position as much as possible. He is not objective in analyzing the potential pitfalls of the case. Is what Bill has done ethical? Is it professional? How should he have handled the situation?

3. David Thomas, a paralegal, is sending out a letter to a client. It is an informative letter advising the client of the status of her case and explaining what the next step in the litigation process will be. David signs the letter without including his title. He mails the letter to the client. The client has questions, and she calls David, thinking that he is the attorney. How should David handle this situation? What should he have done to prevent it?

PRACTICE QUESTIONS AND ASSIGNMENTS

1. Clip an article out of the newspaper or news journal. Then follow the instructions and answer the questions given below:

a. Underline all of the active verbs and circle all of the passive verbs. Did the writer use more active verbs than passive verbs in writing the article?

b. Count the number of words in each sentence. What is the average sentence length? Do short sentences predominate?

c. Locate the topic sentence in each paragraph. Is the writer's paragraph construction effective?

d. Notice how the author uses transitional sentences when moving from one paragraph to the next. Underline the key transitional words or phrases.

2. Analyze the construction of the following paragraphs. How could they be improved?

> The first is knowing of the danger. The second is voluntarily subjecting oneself to the danger. The defense of assumption of risk has two elements.
>
> She did not voluntarily subject herself to the danger when the stadium assigned seats to season-ticket holders. She knew that balls were often hit into the stands. The plaintiff knew of the danger involved in attending a baseball game.

3. Proofread the following paragraph, circling all of the mistakes. Then rewrite the paragraph.

> The defendent was aressted and chrge with drunk driving. Blood alcohol level of .15. He refused to take a breahalyzer test at first. After the police explained to him that he would loose his lisense if he did not take it, he concented. He also has ablood test to verify the results of the breathalyzer.

QUESTIONS FOR CRITICAL ANALYSIS

1. Why is statutory language often difficult to read and understand? What factors must legislators consider when drafting statutes?

2. Why is it important to write to your audience? To what audience should legislators write when drafting legislation?

ROLE-PLAYING EXERCISES

1. Review the *Ethical Concern* presented in this chapter entitled "Objectivity and the Legal Memorandum." Assume that the paralegal conducting the research is Elena Lopez and that her supervising attorney is Allen Gilmore. Further assume that paralegal Lopez has decided to ask attorney Gilmore whether she should mention cases decided in other jurisdictions. Working in pairs, role-play Lopez and Gilmore discussing this issue. Lopez should be curious and concerned about the effect that the adverse

persuasive authority (from the other jurisdiction) may have on the client. Gilmore should inform Lopez of all the reasons why she should mention the case and generally why it is important that relevant case law or statutory law, even though adverse to the client's position, should be discussed in a legal memo. (The student playing the role of Gilmore might want to review the discussion in Chapter 3 of the attorney's duty of candor before beginning this exercise.)

2. Susan Blakely, a paralegal, has just taken her first job with a law firm. One of the firm's clients is suing a department store for negligence, and Susan's supervising attorney has asked her to research case law on the issue. Susan has finished her research and now asks Mary Johansen, a paralegal who has worked for the firm for years, for advice on how to prepare the legal memo. Act out the roles of Susan and Mary as they discuss the preparation of a legal memo.

Susan should ask Mary about the purpose, components, and writing style of a legal memo, as well as other questions, such as the following:

a. "The defendant in this case is Johnson, Galloway, Sterns, Novak & Skinner. How can I abbreviate that name?"

b. "Mary, you've worked for this firm for years, know the attorneys very well, and call them by their first names. Yet you say that when you write a legal memorandum to one of the attorneys, you strike a formal tone. Why is this necessary?"

c. "In my research, I found about twenty cases that seemed to be on point. Should I discuss each case?"

d. "How should I cite the cases that I refer to in the memo? Should I footnote them?"

e. "What if I have no idea about how my research results will affect the client's issue? What do I say in the conclusion section?"

Mary should respond to each question fully. If time allows, reverse roles.

PROJECTS

1. Review the *Practice Questions and Assignments* at the end of Chapter 17. If you did the research required by those questions, use the lemon law and the cases that you found to prepare an internal memorandum analyzing Mr. Consumer's problem and whether the lemon law in your state will help him. Be sure to include your opinion of the strength of his case.

2. If possible, find a copy of a business letter. Identify its component parts. How does it differ from the sample legal letter presented in Exhibit 18.8? How is it similar?

3. Review the hypothetical case discussed in Chapter 17 involving a lawsuit brought by Trent Hoffman against Better Homes Store for negligence. If possible, obtain a copy of the following case (on which that hypothetical example was based): *Ward v. K-Mart Corp.*, 136 Ill.2d 132, 554 N.E.2d 223 (1990). Read through the court's opinion and then do the following:

a. Find at least one statement made by the court that constitutes *dicta.*

b. Brief the case.

ANNOTATED SELECTED READINGS

BLOCK, GERTRUDE. *Effective Legal Writing.* 4th ed. Westbury, N.Y.: Foundation Press, 1992. A text prepared for law students that gives helpful insights into understanding cases. It also discusses grammar (with very helpful practice assignments) and style considerations in legal writing.

BOTEL-SHEPPARD, BONNIE. "Five Quick Tips for Writing Effective Legal Correspondence." *Legal Assistant Today,* January/February 1991. An article containing five helpful tips on writing legal correspondence, from thinking about your reader to being diplomatic when sharing negative information. The article gives the reader a glimpse of the real world of the paralegal.

FAULK, MARTHA. "Fundamentals of Effective Legal Writing." *Legal Assistant Today,* November/December 1991. A useful article that reviews the problems pecu-

liar to legal writing, such as using two legal terms when one is enough. The article also presents "ten commandments" of effective writing.

HURD, HOLLIS T. "Summarizing Cases." *Legal Assistant Today,* January/February 1994. A brief article that offers some practical tips on how to make case summaries just that—summaries. The author offers a simple rule that, if followed, will make summarizing cases easier and the resulting case summary easier to understand: start each case summary with a clear description of "who sued whom for what."

PUTMAN, WILLIAM H. "How to Write an Interoffice Legal Memorandum." *Legal Assistant Today,* November/December, 1993. An article describing how the legal memorandum should be organized and written and that includes numerous tips and practical advice for paralegals.

SHAPO, HELENE S., MARILYN R. WALTER, AND ELIZABETH FAJANS. *Writing and Analysis in the Law.* Westbury, N.Y.: Foundation Press, 1991. An excellent resource for your personal library. It is full of good examples of good legal writing and many examples of how to avoid writing errors. It also includes (in Chapter 2) helpful discussions on reasoning by analogy and synthesizing research results.

TEPPER, PAMELA R. *Basic Legal Writing.* Lake Forest, Ill.: Glencoe, 1992. A good basic text with excellent sections on the mechanics of construction, including grammar and punctuation. It presents clear guidelines for briefing cases and writing various types of legal correspondence.

APPENDIX TO CHAPTER 18

THE APPELLATE BRIEF

APPELLATE BRIEF
A document submitted to an appellate court setting forth legal arguments and supporting law in favor of the appellant or the appellee.

The purpose of the **appellate brief** is to persuade a court of appeals to decide the issue in favor of your client. The brief is filed with the appellate court before the court reviews the case being appealed. The court reviews the briefs submitted by the attorneys for both sides to gain a better understanding of the issues presented in the dispute. Your goal in writing an appellate brief is to convince your readers that the matter must be decided in favor of the client on whose behalf the brief was written.

Although the arguments in an appellate brief should be forceful and convincing, you must not misrepresent or exaggerate the facts and the issues. Always keep in mind that the goal is to persuade the court in favor of the client. If a brief is not credible, or believable, the court will lack confidence in the argument. Arguments must be presented reasonably and be based on the facts of the case and valid law.

Types of Appellate Briefs

Four types of appellate briefs may be filed with the appellate court: the appellant's brief, the appellee's brief, the reply brief, and the *amicus curiae*[1] brief. These briefs are all adversarial—that is, they present arguments on behalf of one of the parties—but they contain distinguishing characteristics.

APPELLANT
The party appealing a case.

APPELLANT'S BRIEF
An appellate brief that argues in favor of the appellant's position. This brief will try to convince the court that the lower court's decision was erroneous.

Appellant's Brief. The **appellant** is the party who appealed the case and who seeks to convince the appellate court to reverse the decision of the trial court. The **appellant's brief** is the first brief filed with the court and, as such, establishes the issues to be addressed. The purpose of the brief is to convince the court that the lower court's decision was erroneous.

APPELLEE
The party against whom an appeal is brought.

APPELLEE'S BRIEF
An appellate brief that argues in favor of the appellee's position. This brief will attempt to rebut (counter) any arguments in the appellant's brief and will emphasize the accuracy of the earlier judgment rendered in its favor.

Appellee's Brief. The **appellee** is the party who prevailed in the lower court and against whom the appeal is brought. The **appellee's brief** will address the issues raised by the appellant's brief. It is filed as a direct response to the claims set forth by the appellant. The purpose of the appellee's brief is to rebut (counter) any arguments in the appellant's brief and to emphasize the accuracy of the earlier judgment rendered in the appellee's favor.

The appellant's brief, because it is the first brief filed with the court, will often contain more background information about the dispute than the appellee's brief. If the attorney for the appellee is satisfied with the appellant's presentation of the procedural history, facts, and issues, he or she may choose to state that the appellee adopts that portion of the appellant's brief.

REPLY BRIEF
An appellate brief filed by the appellant to rebut (counter) arguments made by the appellee in the appellee's brief.

Reply Brief. The **reply brief** is filed by the appellant in response to the appellee's brief. The appellant, as the first party to file a brief, needs an oppor-

1. Pronounced ah-*mee*-cuhs *kur*-ee-ay.

tunity to respond to arguments submitted in subsequent briefs. Although advocating the appellant's cause, the reply brief is narrow in scope and focuses on rebutting whatever arguments were presented in briefs submitted on behalf of the appellee.

***Amicus Curiae* Brief.** The Latin phrase *amicus curiae* means "friend of the court." The phrase refers to individuals or organizations that submit briefs to the appellate court despite the fact that they are not parties to the lawsuit. An individual or organization seeking to file an ***amicus curiae* brief** with the court must petition the court for the right to do so. *Amicus* briefs are usually filed in cases that involve broad public issues, such as civil rights or environmental concerns. The purpose of the *amicus* brief is to convince the court to rule in favor of one of the parties because not to do so would affect a broad interest of society. For example, the American Civil Liberties Union frequently files *amicus* briefs on behalf of parties whose civil rights or liberties have allegedly been violated.

***AMICUS CURIAE* BRIEF**
A brief filed with the court by a third party (that is, a party not directly involved in the lawsuit) that is concerned about the outcome of the litigation. The purpose of such a brief is to convince the court to rule in favor of one of the parties because not to do so would affect a broad interest of society. (*Amicus curiae* is Latin for "friend of the court.")

Writing an Effective Appellate Brief

An appellate brief is an important document and should be presented to the court as a formal piece of legal writing. The court expects a document that presents clear and concise arguments. In addition, each court has procedural rules dictating the general format required of an appellate brief. Because the prescribed format differs from one jurisdiction to another, paralegals should become familiar with the rules of the relevant court. The following sections describe the format required by most courts.

Title Page. The *title page* is the front cover of the appellate brief. The title page provides certain information about the case on appeal. Most title pages identify the court to which the case is being appealed and the lower court from which the case is being appealed. The index or docket number is also listed for easy identification. The names of both the appellant and appellee appear on the title page, but the brief clearly states for which party the document is submitted. Finally, the title page contains the name and address of the attorney or law firm filing the brief and the date of the filing. Exhibit 18.A1 on the following page shows a sample title page of an appellate brief submitted by the appellee (respondent) to the United States Supreme Court.

Courts often have rules specifying the colors to be used for the covers of various types of briefs. For example, a court may require the appellant to submit a blue title page and the appellee to submit a red title page; two other colors may be assigned for reply briefs and *amicus curiae* briefs. The colors assigned may vary from one jurisdiction to another.

Table of Contents. The *table of contents* lists the sections of the appellate brief and gives the page number on which each section begins. The table of contents not only functions as an index to the contents of the brief but also provides the reader with a glimpse of the argument, because it outlines the points being made in the argument. This comprehensive outline allows the reader to locate a particular part of the argument without having to search through the entire document. A sample table of contents is shown in Exhibit 18.A2 on page 749.

EXHIBIT 18.A1
Appellate Brief—Title Page

IN THE SUPREME COURT OF THE UNITED STATES
SPRING TERM 1995
NO. 95-198

John Jeffries Connelly — Petitioner

—AGAINST—

United States of America — Respondent

ON WRIT OF CERTIORARI TO THE UNITED STATES COURT OF APPEALS FOR THE SECOND CIRCUIT

BRIEF FOR RESPONDENT

Joseph P. McCaffrey
U.S. Attorney for the
District of Nita
309 Garden Boulevard,
Suite 321
Capital City, NI 49250
(417) 555-9708

Table of Authorities. The *table of authorities* provides the reader with page references for all authorities cited in the argument. The court and the parties to the dispute will want to refer to the sources of law behind certain arguments, and the table of authorities provides an efficient guide for locating them in the brief. The sources are arranged in a particular order, as shown in Exhibit 18.A3 on page 750. Cases cited in the brief are listed first. The entries are presented alphabetically and contain the full name of the case followed by the proper citations. Following the list of cases are listings of statutory and constitutional provisions referred to in the brief. Additional

EXHIBIT 18.A2
Appellate Brief—Table of Contents

TABLE OF CONTENTS

sources, such as treatises or articles in legal periodicals, may be listed under specific categories or under "miscellaneous."

The table of authorities, which is a crucial part of the brief, is one of the last sections to be completed. When the argument is in final form, the attorney usually asks the paralegal to prepare the table of authorities. Because the court and opposing counsel will rely on the table, accuracy is extremely important. If you prepare a table of authorities, make sure that you are working from the final copy of the brief. If the attorney continues to edit and

EXHIBIT 18.A3
Appellate Brief—Table of Authorities

TABLE OF AUTHORITIES

CASES:
Adams v. Carroll, 875 F.2d 1441 (9th Cir. 1992)........ 15
Chapman v. United States, 953 F.3d 886, 890 (5th Cir. 1994)........ 8
Faretta v. California, 422 U.S. 806 (1975)........ 5
Fitzpatrick v. Wainwright, 800 F.2d 1057 (11th Cir. 1986)........ 17

CONSTITUTIONAL PROVISIONS:
Art. 7, U.S. Constitution........ 14

STATUTES:
Mass. Code Ann., Sec. 24 (1989)........ 12

LAW REVIEW ARTICLES:
Callan, Waiver of Consent and Pro Se Representation, 78 U. Co. L. Rev, 455 (1990)........ 11

make changes to the brief, sources may be deleted or moved, making it very difficult to achieve an accurate listing.

Statement of Jurisdiction. The *statement of jurisdiction* indicates the source of authority for the appellate court's jurisdiction over the dispute. This section of the brief usually refers to the statute granting jurisdiction to the court, as in Exhibit 18.A4.

Questions Presented. The *questions presented* set out the legal issues that will be argued by the parties in the dispute. This section provides the court with a capsule summary of why the decision of the trial court should be reversed or upheld. The number of questions presented to the court reflects the number of legal issues on which the party seeks the court's opinion. When there is more than one issue, each issue raised is numbered separately. In Exhibit 18.A5, which illustrates this section of the appellate brief, there is only one question on appeal.

The questions should be framed in such a way that they lead to a response in the client's favor. The goal is to have the reader nodding his or her head in agreement as the questions are read. The questions should also be clear and concise; they should convince—not confuse—the reader.

EXHIBIT 18.A4
Appellate Brief—Statement of Jurisdiction

STATEMENT OF JURISDICTION

This Court has jurisdiction under 28 U.S.C. Sec. 1298 (1977).

EXHIBIT 18.A5
Appellate Brief—Question Presented

QUESTION PRESENTED

Whether a waiver of a defendant's constitutional right to counsel is knowing and intelligent when a district court judge does not conduct a sweeping inquiry before allowing that defendant to proceed pro se [on his or her own behalf].

Statement of the Claim. The *statement of the claim* usually contains two components: a preliminary statement dealing with the procedural background of the case and a statement of the relevant facts of the case. The preliminary statement is essentially a procedural history of the dispute as viewed from the client's perspective. The procedural information in this section will explain how and from what court the case has been appealed. Additionally, this section includes information regarding the nature of the cause of action, the parties to the suit, the injuries sustained, and the relief sought.

The statement of the facts sets forth the important factual background of the case. The facts are not presented objectively. Rather, they are presented persuasively so that the court is inclined to accept the client's perspective. At the same time, the description of the facts should not be exaggerated or misleading.

The facts that are communicated to the appellate court are limited to the facts that appear in the record of the case.[2] In presenting the facts, the writer must cite the part of the record from which that information was obtained. An excerpt from a statement of the claim is shown in Exhibit 18.A6.

2. The record of the case, or record on appeal, consists of the following: (1) the pleadings, (2) a transcript of the trial testimony and copies of the exhibits, (3) the judge's rulings on motions made by the parties, (4) the arguments of counsel, (5) the instructions to the jury, (6) the verdict, (7) the posttrial motions, and (8) the judgment order from which the appeal is taken.

EXHIBIT 18.A6
Appellate Brief—Statement of the Claim (Excerpt)

STATEMENT OF THE CLAIM (Excerpt)

Three weeks before his trial for charges of violating the National Firearms Act, petitioner, John J. Connelly, filed a motion to proceed pro se with the district court. A week after his motion was filed, the district court held a hearing specifically to consider petitioner's request to represent himself at trial. The trial judge's discussion of the matter with petitioner was thorough, covering the crimes with which he was charged, the statutes he had violated, and the maximum penalties that applied. The judge reiterated petitioner's right to counsel and stressed that the court would appoint counsel should petitioner lack sufficient funds.

During the hearing, petitioner unequivocally stated his intention to proceed pro se and conceded full awareness of the nature of his crimes and the penalties attached. The court cautioned the petitioner, warning that although he had a constitutional right to proceed pro se, self-representation was not the best form of defense.

The petitioner, a thirty-five-year-old college graduate, never wavered in expressing his desire to relinquish the right to counsel and to exercise his constitutional right to proceed pro se. . . .

Summary of the Argument. The *summary of the argument* is a condensed version of the developed argument made in the main text of the brief. This section cannot attempt to match the main body of the argument in detail and depth, but it should present the reader with an overview that mentions each major section of the argument. This section of the brief is relied on heavily by those who have not had an opportunity to review the argument section thoroughly.

The summary is usually one or two pages in length, although the length varies, depending on the size and complexity of the argument. It is not necessary to include citations or quotations in the summary, as they will appear in the main part of the argument. See Exhibit 18.A7 for an excerpt from a sample summary of the argument.

Argument. In the *argument* section, which is the core of the appellate brief, the legal arguments are developed and analyzed in detail. This is the section in which the writer seeks to convince the court that a decision should be rendered in favor of the client. The section sets forth the reasons why the court should decide the case in the client's favor and supports these reasons by referring to case law, statutes, and other legal sources. The argument should be persuasive and convincingly advocate the client's position. The decision of the appellate court is influenced by both the logic and forcefulness of the argument.

Each section of the argument has two main components: the *point heading* and the *body of the argument.* These components are discussed below and illustrated in Exhibit 18.A8.

POINT HEADING
A brief recapitulation of the point being made in a section of an appellate brief. Point headings separate the text into logical sections and make the argument easier to follow.

Point Headings and Subheadings. Each section that discusses one of the legal arguments begins with a point heading, which usually begins with a roman numeral. **Point headings** are brief recapitulations of the argument. Effective point headings enhance the argument's presentation. These head-

EXHIBIT 18.A7
Appellate Brief—Summary of the Argument (Excerpt)

SUMMARY OF THE ARGUMENT (Excerpt)

The Second Circuit correctly affirmed the district court's finding of a knowing and intelligent waiver of counsel. To exercise the right to self-representation, a defendant must voluntarily make the decision and be fully informed of its possible consequences. The circuit courts have split in their interpretation of what constitutes a knowing and intelligent waiver of counsel. There are three approaches. Two approaches are adopted by four circuits, and the other approach is adopted by three circuits. The three approaches are (1) the minimum-inquiry approach, (2) the middle-inquiry approach, and (3) the searching-inquiry approach.

The district court's inquiry and the record as a whole satisfy all three approaches. The inquiry held by the court covered what was essential in evaluating petitioner's understanding: the right being waived, the criminal charges, and the maximum penalties. Additionally, petitioner knowingly and intelligently waived counsel. He is a mature, intelligent adult and a graduate of a four-year college.

No mistreatment or coercion influenced his decision to waive counsel. He made a deliberate choice to represent himself, filing the motion to proceed pro se three weeks before trial. Throughout the court's inquiry, petitioner unequivocally expressed his desire to waive counsel . . . .

EXHIBIT 18.A8
Appellate Brief—Argument (Excerpt)

I. The circuits have split three ways in establishing the level of inquiry necessary for a waiver of counsel to be knowing and intelligent.

A. This court has never set out a specific line of inquiry for a trial judge to conduct when attempting to determine whether a defendant has knowingly and intelligently waived counsel.

In Faretta v. California, this Court held that a defendant in a criminal trial has a constitutional right to proceed without counsel. 422 U.S. 806 (1975). However, the decision to proceed pro se must be the product of an "informed free will." Id. at 835. The Court in Faretta did not establish the level of inquiry a trial judge must make in determining that a defendant has knowingly and intelligently waived counsel:

> Although a defendant need not himself have the skill and experience of a lawyer in order competently and intelligently to choose self-representation, he should be made aware of the dangers and disadvantages of self-representation, so that the record will establish that "he knows what he is doing and his choice is made with his eyes open."

Id. (quoting Adams v. United States ex. rel. McCann, 317 U.S. 269, 279 (1942).

Exactly what the record must reflect and what constitutes a choice made with "eyes open" has been disputed. The circuits are divided three ways in their interpretation of the standard set forth in Faretta . . . .

ings serve as a road map for the reader, setting out the points to be made and separating the text into logical sections. Point headings, if written clearly and concisely, make the argument much easier to follow.

A section of the argument may warrant more than a point heading. If the discussion is particularly complex, the addition of subheadings may help to clarify the structure of the presentation. There should not be too many subheadings under a point heading, however. Excessive divisions in the argument make the argument choppy and confusing. Point headings and subheadings should be distinguishable from one another. It is helpful to review forms for point headings and subheadings, which are on file at most law firms, to gain insight into both organizational and stylistic presentation.

The Body of the Argument. The *body of the argument* develops the reasons why the court should decide in favor of the client. Detailed arguments are set forth in this section. Each argument must thoroughly analyze the legal and factual aspects of the case. Additionally, attorneys and paralegals must address only those issues and facts relevant to the case on appeal. The arguments in this section must be well organized and fully supported by law. Essential sources should be cited and relevant concepts discussed.

EXHIBIT 18.A9
Appellate Brief—Conclusion

CONCLUSION

For the reasons stated above, the middle-inquiry approach is the standard that this court should adopt. The Second Circuit's inquiry standard for the determination of a knowing and intelligent waiver of counsel is sufficient, and therefore appellee respectfully requests that judgment be affirmed.

Respectfully submitted,

Joseph P. McCaffrey

Joseph P. McCaffrey
U.S. Attorney for the District of Nita

Conclusion. The *conclusion*, which follows the argument, is a very brief statement. It is not a summary of the argument but a claim for relief based on the arguments. In an appellant's brief, the conclusion asks the court to reverse the earlier decision of the trial court. In a appellee's brief, the conclusion requests that the earlier decision be upheld. The claim for relief is followed by a closing, typically in the form of "Respectfully submitted," and the name and address of the attorney responsible for the brief. This format is illustrated in Exhibit 18.A9 above.

APPENDIX—KEY TERMS AND CONCEPTS

amicus curiae brief 747
appellant 746
appellant's brief 746
appellate brief 746
appellee 746
appellee's brief 746
point heading 752
reply brief 746

APPENDIX—SUMMARY

1. When a case is appealed to a higher court, attorneys for both sides file appellate briefs with the court of appeals. The purpose of an appellate brief is to convince the appellate court of the merits of a client's position on appeal. A persuasive and forceful writing approach is therefore used.

2. There are four types of appellate briefs: the appellant's brief (filed on behalf of the party appealing the lower court's decision), the appellee's brief (filed on behalf of the party against whom the appeal is being brought), the reply brief (filed by the appellant in response to the appellee's brief), and the *amicus curiae* brief (filed by a "friend of the court" on behalf of one of the parties to the case in the interest of a broadly held public concern).

3. Most courts require that appellate briefs be presented in a format that includes the following sections: title page, table of contents, table of authorities, statement of jurisdiction, questions presented, statement of the claim, summary of the argument, argument, and conclusion.

APPENDIX—QUESTIONS FOR REVIEW

1. What is the purpose of an appellate brief?
2. How does the purpose of an appellate brief differ from the purpose of an internal memorandum?
3. What are the various types of appellate briefs?
4. What are the components of an appellate brief?

PART FOUR

SUBSTANTIVE LAW: EXTENDED COVERAGE

19

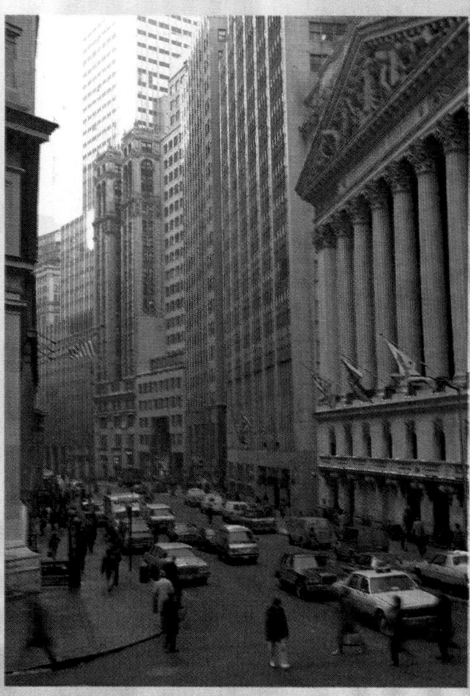

SPECIAL FORMS OF BUSINESS ORGANIZATION

Chapter Objectives

After completing this chapter, you will know:

- What joint ventures are, how they are created, and how they differ from ordinary partnership endeavors.
- The nature and basic structure of some other special forms of business organization.
- The basic laws and procedures relating to the creation and function of franchises.
- Some of the provisions typically included in franchise contracts.

Chapter Outline

INTRODUCTION

In Chapter 9, you read about the three most common types of business organizational structures: the sole proprietorship, the partnership, and the corporation. A business venture does not have to be organized in one of these three forms. Several other organizational forms exist to accommodate special purposes or special needs of businesspersons. For the most part, though, these other forms are hybrid organizations—that is, they have characteristics similar to those of partnerships or corporations, or they combine features of both.

In this chapter, you will read about several of these special forms of business organization. Additionally, you will learn about franchises. The franchise is not really a business *form* but a way of doing business.

JOINT VENTURES

JOINT VENTURE
A relationship in which two or more persons or organizations combine their efforts or their property for a single transaction or project or a related series of transactions or projects.

Paralegals are sometimes asked to assist with work relating to joint ventures. A **joint venture**, which is sometimes referred to as a *joint adventure*, is a relationship in which two or more persons or organizations combine their efforts or their property for a single transaction or project or a related series of transactions or projects. Unless otherwise agreed, joint venturers share profits and losses equally. For example, when several contractors combine their resources to build and sell houses in a single development, their relationship is a joint venture.

Joint ventures range in size from very small activities to multimillion-dollar joint actions engaged in by some of the world's largest corporations. Large organizations often investigate new markets or new ideas by forming joint ventures with other enterprises. For instance, General Motors Corporation and Volvo Truck Corporation were involved in a joint venture—Volvo GM—to manufacture heavy-duty trucks and market them in the United States.

You may be thinking that the joint venture resembles the partnership form of business that you read about in Chapter 9. In fact, it does. The two business forms are similar in many ways. There are some significant differences, though, and you should be aware of them. Here, we look at some of the characteristics of joint ventures, indicating as we go along the ways in which they are similar to partnerships and the ways in which they differ from partnerships.

Characteristics of Joint Ventures

A joint venture resembles a partnership and is taxed like a partnership. The essential difference is as follows:

- **A joint venture typically involves the pursuit of a single project or series of transactions, and a partnership usually concerns an ongoing business.**

Of course, a partnership may also be created to conduct a single transaction. For this reason, most courts apply the same principles to joint ventures as they apply to partnerships. Exceptions include the following:

1. The members of a joint venture have less implied and apparent authority than the partners in a partnership (under partnership law, each partner is an agent of the other partners, as discussed in Chapter 9), because the activities of a joint venture are more limited than the business of a partnership.
2. Although the death of a partner terminates a partnership, the death of a joint venturer ordinarily does not terminate a joint venture.

Duration of Joint Ventures

The members of a joint venture can specify its duration. If the members do not specify a duration, a joint venture normally terminates when the project or the transaction for which it was formed has been completed. Thus, the termination of the joint venture to build and sell houses in a single development would occur once the houses were built and sold. If the members of a joint venture do not specify a particular duration and the joint venture does not clearly relate to the achievement of a certain goal, a joint venture is terminable at the will of any of its members.

Rights and Duties of Joint Venturers

The duties that joint venturers owe to each other are the same as the duties that partners owe to each other, which you read about in Chapter 9. Thus, the contractors in the previous example owe each other fiduciary duties, including a duty of loyalty. If two of the contractors secretly buy the land that was to be acquired by the joint venture, the other joint venturers may be awarded damages for the breach of the duty of loyalty. Each joint venturer is liable to third parties for the actions of the other members of the joint venture in pursuit of the goal of the enterprise.

Each joint venturer has an equal right to manage the activities of the enterprise, just as partners do in a partnership. The members can decide, though, that one member will control the operations of the joint venture without affecting the status of the relationship. For instance, if the contractors agree that one of them will serve as the general contractor to oversee the construction of the houses, it may appear that this contractor is the owner of the business, but this appearance does not affect the members' relationship as joint venturers.

Potential Problems with Joint Ventures

When the members of a joint venture are competitors, they may face conflicting legal obligations. For example, suppose that Company A and Company B, competing pharmaceutical companies, decide to form a joint venture to research and develop a new drug for the treatment of leukemia. Employees of both companies are working together on the project. If an employee of Company A discloses trade secrets (confidential information) to an employee of Company B, the Company A employee breaches a duty owed to his or her firm. At the same time, as a member of a joint venture, Company A has a legal obligation to disclose information relevant to the joint venture to Company B.

ETHICAL CONCERN

Joint Ventures and Client Confidentiality

In the hypothetical situation discussed in the text, suppose that the president of Company A asks his attorney to create the joint-venture agreement. The agreement must contain a condition that certain information relating to its research on other products will not be disclosed to Company B during the course of the joint venture. The final draft of the agreement is now being reviewed by Company B's attorney. He calls Company A's attorney, who is out of the office. He tells Beth, the attorney's paralegal, that Company B objects to the condition. Company B apparently thinks that information about the genetic research being done by Company A to develop a drug to cure cancer will be necessary to the goal of the joint venture—developing a drug for leukemia. Beth tells the attorney that Company A has insisted on the condition specifically to keep the cancer-drug project confidential. Has Beth, by this statement, breached client confidentiality? Yes. Although Company B may already know about the cancer-drug project, it could also be that the attorney is simply on a fishing expedition—seeking verification of rumors that Company B has heard.

DEVELOPING PARALEGAL SKILLS

Scrutinizing Outside Counsel's Bills

Amanda Bryan, a paralegal, works for EnviroClean, Inc. Her supervising attorney has just given her a bill from outside counsel to review. The bill is for legal services relating to a joint venture formed by EnviroClean and ToxicClean, Inc. The purpose of the joint venture is to create a new product that will destroy the toxic components of toxic and hazardous wastes. The bill is for $53,000, and it is itemized as follows:

Documents drafted	$13,000
Expenses	$3,000
Professional Services	$37,000

At EnviroClean, Inc., each department pays for its share of legal services obtained from outside counsel. Amanda must thus find out exactly what types of work were done for the joint venture and by whom. Amanda writes a letter to the attorney at the law firm that submitted the bill. She asks for an itemized bill that indicates the specific documents that were drafted, the names of the attorneys or paralegals who performed the professional services, and the billing rate. She also asks to have the expenses itemized into categories, such as photocopying and fax charges, messenger/courier services, overnight-mail services, and so on.

A week and a half later, Amanda receives the itemized bill that she requested. Her supervising attorney is so impressed with the results that he gives her other bills to handle. Amanda would rather do more legal work, so she creates a sample outside-counsel contract that specifies the categories that must be itemized on bills. Amanda gives the proposed contract to her supervising attorney. The attorney reviews it, suggests some changes, and then forwards it to the general counsel. The general counsel is also impressed and adopts the contract as a model for future outside-counsel arrangements.

As you can see, it may be difficult to draw the line when it comes to deciding which information should or should not be disclosed.

- **To avoid potential legal problems relating to the disclosure of information, joint-venture agreements should specify exactly what information each member will be required to disclose.**

This is something you will want to keep in mind if you are assisting your supervising attorney in drafting or reviewing a joint-venture agreement.

ANTITRUST LAW
The body of federal and state laws protecting trade and commerce from unlawful restraints and anticompetitive practices.

Another potential problem of which you should be aware has to do with antitrust laws in relation to joint ventures. **Antitrust laws** are laws that prohibit anticompetitive practices.[1] If competing companies join forces in a joint venture, the result may be a significant consolidation of power over the

1. The major federal laws prohibiting anticompetitive behavior are the Sherman Antitrust Act of 1890, the Federal Trade Commission Act of 1914, and the Clayton Act of 1914.

market for their products. Suppose, for example, that in the above example Company A and Company B are the two largest pharmaceutical companies in the world and dominate the market for pharmaceutical products. If they joined together in a single enterprise, smaller competitors in the field might find it even more difficult to compete successfully in that market. In such a situation, the joint venture might be held to violate antitrust laws.

SYNDICATES

Another special form of business organization is the syndicate. A **syndicate** is essentially an investment group consisting of firms or individuals that get together to finance a particular project, such as the building of a shopping center or the purchase of a professional basketball franchise. The forms of such groups vary considerably. They may exist as corporations or as general or limited partnerships. In some syndicates, the members merely own property jointly and have no legally recognized business arrangement.

SYNDICATE
An investment group consisting of persons or firms that get together for the purpose of financing a project that they would not undertake independently.

JOINT STOCK COMPANIES

A **joint stock company** is a true hybrid of a partnership and a corporation. It has many characteristics of a corporation in that (1) its ownership is represented by transferable shares of stock, (2) it is usually managed by directors and officers, and (3) it can have a perpetual existence. Most of its other features, however, are more characteristic of a partnership, and it is usually treated like a partnership. Like a partnership, a joint stock company is formed by agreement (not by a state charter). Furthermore, property is usually held in the names of the members, shareholders have personal liability, and generally the company is not treated as a legal entity for purposes of a lawsuit. In a joint stock company, however, shareholders are not considered to be agents of one another, as would be the situation if the company were a true partnership.

JOINT STOCK COMPANY
A hybrid form of business organization that combines characteristics of a corporation (shareholder-owners, management by directors and officers, and perpetual existence) and a partnership (it is formed by agreement, not by state charter; property is usually held in the names of the members; and the shareholders have personal liability for business debts). Usually, the joint stock company is regarded as a partnership for tax and other legal purposes.

BUSINESS TRUSTS

A **business trust** is a special form of business organization that takes the form of a trust. Investors transfer cash or property to trustees in exchange for trust certificates that represent their investment shares. The trustees then manage the trust property for the benefit of—and distribute the business profits to—the investors (who are, in essence, the trust's beneficiaries). The business trust is created by a written trust agreement that sets forth the interests of the investor-beneficiaries and the obligations and powers of the trustees.

The business trust resembles a corporation in many respects. For example, the investor-beneficiaries have limited liability, just as corporate shareholders do. In other words, the investors are not personally liable (beyond the amount that they invested) for the debts or obligations of the trust. Additionally, as in a corporation, the death or bankruptcy of a beneficiary does

BUSINESS TRUST
A form of business organization in which investors (trust beneficiaries) transfer cash or property to trustees in exchange for trust certificates that represent their investment shares. Management of the business and trust property is handled by the trustees for the benefit of the investors. The investors have limited liability and share in the trust's profits.

not terminate the trust. In fact, in a number of states, business trusts must pay corporate taxes.

The business trust was started in Massachusetts in an attempt to obtain the limited liability of corporate status while avoiding certain restrictions that at one time were imposed on a corporation's ownership and development of real property. In the 1800s, some business trusts acquired substantial assets and, in some industries, began to assert significant control over the marketplace. One of the most famous business trusts was John D. Rockefeller's Standard Oil Company. To curb the anticompetitive effects of these trusts, Congress passed the Sherman Antitrust Act of 1890 and other antitrust laws.

COOPERATIVES

COOPERATIVE
A form of business organization that is organized to provide an economic service to its members. It makes distributions of dividends, or profits, to its owners on the basis of their transactions with the cooperative rather than on the basis of the amount of capital they contributed. Examples of cooperatives are consumer purchasing cooperatives, credit cooperatives, and farmers' cooperatives.

A **cooperative** is an association that is organized to provide an economic service without profit to its members (or shareholders). An incorporated cooperative is subject to state laws governing nonprofit corporations. It makes distributions of dividends, or profits, to its owners on the basis of their transactions with the cooperative rather than on the basis of the amount of capital they contributed. Unincorporated cooperatives are often treated like partnerships. The members have joint liability for the cooperative's acts.

This form of business is generally adopted by groups of individuals who wish to pool their resources to gain some advantage in the marketplace. Consumer purchasing cooperatives are formed to obtain lower prices through quantity discounts. Seller marketing cooperatives are formed to control the market and thereby obtain higher sales prices from consumers. Credit cooperatives and farmers' cooperatives are other examples of this form of business enterprise. Cooperatives are often exempt from certain federal laws—for example, antitrust laws—because of their special status.

FRANCHISES

FRANCHISE
A written agreement in which an owner of a trademark, trade name, or copyright licenses another to use that trademark, trade name, or copyright, under specified conditions, in the sale of goods and services.

FRANCHISEE
One who receives a license to use another's (the franchisor's) trademark, trade name, or copyright in the sale of goods and services.

FRANCHISOR
One who licenses another (the franchisee) to use his or her trademark, trade name, or copyright in the sale of goods and services.

Times have changed dramatically since Ray Kroc, the late founder of McDonald's, launched the franchising boom over thirty years ago. Today, over a third of all retail sales in the United States are generated by franchises. A **franchise** is any arrangement in which the owner of a trademark, a trade name, or a copyright has licensed others to use it in selling goods or services. A **franchisee** (a purchaser of a franchise) is generally legally independent of, but economically dependent on, the integrated business system of the **franchisor** (the seller of the franchise). In other words, a franchisee can operate as an independent businessperson but still obtain the advantages of a regional or national organization. Well-known franchises include Hilton Hotels, McDonald's, Holiday Inns, and Burger King.

The Law of Franchising

The growth in franchise operations has outdistanced the law of franchising. There has yet to be developed a solid body of appellate decisions under feder-

DEVELOPING PARALEGAL SKILLS

Verifying Trade Names

Karen Brown is a new paralegal in the law firm of Coleman & Johns. One of the firm's clients is interested in purchasing a "Burger Basket" franchise from J. Michael Robbins, the owner of the franchise. Karen has been asked by her supervising attorney to verify that J. Michael Robbins actually owns the trade name "Burger Basket."

The attorney tells Karen that she can verify Robbins's ownership rights in the trade name by calling Legal Services, Inc., a corporate services company. "Corporate services companies," the attorney explains, "perform many services. They conduct trademark and trade-name searches, register trademarks or trade names with the appropriate state and federal agencies, renew registrations in those states that require annual renewal, and so on. We've used Legal Services, Inc., for years to handle these kinds of tasks for our firm."

Karen is pleased to learn that her task will be so simple—all she has to do is make one phone call, and Legal Services, Inc., will do the rest of the work. Karen calls the company, and her call is answered by Steve Marks. He asks her what services she wants. Karen responds, "Verification of trade-name ownership." Steve then asks Karen for the trade name, and she replies, "Burger Basket." "Who do you believe to be the current owner of the trade name?" asks Steve. "J. Michael Robbins," responds Karen. "The state of registration?" asks Steve. "Kansas," replies Karen. "How soon do you need the information?" asks Steve. "Within three to five days," Karen answers. "Well," Steve says, "we'll see what we can do!"

al or state laws relating to franchises. In the absence of case law precisely addressed to franchising, the courts tend to apply general common law principles and appropriate federal or state statutory definitions and rules. Characteristics associated with a franchising relationship are similar in some respects to those of principal-agent, employer-employee, and employer–independent contractor relationships—yet a franchising relationship does not truly fit into any of these traditional classifications.

Federal Regulation of Franchising. Some statutory requirements specifically relating to franchising have been enacted at the federal level. The Automobile Dealers' Franchise Act of 1956 (also known as the Automobile Dealers' Day in Court Act) protects franchisees from automobile manufacturers who terminate franchises in bad faith. If a manufacturer-franchisor terminates a franchise because of a dealer-franchisee's failure to comply with unreasonable demands (for example, failure to attain an unrealistically high sales quota), the manufacturer may be liable for damages.

Another federal statute is the Petroleum Marketing Practices Act (PMPA), which was passed in 1979 to protect gasoline station franchisees. Before the PMPA's passage, gasoline franchisors sometimes imposed high minimum rents and gallonage requirements. The PMPA prescribes the

grounds and conditions under which a franchisor may terminate or decline to renew a franchise.

Other federal laws also affect franchise operations. Federal antitrust laws may apply if there is an illegal price-fixing agreement affecting the relationship between a franchisor and franchisee. In 1979, the Federal Trade Commission (FTC) issued regulations that require franchisors to disclose material facts necessary for a prospective franchisee to make an informed decision concerning the purchase of a franchise.

State Regulation of Franchising. Most states currently have statutes dealing with franchise law. State legislation tends to be similar to federal statutes and the FTC regulations. That is, state laws are generally designed to protect prospective franchisees from dishonest franchisors and to prohibit franchisors from terminating franchises without good cause. For example, a law might require the disclosure of information that is material to making an informed decision regarding the purchase of a franchise. This could include such information as the actual costs of operation, recurring expenses, and profits earned, along with facts substantiating these figures.

In response to the need for a uniform franchise law, the National Conference of Commissioners on Uniform State Laws drafted a model law that standardizes the various state franchise regulations. Because the uniform law represents a compromise among so many diverse interests, it has met with little success in being adopted as law by the various states.

When a franchise exists primarily for the sale of products manufactured by the franchisor, the law governing sales (Article 2 of the Uniform Commercial Code, which was discussed in Chapter 8) applies.

Types of Franchises

Franchises can take the form of distributorships, chain-style business operations, or manufacturing or processing-plant arrangements.

1. A *distributorship* is established when a manufacturing concern (franchisor) licenses a dealer (franchisee) to sell its product. Often, a distributorship covers an exclusive territory. An example of this type of franchise is an automobile dealership.
2. A *chain-style business franchise* results when a franchise operates under a franchisor's trade name and is identified as a member of a select group of dealers that engages in the franchisor's business. The franchisee is generally required to follow standardized or prescribed methods of operation. In addition, sometimes the franchisee is obligated to deal exclusively with the franchisor to obtain materials and supplies. An example of this type of franchise is McDonald's, along with most other fast-food chains.
3. A *manufacturing or processing-plant franchise* is created when the franchisor transmits to the franchisee the essential ingredients or formula to make a particular product. The franchisee then markets it either at wholesale or at retail in accordance with the franchisor's standards. Examples of this type of franchise are Coca-Cola and other soft-drink bottling companies.

The Franchise Contract

The franchise relationship is created by a contract between the franchisor and the franchisee. To avoid future problems arising from the relationship, prospective franchisees should obtain all of the relevant details of the business and scrutinize carefully the franchise contract and its economic and legal implications. As mentioned above, federal and state disclosure laws require that franchisors supply prospective franchisees with all material facts and information relating to the franchise.

Each franchise relationship and each industry has its own characteristics, so it is difficult to describe the broad range of details a franchising contract may include. The following sections, however, define the essential characteristics of the franchise relationship.

Paying for the Franchise. The franchisee ordinarily pays an initial fee or a lump-sum price for the franchise license (the privilege of being granted a franchise). This fee is separate from the fee for the various products that the franchisee purchases from or through the franchisor. In some industries, the franchisor relies heavily on the initial sale of the franchise for realizing a profit. In other industries, the continued dealing between the parties brings profit to both.

In most situations, the franchisor receives a stated percentage of the annual sales or annual volume of business done by the franchisee. The franchise agreement may also require the franchisee to pay a percentage of advertising costs and certain administrative expenses incurred under the franchise contract.

Location of the Franchise. Typically, the franchisor determines the territory to be served. The franchise contract may specify whether the premises for the business must be leased or purchased outright. In some cases, construction of a building is necessary to meet the terms of the franchise contract.

Certainly the contract will specify whether the franchisor supplies equipment and furnishings for the premises or whether this is the responsibility of the franchisee. When the franchise is a service operation, such as a motel, the contract often provides that the franchisor will establish certain standards for the facility and will make inspections to ensure that the standards are being maintained in order to protect the name and reputation of the franchise.

One area that causes a great deal of conflict is the territorial exclusivity of the franchise. Many franchise agreements, while they do define the territory allotted to a particular franchise, specifically state that the franchise is nonexclusive. That means that the franchisor can establish additional franchises in the same territory. The ramifications of nonexclusivity can be severe.

Price Controls. Franchises provide the franchisor with an outlet for the firm's goods and services. Depending on the nature of the business, the franchisor may require the franchisee to purchase certain supplies from the franchisor at an established price. A franchisor cannot set the prices at which the

ETHICAL CONCERN

Franchise Contracts and the Duty of Competence

Suppose that you are asked to draft a franchise contract for Fabulous Frills, a chain-style clothing store, to use when it sells franchises to others. Using a franchise contract created for another client as a model, you duplicate it on your computer, modify it as necessary, and give it to your supervising attorney for review. She quickly scans it and directs you to make a couple of minor modifications and then send it to Fabulous Frills. No one—not you, your supervising attorney, or the owners of Fabulous Frills—notices that a provision in the contract gives the franchisee exclusive territorial rights. The error only comes to light later—when Fabulous Frills sues your supervising attorney for negligence. Because of this contractual provision, Fabulous Frills has been prevented from expanding in a certain area and has suffered lost profits. This is just one example of the many ethical pitfalls that paralegals must take care to avoid when modifying a document prepared for a previous client to serve a current client's needs.

franchisee will resell the goods, however, as this is a violation of antitrust laws. A franchisor can *suggest* retail prices but cannot insist on them.

Business Organization and Quality Controls. The business organization of the franchisee is of great concern to the franchisor. Depending on the terms of the franchise agreement, the franchisor may set requirements for the form and capital structure of the business. The franchise contract can provide that the franchisee must meet standards of operation relating to such aspects of the business as sales quotas, quality standards, and record keeping. Furthermore, a franchisor may wish to retain stringent control over the training of personnel involved in the operation and over administrative aspects of the business. Although the day-to-day operation of the franchise business is normally left up to the franchisee, the franchise contract may provide for whatever amount of supervision and control the parties agree on.

As a general rule, a provision permitting the franchisor to enforce certain quality standards is valid. Because the franchisor has a legitimate interest in maintaining the quality of the product or service in order to protect its name and reputation, it can exercise greater control in this area than would otherwise be tolerated.

Termination of the Franchise. The duration of the franchise is a matter to be determined between the parties. Often, a franchise starts out for a short period, such as a year, so that the franchisee and the franchisor can determine whether they want to stay in business with each other. Usually, the franchise contract specifies that termination must be "for cause," such as death or disability of the franchisee, insolvency of the franchisee, breach of the franchise contract, or failure to meet specified sales quotas. Most franchise contracts provide that notice of termination must be given. If no set time for termination is given, then a reasonable time with notice is implied. A franchisee must be given reasonable time to wind up the business—that is, to do the accounting and return the copyright, trademark, or any other property to the franchisor.

Much franchise litigation has arisen over termination provisions. The termination provisions of contracts are generally more favorable to the franchisor. This means that the franchisee, who normally invests a substantial amount of time and money in the franchise operation to make it successful, may receive little or nothing for the business upon termination. The franchisor owns the trademark and hence the business.

It is in this area that the lack of statutory law and case law is felt most keenly by the franchisee. Automobile dealerships and gasoline stations subject to franchise contracts now have some statutory protection, however, under the federal laws mentioned earlier. In determining whether a franchisor has acted in good faith when terminating a franchise, the courts need to balance the rights of both parties.

ETHICAL CONCERN

Friends and Franchises—and the UPL

Suppose that your friend Jake is interested in purchasing a franchise. He is about to sign the contract and pay $15,000 to the franchisor. At his request, you read through the contract and notice that while the franchisee's obligations are clearly stated, the franchisor's promises are very vague. You tell Jake that there are many potential pitfalls in franchise relationships and that he really should see an attorney before he signs the contract. Jake, though, cannot see how any problems could arise and doesn't want to spend money for legal assistance that (he thinks) he doesn't need. Should you advise Jake about your specific concerns and suggest that he investigate the franchisor's business more thoroughly, add certain protective provisions to the contract, and the like? No. By advising Jake to seek legal counsel, you've gone about as far as you should in terms of your ethical obligations. If you did give Jake legal advice, you would be engaging in the unauthorized practice of law.

SPECIAL FORMS OF BUSINESS ORGANIZATION AND THE PARALEGAL

Paralegals frequently work on matters relating to corporations, partnerships, and sole proprietorships. The forms of business organization discussed in

SUBSTANTIVE LAW CONCEPT SUMMARY

Special Forms of Business Organizations

Special Business Forms	1. *Joint venture*—A relationship created by two or more persons or organizations in contemplation of a limited activity or a single transaction; otherwise, similar to a partnership. 2. *Syndicate*—An investment group that undertakes to finance a particular project; may exist as a corporation or as a general or limited partnership. 3. *Joint stock company*—A business form similar to a corporation in some respects (shareholder-owners, management by directors and officers, perpetual existence) but otherwise resembling a partnership (it is formed by agreement, property is usually held in the names of the members, shareholders have personal liability for business debts and obligations, and the business is usually taxed as a partnership). 4. *Business trust*—A business form created by a written trust agreement that sets forth the interests of the investor-beneficiaries and the powers and duties of the trustees. It is similar to a corporation in many respects. Investor-beneficiaries receive a share of the profits and are not personally liable for the debts or obligations of the enterprise. 5. *Cooperative*—An association organized to provide an economic service, without profit, to its members; may take the form of a corporation or a partnership.
Franchises	1. *Definition of a franchise*—A franchise is any arrangement in which an owner of a trademark, trade name, or copyright licenses another to use that trademark, trade name, or copyright, under specified conditions, in the sale of goods and services. The seller of the license is the franchisor, and the buyer of the license is the franchisee. 2. *Creation of the franchise relationship*—The franchise relationship is created by a contractual agreement between the franchisor and the franchisee. 3. *Types of franchises:* a. Distributorship (e.g., automobile dealership). b. Chain-style operation (e.g., fast-food chain). c. Manufacturing/processing-plant arrangement (e.g., soft-drink bottling company, such as Coca-Cola). 4. *The franchise contract:* a. Ordinarily requires the franchisee to pay a price for the franchise license. b. Specifies the territory to be served by the franchisee's firm. c. May require the franchisee to purchase certain supplies from the franchisor at an established price. d. May require the franchisee to abide by certain standards of quality relating to the product or service sold by the franchisee, but the franchisor cannot set the retail price of the product or service. e. Usually provides for the date and/or conditions of termination of the franchise agreement.

this chapter are less common, and you may or may not be as extensively involved in work relating to them. Being prepared for any situation, though, is the hallmark of the good paralegal. Depending on the nature of your job, you might be asked to help draft a joint-venture agreement or the paperwork necessary to create a cooperative or other special form of business organization. You might be in charge of reviewing and maintaining the records of a business trust. You might assist with litigation involving special business

TODAY'S PROFESSIONAL PARALEGAL

Reviewing Franchise Agreements

Tom Mansfield, a paralegal, is reviewing a franchise agreement that a client has given to his supervising attorney. The client, Ms. Mulcahey, wants to purchase a franchise called "Yuppies Unlimited," which sells business and casual wear for young professional women. Tom begins to read through the contract for the specifics of the franchise deal.

PRICE AND LOCATION OF THE FRANCHISE

The payment provision requires Ms. Mulcahey to pay $88,000 for the franchise. She must purchase all of the clothing from the franchisor at wholesale cost, and she is encouraged to sell the clothing at the franchisor's "suggested retail price." There are also location requirements. Ms. Mulcahey may lease a building of her choice, but it must be in a business or shopping district that is of high quality—that is, it cannot be in an outlet mall, a discount shopping mall, or a shopping center. The contract is very specific about the design and decor of the retail store, and the contract requires that the store's square-footage be within a certain range.

OTHER PROVISIONS OF THE FRANCHISE CONTRACT

Ms. Mulcahey plans to open the store in a metropolitan area, and there is an exclusivity clause with regard to how many stores can be opened in such an area and the physical distance that must exist between the stores. A business and quality-control provision allows the franchisor to make inspections and requires the franchisee to meet certain quality standards and a sales quota in order to keep the store open. Franchisees also are required to participate in initial and annual training programs at the corporate headquarters of Yuppies Unlimited.

The termination provision sets an initial contract term of two years. If Ms. Mulcahey's store has met the conditions set out in the franchise contract (in terms of quality control and annual sales quotas), then the franchise will be extended for a ten-year period, to be followed by additional ten-year periods. The contract also provides for termination of the franchise for cause.

SUMMARIZING THE CONTRACT

Tom thinks that the contract sounds reasonable and fair. He indicates this in a legal memorandum to his supervising attorney, in which he also summarizes the major provisions of the contract. The attorney will be discussing the contract with Ms. Mulcahey the next day, and the attorney will be relying on Tom's evaluation and summary of the contract provisions when advising the client on the matter.

forms. A knowledge of the basic nature of these business forms will be useful to you in such situations.

A more likely possibility is that, sooner or later, you will be engaged in work relating to a franchise relationship. As you read earlier, franchises are widespread in our society. Also, there is typically a disparity in bargaining power between the franchisor (such as a large oil company or a fast-food restaurant chain) and the franchisee (who may be an individual who has never owned and operated a business before). A franchisee may invest his or her life savings in a franchise operation and then, a few years later, be told that the franchise is being terminated for one reason or another. In such a situation, the franchisee will probably seek legal assistance from an attorney, and litigation may ensue. This is just one example of how disputes between the parties in a franchise relationship can arise. There are many others.

As in other areas of the law, it is impossible to summarize the many types of work that paralegals perform in relation to special business forms and franchises because that work is so varied. The list below will give you

an idea, though, of some specific types of tasks that you might be asked to undertake in this area:

- Research federal and state statutory law governing one of the special business forms discussed or a franchise.
- Research case law to find out how the courts have applied statutes or common law principles governing these types of business forms or relationships.
- Verify ownership rights in a trademark, trade name, or copyright that is subject to a licensing agreement as part of a franchise contract.
- Assist a business trust in the issuance of trust certificates to investor-beneficiaries and create, record, and/or maintain records relating to a business trust.
- Draft a joint-venture agreement and compare it with similar agreements to make sure that the agreement you drafted is thorough and protects the client's interests.
- Assist in reviewing tax records and preparing tax returns for a cooperative or other type of business form discussed in this chapter.
- Assist in out-of-court dispute-settlement procedures, such as mediation, negotiation, and arbitration.
- Assist in litigation relating to a dispute involving members of a special business form or a franchise relationship.
- Assist in litigation relating to claims brought against one of these business forms or a franchise.

KEY TERMS AND CONCEPTS

antitrust law 762
business trust 763
cooperative 764
franchise 764
franchisee 764
franchisor 764
joint stock company 763
joint venture 760
syndicate 763

CHAPTER SUMMARY

1. A joint venture is a relationship in which two or more persons or organizations combine their efforts or their property for a single transaction or project or a related series of transactions or projects. A joint venture is normally not treated as a legal entity and is taxed like a partnership. Joint venturers' duties to one another are the same as those of partners. Each joint venturer has an equal right to manage the activities of the enterprise, and each joint venturer is liable to third parties for the actions of the other members of the joint venture.

2. A syndicate is an investment group consisting of firms or individuals that get together to finance a particular project. The syndicate may exist as a corporation or as a general or limited partnership.

3. A joint stock company is a true hybrid of a partnership and a corporation. It is similar to a corporation because it is owned by shareholders, is managed by directors and officers, and can have a perpetual existence. It is similar to a partnership in that it is formed by agreement (not by state charter), property is usually held in the names of the members, the shareholders have personal liability for business debts and obligations, and it is taxed like a partnership.

4. A business trust is a form of business organization in which investors (trust beneficiaries) transfer cash or property to trustees in exchange for trust certificates that represent their investment shares. Management of the business and trust property is handled by the trustees for the benefit of the investors. The

investors have limited liability and share in the trust's profits.

5. A cooperative is a form of business organization that is organized to provide an economic service to its members. It makes distributions of dividends, or profits, to its owners on the basis of their transactions with the cooperative rather than on the basis of the amount of capital they contributed. Examples of cooperatives are consumer purchasing cooperatives, credit cooperatives, and farmers' cooperatives.

6. A private franchise is not really a form of business organization but rather a way of conducting business. A franchise is any arrangement in which the owner of a trademark, trade name, or copyright licenses another to use that trademark, trade name, or copyright, under specified conditions, in the sale of goods and services. Franchises can take the form of distributorships, chain-style business operations, or manufacturing or processing-plant arrangements. Federal and state statutes provide some protection for franchisees, but there has been little overall regulation of the franchising relationship. The franchise relationship is created by a contract between the franchisor and the franchisee. The franchisee is generally legally independent of the business system of the franchisor. Typically, the franchisor and the franchisee make arrangements relating to payment for the franchise, the location of the franchise, price controls, business organization and quality controls, and termination of the franchise.

QUESTIONS FOR REVIEW

1. What is a joint venture? What are the rights and duties of joint venturers? When might a joint venture be an appropriate way of doing business?

2. What potential problems are associated with joint ventures? How do joint ventures differ from partnerships?

3. What is a syndicate? When is a syndicate used?

4. What is a joint stock company? What is a business trust? When is each of these special business forms used?

5. What is a cooperative? Give examples of businesses that often organize as cooperatives.

6. What is a franchise? How does a franchise relationship arise, and what are the parties to a franchising agreement called?

7. What laws regulate franchising? Name two federal statutes that regulate franchising relationships.

8. List and briefly define the types of franchises discussed in the chapter.

9. List and briefly define the contract provisions typically found in a franchise agreement.

10. List and describe three tasks that a paralegal working with special forms of business organizations may perform.

ETHICAL QUESTIONS

1. Sonoma Vineyards, Inc., and California Vineyards, Ltd., plan to enter into a joint venture to produce a superior brand of champagne. Before signing the agreement, California Vineyards requests confidential financial information from Sonoma Vineyards. Must Sonoma Vineyards supply the confidential financial information?

2. Samantha, a paralegal, is using standard-form trust certificates, which she has stored in the memory of her computer, to draft trust certificates for a client's new business deal. In changing the terms to suit the client's undertaking, she neglects to change the number of investment shares to be received by the investors in the business venture. As a result, the number originally keyed into the document is inadvertently included on the new certificates, and the investors receive fewer shares than they paid for. The investors sue Samantha's supervising attorney for negligence. What will result?

3. Brenda's friend Bob is a paralegal. Brenda has obtained a standard form and has used it to draft an agreement to establish a student bookstore cooperative. The purpose of the cooperative is to obtain lower prices for textbooks through quantity dis-

counts. Brenda asks Bob to review the cooperative agreement that she has drafted. She wants to know if the agreement provides her with adequate protection and, if not, what changes need to be made. How should Bob answer Brenda's questions?

PRACTICE QUESTIONS AND ASSIGNMENTS

1. Which of the following business organizations can be described as an investment group put together to finance a project?

a. Business trust.
b. Joint stock company.
c. Joint venture.
d. Syndicate.

2. Which of the following business entities can be described as an association organized to provide economic services to its members and to gain an advantage in the marketplace?

a. Franchise.
b. Business trust.
c. Cooperative.
d. Joint stock company.

3. Which of the following business organizations can be described as a relationship in which two or more persons combine their efforts or property for a single transaction or project or a related series of transactions or projects?

a. Syndicate.
b. Joint venture.
c. Joint stock company.
d. Franchise.

QUESTIONS FOR CRITICAL ANALYSIS

1. The Automobile Dealers' Franchise Act of 1956 protects a franchisee from having the franchise terminated by the manufacturer in bad faith—for example, for the franchisee's failure to comply with an unrealistically high sales quota. Suppose that a written franchise contract for an automobile dealership explicitly excludes territorial exclusivity but a representative of the manufacturer orally states that the franchisee will have exclusive territorial rights. The manufacturer, acting in accordance with the written contract, then fails to provide exclusive territorial rights. Has the manufacturer acted in bad faith?

2. Why are franchise regulations drafted to protect the franchisee? In other words, why do franchisees need protection?

PROJECTS

1. Go to a library and review several past issues of the *Wall Street Journal*. Find an article discussing a joint venture. Write a one-page, typewritten, double-spaced paper describing the two businesses that are undertaking the joint venture and what is involved—a single project or a series of transactions. Describe the duration of the joint venture, any rights and duties that are apparent or implied, and any potential conflicts.

2. Locate the case *Huang v. Holiday Inns, Inc.*, 594 F.Supp.352 (C.D.Cal. 1984). Describe the franchise relationship that existed between the Huangs and Holiday Inns. Explain why the parties are in court, what remedies the Huangs seek, and why they are seeking them.

3. Review your state's statutes to determine whether your state has a law governing franchising. If so, is it similar to the federal statutes discussed in this chapter? Under the state statute, what type of information must a franchisor disclose to a potential franchisee?

ROLE-PLAYING EXERCISES

1. Review the *Developing Paralegal Skills* feature entitled "Verifying Trade Names." Role-play the conversation between Karen, the paralegal, and Steve, the employee of the corporate services company.

2. Using the bill from outside counsel in the *Developing Paralegal Skills* feature entitled "Scrutinizing Outside Counsel's Bills," role-play a conversation between Amanda Bryan and the office manager at the law firm that submitted the bill. Both Amanda and the office manager should be politely firm and assertive in their conversation.

ANNOTATED SELECTED READINGS

EMERSON, ROBERT W. "Franchise Contract Clauses and the Franchisor's Duty of Care toward Its Franchisees." *North Carolina Law Review,* April 1994. An article that provides a basic discussion of franchise contracts. The article analyzes which provisions should be subjected to the fiduciary, "good cause," "good faith," and "fair dealing" standards of care by the courts in settling disputes between franchisors and franchisees.

GLENN, ROBIN DAY. "Subfranchising." *Franchise Law Journal,* Winter 1994. An interesting discussion of the concept of subfranchising, the legal problems it involves, and the protections not granted to the subfranchisee. (In a subfranchise arrangement, the franchisee grants portions of its franchise to others.)

KLARFELD, PETER J. *Covenants against Competition in Franchising Agreements.* American Bar Association, 1993. A monograph that surveys state laws governing covenants not to compete in relation to franchise agreements. The article contains important information for practitioners in the area of franchising.

NICASTRO, TRACEY A. "How the Cookie Crumbles: The Good Cause Requirement for Terminating a Franchise Agreement." *Valparaiso University Law Review,* Winter 1994. This case note reviews the "good cause" requirement for the termination of a franchise agreement in the context of the Illinois Franchise Disclosure Act. This act is similar to statutes in fifteen other states. The case note provides a basic discussion of the history of these statutes, the problems associated with interpreting "good cause," and a proposed amendment to the franchise statutes to remedy the problems associated with the "good cause" requirement.

ZORN, STEPHEN A. "Couldna Done It Without the Players: Depreciation of Professional Sports Player Contracts under the Internal Revenue Code." *Seton Hall Journal of Sports Law,* 1994. This interesting article on sports-team franchises discusses the multimillion-dollar depreciation deductions available to owners of sports teams for player contracts and other "intangibles."

20

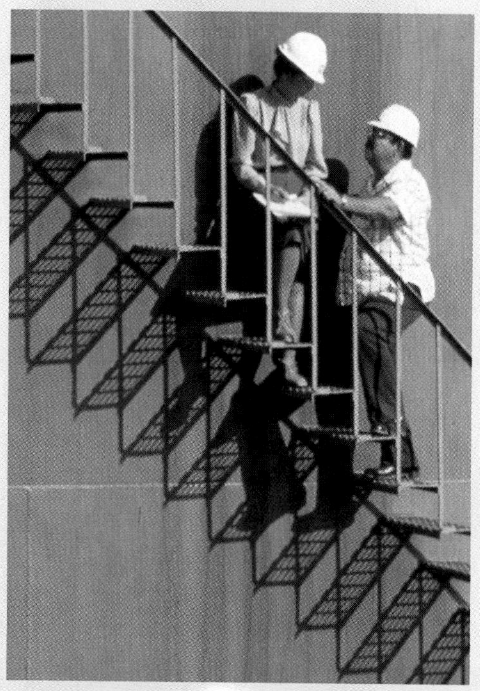

TORTS AND PRODUCT LIABILITY

Chapter Objectives

After completing this chapter, you will know:

- **How certain types of business torts arise, including torts of wrongful interference with contractual or business relationships, appropriation, defamation, and product disparagement.**
- **Some tort actions that can be brought against business polluters.**
- **How landowners can be held liable for injuries incurred by those who enter onto the landowners' premises.**
- **Some negligence doctrines and statutes that govern certain tortious activities.**
- **The various theories under which product-liability actions can be brought.**
- **How the doctrine of strict liability is applied to manufacturers of defective products that injure product users.**

Chapter Outline

INTRODUCTION

The body of tort law is a broad area of civil law, and every paralegal should have at least a basic knowledge of tort concepts and doctrines. Recall from Chapter 8 that a *tort* is a wrongful action that causes another to suffer harm. If the action was intentional, the tort falls into the category of *intentional torts.* Torts of *negligence,* in contrast, result not from intent but from a breach of a duty owed.

BUSINESS TORT
A tort occurring within the business context; typical business torts are wrongful interference with the business or contractual relationships of others, defamation and product disparagement, and appropriation.

In this chapter, we begin by discussing various types of torts related to business activities. **Business torts** are defined as wrongful interferences with others' business rights. You already read about certain types of business torts—those involving the infringement of rights in intellectual property—in Chapter 8. Business torts also include the following causes of action:

1. Wrongful interference with a contractual or a business relationship.
2. Appropriation of another's name or likeness without permission.
3. Defamation and product disparagement.

After examining these business torts, we look at some other types of torts, including the tort of nuisance, toxic torts, torts involving premises liability, and torts governed by special negligence doctrines and statutes. In the final pages of the chapter, we focus on the important area of product liability. Paralegals frequently are involved in some aspect of product-liability litigation, and many paralegals specialize in this area.

WRONGFUL INTERFERENCE

Our economic system of free enterprise is predicated on the ability of business firms to compete for customers and for sales. Unfettered competitive behavior has been shown to lead to economic efficiency and economic progress. Businesses may, generally speaking, engage in whatever behavior is *reasonably* necessary to obtain a fair share of a market or to recapture a share that has been lost. They are not, however, allowed to use the motive of completely eliminating competition to justify certain business activities.

Torts involving wrongful interference with another's business rights generally fall into two categories—interference with a contractual relationship and interference with a business relationship. These two torts and the defenses that can be raised against them are discussed below.

Wrongful Interference with a Contractual Relationship

The body of tort law relating to *intentional interference with a contractual relationship* has increased greatly in recent years. A landmark case in this area involved an opera singer, Joanna Wagner, who was under contract to sing for a man named Lumley for a specified period of years.[1] A man named Gye, who knew of this contract, nonetheless "enticed" Wagner to refuse to

1. *Lumley v. Gye,* 118 Eng.Rep. 749 (1853).

carry out the agreement, and Wagner began to sing for Gye. Gye's action constituted a tort, because it interfered with the contractual relationship between Wagner and Lumley. (Wagner's refusal to carry out the agreement also entitled Lumley to sue Wagner for breach of contract.)

Three basic elements are necessary to the existence of wrongful interference with a contractual relationship:

1. A valid, enforceable contract must exist between two parties.
2. A third party must *know* that this contract exists.
3. This third party must *intentionally induce* either of the two parties to the contract to break the contract, and the interference must be for the purpose of advancing the economic interest of the inducer.

The contract may be between a firm and its employees or a firm and its customers, suppliers, competitors, or other parties. Sometimes a competitor of a firm may attempt to draw away a key employee, even to the extent of paying damages for wrongful interference with a contractual relationship. If the original employer can show that the competitor induced the breach—that is, that the employee would not normally have broken the contract—damages can be recovered.

The highly publicized case of *Texaco, Inc. v. Pennzoil Co.* illustrates how costly the tort of wrongful interference can be for the firm committing the tort. In this case, Pennzoil Company made an offer to buy control of Getty Oil Company and negotiated the offer with Getty Oil's major stockholders. After the deal was made but before the final details of the agreement had been worked out, Texaco, Inc., made an offer to purchase control of Getty Oil that Getty's board of directors accepted. Pennzoil subsequently sued Texaco, alleging tortious interference with its contract with Getty Oil. The trial court found that Texaco had actively induced the breach of the Getty-Pennzoil agreement and awarded over $10 billion to Pennzoil in damages. A Texas appellate court upheld the decision.[2]

Wrongful Interference with a Business Relationship

Individuals devise countless schemes to attract business, but they are forbidden by the courts to interfere unreasonably with another's business in their attempts to gain a share of the market. There is a difference between *competition* and *predatory behavior.* The distinction usually depends on whether a business is attempting to attract customers in general or to solicit only those customers who have already shown an interest in the similar product or service of a specific competitor.

Suppose that a shopping center contains two shoe stores, Store A and Store B. An employee of Store A cannot be positioned at the entrance of Store B for the purpose of diverting customers to Store A. This type of activity constitutes the tort of wrongful interference with a business relationship, often

2. *Texaco, Inc. v. Pennzoil Co.,* 729 S.W.2d 768 (1987). The Supreme Court of Texas also upheld the decision. Other issues in the case were appealed as high as the United States Supreme Court. In 1988, the case was settled for $3 billion. On the day of the payment, Texaco completed its reorganization and emerged from twelve months in bankruptcy proceedings.

referred to as interference with a prospective (economic) advantage, and it is commonly considered to be an unfair trade practice. If this type of activity were permitted, Store A would reap the benefits of Store B's advertising.

Defenses to Wrongful Interference

A person will not be liable for the tort of wrongful interference with a contractual or business relationship if it can be shown that the interference was *justified,* or *permissible.* For example, *bona fide* competitive behavior is a privileged (justified, permissible) interference even if it results in the breaking of a contract. If Harley's Pie Factory advertises so effectively that it induces Sam's Restaurant Chain to break its contract with Jepson's Bakery, Jepson's Bakery will be unable to recover against Harley's Pie Factory on a theory of wrongful interference. After all, the public policy that favors free competition in advertising definitely outweighs any possible instability that such competitive activity might cause in contractual relations. Therefore, although luring customers away from a competitor through aggressive marketing and advertising strategies obviously interferes with the competitor's relationship with his or her customers, such activity is permitted by the courts.

Also, so long as there is no associated *illegal* activity, a businessperson will not incur tort liability for negotiating secretly behind a rival's back, refusing to do business with a competitor, or refusing to deal with third parties until they stop doing business with a rival.

ETHICAL CONCERN

Padding the Bill

John is a new paralegal in a small law firm. He assists Cal, an experienced and competent paralegal who had been with the firm for years. John notices that when Cal's supervising attorney is out of the office, Cal spends a lot of time on personal matters. One day, Cal tells John how many billable hours he had generated in the previous month "without putting in any overtime." John is flabbergasted. He knew that Cal could not have done that much work and suspects that he must be double-billing clients for his work. What should John do? Should he discuss his suspicions with one of the attorneys? Yes. Clearly, it is unethical to "pad" a client's bill (charge a client for work not performed), and, if Cal is doing so, he is causing his supervising attorney to violate the duty to charge clients reasonable fees. John must realize, though, that his ethical action may make life in the workplace difficult for him.

APPROPRIATION

The use of one person's name or likeness by another, without permission and for the benefit of the user, constitutes the tort of **appropriation**. Under the law, an individual's right to privacy includes the right to the exclusive use of his or her identity. A number of cases have arisen concerning the use of a famous person's name for the benefit of the user. One case involved the use of "Here's Johnny," which was the opening line of Johnny Carson's television show. A Michigan corporation that rented and sold portable toilets advertised them as "Here's Johnny" toilets. Carson brought suit, claiming that the Michigan corporation had violated his right to privacy by publicly appropriating his celebrity status for the corporation's commercial benefit. Even though the corporation had not used Carson's name or picture, the court held that the use of "Here's Johnny" was an appropriation of Carson's identity because the phrase was so strongly associated with Carson's public personality.[3]

APPROPRIATION
In tort law, the use of one person's name or likeness by another, without permission and for the benefit of the user.

Other cases have involved the unauthorized use of former world heavyweight boxing champion Muhammad Ali's appellation "The Greatest" to describe a nude male model[4] and the use of professional football wide receiver Elroy Hirsch's moniker "Crazylegs" as the name of a shaving gel.[5] A more

3. *Carson v. Here's Johnny Portable Toilets,* 698 F.2d 831 (6th Cir. 1983).
4. *Ali v. Playgirl, Inc.,* 447 F.Supp. 723 (S.D.N.Y. 1978).
5. *Hirsch v. S. C. Johnson & Son, Inc.,* 90 Wis.2d 379, 280 N.W.2d 129 (1979).

recent case involved Vanna White, the hostess of the popular game show "Wheel of Fortune." Without White's permission, a company, in one of its advertisements, depicted a robot dressed in a wig, gown, and jewelry and posed in a stance for which White is famous next to a game board that resembled the "Wheel of Fortune" set. White sued the company in federal district court, alleging, among other things, that the company had appropriated her celebrity status. Although the trial court granted a motion for summary judgment against White, the appellate court held in her favor.[6]

DEFAMATION AND PRODUCT DISPARAGEMENT

As we stated in Chapter 8, the tort of *defamation* occurs when an individual makes a false statement that injures another's reputation. We also divided defamation into its component parts of libel (defamatory statements in written or printed form) and slander (defamatory statements made orally). Defamation becomes a business tort when the defamatory matter injures someone in a profession, business, or trade or when it adversely affects a business entity in its credit rating and other dealings. For example, when erroneous information from a computer about a person's credit standing or business reputation impairs that person's ability to obtain further credit, *defamation by computer* results.

When economically injurious falsehoods are made not about another's reputation but about another's product or property, disparagement of property occurs. **Disparagement of property** is a general term for torts that can be more specifically referred to as *slander of quality* or *slander of title.*

DISPARAGEMENT OF PROPERTY
Economically injurious falsehoods made about another's product or property. A general term for torts that are more specifically referred to as slander of quality and slander of title.

Slander of Quality

The publication of false information about another's product, alleging that it is not what its seller claims, constitutes a tort of **slander of quality**. This tort is also called **trade libel**. The plaintiff must prove that the slander of quality caused the plaintiff to suffer actual damages. That is, it must be shown that a third person refrained from dealing with the plaintiff because of the improper publication and also that the plaintiff suffered damages as a result. The economic calculation of such damages—they are, after all, conjectural—is often extremely difficult.

SLANDER OF QUALITY
The publication of false information about another's product, alleging that the product is not what its seller claims; also referred to as *trade libel.*

TRADE LIBEL
The publication of false information about another's product, alleging it is not what its seller claims; also referred to as *slander of quality.*

It is possible for an improper publication to be both a slander of quality and a defamation. For example, a statement that disparages the quality of a product may also, by implication, disparage the character of the person who would sell such a product. In one case, for instance, claiming that a product that was marketed as a sleeping aid contained "habit-forming drugs" was held to constitute defamation.[7]

The law of trademarks (discussed in Chapter 8) has, to some extent, made it easier for companies to sue other companies on the basis of purported false advertising. In the past, courts often ruled that companies could

6. *White v. Samsung Electronics America, Inc.*, 971 F.2d 1395 (9th Cir. 1992).
7. *Harwood Pharmacal Co. v. National Broadcasting Co.*, 9 N.Y.2d 460, 174 N.E.2d 602, 214 N.Y.S.2d 725 (1961).

only be liable for false advertising when they misrepresented their own products. It mattered little what such companies claimed about their competitors' brands, particularly in so-called comparative advertisements. Today, false or misleading statements about another firm's products are actionable.

Slander of Title

SLANDER OF TITLE
The publication of a statement that denies or casts doubt on another's legal ownership of particular property, causing financial loss to that property's owner.

When a publication denies or casts doubt on another's legal ownership of property, and when this results in financial loss to that property's owner, the tort of **slander of title** may exist. Usually this is an intentional tort in which someone knowingly publishes an untrue statement about property with the intent of discouraging a third person from dealing with the person slandered. For example, it would be difficult for a car dealer to attract customers after competitors published a notice that the dealer's stock consisted of stolen autos.

PREMISES LIABILITY

As a paralegal, some of the cases on which you work may involve premises liability—that is, the liability of property owners for injuries occurring on their premises. In such situations, liability is based on negligence theory. Recall from Chapter 8 that negligence is generally defined as the failure to use that degree of care that a reasonably prudent person would have used under the circumstances. An action in negligence requires the plaintiff to prove that (1) a duty of care existed, (2) this duty was breached, (3) the plaintiff suffered a legally recognizable injury, and (4) the injury was proximately caused by the breach of due care.

Plaintiffs in cases involving premises liability generally fall into three categories: invitees, licensees, and trespassers. Each of the these three classifications may require a different standard of care on the person in possession of the property.

Invitees

INVITEE
A person, such as a customer or dinner-party guest, who is invited onto another's property for the benefit of the other party.

An **invitee** is one who is invited onto another person's premises for the other person's benefit. Examples of invitees are business customers and dinner-party guests.

Retailers and other firms that explicitly or implicitly invite persons to come onto their premises are usually charged with a duty to exercise reasonable care to protect their business invitees. For example, if you entered a supermarket, slipped on a wet floor, and sustained injuries as a result, the owner of the supermarket would be liable for damages if, when you slipped, there was no sign warning that the floor was wet. A court would hold that the business owner was negligent because the owner failed to exercise a reasonable degree of care in protecting the store's customers against foreseeable risks that the owner knew or *should have known* about. That a customer or other person—it need not be a customer—might slip on the wet floor and be

injured as a result was a foreseeable risk, and the owner should have taken care to avoid this risk or warn the customer of it.[8]

- **Generally, to fulfill the duty of reasonable care owed to invitees, the owner must take steps to remove not only dangers but also to discover and remove any hidden dangers that might injure a customer or other invitee.**

Some risks, of course, are so obvious that the owner need not warn of them. For example, a business owner does not need to warn customers to open a door before attempting to walk through it. Other risks, however, even though they may seem obvious to a business owner, may not be so in the eyes of another, such as a child. For example, a hardware store owner may not think it is necessary to warn customers that a stepladder leaning against the back wall of the store could fall down and harm them. Nonetheless, it is possible that a child could tip the ladder over and be hurt as a result and that the store could be held liable.

Licensees

LICENSEE
A person, such as a theater goer, who receives permission to enter onto another's property for the licensee's benefit.

A **licensee** is one who is invited (or allowed to enter) onto the property of another for the licensee's benefit. Examples of licensees are sales representatives and theater guests. Traditionally, courts have held that the duty of care owed by business owners to licensees is not as great as the duty of care owed to invitees. The underlying rationale for this distinction is that, unlike business customers and others who are invited onto the owner's premises primarily for the owner's benefit, licensees are allowed onto the property primarily for the licensees' benefit. Therefore, "reasonable care" in regard to licensees requires the owner only to correct known dangers. The owner need not inspect the premises for hidden dangers and correct them or warn licensees of them.

At least twenty states have abolished this traditional distinction between invitees and licensees and hold that landowners owe the same duty to licensees as they do to invitees. Nonetheless, other states continue to abide by the distinction. In a recent case, for example, a man slipped on ice when he was attending a Bible study session at a private home and sued the homeowner for negligence. The court held that because the man was a mere licensee, the owner had no duty to inspect the premises for hidden dangers.[9]

Trespassers

TRESSPASSER
In the context of real property, one who enters onto the property of another without permission to do so.

A **trespasser** is one who, without invitation or authorization, enters onto another's property. In some jurisdictions, landowners are held to owe a duty to protect even trespassers against certain known risks. For example, a landowner may have a duty to post a notice that the property is patrolled by

8. See Chapter 17 for a discussion of a hypothetical lawsuit (brought by a customer against a retail business owner) involving premises liability.
9. *Carter v. Kinney*, No. 77487 (Mo. 1995). This case, which was decided by the Missouri Supreme Court, is not published in reporters. It can be retrieved from WESTLAW by keying in the cite 1995 WL 237530.

guard dogs. Under certain circumstances, a landowner might be held liable for injuries sustained by very young children under what is known as the **"attractive nuisance" doctrine.** If children might be expected to be attracted to a dangerous condition on the property, such as an unfenced swimming pool, the landlord may be liable for injuries incurred by the children even though they were trespassing on the property.

"ATTRACTIVE NUISANCE" DOCTRINE
A doctrine under which a landowner may be held liable for injuries incurred by children who are lured onto the property by something on the property that is dangerous and enticing.

TORT ACTIONS AGAINST POLLUTERS

Claims against business polluters today are often brought under state or federal environmental statutes. There are also common law remedies against polluters—remedies that originated centuries ago in England. Those responsible for operations that created dirt, smoke, noxious odors, noise, or toxic substances were sometimes held liable under common law theories of nuisance, negligence, or strict liability. Today, injured individuals continue to rely on the common law to obtain damages and injunctions against business polluters.

Nuisance

NUISANCE
An act that interferes unlawfully with a person's possession or ability to use his or her property.

Under the common law doctrine of **nuisance**, persons may be held liable if they use their property in a manner that unreasonably interferes with others' rights to use or enjoy their own property. In these situations, it is common for courts to balance the harm caused by the pollution against the costs of stopping it.

Courts have often denied injunctive relief (an equitable remedy in which the court grants the plaintiff's petition for an injunction and orders the defendant to discontinue the activity) on the ground that the hardships to be imposed on the polluter and on the community are greater than the hardships to be suffered by the plaintiff. For example, a factory that causes neighboring landowners to suffer from smoke, dirt, and vibrations may be left in operation if it is the core of a local economy. A court may award money damages to an injured party, though. These damages may include compensation for the decreased value of the neighbors' property that results from the factory's operation.

Toxic Torts

TOXIC TORT
A tort that occurs when toxic chemicals are used in a way that causes harm to other persons or their property. Liability for toxic torts may be based on strict liability, as well as negligence and other tort theories.

A developing area of tort law involves **toxic torts**—actions against toxic polluters based on the common law theories of negligence and strict liability. For example, employees might sue an employer whose negligence (failure to use proper pollution controls) resulted in air contamination, causing the employees to suffer respiratory illnesses. Businesses that engage in ultra-hazardous activities—such as the transportation of radioactive materials—are strictly liable for whatever injuries the activities cause. In a strict-liability action, the injured party does not need to prove that the business failed to exercise care.

A landmark case in the area of toxic torts is *Sterling v. Velsicol Chemical Corp.*[10] In 1964, Velsicol Chemical Corporation began operating a chem-

10. 647 F.Supp. 303 (W.D.Tenn. 1986).

DEVELOPING PARALEGAL SKILLS

Gathering Information—Preparing a Form

Several children attending Richard Elementary School became ill, and eventually their illnesses were traced to the school. When the land on which it was built was tested, it was found to be contaminated by wastes used in the paint-making process. A site history of the property was conducted, and it was discovered that the school property had been used as a landfill by Palette Corporation, a paint manufacturer. The parents of children attending the elementary school are holding a meeting tonight to discuss the possibility of taking legal action against Palette Corporation.

Jason Miller, a paralegal with the law firm of Smith & Howard, P.C., will be attending the parent meeting tonight with his supervising attorney, Mason Williams. The attorney was asked to attend the meeting to advise the parents on the possibility of filing a toxic-tort action against Palette Corporation. Jason is to prepare a form for parents to fill out if they want to be included in the case and if they want to be put on a mailing list to be kept updated on the case as it progresses. The form will be handed out at the meeting. Jason will enter the information from the completed forms into a database at the law firm's offices.

Jason sits down at his computer and creates a form that requests the name, address, and telephone number of the family; the names and ages of the children in the family and medical information about them; and the illnesses or injuries suffered by the children as a result of being exposed to the toxic waste at the school. Jason prints out his form, reviews it with his supervising attorney, makes copies of it, and prepares for tonight's meeting.

ical waste burial site on a farm in Tennessee. At the 242-acre site, over the better part of the next decade, Velsicol buried more than 300,000 fifty-five-gallon drums and hundreds of boxes filled with chemical waste. In 1973, the state of Tennessee determined the site to be hazardous and closed it. Local residents sued Velsicol on a number of legal theories, including negligence and strict liability, claiming that the aquifer (underground water) from which they drew their drinking water was contaminated with hazardous chemicals that leaked from the farm. The court awarded the residents damages for a variety of physical and emotional injuries, as well as property damage.[11]

SPECIAL NEGLIGENCE DOCTRINES AND STATUTES

There are a number of special doctrines and statutes relating to negligence. We examine a few of them here.

11. The judgment was upheld on appeal. See *Sterling v. Velsicol Chemical Corp.*, 855 F.2d 1188 (6th Cir. 1988).

Res Ipsa Loquitur

Generally, in lawsuits involving negligence, the plaintiff has the burden of proving that the defendant was negligent. In certain situations, when negligence is obvious, the courts may infer that negligence has occurred. When the courts make such an inference, the burden of proof rests on the defendant to prove that he or she was *not* negligent.

RES IPSA LOQUITUR
A doctrine under which negligence may be inferred simply because an event occurred, if it is the type of event that would not occur without negligence. Literally, the term means "the thing speaks for itself."

The inference of the defendant's negligence is known as the doctrine of ***res ipsa loquitur***, which translates as "the thing speaks for itself." This doctrine is applied only when the event creating the damage or injury is one that ordinarily does not occur in the absence of negligence. *Res ipsa loquitur* has been applied to such events as trains derailing, wheels falling off moving vehicles, and bricks or windowpanes falling from a defendant's premises.

For the doctrine to apply, the event that caused the injury must have been within the exclusive control of the defendant, and it must not have been due to any voluntary action or contribution on the part of the plaintiff. Some courts add still another condition—that the evidence available to explain the event be more accessible to the defendant than to the plaintiff.

Negligence *Per Se*

NEGLIGENCE *PER SE*
An action or failure to act that violates a statutory requirement and that results in harm to another.

Certain conduct, whether it consists of an action or a failure to act, may be treated as **negligence *per se*** ("in or of itself"). Negligence *per se* may occur if

DEVELOPING PARALEGAL SKILLS

"Dep Prep"

Barbara Colfax works as a paralegal for a large corporate law firm in the firm's litigation department. One of the firm's clients, a manufacturing corporation, is being sued by the government for safety-code violations, and the depositions of fifty supervisors, managers, directors, engineers, and corporate vice presidents are being taken by the government. Barbara's supervising attorney, Karen Roth, is defending the corporation, and Karen and Barbara must prepare for and attend each deposition.

Barbara assists Karen by interviewing each deponent two weeks before the deposition. During each interview, Barbara asks the deponent about his or her job duties and responsibilities and how he or she could be alleged to be involved in the safety-code violations. Barbara takes notes during each interview and then prepares a memo to Karen summarizing the deponent-employee's job responsibilities and the role of that employee in regard to the alleged safety violations.

Next, Barbara arranges for a "dep prep"—a meeting in which Karen, Barbara, and the deponent will discuss the upcoming deposition, including the questions that the government is likely to ask, what the answers are, and how the answers will be presented. When the day arrives for the deposition, Karen and Barbara attend the deposition with the client.

an individual violates a statute or an ordinance and that violation causes another to be injured. Numerous federal and state laws impose duties on manufacturers of cosmetics, drugs, foods, toxic substances, and flammable materials. These duties involve appropriate description of contents, labeling, branding, advertising, and selling. In a tort action for damages, a violation of statutory duty is often held to constitute negligence *per se.*

The injured person must prove (1) that the statute clearly sets out what standard of conduct is expected, when and where it is expected, and of whom it is expected; (2) that he or she is in the class intended to be protected by the statute; and (3) that the statute was designed to prevent the type of injury that he or she suffered. The standard of conduct required by the statute is the duty that the defendant owes to the plaintiff, and a violation of the statute is the breach of that duty.

Special Negligence Statutes

A number of states have enacted statutes prescribing duties and responsibilities in certain circumstances, the violation of which will establish civil liability. For example, many states have passed **dram shop acts**. These statutes impose a duty on tavern owners or bartenders not to serve drinks to patrons who are intoxicated or who may become intoxicated. If this duty is breached, liability may be extended to the tavern owner or bartender for injuries caused to a third party by the intoxicated person. In some states, **social-host statutes** impose liability on persons hosting parties for injuries caused by guests who became intoxicated at the hosts' homes.

Most states now also have what are called **Good Samaritan statutes**. Under these statutes, persons who are aided voluntarily by others cannot turn around and sue the "Good Samaritans" for negligence. These laws were passed largely to protect physicians and medical personnel who voluntarily render their services in emergency situations to those in need, such as individuals hurt in car accidents.

DRAM SHOP ACT
A state statute that imposes liability on the owners of bars and taverns for injuries resulting from accidents caused by intoxicated persons when the sellers or servers of alcoholic drinks contributed to the intoxication.

SOCIAL-HOST STATUTE
A state statute that imposes liability on persons hosting parties for injuries caused by guests who became intoxicated at the hosts' homes.

GOOD SAMARITAN STATUTE
A state statute that provides that persons who provide emergency services to, or rescue, others in peril cannot be sued for negligence.

PRODUCT LIABILITY

Manufacturers and sellers of goods can be held liable to consumers, users, and **bystanders** (people in the vicinity of the product) for physical harm or property damage that is caused by the goods. This is called *product liability,* and it encompasses the contract theory of warranty and the tort theories of negligence, misrepresentation, and strict liability—all of which were discussed in Chapter 8.

BYSTANDER
A spectator, witness, or person who was standing nearby when an injury-causing event occurred.

Warranty Law

As you learned in Chapter 8, whenever a seller sells a product, the seller impliedly warrants that the goods sold are reasonably fit for the ordinary purposes for which such goods are used. This is the implied warranty of merchantability. If the goods turn out to be defective, the seller can be sued for breach of warranty.

ETHICAL CONCERN

Efficiency in Research

Research can be time consuming, particularly if you are not sure of what terms to research. For example, suppose that a client alleges that a competitor is making false statements about the client's product. Your job is to research case law on this issue. You remember from your paralegal studies that false statements that injure another's reputation constitute the tort of defamation, so you start by researching that topic. An hour later, you still haven't located any cases that have fact patterns or issues similar to those of the client's case. As mentioned in Chapter 17, an important step in the research process is to define the issue before you start your research. A good place to start the research process is thus to review the basic types of torts, including business torts. If you do this, you will narrow your research to cases involving slander of quality, or trade libel, and you will find a plethora of cases from which to choose, some of which may be on point. Remember that the more time you spend on a task, the more the client must pay—and attorneys have a duty to charge their clients reasonable fees.

At one time, if a person was injured by a defective product, he or she could sue the seller for breach of warranty only if the person was in privity of contract with the seller. **Privity of contract** is the connection that exists between contracting parties, such as a seller and a buyer. If Sam was injured by a defective tool that he purchased from Al's Hardware, for example, Sam could sue Al's Hardware—but not the manufacturer of the tool. This is because Sam's contract of purchase was solely with the hardware store, not with the manufacturer. In other words, no privity of contract existed between Sam and the manufacturer, and therefore, Sam could not recover damages from the tool's manufacturer.

Today, most states have abolished the privity requirement, and warranty law is now an important part of the entire spectrum of laws relating to product liability. Consumers, purchasers, and even users of goods can recover *from any seller* for losses resulting from breach of implied and express warranties. A manufacturer is a seller. Therefore, a person who purchases goods from a retailer can recover from the retailer or the manufacturer if the goods are defective. That is, a product purchaser may sue not only the firm from which he or she purchased a product but also a third party, the manufacturer of the product, in product liability.

Often, plaintiffs in product-liability cases allege that the defendant or defendants should be held liable not only for breach of warranty but also for negligence or in strict liability.

Negligence

As mentioned, negligence is generally defined as the failure to use the degree of care that a reasonable, prudent person would have used under the circumstances.

- **If the failure to exercise reasonable care in the creation or marketing of a product causes an injury, the basis of product liability is negligence.**

The Duty of Care. The manufacturer of a product must exercise due care to make that product safe to be used as intended. Due care must be exercised in designing the product, in selecting the materials, in using the appropriate production process, in assembling and testing the product, and in placing adequate warnings on the label informing the user of dangers of which an ordinary person might not be aware. The duty of care extends to the inspection and testing of products purchased by the manufacturer for incorporation into the final product. The failure to exercise due care, when it results in harm to another, is negligence. Failure to exercise due care must be proved in actions based on the theory of negligence—but not in actions based on the doctrine of strict liability (discussed below).

PRIVITY OF CONTRACT
The connection that exists between the parties to a contract, such as a buyer and a seller.

No Privity Requirement. Just as privity of contract was at one time required for recovery under warranty theory, so was privity required in negligence actions brought against sellers of injury-causing products. During the nineteenth century, exceptions were made to the privity requirement, and during the twentieth century, the requirement that privity of contract must exist

DEVELOPING PARALEGAL SKILLS

Preparing a Video Scrapbook

Deborah Smith, a paralegal with a personal-injury law firm, is working on a product-liability case. The client's wife was killed in an automobile accident when the car was hit by another vehicle and its gas tank exploded upon impact. It appears that the case will go to trial, and Deborah's job is to meet with the client, Jeffrey Roberts, to obtain information from him about his wife's life. She also wants to obtain personal items and photographs of his wife so that she can make a video scrapbook to be shown to the jury.

THE INTERVIEW BEGINS

Deborah meets Jeffrey Roberts at his home. He explains that his wife, Marian, was fifty-eight years old when she died. According to Jeffrey, Marian was a devoted housewife, mother, and grandmother. She liked to cook and always held holiday gatherings at their home for their children and grandchildren. Marian also took care of four of their nine grandchildren three days a week while the children's mother worked. Jeffrey goes on to tell Deborah about the various church activities, community affairs, and volunteer work in which Marian was involved.

OBTAINING ITEMS FOR THE VIDEO SCRAPBOOK

Deborah asks for pictures of Marian, the children, and the grandchildren, as well as any pictures that portray them as the close family that they were. Deborah asks Jeffrey if she may take the photographs and have them copied—using a color photocopy machine—to keep for future use in a video scrapbook about Marian. She assures Jeffrey that the pictures will be kept safe and returned to him in a week or so.

Deborah asks Jeffrey if Marian was as close to all of her grandchildren as she was to the four that she routinely cared for. He tells Deborah that she was and that their oldest granddaughter, Sara, who is fourteen years old, has been quite affected by her grandmother's untimely death. Jeffrey takes out a letter that Sara wrote to him shortly after Marian's funeral. In the letter, Sara describes how sad she is at the loss of her grandmother and at the fact that her grandmother will not be able to see her grow up, attend her wedding, or meet her children. Deborah asks Jeffrey if she can take the letter to include in the scrapbook. He hesitates but decides that it is important to include the letter because it portrays how close the family was.

THE INTERVIEW ENDS

Deborah thanks Jeffrey for his help and tells him that she will return all of the photographs and Sara's letter as soon as they have been copied. Jeffrey tells Deborah that he would like to see the completed video scrapbook but not for a while. It will take him some time to prepare himself to see it.

ETHICAL CONCERN

Personal Opinions and Legal Advice

Virtually every paralegal knows that paralegals are not permitted to give legal advice. If they do, they may be subject to criminal penalties under state statutes that prohibit the unauthorized practice of law. It is often difficult, though, especially for beginning paralegals, to draw the line between the authorized practice of law and the unauthorized practice of law. For example, consider this situation. Claire, a paralegal who works for a firm that specializes in product liability, is conducting her first intake interview. The client she is interviewing wants to sue the manufacturer of an allegedly defective treadmill. He claims that when he was walking on the treadmill, he received an electrical shock that caused him to fall off and seriously injure his hip. Near the end of the interview, the client asks Claire whether she thinks he has a good case. Claire responds, "Well, as you know, I'm a paralegal, and I cannot give legal advice. Personally, though, I think that you do have a good case." Has Claire given "legal advice"? Yes. A paralegal's opinion on any legal matter, even with a disclaimer that it's only a "personal opinion," constitutes legal advice.

between the injured plaintiff and the negligent defendant-manufacturer was abolished. Today, a manufacturer is liable for its failure to exercise due care to any person who sustains an injury proximately caused by a negligently made (defective) product.

Defenses to Negligence. Any manufacturer, seller, or processor who can prove that due care was used in the manufacture of its product has an appropriate defense against a negligence suit, because failure to exercise due care is one of the major elements of negligence. As mentioned earlier, due care includes warning the products' potential users of possible side effects or of the consequences of foreseeable product misuses. Another defense that can be raised by a defendant is that the plaintiff failed to establish *causation*—that is, that the plaintiff's injury was caused by the defendant's acts (see Chapter 8).

Other defenses include contributory negligence, comparative negligence, and, where recognized, assumption of risk. (These defenses were also discussed in Chapter 8.) Any time a plaintiff misuses a product or fails to make a reasonable effort to preserve his or her own welfare, the manufacturer or seller will claim that the plaintiff contributed to causing the injuries. The claim is that the plaintiff's negligence offsets the negligence of the manufacturer or seller. In some states, the contributory negligence of the plaintiff is an absolute defense for the defendant-manufacturer or seller. In many other states, the negligence of both these parties is compared (under the theory of comparative negligence), and damages are based on the proportion of negligence attributed to the defendant.

Misrepresentation

When a fraudulent misrepresentation has been made to a user or consumer and that misrepresentation ultimately results in an injury, the basis of liability may be the tort of fraud.

Fraudulent Misrepresentation. For fraudulent misrepresentation to occur, the misrepresentation must be made knowingly or with reckless disregard for the facts. Examples are the intentional mislabeling of packaged cosmetics and the intentional concealment of a product's defects.

The misrepresentation must also be of a material fact (a fact concerning the quality, nature, or appropriate use of the product on which a normal buyer may be expected to rely). There must also have been an intent to induce the buyer's reliance. Misrepresentation on a label or advertisement is enough to show an intent to induce the reliance of anyone who may use the product. Finally, the buyer must rely on the misrepresentation. If the buyer is not aware of it or if it does not influence the transaction, there is no liability.

- **In contrast to actions based on negligence and strict liability, in a suit based on fraudulent misrepresentation, the plaintiff does not have to show that the product was defective or that it malfunctioned in any way.**

For example, in one case, a plaintiff agreed to have a mechanical heart valve implanted in her heart. About two years later, she learned from her surgeon that the heart valve was one of a group of valves being recalled because of defects and malfunctions. The plaintiff sued the manufacturer

of the valve, but the court found that she had no cause of action under warranty or product-liability theories because the valve in her heart had not yet malfunctioned—that is, there was no evidence that her particular valve was defective. The plaintiff did, however, have a cause of action for fraud because the manufacturer had not disclosed the risks attending the use of its heart valve, of which it was well aware.[12]

Nonfraudulent Misrepresentation. Nonfraudulent misrepresentation, which occurs when a merchant *innocently* misrepresents the character or quality of goods, can also provide a basis of liability. In this situation, it does not have to be proved that the misrepresentation was made knowingly. A famous example involved a drug manufacturer and a victim of addiction to a prescription medicine called Talwin. The manufacturer, Winthrop Laboratories, a division of Sterling Drug, Inc., innocently indicated to the medical profession that the drug was not physically addictive. Using this information, a physician prescribed the drug for his patient, who developed an addiction that turned out to be fatal. Even though the addiction was a highly unusual reaction resulting from the victim's unusual susceptibility to this product, the drug company was still held liable.[13]

Strict Product Liability

Recall from Chapter 8 that under the doctrine of strict liability, people may be held liable for the results of their acts regardless of their intentions or their exercise of reasonable care. For example, a company that uses dynamite in constructing a road is strictly liable for any damages that it causes, even if it takes reasonable and prudent precautions to prevent such damages. In essence, the blasting company becomes liable for any personal injuries it causes and thus is an absolute insurer—that is, the company is liable for damages regardless of fault.

In several landmark cases involving manufactured goods in the 1960s, courts applied strict liability. Today, in many states, the doctrine has become a common method of holding manufacturers liable for injuries to product users or bystanders caused by defective products.

The Restatement of Torts. The Restatement (Second) of Torts[14] designates how the doctrine of strict product liability should be applied. It is a precise and widely accepted statement of the liabilities of sellers of goods (including manufacturers, processors, assemblers, packagers, bottlers, wholesalers, distributors, and retailers) and deserves close attention. Section 402A of the Restatement (Second) of Torts states:

> (1) One who sells any product in a defective condition unreasonably dangerous to the user or consumer or to his property is subject to liability for

12. See *Khan v. Shiley, Inc.*, 217 Cal.App.3d 848, 266 Cal.Rptr. 106 (1990).
13. *Crocker v. Winthrop Laboratories, Division of Sterling Drug, Inc.*, 514 S.W.2d 429 (Tex. 1974).
14. This is the abbreviated title of the *Restatement of the Law of Torts*, Second Edition. Recall from Chapter 17 that the Restatements of the Law logically arrange and summarize common law principles in various areas, such as torts, agency law, and contracts. Although the Restatements are secondary sources of law (and thus not mandatory authorities), they often guide judges in their judicial reasoning.

physical harm thereby caused to the ultimate user or consumer or to his property, if

(a) the seller is engaged in the business of selling such a product, and

(b) it is expected to and does reach the user or consumer without substantial change in the condition in which it is sold.

(2) The rule stated in Subsection (1) applies although

(a) the seller has exercised all possible care in the preparation and sale of his product, and

(b) the user or consumer has not bought the product from or entered into any contractual relation with the seller.

Under this doctrine, a plaintiff does not have to prove that there was a failure to exercise due care, as he or she does in an action based on negligence. If certain requirements are met, the seller's liability to an injured party may be virtually unlimited. Although the drafters of Section 402A did not take a position on bystanders, all courts extend the strict liability of manufacturers and other sellers to injured bystanders. For example, the manufacturer of an automobile was held liable for injuries caused by the explosion of the car's motor while the car was in traffic. A cloud of steam that resulted from the explosion caused multiple collisions, because it kept other drivers from seeing well.[15] In other cases, courts have extended the protections of Section 402A to bystanders whose injuries from defective products are reasonably foreseeable. Thus, someone injured by an exploding bottle in a supermarket was able to recover damages from the manufacturer for an injury caused by the defective product.[16]

Strict liability is imposed by law as a matter of public policy. This public policy rests on the threefold assumption that (1) consumers should be protected against unsafe products, (2) manufacturers and distributors should not escape liability for faulty products simply because they are not in privity of contract with the ultimate users of those products, and (3) manufacturers and sellers of products are in a better position to bear the costs associated with injuries caused by their products—costs that they can ultimately pass on to all consumers in the form of higher prices.

Requirements of Strict Product Liability—Summarized. Section 402A of the Restatement (Second) of Torts indicates the circumstances in which the doctrine of strict liability can be applied. Basically, a cause of action will exist only if the following six basic requirements of strict product liability are met:

1. The product must be in a defective condition when the defendant sells it.
2. The defendant must normally be engaged in the business of selling that product.
3. The product must be unreasonably dangerous to the user or consumer because of its defective condition.[17]

15. *Giberson v. Ford Motor Co.*, 504 S.W.2d 8 (Mo. 1974).
16. *Embs v. Pepsi-Cola Bottling Co. of Lexington, Kentucky, Inc.*, 528 S.W.2d 703 (Ky.App. 1975).
17. This element is no longer required in some states—for example, California.

4. The plaintiff must incur physical harm to self or property by use or consumption of the product.
5. The defective condition must be the proximate cause of the injury or damage.
6. The goods must not have been substantially changed from the time the product was sold to the time the injury was sustained.

Thus, in any action against a manufacturer or seller, the plaintiff does not have to show why or in what manner the product became defective. The plaintiff does, however, have to show that at the time the injury was sustained, the condition of the product was essentially the same as when it left the hands of the defendant manufacturer or seller.

The plaintiff normally must also show that the product was so defective as to be an **unreasonably dangerous product**. A court may consider a product so defective as to be unreasonably dangerous if either (1) the product was dangerous beyond the expectation of the ordinary consumer or (2) a less dangerous alternative was economically feasible for the manufacturer, but the manufacturer failed to produce it.

UNREASONABLY DANGEROUS PRODUCT
In product liability, a product that is defective to the point of threatening a user's health and safety. A product is considered unreasonably dangerous if it is dangerous beyond the expectation of the ordinary user or if a less dangerous alternative was economically feasible for the manufacturer, but the manufacturer failed to produce it.

Under the feasible-alternative approach, courts consider a product's utility and desirability; the availability of other, safer products; the dangers that have been identified prior to an injured user's suit; the dangers' obviousness; the normal expectation of danger, particularly for established products; the probability of injury and its likely seriousness; the avoidability of injury through care in the product's use, including the contribution of instructions and warnings; and the viability of eliminating the danger without appreciably impairing the product's function or making the product too expensive. For example, people often cut themselves on knives, but a court would consider that knives are very useful. Reasoning that there is no way to avoid injuries without making the product useless and that the danger is obvious to users, a court normally would not find a knife to be unreasonably dangerous and would not hold a supplier of knives liable.

At the same time, a court may consider a snowblower without a safety guard over the opening through which the snow is blown to be in a condition that is unreasonably dangerous, even if the snowblower carries warnings to stay clear of the opening. The danger may be within the user's expectations, but the court will also consider the likelihood of injury and its probable seriousness, as well as the cost of putting a guard over the opening and the guard's effect on the blower's operation.

Some products are safe when used as their manufacturers and distributors intend but not safe when used in other ways. Suppliers are generally required to expect reasonably foreseeable misuses and to design products that are either safe when misused or marketed with some protective device—for example, a childproof cap.

Liability Sharing. As with other theories of product liability, a plaintiff using a theory of strict liability in tort has been required to prove that the defective product that caused his or her injury was the product of a specific defendant. In recent years, however, in cases in which plaintiffs could not prove which of many distributors of a harmful product supplied the particular product that caused the plaintiffs' injuries, some courts have dropped this

requirement. This has occurred primarily with cases involving DES (diethylstilbestrol), a drug administered prior to the late 1970s to prevent miscarriages. DES's harmful character was not realized until, a generation later, daughters of the women who had taken DES developed health problems, including vaginal carcinoma, that were linked to the drug. Partly because of the passage of time, a plaintiff-daughter often could not prove which pharmaceutical company—of as many as three hundred firms—had marketed the DES her mother ingested.

In the DES cases, some courts have held that all firms that manufactured and distributed DES during the period in question were liable for the plaintiffs' injuries in proportion to the firms' respective shares of the market. This theory of **market-share liability** was first set out by the California Supreme Court in a 1980 case, *Sindell v. Abbott Laboratories.*[18] Although some states have adopted the theory,[19] many states have not.[20] When recovery is possible under a market-share theory of liability, the plaintiff is normally required to establish the following elements:

MARKET-SHARE LIABILITY
A method of sharing liability among several firms that manufactured or marketed a particular product that may have caused a plaintiff's injury. Each firm's liability is proportional to its respective share of the relevant market for the product. This form of liability sharing is used when the true source of the product is unidentifiable.

1. That the product alleged to be the source of the plaintiff's injury is identical in design and defect to products manufactured and marketed by several firms.
2. That the inability to prove the cause of the harm is not the plaintiff's fault.
3. That the manufacturer of the particular product cannot be identified.

To date, courts have generally been reluctant to apply market-share liability to manufacturers of products other than DES.[21] An interesting exception was made by a Hawaii court in 1991, however, when the court applied market-share liability to the manufacturers of a blood protein, AHF (antihemophilic factor concentrate). A hemophiliac patient who had received AHF injections later tested positive for the AIDS (acquired immune deficiency syndrome) virus. He alleged that he had been exposed to the virus through the AHF injections. Because it was not known which manufacturer was responsible for the particular AHF received by the plaintiff, the court held that all of the manufacturers of AHF could be held liable. In justifying its decision to apply the market-share theory, the court stated that "the problem calls for adopting new rules of causation, for otherwise innocent plaintiffs would be left without a remedy."[22]

Defenses to Strict Liability. Defenses to strict product liability include assumption of risk, product misuse, and comparative negligence.

---

18. 26 Cal.3d 588, 607 P.2d 924, 163 Cal.Rptr. 132 (1980).
19. Including Florida, Washington, New York, Wisconsin, and Hawaii. Most cases in which the market-share liability theory has been applied involved DES.
20. Including Missouri, Illinois, Rhode Island, and Iowa. These states do not apply market-share liability even in DES cases.
21. See, for example, *Pennfield Corp. v. Meadow Valley Electric, Inc.*, 604 A.2d 1082 (Pa.Super. 1992); *Swartzbauer v. Lead Industry Association*, 794 F.Supp. 142 (E.D.Pa. 1992); *Santiago v. Sherwin-Williams Co.*, 782 F.Supp. 186 (D.Mass. 1992); and *Jackson v. Anchor Packing Co.*, 994 F.2d 1295 (8th Cir. 1993).
22. *Smith v. Cutter Biological, Inc.*, 72 Haw. 416, 823 P.2d 717 (1991).

Assumption of Risk. In some states, assumption of risk is a defense in an action based on strict liability in tort. For such a defense to be established, the defendant must show the following basic elements:

1. That the plaintiff voluntarily engaged in the risk while realizing the potential danger.
2. That the plaintiff knew and appreciated the risk created by the defect.
3. That the plaintiff's decision to undertake the known risk was unreasonable.

Product Misuse. Similar to the defense of voluntary assumption of risk is that of **product misuse**. Here, the injured party did not know that the product was dangerous for a particular use, but the use was not the one for which the product was designed. (Contrast this with assumption of risk.) This defense has been severely limited by the courts, however. If the misuse is reasonably foreseeable, the seller must take measures to guard against it.

PRODUCT MISUSE
A defense against product liability that may be raised when the plaintiff used a product in a manner not intended by the manufacturer. If the misuse was reasonably foreseeable, the seller will not escape liability unless measures were taken to guard against the harm that could have been expected to result from the misuse.

Comparative Negligence. Recent developments in the area of comparative negligence are affecting the doctrine of strict liability. Whereas previously the plaintiff's own negligent conduct was not a defense to strict liability, today a growing number of jurisdictions consider the negligent or intentional actions of the plaintiff in the apportionment of liability and damages. This "comparing" of the plaintiff's conduct with the defendant's strict liability results in an application of the doctrine of comparative negligence. Thus, for example, failure to take precaution against a known defect will reduce a plaintiff's recovery. The majority of states have adopted this doctrine, either legislatively or through court decisions.

Limitations on Recovery. Some courts have limited the application of the doctrine of strict product liability to cases in which personal injuries have occurred. Thus, when a defective product causes only property damage, the seller may not be liable under a theory of strict liability, depending on the law of the particular jurisdiction.

As discussed in earlier chapters of this text, statutes of limitations restrict the time within which a certain type of legal action may be brought. A typical statute of limitations provides that an action must be brought within a specified period of time after the cause of action accrues. Generally, a cause of action is held to accrue when some damage occurs. Sometimes the running of the prescribed period is tolled (that is, suspended) until the party suffering an injury has discovered it (or should have discovered it).

Many states have passed laws placing outer time limits on some claims so that the defendant will not be left vulnerable to lawsuits indefinitely. These **statutes of repose** may limit the time within which a plaintiff can file a product-liability suit. Basically, a statute of repose is a statute of limitations that is not dependent upon the happening of a cause of action, such as an injury caused by a defective product. Typically, a statute of repose begins to run earlier and runs longer than a statute of limitations. For example, a statute of repose may bar any claims not brought within twelve years from the date of sale or manufacture of the defective product. Therefore, it is immaterial that the product is defective or causes an injury if the injury occurs after this statutory period has lapsed. In addition, some legislative

STATUTE OF REPOSE
Basically, a statute of limitations that is not dependent upon the happening of a cause of action, such as an injury caused by a defective product. Statutes of repose generally begin to run earlier and run longer than statutes of limitations.

SUBSTANTIVE LAW CONCEPT SUMMARY

Tort Law and Product Liability

Wrongful Interference	1. *Wrongful interference with a contractual relationship*—The intentional interference with a valid, enforceable contract by a third party. 2. *Wrongful interference with a business relationship*—The unreasonable interference by one party with another's business relationship.
Appropriation	The use of one person's name, likeness, or celebrity status by another, without permission and for the benefit of the user.
Defamation and Product Disparagement	Defamation is a business tort when a false statement injures someone in a profession, business, or trade or adversely affects a business entity in its credit rating and other dealings. Product disparagement occurs when a person makes slanderous or libelous statements about another's product or property; more specifically referred to as slander of quality (trade libel) or slander of title.
Tort Actions against Polluters	Although claims against business polluters are often brought under state or federal environmental statutes, such claims may also be brought under the common law theories of nuisance, negligence, and strict liability.
Premises Liability	Landowners are required to exercise a duty of care toward those who enter onto their property. The required standard of care may vary depending on whether the person entering onto the property is an invitee, a licensee, or a trespasser.
Special Negligence Doctrines and Statutes	1. *Res ipsa loquitur*—A doctrine under which a plaintiff need not prove negligence on the part of the defendant because "the thing speaks for itself." *Res ipsa loquitur* has been applied to such events as trains derailing and wheels falling off moving vehicles. 2. *Negligence per se*—A type of negligence that may occur if a person violates a statute or an ordinance providing for a criminal penalty and the violation causes another to be injured. 3. *Special negligence statutes*—State statutes that prescribe duties and responsibilities in certain circumstances, the violation of which will establish civil liability. Dram shop acts, social-host statutes, and Good Samaritan statutes are examples of special negligence statutes.

enactments have limited the application of the doctrine of strict liability to new goods. Some states—for example, Massachusetts—have refused to recognize strict product liability. In these states, recovery is gained mainly under warranty or negligence theory.

TORTS AND PRODUCT LIABILITY AND THE PARALEGAL

As pointed out several times in this text, the law is ever changing. This is particularly true in regard to tort law. The field of tort law continues to expand as new ways to commit wrongs are discovered and new perceptions of what is right and wrong in a social or business context emerge. Further-

SUBSTANTIVE LAW CONCEPT SUMMARY, Continued	
Product Liability Based on Warranty Theory	**1.** All sellers of goods impliedly warrant that their goods are merchantable—that is, reasonably fit for the ordinary purposes for which such goods are used. If the goods are defective, the seller may be sued for breach of warranty. **2.** Privity of contract is not required, and the plaintiff may sue the manufacturer of the product as well as the retailer from which the goods were purchased to recover damages.
Product Liability Based on Negligence	**1.** Due care must be used by the manufacturer in designing the product, selecting materials, using the appropriate production process, assembling and testing the product, and placing adequate warnings on the label or product. **2.** Privity of contract is not required. A manufacturer is liable for failure to exercise due care to any person who sustains an injury caused by a negligently made (defective) product. **3.** Defenses to negligence—Sellers can defend against product-liability claims based on negligence by proving one or more of the following: a. That they exercised due care in the manufacture and marketing of the product. b. That the plaintiff's injuries were not caused by the product. c. That the plaintiff assumed the risk of injury or was also negligent.
Product Liability Based on Misrepresentation	A manufacturer may be liable for either fraudulent misrepresentation or nonfraudulent (innocent) misrepresentation of a product to a user.
Strict Product Liability	**1.** *Requirements of product liability*—Plaintiffs must meet the six requirements listed in this chapter to have a cause of action against a product's manufacturer. **2.** *Market-share liability*—In some cases, courts have held all of the firms that manufactured and distributed a product liable for the plaintiffs' injuries in proportion to the firms' respective shares of the market. **3.** *Limitations on recovery*—State statutes of repose may limit the time within which a plaintiff can file a product-liability suit. **4.** *Defenses to strict product liability*—Defenses to strict product liability include assumption of risk, product misuse, and comparative negligence.

more, tort law is a broad area of civil law; tort claims arise in many different areas of legal work. For these reasons, you can expect, in your work as a paralegal, that sooner or later you will be involved in work that relates to a tort claim.

For example, as discussed in Chapter 2, many paralegals work for attorneys who specialize in personal-injury law. If you work in this area, you will be dealing with tort claims brought by plaintiffs who have been injured in automobile accidents or other incidents as a result of others' negligent actions.

If you work for or on behalf of a corporation, you may be involved in litigation stemming from a business tort, such as wrongful interference, product disparagement, or appropriation, or a lawsuit involving premises liabili-

TODAY'S PROFESSIONAL PARALEGAL

Reviewing Medical Records

Lewis White is a paralegal in a personal-injury defense firm. Today, he is reviewing medical records to verify the extent of the injuries that a plaintiff claims to have incurred in an auto-accident case. The plaintiff in the case is suing both the driver of the other vehicle (for negligence) and the auto manufacturer (under a product-liability theory). The auto manufacturer is a client of Lewis's firm.

REVIEWING THE MEDICAL RECORDS

Lewis will survey the medical records and provide a summary of the plaintiff's physical condition prior to the accident. He will also provide a general summary of the injuries and treatment she received as a result of the accident. This review will be more general than the in-depth medical-records review that is performed in a medical-malpractice case, in which the focus is on the actions taken by the physicians, nurses, and hospital staff who are alleged to have been negligent in their treatment of a patient.

Lewis begins by reviewing the medical records and the summary of the plaintiff's personal physician. Lewis discovers that the plaintiff has suffered from disk problems in the lower part of her spine and that surgery was recommended to treat these problems. Next, Lewis reviews the records of the hospital emergency room. He finds a note indicating that the patient told the emergency-room physician that she had previously experienced back problems. Then Lewis reviews the discharge summary, which does not contain any helpful information.

DISCOVERING A PROXIMATE-CAUSE ISSUE

By reviewing these medical records, Lewis has uncovered a major proximate-cause issue in the case. The plaintiff is alleging that she suffered injuries to her spine as a result of the car accident. In fact, however, the medical records indicate that the plaintiff had back problems prior to the accident. The existence of prior back problems will make it difficult for the plaintiff to prove that she was injured as a result of the accident. Even if she can prove that the accident caused her back problems to become worse, the extent of her damages may be significantly reduced if the majority of her damages were not caused by the accident.

ty. If you specialize in the area of intellectual property, you may be asked to assist in tort litigation concerning the misappropriation of trade secrets or the unauthorized use of other forms of intellectual property.

Additionally, if you are a litigation paralegal, at least some of your work will probably involve product-liability claims. Product-liability cases constitute a significant number of the cases decided in U.S. courts. As mentioned earlier, many paralegals specialize in this area of the law.

Paralegal work related to tort claims varies, of course, depending on the types of torts involved. Generally, tort claims involve litigation, so much of the work you would perform in this area would be as a litigation assistant. Here are a few examples of specific tasks in the area of tort law that a paralegal might be asked to handle:

- Interview a client (plaintiff) to obtain detailed information concerning an allegation made by the plaintiff against a defendant.
- Interview a client (defendant) to obtain information that could be used in the client's defense against a tort claim.
- Locate and interview witnesses to a tortious act.
- Obtain relevant documents, such as medical and employment records, from the parties to the lawsuit or from third parties.

• Research relevant statutory and case law to find out how the law applies to your client's situation, and prepare an internal memorandum for your supervising attorney summarizing your results.
• Draft legal correspondence relating to the claim.
• Prepare documents to initiate or defend against a lawsuit and file them with the court, draft interrogatories, summarize deposition transcripts, prepare the trial notebook, and generally assist with all of the aspects of the litigation process (discussed in Chapters 10 and 11).
• Establish and maintain a system of document control so that important documents are easily retrievable when needed. (In some product-liability cases, there may be thousands of documents to sort through, organize, and track.)

KEY TERMS AND CONCEPTS

appropriation 780
"attractive nuisance" doctrine 784
business tort 778
bystander 787
disparagement of property 781
dram shop act 787
Good Samaritan statute 787
invitee 782
licensee 783
market-share liability 794
negligence *per se* 786
nuisance 784
privity of contract 788
product misuse 795
res ipsa loquitur 786
slander of quality 781
slander of title 782
social-host statute 787
statute of repose 795
toxic tort 784
trade libel 781
trespasser 783
unreasonably dangerous product 793

CHAPTER SUMMARY

1. Business torts are defined as wrongful interferences with others' business rights. Wrongful interference with a contractual relationship is a tort that occurs when a third party intentionally causes either of two parties to a contract to break the contract. Wrongful interference with a business relationship is a tort that occurs when a business firm attempts to solicit customers who have already shown an interest in a similar product sold by a competitor.

2. Other business torts include appropriation, defamation, and product disparagement. Appropriation is defined as the use of one person's name or likeness by another, without permission and for the benefit of the user. Defamation, in the business context, involves libel or slander that injures someone in a profession, business, or trade or that adversely affects a business firm in its credit rating or other dealings. Product disparagement is a general term for torts that are more specifically referred to as slander of quality (the publication of false information about another's product, or trade libel) and slander of title (the publication of information that denies or casts doubt on another's legal ownership of particular property, when the publication results in financial loss to the property's owner).

3. A landowner has a duty to exercise reasonable care toward invitees—those (such as business customers) whom the landowner invites, explicitly or implicitly, onto his or her property for the landowner's benefit. Breach of this duty constitutes negligence and may subject the landowner to liability for injuries occurring on the premises. A landowner also owes a duty of care to licensees—those (such as theater goers) who enter onto the landowner's property primarily for their own benefit. In some circumstances, a landowner may owe a duty of care even to trespassers—those who enter onto the landowner's property without permission to do so.

4. Tort actions against polluters include nuisance actions and toxic torts. Under the common law doc-

trine of nuisance, persons may be held liable if they use their property in a manner that unreasonably interferes with others' rights to use or enjoy their own property. Toxic torts constitute a growing area of tort law. Toxic torts are actions against toxic polluters based on the common law theories of negligence and strict liability.

5. There are a number of special doctrines and statutes relating to negligence. *Res ipsa loquitur* (translated as "the thing speaks for itself") is a doctrine that is applied when negligence can be inferred from the nature of the claim—as when wheels fall off a moving vehicle. Negligence *per se* may occur if a person violates a statute or an ordinance and that violation causes another to be injured. Dram shop acts are statutes that impose a duty on tavern owners or bartenders not to serve drinks to patrons who are intoxicated or who may become intoxicated. If the duty is breached, liability may be extended to the tavern owner or bartender for injuries caused by the intoxicated person. Some states have social-host statutes, which impose liability on persons hosting parties for injuries caused by guests who became intoxicated at the hosts' homes. Good Samaritan statutes prohibit negligence suits against those who voluntarility aid others in emergency situations.

6. Product liability is liability imposed on manufacturers and sellers of goods for injuries caused by defective products to product users or to bystanders. Product-liability suits may be brought under a contract theory of warranty or a tort theory of negligence, misrepresentation, or strict liability. A breach-of-warranty claim can be brought against any seller of the product, including the retailer and the manufacturer. Privity of contract (the connection that exists between contracting parties) is no longer required for recovery under warranty or negligence theory.

7. Product liability based on negligence exists if the plaintiff can prove that the manufacturer breached a duty of care in the manufacture or marketing of the product. Any seller who can prove that due care was used in the manufacture and marketing of its product (including appropriate warnings of the consequences of foreseeable side effects or misuses) or that its product did not cause the plaintiff's injury has a defense against negligence. Other defenses include assumption of risk, contributory negligence, and comparative negligence.

8. Product liability based on misrepresentation occurs when a manufacturer or seller intentionally or unintentionally misrepresents the character or quality of the product being sold. In contrast to cases based on negligence and strict liability, in a case based on fraudulent misrepresentation, the plaintiff does not have to show that the product was defective or that it malfunctioned.

9. Under the doctrine of strict product liability, a plaintiff does not have to prove that there was a failure to exercise due care in the manufacture or marketing of a product. Strict liability is imposed by law as a matter of public policy. To have a cause of action in strict product liability, however, a plaintiff must meet six requirements. Normally, the plaintiff must also show that the product was so defective as to be unreasonably dangerous.

10. In some cases (cases in which plaintiffs cannot prove which of many distributors of a harmful product supplied the particular product that caused the plaintiffs' injuries), courts have dropped the causation requirement and imposed liability on all firms that manufactured and distributed the product during the period in question. Generally, though, courts have been reluctant to apply this theory of "market-share liability."

11. Defenses to strict liability include assumption of risk, misuse of the product, and comparative negligence. Statutes of repose are state statutes that limit the time within which a plaintiff can file a product-liability suit.

QUESTIONS FOR REVIEW

1. What kinds of actions constitute wrongful interference with a contractual or a business relationship? How might a businessperson defend against allegations of wrongful interference with a contractual or a business relationship?

2. How does the tort of appropriation occur? Give one example of this tort.

3. How might defamation occur in the business context? Disparagement of property is a general term for what specific types of torts?

4. What is the difference between an invitee and a licensee? Does the duty of care owed to these two classifications of persons differ? Are landowners ever liable for injuries incurred by trespassers?

5. List and define the tort actions that may be brought against business polluters. Are there any landmark cases? If so, give the case name and citation, a brief description of the facts, and the court's decision for each case.

6. List and define the special negligence doctrines and statutes discussed in the chapter. What effect do these doctrines and statutes have on negligence cases?

7. What is product liability? What are the main theories under which a product-liability action may be brought?

8. Explain the circumstances in which product liability may be based on each of the following: a breach of warranty, negligence, or misrepresentation.

9. What is privity of contract? Is privity of contract required in product-liability cases?

10. Explain the rationale underlying the doctrine of strict product liability. Under what circumstances might a seller be found liable under this doctrine? What is liability sharing, and when is it applied?

ETHICAL QUESTIONS

1. Monica is a legal assistant in a law firm that specializes in representing business defendants in tort cases. Monica's supervising attorney has just been asked to defend a business firm against a toxic-tort claim. The attorney asks Monica to do some legal research on toxic torts—an area with which she is not familiar. It takes Monica twelve hours to complete the research assignment, which is twice as long as the attorney told her to spend on the project. Monica is uncomfortable billing the client for twelve hours of research time. Should Monica allocate some of her research time to two other clients for whom the research will also be used? Why or why not?

2. Rod, a paralegal with a law firm that specializes in defending companies against product-liability claims, is playing cards with some of his friends at their monthly poker game. One of Rod's buddies, Paul, tells Rod that his wife was injured recently at the deli where she works. Paul says that his wife's hand was severely cut when the guard failed on a meat slicer that she was using to slice lunch meat for a customer. Paul goes on to explain that although his wife will miss several weeks of work, she won't qualify for disability and doesn't have enough vacation time left to cover the time that she will be absent from work while her hand heals. Additionally, they will have medical bills, only part of which will be covered by insurance. Paul wants Rod to tell him if his wife can sue for her injuries and lost time at work. How should Rod answer Paul's question?

PRACTICE QUESTIONS AND ASSIGNMENTS

1. Mr. Jones, a patient with good vision, went into the hospital for surgery on his upper spine (just below his neck), which required that he be placed face down on a device that would hold him in position during the surgery. When Mr. Jones regained consciousness after the surgery, he was blind. The experts who have evaluated the case believe that the only possible explanation for Mr. Jones's blindness is the pressure placed on his eyes during the three hours required for the surgery. This is a very difficult theory to prove because blindness occurs so rarely with this type of surgery. Which of the following special negligence doctrines or statutes could be used to help prove that negligence occurred in Mr. Jones's case?

a. Negligence *per se.*
b. *Res ipsa loquitur.*
c. A dram shop act.
d. A Good Samaritan statute.

2. Judy, a nurse, is driving home on the expressway from her shift at the community hospital when freezing rain begins to fall and the roads become extremely icy and slippery. As Judy is driving, she comes upon a serious car accident involving five cars and a

large truck. She stops to aid those injured in the accident. She does what she can to help. Without adequate equipment, bandages, and medication, however, there is little that she can do for one of the victims, and he dies. Several months later, Judy is served with a summons and complaint—she is being sued by the decedent's wife for negligence. Which of the following special negligence doctrines or statutes could Judy use in her defense?

a. Negligence *per se.*
b. *Res ipsa loquitur.*
c. A dram shop act.
d. A Good Samaritan statute.

3. Bill stops at the Good Times Bar at 5:00 P.M. on his way home from work on Friday night. He plays pool, drinks three cans of beer, eats dinner, plays pool, drinks four more cans of beer, and then starts dancing when the band begins to play. By 11:00 P.M., Bill has consumed twelve cans of beer. Although he is obviously intoxicated, the waitress continues to serve him. He leaves the bar at 11:40 P.M. and causes a car accident. Which of the following special negligence doctrines or statutes can the plaintiff use when suing?

a. Negligence *per se.*
b. *Res ipsa loquitur.*
c. A dram shop act.
d. A Good Samaritan statute.

QUESTIONS FOR CRITICAL ANALYSIS

1. In a common law nuisance suit, when would the equitable remedy of injunction be appropriate? When would money damages be preferable as a remedy?

2. Traditionally, privity of contract was required in order for a person injured while using a defective product to sue for damages. Today, most states allow persons injured in this way to sue not only the stores from which they purchased the products (with whom they are in privity of contract) but also the product manufacturers (with whom they are not in privity of contract). Why has the requirement of privity of contract been dropped in product-liability cases?

ROLE-PLAYING EXERCISES

1. Review the facts in the *Developing Paralegal Skills* feature entitled "Preparing a Video Scrapbook." Role-play the meeting between the paralegal, Deborah Smith, and Jeffrey Roberts. The student playing the role of Deborah should be as compassionate, sympathetic, and understanding towards Jeffrey as possible. This student should also try to convince Jeffrey that he can trust Deborah with the photographs and his granddaughter's letter. The student playing the role of Jeffrey should be very emotional when discussing his wife's recent and untimely—and unnecessary, in his view—death. He should require consolation from the student playing the role of Deborah. Reverse roles if time allows.

2. Review the facts in the *Developing Paralegal Skills* feature entitled "Dep Prep." Role-play an initial meeting between the paralegal, Barbara, and a deponent in which the deponent describes his or her job duties and responsibilities to Barbara. The student playing Barbara should be very professional and nonjudgmental. The student playing the deponent should be nervous and should express concern over being found guilty of safety-code violations. Reverse roles if time allows.

PROJECTS

1. Call your county court clerk and find out if mediation is required for tort cases in your state. If it is not required, is it available to litigants as an option?

2. If mediation of tort cases is offered or required by your state courts, ask the clerk if it is possible to observe a mediation proceeding for a few hours.

Observe a proceeding if possible, and write a one-page, double-spaced, typewritten summary of your observations and impressions.

3. Call a county or other local court clerk and find out if there are any product-liability cases on the docket during this semester. If so, arrange to attend the trial and to observe it for as long as possible. Try to obtain a copy of the pleadings before the trial so you are familiar with the product-liability theories involved in the case. Write a two-page, double-spaced, typewritten summary of your observations and impressions.

ANNOTATED SELECTED READINGS

DWIGHT, JENNIFER. "The Nuts and Bolts of Civil Case Organization." *Legal Assistant Today*, March/April 1995. An article providing a good description of the civil litigation file and its contents, as well as sound guidance on how to organize one. The article provides good exposure for students to the realities of law practice and "all the paper."

LIPSON, ASHLEY. "A Short Course in Evidence." *Legal Assistant Today*, September/October 1994. An article offering a good review of the various types of evidence and the objections that may be made to evidence, including the "Perry Mason standards."

MASON, MARILYN. "Finding the Needle in the Medical Records Haystack." *Legal Assistant Today*, September/October 1993. An article providing a smart approach to summarizing medical records. The article suggests techniques based on the detail needed in the summary and the type of case involved.

READE, KATHLEEN M. "The Trial of Wrongful Death Cases." *Legal Assistant Today*, January/February 1995. An eye-opening article for those interested in specializing in personal-injury litigation. The article discusses the type of information that paralegals are often required to obtain from the client in wrongful-death cases, sensitive ways in which to obtain the information, and some of the things paralegals can do to provide emotional support to clients in such cases.

ZEIMET, NAN. "Unlocking the Secrets of Medical Charts." *Legal Assistant Today*, September/October 1994. An informative article describing how to read medical charts. It includes a list of abbreviations commonly found in medical records.

Chapter Objectives

After completing this chapter, you will know:

- **How the law applies to harassment, age discrimination, and disability-based discrimination in the workplace.**
- **Some exceptions made by the courts to the common law employment-at-will doctrine in cases alleging wrongful discharge.**
- **The major provisions of the Family and Medical Leave Act of 1993.**
- **The extent to which the law protects employees' privacy rights.**
- **The major federal and state laws relating to workers' health and safety.**
- **The federal laws that establish employers' obligations in respect to retirement and security income, pension plans, and medical insurance for former employees.**

Chapter Outline

INTRODUCTION

One of the consequences of the extensive government regulation of today's workplace is that employees have more rights than ever before in the history of this nation. Another consequence of regulation is that there are more employment-related claims and lawsuits brought by employees to have these rights enforced. Additionally, firms must comply with employment laws or face potential civil or criminal liability for their failure to do so. To learn what the laws are and how to comply with them, firms need legal counsel. These developments have led to increased work for attorneys and paralegals in this area of the law.

No matter where you work as a paralegal, you will benefit from a basic understanding of the laws governing employment relationships. You read about many of these laws in Chapter 9, in the context of government regulation. You may want to review Chapter 9 in conjunction with your study of this chapter, which covers employment relationships in greater detail.

EMPLOYMENT DISCRIMINATION

Federal laws prohibiting employment discrimination have done much to further employees' rights to fair treatment in the workplace. State laws also protect employees from discriminatory treatment, sometimes to a greater extent than federal laws do. As discussed in Chapter 9, the major federal laws prohibiting employment discrimination are the following:

- Title VII of the Civil Rights Act of 1964 (prohibits discrimination based on race, color, national origin, religion, and gender).
- The Age Discrimination in Employment Act (ADEA) of 1967 (prohibits discrimination based on age).
- The Americans with Disabilities Act (ADA) of 1990 (prohibits discrimination based on disability).

You read about these federal acts and their coverage in Chapter 9. You also learned in that chapter about the Equal Employment Opportunity Commission (EEOC)—the federal agency that enforces federal laws prohibiting discrimination. In this section, we focus on some of the difficulties faced by legal professionals—and the courts—when applying laws prohibiting employment discrimination to particular situations in the workplace.

Sexual Harassment

Title VII prohibits, among other things, discrimination based on gender. Although Title VII does not specifically refer to sexual harassment, the EEOC and the courts have concluded that sexual harassment is a form of gender-based discrimination. Therefore, if a client of your firm alleges that he or she is being sexually harassed, the client—if there is sufficient evidence of the harassment—may have a cause of action against the employer under Title VII.

If you assist your supervising attorney with sexual-harassment cases, you may be faced with a number of questions for which you need answers. Many of these questions will relate to the topics discussed below.

Forms of Sexual Harassment. Recall from Chapter 9 that sexual harassment can take two forms: *quid-pro-quo* harassment and hostile-environment harassment. *Quid pro quo* is a Latin phrase that is often translated to mean "something in exchange for something else." *Quid-pro-quo* harassment occurs when job opportunities, promotions, salary increases, and so on are given in return for sexual favors. Hostile-environment harassment occurs when an employee is subjected to sexual conduct or comments that are perceived as offensive by the employee.

The EEOC's guidelines on harassment, which were revised in 1993, state that the following types of verbal or physical conduct constitute hostile-environment harassment:

- Conduct that has the purpose or effect of creating an intimidating, hostile, or offensive working environment.
- Conduct that has the purpose or effect of unreasonably interfering with an individual's work performance.
- Conduct that otherwise adversely affects an individual's employment opportunities.

Harassment by Managers and Supervisors. What if an employee is harassed by a manager or supervisor of a large firm, and the firm itself (the "employer") is not aware of the harassment? Does the employee nonetheless have a cause of action against the employer? The answer to this question is yes.

- **Generally, an employer is held responsible (liable) for the conduct of certain employees, such as managers or supervisors, even if the employer was unaware of the conduct.**

In a sexual-harassment case, if an employee in a supervisory position did the harassing, the employer is usually held liable *automatically* for the behavior.

Title VII and the statutes discussed in the remaining sections of this chapter impose requirements and liability on employers for statutory violations, even if those violations were committed by employees, such as managers or supervisors. The liability of employers for their employees' wrongful actions—if the actions are undertaken in the scope of employment—is based on the common law doctrine of *respondeat superior.* As stated in Chapter 9, liability is imposed on employers because they have an obligation to direct their business affairs, including the actions of their employees, in such a way as not to harm others. Also, employers are generally in a better financial position to pay damages to those harmed by their employees' wrongful acts.

Harassment by Co-workers and Nonemployees. Often, employees alleging harassment complain that the actions of co-workers, not supervisors, are responsible for creating a hostile working environment. In such cases, the employee still has a cause of action against the employer. Generally, though,

DEVELOPING PARALEGAL SKILLS

Sexual-harassment Claims

Marian Simms recently assisted her supervising attorney, Roberta Magnuson, in the trial of a sexual-harassment case. Marian's supervising attorney represented a legal assistant who sued her employer, a law firm, for sexual harassment. Their client, the legal assistant, won damages of several million dollars—a precedent-setting amount.

The defendant law firm has stated its intention to appeal the trial court's decision. Roberta asks Marian to begin preparing for the appeal by researching the issue that will most likely be appealed—the large punitive-damages award, which comprises a significant portion of the damages awarded to the client.

Marian decides to start her research on WESTLAW because she wants to look for sexual-harassment cases with large punitive-damages awards that have recently been decided by courts in other jurisdictions. Marian knows that no other cases with punitive damages in the multimillion-dollar range have been decided by the courts of her state, so she looks for cases that supply persuasive authority. She chooses WESTLAW because she knows that it is more current than the advance sheets of the reporters or the pocket parts of the digests. Marian enters her query using natural language and begins her research.

the employer will be held liable only if it knew, or should have known, about the harassment and failed to take immediate corrective action.

The EEOC guidelines also make it clear that employers may be liable for harassment by *nonemployees* in certain conditions. For example, if a restaurant owner or manager knows that a certain customer repeatedly harasses a waitress and permits the harassment to continue, the restaurant owner may be liable under Title VII even though the customer is not an employee of the restaurant. The issue turns on the control that the employer exerts over a nonemployee. In the situation just described, a court would likely conclude that the restaurant manager or owner could have taken action to prevent the customer from harassing the waitress.

Proving Sexual Harassment. One of the major problems faced by employees who are sexually harassed is that such harassment can be very difficult to prove. Often, there are no third parties who have witnessed the harassment and no written evidence of it. The question thus comes down to who is more believable, the alleged victim or the alleged offender.

Even if an employee can prove that sexually offensive conduct occurred, at what point does such conduct result in an "intimidating, hostile, or offensive working environment" or otherwise qualify as hostile-environment harassment under the EEOC's guidelines? In other words, how offensive must the conduct be and how many times must it occur before an employee has a cause of action under Title VII for hostile-environment harassment? In recent years, courts have had to struggle with such questions and usually render their decisions on a case-by-case basis. At least one court has con-

cluded that even one incident of sexually offensive conduct can result in a hostile, offensive working environment.[1]

In *Harris v. Forklift Systems, Inc.*,[2] the United States Supreme Court addressed another controversial issue relating to hostile-environment claims. Prior to this decision, many jurisdictions had held that a worker claiming to be a victim of hostile-environment harassment must establish that he or she suffered serious psychological effects as a result of the offensive conduct. In the *Harris* case, the Supreme Court held that "Title VII bars conduct that would seriously affect a reasonable person's psychological well-being, but the statute is not limited to such conduct. So long as the environment would reasonably be perceived, and is perceived, as hostile or abusive, there is no need for it also to be psychologically injurious."

The Applicability of the "Reasonable-person" Standard. Another problem that arises with sexual-harassment claims has to do with the fact that men and women often have different opinions on what constitutes socially offensive conduct. The traditional legal standard for determining what is or is not appropriate behavior is the "reasonable-person" standard (discussed in Chapter 8). If a reasonable person in the same circumstances as the offended employee would have responded similarly to the alleged wrong, then the actual conduct of the offended employee is considered reasonable.

Some courts have held that sexual harassment should be viewed not from the gender-neutral reasonable-person perspective but from a "reasonable-woman" perspective. In *Ellison v. Brady*, for example, the U.S. Court of Appeals for the Ninth Circuit held that a woman's claim of sexual harassment should be viewed in light of a reasonable-woman standard. Any other standard, said the court, "tends to systematically ignore the experiences of women."[3] Other courts have applied a reasonable-man standard to claims of sexual harassment.[4] Still other courts have adopted a gender-sensitive standard in which the gender of the reasonable person mirrors that of the employee-plaintiff.[5]

The EEOC's 1993 guidelines on harassment in the workplace adopted a reasonable-person standard for determining whether harassment in the workplace creates an environment sufficiently hostile or abusive to constitute a Title VII violation. The guidelines provide, however, that in establishing whether the standard has been met, the employee-plaintiff's race, color, religion, gender, national origin, age, or disability must be considered. In the *Harris* case mentioned earlier, the Supreme Court also adopted a broad standard by holding as follows:

- **In cases of alleged sexual harassment, the conduct at issue must be abusive both objectively (as perceived by a reasonable person) and subjectively (as perceived by the victim).**

---

1. See *Radtke v. Everett*, 442 Mich. 368, 501 N.W.2d 155 (1993).
2. __U.S.__, 114 S.Ct. 367, 126 L.Ed.2d 295 (1993).
3. 924 F.2d 872 (9th Cir. 1991).
4. See, for example, *Daniels v. Essex Group, Inc.*, 937 F.2d 1264 (7th Cir. 1991).
5. See, for example, *Lehmann v. Toys 'Я' Us*, 132 N.J. 587, 626 A.2d 445 (1993), in which the court announced a reasonableness standard that applies to "sexual harassment of women by men, men by women, men by men, and women by women."

Same-gender Harassment. Recently, the courts have had to address the issue of whether men who are harassed by other men or women who are harassed by other women are also protected by laws that prohibit gender-based discrimination in the workplace. Although courts have varied in their treatment of such claims, increasingly, this type of harassment is being brought under the protective umbrella of state and federal laws prohibiting gender-based discrimination. For instance, in one case, a California appellate court concluded there was "no basis of support in the statutory language for the contention that the Legislature intended to limit protection from sexual harassment to male-female harassment."[6]

Other Forms of Harassment

Many people are surprised to learn that federal laws prohibiting discrimination in the workplace protect employees who are harassed not only on the basis of gender but also on the basis of race, color, national origin, religion, age, or disability. Increasingly, cases are coming before the courts in which plaintiffs allege harassment based on criteria other than gender.

This is an expanding area of the law, and as a paralegal, you should realize that abusive conduct and comments against members of classes protected under Title VII may constitute hostile-environment harassment. Racial or ethnic slurs against an employee, for example, may create a hostile environment for that employee. The standards set forth in the EEOC's 1993 guidelines indicating the types of verbal and physical conduct that constitute hostile-environment harassment apply to all forms of harassment, not just sexual harassment.

Pregnancy Discrimination

The Pregnancy Discrimination Act of 1978, which amended Title VII, expanded the definition of gender discrimination to include discrimination based on pregnancy. Women affected by pregnancy, childbirth, or related medical conditions must be treated—for all employment-related purposes, including the receipt of benefits under employee-benefit programs—the same as other persons not so affected but similar in ability to work. An employer is required to treat an employee temporarily unable to perform her job owing to a pregnancy-related condition in the same manner as the employer would treat other temporarily disabled employees. The employer must change work assignments, grant paid disability leaves, or grant leaves without pay if that is how other temporarily disabled employees would be treated. Policies concerning an employee's return to work, accrual of seniority, pay increases, and so on must also result in equal treatment.

Discrimination Based on Age

Age discrimination is potentially the most widespread form of discrimination, because anyone—regardless of race, color, national origin, religion, or gender—

6. *Mogilevsky v. Superior Court,* 20 Cal.App.4th 1409, 26 Cal.Rptr.2d 116 (1993).

may be a victim at some point in life. The Age Discrimination in Employment Act (ADEA) of 1967, as amended, prohibits employment discrimination on the basis of age against individuals forty years of age or older. An amendment to the act prohibits mandatory retirement for nonmanagerial workers. For the act to apply, an employer must have twenty or more employees, and the employer's business activities must affect interstate commerce. The ADEA is similar to Title VII in that it offers protection against both intentional (disparate-treatment) age discrimination and unintentional (disparate-impact) age discrimination (see Chapter 9).

Proving Age Discrimination. The burden-shifting procedure under the ADEA is also similar to that under Title VII. The employee must meet several requirements to make a ***prima facie* case** of age discrimination (a case in which the evidence compels the court to accept the plaintiff's conclusion if the defendant produces no evidence to counter it). The plaintiff must prove that he or she (1) was a member of the protected age group, (2) was qualified for the position, and (3) was not hired or was discharged under circumstances that give rise to an inference of discrimination. The burden then shifts to the employer, who must articulate a legitimate reason for the discrimination. If the plaintiff can prove that the employer's reason is only a pretext and that the plaintiff's age was a determining factor in the employer's decision, the employer will be held liable under the ADEA.

***PRIMA FACIE* CASE**
A case in which the evidence compels the court to accept the plaintiff's conclusion if the defendant produces no evidence to counter it.

Cutting Business Costs and Age Discrimination. Numerous cases of alleged age discrimination have been brought against employers who, to cut costs, replaced older, higher-salaried employees with younger, lower-salaried workers. In one case, for example, a fifty-four-year-old manager of a plant who earned approximately $15.75 an hour was temporarily laid off when the plant was closed for the winter. When spring came, the manager was replaced by a forty-three-year-old worker who earned approximately $8.05 an hour. The older manager, who had worked for the firm for twenty-seven years, was given no opportunity to accept a lower wage rate or otherwise accommodate the firm's need to reduce costs. The court, which referred to the firm's dismissal of the manager as an exercise in "industrial capital punishment," held that the manager's dismissal in these circumstances violated the ADEA.[7]

Whether a firing is discriminatory or simply part of a rational business decision to prune the company's ranks is not always clear. Companies will generally defend a decision to discharge a worker by asserting that the worker could no longer perform his or her duties or that the worker's skills were no longer needed. The employee must prove that the discharge was motivated, at least in part, by age bias. Proof that qualified older employees have generally been discharged before younger employees or that co-workers frequently made unflattering age-related comments about the discharged worker may be enough.

7. *Metz v. Transit Mix, Inc.*, 828 F.2d 1202 (7th Cir. 1987).

Discrimination Based on Disability

The Americans with Disabilities Act (ADA) was passed in 1990 and became effective in 1992. When the act was enacted, Congress estimated that about 17 percent of the people in the United States were living with disabilities. Prior to 1990, the major federal law providing protection to those with disabilities was the Rehabilitation Act of 1973. That act only covered federal government employees and those employed under federally funded programs. As of 1994, the ADA extended federal protection against disability-based discrimination to all workplaces with twenty-five or more workers.

According to the EEOC, over 17 percent of the almost 90,000 discrimination cases filed with that office during the first full year of the ADA's implementation related to disability-based discrimination. The EEOC predicts that this percentage will rise over time. For attorneys and paralegals, this means that employers and employees alike will need ever more legal assistance in this area of employment law.

Definition of Disability. As you learned in Chapter 9, which briefly discussed the ADA, the act defines a *person with disabilities* as a person with a physical or mental impairment that "substantially limits" his or her everyday activities. More specifically, the ADA defines *disability* as "(1) a physical or mental impairment that substantially limits one or more of the major life activities of such individuals; (2) a record of such impairment; or (3) being regarded as having such an impairment."

Health conditions that have been considered disabilities under federal law include blindness, heart disease, cancer, muscular dystrophy, cerebral palsy, paraplegia, diabetes, acquired immune-deficiency syndrome (AIDS), and morbid obesity (defined as existing when an individual's weight is two times that of the normal person).[8] The ADA excludes from coverage certain conditions, including homosexuality and kleptomania.

Reasonable Accommodations. The ADA prohibits employers from refusing to hire persons with disabilities who are otherwise qualified for a particular position. It does not, however, require that *unqualified* applicants be hired. That the employer may have to make some reasonable accommodations for an applicant with a disability will not cause the applicant to be considered unqualified. Generally, an employer's accommodation is considered reasonable if the accommodation permits a worker with a disability to perform the essential functions of the job in question.

Employers must modify their job-application process so that those with disabilities can compete for jobs with those who do not have disabilities. For example, a job announcement that lists only a phone number discriminates against potential job applicants with hearing impairments. Therefore, an address must also be provided.

In addition, employers must modify the physical work environment if necessary so that a worker with a disability can perform the essential job functions. Some modifications can be easily made, such as lowering a water

8. *Cook v. Rhode Island Department of Mental Health*, 10 F.3d 17 (1st Cir. 1993).

fountain or installing a ramp to accommodate those in wheelchairs. Reasonable accommodations might also include establishing more flexible working hours, creating new job assignments, and creating or improving training materials and procedures.

In general, the EEOC suggests that employers should give "primary consideration" to an employee's preference in deciding what accommodations should be made. An employee with a disability can, though, reject a reasonable accommodation offered by the employer. Of course, there are limits to the employer's obligation to accommodate an employee under the ADA. If the employee can perform the essentials of his or her job without accommodation, then no violation of the ADA has occurred. Employers who do not wish to accommodate workers with disabilities must demonstrate that the accommodations will cause "undue hardship."

Undue Hardship. When an accommodation would constitute an "undue hardship," the employer is not normally required to undertake it. At what point, though, does an employer's accommodation constitute an undue hardship? As a paralegal, you may be asked to conduct research to find the answer to this question. If so, you will find that the law offers no uniform standards for identifying what is an undue hardship other than the imposition of a "significant difficulty or expense" on the employer. The most you can do is evaluate court decisions that have applied the act to particular situations in the few years since the act went into effect. Consider some examples:

- An employee qualifies as having a disability under the ADA because he has severe bouts of depression. His medication causes drowsiness, and he routinely falls asleep on the job. Can the employer be required to accommodate this employee? The U.S. Court of Appeals for the Seventh Circuit held that "[t]he government may presumably require its employees to stay awake as a matter of decorum. But that is not necessarily to say that an occasional nap would make any federal employee unfit."[9]
- A ski resort owner decides to upgrade the resort's image to obtain a higher rating. One of the resort's chambermaids refuses to wear her dentures because they hurt. Can the owner of the resort fire the worker without liability under the ADA? The answer is, probably not. The ADA protects not only those with disabilities but also those who are *perceived* to have disabilities. In this situation, if the owner of the resort perceives that the employee's refusal to wear her false teeth results in a cosmetic disfigurement (which is a disability under federal law), the employee is a protected individual. If she is fired, that "disability" will substantially limit a major life activity—that is, her job.[10]

Over time, a body of case law will be created as the courts apply the ADA's provisions to specific cases. Legal professionals and others can then turn to case law for guidance on the types of accommodations that may

9. *Overton v. Reilly*, 977 F.2d 1190 (7th Cir. 1992).
10. *Hodgdon v. Mt. Mansfield Co.*, 624 A.2d 1122 (Vt. 1992). Although this case was decided under a state law protecting workers with disabilities, the court looked to federal law—particularly the Rehabilitation Act of 1973—for guidance. The provisions of the ADA closely parallel those of the Rehabilitation Act.

impose undue hardships on employers. In the meantime, it may be difficult, if not impossible, to determine with any accuracy how a court might rule on a particular case.

Preemployment Physicals. Under the ADA, employers are not permitted to ask job applicants about the nature or extent of any known disabilities. Furthermore, they cannot require persons with disabilities to submit to preemployment physicals unless such exams are required of all other applicants. Employers can condition an offer of employment on the employee's successfully passing a medical examination, but disqualifications must result from the discovery of problems that render the applicant unable to perform the job for which he or she is to be hired.

Disabilities and Health-insurance Plans. Employers may wish to hire or refuse to hire workers with disabilities because of their impact on group health-insurance costs. Pursuant to the ADA, the EEOC has developed guidelines that clearly indicate that workers with disabilities must be given equal access to any health insurance provided to other employees. Employers can exclude from coverage preexisting health conditions and certain types of diagnostic or surgical procedures, however. And an employer can put a limit, or cap, on health-care payments in its group-health policy—as long as such caps are "applied equally to all insured employees" and do not "discriminate on the basis of disability."

Whenever a group health-care plan makes a disability-based distinction in its benefits, the plan violates the ADA. The employer must then be able to justify the distinction by doing one of the following:

- Offering proof that limiting coverage of certain ailments is required to keep the plan financially sound.
- Proving that coverage of certain ailments would cause a significant increase in premium payments or their equivalent such that the plan would be unappealing to a significant number of workers.
- Proving that the disparate treatment is justified by the risks and costs associated with a particular disability.

The ADA and Substance Abusers. Many employers and employees are unclear about the protection given by the ADA to substance abusers. Under the ADA, alcoholism is a disability. Consequently, employers cannot legally discriminate against employees simply because they are alcoholics. Thus, employers must treat alcoholics in the same way as they treat other employees. An alcoholic employee who comes to work late because he or she was drinking the night before cannot be disciplined differently than an employee who is late for some other reason. In other words, alcoholics must be held to the same standards of performance as others. Employers do have the right to prohibit the use of alcohol in the workplace. Employers can require that employees not be under the influence of alcohol while working. Finally, employers can either fire or refuse to hire an alcoholic if he or she poses a substantial risk of harm either to himself or herself or to others and the risk cannot be reduced by reasonable accommodation.

Drug addiction is a disability under the act because it is a substantially limiting impairment. Those who are currently using illegal drugs are not

ETHICAL CONCERN

Drug Abuse in the Law Office

What if you are working as a paralegal in a law firm and you suspect that a co-worker (another paralegal) is using drugs and such use is detrimental to the paralegal's work? Do you have an ethical obligation to report your suspicions to your supervisor? Yes—provided that your suspicions are well founded. Paralegals have an ethical duty to serve the clients' best interests. They also, as employees, have a duty of loyalty to their employers, which means that they should act in accordance with their employers' best interests. Drug abuse by one of the firm's paralegals may cause significant harm to the interests of both the clients and the employer.

protected by the act, though. The ADA only protects *former* drug addicts—those who have completed a supervised drug-rehabilitation program or who are currently in a supervised rehabilitation program. Individuals who have used drugs casually in the past are not protected under the act. They are not considered addicts and therefore do not have a disability (addiction).

Dangerous Workers. An employer may defend a decision not to hire a worker with a disability if the applicant would pose a "direct threat to the health or safety" of the other employees. This danger must be substantial and immediate; it cannot be speculative. A worker who suffers from hallucinations that cause him to attack his co-workers would probably be considered to pose such a threat, for example. Other federal regulations also permit employers to terminate the employment of qualified workers whose disabilities are such that they may pose a danger to their own personal well-being.

In the wake of the AIDS epidemic, many employers are concerned about hiring or continuing to employ a worker who has AIDS under the assumption that the worker might pose a direct threat to the health or safety of others in the workplace. Courts have generally held, however, that AIDS is not so contagious as to disqualify employees in most jobs. Therefore, employers must reasonably accommodate job applicants or employees who have AIDS or who test positive for HIV (the virus that causes AIDS).

Affirmative-action Programs

Federal statutes and regulations providing for equal opportunity in the workplace were designed to reduce or eliminate discriminatory practices with respect to hiring, retaining, and promoting employees. **Affirmative-action programs** go a step further and attempt to "make up" for past patterns of discrimination by giving members of protected classes preferential treatment in hiring or promotion. Affirmative-action programs have caused much controversy, particularly when they result in what is frequently called "reverse discrimination"—discrimination against "majority" workers, such as white males.

AFFIRMATIVE-ACTION PROGRAM
A job-hiring program that gives special consideration to minority groups in an effort to overcome present effects of past discrimination.

Although affirmative-action programs have been under attack in recent years, the United States Supreme Court has generally held that they are legitimate if they are designed to correct existing imbalances in the work force and as long as employers consider factors in addition to race or gender when making employment decisions. The Supreme Court usually looks at the special circumstances surrounding each case when determining whether challenged affirmative-action plans are legitimate.

Defenses to Claims of Employment Discrimination

In defending against claims of employment discrimination, including claims of harassment, an employer may attempt to disprove the case by asserting that the plaintiff's allegations are not substantiated by the evidence. Alternatively, the employer may raise a defense (offer a legally acceptable justification) for its actions. We look here at some of the defenses that employers may raise in employment-discrimination cases.

Bona Fide Occupational Qualification. You have already read, in Chapter 9, about the bona fide occupational qualification (BFOQ) defense. This defense applies when discrimination against a protected class is essential to a job—that is, when a particular trait is a bona fide (genuine) occupational qualification. For example, a men's fashion magazine might legitimately hire only male models. Similarly, the Federal Aviation Administration can legitimately impose age limits for airline pilots. Race, however, can never be a BFOQ.

Much controversy has arisen over the BFOQ defense, particularly in gender-based discrimination cases. Some companies have argued that being male is a BFOQ for jobs requiring heavy lifting,[11] whereas others have contended that being female is a BFOQ for flight attendants.[12] Courts have rejected both these arguments and have generally restricted the BFOQ defense to instances in which the employee's gender is essential to the job. In 1991, the United States Supreme Court held that even a fetal-protection policy that was adopted to protect unborn children from the harmful effects of exposure to lead was an unacceptable BFOQ.[13]

Business Necessity An employment practice that discriminates against members of a protected class but that is necessary for job performance.

Business Necessity. An employer may also defend against a claim of discrimination by asserting that a practice that has a discriminatory effect is a **business necessity.** If requiring a high school diploma, for example, is shown to have a discriminatory effect, an employer might argue that a high school education is required for workers to perform the job at a required level of competence. If the employer can demonstrate to the court's satisfaction that there exists a definite connection between a high school education and job performance, then the employer will succeed in this defense.

Seniority System In regard to employment relationships, a system in which those who have worked longest for the company are first in line for promotions, salary increases, and other benefits; they are also the last to be laid off if the work force must be reduced.

Seniority Systems. An employer with a history of discrimination may have no members of protected classes in upper-level positions. Even if the employer now seeks to be unbiased, it may face a lawsuit seeking an order that minorities be promoted ahead of schedule to compensate for past discrimination. If no present intent to discriminate is shown, and promotions or other job benefits are distributed according to a fair **seniority system** (in which workers with more years of service are promoted first or laid off last), however, the employer has a good defense against the suit.

Family and Medical Leave

Nearly two-thirds of women with children now work, by choice or necessity. Also, about a fourth of all adults now provide care for elderly relatives or anticipate the need to provide such care within the next five years. With so many women now working, there is often no caretaker available to attend to medical emergencies or other family needs in the home. The Family and Medical Leave Act (FMLA) of 1993 was passed to protect employees who face these kinds of situations. Although a majority of the states already had

11. *Rosenfeld v. Southern Pacific Co.*, 444 F.2d 1219 (9th Cir. 1971).
12. *Diaz v. Pan American World Airways, Inc.*, 442 F.2d 385 (5th Cir. 1971).
13. *United Automobile Workers v. Johnson Controls, Inc.*, 113 U.S. 158, 111 S.Ct. 1196, 113 L.Ed.2d 158 (1991).

legislation allowing for a leave from employment for family or medical reasons, and many employers maintained private family-leave plans for their workers, the FMLA improves job security for most workers.

Coverage and Applicability of the FMLA

The act requires employers with fifty or more employees to provide their employees with up to twelve weeks of family or medical leave during any twelve-month period. During the employee's leave, the employer must continue the worker's health-care coverage and guarantee employment in the same position or a comparable position when the employee returns to work. An important exception to the FMLA, however, allows the employer to avoid reinstatement of a *key employee*—defined as an employee whose pay falls within the top 10 percent of the firm's work force. Also, the act does not apply to employees who have worked less than one year or less than twenty-five hours a week in the previous twelve months.

Generally, an employee may take family leave to care for a newborn baby, an adopted child, or a foster child. Medical leave may be taken when the employee or the employee's spouse, child, or parent has a "serious health condition" requiring care. The FMLA also allows for intermittent leave when medically necessary.

Remedies for Violations of the FMLA

The FMLA provides a wide array of statutory remedies to the injured employee. Remedies include damages for unpaid wages (or salary), lost benefits, denied compensation, actual monetary losses (such as the cost of providing for care) up to an amount equivalent to the employee's wages for twelve weeks, job reinstatement, and promotion. The successful plaintiff is entitled to court costs, attorneys' fees, and in cases involving bad faith on the part of the employer, double damages.

AT-WILL EMPLOYMENT AND WRONGFUL DISCHARGE

What happens if an employer fires an employee who is not a member of a protected class or otherwise protected under a federal or state statute? In such a situation, the common law applies. As discussed in Chapter 9, under the common law employment-at-will doctrine, either party may terminate an employment contract at any time and for any reason—unless an employment contract specifically provides to the contrary. If there is a written employment contract and the employee's termination violates a contractual provision, then the employee can claim that the employer breached the contract. If no employment contract exists, however, an employee who is discharged from his or her employment may have little legal recourse.

Today, the employment-at-will doctrine has been significantly modified by state and federal statutes regulating the workplace. The doctrine has also been eroded through a series of court rulings that restrict the right of employers to fire workers. Although the rules vary from state to state, the

ETHICAL CONCERN

The Unauthorized Practice of Law—Revisited

Lara, a paralegal, was interviewing a client who was considering petitioning for bankruptcy. The client's right arm was in a sling. After Lara asked him about the injury, the client described how it had happened. He also said that he had been unable to work at his job as a mechanic for two weeks and that he was worried because his employer was threatening to fire him if he couldn't return to work within another week or two. Lara said, "That's odd. Employers are now required by law to give their employees medical leave for up to twelve weeks during any one-year period." Lara said that she would check with her supervising attorney about that matter, and then she continued the interview. In the meantime, what if the client confronted his employer and demanded a twelve-week leave? What if the employer fired him on the spot? What if the employer had only a few employees and was not subject to the leave requirements of the Family and Medical Leave Act of 1993? As you can see, the client might suffer harm by relying on Lara's "legal advice."

trend among the states has been to recognize exceptions to the employment-at-will doctrine in cases brought by employees for wrongful discharge. (Whenever an employer discharges an employee in violation of the law, including federal and state statutory law, the employee may bring an action for **wrongful discharge.**) Exceptions to the employment-at-will doctrine include those based on contract theory, tort theory, and public policy.

Wrongful Discharge
An employer's termination of an employee's employment in violation of common law principles or a statutory law that protects a specific class of employees.

Exceptions Based on Contract Theory

Some courts have held that an *implied* employment contract exists between the employer and the employee. If the employee is fired outside the terms of the implied contract, he or she may succeed in a breach-of-contract action even though no written employment contract exists.

For example, an employer's manual or personnel bulletin may state that, as a matter of policy, workers will be dismissed only for good cause. If the employee is aware of this policy and continues to work for the employer, a court may find that there is an implied contract based on the terms stated in the manual or bulletin. Promises that an employer makes to employees regarding discharge policy may also be considered part of an implied contract. If the employer fires the worker in a manner contrary to the manner promised, a court may hold that the employer has violated the implied contract and is liable for damages.

Exceptions Based on Tort Theory

In a few cases, the discharge of an employee may give rise to an action for wrongful discharge under tort theories. Abusive discharge procedures may result in intentional infliction of emotional distress or defamation. In one case, a restaurant had suffered some thefts of supplies, and the manager announced that he would start firing waitresses alphabetically until the thief was identified. The first waitress fired said that she suffered great emotional distress as a result. The state's highest court upheld her claim as stating a valid cause of action.[14]

Exceptions Based on Public Policy

The most widespread common law exception to the employment-at-will doctrine is the public-policy exception. Under this rule, an employer may not fire a worker for reasons that violate a fundamental public policy of the jurisdiction. For example, a court may prevent an employer from firing a worker who is serving on a jury and therefore cannot work during his or her normally scheduled working hours. Sometimes, an employer directs an employee to do something that violates the law. If the employee refuses to perform the illegal act, the employer might decide to fire the worker. Most states have held that firing the worker under these circumstances violates public policy.

Whistleblowing
Reporting an employer's illegal activity to persons in authority or to the press.

Whistleblowing and Public Policy. **Whistleblowing** occurs when an employee tells a government official, upper-management authorities, or the

14. *Agis v. Howard Johnson Co.*, 371 Mass. 140, 355 N.E.2d 315 (1976).

press that his or her employer is engaged in some unsafe or illegal activity. Employees who expose the wrongdoing of employers often find themselves disciplined or even out of a job. In a few cases, whistleblowers have been protected from wrongful discharge for reasons of public policy. For example, a bank was held to have wrongfully discharged an employee who pressured the employer to comply with state and federal consumer credit laws.[15]

In another case, an at-will employee—a probation officer with the police department of the city of Globe, Arizona—discovered that a man had been arrested for vagrancy under an obsolete statute, had been sentenced to ten days in prison, and had been in jail for twenty-one days. The officer pointed out to a magistrate that this was illegal. The magistrate informed the police chief, the chief fired the officer, and the officer sued the city for wrongful discharge. Holding that the discharge violated public policy, the court said, "So long as employees' actions are not merely private or proprietary, but instead seek to further the public good, the decision to expose illegal or unsafe practices should be encouraged." The court went on to state that "[t]here is no public policy more important or fundamental than the one favoring the effective protection of the lives, liberty, and property of the people. The officer's successful attempt to free the arrestee from illegal confinement was a refreshing and laudable exercise that should be protected, not punished."[16]

Whistleblower Protection Statutes. Although whistleblowers may be protected from retaliatory discharge on the basis of public policy, this public-policy exception to the employment-at-will doctrine is just that—an exception. To encourage workers to report employer wrongdoing, such as fraud, a number of states[17] and the federal government have enacted so-called whistleblower statutes. These statutes protect whistleblowers from retaliation on the part of employers. They may also provide an incentive to disclose information by providing the whistleblower with a monetary reward. For example, the False Claims Reform Act of 1986 requires that a whistleblower who has disclosed information relating to a fraud perpetrated against the U.S. government receive from 15 to 25 percent of the proceeds if the government brings suit against the wrongdoer.[18] Another federal statute, the Whistleblower Protection Act of 1989, protects federal employees who blow the whistle on their employers from employers' retaliatory actions.

ETHICAL CONCERN

Whistleblowing and the Paralegal

Carla had worked for a sole practitioner for nearly a year before she discovered that the attorney routinely added to clients' bills charges for paralegal work that Carla knew she had not performed. What should Carla do? Clearly, she has an ethical obligation not to participate in the attorney's violation of legal ethics. At the same time, she really likes the attorney and her job generally, and she knows that if she confronts the attorney about the matter (or takes other action), she might lose her job. Even though she has evidence of the attorney's unethical actions (her personal time log versus the clients' bills), she doubts whether she can recover damages from the attorney for wrongful discharge—because her employment is "at will," and she has no employment contract. If you ever face such a dilemma, you won't be able to find a solution in a textbook. Unfortunately, there is no simple solution to this kind of problem, and you must decide for yourself what is the "right" thing to do.

PRIVACY RIGHTS

Beginning with the civil rights movements of the late 1950s and 1960s, Americans generally have become more conscious of their constitutional rights. In the last two decades, concerns about the privacy rights of employees have arisen in response to the sometimes invasive tactics used by

15. *Harless v. First National Bank in Fairmont*, 162 W.Va. 116, 246 S.E.2d 270 (1978).
16. *Wagner v. City of Globe*, 150 Ariz. 82, 722 P.2d 250 (1986).
17. At least thirty-seven states now have whistleblower statutes.
18. In one case, an employee of the General Electric Corporation (GE) was awarded $13,387,500 under the False Claims Reform Act. See *U.S. v. General Electric*, 808 F.Supp. 580 (D. Ohio 1992).

employers in their efforts to monitor and screen workers. Lie-detector tests, drug tests, and other practices have increasingly been subject to challenge as violations of employee privacy rights.

Although there is no provision in the U.S. Constitution that guarantees a right to privacy, such a right has been inferred from other constitutional guarantees provided by the First, Third, Fourth, Fifth, and Ninth Amendments to the Constitution. Some states have laws or constitutional provisions relating to privacy rights.

Lie-detector Tests

At one time, many employers required employees or job applicants to take polygraph examinations in connection with their employment. The results of these lie-detector tests are not admissible as evidence in criminal trials, and many persons consider the tests to be an invasion of privacy.

In 1988, Congress passed the Employee Polygraph Protection Act. The act prohibits certain employers from (1) requiring or causing employees or job applicants to take lie-detector tests or suggesting or requesting that they do so; (2) using, accepting, referring to, or asking about the results of lie-detector tests taken by employees or applicants; and (3) taking or threatening negative employment-related action against employees or applicants based on results of lie-detector tests or on their refusal to take the tests.

Employers excepted from these prohibitions include federal, state, and local government employers; certain security service firms; and companies manufacturing and distributing controlled substances. Other employers may use polygraph tests when investigating losses attributable to theft, including embezzlement and the theft of trade secrets.

Drug Testing

Workers whose ability to perform is impaired as a result of drug use can pose a substantial threat to the safety of others. For example, railway or airline employees may seriously endanger the public safety if they perform their jobs under the influence of alcohol or other drugs. Drug and alcohol use also is very costly for employers, who lose billions of dollars each year as a result of absenteeism, impaired performance, and accidents caused by employee drug use. In the interest of public safety and to reduce unnecessary costs, many of today's employers, including the government, require their employees to submit to drug testing.

State laws relating to the privacy rights of private-sector employees as they relate to drug testing vary from state to state. Some state constitutions prohibit private employers from testing for drugs, and state statutes may restrict drug testing by private employers in any number of ways. A collective bargaining agreement may also provide protection against drug testing. In some instances, employees have brought an action against the employer for the tort of invasion of privacy (discussed in Chapter 8).

Constitutional limitations apply to the testing of government employees. The Fourth Amendment provides that individuals have the right to be "secure in their persons" against "unreasonable searches and seizures" conducted by government agents. Drug tests of government employees have

DEVELOPING PARALEGAL SKILLS

Analyzing a Proposed Regulation

Mary Moore works as a paralegal for an oil company that owns several oil pipelines. One of Mary's job responsibilities is to monitor the *Federal Register* for rules proposed by various government agencies that affect the oil industry. As she reads through the *Federal Register,* she spots a proposed regulation from the Department of Transportation (DOT) that would require random drug testing of field employees in the oil and gas pipeline industry.

Mary reads the Notice of Proposed Rulemaking (NOPR) carefully. The proposed rule would have a significant impact on the industry and on her employer's operations. The company is not currently staffed with medical personnel or with facilities at which the testing could be performed. At the end of the NOPR, Mary reads that the DOT will accept public comments on the proposed rule.

Mary turns to her computer and begins to type a memo summarizing the proposed rule and its effects on the company. She indicates that the DOT will accept comments on the proposed rule and asks if the company would be interested in providing comments. She addresses the memo to the general counsel, the vice president of operations, the vice president of engineering, and the vice president of human resources and sends it via E-mail to each of them.

A few days later, Mary receives an E-mail message from the general counsel indicating that he has been approached by the vice presidents to whom she sent her E-mail memo on the DOT NOPR and that they do wish to provide comments. He assigns Mary the task of coordinating a meeting with the vice presidents to obtain their comments. He also asks Mary to prepare a draft of the comments for circulation after the meeting has concluded.

been held constitutional, however, when there was a reasonable basis for suspecting the employees of using drugs. Also, when drug use in a particular government job could threaten public safety, testing has been upheld. For example, a Department of Transportation rule that requires employees engaged in oil and gas pipeline operations to submit to random drug testing was upheld, and the employees need not have been suspected of drug use.[19] The court held that the government's interest in promoting public safety in the pipeline industry outweighed the employees' privacy interests.

AIDS Testing

An increasing number of employers are testing their workers for AIDS. Few public issues are more controversial than this practice, particularly when the testing involves employees who are not in the health-care industry. Some state laws restrict AIDS testing, and federal statutes offer some protection to

19. *Electrical Workers Local 1245 v. Skinner,* 913 F.2d 1454 (9th Cir. 1990).

employees or job applicants who have AIDS or have tested positive for HIV. As discussed earlier in this chapter, the Americans with Disabilities Act of 1990 prohibits discrimination against persons with disabilities, and the term *disabilities* has been broadly defined to include diseases such as AIDS. The law also requires employers to reasonably accommodate the needs of persons with disabilities. Generally, although the law may not prohibit AIDS testing, it may prohibit the discharge of employees based on the results of those tests.

Performance Monitoring

In the last decade, many employers have begun to monitor the performance of their employees through electronic means. Some employers electronically monitor their employees' use of computer terminals or company telephones. In some situations, employers use video cameras to evaluate their employees' performance.

Monitoring Telephone Calls. Employers who listen to employees' telephone conversations may violate the Electronic Communications Privacy Act (ECPA) Act of 1986, which amended existing federal wiretapping law to cover new forms of communications, such as those that take place via cellular telephones or electronic mail (E-mail). This act prohibits the intentional interception of any wire or electronic communication or the intentional disclosure or use of the information obtained by such an interception. The ECPA excludes from coverage, however, any electronic communications through devices that are "furnished to the subscriber or user by a provider of wire or electronic communication service" and that are being used by the subscriber or user, or by the provider of the service, "in the ordinary course of its business." Does this exception to the ECPA—which is often referred to as the "business-extension exception"—permit employers to monitor employee telephone conversations in the ordinary course of their businesses? Some courts have held that it does, so long as the telephone communication does not qualify as a personal call.[20]

Monitoring Computer Files and E-mail. A particularly troublesome issue for many employees is employer monitoring of their computer files, voice mail, E-mail, or other electronic communications. According to a recent survey, 22 percent of the employers sampled monitored such communications, and in firms with less than a thousand employees, the figure was 30 percent.[21] To date, there have been no reported court decisions on whether the business-extension exception applies to monitoring these forms of communications. The Supreme Court of California has suggested, however, in an opinion on a related issue, that if the exception were applied, it would cover only monitoring that was undertaken for a specified purpose and conducted at a particular place and time. The exception would not apply to "surreptitious electronic monitoring."[22]

20. See, for example, *Epps v. St. Mary's Hospital of Athens, Inc.*, 802 F.2d 412 (11th Cir. 1986).
21. Michael Traynor, "Computer E-Mail Privacy Issues Unresolved," *National Law Journal*, January 31, 1994, p. S2.
22. *People v. Otto*, 2 Cal.4th 1088, 831 P.2d 1178, 9 Cal.Rptr.2d 596 (1992).

Potential Consequences of Monitoring Activities. Generally, there is little specific government regulation of monitoring activities, and an employer may be able to avoid what laws do exist by simply informing employees that they are subject to monitoring. Then, if employees later challenge the monitoring practice, the employer can raise the defense of consent by claiming that the employees consented to the monitoring. Employers should be cautious, however, when monitoring employees, because an employee may bring an action for invasion of privacy, and a court may decide that the employee's reasonable expectation of privacy outweighs the employer's need for surveillance. Similarly, an employer should consider alternatives before searching an employee's desk, filing cabinet, or office. If a search is conducted and the employee sues, a court may balance the purposes of the search against its intrusiveness. The court may also consider the availability of less intrusive alternatives that would have accomplished the same purposes.

Screening Procedures

An area of concern to potential employees has to do with preemployment screening procedures. What kinds of questions on an employment application or a preemployment test are permissible? What kinds of questions go too far in terms of invading the potential employee's privacy? Is it an invasion of the potential employee's privacy, for example, to ask questions about his or her sexual inclinations or religious convictions? Although an employer may believe that such information is relevant to the job for which the individual has applied, the applicant may feel differently about the matter. A key factor in determining whether preemployment screening tests violate the privacy rights of potential employees is whether there exists a *nexus*, or connection, between the questions and the job for which an applicant is applying.

For example, in one case, an employer required each job applicant who wished to be hired as a security officer to answer questions that were highly personal and intimate in nature. Some of the questions related to the applicant's religious beliefs ("I believe in the second coming of Christ" and "I believe my sins are unpardonable"). Other questions concerned the job candidate's sexual orientation ("I have often wished that I were a girl" and "Many of my dreams are about sex matters"). Some of the job applicants sued the employer, claiming that the test violated their privacy rights. A California appellate court agreed with the applicants, holding that there was not a clear enough relationship between the questions and the duties of security officers to justify the intrusion of the applicants' privacy rights.[23]

HEALTH AND SAFETY IN THE WORKPLACE

Another area of significant concern to employees has to do with safe working conditions. Under the common law, employees injured on the job had to rely on tort law or contract law theories in suits brought against their

23. *Soroka v. Dayton Hudson Corp.*, 7 Cal.App.4th 203, 1 Cal.Rptr.2d 77 (1991).

employers. Today, numerous state and federal statutes protect employees and their families from the risk of accidental injury, death, or disease resulting from their employment. This section discusses the Occupational Safety and Health Act of 1970 and state workers' compensation acts, both of which are specifically designed to protect employees and their families.

The Occupational Safety and Health Act

The Occupational Safety and Health Act of 1970 was passed in an attempt to ensure safe and healthful working conditions for practically every employee in the country. The act provides for specific standards that must be met by employers, plus a general duty to keep workplaces safe.

Enforcement of the Act. Three federal agencies were created to develop and enforce the standards set by this act. The Occupational Safety and Health Administration (OSHA) is part of the Department of Labor and has the authority to promulgate standards, make inspections, and enforce the act. OSHA has safety standards governing many workplace details, such as the structural stability of ladders and the requirements for railings. OSHA also establishes standards that protect employees against exposure to substances that may be harmful to their health.

The National Institute for Occupational Safety and Health is part of the Department of Health and Human Services. Its main duty is to conduct research on safety and health problems and to recommend standards for OSHA to adopt. Finally, the Occupational Safety and Health Review Commission is an independent agency set up to handle appeals from actions taken by OSHA administrators.

Criminal penalties for willful violation of the federal Occupational Safety and Health Act are limited. Employers may be prosecuted under state laws, however. In 1988, the Justice Department stated its view that criminal penalties in the act did not preempt state and local criminal laws. In other words, the act could not be used to shield employers from state criminal prosecution if they showed willful disregard for worker safety. In 1991, the Court of Appeals for the First Circuit held that the act also did not shield employers from liability under state tort laws.[24]

OSHA Procedures. An employee may file a complaint claiming that a violation of the Occupational Safety and Health Act has occurred. Under the act, an employer cannot discharge an employee who files a complaint or who, in good faith, refuses to work in a high-risk area if bodily harm or death might result. Employers with eleven or more employees are required to keep occupational injury and illness records for each employee. Each record must be made available for inspection when requested by an OSHA inspector. Whenever a work-related injury or disease occurs, employers must make reports directly to OSHA. Whenever an employee is killed in a work-related

24. *Pedraza v. Shell Oil Co.*, 942 F.2d 48 (1st Cir. 1991); *cert.* denied, *Shell Oil Co. v. Pedraza*, 502 U.S.1082, 112 S.Ct. 993, 117 L.Ed.2d 154 (1992). The phrase "*cert.* denied" is short for *certiorari* denied—in this case, by the United States Supreme Court. See Chapter 7.

accident, or when five or more employees are hospitalized in one accident, the Department of Labor must be notified within forty-eight hours. If it is not, the company is fined. Following the accident, a complete inspection of the premises is mandatory.

State Workers' Compensation Laws

As you learned in Chapter 2, state workers' compensation laws establish an administrative procedure for compensating workers injured on the job. Instead of suing, an injured worker files a claim with the administrative agency or board that administers the local workers' compensation claims. Many paralegals assist injured workers in obtaining compensation for on-the-job injuries. Recall from Chapter 13 that some government agencies, including many state workers' compensation boards, allow paralegals to represent clients in negotiations with the agencies or before agency hearings.

Here, we look at some of the typical provisions that are included in state statutes. Bear in mind, though, that these statutes vary in their specific provisions from state to state. If you handle claims for compensation, you will need to familiarize yourself with your state's requirements.

Covered Employees. No state covers all employees. Typically excluded are domestic workers, agricultural workers, temporary employees, and employees of common carriers (companies that provide transportation services to the public). Normally, the statutes cover minors. Usually, the statutes allow employers to purchase insurance from a private insurer or a state fund to pay workers' compensation benefits in the event of a claim. Most states also allow employers to be *self-insured*—that is, employers who show an ability to pay claims do not need to buy insurance.

Requirements for Recovery of Workers' Compensation. In general, to recover workers' compensation benefits, there must be an employment relationship and the injury must be *accidental* and occur *on the job* or *in the course of employment*, regardless of fault. Intentionally inflicted self-injury, for example, is not considered accidental and hence is not covered. If an injury occurs while an employee is commuting to or from work, it is not usually considered to have occurred on the job or in the course of employment and hence is not covered.

Procedures. An employee must notify his or her employer promptly (usually within thirty days) of an injury. Generally, an employee also must file a workers' compensation claim with the appropriate state agency or board within a certain period (ranging from sixty days to two years) from the time the injury is first noticed, rather than from the time of the accident.

- **An employee's acceptance of workers' compensation benefits bars the employee from suing for injuries caused by the employer's negligence.**

By barring lawsuits for negligence, workers' compensation laws also bar employers from raising common law defenses to negligence, such as contributory negligence. For example, an employer can no longer raise such

defenses as contributory negligence or assumption of risk to avoid liability for negligence. A worker may sue an employer who *intentionally* injures him or her, however.

RETIREMENT AND SECURITY INCOME

Federal and state governments participate in insurance programs designed to protect employees and their families by covering the financial impact of retirement, disability, death, hospitalization, and unemployment. A key federal law in this area is the Social Security Act of 1935.

Social Security and Medicare

The Social Security Act provides for old-age (retirement), survivors, and disability insurance. The act is therefore often referred to as OASDI. Under the Federal Insurance Contributions Act (FICA), both employers and employees must "contribute" to help pay for these benefits. The basis for the employee's and the employer's contribution is the employee's annual wage base—the maximum amount of the employee's wages that are subject to the tax. Benefits are fixed by statute but increase automatically with increases in the cost of living.

A health-insurance program, Medicare, is administered by the Social Security Administration for people sixty-five years of age and older and for some under sixty-five who have disabilities (see Chapter 13). It has two parts, one pertaining to hospital costs and the other to nonhospital medical costs, such as visits to doctors' offices. People who have Medicare hospital insurance can obtain additional federal medical insurance if they pay small monthly premiums, which increase as the cost of medical care increases.

As with Social Security contributions, both the employer and the employee contribute to Medicare. Currently, 2.9 percent of the amount of all wages and salaries paid to employees goes toward financing Medicare. There is no cap on the amount of wages subject to the Medicare tax.

Private Retirement Plans

There has been significant legislation to regulate retirement plans set up by employers to supplement Social Security benefits. The major federal act covering these retirement plans is the Employee Retirement Income Security Act (ERISA) of 1974. This act empowers the Labor Management Services Administration of the Department of Labor to enforce ERISA's provisions to regulate individuals who operate private pension funds. ERISA does not require an employer to establish a pension plan. When a plan exists, however, ERISA establishes standards for its management.

VESTING
The creation of an absolute or unconditional right or power.

A key provision of ERISA concerns **vesting**. Vesting gives an employee a legal right to receive pension benefits at some future date when he or she stops working. Before ERISA, some employees who had worked for companies for as long as thirty years received no pension benefits when their employment terminated, because those benefits had not vested. ERISA establishes complex vesting rules. Generally, however, all employee contri-

DEVELOPING PARALEGAL SKILLS

Employee-benefits Specialist

Michael Latham works as a paralegal for an employment law firm. His supervising attorney specializes in employee-benefits law. Michael assists in drafting retirement plans that are regulated under ERISA and various state and federal tax laws. Once certain types of plans, such as 401(k) retirement plans and profit-sharing plans, have been prepared for clients, they must be submitted to the Internal Revenue Service (IRS) for approval as "qualified plans." In such cases, Michael prepares the IRS application and submits it to the IRS. Michael also receives the plan approval from the IRS.

Michael is responsible for following up with the IRS to ensure timely receipt of approval of the retirement plans. He usually has several plans pending before the IRS, which he tracks on a computer calendar. If Michael has not received approval by the calendared date, he contacts IRS personnel to find out when approval can be expected and to see if they have any questions or need any information on the plan.

Today, Michael checks his calendar and notices that he has not received approval of NewCorp's 401(k) plan, which he expected five days ago. Michael picks up the phone and calls the IRS. He speaks with Janet, the IRS agent handling NewCorp's plan. She explains that the approval letter is being prepared and that it will be in the mail late this afternoon. Michael thanks Janet and hangs up the phone, thinking how seldom his problems with the IRS are so easily resolved.

butions to pension plans vest immediately, and employee rights to employer pension-plan contributions vest after five years of employment.

In an attempt to prevent mismanagement of pension funds, ERISA has established rules on how the funds must be invested. Pension-fund managers must be cautious in their investments and refrain from investing more than 10 percent of the fund in securities of the employer. ERISA also contains detailed record-keeping and reporting requirements.

Unemployment Compensation

The Federal Unemployment Tax Act of 1935 created a state system that provides unemployment compensation to eligible individuals. Employers that fall under the provisions of the act are taxed at regular intervals. Taxes are typically paid by the employers to the states, which then deposit them with the federal government. The federal government maintains an unemployment insurance fund, in which each state has an account. Proceeds of this fund are paid out to qualified unemployed workers.

COBRA

Legislation affecting employment relationships addresses a broad range of other issues. One of these issues concerns health insurance for former

SUBSTANTIVE LAW CONCEPT SUMMARY

Employment Law

Employment Discrimination	**1.** *Sexual harassment*—Occurs when employers dole out promotions or other benefits in exchange for sexual favors (*quid-pro-quo* harassment) or when verbal or physical conduct in the workplace "has the purpose or effect of creating an intimidating, hostile, or offensive working environment; has the purpose or effect of unreasonably interfering with an individual's work performance; or otherwise adversely affects an individual's employment opportunities" (hostile-environment harassment). **2.** *Other forms of harassment*—The EEOC's standards as applied to sexual-harassment cases also have been held to apply to harassment based on race, color, national origin, religion, age, or disability. **3.** *Age discrimination*—Under the Age Discrimination in Employment Act (ADEA) of 1967, employers are prohibited from discriminating against individuals forty years of age or older on the basis of their age. **4.** *Disability-based discrimination*—Under the Americans with Disabilities Act (ADA) of 1990, employers are prohibited from discriminating against otherwise qualified workers on the basis of their disabilities. Employers must reasonably accommodate the needs of workers with disabilities unless to do so would create an undue hardship for the employers. **5.** *Affirmative-action programs*—Programs that attempt to make up for past patterns of discrimination by giving members of protected classes preferential treatment in hiring or promotion. These programs have generally been held to be legitimate if they are designed to correct existing imbalances in the work force and as long as employers consider factors in addition to race or gender in making employment decisions. **6.** *Defenses to claims of employment discrimination*—An employer may attempt to disprove the claim or raise one of the following defenses: a. Bona fide occupational qualification (BFOQ). b. Business necessity. c. Seniority system.
Family and Medical Leave	The Family and Medical Leave Act (FMLA) of 1993 requires employers with fifty or more employees to provide their employees (except for key employees) with up to twelve weeks of family or medical leave during any twelve-month period for the following reasons: **1.** *Family leave*—May be taken to care for a newborn baby, an adopted child, or a foster child.

employees. The Consolidated Omnibus Budget Reconciliation Act (COBRA) of 1985 prohibits the elimination of a worker's medical, optical, or dental insurance coverage upon the voluntary or involuntary termination of the worker's employment. The act includes most workers who have either lost their jobs or had their hours decreased and so are no longer eligible for coverage under the employer's health plan. Only those workers fired for gross misconduct are excluded from protection.

The worker has sixty days (beginning with the date that the group coverage would stop) to decide whether to continue with the employer's group insurance plan or not. If the worker chooses to discontinue the coverage,

SUBSTANTIVE LAW CONCEPT SUMMARY, Continued	
	2. *Medical leave*—May be taken when the employee or the employee's spouse, child, or parent has a serious health condition requiring care.
At-will Employment and Wrongful Discharge	Wrongful discharge occurs whenever an employer discharges an employee in violation of the common law or federal or state statutory law. To protect employees from some of the harsh results of the common law employment-at-will doctrine (under which employers may hire or fire employees "at will" unless a contract indicates to the contrary), courts have made exceptions to the doctrine on the basis of contract theory, tort theory, and public policy.
Privacy Rights	A right to privacy has been inferred from guarantees provided by the First, Third, Fourth, Fifth, and Ninth Amendments to the U.S. Constitution. State laws and constitutions may also provide for privacy rights. Employer practices that are often challenged by employees as invasive of their privacy rights include lie-detector tests, drug testing, AIDS testing, performance monitoring, and screening procedures.
Health and Safety in the Workplace	1. The Occupational Safety and Health Act of 1970 requires employers to meet specific safety and health standards that are established and enforced by the Occupational Safety and Health Administration (OSHA). 2. State workers' compensation laws establish an administrative procedure for compensating workers who are injured in accidents that occur on the job, regardless of fault.
Retirement and Security Income	1. *Social Security and Medicare*—The Social Security Act of 1935 provides for old-age (retirement), survivors, and disability insurance (OASDI). Under the Federal Insurance Contributions Act (FICA), both employers and employees must make contributions to help pay for employees' retirement income as provided for under the Social Security Act. The Social Security Administration administers Medicare, a health-insurance program for older or disabled persons. 2. *Private pension plans*—The federal Employee Retirement Income Security Act (ERISA) of 1974 establishes standards for the management of employer-provided pension plans. 3. *Unemployment compensation*—The Federal Unemployment Tax Act of 1935 created a system that provides unemployment compensation to eligible individuals. Covered employers are taxed to help cover the costs of unemployment compensation.
COBRA	The Consolidated Omnibus Budget Reconciliation Act (COBRA) of 1985 requires employers to give employees, on termination of employment, the option of continuing their medical, optical, or dental insurance coverage for a certain period.

then the employer has no further obligation. If the worker chooses to continue coverage, however, the employer is obligated to keep the policy active for up to eighteen months. If the worker is disabled, the employer must extend coverage up to twenty-nine months. The coverage provided must be the same as that enjoyed by the worker prior to the termination or reduction of work. If family members were originally included, for example, COBRA prohibits their exclusion. This is not a free ride for the worker, however. To receive continued benefits, he or she may be required to pay all of the premium, as well as a 2 percent administrative charge.

Employers, with some exceptions, must comply with COBRA if they employ twenty or more workers and provide a benefit plan to those workers. They must inform employees of COBRA's provisions when a group health plan is established. They must also inform any employee who faces termination or a reduction of hours that would affect his or her eligibility for coverage under the plan.

An employer that completely eliminates its group benefit plan is relieved of the responsibility to provide benefit coverage. An employer is also relieved of responsibility to extend coverage for a worker who becomes eligible for Medicare, falls under a spouse's health plan, becomes insured under a different plan (with a new employer, for example), or fails to pay the premium. An employer that fails to comply with COBRA risks substantial penalties, such as a tax of up to 10 percent of the annual cost of the group plan or $500,000, whichever is less.

EMPLOYMENT LAW AND THE PARALEGAL

As mentioned in this chapter's introduction, the extensive regulation of employment relationships has generated substantial legal work for attorneys and paralegals. Today's employers frequently engage in preventive actions to avoid liability for violations of employment laws and regulations. If you work for a corporation—or on behalf of any firm—you may be involved in assisting with the creation of employment policies and guidelines to ensure compliance with employment laws. You may be asked to research current EEOC guidelines on discrimination, for example, or learn what requirements are imposed on business firms by other statutes discussed in this chapter.

No matter where you work or what your paralegal specialty may be, it is likely that sooner or later you will be asked to assist with cases involving employment-related issues. As a litigation paralegal, for example, you might be asked to work on behalf of a plaintiff or a defendant in an employment-discrimination case or a case involving an alleged violation of the Family and Medical Leave Act. As a personal-injury paralegal, you may need to assist an injured client in obtaining benefits—such as medical or disability insurance or unemployment compensation—to which the client is entitled. As an administrative paralegal, you may work for or with a federal or state agency that regulates some aspect of employment relationships. Many paralegals, for example, work closely with—or are employed by—such agencies as the EEOC, OSHA, the Labor Management Services Administration (which implements the provisions of ERISA), state unemployment agencies, and state workers' compensation boards.

Some employment statutes, such as the Occupational Safety and Health Act, impose criminal penalties on violators. A paralegal working in the area of criminal law may thus be asked to assist in defending a firm against a charge brought by OSHA. The corporate paralegal, as indicated above, will likely be involved in work relating to employment policies and employees' claims against the corporation for violation of employment statutes.

As you can see, because employment law touches on so many areas of legal practice, it is impossible to indicate with any degree of specificity the variety of legal work that paralegals undertake in this area. Some examples

TODAY'S PROFESSIONAL PARALEGAL

Handling Workers' Compensation Claims

Cynthia Thomas works in the legal department of a company that makes furniture. One of her jobs is to file workers' compensation injury reports with the insurance company that provides the workers' compensation coverage and with the workers' compensation board, a state agency. If payment is denied, then the injured worker may file a claim and litigate the denial of payment, either formally or informally through the workers' compensation board.

PREPARING AN INJURY REPORT

Today, Cynthia receives a workers' compensation claim from John Smith, who was injured when he cut himself with a saw. He cut his hand and forearm, and nineteen stitches were required to close the wound. Cynthia prepares the injury report, a multi-copy form provided by the state, by inserting the following information: the employee's name and address; the date, time, and location of the accident; a description of the accident; wage information; and various types of employment information, including whether the worker was a full-time or part-time employee, the length of employment, a job description, and an estimate of lost work time. Cynthia has some questions about how long John is expected to be off work while recovering from the accident, so she calls John's supervisor and obtains the answers. Cynthia then adds this information to the injury report.

Cynthia will send a copy of the injury report to the state. The state requires information similar to that requested by the insurance company so that it can monitor the reported injury.

HANDLING MEDICAL RECORDS

Cynthia must also obtain copies of John's medical records to submit to the insurance company and the workers' compensation board. Cynthia prepares a medical-release form and mails it to John Smith for his signature. Once John returns it, Cynthia will request his medical records. Sometimes, the insurance company will require an independent medical exam (IME) to verify the injuries and length of a disability leave. When an IME is required, Cynthia makes the arrangements with the independent physician for the exam.

LITIGATION ASSISTANCE

If a claim is denied, the claimant (John, in this situation) may litigate the matter. When this occurs, Cynthia prepares records on behalf of the company and assists the lawyer who is defending the company. Cynthia's role in assisting outside counsel includes scheduling medical depositions, filing motions with the court, and preparing briefs on legal issues arising during the litigation.

of employment-related tasks undertaken by paralegals were given in the section on employment relationships in Chapter 9 and in the section on employment and labor law in Chapter 2. Others were given in Chapter 13, which covered administrative law.

KEY TERMS AND CONCEPTS

affirmative-action program 815
business necessity 816
***prima facie* case 811**
seniority system 816
vesting 826
whistleblowing 818
wrongful discharge 818

CHAPTER SUMMARY

1. Sexual harassment is a form of gender-based discrimination prohibited under Title VII of the Civil Rights Act of 1964. Employees who can prove that sexual harassment actually occurred—which is often difficult to do—may bring an action against their employers for harassment by supervisors, by co-employees, or by nonemployees (such as customers). To establish the existence of harassment, the reasonable-person standard is used, but the perspective of the victim is also considered. Harassment based on race, color, national origin, religion, age, or disability is also deemed to violate the protections given to these classes of persons under Title VII.

2. The Age Discrimination in Employment Act of 1967 prohibits employers from discriminating against individuals forty years of age or older on the basis of their age. The Americans with Disabilities Act (ADA) of 1990, which went into effect in 1992, prohibits employers from discriminating against otherwise qualified workers on the basis of their disabilities. The ADA requires employers to make reasonable accommodations for the needs of persons with disabilities unless to do so would result in "undue hardship" for the employers. Affirmative-action programs, which attempt to make up for past patterns of discrimination by giving preferential treatment to members of protected classes, are generally considered to be legitimate as long as factors in addition to race or gender are considered in employment decisions.

3. An employer may defend against a claim of employment discrimination by attempting to disprove the claim or raising defenses relating to bona fide occupational qualification, business necessity, or seniority systems.

4. The Family and Medical Leave Act (FMLA) of 1993 requires employers with fifty or more employees to provide their employees with up to twelve weeks of family or medical leave during any twelve-month period. Key employees may be exempted from the act's requirements. An employee may take family leave to care for a newborn baby, an adopted child, or a foster child. Medical leave may be taken when the employee or the employee's spouse, child, or parent has a serious health condition requiring care.

5. Wrongful discharge occurs whenever an employer discharges an employee in violation of the common law or state or federal statutory laws prohibiting discrimination. If the common law doctrine of employment at will applies, employees usually have little recourse if they are discharged arbitrarily from their jobs, unless the discharge breaches an employment contract. Courts sometimes make exceptions to the at-will doctrine, however, including exceptions based on contract theory (implied contracts), tort theory (wrongful actions relating to the discharge), and public policy (whistleblowing).

6. Several employer practices have given rise to complaints by employees that their privacy rights have been violated. Various amendments to the U.S. Constitution have been interpreted as providing for a right to privacy, and state laws and constitutions may provide for privacy rights. Employer practices that are often challenged as invasive of employee privacy rights include lie-detector tests, drug testing, AIDS testing, performance monitoring, and certain types of screening procedures.

7. Under the common law and under various statutes, employers are required to provide safe working conditions for their employees. The key federal statute governing workplace safety is the Occupational Safety and Health Act of 1970. The Occupational Safety and Health Administration (OSHA) establishes specific safety and health standards and procedures by which employers must abide. Workers' compensation statutes establish procedures for compensating workers for accidental on-the-job injuries. An employee who receives workers' compensation forfeits the right to sue the employer for injuries caused by the employer's negligence.

8. Several federal statutes relate to retirement and security income for employees. The Social Security Act of 1935 provides for old-age (retirement), survivors, and disability insurance (OASDI). Under the Federal Insurance Contributions Act (FICA), both employers and employees must make contributions to help pay for employees' retirement income as provided for under the Social Security Act. The Social Security Administration administers Medicare, a health-insurance program for older or disabled persons. The Employee Retirement Income Security Act

(ERISA) of 1974 establishes standards for the management of employer-provided pension plans. The Federal Unemployment Tax Act of 1935 created a system that provides unemployment compensation to eligible individuals. Covered employers are taxed to help cover the costs of unemployment compensation.

9. The Consolidated Omnibus Budget Reconciliation Act (COBRA) of 1985 requires employers to give employees, on termination of employment, the option of continuing their medical, optical, or dental insurance coverage for up to eighteen months (twenty-nine months for employees with disabilities). A former employee who decides to continue his or her insurance coverage may be required to pay all or part of the premium, as well as a 2 percent administrative charge. The act covers all workers whose employment is voluntarily or involuntarily terminated, except workers who are fired for gross misconduct.

QUESTIONS FOR REVIEW

1. What are the different types of employment discrimination? What are affirmative-action programs?

2. What defenses can employers raise against employment discrimination?

3. What is a wrongful-discharge action? What is the employment-at-will doctrine? What are the exceptions to the employment-at-will doctrine?

4. What are the major provisions of the Family and Medical Leave Act of 1993? What remedies are available for violations of this act?

5. What employee privacy rights are protected by law? Are there any areas in which the law does not protect an employee's right to privacy? If so, what are they?

6. What is OSHA? How are OSHA's rules enforced? Can employees file complaints based on OSHA violations by their employers?

7. What are workers' compensation laws? To what employees do they apply?

8. When does an employee have a right to recover workers' compensation? What procedures must an employee follow to obtain such compensation?

9. What is OASDI? What are private retirement plans? What is unemployment compensation?

10. What is COBRA? Are all terminated employees covered by this act? Are the benefits required by COBRA free?

ETHICAL QUESTIONS

1. Roberta works for a sole practitioner as a paralegal. One of Roberta's responsibilities is to do the bookkeeping for the client trust account and for individual trust accounts. These accounts are maintained for several large estates that her supervising attorney, John Bigelow, handles. Over the course of a year, John has purchased a new Ferrari, a new fifty-foot sailboat, and several other "toys." He also took a trip to Hawaii on his vacation. Roberta knows what the firm's income is, and she cannot understand how the attorney can afford these luxuries.

One day, while John is out of the office, Roberta looks through the firm's safe for some important client documents. She discovers that John has been keeping two sets of books for the client trust accounts and that he has been embezzling money from the accounts over the past year. When Roberta confronts John with the second set of books, he tells her that he has just "borrowed" the money and that he intends to pay it back. What should Roberta do?

2. Bill, a paralegal with a large firm, is about to meet with a client to review a draft of a retirement plan that he and his supervising attorney have put together for the client. He is scheduled to meet with Jerry Ackerman, the client's personnel manager. When Bill arrives for the meeting, though, he is met by a different employee of the client. When they sit down in the conference room to review the plan, the employee explains that Jerry Ackerman has taken a medical leave because he has AIDS. The employee says that the company is considering the possibility of requiring AIDS testing of all of its employees to avoid these types of medical leaves in the future. The employee asks Bill if AIDS testing is legal. How should Bill answer?

PRACTICE QUESTIONS AND ASSIGNMENTS

1. Name the laws that govern the following employment-related issues:

a. Sexual harassment.
b. Age discrimination.
c. Wrongful discharge.
d. Racial discrimination.
e. Denial of family leave.
f. Disability-based discrimination.
g. The use of lie-detector tests.
h. Failure to comply with OSHA standards.

2. Which of the following employer practices may be held to violate employee privacy rights?

a. Lie-detector tests (government and security-related employers exempted).
b. Employment at will.
c. Drug testing for reasons of public safety.
d. Retirement-plan investigation.
e. AIDS testing.
f. Listening to employees' telephone conversations.
g. Discharging employees who test positive for HIV.
h. Discrimination based on religion.

QUESTIONS FOR CRITICAL ANALYSIS

1. The Family and Medical Leave Act of 1993 applies to "employees." Does this mean men and women? Should it?

2. Do you think that pension plans are regulated to protect employers or employees? Why?

ROLE-PLAYING EXERCISES

1. Review the facts of Ethical Question 1 above. Role-play the scene in which Roberta, the paralegal, confronts the attorney, John, with the second set of books and accuses him of embezzling client funds. Assume that John tells Roberta not to worry about it, that he will return the funds to the account soon, and so on. Roberta should explain to John her ethical responsibilities in this situation.

2. Role-play Ethical Question 2 above. Have Bill explain to the client's employee why he cannot answer the employee's question.

PROJECTS

1. Does your state have a whistleblower protection act? If so, what protection does it provide to employees who report their employers' violations of the law? Does it provide any rewards for employees who blow the whistle?

2. Use a telephone book or state government directory to find out if your state has an agency parallel to the federal OSHA. If so, what is its function, and how does it differ from the federal agency?

3. What is the citation to your state's workers' compensation statute? Which employees are excluded from the act's coverage?

ANNOTATED SELECTED READINGS

ARNDT, KYLE B., and CHRISTINA A. BULL. "The Impact of the Family and Medical Leave Act of 1993 on the Legal Profession." *U.C.L.A. Law Journal*, Spring 1993. A fascinating article discussing why lawyers who are partners in law firms are not likely to be covered by the Family and Medical Leave Act of 1993.

LUDWIG, STEVEN K. "Complying with the Family and Medical Leave Act." *Practical Lawyer*, September 1993. A blueprint for compliance with the Family and Medical Leave Act.

NADER, RALPH. "Occupational Safety and Health Act." *Houston Law Review*, Symposium, 1994. An interesting article discussing the history of the OSHA statute, including Ralph Nader's involvement in creating it. The article also discusses current problems under the statute and Mr. Nader's recommendations for the future of OSHA.

PERRY, PHILLIP M. "Should You Rat on Your Boss?" *Legal Assistant Today*, March/April 1993. A well-written article that discusses whistleblowing from a practical standpoint and gives advice on what to expect if you "blow the whistle" on your employer. It also includes a section on installing reporting systems in the firm to prevent and report illegal activity.

ROSS, JOHN J. "The Employment Law Year in Review." *Practicing Law Institute—Litigation*, October 1994. An informative article reviewing federal legislation; state developments on the topics of AIDS, smoking, substance abuse, and violence; United States Supreme Court decisions involving employment law; and decisions of other courts.

WALKER, JOHN M. "The Employee Retirement Income Security Act of 1974: An Overview of ERISA Pre-emption." *American Journal of Trial Advocacy*, Fall 1993. An article providing a sound overview of ERISA and its preemption of state law.

22

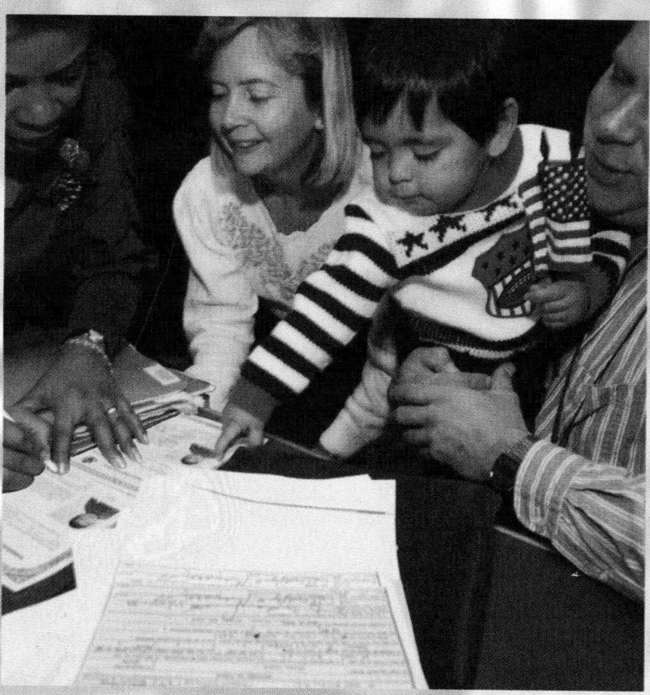

FAMILY LAW

Chapter Objectives

After completing this chapter, you will know:

- **The legal requirements for marriage and the legal obligations of married partners toward each other.**
- **The legal rights and obligations of parents and children.**
- **The procedures involved in terminating a marriage.**
- **How the laws regulate child-custody, child-support, and spousal-support arrangements.**
- **How marital property and debts are divided when a marriage is dissolved.**

Chapter Outline

INTRODUCTION

Family law, as you learned in Chapter 2, deals with family matters. Marriage, divorce, adoption, child support and custody, child and spousal abuse, and parental rights and duties are all areas of family law. Although many families solve their problems internally, sometimes families need outside assistance—from attorneys, paralegals, courts, law-enforcement officers, social workers, and others.

Much of the legal work relating to family law has to do with marriage dissolution. Marriage is a status conferred by state law, and to end a marriage, the state, through the court system, must become involved. Because of the high divorce rate in this country, many attorneys and paralegals are involved in divorce cases. If children are involved, child-support and child-custody issues need to be decided. The property owned by a divorcing couple must also be divided between the spouses. If you are contemplating working as a paralegal in the area of family law, you can probably rest assured that there will be jobs available.

In this chapter, you will read about some important legal concepts and doctrines governing family matters. We look first at the laws governing marriage and then at some legal aspects of parent-child relationships. The remainder of the chapter focuses on marriage termination and related topics, including child custody, child and spousal support, and property settlements.

MARRIAGE

Part of the "American Dream" has always been to marry and have children. In view of the fact that many couples today live together (cohabit) without first marrying, it might seem that this dream has gone by the wayside. In fact, though, more than 90 percent of Americans do marry at least once.

One of the reasons people marry is because marriage confers certain legal and practical advantages.

- **The marital framework establishes the rights and duties of the spouses, as well as of any children born during the marriage.**

Married couples may also have an easier time obtaining insurance and credit, and married couples have more adoption opportunities. Additionally, many companies offer health insurance to spouses but not to unmarried partners. Finally, unmarried couples who live together without marrying may face legal problems in those states that prohibit extramarital cohabitation—although these laws often are not enforced.

Any couple wishing to marry must meet their state's legal requirements for marriage. In this section, you will read about these requirements and the duties that arise when a couple marries.

Marriage Requirements

States place some limitations on who may marry. The betrothed must be man and woman, currently unmarried, not closely related by blood, and over a cer-

tain age—usually eighteen years. State laws vary, and some states prohibit marriages among those who are closely related even if the relation is only by marriage. Persons who are under the required age may marry with parental consent or if they are emancipated from their parents. (**Emancipation** occurs when a child's parent or legal guardian relinquishes the legal right to exercise control over the child. Normally, a child who leaves home to support himself or herself is considered emancipated.) Below a certain age, such as fourteen or sixteen, marriage may be absolutely prohibited by state law except with court approval.

EMANCIPATION
The legal relinquishment by a child's parents or guardian of the legal right to exercise control over the child. Usually, a child who moves out of the parents' home and supports himself or herself is considered emancipated.

Certain procedures are generally required for a legally recognized marriage. The parties must first obtain a marriage license from the state government, usually through the county clerk's office. Some states also require a blood test to check for certain diseases, such as venereal disease and rubella. No state requires a premarital test for AIDS (acquired immune deficiency syndrome), although such a test is offered in some states. Some states require couples to undergo a waiting period before getting the license or between the time of acquiring the license and officially getting married.

In the majority of the states, in addition to a marriage license, some form of marriage ceremony is required. The parties must present the license to someone authorized to perform marriages, such as a justice of the peace, a judge, a court clerk, or a member of the clergy. The marriage ceremony must involve a public statement of the agreement to marry. The remainder of the ceremony is generally within the couple's discretion. After the ceremony, the marriage license must be recorded.

Same-gender Couples

Some of the most controversial family-law topics today involve gay or lesbian couples. Many homosexual couples live in stable, long-term relationships. Sometimes, homosexual couples hold what have become known as "commitment ceremonies," which are similar to marriage ceremonies, to formalize their relationships. No state legally recognizes same-sex marriages, however, and such ceremonies do not invoke the legal protections surrounding marriage. There is no legal provision for community property or alimony (discussed later in this chapter) in such marriages. A homosexual couple may provide for similar protections through a contract, however.

Common Law Marriages

A **common law marriage** is one in which the parties become married solely by mutual consent and without a license or ceremony. At one time, common law marriages were frequent in Europe. Because of the legal difficulties presented by such marriages (particularly the difficulty in establishing whether children were legitimate), they were banned by the Roman Catholic Church in 1545 at the Council of Trent. England abolished the common law marriage in 1753, although it remained lawful in Scotland and in the American colonies. Today in the United States, only fourteen states[1] and the District of Columbia recognize the common law marriage.

COMMON LAW MARRIAGE
A marriage that is formed solely by mutual consent and without a marriage license or ceremony. The couple must be eligible to marry, live together as husband and wife, and hold themselves out to the public as husband and wife. Only fourteen states recognize common law marriages.

1. Alabama, Colorado, Georgia, Idaho, Iowa, Kansas, Montana, Ohio, Oklahoma, Pennsylvania, Rhode Island, South Carolina, Texas, and Utah.

There are four general requirements for a common law marriage:

- The parties must be eligible to marry.
- The parties must have a present and continuing intention and agreement to be husband and wife.
- The parties must live together as husband and wife.
- The parties must hold themselves out to the public as husband and wife.

There are a number of misconceptions about common law marriages. One is that merely by living together, a couple may form a common law marriage. Cohabitation alone, though, cannot produce a common law marriage. The parties must additionally *hold themselves out to others as husband and wife.* Another misconception is that a couple must be living together for a certain number of years. In fact, there is no minimum time period required for a common law marriage. The parties may become married as soon as they live as husband and wife and hold themselves out to the public as a married couple.

While living together is an informal arrangement, a common law marriage is both legal and formal. Once a couple is regarded as married, they have all of the rights and obligations of a traditionally married couple. For example, they are legally obligated to support each other and their children. Furthermore, those states that do not recognize common law marriages nonetheless acknowledge the validity of a common law marriage that was formed in one of the states that do permit common law marriages.

There is no common law divorce. Once a couple is regarded as married—and particularly once a court has recognized them as married by common law—they must obtain a court decree to dissolve the marriage.

Marital Duties

The concept of duties between married partners has a long history. In ancient Rome, marriage was arranged between families through private contracts. Part of the contractual arrangement was that the husband would support and provide for his wife and children. The wife, in turn, had certain duties in the home.

During the Middle Ages, the Roman Catholic Church deemed marriage to be a sacrament. Marriage became subject to canon (ecclesiastical) law and eventually to the governing authorities of the nation or state. In other words, marriage was no longer a private matter. Although we still hear the term *marriage contract,* in fact, marriage is a special type of contract that is not governed by contract law but by the state (in the United States, by the laws governing marriage and divorce in each state), as are the spousal obligations of married partners.

Financial Support. Few of the traditional duties of spouses are enforced by courts today, and generally spouses are allowed to arrange their own affairs however they see fit. Nonetheless, the law still holds that a married person has a duty to financially support his or her spouse and children by providing such basics as food, shelter, and medical care—insofar as the person is able to do so. In many states, this duty lasts throughout the marriage, even if the spouses are living apart. Failure to provide support for a child may be a crim-

inal violation. Additional duties may be created by a separate agreement between the spouses. Some courts will not enforce certain types of agreements, though, such as agreements to dole out sexual relations in return for money or some other consideration.

Interspousal Immunity. The common law traditionally provided that one spouse could not sue the other for torts, such as assault and battery (discussed in Chapter 8). This is the common law doctrine of **interspousal immunity.** Most states have modified this doctrine and now permit one spouse to sue the other for at least intentional torts. Interspousal immunity still means that one partner may not be required to testify against the other in court. A spouse may *voluntarily* so testify, however.

INTERSPOUSAL IMMUNITY
A common law doctrine that prohibited one spouse from suing the other spouse for torts, such as assault and battery, and from testifying against the other spouse in court. The doctrine has been modified. Today, in most states, one spouse may sue the other for at least intentional torts, and a spouse normally may voluntarily testify against the other spouse in court.

In recent years, a number of lawsuits have been brought in which a spouse (or unmarried partner) alleges that the other spouse (or partner) knowingly exposed him or her to AIDS, herpes, or some other sexually transmitted disease. Such an action may qualify as an intentional tort (see Chapter 8). In some states, if a person who knows that he or she is infected with the AIDS virus has sex with an uninformed partner, that person may be subject to criminal prosecution. Paralegals who are assisting in such cases need to check the statutory and case law in their states to find out how the law applies to such situations.

Spousal Abuse. In all states, it is illegal to batter a spouse. Unlawful abuse has been extended to include extreme cases of harassment and threats of physical beating or confinement. If, as a paralegal, you are assisting a client who is a victim of spousal abuse, you should check your state laws governing spousal abuse. Each state creates its own definition of domestic violence through legislation or court decisions. Generally, the local police should be informed. In some cases, an emergency restraining order may be necessary. A **restraining order** is a court order that requires one person (such as an abusing spouse) to stay away from another (such as the victim of spousal abuse). Many shelters are available to assist abused spouses.[2]

RESTRAINING ORDER
A court order that requires one person (such as an abusing spouse) to stay away from another (such as an abused spouse).

PARENTS AND CHILDREN

Traditionally, one of the main purposes of marriage was to have children. In fact, only in the last few decades have childless married couples become as acceptable in the eyes of society as married couples with children. The decision whether to have children is a significant one in every marital relationship. Although the decision should be made mutually, the woman ultimately has the right to use contraceptive devices or to go ahead and bear a child, and she does not need to obtain the husband's permission in either situation.

As a paralegal, you may deal with many issues relating to parenthood and childbearing. You may assist a female client who wants to bring a lawsuit to establish the paternity of a child born "out of wedlock" (born to an

2. See the *Paralegal Profile* in Chapter 7 for a paralegal's description of how she assists battered women who are residents of a women's shelter.

ETHICAL CONCERN

Dealing with Spousal Abuse

Earlier in this text, we touched on some situations in which paralegals face a conflict between personal and legal ethics. Consider another example of this conflict. Lena, a paralegal, is asked to assist in a divorce case. While she is interviewing the client—the divorcing husband—he not only admits to abusing his wife but also acts proud of it. In the husband's mind, he's simply exercising his right as head of the household. Lena cannot stand the man and does not want to have anything further to do with him. What can she do in this situation? One option is to explain her feelings to her supervising attorney and see if another paralegal might handle the work instead. Often, though, either there is no other paralegal available or the attorney will not agree to the replacement. This means that, in Lena's situation, she will have to either work with the client or place her job in jeopardy. If you ever find yourself in this kind of situation, it may help to remind yourself that paralegals have a duty of loyalty to their employers. Additionally, part of the paralegal's job is to be professionally objective.

unmarried woman). You may be asked to investigate the rights of an illegitimate child or research the law governing parental rights in cases involving surrogate parents or artificial insemination. Many family-law paralegals assist in adoptions. Other issues relate to parents' responsibility for their children's wrongful actions or for child abuse. We look at each of these issues here. In the next section, you will read about parental rights and obligations upon marriage termination.

Parental Rights and Obligations

The law has special concern for children and provides many protections for them. Legally, a child is defined as an unmarried minor (under the age of eighteen) who is not emancipated.

General Rights and Duties. Prior to a child's emancipation, parents have certain rights of control over the child. Parents can direct the upbringing of their children and control where they live, what school they attend, and even what religion they practice. Parents also generally control the medical care to be given. Note, though, that a parent's refusal to provide for medical care in life-threatening situations (usually for religious reasons) can be a crime. Parents have broad legal authority to control the behavior of their children and even to physically punish them—so long as the punishment does not constitute child abuse (to be discussed shortly).

Parents also have obligations toward their children. Parents are obligated to provide food, shelter, clothing, medical care, and other necessities for their children. If a couple is married, the law presumes that any newborn child was fathered by the husband, and the husband must support the child unless he can prove that he is not the biological father. (Some states do not allow the husband an opportunity to prove his lack of paternity, however.)

Parents must also ensure that their children attend school (normally until the age of sixteen). Although parental duties to a child generally end when the child reaches the age of eighteen, these duties may continue for a longer period if the child is seriously disabled.

Liability for Children's Wrongful Acts. Under the common law, parents are generally not liable for the wrongful actions of their children. Parents may be liable in some circumstances for their children's actions, however, if the actions resulted from the parents' negligence. For example, suppose that a parent permits her fifteen-year-old son to drive the family car to the grocery store by himself, with no supervision. En route to the store, the boy causes an accident in which a passenger in another car is seriously injured. The passenger would probably succeed in a negligence suit against the boy's parent in this situation.

Parents may also be liable for their children's intentional torts. About half of the states now provide for partial parental liability for their children's intentional torts, up to a limit of about $10,000 (depending on state law).

Child Abuse and Neglect. All states allow parents to physically punish their children within reason. A parent, for example, may slap or spank a child without violating the laws prohibiting child abuse. Although about half of the

states have banned corporal (physical) punishment in the schools, children in the remaining states may endure some form of physical punishment.

- **In all states, however, laws prohibit sexual molestation and extreme punishment of children by anyone.**

For punishment to constitute physical child abuse, the punishment normally must result in injuries—such as broken skin or bones, excessive bruising, or swelling.

Child neglect is also a form of child abuse. Child neglect occurs when parents or legal guardians fail to provide for a child's basic needs, such as food, shelter, clothing, and medical treatment. Child abuse may even extend to emotional abuse, as when a person publicly humiliates a child in an extreme way.

Laws now require doctors, school teachers, day-care workers, social workers, and others who are in frequent contact with children to report suspected cases of child abuse. In serious cases of child abuse or neglect, a government agency may remove the child from his or her parents. Ideally, the child will be reunited with the parents after the parents' problems have been corrected through counseling or otherwise. If the parents are unable to solve their problems, the government agency may ask the court to terminate all parental rights and make the children available for adoption.

Children Born out of Wedlock

People in the ancient world often dealt with illegitimacy expeditiously by simply destroying the pregnant mother of the future illegitimate child. In Biblical days, an adultress was stoned to death. Under Islamic law, too, stoning was the proper punishment for adulteresses. In the Christian world of the Middle Ages, illegitimate children and their mothers were always allowed to live, even though they were usually regarded as outcasts.

Things have changed, of course. Today, an increasing number of children are born to unmarried parents (about one-third of all first births). In response, the law is evolving to provide added rights and protections for children born out of wedlock. One important right is the right to be supported by the biological father.

Financial Support. The biological father of the child has a legal obligation to provide support for the child. This obligation is just as great as for a married father and is determined by the child-support guidelines of the state (discussed later). The obligation usually lasts until the child is no longer a minor. The mother's subsequent marriage to another man does not necessarily extinguish the obligation of the biological father to support the child. In most states, the eventual marriage of the parents of a child born out of wedlock "legitimizes" the child.

Paternity Suits. An unmarried mother may file a **paternity suit** to establish that a certain person is the biological father of her child. If the unwed mother is on public-welfare assistance, the government may file a paternity suit on the mother's behalf—to obtain reimbursement for welfare payments given to the mother. The paternity of a child may be proved scientifically.

PATERNITY SUIT
A lawsuit brought by an unmarried mother to establish that a certain person is the biological father of her child. DNA testing and comparable procedures are often used to determine paternity.

DNA testing and comparable procedures that check for genetic factors can now determine, with almost 100 percent accuracy, whether a person parented a particular child.

Inheritance Rights. While all biological fathers have an obligation to provide child support regardless of marital status, children born out of wedlock still suffer disadvantages. One disadvantage has to do with inheritance rights.

Under the common law, the illegitimate child was regarded as a *filius nullius* (Latin for "child of no one") and had no right to inherit. Today, statutes vary from state to state in regard to the inheritance laws governing illegitimate children. Generally, an illegitimate child is treated as the child of the mother and can inherit from her and her relatives. The child is usually not regarded as the legal child of the father unless paternity is established through some legal proceeding. Many state statutes permit the illegitimate child to inherit from the father, however, if paternity was established prior to the father's death.

A landmark case in establishing the rights of illegitimate children was decided by the United States Supreme Court in 1977. In *Trimble v. Gordon*,[3] an illegitimate child sought to inherit property from her deceased natural father and claimed that an Illinois statute prohibiting inheritance by illegitimate children in the absence of a will was unconstitutional. The Supreme Court agreed. The Court found it hard to perceive any justification for the Illinois statute and held that the section of the Illinois statute "cannot be squared with the command of the Equal Protection Clause of the Fourteenth Amendment."

By declaring the Illinois statute unconstitutional, the Court invalidated similar laws of several other states. That does not mean that all illegitimate children will have inheritance rights identical to those of legitimate children, however. Generally, the courts have upheld state probate statutes that discriminate between legitimate and illegitimate children for valid state purposes.

Adoption

ADOPTION
A procedure by which persons become the legal parents of a child who is not their biological child.

In contrast to children born out of wedlock, adopted children normally have the same legal rights as biological children. **Adoption** is a procedure by which persons become the legal parents of a child that is not their biological child.

- **Once an adoption is formally completed, the adoptive parents have all the responsibilities of biological parents.**

Should they divorce, each adoptive parent has all of the child-support obligations associated with biological parents. Adopted children also have the right to inherit property from their adoptive parents upon the parents' death. Note that adoption is not the same as **foster care,** which is a temporary arrangement in which a family is paid by the state to care for a child for a limited period of time, often pending adoption.

FOSTER CARE
A temporary arrangement in which a family is paid by the state to care for a child for a limited period of time, often pending adoption.

3. 430 U.S. 762, 97 S.Ct. 1459, 52 L.Ed.2d 31 (1977).

Here, we look at some of the basic legal requirements for adoptions. We also examine different types of adoptions and the court's role in the adoption process.

Requirements for Adoption. Adoptions are governed by state laws, and these laws vary substantially from state to state. Generally, however, there are three minimum requirements for an adoption to be legal:

- The legal rights of the biological parents must have been terminated by death or legal decree.
- The adopting parents must follow all procedures required by the state in which the adoption occurs.
- The adoption must be formally approved by a judge.

There may be additional requirements in specific circumstances. For example, adopting a teenage child generally requires the child's official consent.

All states permit single persons to adopt children, but married couples are generally preferred. Although some courts have approved adoptions by same-gender couples, generally such couples find it difficult to adopt children. Two states, Florida and New Hampshire, have explicitly prohibited homosexual adoptions. Some local Florida courts, however, have struck down that state's law as being unconstitutional. Even in the absence of such a law, an Ohio judge held in 1988 that gays and lesbians were ineligible to adopt. Despite the roadblocks, though, over two hundred homosexual couples have successfully adopted children.

Agency Adoptions. Adoption is often done through social-service agencies that are licensed by the state to place children for adoption. The biological parents terminate their parental rights, essentially giving up these rights to the agency and authorizing the agency to find legal parents for their children. Traditionally, in agency adoptions, the identities of the biological and the adoptive parents were kept confidential. Increasingly, though, state laws are allowing for the disclosure of this information in certain circumstances. In some states, for example, if an adopted child wants to meet with his or her birth parent or vice versa, the court will contact the child or parent to see if he or she will agree to such a meeting.

Increasingly, open-adoption procedures are being used. In an **open adoption,** the birth parents and adoptive parents meet with each other at the outset and may continue to meet periodically. The birth mother may "screen" prospective adoptive parents—in the interests of placing her baby with adoptive parents who will provide a cultural or religious background similar to her own, for example, or who meet other criteria. In open adoptions, birth parents and adoptive parents sometimes remain in contact with one another as the child grows. They may agree to exchange pictures and letters, for instance, or to meet with each other at specified intervals.

OPEN ADOPTION
An adoption procedure in which the birth parents and adoptive parents meet with each other at the outset and may continue to meet periodically.

INDEPENDENT ADOPTION
A privately arranged adoption, as when a doctor, lawyer, or other individual puts parents who want to adopt a child in contact with a pregnant woman who has decided to give up her child for adoption.

Independent Adoptions. Prospective adoptive parents may also pursue independent adoption. An **independent adoption** is one that is arranged privately, as when a doctor, lawyer, or other individual puts a couple who wants to have children in contact with a pregnant woman who has decided to give

up her child for adoption. These parties make their own private arrangements. Usually, the adopting parents pay for the legal and medical expenses associated with the childbirth and adoption. The intermediary may also receive a fee. Because this method of adoption has the potential for abuse, it is prohibited by some states.

Stepparent Adoptions. Many adoptions are so-called "stepparent adoptions," which occur when a married partner adopts his or her spouse's children from a former marriage. Usually, in such adoptions, the parental rights of the children's other biological parent are terminated either by consent or through a court proceeding.

Court Approval and Probation. All adoptions, including private, independent adoptions, must be approved in court. The primary standard for approving an adoption is the "best interests of the child." Because this standard is so vague, the courts have a great deal of leeway in deciding whether to place children with prospective adoptive parents. The court considers the financial resources of the adopting parents, their family stability and home environment, their ages, their religious and racial compatibility, and other factors relevant to the child's future health and welfare.

After the adoption, many states place the new parents on probation for a time, usually from six months to one year. The agency or court appoints an individual to monitor developments in the home to ensure that the adoptive parents are caring appropriately for the child's well-being. If they are not, the child may be removed and returned to an agency for placement in another home.

Artificial Insemination and Surrogate Parenting

At one time, couples who wanted to become parents but were unable to have children had only one option: adoption. In recent years, two other ways of becoming parents have emerged—artificial insemination and surrogate parenting. Both of these methods can result in difficult legal issues involving establishment of parental rights.

Artificial Insemination. If a married woman becomes pregnant through artificial insemination with her husband's sperm, there is no legal question as to the paternity of the child. Problems may arise, though, when a pregnancy and birth result from artificial insemination with an anonymous donor's sperm donated to a sperm bank. Usually, in such situations, the husband must consent—in some states, in writing—to the artificial insemination before he will be considered the legal father of the child. Because state laws vary, if you are ever involved in assisting a couple making such arrangements, you should research your state's law carefully to make sure that the couple won't face legal problems later, after the child is born.

Surrogate-parenting Contracts. In 1988, in *In re Baby M*,[4] the New Jersey Supreme Court faced a perplexing issue: whether a surrogate-parenting contract should be enforced. This highly publicized lawsuit involved the first surrogate-parenting contract to reach the courts. The contract was between

4. 109 N.J. 396, 537 A.2d 122 (1988).

William and Elizabeth Stern, who could not have children, and Mary Beth Whitehead. Mrs. Whitehead agreed to be artificially inseminated with Mr. Stern's sperm and to give the baby to the Sterns when it was born. In return, the Sterns agreed to pay Mrs. Whitehead $10,000 for her services as a surrogate parent and to pay all costs associated with the pregnancy and birth. When the baby was born, however, Mrs. Whitehead decided to keep the child and refused to perform her part of the bargain.

The Sterns sued to enforce the contract, and eventually the case came before the New Jersey Supreme Court, which held that the contract was unenforceable. In the court's opinion, surrogate-parenting contracts represented little more than baby selling in disguise. Although the court decided that it was in the best interests of the child to be placed in the Sterns' custody, Mrs. Whitehead's parental rights could not be forfeited by contract. She was thus given visitation rights.

In 1991, a California appellate court faced perhaps an even more challenging issue. In *Anna J. v. Mark C.*,[5] the question before the court was as follows: If a fertilized embryo, formed by a husband's sperm and a wife's egg, was implanted in the womb of a surrogate mother, which of the two women would be the "natural mother" of the child? The court, which admitted that it was journeying "through unchartered territory" in deciding this case, ultimately held that the genetic and biological parents were the "natural" father and mother. The woman who gave birth to the child thus had no legal rights as a "natural mother" to the child.

Because of the legal difficulties that have arisen in regard to surrogate-parenting contracts, this option for becoming a parent is becoming less frequently used. In fact, some states have enacted legislation prohibiting such contracts on the ground that such an arrangement equates to "baby selling." Other states allow surrogate-parenting contracts but do not permit contracts that involve compensation to the surrogate mother for the services rendered. Still other states refuse to enforce such contracts even though they are not prohibited by statute.

MARRIAGE TERMINATION

Just as marital status can only be granted by the state, so can marital status only be terminated by the state. In other words, even though two people want to end their marriage and even though they separate and live apart, they will continue to have the legal rights and obligations of spouses until their marriage is legally terminated.

There are two ways in which a marriage can be terminated: by annulment and by divorce. We look at each of these procedures here.

Annulment

An **annulment** is a court decree that essentially invalidates (nullifies) a marriage. This means that the marriage was never effective in the first place. Today, annulments are rarely granted. To a great extent, this is because no-fault divorce laws (to be discussed shortly) have made divorce a simpler

ANNULMENT
A court decree that invalidates (nullifies) a marriage. Although the marriage itself is deemed nonexistent, children of the marriage are deemed legitimate.

5. 12 Cal.App.4th 977, 286 Cal.Rptr. 369 (1991). The court's ruling was affirmed by the California Supreme Court in *Johnson v. Calvert*, 5 Cal.4th 84, 851 P.2d 776, 19 Cal.Rptr.2d 494 (1993).

option than it once was. Many of those seeking annulments today do so because their religion (such as Roman Catholicism) does not condone divorce. In such situations, an annulment allows a subsequent marriage to be recognized as valid in the eyes of the church.

Grounds for invalidating a marriage through annulment are to some extent similar to those for invalidating other contracts. Recall from Chapter 8 that a contract is not valid unless the parties genuinely assent to it. Genuineness of assent is lacking when a contract is based on fraud or duress. Another requirement for a valid contract is contractual capacity. If one of the parties lacked contractual capacity (was intoxicated, for example) at the time the contract was formed, then the validity of the contract can be challenged. Additionally, an annulment may be granted for other reasons—if the marriage was unconsummated, for example, or if there was **bigamy** (that is, if one party was already married).

BIGAMY
The act of entering into marriage with one person while still legally married to another.

What is the status of the children born to a couple whose marriage is annulled? Even though the marriage is deemed invalid, children born during the marriage are considered legitimate in the eyes of the law. Also, as in a divorce, when a marriage is annulled, child-support, spousal-support, child-custody, and property-settlement issues must be decided by the couple (or the court, if the couple cannot agree) and approved by the court.

Divorce

The other option for terminating a marriage is, of course, a divorce. A **divorce** is a formal court proceeding that legally dissolves a marriage. Divorce laws vary among the states, with some states having much simpler divorce procedures than others. In this area of family law, as in all others, the paralegal must refer to his or her state's laws governing divorce and divorce procedures.

DIVORCE
A formal court proceeding that legally dissolves a marriage.

Fault-based versus No-fault Divorces. Until the 1960s, to obtain a divorce, a petitioning party had to allege reasons for the divorce that were acceptable grounds for divorce under state law. In many states, typical grounds for divorce included adultery, desertion, extreme cruelty, and abuse. Unless the petitioning party could prove that his or her partner was "at fault" for the breakdown of the marriage in one of these ways, a divorce would not be granted.

Changing economic and social conditions in twentieth-century America led to new attitudes toward divorce—attitudes that were reflected in relaxed laws concerning the requirements for divorce. Some states began to grant divorces on other grounds, such as drug addiction and nonsupport. Starting in the late 1960s, states began to allow couples to divorce if they alleged that they had "irreconcilable differences." Thus arose the **no-fault divorce**—a divorce in which neither party is deemed to be at fault for the breakdown of the marriage.

NO-FAULT DIVORCE
A divorce in which neither party is deemed to be at fault for the breakdown of the marriage.

- **Today, all states allow no-fault divorces.**

Generally, there are three grounds on which no-fault divorces may be based: irreconcilable differences (the most common ground), living separately for a period of time specified by state statute (ranging from six months to

three years), and incompatibility. No-fault divorces make it practically impossible for one spouse to prevent a divorce desired by the other. Even in no-fault divorces, however, fault may be taken into consideration by the court in determining a couple's property-settlement and spousal-support arrangements.

The majority of the states permit *both* fault-based and no-fault divorces. Sometimes, a party may seek a fault-based divorce in an attempt to gain a more favorable property settlement than he or she could get in a no-fault divorce.

PETITION FOR DIVORCE
The document filed with the court to initiate divorce proceedings. The requirements governing the form and content of a divorce petition vary from state to state.

Divorce Procedures. Recall from Chapter 10 that a person initiates a civil lawsuit by filing a complaint with the appropriate court. Similarly, a person initiates a divorce action by filing a document—called a **petition for divorce**—with the appropriate state court.

The Petition for Divorce. Although the form and content of the petition vary from state to state and from case to case, generally the petition includes the following:

- The names and addresses of both spouses.
- The date and place of their marriage.
- The names and addresses of any minor children.
- The allegations made by the petitioning party as to why he or she is seeking a divorce.
- A summary of any arrangements made by the divorcing couple as to spousal support, child support, child custody, and visitation rights (usually with reference to one or more separate agreements relating to these matters).
- A prayer for relief (indicating what relief the petitioner seeks from the court).

The petition is served on the other spouse, who must file an answer to the petition within a specified number of days (such as twenty days), depending on state law. Generally, if the spouses are not in complete agreement concerning property settlement, child custody, and other issues, the court will hold a hearing to evaluate the issues and decide which partner should assume what responsibilities temporarily, until the divorce is final. A restraining order, if necessary, may be granted at this hearing. Following the hearing, unless the case is settled through mediation or negotiation, discovery is undertaken (discovery procedures were discussed in Chapter 10), a trial date is set, a trial is held, and the court orders the terms of the parties' divorce settlement.

Negotiation and Mediation. Only about 10 percent of divorces actually go to trial. Usually, the parties settle their differences themselves prior to trial—though often only after lengthy negotiations, which are facilitated by their attorneys.

Divorcing spouses increasingly use mediation to settle disagreements, and in some states, mediation in divorce cases is mandatory. A mediator is typically trained in mediation procedures and meets with the parties in the absence of lawyers. The mediator does not make decisions but tries to guide the parties into agreeing on a mutually satisfactory settlement. Although

ETHICAL CONCERN

Client Information and the Duty of Competence

Paralegals who specialize in divorce law normally have frequent contact with divorcing clients. If you are a specialist in this area, you will probably come to know some of your clients quite well. You will also probably learn all kinds of information from them—about their lives, their spouses, and other things. What do you do with this information? Do you make a note of everything a client tells you? Do you only record what you think is relevant to the case? How do you decide what is or is not relevant? Many paralegals have solved this problem by taking thorough notes during interviews and following casual conversations with clients. They may even tape-record interviews. What may seem irrelevant now may, in light of later developments, be very relevant. If you keep good notes on a case and review them as the case progresses, you can help to ensure that your supervising attorney will not breach the duty of competence.

DEVELOPING PARALEGAL SKILLS

Locating a Spouse

Jean Stemple, a client seeking a divorce, has just left the law offices of Meyers & Meyers after meeting with an attorney, Marshall Lowe, and his paralegal, Terry McCann. Jean and her husband, Bob Stemple, have been separated for almost ten years. Jean now wants a divorce because she has met someone else whom she wants to marry. Because she and Bob have been separated so long, they no longer keep in touch, and they terminated their joint bank accounts years ago. She does not know where Bob lives or works and did not keep his Social Security number. They do have one child, and Jean is entitled to child support, which she would accept.

Terry's job is to locate Jean's husband so that he can be served with divorce pleadings. He needs to find out what assets they may own jointly and what assets Bob Stemple has that could be used to pay child support. According to Jean, she saw one of Bob's friends about a year ago and the friend told her that Bob was living in Oakland, a town about thirty miles away. Terry gets the Oakland telephone directory and finds Bob Stemple's name in it. Terry conveys this information to his supervising attorney.

Because Oakland is located in the same county, the attorney asks Terry to go to the county courthouse to review the voter registration records. The records will give them Bob's full legal name, address, previous addresses, Social Security number, and date of birth. This is a convenient way to get some important, basic information about Bob—information that will help them locate Bob and learn what assets he owns.

paralegals do not assist in negotiating settlements, they often assist divorcing spouses during the the mediation process. Some paralegals are trained mediators and conduct mediation proceedings.[6]

If the parties mutually agree to a settlement concerning contested issues—such as the division of property and any debts owed, child custody, spousal and child support, and so on—the agreement is put in writing and presented to the court for its approval. The court may disapprove the agreement if it appears extremely unfair, although this is a rare occurrence.

***PRO SE* DIVORCE**
A divorce in which the parties represent themselves before the court.

Pro Se *Divorces.* Lawyers are not strictly required for a divorce proceeding. Most states permit "do-it-yourself divorces," sometimes called *pro se* divorces. In a ***pro se* divorce,** the parties represent themselves before the court. Couples can obtain the necessary forms at the local courthouse (or from "forms books"). If a significant amount of money is at stake, however, the divorcing spouses should obtain professional legal advice. Generally, if one or both of the parties did not have legal representation, the court will closely scrutinize the agreement to ensure that it is fair to both spouses.

6. See the discussion of mediation and negotiation in Chapter 7 for additional information on these two methods of dispute settlement. See also the *Featured-Guest* article in that chapter on the role of paralegals in the mediation process.

CHILD CUSTODY

When married partners with children terminate the marriage—by annulment or divorce—the spouses (or the court) must determine who will have custody of the children. As paralegals who work in the area of family law know, in many divorces the issue of child custody—the right to live with and to care for the children on an everyday basis—is the most contentious issue to be resolved. In some cases, a court may appoint a guardian *ad litem* for the child. A **guardian *ad litem*** is a person (often an attorney) appointed by the court to represent the interests of a child or a mentally incompetent person before the court.

GUARDIAN *AD LITEM*
A person appointed by the court to represent the interests of a child or a mentally incompetent person before the court.

Factors Considered in Determining Child Custody

Traditionally, the mother almost always received custody. Forty-four states have now adopted the Uniform Marriage and Divorce Act, which governs custody determinations. Mothers still usually receive custody, but courts now explicitly consider a number of factors when awarding custody. These factors include the following:

- The wishes of the child. A court generally gives more consideration to the wishes of older children.
- The nature of the relationship and emotional ties with each parent. For example, if one of the spouses has never gotten along very well with a child, that spouse will be less likely to receive custody than the other.
- The ability of each parent to provide for the child's needs and education and each parent's interest in doing so.
- The ability of each parent to provide a stable environment for the child.
- The mental and physical health of each parent.

In approving or determining custody decisions, courts may consider other factors. In some recent cases, for example, emphasis was placed on whether one parent was a smoker, because secondary smoke may damage the child's lungs. Custodial arrangements are not permanent and may be changed by a court in view of the parents' changing circumstances.

Types of Custodial Arrangements

The parent who has **legal custody** of a child has the right to make major decisions about the child's life without consulting the other parent. Often, the parent who has legal custody also has physical custody. Many states now provide for **joint custody**—shared custody—of the children of divorcing parents.

LEGAL CUSTODY
Custody that gives a parent the right to make major decisions about a child's life without consulting the other parent.

JOINT CUSTODY
The situation in which the custody of a child or children following the termination of a marriage is shared by both parents.

Joint *legal* custody means that both parents together make major decisions about the child. Some procedure, such as mediation, is usually available in the event of disagreement. In some states, including California, mediation is mandatory in child-custody disputes. Joint legal custody may also involve joint *physical* custody, in which both parents maintain a home for the child and have physical custody of the child for roughly comparable time periods. Joint physical custody usually works best if both parents live in the same school district or if the child attends a private school.

DEVELOPING PARALEGAL SKILLS

Custody Mediation

Katherine Blanchard, a paralegal, is meeting with Mr. Timmis, a client who is in the process of getting a divorce. He and Mrs. Timmis have not been able to agree on child-custody arrangements. He wants to have physical and legal custody of their children, and so does Mrs. Timmis. To avoid having their children endure a custody battle, Mr. and Mrs. Timmis have agreed to mediate their dispute. Katherine is preparing Mr. Timmis for the mediation process.

THE INFORMATION PROFILE

"Mr. Timmis, I have a form here, called a Custody Mediation Information Profile, that you need to fill out. Ms. White, your attorney, has asked that I review it with you in case you have any questions," states Katherine. Mr. Timmis examines the form and says, "This form asks for a lot of personal and confidential information. Will it be kept confidential, or could the mediator be called to testify against me?" Katherine responds, "The mediator must keep the information confidential, and our state court rules prohibit mediators from testifying in custody cases." "Will Ms. White attend the mediation with me?" asks Mr. Timmis. "She may attend, but that's a question you'll have to ask her directly," replies Katherine. "Do you have any other questions about the form?" "No, not now," responds Mr. Timmis.

THE MEDIATION PROCESS

"Now we need to talk about the mediation process," says Katherine. "The mediator will review the pleadings that you and Mrs. Timmis have filed and may contact you with questions. Mediators sometimes find it helpful to talk with the children to find out their concerns, in addition to what you and your wife want, so they may talk to your children," says Katherine. "My wife has brainwashed my kids against me. They'll say what their mother has told them to say. Is there any way to prevent the mediator from talking to my kids?" asks Mr. Timmis. "No, there isn't, but each mediator is different, and your mediator may not feel it necessary to contact your children," responds Katherine.

"We need to know if you would attend mediation with Mrs. Timmis. It is not required, but it would be helpful to the communication process if you'd meet with the mediator together. The mediator is there to try to help you avoid a custody hearing—to rearrange your family in a way that it most beneficial for your children. If you sincerely want to avoid a custody hearing, we strongly urge you to agree to meet with the mediator with Mrs. Timmis present," says Katherine. "Well, I don't know," starts Mr. Timmis. "Please," interjects Katherine, "Remember your children."

"If things get out of hand, will the mediator separate us?" asks Mr. Timmis. "Absolutely," replies Katherine. "The mediator will allow you to go back and forth, as you wish." "Okay, then I'll do it," agrees Mr. Timmis.

"After the mediation, the mediator will write up a summary of the agreement that was reached during mediation and send it to our offices and to the offices of your wife's attorney. Nothing is final until the judge signs an order, which we will prepare with your wife's attorney," says Katherine.

Visitation Rights

When parents do not have joint custody of a child, the noncustodial parent usually receives **visitation rights**—the right to have contact with the child. The parent may get to spend weekends or other time periods with the child. The times and duration of the noncustodial parent's visits are often stated in the divorce settlement.

VISITATION RIGHTS
The right of a noncustodial parent to have contact with his or her child.

In some situations, such as when the custodial parent is concerned about the noncustodial parent's behavior, the court may order supervised visitation. In this situation, a court officer or other person is appointed to supervise the visitation to ensure the child's safety. Only in extreme situations—such as when child abuse is involved or when there is a reasonable fear that the noncustodial parent may kidnap the child—will a court completely deny visitation rights to the noncustodial parent.

CHILD AND SPOUSAL SUPPORT

Regardless of the custody arrangements, a court must make some provision for **child support**—the financial support necessary to provide for the child's needs. In some situations, a divorce decree may also provide that one spouse must provide for the other spouse's support. Generally, issues relating to financial support are considered in conjunction with the division of the spouses' assets and debts (discussed in the next section).

CHILD SUPPORT
The financial support necessary to provide for a child's needs. Commonly, when a marriage is terminated, the noncustodial spouse agrees or is required by the court to make child-support payments to the custodial spouse.

Child Support

States now have official, standardized guidelines determining child-support duties. These guidelines are often percentage formulas based on parental income. Judges must follow the guidelines, unless special circumstances justify a departure or the parents agree to a different arrangement. Children with particularly expensive needs (a child with a disability, for example) may require more support than is provided for under the guidelines. Child-support orders may be revised and adjusted according to the need and ability to pay of the parent providing the child support.

It is a common misconception that if one former spouse fails to meet his or her obligations under a divorce settlement or other court order (for example, if the spouse who has custody withholds visitation rights), the other party can withhold payment of child support.

- **Child support involves a separate court order—it cannot be withheld because an ex-spouse does something that the other ex-spouse does not like.**

(What a parent can do, though, is ask the court to modify the existing order in some way.)

Because so many noncustodial parents failed to make child-support payments in the past, state laws now provide for automatic withholding of support payments from the wages of the parent. To ensure that all states enacted such laws, the federal Family Support Act required that, as of 1994, all new or modified child-support orders had to include automatic wage withholding.

Spousal Support

ALIMONY
Money paid to support a former spouse after a marriage has been terminated. The alimony may be permanent or temporary (rehabilitative).

Alimony is money paid to support a former spouse. Historically, the husband was the wage earner and was expected to pay alimony to his former wife so that she could maintain her standard of living. There are well-known cases involving wealthy entertainers, such as former NBC late-night television host Johnny Carson, who have been directed to pay their ex-wives (or, in a few cases, ex-husbands) hundreds of thousands of dollars per year in alimony. Today, the law governing alimony has changed significantly, largely because in so many couples both partners are income earners. At least one state (Texas) has prohibited court-ordered alimony payments.

Types of Alimony. Alimony may be permanent or temporary. If a court orders one spouse to pay *permanent alimony* to the other, the alimony must be paid until the former spouse receiving the alimony remarries or dies—unless the court modifies the alimony order in light of changing circumstances (for example, if the ex-spouse making the payments loses his or her job or becomes disabled). Although the law permits either spouse to receive alimony, it is almost always the wife who receives it.

A more common form of alimony is temporary alimony, or *rehabilitative alimony.* Rather than providing support payments for an indefinite period of time, rehabilitative alimony is designed to provide the ex-spouse with the education, training, or job experience necessary to support himself or herself. This form of alimony assists spouses who devoted their lives to homemaking or who left lucrative jobs or job opportunities because of the marriage. Rehabilitative support may only last for a limited period, particularly if the spouse finds a good job. In determining whether rehabilitative alimony is appropriate, a court usually considers the recipient's prospects of developing a new career. If the recipient is relatively advanced in age, for example, the court may grant permanent rather than rehabilitative alimony.

Factors Affecting Alimony Awards. In determining the amount of alimony that should be awarded, the courts usually consider the specific circumstances of the parties—their age, education, incomes, and so on. In about half the states, regardless of whether the parties seek a fault-based or no-fault divorce, courts may also consider the reason for the divorce. If one party was more responsible than the other for the breakdown of the marriage, the alimony paid by that spouse might be higher than it would otherwise have been.

Academic Degrees. Often, one spouse supports the other through college or graduate school (such as law school or medical school), and then the couple divorces. The supporting spouse may claim a share of the income subsequently earned by the supported spouse (as a lawyer or a doctor, for example). In such cases, courts have sometimes awarded payments to compensate the supporting spouse for his or her contributions to the other spouse's education. One New York court even held that an academic degree earned by the husband was marital property (property jointly owned by the couple—as will be discussed shortly).

THE LEGAL TEAM AT WORK
Fulfilling the Legal and Emotional Needs of Clients

Because of the personal nature of family law—it often touches on the most intimate aspects of human existence—legal professionals working in this area need to be particularly sensitive to the needs of clients. For many people, divorce is one of the most challenging situations they have ever faced, both financially and emotionally. Parents may be struggling with child-custody decisions or property settlements, the outcome of which will dramatically affect their lives. Battered spouses and abused children face pain and stress that cause them to need significant emotional support. Even adoptions, which generally involve happier clients, can lead to heart-wrenching problems. Adoptive parents may be deprived of their adopted child, for example, for legal or other reasons.

In all areas of legal practice, clients often require emotional support as well as legal services. In the area of family law, clients' emotional needs may be particularly acute. Paralegals, because they usually have more contact with clients than their supervising attorneys do, are in a position to both know these needs and give the needed emotional support. By performing this "hand-holding" function along with their other duties, paralegals free attorneys to concentrate on the legal aspects of the clients' cases. The teamwork approach—paralegals and attorneys working together—thus results in better serving each client's needs in every respect.

PROPERTY DIVISION

When a marriage is terminated, the property owned by the couple and their debts must be divided. **Property settlement**—the division of property at the time of marriage termination—can often be as contentious as child-custody disputes.

PROPERTY SETTLEMENT
The division of property between spouses on the termination of a marriage.

In this section, we look first at the laws governing property ownership by married couples. Then we examine some of the ways in which property and debts may be divided between the spouses when their marriage is terminated.

Property Ownership

Marital property is all property acquired during the course of a marriage (apart from inheritances and gifts made to one of the spouses). **Separate property** is property that a spouse owned before the marriage, plus inheritances and gifts acquired during the marriage. This property belongs to the spouse personally and not to the marital unit. Upon dissolution of the marriage, separate property is not divided but is retained by the owner.

MARITAL PROPERTY
All property acquired during the course of a marriage, apart from inheritances and gifts made to one or the other of the spouses.

SEPARATE PROPERTY
Property that a spouse owned before the marriage, plus inheritances and gifts acquired by the spouse during the marriage.

The ownership right in separate property may be lost during marriage, however. If the spouses combine separate property with that acquired during the marriage, the two properties may be merged into jointly held property. For example, suppose that a wife owns a lot on which the couple builds a house after their marriage. The wife has lost her separate property rights in the land. Merely renovating separately held property (sprucing up a vacation home, for instance) may transform the separate property into joint property.

Placing separate property (money) into a jointly held bank account may transform the money into joint property.

COMMUNITY PROPERTY
Defined in nine states as all property acquired during the marriage, except for inheritances or gifts received by either marital partner.

In nine states,[7] husbands and wives can hold property as community property. In those states, **community property** is all property acquired during the marriage (not including inheritances or gifts received by either party during the marriage). Property owned by either partner before the marriage remains the property of that individual, or separate property. Even if only one party supplied all of the income and assets during the marriage, the spouses share equally in the ownership of that property.

> **ETHICAL CONCERN**
>
> **Sympathy for Clients and the UPL**
>
> Suppose that you are interviewing Mrs. Jaynes, whose husband filed for divorce because he wants to marry someone else. Mrs. Jaynes was the homemaker during the fifteen years the couple was married and faces poor job prospects. She tells you that her husband has refused to give her any alimony even though he earns an excellent income. She also tells you that he will not let her have the family home because it was inherited by him from his parents. During the course of the interview, you learn, among other things, that the husband has contributed to a pension plan at his place of employment for the last fifteen years. You sympathize with the client and are tempted to tell her that she may be able to get alimony (at least rehabilitative alimony), will probably be entitled to half of the pension fund, and may even be given rights to some of the property he inherited. If you told her such things, though, you would be giving legal advice—because these statements relate to her legal rights—and you would thus be engaging in the unauthorized practice of law.

Division of Property

Although most divorcing spouses settle their financial disputes themselves, this settlement is colored by the requirements of the law. In community-property states, courts usually divide the community property equally. Judges may divide separate property as well, though, if necessary to create a fair result.

All of the other states provide for the *equitable distribution* (fair distribution) of property to the divorcing spouses. In some of these states, only the marital property is subject to distribution. In other states, all of the property owned by the couple, including separate property, may be distributed. While in most cases separate property remains with the owner, the courts exercise substantial discretion in deciding which person should receive what property. If one partner's separate property significantly affects the wealth and needs of the divorcing spouses, some of that property may be given to the other partner. Retirement benefits are generally considered to be marital property to be divided between the spouses.

In deciding how to divide property between divorcing spouses, the courts consider a number of factors, including the following:

- The duration of the marriage.
- The health of the parties.
- The individuals' occupations and vocational skills.
- The individuals' relative wealth and income.
- The standard of living during the marriage.
- The relative contributions to the marriage, both financial contributions and homemaker contributions.
- The needs and concerns of any children.
- Tax and inheritance considerations.

A typical property controversy in divorce cases concerns rights to the marital residence. If there are minor children, the house is usually given to the parent with custody of the children. It may be difficult to balance the grant of the house with other property (many families have few substantial assets other than their homes). Once the children are grown, the court may order the house to be sold and the proceeds divided to ensure that the property distribution is equitable.

7. Arizona, California, Idaho, Louisiana, Nevada, New Mexico, Texas, Washington, and Wisconsin.

DEVELOPING PARALEGAL SKILLS

Preparing for Property-settlement Negotiations

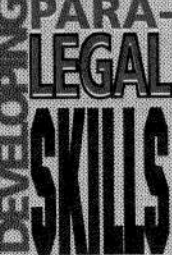

Lea, a paralegal, works for a small law firm that specializes in divorce cases. One of the firm's clients, Mrs. Clark, is seeking a divorce. Tomorrow, her husband and his attorney will meet with Mrs. Clark and Lea's supervising attorney to negotiate a property settlement. Lea is preparing a settlement-agreement checklist for the attorney to take to the settlement meeting.

Lea makes a list of all of the property owned by the Clarks, along with its value and outstanding liens on the property. She also leaves blanks—after "H" for husband and "W" for wife—so that the attorney can write down what division of property the parties agree to. Lea also includes a list of the debts owed by the Clarks. Again, she leaves blanks so that the attorney can write in how much of each debt will be paid by each spouse.

PROPERTY	VALUE	LIEN	DISPOSITION
Home	$300,000	$100,000	H _____ W _____
Cottage	$93,000	—	H _____ W _____
BMW	$32,000	$17,500	H _____ W _____
Savings Account	$7,500	—	H _____ W _____
Retirement (H)	$1,000,000	—	H _____ W _____
IRA (H)	$300,000	—	H _____ W _____
Life Insurance (H)	$800,000	—	H _____ W _____

DEBTS	AMOUNT	DISPOSITION
Visa	$7,300	H _____ W _____
MasterCard	$1,500	H _____ W _____
1995 Taxes (Due)	$3,456	H _____ W _____
1996 Taxes (Estimated)	$9,180	H _____ W _____

Lea goes over the checklist carefully to make sure that all of the Clarks' property and debts are included and that the amounts are accurate. Once she is satisfied that the checklist is accurate and complete, she takes it to her supervising attorney for review.

Division of Debts

Just as property must be divided when a marriage is dissolved, so must the married couple's debts. In most states, each spouse is liable for his or her premarital debts, and those debts are not divided between the spouses when the marriage is dissolved. This law parallels the law that each spouse has separate ownership rights in any property that he or she acquired before the marriage. In most states, one spouse is not held liable for the debts incurred solely by the other spouse (in his or her own name) during the marriage. For example, if one spouse took out a student loan, that spouse would be responsible for the debt, and the debt would not be subject to division when the marriage was dissolved.

In community-property states, however, one spouse may encumber the other with debts as well. Just as all property acquired during the marriage is

shared equally, regardless of which spouse contributed the property, so are any debts acquired during the marriage shared equally by the spouses, regardless of which spouse incurred them.

In all states, spouses are jointly responsible for debts incurred during the marriage for essential family needs, such as food, shelter, clothing, and the like. Both spouses are also jointly responsible for any taxes owed by the marital unit.

Prenuptial Agreements

PRENUPTIAL AGREEMENT
A contract formed between two persons who are contemplating marriage to provide for the disposition of property in the event of a divorce or the death of one of the persons after they have married.

Increasingly, brides and grooms are using prenuptial agreements to avoid problems over property division that may arise in the future. A **prenuptial agreement**—also known as an *antenuptial agreement* or a *premarital agreement*—is a contract between the parties that is entered into before the wedding occurs. A prenuptial agreement generally provides for the disposition of property in the event of a divorce or the death of one of the spouses. Prenuptial agreements must be in writing to be enforceable.

One typical use of the prenuptial agreement is to guarantee that any children from a previous marriage receive a certain share of the remarrying parent's estate. Such contracts also enable the parties to settle possible disagreements in advance and to attain some degree of certainty in regard to their future financial security.

Many states now normally uphold prenuptial agreements even if the agreements eliminate financial support in the event of divorce. Courts do look closely at such agreements for evidence of unfairness, though. Generally, a party must show that a prenuptial agreement was made voluntarily and without threats or unfair pressure. Courts have refused to enforce prenuptial agreements in some circumstances, including the following:

- When the agreement would so impoverish the spouse as to make him or her eligible for welfare assistance.
- When there was unfair bargaining at the time the agreement was formed (for example, when one party failed to disclose all of his or her assets to the other party).
- When one party was not represented by an attorney.
- When the agreement was entered into immediately before the marriage (which may lead a court to suspect that one of the parties was pressured into signing the agreement).

PALIMONY

PALIMONY
A nonlegal term used to describe claims made by a member of an unmarried couple to the property of the other member of the couple after the two have separated.

Palimony is a nonlegal term commonly used to describe claims made by a member of an unmarried couple after the two have separated. After cohabiting for years, a partner may claim some interest in the other's property. There is no statutory provision for such claims, and courts have been reluctant to recognize an automatic right to palimony.

If the members of an unmarried couple enter into a contract that specifies legal rights to certain property should they break up, a court may hold that the contract is valid—although courts have tended to scrutinize such

contracts closely. The California Supreme Court has held that a contract between cohabiting persons may even be implied from conduct or from unspoken understandings. Other states, such as Illinois, are unwilling to recognize palimony actions. Palimony may be especially important for homosexual couples, who are barred from marrying legally.

SUBSTANTIVE LAW CONCEPT SUMMARY

Family Law

Marriage	1. *Requirements:* a. The couple must be man and woman (no state recognizes same-gender marriages), currently unmarried, not closely related by blood, and (usually) eighteen years of age. b. The couple must obtain a marriage license from the state and may be required to take blood tests. c. In most states, the couple must have a wedding ceremony performed. d. In fourteen states, a marriage (common law marriage) may be formed solely by the consent of the parties and without a license or wedding ceremony if the parties live together and hold themselves out to the public as husband and wife. 2. *Marital duties*—A spouse has a duty to support his or her spouse and children and provide for their basic needs (food, clothing, shelter, and medical treatment). Spousal abuse is prohibited.
Parents and Children	1. *Parental rights and obligations*—Parents have the right to control and direct the upbringing of their children as they see fit. They are obligated to provide food, shelter, and other necessities for their children, as well as to make sure their children attend school. Parents are not generally liable for their children's wrongful acts. Parents may be liable if the wrongful acts result from parental negligence or, in some states, if the acts constitute intentional torts. All states prohibit child abuse by parents or anyone else. 2. *Children born out of wedlock*—A child born out of wedlock has a right to be supported by the biological father, and an unwed mother is permitted to bring a paternity suit to establish the father's identity. State laws governing inheritance by illegitimate children vary. Although an illegitimate child can generally inherit from his or her mother and the mother's relatives, the child cannot inherit from the father unless paternity is established through a court proceeding. 3. *Adoption:* a. Agency adoption—An adoption that is arranged through a state-licensed adoption agency. Agency adoptions may be confidential or, as is increasingly the case, open. In an open adoption, the prospective parents and birth parents meet at the outset and may continue to meet over time. b. Independent adoption—An adoption that is privately arranged, as when a doctor or lawyer puts prospective parents in touch with a pregnant woman who wants to give up her baby for adoption. c. Stepparent adoption—An adoption in which a stepparent adopts his or her spouse's children by a previous marriage. 4. *Artificial insemination and surrogate parenting*—Relatively recent methods for having children; may be attended by legal difficulties in terms of parental rights, especially surrogate parenting.
Marriage Termination	1. *Annulment*—The act of declaring a marriage invalid from the outset. Children of an annulled marriage are deemed legitimate, however.

SUBSTANTIVE LAW CONCEPT SUMMARY, Continued	
	2. *Divorce*—Dissolution of a marriage through a formal court proceeding. Traditionally, divorces were only granted on certain grounds, such as adultery. Today, all states have no-fault divorce laws. Many states have both no-fault and fault-based divorce laws.
Child Custody	1. *Legal custody*—A parent who takes legal custody of a child has the right to make major decisions about the child's life without consulting the other parent. 2. *Joint custody*—Exists when custody is shared by the parents; may be joint legal custody and/or joint physical custody. 3. *Visitation rights*—Rights normally given to the noncustodial parent to have physical contact with his or her child.
Child and Spousal Support	1. *Child support*—The payment made by a noncustodial parent to the custodial parent to help support a child's needs following the dissolution of a marriage. The amount of child support is determined by standardized guidelines in each state. State laws provide for automatic withholding of child-support payments from the wages of the parent. 2. *Spousal support*—Money paid by one spouse to support the other following a divorce is called alimony. Permanent alimony is rarely awarded. Sometimes, temporary (rehabilitative) alimony is awarded to help the recipient become educated or retrained so that he or she can support himself or herself.
Property Settlement	1. *Marital property*—Property acquired by a married couple during the course of their marriage (except for inheritances and gifts received separately). In community-property states, both spouses have equal ownership rights in property acquired during the marriage, regardless of which spouse acquired it. 2. *Separate property*—Property owned by a spouse prior to marriage plus inheritances and gifts received by the spouse during marriage. Separate property remains the property of the individual. Separate property may become marital property if it is joined in some way with marital property (such as through a joint bank account). In community-property states, separate property usually remains separately owned, but exceptions are made. In other states, separate property may be divided along with marital property to achieve an equitable distribution of property. Generally, courts exercise broad discretion in dividing property between divorcing spouses. 3. *Debts*—In most states, debts incurred by one spouse prior to marriage or solely in his or her own name during marriage remain that spouse's debts when a divorce occurs. In community-property states, however, debts acquired during marriage are divided between the spouses. 4. *Prenuptial agreements*—Prior to marriage, a couple may form a prenuptial (premarital) contract indicating how their property should be disposed of on divorce or on the death of one of the spouses. These agreements, if they appear to be fair and were voluntarily formed, are generally upheld by the courts.
Palimony	A nonlegal term used to describe claims made by one member of an unmarried couple to property of the other member of the couple after the two separate.

FAMILY LAW AND THE PARALEGAL

The opportunities for paralegals in the area of family law are extensive and probably will continue to be so. The United States has the highest divorce

TODAY'S PROFESSIONAL PARALEGAL

Telling the Children

Brenda Lovitt, a paralegal, receives a telephone call from Linda Robinson, a client. Linda's divorce will be filed tomorrow, and she wants to know if Brenda has any information or suggestions on how she should tell her children about the divorce. Brenda responds, "I do have a list of suggestions, Linda, and if you have a few minutes, I'd be happy to go over them with you on the phone." Linda replies, "That would be great."

HOW TO TELL THE CHILDREN

Brenda finds her list and says to Linda, "First, we suggest that both you and your husband sit down with your children and tell all of them at the same time about the divorce. If they are together, they will be able to support each other. Also, make sure you explain to them that you decided to get a divorce only after you tried all other ways to solve the problem. Remind them that they knew that you and your husband were seeing a marriage counselor to work on your problems. Let them know that, under the circumstances, obtaining a divorce is the best solution to the problem. Also, share your feelings with them. Tell them that you feel sad about the breakup because of how it will affect their everyday lives. Sharing your feelings with them will encourage them to talk about their feelings with you. Also, they will know that it's okay to feel sad.

"Make sure you stress that the divorce is not their fault—that they did nothing to bring it about. And make it clear to them that the divorce will not weaken their relationship with either you or your husband. You must tell them that it's all right for them to continue to love their father, and he should say the same about you. They also need to know that the divorce is a final decision and that you and your husband will not be getting back together.

"We suggest that you discuss the realities with them and explain to them that there will be changes. Tell them that your husband is moving out and that you may sell the house and move. They need to know that the visitation schedule has not been finalized, and perhaps you could involve them in the decisions regarding visitation times. This will help them feel included, and they won't feel so powerless."

WHEN TO TELL THE CHILDREN

Linda responds, "All those suggestions sound helpful. When should we talk to them?" Brenda answers, "Your husband knows that he will be served with the complaint on Friday. Once you know that neither of you will have a change of heart, you should tell the children right away, possibly over the weekend." Linda thanks Brenda and says, "Your advice is so helpful. I don't have anyone to talk to about this—can I call you after we've told them and let you know how it went?" Brenda responds, "I'd be happy to talk to you after you tell the children."

rate in the world (statistically, one out of every two couples who marry end up getting a divorce), and there is no indication that this high rate will decline in the future. Many paralegals work for law practices that specialize in handling divorces and legal work related to divorces, such as child-custody arrangements and property settlements.

Divorce is just one specialty within the broad area of family law, however, and paralegals often specialize in other types of family law, such as adoptions. Paralegals also work for state welfare departments, as well as for publicly sponsored legal-aid foundations and groups that assist persons of low income with family-related legal problems. Paralegals working in the area of probate and estate administration may deal with questions relating to inheritance by children. Finally, paralegals who work for general law practices are often involved in family-related matters, such as prenuptial agreements, adoptions, and divorce cases.

Because family law involves many special legal areas, paralegals working in the area of family law perform many different types of tasks. Here are some examples of the kinds of tasks you might perform if you work in this area of the law:

- Interview a client who is seeking a divorce or an annulment to obtain information about the married couple, their property and debts, the reasons for the marriage breakdown, and their children, if any.
- Draft a petition for divorce.
- File divorce-related documents with the court.
- Assist in pretrial divorce proceedings, such as by drafting interrogatories and deposition questions, summarizing deposition transcripts, and requesting documents in the possession of the opponent or a third party.
- Assist your supervising attorney in preparing a divorcing client for trial and in other trial-preparation matters.
- Assist a divorcing client in mediation procedures (or, if you are a trained mediator, conduct the mediation procedures).
- Draft a settlement agreement.
- Draft a prenuptial agreement.
- Assist in making arrangements for a private adoption.
- Research state laws governing marriage requirements, divorce procedures, child-custody arrangements, property settlements, and other matters.
- Help battered spouses obtain protection from their abusing spouses.
- Draft a restraining order.

KEY TERMS AND CONCEPTS

adoption 844
alimony 854
annulment 847
bigamy 848
child support 853
common law marriage 839
community property 856
divorce 848
emancipation 839
foster care 844
guardian *ad litem* 851
independent adoption 845
interspousal immunity 841
joint custody 851
legal custody 851
marital property 855
no-fault divorce 848
open adoption 845
palimony 858
paternity suit 843
petition for divorce 849
prenuptial agreement 858
***pro se* divorce 850**
property settlement 855
restraining order 841
separate property 855
visitation rights 853

CHAPTER SUMMARY

1. To marry, a couple must meet certain requirements imposed by state law. The couple must be man and woman (no state recognizes same-sex marriages), currently unmarried, not closely related by blood, and over a certain age (usually eighteen) unless an exception applies. The couple must obtain a marriage license from the state (county clerk's office), may be required to undergo blood tests, and (in most states) must have a wedding ceremony performed by a person authorized by the state to perform marriages. Fourteen states recognize common law marriages, which are formed solely by the consent of the parties and without a license or wedding ceremony.

2. A spouse has a duty to support his or her spouse and children. The common law doctrine of interspousal immunity has been substantially modified, but it still means that one partner may not be required to testify in court against the other spouse. Spousal abuse is illegal in all states, and many state and local governments provide shelters and other services for battered women.

3. Until a child is emancipated (free from parental control), parents have the right to direct the upbringing of the child as they see fit. Parents are also obligated to provide food, shelter, medical care, and other necessities for their children. Generally, parents are not liable for their children's wrongful acts, although they may be liable for wrongful acts that result from parental negligence (if such an act causes harm to another) and, in some states, for their children's intentional torts. All states prohibit child abuse by anyone, including parents.

4. A child born out of wedlock (outside a marriage) has the right to be supported by the biological father. Paternity may be established through a paternity suit brought by the child's mother. The inheritance rights of illegitimate children are specified in state statutes and vary from state to state. Generally, an illegitimate child can inherit from the mother and her relatives but cannot inherit from the father unless paternity is established through some legal proceeding.

5. Persons who want to be parents but cannot have children for some physical reason may adopt a child. Adoptions through an agency may be confidential or open. Independent (private) adoptions may also be arranged. A common form of adoption is the "stepparent adoption," through which a stepparent legally adopts his or her spouse's child or children from a previous marriage. All adoptions must be approved by a court, and once a couple adopts a child, the adoptive parents and the child have the same legal rights and duties as biologically related parents and children. Artificial insemination and surrogate parenting are two other options for having children. Both procedures, especially surrogate-parenting arrangements, may give rise to legal difficulties in terms of determining parental rights.

6. Marriages can be terminated by annulment or by divorce. An annulment nullifies (invalidates) the marriage. Children who were born during a marriage that was later annulled are deemed legitimate. Annulments are rarely granted. When an annulment is granted, there must be grounds for the annulment. The most common way of terminating a marriage is through a divorce—a formal proceeding that legally dissolves a marriage. Traditionally, divorces were only granted on certain grounds, such as adultery, extreme cruelty, and desertion. All states now provide for the no-fault divorce (a divorce in which neither party is deemed at fault for the breakdown of the marriage). Many states provide for both no-fault and fault-based divorce.

7. A person initiates a divorce action by filing with the appropriate court a petition for divorce, the required form and content of which vary from state to state. The other party must "answer" the petition within a certain period of time, as established by state law. Unless the case is settled before trial, discovery and other trial-related procedures are undertaken, as in all civil trials. Most divorce cases (about 90 percent) are settled through pretrial mediation and negotiation. Most states permit parties to represent themselves in divorce proceedings.

8. Married couples with children must decide (or the court will decide for them) which parent will have custody of the children following the divorce. Courts consider a number of factors in deciding (or approving) child-custody arrangements. Generally, the court's decision must be in "the best interests of the child." Increasingly, states are providing for the parents' joint custody of the children. If just one parent is given custody, the noncustodial parent normally is allowed visitation rights in all but extreme cases (involving child abuse or the possibility of parental kidnapping, for example).

9. States now have standardized guidelines for determining the amount of child support that should be paid by the noncustodial parent. Usually, the guidelines are percentage formulas based on parental income. State laws also now provide for automatic withholding of child-support payments from the wages of the parent. Spousal support (alimony) used to be awarded frequently by the courts, because women were usually homemakers and had few job prospects after a divorce. Today, because husbands and wives are often both income earners, alimony is given far less frequently and often only on a temporary (rehabilitative) basis—to support a spouse's education or retraining until the spouse is able to support himself or herself.

10. On the termination of a marriage, the couple's property and debts must be divided. The marital property to be divided consists of property acquired during the marriage apart from inheritances and gifts. Property owned by either spouse prior to marriage, as well as any gifts or inheritances received during the marriage, remains separate property—property solely owned by only that spouse. Separate property may become jointly owned, however, if it is joined in some way (such as through a joint bank account) with marital property. In most states, debts incurred by a spouse prior to the marriage or solely in his or her own name during the marriage remain that spouse's debts. In community-property states, however, debts acquired during the marriage are subject to division between the couple at the time of a divorce. Generally, courts seek to obtain an "equitable distribution" of property and may, if it is deemed fair and appropriate, divide separate property as well as marital property.

11. Increasingly, couples are forming prenuptial (premarital) agreements, or contracts, that provide for the disposition of their property should they divorce or should one of the spouses die. These agreements, although closely scrutinized by the courts, are usually upheld unless there is evidence that they are unfair—if they were based on incomplete disclosures, for example, or were made under duress or without legal representation.

12. *Palimony* is a term commonly used to describe claims made by a member of an unmarried couple to certain property of the other member of the couple after the two have separated. State statutes do not provide for palimony, and most courts are reluctant to recognize a right to palimony in the absence of a contractual agreement supporting such a claim.

QUESTIONS FOR REVIEW

1. What are the legal requirements for marriage? What is a common law marriage? What are the legal obligations of married partners toward each other?

2. What are the rights and duties of parents in respect to their children? May parents be held liable for their children's wrongful acts? To what extent may a parent physically punish a child?

3. What are the legal obligations of parents to children born out of wedlock? What are the legal obligations of parents to children they adopt? What are the requirements for a valid adoption?

4. How are parental rights determined in cases involving artificial insemination and surrogate parenting?

5. List and briefly describe the legal methods for terminating a marriage. What legal procedures are involved in a divorce action?

6. List and briefly describe the various types of child-custody arrangements. What factors are considered in determining which parent is awarded custody of minor children? What are visitation rights?

7. Who pays child support, and how is the amount of child support determined? Is automatic wage withholding for child-support payments allowed? What is alimony? On what basis is it awarded? What types of alimony may be awarded?

8. On the termination of a marriage, how are a couple's property and debts divided? What is separate property? What is community property?

9. What is a prenuptial agreement? Under what circumstances have courts refused to enforce prenuptial agreements?

10. What is palimony? Is it recognized in many states? What impact may palimony have on same-gender couples?

ETHICAL QUESTIONS

1. During the course of their twenty-five-year marriage, Mr. and Mrs. Jones have had their family attorney, Mr. Shapiro, prepare their wills, handle their real-estate purchases, and assist them with other

legal matters. On Monday, Mrs. Jones calls Mr. Shapiro and makes an appointment. She explains that she wants to file a divorce action against Mr. Jones. On Wednesday, Mr. Jones calls Mr. Shapiro. He wants to make an appointment to discuss filing a divorce action against Mrs. Jones. May the attorney, Mr. Shapiro, represent both Mr. Jones and Mrs. Jones in the divorce action?

2. Brenda Bates, a paralegal, works for a large, prestigious law firm. Today, Brenda and her supervising attorney, Michael Leason, have an initial client interview with the mayor's wife. During the interview, they learn that the the mayor's wife wants to initiate divorce proceedings against her husband. The mayor's wife shows them evidence, in the form of photographs, of the mayor's infidelity. In addition, they learn that the mayor cheats not only on his wife but also on his tax returns. When Brenda returns home after a busy day at the office, she turns on the television. The lead story is about the mayor and all of the charitable acts that he has performed over the past several months. Brenda starts to tell her husband what she learned about the mayor today from the mayor's wife. Brenda stops mid-sentence, realizing that she has violated an important ethical duty. What ethical duty has she violated?

PRACTICE QUESTIONS AND ASSIGNMENTS

1. Which of the following are required under most state laws for marriage?

a. The couple must be man and woman.
b. The couple must be unmarried.
c. The couple must not be closely related by blood.
d. The couple must obtain a marriage license.
e. A wedding ceremony must be performed by a member of the clergy.
f. The wedding must result in a common law marriage.

2. Which of the following are the currently recognized grounds for divorce:

a. Adultery.
b. Cruelty.
c. Desertion.
d. No-fault.

3. Which of the following are legally recognized methods for dividing marital property at the time of a divorce:

a. Equitable distribution.
b. Community property.
c. Prenuptial agreement.
d. Palimony.

QUESTIONS FOR CRITICAL ANALYSIS

1. In 1988, in *In Re Baby M,* the New Jersey Supreme Court faced a difficult issue: whether a surrogate-parenting contract should be enforced. Make a list of the pros and cons of enforcing such a contract.

2. Until the 1960s, to obtain a divorce, a person had to allege grounds for divorce, such as adultery, desertion, cruelty, or abuse. Today, all states allow no-fault divorces. Since the 1960s, the divorce rate has continually risen. It has now reached 50 percent—in other words, today, one out of every two marriages ends in divorce. Explain how no-fault divorce laws might affect the divorce rate. What other social changes in the past three decades might have contributed to the increase in the divorce rate?

3. Parents are increasingly being awarded joint legal custody and joint physical custody of their children. What are some of the advantages of joint custody? Are there any disadvantages?

ROLE-PLAYING EXERCISES

1. Using the facts from this chapter's *Today's Professional Paralegal* feature, role-play the conversation between the paralegal, Brenda Lovitt, and the client, Linda Robinson, in which Brenda advises Linda on how to tell her children about her upcoming divorce. The students playing the role of Brenda should be emotionally supportive but professional. The students playing the role of Linda should ask questions about the advice that Brenda gives.

2. Using the facts from the *Developing Paralegal Skills* feature entitled "Custody Mediation," role-play the conversation between the paralegal, Katherine Blanchard, and the client, Mr. Timmis, in which Katherine explains the mediation process to Mr. Timmis and tries to persuade him to attend the mediation proceedings with his wife. The students playing the role of Katherine should use persuasive tactics, gently reminding Mr. Timmis that he is attempting custody mediation for the benefit of his children and to avoid a custody hearing. The students playing the role of Mr. Timmis should oppose the idea of attending mediation with Mrs. Timmis but should eventually give in for the sake of the children.

PROJECTS

1. Contact your local divorce court and find out when *pro se* divorces are held, as well as when a divorce trial is scheduled to be held. Try to attend and observe a portion of both a *pro se* divorce and a divorce trial. Write a one-page, double-spaced, typewritten paper summarizing your experience.

2. Review your state's statutes to determine how marital property is distributed at the time of a divorce. Write a one-page, double-spaced, typewritten paper summarizing your findings.

3. Review your state's statutes to determine which of these types of adoptions are allowed by state law: agency adoptions, independent (privately arranged) adoptions, and stepparent adoptions. Write a memo explaining which options are allowed in your state.

4. Research your state's statutory and case law to determine whether surrogate-parenting contracts are enforceable in your state. Prepare a memorandum of law explaining your state's position on this issue.

5. Research your state's law governing the parental rights of husbands in cases involving artificial insemination. What procedure must the husband pursue if he wants to be considered the legal father of the child? Prepare a legal memorandum addressing this issue.

ANNOTATED SELECTED READINGS

ANDRESS, SALLY. "Professional Responsibility: Avoiding Allegations of Misconduct Is Crucial to Your Career." *Legal Assistant Today,* November/December 1994. An article that gives good advice on how to avoid the ethical pitfalls common to family law. The pitfalls concern the unauthorized practice of law, the duty of confidentiality, and conflict of interest.

ANDRESS, SALLY. "Qualified Medical Support Orders." *Legal Assistant Today,* March/April 1995. An informative article that discusses the federal law requiring group health-plan administrators to give medical support to dependent children when ordered to do so by the courts.

MASSEY, LINDI. "In a Sea of Sharks, Fend for Yourself." *Legal Assistant Today,* July/August 1993. An article instructing family-law paralegals and attorneys how to prevent mistakes and problems in court and in related legal proceedings. It also gives some suggestions on what to do when mistakes occur.

MURPHY, JANE C. "Access to Legal Remedies: The Crisis in Family Law." *Brigham Young University Journal of*

Public Law, January 1993. An interesting article that discusses how people with moderate and low incomes lack access to the courts for family-law purposes. The article offers suggestions on what can be done to resolve this problem, including instituting procedural reforms, "relaxing barriers to non-attorney advice and representation," and providing more educational programs to assist people in representing themselves.

WEST, RICHARD. "Putting the Family Back in Family Law Practice: The Small Firm or Solo Practitioner." *Florida Bar Journal,* January 1994. A fascinating review of the family-law practice of Richard Custureri in Ocala, Florida. Custureri's practice is family-oriented. Office organization and services are geared toward the families of not only the clients but also the office staff, many of whom are paralegals.

23

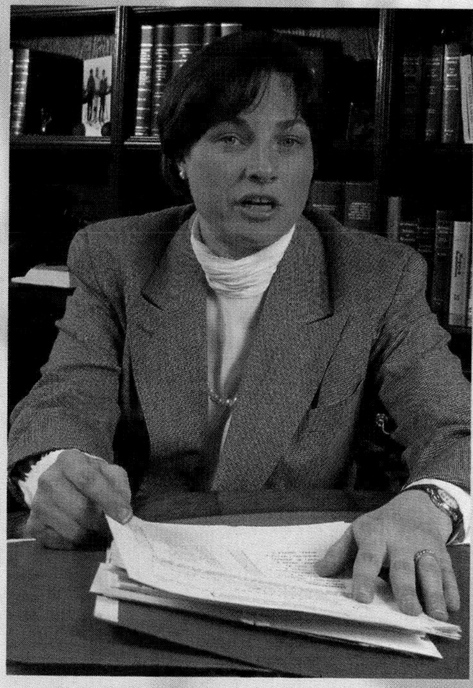

WILLS, TRUSTS, AND ESTATES

Chapter Objectives

After completing this chapter, you will know:

- **What laws govern wills and what requirements must typically be met for a will to be valid.**
- **The types and purposes of various clauses that are usually included in wills.**
- **What a trust is and what different types of trusts can be established.**
- **How property is transferred to heirs and next of kin when a person dies without having made a valid will.**
- **Some of the tasks involved in administering a deceased person's estate.**

Chapter Outline

INTRODUCTION

As you have read elsewhere in this book, there are many forms of property in which people can have ownership rights. What happens to this property and those ownership rights when the property owner dies? The law requires that *someone* own private property. Therefore, upon death, a person's property must be transferred to others.

Many people make plans while they are living regarding how and to whom their property should be transferred when they die. You learned in Chapter 2 that many attorneys and paralegals specialize in assisting clients with this planning process, which is referred to as *estate planning.* One important task involved in estate planning is preparing a will. Other tasks may include establishing a trust or arranging for property to be transferred in other ways, such as by gift or joint ownership.

What happens if a person dies without having made a will? In that situation, the decedent (the person who died) is said to have died **intestate**, and state **intestacy laws** govern the distribution of the property among heirs or next of kin. If no heirs or kin can be found, the property **escheats** (title is transferred to the state).

INTESTATE
The condition of having died without having created a valid will.

INTESTACY LAWS
State laws determining the division and descent of the property of one who dies intestate (without a will).

ESCHEAT
The transfer of property to the state when the owner of the property dies without heirs.

In this chapter, you will learn about wills and other estate-planning devices, particularly trusts. You will also learn how property is distributed under intestacy laws. Additionally, you will read about the kinds of tasks that are typically involved in administering the estate of a deceased person.

WILLS

A *will* is the final declaration of how a person wishes to have his or her property disposed of after death. A will is referred to as a *testamentary disposition* of property, and one who dies after having made a valid will is said to have died **testate**.

TESTATE
Having died with a valid will.

A will is a formal instrument, and paralegals who draft wills must be especially careful to follow exactly the appropriate state statutes. The reasoning behind such a strict requirement is obvious. A will becomes effective only after the maker's death. No attempts to modify it after the death of the maker are allowed, because the court cannot ask the maker to confirm the attempted modifications.

As already mentioned, one of the purposes of a will is to transfer property on death. A will, though, can serve other purposes as well. It can appoint a guardian for minor children or incapacitated adults. It can also appoint a personal representative to settle the affairs of the deceased.

Laws Governing Wills

Laws governing wills come into play when a will is probated. As you learned in Chapter 2, to probate (prove) a will means to establish its validity and to carry the administration of the estate through a special court, which is usually called a probate court but may be called the surrogate court or orphan's court. Statutes governing the requirements for a valid will and probate procedures vary from state to state.

In 1969, the American Bar Association and the National Conference of Commissioners on Uniform State Laws approved the Uniform Probate Code (UPC) for adoption by the states. The UPC codifies general principles and procedures for the resolution of conflicts in settling estates and relaxes some of the requirements for a valid will contained in earlier state laws. Fifteen states have adopted the UPC in full, and nearly all of the other states have enacted some part or section of the UPC and incorporated it into their own probate codes. Because the UPC has affected the probate law in virtually all of the states, references to its provisions will be included in the remainder of this chapter. Nonetheless, the laws do vary from state to state. Therefore, as a paralegal, you should always check the particular laws of the state involved.

The Terminology of Wills

A person who makes out a will is known as a **testator** (from the Latin word *testari*, "to make a will"). When a person dies, a *personal representative* settles the affairs of the deceased. An **executor** is a personal representative named in a will. An **administrator** is a personal representative appointed by the court for a decedent who has died without a will, who has failed to name an executor in the will, who has named an executor lacking the capacity to serve, or who has written a will that the court refuses to admit to probate. A gift of real estate by will is generally called a **devise**, and a gift of personal property under a will is called a **bequest**, or **legacy**. A **devisee** is a person who receives a devise. A **legatee** is a person who receives a legacy.

TESTATOR
One who makes and executes a will.

EXECUTOR
A person appointed by a testator to see that the testator's will is administered appropriately.

ADMINISTRATOR
One who is appointed by a court to handle the probate of a person's estate if that person dies intestate (without a will).

DEVISE
A gift of real property by will.

BEQUEST
A gift by will of personal property (from the verb *bequeath*).

LEGACY
A gift of personal property by will.

DEVISEE
A person who inherits real property under a will.

LEGATEE
A person who inherits personal property under a will.

Gifts by Will

Gifts by will can be specific, general, or residuary. A *specific* devise or bequest (legacy) describes particular property (such as "Eastwood estate" or "my gold pocket watch") that can be distinguished from all the rest of the testator's property. A *general* devise or bequest (legacy) uses less restrictive terminology. For example, "I devise all my lands" is a general devise. A general bequest often specifies a sum of money instead of a particular item of property, such as a watch or an automobile. For example, "I give to my nephew, James, $30,000" is a general bequest.

On occasion, assets are insufficient to pay in full all of the bequests provided for in a will, as well as the taxes, debts, and expenses of administering the estate. When this happens, an *abatement*—by which the legatees receive reduced benefits—takes place. For example, suppose that a client's will leaves "$25,000 each to my children, Sandra and Jacob." Upon the client's death, only $10,000 is available to honor these bequests. By abatement, each child will receive $5,000. If bequests are more complicated, abatement may be more complicated. The testator's intent, as expressed in the will, controls.

If the legatee dies prior to the death of the testator or before the legacy is payable, a *lapsed legacy* exists. At common law, such a legacy failed. Today, under state *antilapse statutes*, a legacy may not lapse if the legatee is in a certain blood relationship to the testator—is the testator's child, grandchild, brother, or sister, for example—and if the legatee left a child or other surviving heir. In this case, instead of lapsing, the legacy passes to the child or other surviving heir.

Sometimes a will provides that any assets remaining after specific gifts have been made and debts paid—called the *residuum*—are to be distributed through a *residuary* clause. A residuary provision is used because the exact amount to be distributed cannot be determined until all other gifts and payouts are made. A residuary clause can pose problems, however, when the will does not specifically name the beneficiaries to receive the residuum. In such a situation, if the court cannot determine the testator's intent, the residuum passes according to state laws of intestacy (discussed later in this chapter).

Requirements for a Valid Will

A will must comply with statutory formalities. Statutory requirements for a valid will are designed to ensure that the testator understood his or her actions at the time the will was made. These formalities are intended to help prevent fraud. Unless they are followed, the will is declared *void* (nonexistent), and the decedent's property is distributed according to state intestacy laws. As mentioned earlier, state laws governing wills are not uniform. Most states, however, uphold the basic requirements discussed below for executing a will.

TESTAMENTARY CAPACITY
The legal capacity to make a valid will. Generally, testamentary capacity exists if the testator is of age and of sound legal mind at the time the will is made.

Testamentary Capacity. Not everyone who owns property necessarily qualifies to make a valid disposition of that property by will. **Testamentary capacity** exists when the testator is of legal age and sound mind *at the time the will is made.* The legal age for executing a will varies, but in most states and under the UPC, the minimum age is eighteen years. Thus, a will of a twenty-one-year-old decedent written when the person was sixteen is invalid if, under state law, the legal age for executing a will is eighteen.

The concept of *sound mind* refers to the testator's ability to formulate and comprehend a personal plan for the disposition of property. Further, a testator must intend the document to be his or her will. Courts have grappled with the requirement of sound mind for a long time, and their decisions have been inconsistent. Mental incapacity is a highly subjective matter and thus is not easily measured. The general test for testamentary capacity requires that the following conditions be met:

- The testator must comprehend and remember the "natural objects of his or her bounty" (usually family members and persons for whom the testator has affection).
- The testator must comprehend the kind and character of the property being distributed.
- The testator must understand and formulate a plan for disposing of the property.

Less mental ability is required to make a will than to manage one's own business affairs or to enter into a contract. Thus, a testator may be feeble, aged, eccentric, or offensive in behavior and still possess testamentary capacity. Moreover, a person can be judged to be mentally incompetent or have delusions about certain subjects and yet, during lucid moments, still be of sound mind and make a valid will.

DEVELOPING PARALEGAL SKILLS

Evaluating Testamentary Capacity

Marie's eighty-seven-year-old mother, Sophie Smithers, wants to change her will, so Marie brings Sophie to the law firm of Smith & Barney. Marie and Sophie meet with Tom Alcott, a paralegal in the firm. Tom is to take down the information from Sophie and communicate the changes that Sophie wants made to the attorney. Tom specializes in probate work and is trained to check clients for testamentary capacity. When Tom hears Sophie repeating her statements about three minutes after she originally makes them, he begins to ask her questions to determine whether she has testamentary capacity.

Tom asks Sophie how many family members she has, how many of them are named in her existing will, and how many other people are named in the will. Sophie tells Tom that she has three children (in fact, she has four) and that she has no grandchildren (in fact, she has seven). She also tells Tom that no one else is named in her will (in fact, her brother and sister are both included in the will). Sophie wants to change her will to leave her cottage to Marie because she believes that her other children are not interested in it. (In fact, Tom knows that all of her children have expressed an interest in receiving their shares of the cottage.) Sophie doesn't know whether she wants to dispose of the cottage upon her death or while she is still living.

Tom explains to Marie and Sophie that he will discuss Sophie's wishes with his supervising attorney. The attorney will then contact Marie and Sophie about the matter. After Marie and Sophie have left the office, Tom prepares a memo to his supervising attorney describing his impressions of Sophie, particularly Sophie's apparent lack of testamentary capacity. He includes in the memo the questions he asked Sophie during the interview and Sophie's answers.

Writing Requirements. Generally, a will must be in writing. The writing itself can be informal as long as it substantially complies with statutory requirements. In some states, a will can be handwritten in crayon or ink. It can be written on a sheet or scrap of paper, on a paper bag, or on a piece of cloth. A will that is completely in the handwriting of the testator is called a **holographic will** (sometimes referred to as an *olographic will*).

HOLOGRAPHIC WILL
A will written entirely in the maker's handwriting and usually not witnessed.

A will also can refer to a written memorandum that itself is not a will but that contains information necessary to carry out the will. For example, Geraldine's will provides that a certain sum of money be divided among a group of charities named in a written memorandum that Geraldine gave to the trustee the day the will was signed. The memorandum will be "incorporated by reference" into the will only if it was in existence when the will was executed (signed) and if it is sufficiently described so that it can be identified.

In some cases, oral wills are found valid. **Noncupative wills** are oral wills made before witnesses. Such wills are not permitted in most states. Even when authorized by statute, a nuncupative will is valid only if made during the last illness or in expectation of the imminent death of the testator, and usually before at least three witnesses. Nuncupative wills are sometimes

NUNCUPATIVE WILL
An oral will (often called a deathbed will) made before witnesses; usually limited to transfers of personal property.

referred to as "deathbed wills." Statutes frequently permit soldiers and sailors to make nuncupative wills when on active duty. In most of the states that do permit nuncupative wills, only personal property may pass in this way, and some of these states set value limits on the personal property that can be transferred.

Signature Requirements. It is a fundamental requirement in almost all jurisdictions that the testator's signature be made with the intent to validate the will. The signature need not be at the end of the will, as long as it appears somewhere in the body of the will. What kind of writing or mark constitutes a signature varies from state to state. Initials, Xs and other marks, and words like "Mom" have all been upheld as valid when it was shown that the testators *intended* them to be signatures.

Witness Requirements. A will must be witnessed by two, and sometimes three, persons. The number of witnesses, their qualifications, and the manner in which the witnessing must be done are generally set out in a state's statute governing wills. A state law may require that a witness be disinterested—that is, not a beneficiary under the will. The UPC, however, provides that a will is valid even if it is witnessed by an interested party. There are no age requirements for witnesses, but they must be mentally competent.

The purpose of requiring a will to be witnessed is to verify that the testator actually executed the will and had the requisite intent and capacity to do so at the time. A witness does not have to read the contents of the will.

Usually, the testator and the witnesses must all sign in the sight or the presence of one another, but the UPC deems it sufficient if the testator acknowledges his or her signature to the witnesses. The UPC thus does not require all parties to sign in the presence of one another.

Publication Requirements. The "publication" of a will is an oral declaration by the maker to the witnesses that the document they are about to sign is his or her "last will and testament." Publication is becoming an unnecessary formality in most states, and it is not required under the UPC.

Clauses Contained in a Will

Every will is a unique document because every person making a will is unique. Thus, the specific contents of a will may vary substantially from one client to another. Typically, though, a will contains the clauses discussed below.

EXORDIUM CLAUSE
The opening, or introductory, clause in a will stating the name of the testator, where the testator resides, the names of the testator's spouse and children, the fact that the document is the testator's last will, and that the document revokes all other wills or codicils previously made by the testator.

***Exordium* Clause.** Usually, a will opens with an ***exordium* clause**. (*Exordium* is a Latin term that means the introduction or beginning of a document.) In this introductory clause, the testator (1) states his or her name and address, (2) declares that the document is his or her "last will and testament," (3) gives the names of his or her spouse and children, and (4) makes a statement to the effect that he or she revokes all prior wills (revocation of wills will be discussed shortly). A typical *exordium* clause, might read as follows:

I, David R. Levine, of the City of Southridge, County of Los Angeles, State of California, do hereby make, publish, and declare this instrument to be my last will and testament and revoke all other wills and codicils previously made by me.

I am married to Louise T. Levine and have two children:

Naomi Jean, born August 30, 1982
Bradley Richard, born September 13, 1984

Clauses Providing for the Disposition of Property. Following the exordium clause may be several clauses that indicate who will receive what under the will.

Devises and Legacies. Usually, the first clauses provide for specific devises and legacies. The following sample clauses provide for a specific devise and a specific legacy, respectively:

I give whatever interest I have in the family home at 3906 Latham Avenue, Southridge, California, to my wife, Louise T. Levine. She is to assume the mortgage. If she predeceases me, then the family home shall be given equally to my two children, or their issue by right of representation, to be divided equally between them. They shall assume any mortgage on the property equally.

I give my stamp collection to my nephew, Jason T. Cassidy.

Often, a testator will incorporate by reference a list (in the testator's handwriting or signed by the testator) of personal property and household possessions, indicating who should receive what property—such as an automobile, furniture, jewelry, and so on.

Then, clauses providing for general devises ("I give all my lands to my son, Eric') and legacies ("I give $10,000 to my sister, Patricia R. Levine") may appear.

Residuary Clauses. Finally, a residuary clause disposes of all of the other assets of the testator. A sample residuary clause might begin as follows:

I give all the rest of my estate of whatever kind and whereever situated to my wife, Louise T. Levine. If she predeceases me, then I give these assets to my children and to the descendants of any deceased children. . . .

The residuary clause usually also provides for the distribution of the testator's assets if no spouse, children, or descendants of children survive the testator.

Limitations on a Testator's Disposition of Property. The law imposes certain limitations on the way a person can dispose of property in a will. For example, a married person who makes a will generally cannot avoid leaving a certain portion of the estate to the surviving spouse. In most states, this is called a "forced share," or "widow's (or widower's) share," and it is often one-third of the estate or an amount equal to a spouse's share under intestacy laws. Children can be excluded as beneficiaries under a will, but if a child is to be excluded, the testator should clearly state that intention in the will.

If the testator ignores blood relatives and names as a beneficiary a nonrelative who is in constant close contact and in a position to influence the making of the will, undue influence may be inferred by the court. When it

DEVELOPING PARALEGAL SKILLS

Drafting a Checklist for a Will

Michael Mann works as a paralegal for a general-practice law firm. He frequently finds himself preparing wills. Because it is such an important job and there is so much information to obtain, Michael has decided to create a will-drafting checklist. He begins by collecting from the files copies of wills that his supervising attorney has prepared for clients over the past six months. Michael reads through the various wills and categorizes the information contained in them. His final checklist contains the following entries:

1. *Client:* Subentries for the client's name, address, telephone number, Social Security number, date of birth, marital status, occupation/position, and employer's name, address, and telephone number.
2. *Client's spouse:* Subentries for the spouse's name, Social Security number, date of birth, and date of marriage.
3. *Client's children:* Subentries for the name, address, sex, and date of birth for each child.
4. *Additional beneficiaries:* Subentries for the name, address, and relationship of possible additional beneficiaries.
5. *Personal representative:* Subentries for the name, address, and relationship of the personal representative, plus whether bond will be required.
6. *Guardian and alternative guardian:* Name, address, and relationship for each.
7. *Trustee and alternative trustee:* Name, address, and relationship for each, plus whether bond will be required.
8. *Property and disposition:* Subentries for assets, debts, specific bequests, general bequests, charitable contributions, trusts, and miscellaneous.

can be shown that the decedent's plan of distribution was the result of improper pressure by another person that had the effect of overriding the maker's intent, the will is declared invalid. For example, if a nurse or friend who was caring for the deceased at the time of death was named as beneficiary to the exclusion of all family members, the validity of the will might well be challenged on the basis of undue influence.

Clause Appointing Fiduciaries. Normally, following the clauses providing for the disposition of the testator's property, the will contains a clause appointing fiduciaries. As discussed earlier in this text, a *fiduciary* is a person who has a duty to act primarily for another's benefit. In the context of wills, the term means one who has a duty to act on behalf of the decedent or persons designated by the decedent.

In this clause, the testator appoints a personal representative, or executor, to act as the testator's representative on his or her death. A personal representative is required to post a bond to ensure honest and faithful performance. Usually, the bond exceeds the estimated value of the personal estate of the decedent. Under most state statutes, the will can specify that the personal representative need not post a bond. The clause appointing a personal

representative might state "I appoint my friend Arthur A. Robe of 3910 Latham Avenue, Southridge, California, to serve as my personal representative. He is to serve without bond." The testator may also designate in this clause a guardian for minor children or a trustee.

***Testimonium* Clause.** At the end of the will, a ***testimonium* clause**, or signature clause, indicates the date on which the will was signed by the testator ("This will was signed by me on the 13th day of February, 1996, at Southridge, California"). Following this clause, the testator's signature appears.

Attestation Clause. Typically, the *testimonium* clause is followed by an **attestation clause**, which indicates the identity of the testator and the date on which the will was signed by the witnesses. If an attestation clause is included, it may also indicate some specific requirement of witnesses, which will serve as a reminder when the will is executed and attested. For example, the following clause includes the phrase "in the presence of each other":

> This last will and testament of David R. Levine, personally known to us, at his request and in his presence of each other, we have signed as witnesses this 13th day of February, 1996.

Other Clauses. Wills may include a number of other types of provisions as well. For example, a testator may want to include in the will a provision relating to funeral or burial arrangements or instructions relating to payment of debts and taxes. Often, a married person's will, if the person's spouse is a beneficiary under the will, contains a clause specifying who would be designated as the "survivor" if both spouses died simultaneously. Such a clause is sometimes called a "common-disaster clause." Most will "forms"—in books or on diskette—contain samples of the various types of clauses that may be included in wills.

Revocation of a Will

An executed last will and testament is not necessarily final. A testator can **revoke** (annul or make void) his or her will at any time during his or her lifetime. Wills can also be revoked by operation of law. Revocation (the act of revoking) can be partial or complete, and it must follow certain strict formalities.

Revocation by the Maker. The maker can revoke an executed will in either of two ways—by a physical act or by another writing.

Revocation by Physical Act. The testator may revoke a will by intentionally burning, tearing, canceling, obliterating, or destroying it or by having someone else do so in the presence of the maker and at the maker's direction. The destruction cannot be inadvertent, or accidental. The maker's *intent* to revoke the will must be shown. When a will has been burned or torn accidentally, it is normally recommended that the maker have a new document created so that it will not falsely appear that the maker intended to revoke the will. When a state statute prescribes the exact methods for

ETHICAL CONCERN

Wills and Paralegal Supervision

It goes without saying that wills must accurately reflect the testator's wishes and that special care must be exercised in preparing a client's will. After all, unless the will is modified or revoked, it is indeed the "final word" on how the testator intends his or her property to be distributed. You will rest easier if you make sure that your supervising attorney reviews carefully any will that you draft, any subsequent modifications that are made, and particularly the document in its final form. Attorneys have a duty to supervise paralegal work. In regard to wills, as a paralegal you should hold your supervising attorney to this duty.

***TESTIMONIUM* CLAUSE**
A clause in a will, just before the testator's signature, that indicates the date on which the will was signed by the testator.

ATTESTATION CLAUSE
A clause in a will, just following the testator's signature and just before the witnesses' signatures, indicating the identity of the testator, the date on which the will was signed by the witnesses, and possibly other information relating to witness requirements.

REVOKE
Annul, or make void. In the context of wills, to nullify a part or all of a will by an act of the maker (tearing up the will, for example, or creating a codicil or second will) or by operation of law (due to a subsequent marriage, divorce or annulment, or the birth of a child).

revoking a will by physical act, those are the only methods by which the will can be revoked by physical act.

In some states, partial revocation by physical act of the maker is recognized. Thus, those portions of a will lined out or torn away are dropped, and the remaining parts of the will are valid. Under no circumstances, however, can a provision be crossed out and an additional or substitute provision be written in. Such altered portions require reexecution (re-signing) and reattestation (rewitnessing).

Revocation by Another Writing. A maker can also revoke a will in writing, either by executing a codicil to the will or by making a second will. A **codicil** is a written instrument separate from the will that amends or revokes provisions in the will or that revokes the entire will. A codicil eliminates the necessity of redrafting an entire will merely to add to it or amend it. The codicil must refer expressly to the will and must be executed with the same formalities that were required for the will. In effect, a codicil updates a will, because the will is "incorporated by reference" into the codicil.

A *second will* can be executed that may or may not revoke the first or a prior will, depending on the language used. The second will must use specific language such as "This will hereby revokes all prior wills." If the second will is otherwise valid and properly executed, it will revoke all prior wills. If the express *declaration of revocation* is missing, then both wills are read together. If any of the dispositions made in the second will are inconsistent with the prior will, the second will controls.

Revocation by Operation of Law. Revocation by operation of law occurs when marriage, divorce or annulment, or the birth of children takes place after a will has been executed.

Marriage. Generally, marriage revokes a will written before the marriage. In most states, when a testator marries after executing a will that does not include the new spouse, the spouse upon the testator's death can receive the amount that he or she would have taken had the testator died intestate (this amount will be discussed later in this chapter, in the section on intestacy laws). In effect, this revokes the will to the extent of providing the spouse with an intestate share. The rest of the estate is passed under the will. If, however, omission of a new spouse from the existing will is intentional or the spouse is otherwise provided for (by transfer of property outside of the will, for example), the omitted spouse will not be given an intestate share.

Divorce or Annulment. At common law and under the UPC, divorce does not necessarily revoke the *entire* will. A divorce or an annulment occurring after a will has been executed, however, revokes those dispositions of property made under the will to the former spouse.

Children Born after a Will Has Been Executed. If a child is born after a will has been executed and if it appears that the testator would have made a provision for the child, then the child is entitled to receive whatever portion of the estate he or she is allowed under state intestacy laws. Most state

---

Ethical Concern

Clarifying Instructions

Attorneys and paralegals are usually busy. Often, attorneys give instructions to paralegals quickly and briefly, assuming that the instructions are understood as intended. Problems arise if the instructions are not, in fact, clear to the paralegal. If you ever find yourself in this position, make sure that the instructions are made clear. For example, suppose that your supervising attorney asks you to draft a will for a client, using "Laura Dunn's" will as a model. The name doesn't ring a bell with you, but you assume that you can find that will. The attorney then leaves the office for the rest of the day, and you spend a miserable hour or so searching in vain through the files and the master client list for "Laura Dunn." The next morning, you explain the problem to the attorney and learn that, in fact, Laura Dunn is the married name of a client whose files are under her maiden name, Laura Jacobson. You are upset, the attorney is displeased, and the signing of the will is delayed—all of which could have been avoided if you had asked the attorney "Who is Laura Dunn?" when he was giving you instructions.

Codicil
A written supplement or modification to a will. Codicils must be executed with the same formalities as a will.

intestacy laws allow a child to receive some portion of the estate if no provision is made in a will—unless it appears from the terms of the will that the testator intended to disinherit the child. Under the UPC, the rule is the same. The effect is to partially revoke the parent's will.

Probate versus Nonprobate

Upon the death of the testator, his or her will is probated. Attorneys and paralegals often become involved in the probate process. Each state has special laws governing the probate process, and paralegals working in this area need to become familiar with the relevant state requirements. Typically, the procedure varies depending on the size of the decedent's estate.

Informal Probate Proceedings. For smaller estates, most state statutes provide for the distribution of assets without formal probate proceedings. Faster and less expensive methods are then used. For example, property can be transferred by affidavit (a written statement taken before a person who has authority to affirm it), and problems or questions can be handled during an administrative hearing. In addition, some state statutes provide that title to cars, savings and checking accounts, and certain other property can be passed merely by the filling out of forms.

A majority of states also provide for *family settlement agreements*, which are private agreements among the beneficiaries. Once a will is admitted to probate, the family members can agree to settle among themselves the distribution of the decedent's assets. Although a family settlement agreement speeds the settlement process, a court order is still needed to protect the estate from future creditors and to clear title to the assets involved.

The use of these and other types of summary procedures in estate administration can save time and money. The expenses of a personal representative's commission, attorneys' fees, appraisers' fees, and so forth can be eliminated or at least minimized through these simpler and less expensive procedures. In some situations, though—such as when a guardian for minor children or for an incompetent person must be appointed and a trust has been created to protect the minor or the incompetent person—probate procedures cannot be avoided.

Formal Probate Proceedings. Normally, for larger estates, formal probate proceedings are undertaken, and the probate court supervises every aspect of the settlement of the decedent's estate. Formal probate proceedings may take several months to complete. As a result, a sizeable portion of the decedent's assets (up to perhaps 10 percent) may have to go toward payment of court costs and fees charged by attorneys and personal representatives.

Property Transfers outside the Probate Process. Commonly, beneficiaries under a will must wait until the probate process is complete—which can take several months if formal probate proceedings are undertaken—to have access to money or other assets received under the will. For this and other reasons, some persons arrange to have property transferred in ways other than by will and outside the probate process. One method of accomplishing this is by establishing a living trust or a Totten trust—as you will read shortly.

Another method is through the joint ownership of property. For example, a person can arrange to hold title to certain property—which may be real or personal property—as a joint tenant with a spouse or other person. Recall from Chapter 8 that in a joint tenancy, when one joint tenant dies, the other joint tenant or tenants automatically inherit the deceased tenant's share of the property.

Yet another way of transferring property outside the probate process is by making gifts to children or others while one is still living. Finally, to make sure that a spouse, children, or some other dependent is provided for, many people take out life-insurance policies. A spouse, child, or other dependent can be named as beneficiary on the policy. Then, on the death of the policyholder, the proceeds of the policy go directly to the beneficiary.

ETHICAL CONCERN

Maintaining a Professional Distance

Paralegals who work in the area of probate and estate administration may end up dealing with emotionally charged situations. A decedent's heirs may maintain that they were treated unfairly under a will, or they may squabble with each other over various items of the decedent's personal property. As a legal professional, you have to learn not to take sides or become emotionally involved in these situations. Wills often are not fair. Many times, children do not inherit equal shares of an estate, and sometimes, a testator specifically excludes a child from the will. If a testator owns a homestead as a joint tenant with his or her spouse, on the testator's death, the spouse inherits the homestead—and the children may eventually end up receiving no real property from their deceased parent. Under the law, a testator has a right to be as unfair as he or she wishes, with certain limitations. As a paralegal, your job is to assist the probate court and your supervising attorney in making sure that the decedent's wishes—whatever they may have been—are carried out during the probate and estate-administration process.

TRUSTS

As discussed in Chapter 2, a *trust* involves any arrangement by which legal title to property is transferred from one person to be administered by a trustee for another's benefit. It can also be defined as a right of property (real or personal) held by one party for the benefit of another. A trust can be created for any purpose that is not illegal or against public policy.

Trusts are important estate-planning devices, and as a paralegal, you may be asked to assist in work relating to the establishment or administration of a trust. In this section, you will read about the essential elements of a trust, the various types of trusts, the powers that are normally conferred on trustees, and finally, how trusts are terminated.

Essential Elements of a Trust

The essential elements of a trust are as follows:

- A designated beneficiary.
- A designated trustee.
- A fund sufficiently identified to enable title to pass to the trustee.
- Actual delivery to the trustee with the intention of passing title.

If Sharp conveys his farm to the Central Bank of Michigan to be held for the benefit of his sons, Sharp has created a trust. Sharp is the *settlor* or *grantor* (the one creating the trust), the Central Bank of Michigan is the trustee, and Sharp's sons are the beneficiaries. This arrangement is illustrated in Exhibit 23.1.

Types of Trusts

There are numerous types of trusts, each with its own special characteristics. Here we look at living trusts, testamentary trusts, charitable trusts, spendthrift trusts, and Totten trusts.

***INTER VIVOS* TRUST**
A trust executed by the grantor and effective during the grantor's lifetime; a living trust.

Living Trusts. A living trust—or ***inter vivos* trust** (*inter vivos* is Latin for "between or among the living")—is a trust executed by a grantor during his

EXHIBIT 23.1
A Trust Arrangement

In a trust, there is a separation of interests in the trust property. The trustee takes *legal* title, which appears to be complete ownership and possession but which does not include the right to receive any benefits from the property. The beneficiary takes *equitable* title, which is the right to receive all benefits from the property.

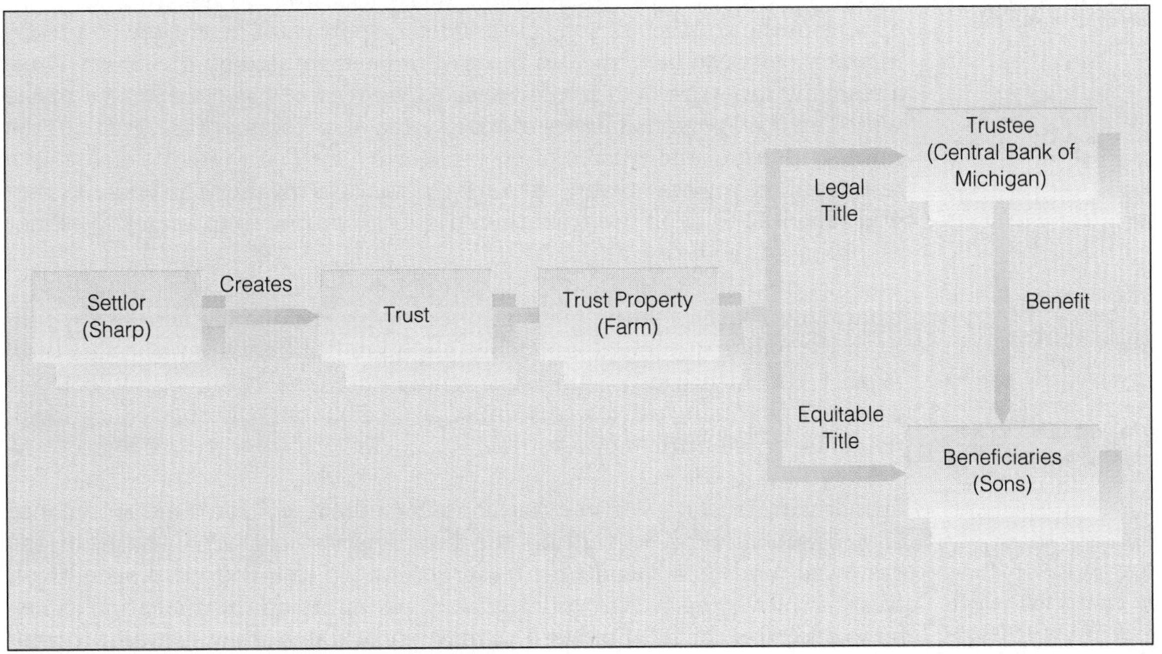

or her lifetime. A living trust may be an attractive estate-planning option for some clients because living trusts are not included in probate property.

There are two types of living trusts: revocable living trusts and irrevocable living trusts. The distinction between these two types of living trusts is an important one for the estate planner. In an irrevocable trust, the grantor permanently gives up control over the property. In a revocable living trust, in contrast, the grantor retains control over the trust property during his or her lifetime.

To establish an *irrevocable* living trust, the grantor executes a "trust deed," and legal title to the trust property passes to the named trustee. The trustee has a duty to administer the property as directed by the grantor for the benefit and in the interest of the beneficiaries. The trustee must preserve the trust property; make it productive; and if required by the terms of the trust agreement, pay income to the beneficiaries, all in accordance with the terms of the trust. Once the *inter vivos* trust has been created, the grantor has, in effect, given over the property for the benefit of the beneficiaries.

To establish a *revocable* living trust, the grantor deeds the property to the trust, but retains the power to amend, alter, or revoke the trust during his or her lifetime. The grantor may also arrange to receive income earned by the trust assets during his or her lifetime. Unless the trust is revoked, the principal of the trust is transferred to the trust beneficiary on the grantor's death.

TESTAMENTARY TRUST
A trust that is created by will and that does not take effect until the death of the testator.

Testamentary Trusts. A trust created by will to come into existence upon the settlor's death is referred to as a **testamentary trust**. Although a testamentary trust has a trustee who maintains legal title to the trust property, actions of the trustee are subject to judicial approval. The trustee of a testamentary trust can be named in the will or be appointed by the court. Thus, a testamentary trust will not fail because no trustee has been named in the will. The legal responsibilities of the trustee of a testamentary trust are the same as those of the trustee of an *inter vivos* trust. If the will setting up a testamentary trust is invalid, then the trust is also invalid. The property that was supposed to be in the trust then passes according to intestacy laws, not according to the terms of the trust.

CHARITABLE TRUST
A trust in which the property held by a trustee must be used for a charitable purpose, such as the advancement of health, education, or religion.

Charitable Trusts. A trust designed for the benefit of a segment of the public or the public in general is a **charitable trust**. It differs from a private trust in that the identities of the beneficiaries are uncertain. Usually, to be deemed a charitable trust, a trust must be created for charitable, educational, religious, or scientific purposes.

SPENDTHRIFT TRUST
A trust created to protect the beneficiary from spending all the money to which he or she is entitled. Only a certain portion of the total amount is given to the beneficiary at any one time, and most states prohibit creditors from obtaining assets of the trust.

Spendthrift Trusts. A trust that contains a provision for the maintenance of a beneficiary by preventing the beneficiary's improvident use of the bestowed funds is a **spendthrift trust**. For a trust to qualify as a spendthrift trust, its provisions must explicitly place restraints on the alienation (transfer to others) of the trust funds. The majority of states allow spendthrift-trust provisions that prohibit creditors from subjecting to the payment of debts the beneficiary's interest in future distributions from the trust.

TOTTEN TRUST
A trust created by the deposit of a person's own money into an account, such as a savings account, in his or her own name as a trustee for another. It is a tentative trust, revocable at will until the depositor dies or completes the gift in his or her lifetime by some unequivocal act or declaration.

Totten Trusts. A special type of trust, called a **Totten trust,**[1] is created when one person deposits money into an account, such as a savings account, in his or her own name as a trustee for another. The Totten trust is also known as a *tentative trust.* The trust is tentative in that it is revocable at will until the depositor dies or completes the gift in his or her lifetime by some unequivocal act or declaration (for example, delivery of the funds to the intended beneficiary). On the depositor's death, if the depositor has not revoked the trust, the beneficiary obtains property rights to the balance in the account. Totten trusts, like *inter vivos* trusts, are not included in probate property.

The Trustee's Role

The trustee is the person who holds the trust property. Anyone legally capable of holding title to and dealing in property can be a trustee. If the settlor of a trust fails to name a trustee or if a named trustee cannot or will not serve, the trust does not fail—a court can appoint a trustee.

1. This type of trust derives its unusual name from *In the Matter of Totten,* 179 N.Y. 112, 71 N.E. 748 (1904).

Duties of the Trustee. A trustee must act with honesty, good faith, and prudence in administering the trust and exercise a high degree of loyalty toward the trust beneficiary. The general standard of care is the degree of care a prudent person would exercise in his or her personal affairs. The duty of loyalty requires that the trustee act in the *exclusive* interest of the beneficiary. Specific duties of the trustee include the following:

- A duty to keep clear and accurate accounts of the trust's administration and furnish complete and accurate information to the beneficiary.
- A duty to keep trust assets separate from his or her own assets.
- A duty to pay to an income beneficiary the net income of the trust assets at reasonable intervals.
- A duty to invest and manage the trust assets as a prudent investor would manage his or her own assets.

Powers of the Trustee. When a settlor creates a trust, he or she may prescribe the trustee's powers and performance. Generally, state law[2] applies only to the extent that it does not conflict with the terms of the trust. When state law does apply, it is most likely to restrict the trustee's investment of trust funds. Typically, statutes confine trustees to investments in conservative debt securities such as government, utility, and railroad bonds and first-mortgage loans on realty. It is common, however, for a settlor to grant a trustee discretionary investment power. In that circumstance, any statute may be considered only advisory, with the trustee's decisions subject in most states to the prudent-person rule.

A difficult question concerns the extent of a trustee's discretion to "invade" the principal (the original amount of the trust fund) and distribute it to an income beneficiary, if the income (interest) earned on the invested trust assets is found to be insufficient to provide for the beneficiary in an appropriate manner. A similar question concerns the extent of a trustee's discretion to retain trust income and add it to the principal, if the income is found to be more than sufficient to provide for the beneficiary in an appropriate manner. Generally, the answer to both questions is that the income beneficiary should be provided with a somewhat predictable annual income, but with a view to the safety of the principal. Thus, a trustee may make individualized adjustments in annual distributions.

Of course, a trustee is responsible for carrying out the purposes of the trust. If the trustee fails to comply with the terms of the trust or the controlling statute, he or she is personally liable for any loss.

Termination of a Trust

The terms of a trust should expressly state the event on which the settlor wishes it to terminate—for example, the beneficiary's or the trustee's death.

2. In eight states, the law consists, in part, of the Uniform Principal and Income Act, published in 1931. The Revised Uniform Principal and Income Act, issued in 1962, has been adopted in thirty-four states. There are other uniform acts that may apply—for instance, about a third of the states have enacted the Uniform Trustees' Powers Act, promulgated in 1964. In addition, most states have their own statutes covering particular procedures and practices. Common law principles have been compiled in the Restatement (Second) of Trusts (1959).

DEVELOPING PARALEGAL SKILLS

Estate Planning

Sara Bloom is a new paralegal for a small law firm. One of the firm's clients, Arnold Thompson, has an appointment today with David Miller, Sara's supervising attorney, to discuss estate-planning options. David asks Sara to sit in on this initial client interview and take thorough notes. He also asks her to bring in a prepared form listing the types of information that the attorney will need from Thompson for estate-planning purposes. When Thompson arrives, Sara introduces herself and escorts him to David's office.

CONDUCTING THE INTERVIEW

The client, a widower, says that when he dies, he wants his three children to inherit his property and all of his other assets. His main concerns are avoiding probate and minimizing the taxes on his estate. He explains that he has a home that is currently valued at $200,000. He also has a life-insurance policy that, on his death, will pay the beneficiaries (his three children) a total of $1 million.

David tells Thompson that there are several possibilities for avoiding probate and minimizing estate taxes. First, David explains that the life-insurance proceeds will be distributed to the children immediately—at least, as soon as the insurance company has completed its investigation of the claim—and will not be subject to probate. "Be aware, though," continues David, "that life-insurance proceeds normally are a part of the taxable estate. One option for avoiding estate taxes on the life-insurance proceeds may be to establish an irrevocable life-insurance trust. I'll look into this possibility and discuss it with you later."

"As far as your residence goes," David says, "there are also some options, including the establishment of a trust, for transferring it to your children outside of probate and with minimal taxation. Why don't we meet next week and discuss the possibilities? In the meantime, I'd like you to meet with Sara and give her detailed information concerning your assets, debts, beneficiaries' names, and so on. Sara will give you a form listing the types of information you should bring with you to the meeting."

CONCLUDING THE INTERVIEW

Sara gives the client the list. "When would it be convenient for you to meet with me?" asks Sara. "Well," Thompson says, "I could come in this Friday, if that works with your schedule." Sara says that day would be fine, and they schedule the appointment. After the client leaves the office, Sara prepares a memo for the file describing what was discussed during today's interview. She will review the memo before meeting with the client on Friday.

If the trust instrument does not provide for termination on the beneficiary's death, the beneficiary's death will not end it. Similarly, without an express provision, a trust will not terminate on the trustee's death.

Typically, a trust instrument specifies a termination date. For example, a trust created to educate the settlor's child may provide that the trust ends when the beneficiary reaches the age of twenty-five. If the trust's purpose is fulfilled before that date, a court may order the trust's termination. If no date is specified, a trust will terminate when its purpose has been fulfilled. Of course, if a trust's purpose becomes impossible or illegal, the trust will terminate.

INTESTACY LAWS

Each state regulates by statute how property will be distributed when a person dies intestate. These statutes are called statutes of descent and distribution or, more simply, intestacy laws, as mentioned in this chapter's introduction. Intestacy laws attempt to carry out the likely intent and wishes of the decedent. Intestacy laws assume that deceased persons would have intended that their natural heirs (spouses, children, grandchildren, or other family members) inherit their property. Therefore, intestacy statutes set out rules and priorities under which these heirs inherit the property. If no heirs exist, then the property will escheat, or revert to the state, and the state will assume ownership of the property.

Surviving Spouse and Children

The rules of descent vary widely from state to state. There is, however, usually a special statutory provision for the rights of the surviving spouse and children. In addition, the law provides that the debts of the decedent must be satisfied out of his or her estate before the remaining assets can pass to the surviving spouse and the children.

A surviving spouse usually receives a share of the estate—one-half if there is also a surviving child and one-third if there are two or more children. Only when no children or grandchildren survive the decedent will a surviving spouse receive the *entire* estate.

Assume that Everett dies intestate—without having made a valid will. He is survived by his wife, Maria, and his children, Augusta and Daniel, and his property passes to his heirs according to intestacy laws. After Everett's outstanding debts have been paid, Maria will receive the homestead (either in fee simple or as a life estate—see Chapter 8) and ordinarily a one-third to one-half interest in all other property, depending on state law. The remaining real and personal property will pass to Augusta and Daniel in equal portions.

Order of Distribution

State statutes of descent and distribution specify the order in which heirs share in the estate of a person who dies intestate. When there is no surviving spouse or child, then grandchildren, brothers and sisters, and (in some states) parents of the decedents are the next in line to share. These relatives are usually called *lineal descendants*. Generally, title will descend before it will ascend. For example, property will pass to the deceased's children before it will pass to his or her parents. Because state statutes differ so widely, few other generalizations can be made about the laws of descent and distribution.

- **Paralegals must refer to the exact terms of the applicable state statutes when addressing any problem of intestacy distribution.**

If there are no lineal descendants, then *collateral heirs* are the next group to share. Collateral heirs include nieces, nephews, aunts, and uncles of the decedent. If there are no survivors in any of the groups already mentioned, most statutes provide that the property is to be distributed among the next of kin of any of the collateral heirs. Stepchildren and other relatives by marriage are not considered kin. Legally adopted children, however, are recognized as lawful heirs of their adoptive parents.

Whether an illegitimate child inherits depends on state statutes. In all states, intestate succession between the mother and the child exists. In some states, intestate succession between the father and the child can occur only when the child is "legitimized" by ceremony or has been "acknowledged" by the father.

Distribution to Grandchildren

When a person who dies intestate is survived by descendants of deceased children, a question arises as to what share the grandchildren of the intestate will receive. Distribution ***per stirpes*** is a method under which the grandchildren take the share that their deceased parent would have been entitled to inherit had that parent lived.

PER STIRPES
A Latin term meaning "by the roots." In the law governing estate distribution, a method of distributing an intestate's estate in which a class or group of distributees take the share to which their deceased ancestor would have been entitled.

Assume that Moran, a widower, has two children, Seth and John. Seth has two children (Bridget and Hallie), and John has one child (Perry). At the time of Moran's death, Seth and John have already died. If Moran's estate is distributed *per stirpes*, the following distribution takes place:

1. Bridget and Hallie: one-fourth each, taking Seth's share.
2. Perry: one-half, taking John's share.

Exhibit 23.2 illustrates the *per stirpes* method of distribution.

PER CAPITA
A Latin term meaning "per person." In the law governing estate distribution, a method of distributing the property of an intestate's estate by which all the heirs receive equal shares.

An estate may also be distributed on a ***per capita*** basis. This means that each person takes an equal share of the estate. If Moran's estate is distributed *per capita*, Bridget, Hallie, and Perry will each receive a one-third share. Exhibit 23.3 illustrates the *per capita* method of distribution.

Under most state intestacy laws and under the UPC, in-laws do not share in an estate. If a child dies before his or her parents, the child's spouse will not receive an inheritance from them. Assume that Moran's two children, Seth and John, are married and that Moran has no grandchildren. If Seth predeceases his father, under most state laws and under the UPC, Moran's entire estate will go to John. Seth's surviving wife will not inherit what would have been Seth's portion of the estate.

ESTATE ADMINISTRATION

When a person dies, someone must identify and collect the assets, pay the debts, and distribute the remaining assets of the decedent's estate. Taking care of these tasks is the subject matter of estate administration—often referred to as probate administration because probate courts normally oversee the management of decedents' estates.

If you are assisting with probate and estate-administration proceedings, you will probably be working closely with personal representatives (execu-

EXHIBIT 23.2
***Per Stirpes* Distribution**

Under *per stirpes* distribution, an heir takes the share that his or her deceased ancestor would have been entitled to inherit, had that person lived. This may mean that a class of distributees—the grandchildren, in this example—do not inherit in equal portions. (Note that Bridget and Hallie only receive one-fourth of Moran's estate, whereas Perry inherits one-half.)

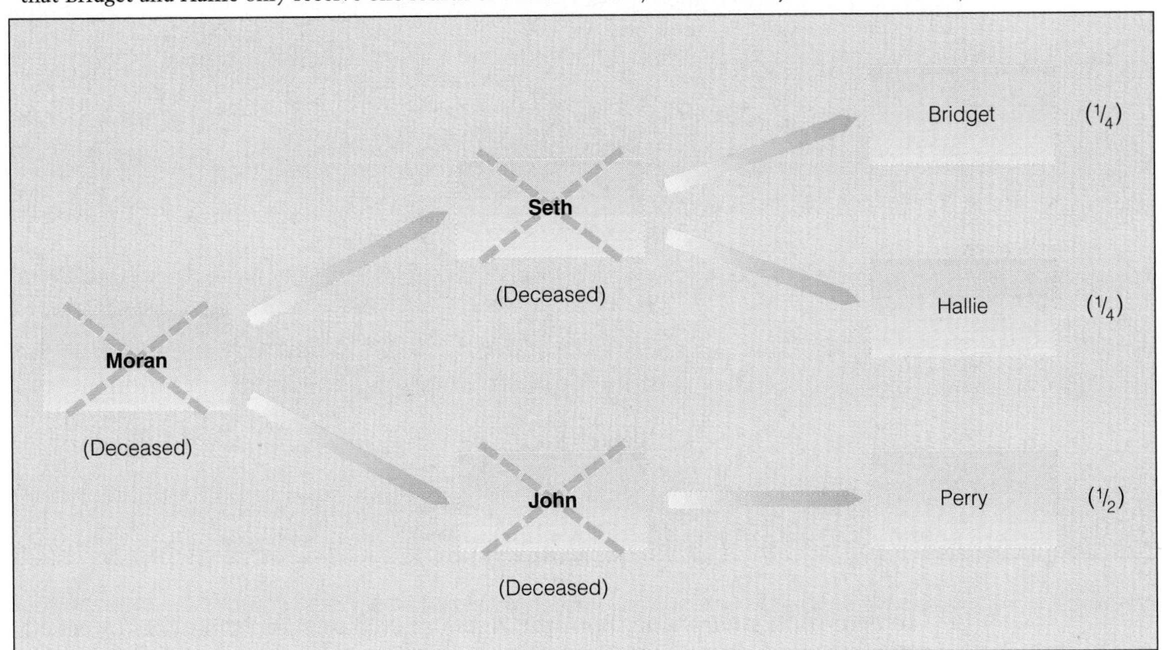

tors or administrators of estates). In some cases, personal representatives play an active role in the estate-administration process. In others, attorneys and paralegals undertake many tasks on behalf of personal representatives. The rules and procedures for managing the estates of deceased persons are controlled by state statute, and these statutes vary from state to state. Because of this, you will need to learn your state's specific requirements. Here, we indicate the general kinds of tasks that are involved in estate administration.

Locating the Will

The first step after a person dies is usually to determine whether or not the decedent left a will. In most cases, the decedent's attorney will have that information. If the firm for which you work prepared the decedent's will, you will have a copy of the will in your files—and the original copy of the will may be in your firm's safe. If there is uncertainty as to whether a valid will exists, the personal papers of the deceased must be reviewed.

Duties of the Personal Representative

The personal representative has a number of duties. The first duty is to collect and inventory the assets of the decedent. If necessary, the assets are appraised

EXHIBIT 23.3
***Per Capita* Distribution**

Under *per capita* distribution, all heirs in a certain class—in this case, the grandchildren—inherit equally. Note that Bridget and Hallie in this situation each inherit one-third of Moran's estate (not one-fourth, as they do under the *per stirpes* method of distribution).

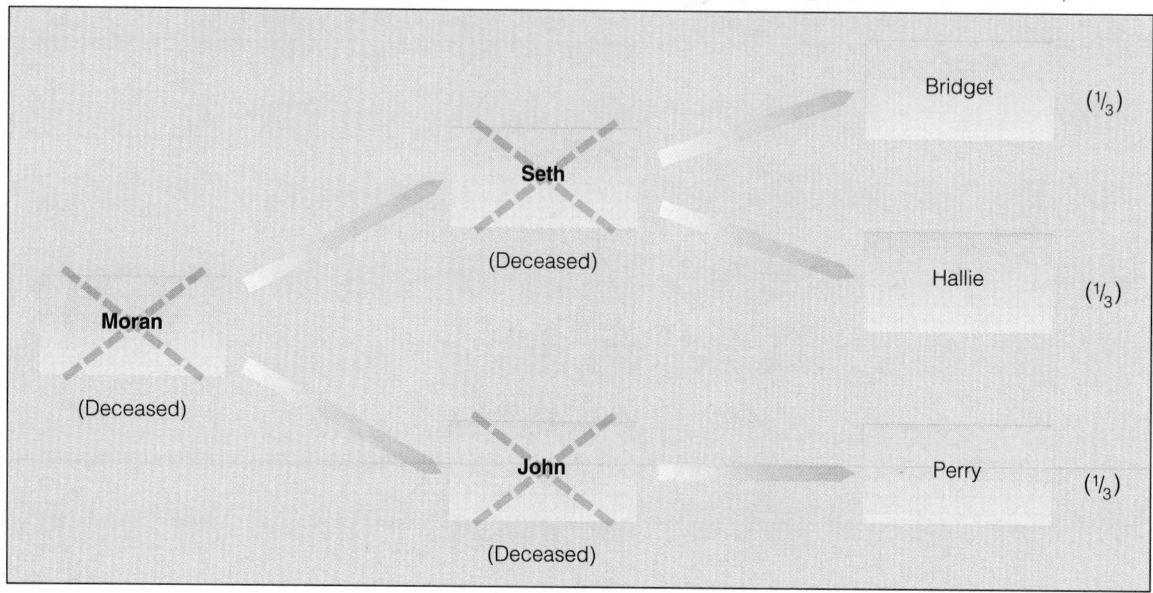

to determine their value. Both the rights of creditors and the rights of beneficiaries must be protected during the estate-administration proceedings. In addition, the personal representative is responsible for managing the assets of the estate during the administration period and for keeping them from being wasted or unnecessarily depleted. The personal representative receives and pays valid claims of creditors and arranges for the estate to pay federal and state income taxes and estate taxes (or inheritance taxes, depending on the state).

Estate and Inheritance Taxes

At the federal level, a tax is levied on the total value of the estate after debts and expenses for administration have been deducted and after various exemptions have been allowed. One important exemption is for property that is left to a surviving spouse. Such property can pass free of estate taxes.

The majority of states assess a death tax in the form of an inheritance tax imposed on the recipient of a bequest rather than on the estate. Some states also have a state estate tax similar to the federal estate tax. In general, inheritance tax rates depend on the type of relationship between the beneficiary and the decedent. The lowest rates and largest exemptions are applied to a surviving spouse and the children of the decedent.

Distribution of Assets

When the ultimate distribution of assets to the beneficiaries has been determined, the personal representative is responsible for distributing the assets of the estate pursuant to the court order. Once the assets have been distributed,

SUBSTANTIVE LAW CONCEPT SUMMARY

Wills, Trusts, and Estates

Wills	1. *Laws governing wills—* a. State statutes (probate laws)—Vary from state to state. b. Uniform Probate Code (UPC)—Codifies general principles and procedures concerning wills and probate; adopted in full by fifteen states and in part by nearly all of the other states. 2. *The terminology of wills—*The maker of the will is the *testator*. A personal representative named in a will is an *executor*, and a personal representative appointed by the court is an *administrator*. A gift of real property under a will is a *devise*, and a gift of personal property is a *bequest* (or *legacy*). A *devisee* is the recipient of a devise, and a *legatee* is the recipient of a legacy. 3. *Gifts by will—*May be specific (identified property, such as house or a watch) or general (unidentified property, such as "all my lands," or a sum of money). 4. *Requirements for a valid will—*The maker must have testamentary capacity and the will must be in writing (except nuncupative wills, valid in some situations), be signed by the testator and the required number of witnesses, and (in some states) be published. Publication occurs when the testator orally declares to witnesses that the will is his or her "last will and testament." 5. *Clauses contained in a will—Exordium* clause, clauses disposing of property, clause appointing fiduciaries, *testimonium* clause, attestation clause, and possibly other clauses, depending on the maker's wishes. 6. *Revocation of a will—*A will can be revoked by the maker (by physical destruction of part or all of the will or by a new writing, which may be a codicil or a second will) or by operation of law (due to marriage, divorce or annulment, or the birth of children). 7. *Probate versus nonprobate:* a. State laws normally provide for informal probate proceedings for smaller estates. For larger estates, formal probate proceedings are undertaken, and the probate court supervises every aspect of the settlement of the decedent's estate. Paralegals working in this area need to become acquainted with their state's specific requirements and procedures relating to probate. b. Property can be transferred outside the probate process through the joint ownership of property, certain types of trusts, gifts, and life-insurance policies.
Trusts	A trust is any arrangement by which property is transferred from one person to be administered by a trustee for another party's benefit. Types of trusts include the following: 1. *Living* (inter vivos) *trust—*A trust executed by the grantor during his or her lifetime. May be revocable or irrevocable. 2. *Testamentary trust—*A trust created by will and coming into existence on the death of the grantor. 3. *Charitable trust—*A trust designed for the benefit of a public group or the public in general. 4. *Spendthrift trust—*A trust created to provide for the maintenance of a beneficiary by allowing only a certain portion of the total amount to be received by the beneficiary at any one time. Creditors cannot reach the trust funds. 5. *Totten (tentative) trust—*A trust created when one person deposits money in his or her own name as a trustee for another.

SUBSTANTIVE LAW CONCEPT SUMMARY, Continued	
Intestacy Laws	1. Vary widely from state to state. Usually, the law provides that the surviving spouse and children inherit the property of the decedent (after the decedent's debts are paid). The spouse usually inherits the entire estate if there are no children, one-half of the estate if there is one child, and one-third of the estate if there are two or more children. 2. If there is no surviving spouse or child, then lineal descendants (grandchildren, brothers and sisters, and—in some states—parents of the decedent) inherit. If there are no lineal descendants, then collateral heirs (nieces, nephews, aunts, and uncles of the decedent) inherit.
Estate Administration	Estate-administration procedures are governed by state statutes. Generally, the process of administering the affairs of a deceased person includes finding the will (if there is one), collecting and inventorying the decedent's assets, paying debts and taxes, and distributing the remaining assets, if any, to the decedent's heirs in accordance with the decedent's wishes.

an accounting is rendered to the court, the estate is closed, and the personal representative is relieved of any further responsibility or liability for the estate.

WILLS, TRUSTS, AND ESTATES AND THE PARALEGAL

Paralegals play a crucial role in assisting clients with estate-planning, probate, and estate-administration procedures. One of the paralegal's important tasks is to collect information about the testator's or decedent's assets and obligations. Another important task performed by paralegals in this area is drafting the documents necessary for these procedures.

During the probate and estate-administration process, the paralegal often functions as a liaison between the court and the personal representative, coordinating the efforts of those involved in the proceedings. If a decedent's property is to be sold, the paralegal frequently assists in making arrangements for the sale or auction of the property. In this situation, the paralegal needs to know the procedures involved in the sale of real estate (discussed in Chapter 8).

In certain areas of legal practice, and especially in the area of probate and estate administration, you can expect that some of the clients with whom you will deal will be suffering emotionally from the loss of a loved one. As a paralegal, you can render invaluable assistance to your supervising attorney by being sensitive to clients' emotional needs. This "hand-holding" function, as it is often called, is part of the process of legal representation. Attorneys increasingly rely on their paralegals to perform this function.

As you might expect, the kinds of work performed by paralegals in the area of law covered in this chapter are too numerous to summarize in a brief space. The tasks listed below are just a few of the many tasks you might perform as a paralegal working in this area:

- Interview a client to find out what property the client owns (solely or jointly with others), how and to whom the client wants to transfer the prop-

TODAY'S PROFESSIONAL PARALEGAL

Meeting with the Personal Representative

Jocelyn Furnow is a paralegal with a small law partnership, West & West. Terrence West, one of the two partners, told Jocelyn yesterday that a friend of his, Bob Milham, would be dropping by today. Bob's brother, Ralph Milham, died a few days ago in a car accident, and Bob, as Ralph's personal representative, wants to know what needs to be done to settle the estate.

JOCELYN'S ASSIGNMENT

Terrence tells Jocelyn that he will be out of the office all afternoon and that when Bob comes by, she should let him know what kinds of documents and information he needs to gather immediately. "Tell Bob," Terrence says to Jocelyn, "to collect these items as quickly as possible and then come in and see me. In fact, see if you can set up an appointment for this Thursday, and tell him he should try to have the necessary information by that time."

MEETING WITH THE CLIENT

That afternoon, Bob Milham enters the office, and Jocelyn greets him. She introduces herself as Terrence West's paralegal and explains that the attorney has authorized her to indicate the kinds of information that Bob should obtain right away. Jocelyn first asks Bob if he brought his brother's will with him. Bob hands Jocelyn the will, which Jocelyn quickly scans. She notes that Bob's name is listed as Ralph's personal representative. She then hands Bob a prepared form—a worksheet that Bob can use to inventory his brother's assets and debts.

GOING OVER THE WORKSHEET

"Basically," explains Jocelyn, "you first need to list your brother's possessions, as the worksheet indicates. Do you know if he owned any real estate, such as a home or land?" Bob states that his brother owned a house and had a car and an airplane. He is fairly sure that Ralph also had some investment securities.

"Well," Jocelyn responds, "look through his personal papers. Try to find the deed to the house, the titles to the car and the airplane, and the certificates or other evidence of the securities he owned. These papers may be in a safe-deposit box, so you need to check with his bank to find out if he had one. Also locate his checkbook and any paperwork indicating whether he had a savings account or owned any certificates of deposit.

"The next step is to find out whether Ralph had any debts outstanding. When you look through his papers, find out how much, if anything, he still owed on the house and on his car and airplane. See if you can find evidence of any other loans that must be paid off."

Jocelyn continues to go over the items listed on the worksheet. Once she is sure that Bob understands what must be done, she schedules an appointment for the coming Thursday. At that time, Terrence can further advise Bob on the probate process and on Bob's duties as personal representative.

erty on his or her death, what arrangements the client wants to make for minor children or other dependents, and so on.

- Draft a will or documents necessary to establish a trust fund or otherwise arrange for property transfer from the client to others.
- Research state statutory laws governing wills and trusts.
- File a will with the probate court to begin probate proceedings.
- Locate a personal representative who is named in a will and help determine whether the person has the desire and legal capacity to represent the deceased.
- Locate beneficiaries named in a will or the next of kin of a person who died intestate.
- Locate, identify, and perhaps have appraised all of the assets of a decedent.
- Assist in determining the liabilities (debts, taxes, and other obligations) owed by a decedent's estate.
- Research federal and state laws relating to estate or inheritance taxes and determine their applicability to a decedent's estate.

KEY TERMS AND CONCEPTS

administrator 871
attestation clause 877
bequest 871
charitable trust 882
codicil 878
devise 871
devisee 871
escheat 870
executor 871
***exordium* clause 874**
holographic will 873
***inter vivos* trust 881**
intestacy laws 870
intestate 870
legacy 871
legatee 871
nuncupative will 873
***per capita* 886**
***per stirpes* 886**
revoke 877
spendthrift trust 882
testamentary capacity 872
testamentary trust 882
testate 870
testator 871
***testimonium* clause 877**
Totten trust 882

CHAPTER SUMMARY

1. Paralegals play an important role in estate planning, probate proceedings, and estate administration. Estate planning normally involves the execution of a will. It may also involve the establishment of a trust or the transfer of property by other means.

2. For a will to be valid, it must meet the requirements set forth by state law. The maker of a will (testator) must have testamentary capacity (be of legal age—in most states, eighteen years of age—and of sound mind). Normally, a will must be in writing, although in some states, nuncupative wills (oral wills, often called "deathbed" wills) are deemed valid. A will must be signed by the testator (what serves as a signature depends on state law) and witnessed by two (and sometimes three) persons. In some states, the will must be "published"—which occurs when the maker orally declares to witnesses that the document is the maker's "last will and testament."

3. Wills are personal documents, and the contents of wills thus vary from person to person. Typically, though, a will contains an *exordium* clause, followed by clauses disposing of the maker's property and appointing fiduciaries (a personal representative, a custodian for minor children or other dependents, a trustee, or others). The will concludes with a *testimonium* clause (indicating when the maker signed the will) and an attestation clause (indicating when witnesses signed the document). One or more provisions of a will can be revoked (made void, or nonexistent)—or the entire will can be revoked—by an act of the maker or through the operation of law. Revocation by the maker can be accomplished by a physical act (destroying all or part of the will) or through another writing—a codicil or a second will. Revocation by operation of law may occur due to marriage, divorce or annulment, or the birth of children.

4. On the death of the testator, the will is probated. Depending on the size of the estate, probate may be informal or formal. State laws normally provide for informal probate proceedings for smaller estates. For larger estates, formal probate proceedings are undertaken, and the probate court supervises every aspect of the settlement of the decedent's estate. To avoid the delays that may be involved in probate proceedings and for other reasons, some people opt to transfer property to their heirs in ways other than by will—for example, through joint ownership of property, living trusts, or gifts.

5. A trust is any arrangement through which property is transferred from one person to be administered by a trustee for another party's benefit. The essential elements of a trust are (1) a designated beneficiary, (2) a designated trustee, (3) a fund sufficiently identified to enable title to pass to the trustee, and (4) actual delivery to the trustee with the intention of passing title.

6. There are many types of trusts. Living (*inter vivos*) trusts are trusts that are executed by the grantor during his or her lifetime. Testamentary trusts come into existence on the death of the grantor. A charitable trust is one designed for the benefit of a public group or the public in general. A spendthrift trust provides for the maintenance of a beneficiary by allowing only a portion of the total amount to be received by the beneficiary at any one time. A Totten (tentative) trust is created when one person deposits money into an account, such as a savings account, in his or her own name as a trustee for another. Usually, a trust instrument specifies the termination date of the trust. If no date is specified, the trust will terminate when its purpose has been fulfilled.

7. When a person dies intestate—without a valid will—state intestacy laws specify who will inherit what share of the decedent's property. These laws vary from state to state. All state laws provide for inheritance of a certain share by a surviving spouse and children. If there is no surviving spouse or child, then the property is inherited by other relatives, in the specific order prescribed by state statutes. If there are no heirs, ownership of the decedent's property reverts to the state (escheats).

8. When a person dies, a personal representative (named in the will or appointed by the court) winds up all of the legal and financial affairs of the decedent on behalf of the beneficiaries or heirs. Paralegals often assist and work closely with personal representatives in this process. All of the assets of the decedent must be located and inventoried, debts and taxes must be paid, and all remaining property must be distributed to the beneficiaries or heirs in accordance with the decedent's wishes and governing laws.

QUESTIONS FOR REVIEW

1. Why is it important to check the law of your specific state when determining the requirements of a will? What laws govern the distribution of the estate of a person who dies without a valid will?

2. In the context of wills, what do the following terms mean?

a. Testator.
b. Personal representative.
c. Executor.
d. Administrator.
e. Devise.
f. Devisee.
g. Legacy.
h. Legatee.
i. Testate.
j. Intestate.

3. How are gifts by will made? What are the requirements for a valid will?

4. What kinds of clauses are contained in a will? What is the purpose or use of each clause? How is a will revoked?

5. When is probate used? What is informal probate? What is formal probate? How can property be transferred outside the probate process?

6. What is a trust? What are the elements required to create a trust? Briefly define the following types of trusts:

a. *Inter vivos* trust.
b. Testamentary trust.
c. Charitable trust.
d. Spendthrift trust.
e. Totten trust.

7. What are intestacy laws? How do they provide for the surviving spouse and the children? How do intestacy laws provide for lineal descendants?

8. What is the difference between *per stirpes* distribution and *per capita* distribution?

9. What procedures are involved in administering an estate? Is a decedent's estate subject to taxation?

10. What are the duties of the personal representative in administering an estate?

ETHICAL QUESTIONS

1. James Simpson, an attorney, has represented Miss Morgan for forty years. She is now eighty-three years old and is revising her will. She instructs the attorney to include in the will a bequest to James Simpson of $50,000. Can Simpson prepare this will? Why or why not?

2. Attorney James Simpson deposits a check in the amount of $225,000 into his law firm's bank account. This check represents the proceeds from the sale of a house that was part of a decedent's estate. The attorney is holding the funds until probate proceedings are completed and the estate is distributed. The attorney periodically borrows some of the funds—$5,000 here and $10,000 there—to cover office expenses. What are the ethical implications of James Simpson's actions?

PRACTICE QUESTIONS AND ASSIGNMENTS

1. Define each of the following terms, as they were used in this chapter:
   a. *Inter vivos.*
   b. Testamentary.
   c. Legacy.
   d. Holographic.
   e. Charitable.
   f. Totten.
   g. *Exordium.*
   h. *Testimonium.*
   i. Spendthrift.

2. Marsha dies without leaving a will. She is survived by her husband, Tom, and their three children. They owned their own home, and Marsha had a bank account, in her name only, containing $30,000. She also owned stock, in her name only, in the amount of $15,000. Marsha had no outstanding debts. Using the laws of intestate succession as discussed in the chapter, determine how much each of Marsha's heirs will inherit.

3. Who would inherit from Marsha in Problem 2 above if Marsha's husband predeceased her and they had no children but Marsha had one brother and one sister?

4. Now assume that Marsha dies intestate and is survived by a daughter and two grandchildren. The grandchildren are the children of her son, who predeceased Marsha. If the *per stirpes* method of distribution is used, what share of Marsha's estate will each grandchild inherit? What share will each grandchild inherit if the *per capita* method of distribution is used?

QUESTIONS FOR CRITICAL ANALYSIS

1. In regard to testamentary capacity, why should less mental ability be required to make a will than to manage one's own business affairs or to enter into a contract?

2. What is a nuncupative will? Should nuncupative wills ever be valid? Explain fully the reasoning behind your answer.

ROLE-PLAYING EXERCISES

1. Using the facts from the *Developing Paralegal Skills* feature entitled "Evaluating Testamentary Capacity," role-play the interview between Tom and Sophie. The students playing the role of Tom should be polite yet assertive in trying to obtain answers from Sophie to determine her testamentary capacity. Students playing the role of Sophie should be very repetitive in their statements and should be confused about the number of children and grandchildren that they have as well as the reason for changing the will.

2. Using the facts from this chapter's *Today's Professional Paralegal,* role-play the conversation between Jocelyn Furnow, the paralegal, and Bob Milham, the client. The students playing the role of Bob should appear distraught and still in a state of shock over Ralph's sudden accidental death. They should also appear to know very little about what is involved in being a personal representative for a decedent. The students playing the role of Jocelyn should be sensitive to the client's emotional needs but forthright about the kinds of information that the client will need to obtain for the upcoming meeting with the attorney.

PROJECTS

1. Obtain a will form reflecting your state's requirements for a valid will. Compare your state's requirements with the requirements discussed in this chapter. Write a two-page, double-spaced, typewritten summary of the ways in which your state's requirements are similar to (or differ from) those discussed in the chapter.

2. Research your state's laws of intestate succession. Summarize how an intestate's estate is distributed under your state's intestacy laws.

3. Review your state's laws governing probate procedures. Describe the alternatives to formal probate proceedings that are allowed in your state and under what conditions these alternative proceedings may be used.

4. Review your state's laws on trusts. Does your state recognize the types of trusts that were discussed in the chapter? If not, which trusts are not recognized in your state? Why?

ANNOTATED SELECTED READINGS

FLEMING, ROBERT B. "Top Ten Changes in the New Uniform Probate Code." *Arizona Attorney,* August/September 1994. An article describing Arizona's recent adoption of changes in Chapter 2 (Intestate Succession and Wills) and Chapter 6 (Nonprobate Transfers) of the Uniform Probate Code.

LEONARD SMITH, JULIE. "Allowing the Probate of Duplicate Wills: Overcoming the Presumption of Revocation and Conflicts with the Statute of Wills." *Connecticut Probate Law Journal,* 1994. A case note that discusses the issue of lost wills and how some states handle the problem—that is, by using testimony to overcome the presumption that the will was revoked and offering a copy of the lost will into evidence.

MILLER, C. DOUGLAS. "Will Formality, Judicial Formalism, and Legislative Reform: An Examination of the New Uniform Probate Code "Harmless Error" Rule and the Movement toward Amorphism." *Florida Law Review,* April 1991. A discussion of the "harmless error" rule. In July 1990, at its annual conference, the National Conference of Commissioners on Uniform State Laws approved and recommended for enactment this rule, which allows defective wills to be admitted into probate when there is a showing of testamentary intent by clear and convincing evidence.

PRATT, KEVIN B. "Environmental Liabilities in Probate: Serious Risks for the Probate Lawyer." *Colorado Lawyer,* October 1994. An interesting article that discusses the problem of estate assets that consist of contaminated property. The article includes a discussion of the "innocent landowner" defense, which is available under the federal Superfund statute, and indicates that the defense is not always easy to prove.

SIGLER, EMY. "Elgar B. Probate Appeal: The Probate Court's Implied Powers to Construe and to Enforce Pre-Nuptial Agreements." *Connecticut Probate Law Journal,* 1994. This interesting article discusses the issue of a probate court's jurisdiction to determine the validity of a prenuptial agreement in order to finalize an estate, as happened in Connecticut in the *Elgar* case.

24

BANKRUPTCY LAW

Chapter Objectives

After completing this chapter, you will know:

- **The law governing bankruptcy procedures.**
- **The various types of relief available for debtors under federal bankruptcy law.**
- **The basic procedures involved in an ordinary, or straight, bankruptcy proceeding.**
- **How bankruptcy law provides relief for corporate debtors and what basic procedures are involved in corporate reorganizations.**
- **Alternative types of relief under bankruptcy law for individuals and family farmers.**

Chapter Outline

INTRODUCTION

Historically, debtors had few rights. At one time debtors who could not pay their debts as they came due faced harsh consequences, including imprisonment and involuntary servitude. Today, in contrast, debtors have numerous rights. One of these rights is the right to petition for bankruptcy relief under federal law.

In the past decade, the number of petitions for bankruptcy filed each year has nearly tripled. Currently, approximately 900,000 bankruptcy petitions are filed each year in the United States. For paralegals, this means that bankruptcy law is an area in which they will be increasingly in demand.

In this chapter, you will read about the law governing bankruptcy. You will also learn about the different types of relief offered under federal bankruptcy law and about the basic bankruptcy procedures required for specific types of relief.

THE BANKRUPTCY CODE

Bankruptcy relief is provided under federal law. Although state laws may play a role in bankruptcy proceedings, particularly state laws governing property, the governing law is based on federal legislation.

Congressional authority to provide bankruptcy relief for debtors is based on Article I, Section 8, of the U.S. Constitution, which gives Congress the power to establish "uniform laws on the subject of bankruptcies throughout the United States." Federal bankruptcy legislation was first enacted in 1898 and since then has undergone several modifications.

Current bankruptcy law is based on the Bankruptcy Reform Act of 1978, as amended. In this chapter, we refer to the current body of bankruptcy law simply as the Bankruptcy Code (or, more simply, the Code). After the passage of the 1978 act, the Code was significantly amended in 1984 and again in 1986. The most recent changes to the Code were made by the Bankruptcy Reform Act of 1994. These changes are included in our discussion in this chapter.

Goals of Bankruptcy Law

As you read in Chapter 2, modern bankruptcy law is designed to accomplish two main goals. The first is to provide relief and protection to debtors who have "gotten in over their heads." The second is to provide a fair means of distributing a debtor's assets among all creditors. Thus, the law attempts to protect the rights of both the debtor and the creditor.

Bankruptcy Courts

Bankruptcy proceedings are held in federal bankruptcy courts, which are under the authority of U.S. district courts, and rulings from bankruptcy courts can be appealed to the district courts. Essentially, a bankruptcy court fulfills the role of an administrative court for the federal district court concerning matters in bankruptcy. The bankruptcy court holds proceedings dealing with the procedures required to administer the estate of the debtor in bankruptcy. Bankruptcy court judges are federally appointed. A bankruptcy court can conduct a jury trial if the appropriate district court has authorized it and the parties to the bankruptcy consent.

Although bankruptcy courts are federal courts, the Federal Rules of Civil Procedure do not apply in bankruptcy cases. Procedures in bankruptcy courts follow instead the Federal Rules of Bankruptcy Procedure.

Types of Bankruptcy Relief

The Bankruptcy Code is contained in Title 11 of the United States Code (U.S.C.) and has eight chapters.[1] Chapters 1, 3, and 5 of the Code include general definitional provisions and provisions governing case administration, creditors, the debtor, and the estate. These three chapters apply generally to all kinds of bankruptcies. The next five chapters of the Code set forth the different types of relief that debtors may seek:

- Chapter 7 provides for **liquidation** proceedings (the selling of all nonexempt assets and the distribution of the proceeds to the debtor's creditors).
- Chapter 9 governs the adjustment of debts of a municipality.
- Chapter 11 governs reorganizations.
- Chapters 12 and 13 provide for the adjustment of debts by parties with regular incomes (family farmers in Chapter 12 and individuals in Chapter 13).

LIQUIDATION
A proceeding under Chapter 7 of the Bankruptcy Code (often referred to as *ordinary*, or *straight*, bankruptcy) in which a debtor states his or her debts and turns all assets over to a trustee, who sells the nonexempt assets and distributes the proceeds to creditors. With certain exceptions, the remaining debts are then discharged and the debtor is relieved of the obligation to pay the debts.

In the following pages, we look at the specific type of bankruptcy relief provided under Chapters 7, 11, and 13 of the Code. To fully inform a **consumer-debtor** (defined as an individual whose debts are primarily consumer debts) of the types of relief available, the Code requires that the clerk of the court give all consumer-debtors written notice of each chapter under which they may proceed prior to the commencement of a bankruptcy filing.

CONSUMER-DEBTOR
Debtors whose debts are primarily consumer debts—that is, debts for purchases that are primarily for household or personal use.

LIQUIDATION PROCEEDINGS

Liquidation under Chapter 7 of the Bankruptcy Code is probably the most familiar type of bankruptcy proceeding and is often referred to as *ordinary*, or *straight*, bankruptcy. Put simply, a debtor in a liquidation bankruptcy states his or her debts and turns all assets over to a trustee. The trustee sells the nonexempt assets and distributes the proceeds to creditors (the trustee's role will be discussed in more detail shortly). With certain exceptions, the remaining debts are then **discharged** (extinguished), and the debtors are relieved of their obligation to pay the debts.

DISCHARGE
The termination of an obligation. A discharge in bankruptcy terminates the debtor's obligation to pay the debts discharged by the court.

Any "person"—defined as including individuals, partnerships, and corporations—may be a debtor in a liquidation proceeding. Railroads, insurance companies, banks, savings and loan associations, investment companies

1. There are no Chapters 2, 4, 6, 8, or 10 in Title 11. Such "gaps" are not uncommon in the U.S.C. This is because chapter numbers (or other subdivisional unit numbers) are sometimes reserved for future use when a statute is enacted. (A gap may also appear if a law has been repealed.)

licensed by the Small Business Administration, and credit unions *cannot* be debtors in a liquidation bankruptcy, however. Rather, other chapters of the Bankruptcy Code or federal or state statutes apply to them. A husband and wife may file jointly for bankruptcy under a single petition.

Filing the Petition

PETITION IN BANKRUPTCY
An application to a bankruptcy court for relief in bankruptcy; a filing for bankruptcy. The official forms required for a petition in bankruptcy must be completed accurately, sworn to under oath, and signed by the debtor.

A straight bankruptcy may be commenced by the filing of either a voluntary or an involuntary **petition in bankruptcy**—the document that is filed with a bankruptcy court to initiate bankruptcy proceedings. The Code requires a consumer-debtor who has opted for liquidation bankruptcy proceedings to state in the petition, at the time of filing, that he or she understands the relief available under other chapters of the Code and has chosen to proceed under Chapter 7. One of your tasks as a paralegal may be to prepare for your supervising attorney's signature an affidavit stating that the attorney has informed the debtor of the relief available under each chapter.

Voluntary Bankruptcy. If a debtor wishes to petition for voluntary bankruptcy, official forms designated for that purpose must be filed with the bankruptcy court. Paralegals normally are entrusted with the task of gathering from the debtor-client the necessary information to include in the bankruptcy forms, or schedules, to be filed with the court.

The Contents of the Petition. Generally, the following information must be entered on schedules, which are then filed with a petition for bankruptcy relief under Chapter 7 of the Code:

- A list of creditors, their addresses, and the amount of debt owed to each.
- A statement of the financial affairs of the debtor.
- A list of all property owned by the debtor, including property claimed by the debtor to be exempt.
- A listing of current income and expenses.

The last item—the listing of current income and expenses—provides creditors and the court with relevant information on the debtor's ability to pay creditors a reasonable amount from future income. This information *could* permit a court, on its own motion, to dismiss a debtor's Chapter 7 petition after a hearing and to encourage the filing of a repayment plan under Chapter 13 of the Code (discussed later in this chapter), when that would substantially improve the chances that creditors would be paid.

The official forms must be completed accurately, sworn to under oath, and signed by the debtor. To conceal assets or knowingly supply false information on these schedules is a crime under the bankruptcy laws.

ORDER FOR RELIEF
A court's grant of assistance to a complainant. In the context of bankruptcy, the order for relief in itself constitutes a discharge of the complainant's (debtor's) debts.

The Order for Relief. If the voluntary petition for bankruptcy is found to be proper, the filing of the petition will itself constitute an order for relief. The **order for relief** effectively discharges the debtor's debts. Once a consumer-debtor's voluntary petition has been filed, the clerk of the court or other appointee must give the trustee and creditors mailed notice of the order for relief not more than twenty days after entry of the order.

Access to Chapter 7 Relief. Anyone liable to a creditor can declare bankruptcy. Debtors do not have unfettered access to Chapter 7 bankruptcy proceedings, however. The Bankruptcy Code allows a bankruptcy court to dismiss a petition for relief under Chapter 7 if the granting of relief would constitute substantial abuse of Chapter 7. The Code does not define "substantial abuse," and usually courts decide the issue on a case-by-case basis, in view of the particular circumstances and needs of the debtor.

Involuntary Bankruptcy. An involuntary bankruptcy occurs when one or more of the debtor's creditors force the debtor into bankruptcy proceedings. An involuntary case cannot be commenced against a farmer or a charitable institution. If the debtor challenges the involuntary petition, a hearing will be held, and the bankruptcy court may enter an order for relief if certain requirements are met. If the court finds that the debtor generally is not paying debts as they become due, for example, it may enter an order for relief. If the court grants an order for relief, the debtor will be required to supply the same information in the bankruptcy schedules as in a voluntary bankruptcy.

An involuntary petition should not be used as an everyday device for collecting debts, and the Code provides penalties for the filing of frivolous petitions against debtors. Judgment may be granted against the petitioning creditors for the costs and attorneys' fees incurred by the debtor in defending against an involuntary petition that is dismissed by the court. If the petition is filed in bad faith, damages can be awarded for injury to the debtor's reputation. Punitive damages may also be awarded.

Automatic Stay

The moment a petition in bankruptcy—either voluntary or involuntary—is filed, there exists an **automatic stay**, or suspension, of virtually all litigation and other action by creditors against the debtor or the debtor's property. In other words, once a petition has been filed, creditors cannot commence or continue most legal actions to repossess property in the hands of the debtor. In some circumstances, a creditor may petition the bankruptcy court for relief from the automatic stay, however. Also, the automatic stay does not apply to paternity, alimony, maintenance, and support debts.

The Code provides that if a creditor *knowingly* violates the automatic stay (a willful violation), any party injured, including the debtor, is entitled to recover actual damages, costs, and attorneys' fees and may be entitled to recover punitive damages as well.

AUTOMATIC STAY
A suspension of all judicial proceedings upon the occurrence of an independent event. Under the Bankruptcy Code, the moment a petition to initiate bankruptcy proceedings is filed, all litigation or other legal action by creditors against a debtor and the debtor's property is suspended.

The Estate in Property

Upon the commencement of a liquidation proceeding under Chapter 7, an estate in property is created. The **estate in property** (sometimes called the *estate in bankruptcy*) consists of all the debtor's interests in property presently held, wherever it is located. Interests in certain property—such as gifts, inheritances, property settlements (divorce), and life-insurance death proceeds—to which the debtor becomes entitled *within 180 days after filing* may also become part of the estate. Thus, the filing of a bankruptcy petition

ESTATE IN PROPERTY
In bankruptcy proceedings, all of the debtor's interests in property presently held and wherever located, as well as interests in certain property to which the debtor becomes entitled within 180 days after filing for bankruptcy.

generally fixes a dividing line: property acquired prior to the filing of the petition becomes property of the estate, and property acquired after the filing of the petition, except as just noted, remains the debtor's.

The Bankruptcy Trustee

BANKRUPTCY TRUSTEE
A person appointed by the bankruptcy court to administer the debtor's estate in the interests of both the debtor and the creditors. The basic duty of the bankruptcy trustee is to collect and reduce to money the estate in property and to close up the estate as speedily as is compatible with the best interests of the parties.

Promptly after the order for relief in the liquidation proceeding has been entered, an interim, or provisional, **bankruptcy trustee** is appointed by the *U.S. Trustee* (a government official who performs certain administrative tasks that a bankruptcy judge would otherwise have to perform). The bankruptcy trustee may be a bankruptcy attorney (one who is not involved in the case).

Trustee's Duties. The basic duty of the bankruptcy trustee is to collect and reduce to money the estate in property and to close up the estate as speedily as is compatible with the best interests of the parties. The trustee is held accountable for administering the debtor's estate in the interests of *both* the debtor and the creditors.

Trustee's Powers. The trustee has the power to require persons holding the debtor's property at the time the petition is filed to deliver the property to the trustee. To enable the trustee to implement this power, the Code provides that the trustee occupies a position equivalent in rights to that of certain other parties. For example, the trustee has the same rights to obtain the debtor's property as certain types of creditors do. The trustee also has rights equivalent to those of the debtor.

In addition, the trustee has specific *powers of avoidance*. That is, the trustee can set aside—void, or avoid (nullify)—a sale or other transfer of the debtor's property, taking it back as a part of the debtor's estate. These powers include voidable rights available to the debtor, preferences, and fraudulent transfers by the debtor. Each is discussed in more detail below. Additionally, certain statutory liens (creditors' claims against the debtor's property) may be avoided by the trustee.

The debtor shares most of the trustee's avoiding powers. Thus, if the trustee does not take action to enforce one of his or her rights, the debtor in a liquidation bankruptcy can nevertheless enforce that right.

Voidable Rights. A trustee steps into the shoes of the debtor. Thus, any reason that a debtor can use to obtain the return of his or her property can be used by the trustee as well. These grounds include fraud, duress, incapacity, and mutual mistake (see Chapter 8 for definitions of these terms).

PREFERENCE
In bankruptcy proceedings, the debtor's favoring of one creditor over others by making payments or transferring property to that creditor at the expense of the rights of other creditors. The bankruptcy trustee is allowed to recover payments made to one creditor in preference over another.

For example, Barry sells his boat to Zenov. Zenov gives Barry a check, knowing that there are insufficient funds in his bank account to cover the check. Zenov has committed fraud. Barry has the right to avoid that transfer and recover the boat from Zenov. Once an order for relief under Chapter 7 of the Code has been entered for Barry, the trustee can exercise the same right as Barry could to recover the boat from Zenov, and the boat becomes a part of the debtor's estate.

Preferences. A debtor is not permitted to transfer property or to make a payment that favors—or gives a **preference** to—one creditor over others. The trustee is allowed to recover payments made both voluntarily and involuntarily to one creditor in preference over another.

To have made a preferential payment that can be recovered, a debtor generally must have transferred property, for a preexisting debt, within *ninety days* of the filing of the petition in bankruptcy. The transfer must give the creditor more than the creditor would have received as a result of the bankruptcy proceedings. Sometimes the creditor receiving the preference is an insider—an individual, a partner, a partnership, or an officer or a director of a corporation (or a relative of one of these) who has a close relationship with the debtor. If this is the case, the avoidance power of the trustee usually is extended to transfers made within *one year* before filing.

If a preferred creditor (one who has received a preference) has sold the transferred property to an innocent third party, the trustee cannot recover the property from the innocent party. The creditor, however, generally can be held accountable for the value of the property.

Fraudulent Transfers. The trustee may avoid fraudulent transfers or obligations if they were made within one year of the filing of the petition or if they were made with actual intent to hinder, delay, or defraud a creditor. For example, suppose that a debtor who is thinking about petitioning for bankruptcy sells his stamp collection, worth several thousand dollars, to a friend for $1,000. The friend agrees that in the future he will "sell" the collection back to the debtor for the same amount of money.

When a fraudulent transfer is made outside the Code's one-year limit, creditors may seek alternative relief under state laws. State laws often allow creditors to recover for transfers made up to three years prior to the filing of a petition.

Exempted Property

The trustee takes control over the debtor's property, but an individual debtor is entitled to exempt certain property from the bankruptcy. The Bankruptcy Code exempts the following from the debtor's estate in property:

1. Up to $15,000 in equity in the debtor's residence and burial plot (the homestead exemption).
2. Interest in a motor vehicle up to $2,400.
3. Interest in household goods and furnishings, wearing apparel, appliances, books, animals, crops, and musical instruments up to $400 in a particular item and $8,000 in total.
4. Interest in jewelry up to $1,000.
5. Interest in any other property up to $800, plus any unused part of the $15,000 homestead exemption up to $7,500.
6. Interest in any tools of the debtor's trade up to $1,500.
7. Any unmatured life insurance contract owned by the debtor.
8. Certain interests in accrued dividends and interest under life-insurance contracts owned by the debtor.
9. Professionally prescribed health aids.
10. The right to receive Social Security and certain welfare benefits, alimony and support, and certain pension benefits.

ETHICAL CONCERN

Divided Loyalties

As a paralegal, if you learn that a fraudulent transfer of property was made by a debtor, you have an ethical obligation to inform your supervising attorney of the debtor's illegal action. But what if the debtor is also your friend? What if you know that the debtor is concealing certain personal property (her grand piano, two valuable paintings inherited from her father, and so on)? When you ask her about these items during the intake interview, she confides in you that she "gave" them to her sister to hold for her so they wouldn't be subject to creditors' claims. What do you do? On the one hand, you know how important these items of personal property are to your friend and are sympathetic to her plight. On the other hand, you know that it is unfair to her creditors to conceal this property and that you would be violating your ethical obligations if you said nothing about it to your supervising attorney. This is another example of how, as a paralegal, your personal loyalties and professional commitments may come into conflict. Harsh as it may sound, you should abide by your professional duties in such situations. Remember, if you do not report the fraudulent concealment of assets, you are, in essence, participating in this wrongdoing.

11. The right to receive certain personal injury and other awards, up to $15,000.

Individual states have the power to pass legislation precluding debtors from using the federal exemptions within that state; a majority of the states have done this. In those states, debtors may use only state, not federal, exemptions. In the rest of the states, an individual debtor (or a husband and wife filing jointly) may choose between the exemptions provided under state law and the federal exemptions.

State laws may provide significantly greater protection for debtors than federal law. For example, under state exemption laws, a debtor may enjoy an unlimited-value exemption on a motor vehicle, even though the federal bankruptcy scheme exempts a vehicle only up to a value of $2,400. A state's law may also define the property coming within an exemption differently than the federal law or may exclude specific things from an exemption, making it unavailable to a debtor who fits within the exception.

Creditors' Meeting

Within a reasonable time after the order for relief has been granted (not less than ten days or more than thirty days), the bankruptcy court must call a meeting of creditors listed in the schedules filed by the debtor. The bankruptcy judge does not attend this meeting.

The debtor is required to attend the meeting (unless excused by the court) and to submit to examination under oath by the creditors and the trustee. At this meeting, the trustee verifies information concerning the nature and extent of the debtor's assets and liabilities and may seek further information. The trustee also ensures that the debtor is aware of the potential consequences of bankruptcy and of his or her ability to file for bankruptcy under a different chapter of the Bankruptcy Code. Creditors may or may not attend—and often do not. If the debtor fails to appear at the meeting or makes false statements under oath, the debtor may be denied a discharge in bankruptcy.

At this first meeting, either a permanent trustee is elected or, as is often the case, the interim trustee becomes the permanent trustee.

Creditors' Claims

PROOF OF CLAIM
A document filed with the bankruptcy court by a creditor to inform a court of a claim against a debtor's property. The proof of claim lists the creditor's name and address, as well as the amount that the creditor asserts is owed to the creditor by the debtor.

In a bankruptcy case in which the debtor has no assets (called a no-asset case), creditors are notified of the debtor's petition for bankruptcy but are instructed not to file a claim. In such a case, the creditors will receive no payment, and most, if not all, of the debts will be discharged. If there are sufficient assets to be distributed to creditors, each creditor must normally file a proof of claim with the bankruptcy court clerk within ninety days of the creditors' meeting to be entitled to receive a portion of the debtor's estate. (This same ninety-day rule applies in Chapter 13 bankruptcies as well.) The **proof of claim** lists the creditor's name and address, as well as the amount that the creditor asserts is owed to the creditor by the debtor. If a creditor fails to file a proof of claim, the bankruptcy court or trustee may file the proof of claim on the creditor's behalf but is not obligated to do so.

Generally, any legal obligation of the debtor is a claim. In the case of a disputed claim, the bankruptcy court will set the value of the claim. Any creditor holding a debtor's obligation can file a claim against the debtor's estate. These claims are automatically allowed unless contested by the trustee, the debtor, or another creditor. A creditor who files a false claim commits a crime.

The Code does not allow claims for breach of employment contracts or real-estate leases for terms longer than one year. Such claims are limited to one year's wages or rent, despite the remaining length of either contract in breach.

Distribution of Property

In the distribution of the debtor's estate in property, secured creditors take priority over unsecured creditors. A **secured creditor** is one who has a security interest in the collateral that secures the debt. For example, a lending institution that finances the purchase of an automobile normally takes a security interest in the automobile—the collateral for the loan.

SECURED CREDITOR
A lender, seller, or any other person in whose favor there is a security interest.

The Code provides that a consumer-debtor, within thirty days of filing a liquidation petition or before the date of the first meeting of the creditors (whichever is first), must file with the clerk a statement of intention with respect to the secured collateral. The statement must indicate whether the debtor will retain or surrender the collateral to the secured party. Also, if applicable, the debtor must specify whether the collateral will be claimed as exempt property and whether the debtor intends to redeem (buy back) the property or reaffirm the debt secured by the collateral. The trustee is obligated to enforce the debtor's statement within forty-five days after it is filed.

If the collateral is surrendered to the secured party, the secured creditor can enforce the security interest either by accepting the property in full satisfaction of the debt or by selling the collateral and using the proceeds to pay off the debt. Thus, the secured party has priority over unsecured parties as to the proceeds from the disposition of the collateral. Indeed, the Code provides that if the value of the collateral exceeds the secured party's claim, the secured party also has priority as to the proceeds in an amount that will cover reasonable fees and costs incurred because of the debtor's default. Any excess over this amount is used by the trustee to satisfy the claims of unsecured creditors. Should the collateral be insufficient to cover the secured debt owed, the secured creditor becomes an unsecured creditor for the difference.

Bankruptcy law establishes an order of priority for classes of debts owed to unsecured creditors, and they are paid in the order of their priority. Each class of unsecured creditors must be fully paid before the next class is entitled to any of the remaining proceeds. If there are insufficient proceeds to pay fully all the creditors in a class, the proceeds are distributed proportionately to the creditors in the class, and classes lower in priority receive nothing. The order of priority among classes of unsecured creditors is as follows:

1. Administrative expenses—including court costs, trustee fees, and attorneys' fees.
2. In an involuntary bankruptcy, expenses incurred by the debtor in the ordinary course of business from the date of the filing of the petition up to the

appointment of the trustee or the issuance by the court of an order for relief.
3. Unpaid wages, salaries, and commissions earned within ninety days of the filing of the petition, limited to $4,000 per claimant. Any claim in excess of $4,000 is treated as a claim of a general creditor (listed as number 9 below).
4. Unsecured claims for contributions to be made to employee benefit plans, limited to services performed during 180 days prior to the filing of the bankruptcy petition and $4,000 per employee.
5. Claims by farmers and fishers, up to $4,000, against debtor operators of grain storage or fish storage or processing facilities.
6. Consumer deposits of up to $1,800 given to the debtor before the petition was filed in connection with the purchase, lease, or rental of property or purchase of services that were not received or provided. Any claim in excess of $1,800 is treated as a claim of a general creditor (number 9 below).
7. Paternity, alimony, maintenance, and support debts.
8. Certain taxes and penalties due to government units, such as income and property taxes.
9. Claims of general creditors.

If any amount remains after the priority classes of creditors have been satisfied, it is turned over to the debtor.

Discharge

From the debtor's point of view, the primary purpose of liquidation is to obtain a fresh start through a discharge of debts. Certain debts, however, are not dischargeable in bankruptcy. Also, certain debtors may not qualify to have all debts discharged in bankruptcy. These situations are discussed below.

Exceptions to Discharge Discharge of a debt may be denied because of the nature of the claim or the conduct of the debtor. Claims that are not dischargeable in a liquidation bankruptcy include the following:

1. Claims for back taxes accruing within three years prior to bankruptcy.
2. Claims for amounts borrowed by the debtor to pay federal taxes.
3. Claims against property or money obtained by the debtor under false pretenses or by false representations.
4. Claims by creditors who were not notified of the bankruptcy; these claims did not appear on the schedules the debtor was required to file.
5. Claims based on fraud or misuse of funds by the debtor while he or she was acting in a fiduciary capacity or claims involving the debtor's embezzlement or larceny.
6. Alimony, child support, and (with certain exceptions) property settlements (to the extent they were not paid on the debtor's distribution of property).
7. Claims based on willful or malicious conduct by the debtor toward another or the property of another.
8. Certain government fines and penalties.
9. Certain student loans, unless payment of the loans imposes an undue hardship on the debtor and the debtor's dependents.

10. Consumer debts of more than $1,000 for luxury goods or services owed to a single creditor incurred within sixty days of the order for relief. This denial of discharge is a rebuttable presumption (that is, the denial may be challenged by the debtor), however, and any debts reasonably incurred to support the debtor or dependents are not classified as luxuries.
11. Cash advances totaling more than $1,000 that are extensions of open-end consumer credit obtained by the debtor within sixty days of the order for relief. A denial of discharge of these debts is also a rebuttable presumption.
12. Judgments or consent decrees against a debtor as a result of the debtor's operation of a motor vehicle while intoxicated.

Objections to Discharge. In addition to the exceptions to discharge previously listed, a bankruptcy court may also deny the discharge based on the debtor's conduct. In such a situation, the assets of the debtor are still distributed to the creditors, but the debtor remains liable for the unpaid portion of all claims. Some grounds for the denial of discharge based on the debtor's conduct follow:

1. The debtor's concealment or destruction of property with the intent to hinder, delay, or defraud a creditor.
2. The debtor's fraudulent concealment or destruction of financial records.
3. The granting of a discharge to the debtor within six years of the filing of the petition.

To encourage creditors' legitimate objections to discharge, the Code provides that even if the creditor loses on the challenge, the creditor is liable for costs and attorneys' fees only if the challenge was not *substantially justified.*

Effect of Discharge. The primary effect of a discharge is to void, or set aside, any judgment on a discharged debt and prohibit any action to collect a discharged debt. A discharge does not affect the liability of a co-debtor.

Revocation of Discharge. The Code provides that a debtor 's discharge may be revoked. Upon petition by the trustee or a creditor, the bankruptcy court may, within one year, revoke the discharge decree if it is discovered that the debtor acted fraudulently or dishonestly during the bankruptcy proceedings. The revocation renders the discharge void, allowing creditors not satisfied by the distribution of the debtor's estate to proceed with their claims against the debtor.

Reaffirmation of Debt

A debtor may voluntarily agree to pay a debt—for example, a debt owed to a family member, family doctor, close friend, or some other party—notwithstanding the fact that the debt could be discharged in bankruptcy. An agreement to pay a debt dischargeable in bankruptcy is referred to as a **reaffirmation agreement**. To be enforceable, reaffirmation agreements must be made before the debtor is granted a discharge. The agreement must be filed with the court. Approval by the court is required unless the debtor's attorney files an affidavit stating that the reaffirmation agreement is voluntarily made, that the debtor understands the consequences of the agreement and of a default under the

REAFFIRMATION AGREEMENT
An agreement between a debtor and a creditor in which the debtor reaffirms, or promises to pay, a debt dischargeable in bankruptcy. To be enforceable, the agreement must be made prior to the discharge of the debt by the bankruptcy court.

agreement, and that the agreement will not result in an undue hardship on the debtor or the debtor's family.

The agreement must contain a clear and conspicuous statement advising the debtor that reaffirmation is not required. The debtor can rescind, or cancel, the agreement at any time prior to discharge or within sixty days of the filing of the agreement, whichever is later. This period of time must be stated *clearly* and *conspicuously* in the reaffirmation agreement.

ETHICAL CONCERN

The Perils of Independent Practice

As you read in Chapter 3, independent paralegals are those who provide services directly to the public (without attorney supervision). Often, independent paralegals assist debtors by selling them "do-it-yourself" bankruptcy kits, typing up bankruptcy forms, and so on. Although this is one way to earn a living, it may be perilous for the paralegal. If you ever contemplate entering into this kind of business, you need to be extremely careful. There have been many cases in which debtors, state bar associations, or other entities have brought legal actions against paralegals for the unauthorized practice of law. It cannot be emphasized enough that practicing as an independent paralegal poses many pitfalls, including potential criminal penalties.

REORGANIZATIONS

The type of bankruptcy proceeding used most commonly by a corporate debtor is the Chapter 11 *reorganization*. In a reorganization, the creditors and the debtor formulate a plan under which the debtor pays a portion of his or her debts and is discharged of the remainder. The debtor is allowed to continue in business. Although this type of bankruptcy is commonly a corporate reorganization, any debtor (except a stockbroker or a commodities broker) who is eligible for Chapter 7 relief is eligible for relief under Chapter 11. Railroads are also eligible.

Prior to 1991, some courts barred individuals from petitioning for reorganization, even though the language of the Code does not limit the use of reorganization to business debtors. The United States Supreme Court, however, has since ruled that a nonbusiness debtor may petition for relief under Chapter 11.[2]

The same principles that govern the filing of a liquidation petition apply to reorganization proceedings. The case may be brought either voluntarily or involuntarily. The same principles govern the entry of the order for relief. The automatic-stay provision is also applicable in reorganizations.

In some instances, creditors may prefer private, negotiated adjustments of creditor-debtor relations, also known as **workouts**, to bankruptcy proceedings. Often these out-of-court workouts are much more flexible and thus more conducive to a speedy settlement. Speed is critical, because delay is one of the most costly elements in any bankruptcy proceeding. Another advantage of workouts is that they avoid the various administrative costs of bankruptcy proceedings.

WORKOUT
An out-of-court negotiation in which a debtor enters into an agreement with a creditor or creditors for a payment or plan to discharge the debtor's debt.

A bankruptcy court, after notice and a hearing, may dismiss or suspend all proceedings in a case at any time if dismissal or suspension would better serve the interests of the creditors. The Code also allows a court, after notice and a hearing, to dismiss a case under reorganization "for cause." Cause includes the absence of a reasonable likelihood of rehabilitation, the inability to effect a plan, and an unreasonable delay by the debtor that is prejudicial to (may harm the interests of) creditors.

Debtor in Possession

DEBTOR IN POSSESSION (DIP)
In Chapter 11 bankruptcy proceedings, a debtor who is allowed, for the benefit of all concerned, to maintain possession of the estate in property (the business) and to continue business operations.

Upon entry of the order for relief, the debtor generally continues to operate his or her business as a **debtor in possession (DIP)**. The court, however, may

2. *Toibb v. Radloff*, 501 U.S. 157, 111 S.Ct. 2197, 115 L.Ed.2d 145 (1991).

appoint a trustee (often referred to as a *receiver*) to operate the debtor's business if gross mismanagement of the business is shown or if appointing a trustee is in the best interests of the estate.

The DIP's role is similar to that of a trustee in a liquidation. The DIP is entitled to avoid preferential payments made to creditors and fraudulent transfers of assets that occured prior to the filing of the Chapter 11 petition. The DIP has the power to decide whether to cancel or assume obligations under executory contracts (contracts that have not yet been performed) that were made prior to the filing.

Collective-bargaining Agreements

The Code attempts to reconcile federal policies favoring collective bargaining with the need to allow a debtor company to reject executory labor contracts while trying to reorganize. The Code sets forth standards and procedures under which collective-bargaining contracts can be assumed or rejected under a reorganization filing. In general, a collective-bargaining contract can be rejected if the debtor has first proposed necessary contractual modifications to the union and the union has failed to adopt them without good cause. The company is required (1) to provide the union with the relevant information needed to evaluate the proposal and (2) to confer in good faith in attempting to reach a mutually satisfactory agreement on the modifications.

Creditors' Committees

As soon as practicable after the entry of the order for relief, a creditors' committee of unsecured creditors is appointed. The committee may consult with the trustee or the DIP concerning the administration of the case or the formulation of the reorganization plan. Additional creditors' committees may be appointed to represent special-interest creditors. Generally, no orders affecting the estate will be entered without either the consent of the committee or a hearing in which the judge hears the position of the committee.

Businesses with debts of less than $2 million that do not own or manage real estate can avoid creditors' committees. In these cases, orders can be entered without a committee's consent.

The Reorganization Plan

A reorganization plan to rehabilitate the debtor is a plan to conserve and administer the debtor's assets in the hope of an eventual return to successful operation and solvency. The plan must be fair and equitable and must do the following:

1. Designate classes of claims and interests.
2. Specify the treatment to be afforded the classes. (The plan must provide the same treatment for each claim in a particular class.)
3. Provide an adequate means for execution.

Only the debtor may file a plan within the first 120 days after the date of the order for relief. If the debtor does not meet the 120-day deadline, however, or if the debtor fails to obtain the required creditor consent within 180

DEVELOPING PARALEGAL SKILLS

Obtaining Creditor's Consent to a Chapter 11 Plan

Marcia Baxter works as a paralegal for a small law firm that specializes in bankruptcy law. One of Marcia's jobs is to send out letters to creditors of her firm's clients in regard to the clients' bankruptcy proceedings.

Today she is preparing two letters, both of which concern bankruptcy proceedings for clients involved in Chapter 11 reorganizations. The first letter accompanies a reorganization plan and requests the creditor to consent to the plan no later than December 3, 1996, which is 180 days from the filing date. Marcia is responsible for calculating the dates as well as for entering the dates, the relevant names and addresses, the case name, and the court's docket number into the letter.

The second letter is a follow-up letter concerning a Chapter 11 plan that was filed several months ago. If a creditor's consent is not received within three months, then Marcia prepares and sends a follow-up letter reminding the creditor that he or she must respond to the request for consent.

Once both letters have been completed and reviewed by her supervising attorney, Marcia makes a copy of each for the file, as well as a copy for the attorney to have close at hand in her office. The creditor's attorney may call to discuss the case and possibly file an objection to the claim.

days, any party may propose a plan. The plan need not provide for full repayment to unsecured creditors. Instead, creditors receive a percentage of each dollar owed to them by the debtor. If a small-business debtor chooses to avoid creditors' committees, the time for the debtor's filing is shortened to 100 days, and any other party's plan must be filed within 160 days.

Once the plan has been developed, it is submitted to each class of creditors for acceptance. For the plan to be adopted, each class that is adversely affected by the plan must accept it. A class has accepted the plan when a majority of the creditors, representing two-thirds of the amount of the total claim, vote to approve it.

Even when all classes of creditors accept the plan, the court may refuse to confirm it if it is not "in the best interests of the creditors." A spouse or child of the debtor can block the plan if it does not provide for payment of his or her claims in cash.

CRAM-DOWN PROVISION
A provision of the Bankruptcy Code that allows a court to confirm a debtor's Chapter 11 reorganization plan even though only one class of creditors has accepted it. To exercise the court's right under this provision, the court must demonstrate that the plan does not discriminate unfairly against any creditors and is fair and equitable.

Even if only one class of creditors has accepted the plan, the court may still confirm the plan under the Code's so-called **cram-down provision**. In other words, the court may confirm the plan over the objections of a class of creditors. Before the court can exercise this right of cram-down confirmation, it must be demonstrated that the plan "does not discriminate unfairly" against any creditors and that the plan is "fair and equitable."

The plan is binding upon confirmation. The debtor is given a reorganization discharge from all claims not protected under the plan. This discharge does not apply to any claims that would be denied discharge under liquidation.

INDIVIDUAL REPAYMENT PLANS

Chapter 13 of the Bankruptcy Code provides for "Adjustment of Debts of an Individual with Regular Income." Individuals (not partnerships or corporations) with regular income who owe fixed unsecured debts of less than $250,000 or fixed secured debts of less than $750,000 may take advantage of bankruptcy repayment plans. This includes salaried employees; individual proprietors; and individuals who live on welfare, Social Security, fixed pensions, or investment income. Many small-business debtors have a choice of filing a plan for reorganization or for repayment. There are several advantages to repayment plans. One is that they are less expensive and less complicated than reorganization proceedings or liquidation proceedings.

Filing the Petition

A repayment-plan case can be initiated only by the filing of a voluntary petition by the debtor. Certain liquidation and reorganization cases may be converted to repayment-plan cases with the consent of the debtor.

A Chapter 13 repayment-plan case may also be converted to a Chapter 7 case at the request of either the debtor or, under certain circumstances, a creditor. A Chapter 13 repayment-plan case may be converted to a Chapter 11 case after a hearing.

Upon the filing of a repayment-plan petition, a trustee, who will make payments under the plan, must be appointed. The automatic stay previously discussed also takes effect. Although the stay applies to all or part of a consumer debt, it does not apply to any business debt incurred by the debtor.

Filing the Plan

Only the debtor may file a repayment plan. This plan may provide either for payment of all obligations in full or for payment of a lesser amount. A plan of rehabilitation by repayment provides for the turnover to the trustee of such future earnings or income of the debtor as is necessary for execution of the plan. The time for payment under the plan may not exceed three years unless the court approves an extension. The term, with extension, may not exceed five years.

The Code requires the debtor to make "timely" payments, and the trustee is required to ensure that the debtor commences these payments. The debtor must begin making payments under the proposed plan within thirty days after the plan has been filed with the court. If the plan has not been confirmed, the trustee is instructed to retain the payments until the plan is confirmed and then distribute them accordingly. If the plan is denied, the trustee will return the payments to the debtor less any costs. Failure of the debtor to make timely payments or to begin payments within the thirty-day period will allow the court to convert the case to a liquidation bankruptcy or to dismiss the petition.

ETHICAL CONCERN

Off-the-job Confidences and the Duty of Loyalty

What if, as a paralegal, you learn—off the job—that one of your firm's clients is planning to petition for bankruptcy? For instance, suppose that you are having dinner with a friend at Tina's Italian Restaurant. Your friend knows the owner, Tina, very well and tells you that Tina is planning to petition for bankruptcy because business is so bad. He asks you to keep this information in the "strictest confidence." You are shocked at the information because the sole practitioner for whom you work has handled Tina's legal affairs for years. You know that Tina not only owes the firm money for previous services but also wants your supervising attorney to defend her in a case of racial discrimination brought by a job applicant. Should you let your employer know about Tina's apparent intention to file for bankruptcy? Yes, you should. Although you have a moral duty to your friend to keep the information confidential, you have a legal duty, as an agent of your employer, to notify your employer of information relevant to the agency (the employment relationship). You also have a duty to be loyal to your employer's interests.

DEVELOPING PARALEGAL SKILLS

Preparing a Proof of Claim

Lee Smith works as a paralegal for a bankruptcy attorney. Today, Lee has been assigned the task of preparing a proof-of-claim form to be filed with the bankruptcy court for a client. The client is a creditor of an individual who has filed for relief under Chapter 13 of the Bankruptcy Code.

Lee turns to his computer. The standard bankruptcy forms are stored in the computer's memory, and Lee retrieves a proof-of-claim form. He keys in the client-creditor's name and address: General Credit Corporation, 1000 Manhattan Drive, New York, NY 10009. Next, he inserts the amount that the debtor owes to the General Credit Corporation for credit-card purchases: $7,583.09. He then enters the date, the debtor's name, and other required data. He prints out the completed form, proofreads it carefully, and gives it to his supervising attorney to review. After the attorney reviews the form, Lee will make copies of it to send to the court for filing.

Confirmation of the Plan

After the plan is filed, the court holds a confirmation hearing, at which interested parties may object to the plan. The court will confirm a plan with respect to each claim of a secured creditor under any of the following circumstances:

1. If the secured creditors have accepted the plan.
2. If the plan provides that creditors retain their claims against the debtor's property and if the value of the property to be distributed to the creditors under the plan is not less than the secured portion of their claims.
3. If the debtor surrenders the property securing the claim to the creditors.

Objections to the Plan

Unsecured creditors do not have a vote to confirm a repayment plan, but they can object to it. The court can approve a plan over the objection of the trustee or any unsecured creditor only in either of the following situations:

1. When the value of the property to be distributed under the plan is at least equal to the amount of the claims.
2. When all the debtor's projected disposable income to be received during the three-year plan period will be applied to making payments. Disposable income is all income received *less* amounts needed to support the debtor and dependents and/or amounts needed to meet ordinary expenses to continue the operation of a business.

Modification of the Plan

Prior to completion of payments, the plan may be modified at the request of either the debtor, the trustee, or an unsecured creditor. If any interested

DEVELOPING PARALEGAL SKILLS

Working for a Bankruptcy Trustee

Rita Hall works as a paralegal for a Chapter 13 bankruptcy trustee, Susan Mitchell. One of Rita's jobs is to monitor the files of the debtors. She must check to verify that the debtors are making timely payments under their Chapter 13 rehabilitation plans so that Susan can make the scheduled payments to the creditors.

Rita has created a database that contains the names, payment schedules, and other information for all of the debtors. She sits down at her computer and prints out the list of payments that are due today. As Rita reviews the list, she finds one debtor who has not commenced payment and two debtors whose payments are two weeks overdue. She types a memo to Susan summarizing her findings and gives the memo to Susan. For the debtor who has not commenced payment, Susan will most likely seek to have the case converted to a Chapter 7 liquidation, as allowed by law. Susan will give Rita instructions on the procedures to be followed when contacting the two debtors whose payments are late.

party objects to the modification, the court must hold a hearing to determine approval or disapproval of the modified plan.

Discharge

After the completion of all payments, the court grants a discharge of all debts provided for by the repayment plan. All debts are dischargeable except for allowed claims not provided for by the plan, certain long-term debts provided for by the plan, and claims for alimony and child support. A discharge of debts under a Chapter 13 repayment plan is sometimes referred to as a "super-discharge." One of the reasons for this is that the law allows a Chapter 13 discharge to include fraudulently incurred debt and claims resulting from malicious or willful injury. Therefore, a discharge under Chapter 13 may be much more beneficial to some debtors than a liquidation discharge under Chapter 7.

Even if the debtor does not complete the plan, a hardship discharge may be granted if failure to complete the plan was due to circumstances beyond the debtor's control and if the value of the property distributed under the plan was greater than creditors would have received in a liquidation proceeding. A discharge can be revoked within one year if it was obtained by fraud.

BANKRUPTCY LAW AND THE PARALEGAL

Although only a small percentage of paralegals (3 to 4 percent) currently specialize in bankruptcy law, there is a growing demand for paralegals in this area. Much of the work previously handled by attorneys can now be done by

Substantive Law Concept Summary

Bankruptcy Law

	Chapter 7	Chapter 11	Chapter 13
Purpose	Liquidation.	Reorganization.	Adjustment of debts.
Who Can Petition	Debtor (voluntary) or creditors (involuntary).	Debtor (voluntary) or creditors (involuntary).	Debtor (voluntary) only.
Who Can Be a Debtor	Any "person" (including partnerships and corporations) except railroads, insurance companies, banks, savings and loan institutions, investment companies licensed by the Small Business Administration, and credit unions. Farmers and charitable institutions cannot be involuntarily petitioned.	Any debtor (except a stockbroker or a commodities broker) eligible for Chapter 7 relief; railroads are also eligible.	Any individual (not partnerships or corporations) with regular income who owes fixed unsecured debts of less than $250,000 or fixed secured debts of less than $750,000.
Procedure Leading to Discharge	Nonexempt property is sold with proceeds to be distributed (in order) to priority groups. Dischargeable debts are terminated.	Plan is submitted; if it is approved and followed, debts are discharged.	Plan is submitted (must be approved if debtor turns over disposable income for a three-year period); if it is approved and followed, debts are discharged.
Advantages	Upon liquidation and distribution, most debts are discharged, and the debtor has the opportunity for a fresh start.	Debtor continues in business. Creditors can accept the plan, or it can be "crammed down" on them. Plan allows for reorganization and liquidation of debts over the plan period.	Debtor continues in business or possession of assets. If plan is approved, most debts are discharged after a three-year period.

TODAY'S PROFESSIONAL PARALEGAL

Gathering Information for a Bankruptcy Petition

Jeff Jones, a paralegal, works for Colin Peters, an attorney who specializes in bankruptcy cases. Today, Jeff is meeting with Mike Hammersmith, a client who wants to file a voluntary petition for bankruptcy under Chapter 7 of the Bankruptcy Code. Mike owns the Corner Liquor Store, a retail liquor and convenience store, and is facing serious financial difficulties. Mike owns the store as a sole proprietor.

The receptionist announces Mike's arrival, and Jeff meets him in the lobby. They walk to the conference room, which Jeff previously reserved, and sit down at the conference table. Jeff removes a checklist from a file folder that he brought with him into the conference room. The same checklist was given to Mike last week, at the end of the initial client interview. Jeff attended that interview with his supervising attorney, so he is already familiar with Mike's case.

REVIEWING THE LIST OF CREDITORS

"First, I'll need a list of your creditors, with their addresses and the amount that you owe to each," says Jeff. Mike hands Jeff a handwritten list, which is somewhat difficult to read. Jeff reviews the list and asks Mike if he owes $5,000 or $8,000 to the National Bank. "It's hard to tell which it is," says Jeff. Mike clarifies that the amount of the debt is $5,000.

REVIEWING THE LIST OF ASSETS

The next item that Jeff needs is a list of all of the assets—both personal and real property—that Mike owns. Mike hands Jeff another handwritten list, and the first thing Jeff notices is that the list is incomplete: it does not include Mike's home or his car. Jeff asks, "Didn't you tell Mr. Peters and me last week that you owned a home and a car?" "That's correct," answers Mike. "But I didn't include that property because Mr. Peters told me that it would be exempt." "We need to list those items here anyway," Jeff says. "We have to disclose all of your property, including exempt property." Mike then gives Jeff the necessary information about the home and the car, and Jeff adds the information to the list.

REVIEWING THE LIST OF INCOME AND EXPENSES

"The last item that I need is the list of your income and expenses," states Jeff. Mike hands his list to Jeff. Jeff reviews it and does not find anything that is inconsistent with what Mike said in the initial client interview.

CONCLUDING THE INTERVIEW

"That's all I need for today. I'll be using this information to draft the bankruptcy petition. After Mr. Peters reviews it, you'll need to stop by and sign it. Can you come by tomorrow—say, at two o'clock?" Jeff asks. "Yes, I think so," Mike responds. Jeff then explains to Mike that once the petition is signed, it will be filed with the bankruptcy court within the next thirty days.

"Thanks for your help," says Mike, as he shakes Jeff's hand. "Come with me and I'll show you out," says Jeff.

paralegals with expertise in this area. For example, whenever a debtor-client wants to petition for bankruptcy relief, numerous forms must be filled out, stating in detail the debtor's assets and liabilities. These forms must be filled out accurately and thoroughly.

Paralegals familiar with the requirements imposed by bankruptcy law know what information must be included with the petition for bankruptcy and can assist attorneys in collecting this information from clients. Paralegals may be involved in evaluating the debtor's financial statements, researching the law governing certain types of contracts, and locating and perhaps appraising certain property belonging to the debtor.

In addition to gathering and analyzing information concerning the debtor's financial status, it is usually the paralegal who drafts the petition in bankruptcy, files the final petition with the bankruptcy court, and pays the appropriate filing fee.

As a paralegal, you may be dealing with bankruptcy cases periodically as part of your work for a general law practice. If you work for a firm that specializes in bankruptcy law, you may be working on behalf of either debtors or creditors who are involved in bankruptcy proceedings. Bankruptcy trustees also require paralegal assistance. In assisting a bankruptcy trustee, you would be working in the interests of both debtors and creditors during the administration of the debtor's estate in property. In any of these situations, a paralegal well trained in the substantive and procedural laws governing bankruptcy can provide invaluable assistance.

The specific types of work handled by bankruptcy paralegals vary, of course, depending on whether they work on behalf of the debtor, a creditor, or the bankruptcy trustee. Here are just a few examples of paralegal tasks that you might be asked to perform in this area of the law if you were assisting a debtor-client (which could be an individual or a corporate representative) in petitioning for bankruptcy relief:

- Conduct an intake interview—and follow-up interviews as necessary—to obtain information concerning the debtor's income, debts, and assets.
- Draft the bankruptcy petition based on the information obtained from the client.
- Verify the validity of creditors' claims that have been submitted to the bankruptcy court.
- Prepare the client for bankruptcy proceedings, such as creditors' meetings.
- Assist in work on the debtor's behalf in any legal actions relating to the bankruptcy proceedings.
- Research the Bankruptcy Code to verify that certain provisions are still effective and keep up to date on bankruptcy law.
- Research state statutes governing property exemptions.
- Research case law to see how the courts have applied a certain provision of the Bankruptcy Code or a state law applicable to the bankruptcy proceedings.

KEY TERMS AND CONCEPTS

automatic stay 901
bankruptcy trustee 902
consumer-debtor 899
cram-down provision 910
debtor in possession (DIP) 908
discharge 899
estate in property 901
liquidation 899
order for relief 900

CHAPTER SUMMARY

1. The two major goals of bankruptcy law are (1) to provide relief for debtors who have "gotten in over their heads" and (2) to provide a fair means of distributing a debtor's assets among all creditors. Current bankruptcy law is based on the Bankruptcy Reform Act of 1978, as amended. The latest revision of the Bankruptcy Code was the Bankruptcy Reform Act of 1994. Bankruptcy cases are held in federal courts, and the Federal Rules of Bankruptcy Procedure apply. State laws, particularly those governing property, may affect bankruptcy cases.

2. The Bankruptcy Code provides for various types of bankruptcy relief, including liquidations (ordinary, or straight, bankruptcy—under Chapter 7 of the Code), reorganizations (under Chapter 11), and individual repayment plans (under Chapter 13).

3. A liquidation under Chapter 7 is initiated by the filing of a bankruptcy petition. In a voluntary liquidation, the debtor petitions the court for relief. In an involuntary liquidation, one or more of the debtor's creditors initiate the proceedings (force the debtor into bankruptcy). In a voluntary bankruptcy, the petition is accompanied by forms, or schedules, that contain information about the debtor's debts, creditors, financial affairs, assets, and current income and expenses. If the petition is found to be proper, it will constitute an order for relief.

4. The moment a petition, either voluntary or involuntary, is filed, an automatic stay on all creditors' actions against the debtor comes into effect. An estate in property (all of the debtor's property subject to distribution to creditors) is created, and a bankruptcy trustee is appointed to administer the estate. The trustee's basic duty is to collect the debtor's available property and reduce it to money for distribution to creditors. The trustee must act in the interests of both the debtor and the creditors in administering the debtor's estate.

5. When a bankruptcy petition is filed, the court notifies the debtor's creditors of the proceedings and calls a creditors' meeting. The debtor is required to attend the meeting and submit to examination under oath by the trustee and the creditors. To be entitled to receive a portion of the debtor's estate, each creditor must normally file a proof of claim with the bankruptcy court within ninety days of the creditors' meeting.

6. The Bankruptcy Code exempts certain property of the debtor from the debtor's estate. The homestead exemption, for example, allows the debtor to retain up to $15,000 in equity in his or her residence and burial plot. There are numerous other exemptions. In some states, debtors may use only state (not federal) exemptions. In the rest of the states, debtors may choose between the exemptions provided under state law and the federal exemptions.

7. In the distribution of a debtor's property to creditors, secured creditors have first priority. The Bankruptcy Code establishes a specific order of priority among classes of unsecured creditors. If any amount remains after the priority classes of creditors have been satisfied, it is turned over to the debtor. Once the debtor's property is distributed, all debts (with certain exceptions) are discharged (extinguished), and the debtor is given a fresh start—unless one or more creditors succeed in an objection to the debtor's discharge. If a debtor voluntarily decides to pay a dischargeable debt (affirm the debt), certain procedures must be followed.

8. A Chapter 11 reorganization is a proceeding that is most commonly used by corporate debtors. In a reorganization, the same principles that govern the filing of a liquidation petition apply, the proceeding may also be brought voluntarily or involuntarily, and the automatic stay comes into effect. Upon entry of the order for relief, the debtor generally continues to operate his or her business as a debtor in possession (DIP). In some cases, such as those involving gross mismanagement, the court may appoint a trustee (receiver) to manage the debtor's estate. The DIP's role and powers are similar to those of a trustee in a liquidation. During the Chapter 11 proceedings, the creditors' committee consults with the DIP or trustee concerning the administration of the case.

9. The reorganization plan in a Chapter 11 proceeding must be fair and equitable and must be approved by the creditors. If the debtor does not submit a plan within a specified period or if creditors fail to consent to the plan, any party may propose a plan. The court may refuse to confirm a plan, notwithstanding the creditors' assent to it, if the plan is not in the best interests of the creditors. In certain circumstances, the court may also force the creditors to accept a plan under the Bankruptcy Code's "cram-down provision."

10. Any individual with regular income who owes fixed unsecured debts of less than $250,000 or secured debts of less than $750,000 may take advantage of a bankruptcy repayment plan under Chapter 13. An individual repayment plan can be initiated only by the filing of a voluntary petition by the debtor. The plan may provide for payment of all obligations in full or for payment of a lesser amount over a period of three years (the court may extend the repayment period to five years in some cases). The debtor turns over to the trustee whatever future income is necessary to execute the plan. The plan must be confirmed by the bankruptcy court, in consultation with creditors. When all payments have been completed in accordance with the plan, the court grants a discharge of all debts provided for by the repayment plan.

QUESTIONS FOR REVIEW

1. What are the two major goals of bankruptcy law? What law governs bankruptcy matters, and in which courts are bankruptcy cases filed? What types of relief are available under the Bankruptcy Code?

2. How is a liquidation proceeding under Chapter 7 initiated? What is the difference between a voluntary bankruptcy and an involuntary bankruptcy?

3. What effect does the filing of a bankruptcy petition have on creditors? What is an automatic stay?

4. What property is included in a bankruptcy estate (estate in property)?

5. When and why are creditors' meetings held? What is a creditor's claim?

6. How is the debtor's estate distributed in a Chapter 7 liquidation? What is the difference between a secured creditor and an unsecured creditor? Is this difference significant in bankruptcy proceedings?

7. What is a discharge in bankruptcy? What is the difference between an "exception to discharge" and an "objection to discharge"?

8. What is a Chapter 11 bankruptcy proceeding? Who is most likely to file for a Chapter 11 bankruptcy? What is a debtor in possession?

9. What role does a creditors' committee play in a Chapter 11 reorganization? What is a reorganization plan?

10. What type of bankruptcy relief is available under Chapter 13? How does a bankruptcy proceeding under Chapter 13 differ from a Chapter 7 proceeding?

ETHICAL QUESTIONS

1. Marla, an independent paralegal, provides a variety of services for the public. Among other things, she provides debtors with bankruptcy forms and types up bankruptcy petitions. Mr. Ford has sought

Marla's services in filing for bankruptcy. He takes home a set of Chapter 7 forms, reads through them, and begins to provide the information needed. He is uncertain whether Chapter 7 will provide him with the type of relief that he needs. He calls Marla and asks her if he has any other options. How should Marla answer Mr. Ford's questions?

2. Tom, a paralegal, meets Mr. Simpson, a client of the law firm for which Tom works, in the elevator. Tom knows that Mr. Simpson has an appointment to see Tom's supervising attorney regarding a bankruptcy petition. There is only one other man on the elevator, whom Tom does not recognize. Tom begins to ask Mr. Simpson about his appointment. Mr. Simpson reveals that he intends to file for bankruptcy. The other passenger on the elevator happens to work for the bank where the client does most of his business. He returns to the bank and informs his supervisor of Mr. Simpson's intention to file for bankruptcy. Have any ethical rules been breached? If so, which one(s)?

PRACTICE QUESTIONS AND ASSIGNMENTS

1. Douglas Worth earns a salary of $20,000 a year as a sales representative. In addition to his salary, he is entitled to a 10 percent commission on what he sells. Over the past five years, Douglas earned annual commissions of $80,000 to $100,000. Because the economy was booming and Douglas was making such large commissions, he purchased a $50,000 Cadillac and a $25,000 boat and incurred credit-card debts totaling $35,000. This year, the economy has slowed down, and Douglas has made only $10,000 in commissions. He still owes $40,000 on the Cadillac and $20,000 on the boat. In all, he owes $95,000 to creditors. Douglas cannot pay his debts as they become due, and it does not appear that his financial situation will improve over the next two years. As a result, he is thinking about filing for bankruptcy. Explain which type of bankruptcy relief would benefit Douglas the most and why.

2. John and Mary Bogen have filed for voluntary bankruptcy under Chapter 7. They own a car, which was financed by the First American Bank and in which the bank took a security interest. They still owe about $10,000 to the bank. They will owe attorneys' fees, trustee fees, and court costs for the bankruptcy action. John owes alimony and child support to his former wife and children. John and Mary also owe income taxes and penalties from 1995. List the priority in which the creditors will be paid.

QUESTIONS FOR CRITICAL ANALYSIS

1. Do you think that people should be able to avoid paying their debts by filing for bankruptcy? Does a person have a moral responsibility to pay his or her debts, even if it takes years and years to pay them off entirely?

2. Why is certain property exempt from the debtor's estate in property? Are these exemptions unduly harsh to creditors? What would result if such exemptions were not allowed?

3. Do you think that our bankruptcy laws are too lenient? Do bankruptcy laws adequately balance the needs of debtors "who have gotten in over their heads" and creditors?

ROLE-PLAYING EXERCISES

1. Using the facts from Ethical Question 2, role-play the encounter between the paralegal, Tom, and the client, Mr. Simpson. Assume for the purposes of this exercise that Tom knows the client fairly well. The students playing the roles of Tom and Mr. Simpson should be friendly with each other and should not act concerned over the presence of the third party on the elevator. The students playing the role of the third party should appear unassuming and should not act as if he is at all concerned in the conversation.

2. Using the facts from the *Today's Professional Paralegal* feature, role-play the client interview between Jeff, the paralegal, and the client, Mike Hammersmith. Jeff should remember to be professional and courteous when asking Mike for the missing information. The students playing the role of the client, Mike Hammersmith, should be nervous about filing for bankruptcy and should be concerned about omitting property.

PROJECTS

1. If there is a federal bankruptcy court located near you, attend a bankruptcy proceeding for a day or part of a day. Write a one-page summary of your experience.

2. Review your state's bankruptcy laws to determine what property is exempt from the debtor's estate in property. Does your state prohibit debtors from using the federal exemptions within the state, or is a debtor allowed to choose between state and federal exemptions? Write a one-page summary of your findings.

3. In 1991, in *Toibb v. Radloff* [501 U.S. 157, 111 S.Ct. 2197, 115 L.Ed.2d 145 (1991)], the United States Supreme Court held that nonbusiness debtors could petition for relief under Chapter 11. Locate the *Toibb* case, brief the case, and write a one-page summary of the court's reasons for allowing nonbusiness debtors to petition for Chapter 11 bankruptcy.

ANNOTATED SELECTED READINGS

BLOCK-LIEB, SUSAN. "A Comparison of Pro Bono Representation Programs for Consumer Debtors." *American Bankruptcy Institute Law Review,* Spring 1994. An article indicating that a "substantial and increasing percentage" of consumer bankruptcies are filed *pro se* by debtors (filed by debtors who are not represented by attorneys). The article compares various *pro bono* programs that allow needy consumer debtors to be represented by attorneys. The article points out that an individual debtor who is not represented by counsel is less likely to obtain a "fresh start" from bankruptcy.

LEITER, RICHARD A., AND LESLIE ANN FORRESTER SHEREN. "Bankruptcy Research." *Legal Assistant Today,* January/February 1994. An article containing a list of research sources compiled by Leslie Ann Forrester Sheren, the law library director at Murphy, Weir & Butler, in San Francisco, California, a leading bankruptcy law firm. It lists a variety of sources, including bankruptcy reporters, on-line research services, and secondary source materials.

MORZAK, KIM. "An Overview of Environmental Claims in Bankruptcy." *Legal Assistant Today,* January/February 1994. A helpful article that discusses various types of environmental claims as to whether they are subject to the automatic-stay provision and whether they are dischargeable in bankruptcy, as well as what priority may be given to these claims.

MORZAK, KIM. "The Automatic Stay—An Overview of Section 362." *Legal Assistant Today,* September/October 1993. An article providing a solid explanation of the automatic-stay provision.

MUND, GERALDINE. "Paralegals: The Good, the Bad, and the Ugly." *American Bankruptcy Institute Law Review,* Winter 1994. An interesting article promoting the use of trained and licensed independent paralegals to handle consumer bankruptcies. The author, a judge, complains that the court's efforts are focused on regulating "the good" (skilled) paralegals, who are unfortunately being grouped together with "the bad" (unskilled) paralegals and "the ugly" (defrauders).

Appendix A

Mastering *West's Paralegal Today*: How to Study Legal Concepts and Procedures

The law sometimes is considered a difficult subject because it uses a specialized vocabulary and also requires substantial time and effort to learn. Those who work with and teach law believe that the subject matter is exciting and definitely worth your efforts. Everything in *West's Paralegal Today: The Legal Team at Work*, including this appendix, has been written for the precise purpose of helping you learn the most important aspects of law and legal procedures.

Learning is a life long process. Your learning of legal concepts and procedures will not end when you finish your paralegal studies. On the contrary, your paralegal studies mark the beginning of your learning process in regard to law and legal procedures. Just as valuable to you as the knowledge base you can acquire from mastering the legal concepts and terms in *West's Paralegal Today* is a knowledge of *how to learn* those legal concepts and terms. The focus in this appendix, therefore, is on developing learning skills that you can apply to any subject matter and any time throughout your career.

The suggestions and study tips offered in this appendix can help you "learn how to learn" law and procedures and maximize your chances of success as a paralegal student. They can also help you build life long learning habits that you can use in other classes and throughout your career as a paralegal.

Mastering Your Text

A mistake commonly made by students is the assumption that the best way to understand the content of written material is to read and reread that material. True, if you read through a chapter ten times, you probably have acquired a knowledge of its contents, but think of the time you have spent in the process. What you want to strive for is using your time *effectively*. We offer here some suggestions on how to study the chapters of *West's Paralegal Today* most effectively.

Read One Section at a Time

A piano student once said to her teacher, "This piece is so complicated. How can I possibly learn it?" The teacher responded, "It's simple: measure by measure." That advice can be applied to any challenging task. As a paralegal student, you are faced with the task of learning complicated legal concepts and procedures. By dividing up your work into manageable units, you will find that before long, you have achieved your goal. Each chapter in *West's Paralegal Today* is divided into several major sections. By concentrating on sections, rather than chapters, you will find it easier to master the chapter's contents.

Assume, for example, that you have been assigned to read Chapter 8 of *West's Paralegal Today.* That chapter covers basic concepts and principles involving various bodies of substantive law, including contract law, sales contracts, torts, property law, and intellectual property. Mastering each of these topics requires you to learn a number of different legal concepts and terms. You will find it easier to master all of these topics if you concentrate on just one topic at a time. For example, you might begin with the section on contract law and focus only on that section.

Once you have read through a section, do not stop there. Go back through the section again and organize the material in your mind. Outlining the section is one way to mentally organize what you have read.

Make an Outline

An outline is simply a method for organizing information. The reason an outline can be helpful is that it illustrates visually how concepts relate to each other. Outlining can be done as part of your reading of each section, but your outline will be more accurate (and helpful later on) if you have already read through a section and have a general understanding of the topics covered within that section.

The Benefits of Outlining. Although you may not believe that you need to outline, our experience has been that the act of *physically* writing an outline for a chapter helps most students to improve greatly their ability to retain and master the material being studied. Even if you make an outline that is no more than the headings in the text, you will be studying more efficiently than you would be otherwise.

Outlining is also a paralegal skill. As a paralegal, you will need to present legal concepts and fact patterns in an outline format. For example, paralegals frequently create legal memoranda to summarize their research results. The legal memorandum is usually presented in an outline format, which indicates how the topics covered in the memo relate to one another logically or sequentially. There is no better time to master the skill of outlining than the present, while you are a student. You can learn this skill by outlining sections and chapters of *West's Paralegal Today.*

Identify the Main Concepts in Each Section. You can use the chapter outlines at the beginning of each chapter as a starting point on your outlines for each section and chapter. The chapter-opening outlines include the headings of each major section within the chapter and the basic subheadings within each section. You use these headings as a guide when creating a more thorough and detailed outline of each section. Be careful, though. To make an effective outline you have to be selective. Outlines that contain all the information in the text are not very useful. Your objective in outlining is to identify main concepts and to arrange more detailed concepts under those main concepts. Therefore, in outlining, your first goal is to *identify the main concepts in each section.* Often the large, first-level headings within your textbook and in the chapter-opening outlines are sufficient as identifiers of the major concepts within each section. You may decide, however, that you want to phrase an identifier in a way that is more meaningful to you.

Outline Format. Your outline should consist of several levels written in a standard outline format. The most important concepts are assigned an upper-case roman numeral; the second most important, a capital letter; the third most important, numbers; the fourth most important, lower-case letters; and the fifth most important, lower-case roman numerals. The number of levels you use in an outline varies, of course, with the complexity of the subject matter. In some outlines, or portions of outlines, you may need to use only two levels. In others, you may need as many as five or more levels.

As an example of how to use numerals and letters in an outline, we present below a partial outline of the contracts section in Chapter 8 of *West's Paralegal Today.*

FUNDAMENTAL LEGAL CONCEPTS: CONTRACTS

I. Definition of a contract
   A. General definition: An exchange of promises that can be enforced in court.
   B. Specific definition: An oral or written agreement formed by two or more parties who promise to perform or refrain from performing some act now or in the future.
II. Breach of contract: Occurs when a party to a contract fails to perform as promised.
III. Requirements of a valid contract
   A. Agreement—divided into two events:
      1. The offer—one party (offeror) makes an offer to another party (offeree) to form a contract.
         a. Requirements of the offer
            i. Must reflect a serious and objective intent on part of offeror to form a contract.
            ii. Must contain sufficiently definite terms so that if accepted, the contract's terms will be clear to a court if a dispute arises.
         b. Offeror may normally revoke (take back) offer at any time prior to acceptance.
      2. Acceptance
         a. Acceptance by offeree creates binding contract (if other requirements for a valid contract are also met).
         b. Acceptance can only be made by offeree, not a third party.
         c. Acceptance must be timely—within time period designated by offeror or within a "reasonable time."
   B. Consideration . . .

Consider Marking Your Text

From kindergarten through high school, you typically did not own your own textbooks. They were made available by the school system. You were told not to mark in them. Now that you own your own text for a course, your learning can be greatly improved by marking your text. There is a trade-off here. The more you mark up your textbook, the less you will receive from your bookstore when you sell it back at the end of the semester. The benefit is a better understanding of the subject matter, and the cost is the reduction in the price you receive for the resale of the text. Additionally, if you want a text that you can mark with your own notations, you necessarily have to buy a new one or a used one that has no markings. Both carry a higher price tag than a used textbook with markings.

The Benefits of Marking. Marking is helpful because it helps you to become an *active* participant in the mastery of the material. Researchers have shown that the physical act of marking, just like the physical act of outlining, helps you better retain the material. The better the material is organized in your mind, the more you will remember. There are two types of readers—passive and active. The active reader outlines and/or marks. Active readers typically do better on exams. Perhaps one of the reasons that active readers retain more is because the physical act of outlining and/or marking requires greater concentration. It is through greater concentration that more is remembered.

Different Ways of Marking. The most commonly used form of marking is to underline important points. The second most commonly used method is to use a felt-tipped highlighter, or marker, in yellow or some other transparent color. Marking also includes circling, numbering, using arrows, brief notes, or any other method that allows you to locate things when you go back to skim the pages in your textbook prior to an exam—or when creating your outline, if you mark your text first and then outline it.

Points to Remember When Marking. Here are two important points to remember when marking your text:

1. *Read through the entire section before you begin marking.* You cannot mark a section until you know what is important, and you cannot know what is important until you read through the whole section.
2. *Do not mark too extensively.* You should mark your text selectively. If you fill up each page with arrows, asterisks, circles, and underlines, marking will be of little use. When you go back to review the material, you will not be able to find what was important. The key is *selective* activity. Mark each page in a way that allows you to see the most important points at a glance.

Memory Devices

During the course of your study of *West's Paralegal Today,* you will encounter numerous legal terms that are, most likely, new to you. Your challenge will be to remember these terms and incorporate them into your own "working" vocabulary. You will also need to remember legal concepts and principles. We look here at some techniques for learning and retaining legal terms and concepts.

Flash Cards. Using flash cards is a remarkably effective method of learning new terms or concepts. Through sheer repetition, or drilling, flash cards force you to recall certain ideas and repeat them. Although published flash cards are available in many bookstores, you should try to create your own by writing terms or concepts on index cards. Write the key term or concept on one side and the definition, process, or description on the other side.

There are several advantages to creating your own flash cards. First, the exercise of actually writing the information will help you insert the term into your permanent memory. Second, you do not need flash cards for terms that you already know or that you will not need to know for your particular course. Third, you can phrase the answer in a meaningful way, with unique cues that are designed just for your purposes. This personalizes the flash card, making the information easier to remember. Finally, you can modify the definition, if need be, so that it matches more closely the particular definition preferred by your instructor.

It is helpful to create your flash cards consistently and routinely at a given point in the learning process. One good moment is when you are reading or outlining your text. Make a flash card for each boldfaced term and write the margin definition on the flash card. Also include pronunciation instructions, if appropriate, on the card.

Take your flash cards with you anywhere. Review them at lunch, while you wait in line, or when your ride on the bus. When a flash card contains a term that is difficult to pronounce, say the term aloud, if possible, as often as you can. When you have a term memorized, set that card aside but save it as an exam-review device for later in the term. Prepare new cards as you cover new terms or concepts in class.

Mnemonics. One method that students commonly employ to remember legal concepts and principles is the use of mnemonic (pronounced "nee-*mahn*-ick) devices. Mnemonic devices are merely aids to memory. A mnemonic device can be a word, a formula, or a rhyme. As an aid to remembering the elements of a cause of action in negligence, for example, you might use the mnemonic ABCD, in which the letters represent the following concepts:

A represents "A duty of care."
B represents "Breach of the duty of care."
C represents "Causation (the breach must cause an injury)."
D represents "Damage (injury or harm)."

Similarly, to remember the basic activities that paralegals may not legally undertake, you might use the mnemonic FACt, in which the letters represent the following concepts:

F represents "fees"—paralegals may not set legal fees.
A represents "advice"—paralegals may not give legal advice.
Ct represents "court"—paralegals, with some exceptions, may not represent clients in court.

Whenever you want to memorize various components of a legal doctrine or concept, consider devising a mnemonic. Mnemonics need not make sense in themselves. The point is, if they help you remember something, then use them. Any association you can make with a difficult term to help you pronounce it, spell it, or define it more easily is a useful learning tool.

Identify What You Do Not Understand

One of the most important things you can do prior to class is clarify in your mind which terms, concepts, or procedures you *do not* understand. You can do this when marking your text by placing check marks or question marks by material that you find difficult to understand. Similarly, you can include queries in your outline. For example, in the sample partial outline of contracts presented above, you might add a query following the subsection on acceptance that reads, "What is considered to be a 'reasonable time'?"

Once you have outlined and marked you text, go back to any problem areas that you have encountered and *think about them.* You will find that it is very exciting to figure out difficult material on your own. If you still do not understand a concept thoroughly, make a note to follow up on this topic later, in the classroom. Perhaps the instructor's lecture will clarify the issue. If not, make a point of asking for clarification.

As a paralegal, you may be frequently asked to undertake preliminary investigations of legal claims. Identifying what facts are *not known* is the starting point for any investigation and focuses investigatory efforts. As a student, you might think about class time as an opportunity to "investigate" further the subject matter of your course. Identifying before class what you do not know about a topic allows you to focus your "investigative" efforts, particularly your listening efforts, during class and to maximize classroom opportunities for learning.

LEARNING IN THE CLASSROOM

The classroom is the heart of your learning experience as a paralegal student. Each instructor develops an overall plan for a course that includes many elements, which are integrated, or brought together, during class sessions. A major element in your instructor's course plan will be, of course, the material presented in your textbook, *West's Paralegal Today.* As discussed in the preceding section, reading your textbook assignments thoroughly, before class, is one way to enhance your chances of truly mastering the subject matter of the course. Equally important to this goal, though, are listening carefully to your instructor and taking good notes.

Be an Active Listener

In Chapter 5 of *West's Paralegal Today,* the authors discuss different types of listening skills. Periodically reviewing that chapter's sections on active listening and retentive listening will help you learn to listen effectively in the classroom. The ability to listen actively is a learned skill and one that will benefit you throughout your career as a paralegal. When your supervising attorney gives instructions, for example, it is crucial that you understand those instructions clearly. If you do not, you will need to ask the attorney to further clarify the instructions until you know exactly what your assignment is. Similarly, when you are interviewing clients or witnesses, you will need to be constantly interacting, mentally, with the information the client or witness is giving you so that you can follow up, immediately if necessary, on that information with further questions or actions.

As a paralegal student, you can practice listening skills in the classroom that you will need to exercise later on the job. The more immediate benefit of listening actively is, of course, a better chance of obtaining an excellent course grade.

In a nutshell, active listening as a student requires you to do the following:

1. *Listen attentively.* For anything to be communicated verbally by one person to another, the listener has to pay attention or no communication will take place. If you find your attention wandering in the classroom, make a conscious effort to become attentive and focus on what is being said.
2. *Mentally interact with what is being said.* Active listening involves mentally "acting" on the information being conveyed by the speaker (your instructor). For example, if your instructor is discussing the elements required for a cause of action in negligence, you do not want simply to write down, word for word, what the instructor is saying. Rather, you first make sure that you *understand* the meaning of what is being said. This requires you to think about what is being said in the context of what else you know about the topic. Does the information make sense within that context? Does what you are hearing raise further questions in your mind? If so, make a note of them.
3. *Ask for clarification.* If you do not understand what the instructor is saying or if something is unclear, ask for clarification. How you do this will depend to some extent on the size of your class and the degree of classroom formality. In some classes, you might feel comfortable raising your hand and questioning the instructor at that point during the lecture or discussion. In other classes, you might make a note to talk to the instructor about the topic after class or later, during the instructor's office hours.

Take Good Notes

The ability to take good notes is another skill that will help you excel both in your paralegal studies and on the job as a paralegal. Ideally, you will understand clearly everything that is being said in the classroom, and note taking will simply consist of jotting down, in your own words, brief phrases and sentences to remind you of what was stated. Often, however, you may not understand fully what the instructor is talking about, or it may take half of the class period before it becomes clear to you where your instructor is going with a certain idea or topic. In the meantime, should you take notes?

The best answer to this question is, of course, "Ask for clarification." But in some situations, interrupting a lecturer may be awkward or perceived as discourteous. In such circumstances, the wiser choice might be to take notes. Write down, to the extent possible, what the instructor is saying, including brief summaries of any examples the instructor is presenting. Later, when you have more knowledge of the subject, what the instructor said during that period may fall into place. If not, find an opportunity to ask for clarification.

Two other suggestions for taking good notes and making effective use of them are the following: (1) develop and use a shorthand system and (2) review and summarize your notes as soon as possible after class.

Develop and Use a Shorthand System. There may be times during a lecture when you want to take extensive notes. For example, your instructor may be discussing a hypothetical scenario to illustrate a legal concept. Because you know that hypothetical examples are very useful in understanding (and later reviewing) legal concepts, you want to include a description of the hypothetical example in your notes. Using abbreviations and symbols can help you include more information in your notes in less time.

In taking notes of a hypothetical example, consider designating a single letter as representative of each person or entity involved in the example. This eliminates the need to write and rewrite the names of each person or entity as they are used. For example, if a hypothetical involves three business firms, you could designate each firm by a letter: *A* could stand for Abel Electronics, *B* for Brentwood Manufacturing, and *C* for Crandall Industries.

Certain symbols and abbreviations, including those listed below, are fairly widely used as a kind of "shorthand" by legal professionals and others to designate certain concepts, parties, or procedures:

Δ	defendant
π	plaintiff
≈	similar to
≠	not equal to, not the same as
∴	therefore
a/k/a	also known as
atty	attorney
b/c or **b/cz**	because
b/p	burden of proof
cert	*certiorari*
dely	delivery
dep	deposition
disc	discovery
JML	judgment as a matter of law
JNOV	judgment *non obstante veredicto* (notwithstanding the verdict)
JOP	judgment on the pleadings
juris	jurisdiction
K	contract
mtg	mortgage
n/a	not applicable
neg	negligence
PL	paralegal
Q	as a consequence, consequently
re	regarding
§ or **sec**	section
s/b	should be
S/F	Statute of Frauds
S/L	statute of limitations

You will want to expand on this short list by creating and using other symbols or abbreviations. Once you develop a workable shorthand system, routinely use it in the classroom and then carry it over to your job. Most firms or corporations you will work for will also commonly use symbols and abbreviations, which you can add to your shorthand system later. It may also be helpful to become familiar with the dictionary's proofing symbols, which are listed under "proofreading" in the dictionary.

Review and Revise Your Notes after Each Class. An excellent habit to form is reviewing and revising your class notes as soon as possible after the class period ends. Often, at the moment you write certain notes, you are not sure of how they fit in the overall design of the lecture. After class, however, you usually have a better perspective and know how the "pieces of the puzzle" fit together. Reviewing and summarizing your notes while the topic is still fresh in your mind—at the end of each day, for example—gives you the opportunity to reorganize them in a logical manner.

If you have a computer available, consider also typing up your notes. That way, when you want to review them, you will be able to read them quickly. Using a basic outline format when typing your notes (or rewriting them, if you do not have a computer available) will be particularly helpful later. You can tell at a glance the logical relationships between the various statements made in class.

Although reviewing and summarizing your notes each day or at other frequent intervals may seem overly time-consuming, in the long run it pays off. First, as with outlining and marking a text, reviewing your notes after class allows you to learn actively—you can think about what was covered during the class period, place various concepts in perspective, and decide what you do or do not understand after you complete your review. Second, you have probably already learned that memory is fickle. Even though we think we will not forget something we learned, in fact, we often do. When preparing for an exam, for example, you will want to remember what the instructor said in class about a particular topic. But, if you are like most people, your memory of that day and that class period may be rather fuzzy several weeks later. If you have taken good notes and summarized them legibly and logically, you will be able to review the topic quickly and effectively.

Networking in the Classroom

Several times in *West's Paralegal Today,* the authors, the featured-guest authors, and the paralegals profiled have all mentioned the importance of networking. The best time to begin networking is in the classroom. Consciously make an effort to get to know your instructor. Let him or her come to know you and your interests. Later, when looking for a job, you may want to ask that instructor for a reference.

Similarly, make an effort to become acquainted with other students in your class. Compared to students who are taking other college courses, such as math courses and history courses, there is a greater likelihood those of you in paralegal studies will be working in the same geographic area and may eventually belong to the same paralegal associations. Establishing connections with your classmates now may lead to networking possibilities later, on the job, which offers many benefits for paralegals. One good way to establish long-term relationships with other students is by forming a study group.

SHOULD YOU FORM A STUDY GROUP?

Many paralegal students join together in study groups to exchange ideas, to share the task of outlining subjects, to prepare for examinations, and to lend support to each other generally. If you want to start a study group, a good way to find potential members is to observe your classmates and decide which students participate actively and frequently in class. Then approach those individuals with your idea of forming a study group. The number of participants in a study group can vary. Ordinarily, three to five members is sufficient for a good discussion. A study group with more than six members may defeat the goal of having each member actively participate, to the greatest extent possible, in group discussions.

Some paralegal students form study groups that meet on an "as needed" basis. For example, any member could call a meeting when there is an upcoming exam or difficult subject matter to be learned. Other students establish ongoing study groups that meet throughout the year (and sometimes for the entire paralegal program). The group works as a team and as such is an excellent preparatory device for working as part of a legal team in a law firm. Study groups can also continue on after course work is completed to prepare for certification exams as paralegals. These groups are also a great way to build relationships with other future paralegals with which you may want to network later, on the job.

Meeting Times and Places. It is helpful to set up a regular meeting time and hold that time sacred. The members must be committed to the meeting times and to completing their assignments, or the group will not serve its purpose. Study groups can meet anywhere. You might meet in a classroom, another school room, a member's home, a park, or a restaurant. Many paralegal schools and colleges have multipurpose rooms or study areas available to students who wish to meet in small groups. Some rooms are equipped with easels or drawing boards, which help facilitate discussions. Audiovisual equipment may also be available for the group's use, such as a television with a VCR for viewing videotaped lectures. The group should select a meeting place that has limited distractions and sufficient space to accommodate each member's opened books, notes, and other materials.

Work Allocation. Teamwork is very important in the paralegal profession. Study groups can help you learn to function as a member of a team by distributing the workload among the group. Work (such as outlining chapters) should be allocated among the group members. It is important to define clearly who will be doing what work. It may be a good idea at the close of each meeting to have each member state out loud what work he or she will be responsible for completing prior to the next meeting. Whatever work one member does, he or she should make copies to distribute to the other members at the meeting.

Evaluating Your Group. You should realize from the outset that your study group will be of little help if you are doing most of the work. You need to make sure that everyone who joins the group is as committed to learning the material as you are and that you make this concern known to the others. The teamwork approach is only effective if everybody does his or her share. As mentioned several times in *West's Paralegal Today,* teamwork involves trust and reliance. If you cannot trust one of the members to form an accurate outline of a topic, you will not be able to rely on that outline. You will end up doing the work yourself, just as a precaution. Therefore, be very selective about whom you invite to join the group. If you joined an already existing group, leave it if it turns out to be a waste of your time.

ORGANIZING YOUR WORK PRODUCT

A part of the learning experience takes place through special homework assignments, research projects, and possibly study-group meetings. For example, if you are studying pretrial litigation procedures, you will read about these procedures in Chapter 10 of *West's Paralegal Today.* Your instructor will also likely devote class time to a discussion of these procedures. Additionally, you may be asked to create a sample complaint or to check your state's rules governing the filing of complaints in state courts. You also might have notes on a study-group discussion of these procedures.

How can you best organize all the materials generated during the coverage of a given topic? Here are a few suggestions that you might find useful. If you follow these suggestions, you will find that reviewing your work prior to exams is relatively easy—most of the work will already have been done.

Consider Using a Three-ring Binder. The authors have found that an excellent way to integrate what you have learned is by using a three-ring binder and divider sheets with tabs for the different topics you cover. As you begin studying *West's Paralegal Today,* for example, consider having a different section in your binder for each chapter. Within that section, you can place your chapter outline (formed while reading the text), notes taken in the classroom or during other reading assignments, samples of projects you have done relating to topics in that chapter, and so on.

Integrate Your Notes into One Document, If Possible. If you have used a computer to key in your chapter outlines and class notes, consider incorporating everything you have learned about a topic into one document—a master, detailed outline of the topic. This can be done relatively easily by using the "cut and paste" feature of word-processing programs. The result will be a comprehensive outline of a particular topic that will make reviewing the topic prior to an exam (and perhaps later, on the job) a simple matter.

THE BENEFITS OF USING A COMPUTER

Many of the paralegals profiled in *West's Paralegal Today* mentioned that if they were a student again, they would spend more time developing computer skills. You should consider acquiring a personal computer, if possible. If not, see if you can arrange with someone else to use his or her personal computer on a routine basis. If your school or college has computers available in the library or other place for student use, you might also use one of those computers. Find out when there is usually a computer available—such as early in the morning—and use the computer routinely at this time.

Using a computer provides many benefits. First, you can practice your keyboarding and word-processing skills (essential paralegal skills) simultaneously as you take notes or work on research or other class projects. Second, if you have a computer available, you can type up and better organize your notes. Such time is well spent because it not only increases your knowledge of the topics but also makes it easy to review what you have learned prior to exams.

Finally, a key benefit of using a computer is the quality of any work product or homework assignment that you submit to your instructor. The editing and formatting features of word-processing programs allow you to correct misspelled words, reorganize your presentation, and generally revise your document with little effort. The spell-checker and grammar-checker features help you avoid glaring errors. The formatting features allow you to present your document in an attractive format. You can change margins, use different fonts (such as italics or boldface) to emphasize certain words or phrases. As a paralegal, you will be using a computer and a word-processing system to generate your work. You will also be expected to know how to use computers to create "quality work products." The more you can learn about computers and word processing as a student, the easier it will be for you to perform your job as a paralegal.

PREPARING FOR EXAMS

Being prepared for exams is crucial to doing well as a paralegal student. If you have followed the study tips and suggestions given in the preceding pages of this appendix, you will have little problem preparing for an exam. You will have at your fingertips detailed outlines of the topics covered, a marked textbook that allows you to review major concepts quickly and easily, and class notes. If you have integrated your outlines and class notes in one comprehensive, detailed outline, you will have an even easier task when it comes time to prepare for an examination.

In addition to mastering the material in *West's Paralegal Today* and in the classroom, if you want to do well on an exam, you should develop an exam-taking strategy. For example, prior to any exam, you should find answers to the following questions:

- What type of exam are you going to take—essay, objective, or both?
- What reading materials and lectures will be covered on the exam?
- What materials should you bring to the exam? Will you need paper to write on, or will paper be provided?
- Will you be allowed to refer to your text or notes during the exam (as in an open-book exam)?
- Will the exam be computerized? If so, you will probably need to bring several no. 2 pencils to the exam.
- How much time will be allowed for the exam?

The more you can find out in advance about an exam, the better you can prepare for it. For example, if you learn that there will an essay question on the exam, one way to prepare for the question is to practice writing timed essays. In other words, find out in advance how much time you will have for each essay question, say fifteen minutes, and then practice writing an answer to a sample essay question during a fifteen-minute time period. This is the only way you will develop the skills needed to pace yourself for an essay exam. Because most essay exams are "closed book," do your timed essay practice without using the book.

Usually, you can anticipate certain essay exam questions. You do this by going over the major concept headings, either in your lecture notes or in your text. Search for the themes that tie the materials together, and then think about questions that your instructor might ask you. You might even list possible essay questions as a review device. Then write a short outline for each of the questions that will most likely be asked. Some instructors give their students a list of questions from which the essay questions on the exam will be drawn. This gives you an opportunity to prepare answers for each of the questions in advance. Even though you cannot take your sample essays to class and copy them there, you will have organized the material in your mind.

TAKING EXAMS

There are several strategies you can employ while taking exams to better your grade, including those discussed below.

Following Instructions

Students are often in such a hurry to start an exam that they take little time to read the instructions. The instructions can be critical, however. In a multiple-choice exam, for example, if there is no indication that there is a penalty for guessing, then you should never leave a question unanswered. Even if there are only a few minutes remaining at the end of the exam, you should guess at the answers for those questions about which you are uncertain.

You also need to make sure that you are following the specific procedures required for the exam. Some exams require that you use a no. 2 lead pencil to fill in the dots on a machine-graded answer sheet. Other exams require underlining or circling. In short, you have to look at the instructions carefully.

Finally, check to make sure that you have all the pages of the examination. If you are uncertain, ask the instructor or the exam proctor. It is hard to justify not having done your exam correctly because you failed to answer all of the questions. Simply stating that you did not have them will pose a problem for both you and your instructor. Do not take a chance. Double-check to make sure.

Use Exam Time Effectively

Examinations are often timed. This can make an otherwise straightforward question more difficult because of the *time pressure* that the student faces. Timed examinations require that a question or cluster of questions be answered within a specified period of time. If you must complete thirty multiple-choice questions in one hour, then you have two minutes to work on each individual question. If you finish fifteen of those questions in one minute instead of two, then you will have banked fifteen minutes that can be spent elsewhere on the examination or used to double-check your answers.

Consider the following example. Assume that you have ninety minutes for the entire exam: thirty minutes to answer the multiple-choice questions, fifteen minutes to answer the true-false questions, and forty-five minutes to answer a long essay question. If you could shave ten minutes off the time it takes to answer the multiple-choice section and five minutes off the time it takes to answer the true-false questions, you will have fifteen additional minutes to complete the long essay question.

Taking Objective Examinations

The most important point to discover initially with any objective test is if there is a penalty for guessing. If there is none, you have nothing to lose by guessing. In contrast, if a point or portion of a point will be subtracted for each incorrect answer, then you probably should not answer any question for which you are purely guessing.

Students usually commit one of two errors when they read objective-exam questions: (1) they read things into the questions that do not exist, or (2) they skip over certain words or phrases.

Most test questions include key words such as:

all
always
never
only

If you miss these key words you will be missing the "trick" part of the question. Also, you must look for questions that are only *partly* correct, particularly if you are answering true/false questions.

Never answer a question without reading all of the alternatives. More than one of them may be correct. If more than one of them seems correct, make sure you select the answer that seems the *most* correct.

Whenever the answer to an objective question is not obvious, start with the process of elimination. Throw out the answers that are clearly incorrect. Even with objective exams in which there is a penalty for guessing, if you can throw out several obviously incorrect answers, then you may wish to guess among the remaining ones because your probability of choosing the correct answer is relatively high. Typically, the easiest way to eliminate incorrect answers is to look for those that are meaningless, illogical, or inconsistent. Often, test authors put in choices that make perfect sense and are indeed true, but they are not the answer to the question you are to answer.

Writing Essay Exams

As with objective exams, you need to read the directions to the essay questions carefully. It is best to write out a brief outline *before* you start writing.

The outline should present your conclusion in one or two sentences, then your supporting argument. You should take care not to include in your essay information that is irrelevant, even if you think it is interesting. It is important to stay on the subject. We can tell you from first-hand experience that no instructor likes to read answers to unasked questions.

Finally, write as legibly as possible. Again speaking from experience, the authors can tell you that it is easier to be favorably inclined to a student's essay if we do not have to reread it several times to decipher the handwriting.

Appendix B

Electronic Legal Research Using the Internet

When you do legal research, you do not necessarily have to go to a law library. Neither do you necessarily have to subscribe to the two specialized legal research electronic systems, WESTLAW and LEXIS. Rather, if you have a computer and a modem you may be able to access sources for legal research from the Internet.

What Internet Is and Is Not

The Internet is a loosely configured web of over 35,000 educational, corporate, and research computer networks around the world. It started in 1969 when the Defense Department wanted to put together a research and development communications network that was designed to survey nuclear war.

There is no central computer on Internet. Rather, with each message that you send there is an address code that allows any computer in the Internet to forward it towards its destination.

There is no governing body for the Internet. The closest thing that resembles one is the Internet Society in Reston, Virginia, which is a volunteer organization of individuals and corporate members. The Internet Society promotes "Net" use and oversees new communications developments.

Getting on the Internet

There are basically two ways to get on the Internet: through your college or university or through a commercial service.

Using Your College or University Gateway

If you are enrolled in a college or university, it is probably connected directly to the Internet and pays thousands of dollars a year for this hookup. One of the uses of a college Internet subscription is typically electronic mail, otherwise known as E-mail or e-mail. Faculty, administrators, and students can get an "**address**" and a "**password**." The address is just like a mailbox at which you receive electronic information. Addresses differ depending on the *gateway* that leads you from your computer through another computer to the person or address you want to reach.

You can get your address now by looking at a copy of the handout that your college or university gives to new users. Then you can start playing with E-mail. One of the first things you can do is roam through the user-friendly **gopher** program. The way you do this is as follows:

- Open your connection the way you would to send or receive E-mail.
- Type "**gopher**."
- Hit return (or enter).
- Now you will see a first-level menu of choices. Pick one by moving the arrow up or down to the item you want to open or type the letter where your cursor is blinking.
- When you are done playing, type "**Q**," and it will **Q**uit.

You may want to contact the so-called "mother of all gophers" site at the University of Minnesota. You can do this the following way:

- Type "**gopher**."
- Then type "**consultant@micro.umn.edu.**"

Accessing Internet Via Commercial Services

Virtually anybody can sign up for commercial on-line service and be able to access the electronic mail (E-mail) part of Internet. These services include Delphi, America On-Line, CompuServe, Prodigy, and others. There is a monthly service charge and then a per-minute usage fee for each of the services.

Alternatively, you can subscribe to a gateway company, such as *The World* in Boston, which charges $20 a month per phone for direct access to the Internet.

HARDWARE AND SOFTWARE

Virtually any computer will work as long as you have a modem attached to it. The faster the modem, usually the better off you are. Most modems sold today have a 14,400 bps speed, and many are being sold with higher speeds.

The communications software that you purchase for accessing the Internet will determine how easy it is for you to use it. For those using IBMs and compatible computers running Windows, there is *WinGopher,* a graphical interface for the Internet. Additional programs include *NetCruiser* by NetCom and *TCP/Connect II* and *WorldLink* by InterCon. For those using Macintosh systems, the latter two are available, as well as a version of *WinGopher* for Macintosh.

By the time you read this, there will undoubtedly be even more "user-friendly" communications software systems for accessing the Internet, including those directly provided by Delphi and other on-line services.

RESEARCH MATERIALS AVAILABLE

Do not expect a library at your fingertips. Rather, think of C-Span that you can watch on cable TV—a lot of raw data. You can, for example, browse through the entire Americans with Disabilities Act of 1990, as well as many other acts. Additionally, you can "chat" with other people because there are **BBSs (bulletin board services)** for every conceivable subject matter, many of which are law related. Nolo Press, which publishes numerous legal materials, may already have its *Nolo News* on-line through Internet.

You can also obtain blank forms, such as simple contracts and tax forms. The forms usually do not come with documentation, however.

Raw Data Available

Virtually all United States Supreme Court decisions, the text of treaties, such as the North American Free Trade Agreement (NAFTA), and many state statutes, such as all of those from California, are available through the Internet.

The White House press releases are available on a daily basis. You are allowed to search through them for a particular topic, such as gun control.

All information from the U.S. Patent and Trademark Office, such as *Patent Office Publications*, are starting to become available on line.

Getting Information on the United States Supreme Court. The United States Supreme Court now makes available its decisions in electronic format within minutes of their release. By using the Internet, you can read the Court's opinions on cases that interest you. To locate Supreme Court rulings, go to the University of Maryland **gopher** at:

info.umde.edu

and choose **Educational Resources/United States/Supreme Court.**

Getting Information on the *United States Code.* If you want information on the *United States Code,* you can go to the Cleveland State University **gopher** at:

gopher.law.csuohio.edu

HyperNet Searching

Through the Internet, you can access Cornell University Law School's computer. Using a "hypertext" research tool, you can pull up a document and then click on a phrase or word. Within seconds you will be linked to other relevant information sources on the Internet.

Independent Bulletin Board Services

There are thousands of independent bulletin board services that are operating from either someone's home or office. Many local BBSs are connected to other BBSs nationwide. Local BBSs are generally listed in the classified-ad section of newspapers or in computer magazines.

If you are in the state of Washington, for example, there is a BBS that allows you to access all of the laws of the state of Washington. FedWorld is a BBS that offers connections to numerous government-run BBSs. They, in turn, provide government documents. You can reach FedWorld through the Internet.

One BBS gives information and discussions of mediation and dispute resolution. It is Conflict-Net. Its BBS direct phone number is 415-322-0162. Its Internet address is **telnet ipc.apc.org**.

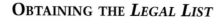

OBTAINING THE *LEGAL LIST*

There is a seventy- to one-hundred-page listing of where to find law on the Internet. It gives you complete instructions on how to access different sources (if you are familiar with the Internet). The following are two ways to obtain this legal list through commercial services:

- On-Line America: Type **"goLEGAL."** Ask for file **NN94INT.TXT.**
- CompuServe: Go to **"LAWSIG, LIBRARY."** Ask for **NN94INT.TXT.**

The following is a way to obtain a general listing of law-related **gophers** throughout the world:

- Select **riceinfo.rice.edu.**
- Then choose **law-gophers**.

This will provide you with a list of **gophers** from around the world that provide law-related information, and it also allows you to access them. This is one way to find out about the laws in any of the fifty states or foreign countries. It also allows you to access **gophers** set up by law schools from around the world.

THE WORLD-WIDE WEB

There is something called a "distributed hypermedia" feature on the Internet called the World-Wide Web. What you do is click on words within a document, and the World-Wide Web will take you to other documents around the world. The two main entries into the World-Wide Web are:

- O'Reilly's Global Network Navigator—It gives you the Declaration of Independence, the U.S. Constitution, and jumping-off points to most of the legal information in the Web. This includes the law libraries at Cornell, Columbia University, Indiana University, and Washington and Lee University.
- Cornell Law School's Legal Information Institute—This allows you to access United States Supreme Court decisions a couple of days after they have been handed down and then allows you to get into the World-Wide Web.

CHOOSING A PASSWORD

It is important that you choose a password that cannot be easily discovered by others. Otherwise you may end up with a huge phone bill, and others may be able to access your electronic mail. Here are some rules for choosing and keeping your password secret:

- Do not use any words that are in any dictionary.
- Use at least eight characters.
- Do not use obvious passwords, such as sports teams or your birthday.

- Mix up numbers, special characters, and letters. Mix upper and lower case.
- Never write your password any place where people can find it.
- Change passwords frequently.
- Do not "lend" your password to anyone else.
- Do not tell your password to someone over the phone.

Appendix C

The NALA Code of Ethics and Professional Responsibility

Preamble

It is the responsibility of every legal assistant to adhere strictly to the accepted standards of legal ethics and to live by general principles of proper conduct. The performance of the duties of the legal assistant shall be governed by specific canons as defined herein in order that justice will be served and the goals of the profession attained.

The canons of ethics set forth hereafter are adopted by the National Association of Legal Assistants, Inc. [NALA], as a general guide, and the enumeration of these rules does not mean there are not others of equal importance although not specifically mentioned.

Canon 1

A legal assistant shall not perform any of the duties that lawyers only may perform nor do things that lawyers themselves may not do.

Canon 2

A legal assistant may perform any task delegated and supervised by a lawyer so long as the lawyer is responsible to the client, maintains a direct relationship with the client, and assumes full professional responsibility for the work product.

Canon 3

A legal assistant shall not engage in the practice of law by accepting cases, setting fees, giving legal advice or appearing in court (unless otherwise authorized by court or agency rules).

Canon 4

A legal assistant shall not act in matters involving professional legal judgment as the services of a lawyer are essential in the public interest whenever the exercise of such judgment is required.

Canon 5

A legal assistant must act prudently in determining the extent to which a client may be assisted without the presence of a lawyer.

Canon 6

A legal assistant shall not engage in the unauthorized practice of law and shall assist in preventing the unauthorized practice of law.

Canon 7

A legal assistant must protect the confidences of a client, and it shall be unethical for a legal assistant to violate any statute now in effect or hereafter to be enacted controlling privileged communications.

Canon 8

It is the obligation of the legal assistant to avoid conduct which would cause the lawyer to be unethical or even appear to be unethical, and loyalty to the employer is incumbent upon the legal assistant.

Canon 9

A legal assistant shall work continually to maintain integrity and a high degree of competency throughout the legal profession.

Canon 10

A legal assistant shall strive for perfection through education in order to better assist the legal profession in fulfilling its duty of making legal services available to clients and the public.

Canon 11

A legal assistant shall do all other things incidental, necessary, or expedient for the attainment of the ethics and responsibilities imposed by statute or rule of court.

Canon 12

A legal assistant is governed by the American Bar Association Model Code of Professional Responsibility and the American Bar Association Model Rules of Professional Conduct.

Adopted May, 1975
Revised November, 1979
Revised September, 1988

Appendix D

The NALA Model Standards and Guidelines for Utilization of Legal Assistants Annotated

Introduction

The purpose of this annotated version of the National Association of Legal Assistants, Inc. (NALA) Model Standards and Guidelines for the Utilization of Legal Assistants is to provide references to the existing case law and other authorities where the underlying issues have been considered. The authorities cited will serve as a basis upon which conduct of a legal assistant may be analyzed as proper or improper.

The Guidelines represent a statement of how the legal assistant may function in the law office. The Guidelines are not intended to be a comprehensive or exhaustive list of the proper duties of a legal assistant. Rather, they are designed as guides to what may or may not be proper conduct for the legal assistant. In formulating the Guidelines, the reasoning and rules of law in many reported decisions of disciplinary cases and unauthorized practice of law cases have been analyzed and considered. In addition, the provisions of the American Bar Association's Model Code of Professional Responsibility and the Model Rules of Professional Conduct, as well as the ethical promulgations of various state courts and bar associations have been considered in development of the Guidelines.

While the Guidelines may not have universal application, they do form a sound basis for the legal assistant and the supervising attorney to follow in the operation of a law office. The Model will serve as a definitive and well-reasoned guide to those considering voluntary standards and guidelines for legal assistants. If regulation is to be imposed in a given jurisdiction the Model may serve as a comprehensive resource document.

I. Preamble

Proper utilization of the services of legal assistants affects the efficient delivery of legal services. Legal assistants and the legal profession should be assured that some measures exist for identifying legal assistants and their role in assisting attorneys in the delivery of legal services. Therefore, the National Association of Legal Assistants, Inc., hereby adopts these Model Standards and Guidelines as an educational document for the benefit of legal assistants and the legal profession.

Comment

The three most frequently raised questions concerning legal assistants are (1) How do you define a legal assistant; (2) Who is qualified to be identified as a legal assistant; and (3) What duties may a legal assistant perform? The definition adopted answers the first question insofar as legal assistants serving attorneys are concerned. The Model sets forth minimum education, training, and experience through standards which will assure that one denominated as a legal assistant has the qualifications to be held out to the public in that capacity. The Guidelines identify those acts which the reported cases hold to be proscribed and give examples of services which the legal assistant may perform under the supervision of an attorney.

The three fundamental issues in the preceding paragraph have been raised in various cases for the past fifty years. In *Ferris v. Snively,* 19 P.2d 942 (Wash. 1933), the Court stated [that] work performed by a law clerk[,] to be proper and not the unauthorized practice of law[,] required supervision by the employing attorney. The Court stated:

> *We realize that law clerks have their place in a law office, and we recognize the fact that the nature of their work approaches in a degree that of their employers. The line of demarcation as to where their work begins and where it ends cannot always be drawn with absolute distinction or accuracy. Probably as nearly as it can be fixed, and it is sufficient to say that it is work of a preparatory nature, such as research, investigation of details, the assemblage of data and other necessary information, and such other work as will assist the employing attorney in carrying the matter to a completed product, either by his personal examination and approval thereof or by additional effort on his part. The work must be such, however, as loses its separate identity and becomes either the product, or else merged in the product, of the attorney himself. (19 P.2d at pp. 945–46.) (See Florida EC3–6, infra, at Section IV.)*

The NALA Guidelines constitute a statement relating to services performed by non-lawyer employees as approved by court decisions and other sources of authority. The purpose of the Guidelines is not to place limitations or restrictions on the legal profession. Rather, the Guidelines are intended to outline for the legal profession an acceptable course of conduct. By voluntary recognition and utilization of the Model Standards and Guidelines the legal profession will avoid many problems.

II. DEFINITION

Legal assistants* are a distinguishable group of persons who assist attorneys in the delivery of legal services. Through formal education, training, and experience, legal assistants have knowledge and expertise regarding the legal system and substantive and procedural laws which qualify them to do work of a legal nature under the supervision of an attorney.

*Within this occupational category some individuals are known as paralegals.

Comment

This definition has been used to foster a distinction between a legal assistant as one working under the direct supervision of an attorney and a broader class of paralegals who perform tasks of similar nature, but not necessarily under the supervision of an attorney. In applying the standards and guidelines it is important to remember that they in turn were developed to apply to the legal assistant as defined therein.

III. STANDARDS

A legal assistant should meet certain minimum qualifications. The following standards may be used to determine an individual's qualifications as a legal assistant:

1. Successful completion of the Certified Legal Assistant ("CLA") certifying examination of the National Association of Legal Assistants, Inc.;
2. Graduation from an ABA approved program of study for legal assistants;
3. Graduation from a course of study for legal assistants which is institutionally accredited but not ABA approved, and which requires not less than the equivalent of 60 semester hours of classroom study;
4. Graduation from a course of study for legal assistants, other than those set forth in (2) and (3) above, plus not less than six months of in-house training as a legal assistant;
5. A baccalaureate degree in any field, plus not less than six months in-house training as a legal assistant;
6. A minimum of three years of law-related experience under the supervision of an attorney, including at least six months of in-house training as a legal assistant; or
7. Two years of in-house training as a legal assistant.

For purposes of these Standards, "in-house training as a legal assistant" means attorney education of the employee concerning legal assistant duties and these Guidelines. In addition to review and analysis of assignments the legal assistant should receive a reasonable amount of instruction directly related to the duties and obligations of the legal assistant.

Comment

The Standards set forth suggested minimum qualifications for a legal assistant. These minimum qualifications as adopted recognize legal related work backgrounds and formal education backgrounds, both of which should provide the legal assistant with a broad base in exposure to and knowledge of the legal profession. This background is necessary to assure the public and the legal profession that the one being identified as a legal assistant is qualified.

The Certified Legal Assistant ("CLA") examination offered by NALA is the only voluntary nationwide certification program for legal assistants. The "CLA" designation is a statement to the legal profession and the public that the legal assistant has met the high levels of knowledge and professionalism required by NALA's certification program. Continuing education requirements, which all certified legal assistants must meet, assure that high standards are maintained. Certification through NALA is available to any legal assistant meeting the educational and experience requirements.

IV. GUIDELINES

These Guidelines relating to standards of performance and professional responsibility are intended to aid legal assistants and attorneys. The responsibility rests with an attorney who employs legal assistants to educate them with respect to the duties they are assigned and to supervise the manner in which such duties are accomplished.

Comment

In general, a legal assistant is allowed to perform any task which is properly delegated and supervised by an attorney, so long as **the attorney is ultimately responsible to the client and assumes complete professional responsibility for the work product.**

The Code of Professional Responsibility of the American Bar Association, EC3–6 states:

ABA Model Rules of Professional Conduct, Rule 5.3 provides:

With respect to a non-lawyer employed or retained by or associated with a lawyer:

(a) a partner in a law firm shall make reasonable efforts to ensure that the firm has in effect measures giving reasonable assurance that the person's conduct is compatible with the professional obligations of the lawyer;
(b) a lawyer having direct supervisory authority over the non-lawyer shall make reasonable efforts to ensure that the person's conduct is compatible with the professional obligations of the lawyer; and
(c) a lawyer shall be responsible for conduct of such a person that would be a violation of the rules of professional conduct if engaged in by a lawyer if:
(1) the lawyer orders or, with the knowledge of the specific conduct ratifies the conduct involved; or
(2) the lawyer is a partner in the law firm in which the person is employed, or has direct supervisory authority over the person, and knows of the conduct at a time when its consequences can be avoided or mitigated but fails to take reasonable remedial action.

The Florida version of EC3–6 provides:

A lawyer or law firm may employ non-lawyers such as secretaries, law clerks, investigators, researchers, legal assistants, accountants, draftsmen, office administrators, and other lay personnel to assist the lawyer in the delivery of legal services. A lawyer often delegates tasks to such persons. Such delegation is proper if a lawyer retains a direct relationship with his client, supervises the delegated work, and has complete professional responsibility for the work product.

The work which is delegated is such that it will assist the employing attorney in carrying the matter to a completed product either by the lawyer's personal examination and approval thereof or by additional effort on the lawyer's part. The delegated work must be such, however, as loses its separate identity and becomes either the product or else merged in the product of the attorney himself.

The Kentucky Paralegal Code defines a legal assistant as:

. . . a person under the supervision and direction of a licensed lawyer, who may apply knowledge of law and legal procedures in rendering direct assistance to lawyers engaged in legal research; design, develop or plan modifications or new procedures, techniques, services, processes or applications; prepare or interpret legal documents and write detailed procedure for practicing in certain fields of law; select, compile and use technical information from such references as digests, encyclopedias or practice manuals; and analyze and follow procedural problems that involve independent decisions.

Kentucky became the first state to adopt a Paralegal Code, which sets forth certain exclusions to the unauthorized practice of law:

For purposes of this rule, the unauthorized practice of law shall not include any service rendered involving legal knowledge or advice, whether representation, counsel or advocacy, in or out of court, rendered in respect to the acts, duties, obligations, liabilities or business relations of the one requiring services where:

A. The client understands that the paralegal is not a lawyer;
B. The lawyer supervises the paralegal in the performance of his duties; and
C. The lawyer remains fully responsible for such representation, including all actions taken or not taken in connection therewith by the paralegal to the same extent as if such representation had been furnished entirely by the lawyer and all such actions had been taken or not taken directly by the attorney. Paralegal Code, Ky. S.Ct. R 3.700, Sub-Rule 2.

While the Kentucky rule is an exception, it does provide a basis for expanding services which may be performed by legal assistants.

There are many interesting and complex issues involving the use of legal assistants. One issue which is not addressed in the Guidelines is whether a legal assistant, as defined herein, may make appearances before administrative agencies. This issue is discussed in Remmer, *Representation of Clients Before Administrative Agencies: Authorized or Unauthorized Practice of Law?*, 15 Valparaiso Univ.L.Rev. 567 (1981). The State Bar of California Standing Committee on Professional Responsibility and Conduct, in opinion 1988–103 (2/8/89)[,] has stated a law firm can delegate authority to a legal assistant employee to file petitions, motions and make other appearances before the Workers' Compensation Appeals Board provided adequate supervision is maintained by the attorney and the client is informed and has consented to the use of legal assistant in such fashion.

In any discussion of the proper role of a legal assistant attention must be directed to what constitutes the practice of law. The proper delegation of work and duties to legal assistants is further complicated and confused by the lack of adequate definition of the practice of law and the unauthorized practice of law.

In *Davis v. Unauthorized Practice Committee,* 431 S.W.2d 590 (Tex., 1968), the Court found that the defendant was properly enjoined from the unauthorized practice of law. The Court, in defining the "practice of law," stated:

> *According to the generally understood definition of the practice of law, it embraces the preparation of pleadings and other papers incident to actions of special proceedings, and the management of such actions in proceedings on behalf of clients before judges in courts. However, the practice of law is not confined to cases conducted in court. In fact, the major portion of the practice of any capable lawyer consists of work done outside of the courts. The practice of law involves not only appearance in court in connection with litigation, but also services rendered out of court, and includes the giving of advice or the rendering of any service requiring the use of legal skill or knowledge, such as preparing a will, contract or other instrument, the legal effect of which under the facts and conclusions involved must be carefully determined.*

The important distinguishing fact between the defendant in *Davis* and a legal assistant is that the acts of the legal assistant are performed under the supervision of an attorney.

EC3–5 of the Code of Professional Responsibility states:

> *It is neither necessary nor desirable to attempt the formulation of a single, specific definition of what constitutes the practice of law. Functionally, the practice of law relates to the rendition of services for others that call for the professional judgment of a lawyer. The essence of the professional judgment of the lawyer is his educated ability to relate the general body and philosophy of law to a specific legal problem of a client; and thus, the public interest will be better served if only lawyers are permitted to act in matters involving professional judgment. Where this professional judgment is not involved, non-lawyers, such as court clerks, police officers, abstractors, and many governmental employees, may engage in occupations that require a special knowledge of law in certain areas. But the services of a lawyer are essential in the public interest whenever the exercise of professional legal judgment is required.*

There are many cases relating to the unauthorized practice of law, but the most troublesome ones in attempting to define what would or would not form the unauthorized practice of law for acts performed by a legal assistant are those such as *Crawford v. State Bar of California,* 355 P.2d 490 (Calif. 1960), which states that any act performed in a law office is the practice of law because the clients have sought the attorney to perform the work because of the training and judgment exercised by attorneys.

See also, Annot. "Layman's Assistant to Parties in Divorce Proceedings as Unauthorized Practice of Law," 12 ALR4 656; Annot. "Activities of Law Clerks as Illegal Practice of Law," 13 ALR3 1137; Annot. "Sale of Books or Forms Designed to Enable Layman to Achieve Legal Results Without Assistance of Attorney as Unauthorized Practice of Law," 71 ALR3 1000; Annot. "Nature of Legal Services or Law-Related Services Which May Be Performed for Others By Disbarred or Suspended Attorney," 87 ALR3 272. See also, Karen B. Judd, CLA, "Beyond the Bar: Legal Assistants and the Unauthorized Practice of Law," *Facts and Findings,* Vol. VIII, Issue 6, National Association of Legal Assistants, May-June, 1982.

V.

Legal assistants should:

1. Disclose their status as legal assistants at the outset of any professional relationship with a client, other attorneys, a court or administrative agency or personnel thereof, or members of the general public;
2. Preserve the confidences and secrets of all clients; and
3. Understand the attorney's Code of Professional Responsibility and these guidelines in order to avoid any action which would involve the attorney in a violation of that Code, or give the appearance of professional impropriety.

Comment

Routine early disclosure of the legal assistant's status when dealing with persons outside the attorney's office is necessary to assure that there will be no misunderstanding as to the responsibilities and role of the legal assistant. Disclosure may be made in any way that avoids confusion. If the person dealing with the legal assistant already knows of his or her status, further disclosure is necessary. If at any time in written or in oral communication the legal assistant becomes aware that the other person may believe the legal assistant is an attorney, it should be made clear that the legal assistant is not an attorney.

The attorney should exercise care that the legal assistant preserves and refrains from using any confidence or secrets of a client, and should instruct the legal assistant not to disclose or use any such confidences or secrets.

DR4–101(D), ABA Code of Professional Responsibility, provides in part that:

A lawyer shall exercise reasonable care to prevent his employees, associates, and others whose services are utilized by him from disclosing or using confidences or secrets of a client. . .

This obligation is emphasized in EC4–2:

It is a matter of common knowledge that the normal operation of a law office exposes confidential professional information to non-lawyer employees of the office, particularly secretaries and those having access to the files; and this obligates the lawyer to exercise care in selecting and training his employees so that the sanctity of all confidences and secrets of his clients may be preserved.

The ultimate responsibility for compliance with approved standards of professional conduct rests with the supervising attorney. *In the Matter of Martinez,* 107 N.M. 171, 754 P.2d 842 (N.M. 1988). However, the legal assistant should understand what he may or may not do. The burden rests upon the attorney who employs a legal assistant to educate the latter with respect to the duties which may be assigned and then to supervise the manner in which the legal assistant carries out such duties. However, this does not relieve the legal assistant from an independent obligation to refrain from illegal conduct. Additionally, and notwithstanding that the Code is not binding upon non-lawyers, the very nature of a legal assistant's employment imposes an obligation not to engage in conduct which would involve the supervising attorney in a violation of the Code. NALA has adopted the ABA Code as a part of its Code of Ethics.

VI.

Legal assistants should not:

1. Establish attorney-client relationships; set legal fees, give legal opinions or advice; or represent a client before a court; nor
2. Engage in, encourage, or contribute to any act which could constitute the unauthorized practice of law.

Comment

Reported cases holding which acts can and cannot be performed by a legal assistant are few:

The legal assistant cannot create the attorney-client relationship. *DeVaux v. American Home Assur. Co.,* 444 N.E.2d 355 (Mass. 1983).

The legal assistant cannot make court appearances. The question of what constitute[s] a court appearance is also somewhat vague. See, for example, *People v. Alexander,* 53 Ill.App.2d 299, 202 N.E.2d 841 (1964), where preparation of a court order and transmitting information to court was not the unauthorized practice of law, and *People v. Belfor,* 611 P.2d 979 (Colo. 1980), where the trial court found that the acts of a disbarred attorney did not constitute an appearance and the Supreme Court of Colorado held that only the Supreme Court could make the determination of what acts constituted an appearance and the unauthorized practice of law.

The following cases have identified certain areas in which an attorney has a duty to act, but it is interesting to note that none of these cases state[s] that it is improper for an attorney to have the initial work performed by a legal assistant. This again points out the importance of adequate supervision by the employing attorney.

Courts have found that attorneys have the duty to check bank statements, preserve a client's property, review and sign all pleadings, ensure that all communications are opened and answered, and make inquiry when items of dictation are not received. *Attorney Grievance Commission of Maryland v. Goldberg,* 441 A.2d 338, 292 Md. 650 (1982). See also *Vaughn v. State Bar of California,* 100 Cal.Rptr. 713, 494 P.2d 1257 (1972).

The legal assistant cannot exercise professional legal judgment or give legal advice. In *Louisiana State Bar v. Edwins,* 540 So.2d 294 (La. 1989) the court held a paralegal was engaged in activities constituting the unauthorized practice of law, which included evaluation of claims and giving advice on settlements. The attorney who delegated the exercise of these acts aided in the unauthorized practice of law. See also, *People of the State of [Colorado] v. Felker,* 770 P.2d 402 (Col. 1989).

Attorneys have the responsibility to supervise the work of associates and clerical staff. *Moore v. State Bar Association,* 41 Cal.Rptr. 161, 396 P.2d 577 (1964); *Attorney Grievance Committee of Maryland v. Goldberg, supra.*

An attorney must exercise sufficient supervision to ensure that all monies received are properly deposited and disbursed. *Black v. State Bar of California,* 103 Cal.Rptr. 288, 499 P.2d 968 (1972); *Fitzpatrick v. State Bar of California,* 141 Cal.Rptr. 169, 569 P.2d 763 (1977).

The attorney must [ensure] that his staff is competent and effective to perform the work delegated. *In re Reinmiller,* 325 P.2d 773 (Ore., 1958). See also, *State of Kansas v. Barrett,* 483 P.2d 1106 (Kan., 1971); *Attorney Grievance Committee of Maryland v. Goldberg, supra.*

The attorney must make sufficient background investigation of the prior activities and character and integrity of his employees to [ensure] that legal assistants have not previously been involved in unethical, illegal, or other nefarious schemes which demonstrate such person unfit to be associated with the practice of law. See *In the Matter of Shaw,* 88 N.J. 433, A.2d 678 (1982), wherein the Court announced that while it had no disciplinary jurisdiction over legal assistants, it directed that disciplinary hearings make specific findings of fact concerning paralegals' collaboration in nefarious schemes in order that the court might properly discipline any attorney establishing an office relationship with one who had been implicated previously in unscrupulous schemes.

VII.

Legal assistants may perform services for an attorney in the representation of a client, provided:

1. The services performed by the legal assistant do not require the exercise of independent professional legal judgment;
2. The attorney maintains a direct relationship with the client and maintains control of all client matters;
3. The attorney supervises the legal assistant;
4. The attorney remains professionally responsible for all work on behalf of the client, including any actions taken or not taken by the legal assistant in connection therewith; and
5. The services performed supplement, merge with and become the attorney's work product.

Comment

EC3–6, ABA Code of Professional Responsibility, recognizes the value of utilizing the services of legal assistants, but provides certain conditions to such employment:

> *A lawyer often delegates tasks to clerks, secretaries, and other lay persons. Such delegation is proper if the lawyer maintains a direct relationship with his client, supervises the delegated work, and has complete professional responsibility for the work product. This delegation enables a lawyer to render legal services more economically and efficiently.*

VIII.

In the supervision of a legal assistant, consideration should be given to:

1. Designating work assignments that correspond to the legal assistant's abilities, knowledge, training and experience.
2. Educating and training the legal assistant with respect to professional responsibility, local rules and practices, and firm policies;
3. Monitoring the work and professional conduct of the legal assistant to ensure that the work is substantially correct and timely performed.
4. Providing continuing education for the legal assistant in substantive matters through courses, institutes, workshops, seminars and in-house training; and
5. Encouraging and supporting membership and active participation in professional organizations.

Comment

Attorneys are responsible for the actions of their employees in both malpractice and disciplinary proceedings. The attorney cannot delegate work to a legal assistant which involves activities constituting the unauthorized practice of law. *See Louisiana State Bar v. Edwins,* 540 So.2d (La. 1989), and *People of the State of Colorado v. Felker,* 770 P.2d 402 (Colo. 1989). In the vast majority of the cases, the courts have not censured attorneys for the particular act delegated to the legal assistant, but rather, have been critical of imposed sanctions against attorneys for failure to adequately supervise the legal assistants. See e.g., *Attorney Grievance Commission of Maryland v. Goldberg, supra.*

The attorney's responsibility for supervision of legal assistants must be more than a willingness to accept responsibility and liability for the legal assistant's work. The attorney must monitor the work product and conduct of the legal assistant to [ensure] that the work performed is substantially correct and completely performed in a professional manner. This duty includes the responsibility to provide continuing legal education for the legal assistant.

Supervision of legal assistants must be offered in both the procedural and substantive legal areas in the law office.

In *Spindell v. State Bar of California,* 118 Cal.Rptr. 480, 530 P.2d 168 (1975), the attorney was suspended from practice because of the improper legal advice given by a secretary. The case illustrates that it is important that both attorneys and legal assistants confirm all telephonic advice by letter.

In all instances where the legal assistant relays information to a client in response to an inquiry from the client, the advice relayed telephonically by the legal assistant should be confirmed in writing by the attorney. This will eliminate claims if the client acts contrary to the advice given. It will establish that the legal advice given is in fact that of the attorney, not the legal assistant, and obviate any confusion resulting from transmission of the advice through the legal assistant.

The *Spindell* case is an example of an attorney's failure to supervise and educate his staff. Not only was the secretary uneducated as to the substantive provisions of the law, but more importantly, she was uneducated as to her duty and authority as an employee of the attorney.

IX.

Except as otherwise provided by statute, court rule or decision, administrative rule or regulation, or the attorney's Code of Professional Responsibility; and within the preceding parameters and proscriptions, a legal assistant may perform any function delegated by an attorney, including but not limited to the following:

1. Conduct client interviews and maintain general contact with the client after the establishment of the attorney-client relationship, so long as the client is aware of the status and function of the legal assistant, and the client contact is under the supervision of the attorney.
2. Locate and interview witnesses, so long as the witnesses are aware of the status and function of the legal assistant.
3. Conduct investigations and statistical and documentary research for review by the attorney.
4. Conduct legal research for review by the attorney.
5. Draft legal documents for review by the attorney.
6. Draft correspondence and pleadings for review by and signature of the attorney.
7. Summarize depositions, interrogatories, and testimony for review by the attorney.
8. Attend executions of wills, real estate closings, depositions, court or administrative hearings and trials with the attorney.
9. Author and sign letters provided the legal assistant's status is clearly indicated and the correspondence does not contain independent legal opinions or legal advice.

Comment

The United States Supreme Court has recognized the variety of tasks being performed by legal assistants and has noted that use of legal assistants encourage cost effective delivery of legal services. *Missouri v. Jenkins,* 491 U.S. 274, 109 S.Ct. 2463, 2471, n. 10 (1989). In *Jenkins,* the court further held that legal assistant time should be included in compensation for attorney fee awards at the prevailing practice in the relevant community to bill legal assistant time.

Except for the specific proscription contained in Section VI, the reported cases, such as *Attorney Grievance Commission of Maryland v. Goldberg, supra,* do not limit the duties which may be performed by a legal assistant under the supervision of the attorney. The Guidelines were developed from generally accepted practices. Each supervising attorney must be aware of the specific rules, decisions and statutes applicable to legal assistants within his jurisdiction.

Appendix E

The NFPA Model Code of Ethics and Professional Responsibility

Preamble

The National Federation of Paralegal Associations, Inc. ("NFPA") is a professional organization comprised of paralegal associations and individual paralegals throughout the United States. Members of NFPA have varying types of backgrounds, experience, education, and job responsibilities which reflect the diversity of the paralegal profession. NFPA promotes the growth, development and recognition of the paralegal profession as an integral partner in the delivery of legal services.

NFPA recognizes that the creation of guidelines and standards for professional conduct are important for the development and expansion of the paralegal profession. In May 1993, NFPA adopted this Model Code of Ethics and Professional Responsibility ("Model Code") to delineate the principles for ethics and conduct to which every paralegal should aspire. The Model Code expresses NFPA's commitment to increasing the quality and efficiency of legal services and recognizes the profession's responsibilities to the public, the legal community, and colleagues.

Paralegals perform many different functions, and these functions differ greatly among practice areas. In addition, each jurisdiction has its own unique legal authority and practices governing ethical conduct and professional responsibility.

It is essential that each paralegal strive for personal and professional excellence and encourage the professional development of other paralegals as well as those entering the profession. Participation in professional associations intended to advance the quality and standards of the legal profession is of particular importance. Paralegals should possess integrity, professional skill and dedication to the improvement of the legal system and should strive to expand the paralegal role in the delivery of legal services.

Canon 1

A paralegal[1] shall achieve and maintain a high level of competence.

---

1. "Paralegal" is synonymous with **"Legal Assistant"** and is defined as a person qualified through education, training, or work experience to perform substantive legal work that requires knowledge of legal concepts and is customarily, but not exclusively performed by a lawyer. This person may be retained or employed by a lawyer, law office, governmental agency or other entity or may be authorized by administrative, statutory or court authority to perform this work.

EC–1.1 A paralegal shall achieve competency through education, training, and work experience.
EC–1.2 A paralegal shall participate in continuing education to keep informed of current legal, technical and general developments.
EC–1.3 A paralegal shall perform all assignments promptly and efficiently.

Canon 2

A paralegal shall maintain a high level of personal and professional integrity.

EC–2.1 A paralegal shall not engage in any *ex parte*[2] communications involving the courts for any other adjudicatory body in an attempt to exert undue influence or to obtain advantage for the benefit of only one party.
EC–2.2 A paralegal shall not communicate, or cause another to communicate, with a party the paralegal knows to be represented by a lawyer in a pending matter without the prior consent of the lawyer representing such other party.
EC–2.3 A paralegal shall ensure that all timekeeping and billing records prepared by the paralegal are thorough, accurate, and honest.
EC–2.4 A paralegal shall be scrupulous, thorough and honest in the identification and maintenance of all funds, securities, and other assets of a client and shall provide accurate accountings as appropriate.
EC–2.5 A paralegal shall advise the proper authority of any dishonest or fraudulent acts by any person pertaining to the handling of the funds, securities or other assets of a client.

Canon 3

A paralegal shall maintain a high standard of professional conduct.

EC–3.1 A paralegal shall refrain from engaging in any conduct that offends the dignity and decorum of proceedings before a court or other adjudicatory body and shall be respectful of all rules and procedures.
EC–3.2 A paralegal shall advise the proper authority of any action of another legal professional which clearly demonstrates fraud, deceit, dishonesty, or misrepresentation.
EC–3.3 A paralegal shall avoid impropriety and the appearance of impropriety.

Canon 4

A paralegal shall serve the public interest by contributing to the delivery of quality legal services and the improvement of the legal system.

EC–4.1 A paralegal shall be sensitive to the legal needs of the public and shall promote the development and implementation of programs that address those needs.
EC–4.2 A paralegal shall support bona fide efforts to meet the need for legal services by those unable to pay reasonable or customary fees; for example, participation in *pro bono* projects and volunteer work.

2. ***"Ex Parte"*** denotes actions or communications conducted at the instance and for the benefit of one party only, and without notice to, or contestation by, any person adversely interested.

EC–4.3 A paralegal shall support efforts to improve the legal system and shall assist in making changes.

Canon 5

A paralegal shall preserve all confidential information[3] provided by the client or acquired from other sources before, during, and after the course of the professional relationship.

EC–5.1 A paralegal shall be aware of and abide by all legal authority governing confidential information.
EC–5.2 A paralegal shall not use confidential information to the disadvantage of the client.
EC–5.3 A paralegal shall not use confidential information to the advantage of the paralegal or of a third person.
EC–5.4 A paralegal may reveal confidential information only after full disclosure and with the client's written consent; or, when required by law or court order; or, when necessary to prevent the client from committing an act which could result in death or serious bodily harm.
EC–5.5 A paralegal shall keep those individuals responsible for the legal representation of a client fully informed of any confidential information the paralegal may have pertaining to that client.
EC–5.6 A paralegal shall not engage in any indiscreet communications concerning clients.

Canon 6

A paralegal's title shall be fully disclosed.[4]

EC–6.1 A paralegal's title shall clearly indicate the individual's status and shall be disclosed in all business and professional communications to avoid misunderstandings and misconceptions about the paralegal's role and responsibilities.
EC–6.2 A paralegal's title shall be included if the paralegal's name appears on business cards, letterhead, brochures, directories, and advertisements.

Canon 7

A paralegal shall not engage in the unauthorized practice of law.

EC–7.1 A paralegal shall comply with the applicable legal authority governing the unauthorized practice of law.

Canon 8

A paralegal shall avoid conflicts of interest and shall disclose any possible conflict to the employer or client, as well as to the prospective employers or clients.

---

3. **"Confidential Information"** denotes information relating to a client, whatever its source, which is not public knowledge nor available to the public. (**"Non-Confidential Information"** would generally include the name of the client and the identity of the matter for which the paralegal provided services.)
4. **"Disclose"** denotes communication of information reasonably sufficient to permit identification of the significance of the matter in question.

EC–8.1 A paralegal shall act within the bounds of the law, solely for the benefit of the client, and shall be free of compromising influences and loyalties. Neither the paralegal's personal or business interest, nor those of other clients or third persons, should compromise the paralegal's professional judgment and loyalty to the client.

EC–8.2 A paralegal shall avoid conflicts of interest which may arise from previous assignments whether for a present or past employer or client.

EC–8.3 A paralegal shall avoid conflicts of interest which may arise from family relationships and from personal and business interests.

EC–8.4 A paralegal shall create and maintain an effective recordkeeping system that identifies clients, matters, and parties with which the paralegal has worked, to be able to determine whether an actual or potential conflict of interest exists.

EC–8.5 A paralegal shall reveal sufficient nonconfidential information about a client or former client to reasonably ascertain if an actual or potential conflict of interest exists.

EC–8.6 A paralegal shall not participate in or conduct work on any matter where a conflict of interest has been identified.

EC–8.7 In matters where a conflict of interest has been identified and the client consents to continued representation, a paralegal shall comply fully with the implementation and maintenance of an Ethical Wall.[5]

5. **"Ethical Wall"** refers to the screening method implemented in order to protect a client from a conflict of interest. An Ethical Wall generally includes, but is not limited to, the following elements: (1) prohibit the paralegal from having any connection with the matter; (2) ban discussions with or the transfer of documents to or from the paralegal; (3) restrict access to files; and (4) educate all members of the firm, corporation or entity as to the separation of the paralegal (both organizationally and physically) from the pending matter. For more information regarding the Ethical Wall, see the NFPA publication entitled "The Ethical Wall—Its Application to Paralegals."

Appendix F

The ABA Model Guidelines for the Utilization of Legal Assistant Services

Preamble

State courts, bar associations, or bar committees in at least seventeen states have prepared recommendations[1] for the utilization of legal assistant services.[2] While their content varies, their purpose appears uniform: to provide lawyers with a reliable basis for delegating responsibility for performing a portion of the lawyer's tasks to legal assistants. The purpose of preparing model guidelines is not to contradict the guidelines already adopted or to suggest that other guidelines may be more appropriate in a particular jurisdiction. It is the view of the Standing Committee on Legal Assistants of the American Bar Association [ABA], however, that a model set of guidelines for the utilization of legal assistant services may assist many states in adopting or revising such guidelines. The Standing Committee is of the view that guidelines will encourage lawyers to utilize legal assistant services effectively and promote the growth of the legal assistant profession.[3] In undertaking this project, the Standing Committee has attempted to state guidelines that conform with the American Bar Association's Model Rules of

---

1. An appendix identifies the guidelines, court rules, and recommendations that were reviewed in drafting these Model Guidelines. [This appendix is not included in *West's Paralegal Today.*]
2. On February 6, 1986, the ABA Board of Governors approved the following definition of the term "legal assistant":

   A legal assistant is a person, qualified through education, training, or work experience, who is employed or retained by a lawyer, law office, governmental agency, or other entity in a capacity or function which involves the performance, under the ultimate direction and supervision of an attorney, of specifically delegated substantive legal work, which work, for the most part, requires a sufficient knowledge of legal concepts that, absent such assistant, the attorney would perform the task.
   In some contexts, the term "paralegal" is used interchangeably with the term legal assistant. [Note: The ABA has since modified this decision. See Chapter 1.]
3. While necessarily mentioning legal assistant conduct, lawyers are the intended audience of these Guidelines. The Guidelines, therefore, are addressed to lawyer conduct and not directly to the conduct of the legal assistant. Both the National Association of Legal Assistants (NALA) and the National Federation of Paralegal Associations (NFPA) have adopted guidelines of conduct that are directed to legal assistants. See NALA, "Code of Ethics and Professional Responsibility of the National Association of Legal Assistants, Inc." (adopted May 1975, revised November 1979 and September 1988); NFPA, "Affirmation of Responsibility" (adopted 1977, revised 1981).

Professional Conduct, decided authority, and contemporary practice. Lawyers, of course, are to be first directed by Rule 5.3 of the Model Rules in the utilization of legal assistant services, and nothing contained in these guidelines is intended to be inconsistent with that rule. Specific ethical considerations in particular states, however, may require modification of these guidelines before their adoption. In the commentary after each guideline, we have attempted to identify the basis for the guideline and any issues of which we are aware that the guideline may present; those drafting such guidelines may wish to take them into account.

Guideline 1

A lawyer is responsible for all of the professional actions of a legal assistant performing legal assistant services at the lawyer's direction and should take reasonable measures to ensure that the legal assistant's conduct is consistent with the lawyer's obligations under the ABA Model Rules of Professional Conduct.

Comment to Guideline 1. An attorney who utilizes a legal assistant's services is responsible for determining that the legal assistant is competent to perform the tasks assigned, based on the legal assistant's education, training, and experience, and for ensuring that the legal assistant is familiar with the responsibilities of attorneys and legal assistants under the applicable rules governing professional conduct.[4]

Under principles of agency law and rules governing the conduct of attorneys, lawyers are responsible for the actions and the work product of the non-lawyers they employ. Rule 5.3 of the Model Rules[5] requires that partners and supervising attorneys ensure that the conduct of non-lawyer assistants is compatible with the lawyer's professional obligations. Several state guidelines have adopted this language. E.g., Commentary to Illinois Recommendation (A), Kansas Guideline III(a), New Hampshire Rule 35, Sub-Rule 9, and North Carolina Guideline 4. Ethical Consideration 3–6 of the Model Code encouraged lawyers to delegate tasks to legal assistants provided the lawyer maintained a direct relationship with the client, supervised appropriately, and had complete responsibility for the work product. The adoption of Rule 5.3, which incorporates these principles, implicitly reaffirms this encouragement.

---

4. Attorneys, of course, are not liable for violation of the ABA Model Rules of Professional Conduct ("Model Rules") unless the Model Rules have been adopted as the code of professional conduct in a jurisdiction in which the lawyer practices. They are referenced in this model guideline for illustrative purposes; if the guideline is to be adopted, the reference should be modified to the jurisdiction's rules of professional conduct.
5. The Model Rules were first adopted by the ABA House of Delegates in August of 1983. Since that time many states have adopted the Model Rules to govern the professional conduct of lawyers licensed in those states. Since a number of states still utilize a version of the Model Code of Professional Responsibility ("Model Code"), which was adopted by the House of Delegates in August of 1969, however, these comments will refer to both the Model Rules and the predecessor Model Code (and to the Ethical Considerations and Disciplinary Rules found under the canons in the Model Code).

Several states have addressed the issue of the lawyer's ultimate responsibility for work performed by subordinates. For example, Colorado Guideline 1.c, Kentucky Supreme Court Rule 3.700, Sub-Rule 2.C, and Michigan Guideline I provide: "The lawyer remains responsible for the actions of the legal assistant to the same extent as if such representation had been furnished entirely by the lawyer and such actions were those of the lawyer." New Mexico Guideline X states "[the] lawyer maintains ultimate responsibility for and has an ongoing duty to actively supervise the legal assistant's work performance, conduct and product." Connecticut Recommendation 2 and Rhode Island Guideline III state specifically that lawyers are liable for malpractice for the mistakes and omissions of their legal assistants.

Finally, the lawyer should ensure that legal assistants supervised by the lawyer are familiar with the rules governing attorney conduct and that they follow those rules. See Comment to Model Rule 5.3; Illinois Recommendation (A)(5), New Hampshire Supreme Court Rule 35, Sub-Rule 9, and New Mexico, Statement of Purpose; see also NALA's Model Standards and Guidelines for the Utilization of Legal Assistants, guidelines IV, V, and VIII (1985, revised 1990) (hereafter "NALA Guidelines").

The Standing Committee and several of those who have commented upon these Guidelines regard Guideline 1 as a comprehensive statement of general principle governing lawyers who utilize legal assistant services in the practice of law. As such it, in effect, is a part of each of the remaining Guidelines.

Guideline 2

Provided the lawyer maintains responsibility for the work product, a lawyer may delegate to a legal assistant any task normally performed by the lawyer except those tasks proscribed to one not licensed as a lawyer by statute, court rule, administrative rule or regulation, controlling authority, the ABA Model Rules of Professional Conduct, or these Guidelines.

Comment to Guideline 2. The essence of the definition of the term legal assistant adopted by the ABA Board of Governors in 1986 is that, so long as appropriate supervision is maintained, many tasks normally performed by lawyers may be delegated to legal assistants. Of course, Rule 5.5 of the Model Rules, DR 3–101 of the Model Code, and most states specifically prohibit lawyers from assisting or aiding a non-lawyer in the unauthorized practice of law. Thus, while appropriate delegation of tasks to legal assistants is encouraged, the lawyer may not permit the legal assistant to engage in the "practice of law." Neither the Model Rules nor the Model Code define the "practice of law." EC 3–5 under the Model Code gave some guidance by equating the practice of law to the application of the professional judgment of the lawyer in solving clients' legal problems. Further, ABA Opinion 316 (1967) states: "A lawyer can employ lay secretaries, lay investigators, lay detectives, lay researchers, accountants, lay scriveners, nonlawyer draftsmen or nonlawyer researchers. In fact, he may employ nonlawyers to do any task for him except counsel clients about law matters, engage directly in the practice of law, appear in court or appear in formal proceedings as part of the judicial process, so long as it is he who takes the work and vouches for it to the client and becomes responsible for it to the client.

Most state guidelines specify that legal assistants may not appear before courts, administrative tribunals, or other adjudicatory bodies unless their rules authorize such appearances; may not conduct depositions; and may not give legal advice to clients. E.g., Connecticut Recommendation 4; Florida EC 3–6 (327 So.2d at 16); and Michigan Guideline II. Also see NALA Guidelines IV and VI. But it is also important to note that, as some guidelines have recognized, pursuant to federal or state statute legal assistants are permitted to provide direct client representation in certain administrative proceedings. E.g., South Carolina Guideline II. While this does not obviate the attorney's responsibility for the legal assistant's work, it does change the nature of the attorney supervision of the legal assistant. The opportunity to use such legal assistant services has particular benefits to legal services programs and does not violate Guideline 2. See generally ABA Standards for Providers of Civil Legal Services to the Poor, Std. 6.3, at 6.17–6.18 (1986).

The Model Rules emphasize the importance of appropriate delegation. The key to appropriate delegation is proper supervision, which includes adequate instruction when assigning projects, monitoring of the project, and review of the completed project. The Supreme Court of Virginia upheld a malpractice verdict against a lawyer based in part on negligent actions of a legal assistant in performing tasks that evidently were properly delegable. *Musselman v. Willoughby Corp.*, 230 Va. 337, 337 S.E.2d 724 (1985). See also C. Wolfram, Modern Legal Ethics (1986), at 236, 896. All state guidelines refer to the requirement that the lawyer "supervise" legal assistants in the performance of their duties. Lawyers should also take care in hiring and choosing a legal assistant to work on a specific project to ensure that the legal assistant has the education, knowledge, and ability necessary to perform the delegated tasks competently. See Connecticut Recommendation 14, Kansas Standards I, II, and III, and New Mexico Guideline VIII. Finally, some states describe appropriate delegation and review in terms of the delegated work losing its identity and becoming "merged" into the work product of the attorney. See Florida EC 3–6 (327 So.2d at 16).

Legal assistants often play an important role in improving communication between the attorney and the client. EC 3–6 under the Model Code mentioned three specific kinds of tasks that legal assistants may perform under appropriate lawyer supervision: factual investigation and research, legal research, and the preparation of legal documents. Some states delineate more specific tasks in their guidelines, such as attending client conferences, corresponding with and obtaining information from clients, handling witness execution of documents, preparing transmittal letters, maintaining estate/guardianship trust accounts, etc. See, e.g., Colorado (lists of specialized functions in several areas follow guidelines); Michigan, Comment to Definition of Legal Assistant; New York, Specialized Skills of Legal Assistants; Rhode Island Guideline II; and NALA Guideline IX. The two-volume Working with Legal Assistants, published by the Standing Committee in 1982, attempted to provide a general description of the types of tasks that may be delegated to legal assistants in various practice areas.

There are tasks that have been specifically prohibited in some states, but that may be delegated in others. For example, legal assistants may not supervise will executions or represent clients at real estate closings in some jurisdictions, but may in others. Compare Connecticut Recommendation 7 and Illinois State Bar Association Position Paper on Use of Attorney Assistants in Real Estate Transactions (May 16, 1984), which proscribe legal assistants conducting real estate closings, with Georgia "real estate job description," Florida Professional Ethics Committee Advisory Opinion 89–5 (1989), and Missouri, Comment to Guideline I, which permit legal assistants to conduct real estate closings. Also compare Connecticut Recommendation 8 (prohibiting attorneys from authorizing legal assistants to supervise will executions) with Colorado "estate planning job description," Georgia "estate, trusts, and wills job description," Missouri, Comment to Guideline I, and Rhode Island Guideline II (suggesting that legal assistants may supervise the execution of wills, trusts, and other documents).

Guideline 3

A lawyer may not delegate to a legal assistant:

- **(a) Responsibility for establishing an attorney-client relationship.**
- **(b) Responsibility for establishing the amount of a fee to be charged for a legal service.**
- **(c) Responsibility for a legal opinion rendered to a client.**

Comments to Guideline 3. The Model Rules and most state codes require that lawyers communicate with their clients in order for clients to make well-informed decisions about their representation and resolution of legal issues. Model Rule 1.4. Ethical Consideration 3–6 under the Model Code emphasized that "delegation [of legal tasks to nonlawyers] is proper if the lawyer *maintains a direct relationship with his client,* supervises the delegated work and has complete professional responsibility for the work product." (Emphasis added.) Accordingly, most state guidelines also stress the importance of a direct attorney-client relationship. See Colorado Guideline 1, Florida EC 3–6, Illinois Recommendation (A)(1), Iowa EC 3–6(2), and New Mexico Guideline IV. The direct personal relationship between client and lawyer is necessary to the exercise of the lawyer's trained professional judgment.

An essential aspect of the lawyer-client relationship is the agreement to undertake representation and the related fee arrangement. The Model Rules and most states require that fee arrangements be agreed upon early on and be communicated to the client by the lawyer, in some circumstances in writing. Model Rule 1.5 and Comments. Many state guidelines prohibit legal assistants from "setting fees" or "accepting cases." See, e.g., Colorado Guideline 1 and NALA Guideline VI. Connecticut recommends that legal assistants be prohibited from accepting or rejecting cases or setting fees "if these tasks entail any discretion on the part of the paralegals." Connecticut Recommendation 9.

EC 3–5 states: "[T]he essence of the professional judgment of the lawyer is his educated ability to relate the general body and philosophy of law to a specific legal problem of a client; and thus, the public interest will be better served if only lawyers are permitted to act in matters involving professional judgment." Clients are entitled to their lawyers' professional judgment and opinion. Legal assistants may, however, be authorized to communicate legal advice so long as they do not interpret or expand on that advice. Typically, state guidelines phrase this prohibition in terms of legal assistants being forbidden from "giving legal advice" or "counseling clients about legal matters." See, e.g., Colorado Guideline 2, Connecticut Recommendation 6, Florida DR 3–104, Iowa EC 3–6(3), Kansas Guideline I, Kentucky Sub-Rule 2, New Hampshire Rule 35, Sub-Rule 1, Texas Guideline I, and NALA Guideline VI. Some states have more expansive wording that prohibits legal assistants from engaging in any activity that would require the exercise of independent legal judgment. Nevertheless, it is clear that all states, as well as the Model Rules, encourage direct communication between clients and a legal assistant insofar as the legal assistant is performing a task properly delegated by a lawyer. It should be noted that a lawyer who permits a legal assistant to assist in establishing the attorney-client relationship, communicating a fee, or preparing a legal opinion is not delegating responsibility for those matters and, therefore, may be complying with this guideline.

Guideline 4

It is the lawyer's responsibility to take reasonable measures to ensure that clients, courts, and other lawyers are aware that a legal assistant, whose services are utilized by the lawyer in performing legal services, is not licensed to practice law.

Comment to Guideline 4. Since, in most instances, a legal assistant is not licensed as a lawyer, it is important that those with whom the legal assistant deals are aware of that fact. Several state guidelines impose on the lawyer responsibility for instructing a legal assistant whose services are utilized by the lawyer to disclose the legal assistant's status in any dealings with a third party. See, e.g., Michigan Guideline III, part 5, New Hampshire Rule 35, Sub-Rule 8, and NALA Guideline V. While requiring the legal assistant to make such disclosure is one way in which the attorney's responsibility to third parties may be discharged, the Standing Committee is of the view that it is desirable to emphasize the lawyer's responsibility for the disclosure and leave to the lawyer the discretion to decide whether the lawyer will discharge that responsibility by direct communication with the client, by requiring the legal assistant to make the disclosure, by a written memorandum, or by some other means. Although in most initial engagements by a client it may be prudent for the attorney to discharge the responsibility with a writing, the guideline requires only that the lawyer recognize the responsibility and ensure that it is discharged. Clearly, when a client has been adequately informed of the lawyer's utilization of legal assistant services, it is unnecessary to make additional formalistic disclosures as the client retains the lawyer for other services.

Most state guidelines specifically endorse legal assistants signing correspondence so long as their status as a legal assistant is indicated by an appropriate title. E.g., Colorado Guideline 2; Kansas, Comment to Guideline IX; and North Carolina Guideline 9; also see ABA Informal Opinion 1367 (1976). The comment to New Mexico Guideline XI warns against the use of the title "associate" since it may be construed to mean associate-attorney.

Guideline 5

A lawyer may identify legal assistants by name and title on the lawyer's letterhead and on business cards identifying the lawyer's firm.

Comment to Guideline 5. Under Guideline 4, above, an attorney who employs a legal assistant has an obligation to ensure that the status of the legal assistant as a non-lawyer is fully disclosed. The primary purpose of this disclosure is to avoid confusion that might lead someone to believe that the legal assistant is a lawyer. The identification suggested by this guideline is consistent with that objective, while also affording the legal assistant recognition as an important part of the legal services team.

Recent ABA Informal Opinion 1527 (1989) provides that non-lawyer support personnel, including legal assistants, may be listed on a law firm's letterhead and reiterates previous opinions that approve of legal assistants having business cards. See also ABA Informal Opinion 1185 (1971). The listing must not be false or misleading and "must make it clear that the support personnel who are listed are not lawyers."

Nearly all state guidelines approve of business cards for legal assistants, but some prescribe the contents and format of the card. E.g., Iowa Guideline 4 and Texas Guideline VIII. All agree the legal assistant's status must be clearly indicated and the card may not be used in a deceptive way. New Hampshire Supreme Court Rule 7 approves the use of business cards so long as the card is not used for unethical solicitation.

Some states do not permit attorneys to list legal assistants on their letterhead. E.g., Kansas Guideline VIII, Michigan Guideline III, New Hampshire Rule 35, Sub-Rule 7, New Mexico Guideline XI, and North Carolina Guideline 9. Several of these states rely on earlier ABA Informal Opinion 619 (1962), 845 (1965), and 1000 (1977), all of which were expressly withdrawn by ABA Informal Opinion 1527. These earlier opinions interpreted the predecessor Model Code and DR 2–102(A), which, prior to *Bates v. State Bar of Arizona,* 433 U.S. 350 (1977), had strict limitations on the information that could be listed on letterheads. States which do permit attorneys to list names of legal assistants on their stationary, if the listing is not deceptive and the legal assistant's status is clearly identified, include: Arizona Committee on Rules of Professional Conduct Formal Opinion 3/90 (1990); Connecticut Recommendation 12; Florida Professional Ethics Committee Advisory Opinion 86–4 (1986); Hawaii, Formal Opinion 78–8–19 (1978, as revised 1984); Illinois State Bar Association Advisory Opinion 87–1 (1987); Kentucky Sub-Rule 6; Mississippi State Bar Ethics Committee Opinion 93 (1984); Missouri Guideline IV; New York State Bar Association Committee on Professional Ethics Opinion 500 (1978); Oregon, Ethical Opinion No. 349 (1977); and Texas, Ethics Committee Opinion 436 (1983). In light of the United States Supreme Court opinion in *Peel v. Attorney Registration and Disciplinary Commission of Illinois,* 496 U.S. 91, 110 S.Ct. 2281 (1990), it may be that a restriction on letterhead identification of legal assistants that is not deceptive and clearly identifies the legal assistant's status violates the First Amendment rights of the lawyer.

Guideline 6

It is the responsibility of a lawyer to take reasonable measures to ensure that all client confidences are preserved by a legal assistant.

Comment to Guideline 6. A fundamental principle underlying the free exchange of information in a lawyer-client relationship is that the lawyer maintain the confidentiality of information relating to the representation. "It is a matter of common knowledge that the normal operation of a law office exposes confidential professional information to non-lawyer employees of the office. This obligates a lawyer to exercise care in selecting and training his employees so that the sanctity of all confidences and secrets of his clients may be preserved." EC 4–2, Model Code.

Rule 5.3 of the Model Rules requires "a lawyer who has direct supervisory authority over the nonlawyer [to] make reasonable efforts to ensure that the person's conduct is compatible with the professional obligations of the lawyer." The Comment to Rule 5.3 makes it clear that lawyers should give legal assistants "appropriate instruction and supervision concerning the ethical aspects of their employment, particularly regarding the obligation not to disclose information relating to the representation of the client." DR 4–101(D) under the Model Code provides that: "A lawyer shall exercise reasonable care to prevent his employees, associates and others whose services are utilized by him from discharging or using confidences or secrets of a client. . . ."

It is particularly important that the lawyer ensure that the legal assistant understands that *all* information concerning the client, even the mere fact that a person is a client of the firm, may be strictly confidential. Rule 1.6 of the Model Rules expanded the definition of confidential information ". . . not merely to matters communicated in confidence by the client but also to all information relating to the representation, whatever its source."[6] It is therefore the lawyer's obligation to instruct clearly and to take reasonable steps to ensure the legal assistant's preservation of client confidences. Nearly all states that have guidelines for the utilization of legal assistants require the lawyer "to instruct legal assistants concerning client confidences" and "to exercise care to ensure that legal assistants comply" with the Code in this regard. Even if the client consents to divulging information, this information must not be used to the disadvantage of the client. See, e.g., Connecticut Recommendation 3: New Hampshire Rule 35, Sub-Rule 4; NALA Guideline V.

Guideline 7

A lawyer should take reasonable measures to prevent conflicts of interest resulting from a legal assistant's other employment or interests insofar as such other employment or interests would present a conflict of interest if it were that of the lawyer.

6. Rule 1.05 of the Texas Disciplinary Rules of Professional Conduct (1990) provides a different formulation, which is equally expansive:

> "Confidential information" includes both "privileged information" and "unprivileged client information." "Privileged information" refers to the information of a client protected by the lawyer-client privilege of Rule 503 of the Texas Rules of Evidence or the Rule 503 of the Texas Rules of Criminal Evidence or by the principles of attorney-client privilege governed by Rule 501 of the Federal Rules of Evidence for United States Courts and Magistrates. "Unprivileged client information" means all information relating to a client or furnished by the client, other than privileged information, acquired by the lawyer during the course of or by reason of the representation of the client.

Comment to Guideline 7. A lawyer must make "reasonable efforts to ensure that [a] legal assistant's conduct is compatible with the professional obligations of the lawyer." Model Rule 5.3. These professional obligations include the duty to exercise independent professional judgment on behalf of a client, "free of compromising influences and loyalties." ABA Model Rules 1.7 through 1.13. Therefore, legal assistants should be instructed to inform the supervising attorney of any interest that could result in a conflict of interest or even give the appearance of a conflict. The guideline intentionally speaks to other employment rather than only past employment, since there are instances where legal assistants are employed by more than one law firm at the same time. The guideline's reference to "other interests" is intended to include personal relationships as well as instances where a legal assistant may have a financial interest (i.e., as stockholder, trust beneficiary or trustee, etc.) that would conflict with the client's in the matter in which the lawyer has been employed.

"Imputed Disqualification Arising from Change in Employment by Non-lawyer Employee," ABA Informal Opinion 1526 (1988), defines the duties of both the present and former employing lawyers and reasons that the restrictions on legal assistants' employment should be kept to "the minimum necessary to protect confidentiality" in order to prevent legal assistants from being forced to leave their careers, which "would disserve clients as well as the legal profession." The Opinion describes the attorney's obligations (1) to caution the legal assistant not to disclose any information and (2) to prevent the legal assistant from working on any matter on which the legal assistant worked for a prior employer or respecting which the employee has confidential information.

If a conflict is discovered, it may be possible to "wall" the legal assistant from the conflict area so that the entire firm need not be disqualified and the legal assistant is effectively screened from information concerning the matter. The American Bar Association has taken the position that what historically has been described as a "Chinese wall" will allow non-lawyer personnel (including legal assistants) who are in possession of confidential client information to accept employment with a law firm opposing the former client so long as the wall is observed and effectively screens the non-lawyer from confidential information. ABA Informal Opinion 1526 (1988). See also Tennessee Formal Ethics Opinion 89–F–118 (March 10, 1989). The implication of this Informal Opinion is that if a wall is not in place, the employer may be disqualified from representing either party to the controversy. One court has so held. *In re: Complex Asbestos Litigation,* No. 828684 (San Francisco Superior Court, September 19, 1989).

It is not clear that a wall will prevent disqualification in the case of a lawyer employed to work for a law firm representing a client with an adverse interest to a client of the lawyer's former employer. Under Model Rule 1.10, when a lawyer moves to a firm that represents an adverse party in a matter in which the lawyer's former firm was involved, absent a waiver by the client, the new firm's representation may continue only if the newly employed lawyer acquired no protected information and did not work directly on the matter in the former employment. The new Rules of Professional Conduct in Kentucky and Texas (both effective January 1, 1990) specifically provide for disqualification. Rule 1.10(b) in the District of Columbia, which became effective January 1, 1991, does so as well. The Sixth Circuit, however, has held that the wall will effectively insulate the new firm from disqualification if it prevents the new lawyer-employee from access to information concerning the client with the adverse interest. *Manning v. Waring, Cox, James, Sklar & Allen,* 849 F.2d 222 (6th Cir. 1988). [As a result of the Sixth Circuit opinion, Tennessee revised its formal ethics opinion, which is cited above, and now applies the same rule to lawyers, legal assistants, law clerks, and legal secretaries.] See generally NFPA, "The Chinese Wall—Its Application to Paralegals" (1990).

The states that have guidelines that address the legal assistant conflict of interest refer to the lawyer's responsibility to ensure against personal, business or social interests of the legal assistant that would conflict with the representation of the client or impinge on the services rendered to the client. E.g., Kansas Guideline X, New Mexico Guideline VI, and North Carolina Guideline 7. Florida Professional Ethics Opinion 86–5 (1986) discusses a legal assistant's move from one firm to another and the obligations of each not to disclose confidences. See also Vermont Ethics Opinion 85–8 (1985) (a legal assistant is not bound by the Code of Professional Responsibility and, absent an absolute waiver by the client, the new firm should not represent client if legal assistant possessed confidential information from old firm).

Guideline 8

A lawyer may include a charge for the work performed by a legal assistant in setting a charge for legal services.

Comment to Guideline 8. The U.S. Supreme Court in *Missouri v. Jenkins,* 491 U.S. 274 (1989), held that in setting a reasonable attorney's fee under 28 U.S.C. §1988, a legal fee may include a charge for legal assistant services at "market rates" rather than "actual cost" to the attorneys. This decision should resolve any question concerning the propriety of setting a charge for legal services based on work performed by a legal assistant. Its rationale favors setting a charge based on the "market" rate for such services, rather than their direct cost to the lawyer. This result was recognized by Connecticut Recommendation 11, Illinois Recommendation D, and Texas Guideline V prior to the Supreme Court decision. See also Fla.Stat.Ann. §57.104 (1991 Supp.) (adopted in 1987 and permitting consideration of legal assistant services in computing attorney's fees) and Fla.Stat.Ann. §744.108 (1991 Supp.) (adopted in 1989 and permitting recovery of "customary and reasonable charges for work performed by legal assistants" as fees for legal services in guardianship matters).

It is important to note, however, that *Missouri v. Jenkins* does not abrogate the attorney's responsibilities under Model Rule 1.5 to set a reasonable fee for legal services and it follows that those considerations apply to a fee that includes a fee for legal assistant services. Accordingly, the effect of combining a market rate charge for the services of lawyers and legal assistants should, in most instances, result in a lower total cost for the legal service than if the lawyer had performed the service alone.

Guideline 9

A lawyer may not split legal fees with a legal assistant nor pay a legal assistant for the referral of legal business. A lawyer may compensate a legal assistant based on the quantity and quality of the legal assistant's work and the value of that work to a law practice, but the legal assistant's compensation may not be contingent, by advance agreement, upon the probability of the lawyer's practice.

Comment to Guideline 9. Model Rule 5.4 and DR 3–102(A) and 3–103(A) under the Model Code clearly prohibit fee "splitting" with legal assistants, whether characterized by splitting of contingent fees, "forwarding" fees, or other sharing of legal fees. Virtually all guidelines adopted by state bar associations have continued this prohibition in one form or another.[7] It appears clear that a legal assistant may not be compensated on a contingent basis for a particular case or paid for "signing up" clients for a legal practice.

Having stated this prohibition, however, the guideline attempts to deal with the practical consideration of how a legal assistant properly may be compensated by an attorney or law firm. The linchpin of the prohibition seems to be the advance agreement of the lawyer to "split" a fee based on a pre-existing contingent agreement.[8] There is no general prohibition against a lawyer who enjoys a particularly profitable period recognizing the contribution of the legal assistant to that profitability with a discretionary bonus. Likewise, a lawyer engaged in a particularly profitable specialty of legal practice is not prohibited from compensating the legal assistant who aids materially in that practice more handsomely than the compensation generally awarded to legal assistants in that geographic area who work in law practices that are less lucrative. Indeed, any effort to fix a compensation level for legal assistants and prohibit greater compensation would appear to violate the federal antitrust laws. See, e.g., *Goldfarb v. Virginia State Bar,* 421 U.S. 773 (1975).

Guideline 10

A lawyer who employs a legal assistant should facilitate the legal assistant's participation in appropriate continuing education and *pro bono publico* activities.

Comment to Guideline 10. While Guideline 10 does not appear to have been adopted in the guidelines of any state bar association, the Standing Committee on Legal Assistants believes that its adoption would be appro-

---

7. Connecticut Recommendation 10; Illinois Recommendation D; Kansas Guideline VI; Kentucky Supreme Court Rule 3.700, sub-rule 5; Michigan Guideline III, part 2; Missouri Guideline II; New Hampshire Rule 35, Sub-Rules 5 and 6; New Mexico Guideline IX; Rhode Island Guideline VIII and IX; South Carolina Guideline V; Texas Guideline V.

8. In its Rule 5.4, which [became] effective on January 1, 1991, the District of Columbia will permit lawyers to form legal service partnerships that include nonlawyer participants. Comments 5 and 6 to that rule, however, state that the term "nonlawyer participants" should not be confused with the term "nonlawyer assistants" and that "[n]onlawyer assistants under Rule 5.3 do not have managerial authority or financial interests in the organization."

priate.[9] For many years the Standing Committee on Legal Assistants has advocated that the improvement of formal legal assistant education will generally improve the legal services rendered by lawyers employing legal assistants and provide a more satisfying professional atmosphere in which legal assistants may work. See, e.g., ABA Board of Governors, Policy on Legal Assistant Licensure and/or Certification, Statement 4 (February 6, 1986); ABA, Standing Committee on Legal Assistants, "Position Paper on the Question of Legal Assistant Licensure or Certification" (December 10, 1985), at 6 and Conclusion 3. Recognition of the employing lawyer's obligation to facilitate the legal assistant's continuing professional education is, therefore, appropriate because of the benefits to both the law practice and the legal assistants and is consistent with the lawyer's own responsibility to maintain professional competence under Model Rule 1.1. See also EC 6–2 of the Model Code.

The Standing Committee is of the view that similar benefits will accrue to the lawyer and legal assistant if the legal assistant is included in the *pro bono publico* legal services that a lawyer has a clear obligation to provide under Model Rule 6.1 and, where appropriate, the legal assistant is encouraged to provide such services independently. The ability of a law firm to provide more *pro bono publico* services will be enhanced if legal assistants are included. Recognition of the legal assistant's role in such services is consistent with the role of the legal assistant in the contemporary delivery of legal services generally and is consistent with the lawyer's duty to the legal profession under Canon 2 of the Model Code.

THE STANDING COMMITTEE ON LEGAL ASSISTANTS
OF THE AMERICAN BAR ASSOCIATION
May 1991

ADOPTED BY ABA HOUSE OF DELEGATES
August 1991

9. While no state has apparently adopted a guideline similar to Model Guideline 10, parts 4 and 5 of NALA Guideline VIII suggest similar requirements. Sections III and V of NFPA's "Affirmation of Professional Responsibility" recognize a legal assistant's obligations to "maintain a high level of competence" (which "is achieved through continuing education") and to "serve the public interest." NFPA has also published a guide to assist legal assistant groups in developing public service projects. See NFPA, "Pro Bono Publico (For the Good of the People)" (1987).

Appendix G

Paralegal Ethics and Regulation: How to Find State-specific Information

NALANet

One resource for state-specific information is NALANet. It is an on-line information service for the legal assistant profession. NALANet captures relevant topics such as ethics, guidelines, membership, case-law updates, legislative activities, bar activities, significant research projects, and articles about the utilization of legal assistants on a state-by-state basis. The Florida example shown below illustrates the type of information available for each state. NALANet is available to members of NALA. For further information, contact NALA at (918) 587-6828.

Florida

Ethics

FL Opinion 86-4 8/1/86
(business cards, letterhead)

FL Opinion 88-15
(solicitation of clients, confidentiality, attorneys fees)

FL Opinion 89-4 8/29/90
(non-lawyers, attorneys fees, solicitation of clients, business cards)

FL Advisory Opinion 74479
(unauthorized practice of law)

FL Bar Re Advisory Opinion Hrs Non-Lawyer Counselor FLA Sup Ct No 70615 5/25/89
(non-lawyers)

FL Ethics Guide for Legal Assistants 86
(definitions, attorneys fees, business cards, supervision, unauthorized practice of law, letterhead, ethics, qualifications)

FL Opinion 88-6 Undated
(initial interview, supervision, non-lawyers)

FL Opinion 87-11
Signing Lawyer Name/Pleadings & Notices
(non-lawyers, unauthorized practice of law, supervision)

FL Bar Advisory Opinion—Non-Lawyer Prep of Living Trusts FL Supreme Court Case No. 78358
(non-lawyers, unauthorized practice of law)

FL Supreme Court Review of Opinion Unauthorized Practice of Law Comm Re Non-Lawyer Prep of Pension Plans 11/29/90
(non-lawyers, unauthorized practice of law)

FL Advisory Opinion 73306 6/1/89
(forms, repr, unauthorized practice of law)

FL Opinion 86-5 8/1/86
(conflict of interest, confidentiality)

FL Opinion 88-6 4/15/88
(supervision, unauthorized practice of law, work product)

FL Opinion 89-5
(real property, non-lawyers)

Rule 10-1.1(B), Rules Regulating Florida Bar (6/20/91) Forms Approved For Use By Lawyers/Non-Lawyers
(non-lawyers, forms)

FL Opinion 92-3 (10/1/92)
(non-lawyers, attorneys fees, solicitation of clients)

Guidelines

FL Ethics Guide For Legal Assistants 86
(definitions, attorneys fees, business cards, supervision, unauthorized practice of law, letterhead, ethics, qualifications)

Membership

FL Family Law Section Florida Bar
(certification, American Bar Association Approved School, experience)

FL Orange County Bar
(affiliate membership)

FL General Practice Section Florida Bar
(certification, American Bar Association Approved School, experience)

FL Local Government Section Florida Bar
(certification, Florida member)

FL Health Law Section Florida Bar
(open)

FL Practice Management & Technology Florida Bar
(certification, American Bar Association Approved School, experience)

FL Real Property Probate & Trust Section
(certification, American Bar Association Approved School, experience)

FL Trial Lawyers Section Florida Bar
(certification, American Bar Association Approved School, experience)

FL Environmental & Land Use Section
(open)

FL Broward County Bar

Cases

The Celotex Corp-Mid Dist. FL 90-10016-8B1 and 90-10017-8B1
(bankruptcy, attorneys fees)

Dube v. Secretary of Dept. Health & Human Serv., 1991 WL 285287 (Cl. Ct. 1991)
(attorneys fees)

FL Bar v. Mitchell, 569 So. 2d 424 (FLA Sup Ct 1990)
(non-lawyers, supervision by lawyer)

Florida Bar v. Carter, 502 So. 2d 904 (FLA Sup Ct 1987)
(supervision)

FL Bar Re Advisory Opinion Hrs Nonlawyer Counselor FLA SupCt No 70615 5/25/89
(non-lawyers)

FL Bar Advisory Opinion-Nonlawyer Prep of Living Trusts FL Supreme Court Case No. 78358
(non-lawyers, unauthorized practice of law)

FL Supreme Court Review of Opinion UPL Comm Re Nonlawyer Prep of Pension Plans 11/29/90
(non-lawyers, unauthorized practice of law)

FL Advisory Opinion 73306 6/1/89
(forms, repr, unauthorized practice of law)

In Re Christopher Backmann, -BR- 1990 (Bkrtcy S.D. FL, No88-04588-BKC-AJC, 3/30/90)
(unauthorized practice of law, supervision, bankruptcy, forms)

United States of America v. Peppers Steel, 742 Supp. 641 (S.D. Fla 1990)
(privilege, discovery, trial practice)

Security First Fed. v. Broom Et Al., DCA No 89-01814, 4/18/90
(qualifications, regulation, real property)

Florida Bar v. Brumbaugh, No. 48803 S.Ct. Florida
(unauthorized practice of law, forms, constitutional law)

Florida Bar v. Furman, No. 51226 SCT Florida
(unauthorized practice of law, constitutional law, non-lawyers, forms)

Std Guaranty Ins. v. Brenda L. Quanstrom, No 72100 Supreme Ct of Florida 1/11/90
(fees, Missouri)

Town of Windermere v. Isleworth Golf & CC Circuit Ct 9th Judicial District, Orange County Florida, CI 87-2677
(attorneys fees)

Ray v. Cutter Labs, 746 F. Supp. (MD FLA 1990)
(privilege waived, unintentional act, privilege)

Corn v. City of Lauderdale Lakes, 794 F. Supp. 364 (S.D. Fla. 1992)
(attorneys fees, market rate fees if prevailing practice)

The Florida Bar v. Daniel E. Shramek, Case No 77,871
(non-lawyers, unauthorized practice of law)

Ippolito v. Florida, Case No. 92-880-Civ.T-99
(non-lawyers, unauthorized practice of law, legal technicians)

Ibanez v. Florida Dept of Bus. & Prof. Regulation, 114 S. Ct. 2084 (1994) 7/18/94
(professional designation)

Legislation

FL Statute 57.104 Computation of Attorney Fee
(definitions, attorneys fees)

FL Senate Bill 2770 10/1/90 Passed Public Law-Paralegal Fees in Guardianship Law
(attorneys fees, supervision)

Articles

Amendment to Rule 4-6.1 of Rules Regulating the Florida Bar Fla SupCt, No 74,538 2/20/92 Pro Bono
(pro bono)

Florida Legal Technician Committee 6/1/92 Preliminary Report Summary
(legal technicians, unauthorized practice of law, regulation)

Rule 10-1.1(B), Rules Regulating Florida Bar (6/20/91) Forms Approved for Use by Lawyers/Nonlawyers
(non-lawyers, forms)

What's in a Name? 8/1/94 Outlines Difference Between Legal Assistant & Technician - Bar News Article Tech
(definitions, certification)

Other

Florida Legal Technician Committee 6/1/92 Preliminary Report Summary
(legal technicians, unauthorized practice of law, regulations)

NFPA REPOSITORY INDEX

Another source of state-specific information is the NFPA Repository Index. It contains statutory and case law information on such state and national issues as the unauthorized practice of law, paralegal fee awards, conflict of interest, the regulation of paralegals, and the utilization of paralegal services. Also included are copies of state and county bar association opinions and their responses to surveys conducted by both the NFPA and the American Bar Association. The repository provides easy access to information by state or by topic. For further information, contact NFPA at (816) 941-4000.

Appendix H

Paralegal Associations

NFPA Associations

Region I

Alaska Association of Legal Assistants
P.O. Box 101956
Anchorage, AK 99510–1956

Arizona Association of Professional Paralegals, Inc.
P.O. Box 25111
Phoenix, AZ 85002

Hawaii Association of Legal Assistants
P.O. Box 674
Honolulu, HI 96809

Los Angeles Paralegal Association
P.O. Box 7803
Van Nuys, CA 91409 [(818) 347–1001]

Oregon Legal Assistants Association
P.O. Box 8523
Portland, OR 97207 [(503) 796–1671]

Sacramento Association of Legal Assistants
P.O. Box 453
Sacramento, CA 95812–0453
[(916) 763–7851]

San Diego Association of Legal Assistants
P.O. Box 87449
San Diego, CA 92138–7449
[(619) 491–1994]

San Francisco Association of Legal Assistants
P.O. Box 26668
San Francisco, CA 94126–6668
[(415) 777–2390]

Washington State Paralegal Association
P.O. Box 232
Ardenvoir, WA 98811 [(509) 784–9772]

Region II

Dallas Association of Legal Assistants
P.O. Box 12533
Dallas, TX 75225 [(214) 991–0853]

Gateway Paralegal Association*
P.O. Box 50233
St. Louis, MO 63105

Illinois Paralegal Association
P.O. Box 8089
Bartlett, IL 60103–8089
[(708) 837–8088]

Kansas City Association of Legal Assistants
P.O. Box 13223
Kansas City, MO 64199
[(913) 381–4458]

Kansas Legal Assistants Society
P.O. Box 1675
Topeka, KS 66601

Legal Assistants of New Mexico
P.O. Box 1113
Albuquerque, NM 87103–1113
[(505) 260–7104]

Manitoba Association of Legal Assistants, Inc.*
22–81 Tyndall Avenue
Winnipeg, Manitoba R2X 2W2

Minnesota Association of Legal Assistants
2626 E. 82nd Street, Suite 201
Minneapolis, MN 55425
[(612) 853–0272]

New Orleans Paralegal Association
P.O. Box 30604
New Orleans, LA 70190

Northwest Missouri Paralegal Association*
Box 7013
St. Joseph, MO 64507

Paralegal Association of Wisconsin, Inc.
P.O. Box 92882
Milwaukee, WI 53202
[(414) 272–7168]

Rocky Mountain Legal Assistants Association
P.O. Box 304
Denver, CO 80201 [(303) 369–1606]

Region III

Baltimore Association of Legal Assistants
P.O. Box 13244
Baltimore, MD 21203
[(301) 576–BALA]

Cincinnati Paralegal Association
P.O. Box 1515
Cincinnati, OH 45201

Cleveland Association of Paralegals
P.O. Box 14247
Cleveland, OH 44114 [(216) 575–6090]

Columbia Legal Assistants Association
P.O. Box 11634
Columbia, SC 29211–1634

Georgia Association of Legal Assistants
P.O. Box 1802
Atlanta, GA 30301 [(404) 433–5252]

Greater Dayton Paralegal Association
P.O. Box 515, Mid-City Station
Dayton, OH 45402

---

*Affiliate member.

Greater Lexington Paralegal Association, Inc.
P.O. Box 574
Lexington, KY 40586

Indiana Paralegal Association
P.O. Box 44518
Indianapolis, IN 46204

Legal Assistants of Central Ohio
P.O. Box 15182
Columbus, OH 43215–0182
[(614) 224–9700]

Louisville Association of Paralegals
P.O. Box 962
Louisville, KY 40201

Memphis Paralegal Association
P.O. Box 3646
Memphis, TN 38173–0646

Michiana Paralegal Association
P.O. Box 11458
South Bend, IN 46634

Mobile Association of Legal Assistants*
P.O. Box 1852
Mobile, AL 36633

National Capital Area Paralegal Association
P.O. Box 19124
Washington, DC 20036–9998
[(202) 659–0243]

Northeastern Ohio Paralegal Association
P.O. Box 9236
Akron, OH 44305

Roanoke Valley Paralegal Association
P.O. Box 1505
Roanoke, VA 24007

Region IV

Central Connecticut Association of Legal Assistants
P.O. Box 230594
Hartford, CT 06123–0594

Central Massachusetts Paralegal Association
P.O. Box 444
Worcester, MA 01614

*Affiliate member.

Central Pennsylvania Paralegal Association
P.O. Box 11814
Harrisburg, PA 17108

Connecticut Association of Paralegals, Inc. (Fairfield County)
P.O. Box 134
Bridgeport, CT 06601

Connecticut Association of Paralegals (New Haven)
P.O. Box 862
New Haven, CT 06504–0862

Delaware Paralegal Association
P.O. Box 1362
Wilmington, DE 19899

Long Island Paralegal Association
c/o Valerie A. Murphy
58 Twin Lawns Ave.
Hicksville, NY 11801

Manhattan Paralegal Association, Inc.
521 Fifth Ave., 17th Floor
New York, NY 10175

Massachusetts Paralegal Association
P.O. Box 423
Boston, MA 02102 [(617) 469–7077]

Paralegal Association of Rochester, Inc.
P.O. Box 40567
Rochester, NY 14604

Philadelphia Association of Paralegals
2 Pen Center Plaza, Suite 200
Philadelphia, PA 19102
[(215) 854–6352]

Pittsburgh Paralegal Association
P.O. Box 2845
Pittsburgh, PA 15230 [(412) 642–2745]

Rhode Island Paralegal Association
P.O. Box 1003
Providence, RI 02901

South Jersey Paralegal Association
P.O. Box 355
Haddonfield, NJ 08033

Southern Tier Association of Paralegals
P.O. Box 2555
Binghamton, NY 13902

West/Rock Paralegal Association
Suite 381–309 Mamaroneck Ave.
White Plains, NY 10601

Western Massachusetts Paralegal Association
P.O. Box 30005
Springfield, MA 01102

Western New York Paralegal Association, Inc.
P.O. Box 207, Niagara Square Station
Buffalo, NY 14202 [(716) 635–8250]

York County Paralegal Association
P.O. Box 2584
York, PA 17405–2584

NALA State and Local Affiliates

(As of August 1994)
For addresses and telephone numbers contact:
NALA Headquarters
1516 South Boston, Suite 200,
Tulsa, OK 74119
Phone: (918) 587-6828
FAX: (918) 582-6772

ALABAMA

Legal Assistant Society of Southern Institute/PJC
President: Douglas Ingram
Birmingham, AL

Alabama Association of Legal Assistants
President: Miriam Rosario, CLA
Birmingham, AL
NALA Liaison: Michael C. Ivey
Birmingham, AL

Samford Paralegal Association
President: Rebecca King
Birmingham, AL

ALASKA

Fairbanks Associations of Legal Assistants
President: Carolyn Bollman, CLA
North Pole, AK
NALA Liaison: Barbara A. Johnson, CLA
Fairbanks, AK

ARIZONA

Arizona Paralegal Association
President: Pamela J. Kieffer, CLAS
Glendale, AZ

NALA Liaison: Marian Johnson, CLA
Tempe, AZ

Legal Assistants of Metropolitan Phoenix
President: Ruth M. Murphy, CLA
Phoenix, AZ
NALA Liaison: Merilyn Ferrara, CLA
Phoenix, AZ

Tucson Association of Legal Assistants
President: Shirley L. Duran, CLA
Tucson, AZ
NALA Liaison: Mary Butera, CLA
Tucson, AZ

ARKANSAS

Arkansas Association of Legal Assistants
President: Patrice Carey
Little Rock, AR
NALA Liaison: Deborah J. Moon
Pine Bluff, AR

CALIFORNIA

Legal Assistants Association of Santa Barbara
President: Sonja B. Youngdahl
Santa Barbara, CA
NALA Liaison: Lana J. Clark, CLA
Santa Barbara, CA

Paralegal Association of Santa Clara County
President: Jean M. Cushman, CLA
San Jose, CA
NALA Liaison: Jo E. Floch, CLA
San Jose, CA

Ventura County Association of Legal Assistants
President: Cynthia J. Adams, CLA
Ventura, CA
NALA Liaison: Pamela K. Jansz, CLA
Oxnard, CA

COLORADO

Association of Legal Assistants of Colorado
President: Donna Coble, CLAS
Greeley, CO

FLORIDA

Florida Legal Assistants, Inc.
President: Donnajeanne B. Halder, CLAS
St. Petersburg, FL
NALA Liaison: Carol D. Holler, CLAS
Ft. Lauderdale, FL

Bay Area Legal Academy Student Association
President: George House, Jr.
Tampa, FL
NALA Liaison: Dr. Darline R. Root
Tampa, FL

Dade Association of Legal Assistants
President: Judith W. Kingman, CLA
Ft. Lauderdale, FL
NALA Liaison: Iris Krinsky, CLAS
Miami, FL

Gainesville Association of Legal Assistants
President: Melissa Flanagan
Gainesville, FL
NALA Liaison: Pamela S. Craig
Gainesville, FL

Jacksonville Legal Assistants
President: Tana J. Stringfellow, CLA
Jacksonville, FL
NALA Liaison: Mary Cathy Cassels, CLA
Jacksonville, FL

Orlando Legal Assistants
President: Jennifer H. Cooper, CLA
Orlando, FL
NALA Liaison: Lisa Vander Weide, CLA
Orlando, FL

Pensacola Legal Assistants
President: Carol G. Skipper
Pensacola, FL
NALA Liaison: Teresa M. Shimek, CLA
Pensacola, FL

Volusia Association of Legal Assistants
President: Mary Joan Harrington
Ormond Beach, FL
NALA Liaison: Theresa J. Thornton-Hill, CLA
Holly Hill, FL

GEORGIA

Georgia Legal Assistants
President: Elaine H. Hall, CLA
Alma, GA
NALA Liaison: Phyllis H. Driver, CLA
Waycross, GA

Professional Paralegals of Georgia
President: Judith W. McCutcheon, CLA
Atlanta, GA
NALA Liaison: Donita C. Berckemeyer, CLA
Atlanta, GA

Southeastern Association of Legal Assistants of Georgia
President: Linda Phipps, CLAS
Savannah, GA
NALA Liaison: Kathy J. Ulmer
Savannah, GA

South Georgia Association of Legal Assistants
President: Perry D. Wendel, CLA
Lake Park, GA
NALA Liaison: Michelle D. Adkins, CLA
Valdosta, GA

IDAHO

Gem State Association of Legal Assistants
President: Susan Carlson, CLA
Kethcum, ID
NALA Liaison: Ruby A. Becker, CLA
Kethcum, ID

ILLINOIS

Central Illinois Paralegal Association
President: Darlene G. Johnson, CLA
Bloomington, IL
NALA Liaison: Carolyn S. Pitts, CLA
Champaign, IL

Heart of Illinois Paralegal Association
President: Amy DeTrempe-Williams
Peoria, IL
NALA Liaison: Sharon R. Moke
Peoria, IL

INDIANA

Indiana Legal Assistants
President: Tina M. Keller
Terre Haute, IN
NALA Liaison: Dorothy M. French, CLA
Evansville, IN

KANSAS

Kansas Association of Legal Assistants
President: Marie T. Martin, CLA
Wichita, KS
NALA Liaison: Sharon K. Engle, CLA
Wichita, KS

KENTUCKY

Western Kentucky Paralegals
President: Lora L. Roberts, CLAS
Murray, KY
NALA Liaison: Lora L. Roberts, CLAS
Murray, KY

LOUISIANA

Louisiana State Paralegal Association
President: Sandra A. Smith, CLAS
Alexandria, LA
NALA Liaison: Karen L. McKnight, CLA
Alexandria, LA

Northwest Louisiana Paralegal Association
President: Karen M. Greer, CLAS
Shreveport, LA
NALA Liaison: Cindy L. Vucinovich, CLAS
Shreveport, LA

MAINE

Maine State Association of Legal Assistants
President: Ann Hartzler, CLA
Portland, ME
NALA Liaison: Judith A. Allen, CLA
Portland, ME

MICHIGAN

Legal Assistants Association of Michigan
President: Darcy L. Dustin
Kalamazoo, MI
NALA Liaison: Charlotte G. Curiston
Dearborn, MI

MINNESOTA

Minnesota Paralegal Association
President: Monica Sveen-Ziebell
Rochester, MN
NALA Liaison: Muriel L. Hinrichs
Rochester, MN

MISSISSIPPI

Mississippi Association of Legal Assistants
President: Debra D. Hammack
Jackson, MS
NALA Liaison: Gail Lucas, CLAS
Hattiesburg, MS

Mississippi College Society of Legal Assistants
President: LaTricia M. Nelson
Jackson, MS
NALA Liaison: Dawn Crosby, CLA
Clinton, MS

Society for Paralegal Studies
University of Southern Mississippi
Jamie B. Thomas, President
Franklinton, LA
Advisor: Gail L. Lucas, CLAS
Hattiesburg, MS

MISSOURI

St. Louis Association of Legal Assistants
President: Stacia Sanders
St. Louis, MO
NALA Liaison: Shirley A. Bettis
Cedar Hill, MO

MONTANA

Montana Association of Legal Assistants
President: Barbara Jo Wilson, CLA
Missoula, MT
NALA Liaison: Myrna L. O'Hare
Missoula, MT

NEBRASKA

Nebraska Association of Legal Assistants
President: Stefanie A. Neisen
Lincoln, NE
NALA Liaison: Lorrie C. Dahl
Lincoln, NE

NEVADA

Clark County Organization of Legal Assistants, Inc.
President: Dorothy C. Lappin, CLA
Las Vegas, NV
NALA Liaison: Betsy Branyan Kidder, CLAS
Las Vegas, NV

Sierra Nevada Association of Paralegals
President: Candace R. Jones, CLAS
Reno, NV
NALA Liaison: Carol A. Hunt
Reno, NV

NEW HAMPSHIRE

Paralegal Association of New Hampshire
President: Lorinda B. Gaillard
Concord, NH
NALA Liaison: Deborah A. West
Concord, NH

NEW JERSEY

The Legal Assistants Association of New Jersey, Inc.
President: Manny Ferrao
Rahway, NJ
NALA Liaison: Wendy Van Duyne
Elizabeth, NJ

NORTH CAROLINA

Coastal Carolina Paralegal Club
President: Nadine Nash
Jacksonville, NC
NALA Liaison: Col. Robert E. Switzer
Jacksonville, NC

North Carolina Paralegal Association, Inc.
President: Mary F. Haggerty, CLA
Charlotte, NC
NALA Liaison: Karen L. Grimes, CLA
Cary, NC

NORTH DAKOTA

Red River Valley Legal Assistants
President: Linda Brastrup Johnson, CLA
Moorhead, MN
NALA Liaison: Eileen Tronnes Nelson, CLA
Grand Forks, ND

Western Dakota Association of Legal Assistants
President: Candy L. Peterson, CLAS
Minot, ND
NALA Liaison: Connie L. Sundby, CLA
Williston, ND

OHIO

Toledo Association of Legal Assistants
President: Denise Wright
Maumee, OH
NALA Liaison: Cynthia L. Getzinger, CLA
Toledo, OH

OKLAHOMA

Oklahoma Paralegal Association
President: Lennis D. Alley, CLA
Ponca City, OK
NALA Liaison: Stephanie K. Mark, CLAS
Tulsa, OK

Rose State Paralegal Association
President: Judy Shaw
Midwest City, OK

Student Association of Legal Assistants
Rogers State College
President: Michelle K. Price
Claremore, OK

TJC Student Association of Legal Assistants
President: Judy Tucker
Tulsa, OK

Tulsa Association of Legal Assistants
President: Judy K. Johnson, CLA
Tulsa, OK
NALA Liaison: Toni Goss Johnson, CLAS
Broken Arrow, OK

OREGON

Pacific Northwest Legal Assistants
President: Perri L. Judd, CLA
Rosenburg, OR
NALA Liaison: Gayla K. Austin, CLA
Albany, OR

PENNSYLVANIA

Keystone Legal Assistant Association
President: Catrina L. Nuss, CLA
Harrisburg, PA
NALA Liaison: JoAnna M. Samosky, CLA
Pottsville, PA

SOUTH CAROLINA

Central Carolina Technical College Paralegal Association
President: Fay Steigerwalt
Sumter, SC
Faculty Advisor: Jim Curzan
Sumter, SC

Greenville Association of Legal Assistants
President: Linda J. Burns, CLAS
Greenville, SC
NALA Liaison: Paula Jones, CLA
Greenville, SC

Paralegal Association of Beaufort County South Carolina
President: Cynthia A. McClelland, CLAS
Hilton Head Island, SC

Tri-County Paralegal Association
President: Sylvia D. Pratt, CLA
Charleston, SC

SOUTH DAKOTA

South Dakota Legal Assistants Association, Inc.
President: Dory M. Maks
Rapid City, SD
NALA Liaison: Beverly McCracken, CLA
Rapid City, SD

TENNESSEE

Greater Memphis Legal Assistants, Inc.
President: Carol Scoggins, CLAS
Bartlett, TN
NALA Liaison: Wanda D. Howard, CLA
Memphis, TN

Tennessee Paralegal Association
President: Caleeta L. Beagles, CLA
Chattanooga, TN
NALA Liaison: Ann S. Burns, CLAS
Jackson, TN

TEXAS

Capital Area Paralegal Association
President: Gail ViDana Maskey
Pflugerville, TX
NALA Liaison: Christine Levy, CLA
Austin, TX

El Paso Association of Legal Assistants
President: Rosella A. Aguayo, CLAS
El Paso, TX
NALA Liaison: Martha G. Parton, CLA
El Paso, TX

Legal Assistant Association/Permian Basin
President: Len Redmon
Odessa, TX
NALA Liaison: Jo T. Behrends, CLA
Odessa, TX

Northeast Texas Association of Legal Assistants
President: Diane Hall, CLA
Longview, TX
NALA Liaison: Barbara J. Hensley, PLS
Longview, TX

Nueces County Association of Legal Assistants
President: Lillie E. Bordelon
Corpus Christi, TX
NALA Liaison: Evelyn Just, CLA
Corpus Christi, TX

Southeast Texas Association of Legal Assistants
President: Brenda E. Jenkins, CLA
Beaumont, TX
NALA Liaison: Lucinda (Cindy) Wagner, CLA
Beaumont, TX

Texarkana Association of Legal Assistants
President: Diane Plunkett, CLA
Texarkana, TX
NALA Liaison: Myra J. Conaway, CLA
Texarkana, TX

Texas Panhandle Association of Legal Assistants
President: Brenda Cole
Amarillo, TX
NALA Liaison: Julie Winkelman
Amarillo, TX

Tyler Area Association of Legal Assistants
President: Carolyn S. Burton, CLA
Tyler, TX
NALA Liaison: Kathy C. Geoffrion, CLAS
Tyler, TX

West Texas Association of Legal Assistants
President: Ruth H. Bagwell, CLA
Lubbock, TX
NALA Liaison: Juanita Fortenberry, CLA
Littlefield, TX

Wichita County Student Association
President: Kathy M. Parker, CLA
Wichita Falls, TX
NALA Liaison: Billie Ruth Goss
Wichita Falls, TX

UTAH

Legal Assistants Association of Utah
President: Marilu Peterson, CLAS
Salt Lake City, UT
NALA Liaison: Jan S. Mahoney, CLA
Salt Lake City, UT

VIRGINIA

Peninsula Legal Assistants, Inc.
President: Victoria Quadros
Poquoson, VA
NALA Liaison: Phyllis T. Anderson, CLAS
Newport News, VA

Richmond Association of Legal Assistants
President: Nellie J. Foley, CLA
Ashland, VA
NALA Liaison: Sheila H. Komito, CLAS
Richmond, VA

Tidewater Association of Legal Assistants
President: Carla L. Nagel, CLA
Poquoson, VA
NALA Liaison: Susan N. Bawtinhimer, CLA
Norfolk, VA

VIRGIN ISLANDS

Virgin Islands Association of Legal Assistants
President: Ann Clayton
Charlotte Amalie, VI
NALA Liaison: Jonetta Darden-Vincent
Charlotte Amalie, VI

WASHINGTON

Association of Paralegals and Legal Assistants of Washington State

President: Sheila M. White, CLAS
Spokane, WA

Columbia Basin College Paralegal Association
President: Regina A. Stevens
Kennewick, WA
NALA Liaison: Kerri Wheeler Feeney, CLAS
Richland, WA

WEST VIRGINIA

Legal Assistants of West Virginia, Inc.
President: Joyce A. Wilson
Charleston, WV
NALA Liaison: Joanne W. Rini, CLA
Charleston, WV

WISCONSIN

Madison Area Legal Assistants Association
President: Beverly A. Potts, CLA
Madison, WI
NALA Liaison: Kristine Caldwell, CLA
Madison, WI

WYOMING

Legal Assistants of Wyoming
President: Anita K. Schroeder, CLAS
Casper, WY
NALA Liaison: Carol D. Martin, CLAS
Rawlins, WY

OTHER LAW-RELATED ASSOCIATIONS

American Association of Law Libraries (AALL)
53 West Jackson Boulevard, Suite 940
Chicago, IL 60604
(312) 939–4764

American Association for Paralegal Education (AAfPE)
P.O. Box 40244
Overland Park, KS 66204
(913) 381–4458

American Bar Association (ABA) Standing Committee on Legal Assistants
750 North Lake Shore Drive
Chicago, IL 60611
(312) 988–5000

Association of Legal Administrators (ALA)
104 Wilmot Road, Suite 205
Deerfield, IL 60015–5195
(312) 940–9240

Legal Assistant Management Association (LAMA)
P.O. Box 40129
Overland Park, KS 66204
(913) 381–4458

National Association for Independent Paralegals
585 5th St. West
Sonoma, CA 95476

National Paralegal Association
P.O. Box 406
Solebury, PA 18963
(215) 297–8333

Appendix I

State and Major Local Bar Associations

Alabama

Alabama State Bar
Founded 1879
10,125 Members
P.O. Box 671
Montgomery, AL 36101
205/269–1515
FAX: 205/261–6310

Birmingham Bar Assn.
Founded 1885
2,698 Members
109 N. 20th St., 2nd Floor
Birmingham, AL 35203
205/251–8006
FAX: 205/251–7193

Alaska

Alaska Bar Assn.
Founded 1955
3,112 Members
P.O. Box 100279
Anchorage, AK 99510
907/272–7469
FAX: 907/272–2932

Arizona

Maricopa County Bar Assn.
Founded 1914
4,500 Members
303 E. Palm Lane
Phoenix, AZ 85004–1532
602/257–4200
FAX: 602/257–0522

State Bar of Arizona
Founded 1933
12,941 Members
111 W. Monroe St.
Phoenix, AZ 85003–1742
602/252–4804
FAX: 602/271–4930

Arkansas

Arkansas Bar Assn.
Founded 1899
4,100 Members
400 W. Markham
Little Rock, AR 72201
501/375–4605
FAX: 501/375-4901

California

Alameda County Bar Assn.
Founded 1877
2,700 Members
360 22nd Street, Suite 800
Oakland, CA 94612
510/893–7160
FAX: 510/893–3119

Beverly Hills Bar Assn.
Founded 1931
3,100 Members
300 S. Beverly Dr.
#201
Beverly Hills, CA 90212
310/553–6644
FAX: 310/284–8290

Lawyers' Club of Los Angeles
Founded 1930
700 Members
3000 S. Robertson Blvd.
Suite 215
Los Angeles, CA 90034–3158
818/305–0124
FAX: 818/568–9758

Lawyers' Club of San Francisco
Founded 1946
2,000 Members
685 Market St.
Suite 750
San Francisco, CA 94105
415/882–9150
FAX: 415/882–7170

Los Angeles County Bar Assn.
Founded 1878
20,000 Members
P.O. Box 55020
Los Angeles, CA 90055
213/896–6424
FAX: 213/896–6500

Orange County Bar Assn.
Founded 1901
6,000 Members
601 Civic Center Drive West
Santa Ana, CA 92701–4002
714/541–6222
FAX: 714/541–1482

Sacramento Cnty. Bar Assn.
Founded 1925
2,400 Members
901 H. St., Suite 101
Sacramento, CA 95814
916/448–1087
FAX: 916/448–6930

San Diego County Bar Assn.
Founded 1920
6,200 Members
1333 Seventh Ave.
San Diego, CA 92101
619/231–0781
FAX: 619/338–0042

Bar Assn. of San Francisco
Founded 1872
9,500 Members
685 Market St.
Suite 700
San Francisco, CA 94105
415/267–0709
FAX: 415/546–9223

Santa Clara County Bar Assn.
Founded 1917
4,000 Members
4 N. Second Street
Suite 400
San Jose, CA 95113
408/287–2557
FAX: 408/287–6083

State Bar of California
Founded 1927
137,103 Members
555 Franklin St.
San Francisco, CA 94102
415/561–8200
FAX: 415/561–8305

Colorado

Denver Bar Assn.
Founded 1891
7,100 Members
1900 Grant St.
#950
Denver, CO 80203-4309
303/860-1115
FAX: 303/894-0821

The Colorado Bar Assn.
Founded 1897
13,500 Members
1900 Grant St. #950
Denver, CO 80203
303/860–1115
FAX: 303/894–0821

Connecticut

Connecticut Bar Assn.
Founded 1875
11,000 Members
101 Corporate Place
Rocky Hill, CT 06067
203/721–0025
FAX: 203/257–4125

Hartford County Bar Assn.
Founded 1783
2,400 Members
61 Hungerford St.
Hartford, CT 06106
203/525–8106
FAX: 203/293–1345

Delaware

Delaware State Bar Assn.
Founded 1923
2,300 Members
1225 King Street
Wilmington, DE 19801
302/658–5279
FAX: 302/658–5212

District of Columbia

Bar Assn. of the Dist. of Columbia
Founded 1871
5,500 Members
1819 H St., NW
12th Floor
Washington, DC 20006–3690
202/223–6600
FAX: 202/293–3388

The District of Columbia Bar
Founded 1972
62,845 Members
1250 H Street, N. W.
6th Floor
Washington, DC 20005–3908
202/737–4700
FAX: 202/626–3473

Florida

Dade County Bar Assn.
Founded 1920
4,000 Members
123 NW First Ave.
#214
Miami, FL 33128
305/371–2220
FAX: 305/539–9749

The Florida Bar
Founded 1950
50,992 Members
650 Apalachee Parkway
Tallahassee, FL 32399–2300
904/561–5600
FAX: 904/561–5827

Hillsborough County Bar Assn.
Founded 1937
2,600 Members
315 E. Madison
Suite 1010
Tampa, FL 33602
813/226–6431
FAX: 813/223–3946

Orange County Bar Assn.
2,200 Members
880 N. Orange Ave., #100
Orlando, FL 32801
407/422–4551
FAX: 407/843–3470

Georgia

Atlanta Bar Assn.
Founded 1888
5,421 Members
2500 The Equitable Bldg.
100 Peachtree St., NW
Atlanta, GA 30303
404/521–0781
FAX: 404/522–0269

State Bar of Georgia
Founded 1964
25,000 Members
800 The Hurt Bldg.
50 Hurt Plaza
Atlanta, GA 30303
404/527–8755
FAX: 404/527–8717

Hawaii

Hawaii State Bar Assn.
Founded 1899
5,290 Members
Penthouse 1, 9th Floor
1136 Union Mall
Honolulu, HI 96813
808/537–1868
FAX: 808/521–7936

Idaho

Idaho State Bar
Founded 1923
3,167 Members
P.O. Box 895
Boise, ID 83701
208/334–4500
FAX: 208/334–4515

Illinois

The Chicago Bar Assn.
Founded 1874
23,000 Members
321 Plymouth Court
Chicago, IL 60604
312/554–2000
FAX: 312/554–2054

Chicago Council of Lawyers
Founded 1969
1,200 Members
220 S. State St., Room 800
One Quincy Court
Chicago, IL 60604
312/427–0710
FAX: 312/427–0181

Illinois State Bar Assn.
Founded 1877
31,000 Members
424 S. Second Street.
Springfield, IL 62701
217/525–1760
FAX: 217/525–0712

Indiana

Indiana State Bar Assn.
Founded 1896
10,450 Members
230 E. Ohio, 4th Fl.
Indianapolis, IN 46204
317/639–5465
FAX: 317/266–2588

Indianapolis Bar Assn.
Founded 1878
3,100 Members
Market Tower, 10 W. Market
Suite 440
Indianapolis, IN 46204
317/269-2000
FAX: 317/464–8118

Iowa

The Iowa State Bar Assn.
Founded 1874
6,900 Members
521 E. Locust
Des Moines, IA 50309
515/243–3179
FAX: 515/243–2511

Kansas

Kansas Bar Assn.
Founded 1882
5,300 Members
P.O. Box 1037
Topeka, KS 66601–1037
913/234–5696
FAX: 913/234–3813

Kentucky

Kentucky Bar Assn.
Founded 1871
11,000 Members
514 West Main Street
Frankfort, KY 40601–1883
502/564–3795
FAX: 502/564–3225

Louisville Bar Assn.
Founded 1900
2,600 Members
707 W. Main St.
Louisville, KY 40202
502/583–5314
FAX: 502/583–4113

Louisiana

Louisiana State Bar Assn.
Founded 1941
16,300 Members
601 St. Charles Ave.
New Orleans, LA 70130
504/566-1600
FAX: 504/566-0930

New Orleans Bar Assn.
Founded 1924
2,300 Members
228 Saint Charles Avenue
Suite 1223
New Orleans, LA 70130
504/525–7453
FAX: 504/525–6549

Maine

Maine State Bar Assn.
Founded 1891
2,850 Members
P.O. Box 788
Augusta, ME 04332–0788
207/622–7523
FAX: 207/623–0083

Maryland

Bar Assn. of Baltimore City
Founded 1880
3,200 Members
111 N. Calvert St., Ste. 627
Baltimore, MD 21202
410/539–5936
FAX: 410/685–3420

Maryland State Bar Assn., Inc.
Founded 1896
16,569 Members
520 W. Fayette St.
Baltimore, MD 21201
410/685–7878
FAX: 410/837–0518

Bar Association of Montgomery County
Founded 1894
2,600 Members
27 W. Jefferson St.
Rockville, MD 20850
301/424–3454
FAX: 301/217–9327

Massachusetts

Boston Bar Assn.
Founded 1761
7,135 Members
16 Beacon St.
Boston, MA 02018
617/742–0615
FAX: 617/523–0127

Massachusetts Bar Assn.
Founded 1911
18,000 Members
20 West St.
Boston, MA 02111–1218
617/542–3602
FAX: 617/426–4344

Michigan

Detroit Bar Assn.
Founded 1836
3,450 Members
2380 Penobscot Bldg.
Detroit, MI 48226
313/961–6120
FAX: 313/965–0842

Oakland County Bar Assn.
Founded 1934
3,500 Members
1760 S. Telegraph
Suite 100
Bloomfield, MI 48302–0181
810/334–3400
FAX: 810/334–7757

State Bar of Michigan
Founded 1936
29,146 Members
306 Townsend St.
Lansing, MI 48933–2083
517/372–9030
FAX: 517/482–6248

Minnesota

Hennepin County Bar Assn.
Founded 1919
6,500 Members
514 Nicollet Mall
#350
Minneapolis, MN 55402
612/340–0022
FAX: 612/340–9518

Minnesota State Bar Assn.
Founded 1883
14,700 Members
514 Nicollet Mall
Suite 300
Minneapolis, MN 55402
612/333–1183
FAX: 612/333–4927

Ramsey County Bar Assn.
Founded 1883
2,800 Members
332 Minnesota Street
E-1312
St. Paul, MN 55101
612/222–0846
FAX: 612/223–8344

Mississippi

The Mississippi Bar
Founded 1905
6,000 Members
P.O. Box 2168
Jackson, MS 39225–2168
601/948-4471
FAX: 601/355–8635

Missouri

Kansas City Metropolitan Bar Association
Founded 1884
3,900 Members
1125 Grand
Suite 400
Kansas City, MO 64106
816/474–4322
FAX: 816/474–0103

Bar Assn. of Metropolitan St. Louis
Founded 1874
6,200 Members
One Metropolitan Square
Suite 1400
St. Louis, MO 63102
314/421–4134
FAX: 314/421–0013

The Missouri Bar
Founded 1944
21,000 Members
P.O. Box 119
Jefferson City, MO 65102
314/635-4128
FAX: 314/635–2811

Montana

State Bar of Montana
Founded 1975
3,030 Members
P.O. Box 577
Helena, MT 59624
406/442–7660
FAX: 406/442–7763

Nebraska

Nebraska State Bar Assn.
Founded 1877
7,550 Members
P.O. Box 81809
Lincoln, NE 68501
402/475–7091
FAX: 402/475–7098

Nevada

State Bar of Nevada
Founded 1928
3,972 Members
201 Las Vegas Blvd.
Suite 200
Las Vegas, NV 89101
702/382–2200
FAX: 702/385–2878

New Hamphsire

New Hampshire Bar Assn.
Founded 1873
4,100 Members
112 Pleasant St.
Concord, NH 03301
603/224–6942
FAX: 603/224–2910

New Jersey

Bergen County Bar
Founded 1898
2,000 Members
61 Hudson St.
Hackensack, NJ 07601
201/488–0044
FAX: 201/488–0073

Essex County Bar Assn.
Founded 1898
2,950 Members
One Newark Center
16th Floor
Newark, NJ 07102
201/622–6207
FAX: 201/622–4341

New Jersey State Bar Assn.
Founded 1899
19,300 Members
New Jersey Law Center
One Constitution Sqr.
New Brunswick, NJ 08901–1500
908/249–5000
FAX: 908/249–2815

New Mexico

State Bar of New Mexico
Founded 1886
5,450 Members
P.O. Box 25883
Albuquerque, NM 87125
505/842-6132
FAX: 505/843-8765

New York

Brooklyn Bar Assn.
Founded 1872
2,300 Members
123 Remsen St.
Brooklyn, NY 11201–4212
718/624–0675
FAX: 718/797–1713

Bar Assn. of Erie County
Founded 1887
3,400 Members
1450 Statler Towers
Buffalo, NY 14202
716/852-8687
FAX: 716/856–7641

Monroe County Bar Assn.
Founded 1892
2,000 Members
One Exchange Street
5th Floor
Rochester, NY 14614
716/546–1817
FAX: 716/546–1807

Bar Assn. of Nassau County, Inc.
Founded 1899
6,000 Members
15th & West Sts.
Mineola, NY 11501
516/747–4070
FAX: 516/747–4147

The Assn. of the Bar of the City of New York
Founded 1871
20,000 Members
42 W. 44th St.
New York, NY 10036
212/382–6620
FAX: 212/302–8219

New York County Lawyers Assn.
Founded 1908
10,200 Members
14 Vesey St.
New York, NY 10007
212/267–6646
FAX: 212/406–9252

New York State Bar Assn.
Founded 1876
60,000 Members
One Elk St.
Albany, NY 12207
518/463–3200
FAX: 518/463–4276

Queens County Bar Assn.
Founded 1876
2,110 Members
90–35 148th St.
Jamaica, NY 11435
718/291–4500
FAX: 718/657–1789

Suffolk County Bar Assn.
Founded 1908
2,840 Members
560 Wheeler Road
Hauppauge, NY 11788–4357
516/234–5511
FAX: 516/234–5899

Westchester County Bar Assn.
Founded 1896
2,572 Members
300 Hamilton Ave.
Suite 400
White Plains, NY 10601
914/761–3707
FAX: 914/761–9402

North Carolina

10th Judicial District Bar Assn.
2,200 Members
P.O. Box 12806
Raleigh, NC 27605
919/677–9903
FAX: 919/677–0761

North Carolina Bar Assn.
Founded 1899
10,150 Members
P.O. Box 12806
Raleigh, NC 27605
919/677–0561
FAX: 919/677–0761

North Carolina State Bar
Founded 1933
14,918 Members
P.O. Box 25908
Raleigh, NC 27611
919/828–4620
FAX: 919/821–9168

North Dakota

State Bar Assn. of North Dakota
Founded 1921
1,740 Members
P.O. Box 2136
Bismarck, ND 58502–2136
701/255-1404
FAX: 701/224–1621

Ohio

Cincinnati Bar Assn.
Founded 1873
3,600 Members
35 E. Seventh St.
8th Floor
Cincinnati, OH 45202–2492
513/381–8213
FAX: 513/381–0528

Cleveland Bar Assn.
Founded 1873
5,200 Members
113 St. Clair Ave., N.E.
Cleveland, OH 44114–1253
216/696–3525
FAX: 216/696–2413

Columbus Bar Assn.
Founded 1869
4,300 Members
175 South 3rd Street
Columbus, OH 43215–5134
614/221–4112
FAX: 614/221–4850

The Cuyahoga County Bar Assn.
Founded 1928
1,300 Members
500 The Terminal Tower
50 Public Square
Cleveland, OH 44113–2203
216/621–5112
FAX: 216/523–2259

Ohio State Bar Assn.
Founded 1880
24,000 Members
P.O. Box 6562
Columbus, OH 43216–6562
614/487–2050
FAX: 614/487–1008

Oklahoma

Oklahoma Bar Assn.
Founded 1939
13,287 Members
P.O. Box 53036
Oklahoma City, OK 73152
405/524–2365
FAX: 405/524–1115

Oklahoma County Bar Assn.
Founded 1902
2,056 Members
119 N. Robinson
Suite 240
Oklahoma, OK 73102
405/236–8421
FAX: 405/232–2210

Tulsa County Bar Assn.
Founded 1903
2,000 Members
1446 South Boston
Tulsa, OK 74119
916/584–5243
FAX: 918/592–0208

Oregon

Multnomah Bar Assn.
Founded 1906
3,400 Members
630 SW Fifth Avenue
Suite 200
Portland, OR 97204
503/222–3275
FAX: 503/243–1881

Oregon State Bar
Founded 1890
11,000 Members
P.O. Box 1689
Lake Oswego, OR 97035
503/620–0222
FAX: 503/684–1366

Pennsylvania

Allegheny Cty. Bar Assn.
Founded 1870
7,500 Members
Kopper's Building, 4th Flr.
Pittsburgh, PA 15219
412/261–6161
FAX: 412/261–3622

Pennsylvania Bar Assn.
Founded 1895
27,750 Members
P.O. Box 186
Harrisburg, PA 17108
717/238–6715
FAX: 717/238–1204

Philadelphia Bar Assn.
Founded 1802
12,500 Members
1101 Market Street, 11th Flr.
Philadelphia, PA 19107–2911
215/238–6338
FAX: 215/238–1267

Puerto Rico

Puerto Rico Bar Assn.
Founded 1840
8,950 Members
P.O. Box 1900
San Juan, PR 00903
809/721–3358
FAX: 809/725–0330

Rhode Island

Rhode Island Bar Assn.
Founded 1898
4,300 Members
115 Cedar Street
Providence, RI 02903
401/421–5740
FAX: 401/421–2703

South Carolina

South Carolina Bar
Founded 1975
8,200 Members
P.O. Box 608
Columbia, SC 29202
803/799–6653
FAX: 803/799–4118

South Dakota

State Bar of South Dakota
Founded 1931
2,077 Members
222 E. Capitol
Pierre, SD 57501
605/224–7554
FAX: 605/224–0282

Tennessee

Nashville Bar Assn.
Founded 1831
2,100 Members
221 Fourth Avenue North
Suite 400
Nashville, TN 37219–2100
615/242–9272
FAX: 615/255–3026

Tennessee Bar Assn.
Founded 1881
7,000 Members
3622 West End Avenue
Nashville, TN 37205–2403
615/383–7421
FAX: 615/297–8058

Texas

Dallas Bar Assn.
Founded 1873
7,600 Members
2101 Ross Ave.
Dallas, TX 75201
214/969–7066
FAX: 214/880–0807

Houston Bar Assn.
Founded 1870
9,600 Members
1001 Fannin, Ste 1300
Houston, TX 77002–6708
713/759–1133
FAX: 713/759–1710

San Antonio Bar Assn.
Founded 1916
2,850 Members
Bexar County Courthouse, 5th Floor
San Antonio, TX 78205
210/227–8822
FAX: 210/271–9614

State Bar of Texas
Founded 1939
62,500 Members
P.O. Box 12487
Austin, TX 78711
512/463–1463 or 800/204–2222
FAX: 512/463–7388

Travis County Bar Assn.
Founded 1914
2,920 Members
700 Lavaca
Suite 602
Austin, TX 78701
512/472–0279
FAX: 512/473–2720

Utah

Utah State Bar
Founded 1931
5,800 Members
645 S. 200 East, #310
Salt Lake City, UT 84111
801/531–9077
FAX: 801/531–0660

Vermont

Vermont Bar Assn.
Founded 1878
1,850 Members
P.O. Box 100
Montpelier, VT 05601
802/223–2020
FAX: 802/223-1573

Virginia

Fairfax Bar Assn.
Founded 1935
2,100 Members
4110 Chain Bridge Road
#303
Fairfax, VA 22030
703/246–2740
FAX: 703/273–1274

Virginia State Bar
Founded 1938
23,300 Members
707 E. Main Street
Suite 1500
Richmond, VA 23219–2803
804/775–0500
FAX: 804/775–0501

Virginia Bar Assn.
Founded 1888
5,300 Members
7th & Franklin Bldg.
701 E. Franklin St. #1515
Richmond, VA 23219
804/644–0041
FAX: 804/644–0052

Virgin Islands

Virgin Island Bar Assn.
Founded 1921
400 Members
P.O. Box 4108
Christiansted, V.I. 00822
809/778–7497
FAX: 809/773–5060

Washington

King County Bar Assn.
Founded 1906
4,500 Members
The Bank of CA Bldg.
Suite 600
900 4th Avenue
Seattle, WA 98164
206/624–9365
FAX: 206/382–1270

Washington State Bar Assn.
Founded 1890
18,546 Members
500 Westin Bldg.
2001 6th Ave.
Seattle, WA 98121–2599
206/727–8200
FAX: 206/727–8320

West Virginia

West Virginia Bar Assn.
Founded 1886
1,300 Members
P.O. Box 346
Charleston, WV 25322–0346
304/342-1474
FAX: 304/345–5864

West Virginia State Bar
Founded 1947
4,000 Members
2006 Kanawha Blvd. E
Charleston, WV 25311
304/558–2456
FAX: 304/558–2567

Wisconsin

Milwaukee Bar Assn.
Founded 1858
2,500 Members
533 East Wells Street
Milwaukee, WI 53202
414/274–6760
FAX: 414/274–6765

State Bar of Wisconsin
Founded 1957
18,000 Members
402 W. Wilson
Madison, WI 53703
608/257–3838
FAX: 608/257–5502

Wyoming

Wyoming State Bar
Founded 1915
1,873 Members
P.O. Box 109
Cheyenne, WY 82003–0109
307/632–9061
FAX: 307/632–3737

Guam

Guam Bar Assn.
350 Members
Suite 101
259 Martyr Street
Agana, Guam 96910
011/671/472–6848
FAX: 011/671/472–1246

Northern Mariana Islands Bar Association
273 Members
February, 1985

Appendix J

Information on the NALA's Certified Legal Assistant (CLA) and Certified Legal Assistant Specialist (CLAS) Examinations*

Certification—A Professional Goal

Certification bestows a measure of professional recognition to those persons who achieve significant competence in the field.

This opportunity for the legal assistant profession is provided by the National Association of Legal Assistants, Inc. [NALA], through its national certification program. The CLA Certifying program consists of successful completion of a comprehensive two day examination. Thereafter, evidence of continuing legal education must be submitted periodically in order to maintain certification. The program is administered by the National Association of Legal Assistants through its Certifying Board which consists of a minimum of five legal assistants who have the Certified Legal Assistant and CLA Specialist designations, two attorneys and two paralegal educators. In 1994, the number of Certified Legal Assistants throughout the nation surpassed 6,500—legal assistants in 49 states, the District of Columbia and the Virgin Islands have been certified by NALA.

Although the goal of becoming a Certified Legal Assistant is a voluntary commitment, the Certified Legal Assistant designation is recognized in the legal field as denoting high standards of professionalism and excellence. The legal community recognizes Certified Legal Assistants have proven that their experience and knowledge are not restricted to a few limited areas but that they have a general knowledge and understanding of the entire profession and capabilities for exceeding minimal requirements.

The NALA CLA Certifying examination program involves successful completion of a two day examination administered in the Spring, in mid-July, and in cooperation with NALA Affiliated Associations in December. The body of knowledge required to attain the Certified Legal Assistant designation is great. Although the NALA Certifying Board recognizes the expertise required of a legal assistant cannot be reduced to a formula, certain basic

*This appendix presents excerpts from NALA's booklet entitled *The Certified Legal Assistant Program.* For information on upcoming CLA and CLAS examination dates and testing centers, contact NALA headquarters at (918) 587-6828.

skills common to the profession are measurable: verbal and written communication skills; judgment and analytical abilities; and an understanding of ethics, human relations, legal terminology, and legal research. The examination covers these areas as well as substantive knowledge of law and procedures. The substantive law section requires each candidate to complete a section on the American legal system and to choose and complete four of eight sections: litigation; estate planning and probate; real estate; criminal law; bankruptcy; contract; business organizations; and administrative law. As a standardized national examination, all sections are on the federal level—no state laws or procedures are tested.

As with all NALA programs, the purpose of the examination program is to help the legal assistant profession by serving as a means of distinguishing and recognizing excellence among legal assistants and by serving as a stabilizing force and directional tool in the growth on the profession. The Certified Legal Assistant program is not rigid—its foundation allows methodical and thoughtful change. It helps by attesting to the competency of certified legal assistants and by serving as a guideline for colleges and schools offering legal assistant programs. While the profession grows the individuals within must, too. Legal assistants are an integral part of the legal team and must strive to improve the profession. NALA's voluntary certification program is one answer to those needs.

Outline—The Certified Legal Assistant Examination

Each section of the examination contains objective questions, such as multiple choice, true/false and matching. The sections on Communications and Judgment and Analytical Ability each contain short answer and/or essay questions.

Communications

This section of the Certified Legal Assistant examination covers the following areas of communications:

Word Usage
Punctuation
Capitalization
Grammar
Nonverbal Communication
Correspondence
Concise Writing
Vocabulary
Rules of Composition

Ethics

This section deals with ethics in the legal assistant's contacts with employers, clients, co-workers and the general public. Unauthorized practice, ethical rules, practice rules and confidentiality are among the topics tested by this section.

Knowledge of the American Bar Association Rules of Professional Conduct and the National Association of Legal Assistants, Inc., Code of Ethics and Professional Responsibility is required by this examination.

Human Relations and Interviewing Techniques

The Human Relations portion encompasses professional and social contacts with the employer, clients and other office visitors, co-workers, including subordinates, and the public outside of the law office. For this reason, the legal assistant should be familiar with: authorized practice, ethical rules, practice rules, delegation of authority, consequences of delegation and confidentiality.

Interviewing Techniques confers basic principles, as agreed upon by most authors on the subject, definitions of terms of basic principles and handling of specialized interviews. Subject areas included in this section of the examination are:

- General considerations for the interviewing situation: courtesy, empathy, physical setting, body language.
- Initial Roadblocks—lapse of time, prejudiced, etc.
- Manner of questions
- Use of checklists for specific matters
- Special handling situations: the elderly, the very young
- Both initial and subsequent interviews are included as are both client and witness interviews.

Judgment and Analytical Ability

The sections of this part deal with (1) analyzing and categorizing facts and evidence; (2) the legal assistant's relationship with the lawyer, the legal secretary, the client, the courts and other law firms; (3) the legal assistant's reaction to specific situations; (4) handling telephone situations; and (5) reading comprehension and data interpretation. The section also contains an essay question which requires analysis of a research request and applicable law and the writing of a responsive memo.

Familiarity with the Rules of Professional Conduct of the American Bar Association and the Code of Ethics and Professional Responsibility of the National Association of Legal Assistants, Inc., will also be helpful. Knowledge of logical reasoning and experience as a legal assistant are valuable assets.

Legal Research

It is extremely important for the legal assistant to be able to use the most important "tool" of the legal profession—the law library. The purpose of the Legal Research section of the CLA Certifying Examination is to test your knowledge of the use of state and Federal codes, the statutes, the digests, case reports, various legal encyclopedias, court reports, Shepardizing and research procedure.

The amount of study and practice you will need to pass this section of the examination will depend on your current knowledge and experience with legal research. You can get excellent practice by researching various topics on your own.

Legal Terminology

The sections of this part deal with (1) Latin phrases; (2) legal phrases or terms in general; and (3) utilization and understanding of common legal terms.

The questions involve legal terminology and procedures used in general practice.

Substantive Law

The Substantive Law section of the CLA Certifying examination is divided into nine parts:

1. General (includes the American Legal System)
2. Administrative Law
3. Bankruptcy
4. Contract
5. Business Organization
6. Criminal
7. Litigation
8. Probate & Estate Planning
9. Real Estate

Each examinee will be required to take the general section and must select four out of the remaining eight specialty tests.

Those persons who are taking the examination, but have not had formal law courses, would benefit from a study of a current textbook in the area.

A great deal of the material covered in this section of the examination is acquired through work experience in the legal field. The Substantive Law mini-tests are designed to test the legal assistant's general knowledge of the fields of law.

STUDY METHODS

Generally, legal assistants study individually for the CLA Certifying Examination. A list of study references for each examination section and sample questions may be found in the Mock Examination and Study Guide available through NALA Headquarters. In addition to providing study references for this examination, this material will aid applicants in developing their own study programs.

Affiliated state and local legal assistant associations of the National Association of Legal Assistants have begun sponsoring study groups or review seminars for those interested in the CLA Certifying Examination. Notices of these programs are included in FACTS & FINDINGS, NALA's quarterly publication, and in the membership newsletter when available. Non-members may call NALA Headquarters for this information or contact state or local associations direct.

The NALA CLA Exam Preparation Manual is available through West Publishing Company. Authored by Attorney Virginia Koerselman, in association with NALA, this manual is a useful tool for preparing to take the NALA Certifying Examination. Copies may be obtained by calling West Publishing Company at (800) 328-9352.

Formal education courses are recommended, especially in assisting a candidate to prepare for the substantive law section. Should you choose this as a study option be sure to keep in mind that all substantive law sections are based on federal rules, codes, practice and procedure. No state laws, codes or procedures are tested.

* * * *

GRADING AND RETAKE POLICY

A passing score of 70% is required for each of the examination sections. The substantive law section is graded as a whole. From a total of 500 points, 350 points is passing regardless of the distribution of points among the five parts.

Results are announced by the Certifying Board in writing to all examinees. Results are not available by telephone or by FAX.

Of the seven sections of the CLA Certifying examination, four sections must be successfully completed in order to retake only those sections failed.

Applicants in retake status may attend a maximum of five retake sessions within a three year period. Applicants in retake status will be allowed to choose which sections will be retaken during any retake session. Again, an applicant can only attend a retake session five times within the three year period. The examination must be successfully completed within five retake sessions in a three year period, or credit for all passed sections will be forfeited. If less than four sections are successfully completed, the applicant must reapply for the full applications.

ELIGIBILITY REQUIREMENTS

An applicant for the Certified Legal Assistant examination must meet at least one of the three eligibility requirements listed on the Certified Legal Assistant application form [in the section of that form presented at the end of this appendix].

* * * *

MAINTENANCE OF CERTIFIED LEGAL ASSISTANT DESIGNATION

In recognition of the continuing change in laws and procedures that have a direct impact on the quality of work performed by legal assistants, Certified Legal Assistants are required to maintain their certified status by submitting proof of continuing education. The CLA Certifying designation is for a period of five years and if the Certified Legal Assistant submits proof of attendance in accordance with the requirements[,] . . . the certificate is renewed for another five years and the process begins again. Lifetime certification is not available.

The Certified Legal Assistant designation may be revoked for any one of the following reasons:

1. Falsification of information on application form.
2. Subsequent conviction of the unauthorized practice of law.
3. Failure to meet continuing legal education requirements as required by the Certifying Board.
4. Divulging the contents of any Examination Questions.
5. Subsequent conviction of a felony.
6. Violation of the NALA Code of Ethics and Professional Responsibility.

Individuals currently serving a prison term are ineligible to sit for the CLA examination.

* * * *

Specialty Certification

NALA has instituted the second phase of the CLA program—certification for those who specialize in a particular area of the law. Specialty Certification involves successful completion of a four hour in-depth examination.

Specialty Examination Descriptions

In July of 1982, the Certifying Board announced the availability of specialty certification in the two areas of Civil Litigation and Probate and Estate Planning to any CLA in good standing. In March 1984 a Corporate and Business Law specialty examination was added, Criminal Law and Procedure was added for the July 1984 testing, Real Estate Specialty examination was added in July 1987 and a Bankruptcy specialty was added in December 1992. These four hour examinations are administered during the same time as the full CLA examination. Specialty certification will be available in other practice areas in the future.

Bankruptcy is a comprehensive examination testing knowledge of the Bankruptcy Code (Title 11 U.S.C. and Title 28 U.S.C.), bankruptcy rules and procedures, including the applicable Federal Rules of Civil Procedure and Federal Rules of Evidence, with regard to debtors and creditors.

Civil Litigation will comprehensively test an applicants' knowledge in the areas of civil procedure, substantive law and litigation techniques. The examination covers the federal rules of civil [procedure], evidence and appellate procedure; civil substantive law (i.e., personal injury, products liability, contracts, etc.); legal terminology; and legal research. Applicants should also be familiar with document control, drafting of pleadings, abstracting information and general litigation techniques.

Probate and Estate Planning covers general probate and trust law, federal estate tax, fiduciary income tax, drafting wills and trusts, and estate planning concepts.

Corporate and Business Law covers the knowledge and applications of those principles of contract, tort, property, agency, employment, administrative, tax as it relates to business organizations, corporate, and partnership law which commonly constitute the subject matter known as business law. Examinees should be thoroughly familiar with the Uniform Commercial Code, Uniform Partnership Act, Uniform Limited Partnership Act, Model Business Corporate Act, as well as with the regulatory authority of those federal agencies which affect the business relationship such as the IRS, SEC, FTC, OSHA and EPA.

Criminal Law and Procedure specialty examination is a comprehensive examination testing an applicant's knowledge in the area of criminal procedure and law from arrest through trial. The examination covers components of substantive criminal law, procedural matters, and constitutional rights guaranteed to defendants. Applicants should be thoroughly familiar with the Federal Rules of Criminal Procedure, Evidence, and major United States Supreme Court Cases. The American Law Institute's Model Penal Code or any nutshell series, such as West, would be a good general reference for this examination.

Real Estate is a comprehensive examination testing the applicant's knowledge in the area of real estate purchases, sales, terminology, actions affecting title, oil, and gas, landlord/tenant relations, easements, abstracts, title insurance, liens, cluster developments, types of conveyances, methods of passing title included in conveyances, legal remedies associated with real estate and legal description of real estate.

The level of testing will require substantial experience in the specialty area. The examinations are offered at the same time as the regular examination.

Legal Assistants are becoming more and more specialized—the CLA Certifying examination tests the broad general skills required of all legal assistants. Specialty certification is a goal for those who want to be recognized for achieving significant competence in a particular field. Further, a legal assistant may want to take more than one specialty examination if a specialty changes over time.

Certified Legal Assistants are awarded two (2) units of continuing legal assistant education (CLAE) credit towards maintenance of the Certified Legal Assistant designation upon successful completion of a specialty examination.

Specialty Eligibility Requirements

The only eligibility requirement for the specialty examination is that an applicant must be a Certified Legal Assistant in good standing. Those who have allowed their certification to lapse through nonadherence to the continuing education requirements or those whose certification has been revoked, are not eligible to sit for a specialty examination.

* * * *

Specialty Grading and Retake Policy

Specialty examinations are four (4) hours in length and are divided into two (2) sections. There is a break after Section 1. An applicant cannot return to the first part of the examination after the break. The examination is graded as a whole and a score of 70% is the passing score for each specialty examination.

Specialty Examination Data: Certified Legal Assistant Specialists (Through April 1994)

Bankruptcy	25
Civil Litigation	286
Probate & Estate Planning	66
Corporate & Business Law	24
Criminal Law & Procedure	27
Real Estate Specialists	96
Total Specialists	524

REQUIREMENTS FOR MAINTAINING CERTIFIED LEGAL ASSISTANT STATUS

All Certified Legal Assistants must submit evidence of completion of five (5) units of Continuing Legal Assistant Education every five (5) years to maintain valid certification. A completed Recertification Audit Verification plus a fee of $50 will also be required at the time of recertification. Notice of one (1) year probation will be given to all Certified Legal Assistants failing to submit evidence of completion of the five (5) units of CLAE within the five (5) year period. If the Certified Legal Assistant fails to complete the above recertification requirements in this time certification will be revoked, with notice to the legal assistant.

All requests for CLAE credit are subject to Certifying Board approval. Relevancy is subject to approval by the NALA Certifying Board who may request employer attestation.

The categories of CLAE with unit values are:

Category A: Successful completion of a NALA Specialty Examination—2 units per Specialty Examination

Category B: Successful completion (Grade C or better) of a relevant course for a minimum of 3 quarter hours or 2 semester hours at an accredited institution of higher education. Relevancy may be requested by employer attestation and NALA Certifying Board approval—2 units per course.

Auditing of a relevant course, or completion of a relevant course not meeting above listed minimums—1 unit per course

(Clarification of hours: Institutions of higher education generally are organized into quarters—10–12 weeks in length and give "quarter hours" as unit of course measurement or into semesters 14–15 weeks in length and give "semester hours" as unit of course measurement. A 2 semester hour course is usually equal to a 3 quarter hour course. Minimums are specified only.

Clarification of "accredited": By any nationally recognized accrediting agency.)

Category C: Attendance at conferences, seminars, workshops, etc., on relevant topics for working legal assistants, with actual hours recorded. Minimum content of one hour required for consideration. Actual educational hours will be recorded and copy of brochure and/or program indicating schedule must be attached (unless a NALA-sponsored event.) Units will be recorded on the basis of ten hours of continuing education equaling one CLAE unit.

Category D: Certified Legal Assistant may petition NALA Certifying Board for credit for unusual experiences which may be considered for credit. Examples: teaching experience; extensive research beyond employment requirements on a topic related to the work of a practicing legal assistant which results in publication—limited to 2 units per petition.

Mechanics: It is the obligation of Certified Legal Assistants to secure supporting data (transcripts, employer and coordinator attestations, articles, etc.) to be submitted to NALA Headquarters as events are attended. These documents will be reviewed by the full Certifying Board for action. Request forms are available from NALA Headquarters, 1516 South Boston, Suite 200, Tulsa, Oklahoma 74119–4464.

NOTE: Effective October 1982, for recertification purposes, except in Category A, units for attending seminars in areas other than substantive law are limited to one unit maximum for any five year period.

Adopted 10/10/77; Amended 6/81; 8/82; 5/85; 5/87; 2/88; 5/88; 10/88; 3/93

CLA is a certification mark duly registered with the U.S. Patent and Trademark Office (No. 1131999). Any unauthorized use is strictly forbidden.

CLA Specialist is a certification mark duly registered with the U.S. Patent and Trademark Office (No. 1751731). Any unauthorized use is strictly forbidden.

Certified Legal Assistant Examination Application Form

NATIONAL ASSOCIATION OF LEGAL ASSISTANTS, INC.
1516 South Boston, Suite 200 Tulsa, Oklahoma 74119
(918) 587-6828 FAX (918) 582-6772

QUALIFICATIONS

Candidates for certification must meet one of the following requirements outlined in Categories 1, 2 or 3 below, at the time of filing this application form. Select the appropriate category based on your experience and training and complete the corresponding parts of this application form, beginning on the next page. Individuals currently serving a prison term are ineligible to sit for the CLA certifying examination.

Category 1

QUALIFICATIONS: Graduation from a legal assistant program that is:

a) Approved by the American Bar Association, or
b) An associate degree program, or
c) A post-baccalaureate certificate program in legal assistant studies, or
d) A bachelor's degree program in legal assistant studies, or
e) A legal assistant program which consists of a minimum of 60 semester (or equivalent quarter)* hours of which at least 15 semester hours (or equivalent quarter hours)** are substantive legal courses.

** 900 clock hours of a legal assistant program will be considered equivalent to 60 semester hours. 90 quarter hours of a legal assistant program will be considered equivalent to 60 semester hours.*
*** 225 clock hours of substantive legal courses will be considered equivalent to 15 semester hours. 22½ quarter hours of legal courses will be considered equivalent to 15 semester hours.*

All applicants applying under this category must submit with this application form a copy of the school's official transcript showing all courses taken and date of graduation. For those applying under "c" a letter or copy of a certificate of completion must be submitted. The letter or certificate must include a statement that the certificate program is a post-baccalaureate program. **The application form will be considered incomplete without a copy of the school's official transcript, and the post-baccalaureate statement if applying under "c".**

Category 2

QUALIFICATIONS: A bachelor's degree in any field plus one (1) year's experience as a legal assistant*. Copy of official transcript showing date of graduation must be attached to the application form.

** Successful completion of at least 15 semester hours (or 22½ quarter hours or 225 clock hours) of substantive legal assistance courses will be considered equivalent to one year experience as a legal assistant.*

All applicants applying under this category must submit with this application form a copy of the school's official transcript showing receipt of a bachelor's degree and date of completion. Those applying under the provision allowing for additional course work in lieu of the one year's work experience, must submit an official school transcript showing complete course work. **The application form will be considered incomplete without a copy of the school's official transcript, along with either verification of experience or official school transcript equivalent courses in lieu of experience.**

Category 3

QUALIFICATIONS: A high school diploma or equivalent plus seven (7) years' experience as a legal assistant under the supervision of a member of the Bar plus evidence of a minimum of twenty (20) hours of continuing legal education credit to have been completed within a two-year period prior to application for the exam.

Within this category, "legal assistant" is defined as: *legal assistants are a distinguishable group of persons who assist attorneys in the delivery of legal services. Through formal education, training and experience, legal assistants have knowledge and expertise regarding the legal system and substantive and procedural law which qualify them to do work of a legal nature under the supervision of an attorney.*

Evidence of continuing education credit is documented by the attorney/employer attestation that must be signed to complete this application form. No further documentation is required.

Appendix K

Specialty Certification Standards for Legal Assistants in Texas

Pursuant to the authority vested in the Legal Assistants Advisory Commission ("the Commission") by the Texas Board of Legal Specialization ("TBLS"), the Commission prescribes the following standards and requirements for legal assistants board certification in civil trial law, personal injury trial law and family law in accordance with the *Texas Plan for Recognition and Regulation of Voluntary Specialty Certification for Legal Assistants in the State of Texas.*

I. General Requirements and Definitions

A. A legal assistant is a person, qualified through education, training, or work experience, who is employed or retained by a lawyer, law office, governmental agency, or other entity in a capacity or function which involves the performance, under the ultimate direction and supervision of a licensed attorney, of specifically delegated substantive legal work, which, for the most part, requires a sufficient knowledge of concepts that, absent such assistance, the attorney would perform.

B. The applicant must be employed in the State of Texas as a legal assistant working under the direct supervision of an attorney duly licensed and doing business in the State of Texas.

C. No person currently under an attorney disciplinary sanction which prohibits that person from practicing law shall be eligible to apply for specialty certification under the *Legal Assistants Plan.*

D. No legal assistant shall be required to be certified in any field of law before being allowed to work under the supervision of a duly licensed attorney as a legal assistant. Any legal assistant shall have the right to work in all fields of law under the supervision of a duly licensed attorney, even though the legal assistant is not board certified in any particular specialty field.

E. All requirements for and benefits to be derived from certification are individual and may not be fulfilled by or attributed to either the attorney under whose supervision the legal assistant is working or to a law firm by whom such legal assistant may be employed.

F. Forms, documents, applications, questionnaires, and examinations involved in the certification process, as well as fees required of applicants for specialty certification or recertification shall be as approved by the Commission and TBLS.

G. Certification shall be for a period of 5 years at the end of which time recertification shall be permitted upon the terms and conditions established by the Commission and TBLS.

H. Definitions of specialty fields:
   1. *Civil Trial Law* involves responsibilities and duties dealing with litigation and mediation of civil controversies in all areas of substantive law before state courts, federal courts, administrative agencies, and arbitrators. In addition to assisting the attorney with the actual pretrial and trial process, "civil trial" includes evaluating, and handling civil controversies prior to the initiation of suit as well as the full course of appellate processes.
   2. *Personal Injury Trial Law* involves responsibilities and duties dealing with trauma or disability, physical or mental, to a person. It includes, by way of definition and not limitation, assisting the attorney with personal injury litigation and mediation involving automobile and other vehicular accident reparations; workmen's compensation; governmental claims; professional malpractice; products liability; statutory claims; Social Security claims; insurance contract claims; or any negligent or intentional tort.
   3. *Family Law* involves responsibilities and duties dealing with, by way of definition not limitation, assisting the attorney with matters involving the Texas Family Code, Titles 1, 2 and 4; Texas Penal Code, Chapter 25 (offenses against the family); the law of homestead and other exempt property; the taxation law of divorce and interspousal transaction; torts against the family; the trial and mediation of cases arising out of the above matters; and the perfection of appeals from both interlocutory and final judgments. For the specific requirements in these areas please refer to Section II(B).

I. Applicants shall furnish satisfactory evidence of their good character, reputation, knowledge and active responsibility to follow the provisions of the attorneys' Texas Disciplinary Rules of Professional Conduct. They shall also furnish a statement as to whether or not they are now or have ever been subject to a unauthorized practice of law complaint by an authorized UPL Committee of the State of Texas or ever been disbarred by the State Bar of Texas or any other state law licensing entity; and if so, the details of such complaint or disbarment including whether or not they had ever been sanctioned by the committee or any court.

   The Commission and TBLS may deny certification or recertification on a finding by the State Bar of Texas Legal Assistants Division Professional Ethics Committee or any legal assistants' organization, a UPL committee or a court that an applicant has been guilty of professional misconduct. The Commission and TBLS may defer certification or recertification based upon the pendency of such proceedings. However, the Commission and TBLS will consider the seriousness of the underlying fact of the misconduct and will consider the passage of time since such misconduct and applicant's experience since that time. Failure to disclose such information is a material misrepresentation and may be cause for rejection or revocation of certification.

J. Applicants shall furnish a statement as to whether or not they have ever been convicted, given probation or fined for a serious crime as hereinafter defined, whether the above resulted from a plea of guilty or nolo contendere or from a verdict after trial or otherwise and regardless of the pendency of an appeal. The term "serious crime" shall include any felony. It shall also include any lesser crime, a necessary element of which as determined by the statutory or common law definition of such crime, involved improper conduct of a legal assistant, interference with the administration of justice, false swearing, misrepresentation, fraud, willful failure to file income tax returns, deceit or bribery, extortion, misappropriation, theft, or an attempt or a conspiracy or solicitation of another to commit a serious crime.

The Commission and TBLS may deny certification or recertification if applicant has been convicted, given probation or fined for a serious crime as defined in this section.

K. Applicants must submit at least 2 written recommendations which must be from:
   1. The legal assistant's present attorney supervisor, or an attorney supervisor who has supervised the legal assistant's work product for a period of at least 1 year during the 5 years immediately preceding application; and
   2. A judge, non-attorney professional, or some supervising attorney with whom the applicant has had special contact work in the particular specialty field during the 5 years immediately preceding application.

   In addition to the names of references supplied by applicants, the Commission and TBLS may, at its option, send recommendation statement forms to other attorneys and/or judges; and the Commission and TBLS may deny certification or recertification based upon information received from written recommendations.

II. MINIMUM STANDARDS FOR CERTIFICATION

A. PROFESSIONAL AND EDUCATIONAL EXPERIENCE
   1. Applicants must have a minimum of 5 years of actual experience as a legal assistant, and
   2. Immediately preceding application, applicants must have a minimum of 3 years of actual Texas experience in the particular field for which the legal assistant applies for specialty certification; and
   3. Applicants must have, in addition to the above, at least one of the following:
      a. Successful completion of the NALA (National Association of Legal Assistants) Certification examination; or
      b. A baccalaureate or higher degree in any field; or
      c. An ABA approved program of education and training for legal assistants; or
      d. A legal assistant program that consists of a minimum of 60 semester credit hours (or equivalent quarter hours) of which at least 18 such credit hours are in substantive legal courses; or
      e. A legal assistant program that consists of at least 18 semester credit hours of substantive legal courses, plus at least 45 semester credit hours (or equivalent quarter hours) of general college curriculum courses; or
      f. Four additional years of actual experience working as a legal assistant under the supervision of a licensed attorney, for a total of 9 years of actual experience.

B. SUBSTANTIAL INVOLVEMENT AND SPECIAL COMPETENCE
Applicants must show substantial involvement and special competence in the specialty field during the 3 years immediately preceding application by showing and providing such information as may be required by the Commission and TBLS.
1. Applicants must submit a written statement demonstrating substantial involvement in the specialty field, evidencing the following:
   a. Applicants must show that during each of the 3 years immediately preceding application they have devoted a minimum of 50% of their legal assistant functions to the specialty field's matters as defined in Section I(H); and
   b. That the applicant has acquired experience and expertise in the specialty field by showing a level of utilization necessary to justify the representation of special competence; and
2. Applicants must show their special competence by providing such information as may be required by the Commission and TBLS to demonstrate the scope, nature, complexity of their Legal Assistant experience.

C. CONTINUING LEGAL EDUCATIONAL EXPERIENCE
Applicants must demonstrate participation in a minimum of 30 hours of continuing legal education in the specialty field, of which 10 hours may be in self-study activities, within the accumulation period which begins 3 years immediately preceding the certification application filing date and ends June 1st of the year in which the certificates are to be issued. Continuing legal education participation includes either:
1. Attendance at and completion of programs of study in the specialty field approved by the Commission and TBLS; or
2. Substantial involvement in continuing legal education in the specialty field through such activity as:
   a. Teaching a course in the specialty field;
   b. Completion of a course in the specialty field;
   c. Participation as a panelist or speaker on a symposium or similar program in the specialty field;
   d. Attendance at a lecture series or similar program, in the specialty field, sponsored by a qualified educational institution or Bar group;
   e. Authorship of a book or article concerning the specialty field, published in a professional publication or journal;
   f. Active participation in the work of a professional committee dealing with a specific problem of the specialty field; and
   g. Such other educational experience as the Commission and TBLS shall approve.

D. PAYMENT OF FEES
Applicants shall timely pay the fees as established from time to time by the Commission and TBLS, including but not limited to the application filing fee, the examination and/or recertification fee.

E. FAILURE TO FURNISH INFORMATION: MISREPRESENTATION
Certification or recertification may be denied because of applicant's failure to furnish the requested information or because of their misrepresentation of any material fact requested by the Commission and TBLS.

F. EXAMINATION
Applicants for certification must pass a written examination applied uniformly to all applicants, and in addition, an oral examination that may be required of some or all of the applicants, to be determined by the Commission and TBLS prior to certification, to demonstrate sufficient knowledge, proficiency and experience in the specialty field to justify the representation of special competence to the legal profession and to the public.

III. RECERTIFICATION

A. Applicants must comply with the Minimum Standards for Certification as set forth in Section II(B) which include:
   1. A satisfactory showing, as determined by the Commission and TBLS, of substantial involvement in the specialty field of law for which certification was granted, during each year of certification;
   2. The payment of any fee prescribed by the Commission and TBLS. In the event a legal assistant's previous certificate is not in effect at the time application is made for recertification, or the legal assistant fails to meet the requirements for recertification, such legal assistant shall be entitled to seek certification by examination as provided in Section II(F) above.
   3. The continued employment and work under the direct supervision of an attorney licensed in the State of Texas.

B. Applicants shall state whether during the preceding 5 year period of certification they have:
   1. Been subject to an unauthorized practice of law complaint by an authorized UPL Committee of the State of Texas or any other state law licensing entity; been found guilty of professional misconduct by State Bar of Texas Legal Assistants Division Professional Ethics Committee or any legal assistants' organization, a UPL committee or a court and if so, the details of such complaint or misconduct including whether or not they had ever been sanctioned by the committee or any court.
   2. Been convicted, given probation, or fined for a serious crime as defined in Section I(J).

C. Applicants must demonstrate participation in a minimum of 75 hours of continuing legal education in the 5 years immediately preceding application. No more than 30 hours of the continuing legal education requirement may be completed in a certification year. Of the 75 total hours, 1 hour of ethics is required per certification year. Applicants are also eligible to receive a maximum of 5 hours of self-study per certification year.

TEXAS BOARD OF LEGAL SPECIALIZATION
November 1, 1993

APPENDIX L

THE CONSTITUTION OF THE UNITED STATES

PREAMBLE

We the People of the United States, in Order to form a more perfect Union, establish Justice, insure domestic Tranquility, provide for the common defence, promote the general Welfare, and secure the Blessings of Liberty to ourselves and our Posterity, do ordain and establish this Constitution for the United States of America.

ARTICLE I

Section 1. All legislative Powers herein granted shall be vested in a Congress of the United States, which shall consist of a Senate and House of Representatives.

Section 2. The House of Representatives shall be composed of Members chosen every second Year by the People of the several States, and the Electors in each State shall have the Qualifications requisite for Electors of the most numerous Branch of the State Legislature.

No Person shall be a Representative who shall not have attained to the Age of twenty five Years, and been seven Years a Citizen of the United States, and who shall not, when elected, be an Inhabitant of that State in which he shall be chosen.

Representatives and direct Taxes shall be apportioned among the several States which may be included within this Union, according to their respective Numbers, which shall be determined by adding to the whole Number of free Persons, including those bound to Service for a Term of Years, and excluding Indians not taxed, three fifths of all other Persons. The actual Enumeration shall be made within three Years after the first Meeting of the Congress of the United States, and within every subsequent Term of ten Years, in such Manner as they shall by Law direct. The Number of Representatives shall not exceed one for every thirty Thousand, but each State shall have at Least one Representative; and until such enumeration shall be made, the State of New Hampshire shall be entitled to chuse three, Massachusetts eight, Rhode Island and Providence Plantations one, Connecticut five, New York six, New Jersey four, Pennsylvania eight, Delaware one, Maryland six, Virginia ten, North Carolina five, South Carolina five, and Georgia three.

When vacancies happen in the Representation from any State, the Executive Authority thereof shall issue Writs of Election to fill such Vacancies.

The House of Representatives shall chuse their Speaker and other Officers; and shall have the sole Power of Impeachment.

Section 3. The Senate of the United States shall be composed of two Senators from each State, chosen by the Legislature thereof, for six Years; and each Senator shall have one Vote.

Immediately after they shall be assembled in Consequence of the first Election, they shall be divided as equally as may be into three Classes. The Seats of the Senators of the first Class shall be vacated at the Expiration of the second Year, of the second Class at the Expiration of the fourth Year, and of the third Class at the Expiration of the sixth Year, so that one third may be chosen every second Year; and if Vacancies happen by Resignation, or otherwise, during the Recess of the Legislature of any State, the Executive thereof may make temporary Appointments until the next Meeting of the Legislature, which shall then fill such Vacancies.

No Person shall be a Senator who shall not have attained to the Age of thirty Years, and been nine Years a Citizen of the United States, and who shall not, when elected, be an Inhabitant of that State for which he shall be chosen.

The Vice President of the United States shall be President of the Senate, but shall have no Vote, unless they be equally divided.

The Senate shall chuse their other Officers, and also a President pro tempore, in the Absence of the Vice President, or when he shall exercise the Office of President of the United States.

The Senate shall have the sole Power to try all Impeachments. When sitting for that Purpose, they shall be on Oath or Affirmation. When the President of the United States is tried, the Chief Justice shall preside: And no Person shall be convicted without the Concurrence of two thirds of the Members present.

Judgment in Cases of Impeachment shall not extend further than to removal from Office, and disqualification to hold and enjoy any Office of honor, Trust, or Profit under the United States: but the Party convicted shall nevertheless be liable and subject to Indictment, Trial, Judgment, and Punishment, according to Law.

Section 4. The Times, Places and Manner of holding Elections for Senators and Representatives, shall be prescribed in each State by the Legislature thereof; but the Congress may at any time by Law make or alter such Regulations, except as to the Places of chusing Senators.

The Congress shall assemble at least once in every Year, and such Meeting shall be on the first Monday in December, unless they shall by Law appoint a different Day.

Section 5. Each House shall be the Judge of the Elections, Returns, and Qualifications of its own Members, and a Majority of each shall constitute a Quorum to do Business; but a smaller Number may adjourn from day to day, and may be authorized to compel the Attendance of absent Members, in such Manner, and under such Penalties as each House may provide.

Each House may determine the Rules of its Proceedings, punish its Members for disorderly Behavior, and, with the Concurrence of two thirds, expel a Member.

Each House shall keep a Journal of its Proceedings, and from time to time publish the same, excepting such Parts as may in their Judgment require Secrecy; and the Yeas and Nays of the Members of either House on any question shall, at the Desire of one fifth of those Present, be entered on the Journal.

Neither House, during the Session of Congress, shall, without the Consent of the other, adjourn for more than three days, nor to any other Place than that in which the two Houses shall be sitting.

Section 6. The Senators and Representatives shall receive a Compensation for their Services, to be ascertained by Law, and paid out of the Treasury of the United States. They shall in all Cases, except Treason, Felony and Breach of the Peace, be privileged from Arrest during their Attendance at the Session of their respective Houses, and in going to and returning from the same; and for any Speech or Debate in either House, they shall not be questioned in any other Place.

No Senator or Representative shall, during the Time for which he was elected, be appointed to any civil Office under the Authority of the United States, which shall have been created, or the Emoluments whereof shall have been increased during such time; and no Person holding any Office under the United States, shall be a Member of either House during his Continuance in Office.

Section 7. All Bills for raising Revenue shall originate in the House of Representatives; but the Senate may propose or concur with Amendments as on other Bills.

Every Bill which shall have passed the House of Representatives and the Senate, shall, before it become a Law, be presented to the President of the United States; If he approve he shall sign it, but if not he shall return it, with his Objections to the House in which it shall have originated, who shall enter the Objections at large on their Journal, and proceed to reconsider it. If after such Reconsideration two thirds of that House shall agree to pass the Bill, it shall be sent together with the Objections, to the other House, by which it shall likewise be reconsidered, and if approved by two thirds of that House, it shall become a Law. But in all such Cases the Votes of both Houses shall be determined by Yeas and Nays, and the Names of the Persons voting for and against the Bill shall be entered on the Journal of each House respectively. If any Bill shall not be returned by the President within ten Days (Sundays excepted) after it shall have been presented to him, the Same shall be a Law, in like Manner as if he had signed it, unless the Congress by their Adjournment prevent its Return in which Case it shall not be a Law.

Every Order, Resolution, or Vote, to which the Concurrence of the Senate and House of Representatives may be necessary (except on a question of Adjournment) shall be presented to the President of the United States; and before the Same shall take Effect, shall be approved by him, or being disapproved by him, shall be repassed by two thirds of the Senate and House of Representatives, according to the Rules and Limitations prescribed in the Case of a Bill.

Section 8. The Congress shall have Power To lay and collect Taxes, Duties, Imposts and Excises, to pay the Debts and provide for the common Defence and general Welfare of the United States; but all Duties, Imposts and Excises shall be uniform throughout the United States;

To borrow Money on the credit of the United States;

To regulate Commerce with foreign Nations, and among the several States, and with the Indian Tribes;

To establish an uniform Rule of Naturalization, and uniform Laws on the subject of Bankruptcies throughout the United States;

To coin Money, regulate the Value thereof, and of foreign Coin, and fix the Standard of Weights and Measures;

To provide for the Punishment of counterfeiting the Securities and current Coin of the United States;

To establish Post Offices and post Roads;

To promote the Progress of Science and useful Arts, by securing for limited Times to Authors and Inventors the exclusive Right to their respective Writings and Discoveries;

To constitute Tribunals inferior to the supreme Court;

To define and punish Piracies and Felonies committed on the high Seas, and Offenses against the Law of Nations;

To declare War, grant Letters of Marque and Reprisal, and make Rules concerning Captures on Land and Water;

To raise and support Armies, but no Appropriation of Money to that Use shall be for a longer Term than two Years;

To provide and maintain a Navy;

To make Rules for the Government and Regulation of the land and naval Forces;

To provide for calling forth the Militia to execute the Laws of the Union, suppress Insurrections and repel Invasions;

To provide for organizing, arming, and disciplining, the Militia, and for governing such Part of them as may be employed in the Service of the United States, reserving to the States respectively, the Appointment of the Officers, and the Authority of training the Militia according to the discipline prescribed by Congress;

To exercise exclusive Legislation in all Cases whatsoever, over such District (not exceeding ten Miles square) as may, by Cession of particular States, and the Acceptance of Congress, become the Seat of the Government of the United States, and to exercise like Authority over all Places purchased by the Consent of the Legislature of the State in which the Same shall be, for the Erection of Forts, Magazines, Arsenals, dock-Yards, and other needful Buildings;—And

To make all Laws which shall be necessary and proper for carrying into Execution the foregoing Powers, and all other Powers vested by this Constitution in the Government of the United States, or in any Department or Officer thereof.

Section 9. The Migration or Importation of such Persons as any of the States now existing shall think proper to admit, shall not be prohibited by the Congress prior to the Year one thousand eight hundred and eight, but a Tax or duty may be imposed on such Importation, not exceeding ten dollars for each Person.

The privilege of the Writ of Habeas Corpus shall not be suspended, unless when in Cases of Rebellion or Invasion the public Safety may require it.

No Bill of Attainder or ex post facto Law shall be passed.

No Capitation, or other direct, Tax shall be laid, unless in Proportion to the Census or Enumeration herein before directed to be taken.

No Tax or Duty shall be laid on Articles exported from any State.

No Preference shall be given by any Regulation of Commerce or Revenue to the Ports of one State over those of another: nor shall Vessels bound to, or from, one State be obliged to enter, clear, or pay Duties in another.

No Money shall be drawn from the Treasury, but in Consequence of Appropriations made by Law; and a regular Statement and Account of the Receipts and Expenditures of all public Money shall be published from time to time.

No Title of Nobility shall be granted by the United States: And no Person holding any Office of Profit or Trust under them, shall, without the Consent of the Congress, accept of any present, Emolument, Office, or Title, of any kind whatever, from any King, Prince, or foreign State.

Section 10. No State shall enter into any Treaty, Alliance, or Confederation; grant Letters of Marque and Reprisal; coin Money; emit Bills of Credit; make any Thing but gold and silver Coin a Tender in Payment of Debts; pass any Bill of Attainder, ex post facto Law, or Law impairing the Obligation of Contracts, or grant any Title of Nobility.

No State shall, without the Consent of the Congress, lay any Imposts or Duties on Imports or Exports, except what may be absolutely necessary for executing its inspection Laws: and the net Produce of all Duties and Imposts, laid by any State on Imports or Exports, shall be for the Use of the Treasury of the United States; and all such Laws shall be subject to the Revision and Controul of the Congress.

No State shall, without the Consent of Congress, lay any Duty of Tonnage, keep Troops, or Ships of War in time of Peace, enter into any Agreement or Compact with another State, or with a foreign Power, or engage in War, unless actually invaded, or in such imminent Danger as will not admit of delay.

Article II

Section 1. The executive Power shall be vested in a President of the United States of America. He shall hold his Office during the Term of four Years, and, together with the Vice President, chosen for the same Term, be elected, as follows:

Each State shall appoint, in such Manner as the Legislature thereof may direct, a Number of Electors, equal to the whole Number of Senators and Representatives to which the State may be entitled in the Congress; but no Senator or Representative, or Person holding an Office of Trust or Profit under the United States, shall be appointed an Elector.

The Electors shall meet in their respective States, and vote by Ballot for two Persons, of whom one at least shall not be an Inhabitant of the same State with themselves. And they shall make a List of all the Persons voted for, and of the Number of Votes for each; which List they shall sign and certify, and transmit sealed to the Seat of the Government of the United States, directed to the President of the Senate. The President of the Senate shall, in the Presence of the Senate and House of Representatives, open all the Certificates, and the Votes shall then be counted. The Person having the greatest Number of Votes shall be the President, if such Number be a Majority of the whole Number of Electors appointed; and if there be more than one who have such Majority, and have an equal Number of Votes, then the House of Representatives shall immediately chuse by Ballot one of them for President; and if no Person have a Majority, then from the five highest on the List the said House shall in like Manner chuse the President. But in chusing the President, the Votes shall be taken by States, the Representation from each State having one Vote; A quorum for this Purpose shall consist of a Member or Members from two thirds of the States, and a Majority of all the States shall be necessary to a Choice. In every Case, after the Choice of the President, the Person having the greater Number of Votes of the Electors shall be the Vice President. But if there should remain two or more who have equal Votes, the Senate shall chuse from them by Ballot the Vice President.

The Congress may determine the Time of chusing the Electors, and the Day on which they shall give their Votes; which Day shall be the same throughout the United States.

No person except a natural born Citizen, or a Citizen of the United States, at the time of the Adoption of this Constitution, shall be eligible to the Office of President; neither shall any Person be eligible to that Office who shall not have attained to the Age of thirty five Years, and been fourteen Years a Resident within the United States.

In Case of the Removal of the President from Office, or of his Death, Resignation or Inability to discharge the Powers and Duties of the said Office, the same shall devolve on the Vice President, and the Congress may by Law provide for the Case of Removal, Death, Resignation or Inability, both of the President and Vice President, declaring what Officer shall then act as President, and such Officer shall act accordingly, until the Disability be removed, or a President shall be elected.

The President shall, at stated Times, receive for his Services, a Compensation, which shall neither be increased nor diminished during the Period for which he shall have been elected, and he shall not receive within that Period any other Emolument from the United States, or any of them.

Before he enter on the Execution of his Office, he shall take the following Oath or Affirmation: "I do solemnly swear (or affirm) that I will faithfully execute the Office of President of the United States, and will to the best of my Ability, preserve, protect and defend the Constitution of the United States."

Section 2. The President shall be Commander in Chief of the Army and Navy of the United States, and of the Militia of the several States, when called into the actual Service of the United States; he may require the Opinion, in writing, of the principal Officer in each of the executive Departments, upon any Subject relating to the Duties of their respective Offices, and he shall have Power to grant Reprieves and Pardons for Offenses against the United States, except in Cases of Impeachment.

He shall have Power, by and with the Advice and Consent of the Senate to make Treaties, provided two thirds of the Senators present concur; and he shall nominate, and by and with the Advice and Consent of the Senate, shall appoint Ambassadors, other public Ministers and Consuls, Judges of the supreme Court, and all other Officers of the United States, whose Appointments are not herein otherwise provided for, and which shall be established by Law; but the Congress may by Law vest the Appointment of such inferior Officers, as they think proper, in the President alone, in the Courts of Law, or in the Heads of Departments.

The President shall have Power to fill up all Vacancies that may happen during the Recess of the Senate, by granting Commissions which shall expire at the End of their next Session.

Section 3. He shall from time to time give to the Congress Information of the State of the Union, and recommend to their Consideration such Measures as he shall judge necessary and expedient; he may, on extraordinary Occasions, convene both Houses, or either of them, and in Case of Disagreement between them, with Respect to the Time of Adjournment, he may adjourn them to such Time as he shall think proper; he shall receive Ambassadors and other public Ministers; he shall take Care that the Laws be faithfully executed, and shall Commission all the Officers of the United States.

Section 4. The President, Vice President and all civil Officers of the United States, shall be removed from Office on Impeachment for, and Conviction of, Treason, Bribery, or other high Crimes and Misdemeanors.

Article III

Section 1. The judicial Power of the United States, shall be vested in one supreme Court, and in such inferior Courts as the Congress may from time to time ordain and establish. The Judges, both of the supreme and inferior Courts, shall hold their Offices during good Behaviour, and shall, at stated Times, receive for their Services a Compensation, which shall not be diminished during their Continuance in Office.

Section 2. The judicial Power shall extend to all Cases, in Law and Equity, arising under this Constitution, the Laws of the United States, and Treaties made, or which shall be made, under their Authority;—to all Cases affecting Ambassadors, other public Ministers and Consuls;—to all Cases of admiralty and maritime Jurisdiction;—to Controversies to which the United States shall be a Party;—to Controversies between two or more States;—between a State and Citizens of another State;—between Citizens of different States;—between Citizens of the same State claiming Lands under Grants of different States, and between a State, or the Citizens thereof, and foreign States, Citizens or Subjects.

In all Cases affecting Ambassadors, other public Ministers and Consuls, and those in which a State shall be a Party, the supreme Court shall have original Jurisdiction. In all the other Cases before mentioned, the supreme Court shall have appellate Jurisdiction, both as to Law and Fact, with such Exceptions, and under such Regulations as the Congress shall make.

The Trial of all Crimes, except in Cases of Impeachment, shall be by Jury; and such Trial shall be held in the State where the said Crimes shall have been committed; but when not committed within any State, the Trial shall be at such Place or Places as the Congress may by Law have directed.

Section 3. Treason against the United States, shall consist only in levying War against them, or, in adhering to their Enemies, giving them Aid and Comfort. No Person shall be convicted of Treason unless on the Testimony of two Witnesses to the same overt Act, or on Confession in open Court.

The Congress shall have Power to declare the Punishment of Treason, but no Attainder of Treason shall work Corruption of Blood, or Forfeiture except during the Life of the Person attainted.

ARTICLE IV

Section 1. Full Faith and Credit shall be given in each State to the public Acts, Records, and judicial Proceedings of every other State. And the Congress may by general Laws prescribe the Manner in which such Acts, Records and Proceedings shall be proved, and the Effect thereof.

Section 2. The Citizens of each State shall be entitled to all Privileges and Immunities of Citizens in the several States.

A Person charged in any State with Treason, Felony, or other Crime, who shall flee from Justice, and be found in another State, shall on Demand of the executive Authority of the State from which he fled, be delivered up, to be removed to the State having Jurisdiction of the Crime.

No Person held to Service or Labour in one State, under the Laws thereof, escaping into another, shall, in Consequence of any Law or Regulation therein, be discharged from such Service or Labour, but shall be delivered up on Claim of the Party to whom such Service or Labour may be due.

Section 3. New States may be admitted by the Congress into this Union; but no new State shall be formed or erected within the Jurisdiction of any other State; nor any State be formed by the Junction of two or more States, or Parts of States, without the Consent of the Legislatures of the States concerned as well as of the Congress.

The Congress shall have Power to dispose of and make all needful Rules and Regulations respecting the Territory or other Property belonging to the United States; and nothing in this Constitution shall be so construed as to Prejudice any Claims of the United States, or of any particular State.

Section 4. The United States shall guarantee to every State in this Union a Republican Form of Government, and shall protect each of them against Invasion; and on Application of the Legislature, or of the Executive (when the Legislature cannot be convened) against domestic Violence.

ARTICLE V

The Congress, whenever two thirds of both Houses shall deem it necessary, shall propose Amendments to this Constitution, or, on the Application of the Legislatures of two thirds of the several States, shall call a Convention for proposing Amendments, which, in either Case, shall be valid to all Intents and Purposes, as part of this Constitution, when ratified by the Legislatures of three fourths of the several States, or by Conventions in three fourths thereof, as the one or the other Mode of Ratification may be proposed by the Congress; Provided that no Amendment which may be made prior to the Year One thousand eight hundred and eight shall in any Manner affect the first and fourth Clauses in the Ninth Section of the first Article; and that no State, without its Consent, shall be deprived of its equal Suffrage in the Senate.

ARTICLE VI

All Debts contracted and Engagements entered into, before the Adoption of this Constitution shall be as valid against the United States under this Constitution, as under the Confederation.

This Constitution, and the Laws of the United States which shall be made in Pursuance thereof; and all Treaties made, or which shall be made, under the Authority of the United States, shall be the supreme Law of the Land; and the Judges in every State shall be bound thereby, any Thing in the Constitution or Laws of any State to the Contrary notwithstanding.

The Senators and Representatives before mentioned, and the Members of the several State Legislatures, and all executive and judicial Officers, both of the United States and of the several States, shall be bound by Oath or Affirmation, to support this Constitution; but no religious Test shall ever be required as a Qualification to any Office or public Trust under the United States.

ARTICLE VII

The Ratification of the Conventions of nine States shall be sufficient for the Establishment of this Constitution between the States so ratifying the Same.

AMENDMENT I [1791]

Congress shall make no law respecting an establishment of religion, or prohibiting the free exercise thereof; or abridging the freedom of speech, or of the press; or the right of the people peaceably to assembly, and to petition the Government for a redress of grievances.

AMENDMENT II [1791]

A well regulated Militia, being necessary to the security of a free State, the right of the people to keep and bear Arms, shall not be infringed.

AMENDMENT III [1791]

No Soldier shall, in time of peace be quartered in any house, without the consent of the Owner, nor in time of war, but in a manner to be prescribed by law.

AMENDMENT IV [1791]

The right of the people to be secure in their persons, houses, papers, and effects, against unreasonable searches and seizures, shall not be violated, and no Warrants shall issue, but upon probable cause, supported by Oath or affirmation, and particularly describing the place to be searched, and the persons or things to be seized.

AMENDMENT V [1791]

No person shall be held to answer for a capital, or otherwise infamous crime, unless on a presentment or indictment of a Grand Jury, except in cases arising in the land or naval forces, or in the Militia, when in actual service in time of War or public danger; nor shall any person be subject for the same offence to be twice put in jeopardy of life or limb; nor shall be compelled in any criminal case to be a witness against himself, nor be deprived of life, liberty, or property, without due process of law; nor shall private property be taken for public use, without just compensation.

AMENDMENT VI [1791]

In all criminal prosecutions, the accused shall enjoy the right to a speedy and public trial, by an impartial jury of the State and district wherein the crime shall have been committed, which district shall have been previously ascertained by law, and to be informed of the nature and cause of the accusation; to be confronted with the witnesses against him; to have compulsory process for obtaining witnesses in his favor, and to have the Assistance of Counsel for his defence.

AMENDMENT VII [1791]

In Suits at common law, where the value in controversy shall exceed twenty dollars, the right of trial by jury shall be preserved, and no fact tried by jury, shall be otherwise re-examined in any Court of the United States, than according to the rules of the common law.

AMENDMENT VIII [1791]

Excessive bail shall not be required, nor excessive fines imposed, nor cruel and unusual punishments inflicted.

AMENDMENT IX [1791]

The enumeration in the Constitution, of certain rights, shall not be construed to deny or disparage others retained by the people.

AMENDMENT X [1791]

The powers not delegated to the United States by the Constitution, nor prohibited by it to the States, are reserved to the States respectively, or to the people.

AMENDMENT XI [1798]

The Judicial power of the United States shall not be construed to extend to any suit in law or equity, commenced or prosecuted against one of the United States by Citizens of another State, or by Citizens or Subjects of any Foreign State.

AMENDMENT XII [1804]

The Electors shall meet in their respective states, and vote by ballot for President and Vice-President, one of whom, at least, shall not be an inhabitant of the same state with themselves; they shall name in their ballots the person voted for as President, and in distinct ballots the person voted for as Vice-President, and they shall make distinct lists of all persons voted for as President, and of all persons voted for as Vice-President, and of the number of votes for each, which lists they shall sign and certify, and transmit sealed to the seat of the government of the United States, directed to the President of the Senate;—The President of the Senate shall, in the presence of the Senate and House of Representatives, open all the certificates and the votes shall then be counted;—The person having the greatest number of votes for President, shall be the President, if such number be a majority of the whole number of Electors appointed; and if no person have such majority, then from the persons having the highest numbers not exceeding three on the list of those voted for as President, the House of Representatives shall choose immediately, by ballot, the President. But in choosing the President, the votes shall be taken by states, the representation from each state having one vote; a quorum for this purpose shall consist of a member or members from two-thirds of the states, and a majority of all states shall be necessary to a choice. And if the House of Representatives shall not choose a President whenever the right of choice shall devolve upon them, before the fourth day of March next following, then the Vice-President shall act as President, as in the case of the death or other constitutional disability of the President.—The person having the greatest number of votes as Vice-President, shall be the Vice-President, if such number be a majority of the whole number of Electors appointed, and if no person have a majority, then from the two highest numbers on the list, the Senate shall choose the Vice-President; a quorum for the purpose shall consist of two-thirds of the whole number of Senators, and a majority of the whole number shall be necessary to a choice. But no person constitutionally ineligible to the office of President shall be eligible to that of Vice-President of the United States.

AMENDMENT XIII [1865]

Section 1. Neither slavery nor involuntary servitude, except as a punishment for crime whereof the party shall have been duly convicted, shall exist within the United States, or any place subject to their jurisdiction.

Section 2. Congress shall have power to enforce this article by appropriate legislation.

AMENDMENT XIV [1868]

Section 1. All persons born or naturalized in the United States, and subject to the jurisdiction thereof, are citizens of the United States and of the State wherein they reside. No State shall make or enforce any law which shall abridge the privileges or immunities of citizens of the United States; nor shall any State deprive any person of life, liberty, or property, without due process of law; nor deny to any person within its jurisdiction the equal protection of the laws.

Section 2. Representatives shall be apportioned among the several States according to their respective numbers, counting the whole number of persons in each State, excluding Indians not taxed. But when the right to vote at any election for the choice of electors for President and Vice President of the United States, Representatives in Congress, the Executive and Judicial officers of a State, or the members of the Legislature thereof, is denied to any of the male inhabitants of such State, being twenty-one years of age, and citizens of the United States, or in any way abridged, except for participation in rebellion, or other crime, the basis of representation therein shall be reduced in the proportion which the number of such male citizens shall bear to the whole number of male citizens twenty-one years of age in such State.

Section 3. No person shall be a Senator or Representative in Congress, or elector of President and Vice President, or hold any office, civil or military, under the United States, or under any State, who having previously taken an oath, as a member of Congress, or as an officer of the United States, or as a member of any State legislature, or as an executive or judicial officer of any State, to support the Constitution of the United States, shall have engaged in insurrection or rebellion against the same, or given aid or comfort to the enemies thereof. But Congress may by a vote of two-thirds of each House, remove such disability.

Section 4. The validity of the public debt of the United States, authorized by law, including debts incurred for payment of pensions and bounties for services in suppressing insurrection or rebellion, shall not be questioned. But neither the United States nor any State shall assume or pay any debt or obligation incurred in aid of insurrection or rebellion against the United States, or any claim for the loss or emancipation of any slave; but all such debts, obligations and claims shall be held illegal and void.

Section 5. The Congress shall have power to enforce, by appropriate legislation, the provisions of this article.

Amendment XV [1870]

Section 1. The right of citizens of the United States to vote shall not be denied or abridged by the United States or by any State on account of race, color, or previous condition of servitude.

Section 2. The Congress shall have power to enforce this article by appropriate legislation.

Amendment XVI [1913]

The Congress shall have power to lay and collect taxes on incomes, from whatever source derived, without apportionment among the several States, and without regard to any census or enumeration.

Amendment XVII [1913]

Section 1. The Senate of the United States shall be composed of two Senators from each State, elected by the people thereof, for six years; and each Senator shall have one vote. The electors in each State shall have the qualifications requisite for electors of the most numerous branch of the State legislatures.

Section 2. When vacancies happen in the representation of any State in the Senate, the executive authority of such State shall issue writs of election to fill such vacancies: *Provided*, That the legislature of any State may empower the executive thereof to make temporary appointments until the people fill the vacancies by election as the legislature may direct.

Section 3. This amendment shall not be so construed as to affect the election or term of any Senator chosen before it becomes valid as part of the Constitution.

Amendment XVIII [1919]

Section 1. After one year from the ratification of this article the manufacture, sale, or transportation of intoxicating liquors within, the importation thereof into, or the exportation thereof from the United States and all territory subject to the jurisdiction thereof for beverage purposes is hereby prohibited.

Section 2. The Congress and the several States shall have concurrent power to enforce this article by appropriate legislation.

Section 3. This article shall be inoperative unless it shall have been ratified as an amendment to the Constitution by the legislatures of the several States, as provided in the Constitution, within seven years from the date of the submission hereof to the States by the Congress.

AMENDMENT XIX [1920]

Section 1. The right of citizens of the United States to vote shall not be denied or abridged by the United States or by any State on account of sex.

Section 2. Congress shall have power to enforce this article by appropriate legislation.

AMENDMENT XX [1933]

Section 1. The terms of the President and Vice President shall end at noon on the 20th day of January, and the terms of Senators and Representatives at noon on the 3d day of January, of the years in which such terms would have ended if this article had not been ratified; and the terms of their successors shall then begin.

Section 2. The Congress shall assemble at least once in every year, and such meeting shall begin at noon on the 3d day of January, unless they shall by law appoint a different day.

Section 3. If, at the time fixed for the beginning of the term of the President, the President elect shall have died, the Vice President elect shall become President. If the President shall not have been chosen before the time fixed for the beginning of his term, or if the President elect shall have failed to qualify, then the Vice President elect shall act as President until a President shall have qualified; and the Congress may by law provide for the case wherein neither a President elect nor a Vice President elect shall have qualified, declaring who shall then act as President, or the manner in which one who is to act shall be selected, and such person shall act accordingly until a President or Vice President shall have qualified.

Section 4. The Congress may by law provide for the case of the death of any of the persons from whom the House of Representatives may choose a President whenever the right of choice shall have devolved upon them, and for the case of the death of any of the persons from whom the Senate may choose a Vice President whenever the right of choice shall have devolved upon them.

Section 5. Sections 1 and 2 shall take effect on the 15th day of October following the ratification of this article.

Section 6. This article shall be inoperative unless it shall have been ratified as an amendment to the Constitution by the legislatures of three-fourths of the several States within seven years from the date of its submission.

AMENDMENT XXI [1933]

Section 1. The eighteenth article of amendment to the Constitution of the United States is hereby repealed.

Section 2. The transportation or importation into any State, Territory, or possession of the United States for delivery or use therein of intoxicating liquors, in violation of the laws thereof, is hereby prohibited.

Section 3. This article shall be inoperative unless it shall have been ratified as an amendment to the Constitution by conventions in the several States, as provided in the Constitution, within seven years from the date of the submission hereof to the States by the Congress.

AMENDMENT XXII [1951]

Section 1. No person shall be elected to the office of the President more than twice, and no person who has held the office of President, or acted as President, for more than two years of a term to which some other person was elected President shall be elected to the office of President more than once. But this Article shall not apply to any person holding the office of President when this Article was proposed by the Congress, and shall not prevent any person who may be holding the office of President, or acting as President, during the term within which this Article becomes operative from holding the office of President or acting as President during the remainder of such term.

Section 2. This article shall be inoperative unless it shall have been ratified as an amendment to the Constitution by the legislatures of three-fourths of the several States within seven years from the date of its submission to the States by the Congress.

AMENDMENT XXIII [1961]

Section 1. The District constituting the seat of Government of the United States shall appoint in such manner as the Congress may direct:

A number of electors of President and Vice President equal to the whole number of Senators and Representatives in Congress to which the District would be entitled if it were a State, but in no event more than the least populous state; they shall be in addition to those appointed by the states, but they shall be considered, for the purposes of the election of President and Vice President, to be electors appointed by a state; and they shall meet in the District and perform such duties as provided by the twelfth article of amendment.

Section 2. The Congress shall have power to enforce this article by appropriate legislation.

Amendment XXIV [1964]

Section 1. The right of citizens of the United States to vote in any primary or other election for President or Vice President, for electors for President or Vice President, or for Senator or Representative in Congress, shall not be denied or abridged by the United States, or any State by reason of failure to pay any poll tax or other tax.

Section 2. The Congress shall have power to enforce this article by appropriate legislation.

Amendment XXV [1967]

Section 1. In case of the removal of the President from office or of his death or resignation, the Vice President shall become President.

Section 2. Whenever there is a vacancy in the office of the Vice President, the President shall nominate a Vice President who shall take office upon confirmation by a majority vote of both Houses of Congress.

Section 3. Whenever the President transmits to the President pro tempore of the Senate and the Speaker of the House of Representatives his written declaration that he is unable to discharge the powers and duties of his office, and until he transmits to them a written declaration to the contrary, such powers and duties shall be discharged by the Vice President as Acting President.

Section 4. Whenever the Vice President and a majority of either the principal officers of the executive departments or of such other body as Congress may by law provide, transmit to the President pro tempore of the Senate and the Speaker of the House of Representatives their written declaration that the President is unable to discharge the powers and duties of his office, the Vice President shall immediately assume the powers and duties of the office as Acting President.

Thereafter, when the President transmits to the President pro tempore of the Senate and the Speaker of the House of Representatives his written declaration that no inability exists, he shall resume the powers and duties of his office unless the Vice President and a majority of either the principal officers of the executive department or of such other body as Congress may by law provide, transmit within four days to the President pro tempore of the Senate and the Speaker of the House of Representatives their written declaration and the President is unable to discharge the powers and duties of his office. Thereupon Congress shall decide the issue, assembling within forty-eight hours for that purpose if not in session. If the Congress, within twenty-one days after receipt of the latter written declaration, or, if Congress is not in session, within twenty-one days after Congress is required to assemble, determines by two-thirds vote of both Houses that the President is unable to discharge the powers and duties of his office, the Vice President shall continue to discharge the same as Acting President; otherwise, the President shall resume the powers and duties of his office.

Amendment XXVI [1971]

Section 1. The right of citizens of the United States, who are eighteen years of age or older, to vote shall not be denied or abridged by the United States or by any State on account of age.

Section 2. The Congress shall have power to enforce this article by appropriate legislation.

Amendment XXVII [1992]

No law, varying the compensation for the services of the Senators and Representatives, shall take effect, until an election of Representatives shall have intervened.

Appendix M

Spanish Equivalents for Important Legal Terms in English

Abandoned property: bienes abandonados
Acceptance: aceptación; consentimiento; acuerdo
Acceptor: aceptante
Accession: toma de posesión; aumento; accesión
Accommodation indorser: avalista de favor
Accommodation party: firmante de favor
Accord: acuerdo; convenio; arregio
Accord and satisfaction: transacción ejecutada
Act of state doctrine: doctrina de acto de gobierno
Administrative law: derecho administrativo
Administrative process: procedimiento o metódo administrativo
Administrator: administrador (-a)
Adverse possession: posesión de hecho susceptible de proscripción adquisitiva
Affirmative action: acción afirmativa
Affirmative defense: defensa afirmativa
After-acquired property: bienes adquiridos con posterioridad a un hecho dado
Agency: mandato; agencia
Agent: mandatorio; agente; representante
Agreement: convenio; acuerdo; contrato
Alien corporation: empresa extranjera
Allonge: hojas adicionales de endosos
Answer: contestación de la demande; alegato
Anticipatory repudiation: anuncio previo de las partes de su imposibilidad de cumplir con el contrato
Appeal: apelación; recurso de apelación
Appellate jurisdiction: jurisdicción de apelaciones
Appraisal right: derecho de valuación
Arbitration: arbitraje
Arson: incendio intencional
Articles of partnership: contrato social
Artisan's lien: derecho de retención que ejerce al artesano
Assault: asalto; ataque; agresión
Assignment of rights: transmisión; transferencia; cesión
Assumption of risk: no resarcimiento por exposición voluntaria al peligro
Attachment: auto judicial que autoriza el embargo; embargo

Bailee: depositario
Bailment: depósito; constitución en depósito
Bailor: depositante
Bankruptcy trustee: síndico de la quiebra
Battery: agresión; física
Bearer: portador; tenedor
Bearer instrument: documento al portador
Bequest or legacy: legado (de bienes muebles)
Bilateral contract: contrato bilateral
Bill of lading: conocimiento de embarque; carta de porte
Bill of Rights: declaración de derechos
Binder: póliza de seguro provisoria; recibo de pago a cuenta del precio
Blank indorsement: endoso en blanco
Blue sky laws: leyes reguladoras del comercio bursátil
Bond: título de crédito; garantía; caución
Bond indenture: contrato de emisión de bonos; contrato del ampréstito
Breach of contract: incumplimiento de contrato
Brief: escrito; resumen; informe
Burglary: violación de domicilio
Business judgment rule: regla de juicio comercial
Business tort: agravio comercial

Case law: ley de casos; derecho casuístico
Cashier's check: cheque de caja
Causation in fact: causalidad en realidad

Cease-and-desist order: orden para cesar y desistir
Certificate of deposit: certificado de depósito
Certified check: cheque certificado
Charitable trust: fideicomiso para fines benéficos
Chattel: bien mueble
Check: cheque
Chose in action: derecho inmaterial; derecho de acción
Civil law: derecho civil
Close corporation: sociedad de un solo accionista o de un grupo restringido de accionistas
Closed shop: taller agremiado (emplea solamente a miembros de un gremio)
Closing argument: argumento al final
Codicil: codicilo
Collateral: guarantía; bien objeto de la guarantía real
Comity: cortesía; cortesía entre naciones
Commercial paper: instrumentos negociables; documentos a valores commerciales
Common law: derecho consuetudinario; derecho común; ley común
Common stock: acción ordinaria
Comparative negligence: negligencia comparada
Compensatory damages: daños y perjuicios reales o compensatorios
Concurrent conditions: condiciones concurrentes
Concurrent jurisdiction: competencia concurrente de varios tribunales para entender en una misma causa
Concurring opinion: opinión concurrente
Condition: condición
Condition precedent: condición suspensiva
Condition subsequent: condición resolutoria
Confiscation: confiscación
Confusion: confusión; fusión
Conglomerate merger: fusión de firmas que operan en distintos mercados
Consent decree: acuerdo entre las partes aprobado por un tribunal
Consequential damages: daños y perjuicios indirectos
Consideration: consideración; motivo; contraprestación
Consolidation: consolidación
Constructive delivery: entrega simbólica
Constructive trust: fideicomiso creado por aplicación de la ley
Consumer-protection law: ley para proteger el consumidor
Contract: contrato
Contract under seal: contrato formal o sellado
Contributory negligence: negligencia de la parte actora
Conversion: usurpación; conversión de valores
Copyright: derecho de autor
Corporation: sociedad anómina; corporación; persona juridica
Co-sureties: cogarantes
Counterclaim: reconvención; contrademanda
Counteroffer: contraoferta
Course of dealing: curso de transacciones
Course of performance: curso de cumplimiento
Covenant: pacto; garantía; contrato
Covenant not to sue: pacto or contrato a no demandar
Covenant of quiet enjoyment: garantía del uso y goce pacífico del inmueble
Creditors' composition agreement: concordato preventivo
Crime: crimen; delito; contravención
Criminal law: derecho penal
Cross-examination: contrainterrogatorio
Cure: cura; cuidado; derecho de remediar un vicio contractual
Customs receipts: recibos de derechos aduaneros

Damages: daños; indemnización por daños y perjuicios
Debit card: tarjeta de dé bito
Debtor: deudor
Debt securities: seguridades de deuda
Deceptive advertising: publicidad engañosa
Deed: escritura; título; acta translativa de domino
Defamation: difamación
Delegation of duties: delegación de obligaciones
Demand deposit: depósito a la vista
Depositions: declaración de un testigo fuera del tribunal
Devise: legado; deposición testamentaria (bienes inmuebles)
Directed verdict: veredicto según orden del juez y sin participación activa del jurado
Direct examination: interrogatorio directo; primer interrogatorio
Disaffirmance: repudiación; renuncia; anulación
Discharge: descargo; liberación; cumplimiento
Disclosed principal: mandante revelado
Discovery: descubrimiento; producción de la prueba
Dissenting opinion: opinión disidente
Dissolution: disolución; terminación
Diversity of citizenship: competencia de los tribunales federales para entender en causas cuyas partes intervinientes son cuidadanos de distintos estados
Divestiture: extinción premature de derechos reales

Dividend: dividendo
Docket: orden del día; lista de causas pendientes
Domestic corporation: sociedad local
Draft: orden de pago; letrade cambio
Drawee: girado; beneficiario
Drawer: librador
Duress: coacción; violencia

Easement: servidumbre
Embezzlement: desfalco; malversación
Eminent domain: poder de expropiación
Employment discrimination: discriminación en el empleo
Entrepreneur: empresario
Environmental law: ley ambiental
Equal dignity rule: regla de dignidad egual
Equity security: tipo de participación en una sociedad
Estate: propiedad; patrimonio; derecho
Estop: impedir; prevenir
Ethical issue: cuestión ética
Exclusive jurisdiction: competencia exclusiva
Exculpatory clause: cláusula eximente
Executed contract: contrato ejecutado
Execution: ejecución; cumplimiento
Executor: albacea
Executory contract: contrato aún no completamente consumado
Executory interest: derecho futuro
Express contract: contrato expreso
Expropriation: expropriación

Federal question: caso federal
Fee simple: pleno dominio; dominio absoluto
Fee simple absolute: dominio absoluto
Fee simple defeasible: dominio sujeta a una condición resolutoria
Felony: crimen; delito grave
Fictitious payee: beneficiario ficticio
Fiduciary: fiduciaro
Firm offer: oferta en firme
Fixture: inmueble por destino, incorporación a anexación
Floating lien: gravamen continuado
Foreign corporation: sociedad extranjera; U.S. sociedad constituída en otro estado
Forgery: falso; falsificación
Formal contract: contrato formal
Franchise: privilegio; franquicia; concesión
Franchisee: persona que recibe una concesión
Franchisor: persona que vende una concesión
Fraud: fraude; dolo; engaño
Future interest: bien futuro

Garnishment: embargo de derechos
General partner: socio comanditario
General warranty deed: escritura translativa de domino con garantía de título
Gift: donación
Gift *causa mortis*: donación por causa de muerte
Gift *inter vivos*: donación entre vivos
Good faith: buena fe
Good-faith purchaser: comprador de buena fe

Holder: tenedor por contraprestación
Holder in due course: tenedor legítimo
Holographic will: testamento olográfico
Homestead exemption laws: leyes que exceptúan las casas de familia de ejecución por duedas generales
Horizontal merger: fusión horizontal

Identification: identificación
Implied-in-fact contract: contrato implícito en realidad
Implied warranty: guarantía implícita
Implied warranty of merchantability: garantía implícita de vendibilidad
Impossibility of performance: imposibilidad de cumplir un contrato
Imposter: imposter
Incidental beneficiary: beneficiario incidental; beneficiario secundario
Incidental damages: daños incidentales
Indictment: auto de acusación; acusación
Indorsee: endorsatario
Indorsement: endoso
Indorser: endosante
Informal contract: contrato no formal; contrato verbal
Information: acusación hecha por el ministerio público
Injunction: mandamiento; orden de no innovar
Innkeeper's lien: derecho de retención que ejerce el posadero
Installment contract: contrato de pago en cuotas
Insurable interest: interés asegurable
Intended beneficiary: beneficiario destinado
Intentional tort: agravio; cuasi-delito intencíonal
International law: derecho internaciónal
Interrogatories: preguntas escritas sometidas por una parte a la otra o a un testigo

***Inter vivos* trust:** fideicomiso entre vivos
Intestacy laws: leyes de la condición de morir intestado
Intestate: intestado
Investment company: compañia de inversiones
Issue: emisión

Joint tenancy: derechos conjuntos en un bien inmueble en favor del beneficiario sobreviviente
Judgment *n.o.v.*: juicio no obstante veredicto
Judgment rate of interest: interés de juicio
Judicial process: acto de procedimiento; proceso jurídico
Judicial review: revisión judicial
Jurisdiction: jurisdicción

Larceny: robo; hurto
Law: derecho; ley; jurisprudencia
Lease: contrato de locación; contrato de alquiler
Leasehold estate: bienes forales
Legal rate of interest: interés legal
Legatee: legatario
Letter of credit: carta de crédito
Levy: embargo; comiso
Libel: libelo; difamación escrita
Life estate: usufructo
Limited partner: comanditario
Limited partnership: sociedad en comandita
Liquidation: liquidación; realización
Lost property: objetos perdidos

Majority opinion: opinión de la mayoría
Maker: persona que realiza u ordena; librador
Mechanic's lien: gravamen de constructor
Mediation: mediación; intervención
Merger: fusión
Mirror image rule: fallo de reflejo
Misdemeanor: infracción; contravención
Mislaid property: bienes extraviados
Mitigation of damages: reducción de daños
Mortgage: hypoteca
Motion to dismiss: excepción parentoria
Mutual fund: fondo mutual

Negotiable instrument: instrumento negociable
Negotiation: negociación
Nominal damages: daños y perjuicios nominales
Novation: novación
Nuncupative will: testamento nuncupativo

Objective theory of contracts: teoria objetiva de contratos
Offer: oferta
Offeree: persona que recibe una oferta
Offeror: oferente
Order instrument: instrumento o documento a la orden
Original jurisdiction: jurisdicción de primera instancia
Output contract: contrato de producción

Parol evidence rule: regla relativa a la prueba oral
Partially disclosed principal: mandante revelado en parte
Partnership: sociedad colectiva; asociación; asociación de participación
Past consideration: causa o contraprestación anterior
Patent: patente; privilegio
Pattern or practice: muestra o práctica
Payee: beneficiario de un pago
Penalty: pena; penalidad
Per capita: por cabeza
Perfection: perfeción
Performance: cumplimiento; ejecución
Personal defenses: excepciones personales
Personal property: bienes muebles
Per stirpes: por estirpe
Plea bargaining: regateo por un alegato
Pleadings: alegatos
Pledge: prenda
Police powers: poders de policia y de prevención del crimen
Policy: póliza
Positive law: derecho positivo; ley positiva
Possibility of reverter: posibilidad de reversión
Precedent: precedente
Preemptive right: derecho de prelación
Preferred stock: acciones preferidas
Premium: recompensa; prima
Presentment warranty: garantía de presentación
Price discrimination: discriminación en los precios
Principal: mandante; principal
Privity: nexo jurídico
Privity of contract: relación contractual
Probable cause: causa probable
Probate: verificación; verificación del testamento
Probate court: tribunal de sucesiones y tutelas
Proceeds: resultados; ingresos
Profit: beneficio; utilidad; lucro
Promise: promesa
Promisee: beneficiario de una promesa
Promisor: promtente
Promissory estoppel: impedimento promisorio
Promissory note: pagaré; nota de pago

Promoter: promotor; fundador
Proximate cause: causa inmediata o próxima
Proxy: apoderado; poder
Punitive, or exemplary, damages: daños y perjuicios punitivos o ejemplares

Qualified indorsement: endoso con reservas
Quasi contract: contrato tácito o implícito
Quitclaim deed: acto de transferencia de una propiedad por finiquito, pero sin ninguna garantía sobre la validez del título transferido

Ratification: ratificación
Real property: bienes inmuebles
Reasonable doubt: duda razonable
Rebuttal: refutación
Recognizance: promesa; compromiso; reconocimiento
Recording statutes: leyes estatales sobre registros oficiales
Redress: reporacíon
Reformation: rectificación; reforma; corrección
Rejoinder: dúplica; contrarréplica
Release: liberación; renuncia a un derecho
Remainder: substitución; reversión
Remedy: recurso; remedio; reparación
Replevin: acción reivindicatoria; reivindicación
Reply: réplica
Requirements contract: contrato de suministro
Rescission: rescisión
Res judicata: cosa juzgada; res judicata
Respondeat superior: responsabilidad del mandante o del maestro
Restitution: restitución
Restrictive indorsement: endoso restrictivo
Resulting trust: fideicomiso implícito
Reversion: reversión; sustitución
Revocation: revocación; derogación
Right of contribution: derecho de contribución
Right of reimbursement: derecho de reembolso
Right of subrogation: derecho de subrogación
Right-to-work law: ley de libertad de trabajo
Robbery: robo
Rule 10b-5: Regla 10b-5

Sale: venta; contrato de compreventa
Sale on approval: venta a ensayo; venta sujeta a la aprobación del comprador
Sale or return: venta con derecho de devolución
Sales contract: contrato de compraventa; boleto de compraventa
Satisfaction: satisfacción; pago
Scienter: a sabiendas
S corporation: S corporación
Secured party: acreedor garantizado
Secured transaction: transacción garantizada
Securities: volares; titulos; seguridades
Security agreement: convenio de seguridad
Security interest: interés en un bien dado en garantía que permite a quien lo detenta venderlo en caso de incumplimiento
Service mark: marca de identificación de servicios
Shareholder's derivative suit: acción judicial entablada por un accionista en nombre de la sociedad
Signature: firma; rúbrica
Slander: difamación oral; calumnia
Sovereign immunity: immunidad soberana
Special indorsement: endoso especial; endoso a la orden de una person en particular
Specific performance: ejecución precisa, según los términos del contrato
Spendthrift trust: fideicomiso para pródigos
Stale check: cheque vencido
Stare decisis: acatar las decisiones, observar los precedentes
Statutory law: derecho estatutario; derecho legislado; derecho escrito
Stock: acciones
Stock warrant: certificado para la compra de acciones
Stop-payment order: orden de suspensión del pago de un cheque dada por el librador del mismo
Strict liability: responsabilidad uncondicional
Summary judgment: fallo sumario

Tangible property: bienes corpóreos
Tenancy at will: inguilino por tiempo indeterminado (según la voluntad del propietario)
Tenancy by sufferance: posesión por tolerancia
Tenancy by the entirety: locación conyugal conjunta
Tenancy for years: inguilino por un término fijo
Tenancy in common: specie de copropiedad indivisa
Tender: oferta de pago; oferta de ejecución
Testamentary trust: fideicomiso testamentario

Testator: testador (-a)
Third party beneficiary contract: contrato para el beneficio del tercero-beneficiario
Tort: agravio; cuasi-delito
Totten trust: fideicomiso creado por un depósito bancario
Trade acceptance: letra de cambio aceptada
Trademark: marca registrada
Trade name: nombre comercial; razón social
Traveler's check: cheque del viajero
Trespass to land: ingreso no authorizado a las tierras de otro
Trespass to personal property: violación de los derechos posesorios de un tercero con respecto a bienes muebles
Trust: fideicomiso; trust

Ultra vires: ultra vires; fuera de la facultad (de una sociedad anónima)
Unanimous opinion: opinión unámine
Unconscionable contract or clause: contrato leonino; cláusula leonino
Underwriter: subscriptor; asegurador
Unenforceable contract: contrato que no se puede hacer cumplir
Unilateral contract: contrato unilateral
Union shop: taller agremiado; empresa en la que todos los empleados son miembros del gremio o sindicato
Universal defenses: defensas legitimas o legales
Usage of trade: uso comercial
Usury: usura

Valid contract: contrato válido
Venue: lugar; sede del proceso
Vertical merger: fusión vertical de empresas
Voidable contract: contrato anulable
Void contract: contrato nulo; contrato inválido, sin fuerza legal
Voir dire: examen preliminar de un testigo a jurado por el tribunal para determinar su competencia
Voting trust: fideicomiso para ejercer el derecho de voto

Waiver: renuncia; abandono
Warranty of habitability: garantía de habitabilidad
Watered stock: acciones diluídos; capital inflado
White-collar crime: crimen administrativo
Writ of attachment: mandamiento de ejecución; mandamiento de embargo
Writ of *certiorari*: auto de avocación; auto de certiorari
Writ of execution: auto ejecutivo; mandamiento de ejecutión
Writ of mandamus: auto de mandamus; mandamiento; orden judicial

Glossary

ABA-approved Program A legal or paralegal educational program that satisfies the standards for paralegal training set forth by the American Bar Association.
Acceptance In contract law, the offeree's notification to the offeror that the offeree agrees to be bound by the terms of the offeror's offer, or proposal to form a contract.
Acquittal A certification or declaration following a trial that the individual accused of a crime is innocent, or free from guilt, in the eyes of the law and is thus absolved of the charges.
Active Listening The act of listening attentively to the speaker's verbal or nonverbal messages and responding to those messages by giving appropriate feedback.
Actus Reus A guilty (prohibited) act. The commission of a prohibited act is one of the two essential elements required for criminal liability, the other element being the intent to commit a crime.
Address Block That part of a letter that indicates to whom the letter is addressed. The address block is placed in the upper left-hand portion of the letter, above the salutation (or reference line, if one is included).
Adjudication The act of resolving a controversy and rendering an order or decision based on a review of the evidence presented.
Administrative Agency A federal or state government agency established to perform a specific function. Administrative agencies are authorized by legislative acts to make and enforce rules relating to the purpose for which they were established.
Administrative Law A body of law created by administrative agencies—such as the Securities and Exchange Commission and the Federal Trade Commission—in the form of rules, regulations, orders, and decisions in order to carry out their duties and responsibilities.
Administrative Law Judge (ALJ) One who presides over an administrative agency hearing and who has the power to administer oaths, take testimony, rule on questions of evidence, and make determinations of fact.
Administrative Process The procedure used by administrative agencies in the administration of law.
Administrator One who is appointed by a court to handle the probate of a person's estate if that person dies intestate (without a will).
Adoption A procedure by which persons become the legal parents of a child who is not their biological child.
Adversarial System of Justice A legal system in which the parties to a lawsuit are opponents, or adversaries, and present their cases in a light most favorable to themselves. The court arrives at a just solution based on the evidence presented by the parties, or contestants, and determines who wins and who loses.
Adverse Witness A witness for the opposing side in a lawsuit or other legal proceeding; a hostile witness.
Advisory Letter A letter from an attorney to a client that contains a legal opinion on an issue raised by the client's question or legal claim; an opinion letter.
Advocate As a verb, to assist, defend, or plead (argue) a cause for another. As a noun, a person (such as an attorney) who assists, defends, or pleads (argues) for another (such as a client) before a court.
Affidavit A written statement of facts, confirmed by the oath or affirmation of the party making it and made before a person having the authority to administer the oath or affirmation.
Affiliate An entity that is connected (affiliated) with another entity. State and local branches of national or regional paralegal associations are often referred to as affiliates.
Affirm An appellate court's decision to uphold the trial court's judgment in a case.
Affirmative-action Program A job-hiring program that gives special consideration to minority groups in an effort to overcome present effects of past discrimination.

Affirmative Defense A response to a plaintiff's claim that does not deny the plaintiff's facts but attacks the plaintiff's legal right to bring an action.
Agency A relationship between two persons in which, by agreement or otherwise, one person (the principal) is bound by the words and acts of another (the agent).
Agency Contacts Notebook A reference guide with names, telephone numbers, and other generalized information about individual contacts working within a particular administrative agency.
Agent A person who is authorized to act for or in the place of another person (the principal).
Aggressive Communication Stating one's opinions without concern for the thoughts, feelings, or rights of the listener.
Agreement A meeting of two or more minds, and a requirement for a valid contract. In contract law, the process of agreement is separated into two distinct events: an offer to form a contract and the acceptance of that offer.
Allegation A party's statement, claim, or assertion made in a pleading to the court. The allegation sets forth the issue that the party expects to prove.
Alimony Money paid to support a former spouse after a marriage has been terminated. The alimony may be permanent or temporary (rehabilitative).
Alternative Dispute Resolution (ADR) The resolution of disputes in ways other than those involved in the traditional judicial process. Mediation and arbitration are forms of ADR.
American Arbitration Association (AAA) The major organization offering arbitration services in the United States.
American Bar Association (ABA) A voluntary national association of attorneys. The ABA plays an active role in developing educational and ethical standards for attorneys and in pursuing improvements in the administration of justice.
Analogy In logical reasoning, an assumption that if two things are similar in some respects, they will be similar in other respects also. Often used in legal reasoning to infer the appropriate application of legal principles in a case being decided by referring to previous cases involving different facts but considered to come within the policy underlying the rule.
Annotation A brief comment, an explanation of a legal point, or a case summary found in a case digest or other legal source.
Annulment A court decree that invalidates (nullifies) a marriage. Although the marriage itself is deemed nonexistent, children of the marriage are deemed legitimate.
Answer A defendant's response to a plaintiff's complaint.
Antitrust Law The body of federal and state laws protecting trade and commerce from unlawful restraints and anticompetitive practices.
Appeal The process of seeking a higher court's review of a lower court's decision for the purpose of correcting or changing the lower court's judgment or decision.
Appellant The party who takes an appeal from one court to another; sometimes referred to as the petitioner.
Appellate Court A court that reviews decisions made by lower courts, such as trial courts; a court of appeals.
Appellate Jurisdiction The power of a court to hear and decide an appeal; that is, the power and authority of a court to review cases that already have been tried in a lower court and the power to make decisions about them without actually holding a trial. This process is called appellate review.
Appellee The party against whom an appeal is taken—that is, the party who opposes setting aside or reversing the judgment; sometimes referred to as the respondent.
Application Software Computer programs designed to instruct the central processing unit on the operation and performance of certain tasks.
Appropriation In tort law, the use of one person's name or likeness by another, without permission and for the benefit of the user.
Arbitration The settling of a dispute by submitting it to a disinterested third party (other than a court), who renders a legally binding decision.
Arbitration Clause A clause in a contract that provides that, in case of a dispute, the parties will determine their rights by arbitration rather than through the judicial system.
Arraignment A court proceeding in which the suspect is formally charged with the criminal offense stated in the indictment. The suspect then enters a plea (guilty, not guilty, or *nolo contendere*) in response.
Arrest To take into custody a person suspected of criminal activity.
Arrest Warrant A written order, based on probable cause and issued by a judge or public official (magistrate), commanding that the person named on the warrant be arrested by the police.
Articles of Incorporation The document filed with the appropriate governmental agency, usually the secretary of state's office, when a business is incorporated. State statutes usually prescribe what kind of information must be contained in the articles of incorporation.
Assault Any word or action intended to make another person fearful of immediate physical harm; a reasonably believable threat.
Assertive Communication Stating one's opinions confidently but tactfully and with concern for the thoughts, feelings, and rights of the listener.
Associate Attorney An attorney who is hired by a law firm as an employee and who has no ownership rights in the firm.

Associate's Degree An academic degree signifying the completion of a two-year course of study, normally at a community college.
Attestation Clause A clause in a will, just following the testator's signature and just before the witnesses' signatures, indicating the identity of the testator, the date on which the will was signed by the witnesses, and possibly other information relating to witness requirements.
Attorney-client Privilege A rule of evidence requiring that confidential communications between a client and his or her attorney (relating to their professional relationship) be kept confidential, unless the client consents to disclosure.
"Attractive Nuisance" Doctrine A doctrine under which a landowner may be held liable for injuries incurred by children who are lured onto the property by something on the property that is dangerous and enticing.
Authentication Establishing the genuineness of an item that is to be introduced as evidence in a trial.
Automatic Stay A suspension of all judicial proceedings upon the occurrence of an independent event. Under the Bankruptcy Code, the moment a petition to initiate bankruptcy proceedings is filed, all litigation or other legal action by creditors against a debtor and the debtor's property is suspended.
Award In the context of ADR, the decision rendered by an arbitrator.

Bachelor's Degree An academic degree signifying the completion of a four-year course of study at a college or university.
Bail The amount or conditions set by the court to ensure that an individual accused of a crime will appear for further criminal proceedings. If the accused person provides bail, whether in cash or by means of a bail bond, then the person is released from jail.
Bankruptcy Court A federal court of limited jurisdiction that hears only bankruptcy proceedings.
Bankruptcy Law The body of federal law that governs bankrupcy proceedings. The twin goals of bankruptcy law are (1) to protect a debtor by giving him or her a fresh start, free from creditors' claims; and (2) to ensure that creditors who are competing for a debtor's assets are treated fairly.
Bankruptcy Trustee A person appointed by the bankruptcy court to administer the debtor's estate in the interests of both the debtor and the creditors. The basic duty of the bankruptcy trustee is to collect and reduce to money the estate in property and to close up the estate as speedily as is compatible with the best interests of the parties.
Battery The unprivileged, intentional touching of another.
Bequest A gift by will of personal property (from the verb *bequeath*).
Beyond a Reasonable Doubt The standard used to determine the guilt or innocence of a person charged with a crime. To be guilty of a crime, a suspect must be proved guilty "beyond and to the exclusion of every reasonable doubt."
Bigamy The act of entering into marriage with one person while still legally married to another.
Bill of Rights The first ten amendments to the Constitution.
Billable Hours The time spent on legal work for a client that requires the legal expertise of an attorney or a paralegal and that is charged directly to the client.
Blue Sky Laws State laws that regulate the offer and sale of securities.
Boilerplate Certain terms or clauses that are normally included in specific types of legal documents.
Bona Fide Occupational Qualification Under Title VII of the Civil Rights Act of 1964, characteristics (such as education, training, and physical strength) that are reasonably necessary to adequate job performance.
Bond A certificate that evidences a corporate debt. It is a security that involves no ownership interest in the issuing corporation.
Bonus An end-of-the-year payment to a salaried employee in appreciation for that employee's overtime work, work quality, diligence, or dedication to the firm.
Booking The process of entering a suspect's name, offense, and arrival time into the police log (blotter) following his or her arrest.
Breach To violate a legal duty by an act or a failure to act.
Breach of Contract The failure of a contractual party to perform the obligations assumed in a contract.
Briefing a Case Summarizing a case. A typical case brief will indicate the case title and citation and then briefly state the factual background and procedural history of the case, the issue or issues raised in the case, the court's decision, the applicable rule of law and the legal reasoning upon which the decision is based, and conclusions or notes concerning the case made by the one who is briefing it.
Bureaucracy The organizational structure, consisting of government bureaus and agencies, through which the government at all levels implements and enforces laws.
Business Invitee A person, such as a customer or client, who is invited onto business premises by the owner of those premises for business purposes.
Business Necessity An employment practice that discriminates against members of a protected class but that is necessary for job performance.
Business Tort A tort occurring within the business context; typical business torts are wrongful interference with the business or contractual relationships of others, defamation and product disparagement, and appropriation.
Business Trust A form of business organization in which investors (trust beneficiaries) transfer cash or property to

trustees in exchange for trust certificates that represent their investment shares. Management of the business and trust property is handled by the trustees for the benefit of the investors. The investors have limited liability and share in the trust's profits.

Bystander A spectator, witness, or person who was standing nearby when an injury-causing event occurred.

Case Law Rules of law announced in court decisions.

Case of First Impression A case presenting a legal issue that has not yet been addressed by a court in a particular jurisdiction.

Case on "All Fours" A case in which all four elements of a case (the parties, the circumstances, the legal issues involved, and the remedies sought by the plaintiff) are very similar.

Case on Point A case involving factual circumstances and issues that are similar to the case at bar (before the court).

Central Processing Unit (CPU) The part of a computer that controls the function of the other computer components, stores the information contained in software programs, and executes the operator's keyboard commands.

Certificate of Incorporation The document issued by a state official (usually the secretary of state) granting a corporation legal existence and the right to function; a corporate charter.

Certification Formal recognition by a private group or a state agency that an individual has satisfied the group's standards of proficiency, knowledge, and competence; ordinarily accomplished through the taking of an examination.

Certified Legal Assistant (CLA) A legal assistant whose legal competency has been certified by the National Association of Legal Assistants (NALA) following an examination that tests the legal assistant's knowledge and skills.

Certified Legal Assistant Specialist (CLAS) A legal assistant whose competency in a legal specialty has been certified by the National Association of Legal Assistants (NALA) following an examination of the legal assistant's knowledge and skills in the specialty area.

Challenge An attorney's objection, during *voir dire*, to the inclusion of a particular person on the jury.

Challenge for Cause A *voir dire* challenge for which an attorney states the reason why a prospective juror should not be included in the jury.

Chancellor An advisor to the king in medieval England. Individuals petitioned the king for relief when they could not obtain an adequate remedy in a court of law, and these petitions were decided by the chancellor.

Charge The judge's instruction to the jury following the attorneys' closing arguments setting forth the rules of law that the jury must apply in reaching its decision, or verdict.

Charitable Trust A trust in which the property held by a trustee must be used for a charitable purpose, such as the advancement of health, education, or religion.

Child Support The financial support necessary to provide for a child's needs. Commonly, when a marriage is terminated, the noncustodial spouse agrees or is required by the court to make child-support payments to the custodial spouse.

Chronologically In a time sequence; naming or listing events in the time order in which they occurred.

Circumstantial Evidence Indirect evidence that is offered to establish, by inference, the likelihood of a fact that is in question.

Citation In case law, a reference to the volume number, name, and page number of the reporter in which a case can be found. In statutory and administrative law, a reference to the title number, name, and section of the code in which a statute or regulation can be found. In criminal procedure, an order for a defendant to appear in court or indicating that a person has violated a legal rule.

Citator A book or on-line service that provides the subsequent history and interpretation of a statute, regulation, or court decision and a list of the cases, statutes, and regulations that have interpreted, applied, or modified a statute, regulation, or court decision.

Civil Law The branch of law dealing with the definition and enforcement of all private or public rights, as opposed to criminal matters.

Civil Law System A system of law derived from that of the Roman Empire and based on a code rather than case law; the predominant system of law in the nations of continental Europe and the nations that were once their colonies.

Closed-ended Question A question that is phrased in such a way that it elicits a simple "Yes" or "No" answer.

Closing A final comment to a letter that is placed above the signature, such as "Very truly yours."

Closing Argument An argument made by each side's attorney after the cases for the plaintiff and defendant have been presented. Closing arguments are made prior to the jury charge.

Code A systematic and logical presentation of laws, rules, or regulations.

Codicil A written supplement or modification to a will. Codicils must be executed with the same formalities as a will.

Codify To collect and organize systematically and logically a body of concepts, principles, decisions, or doctrines.

Common Law A body of law developed from custom or judicial decisions in English and U.S. courts and not attributable to a legislature.

Common Law Marriage A marriage that is formed solely by mutual consent and without a marriage license or ceremony. The couple must be eligible to marry, live

together as husband and wife, and hold themselves out to the public as husband and wife. Only fourteen states recognize common law marriages.
Communication Process The process of sending and receiving verbal and nonverbal messages.
Communication Skills All skills that assist in the communication process. Speaking, reading, writing, and listening skills are all communication skills.
Community Property Defined in nine states as all property acquired during the marriage, except for inheritances or gifts received by either marital partner.
Comparative Negligence A theory in tort law under which the liability for injuries resulting from negligent acts is shared by all persons who were guilty of negligence (including the injured party), on the basis of each person's proportionate carelessness.
Complaint The pleading made by a plaintiff or a charge made by the state alleging wrongdoing on the part of the defendant.
Concurrent Jurisdiction Jurisdiction that exists when two different courts have the power to hear a case. For example, some cases can be heard in either a federal or a state court.
Confirmation Letter A letter that states the substance of a previously conducted verbal discussion to provide a permanent record of the oral conversation.
Conflict of Interest A situation in which two or more duties or interests come into conflict, as when an attorney attempts to represent opposing parties in a legal dispute.
Conflicts Check A procedure for determining whether an agreement to represent a potential client will result in a conflict of interest.
Consideration Something of value, such as money or the performance of an action not otherwise required, that motivates the formation of a contract. Each party must give consideration for the contract to be binding.
Consolidation A process in which two or more corporations join to become a completely new corporation. The original corporations cease to exist, and the new corporation acquires all their assets and liabilities.
Consumer An individual who purchases (or is given) products and services for personal or household use.
Consumer-debtor Debtors whose debts are primarily consumer debts—that is, debts for purchases that are primarily for household or personal use.
Consumer Law Statutes, agency rules, and judicial decisions protecting consumers of goods and services from dangerous manufacturing techniques, mislabeling, unfair credit practices, deceptive advertising, and so on. Consumer laws provide remedies and protections that are not ordinarily available to merchants or to businesses.
Contempt of Court The intentional obstruction or frustration of the court's attempt to administer justice. A party to a lawsuit may be held in contempt of court (punishable by a fine or jail sentence) for refusing to comply with a court's order.
Contingency Fee A legal fee that consists of a specified percentage (such as 30 percent) of the amount the plaintiff recovers in a civil lawsuit. The fee must be paid only if the plaintiff prevails in the lawsuit (recovers damages).
Contract An agreement or bargain struck between parties, in which each party assumes a legal duty to the other party. The requirements for a valid contract are agreement, consideration, contractual capacity, and legality.
Contractual Capacity The threshold mental capacity required by law for a party who enters into a contract to be bound by that contract.
Contributory Negligence A theory in tort law under which a complaining party's own negligence, if it contributed to or caused the injuries complained of, is an absolute bar to recovery. Only a minority of jurisdictions adhere to the doctrine of contributory negligence.
Cooperative A form of business organization that is organized to provide an economic service to its members. It makes distributions of dividends, or profits, to its owners on the basis of their transactions with the cooperative rather than on the basis of the amount of capital they contributed. Examples of cooperatives are consumer purchasing cooperatives, credit cooperatives, and farmers' cooperatives.
Copyright The exclusive right of an author to publish, print, or sell a literary work, an artistic work, or other work of authorship (such as a computer program) for a statutory period of time.
Corporate Chapter The document issued by a state official (usually the secretary of state) granting a corporation legal existence and the right to function.
Corporate Law Law that governs the formation, financing, merger and acquisition, and termination of corporations, as well as the rights and duties of those who own and run the corporation.
Counterclaim A claim made by a defendant in a civil lawsuit against the plaintiff; in effect, a counterclaiming defendant is suing the plaintiff.
Court of Equity A court that decides controversies and administers justice according to the rules, principles, and precedents of equity.
Court of Law A court in which the only remedies that could be granted were things of value, such as money damages. In medieval England, courts of law were distinct from courts of equity.
Cram-down Provision A provision of the Bankruptcy Code that allows a court to confirm a debtor's Chapter 11 reorganization plan even though only one class of creditors has accepted it. To exercise the court's right under this provision, the court must demonstrate that the plan does not discriminate unfairly against any creditors and is fair and equitable.

Crime A broad term for violations of law that are punishable by the state and are codified by legislatures.
Criminal Law The branch of law that governs and defines those actions that are crimes and that subjects persons convicted of crimes to punishment imposed by the government. The objective of criminal law is to protect the public.
Cross-examination The questioning of an opposing witness during the trial.

Damages Money sought as a remedy for a civil wrong, such as a breach of contract or a tortious act.
Database Management System Software that makes it possible to store information in fields, records, and files for easy retrieval and manipulation by the operator.
Debtor in Possession (DIP) In Chapter 11 bankruptcy proceedings, a debtor who is allowed, for the benefit of all concerned, to maintain possession of the estate in property (the business) and to continue business operations.
Deceptive Advertising Advertising that misleads consumers, either by unjustified claims concerning a product's performance or by the failure to disclose relevant information concerning the product's composition or performance.
Deed A document by which title to property is transferred from one party to another.
Defamation Anything published or publicly spoken that causes injury to another's good name, reputation, or character.
Default Judgment A judgment entered by a clerk or court against a party who has failed to appear in court to answer or defend against a claim that has been brought against him or her by another party.
Defendant A party against whom a lawsuit is brought.
Defense That which a defendant offers and alleges in an action or suit as a reason why the plaintiff should not be granted whatever it is the plaintiff is seeking.
Defense of Others The use of reasonable force to protect others from harm.
Defense of Property The use of reasonable force to protect one's property from the harm threatened by another. The use of deadly force in defending one's property is seldom justified.
Delegation Doctrine A doctrine that authorizes Congress to delegate some of its lawmaking authority to administrative agencies. The doctrine is implied by Article I of the U.S. Constitution, which grants specific powers to Congress to enact and oversee the implementation of laws.
Demand Letter An adversarial letter that attempts to persuade the reader that he or she should accept a position that is favorable to the writer's client—that is, demanding that the reader do or not do a certain thing.
Deponent A party or witness who testifies under oath during a deposition.
Deposition A pretrial question-and-answer proceeding, usually conducted orally, in which an a party or witness answers an attorney's questions. The answers are given under oath, and the session is recorded.
Deposition Transcript The official transcription of the recording taken during a deposition.
Devise A gift of real property by will.
Devisee A person who inherits real property under a will.
Dicta A Latin term referring to nonbinding (nonprecedential) judicial statements that are not directly related to the facts or issues presented in the case and thus not essential to the holding.
Digest A compilation in which brief summaries of court cases are arranged by subject and subdivided by jurisdiction and courts.
Direct Evidence Evidence establishing the existence of a fact that is in question without relying on inferences.
Direct Examination The examination of a witness by the attorney who calls the witness to the stand to testify on behalf of the attorney's client.
Director A person elected by the shareholders to direct corporate affairs.
Disbarment A severe disciplinary sanction in which an attorney's license to practice law in the state is revoked because of unethical or illegal conduct.
Discharge The termination of an obligation. A discharge in bankruptcy terminates the debtor's obligation to pay the debts discharged by the court.
Discovery Formal investigation prior to trial. During discovery, opposing parties use various methods, such as interrogatories and depositions, to obtain information from each other to prepare for trial.
Discovery Plan A plan formed by the attorneys litigating a lawsuit, on behalf of their clients, that indicates the types of information that will be disclosed by each party to the other prior to trial, the testimony and evidence that each party will or may introduce at trial, and the general schedule for pretrial disclosures and events.
Disparagement of Property Economically injurious falsehoods made about another's product or property. A general term for torts that are more specifically referred to as slander of quality and slander of title.
Disparate-impact Discrimination In the employment context, discrimination that results from certain employer practices or procedures that, although not discriminatory on their face, have a discriminatory effect. For example, a requirement that all employees have high school diplomas is not necessarily discriminatory, but it may have the effect of discriminating against certain groups.
Disparate-treatment Discrimination In the employment context, intentional discrimination against individuals on the basis of race, color, gender, national origin, or religion.

Dissolution The formal disbanding of a partnership or a corporation.
Diversion Program In some jurisdictions, an alternative to prosecution that is offered to certain felony suspects to deter them from future unlawful acts.
Diversity of Citizenship Under Article III, Section 2, of the Constitution, a basis for federal court jurisdiction over a lawsuit between citizens of different states.
Dividend A distribution to corporate shareholders, disbursed in proportion to the number of shares held.
Divorce A formal court proceeding that legally dissolves a marriage.
Docket The list of cases entered on a court's calendar and thus scheduled to be heard by the court.
Double Billing Billing more than one client for the same billable time.
Double Jeopardy To place at risk (jeopardize) a person's life or liberty at risk twice. The Fifth Amendment to the U.S. Constitution prohibits a second prosecution for the same criminal offense in all but a few circumstances.
Dram Shop Act A state statute that imposes liability on the owners of bars and taverns for injuries resulting from accidents caused by intoxicated persons when the sellers or servers of alcoholic drinks contributed to the intoxication.
Due Process of Law The Fifth Amendment to the U.S. Constitution prohibits the deprivation of "life, liberty, or property without due process of law," meaning that fair, reasonable, and standard procedures must be used by the government in any legal action against a citizen.

E-mail An abbreviation for electronic mail; an electronic message sent over a computer network from one computer terminal to another or others.
Emancipation The legal relinquishment by a child's parents or guardian of the legal right to exercise control over the child. Usually, a child who moves out of the parents' home and supports himself or herself is considered emancipated.
Eminent Domain The power of a government to take land for public use from private citizens for just compensation.
Employee In agency law, one whose physical conduct is controlled by or subject to the control of the employer.
Employment at Will A common law doctrine under which employment is considered to be "at will"—that is, either party may terminate the employment relationship at any time and for any reason, unless the contract specifies otherwise.
Employment Policy Manual A firm's handbook or written statement that specifies the policies and procedures that govern the firm's employees and employer-employee relationships.
Enabling Legislation Statutes enacted by Congress that authorize the creation of an administrative agency and specify the name, purpose, composition, and powers of the agency being created.
Environmental Law All state and federal laws or regulations enacted or issued to protect the environment and preserve environmental resources.
Equitable Principles and Maxims Propositions or general statements of rules of law that are frequently involved in equity jurisdiction.
Escheat The transfer of property to the state when the owner of the property dies without heirs.
Estate in Property In bankruptcy proceedings, all of the debtor's interests in property presently held and wherever located, as well as interests in certain property to which the debtor becomes entitled within 180 days after filing for bankruptcy.
Estate Planning Making arrangements, during a person's lifetime, for the transfer of that person's property or obligations to others on the person's death. Estate planning often involves executing a will, establishing a trust fund, or taking out a life-insurance policy to provide for others, such as a spouse or children, on one's death.
Ethics Moral principles and values applied to social behavior.
Evidence Anything that is used to prove the existence or nonexistence of a fact.
Exclusionary Rule In criminal procedure, a rule under which any evidence that is obtained in violation of the accused's constitutional rights guaranteed by the Fourth, Fifth, and Sixth Amendments, as well as any evidence derived from illegally obtained evidence, will not be admissible in court.
Exclusive Jurisdiction Jurisdiction that exists when a case can be heard only in a particular court.
Executive Agency A type of adminsitrative agency that is either a cabinet department or a subagency within a cabinet department. Executive agencies fall under the authority of the president, who has the power to appoint and remove federal officers.
Executor A person appointed by a testator to see that the testator's will is administered appropriately.
Exordium Clause The opening, or introductory, clause in a will stating the name of the testator, where the testator resides, the names of the testator's spouse and children, the fact that the document is the testator's last will, and that the document revokes all other wills or codicils previously made by the testator.
Expense Slip A slip of paper on which any expense, or cost, that is incurred on behalf of a client (such as the payment of court fees or long-distance telephone charges) is recorded.
Expert Witness A witness with professional training or substantial experience qualifying him or her to testify on a particular subject.

Eyewitness A witness who testifies about an event that he or she observed or has experienced first hand.

Family Law Law relating to family matters, such as marriage, divorce, child support, and child custody.
Federal Question A question that pertains to the U.S. Constitution, acts of Congress, or treaties. A federal question provides jurisdiction for federal courts. This jurisdiction arises from Article III, Section 2, of the Constitution.
Federal Rules of Civil Procedure (FRCP) The rules controlling all procedural matters in civil trials brought before the federal district courts.
Fee Simple A form of property ownership entitling the owner to use, possess, or dispose of the property as he or she chooses during his or her lifetime. Upon death, the interest in the property descends to the owner's heirs.
Feedback A response from the person to whom a message has been sent indicating whether the receiver received and understood the message.
Felony A crime—such as arson, murder, rape, or robbery—that carries the most severe sanctions. Sanctions range from one year in a state or federal prison to life imprisonment or (in some states) the death penalty.
Fiduciary As a noun, a person having a duty created by his or her undertaking to act primarily for another's benefit in matters connected with the undertaking. As an adjective, a relationship founded upon trust and confidence.
Final Order The final decision of an administrative agency on an issue. If no appeal is taken, or if the case is not reviewed by the agency commission, the administrative law judge's initial order becomes the final order of the agency.
Fixed Fee A fee paid to the attorney by his or her client for having rendered a specified legal service, such as the creation of a simple will.
Forms File A reference file containing copies of the firm's commonly used legal documents and informational forms. The documents in the forms file serve as models for drafting new documents.
Foster Care A temporary arrangement in which a family is paid by the state to care for a child for a limited period of time, often pending adoption.
Franchise A written agreement in which an owner of a trademark, trade name, or copyright licenses another to use that trademark, trade name, or copyright, under specified conditions, in the sale of goods and services.
Franchisee One who receives a license to use another's (the franchisor's) trademark, trade name, or copyright in the sale of goods and services.
Franchisor One who licenses another (the franchisee) to use his or her trademark, trade name, or copyright in the sale of goods and services.
Fraud Any misrepresentation, either by misstatement or by the omission of a material fact, knowingly made with the intention of deceiving another and on which a reasonable person would rely and on which an actual person has relied to his or her detriment.
Freelance Paralegal A paralegal who operates his or her own business and provides services to attorneys on a contractual basis. A freelance paralegal works under the supervision of an attorney, who assumes responsibility for the paralegal's work product.
Friendly Witness A witness who gives voluntary testimony at an attorney's request on behalf of the attorney's client; a witness who is prejudiced against the client's adversary.

Garnishment A proceeding in which a creditor legally seizes a portion of a debtor's property (such as wages) that is in the possession of a third party (such as an employer).
General Licensing A type of licensing in which all individuals within a specific profession or group (such as paralegals) must meet licensing requirements imposed by the state before they may legally practice their profession.
Good Samaritan Statute A state statute that provides that persons who provide emergency services to, or rescue, others in peril cannot be sued for negligence.
Grand Jury The group of citizens called to decide whether probable cause exists to believe that a suspect committed the crime with which he or she has been charged.
Guardian *Ad Litem* A person appointed by the court to represent the interests of a child or a mentally incompetent person before the court.

Hard Drive A unit that enables a personal computer to store software programs and data files in permanent memory. The hard drive contains a hard disk.
Hardware The physical components (mechanical, magnetic, electronic, and so on) of the computer, including the computer itself, the keyboard, the monitor, and other peripheral devices attached to the computer.
Headnote A note near the beginning of a reported case summarizing the court's ruling on an issue.
Hearsay An oral or written statement made by an out-of-court declarant that is later offered in court by a witness (not the declarant) concerning a matter before the court. Hearsay is generally not admissible as evidence.
Holding The binding legal principle, or precedent, that is drawn from the court's decision in a case.
Holographic Will A will written entirely in the maker's handwriting and usually not witnessed.
Hornbook A secondary source presented as a single-volume scholarly discussion, or treatise, on a particular legal subject (such as property law).
Hostile Witness A witness for the opposing side in a lawsuit or other legal proceeding; an adverse witness.

Hung Jury A jury whose members are so irreconcilably divided in their opinions that they cannot reach a verdict. The judge in this situation may order a new trial.
Hypothetical Question A question based on hypothesis, conjecture, or fiction. Interviewers sometimes use hypothetical questions to observe how an interviewee might handle a difficult situation.

Impeach To call into question the credibility of a witness by challenging the truth or accuracy of his or her trial statement.
Independent Adoption A privately arranged adoption, as when a doctor, lawyer, or other individual puts parents who want to adopt a child in contact with a pregnant woman who has decided to give up her child for adoption.
Independent Contractor One who works for, and receives payment from, an employer but whose working conditions and methods are not controlled by the employer. An independent contractor is not an employee but may be an agent.
Independent Paralegal A paralegal who offers services directly to the public, normally for a fee, without attorney supervision. Independent paralegals assist consumers by supplying them with forms and procedural knowledge relating to simple or routine legal procedures.
Independent Regulatory Agency A type of administrative agency that is more independent of presidential control than an executive agency. Officials of independent regulatory agencies cannot be removed without cause.
Indictment A charge or written accusation, issued by a grand jury, that probable cause exists to believe that a named person has committed a crime.
Information A formal accusation or complaint, usually issued by a prosecuting attorney, against a criminal suspect. The information initiates the criminal litigation process.
Informative Letter A letter that conveys certain information to a client, a witness, an adversary's counsel, or other person regarding some legal matter (such as the date, time, place, and purpose of a meeting).
Initial Order The decision rendered by an administrative law judge following an administrative hearing. The initial order becomes final unless it is appealed.
Injunction A court decree ordering a person to do or refrain from doing a certain act or activity.
Insider Trading Purchasing or selling securities on the basis of information that has not been made available to the public.
Intellectual Property Property that consists of the products of individuals' minds—products that result from intellectual, creative processes. Copyrights, patents, and trademarks are examples of intellectual property.
Intentional Tort A wrongful act knowingly committed that interferes with the interests of another in a way not permitted by law.
***Inter Vivos* Trust** A trust executed by the grantor and effective during the grantor's lifetime; a living trust.
International Law The law that governs relations among nations. International customs and treaties are generally considered to be two of the most important sources of international law.
Interrogatories A series of written questions for which written answers are prepared and then signed under oath by a party to a lawsuit (the plaintiff or the defendant).
Interspousal Immunity A common law doctrine that prohibited one spouse from suing the other spouse for torts, such as assault and battery, and from testifying against the other spouse in court. The doctrine has been modified. Today, in most states, one spouse may sue the other for at least intentional torts, and a spouse normally may voluntarily testify against the other spouse in court.
Interviewee The person who is being interviewed.
Intestacy Laws State laws determining the division and descent of the property of one who dies intestate (without a will).
Intestate Without having created a valid will.
***Inter Vivos* Trust** A trust executed by the grantor and effective during the grantor's lifetime; a living trust.
Investigation Plan A plan that lists each step involved in obtaining and verifying the facts and information that are relevant to the legal problem being investigated.
Invitee A person, such as a customer or dinner-party guest, who is invited onto another's property for the benefit of the other party.
IRAC Method IRAC is a mnemonic for issue, rule, application, and conclusion. The IRAC method helps legal researchers and writers focus on the four critical elements of a case.

Joint and Several Liability In partnership law, joint and several liability means that a third party may sue one or more of the partners separately or all of them together. This is true even if one of the partners sued did not participate or know about whatever it was that gave rise to the cause of action.
Joint Custody The situation in which the custody of a child or children following the termination of a marriage is shared by both parents.
Joint Liability Shared liability. In partnership law, partners incur joint liability for partnership obligations and debts.
Joint Stock Company A hybrid form of business organization that combines characteristics of a corporation (shareholder-owners, management by directors and officers, and perpetual existence) and a partnership (it is formed by agreement, not by state charter; property is usually held in the names of the members; and the shareholders have personal liability for business debts).

Usually, the joint stock company is regarded as a partnership for tax and other legal purposes.
Joint Tenancy Co-ownership of property in which each party owns an undivided interest in the property. On the death of one of the joint tenants, his or her interest automatically passes to the other joint tenant or tenants and cannot be transferred by the will of the deceased.
Joint Venture A relationship in which two or more persons or organizations combine their efforts or their property for a single transaction or project or a related series of transactions or projects.
Judgment The court's final decision regarding the rights and claims of the parties to a lawsuit.
Judicial Process The procedures relating to the administration of justice through the courts.
Jurisdiction The authority of a court to hear and decide a specific action.
Justiciable Controversy A controversy that is real and substantial as opposed to hypothetical or academic.

Keogh Plan A tax-deferred pension or retirement plan for self-employed taxpayers. The taxpayer funds the plan each year with tax-deductible contributions, which are capped at a certain amount.
Key Number A number (accompanied by the symbol of a key) corresponding to a specific topic within the West Publishing Company's key-number system to facilitate legal research of case law.
Keyboard A computer input device with alpha-numeric characters (arranged similarly to the traditional typewriter) and function keys.

Laches The equitable doctrine that bars a party's right to legal action if the party has neglected for an unreasonable length of time to act upon his or her rights.
Law A body of rules of conduct with legal force and effect, prescribed by the controlling authority (the government) of a society.
Law Clerk In the context of law-office work, a law student who works as an apprentice, during the summer or part-time during the school year, with an attorney or law firm to gain practical legal experience.
Lay Witness A witness who can truthfully and accurately testify on a fact in question without having specialized training or knowledge; an ordinary witness.
Leading Question A question that suggests, or "leads to," a desired answer. Generally, at trial leading questions may be asked only of hostile witnesses. Interviewers may use leading questions to elicit responses from witnesses who otherwise would not be forthcoming.
Lease A transfer by the landlord/lessor of real or personal property to the tenant/lessee for a period of time for consideration (usually the payment of rent). Upon termination of the lease, the property reverts to the lessor.
Legacy A gift of personal property by will.
Legal Administrator An administrative employee of a law firm who manages the day-to-day operations of the firm. In smaller law firms, legal administrators are usually called office managers.
Legal Assistant A person sufficiently trained or experienced in the law and legal procedures to assist, under an attorney's supervision, in the performance of substantive legal work that would otherwise be performed by an attorney. Often referred to as a paralegal.
Legal-assistant Manager An employee who is responsible for overseeing the paralegal staff and paralegal professional development.
Legal Custody Custody that gives a parent the right to make major decisions about a child's life without consulting the other parent.
Legal Ethics The principles, values, and rules of conduct that govern legal professionals.
Legal Reasoning The process of reasoning by which a judge harmonizes his or her decision with previous judicial decisions.
Legatee A person who inherits personal property under a will.
Legislative Rule A rule created by an administrative agency that is as legally binding as a law enacted by a legislature.
Licensee A person, such as a theater goer, who receives permission to enter onto another's property for the licensee's benefit.
Licensing A government's official act of granting permission to an individual, such as an attorney, to do something that would be illegal in the absence of such permission.
Limited Licensing A type of licensing in which a limited number of individuals within a specific profession or group (such as independent paralegals within the paralegal profession) must meet licensing requirements imposed by the state before those individuals may legally practice their profession.
Limited Partnership A partnership consisting of one or more general partners (who manage the business and are liable to the full extent of their personal assets for debts of the partnership) and of one or more limited partners (who contribute only assets and are liable only up to the amount contributed by them).
Limited-liability Company (LLC) A hybrid form of business organization authorized by a state in which the owners of the business have limited liability and taxes on profits are passed through the business entity to the owners.
Limited-liability Partnership (LLP) A hybrid form of business organization authorized by a state that allows professionals to enjoy the tax benefits of a partnership while limiting in some way the normal joint and several liability of partners.
Liquidation The process by which corporate assets are

converted into cash and distributed among creditors and shareholders.

Liquidation A proceeding under Chapter 7 of the Bankruptcy Code (often referred to as *ordinary*, or *straight*, bankruptcy) in which a debtor states his or her debts and turns all assets over to a trustee, who sells the nonexempt assets and distributes the proceeds to creditors. With certain exceptions, the remaining debts are then discharged and the debtor is relieved of the obligation to pay the debts.

Litigation The process of working a lawsuit through the court system.

Litigation Paralegals Paralegals who specialize in assisting attorneys in the litigation process.

Local Area Network (LAN) A system of physically dispersed computers that are interconnected, via telecommunications, within a local area, such as an office building. Users at each connected computer can share information and software with other computers connected to the network.

Long-arm Statute A state statute that permits a state to obtain jurisdiction over nonresident individuals and corporations. Individuals or corporations, however, must have certain "minimum contacts" with that state for the statute to apply.

Magistrate A public civil officer or official with limited judicial authority, such as the authority to issue an arrest warrant.

Mainframe Computer A large, centralized computer processing unit that can service multiple terminals simultaneously and that is capable of storing, handling, and retrieving vast amounts of data (used by large organizations, such as megafirms, government agencies, and universities).

Malpractice Professional misconduct or negligence—the failure to exercise due care—on the part of a professional, such as an attorney or a physician.

Managing Partner The partner in a law firm who makes decisions relating to the firm's policies and procedures and who generally oversees the business operations of the firm.

Mandatory Authority Any source of law that a court must follow when deciding a case. Mandatory authorities include constitutions, statutes, and regulations that govern the issue at bar and court decisions made by a superior court in the jurisdiction.

Marital Property All property acquired during the course of a marriage, apart from inheritances and gifts made to one or the other of the spouses.

Market-share Liability A method of sharing liability among several firms that manufactured or marketed a particular product that may have caused a plaintiff's injury. Each firm's liability is proportional to its respective share of the relevant market for the product. This form of liability sharing is used when the true source of the product is unidentifiable.

Mediation A method of settling disputes outside of court by using the services of a neutral third party, who acts as a communicating agent between the parties; a method of dispute settlement that is less formal than arbitration.

Memorandum of Law A document (known as a brief in some states) that delineates the legal theories, statutes, and cases on which a motion is based.

Mens Rea A wrongful mental state, or intent. A wrongful mental state is a requirement for criminal liability. What constitutes a wrongful mental state varies according to the nature of the crime. For the crime of murder to exist, for example, the required *mens rea* is the intent to take another person's life.

Merger A process in which one corporation (the surviving corporation) acquires all the assets and liabilities of another corporation (the merged corporation).

Mini-trial A private proceeding that assists disputing parties in determining whether to take their case to court. During the proceeding, each party's attorney briefly argues the party's case before the other party and (usually) a neutral third party, who acts as an adviser. If the parties fail to reach an agreement, the adviser renders an opinion as to how a court would likely decide the issue.

Minicomputer A computer with more power and capacity than a microcomputer but less than a mainframe computer. Like the mainframe, the minicomputer (server) can be connected to a number of terminals (clients) simultaneously.

***Miranda* Rights** The constitutional rights of accused persons taken into custody by law-enforcement officials. Following the United States Supreme Court's decision in *Miranda v. Arizona*, on taking an accused person into custody, the arresting officer must inform the person of certain constitutional rights, such as the suspect's right to remain silent or right to counsel.

Misdemeanor A less serious crime than a felony, punishable by a fine or imprisonment for up to one year in other than a state or federal penitentiary.

Modem A device that converts the computer's digital signals into analog sound waves and vice versa so that messages can be transmitted and received over a telephone line. Using a modem and communications software, a user can transfer information from one computer to another via a phone line.

Monitor A black-and-white or multicolor display screen that displays the current activities of the computer.

Mortgage A written instrument giving a creditor an interest in the debtor's property as security for a debt.

Motion A procedural request or application presented by an attorney to the court on behalf of a client.

Motion Challenging the Sufficiency of the Indictment A motion claiming that the evidence submitted by the prosecutor was insufficient to establish probable cause that the defendant committed the crime with which he or she has been charged.

Motion for a Change of Venue A motion requesting that a trial be moved to a different location to ensure a fair and impartial proceeding, for the convenience of the parties, or for some other acceptable reason.

Motion for a Directed Verdict A motion (also referred to as a motion for judgment as a matter of law in the federal courts) requesting that the court grant judgment in favor of the party making the motion on the ground that the other party has not produced sufficient evidence to support his or her claim.

Motion for a New Trial A motion asserting that the trial was so fundamentally flawed (because of error, newly discovered evidence, prejudice, or other reason) that a new trial is needed to prevent a miscarriage of justice.

Motion for Discovery and Inspection A motion requesting permission from the court to obtain evidence in the adversary's possession.

Motion for Judgment as a Matter of Law A motion requesting that the court grant judgment in favor of the party making the motion on the ground that the other party has not produced sufficient evidence to support his or her claim.

Motion for Judgment Notwithstanding the Verdict A motion (also referred to as a motion for judgment as a matter of law in federal courts) requesting that the court grant judgment in favor of the party making the motion on the ground that the jury verdict against him or her was unreasonable and erroneous.

Motion for Judgment on the Pleadings A motion, which can be brought by either party to a lawsuit after the pleadings are closed, for the court to decide the issue without proceeding to trial. The motion will be granted only if no facts are in dispute and the only issue concerns how the law applies to a set of undisputed facts.

Motion for Summary Judgment A motion requesting the court to enter a judgment without proceeding to trial. The motion can be based on evidence outside the pleadings and will be granted only if no facts are in dispute and the only issue concerns how the law applies to a set of undisputed facts.

Motion *in Limine* A motion requesting that certain evidence not be brought out at the trial, such as prejudicial, irrelevant, or legally inadmissible evidence.

Motion to Dismiss A pleading in which a defendant admits the facts as alleged by the plaintiff but asserts that the plaintiff's claim fails to state a cause of action (that is, has no basis in law) or that there are other grounds on which a suit should be dismissed.

Motion to Reduce the Amount of Bail A motion requesting that the bail needed to release the defendant be lowered because it is unreasonably high under the circumstances and may violate the Eighth Amendment's prohibition against excessive bail.

Motion to Suppress Evidence A motion requesting that certain evidence be excluded, or suppressed, from consideration during the trial.

Mouse A device that lets a computer user move the cursor's position on the monitor and give commands to the computer without using a keyboard.

National Association of Legal Assistants (NALA) One of the two largest national paralegal associations in the United States; formed in 1975. NALA offers a certification program for paralegals and is actively involved in paralegal professional developments.

National Federation of Paralegal Associations (NFPA) One of the two largest national paralegal associations in the United States; formed in 1974. NFPA is actively involved in paralegal professional developments.

National Law Law that pertains to a particular nation (as opposed to international law).

Negligence The failure to exercise the standard of care that a reasonable person would exercise in similar circumstances.

Negligence *Per* Se An action or failure to act that violates a statutory requirement and that results in harm to another.

Negotiation A method of alternative dispute resolution in which disputing parties, with or without the assistance of their attorneys, meet informally to resolve the dispute out of court.

Networking Making personal connections and cultivating relationships with people in a certain field, profession, or area of interest.

No-fault Divorce A divorce in which neither party is deemed to be at fault for the breakdown of the marriage.

Nolo Contendere Latin for "I will not contest it." A criminal defendant's plea in which he or she chooses not to challenge, or contest, the charges brought by the government. Although the defendant may still be sentenced or fined, the plea neither admits nor denies guilt.

Nonverbal Communication The sending and receiving of messages without using language. Nonverbal communication includes body language (such as facial gestures) and utterances or sounds that do not consist of words.

Notice-and-comment Rulemaking A three-step administrative rulemaking procedure that involves the publication of a notice of a proposed rulemaking in the *Federal Register*, a comment period for interested parties to express their views on the proposed rule, and the publication of the agency's final rule in the *Federal Register*.

Nuisance An act that interferes unlawfully with a person's possession or ability to use his or her property.

Nuncupative Will An oral will (often called a deathbed

will) made before witnesses; usually limited to transfers of personal property.

Offer A proposal to form a contract with another person or entity (the offeree). The offeree's acceptance of an effective offer creates a legally binding contract, providing all other requirements for a valid contract have been met.
Office Manager An administrative employee who manages the day-to-day operations of a business firm. In larger law firms, office managers are usually called legal administrators.
Officer A person hired by corporate directors to assist in the management of the day-to-day operations of the corporation. Corporate officers include the corporate president, vice president, secretary, treasurer, and possibly others, such as a chief financial officer and chief executive officer. Corporate officers are employees of the corporation and subject to employment contracts.
Open Adoption An adoption procedure in which the birth parents and adoptive parents meet with each other at the outset and may continue to meet periodically.
Open-ended Question A question that is phrased in such a way that it elicits a relatively detailed discussion of an experience or topic.
Opening Statement An attorney's statement to the jury at the beginning of the trial. The attorney briefly outlines the evidence that will be offered during the trial and the legal theory that will be pursued.
Operating-system Software A program allowing the computer to control the sequencing and processing of application software programs so that the computer responds correctly to the operator's commands.
Opinion A statement by the court expressing the reasons for its decision in a case.
Opinion Letter A letter from an attorney to a client that contains a legal opinion on an issue raised by the client's question or legal claim; an advisory letter.
Order for Relief A court's grant of assistance to a complainant. In the context of bankruptcy, the order for relief in itself constitutes a discharge of the complainant's (debtor's) debts.
Ordinance An order, rule, or law enacted by a municipal or county government to govern a local matter unaddressed by state or federal legislation.
Original Jurisdiction The power of a court to take a case, try it, and decide it.
Out Card A large card inserted in a filing cabinet in the place of a temporarily removed file. The out card notifies others who may need the file of the name of the person who has the file and the time and date that the file was removed.
Overtime Wages Wages paid to workers who are paid an hourly wage rate to compensate them for overtime work (hours worked beyond forty hours per week). Under federal law, overtime wages are at least one-and-a-half times the regular hourly wage rate.

Palimony A nonlegal term used to describe claims made by a member of an unmarried couple to the property of the other member of the couple after the two have separated.
Paralegal A person sufficiently trained or experienced in the law and legal procedures to assist, under an attorney's supervision, in the performance of substantive legal work that would otherwise be performed by an attorney. Often referred to as a legal assistant.
Paralegal Certificate A certificate awarded to an individual with a high school diploma or its equivalent who has successfully completed a paralegal program of study at a private, for-profit business school or trade school.
Parallel Citation A second (or third) citation to another case reporter in which a case has been published. When a case is published in more than one reporter, each citation is a parallel citation to the other(s).
Partner A person who has undertaken to operate a business jointly with one or more other persons. Each partner is a co-owner of the business firm.
Partnership An association of two or more persons to carry on, as co-owners, a business for profit.
Party A plaintiff or defendant in a lawsuit. Some cases involve multiple parties (more than one plaintiff or defendant).
Password A predetermined series of numbers and/or letter characters that an authorized user keys in to gain access to a computer system or data contained in computer files; a security code.
Patent A government grant that gives an inventor the exclusive right or privilege to make, use, or sell his or her invention for a limited time period.
Paternity Suit A lawsuit brought by an unmarried mother to establish that a certain person is the biological father of her child. DNA testing and comparable procedures are often used to determine paternity.
Per Capita A Latin term meaning "per person." In the law governing estate distribution, a method of distributing the property of an intestate's estate by which all the heirs receive equal shares.
Per Stirpes A Latin term meaning "by the roots." In the law governing estate distribution, a method of distributing an intestate's estate in which a class or group of distributees take the share to which their deceased ancestor would have been entitled.
Peremptory Challenge A *voir dire* challenge to exclude a potential juror from serving on the jury without any supporting reason or cause. Peremptory challenges based on racial or gender criteria are illegal.
Personal Computer (PC) A desktop computer, or microcomputer, with its own central processing unit, which is

ordinarily used for applications that are tailored to the user's employment, domestic, or educational needs.

Personal Ethics The moral principles and values that individuals apply in their daily lives and decision making.

Personal Liability An individual's personal responsibility for debts or obligations. The owners of sole proprietorships and partnerships are personally liable for the debts and obligations incurred by their business firms. If their firms go bankrupt or cannot meet debts as they become due, the owners will be personally responsible for paying the debts.

Personal Property Any property that is not real property. Generally, any property that is movable or intangible is classified as personal property.

Personal Time Diary A journal or notebook used by paralegals and attorneys to record and track the hours (or fractions of hours) worked and the tasks completed on behalf of each client.

Persuasive Authority Any legal authority, or source of law, that a court may look to for guidance but on which it need not rely in making its decision. Persuasive authorities include cases from other jurisdictions and secondary sources of law, such as scholarly treatises.

Petition for Divorce The document filed with the court to initiate divorce proceedings. The requirements governing the form and content of a divorce petition vary from state to state.

Petition in Bankruptcy An application to a bankruptcy court for relief in bankruptcy; a filing for bankruptcy. The official forms required for a petition in bankruptcy must be completed accurately, sworn to under oath, and signed by the debtor.

Petty Offense In criminal law, the least serious kind of wrong, such as a traffic or building-code violation.

Plain-meaning Rule A rule of statutory interpretation. If the meaning of a statute is clear on its face, then that is the interpretation the court will give to it; inquiry into the legislative history of the statute will not be undertaken.

Plaintiff A party who initiates a lawsuit.

Plea Bargaining The process by which the accused and the prosecutor in a criminal case work out a mutually satisfactory disposition of the case, subject to court approval. Usually, plea bargaining involves the defendant's pleading guilty to a lesser offense in return for a lighter sentence.

Pleadings Statements by the plaintiff and the defendant that detail the facts, charges, and defenses involved in the litigation.

Pocket Part A separate pamphlet containing recent cases or changes in the law that is used to update hornbooks, legal encyclopedias, and other legal authorities. It is called a "pocket part" because it slips into a sleeve, or pocket, in the back binder of the volume.

Portfolio A job applicant's collection of selected personal documents (such as school transcripts, writing samples, and certificates) for presentation to a potential employer.

Postbaccalaureate Certificate A postgraduate certificate awarded by a college or university to an individual who, having already completed a bachelor's degree program, successfully completes a paralegal program of study.

Prayer for Relief A statement at the end of the complaint requesting that the court grant relief to the plaintiff.

Precedent A court decision that furnishes an example or authority for deciding subsequent cases in which identical or similar facts are presented.

Preference In bankruptcy proceedings, the debtor's favoring of one creditor over others by making payments or transferring property to that creditor at the expense of the rights of other creditors. The bankruptcy trustee is allowed to recover payments made to one creditor in preference over another.

Preliminary Hearing An initial hearing in which a magistrate decides if there is probable cause to believe that the defendant committed the crime for which he or she is charged.

Prenuptial Agreement A contract formed between two persons who are contemplating marriage to provide for the disposition of property in the event of a divorce or the death of one of the persons after they have married.

Pressure Question A question intended to make the interviewee feel uncomfortable and respond emotionally. Pressure questions are sometimes used by interviewers to elicit answers from interviewees who may otherwise be unresponsive.

Pretrial Conference A conference prior to trial in which the judge and the attorneys litigating the suit discuss settlement possibilities, clarify the issues in dispute, and schedule forthcoming trial-related events.

***Prima Facie* Case** A case in which the evidence compels the court to accept the plaintiff's conclusion if the defendant produces no evidence to counter it.

Primary Source In legal research, a document that establishes the law on a particular issue, such as a case decision, legislative act, administrative rule, or presidential order.

Principal In agency law, a person who, by agreement or otherwise, authorizes another person (the agent) to act on the principal's behalf in such a way that the acts of the agent become binding on the principal.

Privity of Contract The connection that exists between the parties to a contract, such as a buyer and a seller.

Privileged Information Confidential communications between certain individuals, such as an attorney and his or her client, that are protected from disclosure except under court order.

Pro Bono Publico Legal services provided for free or at a reduced fee by an attorney or paralegal to persons of limited financial means in need of legal assistance.

***Pro Se* Divorce** A divorce in which the parties represent themselves before the court.

Probable Cause Reasonable grounds to believe the existence of facts warranting certain actions, such as the search or arrest of a person.
Probate The process of "proving" the validity of a will and ensuring that the instructions in a valid will are carried out.
Probate Court A court having jurisdiction over proceedings concerning the settlement of a person's estate.
Procedural Law Rules that define the manner in which the rights and duties of individuals may be enforced.
Product Liability The legal liability of manufacturers and sellers to buyers, users, and sometimes bystanders for injuries or damages suffered because of defects in goods purchased. Liability arises when a product has a defective condition that makes it unreasonably dangerous to the user or consumer.
Product Misuse A defense against product liability that may be raised when the plaintiff used a product in a manner not intended by the manufacturer. If the misuse was reasonably foreseeable, the seller will not escape liability unless measures were taken to guard against the harm that could have been expected to result from the misuse.
Profession An occupation requiring knowledge of the arts or sciences and advanced study in a specialized field, such as the law.
Professional Corporation (P.C.) A business form in which shareholders (those who purchase the corporation's stock, or shares) own the firm and share in the profits and losses of the firm in proportion to how many shares they own. Their personal liability, unlike that of partners, is limited to the amount of their investment.
Proof of Claim A document filed with the bankruptcy court by a creditor to inform a court of a claim against a debtor's property. The proof of claim lists the creditor's name and address, as well as the amount that the creditor asserts is owed to the creditor by the debtor.
Property Settlement The division of property between spouses on the termination of a marriage.
Prospectus A document that discloses relevant facts about a company and its operations so that those who wish to purchase stock (invest) in the corporation have the basis for making an informed decision.
Proximate Cause The "next" or "substantial" cause; in tort law, a concept used to determine whether a plaintiff's injury was the natural and continuous result of a defendant's negligent act.
Public Defender A court-appointed attorney who is paid by the state to represent a criminal defendant who is unable to hire private counsel.
Public Law Number An identification number that has been assigned to a specific statute, or public law, following the legislative process.
Public Policy A governmental policy based on widely held societal values.
Public Prosecutor An individual, acting as a trial lawyer, who initiates and conducts criminal cases in the government's name and on behalf of the people.
Punitive Damages Damages that are awarded in a civil lawsuit to punish the wrongdoer. Punitive damages are usually awarded only in cases involving willful or malicious misconduct.

Real Estate Land and things permanently attached to the land, such as houses, buildings, and trees and foliage; real property.
Real Property Immovable property consisting of land, and the buildings and plant life thereon.
Reaffirmation Agreement An agreement between a debtor and a creditor in which the debtor reaffirms, or promises to pay, a debt dischargeable in bankruptcy. To be enforceable, the agreement must be made prior to the discharge of the debt by the bankruptcy court.
Reasonable-person Standard The standard of behavior expected of a hypothetical "reasonable person." The standard against which negligence is measured and that must be observed to avoid liability for negligence.
Record on Appeal The items submitted during the trial (pleadings, motions, briefs, and exhibits) and the transcript of the trial proceedings that are forwarded to the appellate court for review when a case is appealed.
Recross-examination The questioning of an opposing witness following the adverse party's redirect examination.
Redirect Examination The questioning of a witness following the adverse party's cross-examination.
Reference Line The portion of the letter that indicates the matter to be discussed in the letter, such as "RE: Summary of Cases Applying the Family and Medical Leave Act of 1993." The reference line is placed just below the address block and above the salutation.
Reformation An equitable remedy granted by a court to correct, or "reform," a written contract so that it reflects the true intentions of the parties.
Relevant Evidence Evidence tending to make a fact in question more or less probable than it would be without the evidence. Only relevant evidence is admissible in court.
Remand An appellate court's decision to send a case back to the trial court for further proceedings.
Remedy at Law A remedy available in a court of law. Money damages are awarded as a remedy at law.
Remedy in Equity A remedy allowed by courts in situations where remedies at law are not appropriate. Remedies in equity are based on settled rules of fairness, justice, and honesty.
Reporter A publication in which court cases are published, or reported.

Reprimand A disciplinary sanction in which an attorney is rebuked for his or her misbehavior. Although a reprimand is the mildest sanction for attorney misconduct, it is nonetheless a serious one and may significantly damage the attorney's reputation in the legal community.

Res Ipsa Loquitur A doctrine under which negligence may be inferred simply because an event occurred, if it is the type of event that would not occur without negligence. Literally, the term means "the thing speaks for itself."

Rescission A remedy whereby a contract is terminated and the parties are returned to the positions they occupied before the contract was made.

Respondeat Superior In Latin, "Let the master respond." A doctrine in agency law under which a principal or an employer may be held liable for the wrongful acts committed by agents or employees while acting within the scope of their agency or employment.

Responsible Billing Partner The partner in a law firm who is responsible for overseeing a particular client's case and the billing of that client.

Restitution An equitable remedy under which a person is restored to his or her original position prior to loss or injury, or placed in the position that he or she would have been in had the breach not occurred.

Restraining Order A court order that requires one person (such as an abusing spouse) to stay away from another (such as an abused spouse).

Retainer An advance payment made by a client to a law firm to cover part of the legal fee and/or costs that will need to be incurred on that client's behalf.

Retainer Agreement A signed document stating that the attorney or the law firm has been hired by the client to provide certain legal services and that the client agrees to pay for those services in accordance with the terms set forth in the retainer agreement.

Retentive Listening The act of listening attentively to what the speaker is saying for the purpose of remembering, or retaining, the information communicated.

Return-of-service Form A document signed by a process server and submitted to the court to prove that a defendant received a summons.

Reverse An appellate court's decision that is contrary to the trial court's judgment.

Revoke Annul, or make void. In the context of wills, to nullify a part or all of a will by an act of the maker (tearing up the will, for example, or creating a codicil or second will) or by operation of law (due to a subsequent marriage, divorce or annulment, or the birth of a child).

Rule of Four A rule of the United States Supreme Court under which the Court will not issue a writ of *certiorari* unless at least four justices approve of the decision to issue the writ.

Rulemaking The actions undertaken by administrative agencies when formally adopting new regulations or amending old ones. Under the Administrative Procedure Act, rulemaking includes notifying the public of proposed rules or changes and receiving and considering the public's comments.

Rules of Construction The rules that control the judicial interpretation of statutes.

Rules of Evidence Rules governing the admissibility of evidence in trial courts.

Sales Contract A contract for the sale of goods, as opposed to a contract for the sale of services, real property, or intangible property. Sales contracts are governed by Article 2 of the Uniform Commercial Code.

Salutation The formal greeting to the addressee of the letter. The salutation is placed just below the reference line.

Scheduling Conference A meeting (conducted shortly after a plaintiff's complaint is filed) attended by the judge and the attorneys for both parties to the lawsuit. Following the conference, the judge issues a scheduling order for the pretrial events and the trial date.

Search Warrant A written order, based on probable cause and issued by a judge or public official (magistrate), commanding that police officers or criminal investigators search a specific person, place, or property to obtain evidence.

Secondary Source In legal research, any publication that indexes, summarizes, or interprets the law, such as a legal encyclopedia, a treatise, or an article in a law review.

Secured Creditor A lender, seller, or any other person in whose favor there is a security interest.

Security A stock certificate, bond, or other document or certificate that evidences an ownership interest in a corporation or a promise of repayment by a corporation.

Security Code A predetermined series of numbers and/or letter characters that an authorized user keys in to gain access to a computer system or data contained in computer files; a password.

Self-defense The legally recognized privilege to protect oneself or one's property against injury by another. The privilege of self-defense only protects acts that are reasonably necessary to protect oneself or one's property.

Self-incrimination The act of giving testimony that implicates one's own guilt or participation in criminal wrongdoing. The Fifth Amendment to the U.S. Constitution states that no person "shall be compelled in any criminal case to be a witness against himself."

Self-regulation The regulation of the conduct of a professional group by members of the group themselves. Self-regulation usually involves the establishment of ethical or professional standards of behavior with which members of the group must comply.

Seniority System In regard to employment relationships, a system in which those who have worked longest for the company are first in line for promotions, salary increases,

and other benefits; they are also the last to be laid off if the work force must be reduced.
Sentence The punishment, or penalty, ordered by the court to be inflicted on a person convicted of a crime.
Separate Property Property that a spouse owned before the marriage, plus inheritances and gifts acquired by the spouse during the marriage.
Service of Process The delivery of the summons and the complaint to a defendant.
Session Law A law passed by legislators and officially published chronologically by order of legislative session in a multivolume set.
Settlement Agreement An out-of-court resolution to a legal dispute, which is agreed to by the parties in writing. A settlement agreement may be reached at any time prior to or during a trial.
Sexual Harassment In the employment context, the hiring or granting of job promotions or other benefits in return for sexual favors (*quid-pro-quo* harassment) or language or conduct that is so sexually offensive that it creates a hostile working environment (hostile-environment harassment).
Share A unit of stock; a measure of ownership interest in a corporation.
Shareholder Any person or entity that purchases one or more shares of corporate stock, thus giving that person or entity an ownership interest in the corporation.
Slander of Title The publication of a statement that denies or casts doubt on another's legal ownership of particular property, causing financial loss to that property's owner.
Slander of Quality The publication of false information about another's product, alleging that the product is not what its seller claims; also referred to as *trade libel.*
Slip Law The first official publication of a statute that comes out shortly after the legislation is passed (presented as a single sheet or pamphlet).
Slip Opinion A judicial opinion published shortly after the decision is made and not yet included in a case reporter or advance sheets.
Social-host Statute A state statute that imposes liability on persons hosting parties for injuries caused by guests who became intoxicated at the hosts' homes.
Software Computer programs that instruct and control the computer's hardware and operations.
Sole Proprietorship The simplest form of business, in which the owner is the business. Anyone who does business without creating a formal business entity has a sole proprietorship.
Specific Performance An equitable remedy requiring exactly the performance that was specified in a contract; usually granted only when money damages would be an inadequate remedy and the subject matter of the contract is unique (for example, real property).
Spendthrift Trust A trust created to protect the beneficiary from spending all the money to which he or she is entitled. Only a certain portion of the total amount is given to the beneficiary at any one time, and most states prohibit creditors from obtaining assets of the trust.
Spreadsheet Program A computer program that completes calculations, does numerical tracking, and allows the operator to manipulate numeric data for statistical and reporting purposes (such as budget reporting).
Standing to Sue The requirement that an individual must have a sufficient stake in a controversy before he or she can bring a lawsuit. The plaintiff must demonstrate that he or she either has been injured or threatened with injury.
Stare Decisis A flexible doctrine of the courts, recognizing the value of following prior decisions (precedents) in cases similar to the one before the court; the courts' practice of being consistent with prior decisions based on similar facts.
State Bar Association An association of attorneys within a state. Membership in the state bar association is mandatory in over two-thirds of the states—that is, before an attorney can practice law in a state, he or she must be admitted to that state's bar association.
Statute A written law enacted by a legislature under its constitutional lawmaking authority.
Statute of Frauds A state statute that requires certain types of contracts to be in writing to be enforceable.
Statute of Limitations A statute setting the maximum time period within which certain actions can be brought or rights enforced. After the period of time has run, normally no legal action can be brought.
Statute of Repose Basically, a statute of limitations that is not dependent upon the happening of a cause of action, such as an injury caused by a defective product. Statutes of repose generally begin to run earlier and run longer than statutes of limitations.
Statutory Law Laws enacted by a legislative body.
Stock In corporation law, an equity or ownership interest in a corporation, measured in units of shares.
Strict Liability Liability regardless of fault. In tort law, strict liability may be imposed on those who engage in abnormally dangerous activities that cause harm to others, on merchants who introduce into commerce goods that are unreasonably dangerous, and in certain other situations.
Submission Agreement A written agreement to submit a legal dispute to an arbitrator or arbitrating panel for resolution.
Subpoena A document commanding a person to appear at a certain time and place to give testimony concerning a certain matter.
Substantive Law Law that defines the rights and duties of individuals with respect to each other, as opposed to

procedural law, which defines the manner in which these rights and duties may be enforced.
Summary Jury Trial (SJT) A relatively recent method of settling disputes in which a trial is held but the jury's verdict is not binding. The verdict only acts as a guide to both sides in reaching an agreement during the mandatory negotiations that immediately follow the trial. If a settlement is not reached, both sides have the right to a full trial later.
Summons A document served on a defendant in a lawsuit informing a defendant that a legal action has been commenced against the defendant and that the defendant must appear in court on a certain date to answer the plaintiff's complaint.
Support Personnel Those employees who provide clerical, secretarial, or other support to the legal, paralegal, and administrative staff of a law firm.
Supporting Affidavit An affidavit accompanying a motion that is filed by an attorney on behalf of his or her client. The sworn statements in the affidavit provide a factual basis for the motion.
Supportive Listening The act of providing comments, utterances, or gestures that convey to the speaker an interest in what the speaker is saying and that encourage the speaker to continue speaking.
Supremacy Clause The clause in Article VI of the U.S. Constitution that provides that the Constitution, laws, and treaties of the United States are "the supreme Law of the Land." Under this clause, a state law that directly conflicts with a federal law will be rendered invalid.
Suspension A serious disciplinary sanction in which an attorney who has violated an ethical rule or a law is prohibited from practicing law in the state for a specified or an indefinite period of time.
Syllabus A brief summary of the holding and legal principles involved in a reported case, which is followed by the court's official opinion.
Syllogism A form of deductive reasoning consisting of a major premise, a minor premise, and a conclusion.
Syndicate An investment group consisting of persons or firms that get together for the purpose of financing a project that they would not undertake independently.

Table of Cases An alphabetical list of the cases that have been cited or reproduced in a legal text, case digest, or other legal source.
Tenancy in Common Co-ownership of property in which each party owns an undivided interest that passes to his or her heirs at death.
Testamentary Capacity The legal capacity to make a valid will. Generally, testamentary capacity exists if the testator is of age and of sound legal mind at the time the will is made.
Testamentary Trust A trust that is created by will and that does not take effect until the death of the testator.
Testate Having died with a valid will.
Testator One who makes and executes a will.
***Testimonium* Clause** A clause in a will, just before the testator's signature, that indicates the date on which the will was signed by the testator.
Third Parties In the context of legal proceedings, parties who are not directly involved in the proceeding—that is, parties other than the plaintiff and defendant and their attorneys.
Time Slip A record documenting, for billing purposes, the hours (or fractions of hours) that an attorney or a paralegal worked for each client, the date on which the work was done, and the type of work that was undertaken.
Tort A civil (as opposed to criminal) wrong not arising from a breach of contract. A breach of a legal duty, owed by the defendant to the plaintiff, that caused the plaintiff to suffer harm.
Totten Trust A trust created by the deposit of a person's own money into an account, such as a savings account, in his or her own name as a trustee for another. It is a tentative trust, revocable at will until the depositor dies or completes the gift in his or her lifetime by some unequivocal act or declaration.
Toxic Tort A tort that occurs when toxic chemicals are used in a way that causes harm to other persons or their property. Liability for toxic torts may be based on strict liability, as well as negligence and other tort theories.
Trade Journal A newsletter, magazine, or other periodical that provides a certain trade or profession with information (products, trends, or developments) relating to that trade or profession.
Trade Libel The publication of false information about another's product, alleging it is not what its seller claims; also referred to as *slander of quality.*
Trade Name A name used in commercial activity to designate a particular business, a place at which a business is located, or a class of goods. Trade names can be exclusive or nonexclusive. Examples of trade names are Sears, Safeway, and Firestone.
Trade Secret Information or a process that gives a business an advantage over competitors who do not know the information or process.
Trademark A distinctive mark or motto that a manufacturer affixes to the goods it produces to distinguish the goods from goods produced by other manufacturers.
Treatise In legal research, a text that provides a systematic, detailed, and scholarly review of a particular legal subject.
Treaty An agreement, or compact, formed between two independent nations.
Trespasser In the context of real property, one who enters onto the property of another without permission to do so.

Trial Court A court in which most cases usually begin and in which questions of fact are examined.
Trial Notebook A binder that contains copies of all of the documents and information that an attorney will need to have at hand during the trial.
Trust An arrangement in which title to property is held by one person (a trustee) for the benefit of another (a beneficiary).
Trust Account A bank or escrow account in which one party (the trustee, such as an attorney) holds funds belonging to another person (such as a client); a bank account into which funds advanced to a law firm by a client are deposited.

Unauthorized Practice of Law (UPL) Engaging in actions defined by a legal authority, such as a state legislature, as constituting the "practice of law" without legal authorization to do so.
Unconscionable Contract A contract that is void on the basis of public policy because it is so oppressive, one sided, or unfair that it "shocks the conscience" of the court.
Uniform Commercial Code (UCC) A uniform code of laws governing commercial transactions that has been adopted in part or in its entirety by all of the states. Article 2 of the UCC governs contracts for the sale of goods.
Unreasonably Dangerous Product In product liability, a product that is defective to the point of threatening a user's health and safety. A product is considered unreasonably dangerous if it is dangerous beyond the expectation of the ordinary user or if a less dangerous alternative was economically feasible for the manufacturer, but the manufacturer failed to produce it.
User Interface The computer connection, or link, between the software and the hardware that controls the image that an operator views on the monitor and the method of accomplishing a given task.

Venue The geographical district in which an action is tried and from which the jury is selected.
Verbal Communication The sending and receiving of messages using spoken or written words.
Verdict A formal decision made by a jury.
Vesting The creation of an absolute or unconditional right or power.
Vicarious Liability Legal responsibility placed on one person for the acts of another.
Visitation Rights The right of a noncustodial parent to have contact with his or her child.
Voir Dire A French phrase meaning "to speak the truth." The phrase is used to describe the preliminary questions that attorneys for the plaintiff and the defendant ask prospective jurors to determine whether potential jury members are biased or have any connection with a party to the action or with a prospective witness.

Warranty An express or implied promise by a seller that specific goods to be sold meet certain criteria, or standards of performance, upon which the buyer may rely.
Whistleblowing Reporting an employer's illegal activity to persons in authority or to the press.
Wide Area Network (WAN) A system of computers, physically dispersed over a large geographical area, in which the users are able to communicate directly with each other via computer.
Will A document directing what is to be done with the maker's property upon his or her death.
Winding Up The process of winding up all business affairs (collecting and distributing the firm's assets) after a partnership or corporation has been dissolved.
Witness A person who is asked to testify under oath at a trial.
Witness Statement The written transcription of a statement made by the witness during an interview and signed by the witness.
Word-processing Software Specialized application software that allows a computer user to create, edit, revise, save, and generally manipulate textual material and document formatting.
Work Product An attorney's mental impressions, conclusions, and legal theories regarding a case being prepared on behalf of a client. Work product normally is regarded as privileged information.
Workers' Compensation Statutes State laws establishing an administrative procedure for compensating workers for injuries that arise in the course of their employment.
Workout An out-of-court negotiation in which a debtor enters into an agreement with a creditor or creditors for a payment or plan to discharge the debtor's debt.
Writ of *Certiorari* A writ from a higher court asking the lower court for the record of a case.
Wrongful Discharge An employer's termination of an employee's employment in violation of common law principles or a statutory law that protects a specific class of employees.

INDEX

B

C

D

F

J

O

Q

R

S

T

U

V

W

Y

Photo Credits and Acknowledgments

The publisher gratefully acknowledges the contributions provided by the many individuals who appear in the Paralegal Profiles and Featured Guests sections of the book—the cooperation they extended and the photographs they supplied are greatly appreciated.

Part and Chapter Opening Images: 1 © Ron Chapple, FPG International; **3** Photo copyright © UNIPHOTO; **31** © PBJ Pictures, Liason International; **79** © J.A. Kraulis, Masterfile; **123** © Larry Williams, Masterfile; **153** © Sam Sargent, Liaison International; **193** © James Lemas, Liaison International; **195** © John Chiasson, Gamma Liaison; **229** © Jim Craigmyle, Masterfile; **265** © Larry Williams, Masterfile; **316** photo copyright © UNIPHOTO; **365** © Dick Luria, FPG International; **367** © Rommel, Masterfile; **423** © John Chiasson, Gamma Liaison; **457** © Robert E. Daemmrich, Tony Stone Images; **497** © John T. Barr, Gamma Liaison; **537** © Frank Fisher, Liaison International; **567** Photo copyright © UNIPHOTO; **603** © Rommel, Masterfile; **642** © Ed Malitsky, Liaison International; **701** © Paul Figura, Liaison International; **757** © Charles Pefley, Stock Boston; 758 © Rafael Macia, Photo Researchers; **776** © Ray Ellis, Photo Researchers; **804** © David Grossman, Photo Researchers; **836** © Jon Levy, Gamma Liason, **868** © Spencer Grant, Stock Boston; **896** © John Chiasson, Gamma Liason.

Exhibit 16.1 photo courtesy of IBM; **Exhibit 16.2** photo courtesy of DEC Corporation; **Exhibit 16.3** photo courtesy of IBM; **Exhibit 16.4** photo cortesy of Microtech Corporation; **Exhibit 16.7** photo courtesy of 3M Corporation; **Exhibit 16.8** photo by Liane Enkelis; **Exhibit 16.13** courtesy of Micro Craft, Inc. Used with permission; Exhibit 16.14 © Lotus Development Corporation. Used with permission; **Exhibits 17.2, 17.11, 17.12, 17.13, and 17.14** reprinted with permission of Lawyer's Cooperative Publishing, a Division of Thomson Legal Publishing, Inc.; **Exhibit 17.18** Index to Legal Periodicals, Sept. 1991–1992. Copyright © 1992 by the H.W. Wilson Company. Material reproduced with permission of the publisher. **Exhibit 17.28** reproduced by permission of Shepard's McGraw-Hill, Inc. Further reproduction is strictly prohibited.